52ND EDITION

KOVELS'®
ANTIQUES &
COLLECTIBLES
PRICE GUIDE 2020

BLACK DOG
& LEVENTHAL
PUBLISHERS
NEW YORK

Cover design by Carlos Esparza and Katie Benezra

Front cover photographs, from left to right:
Grueby, vase, green, yellow irises, circular stamp
Handel, lamp, water bearer, maiden, kneeling, with water jug
Furniture, chair, Finn Juhl, teak, leather, arms

Back cover photographs, top to bottom:
Hawkes, vase, green cut to clear
Buck Rogers, sign, Popsicle, refreshing
Silver-American, pitcher, water, leafy scrolls
Toy, skittles pin holder, figural, rooster

Spine:
Jewelry, pin, butterfly

Authors' photographs © Kim Ponsky (top) and Alex Montes de Oca (bottom)

Cover copyright © 2019 by Hachette Book Group, Inc.

Black Dog & Leventhal Publishers
Hachette Book Group
1290 Avenue of the Americas
New York, NY 10104

www.hachettebookgroup.com
www.blackdogandleventhal.com

First Edition: September 2019

Black Dog & Leventhal Publishers is an imprint of Perseus Books, LLC, a subsidiary of Hachette Book Group, Inc.
The Black Dog & Leventhal Publishers name and logo are trademarks of Hachette Book Group, Inc.

The publisher is not responsible for websites (or their content) that are not owned by the publisher.
The Hachette Speakers Bureau provides a wide range of authors for speaking events.
To find out more, go to www.HachetteSpeakersBureau.com or call (866) 376-6591.

Print book interior design by Sheila Hart Design, Inc.

LCCN: 2019940021
ISBN: 978-0-7624-6856-0

Printed in the United States of America

WALSWORTH
10 9 8 7 6 5 4 3 2 1

BOOKS BY RALPH AND TERRY KOVEL

American Country Furniture, 1780–1875

A Directory of American Silver, Pewter, and Silver Plate

Kovels' Advertising Collectibles Price List

Kovels' American Antiques 1750–1900

Kovels' American Art Pottery

Kovels' American Collectibles 1900–2000

Kovels' American Silver Marks, 1650 to the Present

Kovels' Antiques & Collectibles Fix-It Source Book

Kovels' Antiques & Collectibles Price Guide (1968–2009)

Kovels' Bid, Buy, and Sell Online

Kovels' Book of Antique Labels

Kovels' Bottles Price List (1971–2006)

Kovels' Collector's Guide to American Art Pottery

Kovels' Collector's Guide to Limited Editions

Kovels' Collectors' Source Book

Kovels' Depression Glass & Dinnerware Price List (1980–2004)

Kovels' Dictionary of Marks— Pottery and Porcelain, 1650 to 1850

Kovels' Guide to Selling, Buying, and Fixing Your Antiques and Collectibles

Kovels' Guide to Selling Your Antiques & Collectibles

Kovels' Illustrated Price Guide to Royal Doulton (1980, 1984)

Kovels' Know Your Antiques

Kovels' Know Your Collectibles

Kovels' New Dictionary of Marks— Pottery and Porcelain, 1850 to the Present

Kovels' Organizer for Collectors

Kovels' Price Guide for Collector Plates, Figurines, Paperweights, and Other Limited Edition Items

Kovels' Quick Tips: 799 Helpful Hints on How to Care for Your Collectibles

Kovels' Yellow Pages: A Resource Guide for Collectors

The Label Made Me Buy It: From Aunt Jemima to Zonkers— The Best-Dressed Boxes, Bottles, and Cans from the Past

BOOKS BY TERRY KOVEL AND KIM KOVEL

Kovels' Antiques & Collectibles Price Guide (2010–2020)

INTRODUCTION

Kovels' Antiques & Collectibles Price Guide 2020 has current, reliable price information and makers' marks. The book has 16,000 prices, 2,500 new color photographs, more than 730 categories, hundreds of dated marks, plus an all-new center section on "Collecting Trends: Iconic Designers of Twentieth-Century Furniture."

We are frequently asked questions like "How old is my grandmother's dish?" Each of the 730 categories includes an introductory paragraph with history, locations, explanations, and other important information to help identify unknown pieces, and some include information about reproductions. We update these introductory paragraphs every year to indicate new owners, new distributors, or new information about production dates. This year we made updates to over 100 paragraphs, many that tell of the sale or closing of a company. This guide includes more than 500 marks. Even more dated marks can be found online at Kovels.com and in our book *Kovels' New Dictionary of Marks, Pottery and Porcelain* available at Kovels.com or at libraries. You will also find more than 200 added facts of interest and tips about care and repair. Each photograph is shown with a caption that includes the description, price, and source, and information about the seller of the piece is listed at the end of the book. The book has color tabs and color-coded categories that make it easy to find listings, and it uses a modern, readable typestyle. All antiques and collectibles priced here were offered for sale during the past year, most of them in the United States, from June 2018 to June 2019. Other prices came from sales that accepted bids from all over the world. Almost all auction prices given include the buyer's premium since that is part of what the buyer paid. Very few include local sales tax or extra charges for things such as phone bids, online bids, credit cards, storage, or shipping.

Most items in our original 1968 price book were made before 1860, so they were more than a century old. Today in *Kovels' Antiques & Collectibles Price Guide*, we list pieces made as recently as 2010. There is great interest in furniture, glass, ceramics, and good design made since 1950 in the midcentury modern style and pieces made after the 1980s.

The 2020 edition is more than 550 pages long and crammed full of prices and photographs. We try to include a balance of prices and do not include too many items that sell for more than $5,000. By listing only a few very expensive pieces, you can realize that a great paperweight may cost $10,000, but an average one is only $25. Nearly all prices are from the American market for the American market. Only a few European sales are reported. These are for items that may be of interest to American collectors. We don't include prices we think result from "auction fever," but we do list verified bargains.

There is an index with cross-references. Use it often. It includes categories and much more. For example, there is a category for Celluloid. Most celluloid will be there, but a toy made of celluloid may be listed under Toy as well as indexed under Celluloid. There are also cross-references in the listings and in the category introductions. But some searching must be done. For example, Barbie dolls are in the Doll category; there is no Barbie category. And when you look at "doll, Barbie," you find a note that "Barbie" is under "doll, Mattel, Barbie" because Mattel makes Barbie dolls and most dolls are listed by maker.

Wherever we had extra space on a page, we filled it with tips about the care of collections and other useful information. Don't discard this book. Old *Kovels'* price guides can be used in the coming years as a reference source for identifying pictures and price changes and for tax, estate, and appraisal information.

The prices in this book are reports of the general antiques market. As we said, every price in the book is new. We do not estimate or "update" prices. Prices are either realized prices from auctions or completed sales. We have also included a few that are asking prices, knowing that a buyer may have negotiated a

lower price. We do not pay dealers, collectors, or experts to estimate prices. If a price range is given, at least two identical items were offered for sale at different prices. Price ranges are found only in categories such as Pressed Glass, where identical items can be identified. Some prices in *Kovels' Antiques & Collectibles Price Guide* may seem high and some low because of regional variations, but each price is what you could have paid for the object somewhere in the United States. Internet prices from individual sellers' ads or listings are avoided. Because so many non-collectors sell online but know little about the objects they are describing, there can be inaccuracies in descriptions. Sales from well-known Internet sites, shops, and sales, carefully edited, are included.

If you are selling your collection, do not expect to get retail value unless you are a dealer. Wholesale prices for antiques are 30 to 40 percent of retail prices. The antiques dealer must make a profit or go out of business. Internet auction prices are less predictable; because of an international audience or "auction fever," prices can be higher or lower than retail.

Time has changed what we collect, the prices we pay, what is "best," and what has dropped in price. There are also laws about endangered species, not a concern when we started, and many changes in tax laws, estate problems, and even more and better reproductions and fakes that make buying more difficult. But there are many more ways to buy and sell. When we started, it was house sales, flea markets, and a few formal antiques shows and auctions. Now, computers and the Internet have made it possible for anyone to buy and sell any day of the week, in every price range. There seem to be more shows closing or joining other shows, auction houses merging, and many more auction bidders. Almost every auction is online as well as available by phone to buyers around the world. And there are frequently live bidders at the more expensive sales. But many auctions end up with unsold pieces, some offered for sale at a set price after the auction. Even eBay is selling only about one-third of the offered antiques. And there are thousands of places to look for prices!

READ THIS FIRST

This is a book for the buyer and the seller. It is an organized, illustrated list of average pieces, not million-dollar paintings and rare Chinese porcelains. Everything listed in this book was sold within the last 12 months. We check prices, visit shops, shows, and flea markets, read hundreds of publications and catalogs, check Internet sales, auctions, and other online services, and decide which antiques and collectibles are of most interest to most collectors in the United States. We concentrate on average pieces in any category. Prices of some items were very high because a major collection of top-quality pieces owned by a well-known collector or expert or celebrity was auctioned. Fame adds to the value. Many catalogs now feature the name, picture, and biography of the collector and advertise the auction with the collector's name in all the ads. This year there were major sales of video games, penny toys, dolls, vinaigrettes, Moorcroft pottery, toys, target balls, canes, Greentown glass, bottles, Dieter Rams designs, tennis collectibles, Ferdinand Martin mechanical toys, Lalique, Disneyana, metal lunch boxes, Western & Canadian collectibles, comic books, comic art, Martinware, Royal Doulton, Fiesta, skating collections, Margaret De Patta jewelry, match safes, Karl Springer designs, antique tools, and Muncie art pottery. Single-collector auctions of dolls, Victorian glass, and Tiffany of all types were well advertised, and prices were high. Some of these prices are reported. The most important bottle auctions are run by major bottle auction companies that feature only bottles, including American flasks. Some of these high prices are also reported, along with less expensive inkwells, bitters bottles, and more.

The biggest item in this year's guide is an advertising sign for crockery by L.C. Baker. It has white letters on a faded gray ground. The sign, 6 by 169 inches, was made in the late 1800s, most likely to use on the front of a building. It sold for only $220, probably because of its unusual long, thin shape. The smallest is a round mother-of-pearl button with purple and pink iridescence and cut-steel accents. It is only 1/2 inch in diameter and sold for $8. The most expensive collectible is a prop from the 1983 Star Wars movie *Return of the Jedi*, Han Solo's DL-44 blaster pistol made of metal and resin. All Star Wars collectibles sell for good prices, but this one-of-a-kind icon was bought for the amazing price of $550,000. And the least expensive collectible in this book is a 1997 Hallmark Keepsake Howdy Doody Christmas ornament that sold for $1. It pictures a colorful Howdy waving and smiling.

There are always some strange and even weird things listed in our price books. We have listed artificial legs several times, usually the plain wooden stump that is pictured in stories of pirates of earlier days. This year we list a prosthetic leg made in the early 1900s. It is made of maple and leather with metal hinges at the knee and a brown shoe on the "foot." It is 31 inches long and sold for $282. We have also learned that old-fashioned medical devices like the legs sell quickly to those who collect health-related things and those who use them in unusual decorative ways or as part of modern sculptures. Also priced and pictured is the historic lightweight wooden leg splint invented by Charles and Ray Eames to use to transport wounded from the battlefield during World War II. The technology that was developed to bend the wood for the splint was used later to make their famous wooden chairs. The splint sold for $625. A strange opium pipe shaped like a dragon with a ball in its mouth sold for $488. It was made of silver with enamel trim and has a special case. The pipe is 7 inches long. We list a lot of sports collectibles and this year there was a remarkable auction of tennis memorabilia with some very rare objects. *Kovels'* has a price listing for a wicker rocking chair with a wicker tennis racket and ball design worked into the 36-inch-high back. It was made in the early 1900s and sold for $3,690. And an 1880s woman's skirt lifter made in the shape of two tennis rackets and balls auctioned for $1,107. But the strangest entry of all was for a decorated trash can from Disneyland made in the 1990s. We don't know who took it out of the park, but it sold at auction for $18,400.

RECORD-SETTING PRICES

ADVERTISING

Red Hat Royal "400" Gasoline sign (image 1): $66,000 for a porcelain gasoline sign with Red Hat graphics, 48-in. diameter. Sold October 8, 2018, by Morphy Auctions, Denver, Pennsylvania.

Houston Gasoline porcelain sign (image 2): $33,600 for a round porcelain Houston Gasoline sign, 47 ½-in. diameter. Sold October 8, 2018, by Morphy Auctions, Denver, Pennsylvania.

Mary Mayo, advertising artist (image 3): $3,000 for a General Mills *Wheaties* advertisement, gouache on board, "I'll have my picture on the box some day," illustrated by Mary Mayo, picturing a young boy in a football uniform, holding his helmet, with his thumb pointing at himself, 1957. Sold December 6, 2018, Swann Galleries, New York.

1.

2.

3.

CLOCKS & WATCHES

E. Howard No. 57 regulator wall clock (image 4): $145,200 for an E. Howard No. 57 wall regulator clock, walnut case, arched crest, carved, reverse painted and gold leaf door, presented to Joseph S. Waterman in 1890, 8-day weight-driven movement, silvered dial, incised Roman numerals, signed E. Howard & Co., Boston. Sold May 19, 2018, by Fontaine's Auction Gallery, Pittsfield, Massachusetts.

FURNITURE

Flaque table by Royere (image 5): $591,000 for a *Flaque* low table made in 1955 by Jean Royere, kidney shaped with straw marquetry-covered wood, 3 round legs, 10 x 49¾ x 25⅞ in. Sold June 6, 2018, by Phillips, New York.

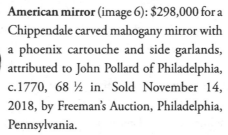

5.

4.

American mirror (image 6): $298,000 for a Chippendale carved mahogany mirror with a phoenix cartouche and side garlands, attributed to John Pollard of Philadelphia, c.1770, 68 ½ in. Sold November 14, 2018, by Freeman's Auction, Philadelphia, Pennsylvania.

Queen Anne stools (image 7): $275,000 (exceptional high price) for a pair of Queen Anne walnut stools, rectangular seat, silk and wool needlework, ring-turned cabriole legs, plastic label, modern paper label, inscribed, c.1710, 18 x 22 x 17 ¼ in. Sold May 9, 2018, by Christie's, New York. From the Collection of Peggy and David Rockefeller.

GLASS

Sand bottle (image 8): $132,000 for sand bottle by Andrew Clemens picturing an American spread-winged eagle underneath a flag with 36 stars on one side and a bouquet of flowers on the reverse with the name Mrs. Eliza B. Lewis, original velvet seal and full label, 6¾ in. Sold October 6, 2018, by Cowan's Auctions, Cincinnati, Ohio.

6.

7.

The previous lot in this sale set a record for a sand bottle as well, but only lasting until the next lot auctioned. An Andrew Clemens inverted sand bottle with nautical scene of sailboats at sea on one side, and an American spread-winged eagle underneath a flag with 42 stars on the reverse, 6 ¼ in. (image 9). It sold for $108,000, October 6, 2018, at Cowan's Auctions.

8.

Most expensive piece of American Pattern glass (image 10): $35,100 for a 19th-century Bakewell, Pears & Co., thumbprint bowl with lid on high-foot compote, colorless, 20 x 11 x 7 ¼ in. Sold September 29, 2018, by Jeffrey S. Evans & Associates, Mount Crawford, Virginia.

9.

10.

MISCELLANEOUS

Chinese Cloisonné enamel urn (image 11): $126,000 for a Chinese Cloisonné enamel on bronze urn with 2 red dragons chasing the flaming pearl of wisdom among clouds, c.1725, 22 in. Sold January 14, 2019, by Pook & Pook, Downingtown, Pennsylvania.

This urn was involved in a competitive bidding battle with more than 403 bids placed and realized a final price at 1,260 times the original estimate ($100-$200).

11.

Tiffany Studios (image 12): $3,372,500 for a rare Tiffany Studios Pond Lily table lamp with leaded glass shade and patinated bronze lily pad base, impressed tag for Tiffany Studios New York, c.1903, 26 ½ x 18 in. Sold December 13, 2018, by Christie's, New York.

12.

Most expensive pearl (image 13): $36,427,000 for Marie Antoinette's 18th-century natural pearl and diamond pendant, set with oval diamonds supporting a diamond bow and a drop-shaped natural pearl, ⅝ x ¾ x 1 in. Sold November 14, 2018, by Sotheby's, Geneva.

13.

Weltron stereo system (image 14): $7,800 for a Weltron GEC-2005 stereo system on pedestal stand with turntable, AM/FM stereo radio, built-in 8-track player, internal speakers and external auxiliary ports, all in a "Space Age" style, 1970s, 27 ½ x 22 ½ in. Sold February 24, 2019, by Urban Culture Auctions, West Palm Beach, Florida.

Most expensive bottle of whisky (image 15): $1,528,800 for Macallan 1926, 60-year-old single malt whisky, bottled in 1986, distilled at the Macallan Distillery, bottle pictures Easter Elchies House hand-painted by Michael Dillon, in wooden presentation case and certificate of authenticity. Sold November 29, 2018, by Christie's, London.

15.

14.

PAINTINGS & PRINTS

Most expensive prewar American work of art (image 16): $91,875,000 for the Edward Hopper (1882-1967) oil on canvas painting "Chop Suey," signed, 1929, 32 x 38 in. Sold November 13, 2018, by Christie's, New York.

16.

17.

18.

19.

David Hockney painting (image 17): $90,312,500 for the 1972 David Hockney painting "Portrait of an Artist (Pool with Two Figures)," acrylic on canvas, 84 x 120 in. Sold November 15, 2018, by Christie's, New York.

Currier & Ives print (image 18): $62,500 for the 1868 Currier & Ives print "Across the Continent/Westward the Course of Empire Takes its Way." Sold December 13, 2018, by Swann Auction Galleries, New York.

Drawing by the artist (image 19): $8,202,000 for the Sir Peter Paul Rubens drawing "Nude Study of a Young Man with Raised Arms," black chalk, white highlights, inscription in brown ink, 1608, 19 ⅜ x 12 ⅜ in. Sold January 30, 2019, by Sotheby's, New York.

René Magritte painting (image 20): $26,830,500 for the oil on canvas painting "Le Principe du Plaisir" (The Pleasure Principle) by René Magritte (1898–1967), signed and dated 1937, 28 ¾ x 21 ½ in. Sold November 12, 2018, by Sotheby's, New York.

20.

21.

PAPER

Movie poster from Star Wars (image 21): $26,400 for a rare Star Wars concept poster for the 1980 sequel *The Empire Strikes Back*, this poster being a trial run featuring art by artist Roger Kastel. Pictures Han Solo and Princess Leia sharing an embrace surrounded by action scenes, 20th Century Fox, 1980, one sheet, 27 x 41 in. Sold July 31, 2018, by Heritage Auctions, Dallas, Texas.

Sutro Baths text-free poster (image 22): $23,400 for the text-free variant of the 1896 poster Sutro Baths, promoting a former San Francisco landmark. Sold August 1, 2018, by Swann Auction Galleries, New York.

Peter Behren poster (image 23): $5,000 for the Peter Behren color woodcut poster "Der Kuss" published by *Pan* magazine, matted and framed, 1898, 15 x 11 ¾ in. Sold August 1, 2018, by Swann Auction Galleries, New York.

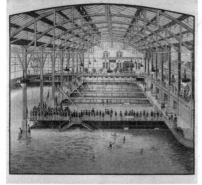

22.

23.

24.

Manuel Orazi poster (image 24): $10,625 for the Manuel Orazi poster "Ligue Vinicole de France," an image showing wine as the answer to the modern world's ills, c.1901, 38 x 53 in. Sold August 1, 2018, by Swann Auction Galleries, New York

Illustrator Eric Carle (image 25): $20,000 for the hand-painted collage for "The Very Hungry Caterpillar" by Eric Carle. Sold December 6, 2018, by Swann Auction Galleries, New York.

25.

Illustrator H.A. Rey (image 26): $17,500 for the color pencil work for "Cecily G and the 9 Monkeys," by H.A. Rey, 1939, the first book to introduce Curious George. Sold December 6, 2018, by Swann Auction Galleries, New York.

26.

27.

Illustrator Helen Craig (image 27): $5,460 for "Angelina Ballerina" by Helen Craig, watercolor and ink alternate version of the title page, 1983. Sold December 6, 2018, by Swann Auction Galleries, New York.

Illustrator Leonard Weisgard (image 28): $5,000 for the double-page illustration for "The Golden Christmas Tree" by Leonard Weisgard, 1988. Sold December 6, 2018, by Swann Auction Galleries, New York.

Illustrator Helen Stone (image 29): $3,500 for Helen Stone's illustrations from "Tell Me, Mr. Owl," 1957, including sketches, studies and composed finished drawings. Sold December 6, 2018, by Swann Auction Galleries, New York.

28.

29.

POTTERY & PORCELAIN

Marblehead vase (image 30): $303,000 for a Marblehead pottery vase with landscape scene band, picturing haystacks in a marsh in brown and beige tones, designed by Annie E. Aldrich, decorated by Sarah Tutt, and made by John Swallow, marked with "M" and partial "P" and sailing ship, also the letters "A" and "T" beneath the Marblehead mark, 8 ½ in. One of four known examples. Purchased by a 19-year-old at a yard sale along with a snowmobile helmet. Sold December 14, 2018, by Skinner, Inc., Boston.

30.

Anna Pottery (image 31): $141,600 for a salt-glazed stoneware snake jug with Albany Slip decoration, inscribed "8 to 7," made in 1877 by Wallace and Cornwall Kirkpatrick, Anna, Illinois, oval body with 12 applied snakes, tall neck and handle in the form of a snake coiled around the neck, each snake is hand incised with crosshatched scaling, flattened diamond-shaped head and impressed eyes, original stopper in the form of a coiled snake, 11 x 9 ¾ x 8 ½ in. Sold November 3, 2018, by Crocker Farm, Sparks, Maryland.

31.

Most expensive 19th Century porcelain (image 32): $1,812,500 for Marly Rouge service of Sevres porcelain iron-red and sky-blue ground, part of dessert service made for Napoleon, 1807-09, iron-red stenciled M. Imple de Sevres mark, date-cyphers 7, 8, and 9 for 1807-09, various incised marks. Sold May 9, 2018, by Christie's, New York. Part of the Collection of Peggy and David Rockefeller.

32.

SPORTS

Heisman trophy (image 33): $435,762 for the Heisman trophy awarded to Tim Brown in 1987 when he played football for Notre Dame. Sold December 10, 2018, by Goldin Auctions, Runnemede, New Jersey.

Mickey Mantle jersey (image 34): $1,320,000 for a Mickey Mantle game-worn jersey from the 1964 World Series. Sold August 18, 2018, by Heritage Auctions, Dallas, Texas.

33.

34.

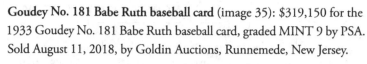

Goudey No. 181 Babe Ruth baseball card (image 35): $319,150 for the 1933 Goudey No. 181 Babe Ruth baseball card, graded MINT 9 by PSA. Sold August 11, 2018, by Goldin Auctions, Runnemede, New Jersey.

Post-World War II trading card (image 36): $2,880,000 for a 1952 Topps Mickey Mantle No. 311 PSA Mint 9 baseball card. Sold April 19, 2018, by Heritage Auctions, Dallas, Texas.

"Shoeless Joe" Jackson baseball card (image 37): $600,000 for the "Shoeless Joe" Jackson 1910 T210 Old Mill baseball card, pictured as a member of the New Orleans Pelicans in his warm-up sweater, 1 ½ x 2 ⅝ in. Sold February 23, 2019, by Heritage Auctions, Dallas, Texas.

35.

36.

37.

TOYS, DOLLS & BANKS

Machine Man robot (image 38): $86,100 for an unboxed Machine Man robot, tin lithographed, battery operated, made in Japan by Masudaya, late 1950s/early 1960s. Machine Man is considered the scarcest member of Masudaya's Gang of Five robot series. Sold March 14, 2019, by Morphy Auctions, Denver, Pennsylvania.

Super Mario Bros. video game (image 39): $100,150 for an unopened copy (sticker sealed) of Super Mario Bros. Nintendo Entertainment System video game, released in 1985, certified by Wata Games as Near Mint, grade 9.4 and seal rating of A++. Sold February 14, 2019, by Heritage Auctions, Dallas, Texas.

38.

Walking Batman toy (image 40): $16,800 for a postwar Japan Walking Batman toy with original Japanese-version box, plastic with cloth cape, battery operated, made by TN, from new old stock, 1960s, 12 in. Sold October 13, 2018, by Milestone Auctions, Willoughby, Ohio.

39.

40.

HOW TO USE THIS BOOK

There are a few rules for using this book. Each listing is arranged in the following manner: CATEGORY (such as silver), OBJECT (such as vase), DESCRIPTION (as much information as possible about size, age, color, and pattern). Some types of glass, pottery, and silver are exceptions to this rule. These are listed CATEGORY, PATTERN, OBJECT, DESCRIPTION, PRICE. All items are presumed to be in good condition and undamaged, unless otherwise noted. In most sections, if a maker's name is easily recognized, such as Gustav Stickley, we include it near the beginning of the entry. If the maker is obscure, the name may be near the end.

- To save space, dollar amounts do not include dollar signs, commas, or cents at the end so $1,234.00 is written 1234.

- You will find silver flatware in either Silver Flatware Plated or Silver Flatware Sterling. There is also a section for Silver Plate, which includes coffeepots, trays, and other plated hollowware. Most solid or sterling silver is listed by country, so look for Silver-American, Silver-Danish, Silver-English, etc. Silver jewelry is listed under Jewelry. Most pottery and porcelain is listed by factory name, such as Weller or Wedgwood; by item, such as Calendar Plate; in sections like Dinnerware or Kitchen; or in a special section, such as Pottery-Art, Pottery-Contemporary, Pottery-Midcentury, etc.

- Sometimes we make arbitrary decisions. Fishing has its own category, but hunting is part of the larger category called sports. We have omitted guns except for toy guns. These are listed in the toy category. It is not legal to sell weapons without a special license, so guns are not part of the general antiques market. Air guns, BB guns, rocket guns, and others are listed in the Toy section. Everything is listed according to the computer alphabetizing system.

- We made several editorial decisions. A butter dish is listed as a "butter." A salt dish is called a "salt" to differentiate it from a saltshaker. It is always "sugar and creamer," never "creamer and sugar." Where one dimension is given, it is the height; if the object is round, it's the diameter. The height of a picture is listed before width. Glass is clear unless a color is indicated.

- Some antiques terms, such as "Sheffield" or "Pratt," have two meanings. Read the paragraph headings to know the definition being used. All category headings are based on the vocabulary of the average person, and we use terms like "mud figures" even if not technically correct. Some categories are known by several names. Pressed glass is also called pattern glass or EAPG (Early American pattern glass). We use the name "pressed glass" because much of the information found in old books and articles use that name.

- This book does not include price listings for fine art paintings, antiquities, stamps, coins, or most types of books. Comic books are listed only in special categories like Superman, but original comic art is listed in Comic Art and cels are listed in Animation Art.

- Prices for items pictured can be found in the appropriate categories. Look for the matching entry with the abbreviation "illus." The color photograph will be nearby.

- Thanks to computers, the book is produced quickly. The last entries are added in June; the book is available in September. But human help finds prices and checks accuracy. We read everything at least five times, sometimes more. We edit more than 35,000 entries down to the 16,000 entries found here. We correct spelling, remove incorrect data, write category paragraphs, and decide on new categories. We proofread copy and prices many times, but there

may be some misspelled words and other errors. Information in the paragraphs is updated each year, and this year more than 145 updates and additions were made.

- Prices are reported from all parts of the United States, Canada, Europe, and Asia, and converted to U.S. dollars at the time of the sale. The average rate of exchange on June 1, 2019, was $1 to about $1.34 Canadian, €0.89 (euro), and £0.78 (British pound). Meltdown price for silver was $14.45 per ounce in June. Prices are from auctions, shops, Internet sales, shows, and even some flea markets. Every price is checked for accuracy, but we are not responsible for errors. We cannot answer your letters asking for price information, or where to sell, but please write if you have any requests for categories to be included or any corrections to the paragraphs or prices. You may find the answers to your other questions at Kovels.com or in our newsletter, *Kovels on Antiques & Collectibles.*

- When you see us at shows, auctions, house sales, flea markets, or even the grocery store, please stop and say hello. Don't be surprised if we ask for your suggestions. You can write to us at P.O. Box 22192, Beachwood, OH 44122, or visit us at our website, Kovels.com.

TERRY KOVEL AND KIM KOVEL
July 2019

ACKNOWLEDGMENTS

The world of antiques and collectibles is filled with people who share knowledge and help, tell stories of record prices, amazing sales, and news, and make books like this possible. Dealers, auction galleries, antiques shops, serious collectors, clubs, publications, and even museum experts have given advice and opinions, sent pictures and prices, and made suggestions for changes. Thank you to all of them! Each picture is labeled with the name of the source. We list a phone number, postal address, and Web address at the end of the book, so you can learn more about any pictured piece. We also include the names of many of the people or places that reported some prices.

And we want to give special thanks to the staff at Kovels' and at Hachette Book Group, our publisher. They deserve the most credit. They helped gather the 16,000 prices, 2,500 pictures, marks, tips on care of collections, and hotlines (bits of information too important to ignore), put it all together, and made it work.

Our thanks to the Hachette staff:

- Lisa Tenaglia, our editor who has worked with us for nine years, who makes sure the book gets finished on time. She is also our advocate and problem solver.

- Lillian Sun, production manager, Melanie Gold, production editor, and the others at Hachette who do all the things we never see that create the quality of the finished product.

- Kara Thornton, publicist who worries about getting stories in newspapers, magazines, book reviews, social media, TV talk shows, and the many online sites that are interested in collecting.

- Mary Flower, Robin Perlow, and Cynthia Schuster Eakin, copyeditors, who seem to find every typo, mislabeled picture, and misspelled name. They make sure the names and dates of every royal family, period of furniture, historic event, the spelling of the Chinese dynasties, and the most misspelled name of them all—Wedgwood—are correct.

- Sheila Hart, who has worked on many editions of the book—redesigning the pages to look great, adapting the layout each time we change the content, adding things such as pages of marks, number of prices, and more color pictures. She also does layout and design of the special features such as the record prices and the yearly fact-filled insert on popular makers and market changes. Somehow she has solved the problem of getting all 16,000 prices and all 2,500 pictures in position in alphabetical order near one another so readers can see both on the same page.

And to those on the Kovels' staff who work on both the digital and print versions of this book:

- Janet Dodrill, our art director, who is able to keep track of all of the pictures and permissions for the items shown in this book as well as extra pictures used for our columns and other publications. She then uses her superior photo editing skills to improve the look and the quality of the pictures by outlining the objects, checking the color, and even working magic with close-ups of details.

- Our in-house price staff, Mozella Colon, Beverly Malone, and Renee McRitchie, who know the vocabulary needed to get prices from all parts of the country and turn them into the proper form to sort into the book.

- Cherrie Smrekar, who takes time from her job running our newsletter to help with prices, tips, hotlines, record prices, and other special features of the book.

- Liz Lillis, a Kovels' staff copyeditor, writer, and researcher, who not only knows all the dates and names but tells us where the commas and periods go and solves other grammar problems. She also writes the online publicity for the book and our homepage.

- Gay Hunter, who is the official boss of the price book production, tracks the prices and pictures in and out, suggests sources for prices at sales and shows, records where and when it was sold, and what the seller said about it. She records the work of the others doing the book prices or paragraphs or reports, runs spell checks on each document, and knows all of our special codes and dating systems. She makes sure we are getting a variety of prices, especially the new ones we seem to see each year when we add new categories (a new category this year is Pyrex). But most of all, she keeps us meeting the book deadlines by reminding us all year that we are way behind.

- And Alberto Eiber, who makes sure we are accurate with articles and reports of the recent things we include that are now called "Design" by art and auction gallery dealers. He also writes about these twentieth-century and contemporary designers.

CONTRIBUTORS

The world of antiques and collectibles is filled with people who have answered our every request for help. Dealers, auction houses, and shops have given advice and opinions, supplied photographs and prices, and made suggestions for changes. Many thanks to all of them:

Photographs and information were furnished by: Abington Auction Gallery, Ahlers & Ogletree Auction Gallery, Alderfer Auction Company, Allard Auctions, American Glass Gallery, AntiqueAdvertising.com, Apple Tree Auction Center, Aspire Auctions, Auction Team Breker, Belhorn Auction Services, Bertoia Auctions, Blackwell Auctions, Bonhams, Brunk Auctions, Bunch Auctions, Burchard Galleries, Charleston Estate Auctions, Christie's, Clars Auction Gallery, Copake Auction, Cordier Auctions, Cottone Auctions, Cowan's Auctions, Crescent City Auction Gallery, Crocker Farm, Doyle Auctioneers & Appraisers, DuMouchelles, eBay, Eldred's, Etsy, Jeffrey S. Evans, Fairfield Auction, Fontaine's Auction Gallery, Forsythes' Auctions, Fox Auctions, Freeman's Auctioneers & Appraisers, Garth's Auctioneers & Appraisers, Glass Works Auctions, Goldin Auctions, Grogan & Company, Hake's Auctions, Hannam's Auctioneers, Harritt Group, Inc., Hartzell's Auction Gallery, Inc., Jack & Jeff Hayes, Heritage Auctions, Hess Auction Group, Homestead Auctions, Humler & Nolan, James D. Julia Auctioneers, Julien's Auctions, Kamelot Auctions, Keystone Auctions LLC, Leland Little Auctions, Leslie Hindman Auctioneers, Locati Auctions, Los Angeles Modern Auctions, Main Auction Galleries, Inc., Martin Auction Co., Matthew Bullock Auctioneers, Milestone Auctions, Morphy Auctions, Nadeau's Auction Gallery, Neal Auction Company, New Orleans Auction Galleries, Norman C. Heckler & Co., Northeast Auctions, Palm Beach Modern Auctions, Period Americana, Phillips, Pook & Pook, Potter & Potter Auctions, Quittenbaum Kunstauktionen GmbH, Rachel Davis Fine Arts, Rago Arts & Auction Center, Rich Penn Auctions, Richard D. Hatch & Associates, Richard Opfer Auctioneering, Inc., Ripley Auctions, Roland Auctioneers & Valuers, Royal Crest Auctioneers, RR Auction, RSL Auction, Ruby Lane, Seeck Auctions, Selkirk Auctioneers & Appraisers, Skinner, Inc., Sotheby's, Soulis Auctions, Strawser Auction Group, Susanin's Auctioneers & Appraisers, Swann Auction Galleries, The Stein Auction Company, Theriault's, Thomaston Place Auction Galleries, Treadway, Treasureseeker Auctions, Turner Auctions & Appraisers, Urban Culture Auctions, Van Eaton Galleries, Weiss Auctions, Willis Henry Auctions, Wm Morford Auctions, Woody Auction, and Wright.

To the others who knowingly or unknowingly contributed to this book, we say thank you: Alex Cooper Auctioneers, Helios Auctions, Kaminski Auctions, Kimballs Auction & Estate Services, Kodner Galleries, Inc., Long Auction Co., Parasel Ltd., Period Americana, Replacements Ltd., and Stony Ridge Auction.

A. WALTER made pate-de-verre glass under contract at the Daum glassworks from 1908 to 1914. He decorated pottery during his early years in his studio in Sevres, where he also developed his formula for pale, translucent pate-de-verre. He started his own firm in Nancy, France, in 1919. Pieces made before 1914 are signed *Daum, Nancy* with a cross. After 1919 the signature is *A. Walter Nancy*.

Bowl, Lizard, Pulled Feather, Iridescent Peacock Eye, Signed, 8 x 4 In. .... *illus*	5843
Tray, Fish, Brown, Green & Blue Fins, Turquoise Spots, Vegetation, Signed, 9¼ x 5¼ In.	3075
Tray, Fish, Swimming, Brown Blue To Pale Yellow, Spots, Signed, 7 x 5 In.	1024
Tray, Lizard, Molded, Green, Yellow Spots, Bright Yellow Outer Rim, Signed, 4¼ In.	3383
Tray, Shield Shape, Blue To Pale Yellow, Moth, Spread Wings, Signed, 4 x 3½ In.	1216

ABC plates, or children's alphabet plates, were most popular from 1780 to 1860 but are still being made. The letters on the plate were meant as teaching aids for children learning to read. The plates were made of pottery, porcelain, metal, or glass. Mugs and other items were also made with alphabet decorations. Many companies made ABC plates. Shown here are marks used by three English makers.

Charles Allerton & Sons
c.1890–1912

Enoch Wood & Sons
1818–1846

William E. Oulsnam & Sons
c.1880–1892

Plate, 2 Men Hunting, Dogs, Blue, Red, Green, c.1875, 7½ In.	149
Plate, Emma, Girl's Face, Amber Glass, Clay's Crystal Works, 1960s, 8 In.	26
Plate, Girls At Tea Party, Blue, Porcelain, c.1880, 6½ In	65
Plate, The Soldiers, Cream, Porcelain, 1800s, 7 In.	149

ABINGDON POTTERY was established in 1908 by Raymond E. Bidwell as the Abingdon Sanitary Manufacturing Company. The company started making art pottery in 1934. The factory ceased production of art pottery in 1950.

Cookie Jar, Humpty Dumpty, On Wall, Yellow, Brown Stripes, Smiling	95
Planter, Cactus, Man Seated, Hat, 1950s, 7 x 3 x 6 In.	65
Sconce, Paneled, Blue, Blond, White, c.1940, 9 x 6 x 4 In., 3 Piece	85
Umbrella Stand, Flared, Green Glaze, Reeds, Heron, Scalloped Rim, 1930s, 14 In.	350
Vase, Acanthus, Blue Matte, Handles, Flared Rim, 1940s, 10 In.	52
Vase, Delta, Jasmine Yellow Matte Glaze, Handles, c.1938, 10 x 6½ In.	85
Wall Shelf, Scalloped, Shell Like, Acanthus Finial, White Gloss, c.1942, 9 x 7 x 3½ In.	79

ADAMS china was made by William Adams and Sons of Staffordshire, England. The firm was founded in 1769 and became part of the Wedgwood Group in 1966. The name *Adams* appeared on various items through 1998. All types of tablewares and useful wares were made. Other pieces of Adams may be found listed under Flow Blue and Tea Leaf Ironstone.

William Adams & Co.
1905–1917

William Adams & Sons
1917–1965

Adams under Wedgwood
1966–1975

Biscuit Barrel, Jasperware, Silver Plated Lid, Handle, Blue & White, Swags, c.1900, 7 In., Pair *illus*	128
Biscuit Jar, Blue & White Fox Hunt Scene, Silver Plated Lid & Bail, Marked, 6½ In.	36
Punch Bowl, Blue, Fairy Villas, Staffordshire, Late 1800s, 7½ x 13¾ In. .... *illus*	176

A. Walter, Bowl, Lizard, Pulled Feather, Iridescent Peacock Eye, Signed, 8 x 4 In.
$5,843

Morphy Auctions

Adams, Biscuit Barrel, Jasperware, Silver Plated Lid, Handle, Blue & White, Swags, c.1900, 7 In., Pair
$128

Neal Auction Company

Adams, Punch Bowl, Blue, Fairy Villas, Staffordshire, Late 1800s, 7½ x 13¾ In.
$176

Jeffrey S. Evans & Associates

ADVERTISING

Advertising, Banner, Sideshow, Mysterious, Magician, Props, Painted Canvas, c.1930, 86 x 112 In. $2,125

Eldred's

Advertising, Box, Post Grape-Nuts Flakes, Baseball Cards On Back, Mickey Mantle, c.1960, 10 x 7 In. $460

AntiqueAdvertising.com

Advertising, Cabinet, Diamond Dyes, Children With Balloon, Embossed, Tin, 24½ x 15¼ In. $915

Wm Morford Auctions

ADVERTISING containers and products sold in the old country store are now all collectibles. These stores, with crackers in a barrel and a potbellied stove, are a symbol of an earlier, less hectic time. Listed here are many advertising items. Other similar pieces may be found under the product name, such as Planters Peanuts. We have tried to list items in logical places, so enameled tin dishes will be found under Graniteware, auto-related items in the Auto category, paper items in the Paper category, etc. Store fixtures, cases, signs, and other items that have no advertising as part of the decoration are listed in the Store category. The early Dr Pepper logo included a period after "Dr," but it was dropped in 1950. We list all Dr Pepper items without a period so they alphabetize together. For more prices, go to kovels.com.

Ad, Everett Pianos, Santa Claus, Children Climbing Ladder, Die Cut, Frame, 13 x 16 In.	840
Anvil, Oliver Tractor 1929, 2½ x 4½ In.	24
Ashtray, Bell Hop, Cast Iron, Carved, Painted, 39 In.	148
Banner, Shoe, Dorothy Dodd Shoe, Faultless Fitting, Paper On Fabric, Victorian, 57 x 40 In.	339
Banner, Sideshow, Mysterious, Magician, Props, Painted Canvas, c.1930, 86 x 112 In. *illus*	2125
Barrel, Compliments Of Guskys, Cast Iron, Nicol Company, Il., c.1890	582
Beer Mug, Budweiser, Clydesdales, Wagon, Snowy Woodlands, 1981, 6½ In.	90
Bench, Brown Shoes, Oak, Scrolled Shape, Cabriole Legs, Early 1900s, 36 x 17 x 58 In.	540
Bicycle Cart, St. Louis Post Dispatch, 20 x 48 x 22 In.	60
Billhook, Parrott Brothers, Trademark Bird, Celluloid, 6¾ In.	153
Bin, Coffee, Celebrated Boston Roasted, Dwinell-Wright Co., Tin, Logo, 21 In.	360
Bin, Coffee, Woolson Spice Companies, Lion, Pine, Slant Hinged Lid, c.1910, 33 x 21 x 22 In.	254
Bin, Diamond Coffees, Metal, Thomson & Taylor Spice Co., c.1890, 22 x 48 x 18 In.	198
Books may be included in the Paper category.	
Bottles are list in the Bottle category.	
Bottle Openers are listed in the Bottle Opener category.	
Box, see also Box category.	
Box, Askew Saddlery Co., Kansas City, Wood, Hinged Lid, c.1910, 19½ x 17 x 32 In.	448
Box, Baum's Castorine, Wood, Paper Labels On 4 Sides, Slide Lid, 50 Lbs., 11 x 22 x 12 In.	51
Box, Breakfast Blend Coffee, Wood, Patina, Toledo, Ohio, 28 x 19 x 16 In.	59
Box, Coffee, Dwinell-Wright Co., No. 44 Blend, Wood, Paper Labels, c.1890, 21 x 15 In.	215
Box, Fairbank's Pure White Floating Soap, Wood, Gold Letters, c.1900s, 8 x 17 x 16 In.	240
Box, Fairmont Dam Waterworks, Schuylkill, Wood, Paper Covered, Engraving, 5¾ In.	236
Box, Post Grape-Nuts Flakes, Baseball Cards On Back, Mickey Mantle, c.1960, 10 x 7 In. *illus*	460
Bucket, Pay Car Tobacco, Wood, Paper Label, Daniel Scotten Co., 12⅜ x 13¾ In.	283
Cabinet, Diamond Dyes, Children With Balloon, Embossed, Tin, 24½ x 15¼ In. *illus*	915
Cabinet, Diamond Dyes, Maypole, Tin Panel, Embossed, 29¾ x 10 x 23 In. *illus*	1829
Cabinet, Humphrey's Veterinary, Wood, Embossed, 27½ x 21 x 7¼ In.	5428
Cabinet, Peerless Dye, Maple, Ash, Roll-Up Back, 21½ x 15 In. *illus*	311
Cabinet, Richardson's Wash Silks, Cherry, Reverse Painted Glass, 33 x 25 x 7 In. *illus*	283
Cabinet, Spool, Clark's O.N.T. Spool Cotton, 6 Drawers, Walnut, 22 x 29 x 19 In.	212
Cabinet, Spool, Clark's O.N.T. Spool Cotton, 4 Drawers, Oak, Gold, Black, 16 x 22 x 15 In. *illus*	545
Cabinet, Spool, Corticelli Silk, Oak, 13 Drawers, Mirror, 35 x 24 x 17½ In.	848
Cabinet, Spool, Goff's Best Braid, Walnut, 3 Drawers, 12 x 18 In.	224
Cabinet, Spool, J. & P. Coats', 26 Drawers, 2 Turned Wood Columns, 2 x 26 x 19¼ In.	732
Cabinet, Spool, John J. Clark's Spool Cotton, Oak, 9 x 21 x 15 In. *illus*	266
Calendars are listed in the Calendar category.	
Can, Wax Beans, New York State Goods, Erie Preserving Co., Barge, Train, 4½ In. *illus*	212
Canisters, see introductory paragraph to Tins in this category.	
Cards are listed in the Card category.	
Case, Display, Dr. M.A. Simmons Liver Medicine, Oak, Glass Shelves, c.1910, 31 x 15 x 15 In. *illus*	509
Case, Display, Freihofer's Quality Cakes, Metal, Glass, Counter, c.1920, 28 x 15 x 17 In.	452
Case, Display, Kiss-Me Gum, Glass Panels, Metal Frame, 9¾ x 16 x 7 In.	270
Case, Display, Paris Garters, Oak, Glass, 2 Garter Boxes, Counter, 16 x 15 In.	283
Case, Display, The Sun, Garters, Wood, Bow Front Glass, Counter, 11 x 8 x 7 In. *illus*	570
Chalkboard, J.C. Penney Co., Metal, Wood Frame, Black Paint, c.1915, 25¾ x 29¾ In.	226
Change Receiver, see Tip Tray in this category.	
Cigar Cutter, Betsy Ross, 5 Cent, A.S. Valentine & Son, Philadelphia, Early 1900s, 7½ In.	510

Advertising, Cabinet, Diamond Dyes, Maypole, Tin Panel, Embossed, 29¾ x 10 x 23 In.
$1,829

Wm Morford Auctions

Advertising, Cabinet, Peerless Dye, Maple, Ash, Roll-Up Back, 21½ x 15 In.
$311

Rich Penn Auctions

Advertising, Cabinet, Richardson's Wash Silks, Cherry, Reverse Painted Glass, 33 x 25 x 7 In.
$283

Rich Penn Auctions

Advertising, Cabinet, Spool, Clark's O.N.T. Spool Cotton, 4 Drawers, Oak, Gold, Black, 16 x 22 x 15 In.
$545

Fontaine's Auction Gallery

TIP
Advertising collectors should check every address, phone number, name, and price information that is on a label, a sticker, or the container. They will help with the research to determine the age of the product.

Advertising, Cabinet, Spool, John J. Clark's Spool Cotton, Oak, 9 x 21 x 15 In.
$266

Hess Auction Group

Advertising, Can, Wax Beans, New York State Goods, Erie Preserving Co., Barge, Train, 4½ In.
$212

AntiqueAdvertising.com

Advertising, Case, Display, Dr. M.A. Simmons Liver Medicine, Oak, Glass Shelves, c.1910, 31 x 15 x 15 In.
$509

Rich Penn Auctions

Advertising, Case, Display, The Sun, Garters, Wood, Bow Front Glass, Counter, 11 x 8 x 7 In.
$570

Morphy Auctions

Advertising, Cigar Cutter, Iron, Tirador, Scrollwork, Spanish Made, Brunhoff Mfg. Co., 7 x 10 x 9 In.
$840

Morphy Auctions

Advertising, Cigar Cutter, Marksman, Older Man, Red, Orange, Gold, Brunoff Mfg. Co., 5 x 8 x 6 In.
$510

Morphy Auctions

Advertising, Cooler, Eskimo Pie, Magic Jar, Metal, Eskimo Figures Feet, c.1930, 15½ In.
$1,808

Rich Penn Auctions

Advertising, Dispenser, Rochester Root Beer, Stoneware, Lid, Spigot, 12½ In.
$396

Rich Penn Auctions

Advertising, Display, Alka-Seltzer, Uncle Ezra Says Try It!, Tin Lithograph, 17 x 7½ x 9 In.
$424

Fontaine's Auction Gallery

Advertising, Display, Big Boy, Fiberglass, Brown Base, Burger On Plate, 56½ x 28½ x 28½ In.
$1,353

Morphy Auctions

Advertising, Display, Hamburglar, Fiberglass, Wood Base, 44 x 27 x 24 In.
$3,075

Morphy Auctions

Advertising, Display, Nobel's Sporting Ammunition, Glasgow & London, 29 x 20 In.
$4,920

Morphy Auctions

Advertising, Display, Poll-Parrot, Shoes, Chalkware, Pair Of Children's Rubbers, 12½ x 7 In.
$113

Rich Penn Auctions

Advertising, Display, Sucker, Watta Pop, Figural Polar Bear, 8½ x 5½ In.
$226

Rich Penn Auctions

Cigar Cutter, Cast Metal, Engraved, Levers, Roi Tan, c.1916, 7¾ x 5 x 4¾ In.	250
Cigar Cutter, Iron, Fernandez Hermano, Scrollwork, Marked, Brunhoff Mfg., 9½ x 5 x 6 In. .	1020
Cigar Cutter, Iron, Tirador, Scrollwork, Spanish Made, Brunhoff Mfg. Co., 7 x 10 x 9 In. *illus*	840
Cigar Cutter, Marksman, Older Man, Red, Orange, Gold, Brunhoff Mfg. Co., 5 x 8 x 6 In. *illus*	510
Clocks are listed in the Clock category.	
Cooler, Eskimo Pie, Magic Jar, Metal, Eskimo Figures Feet, c.1930, 15½ In. .... *illus*	1808
Cooler, Frozen Powerhouse Brand Candy Bars, White, Red, Embossed Metal, 6½ x 15 x 8 In....	2832
Corkscrew, Anheuser-Busch, Walker's Self-Puller, Bell Style, Steel Shaft, 5½ x 3¾ In.	11
Dispenser, Buckeye Root Beer, Stoneware, Tree Trunk, 15½ In.	339
Dispenser, Cardinal Cherry, Green, Cherry Branches, J. Hungerford Smith Co., c.1910, 13 In. .	5664
Dispenser, Fowler's Cherry Smash Syrup, Ruby Red Glass, White Base, Lid, c.1940, 12½ In.	648
Dispenser, Fowler's Cherry Smash, Lid, Dark Red Glass, Chrome Base, c.1940, 15 x 7 In.	324
Dispenser, Hunter's Root Beer Syrup, Lid, Black Text, c.1940, 12¼ x 5½ In.	252
Dispenser, Jim Dandy Root Beer, Soda Fountain, Pump, Hand Painted, 14½ x 9½ In.............	4920
Dispenser, Rochester Root Beer, Stoneware, Lid, Spigot, 12½ In. .... *illus*	396
Dispenser, Soda Fountain, Round Purple Globe, Brass Pump, Counter, 10 x 15 In.	1080
Dispenser, Ward's Orange Crush, Porcelain, Metal Pump, 14½ In.............................	1140
Display, Alka-Seltzer, Uncle Ezra Says Try It!, Tin Lithograph, 17 x 7½ x 9 In. .... *illus*	424
Display, Big Boy, Fiberglass, Brown Base, Burger On Plate, 56½ x 28½ x 28½ In............ *illus*	1353
Display, Blue Label Sign, Beer Bottle, Reverse Glass, Wood Base, Counter, 1950, 9 x 15 x 3 In....	180
Display, Boyemaco, Curtain Fixtures, All Sizes, Mechanical, Oak Case, 16 In............................	59
Display, Cow Ease, Tin Lithograph, Red, Stand, Sprayer, 34¼ x 11 x 16 In.	2006
Display, Eastside Old Tap, Waterfall Motion, Plastic & Cardboard, 1950, 12½ In.	324
Display, Hamburglar, Fiberglass, Wood Base, 44 x 27 x 24 In................................ *illus*	3075
Display, Life Savers, Candy, Counter, Glass, Metal, 3 Tiers, 9½ x 9 x 12 In.	113
Display, Life Savers, Tin Lithograph, 2-Tier Shelf, Glass Panels, 7 x 21 x 9¾ In.	121
Display, Lutted's S.P. Cough Drops, Log Cabin, Handles, Amber Pattern Glass, 7 x 8 x 5 In.......	48
Display, M&M Character, Blue, Fiberglass & Plastic, 54 In.................................	94
Display, National Mazda Lamps, 5 Colored Bulbs, Tin Lithograph, 11 x 17 x 5½ In.	1187
Display, Nobel's Sporting Ammunition, Glasgow & London, 29 x 20 In. .... *illus*	4920
Display, Pabst Blue Ribbon, Barkeep, PBR Bottle, Electric, 13 x 10 x 6 In....................	157
Display, Peanuts, B & W, Salted In The Shell, Fresh, Hot, 16 x 10½ x 14 In.	339
Display, Poll-Parrot, Shoes, Chalkware, Pair Of Children's Rubbers, 12½ x 7 In............... *illus*	113
Display, Quaker Oats Puffed Wheat, Babe Ruth, Hey Kids Join My Baseball Club, 1934, 20 x 31 In.	924
Display, Star, Egg Carrier & Trays, Wood, 1906, 16 x 23 In..................................	230
Display, Sucker, Watta Pop, Figural Polar Bear, 8½ x 5½ In.......................... *illus*	226
Display, Toothbrush, Dr. West's, Miracle Tuft, Red, 18 In...................................	59
Display, Wrigley's Chewing Gum, Metal Lithograph, Hole For Hanging, 6 x 17 In.	198
Dolls are listed in the Doll category.	
Door Push, Come In, Drink Orange Crush, Bottle, Embossed, Tin Lithograph, 12¼ x 3⅛ In. ..	531
Door Push, Drink!, Green Spot Orangeade Beverage, Tin, Decal, Orange Border, 11½ In........	165
Door Push, Orange Crush, Come Again, Thank You, Green, Orange, Yellow, Porcelain, 9½ In.	561
Door Push, Star Naptha Washing Powder, Porcelain, Yellow, Black Text, 6¼ In. .... *illus*	153
Door Push, Vicks VapoRub, Red, Blue Text, Gray Border, Porcelain, 6½ In.	177
Door Push, Wear Finck's Detroit-Special Overalls, Pig, Embossed, Tin, 7 x 3 In. .... *illus*	1416
Fans are listed in the Fan category.	
Figure, Big Boy, Fiberglass, Brown Base, Burger On Plate, 80 In.	9000
Figure, Brownie, Kodak Brownie Camera, Wood, Composition, Clothing, 41 In.	2040
Figure, Burger Beer, The Favorite, Horse, Wood, Rubber, 15 In................................	83
Figure, Drambuie, Prince Charlie, Resin Type Material, Holding Green Cap, 16 In.	71
Figure, Labatt Beer, Man, Standing, 50 On Shirt, Resin Type Material, Round Base, 14 In.......	307
Figure, Mayor McCheese, Fiberglass, Green Leaves Base, 1970, 67 x 34 In....................	3300
Figure, Ronald McDonald, Fiberglass, Red & Yellow, 80½ x 32 In..........................	3000
Figure, Schmidt's, Man Holding 2 Mugs Of Beer, Die Cast, 12 In......................... *illus*	94
Flashlight, Eveready, Felix The Cat, Painted Wood, c.1930, 16 x 27 In..........................	708
Frame, Colonial Club, 5 Cent Cigar, Woman, Big Hat, Early 1800s, 19 x 5 In.	240
Ice Cream Cup, Dairy Queen, Dennis The Menace, Wax Coated, 1969, 3 x 3 In.	18
Iron, Jos. M. Hayes Woolen Co., St. Louis, 3½ In. .... *illus*	180
Jar, Shaker, Blanke's Aerial Globe Pure Spice, Globe Shape, c.1904, 4 In.	39

Advertising, Door Push, Star Naptha
Washing Powder, Porcelain, Yellow,
Black Text, 6¼ In.
$153

Milestone Auctions

Advertising, Door Push, Wear Finck's
Detroit-Special Overalls, Pig, Embossed,
Tin, 7 x 3 In.
$1,416

Wm Morford Auctions

Advertising, Figure, Schmidt's, Man
Holding 2 Mugs Of Beer, Die Cast, 12 In.
$94

Milestone Auctions

A

Advertising, Iron, Jos. M. Hayes Woolen Co., St. Louis, 3 ½ In.
$180

Hartzell's Auction Gallery, Inc.

Advertising, Mirror, Garden City Tailoring Co., Birthstones In Outer Rim, Pocket, c.1920, 2 ⅛ In.
$20

Hake's Auctions

Advertising, Mirror, Got A Headache?, Caf-Fee-No Will Cure It, Bulldog, Celluloid, Oval, 2 x 1 In.
$1,711

Wm Morford Auctions

Tin Trays

The tin advertising tray was first used in the 1880s and is still popular.

Lamps are listed in the Lamp category.	
Lantern, Campbell's Soup, Electric, 1-Light, Hanging, 16 x 9¾ In.	59
Lunch Boxes are also listed in the Lunch Box category.	
Maquette, Mayor McCheese, McDonald's, c.1970, 11 x 15 In.	384

Advertising mirrors of all sizes are listed here. Pocket mirrors range in size from 1 ½ to 5 inches in diameter. Most of these mirrors were given away as advertising promotions and include the name of the company in the design.

Mirror, Garden City Tailoring Co., Birthstones In Outer Rim, Pocket, c.1920, 2 ⅛ In. .... *illus*	20
Mirror, Got A Headache?, Caf-Fee-No Will Cure It, Bulldog, Celluloid, Oval, 2 x 1 In. .... *illus*	1711
Mirror, Humane Horse Collar Co., Celluloid, Oval, 2¾ x 2 In.	45
Mirror, International Shirt & Collar Co., Oriental, Celluloid, Fraternal Theme, 2 In. .... *illus*	177
Mirror, Schaeffer Pianos, Celluloid, Green, Yellow, Parisian Novelty, c.1910, 2¼ In.	64
Mirror, Smith & Sons, Road Making Machinery, Celluloid, c.1900, 4 In.	230
Mirror, Ward Commission Co., Livestock, Pocket, 2¼ In.	141
Mug, Mustache, Jack Daniel's, Old No. 7, Green Vines, 1970s, 3½ In.	15
Pails are also listed in the Lunch Box category.	
Pail, Jackie Coogan, Peanut Butter, Tin Lithograph, Bail Handle, 1 Lb., 3½ In. .... *illus*	142
Pail, Toyland Peanut Butter, Circus Parade, Band, Children, Tin Litho, Pond Co., Lb., 4 x 3 In.	130
Pencil Clip, Drink Regal Beer Text, Round, Red, c.1950	6
Pennant, L.F. Eckert, Dealer, Dodge Bros. & Ford Brand Autos, Triangular, 28¼ x 11 In.	1593
Pin, Anderson Water & Lightning Conductor, House, Slogans, c.1910, 1¾ In.	118
Pin, Bison, American Commission Co., South Omaha, Sioux City, Chicago, Celluloid, 1¾ In.	141
Pin, Celluloid, Famous Stock Saddle, Signed, J.H. Wilson Saddlery Co., 1¼ In.	205
Pin, Central Livestock Market, Kansas City, Cattle, Sheep, Horse, Celluloid, c.1900, 2 In.	205
Pin, Delegate, Convention National Livestock Assoc., Celluloid, Ribbon, 1899, 6½ x 2 In.	90
Pin, Delegate, Metal, National Livestock, Ribbon, Gilt, Longhorn, 1903, 4½ x 2 In.	352
Pin, Hershey Park, Back Paper, Young Child, Cocoa Bean, Pinback, c.1906, 1¼ In. .... *illus*	118
Pin, Lone Star Bar Pin, Longhorns, Stripe, Panther, Engraved, 3 x 2¾ In.	288
Pin, Longhorn, Belt Railroad & Stock Yards Co., Indianapolis, Ribbon, c.1904, 4½ x 2 In.	205
Pin, Longhorn, Metal, Cattle & Horse Growers Assoc., Ribbon, 1904, 5 x 2 In.	115
Pin, Montana Stock Growers, Gilded, Figural Steer's Head, Ribbon, 1921, 4 x 1½ In.	102
Pin, Ship Livestock To Wood Bros., Celluloid, Pig Nursing Litter, c.1900, 2 In.	58
Pin, Sioux City Stock Yards, Indian, Headdress, Celluloid, Whitehead & Hoag, 1¾ In.	448
Pin, St. Paul Winter Carnival, King Boreas, Brown & Bigelow, c.1939, 1¾ In.	15
Pin, Wichita Livestock Exchange, Celluloid Button, Red, Gold, Ribbon, 1901, 6 x 2 In.	58
Pitcher, Tang, Swirl Shape, Orange Plastic Top, Anchor Hocking, c.1965, Qt., 9 In.	21
Plaque, Ronald McDonald, Reclining, Red, Yellow, White, 1970s, 5 x 3 In.	2040
Pot Scraper, Kewpie Soap, National Soap Co., Kewpie Pictured, Blue, White, 2½ x 3 In.	128
Rack, Sunshine Biscuit Co., Metal, 4 Tiers, Tin Lids, 1900s, 39¾ x 30½ x 15 In.	123
Rack, Western Union, Telegraph Blanks, Everywhere, 9¼ x 9 In.	90
Salt & Pepper Shakers are listed in the Salt & Pepper category.	
Scales are listed in the Scale category.	
Sign, 7-20-4 Cigar, Famous For Quality, Red, R.G. Sullivan's, Porcelain, 10¾ x 23 In.	510
Sign, 7Up Likes You, Clerk Holding Case, Cardboard, Counter, c.1948, 12 x 10 In.	132
Sign, 7Up, Lighted Motion, Plastic & Metal Housing, 1950, 12½ x 10½ x 4 In.	360
Sign, A. Nauy & Son Confectioner, Rectangular, Black Molding, 1800s, 17 x 32 In.	400
Sign, Arents, Luggage Shop, Charles Legros, France, c.1930, 40 x 25¾ In.	288
Sign, Aviation, Sinclair Aircraft, Porcelain, 2-Sided, c.1930, 48 In.	17700
Sign, Ballantine, America's Finest Beer, Tin, 1950, 9 x 3½ In.	216
Sign, Billiard & Pool Parlor, Pointing Hand, Painted, E.F. Day, c.1900s, 77 In.	1845
Sign, Brandywine Inn, Entertainment For Men & Horse, Painted, 1900s, 26 x 41 In.	138
Sign, Brasserie Lengrand, Frog, Barstool, Beer, Photolitho, Frame, 1926, 40½ x 36½ In.	468
Sign, Broadside, Louisiana Brand Hams, Sugar Cured, Pig, Chromolithograph, 1800s, 11 x 21 In.	425
Sign, Brown's Jumbo Bread Elephant, Tin, Die Cut, 13 x 15½ In.	677
Sign, Buckeye Beer, Tin, Old Man & Dog, American Art Works Inc., 1950s, 15½ x 20 In.	360
Sign, Budweiser Beer, Bottle, Glass Of Beer, Tray, Tin Lithograph, Frame, 15 x 12 In. .... *illus*	106
Sign, Budweiser, Glass & Bottle Image, Embossed Metal, Self-Framed, 18 x 54½ In.	961
Sign, Buzz Buzz Electric, Cartoon, Tin Litho, Bumblebee, P.D. Eller, 24 x 29 In.	545
Sign, C.H. Wilbur, Dentist, Gilt Letters, Smalted Background, Late 1800s, 17½ x 37 In.	400

Advertising, Mirror, International Shirt & Collar Co., Oriental, Celluloid, Fraternal Theme, 2 In.
$177

AntiqueAdvertising.com

Advertising, Pail, Jackie Coogan, Peanut Butter, Tin Lithograph, Bail Handle, 1 Lb., 3½ In.
$142

AntiqueAdvertising.com

Advertising, Pin, Hershey Park, Back Paper, Young Child, Cocoa Bean, Pinback, c.1906, 1¼ In.
$118

Hake's Auctions

Advertising, Sign, Budweiser Beer, Bottle, Glass Of Beer, Tray, Tin Lithograph, Frame, 15 x 12 In.
$106

Milestone Auctions

Advertising, Sign, California Fair, Woman At Fair, Embossed, Cardboard, 1907, 22 x 13 In.
$767

Wm Morford Auctions

Advertising, Sign, Cincinnati Stove Works, Cast Iron, Woman, On Horse, 2-Sided, Early 1900s, 40 In.
$6,531

Skinner, Inc.

Advertising, Sign, Davis' Pain Killer, Medicine Bottle, People, Tin Lithograph, c.1890, 22 x 28 In.
$3,218

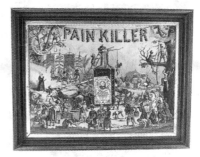

Glass Works Auctions

Advertising, Sign, Dawn Donuts, There's A Difference, Celluloid Over Cardboard, Bastian Bros., 6 x 11 In.
$484

AntiqueAdvertising.com

Advertising, Sign, Dell Comics Are Good Comics, Bookrack Topper, Tin Litho, Late 1940s, 5 x 15 In.
$331

Hake's Auctions

Advertising, Sign, Drink Howel's Root Beer, Embossed, Metal, American Art Works, 24 In.
$509

Rich Penn Auctions

Advertising, Sign, Eveready Flashlights, Hanging From Flashlight, Tin Lithograph, 2-Sided, 10 x 11 In.
$6,254

Wm Morford Auctions

Advertising, Sign, H.V. Dalling, Watchmaker, Painted, Carved Wood, 47 x 34 In.
$1,000

Leslie Hindman Auctioneers

Advertising, Sign, Ice Cream Cone, 3-D, High Relief, Carved, 1900s, 30 ½ x 12 ½ x 9 In.
$500

Rago Arts and Auction Center

Advertising, Sign, It's Always Pure Hires Root Beer, Woman Holding Glass, Black Frame, 15 x 21 In.
$960

Morphy Auctions

Advertising, Sign, J. Kinros, Instrument Maker's Shop, Sextant & Telescope Shape, 1900s, 58 In.
$1,680

Northeast Auctions

Advertising, Sign, Johnny Rockets, Neon Lighting, Side Metal, McBride Co., c.1998, 50 x 53 x 13 In.
$1,210

Fontaine's Auction Gallery

Advertising, Sign, Kellogg's Corn Flakes, Oh! Look Who's Here, Baby, Tin Litho, 2-Sided, 19 x 13 In.
$7,906

Wm Morford Auctions

Advertising, Sign, Nabisco, Made As He Says, Uncle Sam Holding Boxes, Paper Litho, Frame, 34 x 24 In.
$4,484

Wm Morford Auctions

Sign, California Fair, Woman At Fair, Embossed, Cardboard, 1907, 22 x 13 In. .... *illus* 767
Sign, Campbell's Condensed Tomato Soup, Can, Enameled Porcelain, USA, 22 x 12 In. 1765
Sign, Cardboard, Canoe Club Beverage, Kemper Thomas Co., Tin Frame, 1918, 14 x 30 In. 540
Sign, Carhartt Overalls, Flange, Tin Lithograph, Die Cut, 2-Sided, 18½ x 17¾ x 1¾ In. 6136
Sign, Centlivre's, Nickel Plate Bottled Beer, Railroad Interior, c.1910, 26 x 21 In. 254
Sign, Chesterfield Cigarettes, Portraits, 6 Baseball Stars, Cardboard, 1948, 20 x 18 In. 472
Sign, Chew Polar Bear, Luhrman & Wilbern Tobacco Co., Cardboard, 2-Sided, Frame, 12 x 9 In. 1888
Sign, Chisholm Handcrafted Boots, Cowboys, Yellow, Black, Neon, 28 x 27 x 7½ In. 462
Sign, Christian Diehl Brewery, Indian Maiden In Stream, Moonlight, Litho, 19 x 16 In. 660
Sign, Cigar, Cast Iron, Glass Beads, Havana, c.1920s, 60 x 8 In. 582
Sign, Cigars & Tobacco, Wood, Black Paint, Gold Letters, Rectangular, 17 x 39 In. 1180
Sign, Cincinnati Stove Works, Cast Iron, Woman, On Horse, 2-Sided, Early 1900s, 40 In... *illus* 6531
Sign, Colman's Mustard, Polar Bear, Toothache, Yellow, Blue, 1930s, 30 x 20 In. 225
Sign, Columbia Ignitor, Dry Cell Battery, Figural, Tin Litho, Store Display, 27 x 20 In. 4366
Sign, Consult Chular & Anwor, Safe & Special, Wood, Early 1900s, 11½ x 13¼ In. 312
Sign, Crockery, L.C. Baker, Gray Ground, White Lettering, 1800s, 6 x 169 In. 220
Sign, Custer's Last Fight, Anheuser-Busch, Lithograph, Wood Frame, 32 x 42 In. 1239
Sign, Daisy Quinine Hair Tonic, Tin Lithograph, Buerger Bros., 9¾ x 9 In. 151
Sign, Dakota Maid Flour, Female American Indian, Cardboard, Die Cut, 39 x 16 In. 150
Sign, Davis' Pain Killer, Medicine Bottle, People, Tin Lithograph, c.1890, 22 x 28 In. .... *illus* 3218
Sign, Dawn Donuts, There's A Difference, Celluloid Over Cardboard, Bastian Bros., 6 x 11 In. .*illus* 484
Sign, Dell Comics Are Good Comics, Bookrack Topper, Tin Litho, Late 1940s, 5 x 15 In..... *illus* 331
Sign, Destila Cigarettes, Linen Back, Print By Unie-Praha, c.1960, 25 x 37½ In. 115
Sign, Dimsdale Hotel & Bar Entrance, Metal, Shield, Brass, 37½ x 28 In. 390
Sign, Dr. Brown Osteopathic Physician, Wood, Oval, McKeen, 20½ x 41½ In. 590
Sign, Dr. Hyman, Painless Dentist, Yellow Background, No Pain, Sheet Tin, Phila., 19½ In..... 118
Sign, Drink Howel's Root Beer, Embossed, Metal, American Art Works, 24 In. .... *illus* 509
Sign, Drink Wonder Orange, Tin, Cardboard, Litho, Donaldson Art Sign Co., 6 x 9 In. 363
Sign, Dutch Boy Paint Is On The Job, Boy On Ladder, Tin, Donaldson Art Sign, 24 x 36 In. 173
Sign, Early Times Distillery, Kentucky Bourbon Whiskey, Wood Frame, 46 x 37 In. 452
Sign, Eisenlohr's Cinco Cigars, Wood, Painted, Yellow, Red Script, 12½ x 48 In. 561
Sign, Eldorado Music Hall, Woman, 2 Clowns, Black & Gold Frame, 23 x 16 In. 561
Sign, Erin Brew, Wall Hanging, Green Background, Light-Up, 1950, 5 x 10 x 3 In. 252
Sign, Eveready Flashlights, Hanging From Flashlight, Tin Lithograph, 2-Sided, 10 x 11 In. . *illus* 6254
Sign, F.W. Woolworth Co., Reverse Painted, Red, Gold Leaf, Glass, 13 x 71 x 23 In. 908
Sign, Fountain Tobacco, Tin, 4 Vignettes, Lovell & Buffington, 1800s, 28¾ x 21 In. 990
Sign, Frank's Antiques, What's Old I'll Buy It, Sheet Tin, N.Y., 12 x 25 In. 83
Sign, Frostie, Root Beer, Bearded Man Holding Bottle, Crown Cap Shape, Tin, 1950, 12½ In. .. 504
Sign, Gold Bond Stamps, Embossed Metal, 48 x 96 In. 509
Sign, Golden Weeding Coffee, Ennis Hanley Blackburn Coffee Co., Frame, 32 x 33 In. 226
Sign, Grain Belt, Neon, 2 Colors, Everbrite Electric Sign Co., 14½ x 25 In. 198
Sign, Grape-Nuts, To School Well Fed, St. Bernard Dog, Girl, 30 x 20 In. 678
Sign, Grapette Soda, Embossed, Die Cut, Metal, Self-Framed, 16 x 27 In. 339
Sign, H.V. Dalling, Watchmaker, Painted, Carved Wood, 47 x 34 In. .... *illus* 1000
Sign, Hamburglar, McDonald's, Glass Panel, Etched, c.1980, 40 x 42 In. 192
Sign, Hamm's, Neon, Beer Glasses Light-Up, 24 x 36 In. 848
Sign, Hamm's, Starry Night, Twinkling Stars, Beer Glass Constellations, c.1960, 19 x 16 In...... 792
Sign, Harvey Laundry Co., Enamel, Black Background, 2-Sided, Flange, 20 x 12 In. 4838
Sign, HGC, Tin, Embossed, Yellow, Black Letters, Acme Chemical Mfg. Co., 9¾ x 7 In. 151
Sign, Hires Root Beer, Embossed, Metal, Self-Framed, 9¾ x 27½ In. 622
Sign, Hotel, Painted, Wood Panel, Chamfer Corners, Black Background, 11 x 54 x 1 In. 363
Sign, Ice Cream Cone, 3-D, High Relief, Carved, 1900s, 30½ x 12½ x 9 In. .... *illus* 500
Sign, It's Always Pure Hires Root Beer, Woman Holding Glass, Black Frame, 15 x 21 In..... *illus* 960
Sign, J. Kinros, Instrument Maker's Shop, Sextant & Telescope Shape, 1900s, 58 In. .... *illus* 1680
Sign, John Deere Syracuse Chilled Plows, Embossed, Painted, Tin, 1920s, 17⅜ x 29⅞ In. 357
Sign, Johnny Rockets, Neon Lighting, Side Metal, McBride Co., c.1998, 50 x 53 x 13 In...... *illus* 1210
Sign, Kellogg's Corn Flakes, Oh! Look Who's Here, Baby, Tin Litho, 2-Sided, 19 x 13 In. ..... *illus* 7906
Sign, King Leaf Cigars, Cigar Shape, Carved, Painted, Wood, 1800s, 25 x 3½ In. 1652
Sign, Kingfisch Lock Service, Locksmith, Fish Shape, 1940s, 41 In. 420

Advertising, Sign, Oh Boy Gum, Tin Litho, Ebonized Frame, H.D. Beach Co., 15½ x 7¼ x 1 In.
$424

Fontaine's Auction Gallery

Advertising, Sign, Pan Am, Blue, White, Enamel, Convex, 1900s, 24 In.
$5,310

Wm Morford Auctions

Advertising, Sign, Smells Grand, Packs Right, Smokes Sweet, Can't Bite, Embossed, 1950s, 26 x 16 In.
$131

Hake's Auctions

Advertising, Sign, Solemn Pig, John P. Squire & Co., Mayer & Lavenson Co., Tin, 21 x 17 In.
$720

Morphy Auctions

Advertising, Sign, SWP Cover The Earth, Sherwin-Williams, Enamel, Embossed, 35 x 18 In.
$2,360

Wm Morford Auctions

Advertising, Sign, Thirsty? Just Whistle, Early Style Bottle, Embossed, Tin Lithograph, 7 x 9¾ In.
$1,475

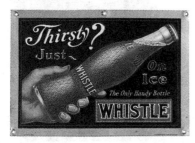

Wm Morford Auctions

Advertising, Sign, Welch's Grape Juice, Tin Over Cardboard, Easel Back, Grapes, Bottle, 6 x 9 In.
$425

AntiqueAdvertising.com

Advertising, Sink, Crane Co., Phila., Pa., Figural, Ceramic, Salesman's Sample, 1904, 3 x 5 In.
$212

AntiqueAdvertising.com

TIP

Any lithographed can with a picture is of more value than a lithographed can with just names. Any paper-labeled can that can be dated before 1875 is rare. Any ad that pictures an American flag or a black person has added value.

Advertising, Spinner, Dr. Daniels' Medicines, Cure Your Horses & Cattle, Hand, Pointing, Tin Litho, 1 x 3 In.
$1,487

AntiqueAdvertising.com

Advertising, Stand, Smoking, Moxie, Hitchie, Butler, Tin Ashtray, Wood, Painted, 32 x 6 In.
$679

Wm Morford Auctions

Advertising, Tin, Cadette Talc, Soldier, Deep Blue, Lithograph, N.J., 7⅜ In.
$661

AntiqueAdvertising.com

Advertising, Tin, Roly Poly, Dixie Queen Tobacco, Satisfied Customer, Pipe, 7 x 6 In.
$1,227

AntiqueAdvertising.com

Sign, Knox Boy Jr., Fancy Gilt Lettering, Black Smalt Ground, Late 1800s, 49 ½ In.		185
Sign, Lightning Mouse Trap, Tin, Embossed, Cardboard, Multicolor Graphics, 6 ⅜ x 9 ½ In.		2242
Sign, Live Lobster, Seafood, Beaver House, Painted, Wood, Frame, Pa., 26 x 37 In.		254
Sign, Marquette Club Ginger Ale, Man, Bottle, Dimensional Eyes, 1940s, 11 ½ In.		58
Sign, Mastercraft Pipes, Man Smoking, Paper, Wood, Painted, 9 x 12 In.		68
Sign, McCormick-Deering Corn Machines, Equipment, Paper Litho, 1931, 31 ⅞ x 21 ⅞ In.		1003
Sign, McDonaldland, Train, Tunnel, Goblins, Hamburger Patch, Canvas, 9 x 4 Ft.		600
Sign, Montana Power, Metal, Red Yellow Block Lettering, 2-Sided, 20 x 36 In.		390
Sign, Mule-Hide Roofs, Painted, Sheet Metal, Raised Lettering, Logo, 11 ½ x 21 ¾ In.		150
Sign, Munyon's, Headache Cure, Home Remedies, Metal, 2-Sided, c.1890, 18 ½ x 4 ½ In.		1652
Sign, N.E. Rum Crystal Spring Distillery, Felton & Son, c.1885, 18 x 24 In.		1680
Sign, Nabisco, Made As He Says, Uncle Sam Holding Boxes, Paper Litho, Frame, 34 x 24 In. *illus*		4484
Sign, Nate Colton Stables, Wood, Painted, Frame, 15 x 43 In.		266
Sign, Niagara Shoes, For Youthful Feet, Metal, American Art Works, 19 x 9 In.		311
Sign, Norman Stoves & Ranges, L.J. Macy, Painted, Yellow Background, 48 x 6 In.		130
Sign, Odorofilat, Formula Unica, Woman Holding Flowers, Argentina, 43 x 29 In.		83
Sign, Oh Boy Gum, Tin Litho, Ebonized Frame, H.D. Beach Co., 15 ½ x 7 ¼ x 1 In. *illus*		424
Sign, Old Topper Snappy Ale, Rochester, N.Y., Yellow Background, Easel Back, 17 ½ In.		161
Sign, Orange Crush, Bottle Cap, Orange, White, Green, Metal, Gas Station, 1950s, 30 In.		799
Sign, Orange Crush, Embossed, Tin, O.C. Co., 1931, 27 x 10 In.		612
Sign, Orme Jeweler's, Tin, Pocket Watch Shape, c.1899, 58 x 32 In.		3120
Sign, Ortlieb's, Brewery Fresh Taste, Beer Bar Light, Henry F. Ortlieb's Brewing Co., 1900s, 7 x 24 In.		103
Sign, Pan Am, Blue, White, Enamel, Convex, 1900s, 24 In. *illus*		5310
Sign, Pentillas Shoe Store & Repairing, White, Black Painted Wood, 24 x 48 In.		240
Sign, Peters Ammo, Moose Head, Gun Wielding Soldier, Forest, Oak Frame, 20 x 13 In.		489
Sign, Peters Shoes, Porcelain, White Border, Red Outline, Early 1900s, 8 x 38 ¾ In.		300
Sign, Pine, 3 Gentlemen, Smoking & Drinking, Tavern, O. Coble, Late 1900s, 20 x 41 In.		1320
Sign, Plus De Pneux Creves, Woman Riding Bicycle, Man Fixing Tire, Frame, France, 45 x 65 In.		576
Sign, Pocket Watch, Suspended Glasses, Watches, Clocks, Jewelry, Cast Iron, Paint, 19 In.		4248
Sign, Porto Ramos Pinto, Man & Woman, Gold Frame, 19 x 13 ½ In.		177
Sign, Poultry Feeds, Enamel, Lay Or Bust, Park & Pollard Co., 7 x 20 In.		649
Sign, Pullman, Applied Letters, Black Text, Tin, 50 In.		58
Sign, R.H. Axline Optician, Ink On Paper, Black Text, Frame, 17 ½ x 22 In.		75
Sign, R.K. Person Jeweller, Clock Shape, Cast Iron, Tin, Late 1800s, 33 In.		480
Sign, Radio, Majestic, Yellow Background, Red & Black Text, Wood Frame, 30 x 25 In.		81
Sign, Red Belt Cigar, Woman Tying Shoe, Frame, Minty Cigar Co., 27 x 22 In.		360
Sign, Red Goose Shoes, Red, Yellow, Enameled Tin, c.1935, 17 x 12 In.		132
Sign, Rooster, Sheet Iron, Painted, 23 x 20 ½ In.		354
Sign, Roslindale, George E. Willard, Gilt Letters, Smalted Background, Late 1800s, 13 x 35 ¼ In.		221
Sign, Schoenling Beer, Electric, Hanging Metal Light, Frosted Glass Panels, 1960, 18 In.		58
Sign, Sherwin-Williams Paints, Cover The Earth, Can, Red Paint, Porcelain, 57 In.		480
Sign, Signs, Multicolor Letters, Electric, Aluminum, Plastic, Florescent Bulbs, 13 x 24 x 11 In.		182
Sign, Smells Grand, Packs Right, Smokes Sweet, Can't Bite, Embossed, 1950s, 26 x 16 In. *illus*		131
Sign, Smoke The Brook Trout Cigar, Currier & Ives, T.R. Harris & Co., Frame, 17 x 23 In.		885
Sign, Soap Box Derby, Red, White, Blue, Car Graphic, Shield Shape, 23 x 22 In.		311
Sign, Solemn Pig, John P. Squire & Co., Mayer & Lavenson Co., Tin, 21 x 17 In. *illus*		720
Sign, Squirt, Quenches Quicker, Embossed, Metal, Self-Framed, 1947, 18 x 40 In.		339
Sign, Stroehmann Bread, Tin, Red Text, Yellow Background, 30 x 12 In.		83
Sign, Sullmanco Inks, Tin Litho, Color Pallet, Sigmund Ullman, 1911, 11 ¼ x 17 In.		91
Sign, Sunbeam Bread, Little Miss Sunbeam, Embossed Metal, 11 ½ x 29 ½ In.		622
Sign, Sunbeam Bread, Wood Frame, Red Background, 25 x 34 In.		81
Sign, Sundries, Trade, Painted, Rectangular, 32 x 90 In.		388
Sign, SWP Cover The Earth, Sherwin-Williams, Enamel, Embossed, 35 x 18 In. *illus*		2360
Sign, Take Home 6 Paks, Electric, Plastic, Litho, Fluorescent Lighting, Schlitz, 10 x 19 In.		130
Sign, Tea Room, Marked Mrs. Hogg's Tea Room, Wood, Minisink Hills, Pa., 7 x 48 In.		226
Sign, Thirsty? Just Whistle, Early Style Bottle, Embossed, Tin Lithograph, 7 x 9 ¾ In. *illus*		1475
Sign, Tingley's Inn, Tavern, Painted Tin, Wrought Iron, Female, Standing, 1800s, 48 In.		2460
Sign, Top Hat Cafe, Sheet Metal, Painted, Top Hat Shape, 28 x 36 In.		118
Sign, Try Our Killer Shrimp, Wood Board, Green, White, 2-Sided, c.1950, 12 x 30 In.		252

Advertising, Tin, Tiger Chewing Tobacco, 5 Cent Packages, Lorillard Co., Round Lid, 11 ⅝ In.
$295

Advertising, Tip Tray, Globe Wernicke Bookcases, Walter R. Miller & Co., Man & Woman, 4 In.
$94

Advertising, Tip Tray, Kenny's Teas & Coffee, 3 Monkeys, See, Hear, Speak No Evil, 4 In.
$153

Advertising, Tray, Hires, 5 Cents, Josh Slinger, Soda Jerk, Round, Tin Lithograph, 1915, 13 In.
$679

Wm Morford Auctions

Advertising, Tray, Hornung's Beer, Beer That Wins Awards, Comic Man Drinking Beer, Round, 12 In.
$68

Hartzell's Auction Gallery, Inc.

Agata, Pitcher, Bulbous, Square Rim, Applied Handle, New England Glass Co., 1800s, 7 In.
$717

Jeffrey S. Evans & Associates

Pringles Can As Burial Wrap
The designer of the container for Pringles potato chips died in 2008, and as he requested, part of his ashes were buried in a Pringles can. The rest of his remains were put into urns given to family members.

Sign, Union Made Overalls, Headlight, Blue, White, Red, Porcelain, 15 x 48 In.	1695
Sign, W.J. Guy, The Place To Go For Implements, Embossed, Tin Litho, 9¾ x 28 In.	2714
Sign, Welch's Grape Juice, Tin Over Cardboard, Easel Back, Grapes, Bottle, 6 x 9 In. .... *illus*	425
Sign, Whalehead Club, Painted, Wood, Ruddy Duck Decoy, 1900s, 22 x 22 In.	48
Sign, William Hounsell & Co., Cardboard, Oak Frame, Late 1800s, 30 x 24 In.	121
Sign, Winchester 1878, Black & Gold, Buffalo, Rifle, Reverse Painted, 1900s, 15 x 36 In.	144
Sign, Wm. A. Kressin, Painter & Decorator, Reverse Painted Glass, c.1925, 17 x 29 In.	156
Sign, Work Shoes, Silver Paint, Block Letters, Parallel Rails, c.1950, 52½ In.	185
Sign, Wrigley's Gum, Delicious, Tin, Cardboard, American Can Co., c.1930, 7 x 11 In.	363
Sign, Yusay Beer, Bullet Shape, Die Cut Glass Bottle, Light-Up, 1950, 16 x 6½ In.	1008
Sink, Crane Co., Phila., Pa., Figural, Ceramic, Salesman's Sample, 1904, 3 x 5 In. .... *illus*	212
Spinner, Dr. Daniels' Medicines, Cure Your Horses & Cattle, Hand, Pointing, Tin Litho, 1 x 3 In. .*illus*	1487
Stand, Horseshoe Brand Clothes Wringer, Wood, Green Paint, Easel Back, 56 In.	136
Stand, Smoking, Moxie, Hitchie, Butler, Tin Ashtray, Wood, Painted, 32 x 6 In. .... *illus*	679
Stickpin, Polly Evans, Comic Strip, Blue, White Enamel, Brass, Oval, 2½ x 1 In.	40
Thermometers are listed in the Thermometer category.	

 Advertising tin cans or canisters were first used commercially in the United States in 1819 and were called tins. Today the word *tin* is used by most collectors to describe many types of containers, including food tins, biscuit boxes, roly poly tobacco containers, gunpowder cans, talcum powder sprinkle-top cans, cigarette flat-fifty tins, and more. Beer Cans are listed in their own category. Things made of undecorated tin are listed under Tinware.

Tin, Biscuit, Carr Delicious, Double Decker Bus Form, Seated Passengers, 8 In.	600
Tin, Biscuit, Christie, Windmill House Form, 4 Blades, Dome Lid, c.1853, 8 In.	300
Tin, Biscuit, Flying Scotsman, W. Crawford & Sons, Locomotive, Tender, 16 In.	570
Tin, Biscuit, Pied Piper, Cart & Co., Tambourine Form, Pied Piper, Drum, Children, 6 In.	390
Tin, Biscuit, Rolls-Royce, Car Shape, Driver, 2 Women Passengers, Lithograph, 12 In.	2280
Tin, Biscuvvtit, Water Witch, Jacob & Co., Houseboat, Windows, People, Lithograph, 10 In.	360
Tin, Breethem, For Your Breath, Woman's Face, Black & Tan, 1931, 2 x 2 In.	24
Tin, Cadette Talc, Soldier, Deep Blue, Lithograph, N.J., 7⅜ In. .... *illus*	661
Tin, Carnation, Malted Milk, Spun Aluminum Top, c.1940, 9 In.	288
Tin, Coffee, Domed & Sliding Lid, McLaughlin's Coffee, 1800s, 22 x 18 In.	215
Tin, Coffee, G.D. Brown, Lyons, Ohio, Clock In Tower, Landscapes, 48 x 19 In.	1476
Tin, Coffee, King Cole, G.E. Barbour, Lid, c.1925, 5¾ In.	235
Tin, Lid, Band-Aid, Red Cross, Johnson & Johnson, 1940s, 3 x 2 In.	45
Tin, Moses Cough Drops, Hinged Lid, Lithograph, E.J. Hoadley, 4¼ x 6 In.	590
Tin, Nye's Celebrated Oil, 38 F.C.T.-B.W. Sperm Oil, Whaling Scene, 6 In.	250
Tin, Popper's Ace Cigars, 10 Cents, Lithograph, Biplane, 50 Count, 5¾ x 5 In.	342
Tin, Roly Poly, Dixie Queen Tobacco, Satisfied Customer, Pipe, 7 x 6 In. .... *illus*	1227
Tin, Sir Walter Raleigh, Tobacco, Orange, Black, White Lettering, 4⅜ In.	28
Tin, Tiger Chewing Tobacco, 5 Cent Packages, Lorillard Co., Round Lid, 11⅝ In. .... *illus*	295
Tin, Tiny-Tot Toilet Powder, Baby, Oval, Gold Cap, United Drug Co., 1921, 3⅝ In.	185

 Advertising tip trays are decorated metal trays less than 5 inches in diameter. They were placed on the table or counter to hold either the bill or the coins that were left as a tip. Change receivers could be made of glass, plastic, or metal. They were kept on the counter near the cash register and held the money passed back and forth by the cashier. Related items may be listed in the Advertising category under Change Receiver.

Tip Tray, Beldings Spool Silks, Reliable, Strong, Bell Image, Canada, Round, 5½ In.	480
Tip Tray, Domestic Sewing Machines, Woman, Tin, Lithograph, 6 In.	45
Tip Tray, El Roi-Tan Perfect Cigars, Couple, Lithograph, Oval, 6 x 4⅜ In.	118
Tip Tray, Globe Wernicke Bookcases, Walter R. Miller & Co., Man & Woman, 4 In. .... *illus*	94
Tip Tray, Kenny's Teas & Coffee, 3 Monkeys, See, Hear, Speak No Evil, 4 In. .... *illus*	153
Tip Tray, King's Pure Malt, Girl Holding Tray Of Malt & Glass, 6 x 5 In.	179
Tip Tray, Leinbach Box Co., Reading, Pa., Woman, Long Hair, 4 In.	118
Tip Tray, Rob Roy Ale Superior Lager Beer, Red, Black, Tin Lithograph, c.1935, 13 In.	611
Tray, Anheuser-Busch, Woman Surrounded By Cherubs, Tin, Oval, c.1900, 16½ In.	259
Tray, Fleischmann Co., Little Girl, Face & Shoulder, Leafy Border, 17 x 14 In.	279
Tray, Goebel's Beer & Porter, Blue & White, Enamel, Brass Rim, 12 In.	5428

Tray, Hall Ice Cream, Woman & Children, Tin Lithograph, Multicolor, 13 ¼ x 10 ½ In. 915
Tray, Hires, 5 Cents, Josh Slinger, Soda Jerk, Round, Tin Lithograph, 1915, 13 In. .... *illus* 679
Tray, Hornung's Beer, Beer That Wins Awards, Comic Man Drinking Beer, Round, 12 In.. *illus* 68
Tray, Tip, see Tip Trays in this category.

AGATA glass was made by Joseph Locke of the New England Glass Company of Cambridge, Massachusetts, after 1885. A metallic stain was applied to New England Peachblow, which the company called Wild Rose, and the mottled design characteristic of agata appeared. There are a few known items made of opaque green with the mottled finish.

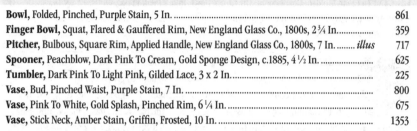

Bowl, Folded, Pinched, Purple Stain, 5 In. 861
Finger Bowl, Squat, Flared & Gauffered Rim, New England Glass Co., 1800s, 2 ¾ In. 359
Pitcher, Bulbous, Square Rim, Applied Handle, New England Glass Co., 1800s, 7 In. .... *illus* 717
Spooner, Peachblow, Dark Pink To Cream, Gold Sponge Design, c.1885, 4 ½ In. 625
Tumbler, Dark Pink To Light Pink, Gilded Lace, 3 x 2 In. 225
Vase, Bud, Pinched Waist, Purple Stain, 7 In. 800
Vase, Pink To White, Gold Splash, Pinched Rim, 6 ¼ In. 675
Vase, Stick Neck, Amber Stain, Griffin, Frosted, 10 In. 1353

AKRO AGATE glass was founded in Akron, Ohio, in 1911 and moved to Clarksburg, West Virginia, in 1914. The company made marbles and toys. In the 1930s it began making other products, including vases, lamps, flowerpots, candlesticks, and children's dishes. Most of the glass is marked with a crow flying through the letter *A*. The company was sold to Clarksburg Glass Co. in 1951. Akro Agate marbles are listed in this book in the Marble category.

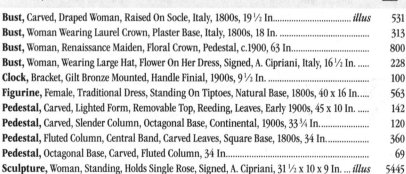

Ashtray Set, Marbleized, 3 Colors, Blue, Jadite & Caramel, Leaf Shape, 1930s, 4 In., 3 Piece.... 35
Ashtray, Green Aventurine, Corkscrew Marbleized, 1920s 26
Flowerpot, Stacked Disc, Green, Marbleized, 1940s, 5 ¼ x 5 ¾ In. 23
Sugar & Creamer, Octagonal, Bright Yellow, Child's 35
Tray, 12 Marbles Set Into Rim, Blue, Yellow, 3 In. 42

ALABASTER is a very soft form of gypsum, a stone that resembles marble. It was often carved into vases or statues in Victorian times. There are alabaster carvings being made even today.

Bust, Carved, Draped Woman, Raised On Socle, Italy, 1800s, 19 ½ In...................... *illus* 531
Bust, Woman Wearing Laurel Crown, Plaster Base, Italy, 1800s, 18 In. 313
Bust, Woman, Renaissance Maiden, Floral Crown, Pedestal, c.1900, 63 In...................... 800
Bust, Woman, Wearing Large Hat, Flower On Her Dress, Signed, A. Cipriani, Italy, 16 ½ In. 228
Clock, Bracket, Gilt Bronze Mounted, Handle Finial, 1900s, 9 ½ In. 100
Figurine, Female, Traditional Dress, Standing On Tiptoes, Natural Base, 1800s, 40 x 16 In..... 563
Pedestal, Carved, Lighted Form, Removable Top, Reeding, Leaves, Early 1900s, 45 x 10 In. 142
Pedestal, Carved, Slender Column, Octagonal Base, Continental, 1900s, 33 ¾ In...................... 120
Pedestal, Fluted Column, Central Band, Carved Leaves, Square Base, 1800s, 34 In.................. 360
Pedestal, Octagonal Base, Carved, Fluted Column, 34 In.. 69
Sculpture, Woman, Standing, Holds Single Rose, Signed, A. Cipriani, 31 ½ x 10 x 9 In. ... *illus* 5445

ALUMINUM was more expensive than gold or silver until the 1850s. Chemists learned how to refine bauxite to get aluminum. Jewelry and other small objects were made of the valuable metal until 1914, when an inexpensive smelting process was invented. The aluminum collected today dates from the 1930s through the 1950s. Hand-hammered pieces are the most popular.

Lamp, Bakelite, Machine Age, c.1930, 14 x 18 In.. *illus* 8750
Sculpture, Abstract, Bolted L-Beams, Signed, Larry Mohr, 1980, 19 ½ x 18 ½ x 18 ½ In.......... 1230
Sign, Rooster, Standing, Gold Paint, Square Red Base, c.1950, 18 In............................ 448
Sink, Vanity, Hinged Top, Mirror & Basin, Black, Modern, 36 x 21 x 16 In. 94
Sled, Duralite, Racer, Tubular, 49 In. 148

AMBER, *see Jewelry category.*

Alabaster, Bust, Carved, Draped Woman, Raised On Socle, Italy, 1800s, 19 ½ In.
$531

Leslie Hindman Auctioneers

Alabaster, Sculpture, Woman, Standing, Holds Single Rose, Signed, A. Cipriani, 31 ½ x 10 x 9 In.
$5,445

Fontaine's Auction Gallery

Aluminum, Lamp, Bakelite, Machine Age, c.1930, 14 x 18 In.
$8,750

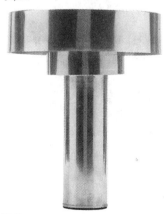

Wright

Amberina, Pitcher, Cream, Diamond-Quilted, Ruffled Edge, Applied Amber Handle, 1900s, 6 In. $406

Garth's Auctioneers & Appraisers

Amberina, Pitcher, Water, Maroon Fuchsia, Globular, Vertical Ribs, Tricornered Mouth, c.1886, 6 In. $6,573

Jeffrey S. Evans & Associates

Amberina, Syrup, Thumbprint, Pewter Lid, Handle, Mt. Washington, 5 ½ In. $226

Hartzell's Auction Gallery, Inc.

 AMBER GLASS is the name of any glassware with the proper yellow-brown shading. It was a popular color just after the Civil War and many pressed glass pieces were made of amber glass. Depression glass of the 1930s–50s was also made in shades of amber glass. Other pieces may be found in the Depression Glass, Pressed Glass, and other glass categories. All types are being reproduced.

Demijohn, Brown Orange, 1800s, 19 In.	60
Jar, Apothecary, Gold Flecked Knop & Pedestal Stem, Italy, Late 1900s, 27 x 13 In.	156
Toothpick Holder, Otter, Lying Down, Pillow Holding Button, Daisy Holder On Belly, 3 ½ In.	48
Vase, Cut To Clear, Molded, Cornucopia, Oil Lamp, Bowl, Pike's Peak Flask, 1900s, 12 x 9 In.	31
Wine, Amber, Zipper Stem, Austria, 1897, 4 In.	468
Wine, Cord Drapery, 1901, 6 ⅛ In.	222

 AMBERINA, a two-toned glassware, was originally made from 1883 to about 1900. It was patented by Joseph Locke of the New England Glass Company but was also made by other companies and is still being made. The glass shades from red to amber. Similar pieces of glass may be found in the Baccarat, Libbey, Plated Amberina, and other categories. Glass shaded from blue to amber is called *Blue Amberina* or *Bluerina*.

Bowl, Swirl, Red On Top, Yellow Green On Bottom, 9 ½ In.	96
Creamer, Ribbed, Ruby To Ivory, Amber Handle, 2 ¼ x 5 ½ In.	2950
Creamer, Squat, Fuchsia To Pale Amber, 12 Vertical Ribs, Handle, c.1886, 2 ⅛ In.	2510
Pitcher, Cream, Diamond-Quilted, Ruffled Edge, Applied Amber Handle, 1900s, 6 In. ...... *illus*	406
Pitcher, Water, Maroon Fuchsia, Globular, Vertical Ribs, Tricornered Mouth, c.1886, 6 In. .. *illus*	6573
Syrup, Thumbprint, Pewter Lid, Handle, Mt. Washington, 5 ½ In. .... *illus*	226
Vase, Lily, Fuchsia To Pale Amber, Trumpet, Vertical Ribs, Polished Pontil, c.1886, 8 In.	2390
Vase, Swirl, Red, Yellow, Polished Pontil, 6 ½ x 5 ½ In.	84

AMERICAN DINNERWARE, *see Dinnerware.*

 AMERICAN ENCAUSTIC TILING COMPANY was founded in Zanesville, Ohio, in 1875. The company planned to make a variety of tiles to compete with the English tiles that were selling in the United States for use in fireplaces and other architectural designs. The first glazed tiles were made in 1880, embossed tiles in 1881, faience tiles in the 1920s. The firm closed in 1935 and reopened in 1937 as the Shawnee Pottery.

Tile, Calvin Coolidge, Gray Green Glaze, Marked, 12 ⅜ x 10 In.	118
Tile, Woman, Scantily Clad, Playing Flute, Yellow & Brown, 1900s, 18 x 6 In.	168

 AMETHYST GLASS is any of the many glasswares made in the dark purple color of the gemstone amethyst. Included in this category are many pieces made in the nineteenth and twentieth centuries. Very dark pieces are called *black amethyst.*

Vase, Cut Glass, Clear, Hobstars & Diamonds, Round Base, 14 ½ x 7 ¼ In. .... *illus*	94
Vase, Tapered, Carved, Gilt Flower, Late 1800s, 11 ¾ In.	531

AMPHORA *pieces are listed in the Teplitz category.*

ANDIRONS *and related fireplace items are included in the Fireplace category.*

 ANIMAL TROPHIES, such as stuffed animals (taxidermy), rugs made of animal skins, and other similar collectibles made from animal, fish, or bird parts, are listed in this category. Collectors should be aware of the endangered species laws that make it illegal to buy and sell some of these items. Any eagle feathers, many types of pelts or rugs (such as leopard), ivory, rhinoceros horn, and many forms of tortoiseshell can be confiscated by the government. Related trophies may be found in the Fishing category. Ivory items may be found in the Scrimshaw or Ivory categories.

Antlers, Antelope, Africa, 10 x 27 In.	50
Birds & Butterflies, On Branches, Glass Dome, Beetles Crawling In Grass, c.1890, 17 In.	2063

Birds, Glass Dome, Ebonized Wood Base, 21 x 21 x 9 In.	2360
Birds, Male & Female Meadowlarks, Glass Dome, Wood Plinth, 14 x 10 In.	430
Birds, Quail, Goldfinch, Black Wood Stand, Glass Dome, 1800s, 11 x 10 x 7 In.	590
Birds, Shellwork, Flowers, Glass Dome, Rosewood Base, 29 x 14 x 10 In.	944
Eland, Head, Shoulder Mount, Africa, 38 x 27 x 64 In.	354
Elk, Antlers, 12-Point Rack, Mounted On Wall Plaque, 52 x 48 In.	173
Fox, Seated, Tail Curled Around Legs, Brown Fur, Square Base, 17 In.	150
Gemsbok Antelope, Shoulder Mount, Horns, Africa, 29 x 20 x 46 In.	118
Kudu, Shoulder Mount, Removable Horns, Africa, 34 x 20 x 60 In.	148
Mountain Lion, Prowling, Roaring, Faux Outdoor Base, 22 x 18 x 80 In.	1200
Red Hartebeest, Elongated Head, Horns, High Forequarters, Africa, 25 x 17 x 39 In.	177
Warthog, Shoulder Mount, 24 x 13 In.	501
Wildebeest, Shoulder Mount, Africa, c.1975, 25 x 36 In. *illus*	420

ANIMATION ART collectibles include cels that are painted drawings on celluloid needed to make animated cartoons shown in movie theaters or on TV. Hundreds of cels were made, then photographed in sequence to make a cartoon showing moving figures. Early examples made by the Walt Disney Studios are popular with collectors today. Original sketches used by the artists are also listed here. Modern animated cartoons are made using computer-generated pictures. Some of these are being produced as cels to be sold to collectors. Other cartoon art is listed in Comic Art and Disneyana.

Cel, Chilly Willy, Blue Ground, 32 x 14 In.	250
Cel, Disney, Jiminy Cricket, Umbrella, Hand Inked, 8½ x 11 In.	500
Cel, Mighty Mouse, Flying Downward, Clouds, Frame, 32 x 14 In.	250
Cel, Pink Panther, Hand Inked, 2 Cel Setup, 13 x 16 In.	300
Cel, Simpsons, Old Money, Entire Family, Fox Seal, 3 x 9 In.	382
Drawing, Pinocchio, I Can Move, I Can Talk, Graphite On Paper, Disney, 12 x 10 In.	1560

ANNA POTTERY was started in Anna, Illinois, in 1859 by Cornwall and Wallace Kirkpatrick. They made many types of utilitarian wares, bricks, drain tiles, and giftware. The most collectible pieces made by the pottery are the pig-shaped bottles and jugs with special inscriptions, applied animals, and figures. The pottery closed in 1894.

Anna Pottery

Figurine, Frog, Seated, Looking Up, Cobalt Blue Highlights, Stoneware, c.1885, 2¾ In.	522
Flask, Hot Spring, Applied Woman, Man, Cobalt Blue Highlights, Hat, Belt, Sword, c.1880, 5⅞ In.	10455
Flask, Pig, Redware, Incised Railroad Map, Wallace & Cornwall Kirkpatrick, c.1865, 7¾ In.	7995
Pitcher, Figural, Fish, Spouting, Salt Glazed, 3 Color Slip, 12¾ In.	1968

ARABIA began producing ceramics in 1874. The pottery was established in Helsinki, Finland, by Rörstrand, a Swedish pottery that wanted to export porcelain, earthenware, and other pottery from Finland to Russia. Most of the early workers at Arabia were Swedish. Arabia started producing its own models of tiled stoves, vases, and tableware about 1900. Rörstrand sold its interest in Arabia in 1916. By the late 1930s, Arabia was the largest producer of porcelain in Europe. Most of its products were exported. A line of stoneware was introduced in the 1960s. Arabia worked in cooperation with Rörstrand from 1975 to 1977. Arabia was bought by Hackman Group in 1990 and Hackman was bought by Iittala Group in 2004. Fiskars Corporation bought Iittala in 2007 and Arabia is now a brand owned by Fiskars.

ARABIA FINLAND

Bowl, Figure On Mule, Playing Instrument, Medieval Women Border, 8¼ x 5½ In.	96
Bowl, Mushrooms, Black & White, 8¼ x 5½ In.	65
Bowl, Vegetable, Blue Rose, 1940-70, Finland, 9 x 7 In.	20
Cup & Saucer, Demitasse, Blue Finn Pattern, Flowers	23
Eggcup, Double, Dark Blue Roses, Leaves, Blue Bands, 4 In., 4 Piece	40
Pitcher, Blue Anemone, 32 Oz., 5 In.	22
Pitcher, Brown Bull, Kaj Franek, Finland, 5 In.	55
Pitcher, Sunflower, Black Handle, K. Franck	175
Pitcher, Yellow Cow, Black Horns, White Ground, 4 In.	45

Amethyst Glass, Vase, Cut Glass, Clear, Hobstars & Diamonds, Round Base, 14½ x 7¼ In.
$94

Cordier Auctions

Animal Trophy, Wildebeest, Shoulder Mount, Africa, c.1975, 25 x 36 In.
$420

Garth's Auctioneers & Appraisers

Architectural, Grill, Elevator, Sunburst, Cast Iron, Rectangles, Holabird & Root Building, c.1928, 11 In.
$500

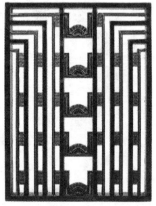

Leslie Hindman Auctioneers

Architectural, Mantel Plate, Iron, Central Spread Wing Eagle, Floral Rosettes, 1800s, 44 In.
$338

Skinner, Inc.

Architectural, Mantel, Flower Sprays, Leafy Scrolls, Pine, Carved, Stained, c.1950, 54 x 66 x 9 In.
$563

Leslie Hindman Auctioneers

> **TIP**
> Be sure copies of lists of valuables, photographs, and other information can be found in case of an insurance loss. Give copies and tell a trusted friend how to find them. Do not keep them in the house.

Architectural, Mantel, Walnut, Carved, Granite Top, Grotesques, Fruit, Flower Pendants, 1800s, 51 x 84 In.
$2,625

Neal Auction Company

Architectural, Model, Cross Section, 2 Stairs, Domed Structure, 1900s, 19 In.
$1,875

Leslie Hindman Auctioneers

Architectural, Overmantel Mirror, Louis XV Style, Fleur-De-Lis, Arched Plate, 1900s, 57 x 29 x 5 In.
$813

Crescent City Auction Gallery

Architectural, Panel, Staircase, Oak, Iron, Cast Leaves, From Palmer Mansion, Chicago, 1880s, 18¾ In.
$1,125

Leslie Hindman Auctioneers

Plate, Boy Playing Trumpet, Wolves, 8 x 8 In.	25
Plate, Owl, Green, Yellow, Red Band, 7 ½ In.	20
Plate, Seal Of County Of Dukes, Blue Transfer, 10 ½ In.	45
Plate, Trees, Shrubs, Flowing River, Archer, Horseman, R. Vosikkinon, 8 x 8 In.	30
Platter, Anemone Brown, Oval, c.1970, 14 x 9 In.	42
Platter, Blue Rose, Banded Rim, 9 x 7 In.	20
Platter, Finn Flower, Blue, 16 ¾ In.	70
Sculpture, Apple, Burgundy, White, Carved Design, 3 ½ In.	68
Teapot, Green Thistle, Green Flowers, Scallop Band, 1955-70, 6 ½ In.	28
Teapot, Lid, Green Flowers, Band & Scallop Design, Gray Ground, 5 Cups, 8 ¼ In.	28

ARCHITECTURAL antiques include a variety of collectibles, usually very large, that have been removed from buildings. Hardware, backbars, doors, paneling, and even old bathtubs are now wanted by collectors. Pieces of the Victorian, Art Nouveau, and Art Deco styles are in greatest demand.

Corbel, Hand Carved, Gilt Painted, Wood, Italy, 1700s, 29 x 22 x 10 In.	1200
Door, Dogon, Granary, Carved, Figures & Animals, 74 In.	272
Door, Mahogany, Starburst, 61 x 24 In.	224
Doorknocker, Bronze, Putti, Shield, 8 In.	134
Doorknocker, Iron, Dolphin, Floral Shape Back Plate, England, c.1850, 9 In.	96
Doorknocker, Iron, Star Shape, Cast, c.1965, 13 ⅝ x 8 ¼ x 1 ⅜ In.	3438
Element, Arched Shape, Carved, Potter Palmer Mansion, 32 ½ x 65 ½ x 3 ½ In.	406
Element, Child's Face, Carved, Wood, 1800s, 6 x 11 In.	58
Element, Eagle, Painted, Wood Base, Cast Iron, Late 1800s, 8 ½ x 15 In.	163
Element, Gothic, Wood, Carved, Painted, 76 x 28 In.	277
Element, Pediment, Terra-Cotta Putto, Mask, Leaves, Scrolls, c.1926, 20 In.	750
Fireplace Surround, Cherry, Burl Elm, Egyptian Revival, Art Deco, c.1915, 95 x 52 In.	2375
Fireplace Surround, Heart Pine, c.1900, 64 ½ x 83 ¾ In.	2880
Gate, Cemetery, Weeping Willow, Sheep, Leafy Scrollwork, Iron, R.H. Parker, 1800s, 41 In.	738
Grill, Elevator, Sunburst, Cast Iron, Rectangles, Holabird & Root Building, c.1928, 11 In. *illus*	500
Key & Fob, Door, Brass, Shield Form, Auditorium Building, Chicago, c.1900, 6 In.	250
Mantel Plate, Iron, Central Spread Wing Eagle, Floral Rosettes, 1800s, 44 In. *illus*	338
Mantel, Flower Sprays, Leafy Scrolls, Pine, Carved, Stained, c.1950, 54 x 66 x 9 In. *illus*	563
Mantel, Mosaic Tile, 2 Mythical Beasts, Fleur-De-Lis, c.1910, 48 ½ x 46 x 10 In.	1625
Mantel, Oak, Baroque Style, France, c.1880, 52 ¼ x 70 x 26 ¼ In.	67
Mantel, Oak, Carved, Leafy Columns, c.1910, 54 ½ x 85 ½ x 11 In.	240
Mantel, Walnut, Carved, Granite Top, Grotesques, Fruit, Flower Pendants, 1800s, 51 x 84 In. *illus*	2625
Model, Cross Section, 2 Stairs, Domed Structure, 1900s, 19 In. *illus*	1875
Model, Spiral Staircase, Carved Wood, Painted, 24 ½ In.	500
Model, Staircase Center, Domed Structure, Tapered Step Base, England, 1900s, 25 In.	531
Ornament, Copper, Scrolls, Central Reserve, Dated 1678-1912, 15 x 24 In.	201
Overmantel Mirror, 3-Piece Plate, Reeded Columns, Classical, Giltwood, 28 x 58 In.	360
Overmantel Mirror, Centered Tinted Photo, Yosemite, 16 x 40 In.	242
Overmantel Mirror, Classical Style, Carved & Gilt, 26 x 66 In.	135
Overmantel Mirror, Classical Style, Medusa, Fruit Frame, Late 1800s, 72 x 37 x 6 In.	861
Overmantel Mirror, Gilt & Gesso, Frame, Louis XV Style, Late 1800s, 36 x 31 ½ x 2 ½ In.	438
Overmantel Mirror, Gilt, Aesthetic Carved, D. Clive Hardy, 77 x 51 In.	1875
Overmantel Mirror, Louis XV Style, Acanthus Leaves, Morning Glory, Arched Top, c.1880, 78 x 52 In.	1750
Overmantel Mirror, Louis XV Style, Fleur-De-Lis, Arched Plate, 1900s, 57 x 29 x 5 In. *illus*	813
Overmantel Mirror, Louis XV Style, Gilt, Trefoil, C-Scrolls & Leaves, 1800s, 41 x 24 In.	469
Overmantel Mirror, Louis XVI Style, Bellflower Border, Beveled Plate, 1900s, 72 x 26 In.	500
Overmantel Mirror, Louis XVI Style, Gilt, Gesso, Musical Instrument, Torch, 70 x 41 In.	615
Overmantel Mirror, Louis XVI Style, Gilt, Gesso, Shell & Flowers, 1800s, 41 x 24 x 2 In.	563
Panel, Carved Wood, Gesso, Pierced, Crown, Leafy Vines, 1800s, 16 ½ x 45 In.	800
Panel, Overdoor, Wood, Oval Cartouche, Leafy Scrolls, Molded Plinth, 1800s, 21 x 57 In.	938
Panel, Staircase, Oak, Iron, Cast Leaves, From Palmer Mansion, Chicago, 1880s, 18 ¾ In. *illus*	1125
Screens are listed in the Fireplace and Furniture categories.	
Valance, Carved, Red Lacquer, Gilt, Archaic Geometric, Chinese, 1800s, 106 x 8 x 1 ¾ In.	84

Arequipa, Vase, Stylized Leaves, Squeezebag, Frederick Rhead, c.1912, 8 ¼ In.
$8,750

Rago Arts and Auction Center

Arts & Crafts, Crucifix, Silver Plate, Enamel, Octagonal Base, 1937, 22 ½ In.
$825

Pook & Pook

TIP
Polish silver by rubbing it with a woolen blanket or piece of carpet.

Auto, Bobblehead, Phillips 66, Figural Cowboy, Station Attendant, Composition, 7 1/4 x 3 1/4 In.
$236

AntiqueAdvertising.com

Auto, Can, Oilzum Motor Oil & Lubricant, Man's Face, Driving Cap, Metal, 9 1/2 In.
$540

Matthew Bullock Auctioneers

Auto, Figurine, Sinclair Gas Service Station, Teal Blue Dinosaur, 48 x 24 x 90 In.
$3,000

Morphy Auctions

 AREQUIPA POTTERY was produced from 1911 to 1918 by the patients of the Arequipa Sanatorium in Marin County, north of San Francisco. The patients were trained by Frederick Hurten Rhead, who had worked at Roseville Pottery.

Vase, Squat, Green, Blue Geometric Band, Oval, Squeezebag, F.H. Rhead, 1912, 5 In.	5625
Vase, Squat, Matte Glaze, Squeezebag, Signed, 1912, 2 1/2 x 5 1/2 In.	5313
Vase, Stylized Leaves, Squeezebag, Frederick Rhead, c.1912, 8 1/4 In. .... *illus*	8750

ARGY-ROUSSEAU, *see G. Argy-Rousseau category.*

 ARITA is a port in Japan. Porcelain was made there from about 1616. Many types of decorations were used, including the popular Imari designs, which are listed under Imari in this book.

Bowl, White Flowers, Blue Ground, Celadon Center, Lobed, Shaped Rim, 11 1/2 In.	593
Charger, Blue, White, Peonies, Plum Blossoms, Chrysanthemums, Japan, 24 In.	154
Charger, White Peonies, Blue Decoration, Circles, Dots, c.1920, 13 1/2 In.	156

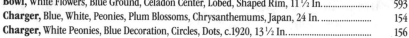 **ART DECO,** or Art Moderne, a style started at the Paris Exposition of 1925, is characterized by linear, geometric designs. All types of furniture and decorative arts, jewelry, book bindings, and even games were designed in this style. Additional items may be found in the Furniture category or in various glass and pottery categories, etc.

Box, Bronze, Footed, Onyx Top, Figural Dog Handle, 4 x 6 1/2 In.	345
Cigarette Case, Hidden Panel, Nude, Lantern, Gilt Silver, Germany, c.1920, 3 1/2 x 3 In.	813
Figurine, Bacchanale, Female Dancer, Nude, Cast Metal, Le Verrier & Janle, c.1925, 12 In.	369
Figurine, Woman, Nude, Arms Out, Holding Crystal, Silvered Metal, Max Le Verrier, 1900s, 10 3/4 In.	234
Figurine, Woman, Seminude, Standing, Head Back, Elbows Out, Plaster, 24 1/4 In.	200
Magazine Rack, Greyhound, Leaping, Cast Iron, 14 x 12 1/4 In.	610
Tray, Carved, Mirror Glass, Handles, Green, Interlocking L Shape, c.1940, 13 x 20 In.	311
Vase, Cylindrical, Brown Branch, Gold Leaves, Signed, Louis Dage, 9 3/4 In.	150

ART GLASS, *see Glass-Art category.*

 ART NOUVEAU is a style of design that was at its most popular from 1895 to 1905. Famous designers, including Rene Lalique and Emile Galle, produced furniture, glass, silver, metalwork, and buildings in the new style. Ladies with long flowing hair and elongated bodies were among the more easily recognized design elements. Copies of this style are being made today. Many modern pieces of jewelry can be found. Additional Art Nouveau pieces may be found in Furniture or in various glass and porcelain categories.

Plaque, Cunningham Coat Of Arms, Walnut, Quatrefoil, Early 1900s, 25 1/2 x 25 In.	181
Vase, Flowers, Woman & Child, Embossed, Marked, Germany, Early 1900s, 17 In.	215

ART POTTERY, *see Pottery-Art category.*

 ARTS & CRAFTS was a design style popular in American decorative arts from 1894 to 1923. In the 1970s collectors began to rediscover Mission furniture, art pottery, metalwork, linens, and light fixtures from this period. The interest has continued. Today everything from this era is collectible, including jewelry, graphics, and silverware. Additional items may be found in the Furniture category and other categories.

Crucifix, Silver Plate, Enamel, Octagonal Base, 1937, 22 1/2 In. .... *illus*	825
Frame, Bleeding Hearts, Inlaid, Wood, Painted, Woman Sitting, Unmarked, 10 x 7 In.	390
Frame, Swallows, Inlaid Wood, 2 Swinging Doors, Painted Birds, 3 3/4 x 5 1/2 In.	313
Vase, Green Matte Glaze, Thistle Flowers, Pottery, 7 x 3 1/2 In.	708
Vase, Rose Matte Glaze, Flowers At Shoulder, 1925, 5 1/2 x 3 1/2 In.	59

AURENE *pieces are listed in the Steuben category.*

AUSTRIA *is a collecting term that covers pieces made by a wide variety of factories. They are listed in this book in categories such as Royal Dux or Porcelain.*

AUTO parts and accessories are collectors' items today. Gas pump globes and license plates are part of this specialty. Prices are determined by age, rarity, and condition. Collectors say "porcelain sign" for enameled iron or steel signs. Packaging related to automobiles may also be found in the Advertising category. Lalique hood ornaments are listed in the Lalique category.

Bobblehead, Phillips 66, Figural Cowboy, Station Attendant, Composition, 7¼ x 3¼ In.. *illus*	236
Bottle, Motor Oil, Tiolene, Clear Glass, Cylindrical, 18 In.	58
Button, Cadillac 30, Dark Blue, Yellow, Spoke Wheels, 1½ In.	177
Button, Overland Cars Early, W&H Back Paper, 1 In.	118
Can, Buffalo Motor Oil, Landscape, Prairie Cities Oil Co., Yellow, Thos. Davidson Co., 1920s, 8 x 3 In.	4484
Can, Oilzum Motor Oil & Lubricant, Man's Face, Driving Cap, Metal, 9½ In. *illus*	540
Car Clock, Oldsmobile, Brass Case, Ansonia Clock Co., c.1915, 4½ In.	118
Clock, Co-Op Oil Co. Label, Red, Green, Light-Up, Round, Electric Neon Clock Co., 26 In.	720
Figurine, Sinclair Gas Service Station, Teal Blue Dinosaur, 48 x 24 x 90 In. *illus*	3000
Gas Pump Globe, Farmco, Glass, Round, Metal Clamp Rims, 1930s, 16 In.	480
Gas Pump Globe, Frontier, Rarin' To Go, Bucking Bronco, Capco-Lite Sleeve, 16 In.	960
Gas Pump Globe, Gold Crown, Milk Glass, Standard Oil Co., Metal Base Rim, 17 In.	600
Gas Pump Globe, Horton's All Power Gasoline, H, Milk Glass, Red & Blue Letters, 16 In.	720
Gas Pump Globe, Laureleaf Auto Fuel, Neon, Made In Montana, Round, 2-Sided, 21 x 18 In..	7380
Gas Pump Globe, Skelly Supreme, 4 Blue Stars, Box, 16 In.	450
Gas Pump Globe, Studebaker, Wheel, Milk Glass, 16 In.	210
Gas Pump Globe, Union Oil Co., Co-Op, Milk Glass, 1920s, 16 In.	600
Gas Pump Globe, Use Co-Op, With Ethyl, Glass, White, Red, Black, 1930s, 16 In.	600
Gas Pump, Super Shell, Brass Nozzle, Red, Yellow, Art Deco, 1930s, 30 x 18 In.	4588
Hood Ornament, Punch, Seated, Cone Hat, 4 x 4 In.	201
License Plate, 1743 OH In White, Blue Ground, Porcelain, 1908-09, 12½ x 5½ In.	633
Mirror, Paterson 30, Write For Territory & Agency, Oval, Pocket, c.1910, 2¾ In.	118
Poster, Delahaye, Man On Horse, Lithograph, c.1925, France, 62 x 48 In.	1875
Poster, Rallye Automobile, Monte Carlo, Icy Cliff, 1930, 47 x 31 In.	6550
Rack, Willard Batteries Co., Service Station Display, Metal, 2 Levels, 41 x 29 x 16 In.	915
Radiator, Oldsmobile, Honeycomb, Harrison, 1930s, 23 x 18 In. *illus*	413
Sign, Firestone Gum-Dipped Tires, Most Miles Per Dollar, Porcelain, 2-Sided, 49 In.	1320
Sign, Gutta Percha Tires, Red, Porcelain, 1930s, 16 x 59 In.	480
Sign, Hood Tires, A.E. Meech Hdw., Man Holding Flag, Tin Lithograph, 11¾ x 23½ In.	3186
Sign, Hood, Sheet Tin, White Letters, Red Background, 2-Sided, 48 x 12 In.	118
Sign, Maserati, Round, Red, White, Blue, Porcelain, 12 In.	343
Sign, Mechanics, Carved, Shield, Surrounded By Stars, c.1850, 38 x 35 In.	1230
Sign, Michelin Tires, Michelin Man, Wood, Dealership, Sand Paint, 11½ x 35 x¾ In.	7198
Sign, Mobilgas Pegasus, Winged Horse, Die Cut, Porcelain, 12 x 12½ In. *illus*	189
Sign, Pennzoil, Metal, Oval Shape, Crested Top, 2-Sided, 11¾ x 16¾ In. *illus*	484
Sign, Texaco Lube, Service Station, Enamel, c.1930s, 8¾ x 38¾ In.	1652
Sign, Trico Wiper Blades & Refills, For Safe Vision, Light-Up, 16½ In.	300

AUTUMN LEAF pattern china was made for the Jewel Tea Company beginning in 1933. Hall China Company of East Liverpool, Ohio, Crooksville China Company of Crooksville, Ohio, Harker Potteries of Chester, West Virginia, and Paden City Pottery, Paden City, West Virginia, made dishes with this design. Autumn Leaf has remained popular and was made by Hall China Company until 1978. Some other pieces in the Autumn Leaf pattern are still being made. For more prices, go to kovels.com.

Bowl, Vegetable, Lid, Oval, 2 Handles, 10 x 6½ x 3 In.	22
Casserole, Lid, c.1935, 2 Qt.	42
Coffeepot, 8½ x 8½ In. *illus*	37
Coffeepot, 8 Cup	42
Cookie Jar, Lid, Big Ear, Gold Trim, Zeisel, 8¼ In.	34
Crock, Bean Pot, Lid	47
Jug, 5¾ In.	29
Platter, Oval, 13½ x 10 In.	19
Relish, 8⅞ In.	20

A

Auto, Radiator, Oldsmobile, Honeycomb, Harrison, 1930s, 23 x 18 In.
$413

Milestone Auctions

Few Cars, Low Wages
When the Model T Ford was invented in 1909, there were only about 8,000 cars in the world. The average wage was 22 cents an hour.

Auto, Sign, Mobilgas Pegasus, Winged Horse, Die Cut, Porcelain, 12 x 12½ In.
$189

Milestone Auctions

Auto, Sign, Pennzoil, Metal, Oval Shape, Crested Top, 2-Sided, 11¾ x 16¾ In.
$484

Fontaine's Auction Gallery

Autumn Leaf, Coffeepot, 8 1/2 x 8 1/2 In.
$37

dnmarti on eBay

Baccarat, Chandelier, 24-Light, Stainless Steel, Red, Green Glass Plume Drop, Signed, 1900s, 39 x 34 In.
$5,500

New Orleans Auction Galleries

Baccarat, Decanter, Huntsman On Horseback, Hounds, Etched, Flowering Vine, Gilt, Marked, c.1950, 8 In.
$319

Leland Little Auctions

Serving Bowl, 2 1/4 x 10 1/2 x 8 In.	15
Teapot, Automobile, 9 x 4 x 4 In.	87
Teapot, Floral, Aladdin Shape, 7 Cup, 1930s	44
Teapot, Marked, 1950	64
Tray, Floral, Wood Frame, 19 1/2 x 12 x 1 1/4 In.	52

AZALEA dinnerware was made for Larkin Company customers from about 1915 to 1941. Larkin, the soap company, was in Buffalo, New York. The dishes were made by Noritake China Company of Japan. Each piece of the white china was decorated with pink azaleas.

Cachepot, 5 1/2 In.	20
Cup & Saucer, 2 1/4 In.	26
Goblet, c.1960, 6 1/4 In.	39
Plate, 9 7/8 In.	25

BACCARAT glass was made in France by La Compagnie des Cristalleries de Baccarat, located 150 miles from Paris. The factory was started in 1765. The firm went bankrupt and began operating again about 1822. Cane and millefiori paperweights were made during the 1845 to 1880 period. The firm is still working near Paris making paperweights and glasswares.

Centerpiece, Empire Style, Gilt Bronze, Glass Columns, c.1850, 12 x 12 1/2 x 7 1/2 In.	1375
Centerpiece, Fluted Cut Glass Bowl, 3-Light Candleholders, c.1880, 23 x 26 x 15 In.	8438
Champagne Cooler, Diamond Point Cut, Gilt Bronze, Lion Head Ring Pulls, c.1950, 9 x 8 In.	688
Chandelier, 24-Light, Stainless Steel, Red, Green Glass Plume Drop, Signed, 1900s, 39 x 34 In. _illus_	5500
Decanter, Huntsman On Horseback, Hounds, Etched, Flowering Vine, Gilt, Marked, c.1950, 8 In. _illus_	319
Decanter, Stopper, Spherical, Acid Etched, Leaves, 9 1/2 In.	151
Decanter, Wine, Stopper, Signed, 9 3/4 In. _illus_	161
Figurine, Cat, Seated, 8 1/2 In.	112
Figurine, Dog, Poodle, Black Glass, Marked, 5 1/4 In. _illus_	130
Inkwell, Silver Lid, Repousse Flowers, Sterling Howard & Co., 1891, 4 x 4 x 3 In.	307
Paperweight, Butterfly, Fuchsia Antennae, Yellow Wings, Red Spots, 1971, 3 In.	155
Paperweight, Butterfly, Globular, Lace Ground, Red & White Millefiori, 2 3/4 x 2 In.	800
Paperweight, Butterfly, Pink, Blue, White, Green & Yellow Flower, Mid 1800s, 2 1/4 In. _illus_	956
Paperweight, Garland, Millefiori, Red, White, Blue, Trefoils, France, 1800s, 2 3/4 In.	299
Paperweight, Globe Shape, Green & Brown Spotted Snake, c.1750, 3 x 2 1/4 In.	1845
Paperweight, Millefiori Mushroom Cap, Cobalt Cut To Clear, Faceted, 2 7/8 In.	3600
Paperweight, Poinsettia, Blue & Opal, Teal Ground, France, 1971, 3 In.	156
Paperweight, Purple & Yellow Wallflower, Stardust Center, Aventurine Leaves, 2 1/2 In.	1320
Paperweight, Red Pompon, Clematis, Petals, Twisted Stem, Star Cut Ground, 3 5/16 In.	3900
Paperweight, Salmon Pompon, Green Leaves, Border Garland Of Cogs, 2 1/2 In.	3300
Paperweight, Silhouette, Globular, 2 Loop Garlands, 2 5/8 x 1 7/8 In. _illus_	215
Paperweight, Sulphide, Louis Philippe, France, 1800s, 2 1/8 In. _illus_	131
Paperweight, Sulphide, Queen Victoria, France, 1800s, 2 3/8 In.	658
Vase, Alternating Leaf, Cut, Signed, 8 1/2 In.	138
Vase, Molded, Acid Etched, Frosted, Clear, Amber, Prunus Tree, Chinoiserie, c.1900, 8 In. _illus_	625
Vase, Octagonal Cut Design, Faceted Rim, Round, Art Deco, 8 1/2 In.	338
Vase, Opaline Glass, Flowers, Branch, Blue, Pink, Bird, France, c.1880, 9 3/4 In. _illus_	192
Vase, Optic Panels, Signed, 10 In.	189
Vase, Stand, Ruby To Green, Flowers, Square Baluster Shape, Signed, c.1915, 4 3/8 In.	598
Vase, Trumpet Shape, Bronze & Marble Base, Footed, 16 In.	173
Vase, Twist, Waisted, Signed, Box, Contemporary, 9 In.	1239

BADGES have been used since before the Civil War. Collectors search for examples of all types, including law enforcement and company identification badges. Well-known prison or law enforcement badges are most desirable. Most are made of nickel or brass. Many recent reproductions have been made.

Chauffeur, Missouri, 1941, Octagonal, Pinback, 1 1/2 In.	12
Chauffeur, New York, Licensed, Pinback, 1920, 1 1/2 x 1 1/8 In. _illus_	24

Baccarat, Decanter, Wine, Stopper, Signed, 9¾ In.
$161

Richard D. Hatch & Associates

Baccarat, Figurine, Dog, Poodle, Black Glass, Marked, 5¼ In.
$130

Leland Little Auctions

Baccarat, Paperweight, Butterfly, Pink, Blue, White, Green & Yellow Flower, Mid 1800s, 2¼ In.
$956

Jeffrey S. Evans & Associates

Baccarat, Paperweight, Silhouette, Globular, 2 Loop Garlands, 2⅝ x 1⅞ In.
$215

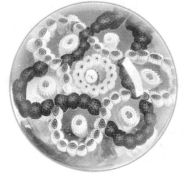

Skinner, Inc.

Baccarat, Paperweight, Sulphide, Louis Philippe, France, 1800s, 2⅛ In.
$131

Jeffrey S. Evans & Associates

Baccarat, Vase, Molded, Acid Etched, Frosted, Clear, Amber, Prunus Tree, Chinoiserie, c.1900, 8 In.
$625

Royal Crest Auctioneers

Baccarat, Vase, Opaline Glass, Flowers, Branch, Blue, Pink, Bird, France, c.1880, 9¾ In.
$192

Eldred's

Badge, Chauffeur, New York, Licensed, Pinback, 1920, 1 ½ x 1 ⅛ In.
$24

Martin Auction Co.

Badge, Employee, 101 Ranch Show, 10 Season, Octagon, Metal, 1911, Miller Bros, 1 ½ In.
$320

Morphy Auctions

Badge, Employee, May I Serve You?, St. Charles Dairy, Name Place, Cardboard, c.1930s, 2 ¾ In.
$12

Hake's Auctions

TIP
Reproduction mechanical banks are usually smaller than the originals because they were made using a real bank as the pattern. But some of the wooden patterns are still available, and banks made from these will be the identical size of an original old bank.

City Marshal, Police, Waverly, Kansas, W.S. Darley & Co., Melrose, Ill.	333
Deputy Sheriff, Custer County, Montana, Eagle, Sterling Silver, 3 x 2 In.	182
Deputy Sheriff, Fresno County, Aero Squadron, Wings At The Center	310
East St. Louis, Largest Horse Mule & Stock Market, Sections, Bar Pin, c.1900, 4 x 2 In.	243
Employee, 101 Ranch Show, 10 Season, Octagon, Metal, 1911, Miller Bros, 1 ½ In. .... *illus*	320
Employee, May I Serve You?, St. Charles Dairy, Name Place, Cardboard, c.1930s, 2 ¾ In.... *illus*	12
Fireman, Cambridge, Amoskeag Fire Engine, Coin Silver, 1860s, 2 ⅛ x 1 ⅜ In.	511
Fireman, Joe Gorton, Hose No. 1, Friendship, N.Y., White Metal, Brass Finish, Wellsville, 1894, 2 In.	38
Fireman, Lanford Eng. Co., East, Fire Department, Silvertone Metal, 1 ¾ In.	18
Guard, Ford, Falcon XT 500, N.O.S. Genuine Sedan Wagon	127
Patrolman, Douglas, Police, Dagget, Eagles, Aircraft	1300
Pilot, Wings, Venezuelan Army, Goldtone Metal, Back Fastening, 3 x 1 In.	26
Police, Bridgeport, Connecticut, 1st Issue, 1850s, 3 ¼ In.	520
Texas Rangers Co., Estados Unidos Mexicanos, Star Center, Lon Willis, 1 ⅝ In.	55

BANKS of metal have been made since 1868. There are still banks, mechanical banks, and registering banks (those that show the total money deposited on the face of the bank). Many old iron or tin banks have been reproduced since the 1950s in iron or plastic. Some old reproductions marked *Book of Knowledge, John Wright,* or *Capron* may be listed. Pottery, glass, and plastic banks are also listed here. Mickey Mouse and other Disneyana banks are listed in Disneyana.

Adding Bank, 5 Cents, Pat'd Aug. 20th, 1889, Metal, Black Paint, Gold Stencils, 5 In.	1920
Apple, On Stem With Leaf, Cast Iron, Painted, Kyser & Rex, 5 ½ In.	1140
Baseball Player, Holding Bat, Red Cap & Socks, A.C. Williams, 6 In.	2210
Bear, Stealing Honey, Cast Iron, Sydenham, 1908, 7 x 4 In.	132
Beehive, Economy Accumulates Wealth, Jos. S. Woodruff's Savings Bank, Chicago, 6 ¾ In.	750
Beehive, Sterling Silver, Putti, 2 Honey Bees, Padlock, c.1900, 2 ½ x 2 ¼ In.	469
Beehive, Yellow Paint, Kyser & Rex, 3 In.	1800
Boat, Battleship Oregon, Brass, J. & E. Stevens, 1895, 5 In.	339
Boy, 2 Faces, Cast Iron, A.C. Williams, c.1910, 2 ¾ In.	60
Buffalo, Wood, Painted, A.C. Williams, c.1925, 3 ⅛ x 4 ⅜ In. .... *illus*	2205
Building, Bank Cupola, Cast Iron, Red & Green Paint, J. & E. Stevens, 5 ½ In.	2700
Building, Belfry, 6 Over 4 Columns, Cast Iron, Yellow Accents, Kenton, 8 In.	1080
Building, Cabin With Shake Roof, Cast Iron, England, 4 In.	900
Building, Castle Tower, Cigar Cutter, Tin, Painted, Gebruder Bing, Germany, c.1900	2083
Building, City Bank, Chimney, Red Paint, 7 In. .... *illus*	4200
Building, City Bank, Eagle Finial, Cast Iron, Red Paint, 12 In.	4500
Building, City Bank, Teller, Cast Iron, H.L. Judd, 5 ½ x 4 ⅜ In.	960
Building, Columbia Bank, Gold Highlights, Combination Lock, Kenton, 7 ½ In. .... *illus*	450
Building, Crown Bank, Scalloped Roof, Cast Iron, White & Gold Paint, 3 ½ In.	1140
Building, Detroit Street Savings Bank Co., Nickel, 4 ¼ In.	12000
Building, Domed Mosque, Grey Iron Casting, 5 In.	450
Building, Flat Iron, Multiple Stories, Cast Iron, Kenton, 8 ½ In.	1200
Building, Globe Savings Fund, 1888, Cast Iron, Red & Gold Trim, Kyser & Rex, 7 In.	1200
Building, Home Bank, Bronze, Green Patina, H.L. Judd, 4 ½ In.	300
Building, Home Savings Bank, Dog Finial, Cast Iron, Gilt, Pat. 1891, 5 ¾ x 4 ⅜ In.	96
Building, House, 2 Story, Cast Iron, Red Roof, A.C. Williams, 3 x 2 In.	60
Building, House, Bay Windows, Cast Iron, Yellow & Green Paint, 4 In. .... *illus*	5700
Building, Independence Hall Tower, Cast Iron, Bronze Finish, Gold Paint, Enterprise, 1876, 9 ½ In.	420
Building, Masonic Temple, Cast Iron, Japanned, 6 In.	5700
Building, Pelican Finial, St. Petersburg, Florida, White Metal, Gilt, 1950s	102
Building, Snappit Still, Snapping Front Door, 8-Sided, H.L. Judd, 4 In.	660
Building, State Bank, Blue & Red Paint, Kyser & Rex, 3 ½ In. .... *illus*	3300
Building, State Bank, Cast Iron, Windows, Marked, 3 x 4 In.	68
Building, State Bank, Fixed Front Door, Painted, Kenton, 9 In.	840
Building, Tower Bank, Red Door, Kyser & Rex, c.1890, 7 In.	510
Building, Westside Presbyterian Church, Germantown, Pa., Silver Paint, 3 ¾ In.	450
Camel, Kneeling, Cast Iron, Kyser & Rex, 1890, 2 ½ x 5 In. .... *illus*	367
Canadian Beaver, Cast Iron, Triangle Mark, W-S S, 7 ½ In.	9600

Bank, Buffalo, Wood, Painted, A.C. Williams, c.1925, 3 1/8 x 4 3/8 In.
$2,205

RSL Auction

Bank, Building, City Bank, Chimney, Red Paint, 7 In.
$4,200

Bertoia Auctions

Bank, Building, Columbia Bank, Gold Highlights, Combination Lock, Kenton, 7 1/2 In.
$450

Bertoia Auctions

Bank, Building, House, Bay Windows, Cast Iron, Yellow & Green Paint, 4 In.
$5,700

Bertoia Auctions

Bank, Building, State Bank, Blue & Red Paint, Kyser & Rex, 3 1/2 In.
$3,300

Bertoia Auctions

Bank, Camel, Kneeling, Cast Iron, Kyser & Rex, 1890, 2 1/2 x 5 In.
$367

RSL Auction

Bank, Cash Register Savings Bank, Round, Footed, Register Window, Embossed, 5 ½ In.
$1,200

Bertoia Auctions

Bank, Dandy-Lion, Nodder, Bobbing, Cat, Ceramic, Holt & Howard, 1959, 6 In.
$127

celebrityresaledc on eBay

Bank, Flower Vendor, Multicolor, Spelter, Germany, c.1925
$1,103

RSL Auction

Bank, Mailbox, Eagle Finial, Brass, Hubley, c.1906, 9 ¼ In.
$424

RSL Auction

Bank, Main Street Trolley, Passengers, Cast Iron, Gold Paint, A.C. Williams, 1900s, 3 x 7 In.
$125

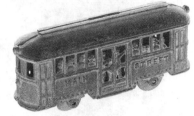

Garth's Auctioneers & Appraisers

TIP

Collector preference has changed in mechanical bank collecting. The rarest banks were the most expensive from the 1950s to the 1980s. Now the collectors want great condition more than rarity and almost perfect paint.

Bank, Mechanical, Eagle & Eaglets, Patina, Cast Iron, J. & E. Stevens, 1883, 6 In.
$452

Rich Penn Auctions

Bank, Mechanical, Rocket Ship, Strato, Duro Mold, Cheltenham Federal Savings, Box, 8 In.
$100

Pook & Pook

Cannon, Cast Iron, Nickel Plated, Hubley, 1914, 3 x 7 In.	3000
Capitalist, Portly Man In Morning Coat, Hat, Cast Iron, 5 In.	840
Car, 4 Passengers, Cast Iron, Red Paint, A.C. Williams, 6½ In.	840
Cash Register Savings Bank, Round, Footed, Register Window, Embossed, 5½ In. .... *illus*	1200
Cat With Ball, Cast Iron, Painted Black & Red, A.C. Williams, 5½ In.	1800
Cat With Toothache, Spelter, Painted, European, 4½ In.	1140
Cat, Chalkware, Sitting, Painted Eyes, Nose & Mouth, c.1900s, 9½ In.	66
Clock, Atlas, Savings, Roman Numerals, Moko, Germany, Box, 4 In.	84
Cottage Money Box, House, Tin, Chad Valley, England, Box, 4½ x 4 In.	120
Dandy-Lion, Nodder, Bobbing, Cat, Ceramic, Holt & Howard, 1959, 6 In.	127
Darkie Sharecropper, Cast Iron, Paint, A.C. Williams, 5½ In.	180
Dog, Bulldog, Gold Paint, Red Collar, Cast Iron, 4½ In.	106
Dog, Newfoundland, Cast Iron, Red Paint, Arcade, 5½ In.	240
Dog, Pug, Cast Iron, Orange Paint, Kyser & Rex, 3½ In.	840
Dog, Spaniel, Redware, Molded, Mottled Glaze, 1800s, 7¼ In.	266
Flower Vendor, Multicolor, Spelter, Germany, c.1925 .... *illus*	1103
Globe, Cast Iron, Eagle Top, Enterprise, 1876, 5¾ In.	136
Horse, Cast Iron, Tin Wheels, Cast Iron, A.C. Williams, c.1920, 5 x 4 In.	108
Horse, Tree, Spelter, Tin, Germany, c.1930	398
Indian, Two Faces, Cast Iron, Red Paint, A.C. Williams, 4¼ In.	480
Liberty Bell, Centennial, Philadelphia, Souvenir, 1876	7200
Lion, Royal, Sitting, Cast Iron, John Harper, England, c.1910, 5 In.	796
Little Miss Muffet, Money Box, Tin, Red & Yellow Paint, England, Box, 4 In.	72
Mailbox, Eagle Finial, Brass, Hubley, c.1906, 9¼ In. .... *illus*	424
Main Street Trolley, Passengers, Cast Iron, Gold Paint, A.C. Williams, 1900s, 3 x 7 In. ... *illus*	125
Mammy With Spoon, Hand On Hip, Cast Iron, Painted, A.C. Williams, 6 In.	900
Mascot, Player Standing On Baseball, American, National, Hubley, 6 In.	1140
McDonald's Big Mac Hamburger, Ceramic, c.1978, 5½ x 5½ In.	20

Mechanical banks were first made about 1870. Any bank with moving parts is considered mechanical. The metal banks made before World War I are the most desirable. Copies and new designs of mechanical banks have been made in metal or plastic since the 1920s. The condition of the paint on the old banks is important. Worn paint can lower a price by 90 percent.

Mechanical, "Jolly Nigger" In Raised Letters, Black Bowtie, Orange Shirt, Cast Iron, 1882, 7 In. ..	509
Mechanical, Ambulance, Red Cross, Need Your Help, Wood, Die Cast, 9½ In.	360
Mechanical, Billy Goat, Ornate Base, Pink Flower, Cast Iron, J. & E. Stevens, 5½ In.	600
Mechanical, Boy Scout Camp, Cast Iron, J. & E. Stevens, c.1915	11400
Mechanical, Boys Stealing Watermelons, Cast Iron, Kyser & Rex, c.1890, 5 x 6⅝ In.	1711
Mechanical, Building, Door Opens, Clerk Holds Tray, Cast Iron, J. & E. Stevens, 1870s, 7 In....	424
Mechanical, Building, Novelty, Gray, Red & White Paint, J. & E. Stevens, c.1876	11025
Mechanical, Cabin, Cast Iron, Yellow, Red, Blue, Black Paint, J.& E. Stevens, c.1900, 4 In.......	216
Mechanical, Creedmoor, Soldier Holds Rifle, Cast Iron, J. & E. Stevens, c.1877, 6¾ In..	198 to 270
Mechanical, Darktown Battery, Baseball Players, Paint, J. & E. Stevens, c.1890	11760
Mechanical, Dentist, Cast Iron, Painted, J. & E. Stevens, c.1880	1920
Mechanical, Dinah, Iron, Old Paint, Green & Maroon Dress, Black, John Harper, c.1900........	492
Mechanical, Dog On Turntable, Cast Iron, Red & Black, H.L. Judd, c.1895, 4¾ In.	330 to 780
Mechanical, Dog On Turntable, Ebony Finish, H. L. Judd, 1895	674
Mechanical, Dog, Bulldog, Coin On Nose, Blue Blanket, J. & E. Stevens, c.1880, 7⅝ In.	900 to 1103
Mechanical, Eagle & Eaglets, Patina, Cast Iron, J. & E. Stevens, 1883, 6 In...... *illus*	452
Mechanical, Frog, Climbing Ladder, Tin, Leaves, 2 Flies, Green, Germany	72
Mechanical, Frogs, Two, Mouth Opens, Cast Iron, J. & E. Stevens, 8½ In.	720
Mechanical, Girl Skipping Rope, J. & E. Stevens, c.1890, 8½ In.	21600
Mechanical, Hall's Excelsior, Cast Iron, Multicolor, J. & E. Stevens, 5½ x 3¾ In.	132
Mechanical, Hall's Excelsior, Cast Iron, Painted Yellow & Red, J. & E. Stevens, c.1869	1200
Mechanical, Hall's Lilliput, Cast Iron, J. & E. Stevens, 1875, 5 In.	531
Mechanical, Hammond's Centennial, Liberty Bell, Black Triangular Stand, 5 In.	780
Mechanical, Hen & Chicks, Bellows, Grassy Base, J. & E. Stevens, Ct., Early 1900s	7963
Mechanical, Home, Crown, Knob, Stairs, J. & E. Stevens, 1870s	2450
Mechanical, Hoop-La Bank, Barrel, Clown, Dog, John Harper, England, c.1897, 7 In.	452
Mechanical, Humpty Dumpty, Cast Iron, Multicolor, Shepard Hardware, c.1882, 7½ In.	510

Bank, Mechanical, Shepherd, Seated Girl & Dog, Cast Iron, 1885, 7 x 7 In. $236

Milestone Auctions

Bank, Mechanical, William Tell, Cast Iron, Painted , Embossed, Patented June 23, 1896, 6¾ x 10 In. $396

Garth's Auctioneers & Appraisers

Bank, Safe, Bank Of Commerce, Nickel Plated, Grey Iron Casting, 1903, 6⅝ In. $215

RSL Auction

TIP
Baking soda and vinegar or lemon juice can be used to remove rust.

B

Bank, Safe, Japanese Safe, Dragon, Nickel Plated, Cast Iron, Kyser & Rex, 1882, 5 In.
$904

RSL Auction

Bank, Safe, Pet, Cast Iron, Silver, Footed, 1910, 4⅜ In.
$158

RSL Auction

Bank, Santa Claus, Ceramic, Napco, 6 In.
$99

Etsy

Mechanical, Humpty Dumpty, Eats Coins, Cast Iron, Porcelain, Ohio Foundry, 7¼ In.		228
Mechanical, I Always Did 'Spise A Mule, Painted, Cast Iron, J. & E. Stevens, c.1915, 10 In.		330
Mechanical, Jonah & The Whale, Cast Iron, Shepard Hardware, c.1890		1320
Mechanical, Jumbo Savings, Elephant, Nods, Tin, Key Lock Trap, 5½ In.		96
Mechanical, Kiltie, Man, Mustache, England, John Harper, 1931		17150
Mechanical, Life-Boats Need Your Help, Contributions, Royal National, Plastic, 12½ In.		84
Mechanical, Lion Bust, Mouth Open, Glazed Bisque, Germany, c.1920		521
Mechanical, Lion Hunter, Teddy Roosevelt, J. & E. Stevens, c.1910, 7½ In.		10413
Mechanical, Little Jocko Musical, Orange, Tin Lithograph, Strauss Mfg. Co., c.1910		4594
Mechanical, Man, Removes Hat, Cast Lead, 5½ In.		390
Mechanical, Minstrel, Black Face, Drum Shape, Tin, Chad Valley, 1930s, 5 In.		108
Mechanical, Mule Entering Barn, Cast Iron, Green Sides, J. & E. Stevens, c.1880, 8½ In.		270
Mechanical, Organ Grinder & Performing Bear, Cast Iron, Kyser & Rex, c.1882, 7 x 5 In.		2700
Mechanical, Owl, Turns Head, Brown, Gray & White, J. & E. Stevens, c.1800		735
Mechanical, Paddy & The Pig, Cast Iron, J. & E. Stevens, c.1882		900
Mechanical, Pay Phone, Wall Phone, Crank, Mouthpiece, Nickel Plated, J. & E. Stevens, 7 In.		570
Mechanical, Pelican, Man Thumbs Nose, Dark Bronze, J. & E. Stevens, c.1880		2328
Mechanical, Rabbit, Standing, Lockwood Mfg. Co., Conn., Late 1880s		398
Mechanical, RMS Titanic, Aluminum, Painted, Sandman Designs Inc., 12 x 8 In.		240
Mechanical, Rocket Ship, Strato, Duro Mold, Cheltenham Federal Savings, Box, 8 In. *illus*		100
Mechanical, Rooster, Push Lever, Head Moves, Cast Iron, Kyser & Rex, 6¼ In.		108
Mechanical, Safe, Watch Dog, Cast Iron, J. & E. Stevens, Cromwell, c.1890		791
Mechanical, Shepherd, Seated Girl & Dog, Cast Iron, 1885, 7 x 7 In. *illus*		236
Mechanical, Speaking Dog, Girl In Blue Dress, Cast Iron, J. & E. Stevens, c.1885		4500
Mechanical, Speaking Dog, Girl In Red Dress, Shepard Hardware		437
Mechanical, Tammany, Brown Coat, Gray Pants, Green Panels, J. & E. Stevens, c.1869		1200
Mechanical, Tammany, Cast Iron, Man Sitting In Chair, J. & E. Stevens, c.1875, 6 In.		270
Mechanical, Teddy & The Bear, Patd. Appld. For, J. & E. Stevens, 7½ x 10½ In.		900
Mechanical, Trick Dog, Clown Holds Hoop, Cast Iron, Hubley		300
Mechanical, Trick Pony, Cast Iron, Blue, White, Red & Black, 7 x 12½ In.		288
Mechanical, Uncle Sam, Drops Coin In Bag, Shepard Hardware, Cast Iron, 11¼ In.		420
Mechanical, Uncle Wiggly, Rabbit, Ribbon, Hat, Tin, Chein, 5 In.		120
Mechanical, William Tell, Cast Iron, Painted , Embossed, Patented June 23, 1896, 6¾ x 10 In. *illus*		396
Merry-Go-Round, Cast Iron, Grey Iron, c.1925, 4¾ x 4⅜ In.		120
Money Bag, 200,000 Dollars, Sack, Rope Twist Cord, Gold Finish, 4 In.		660
Organ, Boy & Girl, Monkey, Crank, Kyser & Rex, c.1882		1960
Organ, Monkey, Cast Iron, Kyser & Rex, 6¼ In.		480
Owl, Cast Iron, Painted Yellow & Gray, Vindex, 4½ In.		120
Red Goose School Shoes, Goose, Cast Iron, Red Paint, Arcade, 4 In.		360
Reindeer, Cast Iron, Orange Paint, Arcade, 6 In.		1020
Rhinoceros, Red Nostrils, White Tipped Horns, Arcade, 5 In.		437
Roof, Cast Iron, Gold Highlights, J.& E. Stevens, c.1887, 5¼ x 3¾ In.		108
Safe, Arched Panel Doors, Beaded Edge, Cast Iron, Japanned, 4 In.		1080
Safe, Army, Cast Iron, Kenton, 1920, 4 In.		170
Safe, Bank Of Commerce, Nickel Plated, Grey Iron Casting, 1903, 6⅝ In. *illus*		215
Safe, Egyptian, Black, Gold Trim, Embossed Symbols, Kyser & Rex, 5 In.		1020
Safe, Eureka Trust, Nickel Plated, Cast Iron, Mudd Mfg. Co., 1895, 5¾ In.		904
Safe, Fidelity Trust Vault, Clock Combination, Barton Smith Co., 6 x 5½ x 6½ In.		83
Safe, Fidelity, Embossed Animal, Cast Iron, Black, Gold Trim, Kyser & Rex, 1881, 3 In.		720
Safe, Floral, Cast Iron, Red, Gold Trim, Combination, J. & E. Stevens, 4½ In.		390
Safe, Globe, Park Bank Variation, Cast Iron, Black, Red, J. & E. Stevens, 4½ In.		660
Safe, Home Safe Deposit, Cast, Iron, c.1900, 3⅞ In.		158
Safe, Japanese Safe, Dragon, Nickel Plated, Cast Iron, Kyser & Rex, 1882, 5 In. *illus*		904
Safe, McKinley Bust, Cast Iron, John Harper, 6 In.		6000
Safe, Moon & Star, Cast Iron, Cream Paint, Gold Trim, 5½ In.		480
Safe, National Safe Deposit, Black, Gold Scrolling Leaves, 4-Footed, Hart, 6 In.		660
Safe, Navy, Cast, Iron, Numbering Lock, Arcade, 1902, 3⅜ In.		396
Safe, New York Bank, Cast Iron, J. & E. Stevens, 1872, 4 In.		113
Safe, Pet, Cast Iron, Silver, Footed, 1910, 4⅜ In. *illus*		158
Safe, Security Safe Deposit, Cast Iron, Kyser & Rex 1881, 8 In.		254

Safe, Security, Cast Iron, Combination Lock, Footed, 1890, 4 In.		124
Safe, Security, Cast Iron, Gold & Copper Highlights, c.1894, 6 x 4¼ In.		156
Safe, Time, Cast Iron, E.M. Roche Novelty Co., 1905, 7 In.		311
Safe, White City, Puzzle, No. 12, Cast Iron, Nicol, 4¾ In.		311
Santa Claus, Ceramic, Napco, 6 In.	*illus*	99
Scotchman, No Verse, Tin Lithograph, Saalheimer & Strauss, Germany, 1930-36		306
Shell Gas Station, Multicolor, Tin, Box, Germany, 6 In.		300
Songbird, On Stump, A.C. Williams, 4¾ In.		510
Steamboat, 6 Holes In Wheel Well, Silver Paint, A.C. Williams, 8 In.		180
Steamboat, Cast Iron, Red & Gold, A.C. Williams, 1910s, 7⅝ In.	*illus*	113
Stop & Save, Red Paint, Dent, 6 In.		420
Streetcar, Oval Roof, Scrolled Sign, Grey Iron Casting, 4½ In.		180
Sundial, On Column, Cast Iron, Arcade Mfg., 4½ In.		720
Teddy Bear, Walking, Cast Iron, Embossed, Arcade, 4 x 2½ In.		55
Thing, Addams Family, Hand Reaches Out, Black, Plastic, Box, 1964, 5 In.		96
Toad, Dark Green, On Stump, J. & E. Stevens, c.1890		11025
Top Hat, Embossed, Pass Around The Hat, Black, Patina, c.1920, 2½ In.		125
Toy, Playland Movies, Mutoscope, Coin-Operated, Plastic, Admiral Toys, Box, 9¾ In.		540
Train, Main Street, Passengers, Cast Iron, Old Gold Paint, A.C. Williams, 1920s, 3 x 7 In.		125
U.S. Air Mail Box, Cast Iron, Red Paint, Pedestal Base, Dent, 6½ In.		780
Wise Owl On Book, Spelter, Painted, European, 4 In.		840

BARBER collectibles range from the popular red and white striped pole that used to be found in front of every shop to the small scissors and tools of the trade. Barber chairs are wanted, especially the older models with elaborate iron trim.

Cabinet, Mug, Wood, 12 Slots, 1960s, 24 x 27 In.		85
Cabinet, Shaving, Golden Oak, Egg & Dart Trim, Tabletop, Drawers, c.1900, 27 x 18 x 8 In.		452
Chair, Belmont, Red Vinyl Upholstery, Chrome & Brass, Hydraulic, c.1950, 51 x 31 x 41 In.		351
Chair, E. Berninghaus Co., Hercules, Leather, Porcelain, Steel, c.1920, 48 x 29 x 40 In.	*illus*	351
Chair, Eugene Berninghaus, Oak, Mauve Upholstery, Reclining Back, c.1880, 47 x 43 In.		452
Chair, Green Porcelain, Leather Upholstery, Round Seat, Koken, 50 x 26½ x 47 In.		1200
Chair, Koken Congress, Hydraulic, Black Leather, Oak Frame, c.1900, 44 x 26 x 42 In.	*illus*	1404
Chair, Paidar, Porcelain & Nickel Plate, Tweed Cloth Upholstery, 48 In.		420
Chair, Theo A. Kochs Co., Reclining Back, Brass Feet, Hydraulic, Chicago, 52½ x 25 In.		452
Fan, Mechanical, Squeeze Handle, 1911, 10 x 4 In.		2065
Pole, Electric Porcelain, Glass Cylinder, Light-Up, Theo A. Kochs Co., c.1920, 77 In.		848
Pole, Hanging, Leaded Glass, White Porcelain Top, Koken, Early 1900s, 34 x 12 In.		1582
Pole, Pine, Red, White, Blue, Painted, Turned, 45 In.		1298
Pole, Porcelain, Wall Mount, Multicolor, Glass, Glass Globe, 30 x 8 x 11 In.		1080
Pole, Wall Mount, Brass Tag, Globe Light, Red, White, Blue, Theo A. Kochs, 27 x 9 x 11 In.	*illus*	351
Pole, Wood, Blue, Red & White Paint, Red Ball Top, 43 In.		224
Pole, Wood, Turned, Carved, Painted, Red & White Spiral Stripes, 80 x 9 In.		944
Pole, Wood, Twisted Red Paint, 30 In.		192
Razor Blade Safe, Ever-Ready Blades, Chest Form, Tin, Lift Lid, 1930s-40s, 2 In.	*illus*	27
Shoeshine Stand, Walnut, Mahogany Stain, 2 Marble Tiers, Cast Iron Rests, 63 x 38 In.		254
Sign, Shop, Red, White, Black, Wood, Painted, 2-Sided, 1900s, 10 x 26 In.		338

BAROMETERS are used to forecast the weather. Antique barometers with elaborate wooden cases and brass trim are the most desirable. Mercury column barometers are also popular with collectors. It is difficult to find someone to repair a broken one, so be sure your barometer is in working condition.

Admiral Fitzroy's, Oak Case, Carved, 1800s, 42 x 9½ In.		472
Aneroid, Brass, Silvered Dial, Selsi Company Inc., England, Early 1900s, 4 x 3 x 1 In.		69
Banjo, Louis XV Style, Bird Finial, Tassels, Leafy Branches, Gilt, Painted, 1900s, 39 In.		431
Banjo, Mahogany, Inlay, Signed, F. Amadio, 39 x 12 In.		720
Banjo, Rosewood, Carved Trim, Silvered Dial, Incised Letters, 40½ x 13 In.	*illus*	182
Empire, Giltwood, Lozenge Shape, Lyre Finial, Selon Torricelli, c.1825, 36 x 19 In.		2125
Mahogany, Mercury Tube, Timby's Patent, Alex Marsh, John Merrick & Co., 38½ In.		185
Nautical, Gimbaled, Mahogany, Brass, Bone Scales, Beveled Glass, 41 In.		3186

Bank, Steamboat, Cast Iron, Red & Gold, A.C. Williams, 1910s, 7⅝ In.
$113

RSL Auction

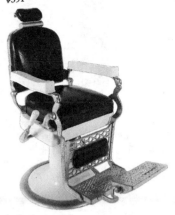

Barber, Chair, E. Berninghaus Co., Hercules, Leather, Porcelain, Steel, c.1920, 48 x 29 x 40 In.
$351

Cordier Auctions

Barber, Chair, Koken Congress, Hydraulic, Black Leather, Oak Frame, c.1900, 44 x 26 x 42 In.
$1,404

Cordier Auctions

TIP
Don't put your name on your mailbox, front door mat, or screen door. It helps burglars find your phone number, then find out when you are away.

27

Barber, Pole, Wall Mount, Brass Tag, Globe Light, Red, White, Blue, Theo A. Kochs, 27 x 9 x 11 In.

$351

Cordier Auctions

Barber, Razor Blade Safe, Ever-Ready Blades, Chest Form, Tin, Lift Lid, 1930s-40s, 2 In.

$27

Jack & Jeff Hayes

Barometer, Banjo, Rosewood, Carved Trim, Silvered Dial, Incised Letters, 40½ x 13 In.

$182

Fontaine's Auction Gallery

Painted Glass Face, Cosulich Line, Lloyd Triestino, 1900s, 14¼ x 9½ In.		188
Stick, Agricultural, Mahogany, Lyman King, N.Y., 1800s, 38 In.		354
Stick, Inlaid, Mercury Tube, Arched, Pediment, Marked, W. Gittens, 1800s, 38 In.		234
Stick, Mahogany, Brass, Spencer Browning & Co., London, 38 In.		480
Stick, Mahogany, Gimballed Arm, Brass, G. Bradford, London, 1800s, 36½ In.		600
Stick, Mahogany, Jas W. Queen, Pa., 1800s, 36¼ In.		1220
Stick, Mercury, Arched Case, Hinged Glazed Door, Brass Dial, Stepped Base, Red, 9 In.		185
Stick, Oak, Brown, Temperature, Signed, F. Robson, 40 x 9½ In.		363
Stick, Walnut, Marked, Charles Wilder, N.H., 1800s, 37¼ In.		1342
Thermometer, Walnut, Acanthus Leaf Carving, Victorian, c.1880, 35 x 10 In.		150
Wheel, Mahogany, Flower & Shell Inlays, George III, London, c.1800, 39 x 10 In.		77
Wheel, Mahogany, Line Inlay, Mercury, Thermometer, England, 1800s, 38 In.		330
Wheel, Nautical, Glass & Porcelain Face, Wood, Brass, Atco Co., Germany, 7 In.		59
Wheel, Thermometer, Mahogany, Swan Neck Pediment, Signed, Riva, Scotland, c.1835, 39 In.		440

BASALT is a special type of ceramic invented by Josiah Wedgwood in the eighteenth century. It is a fine-grained, unglazed stoneware. The most common type is black, but many other colors were made. It was made by many factories. Some pieces may be listed in the Wedgwood section.

Bust, Shakespeare, Collar, Buttons, Convex Base, Impressed Shakespeare, 12 x 8 In.	150
Coffeepot, Lid, Enameled Flowers, Pink, Cream, Green, Hand Painted	275
Creamer, Egyptian Black, Glazed, Lydia Cyples, c.1830, 3 x 4 In.	108
Figurine, Psyche, Seated On Rock, c.1850, 8 In.	395
Paperweight, Head, King Tut, Carved, 1920s, 4 x 2 In.	245

BASEBALL *collectibles are in the Sports category. Baseball cards are listed under Baseball in the Card category.*

BASKETS of all types are popular with collectors. American Indian, Japanese, African, Nantucket, Shaker, and many other kinds of baskets may be found in other sections. Of course, baskets are still being made, so a collector must learn to judge the age and style of a basket to determine its value. Also see Purse.

Bamboo, Food, 2 Tiers, Rectangular, Key-Fret Band, Carved Handle, Chinese, 15¼ In.	*illus*	215
Bee Skep, Rye Straw, Red Paint, Pennsylvania, 1800s, 13 In.		813
Buttocks, Green Paint, Loop Handle, 1800s, 12 x 10 In.		198
Buttocks, Oak Handle & Frame, Tight Weave, 12 x 11½ In.		81
Buttocks, Slit Hickory, Eye-Of-God Binding, Old Red Paint, Handle, 13 x 11 In.	*illus*	176
Buttocks, Splint, Woven, Bentwood Handle, 18 x 17 x 14 In.		47
Cheese, Flat-Sided, Brown, Handle, 17 x 14 x 15½ In.		47
Egg, Wire, Wood Handle, 17¼ x 13½ x 12½ In.		35
Gathering, Lid, Red Paint, Metal Rings, 15 x 16 In.		118
Gathering, Round, Brown Paint, Splint, Woven, Reinforced, Bentwood Handle, 12½ x 13 In.		106
Gathering, Splint, Woven, Bentwood Handle, 21½ x 14 x 10½ In.		47
Hamper, Bamboo Faced, Wood, Hinged Top, 1900s, 21 x 21 x 13 In.		138
Harvest, Grape, Fan Shape, France, 34½ In.		138
Japanese, Heart, Susutake & Hobichiku Bamboo, Rattan, T. Shigeo, 10 x 18 In.	*illus*	17500
Japanese, Ikebana, Bird's Nest, Double Wall, 4 Bamboo Feet, Wrapped Handle, 16 In.		450
Japanese, Ikebana, Cylindrical, Rootwood Handle, c.1900, 23 In.	*illus*	390
Japanese, Ikebana, Flowers, Cone, Flared Rim, 4-Footed, Wisteria Branch Handle, 17 In.		144
Japanese, Purple Bamboo, Dragon Bone Flower, Rattan, S. Shobun, 18 x 10 In.		8750
Longaberger, Green Stripes, Green Knob Lid, 1999, 13 x 19½ x 8 In.		66
Nantucket, Carved Wood Ears, Swing Handles, Copper Pins, Late 1800s, 5 x 9¾ x 8 In.		1260
Nantucket, Lightship, Swing Handle, Round, Wood Bottom, c.1900, 5 x 6½ In.		225
Nantucket, Oval, Swing Handle, Signed, Martha Lawrence, 1990, 6½ x 15 In.		63
Nantucket, Round, Handle, Whalebone, Herbert Sandsbury, 1954, 10½ In.		1080
Nantucket, Round, Swing Handle, High Sides, Turned Base, c.1950, 8 x 9 In.		308
Nantucket, Round, Swing Handle, Signed, Denis Bordeux, 10½ x 19½ In.		125
Pulled Rod, White Oak, Arched Handles, Shenandoah Valley, c.1950, 5 x 12½ In.	*illus*	199

Basket, Bamboo, Food, 2 Tiers, Rectangular, Key-Fret Band, Carved Handle, Chinese, 15 ¼ In.
$215

Clars Auction Gallery

Basket, Buttocks, Slit Hickory, Eye-Of-God Binding, Old Red Paint, Handle, 13 x 11 In.
$176

Forsythes' Auctions

Basket, Japanese, Heart, Susutake & Hobichiku Bamboo, Rattan, T. Shigeo, 10 x 18 In.
$17,500

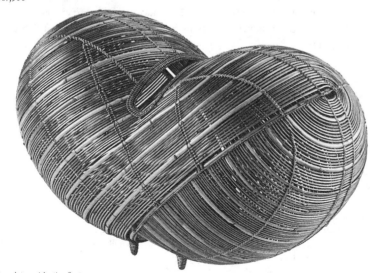

Rago Arts and Auction Center

Basket, Japanese, Ikebana, Cylindrical, Rootwood Handle, c.1900, 23 In.
$390

Eldred's

Basket, Pulled Rod, White Oak, Arched Handles, Shenandoah Valley, c.1950, 5 x 12 ½ In.
$199

Jeffrey S. Evans & Associates

Basket, Splint, Gray Paint, Handle, Rectangular Rim & Base, England, 1800s, 19 x 34 ½ In.
$308

Skinner, Inc.

Basket, Taghkanic, Black Ash, Swing Handle, Late 1800s, 3 ½ x 5 ½ In.
$236

Copake Auction

Basket, Woven, Diamond Patterns, 2 Hinged Lids, Handle, Inverted Saucer Base, 1900s, 7 In.
$156

Garth's Auctioneers & Appraisers

Batman, Comic Book Art, Many Deaths Of Batman, Artboard, Pen & Ink, Jim Aparo, 1989, 11 x 16 In.
$1,356

Hake's Auctions

Batman, Comic Book, Batman, No. 2, Summer Issue, Joker & Catwoman, 1940
$7,148

Hake's Auctions

Batman, Comic Book, Batman, No. 9, 1st Batman Christmas Story, J. Burnley Cover, Feb.-Mar., 1942
$3,764

Hake's Auctions

Rye Straw, Sawtooth Rim, Pennsylvania, 1800s, 3 ½ x 9 ½ In.	281
Splint, Ash, Hemispherical, Bentwood Handle, 1800s, 13 ½ x 16 In.	523
Splint, Ash, Lid, Red Paint, Rectangular, 3 ½ x 5 In.	738
Splint, Cylindrical, Hinged Lid, Painted Red, 1800s, 12 x 17 In.	1107
Splint, Gray Paint, Handle, Rectangular Rim & Base, England, 1800s, 19 x 34 ½ In. ..... *illus*	308
Splint, Market, White Oak, Stave, Arched Handle, Southern, Mid 1900s, 13 ¼ x 12 ½ In.	59
Splint, Melon, Miniature, 1800s, 4 In.	138
Splint, Oak, Kidney Shape, Ribs, Wrapped Rim, Arched Handle, Southern, c.1950, 4 x 4 In.	199
Splint, Red Paint, Circular Rim, Leather Strap & Steel Hook, 1800s, 13 ¼ x 10 ¼ In.	209
Splint, Storage, Woven, Lid, Green Banding, 28 ½ x 17 ½ In.	35
Splint, White Oak, Stave, Arched Handle, Wrapped Rim, Dyed Decoration, c.1915, 7 x 5 In.	82
Splint, White Paint, Swing Handle, Round Rim, Square Bottom, 1800s, 21 x 13 In.	523
Splint, Work, Stave, White Oak, Arched Handle, X-Wrap Rim, Va., c.1915, 16 x 11 In.	82
Splint, Work, White Oak, Ribs, Kidney Shape, Arched Handle, Wrapped Rim, c.1850, 11 x 14 In.	70
Splint, Work, White Oak, Wrapped Handles, Open Weave Button, c.1915, 26 x 13 ¾ In.	70
Splint, Woven, White Oak, Oval, Angular Handle, Va., c.1880, 17 ½ x 14 ½ In.	410
Split Hickory, Market, Brown, Handle, 13 ½ x 25 ¼ In.	71
Split Oak, Painted, Blue & White, Bentwood Handle, 1800s, 11 x 15 In.	625
Taghkanic, Black Ash, Swing Handle, Late 1800s, 3 ½ x 5 ½ In. .... *illus*	236
Tray, Splint, White Oak, Forked Handle, Wrapped Double Rim, c.1850, 15 ½ In.	3393
Willow, Provincial, Woven, Baluster, France, 1800s, 30 x 24 In.	500
Woven, Diamond Patterns, 2 Hinged Lids, Handle, Inverted Saucer Base, 1900s, 7 In. ...... *illus*	156
Woven, Grain, Triangle Pattern, Democratic Republic Of Congo, 19 In.	185
Woven, Ivory Walrus Head Finial, Signed Joe Sikvayugak, Alaska, 3 x 4 In.	360

BATCHELDER
LOS ANGELES
BATCHELDER products are made from California clay. Ernest Batchelder established a tile studio in Pasadena, California, in 1909. He went into partnership with Frederick Brown in 1912 and the company became Batchelder and Brown. In 1920 he built a larger factory with a new partner. The Batchelder-Wilson Company made all types of architectural tiles, garden pots, and bookends. The plant closed in 1932. In 1936 Batchelder opened Batchelder Ceramics, also in Pasadena, and made bowls, vases, and earthenware pots. He retired in 1951 and died in 1957. Pieces are marked *Batchelder Pasadena* or *Batchelder Los Angeles*.

Tile, Arts & Crafts, Peacock, Terra-Cotta, 1920s, 6 x 9 In.	375
Tile, Arts & Crafts, Stylized Pomegranates, Teal Matte Glaze, c.1920, 4 x 4 In.	135

BATMAN and Robin are characters from a comic book created by Bob Kane. Batman first appeared in a 1939 issue of *Detective Comics*. The first Batman comic book was published in 1940. In 1966, the characters became part of a popular television series. There have been radio and movie serials that featured the pair. The first full-length movie was made in 1989.

Action Figure, Mask, Cape, Blue, Box, 12 ½ In.	365
Bank, Heroes, Joker 37, Robber, Dark Knight Trilogy, Funko Pop, Vinyl	97
Button, Batman, Blue Face Mask, DC Comics, Projected Logo, 1989, 1 ¾ In.	10
Button, Nothing Can Stop, Batman, Red Text, Yellow Background, 1 ¾ In.	10
Comic Book Art, Many Deaths Of Batman, Artboard, Pen & Ink, Jim Aparo, 1989, 11 x 16 In. ...*illus*	1356
Comic Book, Batman, No. 2, Summer Issue, Joker & Catwoman, 1940 .... *illus*	7148
Comic Book, Batman, No. 9, 1st Batman Christmas Story, J. Burnley Cover, Feb.-Mar., 1942...*illus*	3764
Comic Book, Batman, No. 36, Cameron & Finger Stories, Dick Sprang Cover, August, 1946	422
Costume, Mask, Outfit, Box, Ben Cooper, 1970	63
Figure, Vinyl, Red Chrome, DC Super Heroes, Funko, Pop, Case	42
Mask, Dark Knight, Soft Helmet, Black, Cosplay, Adults, 8 ¾ x 7 x 6 In.	18
Photograph, Adam West, Glossy, Autograph, 8 x 10 In.	11
Sign, Drink Coke Classic, Batman, Arrow, Metal, Red Ground, White & Yellow Letters	19
Toothbrush, Blister Card, Battery Operated, Janex, 1974	50
Toy, Batcycle, Captain Action, Motorcycle, Plastic, Irwin, 1966	145
Toy, Batman, Walking, Tin, Vinyl Head, Cloth Cape, Battery Operated, T.N., Japan, 12 In.. *illus*	2990
Toy, Batmobile, Batman & Robin, Red & Blue, Battery Operated, Box, Taiwan, 10 In.	637
Toy, Batmobile, Black, Blue Windshield, Yellow Headlight, Battery Operated, Animated Series.	52

BATTERSEA enamels, which are enamels painted on copper, were made in the Battersea district of London from about 1750 to 1756. Many similar enamel boxes, old and new, are mistakenly called Battersea.

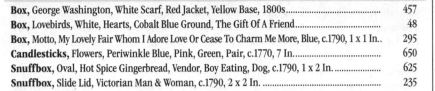

Box, George Washington, White Scarf, Red Jacket, Yellow Base, 1800s	457
Box, Lovebirds, White, Hearts, Cobalt Blue Ground, The Gift Of A Friend	48
Box, Motto, My Lovely Fair Whom I Adore Love Or Cease To Charm Me More, Blue, c.1790, 1 x 1 In.	295
Candlesticks, Flowers, Periwinkle Blue, Pink, Green, Pair, c.1770, 7 In.	650
Snuffbox, Oval, Hot Spice Gingerbread, Vendor, Boy Eating, Dog, c.1790, 1 x 2 In.	625
Snuffbox, Slide Lid, Victorian Man & Woman, c.1790, 2 x 2 In.	235

BAUER pottery is a California-made ware. J.A. Bauer bought Paducah Pottery in Paducah, Kentucky, in 1885. He moved the pottery to Los Angeles, California, in 1910. The company made art pottery after 1912 and introduced dinnerware marked *Bauer* in 1930. The factory went out of business in 1962 and the molds were destroyed. Since 1998, a new company, Bauer Pottery Company of Los Angeles, has been making Bauer pottery using molds made from original Bauer pieces. The pottery is now made in Highland, California. Pieces are marked *Bauer Pottery Company of Los Angeles.* Original pieces of Bauer pottery are listed here. See also the Russel Wright category.

Ashtray, Cowboy Hat, Burgundy, 2½ x 4⅞ In.		28
Bean Pot, Jade Green, 2 Handles, Lid, 1930s, 3 Qt., 8½ In.		43
Bowl, Half Pumpkin, Speckled Beige, No. 514, Tracy Irwin, 10 In.		19
Cal-Art, Flowerpot, Swirl Body, Glossy Yellow, Ray Murray, 1938, 6 x 7 In.		16
Cal-Art, Vase, Robot, Green Matte, Art Deco, Ray Murray, c.1940, 4 x 2⅞ In.		53
La Linda, Pepper Shaker, Gray, Glossy, 2 In.		13
Monterey Moderne, Bowl, Pink, Speckled, 8 In.		21
Monterey Moderne, Cup, Flat, Pink, 2¼ In.		26
Monterey, Casserole, Lid, Pink, Speckled, Brass Cradle, 1950s, 7¾ In.		36
Monterey, Pitcher, Blue, Rings, Ice Lip		31
Plain, Carafe, Orange, Rubber Gasket, Wood Handle, Lid, Finial, 1935, 9 In.	*illus*	133
Plain, Plate, Dinner, Jade Green, Round, Stamped, 11 In.		57
Ring, Casserole, Lid, Yellow, 7¾ In.		55
Ring, Plate, Cobalt Blue, 9½ In.		84
Ring, Refrigerator Jar, Lid, Cobalt Blue, 1930s, 6 In.		37
Swirl, Jardiniere, Green, c.1930, 7 In.		125
Vase, Fan, Orange, Ribbed, Hand Thrown, Matt Carlton, California, 5¾ x 6 In.		70

BAVARIA is a region in Europe where many types of porcelain were made. In the nineteenth century, the mark often included the word *Bavaria.* After 1871, the words *Bavaria, Germany,* were used. Listed here are pieces that include the name *Bavaria* in some form, but major porcelain makers, such as Rosenthal, are listed in their own categories.

Bowl, Lid, The Thelma, Flowers, Gold Trim, Paul Muller, 12 x 8 In.	60
Bowl, Vegetable, Square, White Ground, Gold & Brown Rim, 1950s, 7 x 2 In.	13
Cup & Saucer, Pink Rose, Blue, Flowers, Gold Trim, Crown Mark	31
Plate, Pink Roses, Scalloped Edge, 1930s, 9 In.	18
Relish Tray, Pink Roses, Green Leaves, White Ground, Open Handles, c.1910, 9 x 4 In.	32

BEADED BAGS *are included in the Purse category.*

BEATLES collectors search for any items picturing the four members of the famous music group or any of their recordings. Because these items are so new, the condition is very important and top prices are paid for items in mint condition. The Beatles first appeared on American network television in 1964. The group disbanded in 1971. Ringo Starr and Paul McCartney are still performing. John Lennon died in 1980. George Harrison died in 2001.

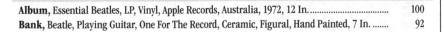

Album, Essential Beatles, LP, Vinyl, Apple Records, Australia, 1972, 12 In.	100
Bank, Beatle, Playing Guitar, One For The Record, Ceramic, Figural, Hand Painted, 7 In.	92

Batman, Toy, Batman, Walking, Tin, Vinyl Head, Cloth Cape, Battery Operated, T.N., Japan, 12 In.
$2,990

Weiss Auctions

Bauer, Plain, Carafe, Orange, Rubber Gasket, Wood Handle, Lid, Finial, 1935, 9 In.
$133

b4y2k! on eBay

Beatles, Lunch Box, Yellow Submarine, Metal, King-Seeley, 1968
$374

Main Auction Galleries, Inc.

Beatles, Poster, Beatle Bar, Ice Cream Bars, Yea! Yea! Yea!, Beatles, Hood, 1965, 20 x 16 In.
$840

Thomaston Place Auction Galleries

Beer Can, Rocky Mountain, Cone Top, Anaconda, Montana, Early 1950s
$66

jkottocans on eBay

Bell, Brass, Hotel, Clockwork, Ornate Detail, Claw Foot, France, 5 ¾ x 5 ¾ In.
$236

AntiqueAdvertising.com

Binder, Band Portrait, Facsimile Signatures, Yellow Vinyl, NEMS Enterprise, 1964	148
Button, I'm A Beatles Fan, Portraits, Red, White, Green Duck Co., 2 ¼ In.	75
Game, Flip Your Wig, 4 Figures, Cards, Box, Milton Bradley, 1964	151
Hanger, Door, We All Live In A Yellow Submarine, Pictures, Cardboard	15
Lunch Box, Yellow Submarine, Metal, King-Seeley, 1968 .... *illus*	374
Ornament, Christmas, Sgt. Pepper's Lonely Hearts Club Band, Beatles On Drum, Kurt Adler ..	11
Pin, I Hate The Beatles, White Ground, Blue & Red Lettering, 3 ½ In.	221
Poster, Beatle Bar, Ice Cream Bars, Yea! Yea! Yea!, Beatles, Hood, 1965, 20 x 16 In. .... *illus*	840
Poster, Let It Be, The Beatles, Movie Daybill, Australia, 1970, 13 x 29 In.	118
Record Case, Disk-Go, Portraits, Green, White Handle, 1966	189
Record, Sgt. Pepper's Lonely Hearts Club, 33 ⅓ RPM, Parlophone, United Kingdom, 12 In.	22
Record, Sgt. Pepper's Lonely Hearts Club Band, 1967, 78 RPM	158
Record, White Album, Pop & Beat, LP, 33 ⅓ RPM, 1960s, 12 In.	480
Scarf, Beatlemania Sweeps Australia, Band Members, Pink, Silk, 1964, 26 x 26 In.	102
Wristwatch, Stainless Steel, 12-Hour Dial, The Beatles, Silver, Raymond Weil, 9 ½ In.	650

BEEHIVE, Austria, or Beehive, Vienna, are terms used in English-speaking countries to refer to the many types of decorated porcelain bearing a mark that looks like a beehive. The mark is actually a shield, viewed upside down. It was first used in 1744 by the Royal Porcelain Manufactory of Vienna. The firm made what collectors call Royal Vienna porcelains until it closed in 1864. Many other German, Austrian, and Japanese factories have reproduced Royal Vienna wares, complete with the original shield or beehive mark. This listing includes the expensive, original Royal Vienna porcelains and many other types of beehive porcelain. The Royal Vienna pieces include that name in the description.

Imperial and Royal Porcelain Manufactory
Vienna, Austria
1749–1827

Bourdois & Bloch
Paris, France
c.1900

Waechtersbach Earthenware Factory
Schlierbach, Hesse, Germany
1921–1928

Bowl, Stylized Poppies, Green, Gilt Rim, 10 In.	20
Charger, Figures, Classical Scene, Banded Border, Scrolled Gilt Leaves, Late 1800s, 14 In.	677
Charger, Portrait, Leonardo Da Vinci, Cobalt Blue Surround, Germany, 1800s, 16 In.	1250
Plate, 2 Young Girls, Whispering, Candlelight, Flowers, Wagner, Austria, 1900s, 10 In.	594
Plate, Bare Breast Beauty, Red Cap, Floral, Una Gitana, Wagner, Austria, 1900s, 10 In.	1140
Plate, Cabinet, Maiden Wearing A Wreath, Epheu, Signed, Wagner, Royal Vienna, 1800s, 9 ½ In.	1063
Plate, Portrait, Woman, Formal Attire, Pearls, Cobalt Rim, Wagner, c.1985, 9 ¾ In.	688
Plate, Woman, Sitting, Bejeweled Headband, La Bella Imperia, c.1850, 9 ½ In.	688
Plate, Woman, Small Frogs, 2 Herons, Vienna, Cobalt Rim, W. Revicha, 8 ¾ In.	390
Potpourri, Royal Vienna, 3 Fluted Legs, Claw Feet, Cylindrical Bowl, Red Body, 17 x 8 In.	1694
Urn, Lid, Figural Transfer, Handle, Plinth Base, Royal Vienna, Kaufmann, 19 ½ In.	94
Urn, Painted, 2 Women, Stepped Base, Cobalt, Gold Gilt, Porcelain, Royal Vienna, 23 x 8 In.	187
Urn, Portrait Of Young Woman, Gilt, Spider, Web, Signed, Kies, 7 ½ x 3 ½ x 5 In.	94
Urn, Women, Putti, Pierced Rim, Signed, Kohler, 1900s, 8 ½ x 8 In.	363
Urn, Young Cupid & Venus, Hand Painted, Oval Panel, H. Pohl, Royal Vienna, 23 x 7 In.	189
Vase, Lid, Cartouches, Portraits, Women, Girls, Gilt, Gorner, c.1890, 17 ½ In.	225
Vase, Oval Cartouche, Maiden, Signed, Wagner, Irrlicht, Royal Vienna, 1800, 7 ⅛ In.	500

BEER BOTTLES *are listed in the Bottle category under Beer.*

BEER CANS are a twentieth-century idea. Beer was sold in kegs or returnable bottles until 1934. The first patent for a can was issued to the American Can Company in September of that year, and Gotfried Kruger Brewing Company, Newark, New Jersey, was the first to use the can. The cone-top can was first made in 1935, the aluminum pop-top in 1962. Collectors should look for cans in good condition, with no dents or rust. Serious collectors prefer cans that have been opened from the bottom.

49er Premium Beer, Flat Top, Atlas Brewery, Totem Pole, Illinois, 1950s, 12 Oz.	1100
81 Beer, Pull Top, Beldo & Willmarth, Red, White Ground, Illinois, c.1969, 12 Oz.	2000
Acme, Flat Top, Grace Bros., Santa Rosa, Calif., Late 1950s, 12 Oz.	125
Alt Heidelberg, Flat Top, Columbia Brewery, Silver Ground, Red, Blue, 1936-37, 12 Oz.	300
Bavarian's Select Beer, Pull Top, International Brewery Co., Covington, Ky., 1964, 12 Oz.	125
Bull Dog Ale, Pull Top, Maier Brewery Co., Los Angeles, Mid 1960s, 12 Oz.	95
Burger, Sparkle Brewed, Light, Flat Top, Cylindrical, Ohio, Mid 1950s	153
Carling Black Label, Bock, Flat Top, White Ground, Red & Black, Cleveland	234
Cook's Gold Blume Beer, Cone Top, F.W. Cook Brewery, Boat, Red, Gold, c.1950, 12 Oz.	650
Crystal Rock Pilsener, Flat Top, White Label, Ohio	93
Drewrys Ale, Old Stock, South Bend, Indiana, Flat Top	21
Eastside, Flat Top, Cylindrical, Breweriana Collection, California	153
Iron City, Cone Top, Red, White, Pittsburgh Brewery Co., 1950s, 12 Oz.	600
Jaguar Malt Liquor, Metallic, Leopard Print, Jaguar Brewery Co., 1960s, 12 Oz.	250
Kaier's Special, Light Lager, Flat Top, Black & Red Lettering, White Ground	22
Krueger Cream Ale, Flat Top, Cylindrical, 1-Sided, Bottom Open, N.Y.	11
Krueger Finest, Light Lager, Flat Top, Red, Yellow, White, 1858	238
Miller High Life, Flat Top, Clean, Cylindrical, Green Ground, 1950s	116
Old Milwaukee, Flat Top, Cylindrical, Rare Gold, Wisconsin	22
Pabst, Old Tankard Ale, Flat Top, Cylindrical, Gray, N.Y.	240
Pickwick Ale, Famous For Flavor, Flat Top, Can, Haffenreffer, Boston, Ma., 1900s	36
Rocky Mountain, Cone Top, Anaconda, Montana, Early 1950s......................*illus*	66
Schlitz, Sunshine, Vitamin D, Cone Top, Crown Cap, 1932	344
Schlitz, Vitamin D, Cone Top, Gold, Red, Jos. Schlitz Brewery, Early 1940s, 12 Oz.	275

BELL collectors collect all types of bells. Favorites include glass bells, figural bells, school bells, and cowbells. Bells have been made of porcelain, china, or metal through the centuries.

Brass, Dinner, Wood Handle, Hanging Ring, 1800s, 11 ¼ In.	111
Brass, Hotel, Clockwork, Ornate Detail, Claw Foot, France, 5 ¾ x 5 ¾ In. ....*illus*	236
Brass, Hotel, Ornate Detail, Figural Nude Supports, Mechanical, 5 ⅝ x 6 In. ....*illus*	354
Bronze, Church, Relief, Jesus & Mary, Flowers, Scrolls, 9 In.	555
Cut Glass, Dinner, Crosscut Diamond, Strawberry Diamond & Fan, 5 In.	150
Iron, Hotel, Figural, Man, Hi-Wheel Bicycle, Turn Knob, 8 ½ x 5 ¾ In.	1416
Porcelain, Tea Rose, Pink Ribbon, Pfaltzgraff, 1990	11
Sleigh, 29 Brass Bells, Graduated, 2-Layer Leather Strap	345

BELLEEK china was made in Ireland, other European countries, and the United States. The glaze is creamy yellow and appears wet. The first Belleek was made in 1857 in the village of Belleek, County Fermanagh, in what is now Northern Ireland. In 1884 the name of the company became the Belleek Pottery Works Company Ltd. The mark changed through the years. The first mark, black, dates from 1863 to 1891. The second mark, black, dates from 1891 to 1926 and includes the words *Co. Fermanagh, Ireland.* The third mark, black, dates from 1926 to 1946 and has the words *Deanta in Eireann.* The fourth mark, same as the third mark but green, dates from 1946 to 1955. The fifth mark (second green mark) dates from 1955 to 1965 and has an *R* in a circle added in the upper right. The sixth mark (third green mark) dates from 1965 to 1981 and the words *Co. Fermanagh* have been omitted. The seventh mark, gold, was used from 1981 to 1992 and omits the words *Deanta in Eireann.* The eighth mark, used from 1993 to 1996, is similar to the second mark but is printed in blue. The ninth mark, blue, includes the words *Est. 1857,* and the words *Co. Fermanagh Ireland* are omitted. The tenth mark, black, is similar to the ninth mark but includes the words *Millennium 2000* and *Ireland.* It was used only in 2000. The eleventh mark, similar to the millennium mark but green, was introduced in 2001. The twelfth mark, black, is similar to the eleventh mark but has a banner above the mark with the words *Celebrating 150 Years.* It was used in 2007. The thirteenth trademark, used from 2008 to 2010, is similar to the twelfth but is brown and has no banner. The fourteenth mark, the Classic Belleek trademark, is similar to the twelfth but includes Belleek's website address. The Belleek Living trademark was introduced in 2010 and is used on items from that giftware line. All pieces listed here are Irish Belleek. The word *Belleek* is now used only on pieces made in Ireland even though earlier pieces from other countries were

Bell, Brass, Hotel, Ornate Detail, Figural Nude Supports, Mechanical, 5 ⅝ x 6 In.
$354

AntiqueAdvertising.com

Belleek, Pitcher, Porcelain, Flowers, White, Loop Handle, 9 ¼ In.
$98

Skinner, Inc.

Belleek, Plate, 13-Star Flag, 13 Kinds Of Flowers, 3 Strands, Box, Bicentennial, 10 In.
$2,500

Leslie Hindman Auctioneers

Bennington, Pitcher, Rockingham Glaze, Molded Ethan Allen Hunt Scene, 1800s, 9¾ In. $125

Selkirk Auctioneers & Appraisers

Betty Boop, Doll, Baby, Red Pajamas, Hearts, Cap, Girl, Big Eyes, Curly Hair, 10 In. $9

saints*vintage on eBay

Betty Boop, Doll, Bimbo, Composition Head, Wood Jointed Body, Decal, Cameo, 1930s, 11 In. $552

Weiss Auctions

sometimes marked *Belleek*. These early pieces are listed in this book by manufacturer, such as Ceramic Art Co., Lenox, Ott & Brewer, and Willets.

Belleek Pottery Co.
1863–1891

Ceramic Art Co.
1894–1906

Willets Manufacturing Co.
1879–1912+

Box, Tobacco, Bacchus Mask, Faces, Grapes, Leaves, 3rd Mark, Black, 1926-46, 6 x 3 In.	150
Cake Plate, Grass Pattern, Handled, 1st Mark, Black, 1863-91, 11½ In.	85
Coffeepot, Bacchus Mask, Grapes, Leaves, Yellow Tint Luster, 3rd Mark, Black, 1926-46, 9 In.	325
Dish, Lid, Tridacna Pink, 2nd Mark, Black, 1891-1926, 8 x 6 x 3 In.	625
Ice Pail, Lid, Putto Blowing Horn, Dolphin, Hippocampi, Mermaids, Prince Of Wales, 19 In.	1250
Pitcher, Porcelain, Flowers, White, Loop Handle, 9¼ In. .... *illus*	98
Plate, 13-Star Flag, 13 Kinds Of Flowers, 3 Strands, Box, Bicentennial, 10 In. .... *illus*	2500
Platter, Round, Mint Green, Scalloped Edges, 2nd Mark, Black, 1891-1926, 16 In.	500
Vase, Flower Encrusted Tree, 2 Birds, Nest Stump, 1900s, 12 In.	63
Vase, Shell, Imperial, Scroll Shape Stand, 1800s, 10 In.	813
Vase, Urn Shape, Flowers & Gilt, 1900s, 18½ In.	154

BENNINGTON ware was the product of two factories working in Bennington, Vermont. Both the Norton Company and Lyman Fenton & Company were out of business by 1896. The wares include brown and yellow mottled pottery, Parian, scroddled ware, stoneware, graniteware, yellowware, and Staffordshire-type vases. The name is also a generic term for mottled brownware of the type made in Bennington.

Billhead, Logo, Wholesale Prices, Bennington Stoneware Pottery, Vt., 1863, 14½ x 8 In.	59
Coffeepot, Lid, Scalloped Rib, Olive Green Glaze, Lyman, Fenton & Co., 1849, 12½ In.	840
Paperweight, Figural, Dog, Spaniel, On Pillow, Impressed Lyman, Fenton & Co., 1800s, 3 x 4½ In.	488
Pitcher, Rockingham Glaze, Molded Ethan Allen Hunt Scene, 1800s, 9¾ In. .... *illus*	125

BERLIN, a German porcelain factory, was started in 1751 by Wilhelm Kaspar Wegely. In 1763, the factory was taken over by Frederick the Great and became the Royal Berlin Porcelain Manufactory. It is still in operation today. Pieces have been marked in a variety of ways.

Bust, Nude Maiden, White, Draped Head Covering, Royal Berlin, c.1890, 12½ In.	1050
Figurine, Man, Pipe In Hand, Animal Skin Sack, Feathered Hat, 1800s, 9 In.	1650
Figurine, Prussian Miner, Military Uniform, Green Hat, 6½ In.	405
Group, Mythological, Bacchanal, Iron Red Orb Mark, c.1860, 10 x 9 x 8 In.	1597
Plate, Woman Buying Bread From Baker, Marked, 1847-49, 10 In.	716

BESWICK started making pottery in Staffordshire, England, in 1894. The pottery became John Beswick Ltd. in 1936. The company became part of Royal Doulton Tableware, Ltd. in 1969. Production ceased in 2002 and the John Beswick brand was bought by Dartington Crystal in 2004. Figurines, vases, and other items are being made and use the name Beswick. Beatrix Potter figures were made from 1948 until 2002. They shouldn't be confused with Bunnykins, which were made by Royal Doulton.

Figurine, Mountain Lion, Snarling, Raised Paw, Brown, Rocky Base, 8½ x 13 In.	61
Teapot, Panda Bear, Seated, Eating Bamboo Stalk, Black, White, Cream, 7 In.	50

BETTY BOOP, the cartoon figure, first appeared on the screen in 1930. Her face was modeled after the famous singer Helen Kane and her body after Mae West. In 1935, a comic strip was started. Her dog was named Pudgy. Although the Betty Boop cartoons ended by 1938, there was a revival of interest in the Betty Boop image in the 1980s and new pieces are being made.

Button, Betty Boop For President, Betty, Campaign Hat, Black & White, c.1984, 1¼ In.	28

Clock, Wall, Neon, Metal, Numerals, Round, Painted Face, 1998, 16 In.	80
Cookie Jar, Top Hat, 3 Paper Labels, Hand Painted, Vandor, 1990, 7 x 5 In.	138
Doll, Baby, Red Pajamas, Hearts, Cap, Girl, Big Eyes, Curly Hair, 10 In. *illus*	9
Doll, Bimbo, Composition Head, Wood Jointed Body, Decal, Cameo, 1930s, 11 In. *illus*	552
Doll, Composition Head, Wood Jointed Body, Red Dress, Heart Decal, Cameo, 1930s, 12 In.*illus*	368
Doll, Composition, Wood, Cotton Clothing, Cameo Doll Co., 1930s, 11¾ In.	177
Figurine, Burlesque, Red Dress & Sandal, Black Round Base, Big Eyes, 6 In.	10
Nodder, Celluloid, Tin Base, Attached Counter Weight, Japan, Box, c.1930, 7 In.	464
Ornament, Betty On Harley-Davidson Motorcycle, Dog.	11
Tote Bag, Plush Fleece, Black, Zipper Top Closure, Dual Straps, Logo & Face, 13 x 13 x 3 In.	19
Toy, Pink Lambretta, Vespa Scooter, Figurine, 12 x 12 In.	60
Toy, Waitress, Rollerskater Diner, Special Edition, Red Hat, 12 In.	40
Trinket Box, Hinged Lid, Porcelain, Top Hat, Pudgy, Midwest Of Cannon Falls, 3½ In.	8
Wall Pocket, Betty & Bimbo, Red Dress, Barn, c.1930	115

BICYCLES were invented in 1839. The first manufactured bicycle was made in 1861. Special ladies' bicycles were made after 1874. The modern safety bicycle was not produced until 1885. Collectors search for all types of bicycles and tricycles. Bicycle-related items are also listed here.

Advertising, Columbia, Girl's Bicycle, Santa Claus, American Flag, Frame, 15¾ x 19 In.	270
Boneshaker, Metal Frame, Wood Wheels, c.1865, 39-In. Front Wheel *illus*	2950
Evans-Carlson, Commander, Girl's, Yellow, Green, c.1954, 37 x 65 In.	501
J.C. Higgins, Colorflow, Woman's, 26-In. Balloon Tires, Batwing Side Skirt, Blue, c.1953	565
Medal, Amateur Bicycle League, Chicago Tribune Award, Bronze, J. Taylor, 1½ In.	40
Motorbike, Solex, Model No. 3800, Black Plastic Gas Tanks, France	150
Packard, Aluminum Gooseneck Handlebar, Bean Son Co., 70 x 39 In.	2185
Poster, Woman Riding Bike, Orient Cycles, Waltham Mfg. Co., Lithograph, 42 x 29 In.	1000
Schwinn, Legacy, Woman's, Red & White, Painted, Helmet Included *illus*	59
Tricycle, Child's, Leather Seat, Spoke Wheels & Paint, 28 x 34 x 20 In. *illus*	141
Tricycle, Iron, High Wheel, Child's, Mustard Paint, Adjustable Handlebars & Seat, 1800s, 28 x 33 x 23 In.	424
Tricycle, Sky King, Red Paint, White Trim, Chrome, Lights, Airflow, 1930s, 26 In. *illus*	424
Tricycle, Wrought Iron, Yellow Paint, 28 x 34 In.	861
Velocipede, Fairy, Tiller Steering, Leather Saddle, Rubber Wheels, 1800s, 23 x 41 In. *illus*	176

BING & GRONDAHL is a famous Danish factory making fine porcelains from 1853 to the present. Underglaze blue decoration was started in 1886. The annual Christmas plate series was introduced in 1895. Dinnerware, stoneware, and other ceramics are still being made today. The figurines remain popular. The firm has used the initials *B & G* and a stylized castle as part of the mark since 1898. The company became part of Royal Copenhagen in 1987.

B. & G.	B&G DANMARK B & G	B&G
Bing & Grondahl 1895+	Bing & Grondahl 1915+	Bing & Grondahl 1983+

Cake Plate, Half Lace, Blue, Fluted, Floral, White Ground, No. 701, 8¼ x 7¼ In.	136
Cake Plate, Sea Gull Handle, Blue On White, Basket Weave Border, 1½ x 9¾ x 10¼ In.	44
Figurine, Antelope, No. 1693, Lauritz Jensen, 7½ In.	135
Figurine, Boy, With Puppy, 7 In.	118
Figurine, Cat, Siamese, No. 2308, Marked, 1980s, 3 x 6 In.	89
Figurine, Else, No. 1574, Girl, Standing, Blue Dress, Purse, 7 In.	50
Figurine, Fox, Seated, No. 1905, Brown, 4¾ x 5 In.	77
Figurine, Girl, Dog, White Ground, Blue Coat, Brown Shoes, Claire Weiss, 4¼ In.	35
Figurine, Man & Child, Riding Dolphin, Kai Nielsen, c.1940, 17½ In.	1600
Figurine, Mary, Girl, Holding Doll, 7⅛ In.	89
Figurine, Monkey, Marked B & G, c.1970, 3⅛ In.	85
Figurine, Polar Bear, Knud Kyhn, 8¼ x 13½ x 7 In. *illus*	210

Betty Boop, Doll, Composition Head, Wood Jointed Body, Red Dress, Heart Decal, Cameo, 1930s, 12 In.
$368

Weiss Auctions

Bicycle, Boneshaker, Metal Frame, Wood Wheels, c.1865, 39-In. Front Wheel
$2,950

Copake Auction

Bicycle, Schwinn, Legacy, Woman's, Red & White, Painted, Helmet Included
$59

Copake Auction

This is an edited listing of current prices. Visit **Kovels.com** to check thousands of prices from previous years and sign up for free information on trends, tips, reproductions, marks, and more.

Bicycle, Tricycle, Child's, Leather Seat, Spoke Wheels & Paint, 28 x 34 x 20 In. **$141**

Rich Penn Auctions

Bicycle, Tricycle, Sky King, Red Paint, White Trim, Chrome, Lights, Airflow, 1930s, 26 In. **$424**

Fontaine's Auction Gallery

Bicycle, Velocipede, Fairy, Tiller Steering, Leather Saddle, Rubber Wheels, 1800s, 23 x 41 In. **$176**

Thomaston Place Auction Galleries

TIP

Be careful handling birdhouses, bird- cages, and bird feeders, old or new. It is possible to catch pigeon fever (psittacosis) through a cut or even from breathing the dust.

Figurine, Rabbit, Brown Glossy Body, White Around Eyes, 5 In.	129
Plate, Christmas, 1937, Arrival Of Christmas, Bus, Snowy Night, 7 In.	30
Plate, Christmas, 1943, Ribe Cathedral, 7 In.	85
Plate, Christmas, 1970, Pheasants In The Snow, 7 1/8 In.	19
Plate, Christmas, 1971, Christmas At Home, 7 In.	18
Plate, Christmas, 1978, A Christmas Tale, 7 1/4 In.	29
Plate, Christmas, 1979, White Christmas, 7 1/4 In.	35
Plate, First Crush, 1986, 8 1/2 In.	27
Plate, Fish, Salmon, Gold Trim, Scalloped, 1950s, 8 In.	54
Plate, Mother's Day, 1983, Raccoons, 5 3/4 In.	20
Plate, Mother's Day, 1988, Mother & Cubs, 6 1/2 In.	25
Plate, Olympic Games, 1972, Munich, 7 1/4 In.	25
Platter, Sea Gull, No. 315, Blue On White, 2 x 16 x 11 In.	36
Serving Bowl, Sea Gull, Seahorse Handle, Fish Scale, 1952-58, 3 1/2 x 8 In.	40
Teapot, Blue, Floral, White Ground, Basket Weave Border, C-Handle, 6 1/2 x 3 x 9 In.	46
Vase, Fish, Salt Glaze Base, 1900s, 11 3/4 In.	175
Vase, Porcelain, Windmill, Globular, Countryside, Royal Copenhagen, 12 In.	77

BINOCULARS of all types are wanted by collectors. Those made in the eighteenth and nineteenth centuries are favored by serious collectors. The small, attractive binoculars called opera glasses are listed in their own category.

Bausch & Lomb, 10x42, Waterproof, Fog Proof, 28-1043	52
Binolux, 10x50, Sporting, Bird Watching, Black, Focusing Wheel	8
Binolux, 7x35, Compass, Leather Case	70
Bushnell, All-Optical, 8x21, Portable, High Times Telescope	13
Huet, 8x30, Wide Angle, 11.4 Degree, Center Focus, Mirapan 200, Paris	586
Leica, Ultravid, 10x42, Blackline, Leather Trim, Focusing Wheel, 5 3/4 x 4 3/4 x 2 1/2 In.	1530
Metal, Leather, Gilt Trim, Presentation, Negretti & Zambra, 1878, 5 1/4 x 5 In.	1020
Nikon, 7x21, Sprint 111, Compact, Lens Caps, Case, 2 Lens, Neck Lanyard	24
Nikon, Aculon A211, 10x42, 6 Dgr Superb Optics, Neck Strap, Turn & Slide Eye Caps	60
Tento, 10x50, Dust Caps, Lens Filter, Case, Strap, Russia	42

BIRDCAGES are collected for use as homes for pet birds and as decorative objects of folk art. Elaborate wooden cages of the past centuries can still be found. The brass or wicker cages of the 1930s are popular with bird owners.

Bamboo, 3 Tiers, Pagoda, Self-Standing Or Hanging, Chinese, 25 In.	22
Bamboo, Circular Base, 3-Footed, Ceramic Pots & Hardstone Rings, 15 1/4 In.	74
Brass, Cloisonne, 3 Birds, Animated, Rotating Ball Clock, Windup, 8 1/2 x 5 In.	156
Brass, Dome Shape, Center Handle, Swing, 17 1/2 x 12 1/2 In.	31
Brass, Metal, Cage, Hook Finial, Round Base, 10 x 6 x 6 In.	12
Brass, Tubular Stand, Cylindrical, Wire, Die Cast, c.1800s, 65 In.	36
Iron, Wire, Door, Drawer, Rectangular, Scrolled Stand, Late 1900s, 66 x 36 x 16 In., 2 Parts	295
Metal, Dark Green, Openwork, Round Holder, Hanging, 17 x 11 In.	15
Metal, Painted, Red, Cream, Green, Latticework, 12 In.	150
Metal, Painted, Swags Mount, Ropes & Tassels, c.1900, 38 In.	313
Metal, Wood Frame, Brass, Painted, c.1900, 21 1/2 x 10 x 13 In.	12
Wire, Hand Carved Wood Birds, Canary Rustic, 1960s, 12 x 8 In.	51

BISQUE is an unglazed baked porcelain. Finished bisque has a slightly sandy texture with a dull finish. Some of it may be decorated with various colors. Bisque gained favor during the late Victorian era when thousands of bisque figurines were made. It is still being made. Additional bisque items may be listed under the factory name.

Bust, Marie Antoinette, Incised Le Tourneur, Sevres Style, 1800s, 20 In.	1250
Bust, Young Woman, Pastel, Gold Highlights, G. Levy, Continental, 1800s, 21 1/2 In.	120
Figure, Organ Grinder, Monkey, Arnart Creation, Japan, 8 3/4 In.	47
Lamp, Disgruntled Man, Figural, Brown Hair, Yellow Jacket & Red Tie, c.1900, 3 1/2 In. *illus*	84
Lamp, Dog, White, Figural, Gold Dot Beading, Yellow Glass Eyes, c.1900, 3 In.	192

Lamp, Figural, Dog, Facial Features, c.1900s, 3¼ In.	203
Lamp, Figural, Young Girl, Blond Hair, Blue Glass Eyes & Bonnet, c.1900, 3½ In. ....*illus*	143
Lamp, Miniature, Skeleton, White Ground, Lavender, Green Glass Eyes, c.1750, 6½ x 2¾ In...	527

BLACK memorabilia has become an important area of collecting since the 1970s. The best material dates from past centuries, but many recent items are also of interest. F & F is the mark used on plastic made by Fiedler & Fiedler Mold & Die Works, Inc. in the 1930s and 1940s. Objects that picture a black person may also be listed in this book under Advertising, Sign; Bank; Bottle Opener; Cookie Jar; Doll; Salt & Pepper; Sheet Music; Toy; etc.

Bottle Holder, Wine, Blackamoor, Holding Shell Basket, Metal, Painted, 14 In.	313
Cookie Jars are listed in the Cookie Jar category.	
Doll, Folk Art, Cotton, Straw Filling, Sunburst Eyelashes, Disc-Jointed, Dress, c.1930, 18 In.	230
Doll, Frozen Charlotte, Porcelain, Painted Child Features, Germany, c.1875, 5 In., Pair	230
Doll, Mammy, Rag, Brown Cotton, Oil Paint, Stitched Joints, Maud Witherspoon, c.1900, 12 In.	1150
Figurine, Boy Playing Dice, Celluloid, 1920s, 3 x 2 In.	129
Mug, Smiling Face, c.1945, 4 x 3 In.	45
Notepad Holder, Mammy, 1950s, 8 x 4 In.	148
Pitcher, Figural Handle, Black Face & Hands, Signed, Willford Dean, 1994, 10½ In.	150
Towel, Mammy Making Pancakes, 26 In.	40
Toys are listed in the Toy category.	

BLENKO GLASS COMPANY is the 1930s successor to several glassworks founded by William John Blenko in Milton, West Virginia. In 1933, his son, William H. Blenko Sr., took charge. The company made tablewares and vases in classical shapes. In the late 1940s it hired talented designers and made innovative pieces. The company made a line of reproductions for Colonial Williamsburg. It is still in business and is best known today for its decorative wares and stained glass.

Ashtray, Cobalt Blue, Waffle Bottom, 1969, 8 In.	38
Ashtray, Free-Form, Glass, Green, Midcentury, 7½ x 5½ In.	10
Bottle, Stopper, Pillow Shape, Amethyst, 13 In.	52
Carafe, 2-Sided Spout, Water Pitcher, Emerald Glass, Label, 8¼ x 6½ In.	22
Carafe, Double Spout, Orange, Rectangular, 9½ In.	89
Decanter, Blue, Crackle, Flame Stopper, Wayne Husted, Blown	78
Lamp, Glass, Bottle Shape, Blue, 1950s-70s, 37 x 8 x 8 In.	68
Pitcher, Etched, Blue, Hand Blown, Wide Spout, Handle, 6 In.	26
Pitcher, Optic Glass, Tangerine, Rough Pontil, Winslow Anderson, Mid 1900s, 12½ In.	187
Pitcher, Tangerine, Yellow, Textured, Marked, c.1960, 6 x 3 In.	58
Serving Bowl, Art, 10 x 4 In.	40
Vase, Amber, Fluted, Optic, Ribbed, c.1950s, 9⅝ x 13 In.	118
Vase, Deep Blue Art Glass Fish, Blown, 12 x 9 x 6½ In.	65
Vase, Flat Top, Blown, Long Neck, Flat Rim, Bulbous Vase, Rough Pontil, 15½ In.	23
Vase, Shouldered, Ruby, Citron, Cobalt Blue Lip, Mottled Green Interior, 10¾ x 9 In.	189
Vase, Trumpet Shape, Purple Bowl, Amber Base, c.1960, 7 x 14 x 14 In.	16

BLOWN GLASS, *see Glass-Blown category.*

BLUE GLASS, *see Cobalt Blue category.*

BLUE ONION, *see Onion category.*

BLUE WILLOW, *see Willow category.*

BOCH FRERES factory was founded in 1841 in La Louvière in eastern Belgium. The pottery wares resemble the work of Villeroy & Boch. The factory closed in 1985. M.R.L. Boch took over the production of tableware but went bankrupt in 1988. Le Hodey took over Boch Freres in 1989, using the name Royal Boch Manufacture S.A. It went bankrupt in 2009.

Centerpiece, Octagonal, Art Deco, Reeded Column, Conforming Base, 8 x 11 In. ......*illus*	188
Platter, Botanical Motif, Marked, B.F.K., 24½ In.	635

Bing & Grondahl, Figurine, Polar Bear, Knud Kyhn, 8¼ x 13½ x 7 In. **$210**

Thomaston Place Auction Galleries

Bisque, Lamp, Disgruntled Man, Figural, Brown Hair, Yellow Jacket & Red Tie, c.1900, 3½ In. **$84**

Jeffrey S. Evans & Associates

Bisque, Lamp, Figural, Young Girl, Blond Hair, Blue Glass Eyes & Bonnet, c.1900, 3 ½ In.
$143

Jeffrey S. Evans & Associates

Boch Freres, Centerpiece, Octagonal, Art Deco, Reeded Column, Conforming Base, 8 x 11 In.
$188

Kamelot Auctions

TIP
Sometimes there are errors in porcelain marks, a misspelled or upside down word. While this type of error on a coin or stamp often adds to the rarity and the price, it does not necessarily raise the value of a piece of porcelain. An error on the front of a plate, like the wrong date on a coronation cup, does add to the rarity and the price.

Urn, Keramis, African Farm Scene, Tan, Browns, Flared, C. Catteau, 1937, 14 x 11 In.	5000
Vase, Birds Of Paradise, Art Deco, Stepped Top & Bottom, C. Catteau, 14 x 11 In.	1500
Vase, Birds, Flowers, Round, Chas Catteau, Marked, 6 ⅛ In. .... *illus*	236
Vase, Blue Crackle, Mounted, Ormolu, c.1880, Pair, 8 ⅝ In.	675
Vase, Flowers, Black & Yellow Stripe, Multicolor, Enamel, 1920, 13 ½ In.	123
Vase, Globe Shape, Geometric, Multicolor, Enamel, 1920, 9 In.	800
Vase, Keramis, Flowers, Oval, Multicolor, Red Ground, Belgium, c.1920, 12 In.	277
Vase, Keramis, Oval, Squirrels, Multicolor, Charles Catteau, c.1930, 12 ¼ In. ... *illus*	2091
Vase, Round, Birds, Flowers, Multicolor, Blue, White Ground, Chas. Catteau, 6 In.	246
Vase, Stylized Bellflowers, Tan, Brown, Blue, Bulbous, Art Deco, C. Catteau, 11 In.	1000
Vase, Stylized Flamingos, Brown & Tan Glaze, Oval, C. Catteau, 10 ½ In.	1500
Vase, Stylized Songbirds, Blue, Green, Brown Striped Ground, Bulbous, Catteau, 10 x 7 In.	1250

BOEHM is the collector's name for the porcelains of Edward Marshall Boehm. In 1953 the Osso China Company was reorganized as Edward Marshall Boehm Inc. In the early days of the factory, dishes were made, but the elaborate and lifelike bird figurines are the best-known ware. Edward Marshall Boehm, the founder, died in 1969, but the firm continued to design and produce porcelain. The Museum of American Porcelain Art bought the assets, including the molds and trademarks, in 2015. The museum is located in South Euclid, Ohio, a suburb of Cleveland. The Boehm Showroom in Trenton, New Jersey, has exclusive use of the molds and trademarks. It also does restoration work and has some retired figures for sale.

Boehm Porcelain, LLC	Boehm Porcelain, LLC	Boehm Porcelain, LLC
1952–1954	1959–1970	1971+

Bald Eagle, Fledgling, Rock Base, 10 In.	47
Ballet, Lovers, Sleeping Beauty, Porcelain, Cream Ground, 11 x 7 x 5 In.	68
Blue Jay, Female, Strawberries, Porcelain, 9 ½ x 15 In.	716
Bluebird, Orange Breast, Metal Branch, Brown Leaves, Flowers, 8 x 7 x 5 In.	158
Cardinal, Male, Red, Black Accents, Wings Spread, On Branch, 15 x 5 ¾ x 8 ½ In.	127
Catbird, Gray, Hyacinths, 1968, 14 In.	130
Hummingbird, Broad Bill, Tree Branch, 8 x 10 x 5 In.	163
Hummingbird, Paphiopedilum, Orchid, 5 x 8 In.	248
Magnolia Grandiflora Rhododendron, Porcelain, Metal, 16 ½ x 7 ½ x 9 In.	369
Pelican, Guarding 2 Chicks, On Rocks, c.1900s, 19 In.	438
Purple Finch, Spread Wings, White Azalea, Green Leaves, Tree Branch, 11 ½ x 7 x 8 In.	339
Robin, Bronze Branches, Porcelain, Pink To Cream White, 10 x 10 x 7 In.	355
Rose, White, Christmas, Tree Branch, Green Leaves, Cherry, 4 x 4 x 6 In.	41
Scarlet Macaw, Metal Stand, Multicolor, 10 x 5 x 3 In.	27
Tumbler, Pigeon, Porcelain, Marked, Pair, 8 x 8 In.	156

BOHEMIAN GLASS, *see Glass-Bohemian*

 BONE includes those articles made of bone not listed elsewhere in this book.

Rattle, Child's, Whalebone, Mallet Shape, Encased Metal Bell, 1800s, 5 ¾ In. ...... *illus*	960
Swift, Whalebone, Expands, Octagonal Walnut Base, Captain Wm. Hussey, 25 In.	1298
Vase, Carved, Stylized Flowers, Metal, Cardeilhac Paris, Minerva Mark, c.1900, 5 In. ...... *illus*	1500

 BOOKENDS have probably been used since books became inexpensive. Early libraries kept books in cupboards, not on open shelves. By the 1870s bookends appeared, especially homemade fret-carved wooden examples. Most bookends listed in this book date from the twentieth century. Bookends are also listed in other categories by manufacturer or material. All bookends listed here are pairs.

Boch Freres, Vase, Birds, Flowers, Round, Chas Catteau, Marked, 6⅛ In.
$236

Bunch Auctions

Boch Freres, Vase, Keramis, Oval, Squirrels, Multicolor, Charles Catteau, c.1930, 12¼ In.
$2,091

Skinner, Inc.

Bone, Rattle, Child's, Whalebone, Mallet Shape, Encased Metal Bell, 1800s, 5¾ In.
$960

Eldred's

Bone, Vase, Carved, Stylized Flowers, Metal, Cardeilhac Paris, Minerva Mark, c.1900, 5 In.
$1,500

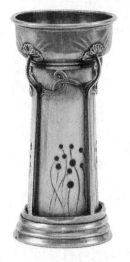

Eldred's

> **TIP**
> Don't cut the price off a book's dust jacket. It will affect the value.

Bookends, Children, Rain & Sunshine, Boy & Girl, Bronze, U Brocia, 6½ x 4 x 3¼ In.
$285

Ruby Lane

Bookends, Kokeshi Doll, Boy & Girl, Wood, Japan, 6½ x 5 x 4½ In.
$160

Ruby Lane

Bookmark, Gold, 9K, Mechanical, Arm Hinged & Sprung, Asprey London, 1934, 2¾ In.
$136

rx8-man on eBay

Bossons, Wall Mask, Coxswain
$36

zebramussel on eBay

Bossons, Wall Mask, Lindbergh, Aviator, 6 x 6 In.
$29

imru2 on eBay

B

Bottle, Bininger, A.M. & Co., 19 Broad St., Peach Brandy, Yellow Amber, Label, Jug, 8 In.
$1,989

Glass Works Auctions

Bottle, Bitters, Doctor Fisch's, W.H. Ware, Patented 1866, Figural, Fish, Golden Amber, 11 In.
$410

Glass Works Auctions

Bottle, Bitters, H. Pharazyn, Phila, Indian Queen, Amber, Gold Paint, Rolled Lip, 1865-70, 12 In.
$1,800

Glass Works Auctions

Asian Women, Bronze & Marble, 1920s, 7 x 4 In.	349
Chelsea Clock, Bronze, Barometer, Ship's Wheel Surround, c.1930, 4¾ x 5½ In.	1920
Children, Rain & Sunshine, Boy & Girl, Bronze, U Brocia, 6½ x 4 x 3¼ In. *illus*	285
Fish, Salmon, Waves, Brass, Onyx Base, 6 x 4 In.	125
Horse Head, Metal, Black Gloss, c.1945, 5¾ x 3 x 6½ In.	65
Isadora Duncan, Scarf Dancer, Bronze Toned Metal, Figural, c.1920, 5 In.	200
Kokeshi Doll, Boy & Girl, Wood, Japan, 6½ x 5 x 4½ In. *illus*	160
Modern Cubes Attached To Form Larger Cubes, Metal, Black, William Curry, 3¾ In.	665
Rabbits, Sitting, Paws Folded, Marble Base, Marked, Hippolyte Moreau, 1920s, 3 x 3 In.	450
Skeleton, Seated, Rests Chin On Knuckles, Signed Milo, 10 x 6 In.	1159
Skyline, Chrome Rods, Curtis Jere, 1977, 7 x 5 In.	695
Thermometer, Art Deco Revere, Chromed Scrolled Metal, Inlaid Wood, c.1937, 5 In.	51
Thinker, Metal, Gold Paint Wash, 1928, 7 x 4 In.	175
Tree Shape, Pots, Coral, 7½ In., Pair	312
Whaleboat, Harpooner, Brass Finish, c.1925, 7 x 4 x 5 In.	720

BOOKMARKS were originally made of parchment, cloth, or leather. Soon woven silk ribbon, thin cardboard, celluloid, wood, silver, tortoiseshell, and metals were used. Examples made before 1850 are scarce, but there are many to be found dating before 1920.

AAA, Brass, Brown Leather, Gilt Lettering, Gucci, Italy, 8¼ x 1½ In.	24
Brass, Butterfly, 2 x 1 In.	12
French Silver, Christmas, Berries, Mistletoe, Silk Tassel, Early 1800s, 4¼ x ½ In.	59
Gilt Metal, Fleur-De-Lis, Letter Opener, Vermeil, Monogram, 4⅝ x ⅝ In.	16
Gold, 9K, Mechanical, Arm Hinged & Sprung, Asprey London, 1934, 2¾ In. *illus*	136
Luminous Silver, Butterfly, Feather, Night-Light, Metal, 5 x ¾ In.	1
Metal, Elephant, Rose Polytechnic Institute, 1940, 4¼ In.	20
Mixed Metal, Hammered, Tree, Flowers, Deer, Fish, Japan, c.1800, 3 x 1 In.	275
Silk, A Birthday Wish, Flowers, Birds, Thomas Stevens, c.1880, 10 x 2 In.	80
Silver Plated, Claw, Egg, Green Agate Stone, Marble Ball, Victorian, 4 In.	25
Sterling Silver, Figural, Edwardian, Adie & Lovekin Ltd., 3½ x 1 In.	265
Sterling Silver, Hand, Pointing Finger, c.1905, 3 x 2 In.	275
Sterling Silver, Horn Of Plenty, Cornucopia, Reed & Barton, 2 x 2 In.	45
Stollwerck Gold Brand Chocolate & Coco, Bastian Bros. Co., 6 x 2 In.	38

BOSSONS **BOSSONS** character wall masks (heads), plaques, figurines, and other decorative pieces of chalkware were made by W.H. Bossons, Limited, of Congleton, England. The company was founded in 1946 and closed in 1996. Dates shown are the date the item was introduced.

Wall Figure, Bald Eagle, Spread Wings, 11 x 9 In.	17
Wall Figure, Pathan, Shield, Sword, Bullets, Yellow, Red, 1967, 10 In.	14
Wall Mask, Bretonne Woman, England, 1982, 5½ In.	6
Wall Mask, Chef, White Hat, England, 1969, 6¼ In.	22
Wall Mask, Coxswain *illus*	36
Wall Mask, Dog, Labrador, Black, England, 1968, 4 x 4 In.	24
Wall Mask, Lindbergh, Aviator, 6 x 6 In. *illus*	29
Wall Mask, Old Salt, Sailor, Raincoat, Pipe, England, 1971, 5¼ In.	11
Wall Mask, Robin Hood, England, 1985	27
Wall Mask, Welsh Woman, Red, Tan, Black Hat, Stone Pendant, Marked, 7 In.	49

BOSTON & SANDWICH CO. *pieces may be found in the Sandwich Glass category.*

BOTTLE collecting has become a major American hobby. There are several general categories of bottles, such as historic flasks, bitters, household, and figural. ABM means the bottle was made by an automatic bottle machine after 1903. Pyro is the shortened form of the word *pyroglaze*, an enameled lettering used on bottles after the mid-1930s. This form of decoration is also called ACL or applied color label. Shapes of bottles often indicate the age of the bottle. For more prices, go to kovels.com.

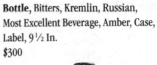

| Calabash flask | Teakettle ink | Case gin bottle |
| 1840-1870 | 1830-1885 | 1650-1920 |

Barber, Coin Dot, Cranberry, Opalescent, Fenton, 8 In. 120

Beam Bottles were made to hold Kentucky Straight Bourbon, made by the James B. Beam Distilling Company. The Beam series of ceramic bottles began in 1953.

Beam, Arkansas Razorback Boar, 1969, 8½ x 8 x 4 In.	54
Beam, Cable Car, Regal China, c.1968, 7¾ x 3 x 4 In.	32
Beam, Car, Corvette, Yellow, 1978, 3¾ x 14 In.	69
Beam, Embossed Dots, Scrolls, Flower, Opalescent Milk Glass, 1957, 11 In.	22
Beam, Preakness, 100th, Pimlico, 1975, 11 In.	35
Beam, Whitetail Deer, Brown, 1982, 10 In.	17
Beer, Kuntz, Label, 1920s, 9¼ In.	87
Bininger, A.M. & Co., 19 Broad St., Peach Brandy, Yellow Amber, Label, Jug, 8 In. .... *illus*	1989
Bitters, Bissell's Tonic, Patented Jany 21, 1868, Orange Amber, Sloping Collar, 1870-80, 9 In. .	450
Bitters, Doctor Fisch's, W.H. Ware, Patented 1866, Figural, Fish, Golden Amber, 11 In. ...... *illus*	410
Bitters, Dr. J. Hostetter's Stomach, Yellow, Olive Tone, Sloping Collar, 1870-80, 9¼ In.............	252
Bitters, E.E. Hall, New Haven, Amber, 9¼ In.	158
Bitters, Greeley's Bourbon, Copper, 1800s, 9 In.	390
Bitters, H. Pharazyn, Phila, Indian Queen, Amber, Gold Paint, Rolled Lip, 1865-70, 12 In. *illus*	1800
Bitters, Kremlin, Russian, Most Excellent Beverage, Amber, Case, Label, 9½ In................ *illus*	300
Bitters, Old Homestead Wild Cherry, Cabin, Shaded Yellow Olive, Sloping Collar, 9⅝ In.. *illus*	7200
Black Glass, Cylindrical, Wine, Deep Yellow Olive, Collared, 10 In.	1080
Black Glass, Mallet, Wine, Dark Olive Green, String Lip, 1700s, 7 In...........................	300
Coca-Cola bottles are listed in the Coca-Cola category.	
Cologne, Cobalt Blue, Embossed Column, Crown & Flowers, Flattened Lip, Pontil, c.1850, 9½ In..	761
Cologne, Cut Glass, Clear Panel, Prism, Arch & Strawberry Diamond, 6 In.	48
Cologne, Cut Glass, Harvard Pattern, Ray Cut Base, 5½ In.	36
Cologne, Cut Glass, Hobstar & Prism, Ray Cut Base, 5 In..................................	48
Cologne, Hindoo Pattern, Tapered, Ray Cut Base, J. Hoare, 7¾ In........................	210
Cosmetic, C.A.P. Mason Alpine Hair Balm, Providence, R.I., Olive Yellow, Label, c.1865, 7 In. ..	2808
Cosmetic, Jerome's Hair Color Restorer, Cobalt Blue, Flared Lip, 1855-65, 6⅜ In.	1170
Cure, Craig's Kidney & Liver, Amber, Double Collar, 1870-80, 9⅝ In........................	156
Cure, Dr. Craig's Cough & Consumption, Amber, Double Collar, 1870-80, 8 In............	600
Cure, Dr. Craig's Kidney, Embossed Kidneys, Amber, Double Collar, 1870-80, 9¾ In.... 420 to	1800
Cure, Warner's Safe, London, Embossed Safe, Lime Green, Squared Lip, 1890-1900, 4⅝ In.	1920
Decanter, Barrel, Yellow Green, 3 Patterned Bands, 3-Piece Mold, 8⅜ In.	2691
Decanter, Cut Glass, Green, Split Concave Leaves, Cut Stopper, Japan, 11 In.	24
Decanter, Donut Shape, Etched, Octagonal Stopper, Finial, 11¾ x 5⅞ x 3 In.	250
Flask, 24 Ribs, Swirled To Left, Yellow Amber, Globular, Outward Rolled Lip, 7⅝ In............	761
Flask, 24 Ribs, Vertical, Yellow Amber, Flattened Teardrop, Disc Mouth, 7¼ In.	702
Flask, Chestnut, Yellow Olive, Applied Rim, Pontil, Early 1800s, 6 In.........................	354
Flask, Concentric Ring Eagle, Yellow Green, Sheared Mouth, Pontil, c.1825, Pt...............	4388
Flask, Corn For The World, Baltimore, Monument, Aqua, Tooled Lip, Pontil, c.1830, ½ Pt. ...*illus*	720
Flask, Cornucopia & Urn, Ice Blue, Sheared Mouth, Pontil, Pt...................................	4095
Flask, Double Eagle, Blue Aqua, Sheared Mouth, Pontil, Pittsburgh, c.1835, Pt. .... *illus*	527
Flask, Double Eagle, Clambroth, Tooled Lip, Pontil, Louisville, 1835-45, Qt...................	1920
Flask, Double Eagle, Olive Amber, Sheared Mouth, Pontil, Stoddard, Qt.....................	2223
Flask, Eagle & Flower Medallion, Green Aqua, Sheared Mouth, Pontil, c.1840, Pt. .... *illus*	1287
Flask, Eagle & Starburst, Blue Aqua, Teal Tone, Tooled Lip, Pontil, Pittsburgh, 1830-40, Pt.	1920
Flask, Eagle & Willington, Amber, Liberty Shield Co., c.1850, 9 In.	120
Flask, Eagle & Willington, Emerald Green, Applied Sloping Collar, 1855-70, Pt................ *illus*	1440
Flask, Eagle, Yellow Amber, Mold Blown, 5¾ In.	183

Bottle, Bitters, Kremlin, Russian, Most Excellent Beverage, Amber, Case, Label, 9½ In.
$300

Bottle, Bitters, Old Homestead Wild Cherry, Cabin, Shaded Yellow Olive, Sloping Collar, 9⅝ In.
$7,200

Bottle, Flask, Corn For The World, Baltimore, Monument, Aqua, Tooled Lip, Pontil, c.1830, ½ Pt.
$720

Bottle, Flask, Double Eagle, Blue Aqua, Sheared Mouth, Pontil, Pittsburgh, c.1835, Pt.
$527

Glass Works Auctions

Bottle, Flask, Eagle & Flower Medallion, Green Aqua, Sheared Mouth, Pontil, c.1840, Pt.
$1,287

Glass Works Auctions

Bottle, Flask, Eagle & Willington, Emerald Green, Applied Sloping Collar, 1855-70, Pt.
$1,440

Glass Works Auctions

Flask, Flag & Stoddard, Olive Amber, Sheared Mouth, Pontil, Pt.	7020
Flask, For Pike's Peak, Prospector, Eagle, Apple Green, Ring Mouth, Pittsburgh, 1865-75, ½ Pt.	192
Flask, Hunter & Stag, Great Western, Aqua, Strapside, Applied Ring Mouth, 1870-80, Pt.	480
Flask, Lafayette & Clinton, Shaded Olive Green, Sheared & Tooled Lip, Pt.	1521
Flask, Lafayette & Eagle, Blue Green, Sheared Mouth, Pontil, Wheeling, Pt. ...... *illus*	4680
Flask, Masonic & Eagle, Amber, 1800s, 7½ In.	250
Flask, Murdock & Cassel, Blue Green, Ribbed Bottom, Zanesville, Pt.	1755
Flask, Pitkin Type, 19 Ribs, Swirled To Right, Moss Green, Sheared Mouth, 6⅝ In.	878
Flask, Pitkin Type, 36 Ribs, Swirled To Left, Amber, Olive Tone, 6⅛ In.	761
Flask, Scroll, Hearts & Flowers, Aqua, Sheared Mouth, Pontil, 1845-60, Qt.	4973
Flask, Scroll, Sapphire Blue, Sheared Mouth, Pontil, Pt.	6435
Flask, Scroll, Yellow Green, Amber Striations, Sheared Mouth, Pontil, Pt.	1755
Flask, Summer Tree, Winter Tree, Orange Amber, Double Collar, Qt.	1287
Flask, Sunburst, Blue Green, Inward Rolled Lip, Pontil, 1825-35, ½ Pt. ...... *illus*	2040
Flask, Sunburst, Copper Puce, Sheared Mouth, Pontil, ½ Pt.	1170
Flask, Sunburst, Green, Ribbed Sides, Tooled Lip, Keene Glass Works, 1815-25, Pt.	450 to 660
Flask, Sunburst, Olive Amber, Sheared Mouth, 1815-30, Pt.	3218
Flask, Swirled Ribs, Deep Aqua, Flattened Sides, 1820-40, 6¾ In.	165
Flask, Union, Clasped Hands & Eagle, Yellow Amber, Applied Ring Mouth, 1860-70, Pt. .... *illus*	480
Flask, Washington & Jackson, Yellow Amber, Pint, Sheared & Tooled Lip, 1825-35, Pt.	300
Flask, Washington & Monument, Light Amethyst, Sheared Mouth, Pontil, Pt.	1521
Flask, Washington & Taylor Never Surrenders, Cobalt Blue, Tooled Lip, Pontil, 1848-55, Qt. . *illus*	4800
Flask, Washington & Taylor Never Surrenders, Shaded Amethyst, Sloping Collar, Qt.	6435
Flask, Washington & Taylor, Cobalt Blue, Sheared & Tooled Lip, Pt.	2106
Flask, Washington, Classical Bust, Light Green, Tooled Lip, Pontil, Bridgeton, 1825-35, Qt.	3600
Flask, Yellow Olive, Melon Form, Vertical Ribs, Round Collar, Keene, c.1820, Pt.	1287
Fruit Jar, Mason, Blue, Bubbles In Glass, Iron Cap, Marked, EA 13, 1858, Pt., 5 In.	69
Fruit Jar, Van Vliet Jar Of 1881, Aqua, Glass Lid, Wire Yoke Clamp, 1881-90, Qt. ...... *illus*	480
Ink, Barrel, Cobalt Blue, Sheared Mouth, Brass Neck Ring, Hinged Cap, 1875-90, 2¼ In.	2808
Ink, Cylindrical, Horse & Rider, Shaded Root Beer Amber, Disc Mouth, 1⅜ x 2⅜ In.	5558
Ink, Fine Black Ink, Prepared By A. Norcross, Boston, Cylindrical, Amber, Master, 4½ In.	246
Ink, Geometric, Deep Olive Amber, Pontil, Keene, 1820-40, 2⅝ In.	5558
Ink, Harrison's Columbian, Cylindrical, Cobalt Blue, Applied Collar, Master, 6 In.	1989
Ink, Hover, Phila., Umbrella, 8-Sided, Blue Green, Inward Rolled Lip, 1¾ In.	293
Ink, J & I E M, Igloo, 6-Sided, Yellow, Olive Tone, Sheared Mouth, c.1875, 1¾ In. ...... *illus*	497
Ink, Jones' Empire, N.Y., 12-Sided, Emerald Green, Applied Collar, Pontil, Master, 6 In.	4973
Ink, Log Cabin, Clear, Sheared Lip, 1860-75, 3⅛ In.	1053
Ink, Petroleum, P.B. & Co., Writing Fluid, Barrel, Aqua, Applied Lip, 1875-90, 2½ In. ...... *illus*	228
Ink, Superior Black Ink, Light Blue, Umbrella, 8-Sided, Flattened Lip, c.1870, 2⅝ In. ...... *illus*	439
Ink, Teakettle, 6-Sided, Canary Yellow, Melon Lobed, Sheared Lip, 1875-90, 2⅞ In. ...... *illus*	510
Ink, Teakettle, 8-Sided, Deep Amethyst, Brass Neck Ring, Hinged Cap, 1875-90, 1¾ In.	644
Ink, Teakettle, Cobalt Blue, Sheared, Brass Cap, 1875-90, 2 In. ...... *illus*	1638
Ink, Teakettle, Ship's Figurehead, Dog In Medieval Dress, Cobalt Blue, 3½ In.	644
Ink, Turtle, Deep Amethyst, Notched Shell, Brass Collar & Cap, 4½ In.	4973
Ink, Umbrella, 8-Sided, Pink Puce, Inward Rolled Lip, 1840-60, 2¾ In.	1404
Ink, W.E. Bonney, Barrel, Aqua, Tooled Lip, Label, 1860-70, 2¾ In.	180
Ink, Wood, Carved, Lacquered, Double Gourd, Metal Screw Lid, Toggle, Japan, 2¼ In.	277
Ink, Zieber & Co.'s Excelsior, 12-Sided, Forest Green, Squared Collar, Master, 7½ In.	3515
Medicine, Apothecary, Cranberry Glass, Molded, 21 In.	438
Medicine, Beekman's Pulmonic Syrup, New York, Olive Green, Double Collar, 7¼ In.	2691
Medicine, Billings & Stover Apothecaries, Cambridge, Mass., Cobalt, 6-Sided, c.1900, 4 In.	556
Medicine, Dr. Hartshorn's, Syrup Of Rhubarb, 38 Cents, Amber, Rounded Shoulder, Label, 6 In.	1170
Medicine, Dr. J. Woodruff's Liniment, Aqua, Cylindrical, Rolled Lip, Pontil, 1840-60, 4 In.	840
Medicine, Dr. J.S. Wood's Compound Elixir, Albany, N.Y., Teal, Tombstone Form, c.1850, 9 In.	5265
Medicine, Dr. S. Anderson's Humor Mixture, Bath, Me., Blue Aqua, Applied Lip, 8¾ In.	410
Medicine, Fenimore's Cough Mixture, Price 50 Cts., Blue Aqua, Paneled, Iron Pontil, 6 In.	761
Medicine, Fisher's Seaweed Extract, Embossed Shrub, Lime Green, 3-Sided, c.1890, 5¼ In.	360
Medicine, Howard's Vegetable Cancer & Canker Syrup, Yellow Olive Amber, c.1855, 7½ In.	4095
Medicine, Newton's Panacea, Purifier Of The Blood, Old Amber, Double Collar, 7½ In.	15210

Bottle, Flask, Lafayette & Eagle, Blue Green, Sheared Mouth, Pontil, Wheeling, Pt.
$4,680

Bottle, Flask, Washington & Taylor Never Surrenders, Cobalt Blue, Tooled Lip, Pontil, 1848-55, Qt.
$4,800

Bottle, Ink, Petroleum, P.B. & Co., Writing Fluid, Barrel, Aqua, Applied Lip, 1875-90, 2½ In.
$228

Norman C. Heckler & Company

Glass Works Auctions

Glass Works Auctions

Bottle, Flask, Sunburst, Blue Green, Inward Rolled Lip, Pontil, 1825-35, ½ Pt.
$2,040

Bottle, Fruit Jar, Van Vliet Jar Of 1881, Aqua, Glass Lid, Wire Yoke Clamp, 1881-90, Qt.
$480

Bottle, Ink, Superior Black Ink, Light Blue, Umbrella, 8-Sided, Flattened Lip, c.1870, 2⅝ In.
$439

Glass Works Auctions

Glass Works Auctions

Glass Works Auctions

Bottle, Flask, Union, Clasped Hands & Eagle, Yellow Amber, Applied Ring Mouth, 1860-70, Pt.
$480

Bottle, Ink, J & I E M, Igloo, 6-Sided, Yellow, Olive Tone, Sheared Mouth, c.1875, 1¾ In.
$497

Bottle, Ink, Teakettle, 6-Sided, Canary Yellow, Melon Lobed, Sheared Lip, 1875-90, 2⅞ In.
$510

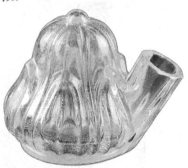

Glass Works Auctions

Glass Works Auctions

Glass Works Auctions

Bottle, Ink, Teakettle, Cobalt Blue, Sheared, Brass Cap, 1875-90, 2 In.
$1,638

Glass Works Auctions

Bottle, Medicine, Phelps's Arcanum, Worcester, Mass., Old Amber, Double Collar, Pontil, c.1850, 9 In.
$4,800

Glass Works Auctions

Bottle, Medicine, Swifts Syphilitic Specific, Cobalt Blue, Applied Squared Lip, 1870-80, 9 In.
$840

Glass Works Auctions

Bottle, Poison, Skull & Crossbones, Demert Drug & Chemical Co., Cobalt Blue, c.1900, 5 In.
$2,160

Glass Works Auctions

Bottle, Sarsaparilla, Dr. J. Townsend's, New York, Blue Green, c.1850, 9 5/8 In.
$936

Glass Works Auctions

Bottle, Seal, Comet Trail, Wine, Olive Green, Tooled Lip, Label, Colnac, France, c.1811, 12 3/4 In.
$1,169

Skinner, Inc.

Bottle, Seal, Rev'd Jn. Moore 1817, Wine, Deep Olive Amber, Dip Mold, Double Collar, 10 In.
$995

Glass Works Auctions

Bottle, Snuff, Agate, Goldfish, Carved, 2-Tone, c.1900s, 2 1/4 In.
$52

Freeman's Auctioneers & Appraisers

Bottle, Snuff, Bat & Fruit, Red & White, Mask & Mock Ring Handles, 1800s, 2 3/4 In.
$120

Eldred's

Medicine, Phelps's Arcanum, Worcester, Mass., Old Amber, Double Collar, Pontil, c.1850, 9 In. ...*illus*	4800
Medicine, Rees Remedy For Piles, Slug Plate, Aqua, Oval, 1840-60, 7 ⅜ In.	819
Medicine, Sanford's Extract Of Hamamelis Or Witch Hazel, Cobalt Blue, Lip, c.1885, 11 In.	1140
Medicine, Smith's Green Mountain Renovator, Vt., Old Amber, Double Collar, 7 In.	2691
Medicine, Swift's Syphilitic Specific, Cobalt Blue, Applied Squared Lip, 1870-80, 9 In....... *illus*	840
Medicine, Swift's Syphilitic Specific, Cobalt Blue, Strapside Flask, Flattened Lip, Qt., 9 In.	1053
Perfume bottles are listed in the Perfume Bottle category.	
Pickle, Cathedral, 4-Sided, Blue Green, Rounded Collar, 11 ½ In..	585
Pickle, Cathedral, 6-Sided, Yellow Amber, Aqua Collar, 13 In.	5265
Pickle, Cathedral, Indented Arches, Blue Green, Rolled Collar, 7 ⅜ In.	1053
Pickle, Cathedral, Square, Deep Olive Amber, Rounded Collar, Willington, 8 ½ In...................	1638
Poison, Cobalt Blue, Raised Crosshatching Overall, Flask, Sheared, 1850-65, 5 ⅝ In.	2223
Poison, Cobalt Blue, Raised Hobnail, Teardrop Flask, Half Post, 1790-1820, 5 ½ In.	1112
Poison, Grass Green, Raised Diamonds, Bulbous, Cylindrical Neck, Rolled Lip, c.1850, 4 In.....	380
Poison, Jacob's Bed Bug Killer, Skull & Crossbones, Amber, Cylindrical, c.1900, 5 ¼ In.	1287
Poison, Jacob's Bichloride Tablets, Poison, Skull & Crossbones, Amber, 8-Sided, 3 ½ In.	2340
Poison, Lattice & Diamond, Amber, Cylindrical, 1890-1910, 7 ¼ In.	1112
Poison, Skull & Crossbones, Demert Drug & Chemical Co., Cobalt Blue, c.1900, 5 In. .... *illus*	2160
Poison, Skull, Raised, Clear, Gold Trim, Cylindrical, Flattened Lip, c.1875, 5 ⅝ In.	4680
Sarsaparilla, Dr. J. Townsend's, New York, Blue Green, c.1850, 9 ⅝ In..........................*illus*	936
Sarsaparilla, Dr. J.S. Rose's, Philadelphia, Deep Teal, Case, Sloping Collar, 1845-60, 9 ¼ In...	4680
Sarsaparilla, Dr. Townsend's, Albany, N.Y., Shaded Yellow Amber, c.1850, 9 ¼ In...................	497
Sarsaparilla, E.R. Clarke's, Sharon, Mass., Aqua, Paneled, Sloping Collar, 7 ½ In...................	322
Sarsaparilla, John Bull Extract, Louisville, Ky., Shaded Teal, Tapered Collar, 9 In.	761
Sarsaparilla, Pelletier's Extract, Hartford, Conn., Aqua, Double Collar, Pontil, c.1855, 10 ¾ In.	1521
Scent, Vinaigrette, Pistol Shape, Cranberry Glass, Hallmark Chain & Ring, 4 ½ In...................	7680
Seal, Comet Trail, Wine, Olive Green, Tooled Lip, Label, Colnac, France, c.1811, 12 ¾ In. .*illus*	1169
Seal, Rev'd Jn. Moore 1817, Wine, Deep Olive Amber, Dip Mold, Double Collar, 10 In.......... *illus*	995
Snuff, Agate, Goldfish, Carved, 2-Tone, c.1900s, 2 ¼ In. ....*illus*	52
Snuff, Agate, Qilong & Bat, Carved, 2 Tone, Chinese, c.1950, 2 ½ x 6 ½ In.	39
Snuff, Amber, Lotus Leaves & Flowers, Shrimp, Carved, Stopper, 1800s, 3 In........................	720
Snuff, Bat & Fruit, Red & White, Mask & Mock Ring Handles, 1800s, 2 ¾ In. .... *illus*	120
Snuff, Black & White Jade, Lohan Sitting, Bat, Fish, Dragon, Red Glass Stopper, c.1790, 2 ½ In.	1375
Snuff, Black Glass, Mother-Of-Pearl, Hardstone Inset, 2 Birds, Jadite Lid, 1900s, 3 In.	1000
Snuff, Black, Elephant, Snowflake Ground, Faux Coral Stopper, 1800s 2 In.	437
Snuff, Celadon, Apple Green Jadite, Oval, Translucent Stone, 1800s, 2 ¼ In.............................	1250
Snuff, Ceramic, Carved Decoration, Mint Green, Chinese, 3 ½ x 2 In....................................	94
Snuff, Circular, Peony Blossom, Green Cap, Carved, Jade, Celadon, Unsigned, 2 ¾ In.	180
Snuff, Jade, Celadon, Basket Weave, Baluster Body, Yellow Quartz Cover, 2 ½ In.....................	375
Snuff, Jade, Celadon, High Shoulder Flattened Shape, Carved, Qilin, Chinese, 3 In.	180
Snuff, Katydid, Green, White Ground, Red Lid, Marked, Chinese, c.1850, 2 ¼ In.	3068
Snuff, Lacquer, Chinese Children Playing, Stone Inlay, Gilt, 1800s, 3 ¾ In.	1003
Snuff, Pine Tree Branches, Carved, Agate, Rectangular, Oval Foot, 1800s, 3 ⅛ In. .... *illus*	1250
Snuff, Porcelain, Blue Medallions, Male Figure, Unglazed Footring, Chinese, 1700s, 2 ½ In. ...	281
Snuff, Snowflake Glass, Red Overlay, Carved, Kuilong, Oval Footring, 2 ⅞ In..........................	125
Snuff, Underglaze Blue & Red, Stopper, Porcelain, 3 ½ In.	313
Snuff, Vase Shape, Taotie Mask, Flower Handles, Malachite, Green, Lid, Chinese, 3 x 7 ½ In. ..	91
Snuff, White Jade, Eagle, Goose, Carved, Oval Foot, 3 In.	469
Snuff, Woman Seated On Tree, Painted, Celadon Hardstone Stopper, Spoon, Chinese, 38 In....	60
Soda, Empire Soda Works San Francisco, Blue, Blob Top, 1861-71, 7 ¾ In............................	600
Soda, J.T. Brown, Chemist, Boston, Double Soda Water, Teal, Torpedo, Blob Top, Stand, 8 ¾ In. ..*illus*	527
Soda, J.V. Dellicker, Richmond, Va., Columbus, O., Aqua, Sloping Collar, 7 In....................*illus*	351
Soda, J.W. Harris, New-Haven Conn, 8-Sided, Blue, 7 ⅜ In.	477
Target Ball, Bogardus, Pat'd Apr 10 1877, Diamond Quilted, Honey Yellow, 2 ⅝ In.................	431
Target Ball, Great Western, Shaded Golden Amber, Sheared, 2 ⅝ In.	2875
Target Ball, Patd Sept 25th 1877, Embossed Shoulder, Teal, Pebbled, 3-Piece Mold, 2 ⅝ In. . *illus*	1725
Whiskey, Cut Glass, Flat Hobstar Plug Stopper, Notched Handle, Ray Cut Base, W.C. Anderson, 9 ½ In..	420
Whiskey, Gold Dust Kentucky Bourbon, N. Van Bergen & Co., Aqua, Double Collar, c.1875, 11 ¾ In..	2520
Whiskey, JT Gayen, Altona, Cannon, Amber, Tapered, Prunts, Blob Top, c.1870, 13 ¾ In. .. *illus*	960
Whiskey, Our Choice, McKinley, Clear, Metal Screw Top, Paper Label, 6 In........................ *illus*	552

B

Bottle, Snuff, Pine Tree Branches, Carved, Agate, Rectangular, Oval Foot, 1800s, 3 ⅛ In.
$1,250

Leslie Hindman Auctioneers

Bottle, Soda, J.T. Brown, Chemist, Boston, Double Soda Water, Teal, Torpedo, Blob Top, Stand, 8 ¾ In.
$527

Glass Works Auctions

Bottle, Soda, J.V. Dellicker, Richmond, Va., Columbus, O., Aqua, Sloping Collar, 7 In.
$351

Glass Works Auctions

Bottle, Target Ball, Patd Sept 25th 1877, Embossed Shoulder, Teal, Pebbled, 3-Piece Mold, 2 ⅝ In.
$1,725

American Glass Gallery

Bottle, Whiskey, JT Gayen, Altona, Cannon, Amber, Tapered, Prunts, Blob Top, c.1870, 13 ¾ In.
$960

Glass Works Auctions

Bottle, Whiskey, Our Choice, McKinley, Clear, Metal Screw Top, Paper Label, 6 In.
$552

Hake's Auctions

Whiskey, Shady Brook, Label, Raised Letters, Frank Jones, c.1906, 11 ½ In.		832
Whiskey, Sherry, Young Woman, Label Under Glass, Backbar, 11 ½ In.	*illus*	7200
Zanesville, 24 Ribs, Swirled To Left, Yellow Orange Amber, Chestnut, 9 x 7 ¼ In.		3218
Zanesville, 24 Ribs, Swirled To Right, Amber, Globular, Applied Lip, c.1825, 7 ½ In.	*illus*	585

BOTTLE CAPS for milk bottles are the printed cardboard caps used since the 1920s. Crown caps, used after 1892 on soda bottles, are also popular collectibles. Unusual mottoes, graphics, and caps from bottlers that are out of business bring the highest prices.

Beverly Hills Sanitorium Milk, Yellow, Green, Metal, Tennessee, 1930s		62
Crown, Black Label, Beer, Black & Gold, Metal, Cork Lined, 1950s		8
Crown, Cuca Ruiva, Beer, Orange Ground, White Letters, Bird Flying, Gold Border, Angola		11
Crown, Frankenmuth Beer, Red Metal, Cork Lined, 1940s		8
Crown, Hires Root Beer, Metal, Brown Lettering, 1960s, 1 ½ In.		13
Crown, Malta Corsair, Red Ground, White Lettering, Guadeloupe Island		7
Crown, Moxie, Cork Lined, Thompsonville, Ct Bottling Works, White, Black, 1930s		3
Crown, Ndlovu, Beer, Elephant, Gold Ground, Tanzania Breweries		16
Crown, Solibra Bock Beer, Kronkorken Chapa, Green, Yellow, Black Border		7
Crown, Squirt, Yellow, Red Lettering, Metal, Cork Lining, Unused		2
Dairy Milk, Bell, Christmas, Green Lettering, Cream Ground, Cardboard, 1 ⅝ In.		18
Dr Pepper, Decatur Bottling Co., Plastic Lined, 1970s		4
Green Acres Farm, Milk, Vitamin D, Approved, Red Border, Middletown, Conn., 1 ⅝ In.		2

BOTTLE OPENERS are needed to open many bottles. As soon as the commercial bottle was invented, the opener to be used with the new types of closures became a necessity. Many types of bottle openers can be found, most dating from the twentieth century. Collectors prize advertising and comic openers.

Budweiser Beer, Cast Iron, Loop Seal Remover, Anheuser Busch Brewing, 1910s, 2 ⅞ In.		28
Cast Iron, Patina, Embossed Pat 1913, c.1913, 4 ½ In.		35
Corkscrew, Knife, Falstaff Beer Choicest, Blade, Celluloid Handle, 1930s, 2 ⅞ In.		40
Donkey, Laughing, Paperweight, Timberjack Machine, Brass, 3 ⅛ In.		41
Goebel Beer, Tin Litho, Early Beer Bottle Image, Goebel Brewing Co., 3 ¼ x 1 ¼ In.	*illus*	401
Starr, Whistle, Long Neck, Wall Mount, Steel, 1925, 4 ¼ In.		56
Storz, Triumph, Beer, Cigar Box, Steel, Engraved, Malt Extract, Key Shape, 1910s, 3 ⅛ In.		25
Teakwood, Stainless Steel, Japan, c.1950, 6 In.		12
Teeth, Bronze, Hand Engraved, Whale Hunting, Azores, 4 ½ In.		150
Woman's Hand With Ring, Brass, 5 ¼ In.		60

BOTTLE STOPPERS are made of glass, metal, plastic, and wood. Decorative and figural stoppers are used to replace the original cork stoppers and are collected today.

Mechanical, Wood, Carved, Anri Hat Tipper, 5 ½ In.		45
Wood, Carved, Bearded Man In Hat, Black Forest, 4 ½ In.		45

BOXES of all kinds are collected. They were made of wood, metal, tortoiseshell, embroidery, or other material. Additional boxes may be listed in other sections, such as Advertising, Battersea, Ivory, Shaker, Tinware, and various Porcelain categories. Tea Caddies are listed in their own category.

Bandbox, Les Trois Jours, Wallpaper, Military Barricade & Flags, c.1832, 13 ½ x 17 In.		180
Bandbox, Wallpaper, Yellow, Lunch From The Hunt Series, Lake On Lid, c.1835, 11 x 15 In.	*illus*	330
Bentwood, Lid, Oval, Pine, Wicker Stitched Seam, c.1875, 8 x 13 ¼ In.	*illus*	150
Bentwood, Oval, Laced Seams, Red & White Tulips, Berks County, c.1800, 5 ½ x 15 In.	*illus*	4680
Bentwood, Twig Handle, Fishtail Lock, Base, 1800s, 12 x 13 x 11 In.		270
Bible Box, Carved, Oak, Plain Lift Top, William & Mary, c.1800, 11 x 29 In.		615
Bible Box, Jacobean, Oak, Carved Facade, Wrought Iron, c.1700, 8 ½ x 25 ½ x 15 In.		531
Bible Box, Pine, Old Red Paint, New Hampshire, c.1715, 9 x 22 x 13 ¼ In.		6600
Black Walnut, Oval, Foster Giesman, c.1994, 5 x 7 ½ x 4 ¾ In.		91
Bone, Carved, Engraved, White, Iron Handle, 1800s, 5 x 9 In.		531

Bottle, Whiskey, Sherry, Young Woman, Label Under Glass, Backbar, 11 ½ In.
$7,200

Glass Works Auctions

Bottle, Zanesville, 24 Ribs, Swirled To Right, Amber, Globular, Applied Lip, c.1825, 7 ½ In.
$585

Glass Works Auctions

Bottle Opener, Goebel Beer, Tin Litho, Early Beer Bottle Image, Goebel Brewing Co., 3 ¼ x 1 ¼ In.
$401

AntiqueAdvertising.com

Box, Bandbox, Wallpaper, Yellow, Lunch From The Hunt Series, Lake On Lid, c.1835, 11 x 15 In.
$330

Garth's Auctioneers & Appraisers

Box, Bentwood, Lid, Oval, Pine, Wicker Stitched Seam, c.1875, 8 x 13 ¼ In.
$150

Garth's Auctioneers & Appraisers

Box, Bentwood, Oval, Laced Seams, Red & White Tulips, Berks County, c.1800, 5 ½ x 15 In.
$4,680

Garth's Auctioneers & Appraisers

TIP
To clean a veneered box or one made of porcupine quills or matchsticks, use a vacuum cleaner hose covered with a nylon stocking.

Box, Bride's, Soft Wood, Brass Rivets, Wood Locking Mechanism, Sweden, 6 x 13 ½ In.
$52

Keystone Auctions LLC LLC

Dual Purpose
Many older bottle openers have a small square hole called a "Prest-O-Lite Key." It was used to turn the valve on automobile gas headlights from about 1910 through the early 1930s, before electric headlights were used.

Box, Document, Papier-Mache, Mother-Of-Pearl, Black Lacquer, Gilt, 1800s, 5 x 6 x 4 In.
$189

Leland Little Auctions

Box, Dome Lid, Wood, Chestnut, Painted, Tulips, c.1850, 3 ¾ x 8 ¾ In.
$3,900

Garth's Auctioneers & Appraisers

Box, Dresser, Beech, Painted, Flowers, Continental, Early 1800s, 4 x 11 ¼ In.
$375

Pook & Pook

Box, Jewelry, Arts & Crafts, Copper Repousse, Leather Tray, Footed, c.1910, 8 x 11 ½ In.
$1,476

Skinner, Inc.

Box, Jewelry, Dome Lid, Rosewood, Brass Leafy Inlay, 3-Section Tray, Key, 5 x 12 x 8 In.
$216

Eldred's

Box, Letter, Cast Bronze, Cutler Mail Chute, American Eagle Seal, 36 x 21 ¼ x 11 ¼ In.
$968

Fontaine's Auction Gallery

Box, Maple, Bleached, Copper & Enamel Mounts, Signed, June Schwarcz, 1975, 3 ½ x 11 x 9 ⅝ In.
$8,750

Los Angeles Modern Auctions

Box, Pantry, Blue Painted, Pointed Finger Joint, Oval, 1800s, 2 ½ x 6 ¼ In.
$400

Skinner, Inc.

Book Shape, Painted, Marbleized, Gilt, Banner, 1839, 3 x 12 ½ In.	531
Book, Hinged Lid, Malachite, Jeweled Butterfly, Russia, Late 1900s, 1 ¾ x 9 x 14 In.	984
Bride's, Bentwood, Painted, Continental, 1800s, 6 ½ x 17 ¾ In.	188
Bride's, Bentwood, Painted, Flowers, Continental, Early 1800s, 4 ⅝ x 11 In.	344
Bride's, Flowers, Blue Top, Brown Trim, Hoop Print, Germany, Late 1800s, 5 x 15 x 9 In.	276
Bride's, Soft Wood, Brass Rivets, Wood Locking Mechanism, Sweden, 6 x 13 ½ In. ...... *illus*	52
Caddy, Bottle, Lid, Dovetailed, Lock, Brass Bail Handle, Early 1800s, 6 ¾ x 10 x 7 ¾ In.	110
Candle, Hinged Lid, Tin, Green, Cylindrical, 2 Strap Brackets, 1800s, 14 In.	277
Candle, Slide Lid, Burl, Hanging, 1800s, 17 ½ In.	125
Candle, Slide Lid, Walnut, Lacquer, 1800s, 7 x 14 ½ In.	275
Card File, Dome Trunk Shape, Brass & Ivory Straps, 3 ½ x 6 ½ x 4 ½ In.	138
Carry, Walnut, Compartments, 2 Lift Tops, Center Handle, Stenciled, 1800s, 2 ½ x 14 ½ In.	138
Champleve, Gilt Bronze, Enamel, 2 Doves, Velvet Fabric, Footed, France, 1800s, 5 x 9 x 5 In.	840
Cigar, Cutting, Painted, Wood, Drawer Base, 17 ½ x 11 ½ x 7 ½ In.	207
Cigar, Doghouse Shape, Wood, Locking, Hinged Roof Opens, c.1900, 6 x 8 x 10 In.	127
Cutlery, Lid, Mixed Wood, Mahogany Inlay, Bone Escutcheon, George III, 13 x 9 x 10 In.	189
Cutlery, Tin, 2 Compartments, Marked, Japan, 1800s, 4 ½ x 13 ¼ x 8 In.	148
Desk, Baroque Style, Embossed Gesso, Metal Figural Strapwork, Doors, c.1900, 14 x 13 x 7 In.	120
Document, Bird's-Eye, Curly Maple, Brass Lock, c.1830, 7 x 12 ½ x 6 ¼ In.	94
Document, Black Paint, Bone Escutcheon, Brass Feet, Navy Emblem, c.1850, 5 x 11 x 6 In.	36
Document, Brass Handle, Cloth Lined, Green Painted, 1800s, 7 ½ x 18 x 10 In.	338
Document, Burl, Satinwood, Marquetry, Ship, 1800s, 5 ¼ x 11 ⅞ x 8 In.	660
Document, Hinged Lid, Lacquer, Red, Gold, Pattern, Japan, 1900s, 18 x 12 In.	504
Document, Mahogany, Inlaid Pinwheels, Hearts & Compass Stars, c.1850, 5 x 9 ½ x 5 In.	1920
Document, Painted, 6-Board Pine, 1800s, 11 x 17 x 11 In.	259
Document, Papier-Mache, Mother-Of-Pearl, Black Lacquer, Gilt, 1800s, 5 x 6 x 4 In. ...... *illus*	189
Document, Poplar, Blue, Red, Ivory, Varnished, Mid 1800s, 4 ½ x 12 ¼ x 9 ½ In.	810
Document, Tin, Red Flowers & Green Leaves, Yellow Scroll, 1800s, 6 ½ x 9 ½ x 5 ¾ In.	738
Document, Toleware, Yellow, Red Stenciled Flowers, 7 x 10 In.	380
Dome Lid, Mustard Paint, Brass Handle, c.1850, 5 ¼ x 10 x 5 ½ In.	369
Dome Lid, Ocher Background, Russet Paint, 1800s, 8 ½ x 18 x 9 In.	338
Dome Lid, Pine, Flowers On Lid, New England, Mid 1800s, 12 x 30 x 14 In.	252
Dome Lid, Pine, Putty Paint, Swirls Mustard & Burnt Sienna, c.1830, 11 x 26 x 13 In.	584
Dome Lid, Pine, Square Nail Construction, Painted Flowers, 1850s, 12 x 30 x 14 In.	660
Dome Lid, Red & Black Painted, England, Early 1800s, 13 ¾ x 32 x 14 ¾ In.	338
Dome Lid, Red Paint, Carved, Wire Hinges, 1799, 5 x 9 ⅞ x 4 In.	369
Dome Lid, Royal Navy, Initials AJE RN, Leather, Brass Mounted, Late 1800s, 7 ½ x 15 In.	400
Dome Lid, Wood, Chestnut, Painted, Tulips, c.1850, 3 ¾ x 8 ¾ In. ...... *illus*	3900
Dovetailed, Hinged Lid, Walnut, Black Paint, Lock, Rectangular, c.1850, 8 x 16 x 8 In.	132
Dowry, Lid, Scrolls, Lines, Wood, Painted, Brass Fittings, India, 1900s, 8 ¾ x 12 x 9 In.	62
Dresser, Beech, Painted, Flowers, Continental, Early 1800s, 4 x 11 ¼ In. ...... *illus*	375
Dresser, Carved, Kingwood, 2nd Boer War, H. Rill Inscription, 1900s, 4 ¾ x 10 ½ In.	610
Dresser, Continental, Carved, Walnut, Bird, Ogee Feet, c.1880, 7 ½ x 9 x 5 ¾ In.	313
Dresser, Gilt Bronze, Pietra Dura, Oval, Beaded Lid, Tahan A Paris, c.1850, 4 x 7 x 5 In.	527
Dresser, Gilt Bronze, Plaque, Young Beauty, Wagner, Oval, 1800s, 1 ½ x 3 ¼ x 3 ¾ In.	900
Dresser, Inlaid Cow, Horse, Figures, Inscribed, Joseph S. Garber, Pa., 1890, 9 x 15 In.	1464
Dresser, Lid, Pine, Painted, Decoupaged Flowers, Watercolor, 1800s, 5 x 11 In.	88
Dresser, Lid, Prison Art, Mahogany, 5 Compartments, Inlay, 1800s, 7 ¾ x 14 ½ x 9 In.	152
Dresser, Pine, Painted, Lakeside Landscape, 4 Side Panels, 1800s, 6 ½ x 13 In.	938
Dresser, Satin, Light Green, Glass, 16 Pointed Stars On Lid, Floral, 5 x 4 ¼ In.	59
Dresser, Swirl Glass, Gilt Bronze, Birds, Nest, Faux Agate, 1800s, 8 x 6 In.	900
Figural, Duck Shape, Hinged Lid, Wood, Painted, Hollow Interior, 1900s, 10 In.	23
Flatware, Horn Veneer, Brass Ball Feet, Maitland Smith Style, 5 x 15 x 14 In.	125
Jewelry, Arts & Crafts, Copper Repousse, Leather Tray, Footed, c.1910, 8 x 11 ½ In. ...... *illus*	1476
Jewelry, Burl, Brass Inlay, Octagonal, Monogram, Satin Interior, 1800s, 4 x 7 x 7 In.	469
Jewelry, Dome Lid, Rosewood, Brass Leafy Inlay, 3-Section Tray, Key, 5 x 12 x 8 In. ...... *illus*	216
Jewelry, Gilt Bronze, Micro Mosaic Plaques, Malachite, c.1950, 3 ¾ x 5 ½ x 4 In.	3120
Jewelry, Gilt, Rococo Flowers, Lion Paw Feet, Divided Shelf, Velvet, 1800s, 6 x 14 x 9 In.	165
Jewelry, Hinged Lid, Hardwood Case, Red Silk, 2 Doors, Chinese, 10 x 14 x 9 In.	94

Box, Pantry, Oval, Bentwood, Peg &
Nails, Signed, Mass., 1874, Miniature,
1 ½ x 4 In.
$313

Pook & Pook

Box, Pipe, Cherry, Wall, Tombstone
Hanger, Drawer, Brass Knob, 1700s,
20 x 4 x 5 In.
$1,112

Thomaston Place Auction Galleries

Box, Pipe, Leaf, Diamond Crest, Heart
Cutout, Thumb Molded Drawer, Conn.,
c.1815, 20 In.
$3,480

Northeast Auctions

Box, Pipe, Wall, Cherry, Inlay, Drawer, 1800s, 19¾ x 8¾ In.
$363

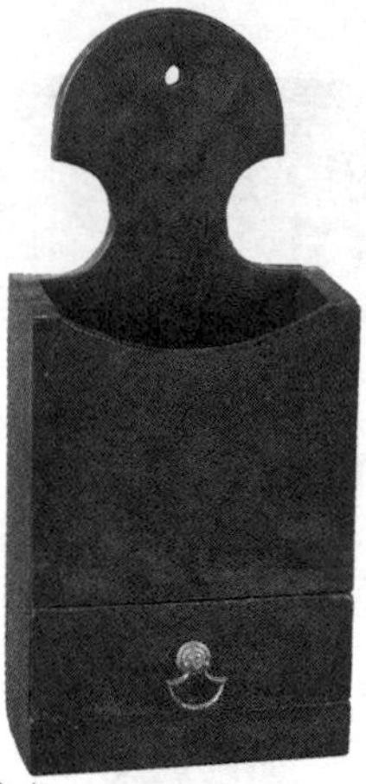

Pook & Pook

Box, Spice, 9 Drawers, Walnut, Thumb Molded, 3 Rows, Wood Pulls, c.1850, 10 x 16 x 6 In.
$400

Skinner, Inc.

Box, Strong, Mahogany, 2 Copper Handles, Metal, Anglo-Colonial, c.1895, 9 x 23 x 14 In.
$525

Heritage Auctions

TIP
Your collectibles will live best at the temperature and humidity that is comfortable for you. Not too hot, cold, wet, or dry.

Jewelry, Hinged Lid, Reclining Nude Woman, Flowers, Gilt, 6 x 11 In.	242
Jewelry, Hinged Lid, Wood, Carved, Flowers, Velvet Lining, 1700s, 4¾ x 9 x 5⅝ In.	72
Jewelry, Mahogany, Hexagonal, Inlaid Diamonds, Brass Bale, 1850s, 10 x 11¾ In.	510
Jewelry, Rosewood, Marquetry Inlaid Borders, Pyramidal, Lock, Key, 6 x 14 x 7 In.	303
Jewelry, Rosewood, Star Inlaid Top, Mirror Inside Lid, 9½ x 13½ x 4 In.	207
Jewelry, Walnut, Carved, 4 Drawers, Ogee Plinth, Early 1900s, 12 x 16 x 6 In.	277
Jewelry, Walnut, Velvet Carved, Signed, J. Camp, Pa., 1973, 16 x 15 x 20 In.	3125
Jewelry, Wood, Carved, Mirror, Key Design, 6 Drawers, Bats, Coins, Chinese, c.1900, 9 x 11 x 15 In.	384
Lapis, Onyx Interior, Gold Plated Ball Feet, 5 x 1¾ x 3½ In.	500
Letter, Brassbound, Burl, Dome Top, Handle, Satin Lined Lid, 1800s, 6 x 8 x 4 In.	156
Letter, Cast Bronze, Cutler Mail Chute, American Eagle Seal, 36 x 21¼ x 11¼ In. *illus*	968
Letter, Oak, Compartments, Slant Front, Hinged, High Relief Carving, 8½ x 9½ In.	104
Letter, Oak, Slant Front, Beveled Glass, Brass Escutcheon, 8¼ x 12¼ x 7½ In.	666
Letter, Wood, Peephole, Carved, Oval Beveled Glass, Locking, Late 1800s, 9 x 12 In.	138
Letter, Wood, Swing Out Doors, Fitted Interior, 2 Inkwells, Drawer, 8 x 15 x 13 In.	184
Lid, Wood, Enameled Metal Panel On Top, A. Ames, J. Ames, c.1960, 3 x 20 x 14 In.	531
Maple, Bleached, Copper & Enamel Mounts, Signed, June Schwarcz, 1975, 3½ x 11 x 9⅝ In. *illus*	8750
Maple, Side Lid, Red Stain, Diamond Shape Handle, 1800s, 8 x 1½ x 2 In.	215
Metal, Sevres Style, Porcelain Mounted, Gilt, Circular, Ball Feet, 1800s, 6¾ In.	688
Pantry, Bentwood, Dry Blue Surface, Oval, 1800s, 2 x 5⅞ In.	875
Pantry, Bentwood, Round, Red Surface, Early 1900s, 12 x 15½ In.	63
Pantry, Blue Painted, Pointed Finger Joint, Oval, 1800s, 2½ x 6¼ In. *illus*	400
Pantry, Lid, Pine, Green, Sundries, Handwritten In Black, J. Burr, 1800s, 3 x 6¾ In.	540
Pantry, Oval, Bentwood, Peg & Nails, Signed, Mass., 1874, Miniature, 1½ x 4 In. *illus*	313
Pantry, Oval, Black Paint, Single Finger Laps, 1800s, 5 In.	226
Pantry, Oval, Red Paint, Single Lap On Lid & Base, Square Cut Tacks, 8¾ x 3½ In.	254
Pantry, Oval, Stamped On Lid, B. Sprague, 1800s, 3 x 6¼ In.	360
Pantry, Pine & Oak, Bentwood, Green Paint, Red & Yellow Star, 1800s, 5 x 10½ In.	594
Pantry, Pine, Green Paint, Interlocking Laps, Canted Sides, Early 1800s, 7 x 10 In.	360
Pantry, Pine, Painted, Black & Blue, Flowers On Lid, Continental, 1828, 5 x 11¾ In.	250
Pantry, Round, Bentwood, Green Paint, Iron Tacks, c.1950, 1½ x 3½ In.	360
Pine, Lid, Sliding, Black Paint, Molded Base, Dovetailed, c.1780, 11 x 20 x 13½ In.	185
Pine, Lid, Sliding, Painted Tulips, Pennsylvania, 4 x 7 x 5 In.	584
Pine, Meeting House, Landscape & Buildings, Massachusetts, 1833, 5 x 10 x 8 In.	6150
Pipe, Cherry, Wall, Tombstone Hanger, Drawer, Brass Knob, 1700s, 20 x 4 x 5 In. *illus*	1112
Pipe, Leaf, Diamond Crest, Heart Cutout, Thumb Molded Drawer, Conn., c.1815, 20 In. *illus*	3480
Pipe, Wall, Cherry, Inlay, Drawer, 1800s, 19¾ x 8¾ In. *illus*	363
Quartz, White, Tiger Eye, Lined Interior, Rectangular, 6 x 4 x 1½ In.	563
Rosewood, Carved Abalone & Bone, Hinged Lid, Brass, Japan, 1900s, 3¾ x 8 x 4¼ In.	60
Rosewood, Mother-Of-Pearl, Footed, Regency, 8 x 12 x 7 In.	316
Shoeshine, Spoon-Carved Flowers, Painted, Brass Handle, Lock, Key, 1800s, 4½ x 8 In.	52
Silver & Copper, Warrior On Top, Green Brown Patina, Wood Lined, Mexico 4¼ In.	115
Spice, 9 Drawers, Walnut, Thumb Molded, 3 Rows, Wood Pulls, c.1850, 10 x 16 x 6 In. *illus*	400
Stationery, Togidashi, Maki-E, Peonies, Rocks, Butterflies, 1800s, 6 x 10½ x 6 In.	1107
Storage, Bentwood, Spruce, Cane Binding, Faded Black Paint, 6½ x 16½ x 10½ In.	143
Strong, Mahogany, 2 Copper Handles, Metal, Anglo-Colonial, c.1895, 9 x 23 x 14 In. *illus*	525
Tantalus, Ebonized Wood, Tortoiseshell, 4 Decanters, 16 Cordials, France, 11 x 13 In. *illus*	840
Tobacco, Tin Lithograph, Green, Red, Black Lettering, Cuba, c.1800s, 8 x 8 x 11 In.	66
Tobacco, Tonkotsu, Pouch Shape, Chrysanthemum, Butterfly, Agate Bead, Japan, c.1850, 4 In.	1680
Tobacco, Tonkotsu, Toad Shape, Brass Tack Eyes, Agate Bead, Suspended Frog Netsuke, 5 In.	204
Valuables, Mirror, Removable Tray, Walnut, Jacob Shaffer, Philadelphia, 1838, 4¼ x 10 In.	300
Vanity, Birchwood, Folding, Mirror, Drawer, Key, Biedermeier, Austria, c.1950, 19 x 13 x 18 In.	369
Vinaigrette, Knight's Helmet, Silver, Gold Accents, 2¾ In. *illus*	5100
Wagon, Slant Lid, Conestoga, Pine, Iron Strap Hinges & Bands, c.1800, 18 x 15½ In. *illus*	2125
Wall, 2 Tiers, Pine, Flattened Arch Crest, Molded Base, Early 1800s, 16 x 12 x 6 In. *illus*	738
Wall, Drawer, Wood, Red, Double Hanger, c.1790, 16 x 14 x 7 In.	2337
Wall, Lift Lid, 3 Tiers, Pine, Iron Wire Hinges, 1800s, 22¼ x 8⅜ x 7½ In.	2337
Wall, Mahogany, Wood, Shaped Backs, Scalloped Sides, 1800s, 20 x 10½ In.	270
Wall, Old Red Paint, 2 Sections For Storage, 16 x 7½ x 3½ In. *illus*	303
Wall, Wood, Red, Lollipop Hanger, Drawer, Brass Knob, 1800s, 12 x 9 x 5½ In.	3075

Box, Tantalus, Ebonized Wood, Tortoiseshell, 4 Decanters, 16 Cordials, France, 11 x 13 In.
$840

Cowan's Auctions

Box, Wall, Old Red Paint, 2 Sections For Storage, 16 x 7½ x 3½ In.
$303

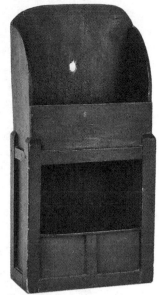

Forsythes' Auctions

TIP
It is said that for the best deals at a flea market or show, you should arrive early (perhaps pay the early bird admission) for best selection and leave late for best deals. But don't forget to look for things displayed on the ground or under shelves. They are often overlooked.

Box, Wagon, Slant Lid, Conestoga, Pine, Iron Strap Hinges & Bands, c.1800, 18 x 15½ In.
$2,125

Garth's Auctioneers & Appraisers

Box, Wedding, Divided Compartments, Wood Handle, Chinese, 11 x 9 x 5 In.
$188

Roland Auctioneers & Valuers

Box, Vinaigrette, Knight's Helmet, Silver, Gold Accents, 2¾ In.
$5,100

Morphy Auctions

Box, Wall, 2 Tiers, Pine, Flattened Arch Crest, Molded Base, Early 1800s, 16 x 12 x 6 In.
$738

Skinner, Inc.

Box, Wood, Lid, Round, Pink Ivorywood, Dale Chase, c.1995, 1¾ x 2 In.
$65

Freeman's Auctioneers & Appraisers

Boy Scout, Wood Carving, Oak, Boy Scout Standing, Wide Brim Hat, c.1910, 30 x 11 x 1 ½ In.
$60

Thomaston Place Auction Galleries

Bradley & Hubbard, Clock, John Bull, Blinking Eye, Cast Iron, Painted, 1800s, 16 ½ In.
$2,124

Cottone Auctions

Bradley & Hubbard, Lamp, Copper, Brass, Figural Handles, Shade, 1900s, 25 In.
$72

Eldred's

Bradley & Hubbard, Lamp, Green Glass Shade, Brass, Receptacle Arm, c.1910, 22 In.
$120

Selkirk Auctioneers & Appraisers

Bradley & Hubbard, Lamp, Rectangular Glass Shade, Metal Overlay, Landscape, Signed, c.1915, 20 ½ In.
$878

Jeffrey S. Evans & Associates

Brass, Bookstand, Pierced, Adjustable, England, 1800s, 7 ¾ x 11 In.
$138

Leslie Hindman Auctioneers

Brass, Casket, Table, Turquoise Glass Cabochons, Mounted Calamander, Rectangular, 1800s, 14 In.
$313

Leslie Hindman Auctioneers

Brass, Chamberstick, Art Nouveau, Circular Base, WMF, c.1800s, 5 In.
$113

Pook & Pook

> **TIP**
> Don't overclean hardware, andirons, or other old brass objects. Clean off the worst, but don't try to make them look brand new.

Brass, Doorknocker, Cannon Shape, Nautical, Harvin Co., c.1900, 9 x 2 In.
$224

Charleston Estate Auctions

Wedding, Divided Compartments, Wood Handle, Chinese, 11 x 9 x 5 In. *illus*	188
Wedding, Wood, Lacquer, Carved, Chinese, c.1900, 17 x 14 x 9 ½ In.	94
Wood, 4 Oil Painted Landscapes, Gilt Trim, Bail Handles, Vienna, c.1820, 18 In.	2588
Wood, Brown Grain, Wrought Iron Handles & Lock, S. Herrick, 30 x 15 In.	142
Wood, Gilt Lacquer, Chrysanthemum Sprays, Japan, c.1800s, 4⅞ x 7⅛ In	260
Wood, Lid, Round, Pink Ivorywood, Dale Chase, c.1995, 1¾ x 2 In. *illus*	65
Wood, Lid, Sliding, 3 Sections, Beehive, Red Table, Roses, White House, 1850s, 6 x 3 x 1⅝ In..	1722
Wood, Lid, Swivel, Geometric Carved Lid, Compartment, 1800s, 2½ x 7⅜ x 3¾ In.	277
Wood, Trunk Shape, Brass Straps, Leather Handles, 8 x 11 x 6½ In.	184

BOY SCOUT collectibles include any material related to scouting, including patches, manuals, and uniforms. The Boy Scout movement in the United States started in 1910. The first Jamboree was held in 1937. Girl Scout items are listed under their own heading.

Armband, Police, Cloth, Blue Print, White Ground, 3 x 17 In.	53
Award, Medal, Bronze, Neck Ribbon, Yellow, Blue	34
Badge, 2 Stripes, Green, Logo, Gold Border, Czechoslovakia, 1¾ x 2½ In.	9
Clip, Roosevelt Council, Metal, 50 Years Protecting Our Freedom, 1921-71, 1⅜ In.	5
Flag, Jamboree, Headquarters, Gear, River Scene, Trees, Black, Green	33
Flag, Troop 23, Dorchester, BSA, Be Prepared, Green Logo, Red & White	19
Neckerchief, Jamboree, Bicentennial, White Ground, Red & Blue Border	5
Paperweight, Eagle, 2 Stars, Shield At Chest, Fish Scale, 3¼ x 3½ In.	7
Patch, Unalachtigo Lodge 168, Order Of The Arrow, Pioneer Trails	28
Sash, Brotherhood, Order Of The Arrow, White & Red, Felt	16
Shirt, Uniform, Webelos, Council Patch, Bicycle Rodeo Logo	16
Spoon, Baden-Powell Centenary, Portrait Finial, 1957, 12½ In.	10
Wood Carving, Oak, Boy Scout Standing, Wide Brim Hat, c.1910, 30 x 11 x 1½ In. *illus*	60

BRADLEY & HUBBARD is a name found on many metal objects. Walter Hubbard and his brother in law, Nathaniel Lyman Bradley, started making cast iron clocks, tables, frames, andirons, bookends, doorstops, lamps, chandeliers, sconces, and sewing birds in 1854 in Meriden, Connecticut. The company became Bradley & Hubbard Manufacturing Company in 1875. Charles Parker Company bought the firm in 1940. There is no mention of Bradley & Hubbard after the 1950s. Bradley & Hubbard items may be found in other sections that include metal.

Clock, Admiral, Blinking Eye, Cast Iron, 1800s, 17 In.	1121
Clock, John Bull, Blinking Eye, Cast Iron, Painted, 1800s, 16½ In. *illus*	2124
Clock, Lion, Blinking Eye, Cast Iron, 1800s, 8 x 10 In.	2832
Clock, Sambo, Blinking Eye, Cast Iron, 1800s, 16 In.	1888
Clock, Topsy, Blinking Eye, Posing, Cast Iron, Painted, 17 In.	1770
Lamp, Art Nouveau, Bronze Plated, Cast Metal, Slag Glass Shade, 23 In.	200
Lamp, Banquet, Openwork Flowers, Electrified Font, Ball Shade, 27 In.	177
Lamp, Brass, Mixed Metals, Satin Glass Shade, Gilt Flowers, Dragons, c.1880, 63 In.	484
Lamp, Cigar Lighter, Urn Shape, 2 Sleeve Holders, Ruby Ball Shade, c.1880, 4⅝ x 3¾ In.	263
Lamp, Copper, Brass, Figural Handles, Shade, 1900s, 25 In. *illus*	72
Lamp, Green Glass Shade, Brass, Receptacle Arm, c.1910, 22 In. *illus*	120
Lamp, Oil, Brass Body, Frosted Pink, Octagonal Base, Electrified, 17 In.	52
Lamp, Rectangular Glass Shade, Metal Overlay, Landscape, Signed, c.1915, 20½ In. *illus*	878

BRASS has been used for decorative pieces and useful tablewares since ancient times. It is an alloy of copper, zinc, and other metals. Additional brass items may be found under Bell, Candlestick, Tool, or Trivet.

Ashtray, Floor, Stand, Fluted Stem, Circular Tray, Man, Matchbox Holder, 1900s	12
Bed Warmer, Hand Chased Lid, Turned Walnut Handle, 1800s, 43 In.	71
Bed Warmer, Punched, Spiral, Maple Handle, 1800s, 47½ In.	25
Bed Warmer, Punched, Tooled Pan, Wood Handle, 1800s, 45 In.	50
Bed Warmer, Wrigglework, Tooled Pan, Turned Wood Handle, 1800s, 40½ In.	50
Bookstand, Pierced, Adjustable, England, 1800s, 7¾ x 11 In. *illus*	138
Bookstand, Pierced, Leaves, Adjustable, Rectangular, 1800s, 7 x 11 In.	138

Brass, Figure, Guanyin, Seated On Double Lotus, Tiara, Holding Vase, Chinese, 1900s, 12 In.
$625

Neal Auction Company

Brass, Hand Warmer, Bowl Shape, Openwork Lid, Double Strap Handle, Chinese, 4½ x 8 In.
$74

Skinner, Inc.

Brass, Jewelry Box, Dome Lid, Walnut, Gilt Handle, Red Velvet, 10 x 12 x 6¾ In.
$1,089

Fontaine's Auction Gallery

This is an edited listing of current prices. Visit **Kovels.com** to check thousands of prices from previous years and sign up for free information on trends, tips, reproductions, marks, and more.

Brass, Letter Holder, Pierced, Tree, Moss, Rosalie Weiner, c.1930, 4 x 4 In. $2,928

Neal Auction Company

Brass, Mortar & Pestle, Stepped Base, Banded Column Support, Flared Opening, c.1710, 11 In. $420

Brunk Auctions

Brass, Signal Cannon, 50 Caliber, Rifled Bore, Iron Carriage, Painted, 1886, 6½ x 13 x 6 In. $468

Forsythes' Auctions

Box, Hammered, Birds Of Prey, Cabochons, Wood, Glass, Velvet, A. Daguet, c.1907, 8 x 11 In.	2250
Box, Marquetry, Mother-Of-Pearl, Wire, Medallion, Leaves, Contoured Border, Lid, 3 x 10 x 7 In.	100
Box, Tobacco, Tavern, Coin Slot, Spring & Latch, Ball Feet, Early 1800s, 5 x 9½ x 5 In.	300
Bucket, Planter, Lion's Head Handles, Footed, Farber, 11 x 12½ In.	23
Bull, Nandi, Seated On A Plinth, India, 1800s, 3 x 2½ In.	400
Casket, Table, Dome Lid, Bronze Appliques, Mounted, Burl, 1800s, 8 In.	250
Casket, Table, Turquoise Glass Cabochons, Mounted Calamander, Rectangular, 1800s, 14 In. *illus*	313
Chamberstick, Art Nouveau, Circular Base, WMF, c.1800s, 5 In. *illus*	113
Chandelier, 6-Light, Brass, Bird Shape Candle Supports, Empire Style, 1900s, 24 In.	660
Chandelier, Basket, Frosted, Flower Shades, 1900s, 28 In.	75
Charger, Embossed, Animals Border, 1700s, 18½ In.	325
Cigarette Dispenser, Donkey, Basket Holder For Cigarettes, Matches On Back, 6 x 8 In.	69
Coal Scuttle, Brass, Relief, Sheet Iron Basket, Tongs, France, c.1900, 21 x 14 x 16 In.	281
Compote, Figural Glass Insects, 6 Insects, Rope Twist Bands, Circular Foot, 1900s, 3 x 12 In.	250
Cooler, Wine, Oval Basin, Applied Legs, Lion Shape Drop Rings, Paw Feet, 1800s, 15 x 18 In.	540
Corbel, 3 Male Heads, Figural, Carved Wood, 9½ x 10 x 6 In.	94
Cover, Clock Window, Father Time, Scythe, Hourglass, Owl, Rooster, 7¼ x 5¼ In.	60
Cup, Fluted, Carved Ball Wood Support, Josef Hoffmann For Wiener Werkstatte, 5¼ In.	1500
Doorknocker, Cannon Shape, Nautical, Harvin Co., c.1900, 9 x 2 In. *illus*	224
Figure, Buddha, Reclining, Head Resting On Hand, Burma, 1⅞ x 8⅞ In.	74
Figure, Girl's Face, Gold, 13 In.	230
Figure, Guanyin, Seated On Double Lotus, Tiara, Holding Vase, Chinese, 1900s, 12 In. *illus*	625
Figure, Horse, Prancing, Hagenauer, Austria, 12 In.	1875
Glove Form, Dessus De Mian, 8½ P, Armand Bonne, Paris, 17 x 3¼ In.	124
Hand Warmer, Bowl Shape, Openwork Lid, Double Strap Handle, Chinese, 4½ x 8 In. *illus*	74
Jardiniere, Islamic Calligraphy, Middle Eastern, c.1950, 9½ x 13¼ In.	150
Jewelry Box, Dome Lid, Walnut, Gilt Handle, Red Velvet, 10 x 12 x 6¾ In. *illus*	1089
Letter Holder, Pierced, Tree, Moss, Rosalie Weiner, c.1930, 4 x 4 In. *illus*	2928
Mortar & Pestle, Stepped Base, Banded Column Support, Flared Opening, c.1710, 11 In. *illus*	420
Ornament, Repousse Grain, Sparrows, Dragonfly, Daisies, Tasseled Ribbon, 2¾ x 2 In.	246
Padlock, Pancake, 2 Keys, Santa Fe Logo, 3 x 2¼ In.	367
Signal Cannon, 50 Caliber, Rifled Bore, Iron Carriage, Painted, 1886, 6½ x 13 x 6 In. *illus*	468
Statue, Woman, Patinated Metal, Marble Base, Victorian, 28 In.	374
Tray, Butler's, Reticulated Gallery, 2¼ x 26 x 16½ In.	219
Tray, Cranes, Acid Etched, Carence Crafters, 5 x 9 In.	425
Tray, Inlay, Scrolls, Central Medallion, Maitland Smith, 31 In.	412

BRASTOFF, *see Sascha Brastoff category.*

BREAD PLATE, *see various silver categories, porcelain factories, and pressed glass patterns.*

BRIDE'S BOWLS OR BASKETS were usually one-of-a-kind novelties made in American and European glass factories. They were especially popular about 1880 when the decorated basket was often given as a wedding gift. Cut glass baskets were popular after 1890. All bride's bowls lost favor about 1905. Bride's bowls and baskets may also be found in other glass sections. Check the index at the back of the book.

Amberina, Scalloped Rim, Victorian, 10 x 11 In.	180
Art Glass, Orange & Yellow Tones, Silver Plated Frame, Victorian, 10 In.	192
Blue Green Glass Bowl, Cut Lip & Plug, Pairpoint, Silver Plate, 13 In.	88
Cased, Ribbed, Square Scalloping, Silver Plated Frame, G.G. Webster & Son, 1900s, 14 In.	156
Cranberry Glass, Delaware, Oval, Gold Highlights, Silver Plate Frame, 10 x 11 In.	102
Cranberry Glass, Flowers, Multicolor, Clear Rim, Rib Optic, c.1890, 4 x 9 In.	234
Light Green Cased, Pink, Hobnail, Ruffled Rim, Silver Plated Frame, 12 In.	168
Orange, Shaded, Threaded Body, Cut Rim, Victorian, Late 1800s, 13 In.	150
Peachblow, Ruffled Lip, Ground Pontil, Cupid, Victorian, 14 x 12 In.	142
Pink Cased, Amber Rim, Ruffled Quatrefoil Edge, Victorian, England, c.1885, 5 In. *illus*	72
Pink Cased, Ribbed, Ruffled Edge, Flowers, Silver Plated Frame, c.1880, 12 In. *illus*	216
Pink Cased, Ruffled, Gold, Blue, White, Floral, Silver Plated Frame, Victorian, 11½ In.	120
Rubina, Overshot, Opalescent, Silver Plated Frame, W. Hammil & Co., c.1885, 10 In. *illus*	168

BRITANNIA, *see Pewter category.*

BRONZE is an alloy of copper, tin, and other metals. It is used to make figurines, lamps, and other decorative objects. Bronze lamps are listed in the Lamp category. Pieces listed here date from the eighteenth, nineteenth, and twentieth centuries. Shown here are marks used by three well-known makers of bronzes.

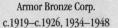

POMPEIAN BRONZE COMPANY

Armor Bronze Corp.
c.1919–c.1926, 1934–1948

Bradley and Hubbard Mfg. Co.
1875–c.1940

Pompeian Bronze Co.
Undated

Aureole, Buddhist, Openwork, Handled, Lacquer & Gilt Front, Plain Back, 10 In. .... *illus*	185
Bottle, Round, Long Neck, Molded Petal Lappet, Beaded, Splayed Stem Foot, India, 11 ½ In.	172
Bowl, Grapes, Leaves, Marked, Chinese, 3 ½ x 12 ½ In. .... *illus*	156
Bowl, Nude Bust, Female, Square Base, Signed G. England, France, 9 x 12 In.	185
Box, Lid, Micro Mosaic, Gilt, Scene, Marble Border, Italy, c.1950, 2 x 2 ¾ In.	540
Brazier, Satyrs, Tripod Base, Cove Molded, Fluted Fire Pot, Italy, c.1815, 32 ½ x 15 ½ In.	2750
Brush Washer, Crane, Wing Around Rim, Round, 4 Jutting Feet, Early 1900s, 2 ¾ x 4 ¾ In.	185
Bust, Aizelin, Eugene Antoine, Diana, Ebonized Pedestal, 1870, 22 x 68 In.	1250
Bust, Bronze, Brown Patina, Wood Base, Bruce Brady, 1994, 17 ½ In.	6250
Bust, Guerra, Patinated, Laminate Base, Signed, 1900s, 8 In.	156
Bust, Mui, J.N., Confederate Soldier, Sword, Walnut Base, Signed, 1981, 10 x 5 ¼ x 5 ½ In.	1029
Bust, Napoleon, Laurel Crown, Square Marble Base, 1800s, 13 In.	523
Bust, Pallas Athena, Goddess Of War, Dore, Marble Base, c.1980, 14 x 6 x 4 In.	1750
Bust, Physician, Naval Doctor, Tapering Square Base, France, 1800s, 13 In. .... *illus*	738
Bust, Pinedo, Emile, Napoleon, Marble Base, 9 In. .... *illus*	375
Bust, Villanis, Young Woman, Head Turned To Side, Hair Up, Marble Base, 11 ½ In.	313
Cachepot, Flowers, Mixed Metal, Gilt, Mount, 12 x 13 x 10 In.	531
Card Holder, Monkey, Standing, Holding Tray Over Head, 7 In. .... *illus*	83
Censer, Circular, 2 Handles, Round Base, Qing, Chinese, Marked, 1800s, 3 ½ x 5 In.	120
Censer, Dragon & Lotus, Patinated, Footed, Chinese, 5 ¼ x 4 x 3 In.	313
Censer, Gilt, Sawasa Ware, Japan, 1800s, 7 x 6 x 3 ½ In.	7800
Censer, Globular, Loop Handles, Tripod Base, Rectangular Panel, Xuande, 9 In.	6875
Censer, Globular, Squat, Pointed Feet, Pierced Dome Lid, Petal, 3 In.	196
Censer, Gold Ornament, Lion's Head Handles, Round, Chinese, 1800s, 3 x 5 ½ In.	120
Censer, Quadruped, Rounded Square Shape, 2 Strap Handles, 8 ½ In.	148
Censer, River Hut Shape, Removable Thatched Roof, Japan, Late 1800s, 6 ¾ x 7 x 4 In.	351
Censer, Urn Shape, Dragon Head Legs, 6-Sided Platform, Japan, Late 1800s, 13 x 6 x 4 In.	146
Clock, Gilt Bronze, Urn Form, Putti, Battery Powered Movement, c.1980, 25 ½ x 31 x 10 ½ In..	3250
Clock, Shelf, Bronze, Figural, Woman, Mirror, Dressing Table, Louis-Philippe, c.1850, 17 x 15 x 8 In.	813
Clock, Shelf, Malachite, Bronze Cupid, Holding Cockerel, E. Coeur A Paris, c.1980, 15 x 11 x 6 In......	2000
Column, Grand Tour, Place Vendome Napoleon, Mount, Black Marble Base, 1800s, 18 In.	1476
Compote, Charles, C., Figural, Putti Holding Bowl, Signed, Deco Foundry, 11 ½ In. .... *illus*	31
Doorknocker, Eagle, Ornate, Carved, Center Medallion, 8 ½ x 9 In.	531
Ewer, Bladder Shape, Panther Form Handle, Verdigris Patina, c.1850, 9 In. .... *illus*	180
Ewer, Gilt, Mounted, Putti Handle, Continental, 1900s, 15 ½ In.	688
Head, Liberty, Half Round, Bold Facial Features, Signed, Yantorno, 1900s, 12 In. .... *illus*	246
Incense Burner, Foo Dog Handle, Dragons, Phoenix, Japan, Late 1800s, 8 x 7 x 5 In.	147
Jardiniere, Champleve Enamel, Flowers, Vines, Sloping Shoulder, Chinese, 10 x 14 In.	254
Jardiniere, Raised Carp, Incised Grasses, Folded In Form, 3-Footed, Asian, 15 x 15 In.............	406
Jewelry Box, Velvet Lined, 4 Side Panels, Hinged Lid, Lock, Spain, 6 x 9 ½ x 7 In.	341
Model, Luxor Obelisk, Hieroglyphics, Bronze Fence, Black Marble Base, 1800s, 11 ½ In.	2337
Pedestal, Bowl, Gilt, Hairy Paw Feet, Caryatids, Oval Ring, 8 ¾ x 9 ½ x 7 ½ In. .... *illus*	875
Planter, Dragon, Foot, Cloud Design, Japan, 1800s, 10 ⅜ x 11 ⅝ In. .... *illus*	303
Plaque, 3 Farmers, Reditio Domum, Return Home, Marble Frame, 12 x 12 In.	47
Plaque, Circular, Neo Romanticism, Male & Female, Countryside Setting, 1920s-50s	36

Bride's Basket, Pink Cased, Amber Rim, Ruffled Quatrefoil Edge, Victorian, England, c.1885, 5 In.
$72

Garth's Auctioneers & Appraisers

Bride's Basket, Pink Cased, Ribbed, Ruffled Edge, Flowers, Silver Plated Frame, c.1880, 12 In.
$216

Garth's Auctioneers & Appraisers

Victorian Glass
Colored Victorian glass like Spanish Lace, cranberry opalescent, and blue and white swirl are bargains today. The glass is selling for two-thirds to half of the prices of eight years ago.

Bride's Basket, Rubina, Overshot, Opalescent, Silver Plated Frame, W. Hammil & Co., c.1885, 10 In.
$168

Garth's Auctioneers & Appraisers

BRONZE

Bronze, Aureole, Buddhist, Openwork, Handled, Lacquer & Gilt Front, Plain Back, 10 In.
$185

Skinner, Inc.

Bronze, Bowl, Grapes, Leaves, Marked, Chinese, 3½ x 12½ In.
$156

Roland Auctioneers & Valuers

Bronze, Bust, Physician, Naval Doctor, Tapering Square Base, France, 1800s, 13 In.
$738

Skinner, Inc.

Bronze, Bust, Pinedo, Emile, Napoleon, Marble Base, 9 In.
$375

Nadeau's Auction Gallery

> **TIP**
> Dust your bronze, then try the Chinese method of polishing. Rub the bronze with the palm of your hand. This puts a little oil on the metal.

Bronze, Card Holder, Monkey, Standing, Holding Tray Over Head, 7 In.
$83

Milestone Auctions

Bronze, Compote, Charles, C., Figural, Putti Holding Bowl, Signed, Deco Foundry, 11½ In.
$31

Selkirk Auctioneers & Appraisers

Bronze, Ewer, Bladder Shape, Panther Form Handle, Verdigris Patina, c.1850, 9 In.
$180

Eldred's

Bronze, Head, Liberty, Half Round, Bold Facial Features, Signed, Yantorno, 1900s, 12 In.
$246

Skinner, Inc.

Bronze, Pedestal, Bowl, Gilt, Hairy Paw Feet, Caryatids, Oval Ring, 8¾ x 9½ x 7½ In.
$875

Susanin's Auctioneers & Appraisers

Bronze, Planter, Dragon, Foot, Cloud Design, Japan, 1800s, 10⅜ x 11⅝ In.
$303

Ahlers & Ogletree Auction Gallery

Bronze, Scroll Weight, Ram, Lying Down, Filed Horns, Chinese, 3 In.
$688

Selkirk Auctioneers & Appraisers

Bronze, Sculpture, Arab Soldier, Riding Camel, Onyx Base, 13 x 14½ x 5 In.
$188

Susanin's Auctioneers & Appraisers

Bronze, Sculpture, Barye, Wildlife, Lion, Antelope, France, 1900s, 5 x 11¼ In.
$192

Selkirk Auctioneers & Appraisers

Bronze, Sculpture, Bertoia, Harry, Tree, Patina, 1970s, 11 x 11 In.
$31,250

Rago Arts and Auction Center

Bronze, Sculpture, Cornwell, Martha Jackson, Girl, Turtle, Marble Base, Signed, 7¾ x 5½ In.
$308

Skinner, Inc.

Bronze, Sculpture, Dancing, Shiva, Arms, Leg Raised, Southeast Asia, 22 In. $113

Pook & Pook

> **TIP**
> *Scratches on bronze cannot be polished off without destroying the patina and lowering the value.*

Bronze, Sculpture, Faun, Dancing, Metal, c.1875, 31 x 12 x 15 In. $813

New Orleans Auction Galleries

Scroll Weight, Ram, Lying Down, Filed Horns, Chinese, 3 In............................*illus*	688
Sculpture, 2 Female Dancers, Seminude, Cold Painted, Rug Covered Base, Austria, 10 x 9 x 5 In.	1000
Sculpture, 2 Girls Dancing, Marble Base, Carl Cauba, Austria, Early 1900s, 4½ x 4 x 2 In.	338
Sculpture, 3 Nude Infants, 1 Blowing Into Cornucopia, Gilt Base, 11 x 7½ In............................	480
Sculpture, Apollo Belvedere, Archer, Black Marble Base, 1800s, 24 x 13 x 7 In.	1188
Sculpture, Arab Soldier, Riding Camel, Onyx Base, 13 x 14½ x 5 In..........................*illus*	188
Sculpture, Augustus Of Prima Porta, Italy, c.1900, 36 In..	4613
Sculpture, Ballerina, Nema, Standing, Skirt Moves, Erotica, Austria, Art Nouveau, c.1920, 7¾ In.	1103
Sculpture, Barye, Dog, Mouse, Naturalistic Ground, France, 1900s, 4¾ x 7¾ In.....................	113
Sculpture, Barye, Wildlife, Lion, Antelope, France, 1900s, 5 x 11¼ In. ....*illus*	192
Sculpture, Basso, Angelo, Horse, Marble Base, Venturi Arte, Italy, Incised Signature, 27¾ In.	246
Sculpture, Beeler, Joe, Into The North Wind, Wood Base, Signed, 1980, 23 x 18 x 9 In.	1573
Sculpture, Bergman, Franz, Slave Girl, Patina, Cold Painted, Marked, Early 1900s, 7 In.	270
Sculpture, Bergman, Franz, Windy Day, Woman, Lifting Skirt, 15 x 7½ In.	1573
Sculpture, Bergman, Pheasant, Cold Painted, Brown, Austria, c.1950, 6½ x 16 In.	563
Sculpture, Bertoia, Harry, Tree, Patina, 1970s, 11 x 11 In. ....*illus*	31250
Sculpture, Bouriane, M., Woman, 2 Dogs, Patina, 12½ x 17 In...................................	200
Sculpture, Boy Pushing Girl On Swing, Squirrel On Rope, Patina, c.1980, 87 In.	3750
Sculpture, Bricard, G., Child, Sitting In Chair, Reading Newspaper, Patina, Signed, 13 x 9 In.	1024
Sculpture, Buddha Of Kamakura, Japan, Late 1900, 6¾ x 5⅞ x 4⅞ In................................	141
Sculpture, Buddha, Seated, Gilt, Double Lotus Pedestal, Chinese, 9 In.	650
Sculpture, Buddha, Seated, Lotus Throne, Painted, Circular Base, Wood Stand, 1600s, 8⅛ In.	1968
Sculpture, Buddha, Teaching Pose, Red & Blue Paint, Crown, Chinese, 1900s, 19 x 12 x 7 In..	584
Sculpture, Buddhist Deity, Standing, Holding Lotus Flower, 10½ In.	125
Sculpture, Chakrasamvara, 4 Heads, 12 Arms, Standing, Double Lotus, 10⅞ In.	308
Sculpture, Cornwell, Martha Jackson, Girl, Turtle, Marble Base, Signed, 7¾ x 5½ In. .....*illus*	308
Sculpture, Dancing Faun, Patinated, Fonderia Sommer Napolii, 10 In.	492
Sculpture, Dancing, Shiva, Arms, Leg Raised, Southeast Asia, 22 In.....................*illus*	113
Sculpture, Diana Victorious Archer, Standing, Bow, Snake Head Hunting Horn, 6 x 2 In.	118
Sculpture, Diana, Winged Putti, Marked, France, 17 x 11½ In.	1080
Sculpture, Dinosaur, Severed Finger In Mouth, 12 In.	295
Sculpture, Dying Gaul, Continental, Marble Base, 1800s, 4¾ x 7 In.	300
Sculpture, Eagle, Gilt, Spread Wings, E Pluribus Unum, 1878, 10½ x 18 In.	1150
Sculpture, Eros, Holding Torch, Raised Arm, Mixed Metal, Octagonal Base, 22½ In.	230
Sculpture, Erzgiesserei, A.G., Socrates, Standing, Gilt, Marble Base, Early 1900s, 6¾ In..........	480
Sculpture, Eule, Charles, Napoleon, Winter Military Attire, France, 1800s, 16 x 5 In.	826
Sculpture, Evans, Carolyn, Female Figure, Dog, Signed, Natick, Mass., 1982, 35 In.	369
Sculpture, Father Time, Wings, Holding Sickle, Hourglass, Yellow Marble Base, c.1910, 7 In....	406
Sculpture, Faun Of Pompei, Square Base, 13 In.	313
Sculpture, Faun, Dancing, Metal, c.1875, 31 x 12 x 15 In.....................................*illus*	813
Sculpture, Ferville-Suan, Charles Georges, Cupid & Swan, Signed, 1881, 15 In.	938
Sculpture, Figural, Icarus Falling, Partial Green Patina, Spiral, 1900s, 47½ In.	780
Sculpture, Fillerup, Peter, Frontiersman, Wood Base, 1985, 11 x 3¼ In.	110
Sculpture, Fischer, Abstract, 5 Tiers, Rectangular Base, Signed F.F., 14 x 5⅝ x 4 In.	861
Sculpture, Fischer, Abstract, Mother & Child, Rectangular Base, Stone, Signed F.F., 10 x 6½ x 3½ In..	246
Sculpture, Fortuna, Holding Cornucopia, Foot On Wheel Of Fortune, 1800s, 42 In...................	1722
Sculpture, Fountain, Aquatic Plants, Putto, Square Pedestal Base, Classical, 66¾ x 13 x 15½ In........	1125
Sculpture, Fox, Carrying Prey, Painted, Geschutzt, Austria, Early 1900s, 8 In.	344
Sculpture, Fugere, H., La Pencee, Gilt, Marble Base, Fitted As Lamp, Signed, 25 In.	1125
Sculpture, Garnier, J., Female, Winter, Wrapped In Shawl, Naturalistic Base, Signed, 8⅛ In. ..	221
Sculpture, Gnome, Cold Painted, Glass Bud Vase, Umbrella, Bundle, c.1900s, 4 In. ....*illus*	213
Sculpture, Guanyin, Seated In Dhyanasana, Flowing Robes, Floral Border, 15 In.	2000
Sculpture, Hagenauer, Franz, African Tribal Figure, Spear & Shield, Signed, 5½ In........*illus*	406
Sculpture, Harvey, Eli, Bear, Standing, Signed, 1900s, 5¼ In.....................................	480
Sculpture, Humphriss, Charles, Indian Brave, Warrior, 11 In....................................	720
Sculpture, Indian, Seated, Cold Paint, Stone Base, After Kauba, Austria, 14¾ In.	2640
Sculpture, Jacobson, A., Couple Embracing, Black Base, Signed, 1900s, 8 x 2¾ x 3 In.	60
Sculpture, Jumping Frog, Catching Dragonfly, On Lily Pad, 1900s, 30 x 21 x 16 In.................	1046
Sculpture, Lanceray, E.A., Soldier, Horseback, Signed, Russia, 9 x 7½ x 3½ In.....................	1452
Sculpture, Lorenzl, Woman & Dog, 14½ In...	125

Bronze, Sculpture, Gnome, Cold Painted, Glass Bud Vase, Umbrella, Bundle, c.1900s, 4 In.
$213

Freeman's Auctioneers & Appraisers

Bronze, Sculpture, Muller, Hans, Harvester, Man, Carrying Tools, Signed, 1873-1937, 18 ⅝ In.
$492

Skinner, Inc.

Bronze, Vase, Trumpet, Gilt Interior, Christofle, c.1900, 6 ½ In.
$469

Royal Crest Auctioneers

Bronze, Sculpture, Hagenauer, Franz, African Tribal Figure, Spear & Shield, Signed, 5 ½ In.
$406

Roland Auctioneers & Valuers

Bronze, Sculpture, Moigniez, Jules, Basset Hound, Mounted, Marble Base, 12 x 21 x 7 In.
$330

Eldred's

Bronze, Sculpture, Spiny Lobster, Gilt, Japan, Late 1800s, 8 ½ In.
$1,786

Grogan & Company

Bronze, Vase, Handles, 2 Peacocks, Archaic Style Bird Supports, Japan, Late 1800s, 19 x 13 In.
$708

Burchard Galleries

Bronze, Vessel, Cooking, Rounded Base, Shallow Sides, Looped Handles, Uruli, India, 24 In.
$461

Skinner, Inc.

TIP
If you buy an Art Deco bronze-and-ivory figure, be very careful to examine the ivory. Even slight cracks or damage lower the value.

Brush, Cookie Jar, Lid, Peter Pumpkin Eater, Marked W24 USA, 10¾ In.
$92

Belhorn Auction Services

Buck Rogers, Sign, Popsicle, Refreshing, Cardboard, c.1939, 14 x 11 In.
$2,053

Milestone Auctions

Buffalo Pottery Deldare, Pitcher, To Demand My Annual Rent, Scenes, Octagonal, 1929, 8 In.
$96

Garth's Auctioneers & Appraisers

Sculpture, Male, Nude, Circular Marble Base, 22 In.	81
Sculpture, Marcello Fantoni, Steel, Torch Cut, Unmarked, 1970, 44 x 10 x 9 In.	800
Sculpture, Mejer, R.J., Cactus, Enameled, Stone Base, Signed, 7½ x 8½ x 8½ In.	125
Sculpture, Mene, Pierre Jules, Horse, Signed, 7¼ x 10 In.	185
Sculpture, Micheal, Claude, Maiden On Goat, Marble Base, Inscribed, 20 x 12 x 8¼ In.	500
Sculpture, Moigniez, Jules, Basset Hound, Mounted, Marble Base, 12 x 21 x 7 In. ..... *illus*	330
Sculpture, Muller, Hans, Harvester, Man, Carrying Tools, Signed, 1873-1937, 18⅝ In. ..... *illus*	492
Sculpture, Napoleon, Standing, Bronze, Messenger & Sons, London, c.1850, 15 x 6 x 6 In.	2000
Sculpture, Napoleon, Standing, Marble Base, 14½ In.	431
Sculpture, Nude Female, Standing, Black Marble Base, Art Nouveau, 15 x 4½ x 2¾ In.	537
Sculpture, Oman, Sheridan, Ram, Standing, Square Base, 7½ In.	200
Sculpture, Parmenter, Ramon, Female Nude, Timeless Innocence, 1954, 16 x 25 In.	563
Sculpture, Parsons, E.B., Lamb, Signed, 4¼ In.	900
Sculpture, Parsons, Edith, Dog, Terrier, With Bone, Rectangular Base, 5 x 7 In.	600
Sculpture, Picciole, Sportsman, Garanti Inlay, Medallion, Marble, Signed, 9¼ In.	115
Sculpture, Pratt, C., Cornstalk, Turquoise, Gilt, Welded Stone Base, Signed, 26½ In.	308
Sculpture, Putto, Seated On Marble Column, Gilt Metal Foot, 1900s, 11½ In.	375
Sculpture, Putto, Seated, Siena Marble Base, France, 1900s, 22 x 10 x 10 In.	1500
Sculpture, Qilin, Mythical Creature, Reclining, Head Turned To Side, 1900s, 1⅛ x 3 In.	197
Sculpture, Remington, Frederic, Horse Head, Rectangular Stand Base, Signed, 11 x 7 In.	1320
Sculpture, Sabin, Hib, Eagle, Painted, Rectangular Base, 7 x 3¼ x 2½ In.	750
Sculpture, Salmones, V., Man, Stylized, Kneeling, Signed, Mexico, 11 x 24 x 12 In.	750
Sculpture, Salmones, Victor, Head Of Woman, Wood Base, Signed, 15 In.	270
Sculpture, Sander, Sherry, Stacked Rocks, Signed, 1900s, 9¾ x 10½ In.	270
Sculpture, Seated Figure, Arms Around Knees, Stamped EW, c.1980, 8 x 9 In.	800
Sculpture, Silenus, Infant Dionysus, Wood Base, Italy, 1800s, 25 x 11 x 10 In.	5250
Sculpture, Spiny Lobster, Gilt, Japan, Late 1800s, 8½ In. ..... *illus*	1786
Sculpture, Stajcar, Pati, Dolphins, Blue Green Patina, Signed, 14¼ x 4¾ x 4¾ In.	343
Sculpture, Stern, Deborah, Coming Together, Signed, c.1981, 16 x 15 x 10 In.	1845
Sculpture, Tuma, Jeannine, Basket Maker, Signed, 1983, 10½ In.	330
Sculpture, Vanderveen, Loet, Sable Antelope, Brown Patina, 5½ x 4 x 9 In.	310
Sculpture, Villanis, E., Nude, Slave Girl, Stone Bench, Removable Blanket, Signed, 16 x 12 In.	1088
Sculpture, Villanis, Emmanuel, Woman, Holding Flowers, Early 1900s, 23 x 14 x 13 In.	767
Sculpture, Walking Carp, Lotus Flower In Forehead, Japan, c.1970, 13½ x 28 In.	154
Sculpture, Wegner, Paul, Pod Of Dolphins, Signed On Base, 22 x 19 x 12 In.	300
Sculpture, Wolff, Albert Moritz, The Kiss, Man On Horse, Kissing Woman, Signed, 10 In.	1560
Sculpture, Zuniga, Francisco, Mother & Child, Black Marble Base, Signed, 1971, 5 In.	1200
Tazza, Barye, Antoine Louis, Gilt, Cat, Owl, Arabesque, Leaves, Vines, Berries, 7 x 6 In.	172
Tazza, Bird & Flower, Painted, Dolphin Supports, France, 1800s, 5½ x 10¾ In.	375
Tazza, Phillippe, Louis, Scroll Base, Paw Feet, Reticulated Basket, Glass Bowl, 1800s, 17 In.	1625
Tray, Marionnet, Albert, Naturalistic, Grapevines, Gold, 13¼ In.	185
Urn, Clodion, Cavorting Putti, Leafy Base, 15 x 18 In.	1563
Urn, Presentation, Gilt, Relief, 2 Handles, Masks, Engraved, France, 1904, 13 x 15 In.	677
Vase, Bamboo Pattern, Cylindrical, Japan, 7 In.	270
Vase, Champleve, Ring Handles, Multicolor, Chinese, 1900s, 12 x 6¾ In.	60
Vase, Handles, 2 Peacocks, Archaic Style Bird Supports, Japan, Late 1800s, 19 x 13 In. ..... *illus*	708
Vase, Lobed Mouth, Dark Brown Patina, Red Highlights, 19th Century, 8½ In.	212
Vase, Mottled, Rounded Body, Flared Neck, Beast Mask Handle, Chinese, c.1700s, 14 In.	502
Vase, Quatrefoil Baluster, Splayed Foot, Ruyi Heads, Leaves, Rectangular Panel, 11 In.	3000
Vase, Suiban, Ikebana, Log Shape Feet, Birds, Branches, Japan, 1800s, 12 x 8 x 3 In.	273
Vase, Tree Trunk, Flowering Prunus, Standing Male, Scholar Riding Donkey, 10¼ In.	938
Vase, Trumpet, Gilt Interior, Christofle, c.1900, 6½ In. ..... *illus*	469
Vase, Warwick, Copper Liner, Base Stamped, Circular Base, 1800s, 6 In.	300
Vessel, Cooking, Rounded Base, Shallow Sides, Looped Handles, Uruli, India, 24 In. ..... *illus*	461

BROWNIES were first drawn in 1883 by Palmer Cox (1840-1924). They are characterized by large round eyes, downturned mouths, and skinny legs. Toys, books, dinnerware, and other objects were made with the Brownies as part of the design.

Bowl, Lid, Brownies Golfing, Flared, Open Handles, Finial, Taylor Smith, England, 8 In.	96
Candlestick, Sailor, Majolica, 7½ In.	150

Candlestick, Uncle Sam, Majolica, 8 In.	180
Candy Container, Man In Top Hat, Composition, Elongated Legs, Separates At Waist, 8 In.	2400
Candy Container, Well-Dressed Man, Emerging From Egg, Composition, 5 In.	390
Sign, If You Like Chocolate Soda Drink Brownie, Tin Lithograph, Embossed, 10 x 28 In.	660
Smoking Set, Sailor, Match, Cigar & Cigarette Holders, Majolica, 8 In.	450
Tea Set, Teapot, Sugar, Lid, Creamer, Finger Bowl, 6 Cups & Saucers, 5-In. Teapot	120
Tobacco Jar, Sailor's Head, Bulging Eyes, Defender On Cap, Majolica, 5 In.	210
Toy, Wagon, Oh What Fun, Brownies All Around, Tin Lithograph, Open Handle, 29 In.	180
Tray, Ice Cream, Brownies Scooping Ice Cream, Tin Lithograph, 13 x 10 ½ In.	108

BRUSH-MCCOY, *see Brush category and related pieces in McCoy category.*

BRUSH POTTERY was started in 1925. George Brush first worked in 1901 in Zanesville, Ohio. He started his own pottery in 1907, but it burned to the ground soon after. In 1909 he became manager of the J.W. McCoy Pottery. In 1911, Brush and J.W. McCoy formed the Brush-McCoy Pottery Co. After a series of name changes, the company became The Brush Pottery in 1925. It closed in 1982. Old Brush was marked with impressed letters or a palette-shaped mark. Reproduction pieces are being made. They are marked in raised letters or with a raised mark. Collectors favor the figural cookie jars made by this company. Because there was a company named Brush-McCoy, there is great confusion between Brush and Nelson McCoy pieces. Most collectors today refer to Brush pottery as Brush-McCoy. See McCoy category for more information.

Bowl, Embossed Flower, Satin Pink, 1962, 2 ½ x 4 ¾ In.	18
Bowl, Pink, Speckled, Pedestal, 8 x 5 In.	22
Cookie Jar, Donkey & Cart, Multicolor, Semimatte, Marked, 10 ½ In.	184
Cookie Jar, Lid, Fish Shape, Cobalt Blue Highlights, 11 ½ x 6 ½ In.	374
Cookie Jar, Lid, Peter Pumpkin Eater, Marked W24 USA, 10 ¾ In. *illus*	92
Cookie Jar, Pig Shape, Green, Gold Trim, Marked, 11 ¼ In.	173
Cookie Jar, Rag Doll, Cream Ground, Marked W16, 11 In.	115
Flowerpot, Pebble Pattern, Attached Saucer, Yellow, 4 In.	14
Jardiniere, Ribbed, Tulips, Burgundy Gloss, 1920s, 4 x 3 ½ In.	45
Jardiniere, Woman, Flowing Drapes, Art Nouveau, Green, Cream, 8 x 10 In.	175
Piggy Bank, Brown Glaze, Speckles, Tan Spots, 1930s, 5 ½ In.	65
Planter, Cat, Spooked, Pale Yellow Gloss, 8 x 6 ¾ In.	45
Planter, Girl, Sun Bonnet, Holding Flower & Basket, 8 x 9 ½ In.	18
Vase, Blue Onyx, Stick Neck, Flared Base, 1920s, 10 ¼ In.	49
Vase, Ear Handles, Jade, Brown, Vellum Glaze, 4 x 6 In.	50
Vase, Pleated, Garland, Bows, Turquoise Glaze, Footed, 1940s, 10 In.	48
Vase, Ring & Leaves, Cone Shape, Ivory Gloss Glaze, 1937, 8 ½ In.	35
Vase, Twist, Ruffled Rim, Orange, Green, c.1935, 4 ½ In.	50

BUCK ROGERS was the first American science fiction comic strip. It started in 1929 and continued until 1967. Buck has also appeared in comic books, movies, and, in the 1980s, a television series. Any memorabilia connected with the character Buck Rogers is collectible.

Button, Club Membership, Cello, Blue, White, Orange, Round, 1937, 1 In.	110
Helmet, Space, Leather, Metal Accessories, 1930, 12 In.	241
Jigsaw Puzzle, Arrow, Outer Space, Box, 1981, 13 ½ In., 200 Piece	20
Lunch Box, No Thermos, Aladdin, Twiki, Wilma Deering, Dr. Huer, 1979	21
Photograph, Colonel Wilma Deering, Signed, Erin Gray, TV Star, 4 x 6 In.	19
Pin, Blue, Buster Crabbe, Space Helmet, Rocket Ship, Back Paper, 1939, 1 ¼ In.	649
Pocket Watch, Mechanical, Comic Scene, 12-Hour Dial, Arabic Numerals, 1920s, 16 In.	64
Sign, Popsicle, Refreshing, Cardboard, c.1939, 14 x 11 In. *illus*	2053
Toy, Atomic Pistol, Gold Metallic, Daisy, Box, 9 ½ In.	673
Toy, Battle Cruiser, Attack Ship, Tootsietoy, Black & Silver, Die Cast Metal, 1937, 5 In.	66
Toy, Disintegrator Gun, Nickel Plated, Daisy Manufacturing, 1920, 10 In.	165
Toy, Ray Gun, Disintegrator, Atomic, Pressed Steel, Engraved, c.1930, 9 ½ In.	133
Toy, Repeller Ray Ring, Solar Scouts, Cream Of Wheat Premium, 1936	785

Buffalo Pottery Deldare, Tray, Court Scene, Building Border, c.1950, 12 x 9 ¼ In.
$88

Garth's Auctioneers & Appraisers

Burmese, Fairy Lamp, Ceramic Base, Tapestryware, Multicolor Flowers, Late 1800s, 6 ¼ x 7 x ½ In.
$389

Jeffrey S. Evans & Associates

Burmese, Fairy Lamp, Clarke's Base, Silver Plated Stand, Meridan, c.1885, 12 In.
$219

Garth's Auctioneers & Appraisers

Burmese, Lamp, Fall Leaves, Multicolor, Globular, c.1900, Miniature, 6 3/8 x 2 1/2 x 3 5/8 In.
$478

Jeffrey S. Evans & Associates

Burmese, Mustard Pot, Ribbed, Barrel Shape, Silver Plate, New England Glass Co., c.1885, 3 In.
$113

Garth's Auctioneers & Appraisers

Buster Brown, Charm, Buster Brown & Tige Portrait, Metal Finish, Gold Luster, Miniature, c.1970
$5

Hake's Auctions

Toy, Rocket Pistol, XZ-35, Pressed Steel, Daisy Mfg., 1935, 7 1/2 In.	104
Toy, Rocket Ship, Tin Lithograph, Multicolor, Windup, Key, Marx, 12 In.	340
Toy, Sonic Ray Gun, Light Beam, High Frequency Buzz, Signal Device, Box, 8 1/2 In.	460

BUFFALO POTTERY was made in Buffalo, New York, after 1902. The company was established by the Larkin Company, famous manufacturers of soap. The wares are marked with a picture of a buffalo and the date of manufacture. Deldare ware is the most famous pottery made at the factory. It has either a khaki-colored or green background with hand-painted transfer designs. The company reorganized in 1956 and was renamed Buffalo China before being bought by Oneida Silver Company.

Buffalo Pottery
1907

Deldare ware
1909

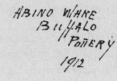

Emerald Deldare
1912

BUFFALO POTTERY

Pitcher, Geranium, Handle, Blue, White, c.1905, 3 1/2 In.	210
Plate, Dinner, Blue Roses, Lune 612, c.1950, 10 In., 5 Piece	55
Platter, Deer, Pound, Oval, Signed R.K. Beck, c.1905, 15 x 11 In.	54
Platter, Oval, Seneca Pattern, Green Flowers, Scalloped Rim, c.1910, 15 In.	25
Platter, Willow, Blue, White, Landscape, Temples, Boats, Trees, Patterns, 10 1/2 In.	12
Teapot, Lid, Argyle, Blue, White, 1914	35

BUFFALO POTTERY DELDARE

Pitcher, 4 Mugs, Ye Olden Days, Black Printed Mark & Date	369
Pitcher, To Demand My Annual Rent, Scenes, Octagonal, 1929, 8 In. .... *illus*	96
Plate, Emerald, Dr. Syntax, Star Gazing, Marked, c.1911, 9 3/8 In.	164
Punch Set, The Fallowfield Hunt, 14 1/2-In. Punch Bowl, 12 Cups	3125
Tray, Court Scene, Building Border, c.1950, 12 x 9 1/4 In. .... *illus*	88

BUNNYKINS, *see Royal Doulton category.*

BURMESE GLASS was developed by Frederick Shirley at the Mt. Washington Glass Works in New Bedford, Massachusetts, in 1885. It is a two-toned glass, shading from peach to yellow. Some pieces have a pattern mold design. A few Burmese pieces were decorated with pictures or applied glass flowers of colored Burmese glass. Other factories made similar glass also called Burmese. Burmese glass was made by Mt. Washington until about 1895, by Gundersen until the 1950s, and by Webb until about 1900. Fenton made Burmese glass after 1970. Related items may be listed in the Fenton category and under Webb Burmese.

Biscuit Jar, Flowers, Silver Plated Lid, Bail, Mt. Washington, 6 In.	96
Fairy Lamp, Ceramic Base, Tapestryware, Multicolor Flowers, Late 1800s, 6 1/4 x 7 x 1/2 In.*illus*	389
Fairy Lamp, Clarke's Base, Silver Plated Stand, Meridan, c.1885, 12 In. .... *illus*	219
Figurine, Buddha, Seated, Painted, Wood, Monastic Robe, Earth Touching Gesture, 17 x 44 In.	200
Lamp, Clarke's Base, Brass & Marble Stand, 1800s, 11 In.	156
Lamp, Fall Leaves, Multicolor, Globular, c.1900, Miniature, 6 3/8 x 2 1/2 x 3 5/8 In. .... *illus*	478
Mustard Pot, Ribbed, Barrel Shape, Silver Plate, New England Glass Co., c.1885, 3 In. .... *illus*	113
Saucer, Lavender Blue Flowers, Mt. Washington, 4 7/8 In.	189
Toothpick Holder, Bud, Multicolor, Leaf & Berry, Square Rim, Pontil, c.1890, 2 7/8 In.	192
Toothpick Holder, Diamond-Quilted, Pink To Yellow, Pinched Rim, Mt. Washington, 2 In.	285
Vase, Rose Bowl, Wishbone Pulled Top, Leaves White Berries, c.1880, 3 x 3 In.	350

BUSTER BROWN, the comic strip, first appeared in color in 1902. Buster and his dog, Tige, remained a popular comic and soon became even more famous as the emblem for a shoe company, a textile firm, and other companies. The strip was discontinued in 1920. Buster Brown sponsored a radio show from 1943 to 1955 and a TV

show from 1950 to 1956. The Buster Brown characters are still used by Brown Shoe Company, Buster Brown Apparel, Inc., and Gateway Hosiery.

Bank, Cast Iron, Goodluck, Horseshoe, Arcade, 1908-32, 4 ¾ x 4 ¼ In.	123
Bank, Still, Painted Cast Iron, Figural, Tige, A.C. Williams, Early 1900s, 5 ½ In.	76
Belt Buckle, Buster & Tige Pulling On Sock, Silver Metal, 1960s, 2 x 3 ½ In.	45
Book, My Resolutions, Hardcover, Red Ground, R.F. Outcault, 1910	156
Button, Brass, Figural, Pointing To His Dog Tige, 1902, ⅝ In.	17
Button, Brown Bilt Club, Buster & Tige, 1930s, ⅞ In.	15
Charm, Buster Brown & Tige Portrait, Metal Finish, Gold Luster, Miniature, c.1970 .... *illus*	5
Clicker, Shoe Shape, Buster Brown Blue Ribbon Shoes, Yellow, Litho, c.1910, 2 ½ In.	35
Figure, Cast Iron, Toy, Standing, Hat, Shoes, Ribbon On Chest, 4 In.	30
Figurine, Automobile, Tige Driving Buster Brown, Green, 5 In.	150
Knife, Hunting, Carbon Steel Blade, Deer Foot Handle, Marble, Sheath, 1930s	79
Knife, Old Marbles, Woodcraft Handle, Blade Engraved, Leather Case, 8 3/16 In.	183
Marionette, Cardstock, Jointed, Winking, 1950s, 10 x 15 ¾ In.	118
Pocket Knife, Kutmaster, 3 Blades, Shoes, Stainless Steel, Black, 2 ¾ In.	21
Pocket Mirror, Tige, Vacation Days Carnival, Round, Celluloid, 1946, 2 3/16 In.	13
Postcard, October Calendar, 2 Pumpkins, Glenville, Minnesota, D.J. Roberts	23
Tin, Buster Brown Cigar, Buster Brown & Tige, Round, 50 Ct., 5 x 5 In. .... *illus*	1121

BUTTER CHIPS, or butter pats, were small individual dishes for butter. They were the height of fashion from 1880 to 1910. Earlier as well as later examples are known.

Blue, Gold Trim, Flowers, Scalloped Edge, c.1901, 3 ⅜ In.	25
Corey Pattern, Ridgway, 3 ¼ In.	20
Dutch Windmill, Elesva Holland Co., c.1950, 3 ½ In.	53
Gray & Black Mulberry Leaves, Gilt Trim, Utzschneider & Co., 1800s, 5 ½ In.	17
Majolica, Begonia Leaf, Brown, Multicolor, 6 Piece	129
Pansy, Yellow, Black, Stangl, c.1960, 4 In.	16
Spatter, Yellow, Red School House, Green, Brown, 3 ¼ In.	82
Violets, Daisies, Purple, White, Green, Cream, Burlington Route, 3 ½ In.	54

BUTTER MOLDS *are listed in the Kitchen category under Mold, Butter.*

BUTTON collecting has been popular since the nineteenth century. Buttons have been used on clothing throughout the centuries, and there are millions of styles. Gold, silver, or precious stones were used for the best buttons, but most were made of natural materials, like bone or shell, or from inexpensive metals. Only a few types favored by collectors are listed for comparison. Political buttons may also be listed in Political.

Bakelite, Flower Like Design, Butterscotch, 1 ⅜ x 1 ⅜ In.	17
Bakelite, Football Shape, Carnelian Red, 1930s, 1 ¼ In., Pair	29
Brass, Geometric Design, Enameled, White Turquoise, Cobalt Blue, Victorian, 1 ¼ In.	55
Brass, Horse, Chariot, Flying Sparrows, c.1900, 1 ½ In.	75
Compressed Wood, Boat, Waves, Clouds & Rope Border, Red Paint, 2 In.	45
Glass, Wildflower, Reversed Painted, Green, Red, 1 ½ In.	6
Lucite, Clear, Square, 2 In.	50
Mother-Of-Pearl, Cut Steel Accents, Purple & Pink Flashes, ½ In.	8
Shell, Abalone, Owl Face, c.1910, ⅝ In.	9
Silver, St. Patrick, c.1890, ¾ x ¾ In.	60

BUTTONHOOKS have been a popular collectible in England for many years and are now gaining the attention of a few American collectors. The buttonhooks were made to help fasten the many buttons of the old-fashioned high-button shoes and other items of apparel.

Brass, Handle, Engraved On Both Sides, Steel, Pat Tomkins, 5 ¾ In.	4
Celluloid Handle, Peach, Metal Hook, 5 ¾ In.	59
Folding, Bow, Faceted, Metal, Late 1800s, 2 ¾ In.	12

Buster Brown, Tin, Buster Brown Cigar, Buster Brown & Tige, Round, 50 Ct., 5 x 5 In.
$1,121

Wm Morford Auctions

Calendar, 1948, Amoco, Eagle Logo, A Great Name, Full Pad, 27 x 19 In.
$90

Matthew Bullock Auctioneers

Calendar, 1954, Carl Dixon & Son Trucking, Tin Lithograph, Stand-Up, Partial Pad, 3 ¾ x 5 In
$177

AntiqueAdvertising.com

Calendar, Perpetual, Wall Hanging, Tin Litho, Koken's Tonique De Lux Card Pocket, 9 x 10 In.
$787

Fontaine's Auction Gallery

> **TIP**
> *Restoring and reusing old things is the purest form of recycling.*

Camark, Vase, Orange Crackle Glaze, Bulbous, Alfred Tetzschner, c.1927, 10 x 8 ½ In.
$1,017

Soulis Auctions

Cambridge, Crown Tuscan, Bowl, Seashell, Flying Lady, Pedestal, c.1936, 7 ¼ x 12 ¾ In.
$140

Jeffrey S. Evans & Associates

Folding, Bow, Silver, Engraved Flowers On Both Sides, Chester Assay Office, 1901	35
Folding, Gold Metal, Flowers & Leaves, 1800s, 1 ⅛ In.	79
Mother-Of-Pearl Handle, Silver Glove, Crisford & Norris, Birmingham	14
Silver Plate, Art Nouveau, Capitol Building, 1890-1910, 6 ½ In.	90
Silver, Figural Feather, No. 1606, Marked, George W. Shiebler, c.1890, 3 ⅜ x ⅜ In.	326
Silver, Figural, Snake Head, Chatelaine, Tubular Handle, 2 ¼ In.	36
Silver, Pocket, Pearlized, Tom & John Cooper, Early 1980s, 2 ⅛ In.	23
Sterling Silver, Adie & Lovekin Ltd., c.1902, 6 ¾ In.	146
Sterling Silver, Aesthetic Design, Double Folding, Gorham, 1800s, ½ x 2 ⅜ In.	175
Sterling Silver, Duck, Leaning, Bulrushes, Steel Shaft, Birmingham, 1907, 9 In.	63

 CALENDARS made to hang on the wall or to be displayed on a desk top have been popular since the last quarter of the nineteenth century. Many were printed with advertising as part of the artwork and were given away as premiums. Calendars illustrated by famous artists or with guns, gunpowder, or Coca-Cola advertising are most prized.

1895, Time Flies, Lithographed, Longfellow Quotations, 6 x 7 In.	30
1899, Antikamnia Quack Med, Skeleton, Cap, Suit, Red Vest, Fountain, 10 x 7 In.	167
1901, Dainty Maidens, Verses Each Page, Ernest Nester, 12 x 9 In.	39
1902, Hood's Sarsaparilla, Columbia's Daughters, 4 Women, Full Pad, 17 x 4 In.	85
1906, Farmers, Fence, Barn, E. Frank Coe's Fertilizer, Full Pad, 9 x 13 In.	26
1906, Women Of Fiction, Life's Gilbert, 6 Female Literary Characters, 12 x 17 ¾ In.	34
1908, Santa Claus, Carrying Honeycomb Tree, Toy, Die Cut, H.C. King, 14 ¼ x 8 In.	960
1909, Lauer Brew'g Co., Red Brick Factory, World Map, Frame, Full Pad, 31 ½ x 23 In.	1280
1910, Milwaukee Harvesting Machines, Doctor, Weighing Baby, Mom, 15 x 23 In.	184
1910, Woman, Lacy Hat, Purple Lilacs, Full Pad, 12 ½ x 8 ¾ In.	49
1912, Oberlin College, Buildings, Black & White, 12 Pages, 8 ⅝ x 11 In.	29
1919, Sunshine Biscuit Girl, Advertising, Pinup, Snow, J. Knowles Hare, 9 ½ x 15 In.	86
1930, Pinup, Advertising, Gene Pressler Lucille, Full Page, 10 ¼ x 16 ¾ In.	51
1931, Blond, Coquette, Pinup, Advertising, Earl Christy, 12 x 24 In.	30
1931, Edison Mazda, Waterfall, Women, Tree, Blue, White, Yellow, 38 ¼ x 18 ½ In.	522
1944, Pinup, Esquire Inc., Vargas, Complete	195
1948, 12 Month, Spiral Bound, Esquire Girl, Pinup, Year Book, 10 x 11 ¾ In.	40
1948, Amoco, Eagle Logo, A Great Name, Full Pad, 27 x 19 In. ....*illus*	90
1949, Beck Engraving Co., Hyacinth Macaws, Salesman's Sample, 13 x 9 In.	40
1949, Pinup, Nude, Skinny Dipper, Tanning, Gil Elvgren, 10 x 13 ¼ In.	86
1949, TWA, Travel, Rex Werner, 26 x 17 In.	45
1954, Carl Dixon & Son Trucking, Tin Lithograph, Stand-Up, Partial Pad, 3 ¾ x 5 In. .... *illus*	177
1955, Pinup, Marilyn Monroe, Golden Dreams & Cowgirl Poses, 4 Pages, 8 ¼ x 12 ½ In.	100
1955, Pinup, Marilyn Monroe, Nude, Red Background, 22 x 12 ½ In.	2596
1958, Playboy, Pinup, Spiral Bound, Envelope, Full Pad, 8 ½ x 12 ¾ In.	74
1960, Hilda, Sleeping, Snack Plate, Pinup, Duane Bryers, Bi-Monthly, 9 ¼ x 14 In.	42
1974, Dog, Scottie, Just To Greet You Every Day, 8 x 7 In.	19
1978, Tasha Tudor, Advent, Bunny Hollow Mice Animals, Rand McNally, 25 x 11 In.	40
Perpetual, Wall Hanging, Tin Litho, Koken's Tonique De Lux Card Pocket, 9 x 10 In. .... *illus*	787

 CALENDAR PLATES were popular in the United States as advertising giveaways from 1906 to 1929. Since then, a few plates have been made every year. A calendar and the name of a store, a picture of flowers, a girl, or a scene were featured on the plate.

1908, Dog, G.W. Hoffman General Merchandise, Shape Rim, Burgundy, 9 In.	16
1908, Dog, Springer Spaniel, Green, Brown, J.A. Mooney, 7 ½ In.	12
1909, Cat, McMahons Dining Rooms Restaurant, Flowers, Chas Renkel, 8 ¼ In.	44
1910, Indian, White Ground, J.M. Chapman, Imperial China, 8 ¼ In.	43
1911, Angel, Sitting, City Drug Store, Shaped Rim, Leaves, Quincy, 8 ½ In.	13
1912, Flowers, Hawley Merchandise Co., Carnation McNicol, 9 In.	67
1912, Indian, Woman Shucking Corn, Dresden, 8 ½ In.	70
1912, Turkey & Hunters, Gold Flowers Sprigs Trimmed Edge, 8 ½ In.	29
1914, Field Bird, Heintz-Speckles Co., Flowers, Advertising, 9 ¼ In.	68
1956, Dutch Windmill Scene, Christmas, Gately's, Gold Gilt, 10 ½ In.	30
1973, Provincial Green, Taylor Smith Taylor, 10 ¼ In.	14

1976, Bicentennial, Bell, Homer Laughlin, 10 In.	18
1979, America The Beautiful, Patriotic, Spencer Gifts Inc., 9 In.	16
1980, African Safari, Wedgwood, 10 In.	31
1982, Wild West, Wedgwood, 10 In.	49
1986, 101 Dalmatians, 25th Anniversary, Disney, 8¾ In.	18
1999, Literary Greats, Millennium Literature, Wedgwood, 10 In.	24

CAMARK POTTERY started out as Camden Art Tile and Pottery Company in Camden, Arkansas. Jack Carnes founded the firm in 1926 in association with John Lessell, Stephen Sebaugh, and the Camden Chamber of Commerce. Many types of glazes and wares were made. The company was bought by Mary Daniel in the early 1960s. Production ended in 1983.

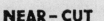

Vase, Orange Crackle Glaze, Bulbous, Alfred Tetzschner, c.1927, 10 x 8½ In. .... *illus*	1017

CAMBRIDGE GLASS COMPANY was founded in 1901 in Cambridge, Ohio. The company closed in 1954, reopened briefly, and closed again in 1958. The firm made all types of glass. Its early wares included heavy pressed glass with the mark *Near Cut*. Later wares included Crown Tuscan, etched stemware, and clear and colored glass. The firm used a *C* in a triangle mark after 1920.

NEAR-CUT

Cambridge Glass Co.	Cambridge Glass Co.	Cambridge Glass Co.
c.1906–c.1920	c.1937	1936–1954

Crown Tuscan, Bowl, Footed, Shell Shape, Rockwell Silver Overlay, Pink, 11 In.	239
Crown Tuscan, Bowl, Seashell, Flying Woman, Pedestal, c.1936, 7¼ x 12¾ In. .... *illus*	140
Crown Tuscan, Bowl, Shell, Gilt, c.1936, 6 x 10 In.	35
Crown Tuscan, Dish, Swan, Gilt, Charleton, c.1936, 5⅞ x 5¾ In.	35
Figurine, Nude Woman, Clear Green Glass, Flower Frog, Bashful Charlotte, 8½ x 4 In.	38
Gloria, Vase, Emerald Green, Etched, Wide Spout, 1930s, 11 In.	189
Nautilus, Decanter, Stopper, Amber, Clear Glass Handle, 6¾ In.	31
Rose Point, Ball Pitcher, Etched, Bulbous Body, Clear, Handle, 11 x 11 In.	59
Rose Point, Ice Bucket, Etched Glass, Swing Handle, Floral, Round Base, 5¾ In.	31
Water Set, Cobalt Blue, Tilt Ball Pitcher, Clear Handle, 6 Geometric Glasses, 1940s	125

CAMBRIDGE POTTERY was made in Cambridge, Ohio, from about 1895 until World War I. The factory made brown-glazed decorated artwares with a variety of marks, including an acorn, the name *Cambridge*, the name *Oakwood*, and the name *Terrhea*.

Vase, Portrait, Native American, Full Headdress, Terrhea Glaze, A. Williams, 23¾ In.	2478

CAMEO GLASS was made in much the same manner as a cameo in jewelry. Parts of the top layer of glass were cut away to reveal a different colored glass beneath. The most famous cameo glass was made during the nineteenth century. Signed cameo glass pieces by famous makers are listed under the glasswork's name, such as Daum, Galle, Legras, Mt. Joye, Webb, and more. Others, signed or unsigned, are listed here. These marks were used by three cameo glass manufacturers.

Albert Dammouse	Ernest–Baptiste Léveillé	François–Eugène Rousseau
1892+	c.1869–c.1900	1855–1885

Compote, Blue Cut, Scalloped Rim, Grape, Leaf, England, Late 1800s, 7¼ In.	300
Dresser Jar, Engraved, Purple, Red, Floral, Gold Trim, Signed, Continental, 1800s, 3 In.	200

Cameo Glass, Vase, Art Deco, Flaring Rim, Botanical, Round Foot, Signed, Charder, 9½ In.
$281

Kamelot Auctions

Cameo Glass, Vase, Blue, Black Cameo Cut Hearts, 6 x 6 In.
$108

Martin Auction Co.

Cameo Glass, Vase, Blue, Roses, Buds, Leaves, Stems, 10¼ x 3½ In.
$2,214

Morphy Auctions

Cameo Glass, Vase, Enamel, Orchids, Twist Shape, Signed, France, 11 In. $748

Richard D. Hatch & Associates

Cameo Glass, Vase, Signed Exterior Of Base, Charder La Verre, 3 x 3 ½ In. $625

Kamelot Auctions

Candelabrum, 3-Light, Figural, Sphinx, Cast Metal, Gothic, Egyptian Revival, 22 x 16 ½ x 8 ½ In. $236

Aspire Auctions

Lamp, Nautical Scene, Palms, Ships, Apocryphal Signature, Matching Glass Shade, c.1980, 15 x 12 In.	201
Vase, Art Deco, Flaring Rim, Botanical, Round Foot, Signed, Charder, 9 ½ In. ....*illus*	281
Vase, Art Nouveau, Lavender, Grapes, France, Rectangular, c.1900, 4 x 7 ½ x 3 ½ In.	308
Vase, Black Alligators, Cream Ground, Signed, 1994, 8 ¼ x 7 In.	219
Vase, Blue, Black Cameo Cut Hearts, 6 x 6 In. ....*illus*	108
Vase, Blue, Roses, Buds, Leaves, Stems, 10 ¼ x 3 ½ In. ....*illus*	2214
Vase, Bottle Shape, Streaks, Yellow Internal, Carved Back, Richard, c.1920, 8 x 2 ½ In.	124
Vase, Brown Flowers & Leaves, Signed, Burgun & Schverer, 4 x 5 In.	984
Vase, Citrine, White, Wheel Carved, Poppies, Stems, Leaves, England, 7 ½ x 3 ¾ In.	1169
Vase, Cone Shape, Yellow White Ground, Orange Circles, Charder, c.1920, 10 In.	950
Vase, Enamel, Orchids, Twist Shape, Signed, France, 11 In. ....*illus*	748
Vase, Forest Scene, Etched On The Bottom, Lamartine, 6 ½ In.	345
Vase, Grapes On Vine, Olive Green Leaves On Lavender, Arsall, 6 In.	142
Vase, Landscape, Windmill, Brown & White Satin Field, Delatte, France, 1921, 7 ½ In.	207
Vase, Narrow Mouth, Flowers, 3 Shades Of Blue, Green, Pink Base, c.1880, 20 In.	1950
Vase, Pale Green, Etched, 3 Unetched Handles, Palm Tree, Vine Cut, Gilt, c.1900, 19 In.	540
Vase, Primerolle Flower Heads, Red, Orange, Stalks, Clambroth, Charder, 17 ½ In.	826
Vase, Signed Exterior Of Base, Charder La Verre, 3 x 3 ½ In. ....*illus*	625
Vase, Waterfront, Landscape, Multicolor, Opalescent Body, 5 ½ In.	316

CAMPAIGN *memorabilia are listed in the Political category.*

CAMPBELL KIDS were first used as part of an advertisement for the Campbell Soup Company in 1904. The kids were created by Grace Drayton, a popular illustrator of the day. The kids were used in magazine and newspaper ads until about 1951. They were presented again in 1966; and in 1983, they were redesigned with a slimmer, more contemporary appearance.

Bank, Penny, Girl & Boy, Cast Iron, A.C. Williams, 1910s-20s, 3 ¼ x 4 In.	25
Doll, Chef, Rubber Squeak, Green Scarf, Pants & Spoon, White Shirt, Hat & Shoes, 8 In.	26
Doll, Girl, Campbell Soup Kid, Cloth, Red Dress & Ribbon, Black Shoes, Yellow Hair, 16 In.	5
Door Stop, Girl Holding Teddy Bear, Cast Iron, 1991, 9 x 5 In.	40
Mug, Kids Gardening, Westwood, c.1983, 3 ½ In., Pair	60
Mug, Soup, White Ground, Girl's Face, Back Of Her Hair Other Side, Applied Handle, 1998	10
Ornament, 3 Kids Sleeping, Soup Bowl Bed, Dog In Spoon, Moon & Stars Hanger, 1993	4
Ornament, Glass Ball, Girl & Boy, Christmas, Collector's Edition, Box, 1990, 3 In.	4
Pillowcase Tubing, Girl Watering Flowers, 1965, 20 x 63 In.	16
Planter, Kid On Each Side, Sitting On Cans, Westwood International, 1997, 8 x 4 In.	32
Spoon, Etched, Kid Image, Mmm Good, Handle, Wm. A. Rogers, Oneida, 5 In.	15
Tie Tack Pin, Spoon Shape, Leaf Wreath, Our 25th Year, c.1985, 3 In.	105
Toy, Farm Truck, Wood, Red & Yellow, Pull Toy, Fisher-Price, No. 845, 1954	27
Toy, K-Line Trains, Single Door, Boxcar K649202, 90th Birthday, 1994	8

CANDELABRUM refers to a candleholder with more than one arm to hold many candles; a candlestick is designed to hold one candle. The eccentricity of the English language makes the plural of candelabrum into candelabra.

2-Light, Box, Woman On Lid, Silver Bronze, Weidlich Brothers, c.1925, 7 x 14 x 5 In.	313
3-Light, Bronze Winged Cherubs, Marble Round Base, Gilt, c.1875, 23 x 8 In., Pair	1000
3-Light, Bronze, Woman Holding Cornucopia-Shape Arms, Gilt, c.1810, 19 x 23 In., Pair	1320
3-Light, Figural, Sphinx, Cast Metal, Gothic, Egyptian Revival, 22 x 16 ½ x 8 ½ In. ....*illus*	236
3-Light, Girandole, Brass, Figural Woman, Cut Crystal Prisms, 14 x 4 x 18 In. ....*illus*	83
3-Light, Porcelain, Mother & Child Standards, Scroll Arms, Roses, Germany, 20 x 10 In., Pair	320
4-Light, Bronze, Marble, Champleve Enamel, Gilt, Stepped Base, Eagle Heads........................	94
4-Light, Cut Glass, Hobstar, Strawberry Diamond, Gilt Silver Plated Arms, Candlesnuffer, 18 x 11 In.	84
4-Light, Cut Glass, Silver Plate Arms, Hobstar, Vesica, Strawberry, Nailhead Diamond, 17 x 13 In. .	84
4-Light, Nickel Plated Brass, Squared Arms, Round Base, K. Hagenauer, 1900s, 20 x 9 In.	2142
4-Light, Porcelain, Mounted, Gilt Bronze, Openwork Base, Sevres Style, c.1900, 21 ½ In.	1250
5-Light, Brass, Clear & Amethyst Prisms, Victorian, 20 ½ x 12 In.	286

6-Light, Brass, Painted Metal, Figural, Robed Woman, 1900s, 32 x 11 In., Pair		320
6-Light, Bronze, Acanthus Capped Stem, Tripod & Marble Base, Paw Feet, 1900s, 40 In.		1250
6-Light, Bronze, Columns, Scrolling Arms, Maison Odiot, Argente, 1800s, 21 x 14 x 7 In.		3500
6-Light, Bronze, Crystal, Spear Finial, Stars & Beads Swags, Scalloped Base, 35 x 15 In.		180
6-Light, Bronze, Geometric Swirls, Patinated, Art Nouveau, Continental, 24 x 2 x 7 In.		182
6-Light, Gilt Bronze, Glass, Lavender Quartz Drops, 2 Tiers, Leaf Feet, c.1875, 43 x 20 In.		2125
6-Light, Putto, Cherub, Marble Plinth, Neoclassical Style, 1800s, 43 x 20 In.		615
7-Light, Altar, Brass, Flowers, Milk Glass, Grapes, Tripodal Base, 1800s, 40 x 16 x 9 In.		246
7-Light, Gilt, Cherub, Leaves, Flowers, 1890, 34 In.		907
7-Light, Silver Plate, Center Flute, Stewart Dawson Co., c.1907, 17 x 16 In.		245
9-Light, Urn Shape, Leafy Handles, Putti, 2 Tiers, Thomire Paris, France, 1800s, 36 In.		12000

CANDLESTICKS were made of brass, pewter, glass, sterling silver, plated silver, and all types of pottery and porcelain. The earliest candlesticks, dating from the sixteenth century, held the candle on a pricket (sharp pointed spike). These lost favor because in times of strife the large church candlesticks with prickets became formidable weapons, so the socket was mandated. Candlesticks changed in style through the centuries, and designs range from Classical to Rococo to Art Nouveau to Art Deco.

Brass, Capstan, 5 x 5 1/2 In. .... *illus*		325
Brass, Capstan, Ring Turned, Circular Drip Pan, Spain, Late 1500s, 5 1/2 In. .... *illus*		420
Brass, Flared Bowl, Tapered Base, Jarvie Style, Arts & Crafts, 13 1/2 x 4 1/2 In.		248
Brass, Mid-Drip, Stepped Circular Base, Shaped Stem, 13 In.		300
Brass, Molded, Push-Up, London, c.1860, 9 In., Pair		145
Brass, Queen Anne, Triangular Stem, Octagonal Base, c.1750, 8 1/4 In., Pair ...... *illus*		168
Brass, Ring Turned Stem, Broad Base, Marked, WH, Late 1700s, 7 3/4 x 6 In.		123
Brass, Round Base, Jarvie, c.1900, 12 1/2 In.		75
Bronze & Brass, Leaves, Animals, Paw Feet, Pricket, Continental, 1800s, 27 x 10 In., Pair ... *illus*		625
Bronze, Urn Shape, Wreathes & Masks, Removable Bobeches, Pair, 9 1/2 In.		330
Copper, Flower Shape Sconce, Tapered Stem, Blue & Green, 8 1/2 In.		215
Cut Glass, Hollow Body, Intaglio Flower, Strawberry Diamond, Ray Cut Base, Rolled Rim, 14 In.		96
Cut Glass, Single-Notched Teardrop Stem, Ray Cut Foot, 6 1/4 In.		18
Figural, Cast Metal, Watch Holder, Socket, 11 x 7 1/2 In.		58
Figural, Woman, Standing, Glass, Multicolor, Circular Base, Italy, c.1960, 14 x 5 x 4 In.		125
Glass, Pink Dolphin Support, Gold Fleck, Blown, Round, Stepped Base, c.1920		67
Glass, Trumpet Shape, Etched, Carved Floral, Flared Bobeche, 1900s, 9 3/4 x 5 In.		30
Iron, Adjustable, 1 Cup, Scrolled Feet, Early 1800s, 17 1/2 In.		469
Iron, Ornate, 3-Footed, Wrought, 18 1/2 In. .... *illus*		24
Iron, Tripod Base, Wrought, Scroll Details, c.1950, 19 1/2 In.		108
Pottery, Frog, Pedestal, Circular Base, Ron Meyers, 10 1/2 In.		138
Sconce, Tin, Round Starburst Reflector, Drip Catcher, 1 Socket, 1800s, 6 1/2 In.		277
Silver, Acanthus Leaves, Footed, 13 1/2 In.		704
Silver, Engraved, Crest Base, Marked, George II, London, 7 In.		500
Silver, George III, Armorial Crest, Marked, John Winter & Co., 1777, 12 In.		2400
Silver, Gilt, Woman, Skirt, Head Is Candle Cup, Arms Over Ears, Lalaounis, 6 1/2 In., Pair		320
Silver, Knopped Stem, George III, Removable Bobeches, 1763, 8 In.		3900
Spelter, Weathered Finish, Rounded Top, 1900s, 5 x 5 In.		46
Wood, 2-Light, Hanging, Wrought Iron, Tin Drip Pans, Trammel, Leather Strap, 22 In.		1320
Wood, Adjustable, Turned Support, 2 Tin Cups, Early 1800s, 25 1/2 In.		469
Wood, Altar, Carved Leaves, Reeded Drip Pans, Paw Feet, c.1825, 36 In.		1937
Wood, Gilt, Silvered, Pricket, Tripod Base, Leafy Borders, Metal Cup, 1800s, 39 In.		240

CANDLEWICK GLASS *items may be listed in the Imperial Glass and Pressed Glass categories.*

CANDY CONTAINERS have been popular since the late Victorian era. Collectors have long favored the glass containers, but now all types, including tin and papier-mache, are collected. Probably the earliest glass container sold commercially was the Liberty Bell made in 1876 for sale at the Centennial Exposition. Thousands of designs were made until the cost became too high in the 1960s. By the late 1970s, reproductions were being made and sold without the candy. Containers listed here are glass unless otherwise described. A

Candelabrum, 3-Light, Girandole, Brass, Figural Woman, Cut Crystal Prisms, 14 x 4 x 18 In.

$83

Charleston Estate Auctions

C

TIP
An "orphan" candlestick is still useful as a holder for bracelets in your bedroom.

Candlestick, Brass, Capstan, 5 x 5 1/2 In.
$325

Copake Auction

Candlestick, Brass, Capstan, Ring Turned, Circular Drip Pan, Spain, Late 1500s, 5 1/2 In.
$420

Northeast Auctions

Candlestick, Brass, Queen Anne, Triangular Stem, Octagonal Base, c.1750, 8¼ In., Pair
$168

Eldred's

Candlestick, Bronze & Brass, Leaves, Animals, Paw Feet, Pricket, Continental, 1800s, 27 x 10 In., Pair
$625

Neal Auction Company

Candlestick, Iron, Ornate, 3-Footed, Wrought, 18½ In.
$24

Copake Auction

Belsnickle is a nineteenth-century figure of Father Christmas. Some candy containers may be listed in Toy or in other categories.

Airplane, Hard Plastic, Santa Claus, Wheels, Arden Pat, 1950s, 4 x 5 x 5½ In.	180
Barney Google, Clear Glass, Comic, Figural, Round Base, Tin Lid	100
Bellboy With Suitcase, Cloth, Yellow & Black Felt Clothes, 9 In.	285
Belsnickle, Composition, Glass Icicle Beard, Tree, Germany, 20 In.	15600
Candlestick Phone, Clear Glass, White Metal Top, Turned Wood Receiver, Sticker, 1920s	28
Cannon, Tin & Glass, Clear, Mounted On 2 Wheels, 5 In.	113
Cash Register, Clear Glass, Wording & Drawer, Tin Base, 1910s, 2¾ x 3 x 1½ In.	154
Chick, Papier-Mache, Yellow, Faux Grass, Germany, 5 x 2 In.	69
Dog, Bulldog, Black Paint, Collar, Seated, Glass, Round Base, Marked, ¾ Oz., 4 In.	170
Dog, Spaniel, Papier-Mache, Painted, Bushy Tail, Amber Glass Eyes, Germany, c.1890, 7 In.	345
Doll, Bisque Head, Shoulder Plate, Blue Inset Glass Eyes, c.1880, 20¾ x 6 In. _illus_	5100
Duck, On Basket, Clear Glass, Original Paint On Beak, Tin Base, Avor, 1920s, 2½ x 4 In.	27
Easter Rabbit, Mohair, Wicker Basket, Fur Tail, Removable Head, 6½ x 4½ x 4 In.	68
Father Christmas, Brown Coat, Fur, Toys Hanging On Belt, Elizabeth Werner, 14 x 5 In. _illus_	187
Jack-O'-Lantern, Tin Lithograph, Metal Toy Co., 1950s, 4 x 4½ In.	23
Little Bo Peep, Lamb, Glass Eyes, Wool Coat, Blue Lace-Trim Dress & Bonnet, 11 x 9 In.	2767
Nodder, Man, Red Derby, Black Shoes, Papier-Mache, 7 In.	198
Rabbit, Composition, Red Dress, Blue Top, Yellow Apron, Germany, 7¼ x 3¼ In. _illus_	23
Rabbit, Fur, Glass Eyes, Papier-Mache Body & Feet, Removable Head, 25 x 9 In. _illus_	1440
Rabbit, Turnip On Its Back, Standing, Round Base, Multicolor, Germany, 5¾ In.	39
Reindeer, Felt Saddle Blanket, Leather Trim, Glass Eyes, Germany, 9½ x 11½ In.	2040
Santa Claus Head, Papier-Mache, Christmas, Germany, 11 x 7½ In.	68
Santa Claus, Bisque Head, Paper Clothes, Sitting On Log, Cotton Legs, Dresden, 9½ In.	1046
Santa Claus, Christmas, Rabbit Fur Beard, Felt Coat, Wood Base, Germany, 20 In. _illus_	186
Santa Claus, Composition, Germany, 8 In.	420
Santa Claus, Glass, Standing, Red Cotton Robe, Circular Base, Marked, 5 In.	124
Santa Claus, Green Faux Fur Robe, Cardboard Tube, Holds Feather Tree, 33 In.	3150
Santa Claus, Green Robe, Miniature, Papier-Mache, Germany, 4¾ In.	339
Santa Claus, Net Bag Body, Celluloid Face & Feet, 8 In.	125
Santa Claus, Papier-Mache, Feather Tree, Sack, Germany, 1900, 6 In.	395
Santa Claus, Red Felt Hooded Robe, Painted Face & Hand, Germany, 9 In.	424
Santa Claus, Spotted Fur Coat, Chef's-Like Hat, Holding Tree, Germany, c.1910, 7 In.	360
Snowman, Papier-Mache, Bobble Head, Bulbous Body, Red Hat, Germany, 11 In.	117
Turkey, Papier-Mache, Feathers, 11 x 8¼ In. _illus_	2280
Vegetable Head, Orange, Red Lips, Papier-Mache, Germany, 5 In.	102
Witch On Rocket, Orange, Black Jack-O'-Lantern Wheels, 8 In.	630
Witch, Composition, Removable Lantern Head, Germany, c.1920, 9 In.	3300

CANES and walking sticks were used by every well-dressed man in the nineteenth century, but by World War I the style had changed. Today canes are used by few but the infirm. Collectors prize old canes made with special features, like hidden swords, whiskey flasks, or risqué pictures seen through peepholes. Examples with solid gold heads or made from exotic materials are among the higher-priced canes. See also Scrimshaw.

Beaver, Carved, Figures, Standing Figure On Shaft, 1800s, 36 In.	561
Bone, Carved, American Eagle, Shield & Flag, 1800s, 33 x 4 In.	1062
Coiled Snakes, Carved, 2 Moving Balls, 1916, 36 In.	106
Dagger, Horn, L-Shape Handle, Inlaid, Double Edge, Pushbutton Release, 34½ In.	495
Girl, Seated, Holding Fan, Carved Bone Handle, 1800s, 35 In.	561
Glass, Twisted, Ribbed, Blue, Red & Lavender, Signed, A. Maretti, Late 1900s, 36 In.	150
Hardwood, Metal, Horn Shape Handle, Bone Dots, 2 Gold Engraved Bands, 1884, 35 In.	154
Ivory, 2 Monkeys, Climbing Cliff, 1800s	688
Ivory, Crook Handle, Baleen Banding, Whalebone Shaft, Metal Ferrule, 1800s, 33 In. _illus_	2280
Ivory, Decaying Tree Stump, 3 Monkeys, Snake, 2 Frogs, Carved, 1800s	875
Ivory, Head, Phrenology, Male Bust, Bamboo Shaft, c.1880, 38 In.	2250
Ivory, Octagonal Handle, Baleen Banding, Oak Shaft, c.1850, 34½ In. _illus_	330
Ivory, Screaming Man's Head, Glass Eyes, 1800s	563

C

Candy Container, Doll, Bisque Head, Shoulder Plate, Blue Inset Glass Eyes, c.1880, 20¾ x 6 In.
$5,100

Candy Container, Father Christmas, Brown Coat, Fur, Toys Hanging On Belt, Elizabeth Werner, 14 x 5 In.
$187

Candy Container, Rabbit, Composition, Red Dress, Blue Top, Yellow Apron, Germany, 7¼ x 3¼ In.
$23

Candy Container, Rabbit, Fur, Glass Eyes, Papier-Mache Body & Feet, Removable Head, 25 x 9 In.
$1,440

Candy Container, Santa Claus, Christmas, Rabbit Fur Beard, Felt Coat, Wood Base, Germany, 20 In.
$186

Candy Container, Turkey, Papier-Mache, Feathers, 11 x 8¼ In.
$2,280

Cane, Ivory, Crook Handle, Baleen Banding, Whalebone Shaft, Metal Ferrule, 1800s, 33 In.
$2,280

Cane, Ivory, Octagonal Handle, Baleen Banding, Oak Shaft, c.1850, 34½ In.
$330

Cane, Walking Stick, Wood, Crutch Shape Handle, Whimsical Faces, Carved, c.1900, 37⅝ In.
$263

Canton, Bidet, Houses, River, Bridge, c.1850, 14 ½ x 23 ½ In. $1,375

Eldred's

Captain Marvel, Patch, Captain Marvel Flying, Felt, c.1943, 3 ½ x 4 ½ In. $118

Hake's Auctions

Card, Baseball, Mickey Mantle, Bowman, No. 65, 1954 $620

Milestone Auctions

TIP

Got bubble gum on your sports cards? Rub them gently with a nylon stocking.

Ivory, Tree Stump, 12 Turtles Climbing Up, 1800s	438
Maple, Carved, Hound Head Grip, Stag & Horse, c.1900, 37 In.	688
Novelty, Action Rifle, Horn Handle, Single Shot, Continental, Early 1900s, 34 In.	1375
Novelty, Cigarette, Bamboo Type Wood, Carved, 35 In.	156
Silver, Knob, Embossed, St. John's Ambulance Brigade, Ebony Shaft, 1917, 30 ½ In.	176
Snake, Chip Carved Scales, Black Painted, 1800s, 36 In.	923
Sword, Horn Handle, Bamboo Shaft, Metal Ferrule, 35 In.	204
Walking Stick, 14K Gold Tip, Tapered, Ebony Shaft, 33 In.	1080
Walking Stick, Bamboo, Bone Handle, Gold Plated Tips, 35 ½ In.	68
Walking Stick, Bone Top, Wood Body, 34 ½ In.	45
Walking Stick, Convertible, Bamboo, Hinged Handle, Opens To Form Seat, Edwardian, 29 In.	182
Walking Stick, Hardwood Shaft, Fitted, Gold Grip, Engraved, John Langdon, 41 ½ In.	4080
Walking Stick, Silver Handle, Maple, Carved Alligator, Hound Chasing Buck, 1900s, 32 ½ In.	527
Walking Stick, Silver, Jester Handle, Opens To Vinaigrette, Hallmarks, c.1883, 32 In.	1107
Walking Stick, Wood, 2 Serpents & Lizard, On Shaft, Tack Eyes, Metal Thimble, 1900s, 36 In.	222
Walking Stick, Wood, 14K Gold Cap, 36 In.	330
Walking Stick, Wood, Carved, Buildings & Bust, Inscribed, POW, 1842, TP, 35 ½ In.	322
Walking Stick, Wood, Carved, Woman's Boot Handle, Snake, Inscribed, POW, 1842, 37 In.	164
Walking Stick, Wood, Crutch Shape Handle, Whimsical Faces, Carved, c.1900, 37 ⅝ In. . *illus*	263
Walking Stick, Wood, Snake, Engraved, 18K Yellow Gold Handle, 36 ¾ In.	1000
Whalebone, Clenched Fist Holding Snake Handle, Wood Bands, c.1850, 35 In.	3600
Whale's Tooth, Scrimshaw, Shark Cartilage Shaft, 19th Century, 31 ½ In.	531
Whimsy, Softwood, Carved & Painted, 3 Balls, Snake, Geometric, 36 ½ In.	96
Wood, Carved Handle, Hand Grasping Spike, Folk Art, 1900s, 36 In.	48
Wood, Carved, Cockatoo, Brass Painted Band, c.1890, 39 ½ In.	300
Wood, Carved, Indian, Head, Dartmouth College Fraternity, c.1873, 36 ½ In.	338
Wood, Eagle's Head Handle, Carved Feathers, c.1800, 35 ½ In.	210
Wood, Fist, Closed, Whale's Tooth On Thumb, Carved Lizard & Coiled Snake On Shaft, 36 In.	354
Wood, Owl's Head, Green Glass Eyes, Gilt Beak, Malacca Shaft, 36 ¾ In.	363
Wood, Snake, Cobra, Carved & Painted, Hollow Iron Pins, 1800s, 28 ¾ In.	677

CANTON CHINA is blue-and-white ware made near the city of Canton, in China, from about 1795 to the early 1900s. It is hand decorated with a landscape, building, bridge, and trees. There is never a person on the bridge. The "rain and cloud" border was used. It is similar to Nanking ware, which is listed in this book in its own category.

Bidet, Houses, River, Bridge, c.1850, 14 ½ x 23 ½ In. .... *illus*	1375
Dish, Leaf Shape, Water, Boat, Willow Tree, c.1890, 8 x 6 In.	155
Platter, Landscape Scene, Rain & Cloud Borders, 1800s, 15 x 12 In.	63
Teapot, Dome Lid, Footed, c.1880, 9 ½ In.	495

CAPO-DI-MONTE porcelain was first made in Naples, Italy, from 1743 to 1759. The factory moved near Madrid, Spain, and operated there from 1771 until 1821. The Ginori factory of Doccia, Italy, acquired the molds and began using the crown and *N* mark. In 1896 the Doccia factory combined with Societa Ceramica Richard of Milan. It eventually became the modern-day firm known as Richard Ginori, often referred to as Ginori or Capo-di-Monte. This company also used the crown and *N* mark. Richard Ginori was purchased by Gucci in 2013. The Capo-di-Monte mark is still being used. "Capodimonte-style" porcelain is being made today by several manufacturers in Italy, sometimes with a factory name or mark. The Capo-di-Monte mark and name are also used on cheaper porcelain made in the style of Capo-di-Monte.

Box, Lid, Cherubs, Trees, Gold Gilt, c.1771-1834, 5 x 2 In.	200
Cake Stand, Bacchanalia Scene, Rim & Center, Hand Painted, 4 x 7 ¾ In.	431
Casket, Temple Shape, Pierced Trim, Bronze Trim & Handles, Enamels, 14 x 14 In.	1375
Dish, Lid, Cherubs, Footed, Lion Handle, 7 x 6 In.	280
Ewer, Neptune, Mermaids, Tropical Fish, Schooling Fish, Seaweed, Dolphin, 16 ½ In.	508
Figurine, Cavalry, Napoleonic War, Hussar, c.1806, 9 ½ In.	150
Figurine, Girl With Bird, Flowers, Bird House, Black Hat, 6 ½ In.	95
Figurine, Woman, Fragrance Dama Con Cesto Rose, Giuseppi Armani, 19 ¾ In.	81
Plaque, Lion Hunt Scene, Hand Painted, Carved Frame, 8 x 10 In.	259

Urn, Children, Raised Relief, Gilt, Figural Handles, 8 x 5 ¼ In.	149
Vase, White Wicker Pattern, Applied Garland, Footed, Shouldered, 15 x 10 In.	18

CAPTAIN MARVEL was introduced in February 1940 in Whiz comic books. An orphan named Billy Batson met the wizard, Shazam, and whenever he said the magic word he was transformed into a superhero. A movie serial was released in 1940. The comic was discontinued in 1954. A second Captain Marvel appeared in 1966, a third in 1967. Only the original was transformed by shouting "Shazam."

Patch, Captain Marvel Flying, Felt, c.1943, 3 ½ x 4 ½ In.	*illus*	118
Picture, Paper, Hand On Hip, Matte Finish, 7 x 10 In.		75
Tie Clip, Embossed Brass, Portrait, Name, Fawcett Publications, 1946		95

CAPTAIN MIDNIGHT began as a network radio show in September 1940. The first comic book appeared in July 1941. Captain Midnight was really the aviator Captain Albright, who was to defeat the Nazis. A movie serial was made in 1942 and a comic strip was published for a short time. The comic book version of Captain Midnight ended his career in 1948. Radio premiums are the prized collector memorabilia today.

Badge, Decoder, Brass, Aluminum, 1948, 2 In.	145
Badge, Decoder, Eagle, Numbers & Letters, Propeller, 1940s	25
Badge, Decoder, Jet Plane, Silver Dart, Plastic, Removable Red Nosepiece, 1957, 2 ½ In.	47
Badge, Decoder, Shield Shape, 1945, 2 ½ In.	75
Medal, Flight Patrol Membership, Spinner, Skelly Oil, Chuck Ramsay, Patsy Donovan, 1940	14
Ring, Shield, Eagle, Globe, Anchor, Brass, Adjustable, Ovaltine, 1942	97
Shake-Up Mug, Portrait, Ovaltine Premium, Plastic, Orange, Blue, 1947, 3 ¾ In.	95
Whistle, Decoder, Code-O-Graph, Numbers & Letters, Blue & Red, 1947	12

CARAMEL SLAG, *see Imperial Glass category.*

CARDS listed here include advertising cards (often called trade cards), baseball cards, playing cards, and others. Color photographs were rare in the nineteenth century, so companies gave away colorful cards with pictures of children, flowers, products, or related scenes that promoted the company name. These were often collected and stored in albums. Baseball cards also date from the nineteenth century, when they were used by tobacco companies as giveaways. Gum cards were started in 1933, but it was not until after World War II that the bubble gum cards favored today were produced. Today over 1,000 cards are issued each year by the gum companies. Related items may be found in the Christmas, Halloween, Movie, Paper, and Postcard categories.

Baseball, Babe Ruth, Sanella Margarine, 1932		165
Baseball, Bill Bailey, Pitcher, St. Louis Amer., Nadja Caramels, 1909		224
Baseball, Dizzy Dean, No. 6, Signed Lou Gehrig Says, Big League Chewing Gum, 1934		130
Baseball, Hank Aaron, All Star, National League, Right Field, Topps, No. 488, 1958		71
Baseball, Heinie Zimmerman, Sweet Caporal, c.1909		3600
Baseball, Larry Doyle, 2nd Base, New York Nat'l, Nadja Caramels, 1909		118
Baseball, Mickey Mantle, 1st Base, Yankees, Topps, Screw-Down Holder, 1968		165
Baseball, Mickey Mantle, All Star, Center Field, American League, Topps, No. 487, 1958		94
Baseball, Mickey Mantle, Bowman, No. 65, 1954	*illus*	620
Baseball, Pee Wee Reese, Brooklyn Dodgers, Topps, No. 30, 1957		59
Baseball, Roger Maris, Rookie, Cleveland Indians, Topps, No. 47, 1958		502
Baseball, Satchel Paige, Pitcher, Cleveland Indians, Topps, No. 220, 1953	*illus*	260
Baseball, Tom Lasorda, Rookie, Pitcher, Brooklyn Dodgers, Signed, 1954	*illus*	59
Baseball, Tris Speaker, Piedmont, 1909		66000
Baseball, Willie Mays, All Star, National League, Center Field, Topps, No. 486, 1958		59
Football, Jim Brown, Cleveland Browns, Topps Rookie, Fullback, 1958		260
Playing, Cigarette Pack Inserts, Victorian Women, Full Deck, 2 ⅝ x 1 ⅜ In.	*illus*	224

CARDER, *see Aurene and Steuben categories.*

C

Card, Baseball, Satchel Paige, Pitcher, Cleveland Indians, Topps, No. 220, 1953
$260

Milestone Auctions

Card, Baseball, Tom Lasorda, Rookie, Pitcher, Brooklyn Dodgers, Signed, 1954
$59

Copake Auction

Card, Playing, Cigarette Pack Inserts, Victorian Women, Full Deck, 2 ⅝ x 1 ⅜ In.
$224

AntiqueAdvertising.com

Carnival Glass Sets

Some carnival glass patterns were made in full sets that include bowls, plates, and accessories in numerous sizes. Other patterns were for novelties made in only one shape.

Carnival Glass, Grape & Cable, Bowl, Ruffled, Stippled, Ribbed Back, 9 In. $275

Seeck Auctions

Carnival Glass, Orange Tree, Plate, Marigold, 9 In. $60

Seeck Auctions

Carnival Glass, Peacocks On The Fence, Plate, Electric Blue, Stippled, Ribbed Back, Northwood, 8¾ In. $350

Woody Auction

CARLTON WARE was made at the Carlton Works of Stoke-on-Trent, England, beginning about 1890. The firm traded as Wiltshaw & Robinson until 1957. It was renamed Carlton Ware Ltd. in 1958. The company went bankrupt in 1995, but the name is still in use.

Pitcher, Cream, Pink & Lavender Flowers, Raspberries, c.1935, 4¾ In. 65

CARNIVAL GLASS was an inexpensive, iridescent pressed glass made from about 1907 to about 1925. More than 1,000 different patterns are known. Carnival glass is currently being reproduced. Here are three marks used by companies that have made 20th-century carnival glass.

Imperial
1910–1924

Northwood Glass Co.
1910–1918

Cambridge Glass Co.
1901–1954, 1955–1958

Big Fish, Bowl, Marigold, Millersburg, 8 In.	225
Blackberry Spray, Ruffled Hat, Amberina, Fenton, 3 x 6¾ In.	100
Cherry & Cable, Spooner, Black Amethyst Handles, 6 x 6 In.	18
Chrysanthemum, Pitcher, Side Handle, Scalloped Rim, 3-Footed, 8¼ x 7 In.	36
Dance Of The Veils, Vase, Green Slag, Footed, Ruffled Rim, Fenton, 1930s, 8 In.	100
Dance Of The Veils, Vase, Mandarin Red, Ruffled, Footed, 1930s, 8 In.	60
Dandelion, Bowl, Spatula Foot, Northwood, 8¼ In.	225
Dandelion, Serving Dish, Amber Marigold, Indiana 1970s, 5 x 2 In.	26
Four Seventy Four, Pitcher, Green, Imperial, 7 In.	50
Good Luck, Bowl, Amethyst, Embossed Horseshoe, Flowers, Northwood, c.1915, 2 x 8¾ In.	76
Good Luck, Bowl, Horseshoe, Flowers, Electric Blue, 1800s, 9 In.	450
Grape & Cable, Bowl, Basketweave Exterior, Green, 8 In.	36
Grape & Cable, Bowl, Centerpiece, Purple, Turned-In Foot	30
Grape & Cable, Bowl, Persian Medallion, Green, Fenton, 5½ x 10 In.	58
Grape & Cable, Bowl, Ruffled, Stippled, Ribbed Back, 9 In. *illus*	275
Grape & Cable, Butter, Purple	45
Grape & Cable, Cuspidor, Aqua Opalescent, Fenton, 4 x 7 In.	50
Holly Sprig, Bowl, Ruffled Edge, Leafy, 9 In.	54
Holly, Plate, Green, Opalescent, Scalloped Rim, Fenton, 10 In.	10
Holly, Vase, Marigold, Ruffled Edge, Green, 2 Handles, 4 x 7 In.	48
Little Fishes, Bowl, Ruffled Edge, Marigold, Open Bubble, 9 In.	40
Nippon, Bowl, Piecrust Edge, Ribbed Back, Ice Blue, 9 In.	80
Orange Tree, Loving Cup, Blue, Fenton, 5¾ In.	90
Orange Tree, Plate, Marigold, 9 In. *illus*	60
Pansy, Bowl, Green, Ruffled Edge	25
Paperweight, Amethyst Dog, Sitting, Iridescent Glass, 3¼ x 3½ In.	18
Peacock At The Fountain, Butter, Cover, Blue, Northwood, 6 x 7½ In.	90
Peacock At Urn, Plate, Amethyst, Millersburg, 6 In.	125
Peacock Tail, Compote, Feather, Green, 5 x 6¼ In.	30
Peacock, Plate, Ribbed Back, Ice Green, 9 In.	110
Peacocks On The Fence, Plate, Electric Blue, Stippled, Ribbed Back, Northwood, 8¾ In. *illus*	350
Peacocks, Bowl, Piecrust Edge, Electric Blue, Northwood, 9 x 2½ In.	321
Persian Medallion, Bowl, Ruffled Edge, Multicolor, 8 In. *illus*	48
Poinsettia, Compote, Banana Boat Shape, Crimped Edge, Plum Opal	225
Poinsettia, Pitcher, Milk, Smoke, Handle	65
Raspberry, Pitcher, Purple, Blue, Northwood, Early 1900s, 7⅜ In.	178
Rising Sun, Tumbler, Aqua, Yellow Gold	225
Stag & Holly, Bowl, 3-Footed, Marigold, Fenton, 10¾ In.	25
Stippled Three Fruits, Bowl, Green, Ruffled, Northwood, 8¾ In.	60
Thistle, Bowl, Ice Cream, Amethyst	42
Three Fruits, Plate, Marigold, Basketweave, 9 In.	15
Wide Rib, Vase, Green, Flared Mouth, 12 x 5 In.	25
Windmill, Bowl, Amethyst, Scalloped Edge, Footed Bottom, Imperial, 1950s, 8 In.	68

CAROUSEL or merry-go-round figures were first carved in the United States in 1867 by Gustav Dentzel. Collectors discovered the charm of the hand-carved figures in the 1970s, and they were soon classed as folk art. Most desirable are the figures other than horses, such as pigs, camels, lions, or dogs. A stander has all four feet on the carousel platform; a prancer has both front feet in the air and both back feet on the platform; a jumper has all four feet in the air and usually moves up and down. Both old and new animals are collected.

Horse, Jumper, Carved Wood, Old Paint, c.1925, 45 x 50 In.		840
Horse, Jumper, Painted Aluminum, Metal Pole, C.W. Parker, 53 x 60 In.	*illus*	339
Horse, Jumper, Teak, Carved, Aluminum, Painted, Coca-Cola Stand, c.1950, 33 x 60 x 11 In.		295
Horse, Jumper, Wood, Carved, Painted, Gustav Dentzel, c.1900, 52 x 60 In.		25960
Horse, Prancer, Black & White, Red Saddle, Philadelphia Toboggan Co., c.1906, 42 x 50 In.		2057
Horse, Prancer, Gilt Mane, Roses, Daffodils, Flowers, Tassels, Ribbons, c.1960, 56 x 64 In.		826
Horse, Prancer, Glass Eyes, White, Philadelphia Toboggan Co., c.1890, 61 x 56 x 11 In.	*illus*	2160
Lion, Strolling, Carved Wood, Painted, D.C. Muller & Bro., c.1920, 54 x 71 In.	*illus*	20400
Rounding Board, Eagle, Flag, Flowers, Rope, Ruffles, Yellow Ground, Carved, 11 x 39 In.		3997
Sign, Catch The Brass Ring & Get A Free Ride, Painted Board, Frame, 23 x 26 In.		1416

CARRIAGE means several things, so this category lists baby carriages, buggies for adults, horse-drawn sleighs, and even strollers. Doll-sized carriages are listed in the Toy category.

Baby, Wood & Iron, Painted Black, Green Velvet Upholstery, Canopy, c.1890, 52 x 25 In.	850
Sleigh, Push, Red Paint, Gold Pinstripes, Handle, Wood, Victorian, Child's, 53 x 12 In.	96
Stroller, Wood Body, Canvas Hood, Wood Spoke Wheels, F.A. Whitney Carriage Co., 38 In.	40
Wood, Reclines, Rubber Wheels, F.A. Whitney, 36 x 42 x 21 In.	75

CASH REGISTERS were invented in 1884 because an eye on the cash was a necessity in stores of the nineteenth century, too. John and James Ritty invented a large model that resembled a clock and kept a record of the dollars and cents exchanged in the store. John Patterson improved the cash register with a paper roll to record the money. By the early 1900s, elaborate brass registers were made. More modern types were made after 1920. Cash registers made by National Cash Register Company are most often collected.

American, Brass, Oak Base, Gilt Housing, Numerical Keys, 26 x 28 x 18½ In.		224
National, Fancy, Brass, Milk Glass, J.C. Olmstead Orfordville, 18 x 10 In.		565
National, Mahogany Case, Carved Trim, Brass Figural Pulls, 19 x 16½ x 15 In.		1210
National, Milk Glass Plate, Cast Floral Scroll Brass, Tape Holder, 19½ x 16 x 17 In.		440
National, Model 36, Brass, Marquee, Registers The Amount, c.1897, 22 x 19 x 15 In.		565
National, Model 39, Brass Case, Oval, Marble Coin Slab, Marquee, 22 x 19 x 16 In.		908
National, Model 52¼, Dolphin Case, Nickel Plated, Marble Top, 1907, 21 x 17 x 15½ In.		510
National, Model 95, 9 Drawers, Marquee, Amount Purchased, 1898, 67 x 27½ x 21 In.	*illus*	565
National, Model 226, Autographic, Brass, Fleur-De-Lis, 1908, 10 x 11 x 16 In.	*illus*	469
National, Model 312, Brass Finish, Black Plastic Coin Tray, Key, 17 x 10 x 16 In.	*illus*	410
National, Model 312, Brass, Top Sign, Dolphins, Lacquered Brass, Key, 21 x 9 x 16 In.	*illus*	819
National, Model 313, Brass, Dolphin Case, 15-Key, Marble Top, 1912, 21 x 10 x 16 In.		861
National, Model 332, Amount Purchased, Brass, Marble Coin Shelf, 22 x 18 x 15 In.	*illus*	380
National, Model 420, Brass, Marble Shelf, Pointing Hand, c.1910, 26 x 15 In.		590
National, Model 442, Brass, Oak Stand, Receipt Box, 28 x 20¼ x 16½ In.		968
National, Model 711, Class 700, 15-Key, Coca-Cola Logo, 16½ x 10 x 21 In.		660
National, Slick Model 328, Race Car Top, DuPont, Jasper Giardina Brass Plate, 19 x 14 x 16 In.		344
Tape Box, National, Cast Iron, 2 Glass Sides, Slot In Lid, 6¾ x 6¾ x 6¼ In.		324

CASTOR JARS for pickles are glass jars about six inches in height, held in special metal holders. They became a popular dinner table accessory about 1890. Each jar had a top that was usually silver or silver plate. The frame, also of a silver metal, had a handle that arched above the jar and a hook that held a pair of tongs. The glass jar was often painted. By 1900, the pickle castor was out of fashion. Many examples found today have reproduced glass jars in old holders. Additional pickle castors may be found in the various Glass categories.

Carnival Glass, Persian Medallion, Bowl, Ruffled Edge, Multicolor, 8 In.
$48

Martin Auction Co.

Carousel Ladies
All horses on a carousel are mares.

Carousel, Horse, Jumper, Painted Aluminum, Metal Pole, C.W. Parker, 53 x 60 In.
$339

Rich Penn Auctions

Carousel, Horse, Prancer, Glass Eyes, White, Philadelphia Toboggan Co., c.1890, 61 x 56 x 11 In.
$2,160

Eldred's

Carousel, Lion, Strolling, Carved Wood, Painted, D.C. Muller & Bro., c.1920, 54 x 71 In.
$20,400

Eldred's

Cash Register, National, Model 95, 9 Drawers, Marquee, Amount Purchased, 1898, 67 x 27 ½ x 21 In.
$565

Rich Penn Auctions

Cash Register, National, Model 226, Autographic, Brass, Fleur-De-Lis, 1908, 10 x 11 x 16 In.
$469

Morphy Auctions

Cash Register, National, Model 312, Brass Finish, Black Plastic Coin Tray, Key, 17 x 10 x 16 In.
$410

Cordier Auctions

Cash Register, National, Model 312, Brass, Top Sign, Dolphins, Lacquered Brass, Key, 21 x 9 x 16 In.
$819

Soulis Auctions

Cash Register, National, Model 332, Amount Purchased, Brass, Marble Coin Shelf, 22 x 18 x 15 In.
$380

Cordier Auctions

Pickle, Amber, Daisy & Button, Silver Plated Frame, Tongs, 10 In.	129
Pickle, Amberina, Coin Spot, Bird, Flowers, Dog Finial, Webster Silver Plated Frame, 9¼ In.	369
Pickle, Aqua Blue, Enamel Flowers, Forbes, Silver Plated Frame, Tongs, 9¾ In.	800
Pickle, Cobalt Blue, Connecticut Plate Co., Double Triple Plate Frame, 1900-09, 12 In.	156
Pickle, Cobalt Blue, Enamel Glass, Optic Ribbed, Brass Lid, c.1800, 6 In.	239
Pickle, Cranberry Coin Spot, Silver Plated Lid, 1800s, 4⅜ In.	195
Pickle, Cranberry Coin Spot, Standard Silver Co., Silver Plated Frame, Tongs, c.1890, 11¾ In.	255
Pickle, Cranberry Glass, Thumbprint, Silver Plated Frame, Lid, Tongs, 13¼ In.	121
Pickle, Cranberry Opalescent, Daisy & Fern, Fenton, Silver Plated Lid, 7 In.	98
Pickle, Cranberry, Thumbprint, Silver Plated Stand, 10¼ In.	150
Pickle, Frosted, Parrot, Grasshopper, Stevens Woodman & Co., Silver Plated Frame, Tongs, 10 In.	165
Pickle, Green Vaseline Glass, Silver Plated Frame, Tongs, 11 In.	299

CASTOR SETS holding just salt and pepper castors were used in the seventeenth century. The sugar castor, mustard pot, spice dredger (shaker), bottles for vinegar and oil, and other spice holders became popular by the eighteenth century. These sets were usually made of sterling silver with glass bottles. The American Victorian castor set, the type most collected today, was made of silver plated Britannia metal. Colored glass bottles were introduced after the Civil War. The sets were out of fashion by World War I. Be careful when buying sets with colored bottles; many are reproductions. Other castor sets may be listed in various porcelain and glass categories in this book.

4 Bottles, Cranberry Glass, W. Briggs & Co., Center Handle, Silver Plated Stand, 8¼ In.	325
4 Bottles, Vaseline Glass, Bicycle Shape Stand, Simpson Hall & Miller, c.1898, 9 x 6 In.	1495
5 Bottles, Cobalt Blue, Footed Stand, Center Handle, 15½ In.	299

CATALOGS *are listed in the Paper category.*

CAUGHLEY porcelain was made in England from 1772 to 1814. Caughley porcelains are very similar in appearance to those made at the Worcester factory.

Urn, Soft Paste, Cobalt Blue, Leaves, Square Base, 1700s, 6 In., Pair	75

CAULDON Limited worked in Staffordshire, Great Britain, and went through many name changes. John Ridgway made porcelain at Cauldon Place, Hanley, until 1855. The firm of John Ridgway, Bates and Co. of Cauldon Place worked from 1856 to 1859. It became Bates, Brown-Westhead, Moore and Co. from 1859 to 1862. Brown-Westhead, Moore and Co. worked from 1862 to 1904. About 1890, this firm started using the words *Cauldon* or *Cauldon Ware* as part of the mark. Cauldon Ltd. worked from 1905 to 1920, Cauldon Potteries from 1920 to 1962. Related items may be found in the Indian Tree category.

CAULDON ENGLAND

Cup & Saucer, Shangri La, Cobalt Blue, Enamel Red, Gold Trim, England	44
Inkwell, Arcadian Chariot, Blue Transfer, Horse, 1930s, 5 x 4 In.	175
Platter, Sylvan Pattern, Blue, White, Cattle, Castle, Brown-Westhead, Moore & Co., c.1890, 15 In.	185

CELADON is the name of a velvet-textured green-gray glaze used by Chinese, Japanese, Korean, and other factories. This section includes pieces covered with celadon glaze with or without added decoration.

Bowl, Famille, Verte, Flared Mouth, Enamel, 1800s, 7½ In.	123
Bowl, Ice Crackle, Turned Rim, Glazed Base, Longquan, Chinese, 1800s, 1⅛ x 4⅜ In.	1020
Bowl, Lotus Scroll, Bisque Foot, Ming Dynasty Style, Chinese, 2½ x 6⅞ In.	86
Bowl, Round, Incised Lotus Exterior, Deep Olive Glaze, Korea, 6½ In.	123
Bowl, Scalloped Rim, Crackle Glaze, 7½ In.	687
Brush Washer, Basin Shape, Straight-Sided, Flanged Rim, 1800s, 1¾ x 5 In. .... *illus*	369
Censer, Crackle Glaze, 3-Legged, Chinese, 4½ x 6⅜ In.	281
Charger, Molded Bat & Cloud, Bisque Foot Ring, c.1900, 2⅜ x 13⅜ In.	523
Charger, Ribbed Cavetto Molding, Barbed Rim, Flowers, Longquan, Chinese, c.1600, 16 In.	4613
Dish, Scalloped Leaves & Geometrics, Chinese, 2 x 9¾ In.	281
Incense Burner, Mythical Creature, Pixiu, Standing, Bulgy Eyes, Bushy Eyebrows, 12 In.	1250

C

Celadon, Brush Washer, Basin Shape, Straight-Sided, Flanged Rim, 1800s, 1¾ x 5 In.
$369

Skinner, Inc.

Celadon, Platter, Birds, Butterflies & Flowers, Porcelain, Oval Chinese, 1800s, 18½ In.
$185

Skinner, Inc.

Celadon, Vase, Baluster Shape, Floral Body & Lid, Plum, Porcelain, 1900s, 33 In.
$1,125

Leslie Hindman Auctioneers

TIP
Decorators say you should think in threes. Accessories on a table look best when grouped in odd numbers.

Celadon, Vase, Yen-Yen, Turned Out Rolled Rim, Molded Peony, Chinese, c.1600, 18½ In.
$4,613

Skinner, Inc.

Chalkware, Figurine, Cat, Seated, Orange Spots, Hind Quarters, Oval Base, 1800s, 9¾ x 5 x 5 In.
$800

Cowan's Auctions

Chalkware, Figurine, Indian, Reclining, Holding Pipe, Painted, 1900s, 13 x 24 x 8 In.
$130

Leland Little Auctions

Lamp Base, Pottery, Art Nouveau, 12 In.	75
Lamp, Vase, Wood Base, Stone Finial, White Silk Shade, 32 x 8½ In.	72
Plate, Flying Crane, Signed, Cliff Lee, Stevens, Pa., 1986, 10 In.	1062
Platter, Birds, Butterflies & Flowers, Porcelain, Oval Chinese, 1800s, 18½ In. ...... *illus*	185
Umbrella Jar, Bamboo & Birds, Mint Green, Japan, 24½ x 12 In.	523
Vase, Baluster Shape, Floral Body & Lid, Plum, Porcelain, 1900s, 33 In. ...... *illus*	1125
Vase, Bottle, Concentric Bands, Grasses, Leaves, Carved Neck, 8⅜ In.	488
Vase, Crackle Glaze, Black, Matte, Chinese, 6⅞ In.	156
Vase, Enamel, 2 Woman, Chinese, 21¼ In.	246
Vase, Hu Shape, Bulbous Bottom, 8-Sided, Green, 8 x 4¾ x 4 In.	281
Vase, Lappets Pattern, Peony Blossom, Swirling Vines, Longquan, Chinese, 1800s, 9¾ In.	266
Vase, Peach Branch, Glazed, Leavy Stand, Signed, 1992, 10½ x 7 In.	5937
Vase, Porcelain, Blue, Dragon, Chinese, 1800s, 12 In.	150
Vase, Porcelain, Light Blue, Ribbed Shape Body & Neck, Molded Mouth, 1800s, 7 In.	625
Vase, Yen-Yen, Turned Out Rolled Rim, Molded Peony, Chinese, c.1600, 18½ In. ...... *illus*	4613
Water Coupe, Famille Rose, Floral Sprigs, Chinese, c.1800, 2¾ In.	2000

CELLULOID is a trademark for a plastic developed in 1868 by John W. Hyatt. Celluloid Manufacturing Company, the Celluloid Novelty Company, Celluloid Fancy Goods Company, and American Xylonite Company all used celluloid to make jewelry, games, sewing equipment, false teeth, and piano keys. The name *celluloid* was often used to identify any similar plastic. Celluloid toys are listed under Toy.

Barrette, 2 Elephants, Trunks Up, Silvertone Clasp, 1¼ In., Pair	14
Box, Repousse, Red Lining, Hinged, 4¼ x 3 x 2¼ In.	53
Buckle, Horse Heads, Green, 4¼ x 3¼ In.	40
Cross, Ivy Leaves, 1920s, 2½ In.	65
Figure, Dog, Sitting, Collar, Base, Japan, c.1930s, 1 x 1½ In.	14
Figures, Lady Duck, Man Chick, Yellow, Red Eyes, Irwin, 5½ In.	95
Hair Comb, Mottled, Open Work, Flowers, Leaves, c.1920, 10 x 9 In.	150
Letter Opener, Ivory Color, Walking Elephants, 6½ In.	12
Memo Pad, Acorn Shape, Days Of The Week, Brass Grommet, 8 Sheets, Early 1900s, 2¾ In.	18
Mirror, Hand Held, JB Ash Co., 1860s, 9¾ In.	16
Pin, Wings, Son In The Service, Shield, Red, White, Blue, 1940s, 1⅜ x ⅝ In.	18
Rattle, Doll, Japanese Style, Red, Blue, Green, 2¼ x 1¼ In.	75
Trinket Box, Humpty Dumpty, Round, 1½ x 1¼ In.	49

CELS *are listed in this book in the Animation Art category.*

CERAMIC ART COMPANY of Trenton, New Jersey, was established in 1889 by Jonathan Coxon and Walter Scott and was an early producer of American belleek porcelain. It became Lenox, Inc. in 1906. Do not confuse this ware with the pottery made by the Ceramic Arts Studio of Madison, Wisconsin.

Bowl, Underplate, Pink, Green, Roses, Blue Ruffled Rim, 4¾ In.	245
Tankard, Red, Pink, Roses, Cream & Red Handle, 14¾ In.	850
Vase, Flowers, Bird In Fight, Gilt Rim & Base, Gilt Handles, c.1901, 8 x 8 In.	450
Vase, Flowers, Hand Painted, Belleek, c.1900, 9½ In.	127
Vase, Poppy Flowers, Red, Orange, Green, Signed M.A. Joyce, 1907, 14½ In.	895
Vase, Wild Carrot, Cream Flowers, Light To Dark Green, c.1915, 10 In.	625

CERAMIC ARTS STUDIO was founded about 1940 in Madison, Wisconsin, by Lawrence Rabbitt and Ruben Sand. Their most popular products were molded figurines. The pottery closed in 1955. Do not confuse these products with those of the Ceramic Art Co. of Trenton, New Jersey.

Figurine, Cat, Sleeping, Light Green Bow, Marked, 2 In.	25
Figurine, Cat, White, Fluffy, Blue Eyes, 5 In.	39
Figurine, Leopard, C In Circle On One Foot, 1950s, 5¾ x 2¾ In.	55
Figurine, Peasant Girl, Blue Head Scarf, Pink Cheeks, 4¾ In.	30
Head Bust, Horse, Stallion, Cream, Brown, High Gloss, 3½ x 3 In.	55

Head Vase, Barbie, Green Bow On Hat, High Gloss, 7 x 5 In.	39
Head Vase, Figurine, Girl, Green Eyes, Pigtails, Brown Hair, 5½ In.	44
Salt & Pepper, Fish, Pink, Green, Big Eyes, 1950s	65
Salt & Pepper, Polar Bears, Mother & Cub, Marked, 4 x 2 In.	20
Salt & Pepper, Poodle On Pillow, Pink, Beige, Green, 3 x 2 In.	64
Shelf Sitter, Boy, Spotted Dog, White Sweater, Yellow Collar, Blue Pants, 4 x 3 In.	22
Shelf Sitter, Dog, Collie, Tail Overhangs, 1949, 4 x 4 In.	36

CHALKWARE is really plaster of Paris decorated with watercolors. One type was molded from Staffordshire and other porcelain models and painted and sold as inexpensive decorations in the nineteenth century. This type is collected today. Figures of plaster, made from about 1910 to 1940 for use as prizes at carnivals, are also known as chalkware. Kewpie dolls made of chalkware will be found in the Kewpie category.

Bank, Dove, Cherry Branch, Painted, Late 1800s, 11 In.	156
Figurine, Cat, Seated, Orange Spots, Hind Quarters, Oval Base, 1800s, 9¾ x 5 x 5 In. ...... *illus*	800
Figurine, Indian, Reclining, Holding Pipe, Painted, 1900s, 13 x 24 x 8 In. .... *illus*	130
Figurine, Will & Son's Fine Shagg, Englishman Standing, Smoking, 13½ x 5¼ x 5 In. .... *illus*	242

CHARLIE CHAPLIN, the famous comedian, actor, and filmmaker, lived from 1889 to 1977. He made his first movie in 1913. He did the movie *The Tramp* in 1915. The character of the Tramp has remained famous, and in the 1980s appeared in a series of television commercials for computers. Dolls, candy containers, and all sorts of memorabilia with the image of Charlie's Tramp are collected. Pieces are being made even today.

Card, Strip, Portrait, Red Ground, Black Line Border, No. 24	6
Chocolate Mold, Figural, Metal, Candy, No. 8, Cane, Hat, Magnet	103
Figure, Leaning On Cane, Black Suit, Hat, Bronze, Cold Painted, 4 In.	65
Figurine, Standing, Holding Flower, Cinema Characters Series, Bisque, Algora, Spain, 1900s, 13 In.	7
Ornament, Blown Glass, Hanging, Black Suit, Shoes & Hat, De Carlini, Italy, 1980	23
Pencil Box, The Tramp, Tin Lithograph, Henry Clive Clanco, 1920s, 7¾ x 2¼ In.	29
Pin, Portrait, Yellow Ground, Promotional, Round, Modern Times Film	28
Token, Gold Rush, Brass, Portrait, Beaded Border, Gaiety Theatre, 1926	9
Toy, Trick Box, The Tramp, Painted, Tin, 1930, 1½ x 1 In.	16

CHARLIE McCARTHY was the ventriloquist's dummy used by Edgar Bergen from the 1930s. He was famous for his work in radio, movies, and television. The act was retired in the 1970s. Mortimer Snerd, another Bergen dummy, is also listed here.

Bank, Figurine, Feed Me & Save Money, 9 In.	45
Charm, Charlie McCarthy, Sitting, Sterling Silver, c.1940, ½ In.	40
Figurine, Standing, Orange Suit, Black Hat & Shoes, Chalkware, c.1950, 16 In.	16
Pencil Sharpener, Bakelite, 1940s, 1½ In.	55
Pin, Charlie McCarthy, Coro Co., 1937, 1 x 1⅝ In.	150
Puppet, Ventriloquist, Composite Head, String Controlled Mouth, 20 In.	42
Puppet, Ventriloquist, Dog Jumpsuit, String Controlled Mouth, 24 In.	32
Puppet, Ventriloquist, K & S, Cloth Body, 1930s, 18 In.	189
Puppet, Ventriloquist, Monocle, Hat, String Controlled Mouth, 20 In.	61
Puppet, Ventriloquist, String Controlled Mouth, 1930s, 20 In.	36
Puppet, Ventriloquist, String Controlled Mouth, Goldberger, 1970s, 30 In.	70
Puppet, Ventriloquist, String Controlled Mouth, Juro Novelty Co., 1977	42
Puzzle, Picture, Charlie McCarthy, Brushing Teeth, Edger Bergen, 1938	40
Radio, Tube, Plays, Brown Case, Majestic, Man Sitting, Electric, 1930s	459
Toy, Benzine Buggy, Charlie McCarthy, Windup, Marx, 1938, 7¼ In.	224 to 400
Toy, Car, Flivver, Mortimer Snerd, Tin Lithograph, Windup, Marx, c.1930, 7 In.	140
Toy, Charlie McCarthy, Walker, Tin, Windup, Marx, 8½ In.	165
Toy, Charlie McCarthy, Walker, Tin, Windup, Marx, Box, 8 In.	271
Toy, Mortimer Snerd, Crazy Car, Tin, Windup, Marx, 7½ In.	201
Toy, Walker, Tin, Windup, Gloss, Marx, Box, 8¾ In. .... *illus*	496

Chalkware, Figurine, Will & Son's Fine Shagg, Englishman Standing, Smoking, 13½ x 5¼ x 5 In.
$242

Fontaine's Auction Gallery

Charlie McCarthy, Toy, Walker, Tin, Windup, Gloss, Marx, Box, 8¾ In.
$496

Milestone Auctions

Chinese Export, Bowl, Famille Rose, 3 Ships, British Flag, Floral Garland Border, c.1785, 11 In.
$8,400

Northeast Auctions

Chinese Export, Bowl, Woman Holding Flowers, 2 Men, Porcelain, 1800s, $4\frac{1}{2}$ x 10 In.
$500

Pook & Pook

Chinese Export, Cider Jug, Lid, Landscape Scene, Blue, White, Gilt, Twist Handle, c.1850, 11 In.
$660

Eldred's

Chinese Export, Plate, Brown Center, Green Fitzhugh, Rim, 1800s, $9\frac{5}{8}$ In.
$1,599

Skinner, Inc.

Chinese Export, Plate, Mythological Scene, 2 Nude Women, Gilt Leaves, Scroll Border, 1800s, 9 In.
$1,107

Skinner, Inc.

Chinese Export, Plate, Raspberry, Center Gilt, Landscape, Horse, Cart, Building, Fitzhugh, c.1815, 7 In.
$4,200

Northeast Auctions

Chinese Export, Platter, Meat, Strainer, Armorial, Gold & Red Enamel Painted, c.1800s, 14 x 12 In.
$208

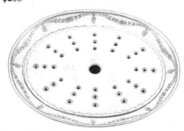

Freeman's Auctioneers & Appraisers

Chinese Export, Platter, Octagonal, Woman, Seated, Flower & Vine Rim Border, Late 1800s, $14\frac{1}{2}$ In.
$1,599

Skinner, Inc.

Chinese Export, Platter, Thousand Butterfly, Porcelain, Multicolor, c.1890, 18 In.
$600

Eldred's

Chinese Export, Teapot, Lid, Rooster, Bird, Butterfly, White Handle, c.1850s, $4\frac{1}{2}$ In.
$207

Copake Auction

CHELSEA porcelain was made in the Chelsea area of London from about 1745 to 1769. Some pieces made from 1770 to 1784 are called Chelsea Derby and may include the letter *D* for *Derby* in the mark. Ceramic designs were borrowed from the Meissen models of the day. Pieces were made of soft paste. The gold anchor was used as the mark, but it has been copied by many other factories. Recent copies of Chelsea have been made from the original molds. Do not confuse Chelsea porcelain with Chelsea Grape, a white pottery with luster grape decoration. Chelsea Keramic is listed in the Dedham category

Figurine, John Milton, Leaning On Pedestal, Gilt Highlights, Multicolor, c.1800, 12 ½ In.	12

CHINESE EXPORT porcelain comprises the many kinds of porcelain made in China for export to America and Europe in the eighteenth, nineteenth, and twentieth centuries. Other pieces may be listed in this book under Canton, Celadon, Nanking, Rose Canton, Rose Mandarin, and Rose Medallion.

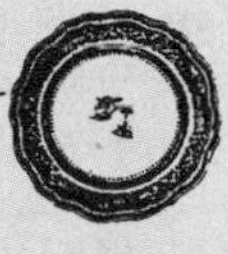

Bowl, Blue & White, Flowers, 1800s, 3 ¼ x 12 x 10 In.	218
Bowl, Famille Rose, 3 Ships, British Flag, Floral Garland Border, c.1785, 11 In. .... *illus*	8400
Bowl, Figural Scene, Blue Border, 1900s, 3 ⅞ x 9 In.	242
Bowl, Glazed, Russet Patches On Black Ground, Cizhou Type, 5 ½ In.	431
Bowl, Porcelain, Silver Mounted, Armorial, Flowers, Crowned Coat Arms, 1800s, 2 ¾ x 5 ½ In.	197
Bowl, Prince Of Orange, Multicolor Enamel, Porcelain, Chinese, Late 1800s, 2 ⅜ x 5 ½ In.	861
Bowl, Woman Holding Flowers, 2 Men, Porcelain, 1800s, 4 ½ x 10 In. .... *illus*	500
Brushpot, Famille Verte, Longevity Flora & Fauna, Tubular Shape, 1800s, 6 x 7 ⅝ In.	7380
Charger, Famille Rose, Cranes & Peonies, c.1700, 17 ¼ In.	1875
Charger, Famille Rose, Figures Under Willow Tree, Flower Border, 1900s, 22 In.	450
Charger, Famille Rose, Phoenix, Dragons, Red Ground, Multicolor, 17 ½ In.	210
Charger, Famille Verte, Alternating Reserves, Birds, Outdoor Pavilions, 13 ½ In.	405
Charger, Famille Verte, Flocks Of Birds, Trees, 1800s, 13 ½ In.	366
Charger, Gilt Decoration, Gold Rim, Grisaille, 1700s, 14 In.	187
Chocolate Pot, Lid, Molded Spout, Handle, Pink Flowers, Blue Trim, Gilt, c.1760, 8 ½ x 9 In...	360
Cider Jug, Lid, Landscape Scene, Blue, White, Gilt, Twist Handle, c.1850, 11 In. .... *illus*	660
Coffeepot, Bulbous, Molded Spout & Handle, Flowers & Ship Decoration, 1800s, 9 In.	277
Cup, Chocolate, Armorial, Portuguese Market, Gilt Rim Border, Ducal Arms, c.1760, 2 ½ In. ...	123
Desk, Cylinder, Roll Top, Writing Slides, Huang Huali, Early 1800s, 41 x 32 x 20 In.	1200
Dish, Flowers & Leaves, White Background, 1700s, 6 ¾ In.	384
Dish, Intertwined Center, 4 Mulberry Medallions, Birds & Landscapes, c.1740, 12 ¾ In.	246
Fishbowl, Flowers & Butterflies, Goldfish, Aquatic Plant, 1800s, 16 In.	308
Jar, Famille Verte, Phoenix, Flower, Bisque Foot Ring, Transitional Period, 5 ⅝ In.	246
Jardiniere, Dogwood, Blue & White, Cylindrical, 1900s, 10 x 10 ¾ In.	60
Jardiniere, Famille Rose, 1800s, 10 x 12 ¼ In.	813
Lamp Base, Electric, Famille Noir, Baluster Shape, Plum Branches, Birds, Wood Stand, 1900s, 15 In.	1046
Lamp Base, Famille Noir, 10 In.	213
Planter, Famille Rose, Blooming Plums, Calligraphy, Octagonal, Late 1800s, 3 ½ x 8 In.	277
Plate, Brown Center, Green Fitzhugh, Rim, 1800s, 9 ⅝ In. .... *illus*	1599
Plate, Mythological Scene, 2 Nude Women, Gilt Leaves, Scroll Border, 1800s, 9 In. .... *illus*	1107
Plate, Octagon, Armorial, Porcelain, Arms Of Aberdeen, c.1760, 8 In.	120
Plate, Raspberry, Center Gilt, Landscape, Horse, Cart, Building, Fitzhugh, c.1815, 7 In. ..... *illus*	4200
Plate, Urn Mysterieuse, Sepia, Green & Black, Leafy Script, c.1795, 9 ½ In.	1560
Platter, Landscape Vignette, Round, 1800s, 13 ¼ x 16 In.	75
Platter, Meat, Strainer, Armorial, Gold & Red Enamel Painted, c.1800s, 14 x 12 In. ..... *illus*	208
Platter, Octagonal, Woman, Seated, Flower & Vine Rim Border, Late 1800s, 14 ½ In. ..... *illus*	1599
Platter, Red Rover, Orange Fitzhugh, c.1832	1920
Platter, Swirling Dragons Amid Clouds, Multicolor, c.1900, 11 ½ x 8 ½ In.	272
Platter, Thousand Butterfly, Porcelain, Multicolor, c.1890, 18 In. ..... *illus*	600
Platter, Tobacco Leaf, Flowers, Enameled, 1800s, 12 x 14 ⅜ In.	1125
Punch Bowl, Famille Rose, Flowers, Footed, 1800s, 5 ⅜ In.	475
Punch Bowl, Famille Rose, Scroll Handles, Stem Foot, Bronze Mounts, 1900s, 12 x 14 In.	813
Saucer, Armorial, Red Enamel, Pomegranate & Grape Border, Landscape, 1800s, 5 ½ In.	197
Teapot, Drum Shape, Floral Cartouches, Gilt, Twig Handle, c.1850, 6 In.	120
Teapot, Lid, Rooster, Bird, Butterfly, White Handle, c.1850s, 4 ½ In. ..... *illus*	207

Chinese Export, Vase, Famille Rose, Courtyard Figures, Foo Dog Handles, Dragons, 1800s, 18 In.
$620

Leland Little Auctions

Chinese Export, Vase, Famille Verte, Batwing Handles, Hunters, Horses, Forest, 1800s, 12 ¾ In.
$438

Leslie Hindman Auctioneers

Chinese Export, Vase, Landscapes, Green Enameled, Lantern Shape, Lobed Rim, Marked, c.1950, 13 ¾ In.
$246

Skinner, Inc.

Chocolate Glass, Cactus, Cake Stand, Shaped Rim, 1901, Greentown, 7 x 10 In.
$527

Jeffrey S. Evans & Associates

Chocolate Glass, Dolphin, Dish, Lid, Beaded Rim, Greentown, c.1902, 4 3/8 x 7 In.
$70

Jeffrey S. Evans & Associates

Chocolate Glass, Racing Deer & Doe, Pitcher, Water, Shaded, Striations, Scalloped Rim, Greentown, 9 In.
$293

Jeffrey S. Evans & Associates

Teapot, Lighthouse Shape, Entwined Handle, Wood Lid, Blue, White, 1800s, 8 In.	84
Teapot, Nephrite, Lid, Carved Frog Finial, 7 1/8 x 4 x 3 1/2 In.	363
Tray, Kidney Shape, Birds, Butterflies, Multicolor, c.1790, 10 1/4 In.	230
Tray, Lotus Leaf, Vines, Scalloped, Red, Green, Pink, c.1740, 10 1/2 In.	704
Vase, Blue & White, Gourd Shape, 1800s, 22 1/2 In.	2750
Vase, Famille Rose, Courtyard Figures, Foo Dog Handles, Dragons, 1800s, 18 In. ...... *illus*	620
Vase, Famille Rose, Flowers, Dragons & Lions, Baluster Shape, 1900s, 14 In.	338
Vase, Famille Rose, Roosters & Insects, 1900s, 17 1/2 In.	100
Vase, Famille Verte, Batwing Handles, Hunters, Horses, Forest, 1800s, 12 3/4 In. ...... *illus*	438
Vase, Famille Verte, Landscape, Baluster Shape, Waisted Bottom, 4 5/8 In.	369
Vase, Landscapes, Green Enameled, Lantern Shape, Lobed Rim, Marked, c.1950, 13 3/4 In. . *illus*	246
Vase, Molded & Carved, Gilt, 2 Meandering Dragons, 9 3/4 In.	215
Vase, Reticulated, Daily Life Scenes, Turquoise Glaze, 1900s, 17 3/8 x 5 3/8 In.	2057

CHINTZ is the name of a group of china patterns featuring an overall design of flowers and leaves. The design became popular with English makers about 1928. A few pieces are still being made. The best known are designs by Royal Winton, James Kent Ltd., Crown Ducal, and Shelley. Crown Ducal and Shelley are listed in their own sections.

Atlas China Co.
c.1934–1939

Old Foley/James Kent
c.1955

Royal Winton
c.1951+

Balmoral, Platter, Oval, 2 Handles, Flowers, Leaves, Black Ground, Royal Winton, 1940s, 10 In.	106
Evesham, Cheese Dish, Lid, Wedge Shape, Fruit, Leaves, Cream Ground, Royal Winton	279
Old English, Eggcup, Double, Blue, Johnson Brothers, 4 1/4 In.	27
Rose, Teapot, Pink, Lid, Johnson Brothers, 4 3/4 In.	49

 CHOCOLATE GLASS, sometimes mistakenly called caramel slag, was made by the Indiana Tumbler and Goblet Company of Greentown, Indiana, from 1900 to 1903. It was also made at other National Glass Company factories. Fenton Art Glass Co. made chocolate glass from about 1907 to 1915. More recent pieces have been made by Imperial and others.

Cactus, Cake Stand, Shaped Rim, 1901, Greentown, 7 x 10 In. ....*illus*	527
Deer & Doe, Pitcher, Swirls, Scalloped Rim, Early 1900s, 9 x 4 3/4 In.	293
Dolphin, Dish, Lid, Beaded Rim, Greentown, c.1902, 4 3/8 x 7 In. ....*illus*	70
Racing Deer & Doe, Pitcher, Water, Shaded, Striations, Scalloped Rim, Greentown, 9 In.........*illus*	293

CHRISTMAS PLATES *that are limited edition are listed in the Collector Plate category or in the correct factory listing.*

CHRISTMAS collectibles include not only Christmas trees and ornaments listed below, but also Santa Claus figures, special dishes, and even games and wrapping paper. A Belsnickle is a nineteenth-century figure of Father Christmas. A kugel is an early, heavy ornament made of thick blown glass, lined with zinc or lead, and often covered with colored wax. Christmas collectibles may also be listed in the Candy Container category. Christmas trees are listed in the section that follows.

Belsnickle, Composition, Cardboard, Rabbit Fur Beard, Fur Coat, Tin Horn, Tree, 19 In.	2700
Belsnickle, Painted Face, White Robe, Holding Tree, Beard, Germany, 10 3/4 In. ...... *illus*	164
Belsnickle, Snow Hound, Holding A Tree, Pink Paint, White, 19 1/2 x 6 1/2 In.	5100
Belsnickle, Yellow Robe, Holding Tree, Composition, Black Base, 14 In.	944
Bench, Iron, Red, Molded Holiday Characters, 15 1/4 x 9 x 6 1/4 In.	625
Candy Containers are listed in the Candy Container category.	
Cup & Saucer, Santa Claus, Sack, Children, Transfer, Gold Border, 1880s, 2 1/2 x 3 In.	78
Decoration, Santa Claus, Paper, Honeycomb Body, Shadowbox Frame, 21 x 23 x 3 In.	704
Doll, Santa Claus, Muslin Face, Side-Glancing Eyes, Straw Stuffing, Stand, 25 1/2 In.	150

Elf, Plastic Face, Soft Body, Red & Green Suit, Knee Hugger, 1960s, 4 In.	15
Figure, Santa Claus, Composition Pants, Blue Mohair Coat, Switches, Sack, Germany, 8 1/4 x 3 1/2 In.	660
Figure, Santa Claus, Movable Head, Arms & Legs, c.1925, Germany, 18 3/4 In.	219
Figure, Santa Claus, On Polar Bear, Painted, Mica Covered, Germany, c.1915, 6 3/4 In.	431
Figure, Santa Claus, Seated In Chair, Sticker, Bendable Arms & Legs, Germany, 13 In. *illus*	3690
Figure, Santa Claus, Sitting On Donkey, Painted, Germany, c.1920, 6 1/2 In.	316
Figure, Santa Claus, Woodcutter, Composition, Felt, Mohair, Mica Covered Base, 15 In.	2160
Game, Santa Claus, Visit, Box, McLoughlin Bros., 20 x 10 1/2 In.	4800
Handkerchief, Santa Claus, Children, Frame, 1859, 16 1/2 x 13 3/4 In. *illus*	150
Lamp, Santa Claus, Standing, On Snow, Red, Black, Gray, c.1894, 9 1/2 x 3 In. *illus*	3510
Mask, Belsnickle, Muslin Face Paint, Crepe Paper Collar, Felt Hat, 15 x 5 1/2 In.	600
Mold, Chocolate, St. Nicholas, Tin, 4 3/4 x 3 x 2 1/4 In.	30
Nodder, Reindeer, Brown Glass Eyes, Metal Antlers, Cloth Collar, Bell, Clockwork, 15 In.	6000
Pitcher, Santa Claus Sledding, Germany, 6 1/4 x 5 1/2 In.	344
Plate, Tin, Girl, Holding Doll, Holly & Ivy, C.D. Kenny Co., 10 1/4 In.	210
Plate, Twelve Days Of Christmas, Tenth Day, Taylor, Smith & Taylor, 11 In.	10
Platter, Santa Claus Head In Center, Merry Christmas On Rim, Kay Finch, 16 In.	63
Postcard, Harp, Holly Leaves & Berries, Kindest Greetings For Christmas, c.1907, 6 x 4 In.	17
Postcard, Santa Claus, Red Suit & Hat, Seated In Green Chair, 1916, 6 x 4 In.	20
Poster, Santa Claus, Yuletide Greetings, Employees Thank You Pep Talk, 1948, 27 x 40 In.	68
Print, Girl In Bed, Book, Mistletoe Over Cat, Frame, c.1890, 22 x 18 3/4 In.	125
Punch Bowl, Santa Claus, Holly, Raised Decoration, Kay Finch, 11 In.	46
Roly Poly, Santa Claus, Toothy Smile, Red Coat, Green Bottom, Schoenhut, 10 In.	504
Sign, Santa Claus Holding Jester, Fur Weihnachten, Cardboard, Germany, 18 1/4 x 13 In.	150
Toy, Lantern, Santa Claus, Figural, Signal, Inside The Glass, Box, 6 1/2 x 3 In.	36
Toy, Puppet Stage, Santa & Children, Die Cut Paper, Fabric, Wood, England, 23 x 15 In.	240
Toy, Santa Claus, Bell Ringer, Red, Black & White, Box, 7 In.	71
Toy, Santa Claus, Horse & Wagon, Filled With Toys, Wheels, Wood, 12 x 27 In.	2400
Toy, Santa Claus, Little Folk From Sunny Slope, Rubber, Rempel Mfg. Co., Box, 11 In. *illus*	29
Toy, Santa Claus, Tin, Windup, Marked, Chein, 1930, 5 3/4 In.	177
Toy, Santa Claus, Walking, Lead Head, Cast Iron Feet, Robe, Sack, Ives, 1893, 10 In.	1560
Wall Pocket, Candy Cane, Green, Red Stripes, Gold Overlay, Swirled, Kay Finch, 10 x 1 In.	65

CHRISTMAS TREES made of feathers and Christmas tree decorations of all types are popular with collectors. The first decorated Christmas tree in America is claimed by many states, including Pennsylvania (1747), Massachusetts (1832), Illinois (1833), Ohio (1838), and Iowa (1845). The first glass ornaments were imported from Germany about 1860. Paper and tinsel ornaments were made in Dresden, Germany, from about 1880 to 1940. Manufacturers in the United States were making ornaments in the early 1870s. Electric lights were first used on a Christmas tree in 1882. Character light bulbs became popular in the 1920s, bubble lights in the 1940s, twinkle bulbs in the 1950s, plastic bulbs by 1955. In this book a Christmas light is a holder for a candle used on the tree. Other forms of lighting include light bulbs. Other Christmas collectibles are listed in the preceding section.

Feather, 7 Tiers, Painted, Turned Wood Base, Germany, 36 In.	295
Feather, Candle Tip & Holders, Paper Bark, Faux Berries, 42 x 24 In.	380
Feather, Dark Green, Red Berries, Round Base, Germany, 30 In.	330
Feather, Green, Cylindrical Base, 34 In.	113
Ornament, Bear On Swing, Cotton, c.1920, Germany, 5 1/2 In.	35
Ornament, Elf, Chenille, Holding Tree, Red & White Hat & Scarf, 1960s, 2 1/2 In.	14
Ornament, Kugel, Cluster Of Grapes, Cobalt Blue, Glass, Baroque Cap, 4 In.	472
Ornament, Kugel, Cluster Of Grapes, Green Glass, Lobed Cap, 7 In.	885
Ornament, Kugel, Cluster Of Grapes, Red Glass, Baroque Cap, 4 3/4 In.	3068
Ornament, Kugel, Cluster Of Grapes, Red, 5-Leaf Cap, 5 In.	3000
Ornament, Kugel, Egg Shape, Olive Glass, Beehive Cap, 3 3/4 In.	224
Ornament, Kugel, Red Pomegranate Cluster, Poland, Blown Glass, 4 In.	50
Ornament, Kugel, Ribbed, Green Glass, 10-Lobed Cap, 4 In.	1121
Ornament, Little Girl, Scrap Tinsel, Fur Muff, Silver, Blue, Green, 7 1/2 In.	44
Ornament, Santa Claus, Purple Clay Face, Chenille, Holding Bottle Brush, 3 5/8 In.	18

Christmas, Belsnickle, Painted Face, White Robe, Holding Tree, Beard, Germany, 10 3/4 In.
$164

Cordier Auctions

Christmas, Figure, Santa Claus, Seated In Chair, Sticker, Bendable Arms & Legs, Germany, 13 In.
$3,690

Morphy Auctions

Christmas, Handkerchief, Santa Claus, Children, Frame, 1859, 16 1/2 x 13 3/4 In.
$150

Morphy Auctions

Christmas, Lamp, Santa Claus, Standing, On Snow, Red, Black, Gray, c.1894, 9 ½ x 3 In.
$3,510

Jeffrey S. Evans & Associates

Christmas Ornaments

Vintage Shiny Brite ornaments sold for about $20 in 2017. The old boxes are also collected and reused for storage each year.

Christmas, Toy, Santa Claus, Little Folk From Sunny Slope, Rubber, Rempel Mfg. Co., Box, 11 In.
$29

Homestead Auctions

Christmas Tree, Stand, Brass, Hand Crafted, Brass Fence, 12 x 8 ½ In.
$430

Morphy Auctions

Ornament, Swing, Baby, Wood & Painted, Sebritz, 3 ¼ In.		23
Stand, Brass, Hand Crafted, Brass Fence, 12 x 8 ½ In.	*illus*	430
Tabletop, Star Light, Non Electric, Box, 1930s-50s, 17 In.		170
Topper, Star, Scrap Tinsel, Foil Feather, 8 x 6 In.		55

 CHROME items in the Art Deco style became popular in the 1930s. Collectors are most interested in high-style pieces made by the Connecticut firms of Chase Brass & Copper Co., Manning-Bowman & Co., and others.

Pitcher, Pinched Edge, Monogram P, Peter Muller-Munk, 12 x 9 ½ In.		937

CIGAR STORE FIGURES of carved wood or cast iron were used as advertisements in front of the Victorian cigar store. The carved figures are now collected as folk art. They range in size from counter type, about three feet, to over eight feet high.

Indian Princess, Feather Headdress, Red Shawl, Blue Dress, Cigars, c.1890, 42 In.	16800
Indian, Hiawatha, Wood, Painted, J. Melchers, Detroit, c.1885, 60 x 15 In.	23600

 CINNABAR is a vermilion or red lacquer. Pieces are made with tens to hundreds of thicknesses of the lacquer that is later carved. Most cinnabar was made in the Orient.

Bowl, Carved Design, Round, Chinese, 11 ½ In.	*illus*	250
Box, Dragon & Leaves, Qianlong, Round, 3 ¼ x 9 ¼ In.		2125
Box, Lid, Carved Relief, Flowers, Fauna, 3 Figures, Black, Red, 1800s, 4 x 8 In.	*illus*	660
Box, Lid, Carved, Daoist Landscape, Black Interior, c.1980, 3 x 4 ¾ In.		62
Box, Lid, Fruit, Insects, Leaves, Vines, Round, 5 x 2 ½ In.		125
Brushpot, Landscape Relief, Carved, 5 ½ x 5 In.		375
Jewelry Box, Casket, Lift Top, Cloisonne Closure & Handles, 8 ½ x 14 ¼ x 9 ¼ In.		735
Plaque, Round, Gilt, Carved Wood Stand, 13 ½ x 16 ¼ In.	*illus*	563
Red, Hinged, Lid, Open Interior, 1900s, 12 ¼ x 23 x 15 ¼ In.		531
Vase, Figures In Landscape, 1800s, 8 ¾ In.	*illus*	360

 CIVIL WAR mementos are important collectors' items. Most of the pieces are military items used from 1861 to 1865. Be sure to avoid any explosive munitions.

Blotter, Flag, 34 Stars, 1861-63, 5 x 7 In.		24
Boots, Cavalry, Lace-Up, Brown Leather, 11 ½ In.		168
Broadside, McClellan, Capture, Richmond, Text, Ornamental Border, c.1861, 4 ¾ In.		780
Cannon Ball, Hollow, Gettysburg Battlefield, 4 ¼ In.	*illus*	127
Canteen, Canvas, Leather, Carved, Selma Arsenal, 1863, 7 In.		420
Saddle, Leather, Brass, Iron Fittings, McClellan, 1861, 19 x 10 ½ In.		168
Snuffbox, Papier-Mache, Rectangular, Dome Lid, Zouave Soldier, 3 x 2 x 1 ¼ In.	*illus*	165
Sword, Cavalry, Wood Handle, Arched Blade, c.1860, 42 In.		96
Sword, Officer's, Brass Hilt, Leather, Brass Wire, Silk Tassel, c.1850, 41 In.		406
Tintype, Sergeant, Seated, Wearing Corps Badge, Gold Color Frame		72
Tintype, Union Soldier, Seated, Holding Rifle, ⅙ Plate		42
Token, Gallery Of American Traitors, Confederate Leaders, Brass, Dewitt, 5, 1 ⅜ In.		496
Token, Jefferson Davis, Death To Traitors, Brass, Dewitt, c.1861, 15/16 In.		674

CKAW, *see Dedham category.*

 CLARICE CLIFF was a designer who worked in several English factories, including A.J. Wilkinson Ltd., Wilkinson's Royal Staffordshire Pottery, Newport Pottery, and Foley Pottery after the 1920s. She is best known for her brightly colored Art Deco designs, including the Bizarre line. She died in 1972. Pieces of some of her early work have been made again by Wedgwood.

Autumn Crocus, Plate, 3 Crocus Bunches, Red, Blue, Purple, Yellow Trim, 9 In.		78
Bizarre, Jug, Central Flower & Berry Clusters, Multicolor, c.1930, 11 ½ In.	*illus*	1169

Cinnabar, Bowl, Carved Design, Round, Chinese, 11 ½ In.
$250

Roland Auctioneers & Valuers

Cinnabar, Box, Lid, Carved Relief, Flowers, Fauna, 3 Figures, Black, Red, 1800s, 4 x 8 In.
$660

Brunk Auctions

Cinnabar, Plaque, Round, Gilt, Carved Wood Stand, 13 ½ x 16 ¼ In.
$563

Susanin's Auctioneers & Appraisers

Cinnabar, Vase, Figures In Landscape, 1800s, 8 ¾ In.
$360

Eldred's

Civil War, Cannon Ball, Hollow, Gettysburg Battlefield, 4 ¼ In.
$127

Keystone Auctions LLC

Civil War, Snuffbox, Papier-Mache, Rectangular, Dome Lid, Zouave Soldier, 3 x 2 x 1 ¼ In.
$165

Forsythes' Auctions

Clarice Cliff, Bizarre, Jug, Central Flower & Berry Clusters, Multicolor, c.1930, 11 ½ In.
$1,169

Skinner, Inc.

Clarice Cliff, Lotus, Jug, Diamonds, Multicolor, Enamel, Band Border In Orange, c.1929, 11 ½ In.
$2,091

Skinner, Inc.

83

Clock, Advertising, American Biscuit Co., Carved, Roman Numerals, Date Ring, c.1910, 37 In.
$1,003

Clock, Advertising, Bulldog Cut Plug, Regulator, Brass, Sessions, 24 x 12 In.
$242

Clock, Advertising, Cat's Paw, Black Cat, Metal, Glass, Red & White, Light-Up, 15 ½ In.
$620

Bizarre, Pot, Marmalade, Orange, Orange Shape, c.1930, 3 In.	342
Bowl, Orange House, Paint, Ceramic, England, 4 x 9 ¼ In.	819
Crocus, Tea Trio, Cup, Saucer, Plate, Windsor, Vivid Colors, Plate 6 ¼ In.	115
Delecia, Jug, Orange, Purple, Blue, Green, Yellow, Dripping Glaze, Dots, 1930, 5 ¾ In.	375
Erin, Jug, Bizarre, Multicolor, Orange Trees, c.1933, 11 ¾ In.	1107
Fantasque, Biscuit Barrel, Orange Lily, Paint, Metal Handle, England, 8 ½ x 5 ½ In.	315
Lotus, Jug, Diamonds, Multicolor, Enamel, Band Border In Orange, c.1929, 11 ½ In. .... *illus*	2091
Lotus, Jug, Fantasque, Wild Rose, Orange & Yellow Central Band Border, c.1930, 11 In.	1353
Lynton, Coffeepot, Lid, Sundew Green, Flowers, Pink, Green, c.1936, 7 ½ In.	328
Rhodanthe, Bowl, Tree, Orange, Brown, Yellow, Crazing, c.1930, 9 In.	547
Tonquin, Platter, Blue & White, Royal Staffordshire, 1950s, 16 x 2 In.	95
Windbells, Jug, Multicolor, Ribbed, Signed, England, 11 x 9 In.	945

 CLEWELL was made in limited quantities by Charles Walter Clewell of Canton, Ohio, from 1902 to 1955. Pottery was covered with a thin coating of bronze, then treated to make the bronze turn different colors. Pieces covered with copper, brass, or silver were also made. Mr. Clewell's secret formula for blue patinated bronze was burned when he died in 1965.

Bowl, Copper Clad, Arts & Crafts, Bronze W Plaque, 4 In.	168
Vase, Bud, Copper Clad, Long Neck, Verdigras Patina, 4 ¼ In.	400
Vase, Copper Clad, Faceted, Signed, 9 ¾ x 4 In.	1062

CLOCKS of all types have always been popular with collectors. The eighteenth-century tall case, or grandfather's, clock was designed to house a works with a long pendulum. The name on the clock is usually the maker but sometimes it is a merchant or other craftsman. In 1816, Eli Terry patented a new, smaller works for a clock, and the case became smaller. The clock could be kept on a shelf instead of on the floor. By 1840, coiled springs were used and even smaller clocks were made. Battery-powered electric clocks were made in the 1870s. A garniture set can include a clock and other objects displayed on a mantel.

Advertising, American Biscuit Co., Carved, Roman Numerals, Date Ring, c.1910, 37 In. .. *illus*	1003
Advertising, Authorized Ford Sales & Services, Neon Spinner, 18 x 18 x 7 In.	2432
Advertising, Bulldog Cut Plug, Regulator, Brass, Sessions, 24 x 12 In. .... *illus*	242
Advertising, Carwalho, One Price Clothier, 8-Day, Bairds, Signed, c.1900, 30 x 1 In.	791
Advertising, Cat's Paw, Black Cat, Metal, Glass, Red & White, Light-Up, 15 ½ In. .... *illus*	620
Advertising, Cat's Paw, Pictures Cat, Metal, Glass, Red, White, Light-Up, Round, 4 x 15 ½ In. .	620
Advertising, Chew Friendship Cut Plug, Animated, Paper, Brass Spring Driven, 1886, 4 In.	970
Advertising, Cigar, 10 Cent, Etch & Gold Leaf Center, Hardwood Galley Case, 16 In.	141
Advertising, Dr Pepper, Logo, Faux Wood Trim, Wall, Howard, 1987, 21 x 17 In.	130
Advertising, Drink Dad's, Bottle Cap Graphic, Cast Aluminum Border, 16 x 16 x 4 In.	339
Advertising, Drink Orange Crush, Plastic, Light-Up, Square, 15 In.	390
Advertising, Ford Motor Co., Gears, Chrome, Enameled Glass, J. Perzel, 1930s, 10 In........ *illus*	6875
Advertising, Henrys Submarine Shop, Neon, Light-Up, 24 In.	3186
Advertising, Herd's Keystone Crackers, Brass, Spade Hands, Baird Clock Co., Pa., c.1892, 26 In.	1331
Advertising, International Harvester, Neon, Square, 18 In. .... *illus*	153
Advertising, Old Barn Auction House, Electric, 2-Sided, Red Metal Frame, 35 x 31 In.	212
Advertising, Old Melrose Whiskey, Records & Goldsborough, Balto., Glass, Wood, 13 In.	424
Advertising, Sun Crest, Orange Soda, Bubble, Pam, 15 In.	236
Advertising, Winchester Repeating Arms, Big Game Rifles, Wood, Baird, 1900s, 32 In. .... *illus*	813
Aitchison Bros., Shelf, Mahogany, Inlaid, Roman Numerals, Ball Feet, 1900s, 16 In.	197
Alarm, Brass, Enamel, Yellow Guilloche Panel, Footed, Loop Handle, 3 x 2 In.	54
Alarm, Rossel & Fils, Carriage, Brass Case, Floral Engraving, 6 ¼ In.	1888
Anniversary, Brass Base, Glass Dome, Germany, 11 ½ In.	88
Ansonia, Art & Commerce, 2 Statues, Sunk Enamel Dial, 8-Day, 21 x 23 In. .... *illus*	819
Ansonia, Bracket, Art Nouveau, Gilt Metal, Door, Faux Mercury Pendulum, 17 x 9 In....... *illus*	856
Ansonia, Don Caesar & Don Juan, Cavaliers, Patinated Metal, Faux Marble, c.1882, 20 x 26 In.	563
Ansonia, Don Juan, Metal, Double Sunk Porcelain Dial, 8-Day, 21 x 19 In.	367
Ansonia, Flowers, Blue, Scrolling Feet, Open Escapement, c.1895, 7 ½ x 9 In.	1210
Ansonia, Jumper, Bobbing Doll, Swing, Nickel Over Brass, 14 In.	383
Ansonia, Mercury, Seated, Bronze Finish, Classical Accents, 15 x 17 In.	226

Ansonia, Regulator, Crystal, Brass, Enamel Dial, Roman Numerals, Pendulum, 11 x 6 In....... 143
Ansonia, Regulator, Crystal, Rosewood, Brass, Ormolu, Porcelain Dial, 16 x 7 In. 248
Ansonia, Regulator, Eastlake, Walnut, Glass Panel Door, Paper Face, c.1800s, 38 x 13 In......... 192
Ansonia, Regulator, Octagonal, Wood, Roman Numerals, 25 x 17 In. 266
Ansonia, Shelf, Artist, Renaissance Painter, Ebonized Wood, Gilt Metal, Porcelain Face, 17 x 21 In.. 270
Ansonia, Swinging Ball, Diana The Huntress, 1880s... 1534
Architectural, Marble Dial, Bronze Egg & Dart Border, Brass Hands, c.1900, 26 x 25 In. 825
Atkins, Wall, Rosewood, Octagonal Bracket, 24½ In... 150
Automaton, Birdcage, Brass, Signed, E. Schmeckenbecher, Germany, 12 x 8 In. .... illus 303
Automaton, Hearth, Brass, Bricked, Lion Mask, Glass Rod, Enamel Dial, France, c.1990, 14 In. 523
Automaton, Man Strikes Bronze Bell, Mahogany, Carved, Roman Numerals, 36 x 13 In..illus 330
Automaton, Napoleon, Rock, Dolphin Mount, Gilt Bronze, Stepped Base, 1800s, 11 In............. 185
Bagues & Fils, Cartel, Louis XVI, Ormolu, Laurel Wreath, Ribbon, Enamel Dial, Paris, 18 In.. 260
Banjo, A. Willard, Mahogany, Roman Numerals, Boston, c.1810, 41 x 10 In. 840
Banjo, Chelsea Clock Co., Mahogany, Painted, Brass Eagle Finial, 1900s, 32 In. .... illus 330
Banjo, E. Howard, Rosewood, Reverse Painted Tablets, Mass., c.1850, 28 In......................... 780
Banjo, Federal, Mahogany, Metal Dial, Roman Numerals, Pendulum, 32 x 10 In. 263
Banjo, Howard & Davis, Faux Rosewood Grain, Glass Panels, Roman Numerals, c.1850, 49 In. 3625
Banjo, Mahogany, Gilt, Ship Portrait, Timepiece, c.1820, 33 In. 1464
Banjo, Mahogany, Iron Dial, Roman Numerals, Early 1800s, 32 In. 590
Banjo, Mahogany, Reverse Painted Panel & Door, Ancient Ruins, Pendulum, 29 In. 295
Banjo, New Haven, Black Walnut, Painted Panel, Gilt Eagle, Art Deco Numerals, 8-Day, 1925, 42 In. 225
Banjo, Oak, Lyre Style, Porcelain Dial, 36½ In.. 222
Banjo, Painted, Wood Works, Roman Numerals, 30-Hour, c.1830, 35 In. .... illus 1298
Banjo, S. Willard, Painted, Convex Dial, 8-Day, Early 1800s, 34 In. 2832
Banjo, William Cummens, Mahogany, Moberg Glass, 8-Day, Brass, c.1820, 32 In. 1652
Banjo, Wood, Reverse Painted Glass, Patinated White Metal, Cowell & Hubbard, 1900s, 41 In. 192
Batchelor, N., Shelf, Girandole, Iron, Black, Gilt, Flowers, N.Y., 21 x 20 In. 424
Birge & Fuller, Steeple, Mahogany Veneer, Wagon Spring, Joseph Ives, 1845, 26 x 13 In. 4798
Black Forest, Shelf, 2 Ibex, Naturalistic Carving, Roman Numerals, 1800s, 28 In. 1750
Black Forest, Shelf, Boy On Top, Carved, Leaves, Acorns, Ovington Bros., 28 x 15 In................. 2541
Black Forest, Wood, Carved, Deer, Oak Tree, 1800s, 29 x 23 In.. 1035
Bracket, Boulle, Louis XIV, Brass, Tortoiseshell Inlay, France, c.1900, 59 x 26 In...................... 7188
Bracket, Boulle, Tortoiseshell, Brass Dial, Rose Gold Filigree, Germany, 1900s, 21 x 15 In. 363
Bracket, James Tregent, Ebonized Oak, Brass Handle, Bell Chime, c.1780, 16 x 10 In. 4095
Bracket, Louis XIV, Kingwood, Tapered Pedestal, Flowers, 5 Gongs, 1900s, 74 x 17 In. 1000
Bracket, Louis XV Style, Ebonized, Gilt Metal, Enamel Dial, Cabriole Legs, 20 x 13 In. 242
Brewster & Ingraham, Shelf, Rosewood, Onion Top, Gothic, Ogee, Frosted Glass, 20 In......... 172
Bronze, Louis XV, Elephant, Figure With Parasol, Gilt Scroll Base, 1800s, 21 In................ illus 3198
Bronze, Marble, Woman, Open Book, The Value Of Knowledge, c.1800, 15 x 24 In................... 570
Brown, J.C., Acorn, Painted Metal Dial, Ships Under Glass, 8-Day, Fusee, 24½ In. 5310
Brown, J.C., Shelf, Beehive, Ripple, Mahogany, Zinc Dial, 8-Day, c.1850, 19 x 10 In. 1275
Bucherer, Bracket, Burl Wood, Steel & Brass Face, Fabric Lining, Late 1900s, 12 In................. 153
Caldwell, Edward F., Shelf, Gilt Bronze, Enamel Face, 2 Cherubs, c.1900 750
Caldwell, J.E., Shelf, Porcelain, Footed, Marti Movement, 14¾ In. 138
Calendar, Walnut, Ebonized Trim, 31 x 19 In.. 2714
Carriage, Brass, Black Porcelain Dial, Red Roman Numerals, c.1890, 8 x 4 In. 4680
Carriage, Brass, Champleve Enamel, Roman Numerals, c.1900, Miniature, 3 x 2 In. 1053
Carriage, Brass, Fluted Columns & Handle, Glass Panels, Ogee Bracket Feet, France, 8 x 4 In. 142
Carriage, Brass, Roman Numerals, Handle, France, 5 In. 275
Carriage, Brass, Sonnerie, Beveled Glass, Arabic Numerals, Shaped Handle, 6 x 4 In. 293
Carriage, Gilt Brass, Engraved, Beveled Glass, Roman Numerals, 1800s, 7 x 3 In...................... 3803
Carriage, Gilt Brass, Floral Frieze, Porcelain Chapter Ring, Key, France, 1900s, 5 In. .... illus 180
Carriage, Gilt Brass, Glass, White Porcelain Dial, Key, France, c.1875, 5 x 3 In. .... illus 1534
Carriage, Henry Et Cie, Gilt Brass, Bell, Double Cherub Handle, Paris, c.1860, 6 In................... 1020
Carriage, Matthew Norman, Brass, Porcelain Dial, Shaped Handle, London, 1900s, 7 x 4 In... 293
Carriage, New Haven, Brass, Beveled Glass Case, 2⅝ x 2 x 1⅜ In.. illus 142
Carriage, Paul Garnier, White Porcelain Dial, Black Numerals, France, c.1860, 6 x 3 In. 1404
Carriage, Sterling Silver, Purple Enamel, Roman Numerals, Miniature, 2⅝ x 2 In.......... illus 761

C

Clock, Ansonia, Art & Commerce, 2 Statues, Sunk Enamel Dial, 8-Day, 21 x 23 In.
$819

Soulis Auctions

Clock, Ansonia, Bracket, Art Nouveau, Gilt Metal, Door, Faux Mercury Pendulum, 17 x 9 In.
$856

Leland Little Auctions

Clock, Automaton, Birdcage, Brass, Signed, E. Schmeckenbecher, Germany, 12 x 8 In.
$303

Ahlers & Ogletree Auction Gallery

Clock, Automaton, Man Strikes Bronze Bell, Mahogany, Carved, Roman Numerals, 36 x 13 In.
$330

Forsythes' Auctions

Clock, Banjo, Chelsea Clock Co., Mahogany, Painted, Brass Eagle Finial, 1900s, 32 In.
$330

Eldred's

Clock, Banjo, Painted, Wood Works, Roman Numerals, 30-Hour, c.1830, 35 In.
$1,298

Cottone Auctions

Clock, Bronze, Louis XV, Elephant, Figure With Parasol, Gilt Scroll Base, 1800s, 21 In.
$3,198

Skinner, Inc.

Clock, Carriage, Gilt Brass, Floral Frieze, Porcelain Chapter Ring, Key, France, 1900s, 5 In.
$180

Brunk Auctions

Clock, Carriage, Gilt Brass, Glass, White Porcelain Dial, Key, France, c.1875, 5 x 3 In.
$1,534

Leland Little Auctions

Clock, Carriage, New Haven, Brass, Beveled Glass Case, 2 5/8 x 2 x 1 3/8 In.
$142

Forsythes' Auctions

Clock, Carriage, Sterling Silver, Purple Enamel, Roman Numerals, Miniature, 2 5/8 x 2 In.
$761

Jeffrey S. Evans & Associates

Clock, Chelsea Clock Co., Carriage, Brass, Porcelain Face, Handle, 5 x 3 x 2 In.
$125

Susanin's Auctioneers & Appraisers

Clock, Chelsea Clock Co., Ship's Wheel, Brass, Steel Dial, Key, Wood Stand, c.1950, 3 In.
$108

Eldred's

Clock, Cuckoo, Black Forest, Carved, Oak Leaves, Bird, Roman Numerals, Germany, 20 x 14 In.
$132

Forsythes' Auctions

Clock, Desk, Art Nouveau, Woman In Gown, Porcelain Dial, Blue Roman Numerals, c.1915, 6 1/2 In.
$556

Jeffrey S. Evans & Associates

Clock, DuTertre, J.B., Shelf, Louis XVI, Gilt Bronze, Ormolu, Laurel, Torches, 15 x 14 In.
$4,160

Susanin's Auctioneers & Appraisers

Clock, Gallery, Thos. Olive, Painted Panel, Couple In Garden, Cranbrook, 1800s, 59 In.
$3,360

Eldred's

Clock, Garnier, Woman With Book, Bronze, Gilt, Patinated, Marble Base, Paris, 1800s, 20 x 28 In.
$3,000

Heritage Auctions

Clock, Gustav Becker, Regulator, Oak, Porcelain Dial, 8-Day, Pendulum, 46 x 14 In.
$424

Fontaine's Auction Gallery

Clock, Howard Miller, Fish, Lacquered Masonite, Enameled Aluminum, G. Nelson, 1965, 11 x 9 In.
$687

Wright

Clock, Howard, E., Regulator, No. 9, Oak, Figure 8, 34 x 11 x 5 In.
$2,375

Leslie Hindman Auctioneers

Carriage, William Comyns & Sons Ltd., Silver, Tortoiseshell, 1906, 4 x 3 x 2 In.		968
Cartel, Bronze, Leaves, Pierced, 8-Day, Porcelain Bezel, Roman Numerals, France, 32 x 20 In.		605
Cartel, J. Meyer, Louis XVI, Gilt Bronze Cartouche, France, Early 1900s, 21 x 9 x 4 In.		750
Cartel, J.E. Caldwell & Co., Patinated Bronze, Pendulum, Key, 1881, 22 x 10 In.		313
Cartel, Louis XV, Gilt Bronze, Lion's Pelt, Ram's Heads, Leaves, Urn Finial, c.1900, 27 x 15 In.		2750
Cartel, Louis XVI, Bronze, Leaves, Cornucopias, Urn Finial, France, c.1890, 31 In.		938
Cartel, Napoleon III, Painted, Gilt Metal Mounts, 1800s, 25 In.		938
Chelsea Clock Co., Carriage, Brass, Porcelain Face, Handle, 5 x 3 x 2 In.	*illus*	125
Chelsea Clock Co., Desk, Ship's Bell, Filigree, Key, Centennial Edition, Box, 1997, 9 In.		1080
Chelsea Clock Co., Desk, Ship's Wheel, Brass, Mahogany Base, Engraved Presentation, 5 In.		151
Chelsea Clock Co., Ship's Bell, Brass Case, Brushed Metal Face, c.1915, 9 x 5 In.		570
Chelsea Clock Co., Ship's Wheel, Brass, Steel Dial, Key, Wood Stand, c.1950, 3 In.	*illus*	108
Cuckoo, Black Forest, Birds, Branches, Corn Cob, Bone Hands, c.1895, 26 x 17 In.		1089
Cuckoo, Black Forest, Carved, Oak Leaves, Bird, Roman Numerals, Germany, 20 x 14 In.	*illus*	132
Cuckoo, Wood, Carved Birds & Leaves, Roman Numerals, Pendulum, 14 In.		40
Desk, Art Nouveau, Woman In Gown, Porcelain Dial, Blue Roman Numerals, c.1915, 6½ In.	*illus*	556
Desk, Bayard, Mahogany, Partial Airplane Propeller, Silver Bolts, Footed, 7 x 15 In.		182
Desk, Luxor, Garden Scene, Rectangular, 7 x 4 x 2 In.		94
Dieter Rams, Alarm, Yellow Plastic, Quartz Movement, Braun, Germany, 1984, 3½ In.		437
DuTertre, J.B., Shelf, Louis XVI, Gilt Bronze, Ormolu, Laurel, Torches, 15 x 14 In.	*illus*	4160
E. Vitoux, Silver, Bulbous Glass Top, Holds Barometer, Thermometer, Compass, 9 In.		1888
Elliott, Bracket, Mahogany, Dome, Tempus Fugit, 7 Chimes, Handle, c.1925, 15 In.		540
Ellis, Harvey, Mahogany, Pewter & Copper Inlay, Porcelain Dial, c.1900, 12 x 17 In.		825
Franz Heiss & Sohne, Shelf, Gilt Bronze, Brass, Inlaid, Vienna, c.1910, 13 x 29 In.		1563
French, Lighthouse, Animated, Porcelain Dial, Balance Wheel, 1800s, 10 In.		3304
French, Lighthouse, Animated, Silver Plate, Gold Wash, Oscillating Light, 1800s, 10 In.		3304
French, Shelf, 3 Men, Brass, Slate & Marble, Marti Movement, France, 17½ In.		200
French, Shelf, Classical, Plato & Euripides, Gilt Bronze, c.1820, 24 x 19 x 7½ In.		3750
French, Shelf, Marble, Ormolu, Bronze Floral Finial, Garland, Pendulum, c.1890, 13 In.		240
Gallery, Thos. Olive, Painted Panel, Couple In Garden, Cranbrook, 1800s, 59 In.	*illus*	3360
Garnier, Woman With Book, Bronze, Gilt, Patinated, Marble Base, Paris, 1800s, 20 x 28 In.	*illus*	3000
Gilbert, Regulator, Walnut, Roman Numerals, Victorian, 52 In.		725
Gilbert, Shelf, Walnut, Arched, Drop Finials, Gilt Flowers On Glass, 22 x 13 In.		110
Gilmore, Jon, Shelf, Lucite Tube, Brass Fittings, Blank Dial, Wood Base, 20 x 12 In.		121
Gilt, Carved, Leaves, Flowers, Roman Numerals, Painted, 1900s, 37 x 11 In.		125
Glass, Venetian, Flower Shape, Etched, Armorial Motifs, 1900s, 25 In.		472
Gustav Becker, Regulator, Mahogany, Brass Dials, Roman Numerals, Pendulum, 56 x 19 In.		495
Gustav Becker, Regulator, Oak, Porcelain Dial, 8-Day, Pendulum, 46 x 14 In.	*illus*	424
Gustav Becker, Wall, Walnut, Crown, Minerva Head, Lion Finial, Pendulum, c.1885, 53 x 16 In.		300
Howard Miller, Ball, Brass, Walnut, Enameled Aluminum, G. Nelson, 1949, 13 x 13 In.		312
Howard Miller, Baroque, Walnut, Brass, Screenprint On Aluminum, G. Nelson, 1957, 15 x 9 In.		1820
Howard Miller, Fish, Lacquered Masonite, Enameled Aluminum, G. Nelson, 1965, 11 x 9 In.	*illus*	687
Howard Miller, String, Enameled Steel, Aluminum, Maple Face, G. Nelson, 18 x 18 In.		1000
Howard Miller, Wall, Aluminum, Acrylic Dial, Chromed Weights & Pendulum, 12 In.		185
Howard, E., Long Drop, Reverse Painted Door, Roman Numerals, 32 x 15 In.		650
Howard, E., Regulator, Astronomical, Riefler Pendulum, c.1875, 57 x 16 In.		5000
Howard, E., Regulator, No. 9, Oak, Figure 8, 34 x 11 x 5 In.	*illus*	2375
Ingraham & Co., Regulator, Oak, Glass Door, Paper Face, c.1915, 33 x 17 In.		180
Ingraham, 2 Glass Doors, Rosettes Between, Painted Tablet, Brass Movement, 1800s, 22 x 13 In.		156
Ingraham, E., Shelf, Wood, Roman Numerals, Late 1800s, 17 x 10¾ x 4½ In.		200
Ingraham, Regulator, Oak, Reverse Painted Glass Door, Brass Pendulum, 38 x 16 In.	*illus*	124
Ingraham, Shelf, Wood, Carved, Gilt On Glass, Roman Numerals, 24 x 15 In.		148
Ithaca, Wall, Calendar, 2 Dials, Paper Over Wood, Glass, Brass, c.1900, 29 x 15 In.		313
Ithaca, Wall, Calendar, Walnut, Painted Tin Faces, Brass Movement, c.1870, 28 In.		360
J. Ellicott, Bracket, George II, Ebony Veneer, Brass Feet, c.1750, 15⅝ In.		6300
Jennings Brothers, Shelf, Winged Cherub Standing, Gilt, Art Nouveau, c.1910, 8 In.		168
Jerome & Co., Wall, Rosewood, Inlaid, 8-Day, Roman Numerals, 29 In.		154
Junghans, Bracket, Mahogany, Brass Dial, Arabic Numerals, Germany, 17 x 12 In.	*illus*	132
Junghans, Bracket, Walnut, Arched Pediment, Laurel Frieze, Brass Dial, 18 x 12 In.		283

Clock, Ingraham, Regulator, Oak, Reverse Painted Glass Door, Brass Pendulum, 38 x 16 In.
$124

Clock, Junghans, Bracket, Mahogany, Brass Dial, Arabic Numerals, Germany, 17 x 12 In.
$132

Clock, LeCoultre, Atmos, Brass & Glass Case, Swiss, 1900s, 9¼ x 8 In.
$744

Clock, LeCoultre, Atmos, Perpetual, Gilt Brass, Glass, Pendulum, 9¼ x 8 In.
$424

TIP
Never use WD40 on the gears or to oil an antique clock. When it is used on brass, it changes and acts like a varnish, gumming up the works.

Clock, LeCoultre, Jaeger, Shelf, Skeleton, Lucite, Gilt Brass, 8-Day, c.1958, 8 x 7 x In.
$550

Clock, Liberty & Co., Shelf, Pewter, Enamel, Stamped, Tudric, c.1910, 6 x 9 In.
$1,750

Clock, Louis Philippe, Shelf, Gilt Bronze, Porcelain, Silk Thread Movement, c.1835, 16 x 8 In.
$500

Clock, National Time Recorder, Oak, Brass, Glass Face, Punch, Locks, 36 x 14 In.
$300

Clock, Pillar & Scroll, Mahogany, 3 Urn Finials, Reverse Painted Tablet, 1800s, 31 x 17 In.
$431

Clock, Seth Thomas, Wall, Mahogany, Molded Cornice, Brass Movement, Early 1900s, 38 x 20 In.
$300

Clock, Shelf, Acorn, Rosewood, Reverse Painted, Merchants Exchange, c.1850, 24 x 15 In.
$1,521

Jeffrey S. Evans & Associates

Clock, Shelf, Art Deco, Veneer, Curved Glass, 4 Chromed Ball Feet, 11 x 21 x 8 In.
$266

Burchard Galleries

Clock, Shelf, Art Nouveau, Bronze, Maiden's Head, Flowing Hair, C. Louchet, c.1900, 10 In.
$995

Jeffrey S. Evans & Associates

Clock, Shelf, Brass, Urn Finial, Animal Ring Handles, French Style, c.1900, 19 ½ In.
$375

Brunk Auctions

Clock, Shelf, Empire, Bronze, Gilt & Patinated, Figural, 1800s, 25 x 16 ⅜ In.
$1,500

Leslie Hindman Auctioneers

Clock, Shelf, Gilt Bronze, Arched Trellis, Maiden, Goat & Baby, France, 1800s, 18 In.
$1,353

Skinner, Inc.

Clock, Shelf, Gilt Bronze, Porcelain, Footed, Pine Finial, c.1875, 20 ½ x 10 In.
$2,250

Heritage Auctions

Clock, Shelf, Gilt Bronze, Winged Female, Footed, 1800s, 19 x 13 ½ In.
$1,016

Nadeau's Auction Gallery

Junghans, Wall, Glazed Ceramic, Plastic, White, Germany, c.1950, 10 x 7 ½ In.	187
Kienzle, Shelf, Mahogany, Arched Columns, Gilt, Germany, 18 ½ In.	113
Le Roy Et Fils, Regulator, Crystal, Rectangular, Bacchus Masks, c.1880, 14 x 8 ⅝ In.	938
LeCoultre, Atmos, Brass & Glass Case, Swiss, 1900s, 9 ¼ x 8 In. *illus*	744
LeCoultre, Atmos, Glass Cover, Bronze, Gilt, 8 ¾ x 6 ½ x 5 ¼ In.	281 to 300
LeCoultre, Atmos, Perpetual, Gilt Brass, Glass, Pendulum, 9 ¼ x 8 In. *illus*	424
LeCoultre, Jaeger, Shelf, Skeleton, Lucite, Gilt Brass, 8-Day, c.1958, 8 x 7 x In. *illus*	550
Lenzkirch, Bracket, Burr Walnut, Dome, Gilt Brass Mounts, 15 x 10 x 7 In.	1187
Liberty & Co., Shelf, Pewter, Enamel, Stamped, Tudric, c.1910, 6 x 9 In. *illus*	1750
Louis Philippe, Shelf, Cathedral, Gilt & Patinated Bronze, 1800s, 25 ¼ In.	2750
Louis Philippe, Shelf, Gilt Bronze, Porcelain, Silk Thread Movement, c.1835, 16 x 8 In. *illus*	500
Lyre, Burl, Gilt Bronze Garlands, Porcelain Dial, France, c.1900, 9 In.	246
Marti, French Art Deco, Marble, Copper Washed Columns, 8-Sided Dial, Pendulum, 22 x 16 In.	424
Mystery, Swinging Ball, Woman Holding Ball, France, 1800s, 34 ½ In.	1440
National Time Recorder, Oak, Brass, Glass Face, Punch, Locks, 36 x 14 In. *illus*	300
New Haven, Calendar, Oak, 2 Dials, Roman Numerals, 1891, 48 x 16 x 7 In.	622
New Haven, Cartel, Round, Chatelaine, Chain, Brass, Porcelain Numbers, c.1890, 9 x 14 In.	185
New Haven, Regulator, Eclipse, Octagonal, Long Drop, Paper On Tin Dial, c.1900, 33 x 18 In.	168
New Haven, Wall, 2 Winding Apertures, Roman Numerals, Pendulum, c.1889, 64 x 22 In.	226
Paillard, Victor, Shelf, Louis XV, Gilt & Patinated Bronze, c.1875, 25 x 31 In.	11250
Painting, Village Blacksmiths, Oil, Porcelain Dial In Tower, Musical, Tharin, Paris, 37 In.	8050
Pillar & Scroll, Mahogany Veneer, Federal House, Mark Lane, Conn., c.1825, 31 x 16 In.	813
Pillar & Scroll, Mahogany, 3 Urn Finials, Reverse Painted Tablet, 1800s, 31 x 17 In. *illus*	431
Pons, Shelf, Bronze, Sultan, Red Griotte Marble Base, Paris, c.1850, 24 x 18 In.	1375
Porcelain, Gilt Bronze, Enamel Dial, Roman Numerals, c.1800, 15 ¾ In.	1625
Porcelain, Gilt Metal, Urn Shape, Plaques, Enamel, Late 1800s, 19 ¼ In.	3500
Portico, Gilt Bronze, Corinthian Columns, Enamel Dial, 1800s, 18 In.	584
Portico, Rosewood, Gilt Brass Inlay, Footed, Roman Numerals, c.1890, 18 In.	197
Portico, Rosewood, Marquetry, Gilt Capitols, Silvered Dial, c.1800, 18 x 9 In.	240
Raingo Freres, Napoleon III, Pedestal, Marble, Gilt Bronze Scrolls, c.1890, 12 x 18 In.	1500
Regulator, Calendar, Double Dial, Gilt Brass, Beveled Glass, c.1890, 14 x 9 In.	1353
Regulator, Oak, White Painted Dial, Arabic Numerals, Pendulum, Key, 30 x 16 In.	165
Regulator, Round Dial, Painted Tablet, Brass Movement, 1900s, 32 ¼ x 18 In.	108
Regulator, Sessions, Reverse Painted Glass Panels, Calendar, c.1915, 36 x 17 In.	108
Regulator, Vienna, Arched Crest, Coved Molding, Porcelain Face, Brass Movement, 38 In.	225
Regulator, Vienna, Biedermeier, Walnut, Porcelain Dial, Dachluhr, 37 x 9 In.	3159
Regulator, Vienna, Carved Case, Gallery Top, Arched Glass Door, 1800s, 35 In.	100
Regulator, Vienna, Eastlake, Walnut, Brass Bezel, Enamel Face, 1900s, 88 x 28 In.	3120
Regulator, Vienna, Mahogany, Arched Crown, Turned Finials, Roman Numerals, 30 x 13 In.	165
Regulator, Vienna, Mahogany, Center Plinth, Finials, Roman Numerals, 40 x 14 In.	198
Regulator, Vienna, Mixed Wood, Brass, Enamel Face, Single Weight, Pendulum, c.1890, 44 x 14 In.	250
Regulator, Vienna, Oak, Broken Arch, Gooseneck Pediment, Brass Movement, c.1800s, 43 x 15 In.	192
Regulator, Vienna, Ornate Case, Half Pilasters, Porcelain Face, Late 1800s, 45 x 17 In.	406
Regulator, Vienna, Walnut Case With Door, Circular Dial, Roman Numerals	185
Regulator, Vienna, Walnut, Arched, Applied Carvings, Painted Face, c.1880, 48 x 17 In.	216
Regulator, Vienna, Walnut, Carved Crown, Turned Pilasters, c.1890, 36 x 16 In.	188
Regulator, Walnut, Arched Top, Turned Finials, Single Weight, Germany, 1800s, 46 x 15 In.	313
Regulator, Walnut, White Metal, Flower, Carved Leaves, 53 x 22 In.	354
Sawin, John, Shelf, Mahogany, Painted, 8-Day, Marked, 1812, 37 In.	2124
Seth Thomas, Clock & Barometer, Brass, Wood Base, Side By Side Mount, 14 x 7 In.	236
Seth Thomas, Maple Case, Hinged Front Door, 21 x 21 x 7 In.	90
Seth Thomas, Regulator, Gilt Brass, Beveled Glass, Porcelain Dial, 11 x 7 In.	170
Seth Thomas, Regulator, Mahogany, Roman Numeral, Late 1800s, 38 In.	1440
Seth Thomas, Regulator, Oak, Painted Dial, Arabic Numerals, Pendulum, 35 x 16 In.	550
Seth Thomas, Shelf, Reverse Painted Glass, Romantic Scene, Roman Numerals, 33 In.	129
Seth Thomas, Shelf, Rosewood, Burl Pilasters, Gilt, Eglomise Panel, Bun Feet, 1800s	106
Seth Thomas, Shelf, Slate, Black, Marble Inlay, 9 ½ x 11 x 6 In.	98
Seth Thomas, Shelf, Wood, Stepped Base, Brass Finial, Pendulum, Key, 12 In.	80

Clock, Shelf, Louis XV Style, Metal, Cherub Top, Tripod Base, Claw Feet, 14 x 7 In.
$305

Nadeau's Auction Gallery

Clock, Shelf, Pink Marble, Bronze, France, Late 1800s, 18 ½ In.
$180

Garth's Auctioneers & Appraisers

Clock, Tall Case, George III, Mahogany, Moon Phase, Brass Face, Plinth Base, c.1800, 92 In.
$1,000

Leslie Hindman Auctioneers

Clock, Tall Case, Herschede, Burl, 3-Weight, 9 Chimes, 1900s, 86 x 24 x 14 In. $2,375

Brunk Auctions

Clock, Tiffany & Co., Shelf, Art Deco, Red Marble, Flowers, Brass Face, 1900s, 6 x 9 In. $1,560

Cowan's Auctions

Clock, United Clock Corp., Joe Louis, Boxing Ring Ropes, Metal, c.1938, 12 x 9 In. $227

Hake's Auctions

Seth Thomas, Ship's, Brass, Round, Gold, Rectangular Base, Ball Feet, 10 ¼ In.	226
Seth Thomas, Wall, Mahogany, Molded Cornice, Brass Movement, Early 1900s, 38 x 20 In.. *illus*	300
Shelf, Acorn, Rosewood, Reverse Painted, Merchants Exchange, c.1850, 24 x 15 In. *illus*	1521
Shelf, Allegorical, Geo. Washington, Bronze Dore, Enamel Dial, Paris, c.1820, 13 x 9 In.	16250
Shelf, Art Deco, Veneer, Curved Glass, 4 Chromed Ball Feet, 11 x 21 x 8 In. *illus*	266
Shelf, Art Nouveau Figure, Gilt, Green Onyx, Porcelain Dial, France, 23 x 13 In.	556
Shelf, Art Nouveau, Bronze, Maiden's Head, Flowing Hair, C. Louchet, c.1900, 10 In. *illus*	995
Shelf, Baby Buddhas, Gilt Bronze, Molded, Scrollwork, Rocaille, c.1875, 10 x 6 In.	1187
Shelf, Beehive, Mahogany Veneer, Birds, Orientalist, Key, Pendulum, Victorian, 17 x 11 In.	112
Shelf, Black Marble, Spelter, Lion's Heads, Disc Feet, Gaitier Fils, Paris, c.1870, 22 x 15 In.	523
Shelf, Brass, Round, Time & Strike Movement, Arabic Numerals, 9 x 10 ½ In.	187
Shelf, Brass, Urn Finial, Animal Ring Handles, French Style, c.1900, 19 ½ In. *illus*	375
Shelf, Bronze, Rectangular, Female Figure, Glass Dome, 1800s, 15 x 13 x 5 In.	11250
Shelf, Bronze, Scrolling Flowers & Leaves, 4-Footed Base, 22 ½ x 16 ¾ In.	531
Shelf, Calendar, Arched Cornice, Finials, Brass Movement, 1800s, 32 x 17 In.	510
Shelf, Carved Leaves & Flowers, Urn Finial, Ram's Head Handles, c.1780, 36 x 18 In.	2750
Shelf, Cathedral, Rosewood, Ripple Front, Etched Glass, c.1860, 19 x 10 x 4 In.	300
Shelf, Charles X, Asian Woman, Scepter, Gilt Bronze, Rococo Base, 1800s, 16 In.	1250
Shelf, Cherub, Floral Swags, Bronze Mount, Birds & Nest Finial, 16 ½ In.	923
Shelf, Cupid, Bow & Arrows, Urn, Bronze, Rectangular Base, c.1890, 15 x 11 In.	540
Shelf, Ducasse Claveau & Co., Demeter, Gilt Metal, Marble Base, France, 1800s, 12 x 17 In.	375
Shelf, Earthenware, Gilt & Enamel, Cobalt Blue Ground, c.1900, 13 ½ In.	172
Shelf, Empire, Bronze, Gilt & Patinated, Figural, 1800s, 25 x 16 ⅜ In. *illus*	1500
Shelf, Empire, Ebonized Wood, Gilt Bronze Mount, Pendulum, Glass Dome, 24 In.	600
Shelf, Empire, Gilt & Patinated Bronze, Marble, Late 1800s, 27 x 16 x 6 In.	2125
Shelf, Fisherman, Throwing Life Preserver, Rocky Base, Patinated Metal, 27 In.	540
Shelf, French Empire, Cupid & Psyche, Bronze Dore, c.1815, 20 x 14 In.	2750
Shelf, George III, Mahogany, Inlaid, 4 Columns, c.1900s, 17 x 13 x 8 In.	250
Shelf, Gilt Brass, Birds, Flowers, Porcelain Dial, Roman Numerals, 15 x 8 In.	2420
Shelf, Gilt Bronze, Arched Trellis, Maiden, Goat & Baby, France, 1800s, 18 In. *illus*	1353
Shelf, Gilt Bronze, Architectural Case, Flowers, Leaves, Cherub Handles, c.1890, 27 In.	2583
Shelf, Gilt Bronze, Blue Enamel, Floral Swags, Urn Finial, Blue, France, 1800s, 13 x 11 In.	625
Shelf, Gilt Bronze, Male & Female Winged Figures, Lyre, Bun Feet, 1800s, 18 In.	2750
Shelf, Gilt Bronze, Muse Of Music, Plucking Lyre, Swans, Roses, France, c.1815, 21 x 13 In.	3000
Shelf, Gilt Bronze, Porcelain, Footed, Pine Finial, c.1875, 20 ½ x 10 In. *illus*	2250
Shelf, Gilt Bronze, Temple, Champleve, Round Dial, Roman Numerals, c.1885, 26 In.	3000
Shelf, Gilt Bronze, Winged Female, Footed, 1800s, 19 x 13 ½ In. *illus*	1016
Shelf, Gilt Bronze, Woman, Middle Eastern Costume, Feather Fan, c.1850, 19 x 16 In.	1000
Shelf, Gothic Revival, Iron Frame, Ogee Crest, Painted, Brass Pendulum, Late 1800s, 20 In.	192
Shelf, Lantern, Brass, Pierced Leaves, Dolphin Frets, England, Early 1900s, 11 x 5 In.	154
Shelf, Louis XV Style, Metal, Cherub Top, Tripod Base, Claw Feet, 14 x 7 In. *illus*	305
Shelf, Mahogany, Maple, Metal Dial, French Feet, 8-Day, c.1810, 43 In.	2655
Shelf, Marble, Gilt Bronze, Footed, France, 9 ½ x 6 ½ x 13 In.	71
Shelf, Marble, Gilt Metal Mounts, Caryatid Supports, France, Late 1800s, 16 x 15 x 6 In.	210
Shelf, Napoleon III, Crouching Venus, Marble, Bronze, Fluted Case, 18 x 9 In.	875
Shelf, Napoleon III, Gilt & Patinated Bronze, Late 1800s, 18 x 22 ½ In.	2125
Shelf, Neoclassical Style, Cavalier, Gilt Bronze, c.1885, 16 In.	221
Shelf, Neoclassical, Grotesque Mask, Shells, Leafy Feet, Roman Numerals, c.1900, 24 In.	938
Shelf, Neoclassical, Urania, Gilt & Patinated Bronze, Marble, c.1830, 18 x 12 In.	1125
Shelf, Pink Marble, Bronze, France, Late 1800s, 18 ½ In. *illus*	180
Shelf, Porcelain, Flowers, Ormolu Mounts, Lenzkirch Works, 20 In.	150
Shelf, Porcelain, Gilt Bronze Mount, Multicolor Enamel, 1800s, 21 In.	3690
Shelf, Rosewood, Filigree Hands, Roman Numerals, 8-Day, 19 x 11 In.	480
Shelf, Sevres Style, Porcelain, Gilt Bronze, Cabochon Mounted, c.1900, 17 x 12 In.	2250
Shelf, Spherical, Cherubs, Marble Base, 1960, 28 x 16 In.	1089
Shelf, Woman Reading Book, Acanthus, Gilt, Honore, Paris, 1827, 18 x 15 In.	2117
Shelf, Wood, Carved, 3 Finials, Roman Numerals, Painted, 10 ¼ In.	1063
Shelf, Wood, Metal Face, Beveled Glass, Brass Numbers, Chimes, Westminster, Trinity, 12 In.	81
Silas Hoadley, Wood Face, Painted, Flowers On Fence, White, Gilt, Conn., 1800s, 16 In.	400

Skeleton, Regulator, Crystal, 3-Quarter, Gilt, Glass, 7¾ x 5 x 5 In.	303
Swinging Arm, Diana The Huntress, Bronze, Patina, France, 1800s, 25 In.	2006
Swinging Arm, Elephant, Arm On Trunk, Spelter, Germany, 1900s, 17 In.	271
Swinging Arm, Youth Holding Lyre, Supports Clock, Spelter, France, c.1900, 20 In.	260
Tall Case, Abraham Edwards, Pine, Pierced Fret Hood, 30-Day, 88 In.	369
Tall Case, Art Deco, Oak, Ebonized, Brass, Arabic Numerals, Germany, Early 1900s, 82 In.	189
Tall Case, Bigelow & Kinard, Scroll Crest, Inlaid Medallions, Pierced Brass, Finials, 96 In.	2200
Tall Case, Burl Wood, Dome Top, Chimes, 51 In.	115
Tall Case, Cherry, Brass, Arched Tombstone Door, 8-Day, c.1810, 84 x 17 x 10 In.	351
Tall Case, Cherry, Wood Dial, Flowers, Roman Numerals, c.1830, 85 In.	380
Tall Case, Chippendale, Flame Birch, Roman Numerals, Painted, c.1800, 89 In.	1000
Tall Case, Chippendale, Mahogany, Engraved Brass & Silver Dial, 8-Day, Late 1800s, 102 In.	3125
Tall Case, Chippendale, Mahogany, Roman Numerals, 8-Day, Brass Finials, 87 In.	2500
Tall Case, Christian Eby, Mahogany, Flat Bonnet, Brass Works, Early 1800s, 75 In.	1440
Tall Case, Colonial Mfg. Co., Mahogany, Arched Top, Beveled Glass, 92 In.	1210
Tall Case, Colonial Mfg. Co., Mahogany, Moon Phase, 3-Weight, 9 Chimes, c.1800, 96 x 26 In.	1800
Tall Case, Colonial, Flowers, Romantic Scene, German Movement, 71 In.	105
Tall Case, Edwardian, Mahogany, Rosettes, 5 Spring Gongs, c.1900, 91 x 21 In.	1250
Tall Case, Federal, Cherry, 2 Sections, String Inlay, c.1825, 97 In.	1188
Tall Case, Federal, Pine, Flat Bonnet, Painted, Roman Numerals, 30-Hour, 1756, 87 In.	5250
Tall Case, Federal, Pine, Painted, Early 1800s, 93½ In.	363
Tall Case, George III Style, Lacquer, Chinoiserie Scenes, Brass Dial, 1900s, 91 In.	594
Tall Case, George III, Mahogany, Moon Phase, Brass Face, Plinth Base, c.1800, 92 In. *illus*	1000
Tall Case, Georgian Style, Moon Face, Painted Dial, Mid 1800s, 94 x 23 x 11 In.	1573
Tall Case, Gustav Becker, Oak, Carved Latticework Crest, Molded Crown, 90 In.	311
Tall Case, Hand-Painted Face, Bird Finial, Roman Numerals, 103 x 18 x 12 In.	161
Tall Case, Hennegen Bates Co., Moon Phase, 3-Weight, 9 Chimes, c.1890, 102 x 25 In.	4200
Tall Case, Herschede, Burl, 3-Weight, 9 Chimes, 1900s, 86 x 24 x 14 In. *illus*	2375
Tall Case, Herschede, Mahogany, Seated Putti, Moon Phase, Brass Dial, Chime, 98 x 29 In.	6000
Tall Case, J. Caperison, K.M. Marnock, Pine, Painted Face, Signed, 81 x 19 In.	456
Tall Case, J. Sands, Walnut, Turned Finials, Carved Rosettes, Ogee Feet, c.1790, 98 In.	6490
Tall Case, J.E. Caldwell & Co., Oak, Early 1900s, 87 In.	588
Tall Case, James Blacklock, Painted Pendulum, Brass Face Marked RB 1800, Lockerbie, 1800	325
Tall Case, John Andrews, Burl, Fretwork, Barley Twist Hood, London, 96 In.	1080
Tall Case, John Fessler, Cherry, Brass, Arched Tombstone Glass Door, c.1850, 109 In.	2900
Tall Case, John Hocken, Pine, Arched Bonnet, Iron Dial, 18-Hour, 1800s, 73 x 19 In.	360
Tall Case, John Warner, Oak, Weights, Pendulum, Roman Numerals, 81 In.	295
Tall Case, L. Furtwangler & Son, Mahogany, Engraved Gilt & Silver Plated Face, 1910, 92 In.	738
Tall Case, Lassel Park, Inlaid Case, Arch, Serve Thy God As I Serve Thee, c.1900, 95 In.	545
Tall Case, Lenzkirch, Baroque, Oak, Coil Spring Gong, Music, Symphonion, c.1880, 87 x 15 In.	8438
Tall Case, Louis XV, Oak, Carved, Pressed Brass Face, Enamel Dial, Early 1800s, 96 In.	313
Tall Case, Mahogany Veneer, Mixed Wood, Carved Urn, Cornucopia, Glass, c.1900, 95 x 26 In.	2706
Tall Case, Mahogany, Arched Bonnet, Brass & Silver Moon Dial, c.1700, 90 x 19 In.	1440
Tall Case, Mahogany, Arched Top, Flowers, Enamel Dial, Roman Numerals, Germany, 80 In.	385
Tall Case, Mahogany, Cherry, Turned Finials, Moon Face, Turned Feet, c.1899, 104 x 21 In.	5100
Tall Case, Mahogany, Paneled, Brass, Silvered Dial, 9 Tubes, c.1905, 104 x 28 In.	4688
Tall Case, Mahogany, Scroll Pediment, Painted Dial, Fluted Pilasters, c.1900, 90 x 21 In.	625
Tall Case, Mahogany, Scrolled Crest, Painted, Flared French Feet, c.1810, 93 In.	923
Tall Case, Mahogany, Swan's Neck, Moon Dial, Fluted Columns, Brass Capitals, c.1780, 92 In.	1875
Tall Case, Oak, Arched Top, Brass Face, Germany, c.1925, 77 x 21 x 12 In.	204
Tall Case, Oak, Floral Spandrels, Metal Rosettes, Bracket Feet, England, 81 In.	510
Tall Case, Oak, Halifax Coat Of Arms, Moon Phase, Finials, Roman & Arabic, c.1800, 85 In.	351
Tall Case, Open Well, Mask, 2-Weight, c.1880, 93 x 24 In.	1512
Tall Case, P. Abbot, George III, Mahogany, Molded Cornice, Brass Dial, London, 95 In.	1875
Tall Case, Painted Arch, Farmers, Horses, Roman Numerals, England, c.1815, 78 In.	468
Tall Case, Pine, Grain Painted, Diagonal Banding, Slat Top, Cove Molding, c.1830, 94 In.	715
Tall Case, R. J. Horner, Chiming, 9 Tubes, Stamped Harris & Harrington, c.1900, 8 x 6 In.	3600
Tall Case, R. Lear Pinhey, Figured Maple, Bracket Feet, England, c.1810, 97 x 18 In.	944
Tall Case, Riley Whiting, Pine, Grain Painted, Tombstone Door, Conn., c.1820, 89 In.	984

Clock, Wall, Mahogany, Round Glass Face, Roman Numerals, Pendulum, 11½ In.

$98

Skinner, Inc.

Clock, Waterbury, Ormolu, Gilt, 3 Cherubs, Flowers, Wave Crest Panel, Pendulum, 14 x 7 In.

$480

Woody Auction

Clock, Welch, E.N., Shelf, Empire Style, Mahogany, Roman Numerals, 25 x 14 In.

$113

Pook & Pook

Clock, Welton, H., Shelf, Column,
Figured Mahogany, Pendulum,
19 x 28 In.
$468

Forsythes' Auctions

TIP
*To set a clock, hold
the minute hand in
the center, turn it
clockwise, wait for
each strike.*

Cloisonne, Bowl, Scrolled Legs, Qilin,
Hooved Creature, Keyfret Border,
Chinese, Late 1800s, 5 x 13 In.
$480

Thomaston Place Auction Galleries

Cloisonne, Bowl, Stem, 3 Foo Dogs,
Lotus Flowerheads, Scrolling Leaves,
1900s, 7¾ In.
$277

Skinner, Inc.

Tall Case, Sheraton, Tiger Maple, 8-Day, Roman Numerals, Penn., c.1820, 101 In.	500
Tall Case, Silas Hoadley, Grain Painted, White Wood Arched Dial, Flowers, 1800s, 82 In.	2091
Tall Case, Silas Hoadley, Mahogany Grain, Tombstone Hood, Scrolled Crest, c.1820, 89 In.	738
Tall Case, Stephen Taber, Mahogany, Pierced Fret, Brass Finials, Ogee Feet, c.1790, 93 In.	8708
Tall Case, Thomas Kefford, Blinking Eye, Roman & Arabic Numerals, 86 In.	585
Tall Case, Thomas Perkins, Hepplewhite, Moon Phase Dial, c.1815, 100 In.	3600
Tall Case, Victorian Style, Mahogany, Carved, Glazed Door, Black, 89 In.	246
Tall Case, W. Wilks, George II, Yew, Brass Face, Inscribed, England, 1700s, 75 In.	225
Tall Case, Walnut, Scrolled Panels, 2 Bells On Top, Italy, 1700s, 117 x 21 In.	2250
Terry, Eli, Mahogany, Lion, Unicorn, Coat Of Arms Crest, Reverse Painted Glass, 42 In.	5310
Terry, Eli, Pillar & Scroll, Mahogany Veneer, Glass Panel, Federal House, c.1825, 31 x 16 In.	600

Tiffany clocks that are part of desk sets made by Louis Comfort Tiffany are listed in the Tiffany category.
Clocks sold by the store Tiffany & Co. are listed here.

Tiffany & Co., Shelf, Art Deco, Red Marble, Flowers, Brass Face, 1900s, 6 x 9 In. .... *illus*	1560
Tiffany & Co., Shelf, Brass, Beveled Glass, Porcelain Face, France, 10 x 6 In.	127
Tower, Bronze, Gilt & Patinated, Columns, Roman Numerals, 1800s, 16 In.	1188
United Clock Corp., Joe Louis, Boxing Ring Ropes, Metal, c.1938, 12 x 9 In. .... *illus*	227
Wall, Art Deco, Walnut, Glass Door, Brass Dial, Arabic Numerals, 33 x 13 In.	220
Wall, Arts & Crafts, Oak, Balloon Shape, Scroll Cut Drop, Old Varnish, c.1910, 31 x 14 In.	468
Wall, German, Oak, Arched, Stylized Buds, Silvered Dial, Pendulum, Chimes, c.1920, 23 x 13 In.	121
Wall, Mahogany Veneer, Rosewood, Painted Face, Pendulum, Late 1800s, 22 In.	156
Wall, Mahogany, Round Glass Face, Roman Numerals, Pendulum, 11½ In. .... *illus*	98
Wall, Marquetry, 8-Day, Roman Numerals, Anglo-American, 1800s, 34 x 17 In.	180
Wall, Napoleon III, Boulle, Walnut, Hexagonal, Late 1800s, 27 x 26 In.	125
Wall, Oak, Painted, Moon Phase Dial, Roman Numerals, Dutch, 1700s, 60 In.	500
Wall, Rococo Style, Gilt Metal Case, Roman Numerals, France, Early 1800s, 20 x 11 In.	189
Wall, Rosewood Veneer, Figure 8 Shape, Painted Face, Paper Label, Late 1800s, 22 In.	156
Wall, Wood, Metal, Sawtooth, Swinging Pendulum, Signed, Anno 1750, 26 x 5 In.	275
Warmink, John, Shelf, Wood, Brass, Moon Phases, Glass Door, Holland, 9 x 8 In.	259
Waterbury, Calendar, Walnut, Carved, Door, 2 Dials, Roman Numerals, 25 x 14 In.	523
Waterbury, Ormolu, Gilt, 3 Cherubs, Flowers, Wave Crest Panel, Pendulum, 14 x 7 In. ...... *illus*	480
Waterbury, Regulator, 2 Reverse Painted Glass Panels, Pendulum, Key, c.1915, 37 x 16 In.	125
Waterbury, Regulator, Calendar, Round Dial, Paper Face, Brass Movement, c.1915, 33 In.	84
Waterbury, Shelf, Mahogany, Brass Bull's-Eye, Victorian, Late 1800s, 27 In.	156
Waterbury, Shelf, Walnut, Carved Crest, Reeded Door, Paper On Tin Dial, Tablet, 23 x 15 In.	248
Welch, E.N., Shelf, Empire Style, Mahogany, Roman Numerals, 25 x 14 In. .... *illus*	113
Welch, Rosewood, Arched Top, Elaborate Turnings, Finials, Tin Dial, Pendulum, 18 x 12 In.	660
Weldon, Oliver, Ogee, Bird's-Eye Maple Case, 25 x 15 In.	236
Welton, H., Shelf, Column, Figured Mahogany, Pendulum, 19 x 28 In. .... *illus*	468

CLOISONNE enamel was developed during the tenth century. A glass enamel was applied
between small ribbons of metal on a metal base. Most cloisonne is Chinese or Japanese.
Pieces marked *China* were made after 1900.

Bead, Ojime, Ball Form, Dragon, Blue Ground, Japan, Late 1800s, ¾ In.	50
Bowl, Red, Blue & White Enamel Leaves, Khlebnikov, Russia, 1884, 1½ x 3½ In.	625
Bowl, Scrolled Legs, Qilin, Hooved Creature, Keyfret Border, Chinese, Late 1800s, 5 x 13 In.*illus*	480
Bowl, Stem, 3 Foo Dogs, Lotus Flowerheads, Scrolling Leaves, 1900s, 7¾ In. .... *illus*	277
Box, Blue, Goldtone Peacock, Peonies & Cherry Blossoms, Signed, 2 x 6½ x 4 In.	424
Box, Tobacco, Hinged Lid, Oval, Gilt, Silver, K. Skvortsov, Moscow, c.1918, 3 In. .... *illus*	750
Censer, Faceted, Flowers, Leaves, Multicolor, Elephant Legs, 1900s, 16 x 21 In.	625
Charger, Crane, Flower On Verso, Mark, Japan, 1900s, 18 In.	545
Charger, Turquoise, Leaves Rim, Birds, Round, 11¾ In. .... *illus*	94
Charger, Wood Stand, Blue Back, Brass String, 20 In.	192
Cigarette Case, Arabesques, Blue Ground, Nikolai Zverev, Russia, 4 In. .... *illus*	4305
Cup, Lid, Ball Finial, Multicolor Scrolls & Flowers, Russia, 3¼ In.	2091
Dish, Medallion, Imperial Eagles, Marked, Cyrillic S.B., Moscow, 4¼ In.	5843
Dish, Quatrefoil Vessel, Fish Scales, Embellishments, Chinese, 1800s, 6 x 9½ x 6 In.	938

Cloisonne, Box, Tobacco, Hinged Lid, Oval, Gilt, Silver, K. Skvortsov, Moscow, c.1918, 3 In. $750

Freeman's Auctioneers & Appraisers

Cloisonne, Charger, Turquoise, Leaves Rim, Birds, Round, 11¾ In. $94

Susanin's Auctioneers & Appraisers

> **TIP**
> *Some disciplined collectors have a rule: Add a new piece to the collection only if you can get rid of a less desirable old one. Most of us just keep adding.*

Cloisonne, Cigarette Case, Arabesques, Blue Ground, Nikolai Zverev, Russia, 4 In. $4,305

Skinner, Inc.

Cloisonne, Goblet, Underplate, Bell Shape, Ivan Lebedkin, 5⅜ x 3 x 5 In. $1,357

Aspire Auctions

Cloisonne, Lamp Base, Electric, Blue, Flower Lappets, Plants, Kyoto School, c.1900, 20 In. $240

Eldred's

Cloisonne, Plate, Song Birds & Peonies, Blue Field, Japan, 1800s, 12 In. $118

Leland Little Auctions

Cloisonne, Teapot, Black Ground, Flower Detail, Miniature, Chinese, 1800s, 3 In. $124

DuMouchelles

Cloisonne, Vase, Baluster Shape, Birds & Flowering Branches, Early 1900s, 44 In. $1,625

Leslie Hindman Auctioneers

Cloisonne, Vase, Birds, Flowering Branches, Carved Wood Stand, Chinese, 1900s, 36 In. $188

Neal Auction Company

Cloisonne, Vase, Bottle Shape, Long Neck, Lipped Mouth, Peach Branches, Early 1900s, 10 In.
$1,188

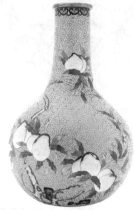

Leslie Hindman Auctioneers

Cloisonne, Vase, Masks, Face, Hooved Creature, Cobalt Blue Ground, Chinese, 18 x 8 In.
$540

Thomaston Place Auction Galleries

Figurine, Bodhisattva, Lotus Tendril, Seated, Chinese, 24 In.	1353
Figurine, Buddha, Sitting, Lotus Flower Base, 47 x 30 In.	1250
Figurine, Dragon Turtle, Coral Red, Turquoise Blue Bead, Gilt, 1900s, 2 5/8 x 6 In.	554
Figurine, Goddess, Blue Dress, Gold Skin, Bare Feet, 48 In.	1230
Figurine, Tara Buddha, Sword, Lotus Flower, Multicolor, Copper, 20 In.	960
Goblet, Underplate, Bell Shape, Ivan Lebedkin, 5 3/8 x 3 x 5 In. .... *illus*	1357
Incense Burner, Gilt, Lion Mask Handles, Lotus Vine, Blue Interior, c.1800	2125
Jar, Goldstone, Dark Green Background, Rooster, Butterfly, 3 1/4 x 3 1/2 In.	79
Jar, Teadust Glaze, Bisque Foot Ring, Recessed Base, Carved Floral Lid, Stand, 2 3/8 In.	2214
Jar, Turquoise, Flowers & Butterflies, Chinese, 13 1/4 In.	500
Jardiniere, Bat, Gourd, Plum, Chinese, 17 x 21 In.	750
Kovsh, Silver Gilt, Textured, Gold, Green, Turquoise, c.1915, 9 In.	10200
Lamp Base, 2-Light, Green, Twisted, Robert Kuo, 1900s, 63 In.	938
Lamp Base, Electric, Bird, Flowers, Tree Bark, Bronze Stand, 23 In.	121
Lamp Base, Electric, Blue, Flower Lappets, Plants, Kyoto School, c.1900, 20 In. .... *illus*	240
Lamp, Multicolor, Cobalt Blue Ball Shade, c.1900s, 9 1/4 x 5 3/8 x 3 3/8 In.	192
Plate, Song Birds & Peonies, Blue Field, Japan, 1800s, 12 In. .... *illus*	118
Sculpture, Horse Head, Blue, Green, Red, 13 In.	258
Snuff Bottle, Stopper, Silver Gilt, Marked, Pyotr Abrosimov, Russia, 3 1/8 x 2 5/8 In.	531
Teapot, Black Ground, Flower Detail, Miniature, Chinese, 1800s, 3 In. .... *illus*	124
Teapot, Dragon, Clouds, Flowers, Waves, Swing Handle, Red, Blue, 7 x 7 1/2 In.	195
Tray, Ape, Baby Ape, Flower, Blue To White Ground, Flowered Border, c.1880, 11 1/2 In.	7380
Tray, Cranes & Peonies, Aventurine Ground, Turquoise Rim, Rectangular, 7 x 8 In.	138
Tray, Rooster, Hen, Chick, Blue To White Ground, Flowered Border, 11 1/2 In.	5227
Urn, Miniature, Round Finial, 1 3/4 x 1 3/4 In.	24
Vase, Baluster Shape, Birds & Flowering Branches, Early 1900s, 44 In. .... *illus*	1625
Vase, Baluster Shape, Painted, Flowers & Leaves, Chinese, 1900s, 24 In.	50
Vase, Birds, Flowering Branches, Carved Wood Stand, Chinese, 1900s, 36 In. .... *illus*	188
Vase, Blue Ground, Flowers, Bird, Silver Rims, Marked, Inaba, Japan, 1900s, 3 x 3 x 7 In.	605
Vase, Bottle Shape, Long Neck, Lipped Mouth, Peach Branches, Early 1900s, 10 In. .... *illus*	1188
Vase, Butterfly & Flower Rondels, 6 Lobes, 6 In.	60
Vase, Chrysanthemums, Transparent Red Ground, Silver Rim, Waisted, Ando, 9 In.	750
Vase, Crane Neck, Floral Sprays, Palmette Scrolls, Ruyi, Tassels, Swirled Roundels, 15 In.	400
Vase, Dragon Decoration, Brick Red Ground, Inverted Pear Shape, 9 1/4 In.	480
Vase, Dragon, Phoenix, Goldstone Ground, Butterfly, Flowers, Japan, c.1950, 12 x 6 In.	156
Vase, Floor, Dark Blue, Flowers & Birds, 45 1/2 In.	188
Vase, Green, Goblet, Robert Kuo, 1900s, 20 In.	375
Vase, Lilies, Sky Blue Ground, Oval, 9 1/2 In., Pair	280
Vase, Masks, Face, Hooved Creature, Cobalt Blue Ground, Chinese, 18 x 8 In. .... *illus*	540
Vase, Oval, Flattened Shoulder, White Orchids, Pale Yellow Ground, Japan, 1900s, 12 In.	123
Vase, Rooster, Dragon, Red, White, Green, 6 In.	58
Vase, Yellow Body, Lotus Tendrils, Marked, Xuande, Chinese, 14 1/2 In.	338

CLOTHING of all types is listed in this category. Dresses, hats, shoes, underwear, and more are found here. Other textiles are to be found in the Coverlet, Movie, Quilt, Textile, and World War I and II categories.

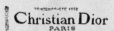

Christian Dior	Norman Norell	Arnold Scaasi
1947–present	1958–1972	1956–2015

Belt, Ammo Style, Woven Canvas, Brass Buckle, 1881	92
Belt, Reversible, Gold Buckle, Red, Brown Box Calf, Hermes, 33 x 1 1/4 In.	313
Belt, Silver, Rectangular Links, Ornate Scrollwork, Cherubs, 1900s, 24 x 1 1/4 In.	210
Blouse, Edwardian, Drawstring Waist, High Collar, Lace, Cotton Organdy, Bust 34	85
Bonnet, Silk, Forest Green, Ruffled, Ribbon, Bow, Neck Flounce, Linen Lining, c.1795, 15 In.	527

Cape, Black, Chantilly Lace, Ruffles, Beaded, Satin Ribbon Bows, c.1880, 19 In.	300
Cape, Evening, Quilted, Mother-Of-Pearl Clasp, 1940s, 29 ½ In.	110
Christening Gown, Ruffled Shoulders, Embroidered, Cotton, c.1890, 2-6 Months	350
Coat, Cotton Serge, Camel Color, Gold Leather, Thierry Mugler, c.1980	8041
Coat, Embroidered, Pointillist Flowers, Givenchy, Haute Couture, 1973	4093
Coat, Leather, Black Breitschwanz, Pierre Cardin, Fall-Winter, 1968	2339
Coat, Lynx, Jay Chester For Gus Mayer, Canada, Full Length, Size 4-6 .... *illus*	1200
Coat, Mink, Black, Satin Lining, 2 Exterior Pockets, 3 Hook & Eye Closures, Full Length	351
Coat, Mink, Dark Brown, Notched Collar, Straight Sleeves, Woman's, 14 x 47 In.	708
Coat, Mink, Lapel Collar, ¾ Length, Revillon, N.Y., 47 In.	369
Coat, Mink, Penn-Fifth Avenue, Woman's	75
Coat, Ranch Mink, Rounded Collar, Full Sleeves, Fully Lined, 38 x 20 In.	319
Coat, Shawl Collar, Embroidered Interior Flower, Canada, Full Length, Size 6-7	1200
Coat, Sheared Mink, Chinchilla, Birger Christensen	650
Coat, Wool, Beige, Pierre Cardin, Haute Couture, 1966-67	3509
Coat, Wool, Dark Gray & Blue, Yohji Yamamoto, c.1985	1754
Coat, Wool, Strawberry Red, Guipure, Romeo Gigli, Fall-Winter, 1990-91	4386
Coatdress, Cotton, Sculptural Sleeves, Blue, Thierry Mugler, Spring-Summer, c.1983	5848
Dress, Asymmetrical, Embroidered, Sequins, Tiger, Kansai Yamamoto, 1978-80 ...... *illus*	3216
Dress, Beaded & Embroidered Lace, Dark Blue Silk, Maison Spinner Couture, c.1918, 54 In.	199
Dress, Black Satin, Lace, Guipure Slip, Yves Saint Laurent, c.1970 .... *illus*	1316
Dress, Blue Beaded, Tiered Skirt, Angel Sleeves, Off-White Silk Bodice, c.1936, 48 In.	129
Dress, Boston Daily Globe Print, Conversation Dress, With Hat, Paper, c.1880s .... *illus*	4680
Dress, Chiffon, Pink Silk Crepe, Shawl Included, Split Butterfly Sleeves, Flapper, 64 x 45 In.	70
Dress, Cocktail, Silk Taffeta, Strapless, Red Dahlias, Black, Green, White Ground, c.1950, 50 In.	495
Dress, Cream, Gray Cashmere, Brushstroke, Cap Sleeves, Silhouette, Chanel, Size 36	531
Dress, Gabardine, Asymmetrical Collar, Train, Black, Red Satin Lining, Thierry Mugler, c.1988	1754
Dress, Gabardine, White & Black, Rhodoid Flowers, Christian Dior, 1969	7017
Dress, Georgette, Navy Blue, Silvery Tubes, Embroidery, Chloe By Karl Lagerfeld, 1973-74	3509
Dress, Gold Silk Taffeta Bodice, Embroidered Lace, Pleats, Edwardian, 43 In.	129
Dress, Golden Guipure, Christian Dior Colifichets, c.1955	2631
Dress, Hooded, Brown, Wool Jersey, Alaia, c.1986	1901
Dress, Ivory Crepe, Rebe Embroidery, Yves Saint Laurent, Haute Couture, c.1966	2631
Dress, Leather, Open Back, Black, Alaia, c.1985	2485
Dress, Muslin, Black, Gold Brocade, Suede Belt, Yves Saint Laurent, c.1976	2778
Dress, Orange Crepe, Circular Panels, Pierre Cardin, 1969-70 .... *illus*	1901
Dress, Organza, Black & Green Stripes, Ostrich Feathers, Christian Dior By Marc Bohan, c.1960	2631
Dress, Oroton, Sleeveless, Silver, Gianni Versace, Size 38	5250
Dress, Pink Silk, Smocked, Satin Rosette Bows, Silk Mesh Lace, Child's, c.1895, 31 In. ..... *illus*	70
Dress, Pioneer Style, Checkered Linen, Wool, Long Sleeves, Brown & Off-White, c.1870, 52 In.	380
Dress, Puffed Tulle Bodice, Taffeta Skirt, Black, Yves Saint Laurent, c.1987	2193
Dress, Rhinestones, Spaghetti Straps, Purple, Yellow, Gianni Versace, 1996, Size 42	813
Dress, Silk Brocade, Salmon, Gold, Green, Shallow Train, Sweetheart Ruched Off Shoulder	152
Dress, Silk Chiffon & Satin, Black, Butterfly Panels, Flowers, Scarf, c.1929, 54 In.	222
Dress, Silk Chiffon, Dark Brown & Black Satin, Metallic Geometric Beading, c.1920, 52 In.	129
Dress, Silk Crepe, Flapper Style, Rose Printed, 1920	115
Dress, Silk, Beige, Copper & Silver Sequins, Pearl Embroidery, Dior, Marc Bohan, c.1977	10234
Dress, Silk, Lace, Blue, Pink Satin Lined, Open Shoulder, Side Zipper, 1940s, 46 In. .... *illus*	129
Dress, Silk, Lime Green, Chiffon, Flowers, Ruffled Bodice, c.1935, 59 In.	497
Dress, Silk, Peach, Buttons Down Back, Satin Ribbon Belt, 1930s, Size 6	95
Dress, Silk, Pleated, White, Jersey Bustier, Gres, Haute Couture, c.1962	4386
Dress, Silk, Red, Royal Blue, Purple, Kelly & Lime Green Flowers, Bonwit Teller, c.1950, 57 In.	351
Dress, Silver Lurex, Hooded, Winged Tunic, Matching Pants, Thierry Mugler, 1979	2631
Dress, Sleeve, Black, Round Neckline, Epaulettes At Shoulder, Celine, Size 38	125
Dress, Sleeveless, Silk, Scoop Neckline, A-Line Silhouette, Spaghetti Straps, Hermes	281
Dress, Summer, Satin, Butterfly Sleeves, Flowers, Velvet Sash, Gored Skirt, c.1939, 52 In.	585
Dress, Taffeta, Asymmetrical Pleated Skirt, Blue, Black & White Underskirt, Gres, c.1975	5848
Dress, Tulle, Black, Layered Tunic Effect, Jean Patou, Couture, c.1930	1754
Dress, Tunic, Orange, Embroidered, Iridescent Sequins, Comme Des Garcons, 1999-2000	2339
Dress, Velvet, Burgundy, Beadwork, Belt, 2 Rhinestone Clips, Hallmarks, c.1930s	103

Clothing, Coat, Lynx, Jay Chester For Gus Mayer, Canada, Full Length, Size 4-6
$1,200

Brunk Auctions

Clothing, Dress, Asymmetrical, Embroidered, Sequins, Tiger, Kansai Yamamoto, 1978-80
$3,216

Sotheby's

Clothing, Dress, Black Satin, Lace, Guipure Slip, Yves Saint Laurent, c.1970
$1,316

Sotheby's

Clothing, Dress, Boston Daily Globe Print, Conversation Dress, With Hat, Paper, c.1880s
$4,680

Cowan's Auctions

Clothing, Dress, Orange Crepe, Circular Panels, Pierre Cardin, 1969-70
$1,901

Sotheby's

Clothing, Dress, Pink Silk, Smocked, Satin Rosette Bows, Silk Mesh Lace, Child's, c.1895, 31 In.
$70

Jeffrey S. Evans & Associates

Clothing, Dress, Silk, Lace, Blue, Pink Satin Lined, Open Shoulder, Side Zipper, 1940s, 46 In.
$129

Jeffrey S. Evans & Associates

Clothing, Jacket, Cotton, Brown, Padded Shoulders, Pockets, Fitted, Martin Margiela, 1989
$5,555

Sotheby's

Clothing, Jacket, Leather, Gold, Belt, Yves Saint Laurent, c.1980
$702

Sotheby's

Clothing, Jacket, Medusa Print, Baroque, Chest Pockets, Cotton, Gianni Versace, 1992
$875

Leslie Hindman Auctioneers

Zippers Tell
Vintage clothing clues: If an item has a metal zipper, it dates from before 1970. A side zipper on a dress was used in the 1940s or '50s. No zipper usually means before the 1940s.

Clothing, Robe, Silk, Dragons, Birds, Clouds, Wave Border, Striped Sleeves, Chinese, c.1950, 54 In.
$2,500

Brunk Auctions

Clothing, Robe, Winter, Silk, Satin Stitch, 8 Dragon Medallions, Chinese, 1800s, 56 In.
$4,500

Leslie Hindman Auctioneers

Clothing, Scarf, Hermes, A La Gloire Des Bataillon De Chasseurs, Frame, 1900s, 38 x 38 In.
$120

Eldred's

Clothing, Scarf, Silk, Baroque, Bird, Green & Yellow, Gianni Versace, 1990s, 35 x 35 In.
$175

Leslie Hindman Auctioneers

Clothing, Scarf, Silk, Christophe Colomb Decouvre L'Amerique, Sailing Ship, Hermes, 36 x 36 In.
$213

Leslie Hindman Auctioneers

Clothing, Scarf, Silk, Rocaille, Shell, Sailor's Valentine, Hermes, Frame, 1900s, 38 x 37 In.
$780

Eldred's

Clothing, Shoes, Stilettos, Kingfisher Feathers, Louis XV Heels, Christian Dior, Delman, c.1953-55
$3,947

Sotheby's

Clothing, Skirt, Leather, Khaki, Side Openings, 3 Metal Ring Closures, Alaia, 1983-84
$2,631

Sotheby's

Clothing, Vest, Blue Fur, Crop, Cap Sleeves, Navy Silk, Gucci, Size 42
$531

Leslie Hindman Auctioneers

Coca-Cola, Bottle, Seltzer, Emerald Green Glass, Acid Etch, Coca-Cola Bottling Co., 12½ In.
$311

Rich Penn Auctions

Dress, Velvet, Satin Neckline, Black, Flowers, Thierry Mugler, 1987-88	5555
Dress, Velvet, Taffeta, Faille Harlequin Patchwork, Belt, Yves Saint Laurent, Riv Gauche, c.1987	2631
Gown, Gold Lurex Knit, Feather Cuffs, Belted Waist, Bill Blass, 1970s, 16¾ In.	300
Hat, Cap, Wool, Yellow Gold, Feather Trim, Rolled Brim, New York, 1940s, 22½ In.	22
Hat, Red & Brown, Cone Shape, Chinese, 8 x 16 In.	35
Hat, Seamed, Velvet, Black, Twist Bow Front, 1930s, 10 In.	135
Jacket, ¾ Length, V Neckline, Pleated Sleeves, Snap Closure, Valentino, Size 40	469
Jacket, Black Mink, Shawl Collar, ¾ Length, Adolfo International, Size 6-8	480
Jacket, Cotton, Brown, Padded Shoulders, Pockets, Fitted, Martin Margiela, 1989 .... *illus*	5555
Jacket, Cropped, Leather, Black, Goldtone Button, Gianni Versace, 1990s	2000
Jacket, Dyed Rabbit Hair, Vibrant Lime Green Color, Fitted, 21½ x 22 In.	89
Jacket, Fur Lined, Cream Wool, Button, Collar, c.1960, 40 In.	142
Jacket, Leather, Gold, Belt, Yves Saint Laurent, c.1980 .... *illus*	702
Jacket, Leather, Light Brown, Polo Ralph Lauren, Man's, Size Large	50
Jacket, Leather, Slash Pockets, Black, Satin Lining, Ivan Grundahl, 38 In.	132
Jacket, Medusa Print, Baroque, Chest Pockets, Cotton, Gianni Versace, 1992 .... *illus*	875
Jacket, Mink, Shawl Collar, Chocolate Brown, Black Satin, Uhlemann Furs, 24 x 22 In.	132
Jacket, Mink, Shawl Collar, Dark Brown, Embroidered, Monogram, Paris, Size 4, 26 In.	1080
Jacket, Ninghai Silk, Matching Pants, Christian Dior By Marc Bohan, 1969	1901
Jacket, Tuxedo, Black, Shawl Collar, Crop Front, Embellished Buttons, Chanel, Size 42	531
Jacket, Wool Boucle, Black, Fur Lined, Ivory Panne Shearling, Chanel, CC, Size 38	2000
Jumper, Ecru Wool, Flannel Asymmetrical, Comme Des Garcons, Tricot, c.1982	5848
Minidress, Cotton, Orange & Red, Woven, Geometrical Pattern, Emanuel Ungaro, c.1966	1901
Minidress, Wool Gabardine, White, Yellow Scalloped Collar, Courreges, 1968	2924
Minidress, Wool, Black, Circular Braided Detail, Pierre Cardin, Haute Couture, 1967	2339
Pullover, Mohair, ¾ Length Sleeves, Green & Brown, Issey Miyake, c.1987	1901
Robe, Embroidered, Butterfly & Flowers, Blue Silk, Chinese, Early 1900s, 55 In.	5500
Robe, Patchwork, Multicolor, Sonia Delaunay, c.1925	1875
Robe, Red Ground, Summer Gauze, Dragon, Flaming Pearl, Chinese, 56½ In.	6875
Robe, Silk, Dragons, Birds, Clouds, Wave Border, Striped Sleeves, Chinese, c.1950, 54 In. . *illus*	2500
Robe, Winter, Silk, Satin Stitch, 8 Dragon Medallions, Chinese, 1800s, 56 In. .... *illus*	4500
Scarf, Hermes, A La Gloire Des Bataillon De Chasseurs, Frame, 1900s, 38 x 38 In. .... *illus*	120
Scarf, Silk, Aux Pays Des Epices, Land Of Spices, A. Faivre, Hermes, 36 x 36 In.	238
Scarf, Silk, Baroque, Bird, Green & Yellow, Gianni Versace, 1990s, 35 x 35 In. .... *illus*	175
Scarf, Silk, Christophe Colomb Decouvre L'Amerique, Sailing Ship, Hermes, 36 x 36 In. .. *illus*	213
Scarf, Silk, Jacquard, Horse, Circles, Multicolor, Black, Michel-Duchene, Hermes, 1987, 35 x 35 In.	375
Scarf, Silk, Les Pivoines, Peonies, Christiane Vauzelles, Hermes, 36 x 36 In.	113
Scarf, Silk, Mosaique Au 24, Mosaic, Letter H, B.P. Emory, Hermes, 36 x 36 In.	281
Scarf, Silk, Opera, Balletto, Teatro Cinema, Faces, Versace, 1991, 34 x 34 In.	163
Scarf, Silk, Rocaille, Shell, Sailor's Valentine, Hermes, Frame, 1900s, 38 x 37 In. .... *illus*	780
Scarf, Silk, Tropiques, Tropics, Birds, Zebras, L. Bourthoumieux, Hermes, 36 x 36 In.	200
Shoes, Stilettos, Kingfisher Feathers, Louis XV Heels, Christian Dior, Delman, c.1953-55 .. *illus*	3947
Skirt, Black, Silk, 5 Layers, Sheer Tulle Overlay, Escada, Size 38	63
Skirt, Leather, Khaki, Side Openings, 3 Metal Ring Closures, Alaia, 1983-84 .... *illus*	2631
Swimsuit, Wool, Modesty Tunic, Trunks, Ultramarine Blue, Rugby, N.Y., Man's, c.1918, Size Large	82
Tie, Silk, Red, Navy, Silk, Hermes, Box	154
Trench Coat, Black, Hermes, Man's, Size 50	90
Vest, Blue Fur, Crop, Cap Sleeves, Navy Silk, Gucci, Size 42 .... *illus*	531
Waistcoat, Gold Silk Brocade, Pomegranate, Mother-Of-Pearl Buttons, Man's, c.1790, 34 In. ..	263
Wedding Dress, Blue Silk, Metallic Gold Embroidered Mesh Lace, Hook & Eye, c.1910, 50 In...	105

> **CLUTHRA** glass is a two-layered glass with small bubbles and powdered glass trapped between the layers. The Steuben Glass Works of Corning, New York, first made it in 1920. Victor Durand of Kimball Glass Company in Vineland, New Jersey, made a similar glass from about 1925. Durand's pieces are listed in the Durand category. Related items are listed in the Steuben category.

Bottle, Perfume, Pink To White, Triangle Shape Stopper, c.1920, 7 In.	702
Bowl, Centerpiece, Green, Footed, 3¼ In.	224
Vase, Blue, Polished Pontil, Signed, Steuben, 8¼ x 7¼ In.	950

COALBROOKDALE was made by the Coalport porcelain factory of England during the Victorian period. Pieces are decorated with floral encrustations.

Basket, Flowers, Cobalt Blue, 10 In.		476
Basket, Lid, Flowers, Multicolor, Basket Weave, 10½ x 5 In.		1036
Bough Pot, Lid, Intertwined Handle, Roses, 8⅛ x 4 In.		325
Perfume Bottle, Flower Stopper, 3-Footed, 19th Century, 10 In.		495
Sugar, Lid, Bird Finial, Flowers, Scalloped Rim, c.1820		175

COALPORT ware was made by the Coalport Porcelain Works of England beginning about 1795. Early pieces were unmarked. About 1810–25 the pieces were marked with the name *Coalport* in various forms. Later pieces also had the name *John Rose* in the mark. The crown mark was used with variations beginning in 1881. The date 1750 is printed in some marks, but it is not the date the factory started. Coalport was bought by Wedgwood in 1967. Coalport porcelain is no longer being produced. Some pieces are listed in this book under Indian Tree.

Coalport Porcelain Manufactory 1820	 Coalport Porcelain Manufactory c.1881	Coalport Porcelain Manufactory 1960

Cake Plate, Hazelton, Burgundy, Gold, 2 Handles, Scalloped Edge, Grapes, 10¾ In.	75
Cup & Saucer, England Rosemary, Flowers, Scalloped Edge, Gold Trim	100
Plate, Dinner, Cobalt Blue, Batwing, Wenham, Signed F. Howard, 1920, 10 In., 11 Piece	1000
Vase, Cobalt Blue, Gilt Scrolled Handles, Oval Vignettes, Landscapes, 15 x 5 In., Pair	563

COBALT BLUE glass was made using oxide of cobalt. The characteristic bright dark blue identifies it for the collector. Most cobalt glass found today was made after the Civil War. There was renewed interest in the dark blue glass in the late 1930s and glass dinnerware was made.

Vase, Smoked Glass Rim, Iridescent Base, Thomas Philabaum, 18½ x 11 x 11 In.	313
Vase, Trumpet, Footed, Flared Top Rim, Polished Pontil Base, 14¼ x 8¼ In.	36

COCA-COLA was first served in 1886 in Atlanta, Georgia. It was advertised through signs, newspaper ads, coupons, bottles, trays, calendars, and even lamps and clocks. Collectors want anything with the word *Coca-Cola*, including a few rare products, like gum wrappers and cigar bands. The famous trademark was patented in 1893, the *Coke* mark in 1945. Many modern items and reproductions are being made.

Banner, Sign Of Good Taste, Die Cut, Metal, Yellow & Red Paint, 10 x 47 In.		339
Bell, Calendar Girl, Centennial Collection, Fostoria, 1909		3
Belt Buckle, Sterling Silver & Gold, Bottle Logo, Retro, 1½ In.		7
Bottle Opener, Red Lettering, Wall Mount, Metal, 3⅛ x 2½ In.		18
Bottle Opener, Starr, White, Cap Catcher, Sprite Boy Logo, Box, 8 In.		47
Bottle, Aluminum, Cap, Do The Dance, Full, Justice, France		12
Bottle, Amber, Marked, Coca-Cola, New York, 7½ In.		68
Bottle, Metal Replica, Loop At Top, Brass Luster, c.1950, 1¼ In.		14
Bottle, Seltzer, Emerald Green Glass, Acid Etch, Coca-Cola Bottling Co., 12½ In.	*illus*	311
Calendar, Sign, Die Cut, Metal, Pad, 1972, 14 x 9½ In.	*illus*	565
Can, Customer Appreciation, Gold Ground, Red & White Label, South Africa, 1993		67
Clock, 5 Cent Sold Here, Sessions Clock Co., Oak, Woolworth Co., c.1925, 36 x 18 In.		850
Clock, Cast Iron, Neon Power Supply, Octagonal, Telechron, 13½ x 13½ x 3 In.		960
Clock, Die Cut Metal, Round, Maroon, c.1951, 17½ In.		226
Clock, Drink Coca-Cola In Bottles, Metal, Wood Case, Selected Devices Co., c.1939, 16 In.		141
Clock, Drink Coca-Cola, Tin Litho, Red, Logo, Black Border, Yellow Numbers, 18 In.		300

Coca-Cola, Calendar, Sign, Die Cut, Metal, Pad, 1972, 14 x 9½ In.
$565

Rich Penn Auctions

Coca-Cola, Clock, Neon, Metal & Glass, Bottle Logo, 15 In.
$1,469

Rich Penn Auctions

Coca-Cola, Clock, Neon, Wall Mount, Round, Red, Black, 17 In.
$108

Martin Auction Co.

This is an edited listing of current prices. Visit Kovels.com to check thousands of prices from previous years and sign up for free information on trends, tips, reproductions, marks, and more.

Coca-Cola, Cooler, Westinghouse
Junior, Holds 51 Bottles, Metal, Bottle
Opener, 35 x 28 x 17 In.
$622

Rich Penn Auctions

Coca-Cola, Gameboard, Folding, Steps
To Health, c.1938, 26½ x 11½ In.
$151

Fontaine's Auction Gallery

Coca-Cola, Mirror, Calendar Girl, Large
Hat, Hamilton King, Celluloid, Pocket,
1910, 2¾ In.
$165

Milestone Auctions

Clock, Neon, Metal & Glass, Bottle Logo, 15 In. .... *illus*	1469
Clock, Neon, Wall Mount, Round, Red, Black, 17 In. .... *illus*	108
Clock, Standard Electric Time Co., Springfield, Mass., Red Circular Frame, 14 In.	177
Clock, Wood, Delicious, Refreshing, Silver Lettering, Baird Clock Co, 1900s, 31 In.	263
Cookie Jar, Lunch Box Shape, Handle, Red, Coca-Cola Labels, Gibson, 8½ x 9½ In.	30
Cookie Jar, Polar Bear, Delivery Truck, Bottles Of Coke, Limited Edition, 1999, 8½ x 10½ x 7 In. .	36
Cooler Bag, New York World's Fair, Red & White Vinyl, c.1964, 10 In.	199
Cooler, Airline, Embossed Metal, Red Paint, 12 x 16½ In.	339
Cooler, Glossy Red Finish, White Text, Chrome Details, Cavalier Corp., c.1948, 12½ x 7 x 17 In.	450
Cooler, Picnic, Metal, Acton Mfg. Co., c.1950, 14 x 13½ x 9 In. .... 198 to 339
Cooler, Portable, Steel, Red, White, Acton Mfg. Co. Inc., c.1950, 18 x 19 x 13 In.	352
Cooler, Westinghouse Junior, Holds 51 Bottles, Metal, Bottle Opener, 35 x 28 x 17 In. .... *illus*	622
Display, Bottle, Lucite, Light-Up, Wood Base, 12½ In.	311
Fountain Dispenser, Metal, Tapper, Curved Lid, Dole Valve Co., 23 x 11 x 16 In.	283
Gameboard, Folding, Steps To Health, c.1938, 26½ x 11½ In. .... *illus*	151
Keychain, Bottle Shape, Metal, Gold Painted, Pair, 2 In.	25
Lighter, Pocket, Zippo Style, Red Ground, White Lettering, Korea	16
Map, United States, Historical Scenes Border, Ohman's, Frame, 29 x 38 In.	59
Match Striker, Drink Coca-Cola, Strike Matches Here, Enamel, 2 Holes, Canada, c.1939, 4 x 4 In..	974
Matchbox, Bottle Machine Shape, Slendo Temp 80, Slant Shelf, 2 x 4½ x 7⁄8 In.	94
Menu Board, Silhouette Girl, Embossed Metal, American Art Works, c.1942, 27 x 19½ In.	198
Mirror, Calendar Girl, Large Hat, Hamilton King, Celluloid, Pocket, 1910, 2¾ In. .... *illus*	165
Pedal Car, Red, White Coca-Cola Logo, White Wall Tires, Murray, 31 In.	177
Pin, Club Member's, Metal Back Bar Pin, Concave c.1930, 1¼ In. .... *illus*	118
Pocket Knife, Coca-Cola Truck, 18 Wheel, 2 Blades, Bottle Opener, Colonial	31
Pocket Mirror, Drink Coca-Cola, Celluloid, Oval, Girl Holding Glass, 1907, 2¾ x 1¾ In.	250
Pretzel Dish, Cast, Aluminum, Brunhoff Mfg. Co., 1935, 4½ x 8 In. .... *illus*	141
Push Bar, Iced Coca-Cola Here, Red, Yellow, 1958, 31½ x 3¼ In.	327
Radio, Cooler Shape, Molded Plastic, Red Paint, 10 x 12½ In.	226
Radio, Figural, Electric, Hobble Skirt Coke Bottle, Embossed, c.1933, 24 x 8 In.	3658
Shade, Hanging, Logo, Green, Red, White, Pittsburgh Mosaic Glass Co., 12 x 22 x 11 In...........	21240
Shade, Leaded Glass, Logo, Pull Cord Socket, Pentagonal Glass Panels, 1920s, 16 x 12 In.	2570
Sign, Bottle Cap Shape, Sheet Metal, Logo, Neon Tubing, Porcelain, 36 x 7 In.	1020
Sign, Bottle Embossed, Tin Litho, Wood Crate, American Art Works, c.1933, 9 In. .... *illus*	1829
Sign, Bottle Shape, Tin, Die Cut, American Art Works Inc., Coshocton, 1932, 9½ x 12 In.. *illus*	900
Sign, Bottle, Wood Box, Embossed, Tin Litho, American Art Works, Early 1930s, 39¼ In.	1829
Sign, Cap, Bottle Of Coke, White Ground, Porcelain, Round, 25 In.	720
Sign, Cap, Drink Coca-Cola In Bottles, Metal, 16 In.	565
Sign, Coca-Cola, Sign Of Good Taste, Tin, 13 x 7 In.	11
Sign, Coke Adds Life To Everything Nice, Metal, Self-Framed, 35½ x 17½ In.	283
Sign, Delicious & Refreshing, Bottle, Porcelain, Mint Green Lettering, 24 x 24 In.	360
Sign, Drink Coca-Cola, Delicious & Refreshing, Cigars, Candy, Porcelain, 1933, 96 In.	3000
Sign, Drink Coca-Cola, Delicious & Refreshing, Tin, Embossed, 1939, 4 x 8 In. .... *illus*	856
Sign, Drink Coca-Cola, Enamel, Red, White Letters, Green & Yellow Border, c.1930, 10 x 30 In.	1947
Sign, Drink Coca-Cola, For The Taste You Never Get Tired Of, Frame, 13½ x 58 In.	58
Sign, Drink Coca-Cola, Ice Cold, Arrow Shape, Wood, Kay Display Co., 1930s, 28 x 23 In.	1475
Sign, Drink Coca-Cola, Sign Of Good Taste, Spinner, Tin Litho, c.1950s, 13⅜ x 14¼ In.	1298
Sign, Enamel Steel, Round, Red & White, c.1947, 47 x 4 x 47 In.	1875
Sign, Ice Cold, Hanging, Flange Bracket, Triangular, 2-Sided, 1937, 33 x 26 In.	1320
Sign, Logo, Red, White, Green, Sheet Aluminum, Wood Edges, Robertson, 1964, 36 x 72 In......	510
Sign, Metal, Logo, Fishtail Shape, 1958, 28 x 60 In.. *illus*	600
Sign, Paper Lithograph, Elaine, Sitting, Holding Umbrella, 1915, 26 x 13 In.	443
Sign, Pause & Refresh, Moving Waterfall, Light-Up, Countertop, 1940s, 8 x 19 x 4 In.	3658
Sign, Sign Of Good Taste, Squirt Boy Logo, Yellow, Green & Red Paint, 26½ In. .... *illus*	622
Sign, Skater Girl Drinking Coke, Cardboard, c.1941, 27 x 16 In.	767
Sign, Tin Lithograph, Embossed, Drink Coca-Cola, Bottle, 1930s, 11 x 35 In.	531
Sign, Tin, Refresh Yourself, Drink A Coca-Cola, 18 x 54 In.	829
Snow Globe, Polar Bear Drinking Cola, Red & White Striped Scarf, Red Skies, 8 In.	52
Stringholder, Take Home In Cartons, Tin Lithograph, 2-Sided, Hanging, 15 x 7⁄8 x 13 x 7 In. ..	1239
Thermometer, Silhouette Girl, Emboss Die Cut Metal, c.1939, 16 x 7 In.	283

Coca-Cola, Pin, Club Member's, Metal Back Bar Pin, Concave c.1930, 1 ¼ In.
$118

Hake's Auctions

Coca-Cola, Pretzel Dish, Cast, Aluminum, Brunhoff Mfg. Co., 1935, 4 ½ x 8 In.
$141

Rich Penn Auctions

Coca-Cola, Sign, Bottle, Embossed, Tin Litho, Wood Crate, American Art Works, c.1933, 9 In.
$1,829

Wm Morford Auctions

Coca-Cola, Sign, Bottle Shape, Tin, Die Cut, American Art Works Inc., Coshocton, 1932, 9 ½ x 12 In.
$900

Morphy Auctions

Coca-Cola, Sign, Drink Coca-Cola, Delicious & Refreshing, Tin, Embossed, 1939, 4 x 8 In.
$856

Aspire Auctions

Coca-Cola, Sign, Metal, Logo, Fishtail Shape, 1958, 28 x 60 In.
$600

Matthew Bullock Auctioneers

Coca-Cola, Sign, Sign Of Good Taste, Squirt Boy Logo, Yellow, Green & Red Paint, 26 ½ In.
$622

Rich Penn Auctions

Coca-Cola, Tip Tray, 1903, Hilda Clark, Tin Lithograph, Gold Border, Round, 6 In.
$974

Wm Morford Auctions

Coca-Cola, Tray, 1939, Springboard, Girl, Metal, Lithograph, 13 x 10 ½ In.
$102

Rich Penn Auctions

Coca-Cola, Tray, 1950, Menu Girl, Holding Bottle, Outdoor Activities Border, 13 In.
$47

Milestone Auctions

Coca-Cola, Vending Machine, Vendo, Model 44, 10 Cent, Wheels, Metal, c.1956, 57½ x 16 x 19 In.
$4,068

Rich Penn Auctions

Coffee Mill, Enterprise, No. 12½, 2 Wheels, Patriotic Decals, Cast Iron, Eagle Finial, 1899, 40 In.
$2,000

Garth's Auctioneers & Appraisers

Thermometer, Tin, Bottle, Marked, Robertson, 23 In.	94
Tip Tray, 1903, Hilda Clark, Tin Lithograph, Gold Border, Round, 6 In. .... *illus*	974
Tray, 1937, Running Girl, Swimsuit, White Cape, Lithograph, 1937, 13 x 10½ In.	130
Tray, 1939, Springboard, Girl, Metal, Lithograph, 13 x 10½ In. .... *illus*	102
Tray, 1950, Menu Girl, Holding Bottle, Outdoor Activities Border, 13 In. .... *illus*	47
Trophy, Cup, Top Area Manager, Dallas, Brass, 2 Handles, Coca-Cola Bottling Co., 9 x 6 In.	54
Trophy, FIFA World Cup, Germany, Box, 2006, 4 In.	51
Truck, Buddy L, Pressed Steel, Yellow & Red, 14 In.	153
Vending Machine, 10 Cent, Red, White, Chrome, Vendo Co., c.1950, 58 x 27 x 17 In.	4200
Vending Machine, Vendo, Model 44, 10 Cent, Wheels, Metal, c.1956, 57½ x 16 x 19 In. ... *illus*	4068
Vending Machine, Vendo, V-81D, Steel, Vends Different Brands, Key, c.1960, 60 x 27 x 19 In...	2034

 COFFEE MILLS are also called coffee grinders, although there is a difference in the way each grinds the coffee. Large floor-standing or counter-model coffee mills were used in the nineteenth-century country store. Small home mills were first made about 1894. They lost favor by the 1930s. The renewed interest in fresh-ground coffee has produced many modern electric mills, hand mills, and grinders. Reproductions of the old styles are being made.

Arcade, Hoffmann's Old Time Coffee, Wood, Tin Litho Face, 13 In.	1169
Arcade, Monarch, Wood, Hanging, Cast Iron Face Plate, Glass Cup, 15¾ In.	1800
Arcade, Telephone Mill, Bronzed Cast Iron, Patented Sept 25 88, 13¼ x 8 In.	338
Arcade, Wall Mount, Lid & Jar, 5 In.	69
Bronson-Walton, Old Glory, Flag, T. Roosevelt, Cast Iron, Tin, Wood, 10 In.	570
Charles Parker, No. 700, Double Wheels, Red Paint, Flowers, 22 In.	1169
Charles Parker, No. 3000, 2 Wheels, Red Paint, Meriden, Conn., 14 x 12 In.	615
Elgin National, 2 Wheels, Red Paint, Cast Iron, Marked Empire, 65 In.	2070
Enterprise, No. 3, Double Wheels & Handle, Red, Yellow & Blue Paint, 14 x 15 In.	1107
Enterprise, No. 7, Double Wheels & Handle, Red Paint, Eagle Finial, 23 x 21 In.	1140
Enterprise, No. 9, 2 Wheels, Eagle & Ball Finial, 27 x 21½ x 19¾ In.	726
Enterprise, No. 12, Cast Iron, Painted, 2 Wheels, 1800s, 25 x 24 x 33 In.	561
Enterprise, No. 12½, 2 Wheels, Patriotic Decals, Cast Iron, Eagle Finial, 1899, 40 In. ..... *illus*	2000
Enterprise, Cast Iron, Brass Hopper, Eagle Finial, Pat. Dec. 9, 73, 28 In.	750
Enterprise, Red, Blue Paint, Yellow Stringing, Decals, Late 1800s, 12½ In.	523
Enterprise, Side Crank Handle, Cast Iron, Wood Drawers & Base, 17 In.	115
Griswold, Clamp, Cast Iron, Black Paint, Tabletop, 1898, 15 In.	1320
J. Fisher, Wood, Pewter Mounted, Stamped, Pennsylvania, 1800s, 9¾ In.	83
John Shultz, Pewter, Iron Mounted, Tiger Maple, Signed, 1837, 10 x 9¼ x 7¼ In.	1003
Landers, Frary & Clark, No. 20, Crown, 2 Wheels, Black Paint, 12¼ In.	1046
Landers, Frary & Clark, No. 70, Crown, 2 Wheels, Red Paint, Eagle, 23 In.	1046
Lane Brothers, No. 14, 2 Wheels, Swift Mill, Red Paint, 21 x 14 In.	861
Peuginox, Brown Bakelite, Stainless Steel, 1950s, 4 x 4 x 4 In.	170
Pine, Finger Jointed, Cast Iron Hardware, Early 1900s, 11 In. .... *illus*	58
Simmons Hardware Co., No. 15, Koffee Krusher, Blue Paint, Pat. Oct. 1 1901, 22 In.	1599
Smith Mill Bros., 2 Wheels, Pinstriping, Tin, Red Paint, Late 1800s, 30 x 18 x 19¼ In.	900
Swift Mill Lane Bros., Iron, 2 Wheels, Wood Handle, 27 x 20 x 15 In. .... *illus*	780
Woodruff & Edwards, No. 44, Elgin National, 2 Wheels, Red Paint, Eagle, 25 In.	660

COIN-OPERATED MACHINES of all types are collected. The vending machine is an ancient invention dating back to 200 B.C., when holy water was dispensed from a coin-operated vase. Smokers in seventeenth-century England could buy tobacco from a coin-operated box. It was not until after the Civil War that the technology made modern coin-operated games and vending machines plentiful. Slot machines, arcade games, and dispensers are all collected.

Arcade, Dickson & Steven, Magic Baseball, 10 Cent, Omaha, Sheldon, c.1966, 65 In.	1728
Arcade, International Mutoscope Reel Co., Punch A Bag, 1 Cent, Oak, c.1910, 80 x 34 In.	5472
Arcade, Mechanical World, Claw Machine, Crane Digger, Oak, Aluminum, 65 x 43 x 26 In. . *illus*	2700
Arcade, Mills, Firefly, Electric Shock, Electricity Is Life, c.1905, 12 x 9 In.	1850
Arcade, Mills, Imperial Shocker, Wood Cabinet, Iron Facade, 1908, 22 x 16 x 12 In. .... *illus*	3600

Arcade, Namco, Ms. Pac Man & Galaga, Cabinet, 1980s, 68 x 25 x 33 In........ 1500
Arcade, National, K.O. Fighters, Boxing, 2 Pistols, 1928, 71 x 40 ½ x 29 In. 3600
Arcade, Strength Tester, 25 Cent, Pine, Cabinet, Keys, c.1980, 77 x 20 x 36 In. 452
Arcade, Totalizer, Basketball Theme, 5 Cent, Countertop, c.1940, 20 x 12 ½ x 12 In........ 545
Arcade, Williams, Baseball, 4 Bagger Deluxe, 10 Cent, c.1956, 25 x 66 x 70 In.............. *illus* 3600
Arcade, Williams, Pennant Fever, Baseball, 67 x 56 In. 960
Bally, Pinball, Bow & Arrow, Indian Theme, 1975, 71 x 30 ½ x 56 In........ 540
Coin Changer, Cast Iron Body, Wood Base, 5 Aluminum Channels, 12 x 10 ½ x 8 ½ In........ 840
Coin Pusher, Silver Falls, Black & White Paint, 71 x 25 ½ x 28 In. 79
Electric Shock, 2 Metal Handles, Wood Case, Meter Measured, c.1940, 11 x 6 x 9 ½ In........... 792
Fortune Teller, 5 Cent, Animated Grandma, Wood Cabinet, Cast Marquee, Iron Base, c.1910.. 7920
Gambling, Skipper Sales, 1 Cent Drop, Red Paint, c.1942...... 288
Game, 25 Cent, Hole Moves, Horse, Sega Jockey Club, Pachinko Style, c.1970.......... 1584
Game, Bingo, Pin, Wood, Glass, 1 Cent, 6-Point Star Playfield, 25 ½ x 16 ½ In......... 254
Game, Electroskill Baseball, Penny Drop, Lock, Key, Evans-Kirk, c.1940, 13 x 8 x 20 In....... 1728
Grip Tester, Great Lakes System, Mercury Athletic Scale, 1950s, 17 x 15 ½ x 12 In. .... *illus* 480
Gum, Adams Gum Co., Glass Globe, Oak Cabinet, Iron Base, 1915, 24 ½ x 14 x 9 ½ In........ 320
Gum, Adams, Chewing Gum, 1 Cent, 4 Column Vendor, 23 x 10 ¼ In......... 198
Gumball, 1 Cent, Oak Mfg., Key Included, 14 In........ 106
Gumball, Abbey Mfg., 1 Cent, Aluminum Base, Lid, Tray, c.1930........ *illus* 130
Gumball, Baseball Theme, Blue Green Sides, Circular Stand, 5 x 15 In........ 308
Gumball, Bluebird, 1 Cent, Cast Aluminum Base & Top, Glass Globe, 14 ½ x 7 ½ x 7 ½ In....... 180
Gumball, Buckley, 1 Cent, Cast Aluminum, c.1935, 12 ½ x 9 ½ In. 396
Gumball, Columbus, Model 45, Aluminum, Octagonal Globe, 2 Locks, Key, c.1946, 14 In........ 311
Gumball, Ford, 1 Cent, Glass Globe, Metal Stand, 42 In. 198
Gumball, Master Novelty, 1 Cent, Ball, Green, Cream, Porcelain, c.1951, 16 x 8 In........ 339
Gumball, Northwestern Corp., Model 33, 1 Cent, Octagonal, Glass Globe, 1933, 15 x 7 In. 240
Gumball, Northwestern, Ball Bubble Gum, Penny Or Nickel, Key, 19 In. 472
Gumball, Oak Mfg. Co., 1 Cent, Cast, Aluminum, Embossed Globe, Stand, c.1947, 46 In. 170
Gumball, Vendors, 1 Cent, Case, Aluminum, Red, Key, 15 In. 102
Movie Viewer, Mills, 10 Cent, Panoram, Wood Body, Lock, Key, c.1941, 80 x 30 In......... 8640
Music Box, Cylinder, Carved Oak, 12 Song Selection, Mermod Freres, 13 x 39 In........ 1830
Music Box, Cylinder, Painted Case, Decal, Penny To Start, 9 x 7 x 20 In. 360
Mutoscope, International Mutoscope Reel, Down For The Count, 1 Cent, Tin, c.1935, 28 In. *illus* 2160
Pinball, A.B.T., 1 Cent, 10 Balls For A Penny, Lock & Key, c.1931, 25 x 15 In. 1872
Pinball, Gottlieb, Minstrel Man, Wood Rail, Yellow, c.1951, 23 x 53 In......... 2914
Pinball, Gottlieb, Shaq Attaq, c.1995, 80 x 27 x 52 In......... 1875
Pinball, Jennings, Sportsman, 5 Cent, Wood Cabinet, c.1934, 40 x 43 x 23 In......... 861
Pinball, Novelty Mfg. Co., Bingo, Mechanical, 1931, 8 ½ x 16 ½ x 25 In. 480
Pinball, Rock-Ola, Jigsaw Puzzle, Mechanical, 1933, 49 ½ x 19 x 41 In........ 900
Pinball, Screwy, Oak Case, Glass, Tabletop, 9 ½ x 16 ½ x 31 In........ 554
Pinball, Williams, Phantom Menace, Star Wars Episode, Keys, 22 ½ x 52 x 72 In........ 2070
Popcorn, Popperette, 10 Cent, Metal & Acrylic, Glass Globe, c.1950, 65 x 18 x 15 In........ 3300
Shocker, Detroit Medical Battery Company, Electricity Is Life, c.1900, 14 x 18 In........ 2736
Shooting Game, A.B.T., Playfield, 1 Cent, Billiard, Lock, Key, Cashbox, c.1931, 25 x 15 In. 3168
Shooting Game, Silver King Novelty Co., Duck, Ball, Gum Vendor, c.1949, 19 x 11 x 24 In. 339
Slot, Baseball, Playing Field, 5 Cents, O.D. Jennings, 1930, 25 x 16 x 15 In........... *illus* 3200
Slot, Caille Bros, 5 Cent, Operator's Bell, Cast Iron, Oak, c.1916, 15 x 15 x 25 In. 4800
Slot, Caille, Grand Prize, 10 Cent, Award Card, Keys, 25 x 16 In........ 904
Slot, Columbia, 5 Cent, Fruit Reels, Award Card, Oak Sides, Cast Iron, c.1936, 18 x 14 ½ In. 452
Slot, Columbia, Nickel, Polished Metal, 1930s, 18 ½ x 14 ½ x 12 In......... 518
Slot, Cowper Mfg. Co., Jackpot Coin Drop, Wood Cabinet, 1898-1911, 25 x 18 x 13 In........ 2700
Slot, Jennings, 1 Cent, 3-Reel, Little Duke, Art Deco, 1930s, 25 x 11 In. 2299
Slot, Jennings, 10 Cent, Club Chief, Claw Foot Stand, Locks & Key, c.1946 1080
Slot, Jennings, Chief, 5 Cent, Wood Cabinet, Metal Marquee, 1937, 6 x 20 x 52 In........ 3075
Slot, Jennings, Sun Chief, 5 Cent, Green, Chrome, 27 x 16 In........ 1815
Slot, Mills, 1 Cent, Castle Front, Wood Base, Aluminum Body, c.1931 1440
Slot, Mills, 5 Cent, Castle Front, Claw Foot Stand, Chicago, c.1935........ 1080
Slot, Mills, 5 Cent, Diamond Front, Lock & Key, Wood Stand, c.1933 .... *illus* 720
Slot, Mills, 25 Cent, Aluminum, Red & Blue Paint, Key, Mid 1900s, 27 x 16 x 15 In. 974

Coffee Mill, Pine, Finger Jointed, Cast Iron Hardware, Early 1900s, 11 In.
$58

Keystone Auctions LLC

Coffee Mill, Swift Mill Lane Bros., Iron, 2 Wheels, Wood Handle, 27 x 20 x 15 In.
$780

Morphy Auctions

Coin-Operated, Arcade, Mechanical World, Claw Machine, Crane Digger, Oak, Aluminum, 65 x 43 x 26 In.
$2,700

Morphy Auctions

Coin-Operated, Arcade, Mills, Imperial Shocker, Wood Cabinet, Iron Facade, 1908, 22 x 16 x 12 In. $3,600

Morphy Auctions

Coin-Operated, Arcade, Williams, Baseball, 4 Bagger Deluxe, 10 Cent, c.1956, 25 x 66 x 70 In. $3,600

Morphy Auctions

Coin-Operated, Grip Tester, Great Lakes System, Mercury Athletic Scale, 1950s, 17 x 15 ½ x 12 In. $480

Morphy Auctions

Slot, Mills, Bandit, 10 Cent, Standing, Circular Base, c.1945 .... *illus*	3168
Slot, Mills, Cherry, 5 Cent, Cast Metal Front, Oak Sides & Base, 25 In.	660
Slot, Mills, Dewey-Chicago, Oak Case, Nickel Plated Mounts, Early 1900s, 66 In.	16520
Slot, Mills, Flasher, 5 Cent, Electro Mechanical, Back Glass, c.1937, 54 x 20 In.	684
Slot, Mills, Q.T. Firebird, Side Vendor Gumballs, Blue, Yellow, 19 x 13 In.	1331
Slot, Watling, 5 Cent, Oak Cabinet, Central Wheel, Countertop, 1910, 20 x 16 x 9 In. .... *illus*	4688
Slot, Watling, Gumball Vender, 1 Cent, Blue Seal, 1931, 24 x 15 ½ x 15 In.	1230
Sobriety Test, Northwestern Corp., Hot Rod, Sheet Metal, Morris, Ill., 1950s, 8 x 18 ½ x 7 In...	1008
Stereo Viewer, Arcade, 5 Cents, Film Strip, c.1931, 12 ½ x 12 ½ In.	288
Stereo Viewer, Mills Novelty, 1 Cent, Oak Cabinet, c.1928, 72 x 20 x 17 In.	2448
Strength Tester, Floor Model, Squeezes 2 Handles, 2 Dimes, Lurid Graphics, c.1930, 40 In.	540
Trade Stimulator, Caille Bros, Jockey Cigar Poker, 5 Cents, Oak, 1905, 35 x 16 x 16 In.	6600
Trade Stimulator, Daval Mfg. Co., Penny Pack, Aluminum, Countertop, 1936, 10 x 9 x 8 In...	330
Trade Stimulator, Fairest Wheel, 5 Cent, c.1890, 21 ½ x 14 x 5 In. .... *illus*	367
Trade Stimulator, Jennings, Poker, 5 Cents, Wood Body, Key, 1930	684
Trade Stimulator, Keystone Novelty, Dice Popper, Nickel, 5 Dice Platform, c.1924	2880
Trade Stimulator, Reliance Novelty Co., 1 Cent, Poker, Nickel Plated, c.1900, 16 ½ x 13 ½ x 11 ½ In..	3600
Trade Stimulator, Rock-Ola, 1 Cent, 3 Jacks, Silver Paint, Chicago, c.1930, 17 ¾ x 12 In........	1080
Trade Stimulator, Rock-Ola, 5-Reel Poker, Hold & Draw, Key, c.1934, 12 ½ x 13 ½ x 9 In.	1029
Trade Stimulator, Rock-Ola, Horse Race, Wood Cabinet, Aluminum, 12 x 15 x 13 In. ...... *illus*	400
Trade Stimulator, Tol Boul, Rotate The Sphere, Insert 1 Franc Coin, 1960, 13 x 12 x 7 In.	144
Trade Stimulator, Trip-L-Jax, Embossed Lettering, Marquee Top, c.1930, 18 x 13 x 10 In.	480
Trade Stimulator, Winner, Spiral, Glass Panels, Wood Body, c.1895, 10 x 10 x 17 In. .... *illus*	1152
Vending, Automat, Chocolate, Mickey Mouse, Key, 6 ½ In.	180
Vending, Ballpoint Pen, Penvend Mfg., Metal Case, 25 Cent, 14 x 8 ½ In.	198
Vending, Bulk, Log Cabin Duplex, 1 Cent, Glass Globes, Cast, Aluminum, c.1930, 16 x 11 In.	396
Vending, Caille, Chocolate, Tin, Girl On Top, Germany, 6 In.	276
Vending, Candy, Hershey's, 1 Cent, Hanging, Orange, Gold Front Grill, 30 ¾ x 4 x 6 In.	363
Vending, Candy, Northwestern Deluxe, Black Porcelain Base, Countertop, c.1936, 7 ½ x 7 x 19 In..	320
Vending, Candy, Star Vendors Los Angeles, 5 Cent, 18 ¼ x 6 ¾ In.	254
Vending, Candy, Stoner, 5 Cent, Red Paint, 1950, 16 x 29 x 55 ¾ In.	1440
Vending, Cigarette, Lucky Strike, Model, Fighter Jet, c.1940, 6 x 4 x 2 In.	226
Vending, Cigarette, Silver, Comet, 1 Cent, Countertop, 1930s, 8 x 6 In.	675
Vending, Cigarettes, Stewart & McGuire, Multi Coin, Floor Model, 28 x 13 x 70 In.	720
Vending, Mills, Gum, Vender, Trade Checks, 5 Cent, 3-Reel, Oak Cabinet, c.1910, 22 ½ x 19 x 56 In..	10200
Vending, National, Cigarettes, Brown, 7 Slots, c.1940, 62 x 23 In..	444
Vending, Nut, Hot, Silver King, 5 Cent, Cast Aluminum, c.1947, 16 In.	311
Vending, Pencil, Harmon Machine Co., 5 Cent, Steel Cabinet, 1940-50, 14 x 9 x 7 In.	240
Vending, Popcorn, Minit Pop, 10 Cents, Red & Yellow Paint, 1948, 63 x 25 x 18 In....................	7200
Vending, Postage, 3 Cent Stamps, Schermack, 10 Cent, 1930s, 13 x 7 In.	325
Vending, Railway, Bahnsteig Karten, Tickets, Tin, Brown, Marklin, Germany, 5 ½ In...............	300
Vending, Stamp, Schermack Products Corp, Model 25, Black, c.1930, 13 x 7 x 8 In.	369
Vending, Stamps, Cast Iron, White, Brown Accents, 14 x 6 ½ x 6 ½ In................................. *illus*	300
Vending, Stollwerck Chocolates, Cherubs, Tin, 10 ¾ In.	252
Vending, Superior Confection Co., Cigarette, Aluminum, c.1930, 12 x 11 x 8 In. .... *illus*	462

COLLECTOR PLATES are modern plates produced in limited editions. Some may be found listed under the factory name, such as Bing & Grondahl, Royal Copenhagen, Royal Doulton, and Wedgwood.

Avon, Betsy Ross, Enoch Wedgwood, 1973, 8 ½ In.	16
Avon, United States Of America, Bicentennial, Oval, Clear, 9 x 6 In....................................	21
Bradford Exchange, Titanic, Hope Survives, Queen Of The Ocean, J. Griffen, 2001, 8 In.	38
Bradford Exchange, Touching The Spirit, Wakan Tanka, Night Sky, Tepees, 8 ¼ In.................	40
Bradford Exchange, Virgin Mary, Visions Of Our Lady Of Guadalupe, 1994, 8 x 6 In........ *illus*	14
Chadwick-Miller Inc., Red Cardinals, 6 In.	68
Enesco, Precious Moments, May Birthday, 1983, 6 ¼ In.	24
Enesco, Raggedy Ann & Andy, Days Of The Week, Gold Edge, 7 In.	24
Exposition De Bruxelles 1888, Coat Of Arms, 13 In.	299
Franklin Mint, La Merveilleuse, Woman, Black & Gold Gown, Jewels, 8 In.............................	125

Coin-Operated, Gumball, Abbey Mfg., 1 Cent, Aluminum Base, Lid, Tray, c.1930
$130

Coin-Operated, Mutoscope, International Mutoscope Reel, Down For The Count, 1 Cent, Tin, c.1935, 28 In.
$2,160

Coin-Operated, Slot, Baseball, Playing Field, 5 Cents, O.D. Jennings, 1930, 25 x 16 x 15 In.
$3,200

Coin-Operated, Slot, Mills, 5 Cent, Diamond Front, Lock & Key, Wood Stand, c.1933
$720

Coin-Operated, Slot, Mills, Bandit, 10 Cent, Standing, Circular Base, c.1945
$3,168

Coin-Operated, Slot, Watling, 5 Cent, Oak Cabinet, Central Wheel, Countertop, 1910, 20 x 16 x 9 In.
$4,688

Coin-Operated, Trade Stimulator, Fairest Wheel, 5 Cent, c.1890, 21 ½ x 14 x 5 In.
$367

Coin-Operated, Trade Stimulator, Rock-Ola, Horse Race, Wood Cabinet, Aluminum, 12 x 15 x 13 In.
$400

Coin-Operated, Trade Stimulator, Winner, Spiral, Glass Panels, Wood Body, c.1895, 10 x 10 x 17 In.
$1,152

Coin-Operated, Vending, Stamps, Cast Iron, White, Brown Accents, 14 x 6½ x 6½ In.
$300

Morphy Auctions

Coin-Operated, Vending, Superior Confection Co., Cigarette, Aluminum, c.1930, 12 x 11 x 8 In.
$462

Morphy Auctions

Collector Plate, Bradford Exchange, Virgin Mary, Visions Of Our Lady Of Guadalupe, 1994, 8 x 6 In.
$14

john-cscollect on eBay

Franklin Mint, Meths, Highlander Series, Portrait, Gold Trim, Leaves, No. 294 .... *illus*	10
Gorham, Life Of Christ Omnibus Muralis, Round, No. 2191, 1977, 12 In.	19
Hamilton Collection, Country Fair, Jane Wooster Scott, 8 In.	30
Hamilton Collection, Table Manners, Mamma Cat, Kittens, On Cabinet, 1988, 8½ In.	24
Hatcheck Girl, 1984, 8½ In.	19
Hibel, The World I Love, Edna's Music Flute Player, No. 2403, 8 In. .... *illus*	5
Holly Hobbie, American Greetings, Happiest Times Shared With Friends, 10 In.	16
Hummel, Heavenly Angel, Pine Trees, Stars Border, No. 264, 1971, 7½ In.	20
Knowles, Erica & Jamie, 1985, 8½ In.	75
Knowles, Fire, 4 Ancient Elements Series, 1985, 9¼ In.	24
Knowles, We've Been Spotted, Dalmatian Puppies, Fire Hose, 8½ In.	10
Lenox, Cottontail Rabbits, Boehm, 1975, 10¾ In.	29
Norman Rockwell, Census Taker, 1984, 8½ In.	19
Norman Rockwell, Grandpa's Gift, 1987, 8½ In.	12
Norman Rockwell, Worlds Away, 1988, 8½ In.	12
Thomas Kinkade, All Friends Are Welcome, Winter, Horse, House, 1993, 8½ In. .... *illus*	7

 COMIC ART, or cartoon art, includes original art for comic strips, magazine covers, book pages, and even printed strips. The first daily comic strip was printed in 1907. The paintings on celluloid used for movie cartoons are listed in this book under Animation Art.

Illustration, Gouache, Southern Gentleman & Belle, John Edwin Jackson, 16 x 12 In.	525
Strip, Donald Duck, Al Taliaferro, 5 Panels, Frame, c.1965, 27 x 10 In.	2500
Strip, Freckles & His Friends, Merrill Blosser, 4 Panels, 1942, 5 x 16¾ In.	100
Strip, The Dailys, Stanley Link, Pen & Ink, 4 Panels, Frame, 1949, 30 x 14 In.	125

 COMMEMORATIVE items have been made to honor members of royalty and those of great national fame. World's Fairs and important historical events are also remembered with commemorative pieces. Related collectibles are listed in the Coronation and World's Fair categories.

Bank, Prince & Princess Of Wales, Portrait Medallion, Cast Metal, 1981, 7 In.	60
Bowl, Teleflora, 75 Years, Holly Berries, Gold Trim, Lenox, 2009, 4 x 7½ x 4¾ In.	6
Pitcher, Queen Victoria, Diamond Jubilee, Stoneware, Doulton, Lambeth, 1837-97, 6 In.	51
Plate, Queen Victoria, Diamond Jubilee, Royal Residences, Castles, Leaves, 1897, 9½ In.	26
Plate, Queen Victoria, Golden Jubilee, Crown, Laurel Leaf Border, Pressed Glass, 1887, 10 In...	30
Poster, Apollo XIV Moon Landing, 25th Anniversary, Gold Shot, 1996, 20½ x 24 In.	13
Tennis Racket, Marriage, King George VI & Queen Elizabeth, Tin Throat Photos, 1923 .. *illus*	1107

COMPACTS hold face powder. A woman did not powder her face in public until after World War I. By 1920, the beauty parlor, permanent waves, and cosmetics had become acceptable. A few companies sold cake face powder in a box with a mirror and a pad or puff. Soon the compact was designed by jewelers and made of gold, silver, and precious materials. Cosmetic companies began to sell powder in attractive compacts of less valuable metal or plastic. Collectors today search for Art Deco designs, famous brands, compacts from World's Fairs or political events, and unusual examples. Many were made with companion lipsticks and other fittings.

Bakelite, Goldtone, Vibrant Green Guilloche Celluloid Design On Lid, 2⅝ In.	16
Cartier, Silver, Engine Turned, Guilloche Enamel Iris, Purple Border, 1900-40......................	217
Coro, Coin Holder, Blue Cabochon Closure, Cohn & Rosenberg, Chain, 3⅜ x 2⅜ In.	55
Elgin, Sterling Silver, Etched Flowers, Monogram, Mesh Wrist Bracelet, 1920s	36
Flato, Goldtone, Lipstick Case, Cover, Pad, Carriage, Mirror Inside, 3 x 2½ In.	62
Frederic Goldscheider, Metal, Gilt, Art Nouveau, Advertising, Paris, c.1890......................	98
Minaudiere, Agme, Mirror, Lipstick, Comb, Cigarette Case, Switzerland, c.1950, 3½ x 4¼ In.	37
Minaudiere, Jeweled Catch, Chain, 2 Winged Wells, 3½ x 2½ x 7½ In.	57
Silver, Hinged Lid, Interior Mirror, Marked For Birmingham By T&S, 1960, 2¾ In.	40
Silver Gilt, Enamel, Woman, Red Cloak, Lipstick Holder, Italy, 1800s, 2¼ x 1¼ In.	171

CONTEMPORARY GLASS, *see Glass-Contemporary.*

COOKBOOKS are collected for various reasons. Some are wanted for the recipes, some for investment, and some as examples of advertising. Cookbooks and recipe pamphlets are included in this category.

American Woman, National Binding, Hard Cover, Ruth Berolzheimer, 1953	11
Betty Crocker's Cooky Book, Hardcover, Spiral Bound, 1963, 10 x 8 In., 156 Pages	28
Betty Crocker's Working Woman's Cookbook, Hardcover, 1982, 10 x 8 In., 160 Pages	32
Charleston Receipts, Syrian-Lebanese, Spiral Bound, Shums Il Bir Club, 1966, 70 Pages	54
Home Comfort, Wrought Iron Range Co., Soft Cover, Black & White Images, c.1933, 223 Pages	26
Instruction In Cooking, By Mrs. John W. Cringan, Hardcover, 1895, 327 Pages	188
Mountain Measures, Junior League, West Virginia, Spiral Bound, 1974, 380 Pages	9
Recipes From The Olde Pink House, 1771, Spiral Bound, Collection Of Secret Recipes, Sava	36
Southern Elegance, Junior League, Gaston County, Hardcover, Spiral Bound, 1987, 360 Pages	14

COOKIE JARS with brightly painted designs or amusing figural shapes became popular in the mid-1930s. They became very popular again when Andy Warhol's collection was auctioned after his death in 1987. Prices have gone down since then and are very low. Many companies made them and collectors search for cookie jars either by design or by maker's name. Listed here are examples by the less common makers. Major factories are listed under their own names in other categories of the book, such as Abingdon, Brush, Hull, McCoy, Metlox, Red Wing, and Shawnee. See also the Disneyana category. These are marks of three cookie jar manufacturers.

Brush Pottery Co.	TWIN-WINTON ©	FITZ AND FLOYD, INC. ©MCMLXXX FF
Brush Pottery Co. 1925–1982	Twin Winton Ceramics 1946–1977	Fitz and Floyd Enterprises LLC 1960–1980

Majorette, Bisque, Pink Cheeks, Red Hat, Black Hair, 11 ¼ In.	35
Monkey, Squat, Holding Banana, Black Hat, California Originals, 10 ½ x 8 ¾ In.	45
Panda, 3-Sided, See, Hear, Speak, Covers Eyes, Ears, Mouth, Black & White, Made In China	19
Train, Engine, Black, Gray, Lionel, Enesco, 6 x 18 x 5 In.	18

COORS dinnerware was made by the Coors Porcelain Company of Golden, Colorado, a company founded with the help of the Coors Brewing Company. Its founder, John Herold, started the Herold China and Pottery Company in 1910 on the site of a glassworks owned by Adolph Coors, the founder of the Coors brewery. The company began making art pottery using clay from nearby mines. Adolph Coors Company bought Herold China and Pottery Company in early 1915. Chemical porcelains were made beginning in 1915. The company name was changed to Coors Porcelain Company in 1920, when Herold left. Several lines of dinnerware were made in the 1920s and 1930s. Marks on dinnerware and cookware made by Coors include Rosebud, Glencoe Thermo-Porcelain, Colorado, and other names. Coors stopped making nonessential wares at the start of World War II. After the war, the pottery made ovenware, teapots, vases, and a general line of pottery, but no dinnerware—except for special orders. In 1986 Coors Porcelain became Coors Ceramics. In 2000, Coors Ceramics changed its name to CoorsTek. The company is still in business making industrial porcelain. For more prices, go to kovels.com.

Coors Porcelain Co. 1920s	Coors Porcelain Co. 1934–1942	Coors Porcelain Co. 1934–1942

Stein, Boat, River, Mountains, 1992, 7 x 3 In.	15
Vase, Beehive Shape, Terra-Cotta, Matte Finish, Green Lip, Ring Handles, c.1925, 5 x 5 In.	45
Vase, Brown Matte, Handles, Green Rim, 1920, 6 In.	75

Collector Plate, Franklin Mint, Meths, Highlander Series, Portrait, Gold Trim, Leaves, No. 294
$10

66slm84 on eBay

Collector Plate, Hibel, The World I Love, Edna's Music Flute Player, No. 2403, 8 In.
$5

treasures(4u) on eBay

Collector Plate, Thomas Kinkade, All Friends Are Welcome, Winter, Horse, House, 1993, 8 ½ In.
$7

davespeanuts on eBay

> **TIP**
> *Put a piece of cardboard between the back of the plate and the wire plate holder to keep the back from scratching.*

Commemorative, Tennis Racket, Marriage, King George VI & Queen Elizabeth, Tin Throat Photos, 1923 $1,107

Morphy Auctions

Copeland, Tureen, Lid, Seaweed, Molded Handles, Flow Blue, Ironstone, c.1850, 11 In. $228

Garth's Auctioneers & Appraisers

Copper, Charger, Seed Pods, Hammered, Gustav Stickley, 1910s, 20 In. $4,062

Rago Arts and Auction Center

COPELAND pieces listed here are those that have a mark including the word *Copeland* used between 1847 and 1976. Marks include *Copeland Spode* and *Copeland & Garrett*. See also Copeland Spode, Royal Worcester, and Spode.

Teapot, Gilt, Green, Portrait Medallion Of John Brown, 5 ½ In.	2440
Tureen, Lid, Seaweed, Molded Handles, Flow Blue, Ironstone, c.1850, 11 In. ...... *illus*	228

COPELAND SPODE appears on some pieces of nineteenth-century English porcelain. Josiah Spode established a pottery at Stoke-on-Trent, England, in 1770. In 1833, the firm was purchased by William Copeland and Thomas Garrett and the mark was changed. In 1847, Copeland became the sole owner and the mark changed again. W.T. Copeland & Sons continued until a 1976 merger when it became Royal Worcester Spode. The company was bought by the Portmeirion Group in 2009. Pieces are listed in this book under the name that appears in the mark. Copeland, Royal Worcester, and Spode have separate listings.

Bowl, Cobalt Blue, Cream, Fox Hunt, Men, Horses, Footed, c.1905, 10 x 4 In.	295
Cake Stand, Greek, Brown, Yellow, 2 Handles, Pedestal, 11 x 4 In.	299
Tureen, Wicker Weave Pattern, Underplate, Red Transfer Lid, Flowers, 13 x 6 In.	325

COPPER has been used to make utilitarian items, such as teakettles and cooking pans, since the days of the early American colonists. Copper became a popular metal with the Arts & Crafts makers of the early 1900s, and decorative pieces, like desk sets, were made. Copper pieces may also be found in Arts & Crafts, Bradley & Hubbard, Kitchen, Roycroft, and other categories.

CHASE U.S.A.

Chase Brass and Copper Co., Inc.
1930s

Craftsman Workshop
Mark of Gustav Stickley
c.1900–1915

POTTER STUDIO

Potter Studio
c.1900–1929

Bed Warmer, Punched, Tooled Pan, Wood Handle, 1800s, 44 In.	25
Bowl, Flower Form, Gold Plated, Lobed Rim, Marie Zimmerman, 1930s, 4 x 12 In.	2125
Bowl, Hammered, Embossed Geometrics, Wurtenbürgische Machin Fabrik Co., Oval, 8 x 12 x 2 ½ In.	413
Bowl, Piecrust Lip, Mixed Metal Flower, Hammer, Gorham, 3 ¼ x 3 ¼ In.	578
Bucket, Apple, Iron Bail Handle, 1800s, 16 x 25 In.	413
Cauldron, Iron Bail Handle, Rounded Bottom, Dovetailed, 1800s, 17 x 25 In.	258
Charger, Seed Pods, Hammered, Gustav Stickley, 1910s, 20 In. ...... *illus*	4062
Dish, Lid, Hammered, Finial, Silver Plated Metal, M. Zimmermann, c.1910, 8 x 7 In. ...... *illus*	1250
Figurine, Crayfish, Articulated, Taisho Period, Japan, 13 ½ In.	540
Fish Poacher, Steel Rack, Handles, 1800s, 24 ¼ In.	75
Jug, Hammered, Dovetailed, 2 Handles, Brass Band, 16 In.	35
Kettle, Apple Butter, Handle, 1800s, 13 ½ x 20 In.	500
Kettle, Apple Butter, Handle, Round, 15 x 23 In.	270
Kettle, Brass & Wood Swing Handle, Marked, E.B. Badger & Sons Co., c.1898, 12 In. ...... *illus*	330
Kettle, Brass, Lid, Handle, 1800s, 11 ½ In.	47
Kettle, Dovetailed, Handle, Brass Knob, 1800s, 14 In.	238
Kettle, Swing Handle, Gooseneck Spout, Stamped, J. Gable, Pennsylvania, 1800s, 14 In. .. *illus*	250
Molds are listed in the Kitchen category.	
Pan, Fish, Poaching, Lift-Out Tray, Toned Handles, France, 1800s, 7 x 26 x 8 In. ...... *illus*	308
Plaque, Electrotype, 4 Metal Roundels, Oak Frame, Samuel H. Black, 1859, 16 x 12 In.	277
Plaque, Round, Courting Couple, Building, 1996, 20 ½ In.	1560
Plaque, Round, Relief, Sacking Of Rome, Square Mahogany Frame, 16 ½ In.	84
Plaque, Woman, Renaissance Style Clothing, Hammered, Greg Ridley, 15 ½ x 7 In.	210
Samovar, Tin Lid, Brass Top Rim, Spigot, P. Daniel, Regency Period, 18 x 15 x 15 ½ In. .... *illus*	136
Sculpture, Face, Triangular, Stamped, K. Hagenauer, Austria, 14 x 6 ½ In.	861
Sculpture, Hanging, Woven Wire, Black Finish, D'Lisa Creager, 2018, 60 x 14 In. ...... *illus*	5325

Copper, Dish, Lid, Hammered, Finial, Silver
Plated Metal, M. Zimmermann, c.1910,
8 x 7 In.
$1,250

Rago Arts and Auction Center

Copper, Kettle, Brass & Wood Swing Handle,
Marked, E.B. Badger & Sons Co., c.1898, 12 In.
$330

Garth's Auctioneers & Appraisers

Copper, Kettle, Swing Handle, Gooseneck
Spout, Stamped, J. Gable, Pennsylvania,
1800s, 14 In.
$250

Pook & Pook

Copper, Pan, Fish, Poaching, Lift-Out Tray,
Toned Handles, France, 1800s, 7 x 26 x 8 In.
$308

Crescent City Auction Gallery

Copper, Samovar, Tin Lid, Brass Top Rim,
Spigot, P. Daniel, Regency Period,
18 x 15 x 15 ½ In.
$136

Soulis Auctions

Copper, Sculpture, Hanging, Woven Wire,
Black Finish, D'Lisa Creager, 2018, 60 x 14 In.
$5,325

Rago Arts and Auction Center

Copper, Vase, Buttressed, Hammered, Angled
Supports, Tookay Shop, Karl Kipp, 1910s, 7 In.
$4,062

Rago Arts and Auction Center

Vintage Copper Is Back

The informal decorating that is
popular today has created a new
demand for vintage copper. Modern copper is often highly polished and shiny. Vintage copper
has a hammered surface or even
etched or applied designs. Look
for copper trays, bowls, kitchen
utensils, and more at flea markets
or house sales. The copper color
will show beneath the dark tarnish
that cleans off quickly.

Copper, Vessel, Hammered, Blackened,
Folded, Male Nude, Signed Leonard Urso,
12 x 37 x 16 In.
$1,000

Rago Arts and Auction Center

Coralene, Vase, Mother-Of-Pearl, Blue, Coin Dot, Yellow Overlay, 3¾ x 4½ In. $150

Woody Auction

Corkscrew, Lady's Leg, Metal, Pink Striped Pants, Black Boots, Germany $415

alexandersantiqueswv on eBay

Corkscrew, Wood Handle, Brass, Wine Bottle Opener, Rotating, Steel Shaft, 6 In. $38

patcap on eBay

Urn, Art Nouveau, Gilt, Silvered, Bronze Mounts, Cherubs, Round Foot, Early 1900s, 29 In.	813
Vase, Buttressed, Hammered, Angled Supports, Tookay Shop, Karl Kipp, 1910s, 7 In. ...... *illus*	4062
Vase, Floor, Hammered, Copper, Wrought Iron Holder, Arts & Crafts, 29 In.	450
Vase, Hammered, Chisel Decoration, Arts & Crafts, 7¾ x 2⅝ In.	246
Vessel, Hammered, Blackened, Folded, Male Nude, Signed Leonard Urso, 12 x 37 x 16 In. *illus*	1000
Wash Boiler, Lid, Wood Handles, 28 x 13¼ x 17 In.	94

COPPER LUSTER *items are listed in the Luster category.*

CORALENE glass was made by firing many small colored beads on the outside of glassware. It was made in many patterns in the United States and Europe in the 1880s. Reproductions are made today.

Vase, Mother-Of-Pearl, Blue, Coin Dot, Yellow Overlay, 3¾ x 4½ In. .... *illus*	150

CORDEY CHINA COMPANY was founded by Boleslaw Cybis in 1942 in Trenton, New Jersey. The firm produced gift shop items. In 1969 it was acquired by the Lightron Corp. and operated as the Schiller Cordey Co., manufacturers of lamps. About 1950 Boleslaw Cybis began making Cybis porcelains, which are listed in the Cybis category in this book.

Bust, Woman, Ringlets, 1940s, 5¼ In.	15
Figurine, Woman, Blue Dress, Flowers In Hair, Ribbon, 14 In.	149
Figurine, Woman, Blue Hat & Shoes, Pink Flower Dress, 11 In.	60
Figurine, Woman, Pitcher On Shoulder, Roses, Curly Blond Hair, 10½ In.	280
Lamp, Figural, Woman, Curled Hair, Hat, Gold Metal Base, 1940s, 34 In.	125

CORKSCREWS have been needed since the first bottle was sealed with a cork, probably in the seventeenth century. Today collectors search for the early, unusual patented examples or the figural corkscrews of recent years.

Bone, Horse Jockey, England, 1900s, 4¼ x 1½ In.	45
Clown, Bottle Opener, Wood, Syroco, Signed, c.1950, 8¾ x 2¾ x 2¾ In.	254
Indian Chief, Wood, Bottle Opener, Multicolor, Syroco, c.1950, 8¾ x 2¾ x 2¾ In.	480
Lady's Leg, Metal, Pink Striped Pants, Black Boots, Germany .... *illus*	415
Metal, Wood Handle, Spring Sides, Hobbyswood Militaria, 5½ x 3 In.	181
Monk, Bottle Opener, Wood, Syracuse Ornamental Co., c.1950, 8 x 2¾ x 2¾ In.	215
Motorcycle, Rider, Bronze Plated, 1930s, 3¾ x 4¼ In.	54
Sommelier, Pierre, Figural, Wine Bottle Opener, Italy, 8 In.	16
Turned Handle, Steel Shaft, Wood Handle, Bottle Opener, Ox Bone, Miniature, 1800s	127
Wood Handle, Brass, Wine Bottle Opener, Rotating, Steel Shaft, 6 In. .... *illus*	38
Wood Handle, Cork Gripper, Steel Shaft, Victorian	15
Wood, Antler Handle, Sterling End Caps, John Hasselbring, c.1935, 6⅛ In.	395
Wood, Pull, Wire Cutter, Knife, c.1890, 6½ In.	145

CORONATION souvenirs have been made since the 1800s. Pottery, glass, tin, silver, and paper objects with a picture of the monarchs and date have been sold at many coronations. The pieces that mention King Edward VIII, the king who was never crowned, are not rare; collectors should be sure to check values before buying. Related pieces are found in the Commemorative category.

Beaker, Czar Nicholas, Queen Alexandra, Geometrics, Khodynka Cup, 1896, 4 x 3¾ In. ... *illus*	310
Cup, Czar Nicholas II, Enamel, Crest, Red, Blue, 1896, 4¼ In.	287
Cup, Saucer, Queen Elizabeth II, Westminster Abby, 1953, 3 x 5 In.	55
Goblet, Queen Elizabeth II, Crown, Etched Rose, Cut Glass, Webb, 1953, 8 In.	130
Group, George VI, Carriage, Gilt, Blue, Horses, Red Saddle Blankets, 1937, 20 In.	295
Jar, King George VI & Queen Elizabeth, Amber Glass, 1937, 2 x 4¼ In.	20
Medal, King Edward VII & Queen Alexandra, Gold Plated, Round, 1902, 1³⁄₁₆ In.	4
Mug, Edward VII, Alexandra, Stoneware, Doulton Lambeth, 4 In.	46
Mug, George V, Bugle Brand, M.B. Foster & Sons Ltd., C-Handle, Guinness, 1910s, 4 x 5 In.	162
Pitcher, William IV, White, Portrait, Crown, Swords, Flowers, 1830, 7 x 4½ In. .... *illus*	47
Plate, King Edward VII & Queen Alexandria, Portrait, Blue Ground, Gold Rim, 1902	11

Thimble, Queen Elizabeth II, Daisy Pattern Top, Reeded Border, Crown, 1952	53
Tray, Queen Elizabeth II, Oval, Crown Handles, Sterling Silver, 1953, 4½ x 3½ In.	40

COSMOS is a pressed milk glass pattern with colored flowers made from 1894 to 1915 by the Consolidated Lamp and Glass Company. Tablewares and lamps were made in this pattern. A few pieces were also made of clear glass with painted decorations. Other glass patterns are listed under Consolidated Lamp and also in various glass categories. In later years, Cosmos was also made by the Westmoreland Glass Company.

Bowl, Spooner, Flowers, Pink Trim, Footed, Lattice Ground, 4 x 4 In.	40
Lamp, Oil, Flowers, Dots On Base, Hurricane Shade, c.1910, 8¾ x 4½ In.	39
Pitcher, Daisies, Pink, Yellow, Blue, Quilted, 1800s, 9 x 6½ In.	70
Salt & Pepper, Flower Grouping, Pink, Yellow, Blue, c.1895-1902, 3¼ x 2¼ In.	38
Salt & Pepper, Pansy Flowers, Purple, Tin Silvertone Tops, 4½ x 2½ In.	36

COVERLETS were made of linen or wool during the nineteenth century. Most of the coverlets date from 1800 to the 1880s. There was a revival of hand weaving in the 1920s and new coverlets, especially geometric patterns, were made. The earliest coverlets were made on narrow looms, so two woven strips were joined together and a seam can be found. The weave structures of coverlets can include summer and winter, double weave, overshot, and others. Jacquard coverlets have elaborate pictorial patterns that are made on a special loom or with the use of a special attachment. Makers often wove a personal message in the corner. Quilts are listed in this book in their own category.

John Henry Meily (1817–1884) 1842–1850s

Matthew Rattray (1796–1872) 1822–1872

Samuel Stinger (c.1801–1879) 1838–1879

Jacquard, Blue & Natural, Eagle Corner Block, Flowerpot Borders, 1850, 72 x 90 In.	625
Jacquard, Blue & Natural, Red, Eagle & House Border, 2 Panel, c.1850, 78 x 88 In.	125
Jacquard, Blue & Red, Repeating Geometric Pattern, c.1850, 98 x 81 In.	554
Jacquard, Blue & White, Flowers, Eagle & Tree Border, Martha Warner, Wool, 1843, 84 x 78 In.	554
Jacquard, Blue & White, Red, Green, Wool & Linen, Vines, Flowers, 88 x 82 In. .... *illus*	143
Jacquard, Blue & White, Wool, Linen, Flowers & Eagle Border, 2 Panel, 1845, 88 x 72 In.	132
Jacquard, Blue, Natural, House Border, Rose Medallions, Newark, Ohio, 1840, 76 x 84 In.	390
Jacquard, Flowers, 3 Colors, Navy & Beige, 2 Panel, 1800s, 75 x 90 In.	90
Jacquard, Flowers, Leaves, Bird Corners, Pennsylvania, 1836	225
Jacquard, Flowers, Sword, Eagle Border, Geo. Washington, Wool & Linen, 1837, 86 x 72 In.	880
Jacquard, Green, Red, Blue, Eagle Corners, Pennsylvania, c.1850	125
Jacquard, Red & Green, Flowers, c.1850, 98 x 82 In.	175
Jacquard, Red, White, Blue, Flowers, Bird, Emanuel Meily, Wool, 1834, 100 x 74 In.	431
Jacquard, Tulips In Urns, Olive Green, Red, Blue, White, Wool & Linen, 1858, 88 x 76 In.	132
Overshot, Blue & White, Geometric Striped Border, Wool, 2 Panel, 1800s, 78 x 74 In.	198
Overshot, Blue & White, Flowers, Bird & Building Border, Wool, S. Balantyne, 1847, 86 x 76 In.	584
Summer & Winter, Blue & White, Bridges, Buildings, 2 Piece, 1850s, 84 x 87 In. .... *illus*	163

COWAN POTTERY made art pottery and wares for florists. Guy Cowan made pottery in Rocky River, Ohio, a suburb of Cleveland, from 1913 to 1931. A stylized mark with the word *Cowan* was used on most pieces. A commercial, mass-produced line was marked *Lakeware*. Collectors today search for the Art Deco pieces by Guy Cowan, Viktor Schreckengost, Waylande Gregory, or Thelma Frazier Winter.

Ashtray, Ram, Blue Glaze, Eckhardt, 5 In.	298
Bowl, Console, Scalloped Bowl, Pedestal, Green Interior, 6 x 16 x 10 In.	400
Candlestick, Etruscan, Yellow Glossy Glaze, c.1930, 1¾ x 4¾ In., Pair	69
Figurine, Tambourine Player, Parchment Gloss Tan Glaze, c.1927, 8½ In.	169
Lamp Base, Raised, Stylized Trees, Branches, Buds, Leaves, Iron Base, c.1925, 12¾ In.	750

Coronation, Beaker, Czar Nicholas, Queen Alexandra, Geometrics, Khodynka Cup, 1896, 4 x 3¾ In.
$310

itsallgood1965 on eBay

Coronation, Pitcher, William IV, White, Portrait, Crown, Swords, Flowers, 1830, 7 x 4½ In.
$47

shazvintage on eBay

Coverlet, Jacquard, Blue & White, Red, Green, Wool & Linen, Vines, Flowers, 88 x 82 In.
$143

Forsythes' Auctions

Coverlet, Summer & Winter, Blue & White, Bridges, Buildings, 2 Piece, 1850s, 84 x 87 In.
$163

Garth's Auctioneers & Appraisers

Cracker Jack, Charm, Movable Dog House, Prize Gumball, Plastic, Green & Red, Mechanical
$16

ginasjunks1 on eBay

Cracker Jack, Pin, Jack The Sailor, Ceramic, Blue & White, Red Flag
$9

foxytwirlygirly on eBay

Match Holder, Seahorse, Ivory Gloss, 3½ In.	38
Vase, Footed, Channeled Fan Shape, Seahorse Base, Green Matte Glaze, c.1926, 7 In.	125
Vase, Globular, Yellow Rose Glaze, Textured, Marked, 1930s, 4½ In.	79

 CRACKER JACK, the molasses-flavored popcorn mixture, was first made in 1896 in Chicago, Illinois. A prize was added to each box in 1912. Collectors search for the old boxes, toys, and advertising materials. Many of the toys are unmarked. New toys are usually paper, older toys are tin, paper, or plastic.

Bank, Box Truck, Hawkeye, Sailor, White, Red, Blue & Black, 1931	8
Box, Tin, Barnum's Animals, Crackers, Red, National Biscuit Company, 1979	8
Charm, Movable Dog House, Prize Gumball, Plastic, Green & Red, Mechanical ..... *illus*	16
Game, Pinball, Bunnies, Butterfly, Red Lettering	3
Globe, Prize, Miniature, Blue & Yellow, Round Stand, Plastic	37
Lunch Box, Metal, Aladdin & Thermos, Jack The Sailor, Bingo, 1978-79	54
Pin, Jack The Sailor, Ceramic, Blue & White, Red Flag ..... *illus*	9
Sign, Red, White & Blue, 4 Grommets, Porcelain Enamel, 1990s, 12 x 6 In.	13
Toy, Sailboat, Tin Lithograph, Stand-Up, 1941	18
Toy, Train, Tin Lithograph, Folded Metal	76

 CRANBERRY GLASS is an almost transparent yellow-red glass. It resembles the color of cranberry juice. The glass has been made in Europe and America since the Civil War. It is still being made, and reproductions can fool the unwary. Related glass items may be listed in other categories, such as Rubina Verde.

Bowl, Ribbed, Turquoise Rim, Sea Form, 2¼ x 2¾ In.	200
Bowl, Thousand Eye, Cut To Clear, Ray Cut Base, 3 x 4¾ In. ..... *illus*	60
Epergne, Enameled, Trumpet Shape, Ruffled Rim, Victorian, 15 x 10½ In.	108
Ewer, Pink, Ruffled Top, Applied Handle, Thumbprint, 5½ x 4½ In.	24
Lamp, Hall, Chain Movement, Cranberry Shade, Brass Fitting, c.1875, 27½ In.	113
Lamp, Kerosene, Milk Glass Base, Ruffled Rim Shade, Electrified, 26 x 6 In.	120
Lamp, Panel Optic, Miniature, Hornet Burner, Plume & Atwood, c.1899, 8 x 3¾ x 3 In.	96
Muffineer, Panel, Pierced Metal Top, 5½ x 2¼ In. ..... *illus*	48
Pitcher, Flowers, Greek Key, Rope Clear Glass, 10 In.	118
Pitcher, Inverted Thumbprint, Twisted Clear Handle, Polished Pontil, c.1880, 7½ In. ..... *illus*	63
Pitcher, Leafy Sprays, Flower, Handle, Silver Collar, Dorflinger, 9¾ x 8 x 5½ In.	2712
Pitcher, Opalescent, Eye Dot Pattern, Clear Ribbed Handle, 10 In.	60
Vase, Cylinder, Gilt, Molded, Base, c.1900, 10¾ In.	263

CREAMWARE, or queensware, was developed by Josiah Wedgwood about 1765. It is a cream-colored earthenware that has been copied by many factories. Similar wares may be listed under Pearlware and Wedgwood.

Coffeepot, Lid, Molded Spout, Slip Shavings, Acorn Knop, England, c.1790, 10 In. ..... *illus*	1476
Jar, Globular Shape, Splayed Bisque Foot, Craquelure, Chinese, 2 x 2¾ In.	677
Jug, Flowers, Cottager Celebration Scene, England, 1700s, 9½ In. ..... *illus*	369
Mug, Brown Slip Marbled, Green Reeded Band, Black Slip, England, c.1800, 4½ In. ..... *illus*	369
Pitcher, Checkered, Slip Shavings, Ribs, Handle, England, c.1790, 4½ In. ..... *illus*	492
Pitcher, Lafayette, Washington, 1824 Visit, Transferware, Early 1800s, 5 x 6 x 4¾ In. ..... *illus*	861
Pitcher, Peace & Plenty, Transferware, Classical Images, England, Early 1800s, 7 x 7¼ x 5 In.	277
Plate Set, Prodigal Son Story, England, 1900s, 9¾ In., 6 Piece	2400
Plate, Elijah & Ravens, Dutch, Pair, c.1700, 10 In.	240
Teapot, Lid, Slip Marbled, Brown, Black, Green Bands, Molded Spout, c.1780, 4¾ In.	1968

 CREIL, France, had a faience factory as early as 1794. The company merged with a factory in Montereau in 1819. It made stoneware, mocha ware, and soft paste porcelain. The name *Creil* appears as part of the mark on many pieces. The Creil factory closed in 1895.

Dish, Compote, Green Transferware, Marked, c.1920, 10 In.	88
Jardiniere, Flowers, Buds, Branches, Leaves, Bouquets, Oval, Gilt Bronze Stand, 6 x 12 In.	218
Plate, Strawberries, Leaves, Tendrils, c.1850, 8½ In.	212

C

C

Cranberry Glass, Bowl, Thousand Eye, Cut To Clear, Ray Cut Base, 3 x 4¾ In.
$60

Woody Auction

Cranberry Glass, Muffineer, Panel, Pierced Metal Top, 5½ x 2¼ In.
$48

Martin Auction Co.

Cranberry Glass, Pitcher, Inverted Thumbprint, Twisted Clear Handle, Polished Pontil, c.1880, 7½ In.
$63

Garth's Auctioneers & Appraisers

Creamware, Coffeepot, Lid, Molded Spout, Slip Shavings, Acorn Knop, England, c.1790, 10 In.
$1,476

Skinner, Inc.

Creamware, Jug, Flowers, Cottager Celebration Scene, England, 1700s, 9½ In.
$369

Skinner, Inc.

Creamware, Mug, Brown Slip Marbled, Green Reeded Band, Black Slip, England, c.1800, 4½ In.
$369

Skinner, Inc.

Creamware, Pitcher, Checkered, Slip Shavings, Ribs, Handle, England, c.1790, 4½ In.
$492

Skinner, Inc.

TIP

If you live in the North and you find your gifts left out in the cold by the front door be careful. Freezing temperatures make glass and ceramics brittle. Bring the package inside, open it, but do not unwrap the contents until everything is room temperature.

Creamware, Pitcher, Lafayette, Washington, 1824 Visit, Transferware, Early 1800s, 5 x 6 x 4¾ In.
$861

Cowan's Auctions

Cruet, Cut Glass, Pyramid Shape, Hobstar & Nailhead Diamond, Double Notched Handle, 9½ In.
$60

Woody Auction

Cruet, Peachblow, Amber Handle, Faceted Stopper, Hobbs, c.1885, 5¼ In.
$448

Jeffrey S. Evans & Associates

Tureen, White, 2 Scrolled Handles, Footed, Marked, 11 x 15 In.	76
Wash Bowl, Brown Pattern, Kingfishers, Dragonfly & Water Lilies, c.1880, 15 In.	283

CROWN DERBY is the name given to porcelain made in Derby, England, from the 1770s to 1935. Andrew Planche and William Duesbury established Crown Derby as the first china-making factory in Derby. Pieces are marked with a crown and the letter *D* or the word *Derby*. The earliest pieces were made by the original Derby factory, while later pieces were made by the King Street Partnerships (1848–1935) or the Derby Crown Porcelain Co. (1876–90). Derby Crown Porcelain Co. became Royal Crown Derby Co. Ltd. in 1890.

Candlestick, Rust Red Transfer, Birds, Applied Gilded Edge, c.1972, 10 x 6 In.	398
Compote, Imari, Cobalt Blue, Peach, Gold, Footed, c.1920, 10⅜ In.	685
Vase, Imari, Cobalt Blue & Peach Flowers, Gold Ground, c.1890, 9 In.	295

CROWN DUCAL is the name used on some pieces of porcelain made by A.G. Richardson and Co., Ltd., of Tunstall and Cobridge, England. The name has been used since 1916. Crown Ducal is a well-known maker of chintz pattern dishes. The company was bought by Wedgwood in 1974.

Cup & Saucer, Chintz, Marked	59
Cup & Saucer, Demitasse, Fruit & Flowers In Blue Urn, c.1928	12
Dish, 3 Sections, Clover Shape, Scalloped, Flowers, Pink, Blue, Yellow, 3-Hole Handle, 9 In.	60
Jug, Hydrangea, Pink & Purple Blossoms, Green Handle & Foot, 1930s, 6 In.	375
Pitcher, Ivy, Pink Transferware, Scalloped Rim, 4½ In.	48
Plate, Flowers, Cobalt Blue Band, Sterling Silver Reticulated Border, 11 In.	77
Serving Dish, Exotic Bird, Rectangular, Scalloped Ends, Blue Trim, 11 In.	45
Sugar, Lid, 2 Handles, Blue Chintz, Black Trim, Octagonal, 4 x 5 In.	139
Tea & Toast Set, Blue, Black Trim, Flowers, Birds, 10¼ In.	119
Teapot, Floral Chintz, Multicolor, Marked, 2 Cups, 6 In.	225
Vase, Bee Eater Birds, Dragonflies, Pine Boughs, Pastel Pink & Green, 1920s, 10 In.	115
Vase, Black, Pink Rose Swags, White Flowers, 1920s, 13 In.	145

CROWN MILANO glass was made by the Mt. Washington Glass Works about 1890. It was a plain biscuit color with a satin finish decorated with flowers and often had large gold scrolls. Not all pieces are marked.

Biscuit Jar, Flowers, Purple, White, Silver Top, Marked W M, c.1893, 7 x 6 In.	1250
Cigar Humidor, Oak Leaves, Acorns, Gold Gilt, Autumn Colors, Hinged Lid, c.1885, 6½ In.	875
Cup & Saucer, Gold Spider Mums, Light Pink Ground, 1891-95, 2 Piece	425
Ewer, Portrait, Man & Woman, Raised, 13 x 5 In.	2995
Pitcher, Bird, Gilt Flower Branch, Gilt Handle, Cream Ground, c.1890, 9 x In.	295
Vase, Round Body, Ring Neck, Matte, Gilt Rose, 22K Gold, c.1890, 10½ In.	1495

CROWN TUSCAN *pattern is included in the Cambridge glass category.*

CRUETS of glass or porcelain were made to hold vinegar, oil, and other condiments. They were especially popular during Victorian times and have been made in a variety of styles since the eighteenth century. Additional cruets may be found in the Castor Set category and also in various glass categories.

Beaded Shell, Blue, Stopper, Dugan Glass Co., c.1904, 7⅝ In.	195
Cut Glass, Bergen Electric Pattern, Ray Cut Base, 6 In.	30
Cut Glass, Cranberry Cut To Clear, Cranberry Buttons, Rayed Base, Russia, 7 In.	720
Cut Glass, Pyramid Shape, Hobstar & Nailhead Diamond, Double Notched Handle, 9½ In.. *illus*	60
Cut Glass, Ray Cut Base, Triple Notched Handle, J. Hoare, 9 In.	24
Cut Glass, Strawberry Diamond, Cane & Fan, Notched Handle, Signed, J. Hoare, 8¾ In.	24
Glass, Overshot, Pale Rose, Bulbous, Reeded Handle, Faceted Stopper, c.1880, 6 In.	70
Hobstar, Strawberry Diamond & Fan, Stopper, Ray Cut Base, 7½ In.	48
Opalescent, White Faceted Stopper, Coin Spot, 1940s, 6 x 3 In.	98
Peachblow, Amber Handle, Faceted Stopper, Hobbs, c.1885, 5¼ In. *illus*	448
Vinegar, Hand Blown, Gold Trim On Bottom & Stopper, Handle, Polished Pontil, 1890s, 10½ In.	129

CT GERMANY was first part of a mark used by a company in Altwasser, Germany (now part of Walbrzych, Poland), in 1845. The initials stand for C. Tielsch, a partner in the firm. The Hutschenreuther firm took over the company in 1918 and continued to use the *CT* until 1952.

C. T.

Biscuit Jar, Lid, Flowers, Lavender, Yellow, Purple, Footed, c.1905, 7 x 4 In.	255
Bowl, 2-Sided, Handle, Pink Flowers, Turquoise Scalloped Edge, Gold Trim, 14 x 11 In.	64
Bowl, Centerpiece, Pink Roses, Victorian Style, Gold Trim, c.1887, 14 In.	82
Platter, Yellow, Black, Orange, Scrollwork, Gold Gilt, 1930s, 12 In.	100
Porcelain, Sunderland Luster Rim, Romantic View, Blue Transfer, Staffordshire, 4 In.	153

CURRIER & IVES made the famous American lithographs marked with their name from 1857 to 1907. The mark used on the print included the street address in New York City, and it is possible to date the year of the original issue from this information. Earlier prints were made by N. Currier and use that name from 1835 to 1847. Many reprints of the Currier or Currier & Ives prints have been made. Some collectors buy the insurance calendars that were based on the old prints. The words *large, small,* or *medium folio* refer to size. The original print sizes were very small (up to about 7 x 9 in.), small (8⅘ x 12⅘ in.), medium (9 x 14 in. to 14 x 20 in.), and large (larger than 14 x 20 in.). Other sizes are probably later copies. Copies of prints by Currier & Ives may be listed in Card, Advertising and in the Sheet Music category. Currier & Ives dinnerware patterns may be found in the Adams or Dinnerware categories.

Home Of Washington, Mount Vernon, Va., 11 x 16 In.	750
Mayflower Saluted By The Fleet, Frame, 22 x 28 In.	390
Regatta Of New York Yacht Club, The Start, Fleet Of Ships, 17 x 28 In.	270
Road Side Cottage Boy Bringing Sheep Through Gate, 9½ x 16¾ In.	725
Rustic Bridge, Central Park, New York, 8⅜ x 12¼ In.	625
Schooner Yacht Magic Of New York Yacht Club, Ship, Frame, 26 x 34 In.	812
Soldiers Dream Of Home, 1862, 8 x 12½ In.	275
Western Farmers Home, 1871, 8½ x 12⅜ In.	800

CUSTARD GLASS is a slightly yellow opaque glass. It was made in England in the 1880s and was first made in the United States in the 1890s. It has been reproduced. Additional pieces may be found in the Cambridge, Fenton, and Heisey categories. Custard glass is called *Ivorina Verde* by Heisey and other companies.

Figurine, Bulldog, Seated, Ears Up, Green, Glass Eyes, 7 x 8 In.	30
Plate, Lions, Trees, Berries, Leaves, Yellow, Green, Shaped Edge, 7½ In.	30
Poppy, Basket, Fenton, 7 In.	68

CUT GLASS has been made since ancient times, but the large majority of the pieces now for sale date from the American Brilliant period of glass design, 1875 to 1915. These pieces have elaborate geometric designs with a deep miter cut. Modern cut glass with a similar appearance is being made in England, Ireland, Poland, the Czech Republic, and Slovakia. Chips and scratches are often difficult to notice but lower the value dramatically. A signature on the glass, usually on the smooth inside of a bowl, adds significantly to the value. Other cut glass pieces are listed under factory names, like Hawkes, Libbey, Pairpoint, Sinclaire, and Stevens & Williams.

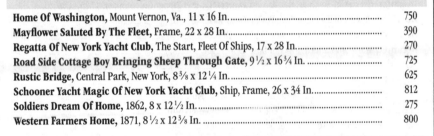

Bonbon, Heart Shape, Hobstar Center, Prism Cut Border, 5½ In.	36
Bottle, Catsup, Hobstar, Cane & Fan, Ray Cut Base, 5½ In.	180
Bottle, Cruet, Hobstar, Strawberry Diamond, Prism & Fan, Signed, J. Hoare, 7 In.	30
Bowl, Eggnog, Lid, Silver Plated Stand, WMF, Germany, 17½ In. .... *illus*	540
Bowl, Hobstar Center, Crosby, J. Hoare, 3½ x 7 In.	36
Bowl, Hobstar Center, Triangular Shape, Block Diamond, Dorflinger, 5 x 9¼ In.	48
Bowl, Hobstar Cluster, 4 x 8 In.	50
Bowl, Hobstar, Fan & Miter Highlights, 2½ x 4½ In.	72
Bowl, Hobstar, Strawberry Diamond, Cane & Fan, 2 x 8 In.	10
Bowl, Hobstar, Strawberry Diamond, Cane, Nailhead & Fan Diamond, Intaglio Leaves, 4 x 8 In.	60

Cut Glass, Bowl, Eggnog, Lid, Silver Plated Stand, WMF, Germany, 17½ In. $540

Cut Glass, Centerpiece, Bisque 4 Seasons Base, Figures, Gilt Bronze, Fluted Column, 16¾ x 14 In. $1,029

Cut Glass, Decanter, Green Cut To Clear, Hobstar, Strawberry, Cane & Zipper Cut, Stopper, 17 In. $600

Cut Glass, Jar, Lid, Green Cut To Clear, Cane, Ray Cut Base, 2½ x 3 In. $180

Woody Auction

Cut Glass, Mug, Bohemian, Amber Cut To Clear, Crosscut Diamond & Pillar, Medallion, 5¾ In. $330

Woody Auction

Cut Glass, Pitcher, Belmont, Crosscut Diamond Handle, Hobstar Base, Dorflinger, 7 In. $360

Woody Auction

Bowl, Hobstar, Vesica, Cane, Strawberry Diamond, Prism & Fan, Clear, 3 x 11 x 10½ In.	300
Bowl, Notched Handles, Hobstar & Cane, Rolled Rim, 4 x 11 In.	15
Bowl, Pansy, Hobstar Multi-Vesica, Strawberry & Nailhead Diamond, Fan, 1 x 7 In.	84
Bowl, Pinto, Blown Mold, Pitkin & Brooks, 6¾ In.	72
Bowl, Queens Type, Emerald Green Cut To Clear, Notched Rim, 3 x 8½ In.	720
Box, Lid, Round, Hobstar Base, Bull's-Eye, Miter On Border, 3¼ x 5 In.	48
Box, Lid, Round, Star, Crosscut Diamond, Fan, Hobstar Base, Silver Lid, 3¾ x 5¼ In.	108
Carafe, Water, Colony, Hobstar Base, Bergen, 8¼ In.	48
Card Tray, Victory, Krantz Smith, 7½ x 5¼ In.	30
Celery Tray, Canoe Shape, Hobstar, Strawberry Diamond, Star, 11½ In.	36
Centerpiece, Bisque 4 Seasons Base, Figures, Gilt Bronze, Fluted Column, 16¾ x 14 In. _illus_	1029
Champagne Bucket, Rookwood Magnum, Silver Plate, Handle, 13 x 14 In.	1437
Cheese Dish, Cane Pattern, Dome Lid, 7½ In.	47
Claret, Gladys, Ray Cut Foot, Hawkes, 4¾ In.	20
Cologne Bottle, Zigzag, Nailhead, Sunburst Base, Birmingham Sterling Stopper, 3½ x 6 In.	59
Compote, Cane & Strawberry Diamond, Notched Air Trap Stem, Scalloped Foot, 10½ x 8 In.	120
Compote, Hobstar, Strawberry Diamond & Fan, Geometrics, Teardrop Stem, J. Hoare, 7 x 6½ In.	48
Compote, Hobstar, Strawberry Diamond & Fan, Notched Teardrop Stem, Foot, 8½ x 5¾ In.	60
Cordial, Blue Cut To Clear, Strawberry Diamond, Block & Fan, Notched Stem, Ray Cut Foot, 5 In.	84
Creamer, Hobstar, Nailhead & Crosscut Diamond, Fan, Ray Cut Base, Notched Handle, 7 In.	36
Cup, Horseradish, St. Louis Diamond, Triple Notched Handle, Ray Cut Base, Silver Rim & Lid, 4 In.	300
Decanter, Crosscut Diamond, Star & Fan, Cut Stopper, Ray Cut Foot, 13½ In.	120
Decanter, Green Cut To Clear, Hobstar, Strawberry, Cane & Zipper Cut, Stopper, 17 In. _illus_	600
Decanter, Green Cut To Clear, Split Vesica, Clear Base, 10¾ In.	150
Decanter, Hobstar & Fan, Step Cut Neck, Ray Cut Base, 10½ In.	108
Decanter, Marlboro Pattern, Ray Cut Base, Dorflinger, 9 In.	108
Ferner, Hobstar & Prism, Brass Rim, 3¾ x 8 In.	50
Finger Bowl, Broadway, Krantz Smith, 2½ x 4½ In.	20
Finger Bowl, Hobstar, Vesica, Strawberry Diamond & Fan, 2¼ x 4½ In.	30
Flask, Blue Cut To Clear, 2-Sided, Petal Center, Ray Center, 6 In.	120
Flask, Cobalt Blue Cut To Clear, Petal Center, Star Border, Notched Border, 6 x 4 In.	120
Goblet, Cranberry Cut To Clear, Engraved, Bird & Flower Branch, Footed, 8 In.	96
Goblet, Hobstar, Nailhead & Strawberry Diamond, Fan, Apple Core Stem, Ray Foot, 7 In.	48
Goblet, Molded, Sulphide Cameo Portrait, c.1860, 5½ x 3½ In.	63
Goblet, Toasting, Green Cut, Diamond & Split Vesica, Notched Stem, Flashed Leaf, Fan Foot, 7 In.	180
Jar, Lid, Green Cut To Clear, Cane, Ray Cut Base, 2½ x 3 In. _illus_	180
Jar, Silver, Lid, Flute Cut, Rose Branch, Monogram, 5¾ In.	84
Jug, Rum, Hobstar, Strawberry Diamond, Prism Cut, Strap Handle, Ray Base, 8¼ In.	180
Knife Rest, Hobstar Ends, Prism Highlights, 4 x ½ In.	24
Muffineer, Waffle & Column, Sunburst Base, Floral Silver Lid, Gorham, 5¼ In.	83
Mug, Bohemian, Amber Cut To Clear, Crosscut Diamond & Pillar, Medallion, 5¾ In. _illus_	330
Mustard, Prism, Glass Lid, Glass Spoon, 2½ In.	36
Mustard, Ray Cut Lid & Base, Hindoo, J. Hoare, 3½ In.	48
Nappy, Hobstar Cluster, Nailhead Diamond Vesica, Strawberry Diamond, 6 In.	24
Nappy, Hobstar, Strawberry Diamond, Fan, 6 In.	36
Pitcher, Belmont, Crosscut Diamond Handle, Hobstar Base, Dorflinger, 7 In. _illus_	360
Pitcher, Blue Cut To Clear, Engraved Rose Branches, Birds, Hobstar Border, 8 In.	1200
Pitcher, Cranberry Cut To Clear, Alternating Rows Of Punty, Ray Cut Base, 7¾ In.	270
Pitcher, Pinwheel, Strawberry Diamond, 2 Notched Handles, Ray Base, 9¼ In.	36
Pitcher, Water, Bulbous Prism, Diamond & Cane Border, Triple Handle, Hobstar Base, 8 In.	120
Pitcher, Water, Strawberry Diamond, Star & Fan, Hobstar Base, Triple Notched Handle, 9 In.	108
Plate, Fredericka Pattern, W.C. Anderson, 6¾ In.	120
Plate, Handgrip, Modified Hobstar Center, Fan Highlights, 6½ In.	84
Plate, Hobstar, Vesica, Nailhead & Strawberry Diamond, 7¾ In.	60
Plate, Parisian, Cranberry Cut To Clear, Notched Rim, Dorflinger, 8 In.	1320
Plate, Parisian, Dorflinger, 7 In.	120
Powder Jar, Hobstar, Crosscut Diamond & Fan, Gorham Silver Cap, 4½ In.	48
Relish, Signed, Maple City, 7½ x 3¾ In.	18
Salt Dip, Royal, Ray Cut Center, Dorflinger, 1½ x 3 In.	24

SELECTED CUT GLASS MARKS WITH DATES USED

J.D. Bergen & Co.
1885–1922
Meriden, Conn.

Tuthill Cut Glass Co.
1902–1923
Middletown, N.Y.

Pairpoint Corporation
1880–1938
New Bedford, Mass.

Libbey Glass Co.
1888–1925
Toledo, Ohio

C. Dorflinger & Sons
1852–1921
White Mills, Pa.

T.B. Clark and Co.
1884–1930
Honesdale, Pa.

Majestic Cut Glass Co.
1900–1916
Elmira, N.Y.

Wright Rich Cut Glass Co.
1904–1915
Anderson, Ind.

T.G. Hawkes & Co.
1880–1962
Corning, N.Y.

H.C. Fry Glass Co.
1901–1934
Rochester, Pa.

H.P. Sinclaire & Co.
1905–1929
Corning, N.Y.

House of Birks
c.1894–1907+
Montreal, Quebec, Canada

Laurel Cut Glass Co.
1903–1920
Jarmyn, Pa.

J. Hoare & Co.
1868–1921
Corning, N.Y.

L. Straus & Sons
c.1894–1917
New York, N.Y.

Cut Glass, Tankard, Cranberry Cut To Clear, Hobstar, Block, Strawberry Diamond, Handle, 12 In.
$210

Woody Auction

Cut Glass, Wine, Gold Enamel, Scrolls, Air Trap Lattice Stem, Continental, 6 ½ In.
$60

Woody Auction

Cut Glass, Wine, Rhine, Yellow Acid Cut To Clear, Flower Branches, Air Twist Stem, Gold Trim, 8 In.
$300

Woody Auction

Czechoslovakia Glass, Bowl, Fruit, Overlay, Cobalt Blue, Hand Cut, 5 ½ x 7 ½ x 12 In.
$112

DuMouchelles

Czechoslovakia Glass, Vase, Cameo, Orange, Yellow, Green, Flared Rim, Carved, Stylized Fruit, c.1910, 15 In.
$369

Brunk Auctions

> **TIP**
> *Always buy the best you can afford. It will keep its value better than less expensive items.*

Czechoslovakia Glass, Vase, Fluted, Swirling Surface, Polished Pontil, 2 Handles, Kralik, 12 x 7 x 4 In.
$1,210

Fontaine's Auction Gallery

Sherry, Cranberry Cut To Clear, Crosscut Diamond Arches, Feathered, Ray Cut Foot, 4 ½ In. ..	84
Stringholder, Prism Cut, Ray Cut Base, Marked, Gorham, 3 ¼ x 3 ½ In..........................	240
Sugar & Creamer, Hobstar & Prism, Ray Cut Base, Double Notched Handles........................	70
Sugar Shaker, Pinwheel, Cane & Fan, Ray Cut Base, Silver Plated Lid, 5 ½ In.	150
Sugar Shaker, Strawberry Diamond & Fan, Silver Plated Lid	24
Tankard, Cranberry Cut To Clear, Hobstar, Block, Strawberry Diamond, Handle, 12 In. .. *illus*	210
Tray, Ice Cream, Hobstar, Nailhead, Vesica & Strawberry Diamond, 14 x 7 ½ In..................	96
Tumbler, Aberdeen, Hobstar Base, Clear Blank, 3 ⅝ In........................	210
Tumbler, Genoa, Hobstar Base, 4 ⅞ In........................	96
Tumbler, Hobstar, Strawberry Diamond, Star & Fan, Pattern Cut Base, 4 ⅞ In........................	36
Vase, Henry VII, Ray Cut Base, Clark, 9 ¾ In........................	48
Vase, Hollow Diamond, Hobstar Base, Dorflinger, 12 ¼ In.	480
Vase, Montrose, Green Cut To Clear, Notched Rim, Dorflinger, 13 ¾ In.	9000
Vase, Pedestal, Starburst, Cane, Strawberry Diamond & Fan, 1980s, 11 x 9 In.	25
Vase, Sunburst, Bulging Prism, Ray Cut Base, 16 In.	720
Vase, Tulip Shape, Nailhead Diamond Petals, Strawberry & Zipper, Scalloped Hobstar Foot.....	330
Wine, Apricot Cut To Clear, Crosscut Diamond Panels, Diamond Stem, Ray Cut Foot, 4 ¾ In....	300
Wine, Apricot Cut To Clear, Vesica, Fan & Tusk, Ray Cut Foot, 6 ½ In........................	108
Wine, Cranberry Cut To Clear, Star & Concave Pillar Design, Diamond Cut Stem, 5 In.	96
Wine, Diamond & Concave Pillar, Green Cut To Clear, Thistle Shape, 4 In................................	180
Wine, Diamond, Split Window, Teardrop Stem, Green Cut To Clear, 4 ⅞ In........................	270
Wine, Gold Enamel, Scrolls, Air Trap Lattice Stem, Continental, 6 ½ In.................. *illus*	60
Wine, Green Cut To Clear, Vesica, Cane, Strawberry Diamond & Fan, Ray Foot, 4 ¾ In.	180
Wine, Parisian, Lime Green Cut To Clear, Hobstar Foot, Dorflinger, 4 ½ In.	688
Wine, Rhine, Amethyst, Hobstar & Lattice, Punty Highlights, Solid Notched Stem, 8 In.	270
Wine, Rhine, Cranberry Cut To Clear, Engraved Floral Branches, Cut Stem & Foot, 8 In..........	210
Wine, Rhine, Yellow Acid Cut To Clear, Flower Branches, Air Twist Stem, Gold Trim, 8 In. *illus*	300
Wine, Rococo & Engraved Flowers, Scalloped Petticoat Foot, 5 ¼ In........................	98
Wine, Turquoise Cut To Clear, Strawberry & Crosscut Diamond, Clear Stem, Ray Cut Foot, 4 ¾ In.	96

CYBIS porcelain is a twentieth-century product. Boleslaw Cybis came to the United States from Poland in 1939. He started making porcelains in Long Island, New York, in 1940. He moved to Trenton, New Jersey, in 1942 as one of the founders of Cordey China Co. and started his own company, Cybis Porcelains, about 1950. It appears Cybis made porcelains until the 1990s and old ones are still selling. See also Cordey.

CYBIS

Figurine, Great Horned Owl, Perched On Branch, Snow, 1975, 20 x 12 In..................................	889
Figurine, Lady Macbeth, Holding Crown, Headband, Belt, Dress, 24K Gold, 1975, 13 In..........	1062
Figurine, Mermaid, Sharmine, Red Hair, Seminude, Rocks, Seashells, c.1980, 13 x 8 In.	250

CZECHOSLOVAKIA is a popular term with collectors. The name, first used as a mark after the country was formed in 1918, appears on glass and porcelain and other decorative items. Although Czechoslovakia split into Slovakia and the Czech Republic on January 1, 1993, the name continues to be used in some trademarks.

CZECHOSLOVAKIA GLASS

Bowl, Fruit, Overlay, Cobalt Blue, Hand Cut, 5 ½ x 7 ½ x 12 In.. *illus*	112
Lamp, Art Deco, Stenciled, Berries, Leaves, Air Brushed, 11 ½ In.	118
Perfume Bottle, Figural Nude Stopper, Octagonal, Black, Art Deco, 6 ¾ In.	236
Vase, Cameo, Orange, Yellow, Green, Flared Rim, Carved, Stylized Fruit, c.1910, 15 In. ...... *illus*	369
Vase, Cameo, Snails, Rounded Base, Flaring Sides, Early 1900s, 11 In.	813
Vase, Fluted, Swirling Surface, Polished Pontil, 2 Handles, Kralik, 12 x 7 x 4 In................. *illus*	1210

CZECHOSLOVAKIA POTTERY

Pitcher, Cat Handle, Iridescent, Black Trim, 4 x 3 ¼ In..........................	34
Pitcher, Lid, Flowers, Dark Green Leaves, Cream Ground, 8 x 6 In..........................	149
Pitcher, Neoclassical Nudes, Lion Handle, Grapevines, Embossed On Base, 9 x 9 In.	46
Vase, Blue To Brown Glaze, 3 Handles, c.1930, 9 In..........................	250
Vase, Reticulated Rim, Circular Base, Eichwald, 12 ½ In..........................	75

C

Daniel Boone, Lunch Box, Metal, Fess Parker, TV Show, Boone, Rifle, Burning Fort, 1965
$42

jogirl2001 on eBay

TIP
Store crystal stemware rim side up on the shelf.

D'Argental, Goblet, Ruby To Frosted, Bell Shape Bowl, Mountain Lake Scene, Signed, c.1915, 7 In.
$658

Jeffrey S. Evans & Associates

Daum, Bowl, Centerpiece, Clear, Daffodil Accents, Pate-De-Verre, Signed, 4 ½ x 12 In.
$984

Clars Auction Gallery

This is an edited listing of current prices. Visit Kovels.com to check thousands of prices from previous years and sign up for free information on trends, tips, reproductions, marks, and more.

Daum, Box, Lid, Berries, Leaves, Enameled, Green, Brown, Mottled Ground, Cameo, Signed, 3 x 5 In. $7,040

Morphy Auctions

Daum, Ewer, Figural, Pate-De-Verre, Mythologie, 1960, 12¼ x 9 x 4½ In. $1,063

Heritage Auctions

Daum, Figurine, Rooster, Clear, Etch Inscribed, France, 1900s, 5 In. $265

Freeman's Auctioneers & Appraisers

TIP
*When moving,
remember there
is no coverage for
breakage if the items
are not packed by
the shipper.*

DANIEL BOONE, a pre–Revolutionary War folk hero, was a surveyor, trapper, and frontiersman. A television series, which ran from 1964 to 1970, was based on his life and starred Fess Parker. All types of Daniel Boone memorabilia are collected.

Knife, Bowie Replica, Stainless Steel Blade, Walnut Handle, Brass Fittings, 8⅜ In.	8
Lunch Box, Metal, Fess Parker, TV Show, Boone, Rifle, Burning Fort, 1965 .... *illus*	42
Lunch Box, Metal, Fight Scene With Indians, c.1955, 8 x 6 In.	99
PEZ Dispenser, Candy, Head Carved, No Feet, Green Body, 1975	66
Pocket Knife, Deldrin Handle, Brass Shield, 3 Blades, Maroon, Schrade Walden, 1976, 4 In.	36
Pocket Knife, Plastic Handle, Blade, Folding, Cowboy, Western, 6 In.	11
Postcard, Homestead, Log House, Old View, Birdsboro, Pa., 3½ x 5½ In.	3
Record, Children's, Vinyl, Adventures Of Daniel Boone, 1949	19
Statue, Bronze, Boy, Racoon Hat, Gun, Patina, 1950s, 6 x 2 In.	45
Thermos, Daniel Boone, Portrait, Red Cup Lid & Handle, 1965	76
Thermos, Fighting Indians, Aladdin, Metal, Plastic Red Top	47

D'ARGENTAL is a mark used in France by the Compagnie des Cristalleries de St. Louis. The firm made multilayered, acid-cut cameo glass in the late nineteenth and twentieth centuries. Cameo glass was made with the D'Argental mark from 1919 to 1925. D'Argental is the French name for the city of Munzthal, home of the glassworks. Later the company made enameled etched glass.

Bowl, Flowers, Red, Green, Amber Ground, 3¾ x 6 In.	215
Goblet, Mountains, Lake, Ruins, Columns, Ruby To Frosted, c.1920, 7 x 3½ In.	693
Goblet, Ruby To Frosted, Bell Shape Bowl, Mountain Lake Scene, Signed, c.1915, 7 In. ...... *illus*	658
Vase, Irises, Buds, Leaves, Brown, Orange, 11½ In.	378
Vase, Mountain Landscape, Lake, Reserve, Blue, Brown, Black, 7½ x 12 In.	1950
Vase, Red Orchids, Yellow & Red Background, Signed, 4 x 8½ In.	813

DAUM, a glassworks in Nancy, France, was started by Jean Daum in 1875. The company, now called *Cristalleries de Nancy,* is still working. The *Daum Nancy* mark has been used in many variations. The name of the city and the artist are usually both included. The term *martele* is used to describe applied decorations that are carved or etched in the cameo process.

Daum
1890

Daum
1960–1971

Daum
1960–1971

Bowl, Art Deco, Smoky Gray, Marked, c.1930, 10 x 8 x 4 In.	1250
Bowl, Centerpiece, Clear, Daffodil Accents, Pate-De-Verre, Signed, 4½ x 12 In. .... *illus*	984
Bowl, Pedestal, Smoky Topaz Color Glass, Etched Border, Signed, 3¼ x 7¾ In.	666
Bowl, Yellow, Etched, 1930s, 6¾ In.	258
Box, Lid, Berries, Leaves, Enameled, Green, Brown, Mottled Ground, Cameo, Signed, 3 x 5 In. *illus*	7040
Centerpiece, Pate-De-Verre, Amethyst Bowl, Purple & Teal Pedestal, 8 x 13 In.	594
Ewer, Figural, Pate-De-Verre, Mythologie, 1960, 12¼ x 9 x 4½ In. .... *illus*	1063
Ewer, Pate-De-Verre, Green & Pink Shading, Box, 1900s, 14½ In.	390
Figurine, African Lion, Seated, Roaring, Pate-De-Verre, Signed, 6 x 10 In.	615
Figurine, Dolphin, Leaping, Chrome Stand, 10 x 18 In.	344
Figurine, Hedgehog, Clear, 2 x 3 In.	225
Figurine, Rooster, Clear, Etch Inscribed, France, 1900s, 5 In. .... *illus*	265
Figurine, Rooster, Pate-De-Verre, Marked, 1960, 3½ x 3 x 2 In.	200
Figurine, Toucan, Pate-De-Verre Amber Beak, Signed, 1970s, 9½ x 5½ In.	344
Lamp, Plafonnier Shade, Brown Leaves, Flowers, Pink, Cream Background, Signed, 19 x 21 In.	5535
Pitcher, Art Deco, Etched, Cross Of Lorraine, Signed, 9¼ In.	250
Pitcher, Japonesque, Pomegranates, Etched, Enameled, Silver Mount, Angular Handle, 5 In.	875
Sugar, Mushrooms, Red, Brown, Green, Yellow Striations, 2 Handles, Cameo, Signed, 4 x 6 In.	7560
Tumbler, Leaves, Berries, Etched, Cylindrical, Cameo, Marked, 4¾ x 2 In.	1000

D

Vase, Amethyst Flowers, Lozenge Shape, 7¾ x 6 x 3½ In.	366
Vase, Amethyst, Flowers, Gilt, Silver Mounts, Cameo, Signed, 5¼ x 2¼ In., Pair	1750
Vase, Amphora Shape, Blue Green, Carved Scarab, 11¾ x 8½ x 7½ In.	995
Vase, Bubbles, Ginger Ale Color, Polished Pontil, 7⅝ x 7½ In. .... *illus*	605
Vase, Bud, Pink, Marbled, Silver, Foil Decor, Marked, c.1915-20, 5 In.	695
Vase, Cabochon, 2 Insects, 2 Jewels, Foil, Maple Leaves, Cameo, 1 x 3¼ In.	1573
Vase, Cylindrical, Winter Landscapes, Brown & White, Signed, Cameo, Trefoil Top Rim, 5¾ x 2 In.	1024
Vase, Daffodil, Wheel Carved, Inlaid, Pedestal Foot, Cameo, Signed, 7 x 6 In.	4225
Vase, Daylily, Brown To Cream, Cameo, Signed, 13 x 4½ In.	1750
Vase, Fig Leaf, Pate-De-Verre, Nancy, France, Late 1900s, 8 x 12 x 10½ In.	2000
Vase, Foxglove, Oval, Red, Orange, Brown, 4¾ x 6 In.	274
Vase, Green & Orange Fruit Trees, Branches, Frosted, Cameo, Cross Of Lorraine, 19 In.	1230
Vase, Hibiscus, Rose & Amber, Carved Flowers, Pate-De-Verre, Signed, 9¼ x 10½ In.	1063
Vase, Lake Scene, Rolling Hills, Orange Background, Cameo, Signed, 16 x 5 In.	2214
Vase, Marsh Scene, Brown, Orange, Cameo, France, c.1900, 9¼ In. ..... *illus*	570
Vase, Molten Green, Iridescent Accents, Etched Base, Early 1900s, 30 In.	5400
Vase, Pillow, Alpine Scene, Frosted Sky, Cameo, Signed, 3⅞ x 4 In.	7380
Vase, Pillow, Mottled Butterscotch & Orange, Cameo, Oval, c.1900, 3¼ x 2 x 3 In.	2749
Vase, Pillow, Oval, Mottled Opal & Amethyst Ground, Cameo, Signed, c.1900, 3¼ In.	1673
Vase, Rectangular, Landscape, Enameled, Cameo, Signed, 2½ x 3½ In.	1500
Vase, Scenic, Autumn, Trees, Lakes, c.1800s, 7 In.	500
Vase, Squat, Long Slender Twisted Neck, Loop Handles, Mottled, Signed, 14 In.	512
Vase, Trees, Brown, Blue Ground, Enamel, Painted, Cameo, c.1910, 2 In.	495
Vase, Triated Pastel, Flared Neck, Micro Bubbles, Flowers, Signed, 4⅝ In.	897
Vase, Wildflowers, Hammered, Wheel Carved, Cameo, Signed, 19 x 5½ In.	3000

DAVENPORT pottery and porcelain were made at the Davenport factory in Longport, Staffordshire, England, from 1793 to 1887. Earthenwares, creamwares, porcelains, ironstone, and other ceramics were made. Most of the pieces are marked with a form of the word *Davenport*.

DAVENPORT LONGPORT STAFFORDSHIRE

Cup & Saucer, Gilt Scrolls & Shells, 1820s	177
Plate, Leaves, Green, Orange, Yellow, Marked, 8¼ In., Pair	385
Platter, Vorwaerts, Ship, Cartouches, Flowers, Birds, Urns, c.1850, 14¾ x 11¾ In.	910

DAVY CROCKETT, the American frontiersman, was born in 1786 and died in 1836. The historical character gained new fame in 1954 when the Walt Disney television show ran a series of episodes featuring Fess Parker as Davy Crockett. Coonskin caps and buckskins became popular and hundreds of different Davy Crockett items were made.

Bank, Shooting Bear, Coonskin Cap, Toytime USA, c.1955, 9 x 7½ In.	132
Button, Indian Fighter, Davy Kneeling, Holding Gun, Litho, Brown, Yellow, c.1955, 1¼ In.	12
Button, Indian Scout, Mountain, Wagon Train, Litho, Black, Red, Yellow, c.1955, 1⅛ In.	20
Clock, Time, Wall, Weight Driven, Pendulum, Number Dial, 7½ In.	26
Cookie Jar, Crossed Arms, Coonskin Cap, Brown, Brush, c.1956, 10½ In.	325
Costume, King Of Pioneers, Top, Pants With Fringe, Belt, Cap, Box, Bland Charnas Co.	100
Jacket, Faux Leather, Pliable Vinyl, Applied Graphics, Fringe, Child's, 1950s, 20 x 34 In.	11
Jackknife, Carbon Steel, Delrin Handle, Celluloid, 3½ In.	8
Lamp, Covered Wagon, Silhouette Shade, Indians Chasing Wagon, c.1955	150
Lamp, Shade, Hunter, Cowboy, Electric, Round Base, 1955, 18 In. .... *illus*	64
Mug, Black Eyes, Red Mouth, Brush, 4¾ In.	45
Mug, White Ground, Davy Crockett On Horse, Rifle, Handle, Signed, 1970s .... *illus*	2
Pistol, Tin Space Click, Flash Gordon, Popeye, Indian, Marx	104
Pocket Knife, Picture On One Side, Blade, Can Opener, Folding, Colonial	13
Puppet, Guitar Playing, Marionette, Unitrol String System, Movable Mouth, 16 In.	26
Sweater, Yarn, Vinyl, Davy Holding Smoking Gun, Indians, Bow, Arrows, Trees, Size 6	50
Toy, Gun, Click Pistol, Tin, Space Ray, Disney, Popeye, Davy Crockett, 1930s-50s	103
Wallet, Frontier Hero, Zipper, Folding, Coin Purse Inside, Leather	16

D

Daum, Vase, Bubbles, Ginger Ale Color, Polished Pontil, 7⅝ x 7½ In.
$605

Humler & Nolan

Daum, Vase, Marsh Scene, Brown, Orange, Cameo, France, c.1900, 9¼ In.
$570

Eldred's

Davy Crockett, Lamp, Shade, Hunter, Cowboy, Electric, Round Base, 1955, 18 In.
$64

treasureray on eBay

DE VEZ

Davy Crockett, Mug, White Ground, Davy Crockett On Horse, Rifle, Handle, Signed, 1970s
$2

Time & Money
According to a study, spending money in a way that saves time makes people happier than spending money on things.

Decoy, Black-Bellied Plover, Tack Eyes, Original Paint, Massachusetts, c.1910, 12 1/2 In.
$188

Decoy, Blue Jay, Miniature, Brown Patina, A. Elmer Cromwell, 3 3/4 In.
$780

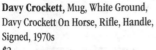 **DE VEZ** was a signature used on cameo glass after 1910. E. S. Monot founded the glass company near Paris in 1851. The company changed names many times. Mt. Joye, another glass by this factory, is listed in its own category.

Vase, Bud, Dandelions & Insects, Teal, Brown, Green, High Round Base, 4 3/4 x 6 1/2 In.	617
Vase, Lake, Mountains, Sky, Trees, Grass, Blue, Green, Marked, 4 3/4 In.	1395
Vase, Lake, Trees, Shades Of Green, Amethyst, c.1912, 5 1/2 In.	1050
Vase, Landscape Scene, Trees, Mountains, Wisteria, Cameo, Signed, 14 1/2 In.	1722
Vase, Landscape, Trees, Mountain, Sun, Brown, Yellow, Angular Mouth, Cameo, 7 1/2 x 2 1/2 In.	227
Vase, Owl, Rocky Perch, Moon, Tree Branches, Leaves, Pink, Purple, Cameo, 5 3/4 x 14 In.	845
Vase, Pear Shape, Stick Neck, Landscape, Trees, River, Ridge, Pink, Green, Cameo, 6 1/2 x 3 In.	260
Vase, Triangular, Trees, House, Landscape, Blue, Pink, Cameo, Signed Cristallerie De Pantin, 4 In.	149
Vase, Violets, Flowers At Shoulder, Stems, Light Green, 10 1/2 x 4 1/2 In.	357

 DECOYS are carved or turned wooden copies of birds, fish, or animals. The decoy was placed in the water or propped on the shore to lure flying birds to the pond for hunters. Some decoys are handmade; some are commercial products. Today there is a group of artists making modern decoys for display, not for use in a pond. Many sell for high prices.

Black Duck, Carved, Painted, Relief Wings, c.1950, 15 1/2 In.	101
Black Duck, Head Turned Right, Glass Eyes, Painted, A. Elmer Crowell, 19 In.	1020
Black Duck, Hollow, Carved Eyes & Wings, Point, Lonnie Ganung, 14 In.	360
Black-Bellied Plover, Tack Eyes, Original Paint, Massachusetts, c.1910, 12 1/2 In. ...... *illus*	188
Blue Jay, Miniature, Brown Patina, A. Elmer Crowell, 3 3/4 In. ...... *illus*	780
Bluebill, Black & White, Wood, Glass Eyes, 1900s, 15 x 7 x 9 In.	94
Bluebill Drake, Hollow Carved, Glass Eyes, Carved PF On Bottom, Late 1900s, 13 In.	240
Blue-Winged Teal Drake, Hollow Carved, Blue Winged, Glass Eyes, 10 3/4 In.	156
Brant, Duck, Black & White, Painted, Carved, c.1900s, 19 1/4 In.	125
Brant, Preening, Painted, Hollow Carved, Harry V. Shourds II ...... *illus*	216
Broadbill Drake, Hollow Body, Tack Eyes, Carved, Painted, Clark Madara, 1900s, 15 x 6 1/2 In.	351
Canada Goose, Carved, Painted, Wood, Brown, 13 1/2 x 23 In.	200
Canada Goose, Glass Eyes, Wood, Chesapeake Bay, Marked, 14 x 26 In.	250
Chickadee, Carved, Black & White Paint, Dome Base, 1900s, 2 1/4 x 3 1/4 In.	215
Duck Drake, Woodstock, Glass Eyes, Head Turned Left, Signed, Jim Keefer, 15 1/2 In.	240
Duck, Black & White, Carved, Wood, Signed, JJS, 1941, 6 x 12 In.	161
Duck, Black, Hollow Carved, Glass Eyes, Marty Collins, 1900s, 14 In.	840
Duck, Carved & Painted, Inset Glass Eyes, Weighted Bottom, 13 In.	77
Duck, Carved, Black & White Paint, 13 In.	123
Duck, Carved, Painted, Mounted, Cedar Lined, Shotgun Shell, 1900s, 9 1/2 x 12 x 6 In.	50
Duck, Carved, Wood, Olive Green, Blue, Red, 13 1/2 In.	54
Duck, Carved, Wood, Painted, Glass Eyes, Wildfowler, 12 1/2 In.	84
Duck, Carved, Wood, Painted, Inset Glass Eyes, Early 1900s, 7 x 15 x 8 In.	130
Duck, Carved, Wood, Painted, J.H. Whitney, 1900s, 20 1/2 In.	446
Duck, Carved, Wood, Painted, Signed, Ed Smith, 14 In.	84
Duck, Hollow Body, Glass Eyes, Carved, Painted, 4 1/4 In.	120
Eider Drake, Original Paint, Nova Scotia, c.1910, 15 In. ...... *illus*	100
Golden Eye Drake, Rectangular Brand On Base, A. Elmer Crowell, 1862-1952, 4 In.	900
Goose, Carved, Straight Neck, Black, White, Brown, 1900s, 16 x 24 In.	246
Goose, Gray With Black, Wood, Painted, 12 x 12 In.	69
Loon, Hand Carved & Painted, Tremblay, 15 x 5 x 5 3/4 In.	59
Mallard Hen, Rectangular Brand On Underside, A. Elmer Crowell, 1862-1952, 4 1/2 In.	1200
Merganser Drake, Wood, Hooded, Glass Eyes, Signed, Steve Brettell, 13 In.	120
Merganser, Carved, Painted, Slim Body, Pointed Head, Black Bead Eyes, Early 1900s, 23 In.	3444
Merganser, Wood, Multicolor, Gold & Black, Overlay, 17 1/2 In.	738
Pigeon, Pine, Painted, Stand, c.1900, 14 x 6 In.	384
Pintail Drake, Glass Eyes, Charles Perdew, Early 1900s, 7 1/2 x 16 x 5 1/4 In.	338
Puffin, Paint Splatter To Back, Signed, Dan Phillips, 1900s, 97 x 12 In.	216
Redhead Drake, Head Turned Right, Glass Eyes, Branded J. Hanson, 14 In.	108
Red-Breasted Merganser, Carved, Painted, Glass Eyes, Jerry Waite, 16 x 5 1/4 x 7 In. ...... *illus*	224
Red-Headed Woodpecker, Circular Wood Base, A. Elmer Crowell, c.1928, 2 In. ...... *illus*	900

Decoy, Brant, Preening, Painted, Hollow Carved, Harry V. Shourds II
$216

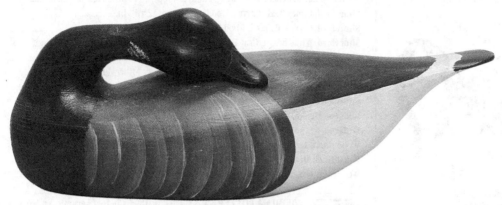

Eldred's

Decoy, Eider Drake, Original Paint, Nova
Scotia, c.1910, 15 In.
$100

Eldred's

Decoy, Red-Breasted Merganser, Carved,
Painted, Glass Eyes, Jerry Waite,
16 x 5¼ x 7 In.
$224

Charleston Estate Auctions

Decoy, Red-Headed Woodpecker, Circular
Wood Base, A. Elmer Crowell, c.1928, 2 In.
$900

Eldred's

Decoy, Surf Scoter Drake, Head Turned, Glass Eyes, Clarence Miller, 1900s, 16½ In.
$360

Eldred's

Decoy, Swan, Preening Position, Glass Eyes, Charles Alsipp, 1900s, 31 In.
$720

Eldred's

Decoy, Widgeon Drake, Glass Eyes, Joe Lincoln, c.1925, 14½ In.
$500

Eldred's

D

Delatte, Pitcher, Silver Leaf Inclusions, Signed Exterior Foot, 9¾ In. $156

Kamelot Auctions

Delft, Tobacco Jar, Cobalt Blue & White, Flowers, Pompadoer, Brass Lid, 1700s, 15 In. $800

POMPADOER

Cowan's Auctions

Delft, Urn, Windmills & Boats, Dolphins Base, Marked, Dutch, c.1800s, 20 x 11 x 9 In. $1,250

New Orleans Auction Galleries

Ruddy Duck, Mounted On Oval Base, A. Elmer Crowell, 2¼ In.		1560
Scoter, Seaduck, Relief Carved Wing, Painted, 1900s, 20½ In.		225
Shorebird, Brown Beak, Carved, Wood, On Stump, 12 x 12 In.		59
Shorebird, Carved, Painted, Wood Base, Contemporary, 15½ In.		50
Shorebird, White Breast, Gray Back, Applied Beak, Metal Stand, c.1899, 5 x 10 In.		431
Shorebird, Wood, Carved, Painted, Mounted, 1900s, 14 In.		369
Surf Scoter Drake, Head Turned, Glass Eyes, Clarence Miller, 1900s, 16½ In.	*illus*	360
Swan, Carved, White, Black Bill, Curved Neck, 1900s, 19 x 29 In.		738
Swan, Preening Position, Glass Eyes, Charles Alsipp, 1900s, 31 In.	*illus*	720
Widgeon Drake, Glass Eyes, Joe Lincoln, c.1925, 14½ In.	*illus*	500
Widgeon Drake, Oval Wood Base, A. Elmer Crowell, c.1930, 3¾ In.		900
Wood Duck Drake, Early Competition Grade, Glass Eyes, Ted Mulliken, 14½ In.		240
Wood Duck Drake, Mount On Wood Circular Base, A. Elmer Crowell, 3¼ In.		1800
Woodcock, Oval Base, Carved Leaf Design, Signed Ben Heinemann, 10½ In.		720

DEDHAM POTTERY was started in 1895. Chelsea Keramic Art Works was established in 1872 in Chelsea, Massachusetts, by members of the Robertson family. The factory closed in 1889 and was reorganized as the Chelsea Pottery U.S. in 1891. The firm used the marks *CKAW* and *CPUS*. It became the Dedham Pottery of Dedham, Massachusetts, in1896. The factory closed in 1943. It was famous for its crackleware dishes, which picture blue outlines of animals, flowers, and other natural motifs. Pottery by Chelsea Keramic Art Works and Dedham Pottery is listed here.

Morning & Night, Pitcher, Rooster, Smiling Sun, Owl, Man In Moon, Rabbit Mark, 5 In.	395
Rabbit, Platter, Blue Ink Mark, 17 x 10 In.	918
Snow Tree, Plate, Blue & White, 8½ In.	395
Swan, Plate, Blue & White, 8 In.	145
Vase, Green, Brown Drip Glaze, Hugh Robertson, Mass., 10½ In.	2583
Vase, Oxblood, Hugh C. Robertson, Chelsea Keramic Art Works, 1880s, 4 x 2 In.	1000
Vase, Tea, Ivory, Green, Glossy, Glaze, Kiln, Incised, H. Robertson, Massachusetts, 6¾ In.	861

DEGUE is a signature acid etched on pieces of French glass made by the Cristalleries de Compiegne beginning about 1925. Cameo, mold blown, and smooth glass with contrasting colored rims are the types most often found. The factory closed in 1939.

Bowl, Metal Stand, Light Blue, Brown, Gray, Marble Design, 2 Piece, 8 x 10 In.	850
Vase, Diane, Nude Woman, Deer, Bird, Clear, Signed, 1930, 10 In.	3850
Vase, Red, Black, Flowers, Leaves, Flowers, Etched, Marked, Cameo, c.1901, 20 In.	1000

DEIaITE NANCY

DELATTE glass is a French cameo glass made by Andre Delatte. It was first made in Nancy, France, in 1921. Lighting fixtures and opaque glassware in imitation of Bohemian opaline were made.

Bowl, Mounted, Blown, Gilt Iron, Orange, Marked, c.1920, 5 x 5 In.		2250
Pitcher, Silver Leaf Inclusions, Signed Exterior Foot, 9¾ In.	*illus*	156
Vase, Acid Etched, Red Leaves, Art Nouveau, Marked Nancy, 1920s, 11 In.		2250
Vase, Art Deco, Berluze, Blue, 1920s, 13 x 4 In.		450
Vase, Nude Maidens, Leaves, Cobalt Blue, Orange Ground, Signed, 9 x 4 In.		461
Vase, Stick, Pink & Blue, Marked, c.1912, 16 In.		475

DELDARE, *see Buffalo Pottery Deldare.*

DELFT is a special type of tin-glazed pottery. Early delft was made in Holland and England during the seventeenth century. It was usually decorated with blue on a white surface, but some was multicolor, decorated with green, yellow, and other colors. Most delftware pieces were dishes needed for everyday living. Figures were made from about 1750 to 1800 and are rare. Although the soft tin-glazed pottery was well-known, it was not named delft until after 1840, when it was named for the city in Holland where much of it was made. Porcelain became more popular because it was more durable, and Holland gradually

stopped making the old delft. In 1876 De Porceleyne Fles factory in Delft introduced a porcelain ware that was decorated with blue and white scenes of Holland that reminded many of old delft. It became popular with the Dutch and tourists. By 1990 all of the blue and white porcelain with Dutch scenes was made in Asia, although it was marked *Delft*. Only one Dutch company remains that makes the traditional old-style delft with blue on white or with colored decorations. Most of the pieces sold today were made after 1891, and the name *Holland* usually appears with the Delft factory marks. The word *Delft* appears alone on some inexpensive twentieth- and twenty-first-century pottery from Asia and Germany that is also listed here.

Clock, Landscapes, Blue & White, Brass Finials, Enamel Dial, Arabic Numerals, 1800s, 26 In..	750
Ginger Jar, Lid, Blue & White Hand Painted, Sailing Scene, Flowers, Dog Finial, 17 In.	196
Lamp, Oil, Bulbous Font, Ribbed Shaft, Square Footed Base, Blue, c.1850, 24 In.	144
Pitcher, Basket Of Fruit, Flowers, Birds, Blue & White, Handle, Spout, 1700s, 9 x 7 In.	2850
Plate, Multicolor, Flowers, Early 1700s, 9 In.	210
Tobacco Jar, Cobalt Blue & White, Flowers, Pompadoer, Brass Lid, 1700s, 15 In. .... *illus*	800
Urn, Windmills & Boats, Dolphins Base, Marked, Dutch, c.1800s, 20 x 11 x 9 In. .... *illus*	1250
Vase, Beaker, Flowers & Garlands, Blue & White, 1700s, 6 x 5 In.	1850
Vase, Octagonal, Landscape Scene, Rider On Horse, Dog, c.1750, 8 x 4½ x 4 In. .... *illus*	152
Wall Pocket, Flattened Cornucopia, Flower Sprays, England, c.1760, 7½ x 5⅞ In.	677

DENTAL cabinets, chairs, equipment, and other related items are listed here. Other objects may be found in the Medical category.

Cabinet, Mixed Wood, 3 Doors, Mirror Back, 22 Drawers, Marble Base, c.1915, 63 x 40 In. *illus*	900
Cabinet, Oak, Beveled Mirror Backsplash, Drawers, Doors, Slide, c.1900, 53 x 29 In. .... *illus*	1380
Compressor, Stand & Arm, Wastebasket, Warmer, DeVilbiss Mfg. Co., 24 x 14 x 27¾ In.	484
Display, Toothbrush, Dr. West Miracle Tuft, Red, 17¾ In.	200
Sign, Tooth Shape, Carved, Painted Wood, c.1950, 15 x 12 In.	354
Tooth Extractor, Metal Crank Shaft, 5 Adjustable Claws, Wood Handle, c.1900, 6 In. .... *illus*	150

DENVER is part of the mark on an American art pottery. William Long of Steubenville, Ohio, founded the Lonhuda Pottery Company in 1892. In 1900 he moved to Denver, Colorado, and organized the Denver China and Pottery Company. This pottery, which used the mark *Denver,* worked until 1905, when Long moved to New Jersey and founded the Clifton Pottery. Long also worked for Weller Pottery, Roseville Pottery, and American Encaustic Tiling Company. Do not confuse this pottery with the Denver White Pottery, which worked from 1894 to 1955 in Denver.

DENVER
C T &
P T Co

Vase, Lonhuda, Molded Tulip Design, Brown Matte Glaze, Marked, 8¼ In.	1416

DEPRESSION GLASS is an inexpensive glass that was manufactured in large quantities during the 1920s and early 1930s. It was made in many colors and patterns by dozens of factories in the United States. Most patterns were also made in clear glass, which the factories called *crystal*. If no color is listed here, it is clear. The name *Depression glass* is a modern one and also refers to machine-made glass of the 1940s through 1970s. Sets missing a few pieces can be completed through the help of a matching service.

Adam, Candy Dish, Pink, Lid, c.1930, 4 x 4 In.	68
American Sweetheart, Bowl, Sherbet, Pink, Footed, 4 In.	10
Aunt Polly, Candy Dish, Blue, Handled, Footed, 1920s, 7½ In.	20
Aunt Polly, Serving Bowl, Blue, Oval, 1920s, 8¼ In.	75
Beaded Block, Celery Dish, Green, 8½ In.	23
Block Optic, Cup & Saucer	11
Brocade, Plate, Oak Leaf, Pink, Bowtie Handles, Fostoria, 6¾ x 7 In.	11
Cameo Ballerina, Bowl, Cereal, 5½ In.	27
Cameo Ballerina, Plate, Dinner, 9½ In.	21
Cathedral, Plate, Luncheon, 8 In.	6
Cherry Blossom, Bowl, Pink, Oval, 9 In.	47
Cherry Blossom, Mug, Green, Jeannette, 2⅞ In.	399
Decagon, Cake Plate, Peach, Open Handles, 12 In.	27

Delft, Vase, Octagonal, Landscape Scene, Rider On Horse, Dog, c.1750, 8 x 4½ x 4 In.
$152

Jeffrey S. Evans & Associates

Dental, Cabinet, Mixed Wood, 3 Doors, Mirror Back, 22 Drawers, Marble Base, c.1915, 63 x 40 In.
$900

Garth's Auctioneers & Appraisers

Dental, Cabinet, Oak, Beveled Mirror Backsplash, Drawers, Doors, Slide, c.1900, 53 x 29 In.
$1,380

Selkirk Auctioneers & Appraisers

Dental, Tooth Extractor, Metal Crank Shaft, 5 Adjustable Claws, Wood Handle, c.1900, 6 In.
$150

Leslie Hindman Auctioneers

Derby, Plate, Shipping Scene, Painted, George Robertson, 10¾ In.
$196

Hannam's Auctioneers

Dick Tracy, Paperweight, Clear Glass, Scalloped Edge, Junior, Comic
$30

lorifitz on eBay

Diana, Bowl, Cereal, Pink, Federal Glass, 5 In.		12
Diana, Creamer, Amber, Federal Glass		9
Dogwood, Cup & Saucer, Pink, MacBeth Evans		16
Doric, Plate, Pink, 6 In.		5
Georgian Lovebirds, Berry Bowl, Green, 4½ In.		8
Madrid, Bowl, Amber, 10 In.		19
Manhattan, Sugar, Handles		7
Mayfair Pink, Shaker, Metal Lid, Anchor Hocking		69
Miss America, Plate, Dinner, Pink, Anchor Hocking, 10 In.		15
Miss America, Wine, Pink, Anchor Hocking, 3¾ In.		89
Moderntone, Sugar & Creamer, Cobalt Blue		17
New Century, Butter, Green, Round		19
Normandie, Berry Bowl, Amber, 5 In.		8
Optic, Sherbet, Paneled, Amber		4
Petalware, Cup & Saucer, Cremax, Gold Trim		5
Princess, Plate, Dinner, Topaz		10
Princess, Sherbet, Pink		12
Quilted Diamond, Sugar, Ice Blue, 2 Handles		8
Ribbon, Cup & Saucer, Green		6
Rose Cameo, Tumbler, Green, Belmont		15
Roulette, Plate, Luncheon, Green, 8½ In.		7
Royal Lace, Sugar, Pink, Handles		14
Shell, Bowl, Cereal, Jadite, 6 In., Pair		28
Shell, Cup & Saucer, Jadite		43
Spiral, Berry Bowl, Green, 5½ In.		18
Spiral, Plate, Green, 6 In.		3
Sylvan, Sugar & Creamer, Green, Federal		71
Thumbprint, Cup & Saucer, Green		10
Twisted Optic, Sherbet, Pink		5
Victory, Plate, Luncheon, Green, 8 In.		5
Windsor Diamond, Berry Bowl, Pink, Jeannette, 4¾ In.		10
Windsor Diamond, Tumbler, Footed, Jeannette, 5 In.		8

DERBY has been marked on porcelain made in the city of Derby, England, since about 1748. The original Derby factory closed in 1848, but others opened there and continued to produce quality porcelain. The Crown Derby mark began appearing on Derby wares in the 1770s.

Figurine, Man, Seated, Bird, Reclining Hound, 1800s, 10⅝ x 5¼ In.		267
Figurine, Minerva, Standing, Shield, Head Of Medusa, 1800s, 13½ In.		394
Plate, Shipping Scene, Painted, George Robertson, 10¾ In.	*illus*	196
Stand, Painted, Twin Handles, Scrolling Neoclassical Plants, 10¼ In.		49
Tazza, 3 Figures, Grapevines, Stevens & Hancock, 13 x 6 In.		77
Vase, Encrusted Flowers, Bulbous, Bottle Neck, Encrusted Flowers, 14½ In.		127
Vase, Twin Handle, Guy's Cliff Warwickshire, 1800s, 13 x 8½ In.		224

DICK TRACY, the comic strip, started in 1931. Tracy was also the hero of movies from 1937 to 1947 and again in 1990, and starred in a radio series in the 1940s and a television series in the 1950s. Memorabilia from all these activities are collected.

Action Figure, Playmates, Yellow Coat & Hat, No. 5797, Special Edition, 15 In.		11
Badge, Detective Club, Pinback, Button, Gold Plated, 1930s, 1¾ x 2 In.		15
Badge, Secret Service Patrol, Member, Star & Face, Embossed, Copper, 1939, 1⅜ In.		14
Gameboard, Detective, Folding, Green, Yellow, White, Blue, Line Border, Whitman, Box, 1937		5
Glass, Frosted, Shaky, Man In Black Suit Holding Phone, c.1945		105
Paperweight, Clear Glass, Scalloped Edge, Junior, Comic	*illus*	30
Pocket Knife, Folding, Black, Blade Marked Comic Strip Classics, Franklin Mint		8
Toy, Baby Sparkle, Lithograph, Pop-Up Hat, Windup, Built-In Key, Marx, 1930, 8½ In.		130
Toy, Car, Police Dept., Tin Lithograph, Windup, Battery Operated, Marx, 1949	*illus*	150
Toy, Gun, Sparkling Pop Pistol, Tin, Black, Marx, 8½ In.		83
Toy, Squad Car, Green Paint, Flashing Light, Louis Marx Co., N.Y., Box, c.1950		674

DICKENS WARE *pieces are listed in the Royal Doulton and Weller categories.*

DINNERWARE used in the United States from the 1930s through the 1950s is listed here. Most was made in potteries in southern Ohio, West Virginia, and California. A few patterns were made in Japan, England, and other countries. Dishes were sold in gift shops and department stores or were given away as premiums. Many of these patterns are listed in this book in their own categories, such as Autumn Leaf, Azalea, Coors, Fiesta, Franciscan, Hall, Harker, Harlequin, Red Wing, Riviera, Russel Wright, Vernon Kilns, Watt, and Willow. For more prices, go to kovels.com. Sets missing a few pieces can be completed through the help of a matching service. Three examples of dated dinnerware marks are shown here.

W.S. George Pottery Co.
Late 1930s–1940

Royal China Co.
1950s+

Salem China Co.
1940s–1960

Autumn Berry, Plate, Dinner, Berries, Brown, Green, Blue Ridge, 9¼ In.	17
Big Apple, Plate, Dinner, Blue Ridge	21
Blossom Time, Bowl, Vegetable, Royal Swan, c.1930, 8¼ In.	20
Blue Garland, Creamer, Blue Flowers, Johann Haviland, 4 In.	19
Boho Chic, Bowl, Vegetable & Dip, Lane & Co., 1961, 12 In.	25
Brier Rose, Tray, Handles, Schumann Bavaria, 1960s, 16½ In.	60
Charm, Cup & Saucer, Forest Green, Fire King, 2⅛ In.	8
Charm, Plate, Luncheon, Royal Red, Fire King, 8¼ In.	10
Christmas, Platinum Trim, Tree, Royal Devon, 1960s, 10½ In., 6 Piece	85
Chrysanthemum, Plate, Salad, Blue, Red, Flowers, Green Leaves, Blue Ridge, 7⅛	12
Dairy Maid, Bowl, Fruit, Crooksville, 5⅜ In.	11
Deck The Halls, Plate, Salad, Poinsettia, Tienshan, 7½ In.	3
French Lily, Plate, Dinner, Jade & Gold, Mikasa, 1995, 10¾ In.	25
French Lily, Soup, Jade, Gold, Mikasa, 1995, 9 In.	21
Harvest Time, Bowl, Gumbo, Iroquois, 7¾ In.	9
Memory Lane, Sugar, Lid, Pink, Royal China, 1960s	8
Noel, Platter, Serving, Oval, Pearl China, c.1950, 14 In.	14
Nova Brown, Gravy Boat, Earthenware, Sango	28
Old Country Roses, Mug, Royal Albert, 3⅛ In.	59
Old Curiosity Shop, Ashtray, Sage Green, Royal China, 1950s, 5½ In.	7
Orange Blossom, Pitcher, Orchard, 9 In.	45
Palm Leaf, Grill Plate, Green, Wallace	45
Pomona, Pitcher, Grapes & Leaves, White Ground, Portmeirion, 8½ In.	26
Pomona, Plate, Dinner, Elsanta, Strawberry, Leaves & Flowers, Portmeirion, 10½ In.	55
Rochelle, Plate, Salad, Nautilus, Eggshell, Square, Homer Laughlin, 1940s, 8 In. 2 Piece	6
Santa Anita, Sugar, Lid, Silver, Gray, White, Marbleized	15
Silhouette, Gravy Boat, Attached Underplate, Lynnbrooke	13
Spring Song, Creamer, Strawberries, Vines, Octagonal Originals, 3¾ In.	14
Vera, Plate, Dinner, Silhouette, Stoneware, Black & White, Mikasa, 1970s, 10 In., 2 Piece	18
Yorktowne, Salt Box, Lid, Pfaltzgraff, 5 x 6 In.	43
Yorktowne, Tureen, Lid, Pfaltzgraff, 8 In.	18

DIONNE QUINTUPLETS were born in Canada on May 28, 1934. The publicity about their birth and their special status as wards of the Canadian government made them famous throughout the world. Visitors could watch the girls play; reporters interviewed the girls and the staff. Thousands of special dolls and souvenirs were made picturing the quints at different ages. Emilie died in 1954, Marie in 1970, Yvonne in 2001. Annette and Cecile still live in Canada.

Basket, Round, Babies, Wood, Openwork, Slant Braces, Madame Alexander	22
Book, Story Of The Dionne Quintuplets, Whitman Co., 1935	22

Dick Tracy, Toy, Car, Police Dept., Tin Lithograph, Windup, Battery Operated, Marx, 1949
$150

ceweed on eBay

D

Dionne Quintuplets, Calendar, 1938, Dietzen's Corn Top Bread, Parrot, Brown & Bigelow, 11½ x 8 In.
$19

impala7 on eBay

Dionne Quintuplets, Doll, Crazy Eyes, Pink Dress, Bonnet, Ribbon Tie, Name Pin, Emilie, Madame Alexander
$57

vom on eBay

TIP
Many types of dolls cannot be washed. Water will melt the material. Water trapped inside may make the doll moldy and produce an unpleasant odor.

D

Dirk Van Erp, Jewelry Box, Brass, Hand Wrought, Jade Panel, Bone Handle, 1900s, 3¼ x 10 x 7 In. $2,625

Pook & Pook

Dirk Van Erp, Vase, Copper, Hammered, Warty, Stamped, Windmill, After 1915, 8½ x 7 In. $7,500

Rago Arts and Auction Center

No Fingers

Mickey Mouse first appeared in 1928. He had black hands and no fingers. In about 1929, he was given white gloves because they were easier to draw and they stood out against his black body.

Disneyana, Alarm Clock, 3 Little Pigs, Big Bad Wolf Face, Ingersoll, 1934, 5 x 5 x 3 In. $5,567

Hake's Auctions

Bowl, Marie In Highchair, Red Band, 5½ In.	40
Calendar, 1938, Dietzen's Corn Top Bread, Parrot, Brown & Bigelow, 11½ x 8 In. *illus*	19
Calendar, 1949, Awrey Bakeries, Fifteen All, 12 Months, Dionne, 7½ x 14½ In.	3
Doll, Composition, Baby Bibs, Hats, Sitting, 1930s, 7½ In., 5 Babies	45
Doll, Crazy Eyes, Pink Dress, Bonnet, Ribbon Tie, Name Pin, Emilie, Madame Alexander *illus*	57
Doll, Madame Alexander, Emilie, 75th Anniversary, No. 12280, Dionne, 1998, 8 In.	25
Doll, Madame Alexander, Marie Pendant, Baby Bib, Open-Close Sleep Eyes, 17 In.	67
Doll, Madame Alexander, Yvonne, Booklet, Dress, Hat, White Shoes, Dionne, 7½ In.	63
Doll, Wood Scooter, Bonnets, Composition, Madame Alexander, 1930s, 8 In., 5 Babies	895
Plate, Girls In Highchairs, Tab Handles, Maple Leaf, 12 In.	104
Postcard, Annette, Yvonne, Cecile, Emilie, Marie, Pink Ground, Portrait, 1930s	2
Postcard, Portrait, Dr. Dafoe, Yvonne, Emilie, Marie, Annette, Cecile, Dionne, 1939	3
Postcard, Teen Portraits, Greetings From Quintland, 1939	15

DIRK VAN ERP was born in 1860 and died in 1933. He opened his own studio in 1908 in Oakland, California. He moved his studio to San Francisco in 1909 and the studio remained under the direction of his son until 1977. Van Erp made hammered copper accessories, including vases, desk sets, bookends, candlesticks, jardinieres, and trays, but he is best known for his lamps. The hammered copper lamps often had shades with mica panels.

Humidor, Copper, Hammered, Hinged Lid, Windmill Mark, 1910, 10 x 6 In.	5625
Jewelry Box, Brass, Hand Wrought, Jade Panel, Bone Handle, 1900s, 3¼ x 10 x 7 In. *illus*	2625
Vase, Copper, Hammered, Oval, Slight Shoulder, Rolled Rim, c.1920, 7 x 6¼ In.	1125
Vase, Copper, Hammered, Warty, Stamped, Windmill, After 1915, 8½ x 7 In. *illus*	7500
Vase, Copper, Hand Hammered, Marked, Arts & Crafts, 9½ In.	431
Vase, Hammered, Shouldered, Rolled Rim, Dovetailed Seam, Marked, 9 x 6 In.	2006

DISNEYANA is a collectors' term. Walt Disney and his company introduced many comic characters to the world. Mickey Mouse first appeared in the short film "Steamboat Willie" in 1928. Collectors search for examples of the work of the Disney Studios and the many commercial products modeled after his characters, including Mickey Mouse and Donald Duck, and recent films, like *Beauty and the Beast* and *The Little Mermaid*.

Alarm Clock, 3 Little Pigs, Big Bad Wolf Face, Ingersoll, 1934, 5 x 5 x 3 In. *illus*	5567
Bank, Donald Duck, Dime Register, Disney Characters, Tin Lithograph, 4 x 2½ In. *illus*	366
Bank, Dopey, Beating Drum, Popeye, Red, Yellow, Marked, Walt Disney, 1939, 7 In.	220
Bank, Figaro, Cat, Smiling Face, Sitting, Black & White, Ceramic	80
Car, Donald Duck, Rubber, Squeak, Convertible, Green, Marked, 1960s, 5 x 3 In.	45
Cel, see Animation Art category.	
Comic Book, Walt Disney's Donald Duck, In The Ghost Of The Grotto, No. 159 *illus*	121
Comic Strip, Donald Duck, Ink & Pencil, Mat, Frame, Signed, 1967, 23 x 30 In.	856
Cookie Jar, Winnie The Pooh, Red Shirt, Bee On Nose, Sitting, Treasure Craft, Box, 10 In.	41
Doll, Mickey Mouse, Velveteen, Oilcloth Eyes, Charlotte Clark, Early 1930s, 13 In. *illus*	1947
Doll, Minnie Mouse, Cowgirl, High Heel Shoes, Neckerchief, Knickerbocker, 1930s, 12 In. *illus*	1162
Donald Duck, Studio Plug, Felt Clothing, Walt Disney Productions, 14 x 14 x 12 In. *illus*	170
Doorstop, Donald Duck, Spinning Sign, Stop & Enter, Painted, Iron, 1971, 8 x 6 x 3 In.	147
Figurine, Belle, Yellow Gown, Round Base, Flower On Hair, Giuseppe Armani, 11⅛ In.	371
Figurine, Mickey Mouse, Bucking Bronco, Celluloid, Windup, Built-In Key, 1940s, 3 In.	591
Game, Mickey Mouse, Pop, Die Cut Cardboard Target, Marks Brothers Co., 11 x 18 In.	195
Hand Puppet, Mickey Mouse, Velvet, Oilcloth Eyes, Knickerbocker, 1935, 11 In.	454
Knife, Souvenir, Blade, Steel, Wood Handle, Compass, Relco, Japan, 1950s, 3 In.	138
Lamp, Mickey Mouse, Scout La Mode, Plaster, La Mode Studios Inc., 9⅜ In. *illus*	201
Lantern, Pluto, Battery Operated, Tin, Linemar, Japan, 6¾ In.	142
Movie Projector, Mickey Mouse, Keystone Mfg. Co., 1934, 6 x 9 x 11½ In. *illus*	227
Nodder, Mickey Mouse, Celluloid Windup, Spring Instrument, Tin Base, Japan, 1930s, 6 In.	156
Pail, Mickey Mouse & Friends, Tin Lithograph, Happynak, 1950, 5¾ x 9¾ In.	106
Pitcher, Pinocchio, Pleasure Island Bound, Tin Lithograph, Handle, 1939, 2¼ x 1¾ In.	51
Pocket Watch, Mickey Mouse, Ingersoll, Celluloid Dial, Metal Case, England, 1933, 2 In. *illus*	447
Scissors, Mickey Mouse, Red Handles, Tin, Marked, W.D. Ent., 1930, 3¼ In. *illus*	153

Disneyana, Bank, Donald Duck, Dime Register, Disney Characters, Tin Lithograph, 4 x 2½ In.
$366

AntiqueAdvertising.com

Disneyana, Comic Book, Walt Disney's Donald Duck, In The Ghost Of The Grotto, No. 159
$121

Clars Auction Gallery

Disneyana, Doll, Mickey Mouse, Velveteen, Oilcloth Eyes, Charlotte Clark, Early 1930s, 13 In.
$1,947

Hake's Auctions

Disneyana, Doll, Minnie Mouse, Cowgirl, High Heel Shoes, Neckerchief, Knickerbocker, 1930s, 12 In.
$1,162

Hake's Auctions

Disneyana, Donald Duck, Studio Plug, Felt Clothing, Walt Disney Productions, 14 x 14 x 12 In.
$170

Rich Penn Auctions

Disneyana, Lamp, Mickey Mouse, Scout La Mode, Plaster, La Mode Studios Inc., 9⅜ In.
$201

Hake's Auctions

Disneyana, Movie Projector, Mickey Mouse, Keystone Mfg. Co., 1934, 6 x 9 x 11½ In.
$227

Hake's Auctions

Disneyana, Pocket Watch, Mickey Mouse, Ingersoll, Celluloid Dial, Metal Case, England, 1933, 2 In.
$447

Hake's Auctions

Disneyana, Scissors, Mickey Mouse, Red Handles, Tin, Marked, W.D. Ent., 1930, 3¼ In.
$153

Milestone Auctions

Disneyana, Snow Shovel, Mickey Mouse & Pluto, Tin Litho, Wood Handle, Ohio, 1930s, 26¾ In.
$422

Hake's Auctions

Disneyana, Souvenir, Hat, Space Mountain, Mickey Mouse Riding, Disneyland, 1970s, 10 In.
$1,265

Van Eaton Galleries

Disneyana, Souvenir, Trinket Box, Dumbo, Flying Elephant, Disneyland, 2005, 10 In.
$805

Van Eaton Galleries

Disneyana, Ticket Book, Child's Entrance, Disneyland, Unused, 1960, 2½ x 6 In.
$4,313

Van Eaton Galleries

Disneyana, Toothbrush Holder, Max Hare Maw, Toby Tortoise Returns, Chinese, c.1936, 4½ In.
$675

Hake's Auctions

Disneyana, Toy, Donald Duck, Dipsy Car, Tin Lithograph, Windup, Marx, 5½ In.
$224

Hess Auction Group

Disneyana, Toy, Dopey, Tin Lithograph, Windup, Marx, 8¼ In.
$177

Hess Auction Group

Disneyana, Toy, Mickey Mouse, On Unicycle, Tin, Windup, Linemar, 5¼ In.
$531

Milestone Auctions

Disneyana, Toy, Mickey Mouse, Rocking On Pluto, Tin Litho, Windup, Linemar, 1950s, 5½ In.
$779

Hake's Auctions

Screenprint, Minnie Mouse In The Pink, David Willardson, 26 ½ x 20 ½ In. 272
Sign, Mickey Mouse, Sunoco Gas & Motor Oil, Porcelain, Gloss, 11 ¾ In. 278
Snow Shovel, Mickey Mouse & Pluto, Tin Litho, Wood Handle, Ohio, 1930s, 26 ¾ In......... *illus* 422
Souvenir, Hat, Space Mountain, Mickey Mouse Riding, Disneyland, 1970s, 10 In. .... *illus* 1265
Souvenir, Trinket Box, Dumbo, Flying Elephant, Disneyland, 2005, 10 In. .... *illus* 805
Sparkler, Mickey Mouse, Tin, Die Cut Opening At Mouth & Eyes, 1930s, 5 ½ In. 443
Tambourine, Mickey & Minnie Mouse, Metal Frame, Noble & Cooley Co., c.1936, 9 x 1 ¼ In. .. 195
Ticket Book, Child's Entrance, Disneyland, Unused, 1960, 2 ½ x 6 In. .... *illus* 4313
Tin, Mickey Mouse, Superfine Mickey Mouse Cocoa, 1930s, 3 x 6 In. 185
Toothbrush Holder, Max Hare Maw, Toby Tortoise Returns, Chinese, c.1936, 4 ½ In....... *illus* 675
Toothbrush Holder, Mickey Mouse, Figural, Ceramic, c.1970, 4 ½ x 4 ¾ x 2 In. 23
Toy, Donald Duck, Dipsy Car, Tin Lithograph, Windup, Marx, 5 ½ In. .... *illus* 224
Toy, Donald Duck, Goofy, Duet, Playing The Drum, Goofy Dances, Tin, Windup, Marx, Box, 11 In. 920
Toy, Dopey, Tin Lithograph, Windup, Marx, 8 ¼ In. .... *illus* 177
Toy, Ferris Wheel, Mickey Mouse, Tin Lithograph, Windup, Chein, 16 ¼ In. 125
Toy, Figaro, Cat, Tin Lithograph, Windup, Marx, 4 ¾ x 2 ¼ x 2 ½ In. 129
Toy, Mickey & Minnie, Handcar, Lionel, Box, 8 x 11 In. 644
Toy, Mickey Mouse, Bimbo Flex, Brown Shirt, Shoes, Wood, 7 In. 406
Toy, Mickey Mouse, Bisque, Movable Arms, Walter E. Disney, Japan, 1928, 4 ¾ In. 216
Toy, Mickey Mouse, Climbing, Die Cut Cardboard, Wire Tail, Dolly Toy Co., 1930s 376
Toy, Mickey Mouse, Dipsy Car, Tin, Windup, Box, Painted, Marx 531
Toy, Mickey Mouse, Fun E Flex Walking Rocker, Wood, Wire Arms & Tail, 7 ½ In. 325
Toy, Mickey Mouse, Guitar, Player, Orchestra Series, Tin Lithograph, Germany, 3 In. 180
Toy, Mickey Mouse, Handcar, Circular Track, Steel, Composition Figures, Box, c.1930, 6 x 9 In. . 565
Toy, Mickey Mouse, On Unicycle, Tin, Windup, Linemar, 5 ¼ In. .... *illus* 531
Toy, Mickey Mouse, Rocking On Pluto, Tin Litho, Windup, Linemar, 1950s, 5 ½ In. .... *illus* 779
Toy, Mickey Mouse, Roller Skater, Tin, Windup, Linemar, 6 ½ In. 496
Toy, Mickey Mouse, Saxophone, Squeeze, Red, Brown & Blue, Germany, 7 In. 130
Toy, Mickey Mouse, Whirling Tail, Windup, Plastic, Marx, Box, 7 In. .... *illus* 184
Toy, Mickey Mouse, Xylophone, Windup, Toy, Plastic, Metal, 11 In. 452
Toy, Minnie Mouse, Knitter, Rocking Chair, Tin, Windup, Linemar, Japan, 7 ½ In. .... 164 to 212
Toy, Pinocchio, Acrobatic, Tin Litho, Rocks Back & Forth, Windup, Marx, Box, 15 x 4 x 3 In..... 234
Toy, Pluto, Drum Major, Tin, Windup, Linemar, Japan, 6 ¼ In. 177
Toy, Professor Von Drake, Tin, Windup, Linemar, Box, 6 In. 496
Toy, Walt Disney Television Car, Tin Lithograph, Friction, Marx, 1950s, 7 ½ In. .... *illus* 358
Wastebasket, Pinocchio, Trash Can, Cylinder, Painted, Walt Disney, 19 x 9 ½ In. 36
Wristwatch, Mickey Mouse, Animated Dial, Metal Case, Ingersoll, 1935, 4 x 6 ¾ x ⅞ In..... *illus* 326

DOCTOR, *see Dental and Medical categories.*

DOLL entries are listed by marks printed or incised on the doll, if possible. If there are
no marks, the doll is listed by the name of the subject or country or maker. Notice that
Barbie is listed under Mattel. G.I. Joe figures are listed in the Toy section. Eskimo dolls
are listed in the Eskimo section and Indian dolls are listed in the Indian section. Doll
clothes and accessories are listed at the end of this section. The twentieth-century clothes listed
here are in mint condition.

A.M., Girl, Mohair Wig, Blue Sleep Eyes, Lace, Floral Hat, Germany, 40 In. 1614
Advertising, GE Band Leader, Composition, Jointed Wood, Maxfield Parrish For Cameo, 19 In.. 922
Advertising, RCA Radiotron Man, Composition Head, Jointed Wood, Cameo, c.1930, 16 In. 633
Alexander dolls are listed in this category under Madame Alexander.
Alt, Beck & Gottschalk, Blue Scarf Lady, Bisque, Blue Glass Eyes, Sculpted Scarf, 18 In.......... 1840
American Character, Betsy McCall, Red Polka Dot Dress, Box, 14 x 32 In........................ *illus* 24
Annalee, Girl, Building Snowman, Blond Hair, Snowy Base, No. 7231, 1994, 7 In. 26
Armand Marseille dolls are listed in this category under A.M.
Automaton, Girl With Surprise Basket, Bisque, Silk Dress, Flower Basket, Bird, Lambert, 20 In. 10063
Automaton, Peasant & Pig, Papier-Mache, Wood, Composition, Painted, Carton Torso, G. Vichy, 34 In. 24150
Automaton, Spanish Dancer, Tambourine, Bisque, Glass, Mohair, Carton Torso, Lambert, 21 In... 5463
Averill, Bonnie Babe, Bisque, Glass Sleep Eyes, Sculpted Hair & Shoes, c.1920, 6 ½ In. 633

Disneyana, Toy, Mickey Mouse,
Whirling Tail, Windup, Plastic, Marx,
Box, 7 In.
$184

Milestone Auctions

Disneyana, Toy, Walt Disney Television
Car, Tin Lithograph, Friction, Marx,
1950s, 7 ½ In.
$358

Hake's Auctions

Disneyana, Wristwatch, Mickey Mouse,
Animated Dial, Metal Case, Ingersoll,
1935, 4 x 6 ¾ x ⅞ In.
$326

Hake's Auctions

SELECTED DOLL MARKS WITH DATES USED

Effanbee Doll Co.
1922+
New York, N.Y.

Lenci
1922+
Turin, Italy

Hertwig & Co.
1864–c.1940
Katzhütte, Thuringia, Germany

K☆R
–39·

Kämmer & Rheinhardt
1886–1932
Waltershausen, Thüringia, Germany

J.D. Kestner Jr.
1805–1938
Waltershausen, Thuringia, Germany

Ideal Novelty & Toy Co.
1961
New York, N.Y.

L.A. & S.

Louis Amberg & Son
1909–1930
Cincinnati, Ohio; New York, N.Y.

BRU. J^NE R
11

Bru Jne. & Cie
c.1879–1899
Paris, France

A M

Armand Marseille
c.1920
Köppelsdorf, Thüringia, Germany

DÉPOSE
TÊTE JUMEAU
6

Maison Jumeau
1886–1899
Paris, France

B ♥ P

Bähr & Pröschild
1871–1930s
Ohrdruf, Thüringia, Germany

DÉPOSE
S.F.B.J.

S.F.B.J. (Société Française de Fabrication de
Bébés & Jouets)
1905–1950+
Paris and Montreuil-sous-Bois, France

ALBEGO
10
Made in Germany

Alt. Beck & Gottschalck
1930–1940
Nauendorf, Thuringia, Germany

Schoenau & Hoffmeister
1901–c.1953
Sonneberg, Thuringia, Germany

Gebruder Heubach
1840–1938
Lichte, Thuringia, Germany

Barbie dolls are listed in this category under Mattel, Barbie.

Bergmann dolls are in this category under S & H and Simon & Halbig.

Black dolls are also included in the Black category.

Boudoir, Girl, Fashion, Gown, High Heels, Paris, c.1920, 30 In.	207
Bru Jne, Fashion, Bisque Swivel Head, Glass Eyes, Blond Mohair, Jointed Wood, 1867, 18 In.	8050
Bye-Lo, Baby, Bisque, Cloth Body, Plastic Hands, Marked, Grace Putman, Germany, 17 In.	68
Cage, Priest, Carved Face & Beard, Articulated Arms, Slatted Base, 1900s, 30¾ In.	813
Charles Twelvetrees, Shebee, Bisque, Bald, O-Shape Eyes, Mouth, Germany, 5½ In.	518
Chase, Mammy, Cloth, Pressed & Painted Features, Fleecy Wig, Stitch-Jointed, Dress, 68 In.	4888
Cloth, Sheppard Baby, Painted Stockinette, Stitched Ears, J.B. Sheppard Linen Co., c.1880, 21 In.	1100
Door Of Hope, Bride & Groom, Wood, Carved, Painted, Silk, Flowers, Beads, c.1919, 12 In., Pair	1265
Door Of Hope, Chang, Chinese Farmer, Wood, Carved, Painted, Woven Straw Over Cloth, 13 In.	805
Door Of Hope, Child, Wood, Painted, Fringe Hair, Cloth Body, Silk, Pompons, 6 In.	575
Door Of Hope, Old Woman, Wood, Painted, Chignon, Brocade Tunic, Silk Pants, c.1920, 11 In.	460
Door Of Hope, Student, Wood Head & Hands, Painted, Cloth Torso, c.1920, 12 In.	460
Freundlich, Sailor, Composition, Painted, Jointed, WWII, 1942, 15½ In.	83

G.I. Joe figures are listed in the Toy category.

Gaultier, Courtier, Bisque Swivel Head, Glass Eyes, Auburn Mohair, Muslin, Costume, 19 In.	2588

Gebruder Heubach dolls may also be listed in this category under Heubach.

Gebruder Heubach, 7246, Bisque Shoulder Head, Glass Eyes, Pouty Face, Scottish Costume, 14 In.	518
Gebruder Heubach, Girl, Bisque, Painted Side-Glancing Eyes, Sculpted Bob, Dress, c.1915, 9 In.	460
German, Baby, Bisque Socket Head, Open Mouth, No Teeth, Bent Limb, 11½ In.	102
German, Bisque Shoulder Head, Glass Eyes, Sculpted Braids & Bodice, Dresden Flowers, 24 In.	1035
German, Bisque Shoulder Head, Sculpted Chignon, Glass Eyes, Gown, c.1870, 18 In.	1955
German, Bisque Shoulder Head, Sculpted Waves, Curls & Jewelry, Muslin, Leather, 22 In.	8625
German, Bisque, Painted Face, Open Mouth, Rabbit Fur, Red Ribbon, 10 In.	147
German, Boy, Bisque Head, Glass Eyes, Open Mouth, Brown Sailor Suit, 13 x 5½ In.	352
German, Gentleman, Bisque, Brown Glass Eyes, Sculpted Wavy Hair, Wool Suit, c.1875, 18 In.	748
German, Papier-Mache Shoulder Head, Painted Features, Jointed Muslin Body, c.1865, 15 In.	3910
Grace Drayton, September Morn, Bisque, Curls, Googly Eyes, Germany, 1915, 5 In.	2070
Greiner, Papier-Mache Shoulder Plate, Cloth Body, Leather Arms, R. Tembleaux, 1850s, 33 In.	178

Half-Dolls are listed in the Pincushion Doll category.

Handwerck, Bisque Head, Blond Mohair Wig, Jointed Limbs, Polka Dot Dress, 17 In. *illus*	70
Handwerck, Bisque, Girl, Blue Eyes, White & Blue Dress, Boots, c.1890, 32 In. *illus*	201
Handwerck, Bisque, Painted Lashes & Eyebrows, Straw Hat, Germany, Marked, 31½ In.	136

Heubach, see Gebruder Heubach.

Ideal, Mighty Mouse, Starched Linen, Felt, Vinyl Hands, Terrytoons, 1950, 16 In. *illus*	2321

Indian dolls are listed in the Indian category.

Japanese, Ichimatsu, Papier-Mache Head, Gofun Finish, Enamel Eyes, Costume, 16 In.	1035
Jumeau, Bebe, Bisque Socket Head, Glass Eyes, Blond Human Hair, Composition, Wood, 11 In.	7480
Jumeau, Bebe, Bisque, Blue Eyes, Blond Hair, 30 In.	1875
Jumeau, Bisque Head, Brown Hair & Eyes, Pierced Ears, Ball-Jointed Body, c.1890, 18 In.	1125
Jumeau, Bisque Head, Brown Skin, Inset Eyes, Open Mouth, Fleecy Wig, Chemise, 11 In.	2645
Jumeau, Fashion, Bisque Swivel Head, Glass Eyes, Blond Mohair, Kid Body, Velvet Dress, 22 In.	4888
K * R, 101, Marie, Bisque Head, Painted Blue Downcast Eyes, Mohair Wig, Ball-Jointed, 11 In.	1610
K * R, 117-55, Mein Liebling, Bisque Socket Head, Glass Eyes, Brunette Mohair, Ball-Jointed, 22 In.	4025
K * R, Girl, Bisque, Brown Glass Googly Eyes, Jointed Wood Toddler Body, 16 In.	6038
Kathe Kruse, Boy, Cloth, Pressed & Painted, Blond Human Hair, Jointed, Type III, 1927, 20 In.	2070
Kathe Kruse, Du Mein, Cloth, Pressed & Painted Features, Stockinet Baby Body, c.1925, 20 In.	1955
Kathe Kruse, Sternschnuppchen, Cloth, Painted, Bonnet Head, Stockinet Baby Body, 14 In.	4600
Kestner, 143, Bisque Socket Head, Brown Complexion, Glass Eyes, Baby Body, 11 In.	575
Kestner, 243, Chinese Baby, Bisque Socket Head, Brown Sleep Eyes, Composition Body, Costume, 13 In.	3910
Kestner, Character Baby Set, Bisque, Composition, Bent-Limb, 3 Heads, Box, 10-In. Doll	1725
Kestner, Hilda, Bisque Dome Head, Blue Glass Eyes, 2 Teeth, 5 Piece Baby Body, 1914, 11 In.	1955
Kestner, Model XI, Child, Bisque Head, Glass Eyes, Brunette Human Hair, Jointed, 16 In.	1955

Kewpie dolls are listed in the Kewpie category.

Lenci, Child, Felt, Pressed & Painted, Side-Glancing Eyes, Ruffled Dress, 21 In.	1955
Lenci, Dutch Girl, Felt, Pressed & Painted, Brown Side-Glancing Eyes, Jointed, 1929, 9 In.	345
Lenci, Felt, Pressed & Painted, Brown Side-Glancing Eyes, Appliqued Dress, 1922, 16 In.	978

Doll, American Character, Betsy McCall, Red Polka Dot Dress, Box, 14 x 32 In.
$24

Copake Auction

Doll, Handwerck, Bisque Head, Blond Mohair Wig, Jointed Limbs, Polka Dot Dress, 17 In.
$70

Cordier Auctions

Doll, Handwerck, Bisque, Girl, Blue Eyes, White & Blue Dress, Boots, c.1890, 32 In.
$201

anniepoojewels on eBay

Doll, Ideal, Mighty Mouse, Starched Linen, Felt, Vinyl Hands, Terrytoons, 1950, 16 In.
$2,321

Hake's Auctions

Doll, Musical, Marotte, Bisque, Glass, Mohair, Wood Wand, Schoenhau & Hoffmeister, c.1910, 15 In.
$271

Auction Team Breker

Doll, Puppet, Giltwood Face & Hands, Velvet, Embroidered, Beaded, Thailand, 33 In.
$123

Skinner, Inc.

Lenci, Golfer, Felt, Pressed, Painted, Fleecy Brunette Hair, Costume, Club, 22 In.	1265
Lenci, Mozart, Felt, Pressed & Painted, Side-Glancing Eyes, Mohair Wig, c.1926, 20 In.	1265
Lenci, Sam, Ebony Felt, Painted, Black Curly Mohair, Sultan Costume, 36 In.	6325
M. Neuhart, Wool, Acrylic, Silk, For Girard's Textiles, c.1961, 13 In.	1690
M. Thompson, Queen Elizabeth, Prince Philip, 2 Children, Bisque, 21 In., 4 Piece	460
Mannequin, Wood, Carved Features, Jointed, Swivel Waist, c.1810, 32 In.	3910
Marseille, Bisque, Painted Eyebrows & Lashes, Sleep Eyes, Hat, Marked, Germany, 20½ In.	113
Mattel, Barbie, Blond Bubble Cut, Blue Bathing Suit, 1960s, 11 In.	225
Mattel, Barbie, Blond Swirl Ponytail, Dressed, No. 1640 Matinee Suit	184
Mattel, Barbie, Brunette Bubble Cut, Dressed, No. 965 Nighty Negligee, Box	489
Mattel, Barbie, No. 1, Brunette Ponytail, Original Accessories & Box, 1959, 11 In.	4600
Mattel, Barbie, No. 1, Brunette Ponytail, Striped Swimsuit, Accessories, Box	5750
Mattel, Barbie, No. 2, Blond Ponytail, Striped Swimsuit, Accessories, Box	2415
Mattel, Barbie, No. 3, Blond Ponytail, Original Swimsuit & Accessories, Box	690
Mattel, Barbie, No. 3, Dressed, Easter Parade, Apple Print Dress	863
Mattel, Barbie, No. 6, Ash Blond Ponytail, Original Red Swimsuit, Accessories, Box	173
Mattel, Barbie's Round The Clock Gift Set, Brunette Bubble Cut, 3 Outfits, Box	431
Mattel, Ken, Brunette, Dressed, Fraternity Meeting Costume, Box, c.1962	431
Mattel, Midge, Brunette, Green & Pink Swim Suit, Box, 1969	195
Mattel, Talking Barbie, Brunette, Vinyl Bikini, Gold Net Cover-Up, Tag, Box	230
Mattel, Twist 'N Turn Barbie, Blond Flip, Checked Swimsuit, Tag, Stand, Box, c.1969	575
Musical, Marotte, Bisque, Glass, Mohair, Wood Wand, Schoenhau & Hoffmeister, c.1910, 15 In. *illus*	271
Paper dolls are listed in their own category.	
Papier-Mache, Painted Features, Black Sculpted Chignon, Kid Body, Germany, c.1840, 8 In.	863
Pincushion dolls are listed in their own category.	
Pottery, Redware Shoulder Head, Sculpted Features, Cloth Body, Penn., 1811, 7 In.	403
Puppet, Giltwood Face & Hands, Velvet, Embroidered, Beaded, Thailand, 33 In. *illus*	123
Raggedy Andy, Cloth, Embroidered Face, Button Eyes, Brown Yarn Hair, Bow Tie, 1900s, 27 In.	395
Rohmer, Fashion, Bisque Swivel Head, Hair Stuffed Kid, Jointed, Dress, c.1860, 13 In.	4025
S & H dolls are also listed here as Simon & Halbig.	
S & H, Bisque, Girl, Sleep Eyes, Teeth, Jointed, 11½ In.	198
S.F.B.J., Jester, Bisque Head, Whitened Complexion, Sleep Eyes, Costume, Mandolin, 16 In.	1840
S.F.B.J., Princess Elizabeth, Bisque Head, Blue Glass Sleep Eyes, Human Hair, Jointed, 18 In.	2415
Sarah Midgley, Cloth, Woman, Black, Aboriginal, Horsehair, Bead Necklace, Belt, Boomerang, c.1930	120
Schoenau & Hoffmeister, Girl, Bisque Socket Head, Blue Eyes, Black Shoes, 1906, 36 In.	747
Schoenhut, Barney Google, Spark Plug, Wood, Painted, Rope Tail, 1922, 8 In.	345
Schoenhut, Boy, Wood, Short Pants, Stockings, Shoes, Toddler, Pat. 1911, 13 In.	124
Schoenhut, Hobo, Wood, Painted, Scruffy Mustache & Beard, Jointed, c.1910, 8 In.	288
Schoenhut, Wood, Carved, Intaglio Eyes, Brunette Mohair, Spring-Jointed, Box, 1911, 14 In.	2300
Shirley Temple dolls are included in the Shirley Temple category.	
Simon & Halbig dolls are also listed here under Bergmann and S & H.	
Simon & Halbig, 1329, Asian Child, Bisque Head, Glass Eyes, Black Mohair, Jointed, Costume, 11 In.	1265
Simon & Halbig, Bisque Socket Head, Human Hair, Glass Sleep Eyes, Ball-Jointed, 25 In.	225
Simon & Halbig, Blue Eyes, Jointed, Composition, Checkered Dress, 1299, 18 In.	396
Simon & Halbig, Lady, Bisque Shoulder Head, Sculpted Coiled Braids, Kid, Silk, c.1875, 23 In.	1380
Simon & Halbig, Sleep Eyes, Lace Outfit, Heinrich Handwerck, Germany, Late 1800s, 30 In.	185
Steiner, Bebe, Bisque Socket Head, Brown Glass Eyes, Blond Mohair Wig, Jointed, 12 In.	3910
Steiner, Jester, Bisque, Painted, Blond Mohair Curls, Composition, Costume, Drum, 9 In.	1955
Ventriloquist Dummy, Man, Wood, Carved, Clothing, Overcoat, Pants, Shoes, 17 In. *illus*	125

DOLL CLOTHES

Accessory, Travel Bag, Leather Handles, Flowers, Gold Plated Lock, 3½ x 3½ In.	40
American Boy, Jacket, White, Cotton, Zipper Lock, 18 In.	3
American Girl, Blouse & Skirt, Lavender, 4 Buttons, Shoes	14
Barbie, Blouse, Skirt & Leggings, Cloth, Black, Sergio Valente, Mattel	21
Barbie, Easter Parade Ensemble, No. 971, Polka Dot Dress, Hat, Gloves, Mattel, Box, 1959	460
Barbie, Gown, Wedding Party, Cloth, Handmade, Adora, Mattel, 11½ In.	2
Barbie, Roman Holiday Ensemble, No. 968, Red, White & Blue Dress, Box, 1959	460
Barbie, Senior Prom Ensemble, No. 961, Green Satin & Tulle, Mattel, Box, 1963	86

Cissy, Dress, Pink Taffeta, Organdy, Lace & Bow At Waist, Rhinestone Button, Mattel	173
Dress, Cotton, Sleeveless, Bow In Back, Lined Bodice, Trimmed, Velcro Closure, 18 In.	5
Tutti, Barbie's Sister, Ship Shape, Blue Dress & Panties, White Cap, Mattel	26
Wayne Gretzky, Suit, Jogging, Hockey Team, Edmonton Oilers, Mattel, 1980s........................	40

DONALD DUCK *items are included in the Disneyana category.*

DOORSTOPS have been made in all types of designs. The vast majority of the doorstops sold today are cast iron and were made from about 1890 to 1930. Most of them are shaped like people, animals, flowers, or ships. Reproductions and newly designed examples are sold in gift shops. These are three marks used by doorstop makers.

B&H	**HUBLEY**	**WILTON PRODUCTS INC WRIGHTSVILLE PA.**
Bradley & Hubbard Manufacturing Co. 1854–1940	Hubley Manufacturing Co. 1894–1965	Wilton Products, Inc. c.1935–1989

Asian Dragon, Cast Iron, Gold Paint, Solid Piece, 4 x 8 In.	95
Baby, Yawning, M.L. Corp., NYC, Cast Iron, c.1931, 9 1/4 In.	113
Basket Of Flowers, Cast Iron, Multicolor Flowers, Leaves, Original Paint, 11 1/2 x 6 In.	47
Basket, Lilies-Of-The-Valley, Phlox, 1-Sided, Multicolor, Hubley, 6 x 4 x 1 1/2 In.	79
Bell, Black Marble, Tall Brass Pole, 1800s, 24 1/2 In.	250
Bird, Cockatiel, Cast Iron, Painted, Multicolor, 14 In.	170
Boy, Whistling Jim, Hands In Pockets, Cast Iron, Bradley & Hubbard, 16 1/4 In.........................	5400
Butler, Bowling Pin Shape, Carrying Tray, Art Deco, 17 1/2 In.	540
Cat, Black, Full Figure, Arched Back, Tail Up, Slotted Screw, Hubley, 10 3/4 x 8 x 2 1/2 In.	203
Cat, Black, Sitting, Cast Iron, Yellow Green Eyes, Hubley, c.1920, 7 In. .... *illus*	156
Cat, Cast Iron, Gray & White, Yellow Eyes, Trapezoid Base, 12 1/2 x 7 1/2 x 2 3/4 In.	339
Cat, Seated, Black Paint, Glass Eyes, Hollow Back, Cast Iron, 10 In.	57
Clown, Solid Cast Iron, Pierrot Harlequin, CJO Judd 1281, 8 1/4 In.	82
Dog, Beagle Puppy, Squatting, Piddling Pup, Cast Iron, Painted, 8 In.	960
Dog, Begging, Cast Iron, Art Deco Style, Orange Paint, Marked, Spencer, c.1950, 15 1/4 In.	240
Dog, Boston Terrier, Brown, White, Cast Iron, 9 3/4 In. .... *illus*	236
Dog, Boston Terrier, Cast Iron, Painted, 10 x 10 In.	58
Dog, Bulldog, Cast Iron, Multicolor, Bradley & Hubbard, England, 9 1/4 x 5 1/2 x 3 1/4 In.	1102
Dog, Fox Terrier, Cast Iron, Hubley, 1930s, 8 x 7 In.	395
Dog, Fox Terrier, Multicolor, Slotted Screw, Hubley, 8 1/2 x 8 x 2 1/2 In.	237
Dog, German Shepherd, Cast Iron, 13 1/2 x 12 1/2 In.	118
Dog, Scottie, Cast Iron, Patinated, Begging, 15 In.	92
Dog, Setter, Cast Iron, Black & White Paint, Green Base, 4 3/4 x 7 3/4 x 1 3/4 In.	90
Dog, St. Bernard, Barrel On Collar, Patinated, Oblong Base, Cast Iron, 8 In...............................	58
Dog, Terrier, Black Paint, Brown Eyes, Slotted Screw, 8 3/4 x 9 1/4 x 3 In....................................	158
Dragon, Sitting, Roland & Manjen, Cast Iron, Ohio, 1900s, 20 In.	600
Drum Major, Square Base, Red, White, Holds Baton, Cast Iron, c.1920, 13 1/2 In........................	1003
Duck, Top Hat, Yellow, Walking, 2-Sided, Cast Iron, 6 x 3 1/2 In..	141
Eagle, Spread Wing, Snake, Handle, Cast Brass, 13 x 7 x 2 1/2 In.	96
Elephant, Hollow, Paint, Cast Iron, Bradley & Hubbard, 10 In.	565
Flower Basket, 1-Sided, Multicolor, Painted, Cast Iron, 11 1/2 x 8 x 2 1/4 In......................... *illus*	45
Flower Basket, Handle, 1-Sided, Multicolor, Waverly Studios, c.1926, 6 x 4 x 2 In.....................	68
Flower Basket, Yellow, Pink & Green Paint, Cast Iron, Hubley, 7 1/2 In...	83
Flowers, Gladiolus, Urn, 1-Sided, Multicolor, Painted, Cast Iron, Hubley, 10 x 8 x 3 In.	79
Flowers, Oval, Cast Iron, 1-Sided, Multicolor, Ring Handle, Bradley & Hubbard, 7 1/2 x 3 1/2 x 3 In...	57
Flowers, Tulips, Planter, Red, Yellow, Cast Iron, Albany Foundry, 8 1/2 x 6 3/4 In.	156
Frog, Cast Iron, Household Patent Co., Early 1800s, 6 x 4 1/2 In.	153
Heron, Perched On Base, Painted, Cast Iron, 1900s, 7 1/2 In. .... *illus*	184

Doll, Ventriloquist Dummy, Man, Wood, Carved, Clothing, Overcoat, Pants, Shoes, 17 In.
$125

Leslie Hindman Auctioneers

Doorstop, Cat, Black, Sitting, Cast Iron, Yellow Green Eyes, Hubley, c.1920, 7 In.
$156

Eldred's

Doorstop, Dog, Boston Terrier, Brown, White, Cast Iron, 9 3/4 In.
$236

Milestone Auctions

Doorstop, Flower Basket, 1-Sided, Multicolor, Painted, Cast Iron, 11 ½ x 8 x 2 ¼ In.
$45

Soulis Auctions

Doorstop, Parrot, Inside Ring, Painted, Cast Iron, Bradley & Hubbard, 13 ¾ In.
$472

Copake Auction

Doorstop, Heron, Perched On Base, Painted, Cast Iron, 1900s, 7 ½ In.
$184

Keystone Auctions LLC

Doorstop, Pig, Multicolor, Rectangular Base, Black Spots, Cast Iron, 1900s, 7 x 8 In.
$173

Keystone Auctions LLC

Doorstop, Monkey, Organ Grinder, Multicolor, 2-Sided, Iron, c.1930, 10 x 6 x 2 ½ In.
$90

Soulis Auctions

Doorstop, Rabbit, Yellow Hat & Coat, Round Base, Cast Iron, c.1920, 10 ¼ In.
$944

Copake Auction

D

Horse, Cast Iron, Wood Base, Hubley, 6 x 7 In.	79
Horse, Standing, Black, Cast Iron, Hubley, 1920s, 10 x 3 In.	283
Horse, Stepped Base, Brass, 10 ½ In.	285
Kitten, Seated, Cushion, Black, 1-Sided, Multicolor, 8 x 6 x 2 In.	68
Lighthouse, Rockery Base, Cast Iron, c.1910, 13 ½ In.	687
Lion, Rampant, Porter, Hollow Back, Cast Iron, 14 ½ In.	90
Lion, Sewer Tile, Rectangular Base, Moore Ceramics, 1900s, 11 x 5 x 7 In.	767
Monkey, Organ Grinder, Multicolor, 2-Sided, Iron, c.1930, 10 x 6 x 2 ½ In. .... *illus*	90
Owl, Perched On A Branch, 1-Sided, Multicolor, Hubley, 7 ½ x 5 x 2 ½ In.	192
Parrot, Inside Ring, Painted, Cast Iron, Bradley & Hubbard, 13 ¾ In. .... *illus*	472
Parrot, Multicolor, Art Deco, Cast Iron, Taylor Cook, 1930, 10 ⅝ In.	660
Parrot, Small Ring, 2-Sided, Multicolor, Bradley & Hubbard, 7 ¾ x 7 x 3 In.	147
Pig, Multicolor, Rectangular Base, Black Spots, Cast Iron, 1900s, 7 x 8 In. .... *illus*	173
Pineapple, Leaves, Iron Base, Cast Brass, 13 ½ x 6 ¼ x 3 In.	60
Pirate, Striped Hat & Belt, Treasure Sack, Cast Iron, c.1900, 12 In.	1062
Rabbit, White, 1-Sided, Cast Iron, 11 ¼ x 6 x 2 In.	136
Rabbit, Yellow Hat & Coat, Round Base, Cast Iron, c.1920, 10 ¼ In. .... *illus*	944
Rattlesnake, Coiled, Multicolor, Cast Iron, 7 ¾ In.	2160
Red Riding Hood, Wolf, Embossed, Cast Iron, Nuydea, 1800s, 7 ½ x 9 ½ In. ... *illus*	295
Sailor, Blue & Red Cap, Blue Pants, Cast Iron, Littco, c.1905, 12 In.	1140
Ship, 3-Masted, Cast Iron, 11 x 11 ¾ In.	59
Ship, Titanic Boat, Gold Trim, Iceberg, Cast Iron, 6 x 11 ½ x 3 ½ In.	21
Snooper, Man, Black Coat, Yellow Pants, Tall Hat, Cast Iron, 13 ¼ In.	170
Squirrel, Branches, Gilt, 1-Sided, Cast Iron, 6 x 9 ¼ x 2 In.	198
Wine Merchant, Green Jacket, Red Pants, Red & Yellow Bottles, Cast Iron, 1920, 10 In.	2829
Woman, Braids, Bun, Crucifix Pendant, Aluminum, 8 x 8 In.	110

DOULTON was founded about 1858 in Lambeth, England. A second factory was opened in Burslem, England, by 1871. The name *Royal Doulton* appeared on the company's wares after 1902 and is listed in the Royal Doulton category in this book. Other Doulton ware is listed here. Doulton's Lambeth factory closed about 1956.

Doulton and Co. 1869–1877	Doulton and Co. 1880–1912, 1923	Doulton and Co. 1885–1902

Bibelot, Dish, Pixie, Elf, No. 8731, Red Hat, Sitting, Lambeth, 4 x 4 ¼ In.	182
Bottle, Water, Lavender, Quants Of Torquay, Stoneware, Lambeth, 2 ¾ In.	12
Cup, 3 Handles, Dogs, Ceramic & Porcelain, No. 2, Lambeth, 1899	28
Flask, Stoneware, Chicks, Pate-Sur-Pate, Florence Barlow, Lambeth, 1885, 10 x 6 ⅝ In.	245
Inkwell, Stoneware, Brown, Isobath, De La Rue Patent, Lambeth, 1885, 4 ¾ In.	264
Jardiniere, Pedestal, Impressed Autumn Leaves, Red, Tan, Lambeth, 24 x 14 ½ In.	632
Jug, Pitcher, Dewar's Whiskey, Stoneware, Queen Victoria, Lambeth, 1800s, 5 ½ In.	107
Jug, Silver, Mounted Mouth & Shoulders, Creamware, Looping Handle, Early 1900s	94
Pitcher, Ewer, Spring, Portrait Medallion, Gilt, Flowers, Burslem, c.1880, 9 ½ In.	305
Pitcher, Stoneware, Slater Patent, Handle, Lambeth, England, 3 ½ x 3 ½ In.	23
Vase, Horses, Grazing, Landscape, Peasant, Incised, Hannah Barlow, Lambeth, 1800s, 11 x 5 ½ In.	345
Vase, Oval Base, Flared Cylindrical Neck, Gilt, Handles, Burslem, 1880, 10 x 5 ¾ In. .... *illus*	72
Vase, Young Woman Holding Yarn, Landscape, Ceramic, JP Hewitt, Burslem, c.1880, 14 In.	355

DRESDEN and Meissen porcelain are often confused. Porcelains were made in the town of Meissen, Germany, beginning about 1706. The town of Dresden, Germany, has been home to many decorating studios since the early 1700s. Blanks were obtained from Meissen and other porcelain factories. Some say porcelain was also made in Dresden in the early years. Decorations on Dresden are often similar to Meissen, and marks were copied. Some of the earliest books on marks con-

Doorstop, Red Riding Hood, Wolf, Embossed, Cast Iron, Nuydea, 1800s, 7 ½ x 9 ½ In.
$295

dakotapaul on eBay

Doulton, Vase, Oval Base, Flared Cylindrical Neck, Gilt, Handles, Burslem, 1880, 10 x 5 ¾ In.
$72

Thomaston Place Auction Galleries

Dresden, Clock, Shelf, Flowers, Hand Painted, Gold Trim, 17 In.
$374

Richard D. Hatch & Associates

Dresden, Urn, Lid, Cherubs, Flowers, Courting Scene, Floral Sprays, 1800s, 24 In.
$1,093

Richard D. Hatch & Associates

Dresden, Vase, Portrait, Woman, Square Body, Richard Klemm, c.1900, 6 x 3 In.
$450

Morphy Auctions

Duncan & Miller, Chanticleer, Vase, Blue Opalescent, Lobed Rim, 1950, 3¼ In.
$60

Jeffrey S. Evans & Associates

fused Dresden and Meissen, and that has remained a problem ever since. The Meissen "AR" mark and crossed swords mark are among the most forged marks on porcelain. Meissen pieces are listed in this book under Meissen. German porcelain marked "Dresden" is listed here. Irish Dresden and Dresden made in East Liverpool, Ohio, are not included in this section. These three marks say "Dresden" although none were used by a factory called Dresden.

Karl Richard Klemm
c.1891–1914

Ambrosius Lamm
c.1887+

Carl Thieme / Saxon Porcelain Manufactory
c.1903

Clock, Shelf, Flowers, Hand Painted, Gold Trim, 17 In............................*illus*	374
Dish, Leaf, Flowers, Crossed Swords, Porcelain, 6 x 7½ In..........................	81
Figurine, Man, Dressed, Oriental Dandy, Flowers, 1800s, 5½ In.....................	210
Figurine, Woman, Holding Swans, 1800s, 5½ x 4¼ In................................	49
Figurine, Woman, Holds Dog, Ballooning Dress, 8½ x 5½ In.........................	280
Group, Courting Couple, Grass, 6¾ x 6 In..	133
Group, Women, Man, Drinking Tea, 10½ x 9½ In.....................................	196
Lamp Base, Oil, Porcelain, Flowers, Medallions, Scrolling, Gilt Highlights, 1800s........	24
Lamp, 3-Light, Portrait, Blue Green Luster, Flowers, Wager, 28 x 11¼ In.............	2118
Lamp, Banquet, Classical Transfer Scenes, Carl Thieme, Germany, 1850s, 34 In.......	510
Urn, Lid, Cherubs, Flowers, Courting Scene, Floral Sprays, 1800s, 24 In............*illus*	1093
Vase, Portrait, Woman, Square Body, Richard Klemm, c.1900, 6 x 3 In............*illus*	450

DUNCAN & MILLER is a term used by collectors when referring to glass made by the George A. Duncan and Sons Company or the Duncan and Miller Glass Company. These companies worked from 1893 to 1955, when the use of the name *Duncan* was discontinued and the firm became part of the United States Glass Company. Early patterns may be listed under Pressed Glass.

Chanticleer, Vase, Blue Opalescent, Lobed Rim, 1950, 3¼ In.......................*illus*	60
Punch Set, Bowl, Tray, Ladle, Cups, Ruby, Blue, Amber Handles, c.1950, 14 x 18 In., 14 Piece..	161
Vase, Roosters, Tall Grass, Opalescent, Lobed Rim, 3¼ x 4¼ In....................	61

DURAND art glass was made from 1924 to 1931. The Vineland Flint Glass Works was established by Victor Durand and Victor Durand Jr. in 1897. In 1924 Martin Bach Jr. and other artisans from the Quezal glassworks joined them at the Vineland, New Jersey, plant to make Durand art glass. They called their gold iridescent glass Gold Luster.

Lampshade, Pyramid Shape, White, Blue, Green Snakeskin Pattern, Wavy Rim, 8¾ x 8¼ x 7¾ In.	1029
Torchiere, Wrought Iron, Pricket Sticks, Tripod Base, 75 In........................	238
Vase, Blue Iridescent, Inside Gold Highlights, Signed, 5¾ In.......................	177
Vase, Blue Iridescent, Thread, Unsigned, 1968, 4½ x 3 In........................	363
Vase, Bulbous, Trumpet Rim, Cobalt Blue, Peacock Feather Design, Splayed Foot, 12½ In...*illus*	424
Vase, Gold Iridescent, Round Rim & Base, Polished Pontil, Unsigned, 10 x 4 In. ....*illus*	203
Vase, Ribbed, Lady Gay Rose, 9 x 10½ In..	826
Wine, Ruby, White Pulled Feather, Amber Stem, Round Base, 4⅜ x 3⅝ In..............	83

DURANT KILNS was founded by Jean Durant Rice in 1910 in Bedford Village, New York. He hired Leon Volkmar to oversee production. The pottery made both tableware and artware. Rice died in 1919, leaving Leon Volkmar to run the business. After 1930 the name Durant Kilns was changed and only the Volkmar mark was used.

Vase, Purple, Lobed, Ridged, 1922, 15½ In..	840
Vase, Turquoise, Crackle Glaze, Brown, Footed, Volkmar, 1917, 8¼ In..............	400
Vase, Turquoise, Crackle Glaze, Wide Shoulders, Brown Unglazed Foot, c.1917, 8 x 6 In...........	540

ELVIS PRESLEY, the well-known singer, lived from 1935 to 1977. He became famous by 1956. Elvis appeared on television, starred in 27 movies, and performed in Las Vegas. Memorabilia from any of the Presley shows, his records, and even memorials made after his death are collected.

Belt Buckle, Solid Brass, Letters, 1978, 1¾ In.	13
Clock, Glass Dome, Dial, Porcelain Base, Rotating Pendulums, Anniversary, 9 In.	11
Cookie Jar, Elvis, Playing Guitar, In Blue Convertible, Vandor, 1997, 10½ x 18 x 8 In.	72
Decanter, Music Box, Porcelain Silver, Miniature, Wood Base, McCormick, 1985	56
Figurine, Doll, Wood Guitar, Red Suit, Black Pants, Oval Base, Signed, 1993, 12 In.	6
Guitar Pick, OK Houck Piano Co., Gibson Guitar, Scotty Moore, 1950s	316
Key Chain, Flasher Images, Elvis Playing Guitar, Microphone, c.1956, 1 x 2 In.	35
Plate, Collector, Portrait, Round, Gold Rim, The King, Susie Morton	17
Scarf, Pink, Dual Signature, White, Black Sign, 1970s	98
Ticket, Concert, Stub, Evening Show, Sec 17 Row F Seat 11, April 13 1972	34
Toy, Figural, White Jumpsuit, McFarlane, Las Vegas, Box, 1970	40
Wristwatch, Direct Reading, Jump Hour, Lord Elgin, 21 Jewel, Lord Elgin, c.1957	332

ENAMELS listed here are made of glass particles and other materials heated and fused to metal. In the eighteenth and nineteenth centuries, workmen from Russia, France, England, and other countries made small boxes and table pieces of enamel on metal. One form of English enamel is called *Battersea* and is listed under that name. There was a revival of interest in artist-made enameling in the 1930s and a new style evolved. There is a recently renewed interest in the artistic enameled plaques, vases, ashtrays, and jewelry. Enamels made since the 1930s are usually on copper or steel, although silver was often used for jewelry. Graniteware, the factory-made household pieces made of tin or iron, is a separate category in this book. Enameled metal kitchen pieces may be included in the Kitchen category. Cloisonne is a special type of enamel using wire dividers and is listed in its own category. Descriptions of antique glass and ceramics often use the term *enamel* to describe paint, not the glass-based enamels listed here. Marks used by three important enamelists are shown here.

Lilyan Bachrach	Kenneth Bates	Edward Winter
1955–2015	1920s–1994	1932–1976

Box, Lid, Hinged, Gilt, Portrait, Woman, Red, France, c.1850, 1 x 2¼ In. .... *illus*	94
Box, Metal, Green, Carved Jade Pendant On Lid, Round, 1900s, 2 x 4 x 3 In.	431
Box, Rosewood, Silver, Copper, Hammered, Ottaviani, c.1965, 2½ x 8 x 12¾ In.	1040
Case, Scent, Bottle & Stopper, Blue, Raised White Flowers, France, c.1800, 2⅜ In.	201
Charger, Prunus Blossom, Multicolor, Gilt Ground, 1900s, 17¾ In.	98
Cigarette Case, Scroll Decoration, Diagonal Stripe, Green, Blue, White, Garnet Clasp, 4 x 3 In.	1375
Mirror, Hand, Brass Frame, Oval, Handle, Flowers, Chinese, 10⅝ In. .... *illus*	74
Plate, Horses, Rearing, Bucking, Teal, Copper, William Hunt Diedrich, c.1925, 7¾ In.	1000
Tray, Puppy Platter, Manor House, Dog Bush, Jeff Koons, 1992, 11 x 15 In.	285
Vase, Champleve, Elephant Head Handles, Shishi Drop Rings, Japan, c.1900, 18 In.	144
Vase, Flowers, Man In Landscape, France, 1800s, 7 In. .... *illus*	230
Vase, Flowers, Translucent Blue, Silver Foil, France, 3½ x 4 In.	316
Vase, Orchids, Multicolor, Leaves, Silver Foil, France, 3 In. .... *illus*	403
Vase, Woman In Garden, Silver Foilwork Gown, Bronze Mounted, France, 1800s, 7½ In.	207

ERPHILA is a mark found on Czechoslovakian and other pottery and porcelain made after 1920. This mark was used on items imported by Ebeling & Reuss, Philadelphia, a giftware firm that was founded in 1866 and went out of business sometime after 2002. The mark is a combination of the letters *E* and *R* (Ebeling & Reuss) and the

Durand, Vase, Bulbous, Trumpet Rim, Cobalt Blue, Peacock Feather Design, Splayed Foot, 12½ In.
$424

Fontaine's Auction Gallery

Durand, Vase, Gold Iridescent, Round Rim & Base, Polished Pontil, Unsigned, 10 x 4 In.
$203

Soulis Auctions

Enamel, Box, Lid, Hinged, Gilt, Portrait, Woman, Red, France, c.1850, 1 x 2¼ In.
$94

Leland Little Auctions

Enamel, Mirror, Hand, Brass Frame, Oval, Handle, Flowers, Chinese, 10⅝ In.
$74

Skinner, Inc.

Enamel, Vase, Flowers, Man In Landscape, France, 1800s, 7 In.
$230

Richard D. Hatch & Associates

first letters of the city, Phila(delphia). Many whimsical figural pitchers and creamers, figurines, platters, and other giftwares carry this mark.

Biscuit Jar, Man, Pink Outfit, c.1880	36
Powder Box, Madame Pompadour Dresser Doll, Green Dress, Fan, 5½ In.	72
Teapot, Figural, Dog, Terrier, Black & White, Pink Bow, Germany, 7½ In.	138
Watering Can, Red Flowers, Leaves, Czechoslovakia, c.1920, 6½ x 9 In.	39

 ES GERMANY porcelain was made at the factory of Erdmann Schlegelmilch from 1861 to 1937 in Suhl, Germany. The porcelain, marked *ES Germany* or *ES Suhl*, was sold decorated or undecorated. Other pieces were made at a factory in Saxony, Prussia, and are marked *ES Prussia*. Reinhold Schlegelmilch also made porcelain. There is no connection between the two factories. Porcelain made by Reinhold Schlegelmilch is listed in this book under RS Germany, RS Poland, RS Prussia, RS Silesia, RS Suhl, and RS Tillowitz.

Hair Receiver, Flowers, Multicolor, Gilt Highlights, 4¼ x 2½ In.	24
Plate, Roses, Yellow, Scalloped Gilt Rim, c.1905, 8⅝ In.	65
Tray, Orange Flowers, Green Leaves, Gilt Handle & Trim, Scalloped, 8 x 7 In.	111

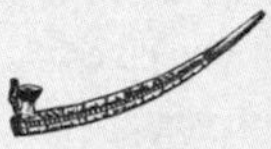

ESKIMO artifacts of all types are collected. Carvings of whale or walrus teeth are listed under Scrimshaw. Baskets are in the Basket category. All other types of Eskimo art are listed here. In Canada and some other areas, the term *Inuit* is used instead of Eskimo. It is illegal to sell some whale parts that are used to made decorative items. The law has changed several times, so check the legality before you buy or sell.

Figurine, Face, Carved, Bone, Stand, c.1900, 2½ In.	593
Group, Polar Bears, Soapstone, Peter Robert Kapakatoak, Canada, 6½ x 8½ x 8½ In.	168
Sculpture, Stone, Serpentine, Brown Speckled, Inukshuk, c.1985, 14½ x 14 x 6 In.	210
Tusk, Walrus, Happy Jack, Kayak, Harpooning Walrus, Ice, Engraved, c.1950, 23 In.	1800
Tusk, Walrus, Hunting Scenes, Otter, Polar Bear, Caribou, Marked, 1939, 16½ In.	1020
Tusk, Walrus, Polar Bear Shape, Carved, Petrified, c.1820, 2 x 6 In.	720
Tusk, Walrus, Salmon Shape, 4 Ivory Pegs, Engraved, c.1950, 12 In.	600

ФАБЕРЖЕ
КФ **FABERGE** was a firm of jewelers and goldsmiths founded in St. Petersburg, Russia, in 1842, by Gustav Faberge. Peter Carl Faberge, his son, was jeweler to the Russian Imperial Court from about 1870 to 1917. The rare Imperial Easter eggs, jewelry, and decorative items are very expensive today. The name *Faberge* is also used for art made of precious metals and jewels by Peter Carl Faberge's grandson. Theo Faberge launched a collection of artistic things made of expensive materials in 1895. He made jeweled eggs in several sizes. The collection is sold in several museums.

Bowl, Silver, Gold Wash, Scalloped Foot, Gadroon, Enameled, 1920s, 2 x 3 In.	756
Egg, Imperial Crown Of Russia, Cobalt Blue, Sterling Silver, England, 1986	600
Egg, Swan Lake, Red & Clear Crystal, Imperial Crown Of Russia, Gilt Dancers, c.1985	938
Vase, Flower, Diamond, Raspberries, Nephrite Leaves, Gold Stem, 6¼ In.	1599

 FAIENCE refers to tin-glazed earthenware, especially the wares made in France, Germany, and Scandinavia. It is also correct to say that faience is the same as majolica or Delft, although usually the term refers only to the tin-glazed pottery of the three regions mentioned.

Bowl, Portrait, Warrior, Black Ground, Renaissance Revival, Italy, 17 In. .... *illus*	130
Centerpiece, Handles, Woman's Head, Crown, Neoclassical Scenes, Deruta, 1800s, 22 x 23 In.	531
Charger, Mythological Scene, Bacchus, Ulisse Cantagalli, 1800s, 20 In.	1560
Charger, Woman On Horse, Farmer, Cow, Blue & White, Blue & Yellow Flowers Border, 1800s, 24 In.	605
Figure, Holding Farming Implements, 9 Horizontal Bands, Egypt, 8½ In.	6765
Figure, Lion, Walking, Cobalt Blue Glaze, c.1700s, 5½ In.	281
Jardiniere, Oval, Dragon Handles, Gilt, Floral Body, Continental, 1800s, 10 x 15 In. .... *illus*	250
Jardiniere, Stand, Turquoise, Sunflower & Bamboo, Burmantofts, c.1890, 58 In. .... *illus*	793
Platter, Palissy Style, Greek Scene, Hercules, France, 15⅝ x 19 x 2½ In. .... *illus*	531

Enamel, Vase, Orchids, Multicolor, Leaves, Silver Foil, France, 3 In.
$403

Richard D. Hatch & Associates

Faience, Bowl, Portrait, Warrior, Black Ground, Renaissance Revival, Italy, 17 In.
$130

Aspire Auctions

Faience, Jardiniere, Oval, Dragon Handles, Gilt, Floral Body, Continental, 1800s, 10 x 15 In.
$250

Leslie Hindman Auctioneers

Faience, Jardiniere, Stand, Turquoise, Sunflower & Bamboo, Burmantofts, c.1890, 58 In.
$793

Neal Auction Company

Faience, Platter, Palissy Style, Greek Scene, Hercules, France, 15 5/8 x 19 x 2 1/2 In.
$531

Roland Auctioneers & Valuers

Faience, Vase, 2 Gourd Shape, Applied Dragon, Burmantofts, England, 1900s, 22 x 12 In.
$406

Rago Arts and Auction Center

Fairing, Match Holder, Pink Pig, Vase, Anthropomorphic, German, 1800s, 4 x 3 x 2½ In.

$26

antique*picnic on eBay

Fan, Abalone, Painted, Metal Overlay, Frame, 13¾ x 22 x 2 In.

$219

Susanin's Auctioneers & Appraisers

Fan, Electric, Adams-Bagnall Jandus, Wire Yoke Arms, Brass Windmill Blades, c.1901, 12 In.

$480

Soulis Auctions

Vase, 2 Gourd Shape, Applied Dragon, Burmantofts, England, 1900s, 22 x 12 In............... *illus*	406
Vase, Multicolor, Fleur-De-Lis Shape, 13 x 8 In..	220

 FAIRINGS are small souvenir boxes and figurines that were sold at country fairs during the nineteenth century. Most were made in Germany. Reproductions of fairings are being made, especially of the famous *Twelve Months after Marriage* series.

Figurine, Boot, Cat, 1¾ In.	35
Figurine, Couple, The Lovers Disturbed, White Ground, Black Trim, 4 x 2¼ x 3½ In.	25
Figurine, Pink Pig Porker, Mounted, Porcelain, 3 x 4½ x 3½ In..	179
Match Holder, Pink Pig, Vase, Anthropomorphic, German, 1800s, 4 x 3 x 2½ In. .... *illus*	26
Striker, Match, Girl & Dog, Porcelain, Conta Boheme, Victorian..	28
Trinket Box, 12 Months After Marriage, Victorian, c.1840s, 3¼ x 3½ x 2¼ In.	75
Trinket Box, Bonzo The Dog, Ashtray, Bowl, Spring Tail, 1920s, 5⅞ In..................................	18
Trinket Box, Figural, Girl, Tea Set, Staffordshire, 1800s..	30

FAIRYLAND LUSTER *pieces are included in the Wedgwood category.*

FAMILLE ROSE, *see Chinese Export category.*

 FANS have been used for cooling since the days of the ancients. By the eighteenth century, the fan was an accessory for the lady of fashion and very elaborate and expensive fans were made. Sticks were made of ivory or wood, set with jewels or carved. The fans were made of painted silk or paper. Inexpensive paper fans printed with advertising were giveaways in the late nineteenth and early twentieth centuries. Electric fans were introduced in 1882. There are collectors of electric fans who like to buy damaged ones to repair.

Abalone, Painted, Metal Overlay, Frame, 13¾ x 22 x 2 In.. *illus*	219
Advertising, Columbia Grafonola, Spinning Dial, Singers & Hit Songs, c.1925, 8 x 11 In.	108
Advertising, Drink Moxie, 2-Sided, Man, Woman, 1920s, 7 x 8 In.	75
Bamboo, Folding, Silk Hand, Flower, Rose, White, Red, 9¼ x 15¼ In....................................	6
Bone, Hand Carved, Abalone & Silk, 1890s, Frame..	53
Celluloid, Ostrich Feather, Black, Silver Scrolls On Holder, Rodien, c.1880, 25 x 16 In.	375
Celluloid, Painted, Tassel, Guards, Art Deco, 1920s	21
Electric, 6 Blades, Painted, Army Green, Brass, General Electric, 20 In.	141
Electric, Adams-Bagnall Jandus, Wire Yoke Arms, Brass Windmill Blades, c.1901, 12 In... *illus*	480
Electric, Ceiling, Victor Zephyr, Breeze Spreader Louvers, Black, c.1939, 16 In.	102
Electric, Ceiling, Zeppelin, Aluminum Wings, Blade, Leland Electric Co., 27 x 20 x 34½ In. ...	9680
Electric, Dayton Fan & Motor Co., Brass Windmill Blades, Iron Base, c.1910, 8 In. .... *illus*	339
Electric, Emerson, 3-Speed, Parker Blades, Step Base, Oscillator, c.1914, 12 In........................	215
Electric, Emerson, 6 Brass Parker Blades, Brass Cage, Yoke, Wing Nuts, c.1914, 16 In.	256
Electric, Emerson, Parker Blades, Iron Base, S-Type Guard, Oscillating, c.1923, 12 In.	181
Electric, Emerson, Parker Blades, Iron Step Base, 3-Speed, S-Type Guard, c.1941, 9 In.	311
Electric, Emerson, Rib Base, Brass Cage, Parker Blades, Auto Start, c.1910, 12 In............. *illus*	819
Electric, Emerson, Yoke Assembly, 4 Park Blades, 3-Speed, Brass Cage, Desk Model, c.1912, 16 In. *illus*	203
Electric, General Electric, Brass Blades, 3-Speed Motor, Signed, c.1901, 8 In............................	226
Electric, General Motors, Black, Delco Appliance Co., 18 x 21 In...	179
Electric, Gilbert, Aluminum, Black Metal Base, Toggle Switch, Art Deco, c.1930, 10 In.	218
Electric, Hawthorn Victor Style, Tank Motor, Brass Screws, Cage, Blades, c.1906, 12 In.	367
Electric, Menominee, Iron Step Base, Universal Ball Motor, Brass Windmill, c.1912, 8 In........	339
Electric, Metal Bell, Slotted Cage, Wood Grain Effect, Electro Dental Mfg., 9 In. .... *illus*	192
Electric, Oscillating, Cast Iron, Brass, Canada, 1920s, 14 x 15 In...	296
Electric, Oscillator, Dayton, Tab Base, Brass Windmill Blades, Dayton, 12 In.	367
Electric, Robbins & Myers, Brass Cage, Windmill Blade, Lollipop Vane, Oscillating, 16 In........	1978
Electric, Robbins & Myers, S-Type Guard, Iron Base, Brass Windmill Blades, c.1915, 9 In.	254
Electric, Singer Simanco, Ribbonaire, Bakelite, 2-Speed	87
Electric, Vertical Rod, V Shape Vanes Oscillating, Westinghouse, 16 x 11 x 12½ In..................	706
Electric, Westinghouse, 4 Brass Windmill Blades, S-Type Guard, c.1912, 8 In.	203
Electric, Westinghouse, Tesla, 4 Windmill Blades, Brass Cage, 1991, 12 In.	2599
Folding, Black, Spanish Style, Dance Party, Wedding Lace Silk, Flower....................................	2

F

Fan, Electric, Dayton Fan & Motor Co., Brass Windmill Blades, Iron Base, c.1910, 8 In.
$339

Soulis Auctions

Fan, Electric, Emerson, Rib Base, Brass Cage, Parker Blades, Auto Start, c.1910, 12 In.
$819

Soulis Auctions

Fan, Electric, Emerson, Yoke Assembly, 4 Park Blades, 3-Speed, Brass Cage, Desk Model, c.1912, 16 In.
$203

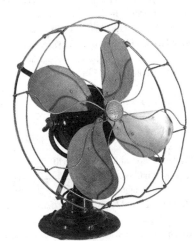

Soulis Auctions

Fan, Electric, Metal Bell, Slotted Cage, Wood Grain Effect, Electro Dental Mfg., 9 In.
$192

Soulis Auctions

Fan, Luminaire, Floor, Tripod Harp Style Base, Candle Socket Arms, 58 x 17 x 17 In.
$968

Fontaine's Auction Gallery

Fan, Painted, Shadowbox, Scene Of Women Gathered In Forest, 13 ¼ x 23 ¼ x 1 ½ In.
$242

Fontaine's Auction Gallery

F

Fenton, Burmese, Pitcher, Leaves, Apple Green, Handle, 4 1/4 x 4 In.
$72

Martin Auction Co.

Fenton, Burmese, Vase, Satin Pink, Jack-In-The-Pulpit, 7 x 4 In.
$96

Martin Auction Co.

Fenton, Hobnail, Cruet, Cranberry, Opalescent, Stopper, 6 1/2 x 4 1/2 In.
$42

Martin Auction Co.

Folding, Hand Painted, Spanish Theme, Paper, Casa De Diego, El Pepepe, 1970s	8
Luminaire, Floor, Tripod Harp Style Base, Candle Socket Arms, 58 x 17 x 17 In. ...... *illus*	968
Painted, Hand, Celluloid, Crocheted Tassel, Floral, Ivory, 11 1/4 x 6 1/8 In.	3
Painted, Shadowbox, Scene Of Women Gathered In Forest, 13 1/4 x 23 1/4 x 1 1/2 In. .... *illus*	242
Satin, Red, Decorative, Wall, Wood Sticks, Floral, 2 Birds, Oriental Style, 30 In.	6
Shell, Ostrich Feather, Faux Tortoiseshell Spine, Green, J Duvelleroy, 16 In.	158
Silk & Wood, Lace Trim, Ivory, Hand Painted Flowers, 18 x 10 In.	78
Silk, Handheld, Folding, Ornate Floral, Silver, Carved Bone Bovine, 21 x 13 In.	22

FAST FOOD COLLECTIBLES *may be included in several categories, such as Advertising, Coca-Cola, Toy, etc.*

FEDERZEICHNUNG, *see Loetz category.*

FENTON ART GLASS COMPANY was founded in 1905 in Martins Ferry, Ohio, by Frank L. Fenton and his brother, John W. Fenton. They painted decorations on glass blanks made by other manufacturers. In 1907 they opened a factory in Williamstown, West Virginia, and began making glass. The company stopped making art glass in 2011 and assets were sold. A new division of the company makes handcrafted glass beads and other jewelry. Copies are being made from leased original Fenton molds by an unrelated company, Fenton's Collectibles. The copies are marked with the Fenton mark and Fenton's Collectibles mark. Fenton is noted for early carnival glass produced between 1907 and 1920. Some of these pieces are listed in the Carnival Glass category. Many other types of glass were also made. Spanish Lace in this section refers to the pattern made by Fenton.

Fenton Art Glass Co.
1970–1975

Fenton Art Glass Co.
1980s

Fenton Art Glass Co.
1983+

Basket, Green, Center Handle, Flowers, Leaves, Hexagonal Base, Signed, George Fenton, 11 x 5 In. ...	30
Bowl, Hen Shape Lid, Pink, 4 x 5 In.	46
Burmese, Basket, Satin, Center Handle, Ruffled Top, Floral, Vines, 8 x 5 In.	96
Burmese, Egg, Satin Glass, Hanging Hearts, Yellow, Pink, 4 7/8 x 10 3/4 In.	48
Burmese, Pitcher, Leaves, Apple Green, Handle, 4 1/4 x 4 In.	*illus*	72
Burmese, Vase, Ruffled Rim, Flowers, 5 x 6 In.	132
Burmese, Vase, Satin Pink, Jack-In-The-Pulpit, 7 x 4 In.	*illus*	96
Coin Dot, Lampshade, Cranberry, Ruffled Edge, Hand Blown, 10 In.	155
Diamond Lace, 3 Jack-In-The-Pulpit Vases, Ruffled Rim Bowl, 10 1/2 x 13 In.	263
Epergne, Opalescent, 4 Branch, Vaseline Glass, Molded, Crystal, Ruffled Rims, 17 x 12 In.	300
Fairy Lamp, Embossed Roses, Ruffled, Satin Green, 6 1/2 x 5 1/2 In.	24
Fairy Lamp, Iridescent, Dome, Floral, Hand Painted, 5 x 3 1/4 In.	48
Figurine, Butterfly, Resting On A Branch, Flowers, Wing Detail, White, 5 x 4 In.	18
Hanging Hearts, Rose Bowl, Murrhina Overlay, Freehand Design, Dave Fetty, 5 x 5 In.	109
Hobnail, Beer Stein, Milk Glass, 7 x 4 In.	119
Hobnail, Candy Dish, Lid, Plum Purple, Opalescent, Footed, 8 1/2 x 5 In.	175
Hobnail, Compote, White Custard Glass, Ruffled Rim, 5 1/2 x 6 1/4 In.	24
Hobnail, Cruet, Cranberry, Opalescent, Stopper, 6 1/2 x 4 1/2 In.	*illus*	42
Hobnail, Fairy Lamp, Amber, Opalescent, 4 1/2 x 3 1/2 In.	30
Hobnail, Sugar, Lid, Scalloped, Milk Glass, 4 3/4 x 4 In.	25
Hobnail, Vase, Yellow, Ruffled Edge, Vaseline, 8 x 3 5/8 In.	313
Honeycomb, Vase, Cranberry, Opalescent, Urn Shape, Tooled Rim, 11 1/4 x 8 In.	176
Lampshade, Turquoise, Silver Crest, Hurricane, Blown Glass, Round Base	52
Mosaic, Egg, Hand Blown, Pulled Swirl, Hollow, Paperweight, Dave Fetty, 5 In.	88
Silver Crest, Cake Stand, White Milk Glass, Crimpled Edge, 12 1/2 In.	150
Silver Crest, Compote, 1940s, 4 x 8 In.	25
Swirl, Vase, Blue Crest, Scalloped Rim, Flowers, 6 x 4 In.	30
Vista Pink, Jug, Pink Leaves, Landscape, Handle, Mason's, 4 x 4 In., 12 Oz.	29

F

FIESTA, the colorful dinnerware, was introduced in 1936 by the Homer Laughlin China Co., re-designed in 1969, and withdrawn in 1973. It was reissued again in 1986 in different colors and is still being made. New colors, including some that are similar to old colors, have been introduced. One new color is introduced in March every year. The simple design was characterized by a band of concentric circles beginning at the rim. Cups had full-circle handles until 1969, when partial-circle handles were made. Harlequin and Riviera were related wares. For more prices, go to kovels.com.

Fiesta
1936–1970

Fiesta Kitchen Kraft
1939–c.1943

Fiesta Casual
1962–c.1968

Chartreuse, Ashtray	47
Chartreuse, Vase, Millennium II, Round Body, 8 x 8 ½ In.	26
Clock, Tune Times, Bugs Bunny, Tweety Bird, Sylvester, White, Blue, 1998, 10 ¼ In.	71
Cobalt Blue, Bowl, Fruit, 1938-51, 4 In.	20
Cobalt Blue, Creamer, Stick Handle, 3 In.	49
Cobalt Blue, Mixing Bowl, No. 3, Inside Rings, 1936-37	78
Cobalt Blue, Mug, Lazarus, 86th Anniversary, 1851-1937, Department Store	177
Cobalt Blue, Utility Tray, Oval	24
Cobalt Blue, Water Carafe, Handle	118
Gray, Plate, Bread & Butter, 6 ½ In.	11
Green, Plate, Dessert, Round, 6 In.	295
Green, Eggcup, 89th Anniversary, Lazarus, 1851-1940	94
Ivory, Mixing Bowl, No. 7, Inside Bottom Rings, 1936-38, 7 x 11 In. *illus*	435
Light Green, Mixing Bowl, Nesting, No. 2, Inside Rings	24
Medium Green, Pitcher, Water, Disc	489
Medium Green, Sugar, Lid, Scroll Handles, Concentric Rings, 1950s, 5 In. *illus*	73
Medium Green, Utility Tray, Oval	24
Red, Ashtray, Round *illus*	59
Red, Compote, Footed, Round	118
Red, Grill Plate, 3 Sections, 11 ⅝ In.	59
Red, Mixing Bowl, No. 1, 3 ½ x 5 In.	88
Red, Pitcher, Lid, Kitchen Kraft, 6 ½ In.	279
Rose, Gravy Boat, Footed, Handle, 8 x 4 ¾ x 3 ½ In.	13
Rose, Server, Coffee	649
Turquoise, Carafe, Lid, Finial, 10 In.	81
Turquoise, Plate, Salad, 7 ⅜ In.	15
Turquoise, Vase, Bud, Footed	53
White, Plate, Reindeer, Christmas Lights Around Head & Back, Prototype, 9 In.	130
Yellow, Cake Plate	826
Yellow, Candleholder, Bulb, Square Base, 3 ¾ x 2 ½ In., Pair *illus*	53
Yellow, Compote, Sweets, Fruit, Footed, Pedestal Bowl	105
Yellow, Pitcher, Sunflower, Sample, 1871	266

FINCH, *see Kay Finch category.*

FINDLAY ONYX AND FLORADINE are two similar types of glass made by Dalzell, Gilmore and Leighton Co. of Findlay, Ohio, about 1889. Onyx is a patented yellowish white opaque glass with raised silver daisy decorations. A few rare pieces were made of rose, amber, orange, or purple glass. Floradine is made of cranberry-colored glass with an opalescent white raised floral pattern and a satin finish. The same molds were used for both types of glass.

Celery Vase, Onyx, Lid, Ribbed Neck, Opal Iridescent, 8 ½ In.	189
Sugar, Floradine, Lid, Flowers, 5 ½ In.	472
Syrup, Onyx, Opal Glass Handle, Thumblift, 7 In.	83

Fiesta, Ivory, Mixing Bowl, No. 7, Inside Bottom Rings, 1936-38, 7 x 11 In.
$435

karen98northern on eBay

Fiesta, Medium Green, Sugar, Lid, Scroll Handles, Concentric Rings, 1950s, 5 In.
$73

bybeetoo on eBay

TIP
Never stack cups or bowls inside each other.

Fiesta, Red, Ashtray, Round
$59

Strawser Auction Group

Fiesta, Yellow, Candleholder, Bulb, Square Base, 3 ¾ x 2 ½ In., Pair
$53

Strawser Auction Group

Firefighting, Fire Mark, Liberty Tree, No. 852, Wood, Metal, c.1790, 16½ x 11 In. $720

Eldred's

Firefighting, Helmet, Brass Eagle, Red, 12, KCKFD, Cairns & Brother, 8½ x 13½ x 11 In. $600

Soulis Auctions

Firefighting, Helmet, Leather Plate, Elk Ridge Fire Dept, Metal Tag, Cairns & Brother $373

Keystone Auctions LLC

TIP

Beware of fire. Never put a heavy object on top of an electric cord. Never put the cord under a rug.

FIREFIGHTING equipment of all types is collected, from fire marks to uniforms to toy fire trucks. It is said that every little boy wanted to be a fireman or a train engineer 75 years ago and the collectors today reflect this interest.

Bucket, H & L 2, Gold Lettering, Red Black, Handle, 1800s, 12½ In.	250
Bucket, Leather, Painted, Clasping Hands, Mutual Fire Society, 13 In., Pair	7200
Bucket, Leather, Yellow, Concord Bank, Painted, Handle, c.1910, 13 x 7 In.	1337
Extinguisher, Brass, Coulter Copper & Brass Co., Canada, 24 x 7 In.	156
Fire Mark, Liberty Tree, No. 852, Wood, Metal, c.1790, 16½ x 11 In. *illus*	720
Helmet, Brass Eagle, Red, 12, KCKFD, Cairns & Brother, 8½ x 13½ x 11 In. *illus*	600
Helmet, Leather Plate, Elk Ridge Fire Dept, Metal Tag, Cairns & Brother *illus*	373
Helmet, Leather, Black, Eagle Finial, Firemens Active Phila, 1800s, 10 In.	1800
Helmet, Leather, White, Crown & Brim, Eagle Crest, New York, 1800s, 14 x 10⅞ In.	923
Plaque, Germantown Mutual Fire, Raised Lettering, Handshake, Iron, 1800s, 8 x 12 In.	360
Trumpet, Tin, Chief Engineer, Black Lettering, c.1820, 18 In.	812

FIREPLACES were used to cook food and to heat the American home in past centuries. Many types of tools and equipment were used. Andirons held the logs in place, firebacks reflected the heat into the room, and tongs were used to move either fuel or food. Many types of spits and roasting jacks were made and may be listed in the Kitchen category.

Andirons, Brass, Steeple Finial, Ball, Scrolling Legs, Ball Feet, 22 In.	480
Andirons, Bronze, Figural, Man, Kneeling, Louis McClellan Potter, Marked, 23 In.	4063
Andirons, Cherub, Architectural Pediment, Wheat, Flower Spray, Fruit, 21 x 14 In.	300
Andirons, Federal, Double Lemon Tops, Hexagonal Pedestals, Ball Feet, Brass, c.1900, 18 In.	780
Bellows, Ship Portrait, Painted, Brass Nozzle, 18 In.	738
Coal Bucket, Hepplewhite Style, Wood, Inlays, Compartment, England, c.1915, 19 x 15 In.	120
Coal Scuttle, Mahogany, Fall Front Door, Metal Interior, Art Deco, 19 x 13 x 12 In.	65
Crane, Arts & Crafts, Iron, Serpent Terminal, Samuel Yellin, 10½ x 16½ In.	2000
Fender, Brass & Iron, Wirework, Gothic Arches, 1800s, 9¼ x 42 In.	554
Fender, Brass, Curved, Openwork, 40 x 9½ In.	106
Fender, Brass, Curved, Paw Footed, c.1880, 8 x 36 x 13 In.	108
Fender, Brass, Pierced, Urns, Thistles, Leaves, Ring Pull, 1800s, 9 x 48 In.	147
Fender, Brass, Wire, Curved, Finials, c.1825, 12½ x 45 x 11 In. *illus*	439
Fender, Bronze, Balustrade Garden, Urn Chenets, Bellflowers, Molded, c.1980, 14 x 42 In.	563
Fender, Louis XV Style, Bronze, Urn Chenets, Flame Finials, Crest, c.1980, 21 x 57 In.	500
Fender, Wire, Brass, Serpentine Front, Wings, 63 x 11 x 10 In.	59
Fender, Wrought Iron, Leather Seat, Black Paint, Early 1900s, 25 x 59 x 23 In. *illus*	420
Fireback, Figural, Cast Iron, Black, 32¾ x 22 In. *illus*	308
Fireplace Dummy, Poodle, Orange Bell, Sitting, Tin, 1800s, 25 In. *illus*	438
Footman, Brass, Iron, Cabriole Legs, Star, Handles, 18 x 14 x 16 In. *illus*	71
Insert, Brass, Iron, Serpentine Front, 2 Ball Feet, 31 x 30 x 13 In.	160
Mantel is listed in the Architectural category.	
Screens are also listed in the Furniture category.	
Screen, Brass, Fan Shape, 1900s, 27 In.	100
Screen, Brass, Fan Shape, Peacock Tail Shape, Woman Carrying Ball, Finial, 33 In.	148
Screen, Brass, Iron, Cast Paw Feet, c.1875, 16¾ x 49 In.	123
Screen, Brass, Iron, Wirework, Scrolled Embellishments, c.1825, 14¾ x 39 In.	369
Screen, Brass, Iron, Wirework, Scrolled Embellishments, c.1825, 24¼ x 41 In.	1046
Screen, Brass, Scrolled Feet, Vine Finial, 31½ x 25 In.	540
Screen, Brass, Wirework, Black, 30 x 44 In.	523
Screen, Bronze, Gilt, Louis XV Style, Cartouche, Leafy Scroll Feet, c.1900, 49 In.	625
Screen, Carved Frame, Angel, Young Child, Late 1800s, 34 x 22½ In. *illus*	60
Screen, Embroidered, Turned Sides, Carved Scroll Top, Finials, 1800s, 50 x 26 x 12 In.	644
Screen, Garden, Semicircular, Plywood, 2-Sided, Ships, Nancy Whorf, 17¼ x 34 In.	375
Screen, Glass, Copper Frame, 18¾ x 36 x 8½ In.	1000
Screen, Mahogany, Gilt Bronze Mounts, Silk Panel, Caster Feet, Empire, 38 x 24 In.	300
Screen, Mounted, Winged Angels, Claw Feet, Louis XV Style, 33 x 31 In. *illus*	1342

F

Fireplace, Fender, Brass, Wire, Curved, Finials, c.1825, 12 ½ x 45 x 11 In.
$439

Jeffrey S. Evans & Associates

Fireplace, Fender, Wrought Iron, Leather Seat, Black Paint, Early 1900s, 25 x 59 x 23 In.
$420

Brunk Auctions

Fireplace, Fireback, Figural, Cast Iron, Black, 32 ¾ x 22 In.
$308

Skinner, Inc.

Fireplace, Fireplace Dummy, Poodle, Orange Bell, Sitting, Tin, 1800s, 25 In.
$438

Pook & Pook

Fireplace, Footman, Brass, Iron, Cabriole Legs, Star, Handles, 18 x 14 x 16 In.
$71

Copake Auction

Fireplace, Screen, Carved Frame, Angel, Young Child, Late 1800s, 34 x 22 ½ In.
$60

Garth's Auctioneers & Appraisers

Fireplace, Screen, Mounted, Winged Angels, Claw Feet, Louis XV Style, 33 x 31 In.
$1,342

Nadeau's Auction Gallery

Fireplace, Screen, Paint, Porcelain Panels Of Birds, Mount Frame, c.1900, 34 x 25 ½ In.
$396

Garth's Auctioneers & Appraisers

Fireplace, Screen, Pole, Fern Decoration, Turned Stem, Finial, Arched Carved Legs, c.1750, 56 In.
$390

Eldred's

F

149

Fireplace, Screen, Steel, Black Paint, Pinecones, Trifold, Arts & Crafts, 32 x 40 In.
$246

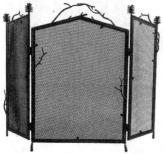

Skinner, Inc.

TIP

Rub soap on noisy door hinges.

Fischer, Candlestick, Gilt, 2 Cherubs, Reticulated Base, 9¾ x 5½ In.
$72

Thomaston Place Auction Galleries

Fischer, Figurine, Antelope, Rust Fishnet, Gilt Horns & Feet, 1900s, 7 In.
$344

Leslie Hindman Auctioneers

Screen, Paint, Porcelain Panels Of Birds, Mount Frame, c.1900, 34 x 25½ In.	*illus*	396
Screen, Pole, Brass, Octagonal Base, Adjustable, Gilt Wood Frame, c.1950, 55 In.		47
Screen, Pole, Fern Decoration, Turned Stem, Finial, Arched Carved Legs, c.1750, 56 In.	*illus*	390
Screen, Pole, Rosewood, Lacquer Floral, 1800s, 57½ In.		125
Screen, Regency, Gilt, Mahogany, Embroidered, Children, c.1800, 62 In., Pair		875
Screen, Steel, Black Paint, Pinecones, Trifold, Arts & Crafts, 32 x 40 In.	*illus*	246
Spit, Bell Form, Gold, Brass, Signed, G. Salter, 1800s, 13½ In.		47
Striker, Steel, Strike-A-Lite, Hand Forged, Snake Shape, 4 In.		254
Trammel, Cross Base, Adjustable, Single Candle, England, 38 In.		1107
Trammel, Wrought Iron, Heart Finial, Scrolled Terminals, c.1825, 14 In.		625

FISCHER porcelain was made in Herend, Hungary. The wares are sometimes referred to as Herend porcelain. The pottery was originally founded in Herend in 1826 and was bought by Moritz Fischer in 1839. Fischer made replacement pieces for German and Far Eastern dinnerware and later began making its own dinnerware patterns. Figurines were made beginning in the 1870s. The company was nationalized in 1948. Martin's Herend Imports, Inc., began importing Herend china into the United States in 1957. The company was privatized in 1993 and is now in business as Herend.

Cachepots, Birds, On Branch, Butterflies, Gilt Rim, 1900s, 6 x 7 In., Pair		206
Candlestick, Gilt, 2 Cherubs, Reticulated Base, 9¾ x 5½ In.	*illus*	72
Centerpiece, Dolphin, 4 Scallop Shells, Bird, Floral On Black, Square Base, 9½ x 16 In.		460
Figurine, Antelope, Rust Fishnet, Gilt Horns & Feet, 1900s, 7 In.	*illus*	344
Figurine, Deer, With Fawn, Seated, Green Fishnet, White, Gilt Highlights, Signed, 3½ x 5 In.		393
Figurine, Eagle, Wings Up, Curved Sword At Feet, White Glaze, 1900s, 13 In.		125
Figurine, Matador, Wrestling White Bull, Red Jacket, Blue Pants, 7 x 11 In.		126
Figurine, Rabbit, Blue & White, Fishnet, 5¼ In.		81
Figurine, Rooster, Blue Fishnet, Gilt, 1900s, 5¼ In.		108
Trinket Box, Blue Garland, Bunny Finial, Painted Flowers, 6 In.		52
Vase, Nude Woman, Butterfly, Hand Painted, Cylindrical, 11 In.	*illus*	203

FISHING reels of brass or nickel were made in the United States by 1810. Bamboo fly rods were sold by 1860, often marked with the maker's name. Lures made of metal, or metal and wood, were made in the nineteenth century. Plastic lures were made by the 1930s. All fishing material is collected today and even equipment of the past 30 years is of interest if in good condition with original box.

Creel, Wicker, Leather Strap & Latch, 14 x 6 x 9 In.	*illus*	60
Harpoon, Whalers, Toggle Iron Head, Mount, Oak Shaft, Attach Ropes, c.1870, 86 In.		330
Harpoon, Wrought Iron, Wood, 1800s, 157 In.		1230
License, Angling, Connecticut, Resident, c.1940, 1¾ In.	*illus*	40
Lure, 3 Hooks, Wood, Heddon Vamp, Frog Spot, 4¾ In.		24
Lure, Chippewa, Fancy Sienna, Imell Bait & Tackle Co., 1910s, 4 In.		327
Lure, Edon Bait Co., Strausborger, Green, Yellow, Wood, 3 In.		65
Lure, Glass Eye, Wood, Heddon Dowagiac, 3 Hooks, 4½ In.	*illus*	60
Lure, Glass Eyes, Back Spinner, Yellow, 2 Hooks, 4¾ In.		12
Lure, Heddon Lucky 13, Red, Yellow, 4¼ In.		10
Lure, Jitterbug, Fred Arbogast, White, Hooks, 2½ In.		66
Lure, Wood, Glass Eyes, Front Spinner, 2 Hooks, Green Stripes, 4¼ In.		30
Lure, Wood, Yellow, Black Stripe Body, Front Spinner, 5½ In.		72
Outboard Motor, Elgin, 1.25 HP, Air Cooled Motor, Sears & Roebuck, 34 x 7½ x 18 In.		151
Plaque, Fish, Wall, Frame, Signed, Ken Sprague, c.1950, 14½ In.		300
Reel, Baitcasting, Right Hand Retrieve, Abu Garcia Ambassadeur, 5500-C3, Sweden		63
Reel, Side Cast, Mallochs, Scotland, 1900s, 4¼ x 4¼ In.		130
Sign, Fishing Parties Day Or Night Capt. A. Moeller, Wood, Painted, 14 x 21½ In.		767
Sign, South Bend & Oreno Fishing Tackle, 3-Fold, 34 x 38½ In.		79

FLAGS *are included in the Textile category.*

FLASH GORDON appeared in the Sunday comics in 1934. The daily strip started in 1940. The hero was also in comic books from 1930 to 1970, in books from 1936, in movies from 1938, on the radio in the 1930s and 1940s, and on television from 1953 to 1954. All sorts of memorabilia are collected, but the ray guns and rocket ships are the most popular.

Action Figure, Mego, Plastic, Red Shirt, Navy Blue Pants, 1976, 10 In.	18
Action Figure, Ming The Merciless, Space Ship, Mattel, 1979, 3 ¾ In.	22
Cocktail Shaker, Rocket Ship, Stainless Steel, Red Plastic Base, c.1950, 12 In. *illus*	16
Compass, Portrait, Spaceships, Planets, Vinyl Strap, Esquire Novelty Co., c.1951	60
Game, Board, Space Target & On The Beam, Tin Lithograph, 1952, 15 x 12 In.	64
Knife, Jack, Novelty, Carbon Steel, Delrin, Celluloid, Folding, 3 ½ In.	5
Puzzle, Boy & Girl, 3 Sets, Milton Bradley, 12 In.	127
Toy, Arresting Ray Clicker Gun, Tin Lithograph, Multicolor, Marx, 1950s, 10 In. *illus*	128
Toy, Rocket Fighter Ship, Sparkling, Red, Yellow, White, Tin, Schylling, 12 x 4 In.	53
Toy, Signal Pistol, Blue, Red, Marx, 1935	146
Toy, Sparkling Rocket, Fighter Ship, Red, Yellow, Box, Marx, 12 In.	439

FLORENCE CERAMICS were made in Pasadena, California, from the 1940s to 1977. Florence Ward created many colorful figurines, boxes, candleholders, and other items for the gift shop trade. Each piece was marked with an ink stamp that included the name *Florence Ceramics Co.* The company was sold in 1964 and although the name remained the same, the products were very different. Mugs, cups, and trays were made.

Bust, Gigi, Ponytail, White Matte Glaze, Porcelain, 1960s, 13 x 5 In.	27
Figurine, Angel, Blue Dress, Closed Wings, Red Lips, Blond Hair	42
Figurine, Betsy, Youth, White Dress & Hat, Gold Trim, 7 ½ In.	16
Figurine, Charles, White Suit & Cape, Black Shoes, Red Lips, 8 ½ In.	22
Figurine, Juliet, High Waisted Dress, White Hat, 1950s, 8 ¾ In.	88
Figurine, Peter, Standing, Turquoise Top Coat, 9 ⅜ In.	45
Figurine, Sherri, Teal Gown, Hat, Gold Leaf, Semi Porcelain, 8 ⅜ In. *illus*	81
Figurine, Story Book Hour, Mother, Boy, Girl, Multicolor, 6 ¾ x 8 x 5 ½ In.	65
Figurine, Woman, Dealer Sign, Pink Dress, 6 ½ In. *illus*	97
Figurine, Woman, Hand Muff, Spaghetti Trim, Cream, Gold, 7 ½ In.	34
Figurine, Woman, Holding Yorkshire Dog, Brown Wrap, Box, G. Armani, 1900s, 13 In. *illus*	75

FLOW BLUE ceramics were made in England and other countries about 1830 to 1900. The dishes were printed with designs using a cobalt blue coloring. The color flowed from the design to the white body so that the finished piece has a smeared blue design. The dishes were usually made of ironstone china. More Flow Blue may be found under the name of the manufacturer. These three marks are used on flow blue dishes.

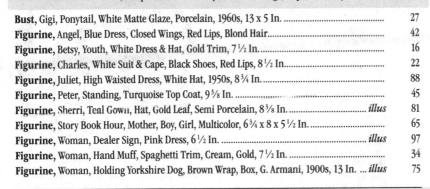

W.H. Grindley & Co. (Ltd.)
c.1880–1891

Johnson Brothers
c.1913+

Wood & Son(s) (Ltd.)
1891–1907

Platter, Ancient Ruins, Oval, Scallop Edges, Staffordshire, c.1850, 20 x 16 ½ In.	164
Platter, Cashmere, Ink Stamp, Nice, Signed, F. Morley & Co., 15 In.	181
Platter, Flowers, Multicolor, Gold Highlights, Ironstone, England, c.1875, 17 x 14 In.	120
Platter, Oriental Pattern, Mahogany Stand, Bamboo Turnings, England, c.1850, 22 x 25 x 21 In. *illus*	150
Platter, Serving, Non Pareil, Burgess & Leigh, Signed, Ink Stamp, c.1890, 13 ½ In.	40
Platter, Serving, Shell, Trees, Flowers, E. Challinor, 12 ½ In.	136
Platter, Serving, Transfer, Cobalt Blue, Underglaze, Chinoiserie, Flowers, 20 x 16 In.	53
Platter, Well & Tree, Woman, Flower Border, Marked, c.1850, 19 ½ x 16 In. *illus*	228
Teapot, Peking, Signed, British Ceramic Registry, c.1845, 9 In.	68

Fischer, Vase, Nude Woman, Butterfly, Hand Painted, Cylindrical, 11 In.
$203

Hartzell's Auction Gallery, Inc.

Fishing, Creel, Wicker, Leather Strap & Latch, 14 x 6 x 9 In.
$60

Alderfer Auction Company

Fishing, License, Angling, Connecticut, Resident, c.1940, 1 ¾ In.
$40

Hake's Auctions

Fishing, Lure, Glass Eye, Wood, Heddon Dowagiac, 3 Hooks, 4½ In.
$60

Martin Auction Co.

Flash Gordon, Cocktail Shaker, Rocket Ship, Stainless Steel, Red Plastic Base, c.1950, 12 In.
$16

wagsoto on eBay

Flash Gordon, Toy, Arresting Ray Clicker Gun, Tin Lithograph, Multicolor, Marx, 1950s, 10 In.
$128

jaysbeard525 on eBay

> **TIP**
> Put fresh flowers in view when you're away for a short period of time. Fresh flowers indicate owners aren't away for long.

Florence Ceramics, Figurine, Sherri, Teal Gown, Hat, Gold Leaf, Semi Porcelain, 8⅜ In.
$81

bonswe_46 on eBay

Florence Ceramics, Figurine, Woman, Dealer Sign, Pink Dress, 6½ In.
$97

sunlitadelaide on eBay

Florence Ceramics, Figurine, Woman, Holding Yorkshire Dog, Brown Wrap, Box, G. Armani, 1900s, 13 In.
$75

Selkirk Auctioneers & Appraisers

Flow Blue, Platter, Oriental Pattern, Mahogany Stand, Bamboo Turnings, England, c.1850, 22 x 25 x 21 In.
$150

Garth's Auctioneers & Appraisers

Flow Blue, Platter, Well & Tree, Woman, Flower Border, Marked, c.1850, 19½ x 16 In.
$228

Garth's Auctioneers & Appraisers

Folk Art, Bottle, Whimsy, Fence-Like Pieces Inside, Painted, Alexander Co., N.C., c.1815, 9 In.
$129

Jeffrey S. Evans & Associates

Tureen, Ironstone, Peking, England, c.1850, 13 In.	96
Tureen, Madras, Flowers, Rosebud Finial, Open Handles, England, 1800s, 11 In.	120
Vase, Chinoiserie, Willow Type, Cobalt Flow, Porcelain, Signed, Mintons, 12 In.	192

FOLK ART is also listed in many categories of this book under the actual name of the object. See categories such as Box, Cigar Store Figure, Paper, Weather Vane, Wooden, etc.

Airplane, Wood, Sheet Metal, Yellow & White Paint, Vollis Simpson, 20 x 33½ In.	156
Bird Tree, Carved, Song Bird, Painted, Dewalt, 25 x 28 In.	180
Bottle, Whimsy, Fence-Like Pieces Inside, Painted, Alexander Co., N.C., c.1815, 9 In. *illus*	129
Cat, Crouching, Striped, Tail Up, Gregory Gorby, 22 In.	317
Crab Claw, Fossil, Composite, Carved, Wood Stand, JL Heatwole, c.1985, 5½ x 3¾ In.	234
Eagle, Head, Carved, Hardwood, Painted, 22 In.	236
Eagle, Spread Wings, Open Beak, Flag, Shield, Multicolor, 42 x 24 In.	2214
Eagle, Spread Wings, Wood, Carved, Red & Black Paint, Yellow Highlights, W. Schimmel, 6 x 9 In. *illus*	2760
Eagle, Wood, Carved, Brown & White Paint, Wood Base, c.1950, 16 In.	363
Flag, American, 48 Stars, Crocheted Crepe Paper, Wood Pole, Meta Schmitt, 33 x 54 In.	344
Frame, Oval, Pine, Carved, Daisies, Diamonds, Horseshoe, Good Luck 1923, 15 x 12 In. *illus*	390
Hand, Pointing, Carved Wood, 1800s, 25 x 9 x 6 In. *illus*	1534
Head, Man, Mounted, Carved, Black Painted, Circular Base, Wood Stand, 1800s, 14 In.	861
Jesus, Arms Out, Small Men Attached To Hands, Ronald Cooper, 23½ x 24½ In.	600
Man, Captain, Blackbeard, Blue Uniform, Red Trim, Wood, 55 x 12½ x 11 In.	177
Man, Hands In Pockets, Standing, Carved, Green, Square Base, 20 In.	118
Man, Holding Ax, Child, Carved, Painted, Wood, Contemporary Base, 12 In.	163
Man, Holding Pipe, Carved, Square Base, Signed, Continental, 1937, 11½ In.	177
Man, Seated, Drinking, Smoking, Straw Hat, Wood, Carved, 14 x 5 x 5¼ In.	375
Man, Standing, Painted Eyes, Hair & Mustache, Wood, c.1900, 37½ In.	293
Model, Carriage, 4 Horses, 2 Riders, Carved Wood, Painted, 35 x 6 x 12 In.	12
Mountain Man, Apple For The Educator, Carved, Painted, JL Heatwole, 1986, 3 In. *illus*	878
Owl, Standing, Walnut, Carved, Round Base, c.1825, 7¼ In.	615
Painting, Eve In The Garden Of Eden, Oil On Canvas, Signed, A. Merriweather, 24 x 32 In.	46
Parrot, Carved, Perch, Blue, Red, Green, Yellow, Schimmel, John R. Dierwechter, 19 x 13 In. *illus*	410
Parrot, Wood, Carved, Painted, Incised Tail Feathers, Cylindrical Base, Late 1900s, 8 In.	3600
Picture, Horse, Wood, Painted, Frame, 1800s, 9 x 7 In. *illus*	590
Plaque, Eagle, Flags, Stars, Painted, Carved, Mounted, Oval Board, 39 x 18½ In. *illus*	770
Preacher, Standing, Suit, Podium, 10 x 5 In.	396
Rabbit, Puppet, White Painted, Wood	71
Rack, Hat, Bird Top, Signed Sticks, 72 In.	191
Rooster, Metal, Standing, Articulated Figures, 17½ In.	188
Sailor, Sad, Carved, Holding Bottle & Bag, 13¾ In.	35
Stick, Instrument, Carved Devil Head, Wood, 66 In.	413
Stork, 1 Foot On Ball, Painted, 39 x 31 In.	148
Talisman, Bird Head, Gypsy Witch, Skull Incised, Signed, JL Heatwole, c.1985, 2¾ In.	293
Tiger, Wood, Jointed Legs, Painted, Wood Base, 14½ x 12 x 3¾ In.	163
Uncle Sam, Silhouette, Striped Pants, Wood, Painted, Weathered, 78 x 14 In.	354
Whirligig, 2 Workers, Sharpen Blade, Wood, Carved, Fiber Board, Fabric, Stand, 1900s, 38 x 29 In.	266
Whirligig, Adam, Eve, Apple Tree, Snake, Signed, N. Arena, Contemporary, 20 x 8½ In.	307
Whirligig, Dapper Gentleman, Bicycle, Tin, Wood, Painted, Counterbalance, c.1925, 20 x 24 In. *illus*	720
Whirligig, Dracula, Wing Arms, Tumbstone Plinth, Nicholas Arena, 1989, 22¾ In.	307
Whirligig, Lady Liberty, Stars & Stripes Dress, Painted, Signed, Nicholas Arena 91, 21 In. *illus*	354
Whirligig, Man With Top Hat, Jacket, Red Buttons, Pine, 2-Sided, c.1920, 14 In.	1800
Whirligig, Man, Reading Newspaper, Woman, Doing Laundry, Wood, Painted, c.1950, 21 In.	188
Whirligig, Man, Sawing, Red & Grey, Wood, Early 1900s, 25 In.	88
Whirligig, Man, Top Hat, Monocle Riding, Tin, Wood, c.1925, 19½ x 24 In.	720
Whirligig, Rooster, Multicolor, Wood, Sheet Metal, c.1950, 34 In. *illus*	188
Whirligig, Train, Men On Handcar, Painted, Wood, Rectangular Base, 30 In. *illus*	266

FOOTBALL collectibles may be found in the Card and the Sports categories.

Folk Art, Eagle, Spread Wings, Wood, Carved, Red & Black Paint, Yellow Highlights, W. Schimmel, 6 x 9 In. $2,760

Garth's Auctioneers & Appraisers

Folk Art, Frame, Oval, Pine, Carved, Daisies, Diamonds, Horseshoe, Good Luck 1923, 15 x 12 In. $390

Garth's Auctioneers & Appraisers

TIP

Don't put wood or paper or textiles near heating vents or fireplaces. Heat will harm them.

Folk Art, Hand, Pointing, Carved Wood, 1800s, 25 x 9 x 6 In. $1,534

Cottone Auctions

Folk Art, Mountain Man, Apple For The Educator, Carved, Painted, JL Heatwole, 1986, 3 In.
$878

Jeffrey S. Evans & Associates

Folk Art, Parrot, Carved, Perch, Blue, Red, Green, Yellow, Schimmel, John R. Dierwechter, 19 x 13 In.
$410

Cordier Auctions

Folk Art, Picture, Horse, Wood, Painted, Frame, 1800s, 9 x 7 In.
$590

Copake Auction

Folk Art, Plaque, Eagle, Flags, Stars, Painted, Carved, Mounted, Oval Board, 39 x 18 ½ In.
$770

Copake Auction

Folk Art, Whirligig, Dapper Gentleman, Bicycle, Tin, Wood, Painted, Counterbalance, c.1925, 20 x 24 In.
$720

Garth's Auctioneers & Appraisers

Folk Art, Whirligig, Lady Liberty, Stars & Stripes Dress, Painted, Signed, Nicholas Arena 91, 21 In.
$354

Leland Little Auctions

Folk Art, Whirligig, Rooster, Multicolor, Wood, Sheet Metal, c.1950, 34 In.
$188

Pook & Pook

Folk Art, Whirligig, Train, Men On Handcar, Painted, Wood, Rectangular Base, 30 In.
$266

Copake Auction

Fostoria, Berry, Bowl, Berries & Leaves, Pink Milk Glass, Pedestal, 1950s, 4 ½ x 7 ¼ In.
$29

oldfoundobjects on eBay

FOSTORIA glass was made in Fostoria, Ohio, from 1887 to 1891. The factory was moved to Moundsville, West Virginia, and most of the glass seen in shops today is a twentieth-century product. The company was sold to Lancaster Colony Corporation in 1983 and closed in 1986. Additional Fostoria items may be listed in the Milk Glass category.

American, Porch Vase, Ruffled Rim, Round Base, 8 x 6 1/4 x 6 1/2 In.	1374
Berry, Bowl, Berries & Leaves, Pink Milk Glass, Pedestal, 1950s, 4 1/2 x 7 1/4 In. ....*illus*	29
Candy Jar, Urn Shape, Aqua Blue, Footed, 15 In.	41
Heirloom, Bonbon, Ruby Red, Oval, 9 1/2 In. ....*illus*	13
Loop Optic, Pitcher, Clear Glass, Amber Foot, Handle	17
Loop Optic, Vase, Azure Blue, Round Rim & Base, 1928-30, 6 x 4 1/2 In.	13
Versailles, Goblet, Azure Blue, Stem, 8 1/2 In.	16

FOVAL, *see Fry category.*

FRAMES *are included in the Furniture category under Frame.*

FRANCISCAN is a trademark that appears on pottery. Gladding, McBean and Company started in 1875. The company grew and acquired other potteries. It made sewer pipes, floor tiles, dinnerware, and art pottery with a variety of trademarks. It began using the trade name *Franciscan* in 1934. In 1936, dinnerware and art pottery were sold under the name *Franciscan Ware.* The company made china and cream-colored, decorated earthenware. Desert Rose, Apple, El Patio, and Coronado were best sellers. The company became Interpace Corporation and in 1979 was purchased by Josiah Wedgwood & Sons. The plant closed in 1984, but production of a few patterns shifted to China and Thailand. For more prices, go to kovels.com.

Gladding, McBean & Co.
1934–1963

Gladding, McBean & Co.
c.1940

International Pipe and
Ceramics
1963+

Apple, Creamer, 3 In.	26
Desert Rose, Plate, Dinner, 10 5/8 In.	35
Desert Rose, Toast Cover	104
Fresh Fruit, Creamer, 8 Oz., 4 1/8 In.	19
Hacienda Gold, Soup, 6 3/8 In.	19
Madeira, Plate, Salad, Tan Flowers, Green & Brown Band, 8 1/2 In.	11
October, Bowl, Cereal, Brown & Yellow Leaves, 7 In.	11
Starburst, Plate, Dinner, 1950s, 10 7/8 In.	43
Tile, Beads On String Repeating Pattern, Blue, Green, Brown, Yellow, 1973, 12 In.	80

FRANKOMA POTTERY was originally known as The Frank Potteries when John F. Frank opened shop in 1933. The name "Frankoma," a combination of his last name and the last three letters of Oklahoma, was used beginning in 1934. The factory moved to Sapulpa, Oklahoma, in 1938. Early wares were made from a light cream-colored clay from Ada, Oklahoma, but in 1956 the company switched to a red clay from Sapulpa. The firm made dinnerware, utilitarian and decorative kitchenwares, figurines, flowerpots, and limited edition and commemorative pieces. John Frank died in 1973 and his daughter, Joniece, inherited the business. Frankoma went bankrupt in 1990. The pottery operated under various owners for a few years and was bought by Joe Ragosta in 2008. It closed in 2010. The buildings, assets, name, and molds were sold at an auction in 2011.

Figurine, Pacing Ocelot, Crystalline Black Matte Glaze, 5 x 8 1/2 In.	1008
Wagon Wheel, Creamer, Onyx Black, 2 In.	48

Fostoria, Heirloom, Bonbon, Ruby Red, Oval, 9 1/2 In.
$13

pattyswitchercreekvintage on eBay

Fraternal, Clock, Tall Case, S. Hoadley, Grain Painted, Wood Movement, Masonic Symbols, 1800s, 85 In.
$888

Jeffrey S. Evans & Associates

Fraternal, Elks, Humidor, Lid, Green, Cream, Elk, Inscribed Tobacco, Nakara, 7 x 5 In.
$1,020

Woody Auction

F

Fraternal, Odd Fellows, Ballot Box, Wood, Dovetailing, Black & White Marbles, Early 1900s, 4 x 14 In. $500

Garth's Auctioneers & Appraisers

Fraternal, Odd Fellows, Banner, Embroidered Symbols, Painted, Gold Thread, c.1880, 42 x 29 In. $246

Skinner, Inc.

Furniture, Bed, Four-Poster, Chippendale, Mahogany, Carved, Feather & Fern, 1800s, 79 x 60 x 82 In. $351

Thomaston Place Auction Galleries

TIP

A decorator's trick for a small bedroom: keep the bed 19 inches high so it can be used as a chair, too.

FRATERNAL objects that are related to the many different fraternal organizations in the United States are listed in this category. The Elks, Masons, Odd Fellows, and others are included. Also included are service organizations, like the American Legion, Kiwanis, and Lions Club. Furniture is listed in the Furniture category. Shaving mugs decorated with fraternal crests are included in the Shaving Mug category.

Clock, Tall Case, S. Hoadley, Grain Painted, Wood Movement, Masonic Symbols, 1800s, 85 In... *illus*	888
Elks, Humidor, Lid, Green, Cream, Elk, Inscribed Tobacco, Nakara, 7 x 5 In.....................*illus*	1020
Knights Templar, Dagger, Gold Hilt, Masonic Symbols, Black Sheath, 15 ½ In.	24
Masonic, Razor, Blade Marked Wade & Butcher, Sheffield, Masonic Symbols, 6 ¼ In...............	72
Odd Fellows, Ark Of The Covenant, Gold Paint, Iron Stand, Tablets, Early 1900s, 25 In...........	180
Odd Fellows, Ballot Box, Wood, Dovetailing, Black & White Marbles, Early 1900s, 4 x 14 In...*illus*	500
Odd Fellows, Banner, Embroidered Symbols, Painted, Gold Thread, c.1880, 42 x 29 In. ...*illus*	246
Odd Fellows, Bookends, Rebekahs, Gold Crescent Moon, Bird, Iron, c.1920, 7 x 6 x 2 ¾ In...............	108
Odd Fellows, Sign, Carved, 3 Chain Links, Crossed Staffs, Heart-In-Hand, 1800s, 94 x 30 In...	2460
Odd Fellows, Torch, Carved, Red & Gold Painted, 1800s, 32 ¾ In.	431
Order Of Eagles, Sign, Wood, Red Black, White, Edge Strip, Iron Hanging Chains, 18 x 73 In.	198

FRY GLASS was made by the H.C. Fry Glass Company of Rochester, Pennsylvania. The company, founded in 1901, first made cut glass and other types of glasswares. In 1922 it patented a heat-resistant glass called Pearl Ovenglass. For two years, 1926–1927, the company made Fry Foval, an opal ware decorated with colored trim. Reproductions of this glass have been made. Depression glass patterns made by Fry may be listed in the Depression Glass category. Some pieces of cut glass may also be included in the Cut Glass category.

FRY FOVAL

Vase, Trumpet Shape, White Pulled Feathers, Blue Foot, Blue Rim, 18 In.....................................	1260

FULPER POTTERY COMPANY was incorporated in 1899 in Flemington, New Jersey. It made art pottery from 1909 to 1929. The firm had been making bottles, jugs, and housewares since 1805. Vasekraft is a line of art pottery with glazes similar to Chinese art pottery that was introduced in 1909. Doll heads were made about 1928. The firm became Stangl Pottery in 1929. Stangl Pottery is listed in its own category in this book.

Bowl, Bulb, Blue Matte & Green Oyster Glaze, Rolled Rim, c.1915, 3 In.................................	195
Incense Burner, Mahogany, Ivory, Green Flambe Glaze, 6 Handles, 1910s, 12 x 7 In...............	1250
Jug, Brown, Tan Flambe Glaze, Green Crystalline Glaze, Braided Handle, c.1920, 10 In.	189
Lamp Base, 2-Light, Green Crystalline Flambe Glaze, Early 1900s, 30 In..............................	204
Vase, Brown, Green, Blue, Glazed, Rim Handles, Signed, 3 x 3 In.......................................	175
Vase, Drilled Out, Molded Rim & Base, Glaze, 9 x 11 In.	83
Vase, Dust Glaze, Brown, Molded Rim, 5 ½ In.	221
Vase, Flemington Green Flambe Glaze, Ink Stamp, 14 x 7 ½ In...	531
Vase, Green Crystalline Glaze, Square Handles, Signed, c.1925, 8 x 5 In.	250
Vase, Trumpet Shape, Flamble Glaze, Dark Brown To Light Tan, 8 x 3 In................................	175

FURNITURE of all types is listed in this category. Examples dating from the seventeenth century to the 1970s are included. Prices for furniture vary in different parts of the country. Oak furniture is most expensive in the West; large pieces over eight feet high are sold for the most money in the South, where high ceilings are found in the old homes. Modern is popular in New York, California, and Chicago. Condition is very important when determining prices. These are NOT average prices but rather reports of unique sales. If the description includes the word *style*, the piece resembles the old furniture style but was made at a later time. It is not a period piece. Small chests that sat on a table or dresser are also included here. Garden furniture is listed in the Garden Furnishings category. Related items may be found in the Architectural, Brass, and Store categories.

Armchairs are listed under Chair in this category.

Armoire, Fruitwood, Paneled Frieze, 2 Doors, Chevron Veneered Panels, Late 1800s, 100 x 59 In...	1750
Armoire, Louis Philippe Style, Walnut, Carved, 2 Triple Panel Doors, 1800s, 95 x 66 In.	750
Armoire, Louis XV Style, Rectangular Top, 3 Drawers, Cabriole Legs, 1900s, 50 x 61 In.	313

Armoire, Louis XV Style, Rosewood, Parquetry Veneer, Mirror, c.1900, 98 x 63 x 18 In.	625
Armoire, Louis XV, Flowers, 2 Long Doors, 2 Panels, Carved Feet, Late 1700s, 92 x 63 In.	3000
Armoire, Mahogany, Carved, Ogee Frame, Mirror, Plinth Base, Bracket Feet, 1800s, 87 x 44 x 22 In.	246
Armoire, Pine, Bonnet Top Case, 2 Doors, Carved Base, France, c.1800, 83 x 54 In.	500
Armoire, Provincial, Oak, 2 Doors, Carved Design, French, 76 ½ x 57 x 23 In.	187
Armoire, Rosewood, Carved, Floral Crest, Molded Cornice, Mirrored Door, Mid 1800s, 99 x 44 x 21 In.	7188
Bar Cart, Compartments, Removable Metal Liners, Baker Furniture Co., 27 x 44 x 14 In.	1092
Bar Cart, Rosewood, Sliding Compartments, Casters, Denmark, 29 x 35 In.	889
Bar, Mahogany, Box Type Top, 2 Gothic Panel Doors, Open Compartment, 1800s	144
Bed Corona, For Canopy, Crown, Carved, Painted, Draped Fabric, Gilt, c.1780, 20 x 18 x 14 In.	2750
Bed, Burl, Carved, Scrolls, Fan, Flowers, Headboard, Footboard, c.1900, 65 In.	313
Bed, Campaign, William IV, Mahogany, Folding, Cane, Handles, c.1810, 23 x 73 In.	512
Bed, Canopy, Carved, Mahogany, Reeded Acanthus Post, Pegged, Early 1800s, 87 x 75 x 58 In.	1125
Bed, Canopy, Curly Maple, Cherry, Scrolled Headboard, Mid 1800s, 75 x 57 x 72 In.	625
Bed, Canopy, Hangings, Blue & White Paint, Shaped Headboard, Rails, 1900s, 88 x 65 In.	1375
Bed, Directoire Style, Mahogany, Ormolu Mount, Early 1900s, 58 x 28 x 89 In.	2299
Bed, Four-Poster, Chippendale, Mahogany, Carved, Feather & Fern, 1800s, 79 x 60 x 82 In. *...illus*	351
Bed, Four-Poster, Federal, Mahogany, Turned, Paneled Headboard, Rosettes, 1800s, 88 x 87 x 80 In.	1200
Bed, Four-Poster, Federal, Reeded Posts, Mahogany, Headboard Panels, Carved, c.1915, 95 x 54 x 72 In.	875
Bed, Four-Poster, G. Crespi, 3 Fluted Posts, Bamboo, Brass, Upholstered, 96 x 67 In.	2898
Bed, Four-Poster, Mahogany, Turned Legs, Scroll Headboard, Twin, 63 x 43 x 77 In.	224
Bed, Geometric, Pierre Cardin, Bronze, Italy, Queen Size, c.1960, 37 x 69 x 78 In.	1125
Bed, Henri II Style, Walnut, Carved, Geometric, Flowers, Bun Feet, Early 1900s, 73 x 52 x 73 In.	188
Bed, J. Camp, Walnut, Carved Headboard, Stylized Figures, Signed, Pa., 1994, 48 x 98 x 84 In.	5938
Bed, Jenny Lind, Spool Carved, Peaked Pediment, Turned Legs, 1800s, 78 x 77 x 54 In.	36
Bed, Louis XV Style, Painted, Upholstered, Headboard, Footboard, 1900s, 51 x 82 x 76 In.	813
Bed, Louis XV, Painted, Upholstered, Curved Headboard, Footboard, 51 x 82 In.	819
Bench, Black Forest, Bears, Standing, Holding Seat, Carved, c.1890, 23 x 39 In.	5860
Bench, Bucket, Pine, Blue Gray Paint, 2 Shelves, 29 x 33 x 11 ¾ In.	106
Bench, Bucket, Pine, Paint Traces, Single Board Shelf Back, Pennsylvania, 1800s, 42 x 43 In.	813
Bench, Carved Wood, Painted, White Goat Hair, Mongolia, 1900s, 17 x 39 x 24 In.	3125
Bench, Contemporary, Leather, Chrome Steel, X-Shape Base, Greek Key, 22 x 42 x 17 In.*...illus*	531
Bench, Contemporary, Tufted Seat, Scalloped Skirt, Overupholstered, Velveteen, 23 x 56 x 18 In.	366
Bench, Deacon's, Painted, Half Spindles, Fruit Decoration, 72 x 21 x 34 In.	254
Bench, Deacon's, Pine, Mustard Yellow Paint, Spindle Back, Arms, 1800s, 78 In.	840
Bench, Elm, 1-Board, Round Ends, Hourglass Shape Legs, Bracket Feet, 1800s, 19 x 5 x 80 In.	240
Bench, Finn Juhl, Rosewood, Enameled Steel, Brass, Upholstered, Leather, 1959, 17 x 18 x 59 In.	9375
Bench, G. Nelson, Slat, Wood, Chrome Plated Steel, Herman Miller, 1945, 72 x 18 x 14 In.	2750
Bench, G. Nelson, Vertical Slats, 2 Black Legs, Unmarked, c.1950, 14 x 68 x 18 In.	1599
Bench, H. Bertoia, Ash, Matte Chrome Plated Steel, Knoll, 1952, 82 x 18 x 15 In.	1500
Bench, H. Bertoia, Teak, Slat Teak, Steel Base, Knoll, 1952, 15 ½ x 72 In.	1062
Bench, Hardwood, Carved, False Bamboo, Paneled Seat, Outswept Arms, 29 x 32 In.	875
Bench, Hardwood, Reticulated Back, Dowels, Arms, 1900s, 37 x 50 x 21 In.*...illus*	968
Bench, High Back, 3 Boards, Shaped Sides, Painted, Cushion, 47 x 48 In.	183
Bench, Jacobean Oak, Carved, 4-Panel Back, Front & Back Stretcher, Upholstered Seat, 44 x 74 In.	375
Bench, Louis Philippe, Walnut, Carved, Reeded Arms, False Leather, c.1850, 34 x 75 x 18 In.	584
Bench, Louis XV Style, Gilt, Wood, Tufted Upholstery, Cabriole Legs, 20 x 41 x 19 In.	215
Bench, Louis XVI Style, Needlepoint Upholstery, Aubusson Style, 1800s, 15 x 48 x 26 In.	118
Bench, M. Nakashima, Cone Shape, Black Walnut, Spindle Back, Signed, Pa., 1992, 32 x 71 x 35 In.	5625
Bench, M. Nakashima, R Bench, English Walnut, Black Walnut, Signed, 1994, 14 x 68 x 27 In.	3625
Bench, Mahogany, Padded Back, Cushion Seat, Saber Legs, Italy, 1800s, 36 x 46 x 19 In.	875
Bench, Mammy's, Mixed Wood, Painted, Stenciled, Floral, c.1800, 30 x 53 x 22 In.*...illus*	438
Bench, Oak, 4-Panel Carved Back, Downswept Arms, Cabriole Legs, c.1700s, 36 x 58 x 26 In.	960
Bench, Oak, Lift Seat, Gingerbread Accents, Lacquer, 38 x 42 x 16 In.	92
Bench, Painted, Old Ocher Grain Decoration, Wood, Pennsylvania, 1800s, 18 x 92 x 10 In.	188
Bench, Piano, Baroque Style, Carved, Upholstered, Gilt, 20 x 13 x 41 ½ In.	960
Bench, Piano, Louis XVI Style, Parcel Gilt, Oval, Overstuffed Cushion, 21 x 39 x 16 In.	813
Bench, Pine, Camel Color Paint Over Red, 2 Shelves, 1800s, 25 ½ x 38 x 12 In.	450
Bench, Portfolio Cognita, Storage, Red & White, Herman Miller, 18 x 54 x 18 In.	625
Bench, Rectangular, Carved Apron, Cabriole Legs, Needlepoint, Flowers, Continental, 20 x 39 x 16 In.	125

Furniture, Bench, Contemporary, Leather, Chrome Steel, X-Shape Base, Greek Key, 22 x 42 x 17 In. $531

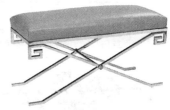

New Orleans Auction Galleries

Furniture, Bench, Hardwood, Reticulated Back, Dowels, Arms, 1900s, 37 x 50 x 21 In. $968

Ahlers & Ogletree Auction Gallery

Furniture, Bench, Mammy's, Mixed Wood, Painted, Stenciled, Floral, c.1800, 30 x 53 x 22 In. $438

Garth's Auctioneers & Appraisers

Furniture, Bookcase, George III, Mahogany, Fitted, Glass Pane Doors, England, c.1780, 95 x 53 x 24 In.
$2,000

Rago Arts and Auction Center

Furniture, Bookcase, Revolving, Mixed Wood, Cutouts, Red Brown Paint, Tripod Base, c.1865, 32 x 24 In.
$175

Garth's Auctioneers & Appraisers

Furniture, Bookshelf, S. Marx, Crackle Lacquered Wood, Glass Shelves, c.1955, 41 x 12 x 30 In.
$10,000

Wright

Furniture, Buffet, Louis XV, Oak, 4 Drawers, Scalloped Apron, Cabriole Legs, 1800s, 37 x 66 x 22 In.
$875

New Orleans Auction Galleries

Furniture, Cabinet, Burl, Gilt, Marble Top, Doors, Fitted Interior, France, 1900s, 41 x 40 In.
$500

Brunk Auctions

Furniture, Cabinet, Display, Mixed Wood, Brass, Curved Glass, Glass & Fabric Shelves, c.1985, 68 x 28 In.
$252

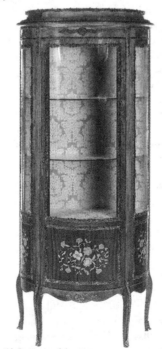

Garth's Auctioneers & Appraisers

Furniture, Cabinet, Elm, 4 Drawers, 2 Doors, Butterfly Lockplate, Korea, 1900s, 37 x 38 x 17 In.
$438

Leslie Hindman Auctioneers

Furniture, Cabinet, Filing, Oak, 4 Drawers, Paneled Sides, Brass Hardware, c.1915, 52 x 16 x 28 In.
$252

Garth's Auctioneers & Appraisers

Furniture, Cabinet, Gilt, Marble Top, Painted Scenes, Fin De Siecle, Vernis Martin, c.1900, 36 x 45 In.
$2,500

Heritage Auctions

Bench, Savonarola Style, Inlay, Outscrolled Arms, Openwork, X-Brace, Syria, c.1920, 28 x 36 In.	813
Bench, Shell Carved, Aprons, Cabriole Legs, Ball & Claw Feet, Berkey & Gay, c.1930	263
Bench, Stickley Bros., 3 Square Spindles, 5-Slat Seat, Oak, 27 x 18½ x 14½ In.	605
Bench, Telephone, Carved Oak, Arm Crest, Brass Tacks, Filigree & Grapes, 28 x 32 x 18 In.	393
Bench, Walnut, Upholstered, Carved, Fluted Legs, c.1930, 19 x 38 x 16 In.	250
Bench, Waterfall, U-Shape, Upholstered, Blue, Black & Red, 20 x 38 x 20 In.	125
Bench, Window, Holly Hunt, Leather Seat, Metal Base, Tapered Legs, C. Liaigre, 18 x 48 x 16 In.	4235
Bench, Window, Louis XV Style, Upholstered, Arms, 27 x 43 In.	300
Bench, Window, Rattan, Woven Cushion, Curved Legs, Wood, 18 x 41 x 19 In.	322
Bench, Windsor, Triple Bow Back, Single-Board Seat, Turned Legs & Stretcher, 1900s, 39 x 71 In.	1080
Bin, Pine, Divided, Lift Top, Turned Feet, Grain Paint, Mid 1800s, 20 x 49 x 16 In.	240
Bookcase, Barrister, Empire Style, Glazed Mahogany Veneer, 4 Tiers, Black, 59 x 51 x 14 In.	584
Bookcase, Barrister, Glass Door, Drop Front Desk, Drawer, Globe-Wernicke, c.1915, 77 In.	1000
Bookcase, Barrister, Oak, 3 Shelves, Stacking, Humphrey Widman, Early 1900s, 52 x 34 In.	225
Bookcase, Barrister, Oak, 4 Stacks, Top & Base Section, Globe-Wernicke, 64 x 34 x 11 In.	550
Bookcase, Barrister, Oak, 6 Sections, Stacking, Globe-Wernicke, 92 x 34 In.	671
Bookcase, Chippendale, Walnut, Raised Panels, Reeded Quarter Columns, Pennsylvania, 42 x 37 In.	375
Bookcase, Edwardian, Satinwood, Grill Paneled Doors Over Bowed Doors, Shelves, 1900s, 92 x 64 In.	2750
Bookcase, George III, Mahogany, Fitted, Glass Pane Doors, England, c.1780, 95 x 53 x 24 In. ...... *illus*	2000
Bookcase, Georgian Style, Mahogany, Ogee Cornice, Glazed Doors, Bracket Feet, 84 x 39 x 13 In.	750
Bookcase, Georgian, Breakfront, Mahogany, Glazed Doors, Drawers, c.1800, 92 x 112 In.	6765
Bookcase, H. Glass, Swingline, Painted Blue, Yellow, Birch, Plywood, Fleetwood, 1952, 32 x 28 In.	2470
Bookcase, Hale, Mahogany, 2 Glass Doors, Adjustable Shelves, 60 x 46 x 14 In.	136
Bookcase, Library, Oak, Carved, Mirror In Top, Shelves, Glass Doors, Drawers, c.1915, 70 x 43 In.	480
Bookcase, Library, Oak, Routed Top Edge, 2 Glass Doors, Casters, 1900s, 63 x 41 x 13 In.	281
Bookcase, Louis XV Style, Cherry, Ogee Crown, Arched Doors, Plinth Base, 1800s, 80 x 79 x 17 In.	750
Bookcase, Mahogany, 2 Doors, Glass Panels & Sides, 1800s, 60 x 46 x 17 In.	127
Bookcase, Mahogany, Brass Handle, Federal Glazed, 1800s, 70 x 40 In.	246
Bookcase, Mahogany, Glass Doors, 4 Graduated Drawers, Ogee Bracket Base, 77 x 45 x 23 In.	492
Bookcase, Oak, 2 Doors, 3 Interior Shelves, Fluted Columns, 1900s, 52 x 58 x 16 In.	250
Bookcase, Oak, 2 Glass Doors, 24 Panes, Painted, 48½ x 12½ x 48½ In.	413
Bookcase, Oak, Carved, 2 Drawers, 6 Shelves, Portsmouth, 1906, 43 x 57 x 13 In.	910
Bookcase, Oak, Carved, Lion's Head Corbels, Arched Crest, Glass Panel, 67 x 35 x 15 In.	1210
Bookcase, Oak, Carved, Northwind Borders, Spain, 58 x 74 x 16 In.	700
Bookcase, Open, Carved, Stripped Pine, 2 Shelves, Twist Turned Columns, c.1890, 89 x 58 x 32 In.	1188
Bookcase, Ornate Turned Spindles, Bentwood, 4 Shelves, Victorian, 38 x 19 x 15 In.	52
Bookcase, Revolving, Mixed Wood, Cutouts, Red Brown Paint, Tripod Base, c.1865, 32 x 24 In. ... *illus*	175
Bookcase, Secretary, Fruitwood, Swan Neck, 2 Doors, 2 Shelves, 2 Drawers, 1800s, 17 In.	875
Bookcase, Secretary, Regency Style, Mahogany, Cylindrical, Drawers, 97 x 68 x 23 In.	938
Bookcase, Stickley, Oak, 2 Doors, Leaded Glass Panels, 8 Adjustable Shelves, 58 x 46 x 14 In.	1380
Bookcase, Walnut, Doors, Drawers, Bracket Base, 2 Piece, Victorian, 73 x 37 x 22 In.	165
Bookcase, Walnut, Glass Doors, Interior Shelves, Cupboard Doors, 1950s, 86 x 81 In.	468
Bookshelf, Mahogany, V-Shape Bin, X-Brace, Bamboo Turned Legs, Shelf, 34 x 35 x 16 In.	185
Bookshelf, Pine, False Bamboo, Swing Handle, 3 Shelves, Drawer, 1900s, 30 x 15 x 10 In.	188
Bookshelf, S. Marx, Crackle Lacquered Wood, Glass Shelves, c.1955, 41 x 12 x 30 In. .... *illus*	10000
Bookshelf, Walnut, 4 Open Shelves, Carved Rosettes, Scalloped Top, c.1900, 40 x 17 x 10 In.	150
Bookstand, Revolving, Mahogany, Glass Top, Bins, Pedestal Base, 28 x 21 In.	671
Breakfront, Chippendale Style, Mahogany, Upholstered Interior, Doors, Baker Furniture, 85 x 96 In.	3105
Breakfront, George III, Mahogany, Doors, 4 Drawers, Ogee Bracket Foot, c.1790, 87 x 91 In.	2500
Breakfront, George IV, Mahogany, 2 Glazed Doors, Drawers, Pullout, 88 x 67 x 22 In.	1680
Breakfront, Georgian Style, Bubble Design Glass Panes, Drawers, Desk, 82 x 66 x 16 In.	250
Bucket Sink, Pine, Scalloped Fascia, c.1900, 22 x 24 x 13 In.	104
Buffet, Bowfront, Inlay, Drawer, 2 Cupboards, Mahogany, 36 x 54 x 21 In.	195
Buffet, Fruitwood, Carved Flowers, 3 Panel Doors, Scalloped Apron, 1800s, 48 x 80 x 21 In.	1000
Buffet, Henri II Style, Deaux Corps, Carved, Oak, Female Mask, Columns, 1800s, 89 x 65 x 24 In.	861
Buffet, Louis XV, Oak, 4 Drawers, Scalloped Apron, Cabriole Legs, 1800s, 37 x 66 x 22 In. *illus*	875
Buffet, Renaissance Revival, Deux Corps, 4 Doors, Early 1900s, 80 x 45 In.	277
Bureau, Chippendale, Cherry, 4 Drawers, Ogee Bracket Feet, c.1780, 39 x 46 x 20 In.	780
Bureau, George III, Walnut, Banded & Rectangular, 5 Drawer, Bracket Feet, c.1890, 39 x 33 In.	1500
Bureau, Walnut, Oval Mirror, 3 Drawers, Marble Top, c.1870, 60 x 42 x 20 In.	199

Furniture, Cabinet, Gio Ponti, Walnut, Hidden Drawers, Singer & Sons, Italy, c.1950, 36 x 47 In.
$25,000

Rago Arts and Auction Center

Furniture, Cabinet, Oak, Carved Crest, Curved Glass, Door, Reeded Columns, Paw Legs, c.1915, 68 x 39 In.
$250

Garth's Auctioneers & Appraisers

Furniture, Cabinet, P. Evans, Directional, Sculptured Bronze, Wood, 2 Drawers, 1974, 28 x 13 In.
$2,625

Rago Arts and Auction Center

Furniture, Cabinet, Pine, Blind Door, Grain Painted, Interior Shelves, Vermont, c.1825, 24 x 19 In.
$12

Garth's Auctioneers & Appraisers

Furniture, Cabinet, Renaissance Revival, Rosewood, Arched, Shelves, Inlay, 1800s, 65 x 61 In.
$6,250

Neal Auction Company

Furniture, Candlestand, Maple & Pine, Spanish Brown, Adjustable, Tripod, Late 1700s, 46 In.
$813

Pook & Pook

Cabinet, 2 Doors, 4 Drawers, Brass Handle, Mahogany, Tansu Chest, 37 x 16 x 40 In.	1003
Cabinet, 2 Doors, Gesso Scene, Gilt Stand, Cabriole Legs, Continental, 1900s, 62 x 42 x 25 In.	4000
Cabinet, 2 Doors, Glass Shelves, Oak, Chinese, 59 ½ x 39 In.	125
Cabinet, 2 Drawers, Brass Pulls, Oak, File, Signed, Yawman & Erbe, c.1900, 11 x 21 x 11 In.	254
Cabinet, Art Deco, Ebonized Wood, Lucite Columns & Leaf, c.1950, 33 x 44 x 22 In.	375
Cabinet, Art Deco, Mahogany, 4 Doors, Marble Inset, Beveled Glass, 41 x 62 x 20 In.	313
Cabinet, Bamboo, Painted, Floral, 2 Doors, 3 Shelves, 37 x 15 x 42 In.	295
Cabinet, Belle Epoque, Marble Top, 3 Drawers, Fluted Tapering Legs, Early 1900s, 35 x 25 x 13 In.	875
Cabinet, Bench Seat, 2 Doors, Painted Deer Scenes, Leaves, Flowers, Tibet, 23 x 22 x 12 In.	125
Cabinet, Brittany Style, Painted, 4 Doors, 82 x 42 x 14 ½ In.	125
Cabinet, Burl Walnut, Curio, Arched Crown, Mullioned Door Legs, Paw Feet, c.1900, 82 x 21 x 17 In.	615
Cabinet, Burl, Gilt, Marble Top, Doors, Fitted Interior, France, 1900s, 41 x 40 In. ....*illus*	500
Cabinet, Carved, Birds, Flowers, Arched Pediment, Shelves, Drawers, c.1900, 70 x 40 x 13 In.	2583
Cabinet, Colonial Style, Carved Wood, Iron Hinges, Mexico, Late 1900s, 74 x 42 ½ x 22 In.	281
Cabinet, Curved Glass, Oak, Leaded & Beveled Glass, Door, 1900s, 78 ½ x 44 ½ In.	1920
Cabinet, Danish Modern, 3 Adjustable Shelves, 2 Doors, 56 x 47 x 16 ½ In.	242
Cabinet, Display, Chimney Style, Glass Shelves, Home Meridan, 69 x 18 x 11 In.	138
Cabinet, Display, French Provincial, Walnut, Shaped Glass Panels, 3 Shelves, 58 x 22 In.	308
Cabinet, Display, Glass Doors, Shelves, Scroll Feet, Pulaski, 59 x 33 x 15 In.	81
Cabinet, Display, Inlay, 7 Drawers, Sliding Doors, Open Shelves, c.1900, 46 x 20 In.	900
Cabinet, Display, Mirror Back, Yellow, Glass Doors, Adjustable Shelves, 1800s, 91 x 58 x 17 In.	322
Cabinet, Display, Mixed Wood, Brass, Curved Glass, Glass & Fabric Shelves, c.1985, 68 x 28 In. .*illus*	252
Cabinet, Display, Oak, 3 Shelves, Doors, Plinth Base, Bracket Feet, Early 1900s, 86 x 71 x 16 In.	369
Cabinet, Domed Molded Cornice, 2 Doors, 3 Shelves, Plinth Base, Oak, 1800s, 106 x 36 In.	500
Cabinet, Edwardian, Satinwood, Painted, 2 Doors, Ball Feet, Late 1800s, 36 x 44 x 20 In.	875
Cabinet, Elm, 2 Panel Doors, 2 Shelves, Openwork Apron, Early 1900s, 81 x 42 x 20 In.	123
Cabinet, Elm, 4 Drawers, 2 Doors, Butterfly Lockplate, Korea, 1900s, 37 x 38 x 17 In. ....*illus*	438
Cabinet, Empire, Drop Front, Concave Front, 4 Doors Over 2, 6 Drawers, 94 x 75 x 21 In.	878
Cabinet, Etagere, Carved, Rosewood, Marble Top, Serpentine Apron, c.1850, 99 x 47 x 21 In.	3750
Cabinet, Filing, Oak, 4 Drawers, Paneled Sides, Brass Hardware, c.1915, 52 x 16 x 28 In. ..*illus*	252
Cabinet, Filing, Single Tambour Drawer Case, 10 Document Slots, 59 x 19 ½ x 15 In.	151
Cabinet, Fruitwood, Brass Mounts, Inlay, Pane Door, Shelf, Block Feet, 1800s, 20 x 27 x 12 In.	180
Cabinet, G. Nakashima, Kornblut, Walnut, Rosewood, Maple Burl, Drawer, 22 x 21 In.	17500
Cabinet, G. Nelson, Steel Frame, Laminate, Lacquered Wood, Herman Miller, 1950, 33 x 18 x 29 In.	1430
Cabinet, G. Nelson, Thin Edge, Rosewood, Enameled Aluminum, Herman Miller, 40 x 40 In.	5312
Cabinet, Galle Style, Walnut, Drawer, Square Marble Top, France, 31 x 14 x 14 In.	130
Cabinet, Georgian Style, Mahogany, Serpentine, Doors, Drawers, Scrolled Stiles, 38 x 55 x 23 In.	500
Cabinet, Gilt, Marble Top, Painted Scenes, Fin De Siecle Vernis Martin, c.1900, 36 x 45 In. ...*illus*	2500
Cabinet, Gio Ponti, Walnut, Hidden Drawers, Singer & Sons, Italy, c.1950, 36 x 47 In. ......*illus*	25000
Cabinet, H. Solvsten, Hanging, Pine, Lacquered Wood, Denmark, c.1955, 19 x 39 In.	2250
Cabinet, Hanging, Gothic Revival, Birch, 2 Doors, c.1850, 25 ½ x 23 ½ In.	219
Cabinet, Hanging, Spice, Oak, Branded Drawer Fronts, c.1900, 12 ¾ x 27 x 8 In.	104
Cabinet, J. Camp, Carved, Walnut, Signed, Pa., 1994, 34 x 62 x 21 In.	5625
Cabinet, Jewelry, Chippendale Style, Doors, Interior Drawers, Bracket Feet, 1983, 13 x 16 x 10 In.	120
Cabinet, Knoll & Drake, Rosewood, Aluminum, 4 Doors, 2 Drawers, Signed, c.1955, 40 x 79 In.	1375
Cabinet, Leaf Scrolls, Talon & Ball Feet, Marquetry, Dutch, 1800s, 33 x 24 x 11 In.	500
Cabinet, Liquor, Boulle Style, Decanters, 7 Shots, Tahan, Paris, 1800s, 13 x 9 x 10 In.	325
Cabinet, Louis XV Style, Gilt Metal Gallery, Cabriole Legs, 44 x 23 ½ x 14 In.	826
Cabinet, Louis XV, Gilt Bronze, Tulipwood, Parquetry, Marble Top, 38 x 33 ½ x 15 In.	1625
Cabinet, Louis XVI Style, Marble Top, Veuve Paul Sormani & Fils, c.1890, 42 x 29 x 21 In.	2500
Cabinet, Mahogany, Carved Torches & Leaves, Stepped Base, Late 1800s, 62 x 71 x 19 In.	523
Cabinet, McCobb, Brass Label, Drawers, 1952, 49 x 71 x 14 In.	1625
Cabinet, Multicolor, Ebonized, Oriental Landscape, Square Legs, 38 ½ x 62 ½ x 21 In.	2000
Cabinet, Mummenthaler & Meier, Magic Box, Fold-Out Desk, Rosewood, Swiss, 1928, 45 x 64 x 21 In.	1640
Cabinet, Neoclassical Style, Mahogany, Satinwood Veneers, c.1900, 37 x 28 x 19 In.	369
Cabinet, Neoclassical, Arch Panel Glass Door, Columns, 1900s, 93 x 52 x 25 In.	1310
Cabinet, Oak, 10 Drawers, Cast Iron Pulls, Cove Molded Crest, c.1910, 62 x 24 x 16 In.	443
Cabinet, Oak, 8 Drawers, Roll Front, Inset Paneled Sides, Brass Pulls, 47 x 18 x 24 In.	545
Cabinet, Oak, Carved Crest, Curved Glass, Door, Reeded Columns, Paw Legs, c.1915, 68 x 39 In.....*illus*	250
Cabinet, Oak, Carved Scene, Abraham Sacrifice Isaac, Turned Legs, Dutch, 1800s, 56 In.	500

Furniture, Candlestand, Painted, Salmon Swirl, Round Top, Pennsylvania, c.1830, 29 x 20 In.
$1,750

Pook & Pook

Furniture, Candlestand, Queen Anne, Mahogany, Tilt Top, Tripod Legs, Slipper Feet, Late 1700s, 28 In.
$156

Eldred's

Furniture, Canterbury, Mahogany, Mushroom Finials, 3 Sections, England, c.1830, 22 x 19 x 14 In.
$84

Thomaston Place Auction Galleries

Furniture, Canterbury, Sheraton, Mahogany, Drawer, c.1815, 20 ½ x 20 ¼ In.
$475

Pook & Pook

Furniture, Cart, Carving, Silver Plate, Revolving Domed Cover, Faux Alligator Skin, Gilt Metal, 46 x 31 In.
$1,125

Neal Auction Company

Furniture, Cart, Flower, Painted, Wood & Iron, 2 Wheels, Handle, 27 x 48 In.
$197

Skinner, Inc.

Furniture, Cellarette, Mahogany, Brass Bail Handle, Compartments, Casters, c.1900, 31 x 16 x 11 In.
$523

Skinner, Inc.

Furniture, Chair, A. Pearsall, Model 2466C, Walnut Frame, Upholstery, c.1960, 33 x 32 In.
$1,750

Wright

Furniture, Chair, Aalto, Lounge, Birch, Curved Frame, Upholstered Seat & Back, 1936, 29 x 32 In.
$1,476

Skinner, Inc.

Furniture, Chair, Arne Jacobsen, Egg, Swivel, Tilt, Aluminum, Leather, F. Hansen, 2005, 42 In.
$4,062

Rago Arts and Auction Center

Furniture, Chair, Banister Back, 5 Spindles, Scroll Handholds, Arms, c.1750, 45 In.
$1,046

Skinner, Inc.

Furniture, Chair, Belter, Fountain Elms, Laminated Rosewood, S-Scrolls, Cabriole Legs, 38 In.
$4,840

Fontaine's Auction Gallery

Cabinet, Oak, Carved, Relief Hunters, Square Bun Feet, Shelves, c.1900, 60 x 44 x 17 In..........	880
Cabinet, Open Back Top Unit, Cupboard Doors Below, Pine, c.1900	120
Cabinet, P. Evans, Directional, Sculptured Bronze, Wood, 2 Drawers, 1974, 28 x 13 In......*illus*	2625
Cabinet, Parlor, D-Shape Top, Scrolling Leafy Urn Panels, Top Shape Feet, 43 x 71 x 17 In......	1188
Cabinet, Parlor, French Style, Marble Top, Mahogany, Painted, Floral, 1900s, 40 x 41 In..........	438
Cabinet, Parlor, Gilt Incised, Ebonized, Ribbons, Flowers, Mid 1800s, 45¾ x 55 x 20 In.	1563
Cabinet, Pine, 3 Doors, Wave Skirt, Flat Top, Circle Handle, 1900s, 27 x 51 x 19 In.	125
Cabinet, Pine, 4 Drawers, Roll Top, Knob Handle, Flat Based, Wood, 13 x 11 x 6 In.	313
Cabinet, Pine, Blind Door, Grain Painted, Interior Shelves, Vermont, c.1825, 24 x 19 In....*illus*	12
Cabinet, Regency Style, Rosewood, Grillwork Doors, England, 1800s, 37 x 72 x 17½ In.	438
Cabinet, Renaissance Revival, Rosewood, Arched, Shelves, Inlay, 1800s, 65 x 61 In..........*illus*	6250
Cabinet, S. Smith, Mahogany, Walnut, 2 Compartments, Pigeonholes, c.1840, 22 x 18 x 10 In.	369
Cabinet, Scroll Finial, Gallery, Rosewood, Mirrored Center, 1800s, 44 x 17 x 51 In.	106
Cabinet, Sevres Style, Bird's-Eye Maple, Satinwood Inlay, Napoleon III, c.1865, 57 x 47 x 21 In..	2000
Cabinet, Shaped Back & Sides, 2 Doors, Painted, Pa., 1800s, 33 x 30 In.	800
Cabinet, Stand, Lacquer, Brass Mounts, Drawers, Doors, Multicolor Panels, 46 x 30 x 16 In.....	484
Cabinet, Wall, 4 Lattice Doors, Continental, Footed, 75 x 13 x 69 In.	177
Cabinet, Walnut, Drawer, 2 Doors, Burl Panels, Victorian, 56 x 39 In.............................	219
Cabinet, Walnut, Pine, Poplar, Frame, Chamfered Edges, c.1950, 24 x 24 x 13 In.	163
Cabinet, Wegner, Rosewood, Chrome Plated Steel, Doors, Ry Mobler, Denmark, 1965, 31 x 79 In. ..	5937
Cabinet, Wegner, Teak, Glass, Drawer, Shelves, Ry Mobler, Denmark, c.1958, 71 x 71 In.	1500
Candlestand, 2-Light, Iron, Adjustable, Brass Nozzles, Bobeche, 66 x 18½ In.	118
Candlestand, 2-Light, Iron, Adjustable, Tapering Rod, Tripod Base, Penny Feet, 23 x 11 In.....	492
Candlestand, 2-Light, Red, Screw Adjustable, Ring Turnings, 1800s, 45 In.	431
Candlestand, Birch, Inlaid Fan, Pedestal, Tripod Legs, New England, Mid 1800s, 28 x 17 x 17 In...	380
Candlestand, Cherry & Birch, Oval Top, New England, 1800s, 28 x 24 In.	125
Candlestand, Federal, Cherry, Square Top, Turned Support, Tripod Base, 26 x 18 In.	154
Candlestand, Federal, Mahogany, Shaped Top, New England, 1800s, 28¾ x 26 In.	163
Candlestand, Federal, Round Top, Applewood, Pennsylvania, 1800s, 28½ x 21 In.	263
Candlestand, Federal, Walnut, Round, Tripod Based, c.1800, 27 x 16 x 23 In.	100
Candlestand, Forged Iron, Tripod, Brass Drip Pans, c.1800, 67 In..................................	1107
Candlestand, Hepplewhite, Cherry, Square Top, Round Corners, Spider Legs, c.1820, 27 x 18 In. ...	99
Candlestand, Mahogany, Cut Corners, Turned Post, Cabriole Legs, England, c.1810, 29 x 20 In.....	308
Candlestand, Maple & Pine, Spanish Brown, Adjustable, Tripod, Late 1700s, 46 In..........*illus*	813
Candlestand, Maple, Faceted Standard, Mortised T-Base, Round Top, c.1800, 26 x 17 In.	531
Candlestand, Octagonal Top, Tripod Base, Carved Feet, England, 1900s, 29 x 23 x 16 In.	554
Candlestand, Painted, Salmon Swirl, Round Top, Pennsylvania, c.1830, 29 x 20 In.........*illus*	1750
Candlestand, Queen Anne Style, Nantucket Basket Top, Swing Handle, Cherry, 27 x 18 In.	3600
Candlestand, Queen Anne, Burl, Birdcage Support, Cabriole Legs, Pad Feet, c.1800, 28 x 22 In.	250
Candlestand, Queen Anne, Mahogany, Tilt Top, Cabriole Legs, Va., c.1780, 26½ x 19½ In.....	7605
Candlestand, Queen Anne, Mahogany, Tilt Top, Tripod Legs, Slipper Feet, Late 1700s, 28 In...*illus*	156
Candlestand, Serpentine Top, Snake Foot Base, 1700s, 16½ x 16 x 27 In............................	177
Candlestand, Serpentine, Walnut, Tilt Top, Splay Legs, 27 x 16½ x 16¾ In.	431
Candlestand, Walnut, Red, Yellow Pinstripes & Bands, Tripod Feet, 1800s, 26 x 14 In............	469
Candlestand, Walnut, Round Top, Tripod Base, Slipper Feet, Pennsylvania, 1800s, 26½ In.....	123
Candlestand, Wood, Black, Fixed Top, Iron Spider, Pedestal, c.1825, 25 x 16 x 16 In.	810
Candlestand, Wrought Iron, Adjustable, Cup, Rush Holder, Penny Feet, c.1800, 44¾ In.	875
Canterbury, Georgian Style, Ebonized, Gilt, Greek Key, Drawer, Brass Casters, 22 x 25 In.	438
Canterbury, Mahogany, Mushroom Finials, 3 Sections, England, c.1830, 22 x 19 x 14 In..*illus*	84
Canterbury, Mahogany, Turned Legs, Casters, England, 21¾ x 18 x 11¾ In.	369
Canterbury, Sheraton, Mahogany, Drawer, c.1815, 20½ x 20¼ In.................................*illus*	475
Canterbury, Walnut, Lyre Supports, Brass Caster Feet, c.1835, 21 x 19 In.	519
Cart, Carving, Silver Plate, Revolving Domed Cover, Faux Alligator Skin, Gilt Metal, 46 x 31 In. *illus*	1125
Cart, Flower, Painted, Wood & Iron, 2 Wheels, Handle, 27 x 48 In.............................*illus*	197
Cart, Serving, R. Schultz, Aluminum, Stainless Steel, Rubber, c.1990, 26¼ x 24 x 39 In..........	1170
Cassone, Walnut, Hinged Lid, Fitted Interiors, Tin Liners, Italy, 1800s, 19 x 58 x 19 In.	625
Cassone, Walnut, Relief Carved, Penwork Top, Front Panels, Italy, 1700s, 27 x 80 x 24 In........	1750
Cellarette, Bombay Form, Oak, Carved, Pyramidal & Wavy, Edge, 16 x 30½ x 17½ In.	303
Cellarette, Dome Lid, 10 Fitted Compartments, 1800s, 6 x 10 x 6 In..............................	104
Cellarette, Mahogany, Brass Bail Handle, Compartments, Casters, c.1900, 31 x 16 x 11 In..... *illus*	523

Cellarette, Mahogany, Sarcophagus Form, Leaf-Carved Paw Feet, c.1825, 27½ x 26 x 19½ In.	1250
Chair Set, Neoclassical, Curly Maple, Vase Shape Splat, Rolled Crest, Saber Legs, 34 In., 8	660
Chair, A. Pearsall, Model 2466C, Walnut Frame, Upholstery, c.1960, 33 x 32 In. ....*illus*	1750
Chair, Aalto, Lounge, Birch, Curved Frame, Upholstered Seat & Back, 1936, 29 x 32 In. .....*illus*	1476
Chair, Adirondack, Twig, Wood, Painted, 54 In.	177
Chair, Ant, Bent Plywood, 3 Metal Tube Legs, F. Hansen, Denmark, 30 x 20 In.	246
Chair, Arne Jacobsen, Egg, Swivel, Tilt, Aluminum, Leather, F. Hansen, 2005, 42 In. ....*illus*	4062
Chair, Arrow Back, Plank Seat, Turned Legs & Supports, Painted, Child's, 15 In.	1062
Chair, Art Deco, Ostrich, Lobed Back, Cabriole Legs, Scroll Feet, France, c.1930s, 41 In.	2500
Chair, Arts & Crafts, Oak, Carved, Leather Upholstery, Arms, 39 x 26½ x 24 In.	185
Chair, Banister Back, 5 Spindles, Scroll Handholds, Arms, c.1750, 45 In. ....*illus*	1046
Chair, Barrel Back, Contemporary, Upholstered, Arms, Baker Furniture	175
Chair, Barrel Back, Open Slats, Flared Arms, 3 Legs, Mahogany, Art Deco, 1900s, 31 In.	677
Chair, Belter, Fountain Elms, Laminated Rosewood, S-Scrolls, Cabriole Legs, 38 In. ....*illus*	4840
Chair, Bergere, French Provincial Style, Upholstered, Closed Arms, Karges, c.1970, 38 In.	507
Chair, Bergere, Louis Philippe, Mahogany, Saber Legs, Paw Feet, Closed Arms, 1800s, 36 In.	1875
Chair, Bergere, Louis XV Style, Upholstered, Closed Arms, 1800s, 45 x 33 x 32 In.	431
Chair, Bergere, Louis XVI Style, Fruitwood, Ribbon Carved Crest, Closed Arms, Early 1900s, 36 In.	313
Chair, Bergere, Louis XVI Style, Upholstered, Cabriole Legs, Closed Arms, 1800s, 30 In.	625
Chair, Bergere, Louis XVI Style, Walnut, Upholstered, Closed Arms, 33½ In.	94
Chair, Black Lacquer, Upholstered, Chinese Style, Arms, c.1960, 30 x 30 In.	189
Chair, Black Paint, Gilt Stencil, Straight Crest Rail & Splat, Rush Seat, 1800s, 33 In. ....*illus*	30
Chair, Black Paint, Stencil, Cane Seat, Gilt, Baltimore, 1800s, 33½ In.	24
Chair, Bugatti, Ebonized Wood, Parchment, Copper, Pewter, Bone Inlay, c.1900, 46 x 32 In.	7500
Chair, Butterfly, Mahogany, Carved, Cushion, Cabriole Legs, Upholstered, Arms, c.1940, 42 In.	469
Chair, Captain's, Esherick, Walnut, Woven Leather Seat, 1951, 30 In..............*illus*	9375
Chair, Captain's, Old Bittersweet Paint, Columbus Marble, Wilmington, Mid 1800s, 29 In.......	120
Chair, Carved Hardwood, Inset, Porcelain Plaques, Chinese, 39 x 26 In.	2750
Chair, Chamber, Red Paint, Hinged Door, Potty Seat, England, Early 1800s, 29 In............*illus*	431
Chair, Channel Back, Wood, Cabriole Legs, Christopher Guy, 29½ x 44½ x 37 In.	605
Chair, Chippendale Shape, Laminate, Plywood, Venturi & Scott, Knoll, 1985, 37 In. ....*illus*	3250
Chair, Chippendale Style, Mahogany, Ball & Claw Feet, Upholstered, Arms, Late 1900s, 36 In..	344
Chair, Chippendale Style, Walnut, Upholstered Seat, Shaped Splat, Arms	150
Chair, Chippendale, Mahogany, Cushion Seat, Cabriole Legs, Arms. 1700s, 39 x 30 In.	875
Chair, Chippendale, Walnut, Carved Shell Crest, Scrolled Splat, Cabriole Legs, c.1775	2250
Chair, Club, Art Deco Style, Barrel Back, Slats, 3 Legs, Upholstered Seat, 30 In. ....*illus*	677
Chair, Club, Modern, Fourtuny Upholstered, Tufted Back, 35 In.	121
Chair, Club, Swivel, Dunbar, c.1950s, 32 x 30¾ In.	438
Chair, Cockfighting, Mahogany, Carved, Red Leather, Iron Tack, 1800s, 37 In............*illus*	813
Chair, Continental Style, Revolving, Upholstered, Carved Ram's Heads, 30 In.	660
Chair, Corner, Bamboo Design, Carved, Square, 1800s, 31 In.	98
Chair, Corner, Colonial Revival, Mahogany, Carved, Spindles, Cabriole Legs, 1800s, 29 In... *illus*	240
Chair, Corner, Mahogany, Cabriole Legs, Vase Shape Splats, Bellflower, Va., c.1780, 31 In.	1900
Chair, Corner, Queen Anne, Maple, Cushion Back, Curved Arms, Turned Legs, 34 In.	600
Chair, Corner, Windsor, Comb Back, Banister, Shaped Slats, Black, Arms, 1800s, 45½ In.	1020
Chair, Craftsman, Slab Seat & Back, Arms, T-Shape Base, Signed, Fisher 80, 1980, 47 In..*illus*	431
Chair, Crest Rail, Carved Splat, Walnut, Foliate Scrolls, Bun Feet, Early 1900s, 50¾ In.	100
Chair, Cube, Oak, Prairie Style, Blue Leather Cushions, 29 x 42 x 37½ In. ....*illus*	518
Chair, Curved, Tufted Upholstered Seat, Wood Frame, Open Arms, 36 In.	148
Chair, D. Johnson, Lounge, Enameled Steel, Jute, Calif., c.1950, 28 x 35 x 32¾ In. ....*illus*	1625
Chair, Desk, Red Paint, Adjustable, Caster Wheel, Metal, Marked, Kevi, 31½ In.................*illus*	94
Chair, Desk, Regency, Mahogany, Leather Covered, Swivel Base, c.1850, 35 x 22 x 25 In.	3000
Chair, E. Eiermann, E 11, Wicker, Fabric Cushion, Germany, 1968, 33 x 34 In.	907
Chair, E. Eiermann, SE 69, Chrome Steel, Plywood, Nut Veneer, 3 Legs, Germany, c.1952, 29 In.. *illus*	2268
Chair, Eames, Birch Plywood, Aniline Dyed, Chrome Plated Steel, Rubber, 22 x 25 x 27 In.......	1250
Chair, Eames, Birch Plywood, Dyed, Heart Cutout, 1944, Child's, 14 x 14 In....................*illus*	10625
Chair, Eames, Drafting, Vinyl, Fiberglass Shell, Steel Base, Herman Miller, 1970, 40 In. ...*illus*	455
Chair, Eames, Wire Mesh, Upholstery Tag, c.1952, 32 x 18½ x 16½ In.	2500
Chair, Empire Style, Gilt Metal, Mounted, Mahogany, Early 1900s, 39 In.	63
Chair, F. Henningsen, Mahogany, Upholstered, Arms, Denmark, c.1935, 35 x 26 x 25 In.	1500

Furniture, Chair, Black Paint, Gilt Stencil, Straight Crest Rail & Splat, Rush Seat, 1800s, 33 In.
$30

Cowan's Auctions

Furniture, Chair, Captain's, Esherick, Walnut, Woven Leather Seat, 1951, 30 In.
$9,375

Wright

Furniture, Chair, Chamber, Red Paint, Hinged Door, Potty Seat, England, Early 1800s, 29 In.
$431

Skinner, Inc.

Furniture, Chair, Chippendale Shape, Laminate, Plywood, Venturi & Scott, Knoll, 1985, 37 In.
$3,250

Wright

Furniture, Chair, Club, Art Deco Style, Barrel Back, Slats, 3 Legs, Upholstered Seat, 30 In.
$677

Skinner, Inc.

Furniture, Chair, Cockfighting, Mahogany, Carved, Red Leather, Iron Tack, 1800s, 37 In.
$813

Crescent City Auction Gallery

Chair, Fauteuil, Louis VX Style, Walnut, Padded Back, Sides, Overstuffed Seat, 1800s, 42 In. ...	938
Chair, Fauteuil, Louis XV Style, Flowers, Molded Back Crest, Shell & Leaf Carved, 37 3/8 In.	750
Chair, Fauteuil, Louis XV Style, Upholstered, Flat Back, Arms, c.1900, 34 1/2 In.	188
Chair, Fauteuil, Louis XV, Walnut, Upholstered, Curved Back, 1700s, 44 x 26 x 27 In.	400
Chair, Fauteuil, Mahogany, Upholstered, Lion's Head Arms, Turned Stretchers, Hairy Paw Feet.	250
Chair, Fernando & Humberto Campana, Stainless Steel, Plastic Tubing, Brazil, 1995, 29 In.*illus*	500
Chair, Finn Juhl, Lounge, Walnut, Brass, Upholstered, Denmark, 1960s, 31 x 28 1/2 x 33 In.	3250
Chair, Finn Juhl, Teak, Leather, Arms, Denmark, 1948, 31 1/2 x 27 1/2 In.............*illus*	5000
Chair, Floral Crest, Cabriole, Legs, Brown Leather Upholstery, France 57 x 29 x 32 In.	350
Chair, Folding, Cane Seat, Wood, Lacquered, England, 1800s............	177
Chair, G. Nakashima, Lounge, Walnut, Hickory, Spindles, Upholstered Seat, 1974, 35 x 34 In. ..	13750
Chair, George III, Mahogany, Barrel Back, Channeled, Cushion, Tapered Legs, 1800s, 43 x 30 x 20 In...	688
Chair, George III, Mahogany, Box Stretcher, Upholstered, Late 1700s	850
Chair, George III, Mahogany, Molded Tapered Legs, Stretchers, 43 x 32 x 24 In.	375
Chair, Georgian Style, Mahogany, Leaf Carved, Claw Feet, Arms, Late 1900s, 27 x 24 In.	234
Chair, H. Bertoia, Lounge, Diamond, Stainless Steel Base, Knoll, 1952, 27 x 44 x 34 In.	1500
Chair, H. Probber, Suspension, Laminated Birch, Upholstered, 1949, 27 x 43 x 28 In.	2000
Chair, Half-Spindle Back, Painted, American Eagle, Flags, Plank Seat, Mid 1800s, 32 In. .*illus*	600
Chair, Hall, Walnut, Heavily Carved Scrolling, Upholstered, Continental, 47 In.	1188
Chair, Harp, Walnut, Shell Shape Seat, 3 Legs, Paw Feet, Venetian Baroque Style, Italy, 1800s, 23 In.	688
Chair, Hepplewhite, String Inlay, Fan Shape, Upholstered, Cushion, Arms, 22 x 23 In............	96
Chair, Hinged Seat, Storage Box Beneath, Walnut Panels, Crest, 40 x 22 x 19 In.	182
Chair, Horns, Longhorn, Upholstered, Padded Headrest, Arms, c.1910, 38 x 32 In. ....*illus*	1188
Chair, J. Caruso, Molded Plastic, Stackable, U-Shape Steel Rod Legs, c.1950, 30 x 18 In.	12
Chair, J.B. Van Sciver, Carved, Needlework Tapestry Upholstered, Arms, 47 In............	60
Chair, Jansen Curule Savonarola, Leather, Iron Base, Claw Feet, 31 In.	210
Chair, Knoll, Upholstered, Shelton Mindel, 32 x 22 x 23 In............*illus*	63
Chair, Lacquer, Carved, Phoenix Bird, Dragon, Bat, Arms, Chinese, 34 In.	325
Chair, Ladder Back, Square Nails, Woven Birch Seat, Turned Acorn Finials, Arms, New England, 44 In.	165
Chair, Ladder Back, Turned Posts, Bulbous Stretcher, Scroll Arms, Late 1700s, 16 x 44 In.......	336
Chair, Ladder Back, Welsh Style, Rush Seat, Turned Legs, Arms, 41 x 23 x 22 In.	100
Chair, Ladder Back, William & Mary, Sausage Turned Stretchers, New York, Arms, c.1750	438
Chair, Ladder Back, Yellow Seat, Wood, Carved, Arms, 1800s, 16 x 46 In.	590
Chair, Leather, Brown, Longhorn Back, Arms & Legs, Texas, Early 1900s, 36 x 29 x 26 In.	1188
Chair, Leather, Upholstered, Ball Feet, Mexico, 43 1/2 In.	31
Chair, Library, Mahogany, Arched Crest, Padded Seat & Back, Arms, c.1850, 40 In.	688
Chair, Lolling, Hepplewhite, Canted Back, Serpentine, Curved Arms, Molded Legs, 46 In.	3000
Chair, Lolling, Hepplewhite, Mahogany, Inlay, Canted Back, Upholstered Seat, 45 In.	1020
Chair, Lolling, Hepplewhite, Mahogany, Striped Upholstery, New England, 1800s, 43 x 17 In...	450
Chair, Longhorn, Fur, Horn Shape Back, Cushion, Texas, Arms, 1950s, 39 x 33 x 23 In.....*illus*	500
Chair, Longhorn, Upholstered, Padded Arms & Headdress, c.1910, 38 x 32 In............	1188
Chair, Louis XIV Style, Ormolu Mounts, Gold Gilt, Upholstered, Arms, 36 In.	313
Chair, Louis XV Style, Barrel Shape Crest, Arm Terminals, Cabriole Legs, Arms, 34 x 30 x 36 In.	123
Chair, Louis XV, Carved, Beech Frame, Upholstered, Arms, France, 1700s, 41 x 26 x 23 In........	720
Chair, Louis XVI Style, Barrel Back, Fruitwood Frame, Upholstered, Cabriole Legs, Arms, 35 x 31 In.	527
Chair, Lounge, S. Karpen Bros., Turned Wood, Aluminum, Upholstered, 1960s, 29 x 36 In., Pair.....*illus*	5937
Chair, Lounge, Swing Back, Walnut, Cumberland Furniture Co., c.1960, 30 x 25 x 25 In.	185
Chair, Lounge, Upholstered, Brass Feet, c.1965, 34 x 37 1/2 x 37 1/2 In............	250
Chair, Mahogany, Carved, Green Chintz Upholstery, Arms, Victorian, c.1860, 41 x 25 In...........	188
Chair, Mahogany, Crest, Urn Shape Splat, Needlepoint Seat, Fluted Leg, Arms, c.1900, 53 In....	132
Chair, Mahogany, Marquetry, Curved Crest Rail, Slip Seat, Arms, 1900s, 43 x 19 x 24 In.	369
Chair, Mahogany, Rush Seat, Spindle, Carved, 24 x 29 x 24 1/2 In............	177
Chair, Mahogany, Upholstered, Arch Padded Back, Cabriole Legs, Arms, 1700s, 37 x 18 x 24 In.	615
Chair, Maple, Oak, Green, River Cane Splint Seat, Southern Appalachia, 1800s, 32 x 17 In.	70
Chair, McCobb, Predictor Group, Lacquered Wood, Cowhide, Arms, 1951, 24 x 25 In.......*illus*	2000
Chair, Mies Van Der Rohe, Brno, Aluminum, Upholstered, c.1965, 32 x 24 x 22 In.............*illus*	437
Chair, Mixed Wood, Gilt Metal, Applied Spools, Pierced Crest, Padded Arms & Seat, 54 In.	492
Chair, Molesworth, Burl, Patinated Brass, Leather, 1932-33, 36 x 32 In................*illus*	37500
Chair, Mother-Of-Pearl, Marble Inlay, Carved, Shou Symbols, Arms, 1900s, 38 x 25 x 17 In. *illus*	185
Chair, Needlepoint, Carved, Woman & Bird Motif, Arms, Victorian, 24 x 20 x 36 In.................	45

Chair, Oak, Griffin Mask, Crest, Spindle Back, Saddle Seat, Taper Legs, 16 x 15 x 38 In.	99
Chair, P. Evans, Directional, Bronze, Sculptured, Upholstered, 1970s, 31 In., Pair	33750
Chair, P. Evans, Lounge, Argente, Swivel, Steel, Aluminum, Welded, 1970s, 29 x 30 In. .....*illus*	12500
Chair, P. Lissoni, Lounge, Chrome Metal, Upholstered, Back Pillow, Knoll, 24 x 35 x 34 ½ In...	308
Chair, P. Paulin, Tongue, Latex Foam, Tubular Steel, Artifort, Dutch, c.1960, 35 In. ....*illus*	406
Chair, Painted, Carved, Velvet Covered Seat & Back, Cabriole Legs, Continental, 36 x 21 In......	246
Chair, Patrick Norguet, Acrylic, Rainbow Stripes, Translucent, Italy, 31 ¾ x 15 ¼ In.	4725
Chair, Pedro Friedeberg, Hand Shape, Carved, Gesso, Gilt, Mahogany, 1960s, 37 x 21 In...*illus*	28750
Chair, Piano, Empire, Mahogany, Swivel, Curved Back, Inlay, Upholstered, c.1835, 32 In.	813
Chair, Piano, Empire, Mahogany, Swivel, Fan Veneers, 3 Legs, Ormolu Mounts, c.1850, 32 x 14 In...*illus*	813
Chair, Queen Anne Style, Upholstered, Toile Fabric, 42 ½ In.	413
Chair, Queen Anne, Cherry, Vase Shape Splat, Cabriole Legs, Pad Feet, Arms, 42 x 24 In.	240
Chair, Queen Anne, Mahogany, Burl Slat Back, Balloon Seat, Arms, Ireland, 42 x 26 In.	198
Chair, Queen Anne, Mahogany, Canted Back, Damask Upholstery, Cabriole Legs, 1700s, 44 In.	8880
Chair, Queen Anne, Mahogany, Vase Shape Splat, Duck Feet, Cabriole Legs, c.1750, 40 In.	1920
Chair, Queen Anne, Red Paint, Pierced Splat, Rush Seat, Pad Feet, 40 In..........................	246
Chair, Queen Anne, Vase Shape Splat, Medial Stretcher, Ring-Turned Front Legs, 42 In....*illus*	132
Chair, Queen Anne, Walnut, Vase Shape Splat, Cabriole Legs, Open Arms, 1700s, 43 x 30 x 21 In.	375
Chair, Reading, Mahogany, Yoke Crest Rail, Pad Seat, Reeded Legs, Late 1800s, 31 x 23 x 18 In.	156
Chair, Reclining, Oak Frame, Upholstered, Footrest, Arms, c.1900, 44 In..........................*illus*	375
Chair, Regency Style, Book Holder, Drink Holder, Brass Swing Arms, Cane Sides, 41 x 27 In. ...	805
Chair, Regency, Walnut, Domed Padded Back, Cabriole Legs, Scroll Feet, Arms, 1700s, 44 In...	1250
Chair, Relief Carved Lion, Wood, 4-Part Shape, Snake, Turtle, Africa, c.1950, 43 x 26 x 30 In. .	130
Chair, Renaissance Revival, Oak, Dolphins, Grotesque, Hairy Paw Feet, Arms, 1900, 38 x 13 x 20 In.	208
Chair, Rococo Revival, Mahogany, Serpentine Crest Rail, Cabriole Legs, Claw Feet, 40 x 17 In.	3840
Chair, Rohlfs, Oak, Tall Narrow Back, Cutout Design, Carved R Cipher, 57 x 19 In............*illus*	10625
Chair, Rosewood, Black Leather, Niels Koefoed, Denmark, 37 x 15 x 20 In.	177
Chair, Rosewood, Cushion Seat, Upholstered, Arms, Casters, England, c.1815, 40 x 29 x 30 In.	438
Chair, Roycroft, Meditation, Quartersawn Oak, Leather Seat, Orb & Cross, c.1905, 34 In...*illus*	1875
Chair, Shaker, Tilters, Maple & Hickory, Wood Pegs, Box Stretcher Frame	161
Chair, Slat Back, Maple & Ash, Pennsylvania, Arms, 1800s, 50 x 23 x 18 In.	38
Chair, Slipper, Regency, Rosewood, Inlay, Serpentine Back, Early 1800s, 34 x 20 x 20 In.........	250
Chair, Slipper, Rococo Revival, Carved, Fruit, Turned Legs, Upholstered, c.1875, 41 x 18 x 18 In..	250
Chair, Stickley Bros., Morris, Oak, Horizonal Slat Sides, Round Seat, 42 x 30 x 34 In.	143
Chair, Thonet, Lounge, Adjustable Back, Bentwood, Scroll Arms, c.1940, 42 x 27 x 60 In. .*illus*	875
Chair, Throne, Baroque Style, Gilt, Silvered Wood, Carved, Paris, Late 1800s, 53 In.	1250
Chair, Tufted Leather, Walnut, Dog Head Arms, 1800s, 37 x 31 In.	2832
Chair, Vermelha, Red, Steel Feet, Fernando & Humberto Campana, 1998, 30 x 31 In........*illus*	3750
Chair, Walker Weed, Leather, Walnut, Signed, New Hampshire, c.1957, 33 x 26 In.	2125
Chair, Walnut, Black Leather, H-Stretcher, Scroll Arms, England, 1700s, 37 x 22 In.	99
Chair, Walnut, Vase Shape Splat, Cabriole Legs, Chippendale, Pa., c.1765, 37 ½ In.	322
Chair, Windsor Oak, Elm, Ash, Tipped Feet, Arm, 1900s, 43 ¾ x 30 In.	281
Chair, Windsor, 9 Spindles, Continuous Arm, Rhode Island, c.1790, 40 In.	590
Chair, Windsor, 10 Spindles, Green Surface, H-Stretcher, Arms, Pennsylvania, c.1790	500
Chair, Windsor, Arrow Back, Board Seat, Turned Legs, Arms, c.1800............................*illus*	288
Chair, Windsor, Black Paint, Continuous Arm, 1800s, 35 ½ In.	228
Chair, Windsor, Black, Small Drawer, Writing Arm, Pennsylvania, c.1790 ....*illus*	2000
Chair, Windsor, Bow Back, 9 Spindles, Vase Turnings, c.1790, 36 In. ....*illus*	708
Chair, Windsor, Bow Back, Bamboo Turnings, Scrolled Handholds, Pa., c.1800, 37 In. ....*illus*	1046
Chair, Windsor, Bow Back, Beaded Crest, Turned Legs, Arms, 1790s, 35 In.	554
Chair, Windsor, Bow Back, Braced, Turned Legs, Continuous Arm, 36 In.	360
Chair, Windsor, Bow Back, Mustard Painted, Splayed Legs, Arms, England, 1800s, 36 In.	1845
Chair, Windsor, Bow Back, Spindles, Black, Bead Crest, Continuous Arm, 36 ½ In.	3774
Chair, Windsor, Brace Back, 7 Spindles, New York, c.1790, 38 In...........................*illus*	472
Chair, Windsor, Brace Back, 9 Spindles, Continuous Arm, New York, c.1790, 36 In.	708
Chair, Windsor, Brace Back, Beaded Crest, Black Paint, Carved Saddle Seat, 38 In...................	923
Chair, Windsor, Comb Back, Carved Ears, Bulbous Turnings, Arms, Late 1800s.................*illus*	625
Chair, Windsor, Comb Back, Marked Under Seat, Walter Steeley, Arms, 45 In.	590
Chair, Windsor, Comb Back, Spindle Back, Scroll Top Rail, Saddle Seat, Arms, 1780, 43 In......	780
Chair, Windsor, Comb Back, Writing Arm, Drawer, Fitted Interior, Red Paint, c.1850 ....*illus*	240

Furniture, Chair, Corner, Colonial Revival, Mahogany, Carved, Spindles, Cabriole Legs, 1800s, 29 In.
$240

Garth's Auctioneers & Appraisers

Furniture, Chair, Craftsman, Slab Seat & Back, Arms, T-Shape Base, Signed, Fisher 80, 1980, 47 In.
$431

Skinner, Inc.

Furniture, Chair, Cube, Oak, Prairie Style, Blue Leather Cushions, 29 x 42 x 37 ½ In.
$518

Keystone Auctions LLC

TIP
Glue weather stripping to the bottom of a chair rocker to protect the floor.

FURNITURE

Furniture, Chair, D. Johnson, Lounge, Enameled Steel, Jute, Calif., c.1950, 28 x 35 x 32¾ In.
$1,625

Wright

Furniture, Chair, Desk, Red Paint, Adjustable, Caster Wheel, Metal, Marked, Kevi, 31½ In.
$94

Copake Auction

Furniture, Chair, E. Eiermann, SE 69, Chrome Steel, Plywood, Nut Veneer, 3 Legs, Germany, c.1952, 29 In.
$2,268

Quittenbaum Kunstauktionen GmbH

Furniture, Chair, Eames, Birch Plywood, Dyed, Heart Cutout, 1944, Child's, 14 x 14 In.
$10,625

Wright

Furniture, Chair, Eames, Drafting, Vinyl, Fiberglass Shell, Steel Base, Herman Miller, 1970, 40 In.
$455

Wright

Furniture, Chair, Fernando & Humberto Campana, Stainless Steel, Plastic Tubing, Brazil, 1995, 29 In.
$500

Wright

Furniture, Chair, Finn Juhl, Teak, Leather, Arms, Denmark, 1948, 31½ x 27½ In.
$5,000

Freeman's Auctioneers & Appraisers

Furniture, Chair, Half-Spindle Back, Painted, American Eagle, Flags, Plank Seat, Mid 1800s, 32 In.
$600

Garth's Auctioneers & Appraisers

Furniture, Chair, Horns, Longhorn, Upholstered, Padded Headrest, Arms, c.1910, 38 x 32 In.
$1,188

New Orleans Auction Galleries

Furniture, Chair, Knoll, Upholstered, Shelton Mindel, 32 x 22 x 23 In.
$63

Susanin's Auctioneers & Appraisers

Furniture, Chair, Longhorn, Fur, Horn Shape Back, Cushion, Texas, Arms, 1950s, 39 x 33 x 23 In.
$500

New Orleans Auction Galleries

Furniture, Chair, Lounge, S. Karpen Bros., Turned Wood, Aluminum, Upholstered, 1960s, 29 x 36 In., Pair
$5,937

Rago Arts and Auction Center

Furniture, Chair, McCobb, Predictor Group, Lacquered Wood, Cowhide, Arms, 1951, 24 x 25 In.
$2,000

Wright

Furniture, Chair, Mies Van Der Rohe, Brno, Aluminum, Upholstered, c.1965, 32 x 24 x 22 In.
$437

Wright

Furniture, Chair, Molesworth, Burl, Patinated Brass, Leather, 1932-33, 36 x 32 In.
$37,500

Rago Arts and Auction Center

Furniture, Chair, Mother-Of-Pearl, Marble Inlay, Carved, Shou Symbols, Arms, 1900s, 38 x 25 x 17 In.
$185

Skinner, Inc.

Furniture, Chair, P. Evans, Lounge, Argente, Swivel, Steel, Aluminum, Welded, 1970s, 29 x 30 In.
$12,500

Rago Arts and Auction Center

Furniture, Chair, P. Paulin, Tongue, Latex Foam, Tubular Steel, Artifort, Dutch, c.1960, 35 In.
$406

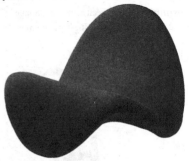

Freeman's Auctioneers & Appraisers

F

Furniture, Chair, Pedro Friedeberg, Hand Shape, Carved, Gesso, Gilt, Mahogany, 1960s, 37 x 21 In.
$28,750

Rago Arts and Auction Center

Furniture, Chair, Piano, Empire, Mahogany, Swivel, Fan Veneers, 3 Legs, Ormolu Mounts, c.1850, 32 x 14 In.
$813

New Orleans Auction Galleries

Furniture, Chair, Queen Anne, Vase Shape Splat, Medial Stretcher, Ring-Turned Front Legs, 42 In.
$132

Eldred's

Furniture, Chair, Reclining, Oak Frame, Upholstered, Footrest, Arms, c.1900, 44 In.
$375

Garth's Auctioneers & Appraisers

Furniture, Chair, Rohlfs, Oak, Tall Narrow Back, Cutout Design, Carved R Cipher, 57 x 19 In.
$10,625

Rago Arts and Auction Center

Furniture, Chair, Roycroft, Meditation, Quartersawn Oak, Leather Seat, Orb & Cross, c.1905, 34 In.
$1,875

Rago Arts and Auction Center

Furniture, Chair, Thonet, Lounge, Adjustable Back, Bentwood, Scroll Arms, c.1940, 42 x 27 x 60 In.
$875

Kamelot Auctions

Furniture, Chair, Vermelha, Red, Steel Feet, Fernando & Humberto Campana, 1998, 30 x 31 In.
$3,750

Los Angeles Modern Auctions

Furniture, Chair, Windsor, Arrow Back, Board Seat, Turned Legs, Arms, c.1800
$288

Keystone Auctions LLC

Chair, Windsor, Fanback, 7 Spindles, Brown Paint, 37 In.	338
Chair, Windsor, Fanback, 7 Spindles, Pennsylvania, c.1790	1125
Chair, Windsor, Fanback, 7 Swell Spindles, Black Paint, Late 1700s, 37¾ In.	290
Chair, Windsor, Fanback, Black Paint, Carved, Ears, Arms, Knuckles, c.1790, 47½ In.	10455
Chair, Windsor, Fanback, Bowed Crest, Plank Seat, Splayed Turned Legs, 35 In.	212
Chair, Windsor, Fanback, Scroll Ears, Blunt Arrow Feet, Arms, c.1790 ....*illus*	2000
Chair, Windsor, Maple, Pine, Triple Comb, Continuous Arm, Ring-Turned Legs, 40 x 25 In.	1080
Chair, Windsor, Rod Back, Bamboo Turnings, Brown, Arms, England, 1800s, 36 In. ....*illus*	400
Chair, Windsor, Rod Back, Bamboo Turnings, Outward Bending Arms, Early 1800s, 38 In.	182
Chair, Windsor, Sack Back, 7 Spindles, Arms, Brown Paint, D.R. Dimes	175
Chair, Windsor, Sack Back, 7 Spindles, Black Paint, New York, c.1790, 35½ In.	236
Chair, Windsor, Sack Back, Mixed Wood, Ebenezer Tracy, Arms, Late 1700s, 36 In. ....*illus*	1375
Chair, Windsor, Sack Back, Red Paint, H-Stretcher, New England, Late 1700s, Child's, 19 In.	509
Chair, Windsor, Sack Back, Saddle Seat, Black, Continuous Arm, England, Late 1700s, 41 In.	246
Chair, Wing, Black, Roy McMakin, c.1988, 34½ x 36 x 34 In.	2000
Chair, Wing, Chippendale Style, Upholstered, Carved Legs, Ball & Claw Feet, 46 In.	127
Chair, Wing, Chippendale, Mahogany, Canted Back, Arched Chest, Frontal Legs, 43½ In.	1200
Chair, Wing, French Provincial Style, White Paint, Upholstered, Arms, 41 In.	277
Chair, Wing, George III Style, Leather Upholstery, Nailheads, c.1900, 45 x 33 In. ....*illus*	688
Chair, Wing, Green Leather, Tapered Legs, Ethan Allen..............*illus*	275
Chair, Wing, Mahogany, Damask Upholstery, Arms, Early 1800s, 46½ In.	1125
Chair, Wood, Turned Posts, Half Back, Rush Seat, Arms, c.1850, Child's, 21 In.	192
Chair, Y. Ekstrom, Lamino, Highback, False Reindeer Upholstery, Sweden, 1956, 41 In.....*illus*	875
Chair, Rocker, is listed under Rocker in this category.	
Chair-Table, Maple, Pine, Red, Round, 3-Board Top, Square Base, 1800s, 19 In.	1230
Chair-Table, Oak, Shoefoot, Red, Pine, Oval Top, Beaded Stretcher, 1750, 27 x 35 x 41 In. ..*illus*	1016
Chair-Table, Pine, Black Paint, Shoefoot, Circular Top, 27 x 47½ In.	2091
Chair-Table, Pine, Scrub Top, Shoefoot Base, Pennsylvania, Late 1800s, 27 x 59 x 43 In.	2640
Chair-Table, Red Paint, Pine, Oval Top, Chamfered Edges, Early 1800s, 64 In.	3075
Chair-Table, Walnut & Pine, Green Paint, Oval Top, Shoefoot Base, 25 x 39 x 33 In.	900
Chair-Table, William & Mary, Cherry, Shoefoot, Circular Top, c.1740, 27 x 41 In..............*illus*	8125
Chaise Longue, Brayton International, Chrome & Leather, 34 x 64 x 23 In.	1500
Chaise Longue, Louis XV Style, Gilt, Curved Crest Rail, Scrolls, c.1900, 32 x 76 In.	750
Chaise Longue, Victorian, Walnut, Carved, Upholstered, 1800s, 72 In.	563
Chest, 2 Drawers, Onion Feet, 1800s, 14 x 14 x 9 In.	115
Chest, 2 Short Drawers, 3 Long Drawers, Brass Mounts, Turned Feet, c.1850, 42 x 39 In....*illus*	1845
Chest, 4 Drawers, Crotch Mahogany Front, Ball Pulls, c.1850, 23½ x 17 x 12½ In.	189
Chest, 5 Drawer, Labeled, Maurice Villency, 39½ x 19½ x 39¾ In.	118
Chest, 5 Drawers, Grain Painted, Molded Cornice, Vermont, Late 1700s, 46 x 35 x 19 In.	3919
Chest, 6 Thumb Drawers, Carved, Pendant, New Hampshire, 1700s, 59¾ x 36 x 19 In.	2091
Chest, American Empire, Striped Maple, Drawers, Turned Pilasters & Legs, 1800s, 42 In...*illus*	252
Chest, Bachelor's, George III, Mahogany, Brush Board, England, 1800s, 34 x 36 x 19½ In.	438
Chest, Bamboo & Lacquer, 3 Drawers, Splayed Legs, Late 1800s, 36 x 30 x 17 In. ....*illus*	1500
Chest, Bedside, Walnut, Marble Top, Carved, Drawer, Door, Bun Feet, c.1890, 32 x 10 x 18 In.	813
Chest, Bedside, Zelkova Wood Frame, 4 Drawers, 2 Doors, Korea, Late 1800s, 34 x 40 x 18 In.	123
Chest, Blanket, 2 Drawers, Dovetailed, Grain Painted, Turned Legs, 22½ x 45 x 19 In.	203
Chest, Blanket, Bracket Feet, Wrought Iron, Strap Hinges & Handles, 1850, 25 x 47 x 23 In.	938
Chest, Blanket, Carved, Mother-Of-Pearl Inlay, Ottoman Syria, 1800s, 29 x 43 In...........*illus*	813
Chest, Blanket, Carved, Oak, Sunflower, 2 Drawers, Peter Blin, 40 x 44½ x 20 In.	6300
Chest, Blanket, Chippendale, Walnut, 3 Drawers, Ogee Bracket Feet, Late 1700s, 35 x 51 In.	1188
Chest, Blanket, Chippendale, Walnut, Bracket Base, Scalloped Apron, 1800s, 16 x 25 In.	780
Chest, Blanket, Eagle, Union Shield, Banner, Bracket Feet, 1807, 26 x 50 x 23 In. ....*illus*	4718
Chest, Blanket, Federal, Walnut, Turned Feet, Va., c.1830, 14½ x 21 x 10½ In.	439
Chest, Blanket, Hinged Top, Dovetailed, Base Molding, England, 1800s, 19 x 38 x 18¾ In.	861
Chest, Blanket, Hinged Top, Molded Edge & Base, Soap Hollow, c.1810, 27 x 44 In.	2214
Chest, Blanket, Lift Lid, Painted, Wood, Brass Handle, 42 x 18 x 18 In.	118
Chest, Blanket, Paint Decorated, Yellow, Green, Red, Tapering Legs, c.1810, 23 x 32 In.	4920
Chest, Blanket, Painted, Pine, Decorated Blue Sponge, c.1800, 21½ x 37 In.	700
Chest, Blanket, Painted, Pine, Red Grain, Pennsylvania, 1800s, 20 x 30 In.	188
Chest, Blanket, Painted, Pine, Yellow Grained Surface, Pennsylvania, c.1850, 21 x 37 In.	163

Furniture, Chair, Windsor, Black, Small Drawer, Writing Arm, Pennsylvania, c.1790
$2,000

Pook & Pook

Furniture, Chair, Windsor, Bow Back, 9 Spindles, Vase Turnings, c.1790, 36 In.
$708

Cottone Auctions

Furniture, Chair, Windsor, Bow Back, Bamboo Turnings, Scrolled Handholds, Pa., c.1800, 37 In.
$1,046

Skinner, Inc.

F

Furniture, Chair, Windsor, Brace Back, 7 Spindles, New York, c.1790, 38 In.
$472

Cottone Auctions

Furniture, Chair, Windsor, Comb Back, Carved Ears, Bulbous Turnings, Arms, Late 1800s
$625

Pook & Pook

Furniture, Chair, Windsor, Comb Back, Writing Arm, Drawer, Fitted Interior, Red Paint, c.1850
$240

Garth's Auctioneers & Appraisers

Furniture, Chair, Windsor, Fanback, Scroll Ears, Blunt Arrow Feet, Arms, c.1790
$2,000

Pook & Pook

Furniture, Chair, Windsor, Rod Back, Bamboo Turnings, Brown, Arms, England, 1800s, 36 In.
$400

Skinner, Inc.

Furniture, Chair, Windsor, Sack Back, Mixed Wood, Ebenezer Tracy, Arms, Late 1700s, 36 In.
$1,375

Garth's Auctioneers & Appraisers

Furniture, Chair, Wing, George III Style, Leather Upholstery, Nailheads, c.1900, 45 x 33 In.
$688

Leslie Hindman Auctioneers

Furniture, Chair, Wing, Green Leather, Tapered Legs, Ethan Allen
$275

Nadeau's Auction Gallery

Furniture, Chair, Y. Ekstrom, Lamino, Highback, False Reindeer Upholstery, Sweden, 1956, 41 In.
$875

Freeman's Auctioneers & Appraisers

Chest, Blanket, Pine, 6 Drawers, 2 False, Yellow, Brown Grain Finish, Lift Top, c.1850, 36 In....	1320
Chest, Blanket, Pine, Bootjack Cutout Base, 43 x 15 ½ x 17 ½ In.	148
Chest, Blanket, Pine, Dovetailed, Painted, Blue, Green, 1800s, 17 x 43 x 20 ½ In.	106
Chest, Blanket, Pine, Drawers, Dovetailed, Grain Painted, Footed, Till, Pa., c.1825, 25 x 39 In. *illus*	1750
Chest, Blanket, Poplar, Compartments, Blue, White, S.B., Early 1800s, 22 x 37 x 20 In.	2177
Chest, Blanket, Poplar, Painted, Turned Feet, Ocher, Red, Pa., Early 1800s, 26 x 38 x 20 In. *illus*	738
Chest, Blanket, Pumpkin Pine, Drawer, Ogee Shape, England, 1800s, 24 ½ x 25 x 13 In.	132
Chest, Blanket, Shaker, Walnut, Dovetailed, Lift Top, Open Interior, 1800s, 21 x 44 In. *illus*	390
Chest, Blanket, Sheraton, Mahogany, Dovetailed, Turned Legs, 1800s, 24 x 46 x 20 In.	288
Chest, Blanket, Sheraton, Pine, Applied Edge, Lid, Mid 1800s, 23 x 38 x 20 In.	96
Chest, Blanket, Softwood, 2 Drawers, Rectangular Top, 1800s, 29 x 45 x 22 ½ In.	165
Chest, Blanket, Stickley, Oak, Fox Tail Decoration, Cedar Bottom, 25 x 42 x 21 In.	546
Chest, Blanket, Tiger Maple, Cedar, Logo, Lane, 17 x 48 x 25 In..	127
Chest, Blanket, Yellow Pine, Hinged Lid, Till, Cherry Stand, Early 1800s, 24 x 22 In.........*illus*	189
Chest, Brass Corners, Bindings, Pulls, 5 Drawers, Turned Feet, 1800s, 42 x 20 x 4 In.	2457
Chest, Butler's, American Empire, Mahogany, Doors, Drawers, 1800s, 68 x 48 x 21 In.	594
Chest, Butler's, Mahogany, Pullout Desk, Pigeonholes, Paneled Doors, c.1800s, 43 x 45 In. *illus*	360
Chest, Campaign, Mahogany, 2 Half Drawers, Brass Pulls, England, 1900s, 32 x 30 x 15 In.	1020
Chest, Campaign, Mahogany, Brass, 5 Drawers, 1800s, 35 ½ x 41 x 20 In.	181
Chest, Camphor, Red Paint, Floral & Brass Mounts, c.1850, 13 x 29 In............................*illus*	510
Chest, Carved, Painted, Roses On Drawer, 3 Drawers, c.1900, 16 x 12 x 7 In.	330
Chest, Charles II, Rectangular Top, 3 Drawers, Paneled, Ball Feet, 1700s, 35 x 33 x 19 In.	1188
Chest, Cherry, 4 Drawers, Flute Quarter Columns, Ogee Bracket Base, Late 1700s, 37 ½ x 38 x 20 In.	2322
Chest, Cherry, Bird's-Eye Maple, 4 Drawers, Backsplash, Corinthian Capitals, 1800s, 52 x 43 x 24 In.	450
Chest, Cherry, Bracket Feet, Henkel Harris, 55 ½ x 36 ½ x 31 In.	369
Chest, Cherry, Carved, 9 Drawers, Bracket Base, Connecticut, 1700s, 85 x 38 x 19 In.	1353
Chest, Cherry, Drawers, Brass, Wood Pulls, Turned Legs, 1800s, 51 x 42 x 19 In.	360
Chest, Chippendale Style, Mahogany, 4 Drawers, Brass Pulls, Bracket Feet, 31 x 40 x 19 In.	142
Chest, Chippendale Style, Mahogany, Thomasville High, 62 ¾ x 40 x 19 ½ In.	138
Chest, Chippendale Style, Pine, 4 Drawers, Bracket Feet, 1900s, 30 x 36 x 21 In. ....*illus*	1375
Chest, Chippendale, 14 Drawers, Scalloped Skirt, Cabriole Legs, Claw Feet, 80 x 41 In.	9375
Chest, Chippendale, Cherry, Molded Top, 5 Graduated Drawers, Dovetailed, 45 x 39 In.	708
Chest, Chippendale, Mahogany, 4 Cock-Beaded Drawers, Brass Pulls, Late 1800s, 30 x 25 x 17 In.	480
Chest, Chippendale, Maple, 4 Drawers, Ogee Feet, c.1800, 32 ½ x 37 x 19 In.	840
Chest, Chippendale, Tiger Maple, Ogee Bracket Feet, 6 Drawers, c.1770, 52 x 35 In.	1000
Chest, Chippendale, Walnut, 4 Drawers, Ogee Bracket Feet, Pa., c.1770, 36 x 36 In.	1500
Chest, Chippendale, Walnut, Quarter Columns, Ogee Bracket Feet, c.1770, 67 x 38 In.	2750
Chest, Cigar, Carved Walnut, Black Forest, c.1880, 13 x 14 ½ x 8 ¼ In............................*illus*	938
Chest, Colonial Revival, Carved, Leafy Design, 1800s, 14 x 25 ½ x 13 In.	281
Chest, Curly Maple, Mahogany, Turned Pulls & Feet, c.1850, Miniature, 25 x 18 x 11 In.	1534
Chest, Dower, Pine, Black & Ocher Paint, Drawers, Pennsylvania, c.1810, 29 x 46 ½ In.	594
Chest, Dower, Pine, Blue Paint, Tulips, Sun Faces, Birds, Late 1700s, 22 x 48 In.............*illus*	4250
Chest, Drawers, Contemporary, Painted, Yellow, Flowers, 30 x 26 x 16 In..............................	250
Chest, Drawers, Flame Burl Facades, Turned Legs, Empire Style, c.1950, 24 x 19 x 13 In...........	408
Chest, Empire Style, Mahogany, 5 Drawers, Marble Top, 1800s, Miniature, 19 x 12 x 7 In.	688
Chest, Federal Style, Mahogany, Dentil Inlaid Top, 4 Drawers, Shaped Skirt, 32 x 31 x 16 In.	688
Chest, Federal, Tiger Maple, Cherry, 5 Over 3 Drawers, Spiral Twist Columns, 56 x 42 In.	1250
Chest, Federal, Tiger Maple, Cherry, 5 Upper Drawers, 3 Long Drawers, c.1815, 56 x 42 In.... *illus*	1250
Chest, G. Nelson, 3 Drawers, Aluminum Pulls, Foil Label, c.1950, 29 ¾ x 18 In........................	984
Chest, G. Nelson, 4 Drawers, Black Vinyl Top, 6 Compartments, Herman Miller, 24 x 34 x 18 ½ In.	546
Chest, George III Style, Chinoiserie Themes, England, 1800s, 31 ½ x 37 ½ x 21 In.	1125
Chest, George III, Mahogany, 7 Drawers, Knob Handles, 70 x 44 x 23 In.	593
Chest, George III, Mahogany, Dentil Cornice, 7 Drawers, Brass Bail Pulls, 67 x 44 x 22 In.......	1968
Chest, Georgian Style, Brass Handles, Mahogany, Plinth Base, 1800, 37 x 30 x 18 ⅜ In.	3500
Chest, Hepplewhite, Cherry, Drawers, Line Inlay, Early 1800s, 39 x 39 ½ In.............................	750
Chest, Hepplewhite, Mahogany, 5 Drawers, Splayed Feet, c.1800, 43 x 44 x 19 ¾ In..................	240
Chest, Hepplewhite, Walnut, 4 Graduated Drawers, c.1800, 36 x 39 x 21 In.	238
Chest, Hollywood Regency, Mirrored, Rectangular Top, 3 Drawers, White, 30 x 30 x 20 In.	272
Chest, Lift Top, Swedish Painted, Molded Frame, Iron Handles, 1839, 18 x 42 x 22 In.	144
Chest, Louis XV Style, Walnut, Drawers, Porcelain Pulls, Scenes, c.1910, 39 x 21 In.	677

Furniture, Chair-Table, Oak, Shoefoot, Red, Pine, Oval Top, Beaded Stretcher, 1750, 27 x 35 x 41 In.
$1,016

Skinner, Inc.

Furniture, Chair-Table, William & Mary, Cherry, Shoefoot, Circular Top, c.1740, 27 x 41 In.
$8,125

Pook & Pook

Furniture, Chest, 2 Short Drawers, 3 Long Drawers, Brass Mounts, Turned Feet, c.1850, 42 x 39 In.
$1,845

Skinner, Inc.

Furniture, Chest, American Empire, Striped Maple, Drawers, Turned Pilasters & Legs, 1800s, 42 In.
$252

Selkirk Auctioneers & Appraisers

Furniture, Chest, Bamboo & Lacquer, 3 Drawers, Splayed Legs, Late 1800s, 36 x 30 x 17 In.
$1,500

Leslie Hindman Auctioneers

Furniture, Chest, Blanket, Carved, Mother-Of-Pearl Inlay, Ottoman Syria, 1800s, 29 x 43 In.
$813

Neal Auction Company

Furniture, Chest, Blanket, Eagle, Union Shield, Banner, Bracket Feet, 1807, 26 x 50 x 23 In.
$4,718

Skinner, Inc.

Furniture, Chest, Blanket, Pine, Drawers, Dovetailed, Grain Painted, Footed, Till, Pa., c.1825, 25 x 39 In.
$1,750

Garth's Auctioneers & Appraisers

Furniture, Chest, Blanket, Poplar, Painted, Turned Feet, Ocher, Red, Pa., Early 1800s, 26 x 38 x 20 In.
$738

Skinner, Inc.

Furniture, Chest, Blanket, Shaker, Walnut, Dovetailed, Lift Top, Open Interior, 1800s, 21 x 44 In.
$390

Cowan's Auctions

Furniture, Chest, Blanket, Yellow Pine, Hinged Lid, Till, Cherry Stand, Early 1800s, 24 x 22 In.
$189

Leland Little Auctions

Furniture, Chest, Butler's, Mahogany, Pullout Desk, Pigeonholes, Paneled Doors, c.1800s, 43 x 45 In.
$360

Cowan's Auctions

Furniture, Chest, Camphor, Red Paint, Floral & Bass Mounts, c.1850, 13 x 29 In.
$510

Eldred's

TIP
Don't wax a piece of furniture that has not been cleaned in the past year.

Furniture, Chest, Chippendale Style, Pine, 4 Drawers, Bracket Feet, 1900s, 30 x 36 x 21 In.
$1,375

Leslie Hindman Auctioneers

TIP
When moving a large chest, always remove the top drawers first. If you pull out the bottom drawers and then move the chest, it is likely to tip over.

Furniture, Chest, Cigar, Carved Walnut, Black Forest, c.1880, 13 x 14½ x 8¼ In.
$938

Heritage Auctions

Furniture, Chest, Dower, Pine, Blue Paint, Tulips, Sun Faces, Birds, Late 1700s, 22 x 48 In.
$4,250

Pook & Pook

Furniture, Chest, Federal, Tiger Maple, Cherry, 5 Upper Drawers, 3 Long Drawers, c.1815, 56 x 42 In.
$1,250

New Orleans Auction Galleries

Furniture, Chest, Mahogany, 3 Short & 3 Long Drawers, Inlay, Henredon, Aston Court, 31 x 30 In.
$305

Nadeau's Auction Gallery

Furniture, Chest, Metal, Tortoiseshell, Lacquer Wood, Bird, Japan, 1800s, 21 x 14½ x 17 In.
$715

Freeman's Auctioneers & Appraisers

Furniture, Chest, Parzinger, 6 Drawers, Mahogany, Bleached, Brass Handles, 1940s, 33 x 80 x 18 In.
$2,000

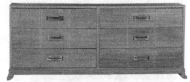

Rago Arts and Auction Center

Furniture, Chest, Pine, Mustard Paint, Black Decoration, Red Border, Early 1800s, 23 x 42 x 17 In.
$1,089

Skinner, Inc.

Furniture, Chest, Sheraton, Bird's-Eye Maple, Mahogany, Drawers, Doors, 1800s, 48 x 52 In.
$3,600

Eldred's

TIP
Don't ignore signs of "wildlife." Use sprays and exterminators. Moths and carpet beetles eat upholstery and fabrics; termites eat wood; powder post beetles and dry wood termites eat wood.

FURNITURE

Furniture, Chest, Walnut, Quarter Columns, Turned Feet, Pennsylvania, Early 1800s, 49 x 38 x 22 In.
$1,063

Pook & Pook

Handles

Many Victorian chests had mushroom-turned wooden knobs. But by the later part of the Victorian era, the leaf-carved handle or the molded, mass-produced leaf handle was used.

Furniture, Chest-On-Chest, Mahogany, Broken Arch, c.1900, 81 x 37 In.
$550

Nadeau's Auction Gallery

Chest, Mahogany, 3 Short & 3 Long Drawers, Inlay, Henredon, Aston Court, 31 x 30 In.....*illus*	305
Chest, Mahogany, Block Front, 4 Drawers, Rectangular Top, 31 ½ x 36 ½ x 16 In.	366
Chest, Mahogany, Gilt Outline, Drawers, Painted Columns, c.1830, Miniature, 14 x 13 In.	3660
Chest, Mahogany, Oak, 3 Drawers, Apron, Cabriole Legs, Henkel Harris, 1900s, 40 x 22 x 17 In.	576
Chest, Mahogany, Outset Upper Drawers, Brass Handles, c.1830, 43 x 38 x 21 ½ In.	594
Chest, Maple, Ogee Front, 4 Drawers, Canted Corners, Cutout Bracket Base, c.1820, 37 x 34 x 19 In..	201
Chest, Metal, Tortoiseshell, Lacquer Wood, Bird, Japan, 1800s, 21 x 14 ½ x 17 In.....*illus*	715
Chest, Mule, Oak, Coffer, 2 Drawers, Half Columns, Chamfered Back, 1700s, 36 x 59 In.	424
Chest, Mule, Pine, Drawer, Bracket Feet, Molded Edge Lid, c.1850, 27 x 29 x 17 In.	780
Chest, Oak, 6 Drawers, Brass Handles, Ogee Bracket Feet, Miniature, 11 x 6¾ x 4¾ In.	625
Chest, Oak, Hinged Lid, Forged Lock, Escutcheon, Key, 1800s, 23 ½ x 23 x 14 In.	936
Chest, Parzinger, 6 Drawers, Mahogany, Bleached, Brass Handles, 1940s, 33 x 80 x 18 In. *illus*	2000
Chest, Pine, Blanket, Red Paint, c.1950, 20 x 32 x 15 In.	600
Chest, Pine, Grain Painted, Scroll Feet, 4 Glued Drawers, c.1850, 10 x 11 x 7 In.	188
Chest, Pine, Mustard Paint, Black Decoration, Red Border, Early 1800s, 23 x 42 x 17 In....*illus*	1089
Chest, Pine, Painted, 4 Drawers, Yellow Grained Surface, 1800s, 36 x 37 ½ In.	250
Chest, Pine, Painted, Knob Handle, Alligator Finish, 5 Drawers, 43 x 31 x 19 In.	125
Chest, Queen Anne Style, Cherry, 2 Short Over 3 Long Drawers, Pennsylvania, 31 x 32 In.	675
Chest, Queen Anne, Cherry, 8 Drawers, Bracket Feet, c.1750, 71 x 37 ½ x 19¾ In.	480
Chest, Red Paint, 4 Drawers, Rectangular Top, Cutout Base, 1800s, 40 x 36 x 19 In.	2706
Chest, Red Walnut, 5 Graduated Drawers, Brass Ring Drop Pulls, 48 x 33 ½ x 20 In.	761
Chest, Rosewood, 4 Drawers, Plinth Base, Ralph Lauren, 1900s, 32 x 35 x 20 In.	369
Chest, Sheraton, Bird's-Eye Maple, Mahogany, Drawers, Doors, 1800s, 48 x 52 In.....*illus*	3600
Chest, Sheraton, Cherry, 3 Dovetailed Drawers, Turned Feet, c.1850, 42 x 40 x 21¾ In.	2460
Chest, Sheraton, Cherry, Maple, 4 Drawers, c.1835, 43 ½ x 42 In.	338
Chest, Sheraton, Grain Painted, 2 Short Over 3 Long Lip Drawers, 1800s, 46 x 36 x 19 In.	177
Chest, Sheraton, Tiger Maple, Cherry, Butternut, 3 Drawers, 1850, 36 x 32 In.	700
Chest, Shiro Kuramata, Side One, Ash, Steel, Curved, Drawers, 1992, 67 x 24 In.	13750
Chest, Sugar, Cherry, 2-Board Top, Lower Drawer, Tapered Feet, c.1850, 27 x 38 In.	761
Chest, Sugar, Cherry, Peg & Panel Construction, Lift Top, Kentucky, 33 x 39 In.	1800
Chest, Sugar, Cherry, Solid Board Front, Back & Sides, Lock, 27 x 18 x 35 In.	176
Chest, Tansu, Hardwood, Brass, Footed, Japan, 1900s, 30 x 32¾ x 13 In.	185
Chest, Teak, Dark Wood Accents, Henning Jorgensen, c.1950, 48 x 39 In.	1476
Chest, Tiger Maple Frame, 5 Drawers, 4 Cabriole Legs, 1800s, 56 x 37 x 14 In.	1599
Chest, Tiger Maple, 4 Drawers, Turned Stiles, Ball Feet, c.1835, Miniature, 21 x 17 In.	1770
Chest, Victorian Style, Mahogany, Drop Front Drawers, 76 x 34 ½ x 17 ½ In.	720
Chest, Walnut, 4 Drawers, Painted, 1800s, 38 x 19 x 32 ½ In.	2124
Chest, Walnut, 5 Drawers, Ogee Bracket Feet, Chippendale, c.1800, 47 x 46 x 22 In.	1062
Chest, Walnut, Molded Edge, 3 Drawers, Ogee Bracket Feet, Italy, c.1750, 36 x 37 x 20 In.	875
Chest, Walnut, Quarter Columns, Turned Feet, Pa., Early 1800s, 49 x 38 x 22 In. ....*illus*	1063
Chest, White Paint, 5 Drawers, Rifle & Sword Stencil, Continental, 1800s, 41 x 21 x 41 In.	177
Chest, Widdicomb, Rectangular Top, Venetian Style, 32¾ x 50 x 24 ½ In.	250
Chest, William & Mary Style, Drawers, Walnut, Rectangular Top, Mervin Martin, 39 x 38 In...	650
Chest, Wood, Maple, Chestnut, Pine, 4 Drawers, Flowers, Miniature, 10¾ x 5 ½ x 10 In.	880
Chest, Yellow Grain, Pine, Hinged Lift Top, 2 Panel Doors, Bracket Feet, 1800s, 40 x 47 x 21 In.	840
Chest, Yellow, Green Paint, Pine, Lift Top, 2 Secret Drawers, Bracket Feet, 1800s, 24 x 52 x 22 In.	308
Chest-On-Chest, 2 Parts, Mahogany, Broken Arch, c.1900, 81 x 37 In.....*illus*	550
Chest-On-Chest, Tiger Maple, 8 Drawers, Molded Top, Bracket Feet, 70 x 39 ½ In.	4800
Chest-On-Chest, Tiger Maple, Molded Cornice, 9 Drawers, Brass, 77 x 38 x 18¾ In.	5443
Coat Rack, Bentwood, 8 Hooks, 3 Splayed Legs, 76 In.	110
Coat Rack, Bird's-Eye Maple, Lyre Shape Arms, Pegs, c.1840, 82 In.	488
Coffer, Oak, Carved Flowers, Iron Grip Lock, Strap Hinges, 1767, 29 x 55 ½ In.	288
Coffer, Oak, Hinged Lid, Linenfold, Carved Panels, England, c.1600s, 22 x 44 In.	431
Coffer, Provincial, Fruitwood, Hinged Top, Tri-Panels, Cabriole Feet, Late 1700s, 28 ½ x 61 x 29 In..	1188
Commode, Biedermeier, Fruitwood, Inlay, Drawer, Door, Square Legs, 1800s, 32 x 15 In.	375
Commode, Birch, 3 Drawers, Cylindrical Pilasters, Bracket Feet, c.1850, 32 x 35 x 19 In.	875
Commode, Burl, Oak, 2 Drawers, Cock-Beaded Edge, Relief Carved, Italy, c.1910, 31 x 36 x 20 In. ..	413
Commode, Carved, Frieze Drawer, Panel Doors, Marble Top, Late 1900s, 31 x 21 x 18 In.	469
Commode, Drawer, Cabinet Base, Grand Rapids, Johnson Furniture Co., 34 x 44 x 18 In.	558
Commode, George III, Mahogany, Square Top, Straight Legs, 1700s, 30 x 21 x 17 In.....*illus*	531

Commode, Kidney Shape, Marble Top, Jasperware Plaques, Gallery, France, 29 x 21 x 11 In....	250
Commode, Louis Philippe, Mahogany, Marble Top, 3 Drawers, Block Feet, 1800s, 38 x 50 x 22 In. .	875
Commode, Louis XV Style, Bombe, Marble Top, Mahogany, Inlay, Breche D'Aleps, 38 x 48 x 21 In..	677
Commode, Louis XV Style, Marble, Sunburst, Inlay, Ormolu, Spain, c.1985, 32 x 33 x 16 In...*illus*	319
Commode, Louis XV Style, Marble Top, Inlay, Bronze Mounts, France, c.1900, 41 x 44 In. ..*illus*	1020
Commode, Louis XV Style, Marble Top, Kingwood, Gilt Bronze, Painted, 35 x 40 x 18 In.	813
Commode, Louis XV Style, Marble Top, Scroll Apron, Finial, Auffray & Co., 33 In.	200
Commode, Louis XV Style, Marble Top, Tulipwood, Mahogany Veneer, 1800s, 34 x 44 x 23 In.	308
Commode, Louis XV Style, Stone Top, Acanthus, Maitland Smith, 35 ½ x 61 x 25 In.	726
Commode, Louis XV Style, Walnut, 3 Drawers, Cabriole Legs, Early 1900s, 33 x 43 x 18 In.	1625
Commode, Louis XV, Rosewood, Pink Marble Top, Drawers, Brass Handles, 36 x 41 x 23 In.....	3025
Commode, Louis XVI Style, Marble Top, Mahogany, Gilt Bronze, 33 x 43 ½ x 18 In.	1188
Commode, Louis XVI Style, Oak, Parquetry Veneer, Gilt Brass, Early 1900s, 30 x 42 x 18 In.	750
Commode, Louis XVI, Breakfront, Marble Top, Inlay, France, 36 x 50 x 21 In.	938
Commode, Louis XVI, Burl Walnut, Marble, 3 Drawers, Tapered Legs, Brass, 1800s, 35 x 49 In..	1800
Commode, Louis XVI, Ebonized, Black, Brass, Gray Marble Top, France, 1800s, 34 x 49 x 23 In.	1063
Commode, Marquetry, Marble Top, Bronze Mounts, 4 Drawers, Flared Legs, 1800s, 33 x 25 x 17 In.	1250
Commode, Neoclassical, Mahogany, Green Marble Top, Drawer, 1900s, 35 x 15 x 14 In.	308
Commode, Provincial, 3 Drawers, Walnut, Paris, 1700s, 38 x 52 x 25 In.	2750
Commode, Regency, Fruitwood, 3 Long Drawers, Cabriole Legs, Scroll Toes, c.1800, 33 x 47 x 24 In.	1625
Commode, Rococo Revival, Serpentine, Walnut, Paw Feet, Late 1700s, 33 ½ x 26 ½ In.	500
Cradle, Hooded, Mahogany, Dovetailed Case, Cutout Heart Handles, c.1850, 29 x 40 In.	120
Cradle, Shaker, Walnut, Dovetailed, Oval Cutouts, Union Village, c.1890, 22 x 24 In.........*illus*	330
Credenza, V. Kagan, Cherry, Drawers, Arched Leg Base, Grosfeld House, c.1955, 32 x 80 In.	6400
Crib, Empire Style, Mahogany Inlay, Outscrolled Head & Footboard, 38 x 40 In.................*illus*	250
Cupboard, 12-Pane Door, Plate Rails, 2 False Drawers, 2 Doors, 1800s, 83 x 43 x 21 In....*illus*	374
Cupboard, 2 Doors, Diamond Panels, Painted, Shelf, Drawers, Continental, c.1890, 45 x 47 In.	750
Cupboard, Cherry, 4 Shelves, Glass Panel Doors, Early 1800s, 86 x 53 In.	313
Cupboard, Cherry, Step Back, 2 Doors, Glass Panes, Brass Knob, c.1830, 89 x 56 x 20 In. .*illus*	1870
Cupboard, Cherry, Step Back, Fan & Star Carved, Va., c.1850, 86 x 43 x 22 In.	1872
Cupboard, Chinese Style, Hardwood, Marble Top, Brass Pulls, 22 x 22 x 16 In......................	492
Cupboard, Chippendale, 2 Sections, Walnut, 6 Drawers, 2 Doors, c.1780, 83 ½ x 46 In.	2500
Cupboard, Chippendale, Walnut, Fan Carved Doors, Scalloped Shelf, c.1780, 89 x 37 In.	2750
Cupboard, Corner, Cherry, 2 Doors, 12-Pane, 1800s, 89 x 45 x 22 In.	1243
Cupboard, Corner, Cherry, 2 Sections, Molded Cornice, Glass Pane Door, Shelves, 1900s, 80 x 42 In.	400
Cupboard, Corner, Chippendale, Tiger Maple, Brass Knobs, Eldred Wheeler, 81 x 35 x 20 In.....	3276
Cupboard, Corner, Federal Style, Glazed Walnut, 2 Sections, Carved, 82 x 39 x 19 In................	461
Cupboard, Corner, Hanging, Cherry, Double Paneled Door, 3 Shelves, 1800s, 34 x 22 x 12 In..	300
Cupboard, Corner, Hanging, Open Fretwork, Hinged Door, Early 1900s, 27 x 22 x 15 In...........	142
Cupboard, Corner, Mahogany, Inlay, Bracket Feet, Pennsylvania, Early 1800s, 103 x 49 x 22 In.....	4320
Cupboard, Corner, Pine, 2 Glass Pane Doors Over 2 Doors, Blue Paint, c.1850, 85 x 51 In..*illus*	4500
Cupboard, Corner, Pine, Grain Painted, 4 Open Shelves, Door, 1800s, 91 x 44 x 19 In. ......*illus*	250
Cupboard, Corner, Walnut, 2 Sections, Blind Door, 1800s, 51 x 21 x 90 In.	207
Cupboard, Corner, Walnut, String Inlay, Bracket Feet, Arch Door, c.1800, 88 x 38 In................	1112
Cupboard, Court, Oak, Gallery Top, Glass, 2 Drawers, England, Late 1800s, 96 x 45 In.....*illus*	336
Cupboard, Crest, Brass Hinges, Arched Top, Maple, Bracket Base, c.1800, 79 x 44 x 22 In.	826
Cupboard, French Provincial, Pine, Panel Doors, 3 Shelves, Canada, c.1790, 76 x 60 In. ..*illus*	600
Cupboard, Hanging, Pine, Apple Green Paint, Doors, Pa., 1800s, 25 x 26 x 8¾ In......................	1125
Cupboard, Hanging, Red Painted Surface, Pennsylvania, Late 1800s, 26 x 20¼ In....................	688
Cupboard, Jelly, Ocher Grain, 2 Drawers, Block Foot, Pennsylvania, 1800s, 54 x 48 In.	488
Cupboard, Jelly, Pine, Single-Board Top, Square Nail Construction, 44 x 51 In.	600
Cupboard, Linen, William & Mary Style, Carved, Oak, Inlay, Drawer, Doors, 1800s, 40 x 43 In...*illus*	527
Cupboard, Louis XV Style, Carved Oak, Shelves, Cabriole Legs, 1800s, 92 x 60 x 22 In.	1000
Cupboard, Oak, Panel Doors, Gothic Arches, Bracket Feet, Late 1800s, 66 x 26 x 17 In............	584
Cupboard, Open Shelves, Dovetailed Drawer, Red Wash, 1900s, 77 x 28 x 14 In........................	300
Cupboard, Pine, 5 Drawers, Old Blue Paint, Late 1800s, 56 x 32 In.	750
Cupboard, Pine, Backsplash, 2 Drawers, Open Shelf, 2 Doors, c.1865, 52 ½ x 47 In. ....*illus*	450
Cupboard, Pine, Corner, Blue Gray Paint, Shelves, Paneled Door, 1790s, 87 ½ In......................	2214
Cupboard, Pine, Cornice, Door, 12 Panes, Shelves, Brass Pulls, Bun Feet, France, 1800s, 86 x 32 x 16 In.	390
Cupboard, Pine, Red, Step Back, 4 Doors, 5 Drawers, 1800s, 80 x 52 x 17 In.	3198

Furniture, Commode, George III, Mahogany, Square Top, Straight Legs, 1700s, 30 x 21 x 17 In.
$531

Leslie Hindman Auctioneers

Furniture, Commode, Louis XV Style, Marble, Sunburst, Inlay, Ormolu, Spain, c.1985, 32 x 33 x 16 In.
$319

Leland Little Auctions

Furniture, Commode, Louis XV Style, Marble Top, Inlay, Bronze Mounts, France, c.1900, 41 x 44 In.
$1,020

Brunk Auctions

Furniture, Cradle, Shaker, Walnut, Dovetailed, Oval Cutouts, Union Village, c.1890, 22 x 24 In.
$330

Cowan's Auctions

Furniture, Crib, Empire Style, Mahogany Inlay, Outscrolled Head & Footboard, 38 x 40 In.
$250

Neal Auction Company

Furniture, Cupboard, 12-Pane Door, Plate Rails, 2 False Drawers, 2 Doors, 1800s, 83 x 43 x 21 In.
$374

Keystone Auctions LLC

Cupboard, Queen Anne Style, Drawers, Shelves, Turned Finials, Ireland, 33 x 82 x 21 In........	797
Cupboard, R. Treat Hogg, Walnut, Glass Doors, Shelves, Pullout, 2 Drawers, Brass, 87 x 42 x 21 ½ In....	369
Cupboard, Shaker, Walnut, 4 Paneled Doors, 3 Inside Shelves, 1800s, 79 x 47 In..............*illus*	600
Cupboard, Step Back, 2 Sections, Pie Shelf, Doors, Drawers, 1850s, 84 x 50 ½ x 20 ¾ In..........	510
Cupboard, Step Back, Arched Glass Paned Doors, Dovetailed Drawers, 1800s, 89 x 46 x 20 In.	270
Cupboard, Step Back, Open Top, Blue Green Paint, 2 Doors, 1800s, 72 x 37 x 21 In.	944
Cupboard, Step Back, Pine, 3 Dovetailed Drawers, Red Paint, c.1850, 79 x 49 x 20 ½ In..........	900
Cupboard, Step Back, Pine, Blind Doors, Drawers, Blue Paint, Cornice, c.1850, 89 x 52 In...*illus*	2040
Cupboard, Step Back, Walnut, Pine, 12 Glass Panels, Interior Shelves, c.1850, 51 x 19 In.......	1080
Cupboard, Step Back, Walnut, Pine, Glass Doors, Drawers, Doors, Ohio, c.1850, 89 In............	2500
Cupboard, Tiger & Bird's-Eye Maple, Hanging, Scrolled Pediment, c.1840, 39 x 31 x 11 In......	176
Cupboard, Tiger Maple, 8 Drawers, Bracket Base, England, 1700s, 72 x 38 x 18 In..................	3510
Cupboard, Wall, Red Painted, Pine, 2 Doors, New England, Early 1800s, 35 x 43 ½ x 9 ½ In...	738
Cupboard, Wall, Red, 2 Interior Drawers, 2 Shelves, c.1810, 36 ¼ In.	2091
Cupboard, Walnut, Carved Pediment, 2 Hinged Doors, 8 Panes, 1800s, 11 x 54 x 36 In.	1062
Cupboard, Welsh, Pine, Top Plate Racks, Cup Hooks, 2 Sections, 1800s, 94 x 102 x 23 In......	600
Cupboard, Wood, Red, 2 Sections, 4 Doors, Turned Feet, 1800s, 67 x 37 x 16 In.	1107
Daybed, G. Nakashima, Upholstered, Black Walnut, Pa., c.1960, 15 ½ x 72 ½ x 30 In..............	4688
Daybed, G. Songia, Rosewood, Tufted Leather, Curved Arms, Italy, c.1960, 16 x 78 x 34 In.......	1875
Daybed, Rattan Ends, Yellow Green, Bun Feet, c.1950, 76 x 30 x 27 In.................................	24
Daybed, Wegner, Oak, Cane Back, Getama, Denmark, c.1975, 29 x 81 x 36 In........................	800
Desk, 2 Pedestals, 4 Drawers, 3 Drawer Frieze, Chinese, c.1910, 31 x 65 x 26 In...................	3125
Desk, Arts & Crafts, Slant Front, Oak, Wa-Man-Co, Waller Mfg., c.1925, 40 x 32 In.............*illus*	252
Desk, Arts & Crafts, Trestle, Rectangular Glass Top Over Wood, 30 x 48 x 29 ½ In.	826
Desk, Bombe, Drop Front, Burl Walnut, 3 Drawers, Fitted Interior, Ball & Claw Feet, 1700s, 41 x 50 In....	1188
Desk, Butler's, Mahogany, Cherry, Inlay, Maryland, c.1700s, 43 x 35 x 22 In......................	1080
Desk, Carved, Foo Dogs, Dragons, Drawers, 2 Doors, Fitted, c.1885, 50 x 30 x 62 In.	1000
Desk, Chippendale, Drop Front, Mahogany, Cock-Beaded Drawers, Bracket Feet, c.1890, 30 x 25 In..	523
Desk, Chippendale, Slant Front, 4 Drawers, c.1770, 42 ½ x 40 In....................................	575
Desk, Chippendale, Slant Front, Walnut, 4 Drawers, Ogee Bracket Feet, 44 x 40 x 23 In.	1875
Desk, Collinson, Hepplewhite, Tiger Maple, Square Tapered Legs, c.1900, 31 x 54 x 27 In.	242
Desk, Danish Modern, G. Petersen, Rosewood, Chrome H Base, 28 x 55 x 26 In.	800
Desk, Drop Front, Mahogany, Block Feet, Brass Hardware & Mounts, c.1800, 43 x 42 x 19 In....	3422
Desk, Drop Front, Molded Edge, Ornate Hinges, Ball & Claw Feet, c.1975, 44 x 33 x 17 In.........	330
Desk, Eastlake, Walnut, Roll Top, Drawers, Brass Pulls, Fitted Interior, 1800s, 45 x 36 In..*illus*	585
Desk, Empire Style, Roll Top, C Roll, Mahogany, Marble Top, Bronze, c.1890, 50 x 64 In...*illus*	4688
Desk, Federal Style, Glazed & Inlaid, Mahogany, 2 Drawers, 63 ½ x 30 x 20 ½ In.	234
Desk, Federal, Mahogany, Tambour, 2 Drawers, Brass, Mass., c.1810, 43 x 37 In.	363
Desk, Federal, Walnut, Slant Front, Eagle Inlay, c.1800, 43 In. ....*illus*	915
Desk, George II Style, Mahogany, Inlay, 4 Drawers, Cabriole Legs, 30 x 58 x 32 In.	188
Desk, George III, Slant Front, Oak, 3 Drawers, c.1770, Miniature, 17 x 12 In........................	563
Desk, Georgian Style, Mahogany, Burl Veneer, 1900s, 31 x 42 ½ x 20 ¾ In............................	400
Desk, H. Magg, Blockboard, Elm Veneer, Black Formica, Germany, 1955, 31 x 39 In..........*illus*	2268
Desk, Hepplewhite Style, Slant Front, Drawers, Fitted Interior, 1900s, Miniature, 16 x 11 In. *illus*	175
Desk, Hepplewhite, Mahogany, 3 Drawers, Bellflower, c.1795, 45 x 37 x 19 In......................	360
Desk, Lady's, Louis XVI Style, Mahogany, Grillwork Doors, Marble Top, 1900s, 54 x 31 x 20 In.	594
Desk, Lady's, Serpentine Drawers, Cabriole Legs, France, c.1900, 42 x 27 In.....................*illus*	339
Desk, Larkin Type, Oak, Beveled Mirror, Bowfront, Lead Glass Door, 71 x 39 x 13 In................	81
Desk, Louis XV Style, Pedestal, Painted, White, 7 Drawers, Brass Handles, 30 x 49 x 27 In.	1062
Desk, Luther Conover, Mahogany, Steel, Lacquered Wood, Drawers, c.1950, 28 x 48 x 24 In......	1625
Desk, Maple, Black, Slant Front, Thumb-Molded Lid, 4 Drawers, 1790s, 42 x 36 x 19 In.	2337
Desk, Napoleon III, Boulle, Ebonized, 2 Drawers, Cabriole Legs, Ormolu, 1900s, 54 x 35 x 19 In.	2250
Desk, Neoclassical, Frieze Drawer, Festoons, Top Shape Feet, 1800s, 30 x 42 x 26 In.	1125
Desk, Oxbow, Slant Front, Mahogany, Drawers, Ball & Claw Feet, c.1780, 44 x 41 x 22 In.	540
Desk, Partners, Campaign Style, Satinwood, 8 Drawers, Bail Handles, 1900s, 27 x 72 In.	3000
Desk, Partners, Leather, Drawers, False Drawers, Door Fronts, England, 1700s, 31 x 67 In... *illus*	1440
Desk, Partners, Mahogany, Leather Inlay, 9 Drawers, Brass Handle, 31 x 72 x 40 In.	345
Desk, Partners, Regency Style, Tooled Leather, Drawers, Curved X-Brace, 31 x 60 In.	1625
Desk, Plantation, American Sheraton, Cherry, Poplar, 2 Sections, 59 x 28 In.....................*illus*	406
Desk, Queen Anne, Drop Front, Cherry, Carved, 4 Drawers, c.1760, 48 x 39 In.	1875

Furniture, Cupboard, Cherry, Step Back,
2 Doors, Glass Panes, Brass Knob, c.1830,
89 x 56 x 20 In.
$1,870

Forsythes' Auctions

Furniture, Cupboard, Corner, Pine, 2 Glass
Pane Doors Over 2 Doors, Blue Paint, c.1850,
85 x 51 In.
$4,500

Garth's Auctioneers & Appraisers

Furniture, Cupboard, Corner, Pine, Grain
Painted, 4 Open Shelves, Door, 1800s,
91 x 44 x 19 In.
$250

Doyle Auctioneers & Appraisers

Furniture, Cupboard, Court, Oak, Gallery
Top, Glass, 2 Drawers, England, Late 1800s,
96 x 45 In.
$336

Garth's Auctioneers & Appraisers

Furniture, Cupboard, French Provincial,
Pine, Panel Doors, 3 Shelves, Canada, c.1790,
76 x 60 In.
$600

Cowan's Auctions

Furniture, Cupboard, Linen, William &
Mary Style, Carved, Oak, Inlay, Drawer, Doors,
1800s, 40 x 43 In.
$527

Jeffrey S. Evans & Associates

Furniture, Cupboard, Pine, Backsplash,
2 Drawers, Open Shelf, 2 Doors, c.1865,
52 ½ x 47 In.
$450

Garth's Auctioneers & Appraisers

Furniture, Cupboard, Shaker, Walnut,
4 Paneled Doors, 3 Inside Shelves, 1800s,
79 x 47 In.
$600

Cowan's Auctions

Furniture, Cupboard, Step Back, Pine,
Blind Doors, Drawers, Blue Paint, Cornice,
c.1850, 89 x 52 In.
$2,040

Garth's Auctioneers & Appraisers

Furniture, Desk, Arts & Crafts, Slant Front, Oak, Wa-Man-Co, Waller Mfg., c.1925, 40 x 32 In.
$252

Garth's Auctioneers & Appraisers

Furniture, Desk, Eastlake, Walnut, Roll Top, Drawers, Brass Pulls, Fitted Interior, 1800s, 45 x 36 In.
$585

Thomaston Place Auction Galleries

Furniture, Desk, Empire Style, Roll Top, C Roll, Mahogany, Marble Top, Bronze, c.1890, 50 x 64 In.
$4,688

Neal Auction Company

Furniture, Desk, Federal, Walnut, Slant Front, Eagle Inlay, c.1800, 43 In.
$915

Nadeau's Auction Gallery

Furniture, Desk, H. Magg, Blockboard, Elm Veneer, Black Formica, Germany, 1955, 31 x 39 In.
$2,268

Quittenbaum Kunstauktionen GmbH

Furniture, Desk, Hepplewhite Style, Slant Front, Drawers, Fitted Interior, 1900s, Miniature, 16 x 11 In.
$175

Garth's Auctioneers & Appraisers

Furniture, Desk, Lady's, Serpentine Drawers, Cabriole Legs, France, c.1900, 42 x 27 In.
$339

Soulis Auctions

Furniture, Desk, Partners, Leather, Drawers, False Drawers, Door Fronts, England, 1700s, 31 x 67 In.
$1,440

Selkirk Auctioneers & Appraisers

Furniture, Desk, Plantation, American Sheraton, Cherry, Poplar, 2 Sections, 59 x 28 In.
$406

Garth's Auctioneers & Appraisers

F

Desk, Roll Top, 2 Doors, Bone Inlay, Leaves, 47 x 20 x 13 ½ In.	250
Desk, Roll Top, C Roll, Oak, 2 Banks Of 3 Drawers, Center Drawer, c.1915, 43 x 61 In. .... *illus*	510
Desk, Roll Top, Mechanical, Satinwood, Drawers, Tapered Legs, c.1880, 42 x 36 x 20 In. .... *illus*	2299
Desk, Roll Top, Oak, Tambour Front, Drawer, Lower Shelves, 1900s, 46 x 29 In.	165
Desk, School, Openwork Metal, Wood, c.1900, Child's, 24 x 33 x 27 In. .... *illus*	65
Desk, Schoolmaster's, Federal, Softwood, Slant Front, Grain Painted, Pa., 39 x 27 In. .... *illus*	165
Desk, Schoolmaster's, Sheraton, Softwood, Lift Lid, 1800s, 47 x 37 x 25 In.	177
Desk, Shaker Style, Cherry, Maple, Side & Front Drawers, Robert Whitley, 38 ½ x 28 In.	675
Desk, Slant Front, Inlay, Mahogany, 3 Drawers, Ball & Claw, Feet, 42 x 34 x 19 In.	545
Desk, Slant Front, Mahogany, Drawers, Bracket Feet, Brass Handle, c.1790, 43 x 38 x 20 In. ... *illus*	523
Desk, Slant Front, Mahogany, Shell Carved Drawer, Compartments, 1800s, 43 x 40 x 22 In. ..... *illus*	1451
Desk, Slant Front, Pine, Painted, Dry Red Surface, Turned Feet, c.1830, 44 x 38 In.	1000
Desk, Slant Front, Tiger Maple, 4 Graduated Drawers, Bracket Base, 39 x 32 x 18 In.	3159
Desk, Spinet, Mahogany, Drawers, Pigeonholes, Turned Legs, Colonial Mfg. Co., c.1950, 32 x 44 x 21 In.	308
Desk, Stickley, Drop Front, Oak, Drawer, Shelf, Marked, 1994, 47 x 27 In. .... *illus*	1150
Desk, Student, Double Wide, Iron Frame, Lift Top, 3 Inkwells, c.1900, 41 x 59 x 23 In. .... *illus*	270
Desk, Svend & Madsen, Teak, 3 Drawers, Tapered Legs, Denmark, c.1965, 29 x 62 x 30 In.	677
Desk, Tabletop, Rosewood, String Inlay, Tooled Leather, 2 Inkwells, 10 x 18 x 5 In.	161
Desk, Tabletop, Writing, Mahogany, Brassbound, 7 x 19 ½ x 9 ¾ In.	150
Desk, Tiger Maple, Slant Front, Drawers, Central Pendant, Late 1700s, 40 x 36 x 18 In.	2758
Desk, Tiger Maple, Slant Front, Pigeonholes, Drawers, Brass Bail Pulls, Bracket Feet, c.1780, 42 x 36 In.	875
Desk, Vargueno, Drop Front, Gilt, Iron Mounts, Taquilon Base, Spain, c.1890, 59 x 47 In. ... *illus*	10625
Desk, Vittorio Dassi, Mahogany, Smoked Glass Top, 4 Drawers, Key, c.1960, 31 x 71 In.	1968
Desk, Walnut, Carved Flowers, Block & Bun Feet, Spain, c.1800s, 31 x 66 x 30 In. .... *illus*	1188
Desk, Walnut, Carving, Inlay, Shelves, Drop Down Doors, Ornate Brackets, c.1890, 56 x 47 In.	2375
Desk, Walnut, Slant Front, Gallery Top, Fitted Interior, Twist Legs, Continental, 1800s, 48 x 50 In. ... *illus*	3600
Desk, William & Mary, Slant Front, Mahogany, Oak, Turned Onion Feet, 1700s, 40 x 36 x 21 In.	389
Desk, Wooton, Walnut, Carved, Doors, Ebonized, Label, c.1874, 69 x 42 In. .... *illus*	6100
Desk, Wooton, Walnut, Doors, Carved, Fitted Interior, Spindle Gallery, 74 x 42 x 31 In.	7260
Desk, Yew, Veneer, Tooled Leather, Drawers, Bail Pulls, Early 1900s, 30 x 50 x 34 In. .... *illus*	1968
Dining Set, E. Saarinen, Table, 6 Chairs, 1 Shown, Fiberglass, Upholstered, Knoll, 1956 .... *illus*	3000
Dresser, Corner, Anglo-Indian, Bamboo, Seagrass, Mirror, Drawers, Shelves, c.1890, 63 In. ... *illus*	1250
Dresser, Duckloe Bros. Inc., 4 Drawers, Cherry, Pullout Top, 31 x 18 x 35 In.	113
Dresser, Empire, Cherry, Maple, 4 Drawers, Turned Stiles, Pa., Miniature, 21 x 17 In. .... *illus*	1770
Dresser, G. Nelson, Walnut, Door, 4 Drawers, Foil Label, 1950, 30 x 56 x 18 In.	1476
Dresser, Marble Top, Inlay, 2 Drawers, Brass Handle, Signed Albert L, Miniature, 11 x 7 x 11 In.	384
Dresser, Mirror Top, 6 Drawers, Steel, Tapered Legs, Casters, c.1950, 71 x 32 x 19 In. .... *illus*	438
Dresser, Mirror, Marble Shelf, 4 Drawers, Carved Harp, Bracket Feet, 39 ½ x 39 x 18 In.	152
Dresser, Neoclassical, Mahogany, Stenciled, 5 Drawers, Mirror, S Supports, 64 x 36 In.	2832
Dresser, North Shore, Pine, 3 Open Shelves, Scalloped Edge, Drawer, 87 x 76 x 18 In.	2400
Dresser, Overhanging Top, Diamond Escutcheons, Turned Pulls, c.1830, 44 x 21 x 42 In.	220
Dresser, Pine, Burl Accents, 5 Drawers, Columns, 1800s, 7 x 32 x 19 In.	92
Dresser, Sheraton, Bird's-Eye Maple, Drawers, Glass Pulls, Turned Feet, c.1820, 64 x 44 In.	2125
Dresser, Welsh, Oak, Breakfront Base, Drawers, Upper Shelves, Doors, 1800s, 78 x 81 In. *illus*	1250
Dry Sink, Copper Lined Top, 2 Doors, Rolling Apron, 1950s, 44 ½ x 42 x 20 In.	216
Dry Sink, Pine, Backsplash, Drawer, Lower Shelf, Shaped Ends, c.1865, 42 ½ x 65 In. .... *illus*	480
Dry Sink, Pine, Nailed Construction, 2 Doors, Miniature, 21 x 27 x 10 ½ In.	161
Dry Sink, Pine, Square Nail Construction, Zinc Lined Well, Doors, Mid 1800s, 37 x 48 x 19 In.	1440
Dry Sink, Poplar, 2-Level Well, Hinged Lid, 2 Doors, Brass Latches, 1800s, 31 x 29 In.	600
Dry Sink, Well, Pine, Poplar, Zinc Liner, Drawer, 2 Doors, c.1875, 36 x 44 x 19 In.	750
Dry Sink, Well, Walnut, 2 Doors, Beveled Corners, Cutout Feet, c.1885, 38 x 48 x 17 In. .... *illus*	420
Dumbwaiter, Hepplewhite Style, Tiered, Curly Maple, 3 Round Dish Tops, Spider Legs, 52 x 19 ½ In.	165
Dumbwaiter, Mahogany, 3 Tiers, 3-Part Lobed Urn Shape, Snake Pad Feet, 40 x 20 In. .... *illus*	113
Easel, Adjustable, French Rococo Revival Style, Mahogany, Gilt, Late 1900s, 88 x 36 x 48 In. ...	649
Easel, Adjustable, Renaissance Revival, Walnut, Cross Bar Shelf, c.1980, 78 x 24 x 28 In. ... *illus*	2125
Easel, Rococo Revival, Gilt, Wood, Carved, 1800s, 77 x 27 x 33 In. .... *illus*	875
Easel, Walnut, Adjustable, Hand Crank Mechanism, Anco, 1900s, 70 x 28 In.	531
Etagere, 3 Tiers, Drawer, Shelves, Spindles, Bell Shape Legs, c.1850, 37 x 19 x 14 In.	322
Etagere, Anglo-Indian, Bamboo, Lacquered, Drawer, Shelves, 2 Tiers, 1900s, 66 x 25 x 16 In.	1375
Etagere, Carved, Dragons, Doors, 3 Drawers, Hardwood, Japan, c.1890, 65 x 32 x 11 In. .... *illus*	1063

Furniture, Desk, Roll Top, C Roll, Oak, 2 Banks Of 3 Drawers, Center Drawer, c.1915, 43 x 61 In.
$510

Garth's Auctioneers & Appraisers

Furniture, Desk, Roll Top, Mechanical, Satinwood, Drawers, Tapered Legs, c.1880, 42 x 36 x 20 In.
$2,299

Fontaine's Auction Gallery

TIP
Mahogany furniture can be cleaned with a sponge dipped in equal parts of warm water and white vinegar. Dry with a soft cloth.

Furniture, Desk, School, Openwork Metal, Wood, c.1900, Child's, 24 x 33 x 27 In.
$65

Copake Auction

Furniture, Desk, Schoolmaster's, Federal, Softwood, Slant Front, Grain Painted, Pa., 39 x 27 In.
$165

Hess Auction Group

Furniture, Desk, Slant Front, Mahogany, Drawers, Bracket Feet, Brass Handle, c.1790, 43 x 38 x 20 In.
$523

Skinner, Inc.

Furniture, Desk, Slant Front, Mahogany, Shell Carved Drawer, Compartments, 1800s, 43 x 40 x 22 In.
$1,451

Skinner, Inc.

Furniture, Desk, Stickley, Drop Front, Oak, Drawer, Shelf, Marked, 1994, 47 x 27 In.
$1,150

Keystone Auctions LLC

Furniture, Desk, Student, Double Wide, Iron Frame, Lift Top, 3 Inkwells, c.1900, 41 x 59 x 23 In.
$270

Garth's Auctioneers & Appraisers

Furniture, Desk, Vargueno, Drop Front, Gilt, Iron Mounts, Taquilon Base, Spain, c.1890, 59 x 47 In.
$10,625

Heritage Auctions

Furniture, Desk, Walnut, Carved Flowers, Block & Bun Feet, Spain, c.1800s, 31 x 66 x 30 In.
$1,188

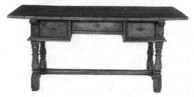

New Orleans Auction Galleries

Furniture, Desk, Walnut, Slant Front, Gallery Top, Fitted Interior, Twist Legs, Continental, 1800s, 48 x 50 In.
$3,600

Eldred's

Furniture, Desk, Wooton, Walnut, Carved, Doors, Ebonized, Label, c.1874, 69 x 42 In.
$6,100

Neal Auction Company

Furniture, Desk, Yew, Veneer, Tooled Leather, Drawers, Bail Pulls, Early 1900s, 30 x 50 x 34 In.
$1,968

Skinner, Inc.

Furniture, Dining Set, E. Saarinen, Table, 6 Chairs, 1 Shown, Fiberglass, Upholstered, Knoll, 1956
$3,000

Wright

Furniture, Dresser, Corner, Anglo-Indian, Bamboo, Seagrass, Mirror, Drawers, Shelves, c.1890, 63 In.
$1,250

New Orleans Auction Galleries

Furniture, Dresser, Empire, Cherry, Maple, 4 Drawers, Turned Stiles, Pa., Miniature, 21 x 17 In.
$1,770

Hess Auction Group

Furniture, Dresser, Mirror Top, 6 Drawers, Steel, Tapered Legs, Casters, c.1950, 71 x 32 x 19 In.
$438

Rago Arts and Auction Center

Furniture, Dresser, Welsh, Oak, Breakfront Base, Drawers, Upper Shelves, Doors, 1800s, 78 x 81 In.
$1,250

New Orleans Auction Galleries

Furniture, Dry Sink, Pine, Backsplash, Drawer, Lower Shelf, Shaped Ends, c.1865, 42½ x 65 In.
$480

Garth's Auctioneers & Appraisers

Furniture, Dry Sink, Well, Walnut, 2 Doors, Beveled Corners, Cutout Feet, c.1885, 38 x 48 x 17 In.
$420

Garth's Auctioneers & Appraisers

> **TIP**
> *Stained marble tabletops can be touched up by using paste wax and steel wool.*

Furniture, Dumbwaiter, Mahogany, 3 Tiers, 3-Part Lobed Urn Shape, Snake Pad Feet, 40 x 20 In.
$113

Soulis Auctions

Furniture, Easel, Adjustable, Renaissance Revival, Walnut, Cross Bar Shelf, c.1980, 78 x 24 x 28 In.
$2,125

New Orleans Auction Galleries

Furniture, Easel, Rococo Revival, Gilt, Wood, Carved, 1800s, 77 x 27 x 33 In.
$875

Susanin's Auctioneers & Appraisers

Furniture, Etagere, Carved, Dragons, Doors, 3 Drawers, Hardwood, Japan, c.1890, 65 x 32 x 11 In.
$1,063

Leslie Hindman Auctioneers

Etagere, Cherry, 3 Mirrors, Single Door, Spindles, Carved, Shelves, c.1900, 16 x 35 x 12 In.......	252
Etagere, Mahogany, Adjustable Book Rest, Tooled Leather, Drawers, 40 x 22 x 18 In..............	496
Etagere, Modern, 3 Tiers, Bird's-Eye Maple, Glass Shelves, 80 x 33¾ x 21 In.................	563
Etagere, Multi Level, Drawer, Carved, Painted, Chinese, 59 x 27½ x 11½ In................	94
Etagere, Regency Style, 2 Shelves, Mahogany, Late 1800s, 31 x 24 x 17¾ In............	188
Etagere, Rosewood, 3 Tiers, Carved, Drawer, 1800s, 24 x 16 x 46½ In..............	531
Etagere, Rosewood, Barley Twist Supports, Drawer, Casters, 54 x 29¾ x 15½ In............	390
Etagere, Walnut, Carved Pull, Drawer, Late 1800s, 33 x 44 In. ....*illus*	50
Etagere, William IV Style, Teak, 3 Tiers, 3 Long Shelves, 52 x 42 x 16½ In.	1188
Footstool, Apron, Cabriole Legs, Upholstered, Yellow Bees, Italy, 1900s, 17 x 21 x 15 In.	303
Footstool, Baroque, Walnut, Curved Legs, Upholstered, Brass Tacks, Early 1800s, 18 x 19 x 17 In..	300
Footstool, Birch, Classical, False Grain Painted, Mid-Atlantic Region, c.1840, 15 x 20 In..........	138
Footstool, Bird, Heart, Rose, White Ground, Nancy Whorf, 17¾ x 21 x 9 In......................*illus*	270
Footstool, Centennial, Carved Walnut, Needlework Seat, 1800s, 19 x 19¾ In................	225
Footstool, Chippendale Style, Mahogany, Upholstered, Ball & Claw Feet, c.1950, 18 x 22 In... *illus*	1250
Footstool, Chippendale Style, Upholstered, Ball & Claw Feet, 19 x 19 x 19 In..............	120
Footstool, Cow Horn, Cowhide Cover, Iron Tacks, Late 1800s, 12 x 17 In. ....*illus*	523
Footstool, Crewel Top, Blue Ground, 4 Turned Legs, 1800s, 8½ x 13½ In......................*illus*	123
Footstool, George II Style, Upholstered, Ball & Claw Feet, 19 x 18 x 23 In.	270
Footstool, Painted, Splayed Arched Bootjack Ends, England, c.1890, 5 x 10 x 5 In............	431
Footstool, Parquetry, Carved, Wood, Painted, 4¾ x 13 In............	13
Frame, Brass, Art Deco, Jeweled, Filigree, 6 x 8 In............	173
Frame, Bronze, Figural, Woman In Gown, Standing, Palm Trees, c.1900, 9¾ x 4 x 8 In..........	198
Frame, Fruitwood, Carved Trees, Reeded Sides, Initials BG, Late 1800s, 10 x 7½ In.	431
Frame, Italian Style, Carved, Scroll & Shell, Early 1900s, 34 x 29 In.	330
Hall Stand, Cast Iron, Mirror, 6 Hooks, Umbrella Pan, 1800s, 77 x 24 x 13 In.	413
Hall Stand, Iron, Mirror, Hooks, Marble, Drawer, Wells, Coalbrookdale, c.1890, 90 x 50 x 20 In....	3540
Hall Stand, Oak, Bevel Mirror, Iron Hooks, Carved, Saber Legs, c.1890, 79 x 33 In. ....*illus*	480
Hall Stand, Oak, Carved, Lift Seat, Mirror, Hooks, Umbrella Holder, c.1915, 78 x 35 In. .....*illus*	330
Hall Stand, Oak, Carved, Mirror, Bronze Hooks, Marble Top, Trays, France, c.1900, 93 x 54 x 15 In.	750
Hall Stand, Rococo Revival, Walnut, Carved, Mirror, 105 x 60 x 16 In............	523
Hall Tree, 4 Tiers, Glass & Marble Shelves, Brass Casement, Outswept Feet, 1900s, 57 x 27 x 10 In.	308
Hall Tree, Iron, Drop Pans, Coat Hooks, Coalbrookdale Style, 82 x 33 x 11 In............	469
Hat Rack, Hanging, Folding, 13 Porcelain Tipped Hooks, 33 x 36 In.	47
Hat Rack, Horse, Dog Heads, Iron, 19 x 13 In............	590
Headboard, Dark Green, Velvet Fabric, Bevilacqua, 80 x 72 In.	475
Headboard, G. Nakashima, Black Walnut, Rosewood, 1969, 34 x 3½ x 90½ In.......................	8750
Headboard, G. Nelson, Thin Edge, Rosewood, Vinyl, Aluminum, Herman Miller, 1956, 116 x 39 In.	5312
Headboard, Rococo Revival, 2 Cherubs, Flowering Urn, Parcel Gilt, c.1900, 66 x 75 In.............	531
Headboard, Upholstered, Custom, Tufted White, Linen, Carved, 72 x 90 In.	142
Highboy, 8 Drawers, Brass Handles, Chippendale Style, Andy May, 1900s, 39 x 19 x 74¾ In......	177
Highboy, Berkey & Gay, 10 Drawers, Acanthus Pediment, Drawers, Ball & Claw Feet, c.1930	372
Highboy, Bonnet Top, Cabriole Legs, Pad Feet, Brass Handle, Drawers, c.1770, 37 x 19 x 78 In....*illus*	1888
Highboy, Chippendale Style, Walnut, Carved, Molded, A.F. Hackman, Repro, c.1960, 82 x 39 x 23 In.	2478
Highboy, Queen Anne Style, Cherry, 3 Side Drawers, Eldred Wheeler, 1900s, 71 x 35 x 19 In.....	1680
Highboy, Queen Anne Style, Tiger Maple, Molded Cornice, Cabriole Legs, 1900s, 58 x 25 x 15 In.	1020
Highboy, Queen Anne, Maple, Fan Carved Drawer, c.1765, 74 x 37¾ In.	3250
Highchair, Slat Back, Rush Seat, Serpentine Slats, Green, Late 1800s, 23 x 41 x 17 In.	510
Highchair, Windsor, Gouged Carved, Saddle Seat, H-Stretcher, c.1780, 35 In....................*illus*	2645
Highchair, Wood, Red, Ball Finials, Turned Arms, Double Stretchers, 1700s, 37 x 21 In............	523
Huntboard, Federal, Mahogany, 3 Drawers, Inlaid Fan Corners, Tapered Legs, c.1815, 41 x 57 x 25 In..	1125
Huntboard, Georgian, Mahogany, Serpentine Top, Tapered Legs, Spade Feet, 35 x 47 x 26 In..	1250
Huntboard, Queen Anne Style, Cherry, 4 Drawers, Lancaster, Pennsylvania, 34 x 56 In..........	450
Hutch, Maple, Glazed Doors, Shelves, 2 Drawers Over 2 Cupboard Doors, 1800s	450
Kas, Cherry, Pine Secondary, Bracket Feet, Interior Shelves, 2 Doors, 1850s, 81 x 50 x 19 In.....	900
Kneeler, Prie-Dieu, Carved Walnut, Cross Splat, Needlework, Paris, c.1870, 36 x 18 x 18 In......	308
Kneeler, Prie-Dieu, Louis XV Style, Walnut, Cross Back Splat, Cabriole Legs, 1800s, 36 x 18 x 22 In..	438
Kneeler, Prie-Dieu, Walnut, Trapezoid Seat, Needlepoint, 1700s, 35 x 18 x 17 In...............*illus*	406
Kneeler, Prie-Dieu, Walnut, Upholstered, Turned Legs, Dolphin Splat, 1800s, 30 In.................	188
Lap Desk, Abalone & Wood Inlay, Inkwell, Compartments, 1800s, 9 x 12 x 6 In.................	219

Furniture, Etagere, Walnut, Carved Pull, Drawer, Late 1800s, 33 x 44 In.
$50

Pook & Pook

Furniture, Footstool, Bird, Heart, Rose, White Ground, Nancy Whorf, 17¾ x 21 x 9 In.
$270

Eldred's

Furniture, Footstool, Chippendale Style, Mahogany, Upholstered, Ball & Claw Feet, c.1950, 18 x 22 In.
$1,250

Brunk Auctions

Furniture, Footstool, Cow Horn, Cowhide Cover, Iron Tacks, Late 1800s, 12 x 17 In.
$523

Crescent City Auction Gallery

Furniture, Footstool, Crewel Top, Blue Ground, 4 Turned Legs, 1800s, 8½ x 13½ In.
$123

Skinner, Inc.

Furniture, Hall Stand, Oak, Bevel Mirror, Iron Hooks, Carved, Saber Legs, c.1890, 79 x 33 In.
$480

Soulis Auctions

Furniture, Hall Stand, Oak, Carved, Lift Seat, Mirror, Hooks, Umbrella Holder, c.1915, 78 x 35 In.
$330

Garth's Auctioneers & Appraisers

Furniture, Highboy, Bonnet Top, Cabriole Legs, Pad Feet, Brass Handle, Drawers, c.1770, 37 x 19 x 78 In.
$1,888

Copake Auction

TIP
Be sure the big furniture you buy is small enough to go through the door into your room.

Furniture, Highchair, Windsor, Gouged Carved, Saddle Seat, H-Stretcher, c.1780, 35 In.
$2,645

Keystone Auctions LLC

Furniture, Kneeler, Prie-Dieu, Walnut, Trapezoid Seat, Needlepoint, 1700s, 35 x 18 x 17 In.
$406

Crescent City Auction Gallery

Furniture, Lowboy, Queen Anne Style, Tiger Maple, Slate Center, Brass, 1900s, 31 x 31 ½ x 20 In.
$1,755

Thomaston Place Auction Galleries

Furniture, Mirror, Brass, Cartouche, Gold, 1900s, 35 x 25 In.
$406

Leslie Hindman Auctioneers

Furniture, Mirror, Cheval, Federal, Mahogany, Inlaid Frame, Arched Saber Legs, 1800s, 76 In.
$246

Cowan's Auctions

Furniture, Mirror, Chippendale, Mahogany, Gilt, Painted Liner, Pine Back, c.1790, 25 x 13 ¼ In.
$143

Forsythes' Auctions

Furniture, Mirror, Fornasetti, Cammei, Lacquered Wood, Glass, Milano, Italy, c.1955, 19 x 9 In.
$7,000

Wright

Furniture, Mirror, Grain Painted, Rosette Cresting, 2 Shallow Drawers, Late 1800s, 33 x 15 In.
$400

Skinner, Inc.

Furniture, Mirror, Louis XV, Giltwood, Carved, Flower Head Accents, 1900s, 55 x 38 ½ In.
$500

Leslie Hindman Auctioneers

Furniture, Mirror, Pier, Louis XVI Style, Giltwood, Carved, Painted Panel, 1800s, 67 x 41 In.
$1,188

Neal Auction Company

Lap Desk, Brass, Calamander, Slant Front Opening, Victorian, 4 x 14 x 9 In.	500
Lap Desk, Pine, Mixed Wood, Reticulated Brass Mounts, Hinged Lids, Inkwells, 1800s, 4 x 13 x 10 In.	319
Lectern, Eagle, Spread Wings, Atop An Orb, Stand, 1700s, 73 ½ x 25 ¾ x 23 In.	3125
Lectern, George III, Ratcheted Top, Tripod Base, Mahogany, c.1950, 29 x 22 x 17 In.	615
Library Steps, Folding, Carved, Mahogany, 4 Steps, Hand Support, 1900s, 59 x 16 x 28 In.	1169
Linen Press, Cherry, Pine, Poplar, 2 Piece, c.1850, 74 ¾ x 50 x 20 In.	1750
Linen Press, Chippendale, Tiger Maple, 2 Doors, 4 Drawers, Pa., c.1800, 77 x 45 In.	5750
Linen Press, Flame Mahogany, 4 Drawer Pulls, Brass Handle, Gillows, Lancaster, 79 x 50 ½ x 25 In.	500
Linen Press, George III Style, Mahogany, Splayed Legs, 2 Parts, 1800s, 78 x 54 x 22 In.	531
Linen Press, George III, Mahogany, Bowfront, 2 Doors, 2 Drawers, 81 x 43 x 21 In.	281
Linen Press, Mahogany, Molded Cornice, 2 Doors, Shelves, 4 Drawers, Brass Pulls, 1800s, 80 x 45 In.	420
Linen Press, Regency, Mahogany, 4 Drawers, Banded, Splayed Legs, Early 1800s, 83 x 50 x 24 In.	1250
Linen Press, White Pine, Applied Molded Cornice, 2 Doors, 8 Drawers, 1800s, 82 x 68 In.	1107
Love Seat, Federal Style, Rounded Back, Pink, 1900s, 73 In.	200
Love Seat, French Style, Walnut, Carved Frame, Columns, Upholstered, 33 x 53 In.	620
Love Seat, Leather, Iron Tack, Removable Cushions, 1900s, 32 x 70 x 34 In.	1200
Love Seat, Leather, Upholstered, Throw Pillows, Bernhardt, 34 x 72 x 32 In.	158
Love Seat, Mahogany, Arched Floral, Mother-Of-Pearl Inlay, c.1900, 35 x 43 x 20 In.	431
Love Seat, Queen Anne Style, Walnut, Upholstered, Lancaster, Pennsylvania, 1900s, 35 x 60 In.	425
Lowboy, Chippendale Style, Mahogany, Cabriole Legs, Ball & Claw Feet, 30 x 35 In.	832
Lowboy, Chippendale Style, Mahogany, Carved, Pierced Brasses, Kindel, 29 x 37 x 19 In.	1416
Lowboy, Queen Anne Style, Maple, 2 Drawers, Brass, Eldred Wheeler, Late 1900s, 27 x 32 x 19 In.	1320
Lowboy, Queen Anne Style, Tiger Maple, Slate Center, Brass, 1900s, 31 x 31 ½ x 20 In. *illus*	1755
Mirror, Applied Glass Jewels, Beads, Silvered, Ebonized, Oval, Italy, 1800s, 29 x 23 In., Pair	1750
Mirror, Arts & Crafts, Hammered Copper, Scalloped Repousse Surround, Early 1900s, 22 In.	248
Mirror, Baroque, Eagle Carved Crest, Harvest Scene, Ogee-Molded Fake Wood, Giltwood, 31 x 25 In.	1250
Mirror, Baroque, Giltwood, Angle Frame, Pierced Scrollwork, Spain, c.1980, 45 x 38 ½ In.	938
Mirror, Baroque, Giltwood, Guilloche Frame, Half-Round Crest, Bellflower, Italy, c.1915, 76 x 44 In.	1625
Mirror, Beveled Glass, Bronze, Bark Frameworks Inc., 1990s, 19 ½ x 14 In.	1000
Mirror, Black Painted, Wood Frame, 1900s, 64 ½ x 44 In.	531
Mirror, Black, Bronze Border, Sherle Wagner, 1900s, 27 x 21 ½ In.	228
Mirror, Brass, Cartouche, Gold, 1900s, 35 x 25 In. *illus*	406
Mirror, Brass, Octagonal, Baroque Style, Dutch, 1900s, 60 x 49 ½ In.	500
Mirror, Bronze, Beast & Grapevine, Circular, Flowerheads, 5 ½ In.	938
Mirror, Cartouche, Giltwood, Carved, Continental, 1800s, 69 x 34 ¼ In.	1815
Mirror, Carved Frame, Figural Bearded Man, Arms Raised, Continental, c.1975, 34 x 26 In.	360
Mirror, Cast Iron Frame, Etched, Flowers Finial, 34 x 23 In.	35
Mirror, Cast Resin, Gilt, Double Dolphin Shape, Convex, Carver's Guild, 40 x 23 In.	945
Mirror, Cheval, Carved, Flowers & Leaves, Beveled, Legs, c.1925, 70 ½ x 30 In.	330
Mirror, Cheval, Federal, Mahogany, Inlaid Frame, Arched Saber Legs, 1800s, 76 In. *illus*	246
Mirror, Chinese Chippendale, Giltwood, Flowers, England, 1800s, 48 x 54 In.	1521
Mirror, Chippendale, Backboard & Glass, Mahogany, Veneer, 1700s, 23 x 13 ½ In.	106
Mirror, Chippendale, Mahogany, Gilt, Painted Liner, Pine Back, c.1790, 25 x 13 ¼ In. *illus*	143
Mirror, Chippendale, Mahogany, Gilt, Phoenix Bird, Leaf & Fruit Fillets, 40 x 19 In.	1560
Mirror, Classical Style, Giltwood, Gesso, Surmounted Shell, Carved Laurels, c.1950, 40 x 31 In.	406
Mirror, Crown, Shells, Putti, Pink, Teal, Porcelain, c.1850, 30 x 20 In.	2160
Mirror, Eastlake Style, Wood Inlay, Stenciled Label, Meeks, 65 ½ x 24 In.	360
Mirror, Empire Style, Parcel Gilt, Reverse Painted, Late 1800s, 37 x 55 In.	500
Mirror, Federal Style, Bull's-Eye, Eagle Crest, Giltwood, Oval, 23 x 35 x 4 In.	527
Mirror, Federal, Giltwood, Reverse Painted, Cove Molded Top, Dart Base Molding, 43 x 24 In.	840
Mirror, Federal, Mahogany, Parcel Gilt, Phoenix Crest, Flowers & Fruits, 1800s, 50 x 30 In.	1375
Mirror, Federal, Reverse Painted Fruit, Gold & Black Border, c.1840, 20 ½ x 11 In.	198
Mirror, Federal, Woman At Piano Forte, Flowers, Painted, Brass Floral Rosettes, 40 x 19 In.	248
Mirror, Fornasetti, Cammei, Lacquered Wood, Glass, Milano, Italy, c.1955, 19 x 9 In. *illus*	7000
Mirror, Fornasetti, Lacquered Wood, Glass, Circle Of 9 Convex Mirrors, 1950, 11 In.	1534
Mirror, G. Nakashima, Walnut, Widdicomb, 42 ½ x 52 x 4 ½ In.	2337
Mirror, George II Style, Giltwood, Carved, Floral, Phoenix Crest, c.1900, 51 x 26 x 7 In.	400
Mirror, George III Style, Carved, Giltwood, Rocaille Frame, Chinoiserie Panels, 62 x 32 In.	3625
Mirror, Georgian Style, Carved & Painted, Shell Pediment, 1900s, 53 ½ x 31 ½ In.	1000
Mirror, Gesso Giltwood Frame, Carved, Signed, 1954, 23 x 20 In.	35

Furniture, Mirror, Pier, Rococo Revival, Giltwood, Lunette Top, Pierced Scrollwork, 1850s, 86 x 37 In.
$1,125

New Orleans Auction Galleries

Furniture, Mirror, Regency Style, Giltwood, Bronze, Pierced Scrollwork, France, c.1880, 65 x 32 In.
$1,250

New Orleans Auction Galleries

Furniture, Mirror, Reverse Painted, Giltwood, Flowers, Continental, 1900s, 19 ½ x 15 In.
$120

Brunk Auctions

Furniture, Pedestal, Bugatti, Walnut, Copper, 4 Columns, Portrait, c.1900, 58 x 18 In.
$16,250

Rago Arts and Auction Center

Furniture, Pedestal, Marble, Walnut, Bevel Edge Top, Octagonal Base, Late 1800s, 28½ x 15 In.
$252

Garth's Auctioneers & Appraisers

Furniture, Pedestal, Rosewood, Carved, Marble Top, Fretwork, Barley Twist, c.1850, 33 x 16 In.
$1,250

Neal Auction Company

Mirror, Giltwood Frame, Gesso, Oval, Bronze Border, Laurel Leaf, 31 In.	260
Mirror, Giltwood, 2 Dolphins, Convex, Carver's Guild, 1900s, 40 x 23 In.	938
Mirror, Giltwood, Carved, Floral & Basket, France, 63 x 36 In.	313
Mirror, Giltwood, Carved, Monumental, Fin De Siecle, 1800s, 79 x 40 x 2½ In.	1000
Mirror, Giltwood, Carved, Walnut, Crest, Urn, Flowers, France, 53½ x 23½ In.	123
Mirror, Giltwood, Convex, Ebonized Eagle Crest, Carved Acanthus, c.1800, 55 x 29 In.	1250
Mirror, Giltwood, Gesso, Wood, Eagle Finial, c.1900, 76 x 38 In.	259
Mirror, Giltwood, Oval, Lovebirds Carrying Quiver Arrows & Torch, Laurel Sprays, 1800s, 54 x 38 In.	1500
Mirror, Giltwood, Reeded, Frame, Rectangular, c.1950, 46½ x 30½ In.	185
Mirror, Girandole, Carved, Eagle, Filigree, Pendent Crest, Round Frame, 36 x 24 x 4 In.	363
Mirror, Grain Painted, Rosette Cresting, 2 Shallow Drawers, Late 1800s, 33 x 15 In. .....*illus*	400
Mirror, Grain Painted, Split Baluster Frame, Tiger Maple, Rosette Block, 1800s, 24 x 12 In.	308
Mirror, Half Pilasters, Corner Blocks, Empire Gold Leaf, Mid 1800s, 26½ x 18½ In.	60
Mirror, Hepplewhite, Mahogany, George III, 3 Drawers, 22 x 17 In.	250
Mirror, Horizontal Beveled Plate, Leaf Frame, Victorian Style, 1900s, 39 x 50 In.	281
Mirror, La Barge Style, Black Glass Frame, Floral, 41 x 51 In.	125
Mirror, La Barge, Giltwood, Carved, Glass, Plumes, 50½ x 63 In.	400
Mirror, La Barge, Italian Style, Giltwood, Carved, Leaves, 1900s, 61 x 41 In.	424
Mirror, Louis XIV, Gilt Metal Repousse, False Tortoiseshell, Mask, Acanthus, Beveled, 45 x 28 In.	381
Mirror, Louis XV, Giltwood, Carved, Flower Head Accents, 1900s, 55 x 38½ In. ....*illus*	500
Mirror, Louis XVI Style, Frame, Giltwood, Early 1900s, 55 x 45½ In.	1063
Mirror, Louis XVI Style, Giltwood Frame, Egg & Dart Border, Floral Garland, 35 x 30 In.	188
Mirror, Louis XVI Style, Giltwood, Palmette Crest, Urn Finials, Acanthus Mount, 68 x 43 In.	813
Mirror, Mahogany, Inlay, Prince Of Wales, Mid 1900s, 49½ x 26 In.	177
Mirror, Mahogany, Marble Shelf, Victorian, 26½ x 10 x 82 In.	136
Mirror, Make Do, Rectangular, Multicolor, Crest, Giltwood Molding, c.1910, 14 x 7 In.	2460
Mirror, Metal, Giltwood, Glass, Signed, La Barge, Chinoiserie, 1900s, 42½ x 32½ In.	185
Mirror, Murano Glass, Faceted, Ribbons, Flowers, Beads, Etched, c.1900, 57 x 33 In.	1020
Mirror, Neoclassical Style, Carved, Wood Frame, Flower & Vase Finial, 55 x 33 In.	677
Mirror, Oak, Carved, Seashell Crest, Wolf Heads, Cattails & Reeds, 49 x 26 x 5½ In.	424
Mirror, Painted, Blue & Green, Floral, Glass, Venetian Style 1900s, 38¼ x 18 In.	250
Mirror, Painted, Leaves, Molded Frame, Contemporary, 1900s, 44½ x 29½ In.	125
Mirror, Parzinger, Enameled Metal, 53 x 53 In.	369
Mirror, Pier, Carved, Multicolor, Giltwood, Leaves & Urn, 49½ x 32 In.	438
Mirror, Pier, Chippendale, Giltwood, Walnut, Carved, Bird Finial, Flowers, Leaves, 53 x 26 In.	4200
Mirror, Pier, Federal, Brass, Mahogany, 1815-20, 38 x 19½ In.	125
Mirror, Pier, Giltwood, Depicting Biblical Scene, Plate, Paris, 1800s, 67 x 31 x 1¾ In.	750
Mirror, Pier, Louis XV Style, Pastoral Scene, Parcel Gilt, Carved, 1700s, 59 x 40 In.	1063
Mirror, Pier, Louis XVI Style, Giltwood, Carved, Painted Panel, 1800s, 67 x 41 In. ....*illus*	1188
Mirror, Pier, Rococo Revival, Giltwood, Lunette Top, Pierced Scrollwork, 1850s, 86 x 37 In...*illus*	1125
Mirror, Plateau, Beveled Edge, Silver Plated Border, 1950s, 10 In.	30
Mirror, Queen Anne, Mahogany, Arched & Shell Carved Crest, Gilt, c.1750, 25 x 11 In.	413
Mirror, Queen Anne, Pine, Rectangular, Molded Frame, Scroll Crest, 1700s, 19 x 11 In.	3444
Mirror, Regency Style, Crest Rail, Giltwood, Flowers, Scrolls, Carved Frame, 1900s, 62 In.	875
Mirror, Regency Style, Giltwood, Bronze, Pierced Scrollwork, France, c.1880, 65 x 32 In. ..*illus*	1250
Mirror, Regency Style, Rectangular Wood Frame, Giltwood, c.1940, 34 x 39 In.	372
Mirror, Regency, Giltwood, Bronze, Carved Acanthus Leaves, Shells, Flower Heads, 40 x 21 In.	1125
Mirror, Renaissance Revival, Flowers, Glass, c.1870, 22 x 21 In.	91
Mirror, Reverse Painted, Giltwood, Flowers, Continental, 1900s, 19½ x 15 In. ....*illus*	120
Mirror, Rococo Revival, Carved, Painted, Rocaille Surround, Oval Plate, 1800s, 41 x 35 In.	250
Mirror, Shaving, Mixed Wood, Scalloped Post, Geometric Inlay, c.1900, 13 x 15¾ In.	120
Mirror, Shaving, Oval, Drawer, Mahogany, Adjustable Height, 62 In.	330
Mirror, Shaving, Walnut, Inlay, Drop Down Magnifying Lens, Bone Finials, 1800s, 25 x 10 In.	263
Mirror, Silver Frame, Scalloped, Hammered, Wiener Werkstatte, Vienna, 1903-32, 16 x 12 In.	2214
Mirror, Split Baluster, Woman, White Dress, Red Drapery, England, c.1830, 30 x 14 In.	185
Mirror, Starburst, Silver, Wood, Convex, Midcentury, 58 In.	875
Mirror, Table, Beveled, Brass Frame, Scrolling Branches, Chicken & Bird, 15 x 12 x 6 In.	212
Mirror, Tortoiseshell, Ripple Moldings, Continental, Ebonized, 1800s, 34 x 40 In.	1063
Mirror, Urn & Ribbon Top, Giltwood, Continental, 1800s, 58 x 24 In.	2520
Mirror, Vanity, Cloisonne, Enameled & Jade Inlaid Silver, Chinese, c.1910, 10¼ x 5¼ x ¾ In..	2500

F

Mirror, Vanity, Gilt Bronze, Footed, Ribbon Finial, Lapis Lazuli, Pietra Dura, 16 x 12 x 8 In....	1500
Mirror, Venetian Style, Oval Center, Octagonal Rim, Sequins, c.1950, 33 x 28 ½ In................	475
Mirror, Walnut & Mahogany, Molded Frame, c.1870, 40 x 26 In................	120
Mirror, Walnut Frame, Carved, Decorated Crest, Gilt Feather, 1800s, 46 x 29 In........	300
Mirror, Walnut, Veneer, Carved, Giltwood Leaf, Crest, c.1740, 55 x 19 In.........	1440
Mirror, Walnut, Veneer, Sarcophagus Crest Shape, Pine Box, Late 1700s, 16 x 10 In....	187
Ottoman, Knoll, Grasshopper, Walnut, Upholstered, Signed, 1948, 16 x 17 x 23 In..............	937
Ottoman, Moller, Teak, Cord Cushion, Oval Tapered Legs, Marked, Denmark, 1900s, 18 x 19 x 14 In..	338
Overmantel Mirror, see Architectural category.	
Pedestal, Black Marble, Non Tapered Tuscan Round Column, 14 x 14 x 37 In.	330
Pedestal, Bugatti, Walnut, Copper, 4 Columns, Portrait, c.1900, 58 x 18 In..................*illus*	16250
Pedestal, Carved, Cherry, Claw Foot, Gadroon Edge, Apron, Pendant Finials, 26 In.	908
Pedestal, Circular Top, Gilt, Mask Form Mounts, Empire Style, 1900s, 31 ¾ In.	406
Pedestal, Column, Green Marble, Spiral, Caesar Scheggi Scultori Firenze, Late 1800s, 44 In....	360
Pedestal, Ebonized, Wood & Ceramic, Square Top, Tapering Leaves, 1800s, 44 ½ In.........	200
Pedestal, Figural, Seated Winged Lion, Mahogany, 1900s, 46 ½ In.	1375
Pedestal, Fruitwood, Gilt, Leafy Brackets, Panel Side, Continental, 31 x 25 x 24 In.	688
Pedestal, George III Style, Mahogany, Tripod Feet, Carved, 43 x 11 In.	125
Pedestal, Louis XIII Style, Twist Supports, Shelf, Square Base, Disc Feet, 1800s, 69 x 16 x 16 In.	406
Pedestal, Louis XV Style, Vernis Martin, Gilt Bronze, Scenic, France, c.1900, 43 x 18 x 18 In....	938
Pedestal, Louis XVI Style, Walnut, Carved, Circular Top, 3 Cabriole Legs, Late 1800s, 43 x 16 In.....	375
Pedestal, Marble, Bronze Mounts, Rotating Square Top, Molded Square Base, 43 x 11 In.........	293
Pedestal, Marble, Walnut, Bevel Edge Top, Octagonal Base, Late 1800s, 28 ½ x 15 In. ......*illus*	252
Pedestal, Onyx, Rectangular, Swirling, Red & Rusty Orange, Brazil, 30 x 12 x 12 In.	1000
Pedestal, P. Evans, Cityscape, Chrome Plated Steel, Brass, Signed, 48 x 15 x 15 In...............	1968
Pedestal, Rope Twist Column, Gray Marble, 15 x 15 x 41 In.	330
Pedestal, Rosewood, Carved, Marble Top, Fretwork, Barley Twist, c.1850, 33 x 16 In........*illus*	1250
Pedestal, Stand, Circular Top & Base, Carved Column, Alabaster, Late 1800s, 27 In.	108
Pedestal, Teak, Hand Carved, Inset Marble, Hexagonal Top, Chinese, 1800s, 36 x 18 In.	465
Pie Safe, Cherry, 2 Drawers Over 2 Doors, Punched Tin Panels, Stars, c.1885, 51 x 40 In..*illus*	570
Pie Safe, Cherry, Red & Black, Cathedral Tin Panels, 2 Doors, 1800s, 52 x 41 In.............*illus*	938
Pie Safe, Hanging, Black Paint, Pegs, Punched Tin Panels, Geometrics, Pinwheels, 34 x 30 In..	600
Pie Safe, Maple, Doors, Wrought Iron Base, Punched Tin Panels, Compass Stars, c.1850, 62 x 37 In.	450
Pie Safe, Poplar, Pine, 3 Shelf Interior, Panels, Hearts, Star, 1800s, 46 x 37 x 17 In..................	540
Pie Safe, Walnut, 2 Drawers, 2 Doors, Punched Tin Panels, Wythe Co., c.1850, 53 x 52 In. *illus*	4388
Pie Safe, Walnut, Drawers, Doors, Punched Tin Panels, Diamond Design, c.1850, 51 x 48 In...	1140
Planter, Louis XV Style, Gilt Cane, Demilune, Carved, Sabot Feet, 1900s, 35 x 31 x 13 In...*illus*	338
Rack, Baking, 3 Shelves, Iron & Brass, 84 x 50 In.	125
Rack, Baking, 4 Tiers, Oak, Mortise & Peg Frame, Spindle Shelves, 52 x 42 x 12 In.	236
Rack, Baking, Footed, 2-Tone Steel, Arrows, 2 Doors, c.1900, 84 x 50 ½ x 14 In.........	188
Rack, Baking, Iron & Brass, 3 Levels, Contemporary, c.1900, 94 x 24 In.	138
Rack, Baking, Old Yellow Paint, 3 Shelves, 1800s, 72 x 13 ¾ x 26 ½ In.....................*illus*	132
Rack, Baking, Victoria Style, Iron & Brass, D-Shape Shelves, Tubular Legs, 86 x 60 x 18 In.	625
Rack, Drying, 4 Sections, Caster Feet, Black Paint, c.1900, 58 x 28 In.................	138
Rack, Iron, 5 Hooks, Wall, Scrollwork Back, 24 x 17 ½ In.................	148
Rack, Magazine, Oak, Townshend Furniture, c.1920, 40 ½ x 36 In.................	122
Rack, Magazine, Stick & Ball, Turnings, c.1915, 52 ½ x 23 In.................	114
Rack, Plate, Hanging, Georgian Style, Pine, 3 Shelves, c.1980, 38 x 47 x 6 In. ....*illus*	283
Rack, Wall, 3 Brass Hooks, Wood, c.1900, 26 In.................	71
Recamier, Directoire Style, Outscrolled Arm, Painted, Cushion, 32 x 45 In.	156
Recamier, William IV, Floral, Carved & Brass Inlay, Mahogany Veneer, 37 x 76 x 25 In...........	154
Rocker, Cane Seat, Tiger Maple, Rattan Back, 1800s, 39 x 19 In......................*illus*	118
Rocker, Carved, Man Of The North Wind, C-Scroll Splat, Late 1800s, 33 x 25 x 26 In.	339
Rocker, Cushion, Arts & Crafts Period, 37 x 22 In.	83
Rocker, Jugendstil Shape, Geometric Top Rail, Backrest, Round Bentwood Stile, Vienna, c.1900, 34 In.	800
Rocker, Kem Weber, Art Deco, Chrome Plated Steel, Karl Springer, 35 x 25 x 30 In.	956
Rocker, L. & J.G. Stickley, Oak, Drop Arm, Ladder Back, 5 Slats, 40 x 32 x 36 ¾ In.................	1210
Rocker, Ladder Back, Painted, Wood, Woven Birch Seat, Birds, Virginia, 39 In.	94
Rocker, Ladder Back, Shaker, No. 3, Youth, Rush Seat, Stamped Back, 33 x 19 x 15 In.	143
Rocker, Ladder Back, White Oak, 3-Slat Back, Splint Seat, Shenandoah Co., c.1850, 37 In.	82

Furniture, Pie Safe, Cherry, 2 Drawers Over 2 Doors, Punched Tin Panels, Stars, c.1885, 51 x 40 In.
$570

Garth's Auctioneers & Appraisers

Furniture, Pie Safe, Cherry, Red & Black, Cathedral Tin Panels, 2 Doors, 1800s, 52 x 41 In.
$938

Pook & Pook

Furniture, Pie Safe, Walnut, 2 Drawers, 2 Doors, Punched Tin Panels, Wythe Co., c.1850, 53 x 52 In.
$4,388

Jeffrey S. Evans & Associates

F

Furniture, Planter, Louis XV Style, Gilt Cane, Demilune, Carved, Sabot Feet, 1900s, 35 x 31 x 13 In.
$338

Skinner, Inc.

Furniture, Rack, Baking, Old Yellow Paint, 3 Shelves, 1800s, 72 x 13¾ x 26½ In.
$132

Forsythes' Auctions

Furniture, Rack, Plate, Hanging, Georgian Style, Pine, 3 Shelves, c.1980, 38 x 47 x 6 In.
$283

Leland Little Auctions

Rocker, Pine, Painted, Scroll Splat, Needlepoint Seat, Arms, 1800s	263
Rocker, Shaker, Ladder Back, Maple, 5-Splat Back, Acorn Finials, Leather Seat, Arms, 43 In...*illus*	900
Rocker, Shaker, Shawl Back, Maple, Rush Seat, Mushroom Arm Caps, c.1875, 37½ In.	450
Rocker, Shaker, Shawl Back, No. 7, Woven Tape Seat, Arms, 40 x 31 In....*illus*	104
Rocker, Stickley & Brandt Co., Slat Back, Fabric Seat, Armrests, 32½ x 27 x 29 In.	129
Rocker, W.R. Winfield Style, Leather, Tubular Brass Frame, Late 1800s, 37 x 27 x 39 In.	188
Rocker, Walker Weed, Walnut, V Back, Signed, New Hampshire, c.1959, 29 x 17 x 27 In.	875
Rocker, Wicker, Starburst Back, Woven Cane Seat, Roll Arms, Victorian, 25 x 36 In.	84
Rocker, Windsor, Arrow Back, Yellow Paint, Arms, 43 In.	185
Room Divider, 3-Panel, Hinged, Wood, 9 Barley Twist Turned Spindles, 90 In.	121
Screens are also listed in the Architectural and Fireplace categories.	
Screen, 2-Panel, Ebonized Mahogany, Carved, Chinoiserie Wallpaper, c.1890, 69 x 61 In..*illus*	113
Screen, 3-Panel Wood, Book Spines, Painted Tiles, 61 x 41 In.	224
Screen, 3-Panel, Embossed Leather, Aesthetic Revival, Italian, Mid 1800s, 72 x 20 In.	908
Screen, 3-Panel, Georg Jensen, Wood, Persian Panorama, c.1950, 69 x 64 In.	1107
Screen, 3-Panel, Leaf Scrollwork, Fanned Caning, Carved, Oak, Late 1800s, 72 x 72 In.	293
Screen, 3-Panel, Louis XV Style, Gilt, Bevel Glass Top, Silk Panels, 68 x 61 In.	2520
Screen, 3-Panel, Louis XV Style, Gilt, Rocaille & Scrolls, Upholstered Panel, c.1900, 75 In.	375
Screen, 3-Panel, Mahogany, Rattan & Mirror, 1900s, 89 x 66½ In. ...*illus*	375
Screen, 3-Panel, Metal, Composition, Gilt Relief, Italy, Contemporary, 72 x 50 In.	224
Screen, 3-Panel, Mirror Inset, Painted, Bird, Flowering Branches, 1900s, 66 x 56 In.	250
Screen, 3-Panel, Mirrors, Rococo & Classical Style, 1900s, 70¾ x 59 In.	211
Screen, 3-Panel, Painted Leather, Classical Scenes, Fruit, Flowers, Brass Nailhead Trim, 70 In.	750
Screen, 3-Panel, Rockwell Carey, Oil On Wood, 3 Leaping Deer, Trees, c.1930, 70¾ In.	4000
Screen, 3-Panel, William H. Wheelwright, Oak, Fox Hunt Scene, Signed, 1700s, 60 x 54 In..*illus*	4063
Screen, 4-Panel, Arts & Crafts, 5 White Cranes Scene, Moon, Silk, 1900s, 36 x 70 In.	378
Screen, 4-Panel, Carved, Gold Leaf, Peonies, Morning Glories, Chinese, 72 x 66 In.	310
Screen, 4-Panel, Carved, Pierced Greek Key Upper Panels, Chinese, c.1900, 92 x 81 In.......*illus*	113
Screen, 4-Panel, Contemporary, Limed Oak, Square Cutout Grid, 79 x 72 In.	250
Screen, 4-Panel, Coromandel, Lacquer, Gilt Floating, Landscape Vignettes, 1900s, 72 x 64 In.	250
Screen, 4-Panel, Dressing, Mahogany, Gold Silk Panels, Griffin Heads, Claw Feet, 70 In.	1089
Screen, 4-Panel, Folding, Painted Leather, Leafy Cartouche, Brass Trim, 72 x 60 In.	1000
Screen, 4-Panel, Heron & Fauna, Continental, 1900s, 72 x 113 In.	313
Screen, 4-Panel, Lacquer, Animals In A Landscape, Chinese, Late 1800s, 67½ x 66 In.	188
Screen, 4-Panel, Oil On Canvas, Village Scene, River, Floral, Late 1900s, 73 x 78 In.........*illus*	500
Screen, 4-Panel, Silk, Peacocks, Rocks & Flowers, Japan, 1900s, 59½ x 73 In.	469
Screen, 4-Panel, Tapestry, Leather, Nailheads, France, c.1900, 75¾ x 92 In.	212
Screen, 6-Panel, Coromandel, Lacquer, Multicolor, Court Figures, 1800s, 71½ x 94½ In.	688
Screen, 6-Panel, Jacobean, Oak, Carved, Female Heads, Leafy Panels, Iron Hinges, 79 x 90 In..	1298
Screen, 6-Panel, Louis XVI Style, Painted, Acanthus Borders, 1800s, 96 x 162 In.	4125
Screen, 6-Panel, Multicolor, Exotic Birds, Flowering Trees, Chinese, 1900s, 84 x 120 In.	1625
Screen, 6-Panel, Peacock, Acrylic, Gold Leaf, Silk Fabric, Wayne E. Smyth, 1900s, 81 x 114 In.	1500
Screen, Bamboo Forest, Black Lacquer, Silver Leaf, Brocade Border, Japan, 1800s, 38 x 68 In.	293
Screen, Wood, Decoupage, Flower Basket, 1900s, 24 x 24 In.	281
Secretary, 3 Drawers, Fitted Interior, Keys, Biedermeier, 66½ x 43 x 22½ In.	1600
Secretary, Biedermeier Style, Drawers, Cubbyholes, Mellow Color, c.1900, 65½ In.	199
Secretary, Burl Ash, Ebonized, Drop Front, Columns, 1800s, 55 x 39 x 20 In.	875
Secretary, Burl Veneer, Slant Front, Cabinet, 2 Doors, 83 x 36½ x 19 In.	250
Secretary, Burl Walnut, Granite Top, England, Early 1800s, 39 x 51 x 23½ In.	525
Secretary, Charles X, Drop Front, Walnut, Fitted Interior, 38½ x 17 x 57½ In.	277
Secretary, Chippendale, Mahogany, Key Cornice, Glazed Doors, c.1770, 88¾ x 43 In.	4500
Secretary, Drop Front, 3 Drawers, Granite Top, France, 55 x 37 In.	458
Secretary, Drop Front, Mahogany, 5 Drawers, Inlaid Writing Surface, 63 x 38 x 22 In.	488
Secretary, Drop Front, Maple, Fitted Interior, Glazed Doors, Drawers, Inverted Pawn Foot, 1800s..	312
Secretary, Federal Style, Mahogany, Inlay, Early 1900s, 79 x 36 In.	388
Secretary, Fruitwood, Mahogany, Inlay, Drawers, Fitted Interior, London, c.1904, 61 x 40 x 16 In..	4613
Secretary, George III, Mahogany, Top Drawer Fitted For Writing, c.1790, 89 x 40 x 21 In.	1000
Secretary, Georgian Style, Flip Top, Burl Veneer, Tambour Doors, 48 x 39 x 22 In.	780
Secretary, Georgian Style, Mahogany, Drawers, Bracket Feet, 1800s, 90 x 53 x 22 In.	861
Secretary, Gothic Revival, Mahogany, Glass Pane Doors, Black Marble, c.1950, 92 x 49 In.	908

F

Furniture, Rocker, Cane Seat, Tiger Maple, Rattan Back, 1800s, 39 x 19 In.
$118

Copake Auction

Furniture, Rocker, Shaker, Ladder Back, Maple, 5-Splat Back, Acorn Finials, Leather Seat, Arms, 43 In.
$900

Cowan's Auctions

Furniture, Rocker, Shaker, Shawl Back, No. 7, Woven Tape Seat, Arms, 40 x 31 In.
$104

Bunch Auctions

Furniture, Screen, 2-Panel, Ebonized Mahogany, Carved, Chinoiserie Wallpaper, c.1890, 69 x 61 In.
$113

Neal Auction Company

Furniture, Screen, 3-Panel, Mahogany, Rattan & Mirror, 1900s, 89 x 66½ In.
$375

Leslie Hindman Auctioneers

Furniture, Screen, 3-Panel, William H. Wheelwright, Oak, Fox Hunt Scene, Signed, 1700s, 60 x 54 In.
$4,063

Rago Arts and Auction Center

Furniture, Screen, 4-Panel, Carved, Pierced Greek Key Upper Panels, Chinese, c.1900, 92 x 81 In.
$113

Selkirk Auctioneers & Appraisers

Furniture, Screen, 4-Panel, Oil On Canvas, Village Scene, River, Floral, Late 1900s, 73 x 78 In.
$500

New Orleans Auction Galleries

Furniture, Secretary, Slant Front, Blue Paint, 2 Upper Doors, c.1810, 66 x 28 x 23 In.
$3,483

Skinner, Inc.

F

Furniture, Server, Majorelle, Rosewood, Doors, Drawers, Mother-Of-Pearl Inlay, 1920, 53 x 49 x 17 In.
$938

Kamelot Auctions

Furniture, Settee, Black Stain, Double Back Splats, Carved, Lift Top Seat, 1800s, 48 x 37 In.
$125

Eldred's

Furniture, Settee, Wing, Splayed Legs, Rolled Arms, Italy, c.1950, 38 x 55 In.
$750

Kamelot Auctions

Secretary, Hanging, Oak, Paneled Door, Fitted Interior, 4 Drawers, 1800s, 23 x 22 x 15 In.	307
Secretary, Hekman, Mahogany, Pediment Top, Glass Doors, Inlay, Late 1900s, 88 x 38 x 19 In.	336
Secretary, Louis Philippe Style, Walnut, Inset Leather, Maple, Plinth Base, c.1860, 35 x 45 x 23 In.	615
Secretary, Louis Philippe, Drop Front, Cherry, Carved, Drawers, Bun Feet, 1800s, 58 x 38 In.	431
Secretary, Louis XV Style, Mahogany, Carved, Leather, Cabriole Legs, Early 1900s, 41 x 31 In.	369
Secretary, Louis XV Style, Mahogany, Marquetry, Ormolu, Drawers, Cabriole Legs, 1900s, 34 x 28 In.	338
Secretary, Mahogany, Doors, 8 Drawers, Bracket Feet, c.1800, 82 x 45 x 23 In.	984
Secretary, Mahogany, Drawer, Reeded Legs, Mass., Early 1800s, 46 x 34 x 17 In.	338
Secretary, Mahogany, Turned Finials, 3 Glass Shelves, 4 Drawers Chest, 88 x 42 x 22 In.	1121
Secretary, Mahogany, Walnut, Bracket Feet, Mirrored, George III, c.1780, 82 ½ x 30 x 21 In.	1125
Secretary, Multicolor, Ball Finials, Arched Doors, Bun Feet, Continental, 1800s, 96 x 49 x 23 In.	5000
Secretary, Queen Anne Style, Chinoiserie, Arched Crest, Mirror Doors, Compartments, 86 x 36 In.	4688
Secretary, Queen Anne, Multicolor, 2 Paneled Doors, Squat Bun Feet, 1900s, 92 x 45 x 21 In.	6875
Secretary, Renaissance Revival, Desk, Walnut, 2 Glass Pane Doors, 1800s, 84 x 44 x 20 In.	338
Secretary, Roll Top, Walnut, Victorian, Glass Doors, 82 x 36 In.	275
Secretary, Sheraton, 8-Pane Bookcase, 2 Dovetailed Drawers, 1850, 74 x 40 x 22 In.	1625
Secretary, Sheraton, Mahogany, Glazed Doors, Drawers, Hinged Top, c.1810, 77 In.	270
Secretary, Slant Front, Blue Paint, 2 Upper Doors, c.1810, 66 x 28 x 23 In. .... *illus*	3483
Secretary, Walnut, Panel Doors, Cubbyholes, Plinth Base, 1800s, 85 x 49 x 16 In.	500
Semainier, Mahogany, Maple, 7 Drawers, Brass Handles, Contemporary, 53 x 23 x 17 In.	92
Server, Burl, Inlay, Mirror, Gilt Bronze, Marble, Drawers, Doors, Shelves, France, 63 x 50 In.	500
Server, Flip Top, Wheels, 3 Drawers, Catlin Plastic Handles, 1930, 32 x 42 x 60 In.	424
Server, Louis XV Style, Oak, Iron Escutcheons, Cabriole Legs, French, 1900s, 51 x 54 x 19 In.	984
Server, Mahogany, Marble Top, Carved Frieze, 2 Drawers, Paneled Doors, c.1880s, 38 x 80 x 25 In.	2706
Server, Majorelle, Rosewood, Doors, Drawers, Mother-Of-Pearl Inlay, 1920, 53 x 49 x 17 In.....*illus*	938
Server, Nils Jonsson, Teak, 2 Sliding Panel Doors, Tapered Legs, 1960, 28 x 37 x 16 In.	472
Server, Oak, 2 Tiers, Marble Top, Open Shelf, c.1880, 41 x 46 x 16 In.	338
Server, Paolo Buffa, Maple & Elm, Doors, Drawers, Carved Animals, c.1950, 38 x 63 x 19 In.	1500
Server, Queen Anne, Brass Handles, 4 Drawers, 40 x 22 x 37 In.	502
Server, Red Paint, Long Drawer, 2 Panel Doors, Bracket Base, 1900s, 39 x 41 ½ x 20 In.	236
Server, Walnut, 2 Doors, Drawers, Shelves, Claw Feet, c.1836, 59 x 38 x 19 In.	153
Settee, Adam Style, Painted, Cane Seat, Crest Rail, 4 Grisaille Panels, c.1810, 34 x 74 In.	1586
Settee, Arts & Crafts Style, Warren Hile Studio, Block Foot, c.1900, 76 x 32 x 29 In.	620
Settee, Arts & Crafts, Oak, Lift Top Seat, 45 x 48 x 18 In.	126
Settee, Arts & Crafts, Oak, Vertical Slats, 5 Pillows, Limbert c.1925, 36 x 67 x 26 In.	531
Settee, Black Stain, Double Back Splats, Carved, Lift Top Seat, 1800s, 48 x 37 In. ....*illus*	125
Settee, C. Malmsten, Upholstered, Beech, Signed, Sweden, c.1945, 28 x 29 x 55 In.	1500
Settee, Edwardian, Mother-Of-Pearl Inlay, Upholstered, 37 ¾ x 51 x 23 In.	156
Settee, Federal Style, Mahogany, Upholstered, Closed Arms, 36 x 53 In.	123
Settee, G. Nakashima, Black Walnut, Upholstered, Signed, Ottenberg, c.1958, 30 x 48 x 33 In.	5000
Settee, Louis XV Style, Upholstered, Walnut, Carved, Tapestry, c.1900, 42 x 17 x 74 In.	197
Settee, Painted, Plank Bottom, c.1800s, 70 In.	238
Settee, Reeded Crest Rail, Cushion Seat, Pillows, Rosewood, Early 1800s, 36 x 90 x 23 In.	1188
Settee, Sheraton, Rush Seat, Black & Red Paint, Scroll Arms, c.1810, 34 x 78 In.	720
Settee, Venetian, Padded Seat, Molded Cabriole Legs, Gilt Accents, 1800s, 39 x 88 x 26 In.	1500
Settee, White Paint, Gilt, Upholstered, Continental, 1900s, 37 x 67 ½ x 29 In.	593
Settee, William & Mary, Turned Walnut, Upholstered, 40 ½ x 52 ½ x 30 In.	840
Settee, Wing, Splayed Legs, Rolled Arms, Italy, c.1950, 38 x 55 In....................*illus*	750
Settee, Wood Frame, Cream Fabric, Upholstered, Victorian, 1800s.	130
Settle, Oak, 14 Slats, Dark Brown Leather Cushion, Arts & Crafts, Unsigned, 36 x 77 In.	726
Shelf, Bamboo Stick, 4 Tiers, c.1900, 28 x 12 x 59 In. ....*illus*	94
Shelf, Esherick, Cherry, Wall Mounted, 1960, 9 x 9 x 44 In.	5312
Shelf, Gallery Top, Fretwork, Mirror Panel, Drop Shelf Below, 1800s, 41 x 27 In.	188
Shelf, Hanging, 3 Tiers, Wood, Black Paint, 22 ½ x 33 In.	135
Shelf, Mahogany, Cutout Sailor & Flag, Horse, Carved & Painted, 1872, 11 ½ In.	800
Shelf, Mahogany, Stepped Sides, c.1800, 37 x 35 ¾ In.	625
Shelf, Mixed Wood, Pine, Framework, Late 1800s, 27 x 20 x 9 In.	540
Shelf, Oak, Gargoyle Mask, Oak, Painted, 9 In. ....*illus*	236
Shelf, Pine, Drawer, Red Stain Paint, Mid 1800s, 12 ½ x 23 In.	1375
Shelf, Pine, Whale Tail, Wood, 1800s, 29 ½ x 28 ½ In.	200

F

Shelf, Sliding, Pine, 6 Drawers, Wood Pulls, Molded Base, Bun Feet, 1800s, 44 x 34 x 23 In......	384
Shelf, Wall, Art Nouveau Style, Bust, Woman, Wood, 21 x 23 In..	173
Shelf, Whaleback, Walnut, 2 Drawers, Brass Knob, New England, 1800s, 31 x 25 x 8 In.	540
Sideboard, 4 Doors, 3 Drawers, Carved Accent, Feet, Brass Pulls, c.1900, 70 x 24 x 40 In.	83
Sideboard, A. Quervelle, Bookend Mahogany, Marble Top, Acanthus Knees, 57 x 70 In.	3304
Sideboard, Acajou, Marquetry, Marble Top, Glass Vitrine, c.1950, 85 x 78 x 24 In.	1125
Sideboard, Aco Mobler, 3 Sliding Doors, Shelf, 6 Drawers, Denmark, c.1950, 31 x 59 In.	492
Sideboard, Arne Hovmand Olsen, 4 Sliding Door, 5 Drawers, c.1950, 32 x 78 ½ In.	1722
Sideboard, Beech, 2 Doors, Arched Pilasters, Serpentine Skirt, 1800s, 40 x 56 x 13 In.	984
Sideboard, Cherry, Banded Inlay Top, Tapered Leg, 2 Front Drawers, 38 x 66 x 23 In.	748
Sideboard, Cherry, Serpentine Front, Drawers, Cupboards, Bellflower, c.1800, 38 x 60 x 22 In.	2177
Sideboard, Directoire Style, 4 Doors, 4 Drawers, Curved Marble Top, c.1920, 43 x 75 x 20 In. ..	938
Sideboard, Directoire Style, Brass Bound, Rectangular Top, 32 x 75 x 18 ½ In.	313
Sideboard, Drawer, Ribbon Border, Leaf Handles, Scrolling Legs, 36 x 35 x 23 In.	118
Sideboard, Drexel, Walnut, 2 Doors, 4 Drawers, Round Pulls, c.1960, 31 x 66 x 20 In.	497
Sideboard, Federal Style, Ferdinand Keller, Inlay, Mahogany, Philadelphia, 1920s, 39 ½ x 68 In. .	463
Sideboard, Federal Style, Mahogany, 3 Drawers, Panel Door, c.1925, 40 x 72 x 21 In. ....*illus*	120
Sideboard, Federal Style, Mahogany, Drawers, Curved Doors, Baker Furniture, 37 x 65 x 26 In.	390
Sideboard, Federal, Mahogany, Bellflower Inlay, 1800s, 40 ½ x 68 ½ x 23 In. ....*illus*	750
Sideboard, Federal, Mahogany, Inlay, Shell Inlaid Doors, Tapered Legs, c.1810, 38 x 75 x 27 In.	938
Sideboard, Federal, Tiger Maple, Square Tapering Legs, N.Y., 1800s, 41 x 70 x 24 In.	2337
Sideboard, Floral Inlay, Molded Top Edge, 2 Dovetailed Drawers, Base Molding, 34 x 85 x 21 In.	120
Sideboard, Fratelli Alesini, Rectangular Marble Top, 3 Drawers, Marked, 81 x 53 x 22 In.	308
Sideboard, George III Style, Mahogany, Serpentine Front, Inlay, 36 x 51 x 20 In.	234
Sideboard, George III, Banded Mahogany, 4 Drawers, 36 x 90 x 30 In.	1250
Sideboard, George III, Carved & Painted, Mahogany, Marble Top, 38 x 25 x 64 In.	2375
Sideboard, George III, Mahogany, Satinwood, Brass Gallery, 36 x 84 x 30 In.........................	406
Sideboard, Georgian Style, Mahogany, 4 Drawers, Square Legs, 1900s, 33 x 60 x 16 In.	188
Sideboard, Hepplewhite, Mahogany, Drawer, 2 Doors, c.1800, 41 ½ x 72 x 25 ½ In.	570
Sideboard, Horner Style, Oak, Barley Twist Column Supports, Paw Feet, 38 x 66 x 27 In.	1300
Sideboard, Ib Kofod-Larsen, 4 Doors, Rosewood, Denmark, 1950s, 42 x 86 ½ x 18 In.......*illus*	1750
Sideboard, Irish Regency, Mahogany, 3 Drawers, Bracket Feet, c.1815, 52 x 75 x 26 In.	5750
Sideboard, Jacobean Style, Drawer, Paneled Doors, Bun Feet, Continental, 1900s, 39 x 64 x 25 In.	313
Sideboard, James Mont, 4 Doors, Wood & Bronze, Mounted, c.1965, 37 x 69 ½ x 23 ½ In..........	1375
Sideboard, L. & J.G. Stickley, Oak, Overhanging, 4 Drawers, Copper Pulls, 34 x 54 x 24 In.......	847
Sideboard, Louis XV Style, Walnut, Carved, Panel Doors, Cabriole Legs, 1800s, 40 x 62 x 19 In.	1625
Sideboard, Louis XVI Style, Marble Top, Putty Color Paint, France, c.1915, 37 x 41 x 17 In.......	360
Sideboard, Mahogany & Satinwood, Serpentine Front, Lion's Head Handle, 33 ¾ x 46 x 23 ¾ In....	625
Sideboard, Mahogany, Central Drawer, Brass Lion's Head Pull, 1700s, 35 x 56 x 24 ½ In.	375
Sideboard, Mahogany, Rectangular Case, Lightwood Inlay Border, 6 Legs, c.1800, 41 x 70 x 27 In.	2950
Sideboard, Majorelle, Mahogany, Drawer, Door, Raised Panels, Shelves, 1900s, 59 x 61 In..*illus*	1875
Sideboard, Marble Top, Ornate, Openwork Design, France, 1900s, 36 x 74 x 20 ½ In...............	531
Sideboard, Marble Top, Scrolled Crest, Shelf, Fluted Columns, Drawers, Victorian, 87 x 61 x 27 In. .	810
Sideboard, Mirror, Leaf Inlay, 2 Doors, Footed, Italian Style, 1900s, 87 x 105 x 24 In.	210
Sideboard, Nils Jonsson, Teak, 5 Drawers, Sliding Panel Doors, Denmark, 1960, 31 x 75 In.....	944
Sideboard, Oak, Drawers, 2 Doors, Ogee Feet, Turn Knobs, Miniature, 9 ½ x 5 x 11 ½ In.	198
Sideboard, Osvaldo Borsani, Art Deco, Walnut, Black Lacquer, Glass Top, Italy, 35 x 69 x 17 In.	1978
Sideboard, P. Evans, Cityscape, Burl, 2 Cabinets, Shelf, Chrome Ends, c.1975, 33 x 84 In..*illus*	5043
Sideboard, Paolo Buffa, Maple & Elm, Turned Legs, Carved Egrets, c.1950, 38 x 92 x 21 In.	1500
Sideboard, Provincial, Fruitwood, 3 Drawer Pulls, 3 Doors, Brass Handles, 40 x 89 x 20 In.....	500
Sideboard, Regency, Mahogany, Carved, Leaves, Scrolls, Drawers, c.1850, 67 x 77 In.............	2125
Sideboard, Rosewood, 4 Sliding Doors, 3 Drawers, Compartments, Denmark, 1960, 31 x 79 x 18 In.	1062
Sideboard, S. Young, Walnut, Steel, 5 Drawers, Calif., c.1960, 32 ½ x 19 x 64 ¾ In.	500
Sideboard, Scottish Regency, Mahogany, Breakfront, Plate Shelf, c.1805, 53 x 90 x 30 In.	2375
Sideboard, Tibbenham, Mahogany, Serpentine, Brass Gallery, Walnut Inlay, 48 x 67 x 48 In. .	351
Sideboard, Walnut, Marble Top, Corbel Supports, Drawers, Victorian, 76 x 53 ¾ x 27 In.	1029
Sofa, 2 Bow Back, Curved Frame, Cabriole Legs, Orange Velvet, c.1860, 38 x 80 x 30 In.	199
Sofa, Alberto Rosselli, Brown Leather, 2 Sections, Plastic Base, c.1990, 20 x 90 x 32 In.	4484
Sofa, Art Deco, Velvet Upholstery, Loose Cushion, Curved Legs, 1900s, 34 x 72 x 41 In.......*illus*	1188
Sofa, Barcelona Style, Futon, Black Leather, Chrome Frame, Adjustable, Reclining, 34 x 77 In. .	288

Furniture, Shelf, Bamboo Stick, 4 Tiers, c.1900, 28 x 12 x 59 In.
$94

Copake Auction

Furniture, Shelf, Oak, Gargoyle Mask, Oak, Painted, 9 In.
$236

Hess Auction Group

Furniture, Sideboard, Federal Style, Mahogany, 3 Drawers, Panel Door, c.1925, 40 x 72 x 21 In.
$120

Garth's Auctioneers & Appraisers

FURNITURE

Furniture, Sideboard, Federal, Mahogany, Bellflower Inlay, 1800s, 40 ½ x 68 ½ x 23 In.
$750

Rago Arts and Auction Center

Furniture, Sideboard, Ib Kofod-Larsen, 4 Doors, Rosewood, Denmark, 1950s, 42 x 86 ½ x 18 In.
$1,750

Rago Arts and Auction Center

TIP

Try this method to remove white water stains from wood. Put a piece of blotter paper over the spot and press with a warm iron. The spot should vanish. If it does not, rub it with lemon oil.

Furniture, Sideboard, Majorelle, Mahogany, Drawer, Door, Raised Panels, Shelves, 1900s, 59 x 61 In.
$1,875

Rago Arts and Auction Center

Sofa, Biedermeier, Fruitwood, Curved, Inlay, Shaped Crest, Tubular Arms, 1800s, 78 In...*illus*	240
Sofa, Camelback, Mahogany, Reeded Front Legs, Upholstered, 1800s, 34 x 82 In.	438
Sofa, Camelback, Mahogany, Scroll Arms, Square Legs, Stretchers, 37 x 83 x 30 In.	375
Sofa, Carved, Floral & Scrolling Leaves, Cabriole Legs, Upholstered, Victorian, 45 x 74 x 35 In.	2478
Sofa, Carved, Scrolled Crest, Serpentine Seat, Cabriole Legs, Rosewood, Mid 1800s, 48 x 66 x 30 In.	3438
Sofa, Chesterfield, Red Leather, Armrest, Button Cushion, Bun Feet, 82 In.	3250
Sofa, Chesterfield, Upholstered, Scroll Arms, c.1970, 28 x 89 In.	1250
Sofa, Chippendale Style, Camelback, Oak, Tweed Upholstery, Scroll Arms, 1800s, 36 x 33 In.	73
Sofa, Chippendale, Camelback, Mahogany, Scroll Arms, Upholstered, c.1800, 40 x 96 In. *illus*	4500
Sofa, Chippendale, Camelback, Scroll Arms, Damask Upholstery, 1700s, 34 x 89 x 35 In.	4320
Sofa, Christopher Guy, Channel Back, Gray Velvet, 89 x 37 x 29 ½ In.	1573
Sofa, Curved, Upholstered, Iron, Brass Legs, Italy, c.1950, 37 x 75 x 29 In.	1125
Sofa, David Masterson, Upholstered, Silk, Filled Cushion, 30 x 86 x 35 In.	1800
Sofa, E.O. Jorgensen, Pine, Enameled Steel, Upholstered, Brass, Denmark, c.1960, 37 x 34 x 88 In.	1625
Sofa, Eames, Compact, Upholstered, Chrome & Steel Legs, 1959, 72 ½ x 30 In.	923
Sofa, Empire Style, Velvet Upholstery, Paw Feet, 31 x 84 In.	185
Sofa, Empire, Mahogany, Carved, Outscrolled Arms, Paw Feet, c.1825, 90 In. *illus*	4500
Sofa, Empire, Mahogany, Scroll Back & Arms, Lobed Feet, c.1840, 33 x 77 x 25 In.	438
Sofa, F. Hansen, Ax, Laminated Teak & Beech, Plywood, Leather, Denmark, 1950, 29 x 28 x 64 In.	315
Sofa, F. Schlegel, Beech, Upholstered, Denmark, c.1935, 30 x 33 x 80 In. *illus*	2375
Sofa, Federal Style, Mahogany, Reeded Front Legs, Upholstered, 1900s, 34 x 74 In.	120
Sofa, Federal, Arched Crest, Seat Rail, Turned Supports, Upholstered, Mass., c.1810, 76 In.	492
Sofa, Federal, Cornucopia Arms, Claw Feet, c.1830, 33 x 82 x 16 In.	944
Sofa, Federico Munari, Curved, Cream Upholstered, Bronze Legs, Italy, 31 x 106 In.	4375
Sofa, France & Sons, Teak, Chromed Metal, Upholstered, Rubber Coated, Denmark, 30 x 80 x 30 In.	1599
Sofa, G. Nelson, Sling, Leather, Chrome Plated Steel, Herman Miller, 1963, 87 x 32 x 29 In.	3000
Sofa, George III, Camelback, Mahogany, Damask Upholstery, c.1800, 36 x 67 x 26 In.	2040
Sofa, H. Acton, Leather Upholstery, Chrome Plated Steel, c.1955, 28 x 31 x 80 In.	1170
Sofa, Hardwood, Carved, Scrolls & Leaves, Cane Back, Cushion, Paw Feet, c.1815, 36 In....*illus*	523
Sofa, Hepplewhite Style, Curved, Mahogany, Tapered Legs, Asian Pattern, 1900s, 36 x 53 In.	96
Sofa, J. Kensley McKie, Carved Antelope Horns, Cushion, Marked JKM, 1978, 27 x 82 In.	33210
Sofa, J. Risson, Slant Back, Black, Upholstered Seat, Geometric Arms, 32 x 90 x 27 In.	1170
Sofa, Jean-Michel Frank, Upholstered, Lacquered, Cushion, France, c.1930, 30 x 36 x 91 In.	975
Sofa, Jydsk Mobelvaerk, Rosewood, Chromed Steel, 3 Seats, Denmark, 1970s, 25 x 88 x 30 In.	1750
Sofa, Kittinger, Sheraton Style, Mahogany, Upholstered, 36 x 77 In. *illus*	445
Sofa, Le Corbusier, Tubular Chrome Plated Frame, Black Leather, Down Filled, 1928, 26 x 71 x 28 In.	1770
Sofa, Louis XV Style, Walnut, Carved, Serpentine, Cabriole Legs, Floral, 1800s, 38 x 82 x 29 In.	800
Sofa, Louis XVI Style, Carved, Crest Rail, Fluted Tapering Leg, 1800s, 38 x 50 x 24 In.	750
Sofa, Louis XVI Style, Mahogany, Striped Silk, Fluted Legs, Mid 1900s, 34 x 53 x 28 In.	271
Sofa, M. Zanuso, Upholstered, Steel, Rubber, Adjustable, Italy, 1951, 29 x 35 x 76 In.	2000
Sofa, Mahogany, Leather Upholstery, Tufted, 3-Cushion Seat, Bun Feet, 1900s, 86 In.	2000
Sofa, Mahogany, Scroll Arms, Carved Rosettes, Paw Feet, Va., c.1825, 90 x 25 x 33 In.	1287
Sofa, Metallic Thread, Damask Upholstery, 3-Cushion Seat, 1900s, 82 In.	1875
Sofa, Molesworth, 3 Seats, Burl, Patinated Brass, Leather, 38 x 83 In...*illus*	38750
Sofa, Ornate, Hardwood, 3 Upholstered Panels, Carved, Chinese, 42 x 67 In. ...*illus*	313
Sofa, Poul Kjaerholm, Leather Upholstery, Brushed Chrome Frame, 1900s, 30 x 78 x 27 In.	6875
Sofa, Roy McMakin, 3 Cushions, Black, c.1988, 31 ⅝ x 83 x 30 In.	8750
Sofa, Sectional, 3-Piece, Regal Blue, Leather, Brushed Finish, 1900s, 91 x 101 In.	600
Sofa, Sheraton, 8 Mahogany Legs, Reeded Legs, Upholstered, c.1805, 34 x 16 x 79 In.	1080
Sofa, Sheraton, Flame Birch Panels, New England, Early 1800s, 34 x 76 x 24 In.	826
Sofa, Stained Beech, Teak, Stripes, Ash, Upholstered, Denmark, c.1950, 24 x 32 x 90 In.	812
Sofa, Stendig, Leather Upholstery, 9 Flexible Segments, Italy, 29 x 89 x 39 In.	4920
Sofa, Tuxedo, Renaissance Revival, Walnut, Upholstered, 18 x 25 x 34 In.	322
Sofa, Upholstered, Loose Cushions, 3 Seats, 20th Century, 89 In.	281
Sofa, Victorian, Carved, Black Seat, Jeliff, 1860s, 67 In. *illus*	207
Sofa, Victorian, Mahogany, Scroll Arms, Feathered Skirt, Paw Feet, 34 x 83 x 25 In.	161
Sofa, Wormley, Leather, Tufted Black, Armrest, Dunbar Tag, c.1960, 24 x 98 x 35 In.	4235
Stand, 2 Drawers, Tiger Maple, Brass Pulls, Turned Legs, 1800s, 28 x 21 ½ x 17 In.	615
Stand, 2 Maple Drawers, Lower Shelf, 1800s, 35 x 17 x 35 In.	177
Stand, 3 Tiers, Pierced, Lotus, Chinese, Early 1900s, 20 x 6 x 5 ½ In.	390

Furniture, Sideboard, P. Evans, Cityscape, Burl, 2 Cabinets, Shelf, Chrome Ends, c.1975, 33 x 84 In.
$5,043

Skinner, Inc.

Furniture, Sofa, Art Deco, Velvet Upholstery, Loose Cushion, Curved Legs, 1900s, 34 x 72 x 41 In.
$1,188

Rago Arts and Auction Center

Furniture, Sofa, Biedermeier, Fruitwood, Curved, Inlay, Shaped Crest, Tubular Arms, 1800s, 78 In.
$240

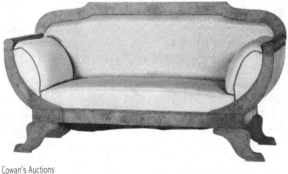

Cowan's Auctions

Furniture, Sofa, Chippendale, Camelback, Mahogany, Scroll Arms, Upholstered, c.1800, 40 x 96 In.
$4,500

Brunk Auctions

Furniture, Sofa, Empire, Mahogany, Carved, Outscrolled Arms, Paw Feet, c.1825, 90 In.
$4,500

New Orleans Auction Galleries

Furniture, Sofa, F. Schlegel, Beech, Upholstered, Denmark, c.1935, 30 x 33 x 80 In.
$2,375

Wright

Furniture, Sofa, Hardwood, Carved, Scrolls & Leaves, Cane Back, Cushion, Paw Feet, c.1815, 36 In.
$523

Skinner, Inc.

Furniture, Sofa, Kittinger, Sheraton Style, Mahogany, Upholstered, 36 x 77 In.
$445

Nadeau's Auction Gallery

F

Furniture, Sofa, Molesworth, 3 Seats, Burl, Patinated Brass, Leather, 38 x 83 In.

$38,750

Rago Arts and Auction Center

Furniture, Sofa, Ornate, Hardwood, 3 Upholstered Panels, Carved, Chinese, 42 x 67 In.

$313

Roland Auctioneers & Valuers

Furniture, Sofa, Victorian, Carved, Black Seat, Jeliff, 1860s, 67 In.

$207

Copake Auction

Furniture, Stand, Art Nouveau Style, Carved, Hardwood, Chinese, 6 In.

$113

Leslie Hindman Auctioneers

Stand, Aesthetic Revival, 3 Tiers, Ornate Appliques, Black Paint, Ball & Claw Feet, 34 x 15 x 15 In. .	156
Stand, Art Nouveau Style, Carved Fruitwood, Rosewood, Shelves, Late 1900s, 47 x 19 x 19 In. ...	500
Stand, Art Nouveau Style, Carved, Hardwood, Chinese, 6 In...*illus*	113
Stand, Bradley & Hubbard, Gilt, 3 Tiers, Floral Medallions, Griffin Feet, c.1880, 32 x 16 x 12 In.	394
Stand, Carved, Marble Inset Top, Chinese, c.1900, 18 In.	113
Stand, Egyptian Goddess, Cobra, Bowl, Gold, Silver, Scarab & Vulture Base, 73 x 25 x 23 In. ...	200
Stand, Empire Style, Marble Stand, 3 Legs, Plinth, Circular Base, 1900s, 34 In......................	465
Stand, Federal, 2 Drawers, Mahogany, Urn Column, Scroll Feet, c.1840, 22 x 17 x 27 In. .	142
Stand, Federal, Pine, Red Paint, Cut Corners, 1800s, 26 ½ x 22 x 16 In..........................	111
Stand, Fern, Brass, Leaves, Marble Inserts, 2 Layers, Square, Continental, 1900s, 27 x 13 In....	30
Stand, Fern, Tiered Base, Alligatored Varnish, Turned Knobs & Drops, Early 1900s, 33 In........	390
Stand, Folio, Renaissance Revival, Walnut, Cheval Base, c.1875, 46 x 24 x 28 In.............*illus*	1625
Stand, G. Nelson, Thin Edge, Teak, Steel, Chrome Plated, Herman Miller, 1952, 18 x 19 x 22 In.	1250
Stand, George III, Mahogany, Reddish Brown Timber, 28 x 12 x 13 In.	500
Stand, Hardwood, Carved Skirt, Square, Chinese, c.1900, 44 x 13 In.	472
Stand, Hardwood, Inlay, Mother-Of-Pearl, Chinese, 1800s, 27 ½ In.	200
Stand, Henri II Style, Walnut, Marble Top, Rope Twist, Plinth Base, Early 1900s, 38 x 16 x 13 In. ...	369
Stand, Hepplewhite, Drawer, Molded Edge, Brass Pull, Tapered Legs, c.1820, 18 x 16 x 26 In....	220
Stand, Hepplewhite, Pine, Tall Back, Splay Leg, 32 x 13 x 13 In...	224
Stand, Hepplewhite, Walnut, Square Overhanging Top, Tapered Legs, 28 x 20 x 20 In.	176
Stand, Kettle, Maple, Octagonal Top, Cross Base, Late 1700s, 21 x 9 In.........................	3750
Stand, Kilian Brothers, Walnut, Carved, Ebonized, Circular Top, N.Y., Late 1800s, 31 x 14 In...	88
Stand, Louis XIV Style, Gilt, Carved, 3 Lion's Paw Feet. France, 1800s, 18 x 21 In...............	625
Stand, Louis XVI Style, Cherry, Marble Top, Drawers, 1800s, 34 x 26 x 14 In.	531
Stand, Magazine, Oak, 4 Shelves, 3 Slat Sides, 42 x 21 x 12 In...	1210
Stand, Mahogany, 2 Drawers, Inlaid Top, Turned Legs, Stretcher Base, Continental, 29 x 17 x 27 In.	286
Stand, Mahogany, Molded Top, Twist Turnings, White Metal Feet, 1900s, 29 x 16 In...........	210
Stand, Maple, Drawer, Red, Turned Legs, Box Stretcher, Late 1700s, 24 x 27 x 19 In..............	5000
Stand, Maple, Tiger, 2 Drawers, Brass Pulls, Turned Legs, c.1810, 27 x 19 x 19 In.	480
Stand, Mazarin, Mahogany, Floral Cornucopia, Cloud, Chinese, Early 1800s, 18 x 15 x 12 In. .	201
Stand, Modern, Mahogany, Twisted Shape, 22 ¾ x 11 ½ x 11 ¾ In...............................*illus*	219
Stand, Music, Baroque Style, Tripod Base, Scroll Feet, Continental, 1900s, 53 x 20 In..............	277
Stand, Music, Carved, Wood, Tripod, 1900s, 49 In.	194
Stand, Pine, Alligator Surface, 2 Drawers, Pullout Writing Slide, 1800s, 32 ½ x 21 In.	325
Stand, Pine, Drawer, Red & Black Paint, Bennington Knob, Turned Legs, 1800s, 29 x 25 x 25 In...	625
Stand, Plant, 4 Tiers, Green Paint, Cross Bracing, New England, 1800s, 27 x 40 x 25 In.	677
Stand, Plant, Amish, Pine, 3 Tiers, Scalloped Sides, Green, 1950s, 37 ½ x 48 x 22 ¼ In.............	420
Stand, Plant, Carved, Hardwood, Square Top, Chinese, 48 x 14 x 14 In.............................	277
Stand, Plant, Iron, Circular Holders, 9 Adjustable Arms, Tripod Base, Victorian, 42 In.	543
Stand, Plant, Teak, Marble Top, Aprons, Lotus, Mythical Faces, Claw Feet, 34 x 18 In.	182
Stand, Plant, Walnut, Carved Top, Gadroon Apron, Floral Clusters, Cabriole Legs, 32 In..........	1573
Stand, Plant, Wire, 2 Tiers, White Paint, Rolling Foot, Victorian, 32 x 33 In.......................	125
Stand, Reading, Arts & Crafts, Oak, Trestle, Adjustable Easel, Shoefeet, 27 x 36 x 10 In.	36
Stand, Round, Marble Top, Floral Carved Frame, Cabriole Legs, Claw & Pearl Feet, c.1900, 27 x 19 In...	338
Stand, Roycroft, Drawer, Shelf, Door, White Furniture Co., Orb & Cross, c.1910, 31 x 18 In...*illus*	4062
Stand, Shaving, Adjustable, Industrial, Cast Iron, Steel & Copper Patina, 63 ½ In.....................	625
Stand, Shaving, Empire, Mahogany, Mirror, Drawer Shelf, Turned Pedestal, 61 x 15 In. ...*illus*	153
Stand, Shaving, Mahogany, Lyre Shape Frame, Mirror, Bronze Mounts, c.1910, 68 x 15 In.	1029
Stand, Sheraton, Birch & Bird's-Eye Maple, 2 Drawers, c.1820, 28 x 18 In.............................	388
Stand, Sheraton, Cherry, Drawer, Square Top, Cylindrical Feet, 1800s, 29 x 21 In.	250
Stand, Sheraton, Drawer, Green Surface, Ball Foot, Pennsylvania, 1800s, 30 x 23 In.	288
Stand, Sheraton, Drawer, Walnut, Reeded Legs, Turned Foot, New England, 1800s, 29 x 19 In.	388
Stand, Sheraton, Mahogany, Dovetailed Drawer, Quatrefoil Shelf, c.1850, 32 x 18 x 17 In........	156
Stand, Sheraton, Mahogany, Drawers, Spool Turnings, Boston, c.1810, 29 x 22 x 19 In............	120
Stand, Sheraton, Mahogany, Thin Turret Corner Top, Drawer, Tapered Legs, c.1840, 28 x 17 x 16 In.	210
Stand, Sheraton, Maple, Glass Top, Drawers, Reeded Legs, Brass Pulls, 29 x 23 x 19 In.	153
Stand, Sheraton, Maple, Walnut, Poplar, 2 Dovetailed Drawers, c.1850, 29 x 18 x 17 In.	594
Stand, Sheraton, Pine, Grain Painted, Drawer, Square Nails, c.1850, 29 x 23 x 17 In.........*illus*	720
Stand, Sheraton, Smoke Painted, Drawer, Mushroom Pull, Ball Feet, c.1820, 30 x 23 In............	277
Stand, Slab, Wood, 4 Legs, Uneven Top Shape, 1900s, 20 x 25 In....................................	125

F

Furniture, Stand, Folio, Renaissance Revival, Walnut, Cheval Base, c.1875, 46 x 24 x 28 In. $1,625

New Orleans Auction Galleries

Furniture, Stand, Modern, Mahogany, Twisted Shape, 22¾ x 11½ x 11¾ In. $219

Roland Auctioneers & Valuers

Furniture, Stand, Roycroft, Drawer, Shelf, Door, White Furniture Co., Orb & Cross, c.1910, 31 x 18 In. $4,062

Rago Arts and Auction Center

Furniture, Stand, Shaving, Empire, Mahogany, Mirror, Drawer Shelf, Turned Pedestal, 61 x 15 In. $153

Nadeau's Auction Gallery

Furniture, Stand, Sheraton, Pine, Grain Painted, Drawer, Square Nails, c.1850, 29 x 23 x 17 In. $720

Garth's Auctioneers & Appraisers

Furniture, Stand, Smoking, Glass Front, Ashtray Holder, Splay Cutout Legs, c.1920, 27 x 20 x 14 In. $154

Forsythes' Auctions

TIP
Use one type of furniture polish. If you switch from an oil polish to a wax polish, the surface will appear smudged.

Furniture, Stand, Wood, Carved, Flat Top, 2 Swirling Feet, 2 Stretchers, 2½ x 10 x 4½ In. $62

Skinner, Inc.

Furniture, Stool, Cricket, Windsor, 3 Turned Legs & Back, 1800s, 9½ In. $92

Keystone Auctions LLC

Furniture, Stool, G. Nakashima, Walnut, Triangular Top, 3 Legs, c.1960, 12 ½ x 18 x 16 In.
$2,160

Brunk Auctions

Furniture, Stool, George II, Carved, Mahogany, Cabriole Legs, 18 x 21 ½ In.
$238

Pook & Pook

Furniture, Stool, McCobb, Metal Frame, Leather Upholstery, Square, c.1965, 17 ¾ x 20 ½ In.
$369

Skinner, Inc.

Furniture, Stool, Mies Van Der Rohe, Barcelona, Cowhide Sling, Knoll Chrome, 1930, 12 x 23 x 23 In.
$1,063

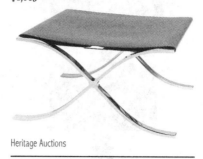

Heritage Auctions

Furniture, Stool, Neoclassical, Rosewood, Beech, Needlepoint, England, 1800s, 17 x 21 In.
$300

Brunk Auctions

Furniture, Stool, Piano, Rotating, Mahogany, Upholstered Back, Circular Seat, Splayed Legs, 1900s, 28 In.
$163

Leslie Hindman Auctioneers

Furniture, Stool, Savonarola Style, X-Shape, Oak, Carved, Slatted Legs, c.1890, 15 x 15 In.
$180

Eldred's

Furniture, Table, Adam Style, Mahogany, Drawer, Floral Medallion, Tapered Square Legs, 35 x 30 In.
$369

Crescent City Auction Gallery

Furniture, Table, Bamboo & Ebonized, Lacquered, Victorian Style, 1900s, 29 x 21 In.
$344

Leslie Hindman Auctioneers

Stand, Smoking, Glass Front, Ashtray Holder, Splay Cutout Legs, c.1920, 27 x 20 x 14 In. ...*illus*	154
Stand, Smoking, Maple, Pipe Rack, Cups Of Tobacco, Cigar, Cigarettes, 3 Legs, 34 x 15 x 9 In.	42
Stand, Splay Leg, Red Board Top, Box Stretcher, Green Paint, 1800s, 29 x 25 x 17 In.	207
Stand, Walnut, Splay Leg, Square Top, Pennsylvania, Early 1800s, 27 x 15 In.	125
Stand, Walnut, Twisted Column, Carved Faces, c.1890, 37 ½ x 15 ¾ In.	1296
Stand, Widdicomb, Stained Walnut, Brass Legs, Wicker, Label, 1950s, 24 x 21 x 22 In., Pair	3250
Stand, Wood, Carved, Flat Top, 2 Swirling Feet, 2 Stretchers, 2 ½ x 10 x 4 ½ In. ...*illus*	62
Stand, Wood, Square Top, Mother-Of-Pearl Inlay, Flowers, Apron, Chinese, 20 In.	308
Stool, Black Paint, Lion Embroidered, Felt Cushion, Splayed Legs, 1800s, 12 x 12 In.	277
Stool, Carved, Teak, 4 Legs, Sori Yanagi, Japan, 1990, 16 x 14 ½ In.	1500
Stool, Chippendale Style, Mahogany, Round, Carved, Pad Foot, c.1900, 19 x 23 In.	138
Stool, Chippendale, Mahogany, Pink, Gray, Ball & Claw Feet, Eagle, 1700s, 20 x 34 x 18 In.	259
Stool, Cricket, Windsor, 3 Turned Legs & Back, 1800s, 9 ½ In. ...*illus*	92
Stool, Curule, Rosewood, Carved, Upholstered, Turned Stretcher, X-Brace, c.1850	438
Stool, Erik Buck, Teak, Bar, Leather Seat, Lumbar Support, Footrest, Denmark, 33 x 15 x 17 In.	154
Stool, Esherick, Walnut, Hickory, 3 Legs, Carved, 1960, 18 ¾ x 13 x 14 In.	6875
Stool, G. Nakashima, Walnut, Triangular Top, 3 Legs, c.1960, 12 ½ x 18 x 16 In. ...*illus*	2160
Stool, George II, Carved, Mahogany, Cabriole Legs, 18 x 21 ½ In. ...*illus*	238
Stool, George III Style, Mahogany, Overstuffed Cushion, Ball & Claw Feet, c.1900, 19 x 19 x 14 In.	213
Stool, George III, Mahogany, Carved Marlboro Legs, Stretcher, c.1775, 17 x 19 x 15 In.	671
Stool, Grotto Style, Shell Shape Seat, Mahogany, Dolphin Supports, 1900s, 18 x 19 x 18 In.	625
Stool, Industrial, Metal Base On Wheels, Footrest Ring, False Leather Seat, c.1900	46
Stool, Jacobean Style, Oak, Joint, Wood Stretchers, Square Foot, 18 x 17 In.	475
Stool, K. Thomsen, Teak, Mogens Lassen, 3 Legs, Signed, Denmark, 1942, 18 x 14 x 19 ½ In.	3750
Stool, Louis XV Style, Walnut, Rectangular, Cabriole Legs, Scrolled Toes, Late 1800s, 20 In.	94
Stool, M. Nakashima, Plank, Walnut, Signed, Pa., 1992, 12 ½ x 21 x 16 In.	875
Stool, McCobb, Metal Frame, Leather Upholstery, Square, c.1965, 17 ¾ x 20 ½ In. ...*illus*	369
Stool, Mies Van Der Rohe, Barcelona, Cowhide Sling, Knoll Chrome, 1930, 12 x 23 x 23 In. ...*illus*	1063
Stool, Milking, Rectangular Seat, 4 Splayed Legs, 1800s, 10 ½ In.	246
Stool, Mother-Of-Pearl, Square, Inlay, Square Legs, c.1900, 18 x 14 x 14 ½ In.	188
Stool, Napoleon III, Rosewood, Kingwood, Pad Seat, Cabriole Legs, Brass Feet, c.1890, 19 x 17 x 15 In.	313
Stool, Neoclassical, Rosewood, Beech, Needlepoint, England, 1800s, 17 x 21 In. ...*illus*	300
Stool, Organ, Cast Iron, Octagonal, Adjustable, 3 Scrolling Feet, 19 x 13 x 13 In.	545
Stool, P. Evans, Patchwork, Brass, Nailheads, Upholstered, Directional, 1970s, 22 x 20 In.	2625
Stool, Piano, Carved, Revolving, Walnut, Upholstered, Tripod Feet, 1800s, 15 x 20 In.	177
Stool, Piano, Rotating, Mahogany, Upholstered Back, Circular Seat, Splayed Legs, 1900s, 28 In. ...*illus*	163
Stool, Rectangular, Molded Top, Turned Splayed Legs, 1800s, 19 ½ x 15 ½ x 12 In.	283
Stool, Red Leather, Upholstered, Indian Medallion, Ottoman, 9 ½ x 17 x 11 ½ In.	156
Stool, Regency Style, Ebonized, Cane Square Seat, X-Stretcher, 1800s, 18 x 17 x 17 In.	625
Stool, Risom, Maple, Nylon Strapping, Knoll, c.1947, 16 ½ x 15 x 17 ½ In.	437
Stool, Round, Through Tenon Legs, Old Paint Surface, 30 x 14 In.	106
Stool, Savonarola Style, X-Shape, Oak, Carved, Slatted Legs, c.1890, 15 x 15 In. ...*illus*	180
Stool, Turned Legs, Stretcher Base, Curly Maple Top, 1800s, 21 x 17 ¾ x 14 ½ In.	1094
Stool, Vinyl, Laminated Maple, Lavender, c.1960, 19 x 14 ¾ x 19 ¾ In.	65
Stool, Walnut, Mortise Top, Fox Tails, Deep Skirt, Splayed Legs, 1800s, 6 ½ x 13 x 7 In.	115
Stool, Walnut, Wood, Rectangular Top, Ball Feet, Continental, 19 x 21 In.	388
Stool, Wood, Oak, Painted, Carved, Stretchers, Square Foot, 17 x 18 In.	350
Stool, Zigzag, F&H Campana, Steel Frame, Green, Plastic Wrapped Seat, 2001, 25 ½ x 17 In.	212
Table, Adam Style, Mahogany, Drawer, Floral Medallion, Tapered Square Legs, 35 x 30 In. ...*illus*	369
Table, Altar, Carved, Dragons, Spandrels, Square Legs, 36 x 60 x 15 In.	1750
Table, Altar, Hardwood, 8 Buddhists, Daoist Emblems, Scroll Feet, 1900s, 33 x 62 x 14 In.	923
Table, Altar, Rectangular, Geometric, Club Legs, Chinese, 1900s, 33 x 55 x 20 In.	132
Table, Altar, Softwood, Rectangular, Chinese, 1700s, 33 x 52 ¾ In.	200
Table, Art Deco, Adjustable, Brass Capped Feet, Leaves, France, 1920, 44 In.	153
Table, Art Deco, Glass & Brass, Early 1900s, 15 x 12 x 24 In.	338
Table, Art Deco, Onyx Top, Iron, Stretcher Design, 30 x 29 ¼ In.	250
Table, Arts & Crafts Style, Oak, Octagonal Top, Mortise & Tenon, Carved, 22 x 24 x 24 In.	156
Table, Baker's, Cast Iron, Marble Top, Scroll Trestle Supports, France, 1800s, 30 x 69 x 32 In.	861
Table, Bamboo & Ebonized, Lacquered, Victorian Style, 1900s, 29 x 21 In. ...*illus*	344
Table, Bamboo, Painted, Floral, 3 Tiers, 21 x 15 x 29 ¾ In.	207

Furniture, Table, Bronze, Gilt, Flowers & Leaves, Glass Top, Early 1900s, 20 ¾ x 25 ½ x 18 In.

$250

Leslie Hindman Auctioneers

Furniture, Table, Center, Fruitwood, Circular Top, Tripod Base, Pedestal, 1900s, 29 x 35 In.

$750

New Orleans Auction Galleries

TIP
Don't store dining table leaves on end. They may warp. Flat under the bed is an ideal storage location.

Furniture, Table, Center, Mahogany & Fruitwood, Marquetry, Adjustable, Dutch, 1900s, 31 x 41 In.

$500

Leslie Hindman Auctioneers

F

Furniture, Table, Center, Victorian, Marble Top, Carved Dog, Shelf, Shaped Legs, 28 x 36 In.
$240

Cowan's Auctions

Furniture, Table, Chippendale Style, Drum Shape, Walnut, Pedestal, Claw Foot, c.1920, 30 x 28 In.
$406

Leslie Hindman Auctioneers

Furniture, Table, Coffee, Buckeye, Burl, 2 Sections, Organic Shape, Mid 1900s, 14 x 38 In.
$960

Selkirk Auctioneers & Appraisers

Cocktail or Coffee

When Prohibition ended in 1933, furniture makers started to sell low "cocktail tables" to be used in front of sofas to serve the newly legal mixed drinks. The public objected to the name, so it was renamed a "coffee table."

Table, Bamboo, Square Top, Lacquer, Gilt Leaves, Shelf, Late 1800s, 28 x 26 x 26 In.	406
Table, Baroque Style, Gilt Stand, Round Marble Top, 3-Sided Base, 1800s, 30 x 20 In.	793
Table, Birch, 5 Drawers, Pullout Candlesticks, Tapered Legs, 29 x 29 x 21 In.	406
Table, Blackamoor Base, Carved Wood, Paint & Gilt, Round Glass Top, 19 x 18 In.	715
Table, Breakfast, Mahogany, Fall Leaf, Baltimore Classical, c.1825, 29 x 21 In.	222
Table, Breakfast, Pembroke, Mahogany, Drawer, Square Legs, 1700s, 28 x 24 x 29 In.	72
Table, Breakfast, Tilt Top, Mahogany, Bird's-Eye Maple Veneer, Brass-Capped Feet, 27 x 60 x 41 In.	720
Table, Bronze, Gilt, Flowers & Leaves, Glass Top, Early 1900s, 20¾ x 25½ x 18 In. ....*illus*	250
Table, Burl, Round, Low, Bow Shape, Curved Metal Support, Mastercraft, 15 x 23 In.	236
Table, Cafe, Marble Top, Cast Iron, Trestle Base, X-Shape Ends, 1900s, 28 x 39 x 23 In.	1112
Table, Card, 3 Legs, Mahogany, D-Shape Top, Fluted Post, Brass Casters, c.1800, 29 x 36 x 18 In.	3774
Table, Card, Carved, Rectangular Top, Mahogany, Rounded Corners, Tapering Legs, 30 x 36 x 17 In.	209
Table, Card, Cherry, Inlay, Reeded Tapered Legs, Early 1800s, 29 x 36 x 17 In.	738
Table, Card, Federal Style, Inlay, Mahogany, Charak, 31½ x 36 In.	275
Table, Card, Federal, Inlay, Mahogany, 2 Drawers, 1800s, 29½ x 33 x 15¾ In.	861
Table, Card, Federal, Mahogany, Grained Top, Square Legs, c.1800, 29 x 35 x 17 In.	1800
Table, Card, George III, Foldover, Mahogany, Inlay, Demilune, 29 x 36 x 18 In.	437
Table, Card, H. Tanner, Walnut, Inlay, Birch & White Pine, England, 30 x 36 x 19 In.	1080
Table, Card, Hepplewhite, Mahogany, Curved Top & Leaf, Swing Leg, 1800s, 29 x 37 x 18 In.	120
Table, Card, Hepplewhite, Mahogany, Satinwood Panels, c.1790, 28 x 36 x 17 In.	360
Table, Card, Hepplewhite, Maple, Birch, Square Legs, Gateleg, 1800s, 29 x 34 x 17 In.	527
Table, Card, Mahogany, D-Shape Top, Mitered Panel, Herringbone Legs, c.1808, 29 x 35 x 17 In.	1815
Table, Card, Mahogany, Lift Top, Brass Paw Feet, c.1850, 29½ x 36 x 17¾ In.	469
Table, Card, Mahogany, Square Tapering Legs, c.1800, 28 x 34 x 16 In.	461
Table, Carved, Wood, France, 1900s, 28 x 33½ In.	94
Table, Cast Metal, Black Paint, Glass Top Patio, 30 x 48 x 48 In.	188
Table, Center, Biedermeier Style, Gilt Bronze, Ebonized, Austria, 1800s, 29 x 43¾ In.	938
Table, Center, Eastlake, Square Top, Walnut, 4 Stretcher Feet, Victorian, 29 x 21 x 29 In.	59
Table, Center, Empire Style, Carved, Mahogany, Marble Top, Columnar Legs, 1900s, 29 x 32 In.	492
Table, Center, False Marble Top, Painted, Louis XVI Style, 1900s, 33½ x 52 x 24½ In.	2000
Table, Center, Fruitwood, Circular Top, Tripod Base, Pedestal, 1900s, 29 x 35 In. ....*illus*	750
Table, Center, Gilt, Metal Round Base, Malachite Veneer Top, 30 x 33 In.	500
Table, Center, Gothic Revival, Oak, Early 1900s, 30 x 36 x 36 In.	175
Table, Center, Louis XVI Style, Marble Top, Oval, 2 Shelves, Early 1900s, 29¾ x 35 x 23½ In.	615
Table, Center, Low, Circular Glass Top, Marble Lower Shelf, 1900s, 16 x 40 In.	688
Table, Center, Mahogany & Fruitwood, Marquetry, Adjustable, Dutch, 1900s, 31 x 41 In. ...*illus*	500
Table, Center, Mahogany, Circular Legs, Greek Key, Ormolu Bulb Feet, Louis XVI, 32 x 31½ In.	2125
Table, Center, Mahogany, Gilt, Viennese, c.1820, 28¾ x 40 In.	1250
Table, Center, Mahogany, Oval Top, Single Drawer, Squat Bun Feet, c.1880, 29 x 38 x 26 In.	1188
Table, Center, Marble Top, Mahogany, Reeded Cabriole Legs, Urn Finial, 1800s, 29 x 38 x 26 In.	308
Table, Center, Medallion, Inlaid Musical Theme, Lion's Head Ormolu Mounts, 32 x 30 In.	173
Table, Center, Neoclassical Style, Carved, Pine Marble Top, 28½ x 38 In.	593
Table, Center, Neoclassical Style, Pietra Dura Gilt, Marble Top, 1900s, 35 x 58 x 27 In.	2460
Table, Center, Oak, Round, Stubby Paw Feet, 2-Tier Shelves, Carved Skirt, c.1900, 31 x 48 In.	468
Table, Center, Parquetry, Gilt Bronze, Paris, 30 x 44 x 27 In.	1500
Table, Center, Regency, Mahogany, Octagonal, Drawers, Splayed Legs, Casters, 1800s, 30½ x 41 x 34 In.	1500
Table, Center, Tooled Leather, Brass Mounts, Twist Pedestal Base, 31½ x 40 In.	549
Table, Center, Victorian, Marble Top, Carved Dog, Shelf, Shaped Legs, 28 x 36 In. ....*illus*	240
Table, Center, Victorian, Marble Top, Quadruped Base, Rosette, 29 x 29 x 21 In.	96
Table, Center, Victorian, Marble Top, Shaped Corners, Casters, 30½ x 23 x 22½ In.	150
Table, Center, Walnut, Gray Marble Top, 4 Flat Legs, Victorian, 30 x 35 x 24 In.	424
Table, Charles X Style, Birch Center, Dished Gray Marble Top, France, 30 x 38½ In.	625
Table, Cherry & Walnut, Oval Top, Button Feet, 1700s, 26 x 29 In.	163
Table, Cherry, Single Drawer, Turned Legs, c.1850, 19½ x 19 In.	270
Table, Chippendale Style, Drum Shape, Walnut, Pedestal, Claw Foot, c.1920, 30 x 28 In. ....*illus*	406
Table, Chippendale Style, John Stuart, Mahogany, Piecrust, Cabriole Legs, 28 x 28 In.	236
Table, Chippendale, Tilt Top, Mahogany, Ball & Claw Feet, c.1800, 24½ x 24¾ x 24½ In.	165
Table, Circular Marble Top, Flared Base, Bentwood, Continental, Early 1900s, 30 x 36 In.	125
Table, Circular Marble Top, Inlaid, Gothic Arches, Quatrefoils, Plinth Base, Italy, 1800s, 37 In.	1000
Table, Circular, 2 Tiers, Low, 1900s, 17 x 48 In.	875

F

Table, Coffee, Adrian Pearsall, Walnut, Square Glass Top, 36 x 15¾ In.	303
Table, Coffee, Aldo Tura, Goatskin, Brass Inlay, Brass Bottle Insert, 14 x 63 x 39 In.	3000
Table, Coffee, Alessandro Albrizzi, Acrylic, Chrome Metal, Glass, 1900s, 15 x 60 x 25 In.	553.5
Table, Coffee, Asian Style, Mahogany, 1900s, 17 x 59 x 22 In.	281
Table, Coffee, Bertha Schaefer, Walnut, Granite Top, c.1955, 15¼ x 17 x 48 In.	687
Table, Coffee, Beveled Edge, Tapered Legs, Brass Accents Feet, c.1985, 15¾ x 39½ In.	154
Table, Coffee, Buckeye, Burl, 2 Sections, Organic Shape, Mid 1900s, 14 x 38 In. ......*illus*	960
Table, Coffee, Chippendale Style, Square, Shaped Apron, Ball & Claw Feet, 1900s, 18½ x 42 In.	125
Table, Coffee, Ettore Sottsass, Park Lane, Marble, Fiberglass, Round, Memphis, 1983, 14 x 41 In.	3250
Table, Coffee, Fontana Art, Pietro Chiesa, Curved Glass, Decal, 1900s, 13 x 51 x 27 In.	660
Table, Coffee, Frankl, Lacquered Cork, Mahogany, Johnson, c.1948, 71 x 21 x 13 In.	3750
Table, Coffee, G. Frattini, Kyoto, Beech, Ebony, Openwork Grid, c.1974, 14 x 36 In.	2928
Table, Coffee, Gilt Bronze, Green Marble Base, Glass Top, Pedestal, France, 1900s, 23¾ x 61 x 20 In.	1000
Table, Coffee, Gilt, Glass Top, Nude Figure Supports, Marked ARP, 16 x 44 x 28 In.	263
Table, Coffee, Glass Top, 2 Bronze Blackamoor Supports, 20 x 66 x 18 In.	375
Table, Coffee, Glass Top, 2-Tone Steel, X-Form Base, 18 x 36 x 36 In. ......*illus*	188
Table, Coffee, Greta Magnusson Grossman, 3 Drawers, Walnut, 1952, 16 x 18 x 65 In.	1250
Table, Coffee, Hvidt, Teak, Brass, 6 Sections Make A Circle, Denmark, c.1952, 51 In. ......*illus*	5100
Table, Coffee, I. Noguchi, Walnut, Glass, c.1950, 16 x 41½ x 45 In. ......*illus*	937
Table, Coffee, Industrial, Oak, Patinated Metal, Black Painted, 17½ x 60 x 35 In. ......*illus*	187
Table, Coffee, Iron, Painted, Glass Top, Red & Gold Undertones, 1900s, 20 x 65 x 45 In.	69
Table, Coffee, Jeanneret, Teak, Circular Top, 3 Legs, c.1966, 16 x 25 x 26½ In.	8125
Table, Coffee, Jules Leleu, Lacquered Wood Top, Patinated Steel, Bronze, 1940s, 18 x 35 In.	1250
Table, Coffee, Kittinger, Marble Top, Inlay, Depicting A Man, Holding Horn, 20 x 36 In. ......*illus*	715
Table, Coffee, Louis XVI Style, Glass Top, Bronze Border, Carved, c.1950, 17 x 39 x 19 In.	125
Table, Coffee, Luther Conover, Mahogany, Enamel Steel, c.1955, 58½ x 35 x 12 In.	4550
Table, Coffee, Mahogany, Rectangular Top, 21 x 48 In.	100
Table, Coffee, Marzio Cecchi, Marble, Cantilever, c.1950, 53½ x 20¾ x 15 In.	210
Table, Coffee, Milo Baughman, Chrome, Marble Top, 16 x 36 In.	250
Table, Coffee, Mirrored Rectangular Base, Kilim Top, 18 x 61 x 36 In.	156
Table, Coffee, Oak, Carved, Rectangular Top, Turned Legs, Early 1900s, 17 x 50 x 33 In.	250
Table, Coffee, P. Evans, Argente, Aluminum, Glass Top, Welded, Textured, 1970s, 16 x 36 In.*illus*	16250
Table, Coffee, Philip & Kelvin LaVerne, Bronze & Pewter, Etched, Patinated, c.1950s, 17 x 42 In.	3750
Table, Coffee, Philip & Kelvin LaVerne, Brutalist, Acid, Bronze, Nude Women, Cherub, 22 x 40 In.	2875
Table, Coffee, Philip & Kelvin LaVerne, Chan, Bronze, Painted, Patinated, 1960s, 17 x 47 In.	6250
Table, Coffee, Pine, Sand Work, Pottery Fragment Border, Navajo Style, 16 x 61 x 29 In.	175
Table, Coffee, Richard Schultz, 8-Petal Top, Teak, White Painted Aluminum Base, 1960s, 15 x 42 In.	1770
Table, Coffee, Robsjohn-Gibbings, Walnut, 3 Legs, Athens, Greece, 17½ x 24 In.	2952
Table, Coffee, S. Hansen Jr., Stoneware, Lacquered Wood, Denmark, c.1965, 20 x 38 x 38 In.	312
Table, Coffee, Silas Seandel, Lily Pads, Mixed Metals, Glass Top, 1973, 16½ x 37 x 66 In.*illus*	3625
Table, Coffee, Tavola, Oggetti, Glass Top, Round, Black, 16 x 50 x 47 In.	496
Table, Coffee, V. Kagan, 3 Sections, Mosaic, Glass, Brass, N.Y., c.1955, 15 x 48 In. ......*illus*	5313
Table, Coffee, Walnut, Brass Gallery, Oval, Baker Furniture Co., 23 x 22 x 30 In. ......*illus*	620
Table, Coffee, Walnut, Inset Plaque, Woman On Horse, Cupid Running Alongside, 16 x 42 In.	923
Table, Coffee, Walnut, Stone, Rectangular Top, c.1980, 53 x 32¼ In.	32
Table, Coffee, Wormley, Walnut, Planks, Hairpin Legs, Dunbar, 11¾ x 72 In. ......*illus*	861
Table, Coffer, Elm, Shanghai, Drawers, Iron Hardware, Red Lacquer, 1800s, 38 x 76 x 17 In.	246
Table, Console, 2 Pedestals, Glass Top, Egyptian Style, Contemporary, 36 x 60 x 19 In.	106
Table, Console, Bird Inlay, Mahogany Veneer, Oak, 4 Cabriole Legs, c.1850, 28 x 28 x 15 In.	413
Table, Console, Brown Paint, Rope Clad, 1900s, 32¼ x 60 x 18 In.	500
Table, Console, Edgar Brandt Style, Scalloped Marble Top, Iron, Art Deco, 1900s, 31 x 30 x 25 In.	39
Table, Console, Empire, Gallery, Marble Inset, 1800s, 41 x 50 x 21 In.	1625
Table, Console, George III Style, Parcel Gilt, Demilune Marquetry Top, 35 x 65 x 26 In.	1125
Table, Console, George III, Gilt, Marble Top, Serpentine, Rococo, c.1760, 36 x 43 x 24 In.*illus*	6500
Table, Console, Gilt, Marble Top, Floral Carved Swags, Tapered Legs, 36 x 57 x 19 In.	3125
Table, Console, Gio Ponti, 3 Drawers, Tapered Legs, c.1960, 30 x 39½ x 12½ In.*illus*	688
Table, Console, Jean-Michel Frank Style, Iron Case, Leather, Drawers, Bronze Pulls, 31 x 49 x 16 In.	2250
Table, Console, Leather Top & Base, Iron, Copper Leaves, Gilt, Art Deco, 1900s, 34 x 55 x 77 In.	300
Table, Console, Louis XV Style, Marble Top, Acanthus Apron, Cabriole Legs, c.1900, 31 x 52 x 17 In.	1000
Table, Console, Louis XV Style, Demilune, False Marble Top, Gilt, 1800s, 37 x 35 x 15 In.	1500
Table, Console, Louis XV Style, Marble Top, Parcel Gilt, Rose, 1800s, 33 x 58 x 27 In.	3750

F

Furniture, Table, Coffee, Glass Top, 2-Tone Steel, X-Form Base, 18 x 36 x 36 In. $188

Roland Auctioneers & Valuers

Furniture, Table, Coffee, Hvidt, Teak, Brass, 6 Sections Make A Circle, Denmark, c.1952, 51 In. $5,100

Cowan's Auctions

TIP
Don't put a runner or a vase on your wooden table if it is in sunlight. Eventually the finish will fade around the ornaments and leave a shadow of the items on the wood.

Furniture, Table, Coffee, I. Noguchi, Walnut, Glass, c.1950, 16 x 41½ x 45 In. $937

Wright

Furniture, Table, Coffee, Industrial, Oak, Patinated Metal, Black Painted, 17½ x 60 x 35 In. $187

Doyle Auctioneers & Appraisers

FURNITURE

Furniture, Table, Coffee, Kittinger, Marble Top, Inlay, Depicting A Man, Holding Horn, 20 x 36 In.
$715

Susanin's Auctioneers & Appraisers

Furniture, Table, Coffee, P. Evans, Argente, Aluminum, Glass Top, Welded, Textured, 1970s, 16 x 36 In.
$16,250

Rago Arts and Auction Center

Furniture, Table, Coffee, Silas Seandel, Lily Pads, Mixed Metals, Glass Top, 1973, 16½ x 37 x 66 In.
$3,625

Rago Arts and Auction Center

The Skyscraper

Paul T. Frankl, the American furniture designer, hired cabinetmakers to make his furniture. Pieces from the 1920s and '30s are rare and high-priced. Skyscraper bookcases can sell for over $50,000. In the late 1930s, he had his designs mass-produced, and these pieces are less expensive. His designs were often copied.

Table, Console, Louis XVI Style, Bronze, Gilt, Marble, Acanthus Knees, c.1950, 36 x 66 x 23 In.	2500
Table, Console, Louis XVI, Walnut, Ormolu Rim, Bronze Edges, Reeded Legs, 57 x 16 x 31 In. .	36
Table, Console, Mahogany, Marble Top, Gilt, Eagle Base, Columns, 1900s, 37 x 50 In........*illus*	750
Table, Console, Marble Top, Paw Feet, England, c.1825, 34 x 27 x 17 In..................................	2706
Table, Console, Marble, Inlaid Decoration, Stepped Base, Italy, 30 x 24 x 11 In. ....*illus*	594
Table, Console, Modern, White, Mosaic, Veneer, Apron, 4 Drawers, 31 x 53 x 18 In....................	424
Table, Console, Neoclassical, Mahogany, Marble, Leaf Carved Scrolls, Phila., c.1850, 32 x 48 x 22 In.	2750
Table, Console, Neoclassical, Painted, Marble Inset Top, X-Stretcher, c.1820, 31 x 39 x 19 In.	1625
Table, Console, Osvaldo Borsani, Rosewood, Painted, Tooled Leather, Brass, 1930s, 33 x 63 x 18 In..	2250
Table, Console, Regency Style, Mahogany, Shelves, Doors, Top Shape Feet, 1900s, 34 x 60 x 16 In...	1063
Table, Console, Renaissance Revival Style, Parquetry, Barley Twist Legs, 32 x 42 x 18 In.	154
Table, Console, Rene Drouet, Gilt Metal, Marble, France, 1900s, 29 x 47½ x 25½ In.	2706
Table, Console, Wood, 2 Rams Support, Carved, Painted, Glass Top, Ball Feet, 28 x 55 x 18 In.	375
Table, Corner, Mahogany, Lower Shelf, c.1950, 19 x 11¾ In.....................................*illus*	62
Table, Danish Modern, Drop Leaf, Teak, 2 Swing Legs, 28½ x 5 x 54 In.	333
Table, Dining, Biedermeier, Cherry, Tilt Top, Turned Pedestal, Saber Legs, Paw Feet, 28 x 47 In.	660
Table, Dining, Borge Mogensen, Drop Leaf, Gateleg, Breadboard Top, 1958, 28 x 49 x 36 In....	878
Table, Dining, Burl Walnut Panels, Octagonal Split, Pedestal Base, Rosettes, 29 x 48 In....*illus*	1029
Table, Dining, Carved, Oak, Claw Foot, Chamfered Corners, Scroll Legs, 29 x 66 x 38 In.	726
Table, Dining, Center, Rattan, Octagonal Beveled Glass Top, 32 x 72 In.	813
Table, Dining, Colonial Revival, Carved, Mahogany, 31 x 54 In.......................................	400
Table, Dining, Drop Leaf, 3 Part, Removable D-Shape Ends, c.1815, 30 x 94 x 50 In. ....*illus*	594
Table, Dining, Drop Leaf, J. Hansen, Rosewood, Matte, Denmark, c.1950, 28 x 39 x 73 In.	2750
Table, Dining, Duncan Phyfe Style, Drop Leaf, Triple Pedestal, 3 Leaves, 97 In.	130
Table, Dining, E. Saarinen, Marble, Enamel Aluminum, Knoll, 1957, 54 x 28 In......................	2250
Table, Dining, E. Saarinen, Tulip, White Laminate Top, Aluminum, Knoll, 1950s, 29 x 42 In. .	767
Table, Dining, Empire Revival Style, Circular Top, Carved Frieze, Bun Feet, 30 x 45 In.	277
Table, Dining, Esherick, Walnut, Cherry, Carved, 1956, 28½ x 48 x 93 In...........................	9100
Table, Dining, Ferdinand Keller, Federal Style, Mahogany, Crossbanded, Inlay, Leaves, 1920s, 144 In.	200
Table, Dining, French Provincial Style, Oval, Cabriole Legs, 2 Leaves, Italy, 30 x 66 In......*illus*	492
Table, Dining, Glass Top, Acanthus Scroll Legs, Curved Stretcher, Late 1900s, 29 x 96 x 48 In..	344
Table, Dining, Jacobean Style, Drop Leaf, England, 30½ In.	767
Table, Dining, Jacobean Style, Oak, Carved, Pullout Leaves, Turned Legs, c.1935, 30 x 93 x 38 In. ..	312
Table, Dining, Jeanneret, Teak, Square Top, 4 Legs, c.1959, 35¾ x 35¾ x 28 In.......................	8125
Table, Dining, John Vesey, Polished Aluminum, Steel, Glass, 1900s, 30 x 87 x 44 In.	1968
Table, Dining, Karl Springer, Lacquer, Green, 29½ x 54 In.	923
Table, Dining, Leon Rosen, Glass Top, 2 Glass Chrome Base, 29 x 108 x 44 In.......................	130
Table, Dining, Louis XIII Style, Walnut, Ring-Turned Legs, 2 Leaves, c.1910, 30 x 122 In.	625
Table, Dining, Mahogany, Round, Pedestal, Art Deco, 30¼ x 48 In.	437
Table, Dining, P. Evans, Chrome, Steel, Rosewood, Signed, 1970s, 29 x 84 x 40 In.	1875
Table, Dining, P. Evans, Cityscape, Glass Top, Burl & Chrome Base, 1970, 96 x 47 In.........*illus*	3075
Table, Dining, P. Evans, Skyline, Glass Top, Bronzed Resin, Wood, 29 x 96 In.	10710
Table, Dining, Pine, Rectangular Top, X-Brace, Iron Trestle, 1900s, 29½ x 96 x 48 In.............	469
Table, Dining, Plywood, Pedestal, 4-Footed, 2 Leaves, Gudme Mobelfabrik, c.1975, 48 To 86 In.	246
Table, Dining, Poul Kjaerholm, Marble, Steel, E. Kold Christensen, Denmark, 1963, 24 x 55 In..*illus*	8750
Table, Dining, Queen Anne, Drop Leaf, Trifid Feet, c.1765, 29 x 16 x 40 In.	750
Table, Dining, R. Schultz, Petal, Redwood, Aluminum, Knoll, c.1980, 41 x 28 In.	2750
Table, Dining, Regency Style, Extension Leaf, Turned Pedestals, Brass Paw Feet, 29 x 97 x 43 In.	938
Table, Dining, Regency, Mahogany, Circular Top, 4 Splayed Legs, 1800s, 30 x 72½ In.............	3000
Table, Dining, Round Glass Top, Chrome Metal, Pedestal Stand, Pace Collection, 30 x 54 In. ..	2091
Table, Dining, Ship's Wheel, Mahogany, 9 Spokes, Glass Top, c.1890, 27 x 76 In.............*illus*	3900
Table, Dining, Wegner, Oval, Teak, Oak, Folding Leg, J. Hansen, Denmark, c.1960, 28 x 70 x 51 In.	8125
Table, Dining, Wegner, Walnut, Oak, J. Hansen, Denmark, 1953, 41 x 116 In. ....*illus*	8750
Table, Dining, William & Mary Style, Drop Leaf, Maple, Gateleg, Rhode Island, 29 x 54 x 53 In.	263
Table, Dining, Wormley, Rectangular, 2 Leaves, Casters, Dunbar, 1950s, 40 x 76 x 29 In.	813
Table, Drawer, Wood, Tapered Leg & Banding, 1800s, 28½ x 33 x 22 In.	92
Table, Dressing, 2 Drawers, Scrolled Backsplash, Painted, c.1825, 35 x 36 x 17 In.	461
Table, Dressing, 2 Tiers, Yellow, Green Trim, Fruit, Flowers, 3 Drawers, Brass Pulls, c.1820, 32 In.	2520
Table, Dressing, Chippendale Style, Drawers, Apron, Cabriole Legs, Late 1900s, 30 x 36 x 20 In.	330
Table, Dressing, Chippendale, Walnut, Carved, Scroll Apron, c.1765, 30 x 32 In.................*illus*	4500

F

Furniture, Table, Coffee, V. Kagan, 3 Sections, Mosaic, Glass, Brass, N.Y., c.1955, 15 x 48 In.
$5,313

Freeman's Auctioneers & Appraisers

Furniture, Table, Console, Mahogany, Marble Top, Gilt, Eagle Base, Columns, 1900s, 37 x 50 In.
$750

Crescent City Auction Gallery

Furniture, Table, Coffee, Walnut, Brass Gallery, Oval, Baker Furniture Co., 23 x 22 x 30 In.
$620

DuMouchelles

Furniture, Table, Console, Gio Ponti, 3 Drawers, Tapered Legs, c.1960, 30 x 39 ½ x 12 ½ In.
$688

Kamelot Auctions

Furniture, Table, Console, Marble, Inlaid Decoration, Stepped Base, Italy, 30 x 24 x 11 In.
$594

Kamelot Auctions

Furniture, Table, Coffee, Wormley, Walnut, Planks, Hairpin Legs, Dunbar, 11 ¾ x 72 In.
$861

Cowan's Auctions

TIP
Felt tops on card tables and desks attract moths. Vacuum tops carefully at least once a year.

Furniture, Table, Corner, Mahogany, Lower Shelf, c.1950, 19 x 11 ¾ In.
$62

Wright

Furniture, Table, Console, George III, Gilt, Marble Top, Serpentine, Rococo, c.1760, 36 x 43 x 24 In.
$6,500

Susanin's Auctioneers & Appraisers

FURNITURE

Furniture, Table, Dining, Burl Walnut Panels, Octagonal Split, Pedestal Base, Rosettes, 29 x 48 In.
$1,029

Fontaine's Auction Gallery

Furniture, Table, Dining, Drop Leaf, 3 Part, Removable D-Shape Ends, Rectangular, c.1815, 30 x 94 x 50 In.
$594

Roland Auctioneers & Valuers

Furniture, Table, Dining, French Provincial Style, Oval, Cabriole Legs, 2 Leaves, Italy, 30 x 66 In.
$492

Skinner, Inc.

Furniture, Table, Dining, P. Evans, Cityscape, Glass Top, Burl & Chrome Base, 1970, 96 x 47 In.
$3,075

Skinner, Inc.

Furniture, Table, Dining, Poul Kjaerholm, Marble, Steel, E. Kold Christensen, Denmark, 1963, 24 x 55 In.
$8,750

Wright

Furniture, Table, Dining, Ship's Wheel, Mahogany, 9 Spokes, Glass Top, c.1890, 27 x 76 In.
$3,900

Eldred's

Furniture, Table, Dining, Wegner, Walnut, Oak, J. Hansen, Denmark, 1953, 41 x 116 In.
$8,750

Wright

Furniture, Table, Dressing, Chippendale, Walnut, Carved, Scroll Apron, c.1765, 30 x 32 In.
$4,500

Pook & Pook

Furniture, Table, Drop Leaf, Chippendale, Rounded Edges, Square Legs, c.1810, 28 x 53 x 22 In.
$192

Garth's Auctioneers & Appraisers

Furniture, Table, Drop Leaf, Envelope, Bird's-Eye Maple, Bamboo Turnings, c.1890, 28 x 27 In.
$1,125

Neal Auction Company

Furniture, Table, Drop Leaf, Hepplewhite, Walnut, Chevron Inlay, c.1815, 28 x 38 ½ x 19 In.
$180

Garth's Auctioneers & Appraisers

Furniture, Table, Drop Leaf, Regency, Mahogany, Boxwood Inlay, Drawer, c.1800, 29 x 30 In.
$1,440

Eldred's

Furniture, Table, Drop Leaf, Tiger Maple, Square Tapered Legs, 1800s, 28 x 37 x 18 In.
$270

Eldred's

Furniture, Table, Empire Style, Iron, Lyre, Anthemion, Rosettes, Stone Top, 1900s, 32 x 100 In.
$1,320

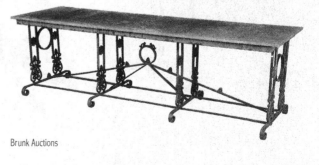

Brunk Auctions

F

Furniture, Table, First Period Napoleonic, Half Round Mahogany Top, Pedestal, 29 x 38 In.
$170

Soulis Auctions

Furniture, Table, Florence Knoll, Chromed Steel & Rosewood Oval, 1960, 28 x 78 x 48 In.
$1,125

Rago Arts and Auction Center

Furniture, Table, French Style, Round, Gilt Marble Top, Carved, Cabriole Legs, c.1900, 32 x 24 In.
$431

Crescent City Auction Gallery

Furniture, Table, Game, Chess, Backgammon, Drexel, Embossed Leather, Flip Top, 30 x 37 In.
$374

Burchard Galleries

Furniture, Table, Game, Georgian, Mahogany, Turret Top, Cabriole Legs, 1700s, 27 x 32 x 16 In.
$677

Skinner, Inc.

Furniture, Table, Game, S. McIntire, Mahogany, Carved, Turned Pedestal, c.1790, 30 x 36 In.
$510

Eldred's

Furniture, Table, Glass Top, Magazine Rack, Mathieu Matégot, France, c.1950, 19 x 16 x 24 In.
$1,063

Rago Arts and Auction Center

Furniture, Table, I. Noguchi, Glass Top, Wood Base, 1940s, 16 x 50 x 36 In.
$1,625

Susanin's Auctioneers & Appraisers

Furniture, Table, Iron & Bronze Arrow, Marble Top, Manner Of Jansen, 23 x 15 In.
$281

Kamelot Auctions

Furniture, Table, Japonesque, Lacquered Wood, Painted Top, Splayed Supports, Footed, 31 x 25 In.
$1,250

Neal Auction Company

Table, Dressing, Chippendale, Walnut, Drawers, Ball & Claw Feet, Pa., c.1770, 28 x 31 x 19 In..	1320
Table, Dressing, Georgian, Ribbon Mahogany, Compartments, Mirror, 1686, 10 x 17 x 34 In...	620
Table, Dressing, Louis Philippe, Mahogany, Oval Mirror, Marble, Paw Feet, 1800s, 55 x 33 x 17 In..	438
Table, Dressing, Neoclassical, Gilt, Stencil, Mahogany, Paw Feet, New York, c.1825, 35 x 37 x 19 In.	1250
Table, Dressing, Pine, Basswood, Red Grain Painted, 2 Tiers, c.1830, 34 x 30 In.	450
Table, Dressing, Pine, Scroll Backsplash, 2 Tiers, Drawers, Smoke Painted, 1800s, 38 x 33 In..	563
Table, Dressing, Queen Anne, Walnut, Fan Carved Drawer, Brass Handle, c.1730, 30 x 30 x 19 In.	2214
Table, Dressing, Rococo Revival, Glass Door, Drawers, Pullout Slide, Italy, c.1910, 53 x 36 x 23 In...	300
Table, Dressing, Rosewood, Grain Painted, 1800s, 38 ½ x 36 In.	113
Table, Dressing, Sheraton, Curly Maple, Pine, 2 Drawers, Rosettes, c.1850, 31 x 35 x 18 In.	594
Table, Dressing, Sheraton, Pine, Yellow Paint, Shaped Backsplash, Fruit, Drawer, 34 In.	600
Table, Dressing, Walnut, 3 Drawers, Cabriole Legs, Slipper Feet, c.1700, 28 x 30 x 19 In.	5806
Table, Dressing, Walnut, Scalloped Apron, Bench Made, 1900s, 27 ½ x 26 In.	138
Table, Drop Leaf, Chippendale, Rounded Edges, Square Legs, c.1810, 28 x 53 x 22 In........*illus*	192
Table, Drop Leaf, Envelope, Bird's-Eye Maple, Bamboo Turnings, c.1890, 28 x 27 In.........*illus*	1125
Table, Drop Leaf, Federal, Paw Foot, Mahogany, c.1840, 28 x 22 x 40 In.	125
Table, Drop Leaf, French Provincial Style, Oak, Cabriole Legs, 29 x 35 x 23 In.	154
Table, Drop Leaf, George I, Oak, Gateleg, c.1730, 30 x 24 x 60 In.	397
Table, Drop Leaf, Harvest, Pine, Pennsylvania, Early 1800s, 29 x 39 x 84 In.	1150
Table, Drop Leaf, Hepplewhite, Cherry, Tapered Legs, Drawer, 1800s, 17 ½ x 35 ½ In.	148
Table, Drop Leaf, Hepplewhite, Walnut, Chevron Inlay, c.1815, 28 x 38 ½ x 19 In. ....*illus*	180
Table, Drop Leaf, Mahogany, Drawers, Baluster Shape Legs, 1800s, 27 x 37 In.	1107
Table, Drop Leaf, Mahogany, Tapered Legs, Massachusetts, c.1795, 28 x 48 x 48 In.	800
Table, Drop Leaf, Neoclassical, Mahogany, Pedestal, Reeded Legs, Baltimore, c.1825, 29 x 65 In.	222
Table, Drop Leaf, Queen Anne, Mahogany, Mass., c.1760, 27 ½ x 13 ¾ x 35 ¾ In.	625
Table, Drop Leaf, Queen Anne, Mahogany, Swing Leg, Padded Feet, c.1750, 28 x 38 x 13 In.	240
Table, Drop Leaf, Rectangular, Dovetailed Drawer, Wood, Turned Leg, 1800s, 28 x 18 x 36 In.	138
Table, Drop Leaf, Regency, Mahogany, Boxwood Inlay, Drawer, c.1800, 29 x 30 In. ....*illus*	1440
Table, Drop Leaf, Sheraton, Curly Maple, Turned Legs, Brass Ball Feet, c.1840, 31 x 25 x 36 In.	384
Table, Drop Leaf, Sheraton, Mahogany, Drawers, Turned Legs, c.1820, 30 x 20 x 19 In.	144
Table, Drop Leaf, Sheraton, Maple, Pine, 2 Drawers, Curved Leaves, c.1850, 28 x 18 In.	458
Table, Drop Leaf, Tiger Maple, Drawer, Single-Board Top, Rounded Leaves, c.1835, 39 x 19 In.	344
Table, Drop Leaf, Tiger Maple, Square Tapered Legs, 1800s, 28 x 37 x 18 In......................*illus*	270
Table, Drop Leaf, William & Mary, Maple, Drawer, Gateleg, 1700s, 27 x 36 ¾ x 14 In.	450
Table, Eames, Laminate, Plywood, Chrome Plated Steel, Herman Miller, c.1995, 9 x 29 x 89 In.	1250
Table, Edwardian, Oak, Circular Top, Molded Edge, Claw Feet On Casters, c.1900, 30 x 55 x 12 In...	507
Table, Eero Saarinen, Marble Top, Tulip Shape, Knoll, c.1960, 14 x 20 In.	563
Table, Eero Saarinen, Tulip, Rounded Wood Top, Black Pedestal Base, Knoll, 29 x 54 In.	1170
Table, Elm, Carved, Square Edge Frame, Openwork Apron, Recessed Leg, 1800s, 34 x 37 x 15 In.	123
Table, Empire Style, Iron, Lyre, Anthemion, Rosettes, Stone Top, 1900s, 32 x 100 In. ....*illus*	1320
Table, Empire Style, Pedestal Base, Carved Gilt Dolphins, Marble Top, 1800s, 28 x 43 In.	2400
Table, Farm, Oak, Carved, Plank Top, Drawer, Turned Legs, H-Stretcher, 1900s, 30 x 87 x 31 In..	800
Table, Farm, Pine, Oval, Late 1800s, 28 ½ x 64 x 40 In.	750
Table, Federal, Cherry, Painted Top, Early 1800s, 30 x 36 x 28 ½ In.	200
Table, First Period Napoleonic, Half Round Mahogany Top, Pedestal, 29 x 38 In.............*illus*	170
Table, Florence Knoll, Chromed Steel & Rosewood Oval, 1960, 28 x 78 x 48 In..................*illus*	1125
Table, Frederic Schmit, Mahogany, Veneer, Ormolu Trim, French Inlay, c.1920, 29 x 32 x 20 In.	649
Table, French Style, Round, Gilt Marble Top, Carved, Cabriole Legs, c.1900, 32 x 24 In......*illus*	431
Table, Galle, Mahogany, Fruitwood Inlay Of Magpie, Oak Branch, c.1900, 22 x 25 In.	2875
Table, Game, Chess Pieces, Fruitwood & Maple, Adirondack, 28 x 28 ½ x 29 In.	177
Table, Game, Chess, Backgammon, Drexel, Embossed Leather, Flip Top, 30 x 37 In. ....*illus*	374
Table, Game, Chess, Octagonal, Steel Base, Marble Top, Italy, 1900s, 26 ½ x 27 In.	438
Table, Game, Edwardian, Rosewood, Envelope, Inlay, Reeded Supports, c.1910, 30 x 30 x 30 In.	1250
Table, Game, Empire, Foldover Top, Mixed Wood, Pedestal Base, c.1850, 30 x 36 x 17 In.	192
Table, Game, Foldover Top, Fluted Tapered Legs, Spade Feet, Marquetry, 1800s, 30 x 42 x 31 In.	375
Table, Game, George III, Mahogany, Inlay, Tapered Legs, England, 1800s, 28 x 40 x 18 In.	780
Table, Game, George III, Mahogany, Shaped Top, Trifid Feet, c.1740, 29 x 34 In.	375
Table, Game, Georgian, Mahogany, Turret Top, Cabriole Legs, 1700s, 27 x 32 x 16 In........*illus*	677
Table, Game, Hepplewhite, Demilune, Inlay, Square Legs, Arrow Feet, 1800s, 28 x 36 x 17 In. .	300
Table, Game, Louis XV Style, Bronze Mounts, Foldover Top, Cabriole Legs, 1800s, 30 x 34 x 18 In.	1188

Furniture, Table, Knoll, Elliptical, Oval Top, 4 Splayed Legs, 28 ½ x 78 x 47 ½ In. $293

Susanin's Auctioneers & Appraisers

TIP
Use a credit card to scrape hardened candle wax from a table.

Furniture, Table, Library, Regency Style, Mahogany, Single-Board Top, Trestle, 1800s, 29 x 57 In. $1,140

Brunk Auctions

Furniture, Table, Louis XVI Style, Kingwood, Brocatelle Marble Top, France, 1800s, 33 x 47 In. $677

Skinner, Inc.

Furniture, Table, Mahogany, Mixed Wood, Round, Inlaid Panel, Birds, Flowers, 1800s, 29 x 62 In. $5,250

New Orleans Auction Galleries

F

Furniture, Table, Maple, Black Over Red Paint, Oval, Gateleg, Ball Feet, Mass., 27 x 46 x 53 In.
$4,440

Northeast Auctions

Furniture, Table, McCobb, Enameled Steel, Mahogany, 200 Series, 1950, 22 x 20 x 32 In.
$500

Wright

Furniture, Table, Oval, Shoefoot, Square Stretchers, England, 1700s, 26 ½ x 28 ¾ x 17 ½ In.
$7,380

Skinner, Inc.

Furniture, Table, Pembroke, George III, Painted Border, Vine, Ribbon, Drawer, c.1800, 39 x 26 In.
$800

Skinner, Inc.

Furniture, Table, Peter Hunt, Paint Decorated, Hearts, Fruit, Oval, Signed O'Vince, 18 x 29 x 22 In.
$480

Eldred's

Furniture, Table, Pier, Marble Top, Carved Feet, Gilt, Ebonized, Mirror Plate, c.1820, 36 x 39 In.
$2,500

Brunk Auctions

Table, Game, Mahogany Inlay, Foldover Top, England, 1800s, 30 x 36 ½ x 17 ½ In.	438
Table, Game, Maple, Veneered Top, Ball Foot, Late 1700s, 29 x 34¾ In.	7500
Table, Game, Regency Style, Mahogany, Leather Backgammon Board, 1800s, 30 x 26 x 16 In.	1063
Table, Game, S. McIntire, Mahogany, Carved, Turned Pedestal, c.1790, 30 x 36 In...........*illus*	510
Table, George II Style, Gilt, Marble Top, 1900s, 36 x 70 x 28 ½ In.	7500
Table, George II Style, Oak, Tilt Top, Tripod Feet, 1800s, Miniature, 14 x 12 In.	125
Table, George III, Oak, Pine Secondary, Cock-Beaded Drawer, Late 1700s, 28 x 29 x 17 In.......	142
Table, George III, Satinwood, Bowfront Top, Spade Feet, Late 1700s, 31 x 32 x 19 In.................	138
Table, Georgian Style, Mahogany, Octagonal, Tilt Top, Ball & Claw Feet, 1900s, 29 x 31 In.......	492
Table, Georgian Style, Tilt Top, Mahogany, 8-Point Star, Tripod Base, c.1900, 28 x 30 In.	813
Table, Georgian, Pembroke, Frieze Drawer, Square Tapered Legs, Early 1800s, 29 x 37 In.	281
Table, Gilt, False Marble Top, Carved, Ball & Claw Feet, Porphyry Pedestal Base, 1700s, 37 x 40 In.	1875
Table, Gilt, Marble Top, Square Legs, Stretcher, Carved Feet, Italy, 1900s, 33 x 39 x 21 In...............	1750
Table, Glass Top, Bronze Rings, Downswept Legs, c.1970, 30 ½ x 98 ½ x 43 ½ In.	1750
Table, Glass Top, Magazine Rack, Mathieu Mategot, France, c.1950, 19 x 16 x 24 In.........*illus*	1063
Table, Hall, White Marble Top, Carved Bowed Cabriole Legs, Italy, 1900s, 36 x 78 x 22 In.	761
Table, Hardwood, Octagonal, Carved, Bamboo, Early 1900s, 22¾ In.	154
Table, Harvest, Poplar, Grain Painted, Plain Skirt, Turned Legs, 1800s, 28 x 96 x 33 In.	468
Table, Hepplewhite, Cherry, Pegged, 2-Board Top, Drawer, Tapered Legs, 1800s, 25 x 26 In.	270
Table, Hepplewhite, Pembroke, Mahogany, D-Shape Leaves, c.1800s, 28 x 32 x 11 In.	1560
Table, Hollywood Regency, Brass, Enamel, Reverse Painted, Early 1900s, 19 ½ x 27 ½ In.........	813
Table, Huntboard, Pine, Rectangular Top, 2 Drawers, Stretchers, 1800s, 36 x 21 In.	3567
Table, I. Noguchi, Glass Top, Wood Base, 1940s, 16 x 50 x 36 In...............................*illus*	1625
Table, Inset Marble Top, Hardwood Frame, Chinese, Early 1900s, 19 x 15 In.	189
Table, Iron & Bronze Arrow, Marble Top, Manner Of Jansen, 23 x 15 In.............................*illus*	281
Table, Iron, Black, Glass Top, Acid Etched, Gold, Iron Base, Finials, Tassels, 32 x 27 x 14 In.....	484
Table, Jacobean Style, Oak, Rectangular Top, Cylindrical Legs, 1800s, 30 x 65 x 27 In.............	1063
Table, Japonesque, Lacquered Wood, Painted Top, Splayed Supports, Footed, 31 x 25 In....*illus*	1250
Table, Karl Springer, Cylindrical, Snakeskin, 1900s, 17 ¼ x 18 In.	923
Table, Karl Springer, Lucite Base, Bamboo Shape, Glass Top, 1900s, 16 x 51 x 29 In.	375
Table, Karl Springer, Snakeskin, Yellow, 1900s, 19 x 20 x 16 In.	2091
Table, Knoll, Elliptical, Oval Top, 4 Splayed Legs, 28 ½ x 78 x 47 ½ In..........................*illus*	293
Table, Knoll, Teak, Square Top, Tapered Legs, Label, 27 x 27 x 19 In.	148
Table, L. & J.G. Stickley, Double Trestle, Lower Shelf, c.1915, 60 x 36 In.	2125
Table, L. & J.G. Stickley, Oak, Drawer, Copper Pulls, Square Legs, 29 x 42 x 28 In.	1452
Table, L. & J.G. Stickley, Overhanging Top, Crossed Stretchers, c.1917, 20 x 20 In.	424
Table, Library, Edwardian, Carved, Oak, Rectangular, Leaves, 2 Drawers, c.1910, 29 x 48 x 30 In. .	94
Table, Library, Neoclassical Style, Leather Top, Tapered Legs, Birch, 1800s, 30 x 74 x 33 In......	750
Table, Library, Regency Style, Mahogany, Single-Board Top, Trestle, 1800s, 29 x 57 In. ....*illus*	1140
Table, Library, Walnut, Short Tapered Feet, Flat Stretcher, Early 1900s, 30 x 96 x 48 In.	1599
Table, Louis XIV Style, Pietra Dura & Silver, Pendant Cartouches, Acanthus Legs, 33 x 74 x 38 In.	8438
Table, Louis XV Style, Drawers, Marquetry, Cabriole Legs, 1900s, 32 x 54 x 29 In.	1375
Table, Louis XV Style, Gilt, Marble Top, Cabriole Legs, Turtle Form, c.1900, 21 x 27 x 21 In.	1063
Table, Louis XV Style, Kingwood, Leather, 2 Drawers, Cabriole Legs, 1800s, 31 x 48 x 25 In......	2125
Table, Louis XV Style, Leather Top, Drawers, Cabriole Legs, 1800s, 29 x 53 x 29 In.................	2500
Table, Louis XV Style, Mahogany, Gilt Bronze, Kidney Shape, 1900s, 32 ½ x 68 ½ x 40 In.........	1188
Table, Louis XV Style, Onyx Top, Carved Edge, Frieze, Cabriole Legs, 1800s, 31 x 26 In.............	732
Table, Louis XV, Marble Top, 2 Drawer, Burl, Ormolu, Veining, France, 28 x 23 x 15 In.	288
Table, Louis XV, Tulipwood, Writing, Leather, France, 1800s, 28 ½ x 25 x 18 ½ In.	438
Table, Louis XVI Style, Dining, Mahogany, Bronze, Fluted Legs, c.1940, 29 x 70 x 43 In.	250
Table, Louis XVI Style, Kingwood, Brocatelle Marble Top, France, 1800s, 33 x 47 In..........*illus*	677
Table, Low, Rosewood, Carved Rim, Scroll Legs, Chinese, 6 x 25¾ x 12 In.	425
Table, M. Berthier & J. Magis, Circular Top, Chrome, Tripod Base, Italy, 24 x 20 In.	182
Table, M. Nakashima, Wepman, Black Walnut, Burl Maple, 3 Legs, 1993, 17 x 17 x 18 In.	2500
Table, Mahogany, Marble Top, Ogee Frieze, Drawer, Paw Feet, 1800s, 37 x 43 x 18 In.	875
Table, Mahogany, Mixed Wood, Round, Inlaid Panel, Birds, Flowers, 1800s, 29 x 62 In.....*illus*	5250
Table, Maple, Black Over Red Paint, Oval, Gateleg, Ball Feet, Mass., 27 x 46 x 53 In. ....*illus*	4440
Table, Marble & Square Top, Victorian, Carved, 27 x 18 x 29 In..	118
Table, Marble Top, Black, Pietra Dura, White, Green, Floral, Victorian, 23¾ x 30 ½ In.	688
Table, Marble Top, Serpentine, Cabriole Legs, Filigree Bronze Mount, 19 x 43 x 25 In.	726

Furniture, Table, Renaissance Revival Style, Walnut, Frieze Drawer, Carved, 1900s, 19 x 32 In.
$250

Neal Auction Company

Furniture, Table, Rustic, Hand Carved, Heart Shape Top, Tripod Legs, 21 x 10 x 26 In.
$35

Copake Auction

Furniture, Table, Sewing, Neoclassical, Mahogany, Carved, Lift Top, Pedestal, 1800s, 29 x 19 In.
$500

Neal Auction Company

F

Furniture, Table, Sewing, Sheraton, Mahogany, 2 Drawers, Reeded Legs, c.1805, 30 x 20¾ x 15 In.
$330

Eldred's

Furniture, Table, Tea, Kittinger, Queen Anne Style, Cabriole Legs, Williamsburg Series, c.1985, 26 x 29 In.
$263

Garth's Auctioneers & Appraisers

Furniture, Table, Tilt Top, 8-Sided Top, Fruitwood, Inlay, Tripod Base, Italy, 1900s, 30 x 25 In.
$438

Neal Auction Company

Table, Marble, Iron, Scrolling Acanthus Leaves On Stand, Maitland Smith, 1900s, 30 x 22 In.	242
Table, Marquetry, Circular Top, Wrought Iron, Tripod Feet, Italy, 1800s, 25 x 14½ In.	125
Table, McCobb, Enameled Steel, Mahogany, 200 Series, 1950, 22 x 20 x 32 In. ....*illus*	500
Table, Molded Top, Scalloped Frieze, Cabriole Legs, Hoof Feet, Fruitwood, 1800s, 27 x 29 x 23 In.	500
Table, Multicolor, Marble Top, Portrait Medallion, Circular Legs, c.1850, 37 x 52½ x 26½ In.	4500
Table, Nakashima Woodworkers, Slab Top, Order Card, Sketch, Delorenzo, N.Y., 1950, 21 x 37 x 22 In.	2829
Table, Neoclassical, Marble Top, Gilt, X-Stretcher, Leafy Feet, 1800s, 32 x 37 x 26 In.	3250
Table, Neoclassical, Walnut, Drawers, Ebonized Band, 3 Pad Feet, Italy, c.1800, 30 x 47 In.	303
Table, Nicholas Petit, Leather Inset Slides, False Drawers, c.1780, 30 x 64 x 30 In.	4500
Table, Oak, Baluster Legs, Central Stretcher, Parquet Top, Mortise & Tenon, 1900, 32 x 36 x 15 In.	1188
Table, Oak, Gadroon Carved Frieze, X-Stretcher, Block Feet, Late 1800s, 30½ x 37½ In.	1750
Table, Oak, Pedestal, 4 Paw Feet, 2 Leaves, Early 1900s, 42 x 11 In.	60
Table, Octagonal, Grape Branches, Scrolling Vines, Mid 1800s, 24¾ x 24 x 24 In.	438
Table, Oval, Shoefoot, Square Stretchers, England, 1700s, 26½ x 28¾ x 17½ In. ....*illus*	7380
Table, P. Evans, Chrome Plated Steel, Brass, 1900s, 22 x 30 x 30 In.	1968
Table, P. Evans, Steel, Patinated Copper, Slate, Brass, 1900s, 29½ x 32 x 32 In.	2214
Table, Painted, Old Spanish Brown Surface, Circular Top, c.1800, 26½ x 60 In.	2500
Table, Pedestal, Stone Top, Gilt, Pierre Ouvrier E. Ringuet Sr. Paris, c.1900, 27 x 26 In.	480
Table, Pembroke, Chippendale, Mahogany, Scalloped Leaves, c.1790, 28 x 20 x 33 In.	750
Table, Pembroke, Federal, Mahogany, Early 1800s, 28 x 21 x 30 In.	75
Table, Pembroke, George III, Mahogany, Tulipwood Band, Tapered Legs, c.1790, 28 x 20 x 31 In.	438
Table, Pembroke, George III, Painted Border, Vine, Ribbon, Drawer, c.1800, 39 x 26 In.....*illus*	800
Table, Pembroke, Hepplewhite, Cherry, Scalloped Apron, X-Stretcher, Late 1700s, 27 x 18 x 8 In.	360
Table, Pembroke, Regency, 2 Drawers, Early 1800s, 28 x 26½ x 46 In.	163
Table, Pembroke, Sheraton, Mahogany, Round, Drawer, c.1810, 21 x 10 x 31 In.	510
Table, Peter Hunt, Paint Decorated, Hearts, Fruit, Oval, Signed O'Vince, 18 x 29 x 22 In. ..*illus*	480
Table, Pier, Louis Philippe, Mahogany, Marble Top, Paw Feet, c.1850, 36 x 51 In.	875
Table, Pier, Mahogany, Marble Top, Scroll Feet & Uprights, c.1835, 37 x 43 x 19 In.	1375
Table, Pier, Marble Top, Carved Feet, Gilt, Ebonized, Mirror Plate, c.1820, 36 x 39 In.......*illus*	2500
Table, Pier, Meeks, Classical, Mahogany, Parcel Gilt, Stencil, New York, c.1850, 38 x 44 x 20 In.	4000
Table, Porcelain, Rotating, Gold, White, Hand Painted, France, 1900s, 21 x 15 In.	88
Table, Queen Anne Style, Mahogany, Tilt Top, 1900s, 28¾ x 34½ In.	500
Table, Queen Anne, Drop Leaf, Oak, Carved Mahogany, England, c.1750, 28 x 36 x 13 In.	649
Table, Queen Anne, Oval Top, Red, Splayed Legs, Turned Button Feet, 1700s, 26 x 31 x 23 In.	840
Table, Red Painted, Butterfly, Drop Leaf, Diminutive, 1900s, 23 x 16 x 28 In.	238
Table, Regency, Rosewood, Egyptian Marble Top, Acanthus Carved Legs, c.1850, 38 x 38 x 20 In.	1000
Table, Renaissance Revival Style, Walnut, Frieze Drawer, Carved, 1900s, 19 x 32 In. ....*illus*	250
Table, Renaissance Revival, Walnut, Inlaid Top, Gilt, Fluted Legs, Stretcher, c.1870, 29 x 45 In.	2500
Table, Rohde, Walnut, Serpentine Edge Top, Herman Miller, 1900s, 15 x 44 x 44 In.	2706
Table, Rosewood, Carved, Frieze Drawer, Trestle Base, Stretchers, Continental, 1900s, 30 x 41 x 27 In.	563
Table, Rosewood, Serpentine Top, Shell Carved Frieze, Scroll Legs, Shoefeet, c.1830, 29 x 42 x 26 In.	1125
Table, Rustic, Hand Carved, Heart Shape Top, Tripod Legs, 21 x 10 x 26 In. ....*illus*	35
Table, Sawbuck, Oak, Rectangular Top, 1900s, 29½ x 72 x 35¾ In.	513
Table, Sawbuck, Pine, Scrubbed Top, Light Green Base, 1800s, 30½ x 79 x 24¾ In.	2125
Table, Scroll Legs, Carved, Penwork, Leaves, Ireland, 1700s, 38 x 22 x 30 In.	1015
Table, Server, 2 Tiers, Mahogany, Serpentine, Brass Trim, Side Handles, 33 x 34 x 19 In.	242
Table, Server, Birch & Yellow Pine, Square Tapered Legs, c.1800, 34 x 31 x 24 In.	222
Table, Sewing, Carved, Upholstered, Mahogany, Early 1800s, 32 x 20½ x 17½ In.	308
Table, Sewing, Drop Leaf, Federal Style, Mahogany, Drawers, Scrolled Feet, c.1920, 27 x 20 x 18 In.	94
Table, Sewing, Drop Leaf, Walnut, Drawer, Tapered Legs, Pa., c.1890, 27 x 31 In.	300
Table, Sewing, Empire Style, Mahogany, Gilt Bronze, 1800s, 30 x 22 x 17 In.	238
Table, Sewing, Federal, Rotating, Walnut, 2-Board Top, Cabriole Legs, 1800s, 28 x 23 x 23 In.	5400
Table, Sewing, Louis XV Style, Gilt Bronze, Kingwood, Cabriole Legs, Early 1900s, 28 x 24 x 17 In.	531
Table, Sewing, Mahogany, 3 Convex Drawers, Turned Legs, Boston, 28 x 20 In.	322
Table, Sewing, Martha Washington, Mahogany, 3 Drawers, Turned Legs, c.1920, 17¾ x 17 x 10 In.	72
Table, Sewing, Neoclassical, Mahogany, Carved, Lift Top, Pedestal, 1800s, 29 x 19 In........*illus*	500
Table, Sewing, Sheraton Style, Drawer, Square Cut Top, Turned Legs, 1800s, 29 x 19 x 17 In.	96
Table, Sewing, Sheraton, 2 Tiers, Mahogany, Brass Knob, c.1830, 31½ x 21 x 17¾ In.	163
Table, Sewing, Sheraton, Cherry, 2-Board Top, Drawer, Turned Legs, Mid 1800s, 29 x 25 x 19 In.	132

Table, Sewing, Sheraton, Dovetailed Drawer, Turned Legs, 1800s, 28 x 22 x 18 In.	150
Table, Sewing, Sheraton, Mahogany, 2 Drawers, Reeded Legs, c.1805, 30 x 20¾ x 15 In.....*illus*	330
Table, Sewing, Wicker, Wood Top, White Paint, Openwork, 17 x 11½ x 28 In.	24
Table, Shang Ti, Round Top, Philip & Kelvin LaVerne, 19⅝ x 17¾ In.	5000
Table, Shaped, Marble Top, Victorian, 21 x 24 x 38 In.	100
Table, Sheraton, Half Round, Applied Beading, Turned Legs, c.1850, 27 x 39 x 19 In.	120
Table, Sheraton, Pine, Yellow Paint, Fruit On Crest, c.1850, 38½ x 32 x 15 In.	240
Table, Sheraton, Rounded Corners, Drop Leaf, 2 Drawers, Turned Legs, c.1850, 28 x 17 In.	108
Table, Side, Decoupage Top, Bamboo Legs, Shelf, Floral, Early 1900s, 26 x 40 x 24 In.	625
Table, Side, Empire Style, Drawers, Carved, Floral, Paw Feet, c.1880, 33 x 15 x 13 In.	188
Table, Side, Gilbert Martin, Stainless Steel, Geometric, 1960s, 16 x 20 In.	3750
Table, Side, Glass Oval Top, Pedestal Base, 4 Feet, 1800s, 11 x 22 x 22 In.	403
Table, Side, Lawrence Laske, Saguaro Cactus, Wood, Chromed Metal, Knoll, 1993, 20 x 26 In. ..	369
Table, Side, Louis XIV Style, Carved, Wood, France, c.1950, 31 x 35 x 20 In.	113
Table, Side, Louis XV Style, Gilt Bronze, Lacquer Top, Chinoiserie, 1800s, 25 x 22½ x 16 In.....	250
Table, Side, Louis XVI Style, Marquetry, Oval Marble Top, Brass Gallery, 1900s, 30 x 20 x 15 In.	500
Table, Side, M. Nakashima, Minguren, Buckeye Burl, Black Walnut, Pa., c.1998, 18 x 23 x 20 In.....	5625
Table, Side, Mahogany, Circular Top, Drawer, 4 Straight Legs, Baker Furniture, 26½ In..........	217
Table, Side, Mahogany, Gilt Bronze, Inset Sevres Panels, France, c.1900s, 29 x 21 x 14 In.	2000
Table, Side, Octagonal, Classical Arabic, Inlay, 4 Plank Legs, Morocco, 20 x 16 x 16 In.	300
Table, Side, Octagonal, Lower Shelf, Tapered Legs, Early 1900s, 22 x 28½ In..........................	153
Table, Side, Round Top, Marble, Carved Apron, Bamboo Leaves, Cabriole Legs, c.1930s, 20 x 16 In. ..	313
Table, Side, Walnut, Round, 4 Legs, Cumberland, 1960, 20 x 29 In.	185
Table, Side, Wendell Castle, Maple, Jelutong Wood, Lacquer, c.1980, 24 x 16 In., Pair	7500
Table, Side, Wood, Frieze Drawer, Saber Legs, Dutch Marquetry, Late 1700s, 29 x 23 x 23 In. ...	375
Table, Silas Seandel, Bronze, Patinated, Signed & Dated, 1970, 14¾ x 29 In.	5228
Table, Softwood, Sawbuck Base, X-Legs, Rectangular Top, 28 x 42 x 23½ In.	201
Table, Tavern, 2 Drawers, Ring-Turned Legs, H-Stretcher, 1700s, 29 x 64 x 34 In......................	1089
Table, Tavern, Drawer, Rectangular Top, 1700s, 28½ x 58½ x 32 In.	594
Table, Tavern, Oval Top, Splay Tapered Leg Base, Tan Paint, Early 1800s, 26 x 23 x 32 In.	1306
Table, Tavern, Painted, Pine, Black Surface, Turned Legs, c.1780, 22 x 29 x 23 In.	1375
Table, Tavern, Pine, 2 Drawers, Pinned Top, Stretcher Base, Pa., 1800s, 30 x 48 x 30 In.	200
Table, Tavern, Pine, 3-Board Top, Breadboard Ends, Stretcher, Early 1800s, 26 x 42 x 29 In.	570
Table, Tavern, Pine, Rectangular, Scalloped Apron, c.1800, 28 x 25 In.	3120
Table, Tavern, Pine, Ring-Turned Legs, Stretcher, Red Surface, 29½ x 30½ x 24 In..................	1625
Table, Tavern, Queen Anne, Pine & Maple, Oval Top, Turned Legs, 1700s, 28 x 34¾ In.	1500
Table, Tea, Georgian Style, Mahogany, Tilt Top, Scalloped Edge, 29 x 32 In...............................	687
Table, Tea, Hardwood, Rectangular, Carved, Chinese, Late 1800s, 26 x 26 x 18 In.	540
Table, Tea, Kittinger, Queen Anne Style, Cabriole Legs, Williamsburg Series, c.1985, 26 x 29 In..*illus*	263
Table, Tea, Queen Ann Style, Mahogany, Scalloped Apron, Cabriole Legs, 1900s, 26 x 30 x 20 In.	96
Table, Tea, Queen Anne Style, Cherry, Round Top, Birdcage Baluster Shaft, c.1770, 29 x 33 In.	500
Table, Tea, Queen Anne, Birdcage, Round Tilt Top, Mahogany, Pad Feet, Pa., c.1800, 28 x 33 In.	210
Table, Tea, Queen Anne, Mahogany, Cabriole Legs, Va., c.1760, 26 x 34½ In.	1872
Table, Tea, Queen Anne, Rectangular, Tray Top, Scalloped Apron, Pad Feet, 1700s, 28 x 30 x 24 In..	6875
Table, Tea, Queen Anne, Walnut, Tilt Top, Tripod Base, Dauphin Co., Pa., c.1770, 32 x 28 In....	380
Table, Tea, Tilt Top, Chippendale, Walnut, Ball & Claw Feet, Pa., c.1770, 29 x 33½ In..............	3750
Table, Tea, Tilt Top, George III Style, Mahogany, Piecrust, Fluted Stem, Tripod, 1800s, 29 x 28 In. .	438
Table, Tea, Tilt Top, Turned Column, Tripod Base, Cabriole Legs, Pad Feet, c.1850, 29 x 27 In.	120
Table, Telephone, Painted, Tray Top, Columnar, 1900s, 22 In.	138
Table, Tilt Top, 8-Sided Top, Fruitwood, Inlay, Tripod Base, Italy, 1900s, 30 x 25 In. ....*illus*	438
Table, Tilt Top, Chippendale, Walnut, Birdcage Support, Tripod Base, Late 1700s, 8½ x 22 In.	188
Table, Tilt Top, Mahogany, Round Top, 3-Part Base, Japan, Mid 1800s, 28 x 48 In....................	3198
Table, Travertine, Brass Coated Steel, Italy, c.1960, 18 x 30 In.	437
Table, Tray, Black Lacquer, Inlay, Shaped Apron, Scroll Feet, 1900s, 5 x 17 x 10 In.	94
Table, Tray, Butler's, George III Style, Mahogany, Segmented, 1800, 24 x 32 x 21 In.	688
Table, Tray, On Stand, Cherry, X-Stretcher, 23½ x 22 x 34 In..	183
Table, Tray, Queen Anne Style, Chinoiserie, England, Early 1900s, 18 x 30 x 21 In.	240
Table, Trestle, Baroque Style, Rectangular Top, Iron Stretchers, Spain, 1900s, 31 x 80 x 27 In. ..	813
Table, Trestle, Hardwood, Leafy Edge Top, Twist Legs, Scalloped Stretcher, 1800s, 31 x 54 x 35 In. .	1125
Table, Trestle, Oak, Breadboard Top, Weathered, Stretcher Base, 29 x 61 x 27 In.	2188

Furniture, Table, Walter Von Nessen, Steel, Tiers, Enameled Wood, Bakelite, 1930s, 30 x 30 In.

$12,500

Rago Arts and Auction Center

Furniture, Tabouret, Inset Marble Top, Bat Carved Legs, Pierced Skirt, Chinese, Late 1800s, 23 x 17 In.

$420

Brunk Auctions

TIP

If you have an old, perhaps 18th-century, piece of furniture, try this dating tip. Pull the drawers out and put them back upside down. Each drawer should move back and forth as easily as it did in the right-side-up position. Old-time cabinetmakers made both the drawer and the opening exactly square. Later repairs may not be as exact.

Furniture, Umbrella Stand, Brass, Strap Handle, Cone Shape, 1900s, 34¾ In.
$88

Freeman's Auctioneers & Appraisers

Furniture, Umbrella Stand, Iron, Figural, Man In Khaki, British Soldier, c.1910, 27½ x 15 In.
$390

Eldred's

Borax

Borax is the slang name for very cheap furniture. It originally referred to cheap, poorly made but flashy furniture made for the bottom of the market during the Depression. It was often made of inexpensive gum or poplar wood with a printed veneer pattern. The term is still used today.

Table, Trestle, Renaissance Revival, 3 Drawers, Iron Stretchers, 1900s, 31 x 56 x 27 In.		813
Table, Venetian, Blackamoor Base, Wood, Malachite Veneer, 40 x 27½ In.		6250
Table, Wall Mounted, Gilt Metal, Lion's Head, Gray Marble Top, 8 x 22 x 12 In.		344
Table, Wall, Marble Top, Carved, Victorian, 34 x 35 x 15 In.		104
Table, Walnut Veneer, Carved, Spindled Legs, Slab Marble Top, Victorian, 36 x 24 x 28 In.		189
Table, Walnut, Breadboard Top, Germantown Black Paint, Tapered Legs, c.1810, 28 x 37 x 26 In.		230
Table, Walnut, Carved, Frieze Drawers, Serpentine Apron, Ball & Claw Feet, 1700s, 31 x 47 x 30 In.		1500
Table, Walnut, Marquetry Top, Fluted Legs, Stretcher, c.1870, 29½ x 45 x 32 In.		2500
Table, Walnut, Octagonal Top, Leather Inset, Splayed Legs, Casters, Italy, 1900s, 30 x 30 In.		847
Table, Walnut, Oval Top, Flowers, Serpentine Frieze, Cabriole Legs, c.1850, 28 x 40 x 29 In.		1188
Table, Walter Von Nessen, Steel, Tiers, Enameled Wood, Bakelite, 1930s, 30 x 30 In.	*illus*	12500
Table, Wegner, Andreas Tuck, Folding Tray, Teak, Oak, Marked, c.1960, 19 x 28 x 28 In.		1875
Table, Wegner, Model AT35, Teak, Removable Tray, Marked Underside, 18 x 21 x 24 In.		1287
Table, William IV, Mahogany, Tooled, Leather Inset Top, c.1835, 29 x 60 x 35 In.		1125
Table, William IV, Tilt Top, Rosewood, Square Top, 28 x 52½ x 40 In.		2000
Table, Wood Framed Glass Top, Square Wrought Iron Base, Openwork, 47 x 21 x 29 In.		236
Table, Work, Cherry, Dovetailed Drawers, Turned Legs, c.1935, 29 x 19 In.		240
Table, Work, Drop Leaf, 2 Drawers, Turned Legs, 1800s, 27½ x 18 x 20 In.		180
Table, Work, Meeks, Carved Mahogany, Foldover Top, Ogee Feet, 1850s, 30 x 23 x 15 In.		438
Table, Work, Neoclassical Style, Inlay, Walnut, 3 Drawers, 31 x 18 x 14 In.		492
Table, Work, Neoclassical, Hinged Top, 3 Drawers, Acorn Drops, N.Y., 1800s, 29 x 22 In.		117
Table, Work, Painted, Pine, Old Red Surface, Pennsylvania, 29 x 28½ In.		263
Table, Work, William & Mary, Drawer, Walnut, Concord Leg, 27 x 27 x 26½ In.		150
Table, Writing, G. Stickley, Quartersawn Oak, Drawers, Fitted Back, 1904, 37 x 38 In.		984
Table, Writing, Gothic Revival, Walnut, Poplar, Fitted Drawer, 1800s, 30 x 34 x 21 In.		960
Table, Writing, Henri II Style, Walnut, Leather, Twist Legs, H-Stretcher, Early 1900s, 31 x 55 x 30 In.		492
Table, Writing, Rectangular Top, Silver Metal, Drawer, Curule Shape Base, 30 x 42 x 30 In.		375
Table, Yew, Round Top, Triangle Leg Support, Late 1700s, 26 x 27 In.		1000
Tabouret, Inset Marble Top, Bat Carved Legs, Pierced Skirt, Chinese, Late 1800s, 23 x 17 In.	*illus*	420
Tabouret, Napoleon III, Leopard Skin Upholstery, 6 Legs, Ebonized, c.1865, 15 In.		438
Tea Cart, 2 Tiers, Brass, Mahogany, Handles, Wheels, Casters, France, c.1940, 33 x 36 In.		492
Tea Cart, Folding, Tan Veneer, Tray Insert, 1900s, Denmark, 29¾ x 43½ In.		236
Teapoy, Regency Style, Mahogany, Tripod Base & Ball Feet, 1800s, 28 In.		406
Teapoy, Regency Style, Maple, Rectangular Casket, Ribbed Edges, Late 1800s, 28 x 21 x 14 In.		563
Teapoy, Regency, Mahogany, Caddy, Sarcophagus, Quatrefoil Base, c.1825, 26 x 20 x 14 In.		570
Tete-A-Tete, Padded Back & Arms, Round Seats, Spindled Legs, Belle Epoque, c.1900, 27 x 35 x 19 In.		219
Umbrella Stand, Brass, Lion's Head Bail Handles, Round Base, 24½ x 11½ In.		289
Umbrella Stand, Brass, Repousse, Domed Base, Arabic Inscriptions, Mamluk, Cairo, 25 x 7 In.		96
Umbrella Stand, Brass, Strap Handle, Cone Shape, 1900s, 34¾ In.	*illus*	88
Umbrella Stand, Cane Holder, Painted False Bamboo, France, c.1880, 27½ x 24 In.		625
Umbrella Stand, Cast Iron, Dog & 2 Canes, Footed, Early 1900s, 26 In.		115
Umbrella Stand, Cast Iron, Removable Tray, Arch Top, Flower Motif, 15 x 8¾ x 25¾ In.		39
Umbrella Stand, Iron, Figural, Man In Khaki, British Soldier, c.1910, 27½ x 15 In.	*illus*	390
Vanity, Rococo Revival, Walnut, Marble Top, Oval Mirror, Scroll Legs, 72 x 45 x 20 In.	*illus*	1029
Vitrine, Carved Gilt, Wood Legs, Serpentine Glass Shelves, Electrified, 66 x 32 x 23 In.		378
Vitrine, French Art Deco, Enameled Wrought Iron, Brass, Glass, 1920-30, 55 x 24 In.		1375
Vitrine, Georgian Style, Mahogany, Hanging, 1800s, 49¾ In.		375
Vitrine, Gilt Bronze, Mahogany, Arched Door, Flowers, Swags, Mirror, Continental, 38 x 25 In.	*illus*	448
Vitrine, Louis XV Style, Bombe, Glazed, Vernis Martin, Late 1800s, 71 x 31 x 14 In.	*illus*	813
Vitrine, Louis XVI Style, Mahogany, Brass Doors, Shelves, Rosettes, Bellflowers, 1900s, 54 x 51 x 16 In.		308
Vitrine, Louis XVI Style, Mahogany, Glass Shelves, Sabot Feet, 63 x 25 x 13 In.		369
Vitrine, Louis XVI Style, Mahogany, Marble Top, Ormolu, Bevel Glass, c.1925, 63 x 28 x 14 In.		688
Vitrine, Louis XVI Style, Parquetry, Shelves, Square Legs, 1900s, 31 x 15 x 11 In.		308
Vitrine, Louis XV-XVI Style, Kingwood, Marble, Ormolu, Glass Doors, c.1890, 67 x 47 In.		2500
Vitrine, Louise XVI, Mahogany, Brass Mounts, Mirror, Marble Top, 50¾ x 28 x 13 In.		500
Vitrine, Mahogany, Inlay, Glass, Early 1900s, 28 x 25¾ x 16¾ In.		150
Vitrine, Oak, Quatrefoil, Beveled Doors, Gothic Arches, Late 1800s, 96 x 34 x 18 In.		1500
Vitrine, Vernis Martin, 2 Quarter Round Doors, Shelves, 1900s, 53 x 34 x 16 In.		750
Vitrine, Vernis Martin, Wood, Glass Front, Shelves, 1900s, 85 x 40 x 22 In.		1063
Wardrobe, Chinese Scenes, Bonsai Tree, Red, Gilt, Continental, 1900s, 72 x 54 x 13 In.		120

F

Furniture, Vanity, Rococo Revival, Walnut, Marble Top, Oval Mirror, Scroll Legs, 72 x 45 x 20 In.
$1,029

Fontaine's Auction Gallery

Furniture, Vitrine, Gilt Bronze, Mahogany, Arched Door, Flowers, Swags, Mirror, Continental, 38 x 25 In.
$448

Neal Auction Company

Furniture, Vitrine, Louis XV Style, Bombe, Glazed, Vernis Martin, Late 1800s, 71 x 31 x 14 In.
$813

Heritage Auctions

Furniture, Washstand, Sheraton, Cherry & Tiger Maple, Low Shelf, Drawer, Pa., c.1825, 33 x 21 In.
$225

Pook & Pook

Furniture, Wardrobe, Pine, Painted, Red Surface, Floral Panels, Continental, 1815, 68 x 50¾ In.
$813

Pook & Pook

F

211

FURNITURE

G.Argy-Rousseau, Ashtray, Open
Flower, Red & Purple, Pate-De-Verre,
Signed, 4 x 2 In.
$768

Morphy Auctions

Galle, Jardiniere, Egyptian Revival,
Winged, Multicolor Faience, 1800s,
14 x 4¾ x 4½ In.
$2,125

Royal Crest Auctioneers

Galle, Vase, Inset Marquetry, Wheel-
Carved Flowers, Swirling Background,
Cameo, Signed, 6 x 4 In.
$21,420

Morphy Auctions

TIP
*Put a rubber collar
on the faucet spout
over the sink. This
may keep you from
breaking a piece
of glass or china you
are washing.*

Wardrobe, Edwardian, Mahogany, Pine, 3 Parts, Dentil Molded Cornice, 80 x 45 x 21 In........	212
Wardrobe, Knock Down, 2 Doors, Drawers, Walnut, Brass Handle, Late 1800s, 84 x 52 x 15 In..	69
Wardrobe, Pine, Painted, Red Surface, Floral Panels, Continental, 1815, 68 x 50¾ In. .....*illus*	813
Wardrobe, Schrank, 2 Doors, Inlay, Wood Grain Veneers, Germany, 1800s, 82 x 81 x 29 In.....	1695
Wardrobe, Thomas Day, Walnut Veneer, 2 Panel Doors, Bracket Scroll Base, c.1850, 83 x 60 x 20 In.	1416
Washstand, Cherry, Poplar, Scroll Swan Neck Pilasters, Turned Feet, c.1800, 33 x 21 x 20 In..	188
Washstand, Gallery Top, Bowl Hole, Shelf, Frieze Drawer, Turned Legs, 1800s	113
Washstand, George III Style, Mahogany, Drawer, 40¾ x 16½ x 15 In.	135
Washstand, Hole In Top, Medial Shelf, Drawer, Smoke Finish, England, 1800s, 35 x 17 In.......	338
Washstand, Ralph Lauren, Mahogany, Drawer, 35 x 37 x 22 In.	90
Washstand, Sheraton Tiger, Maple, Scroll Gallery, Upper & Lower Drawer, 1800s, 35 x 23½ In.	900
Washstand, Sheraton, Cherry & Tiger Maple, Low Shelf, Drawer, Pa., c.1825, 33 x 21 In...*illus*	225
Washstand, Sheraton, Painted, Shaped Back, Drawer, Cylindrical Foot, c.1825, 37 x 17 In.	213
Washstand, Sheraton, Softwood, Painted, Bird, Floral, Multicolor, Brown Ground, 35 x 25 In.	189
Washstand, Sheraton, Softwood, Red Paint, Ring-Turned Legs, Lower Drawer, Pa., 31 x 25 In..	200
Washstand, Sheraton, Walnut, Scalloped Backsplash, Glass Pulls, 1800s, 37 x 23 x 18 In........	236
Washstand, Tiger Maple, 2 Shelves, Shaped Front Legs, England, Early 1800s, 37 x 17 x 15 In.	185
Window Seat, Louis XVI Style, Oval Cane Seat, Cushion, Gilt, Fluted Legs, 1800s, 39 In. Wide...	250

G. ARGY-ROUSSEAU is the impressed mark used on a variety of glass objects in the Art Deco style. Gabriel Argy-Rousseau, born in 1885, was a French glass artist. In 1921, he formed a partnership that made pate-de-verre and other glass. The partnership ended in 1931 and he opened his own studio. He worked until 1952 and died in 1953.

Ashtray, Open Flower, Red & Purple, Pate-De-Verre, Signed, 4 x 2 In.................................*illus*	768
Cup, 3 Open Handles, Lotus, Pate-De-Verre, 4 In.	3933
Pendant, Pate-De-Verre, Parrot, Red Head, Purple Blossoms, 3½ In. Diam..............................	1416
Vase, Prunus, Dark Pink Blossoms, Green Leaves, Signed, 6½ x 3½ In....................................	5535

GALLE was a designer who made glass, pottery, furniture, and other Art Nouveau items. Emile Galle founded his factory in France in 1874. After Galle's death in 1904, the firm continued to make glass and furniture until 1931. The *Galle* signature was used as a mark, but it was often hidden in the design of the object. Galle cameo and other types of glass are listed here. Pottery is in the next section. His furniture is listed in the Furniture category.

Bottle, Irises, Yellow Shaded To Tan, Silver Inclusions & Overlay, Stopper, 7 x 3 In....................	875
Bowl, Oval, 2 Handles, Light Blue Glaze, Hand Paint, Floral, Gold, Faience, Marked, 1800s......	531
Box, Amber, Pond Lilies, Light Blue, Cameo Flowers, Blue & Green Background, 6 x 3 In.	2460
Chandelier, Coupe, Frosted Icicles, Flowers, Ribbon, 3 Bronze Candle Arms, c.1890, 34 x 24 In.	8000
Jardiniere, Egyptian Revival, Winged, Multicolor Faience, 1800s, 14 x 4¾ x 4½ In.........*illus*	2125
Lamp, 1-Light, Salmon Shading, Cream Background, Signed, 18 x 7½ In.	1408
Lamp, Domed Shade, Rose, Violet, Green Ground, Leaf, Berry, 23 x 10¼ In.	3198
Lamp, Orange Brown, Spherical, Leaves, Metal Stand, Cameo, France, Signed, c.1900, 6 In.	1076
Planter, Basket Weave, Raised Ferns, Pink Flowers, Wall Mount, 19th Century, 12 x 6 In..........	612
Tray, White Chrysanthemums, Brown, Amber Leaves, Signed, 6½ x 4½ In.	1764
Vase, 4-Color Trumpets, Lilies & Orchids, Blue, Green, Matte, Cameo, 4¾ In............................	330
Vase, Amber, Dragonfly, Lily Pond, Blue & Cream Background, Cameo, Signed, 10 x 5 In........	4305
Vase, Barrel Shape, Violets, Leaves, Cameo Over Frosted Citron, 4 In.	295
Vase, Bleeding Hearts, Red Leaves, Cameo, Signed, 8 x 3½ In..	1250
Vase, Bottle Shape, Orchids, Leaves, Matte Finish, Signed, 6⅜ In.	366
Vase, Bud, Amethyst To Frosted Color, Flowers, Cameo, Signed, c.1900, 5⅜ In.	329
Vase, Bud, Flowers, Leaves, Banjo Shape, Red, Brown, Amber, 7 In.	1197
Vase, Chrysanthemum, Vines, Leaves, Scalloped Rim, Green Hue Base, c.1880, 13½ In.	5000
Vase, Citrus Fruit, Broad Leaves, Round, Short Neck, Cameo, 7½ In.	120
Vase, Cylindrical, Trees, Lake, Red, Yellow, Blue, Green, Cameo, 23½ x 8 In.	96
Vase, Dark Amber, Trees, Lake, Pastel Yellow Background, Cameo, Signed, 14 x 4 In.	3383
Vase, Dark Red To Rose, Pale Yellow Background, Cameo, Signed, 6½ x 5½ In.	1250
Vase, Emerald, Hexagonal Neck, Serpentine Rim, Handle, 3½ x 5¼ In.	1682
Vase, Flowers, Brown, Yellow Background, 6½ In.	489

Vase, Flowers, Green, Purple, Pear Shape, 9 In.		1386
Vase, Flowers, Japanese Cherry Blossoms, Red Cameo, Pastel Yellow Background, Signed, 7¼ x 5 In.		1680
Vase, Flowers, Pink, Red, Cream, Gilt Leaves, Transparent Amber Glass, Signed, 9 x 4 In.		2016
Vase, Flowers, Red To Pink, Yellow, Cameo, Bulbous, Marked, France, 4⅜ In.		861
Vase, Inset Marquetry, Wheel-Carved Flowers, Swirling Background, Cameo, Signed, 6 x 4 In.	*illus*	21420
Vase, Lily Pond, Aquatic Flowers, Red Cameo, Pastel Yellow Ground, Signed, 11 x 3 In.		1476
Vase, Narrow Mouth, Flowers, Pale Lavender & Green, Cameo, c.1910, 8½ In.		1495
Vase, Purple Pine Trees, Blue Mountains, Yellow Sky, 23½ In.		5120
Vase, Purple, Blue Flowers, Leaves, White, Peach, Cameo, Signed, 5½ x 5 x 2¾ In.	*illus*	488
Vase, Red Clematis Flowers & Leaves, Pink Frosted Ground, Mold Blown, Signed, 7 x 3 In.		1920
Vase, Red Magnolias, Pastel Yellow Ground, Cameo, Signed, 20 x 4 In.	*illus*	6765
Vase, Round, Hydrangea Blossoms, Frosted Lug Handles, Lilac, Gray, Apricot, 11 x 10 In.		2360
Vase, Seaweed, Fire Polished, Red Overlay, Cameo, Signed, 4 x 4 In.		5000
Vase, Shouldered, Orange Blossoms, Frosted Opal, Cameo, 3 In.		142
Vase, Spiderweb, Red Cameo Leaves, Yellow & Blue Leaves, Clear Ground, Signed, 8 x 2 In.		1560
Vase, Spiderweb, Red Maple Leaves, Cameo, Wheel Carved, Signed, 3 x 3 In.		3500
Vase, Stick, Flower Sprays, Gourds, Red, Green, Amber, Etched, Enamel, c.1900, 13½ In.		1280
Vase, Tiger Lily, Tan & Brown On Light Blue Ground, Cameo, 23¼ In.		4160
Vase, Yellow, Amethyst Ground, Pond Lily, Signed, France, c.1900, 8⅞ In.	*illus*	956

GALLE POTTERY was made by Emile Galle, the famous French designer, after 1874. The pieces were marked with the initials *E. G.* impressed, *Em. Galle Faiencerie de Nancy,* or a version of his signature. Galle is best known for his glass, listed above.

Candleholder, Figural Lion, Rook Shape Holder, Blue & White, Signed, 16 x 9 x 7 In.		2057
Chandelier, Dome, Flowers, Ribbons, Pendant Icicles, 3 Spelter Arms, 34 x 23 In.		2420
Figurine, Dog, Seated, Blue & White, Glass Eyes, Faience, 12¾ In.		720
Pitcher, Aesthetic Movement, Bird Shape, Egyptian Bird Handle, Marked, 12 In.		720
Tureen, Soup, Lid, Blue & Amber Flowers, Leeks In Relief On Top, 10 In.		300
Vase, 4 Snowballs, White, Flower Highlights, Signed, 4¾ x 5½ In.		95
Vase, Figural, Rabbit, Flowers, Ribbon, Glass Eyes, 8 x 7 In.		396
Wall Pocket, Rooster, Butterfly, Grapevine, Clouds, Faience, Signed, 14 In.	*illus*	4410

GAME collectors like all types of games. Of special interest are any board games or card games. Transogram and other company names are included in the description when known. Other games may be found listed under Card, Toy, or the name of the character or celebrity featured in the game. Gameboards without the game pieces are listed in the Gameboard category.

Addams Family, Filmways TV Productions, Ideal, Board, 1964, 10 x 19¾ In.		389
Backgammon, Bakelite, Yellow Chips, Cups, Dice, Cork Surface, Flowered Case, 19 x 14 In.		92
Baseball, Great American Game, Tin, Mechanical Reel, Pushbutton, Frantz, 13½ In.		201
Bean Bag, Carnival, Painted, Plywood, Clown, Canvas Backing, 1900s, 50 x 31¾ In.	*illus*	313
Bean Bag, Regulation, Yellow, Red, Wood, Particle Board, Eagle Toys, 1900s, 26 x 15 x 3 In.	*illus*	72
Bezique & Piquet, Circassian Walnut, Cards, Rules & Counters, Box, 8½ In.		72
Carnival, Huckleberry Hound, Huckle Chuck, Nodding Head, 31 x 15¼ In.	*illus*	121
Chess, Black, Beige, Inlay, Hinged Box, Pieces, Asian Style, 4 x 14 x 14 In.		250
Chess, Lapis Lazuli, White Marble, White Border, Fitted Case, Morita Gil, 10¾ x 10¾ In.		258
Dinner, Turkey, Woman, Santa, Elves, Parker Brothers, Box, 17 x 11 In.		3300
Dominoes, Cribbage, POW, Whalebone, Dot & Circle, Box, 1800s, 1¾ x 2½ x 6⅞ In.	*illus*	584
Fish Pond, Gnome, Milton Bradley, Board, 21 x 13½ In.		125
Flying Nun, Screen Gems Inc., Milton Bradley, Board, 1968, 19 x 9⅝ In.	*illus*	555
Horse Race, Jeu De Course, Mechanical, Canvas & Wood Box, 8 Painted Horses, 16 x 13 x 13 In.		182
Horse Race, Mechanical, Mahogany Case, Brass Gates, c.1895, 19¾ x 11 In.		500
Horse Race, Wood, Painted, Iron, Multicolor, Circular Base, 17 In.		431
Jigsaw Puzzle, Essolube Motor Oil, Dr. Seuss, Family In Car, 50 Pieces, Envelope, 11 x 17 In.	*illus*	83
Lawn Tennis, Net, Posts, Mallet, Stakes, Victorian Scene On Box, Horsman, 1880s	*illus*	2768
Mahjong, Bamboo Backed Game Pieces, Accessories, Booklet, Chinese, 1900s, 2 x 13 x 8 In.		84
Mahjong, Carved Case, 146 Bone & Bamboo Tiles, Chinese, 1900s, 9½ x 7 x 10 In.		393
Mother Hubbard's Party, Winter Scenes, Paper Litho, Wood, Target, c.1880, 18¼ x 11½ In.		1560

Galle, Vase, Purple, Blue Flowers, Leaves, White, Peach, Cameo, Signed, 5½ x 5 x 2¾ In.
$488

Susanin's Auctioneers & Appraisers

G

Galle, Vase, Red Magnolias, Pastel Yellow Ground, Cameo, Signed, 20 x 4 In.
$6,765

Morphy Auctions

Galle, Vase, Yellow, Amethyst Ground, Pond Lily, Signed, France, c.1900, 8⅞ In.
$956

Jeffrey S. Evans & Associates

Galle Pottery, Wall Pocket, Rooster, Butterfly, Grapevine, Clouds, Faience, Signed, 14 In.

$4,410

Morphy Auctions

Game, Bean Bag, Carnival, Painted, Plywood, Clown, Canvas Backing, 1900s, 50 x 31¾ In.

$313

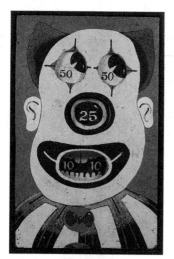

Rago Arts and Auction Center

Game, Bean Bag, Regulation, Yellow, Red, Wood, Particle Board, Eagle Toys, 1900s, 26 x 15 x 3 In.

$72

Eldred's

My Favorite Martian, Transogram, Jack Terchock Television, Board, 1963, 17 x 9 In. ...... *illus*	577
Night Before Christmas, Santa Claus, Box, 1896, 16½ x 14½ In.	3600
Pinball, Atlas, World Maps, Tin, Wood, Lindstrom's Toy Co., Copyright 1934, 14 x 24 In.	110
Puzzle Cube, Aunt Louisa's, Santa Claus, Box, 11½ x 10 In. ...... *illus*	4800
Puzzle, Chevrolet School Buses, 2-Sided, Compliments Of Chevy Dealer, 1932, 8 x 13 In.	85
Puzzle, Dissected Map Of The United States, McLoughlin Bros., Box. ...... *illus*	46
Puzzle, Frame, Santa, Smoking Pipe, Pointing His Finger, McLoughlin, 26¾ x 22½ In.	2000
Ring Ball Toss, Paper Lithograph, American Indian, 2 Wood Rings, 13 In.	58
Roulette Wheel, Flat Circular Discs, Interior Holes, 3½ x 11½ In.	90
Roulette Wheel, Lithograph, Wood, Iron, Yellow, Red & Black Paint, 13 x 13 x 4¼ In.	584
Secret Agent, Cardboard, John Drake, Milton Bradley, Board, 1966, 19 x 9½ In.	156
Skittles, 9 Animals, Shoebutton Eyes, On Wood Kegs, Steiff, Germany, c.1895, 8 To 10 In.	10350
Skittles, Dog, Dachshund, Glass Eyes, Wheeled Base, Holds 9 Pin Dogs, Germany, 21 In.	12000
Steeplechase, Glass, Wood Case, Countertop, 1 Cent, Early 1900s, 17½ x 14 x 8½ In.	554
Target, Punch & Judy, Paper Lithograph Over Wood, 13 x 11 In.	461
Target, Wood, 2 Balls, Mother Goose Rhyme Theme, Paper Lithograph, c.1880, 11 x 18 x ¼ In..	544
Wheel Of Chance, Metal Hub, Yellow, Red & Black Paint, H.C. Evans, Late 1800s, 20½ In.	923
Wheel Of Chance, Red, Yellow, Blue, Number Sections, Cross Bracket, c.1905, 24 In. ...... *illus*	871
Wheel Of Chance, Stenciled Red & Black Paint, Numbers 1 To 30, Early 1900s, 30 In.	120
Wheel Of Chance, Wood, Painted, E.J. Loddell, 31 In. ...... *illus*	277

 GAME PLATES are plates of any make decorated with pictures of birds, animals, or fish. The game plates usually came in sets consisting of 12 dishes and a serving platter. These sets were most popular during the 1880s.

Grouse, Rutherford B. Hayes Pattern, Leaves, Plants, T.R. Davis, 1880, 9 In.	1920
Trout, Scalloped Rim, Tressemann & Vogt, Limoges, c.1890, 9½ In.	135
Woodcock, Brown To Green, Blue Rim, Scalloped, Bavaria, 12 In.	140

GAMEBOARD collectors look for just the board without the game pieces. The boards are collected as folk art or decorations. Gameboards that are part of a complete game are listed in the Game category.

Backgammon, Checkers, Black & Light Green, Raised Edge, Late 1800s, 15 x 15¾ In.	308
Backgammon, Checkers, Wood, Edging, Central Divider, 2-Sided, 1900s ...... *illus*	165
Backgammon, Checkers, Yellow & Black, Green Lined, Red Background, 1800s, 20 x 16 In. ...	1107
Checkers, Baseball Diamond, 2-Sided, Red & Black Paint, c.1890, 14 x 14 In.	1845
Checkers, Carved, Red & Yellow, Blue Background, Stars, 1800s, 20 x 16½ In.	3198
Checkers, Department Store, 2-Sided, Spinner, 22 x 14½ In. ...... *illus*	64
Checkers, Hand Painted, Black & Orange, Black Border, 1900s, 21 x 18 In.	58
Checkers, Marquetry, Hardwoods, Chain & Geometric Border, Late 1800s, 20 x 20 In.	197
Checkers, Mixed Wood, Bone Inlays, Egypt, c.1950, 16 x 16 In.	41
Checkers, Octagonal, Brown Paint, Square, Crokinole, 30 In.	71
Checkers, Painted, Walnut, Black & White Border, c.1900, 14¼ x 14¼ In.	163
Checkers, Parcheesi, 2-Sided, Compass Corners, Late 1800s, 19 x 19 In.	615
Checkers, Parcheesi, Paint Decorated, 2-Sided, Molding, White Ground, c.1890, 16½ x 16 In.	3998
Checkers, Parcheesi, Painted, 2-Sided, 18¼ x 18¾ In.	277
Checkers, Parcheesi, Red Ground, Red, Blue, Green, Black, 2-Sided, c.1890, 19 x 18 In. ..... *illus*	3048
Checkers, Parcheesi, White & Black, White & Blue, 2-Sided, Frame, c.1890, 20 x 20 In.	1016
Checkers, Peg, Red, Black, Spade, Diamond, Heart & Flower, Early 1900s, 23½ x 23½ In.	270
Checkers, Red & Black Paint, Card Suit Symbols In Corners, c.1900	201
Checkers, Wood, Black & White Paint, c.1900, 12 x 23½ In.	472
Checkers, Wood, Painted, Red & White, c.1905, 23 x 16 In.	437
Chess, Wood, Painted, Black & White, 21 x 16½ In.	88
Chinese Checkers & Checkers, 2-Sided, Multicolor, Late 1800s, 19 x 17 In. ...... *illus*	861
Cribbage, Carved Ivory Tusk, Seals, Sled Dog Team, Artic Fox, Walrus, Inuit, 15 In.	113
Cribbage, Monkeys, 2 Flowers, Ivory, Carved, Japan, 3 x 8¼ In.	120
Cribbage, Walrus, Ivory, Carved, Bone, Eagle, Inuit, Signed, Exem, 9 In.	213
Painted, Red, Yellow, Green, 8-Point Star, 1900s, 12 x 11¾ In.	215
Parcheesi, Painted, Pine, Multicolor Blocks, Blue Background, 1800s, 21 x 21 In. ...... *illus*	3000

Game, Carnival, Huckleberry Hound, Huckle Chuck, Nodding Head, 31 x 15 ¼ In.
$121

Fontaine's Auction Gallery

Game, Dominoes, Cribbage , POW, Whalebone, Dot & Circle, Box, 1800s, 1 ¾ x 2 ½ x 6 ⅞ In.
$584

Skinner, Inc.

Game, Flying Nun, Screen Gems Inc., Milton Bradley, Board, 1968, 19 x 9 ⅝ In.
$555

Hake's Auctions

Millions of "Yahtzee"
Edwin Lowe, the man who first marketed Bingo, was asked to promote a new game called Yacht Game in 1956. Lowe renamed it Yahtzee. He filed for a trademark in April 1957 and eventually sold over 40 million Yahtzee games.

Game, Jigsaw Puzzle, Essolube Motor Oil, Dr. Seuss, Family In Car, 50 Pieces, Envelope, 11 x 17 In.
$83

AntiqueAdvertising.com

Game, Lawn Tennis, Net, Posts, Mallet, Stakes, Victorian Scene On Box, Horsman, 1880s
$2,768

Morphy Auctions

Game, My Favorite Martian, Transogram, Jack Terchock Television, Board, 1963, 17 x 9 In.
$577

Hake's Auctions

TIP
Bright sunlight may fade colors of gameboard boxes.

Game, Puzzle Cube, Aunt Louisa's, Santa Claus, Box, 11 ½ x 10 In.
$4,800

Morphy Auctions

Game, Puzzle, Dissected Map Of The United States, McLoughlin Bros., Box
$46

Keystone Auctions LLC

Game, Wheel Of Chance, Red, Yellow, Blue, Number Sections, Cross Bracket, c.1905, 24 In.
$871

Skinner, Inc.

G

Game, Wheel Of Chance, Wood, Painted, E.J. Loddell, 31 In.
$277

Skinner, Inc.

Gameboard, Backgammon, Checkers, Wood, Edging, Central Divider, 2-Sided, 1900s
$165

Forsythes' Auctions

Gameboard, Checkers, Department Store, 2-Sided, Spinner, 22 x 14½ In.
$64

Morphy Auctions

Gameboard, Checkers, Parcheesi, Red Ground, Red, Blue, Green, Black, 2-Sided, c.1890, 19 x 18 In.
$3,048

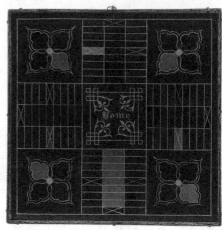

Skinner, Inc.

Gameboard, Chinese Checkers & Checkers, 2-Sided, Multicolor, Late 1800s, 19 x 17 In.
$861

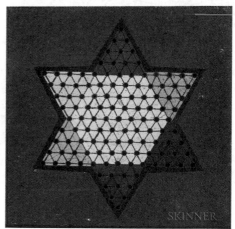

Skinner, Inc.

Gameboard, Parcheesi, Painted, Pine, Multicolor Blocks, Blue Background, 1800s, 21 x 21 In.
$3,000

Pook & Pook

Parcheesi, Rectangles, Circles & Stars, Custom Frame, Painted, c.1900, 24 x 24 In. 9840
Parcheesi, Wood, Breadboard Ends, Painted, Stars On Back, c.1910, 21 ½ In. ....*illus* 6840

GARDEN FURNISHINGS have been popular for centuries. The stone or metal statues, urns and fountains, sundials, small figurines, and wire, iron, or rustic furniture are included in this category. Many of the metal pieces have been made continuously for years.

Arbor, Green Paint, Metal, Latticework, Half Circles Arch, 89 x 50 x 22 In.	98
Arbor, White Paint, Scrolled Sides, Arched Metal Supports, 100 x 63 x 18 In.	293
Armillary, Neoclassical Style, Bronze, Claw Feet, Ram's Head Mounts, c.1940, 33 x 11 x 7 In....*illus*	1188
Bench, Carved, Marble, Winged Griffin Supports, 51 x 87 x 28 In.	3750
Bench, Cast Iron, Ferns, Black Paint, 33 x 53 ½ x 13 In.	330
Bench, Cast Iron, Figural Reserves, Slatted Wood Seat, Scroll Arms, England, 35 x 41 In...*illus*	688
Bench, Cast Iron, Neoclassical Style, White Paint, Scroll Arms, Mid 1900s, 31 x 46 x 20 In.	944
Bench, Cast Iron, Wood Slat Seat, Arched Supports, Shells, Seahorses, 1900s, 33 In.	575
Bench, Cement, Faux Wood, Arms, Carlos Cortes, 35 x 75 In. ....*illus*	775
Bench, Fern Pattern, Black Paint, Green, Cast Iron, James W. Carr, Va., c.1880, 30 x 43 x 14 In..	1521
Bench, Fern, Blackberry Design, 1800s, 34 x 17 x 5 ½ In.	540
Bench, Fern, Cast & Black Painted Iron, Victorian, Late 1800s, 33 x 55 x 6 In.	1180
Bench, Greek Medallion, Birds, Branch Arms, Iron, 72 ½ In.	508
Bench, Metal, Arched Scroll & Fleur-De-Lis Back, Outscrolled Arms, 1900s, 36 x 59 In.	395
Bench, Peacock, Fan Back, Pierced, Scrolls, Cast Iron, Colebrookdale, c.1885, 37 In., Pair	1250
Bench, Terra-Cotta, Griffin Ends, Wood Slat Seat & Back, Italy, 46 x 80 x 36 In.	1500
Bench, Winged Griffin, Cast Iron, Wood Seat, Colebrookdale, 28 x 43 x 31 In. ....*illus*	281
Bench, Wrought Iron, White Paint, Shell Back, Nautilus, 56 ¾ x 50 In.	246
Birdbath, Birds, Round, Column Support, Pierced Base, 34 x 21 In.	584
Birdbath, Scalloped Rim, Hummingbird On Edge, Circular Base, Cast Iron, 24 In..........*illus*	115
Birdhouse, Chimney Top, White Paint, Star, Wood, 27 x 13 x 24 In.................*illus*	266
Boots, Iron, Green Paint, 1800s, 7 x 8 In.	123
Chair, Gothic Style, Pointed Arch Back, Cast Iron, Victorian, 42 x 20 x 16 In.	212
Chair, Scroll Back, Leafy Apron & Legs, Rococo Style, Iron, Late 1800s, 32 x 25 x 15 In.	500
Figure, Boy, On Bale, Hitching Post, Attributed To J.W. Fiske, c.1875, 46 In.	2125
Figure, Lion, Curly Mane, Seated, Mouth Open, Stone, Cut, 25 In., Pair	861
Fountain, Ball Top, Rounded Base, Marble, 24 In.	188
Fountain, Bronze, Putti, Swordfish, Circular Shell, Dolphin Support, 1900s, 47 x 33 In...*illus*	1250
Fountain, Cherub, Pan, Hoofed Feet, Cast Lead, Marble Carving, 37 x 16 In.	4750
Fountain, Wall Mount, 3 Zinc Birds, Zinc Bowl, Cast Iron, 84 x 47 x 13 In.................*illus*	1625
Gate, Arched Top, Scroll Design, Iron, 90 x 39 ¾ In.	63
Gnome, Standing, Holding Stick, Wood, Carved, Black Forest, 7 ½ In................*illus*	630
Group, Boy Pushing Girl On Swing, Squirrel, Bronze, Patina, Life Size, 87 x 48 In.	3750
Hitching Post, Eagle, Spread Wing, Iron, Early 1900s, 39 x 30 ½ In.	438
Hitching Post, Horse Head, Holding Chain, Ring, Iron, 1800s, 48 In.	708
Hitching Post, Horse Head, Cast Iron, c.1900, 13 ¼ In., Pair	360
Hitching Post, Horse Head, Iron, Tapered & Fluted Post, Leaf & Scroll Base, c.1890, 38 In.	400
Hitching Post, Man, Figural, Outstretched Arms, Iron, Metal Base, 1800s, 13 In.	1140
Pedestal, Sphere Top, Blue, Glazed, Porcelain, 39 In.	83
Plant Stand, see also Furniture, Stand, Plant	
Plant Stand, Wirework, Brass Casters, Victorian, Late 1800s, 33 x 23 x 14 In.	344
Planter, Cartouche, Floral Medallions, Concrete, 8 x 37 ½ x 10 ¾ In.	24
Planter, Iron Base, Wire & Pressed Tin Frame, Blue Paint, 23 x 18 In...................*illus*	69
Planter, Painted Yellow Ocher, Wood, Adirondack, Mid 1700s, 33 x 35 x 12 In. ....*illus*	375
Seat, Barrel Shape, Birds & Flowers, White Background, Ceramic, 8 x 12 In.	188
Seat, Barrel Shape, Blue Ground, Lotus, Porcelain, Wood Stand, Late 1800s, 19 x 12 In.	554
Seat, Barrel Shape, Flowers, Porcelain, Red Mark, Chinese, c.1975, 19 ½ x 12 In..............*illus*	270
Seat, Barrel Shape, Lion, Pink & White, Ceramic, 1900s, 18 ½ In.	688
Seat, Barrel Shape, Trellis Ground, Porcelain, 1800s, 18 ⅞ x 12 In.	1353
Seat, Blue & White, Flowers, Porcelain, Chinese Style, 1900s, 20 x 13 In.............*illus*	150
Seat, Blue & White, Transfer, Mountain & River, Porcelain, 1900s, 17 In. ....*illus*	125
Seat, Butterflies, Blossoms, Red Cracked Ice, Porcelain, Asian, 1900s, 17 In.	236
Seat, Cast Metal, Tree Surround, Open Pierce, Urns, Flowers, 1900s, 32 x 60 In. ....*illus*	813
Seat, Drum Shape, Famille Rose, Fruit, Birds, Butterflies, Coins, Chinese, 1800s, 18 In.	1298

Gameboard, Parcheesi, Wood, Breadboard Ends, Painted, Stars On Back, c.1910, 21 ½ In.
$6,840

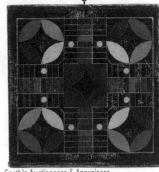

Garth's Auctioneers & Appraisers

G

Garden, Armillary, Neoclassical Style, Bronze, Claw Feet, Ram's Head Mounts, c.1940, 33 x 11 x 7 In.
$1,188

Kamelot Auctions

Garden, Bench, Cast Iron, Figural Reserves, Slatted Wood Seat, Scroll Arms, England, 35 x 41 In.
$688

Neal Auction Company

Garden, Bench, Cement, Faux Wood, Arms, Carlos Cortes, 35 x 75 In.
$775

Pook & Pook

Garden, Bench, Winged Griffin, Cast Iron, Wood Seat, Colebrookdale, 28 x 43 x 31 In.
$281

Kamelot Auctions

Garden, Birdbath, Scalloped Rim, Hummingbird On Edge, Circular Base, Cast Iron, 24 In.
$115

Keystone Auctions LLC

Garden, Birdhouse, Chimney Top, White Paint, Star, Wood, 27 x 13 x 24 In.
$266

Copake Auction

Garden, Fountain, Bronze, Putti, Swordfish, Circular Shell, Dolphin Support, 1900s, 47 x 33 In.
$1,250

Crescent City Auction Gallery

Garden, Fountain, Wall Mount, 3 Zinc Birds, Zinc Bowl, Cast Iron, 84 x 47 x 13 In.
$1,625

Kamelot Auctions

Garden, Gnome, Standing, Holding Stick, Wood, Carved, Black Forest, 7½ In.
$630

Morphy Auctions

Garden, Planter, Iron Base, Wire & Pressed Tin Frame, Blue Paint, 23 x 18 In.
$69

Keystone Auctions LLC

Garden, Planter, Painted Yellow Ocher, Wood, Adirondack, Mid 1700s, 33 x 35 x 12 In.
$375

Rago Arts and Auction Center

G

Seat, Famile Rose, Dish Top, Birds, Flowers, Cartouches, Oval, Chinese, c.1850, 18 In.	*illus*	2520
Seat, Hexagonal, Barrel Shape, Blue & White Transfer, Birds, Flowers, Porcelain, 18 x 11 In.		2091
Seat, Octagonal, Barrel Shape, Pink & Chinoiserie, Ceramic, 1900s, 18¾ In.		138
Seat, Peacock, Flowers, Red Ground, Openwork Symbols, Porcelain, Chinese, 1900s, 18 In.		132
Seat, Round Pillow Top, Wickerwork Base, Ceramic, 1900s, 20 In.		125
Settee, Splat, 2 Faces, Heart, Metal, Patinated, 38 x 58 x 19 In.	*illus*	293
Settee, Trapezoidal Seat, Curving Legs, White, Cast Iron, Late 1800s, 35½ x 44 In.		400
Stand, Plant, Square Top, Bentwood, Twig, 2 Layers, 12 x 12 x 30 In.	*illus*	68
Sundial, Iron, Carved Stone Base, Circular Foot, Virginia Metal Crafters, c.1910, 30 In.	*illus*	375
Table, Iron, Scroll-Edge Base, 5 Leafy Downswept Legs, Crown, 30 x 42 In.		188
Table, Patio, Lozenge Shape, Chain Base, Plate Metal Top, Glass Top, 29 x 64 In.		234
Table, Patio, Teak, Rectangular Top, 39 x 65 x 30 In.		207
Table, Potting, Pine, 3 Drawers, c.1890, 31½ x 41½ x 25½ In.		375
Urn, Campana, Rolled Rim, Egg & Dart, Fluted Support, Black, Iron, 1800s, 20 x 19 In., Pair .		1230
Urn, Handles, Curled, Separate Plinth, c.1890, 40 x 40 x 27 In.		1375
Urn, Red Painted, Classical Shape, Square Base, 16½ x 12¾ In.		135
Wheelbarrow, Eastern Garden, Painted Blue, Lansing Company, Boston		575
Wheelbarrow, Red, Green, Blue, Wood, Iron Wrapped Wheel, Primitive, 22 x 20 x 55 In.		83
Windmill, Wood, Wire Mesh Blades, Copper Roof, England, c.1900, 33 x 25 x 13 In.	*illus*	351

GAUDY DUTCH pottery was made in England for the American market from about 1810 to 1820. It is a white earthenware with Imari-style decorations of red, blue, green, yellow, and black. Only sixteen patterns of Gaudy Dutch were made: Butterfly, Carnation, Dahlia, Double Rose, Dove, Grape, Leaf, Oyster, Primrose, Single Rose, Strawflower, Sunflower, Urn, War Bonnet, Zinnia, and No Name. Other similar wares are called Gaudy Ironstone and Gaudy Welsh.

Grape pattern
1810–1820

Single Rose pattern
1810–1820

War Bonnet pattern
1810–1820

Bowl, Single Rose, c.1850, 9 In.	295
Cup & Saucer, Primrose, c.1820	1933
Plate, War Bonnet, Flowers, Grapes, c.1850, 8⅜ In.	275
Sugar, Lid, Leaf, c.1850, 5½ In. .... *illus*	3625
Sugar, Lid, Sunflower, Clamshell Handles, c.1850, 4¾ In.	150

GAUDY IRONSTONE is the collector's name for the ironstone wares with the bright patterns similar to Gaudy Dutch. It was made in England for the American market after 1850. There may be other examples found in the listing for Ironstone or under the name of the ceramic factory.

Jug, Ribbed Handle, Paneled, 4¼ In.	100

GAUDY WELSH is an Imari-decorated earthenware with red, blue, green, and gold decorations. Most Gaudy Welsh was made in England for the American market. It was made from 1820 to about 1860.

Bowl, Footed, Blue Leaves, Gold Dots, Blossoms, 5 x 10 In.	69
Bowl, Square, Green, Yellow, Red, Scalloped Edge, 8 In.	170

GEISHA GIRL porcelain was made for export in the late nineteenth century in Japan. It was an inexpensive porcelain often sold in dime stores or used as free premiums. Pieces are sometimes marked with the name of a store. Japanese ladies in kimonos

Garden, Seat, Barrel Shape, Flowers, Porcelain, Red Mark, Chinese, c.1975, 19½ x 12 In.
$270

Garth's Auctioneers & Appraisers

Garden, Seat, Blue & White, Flowers, Porcelain, Chinese Style, 1900s, 20 x 13 In.
$150

Leslie Hindman Auctioneers

Garden, Seat, Blue & White, Transfer, Mountain & River, Porcelain, 1900s, 17 In.
$125

Eldred's

Garden, Seat, Cast Metal, Tree Surround, Open Pierce, Urns, Flowers, 1900s, 32 x 60 In.
$813

Kamelot Auctions

Garden, Seat, Famile Rose, Dish Top, Birds, Flowers, Cartouches, Oval, Chinese, c.1850, 18 In.
$2,520

Eldred's

Garden, Settee, Splat, 2 Faces, Heart, Metal, Patinated, 38 x 58 x 19 In.
$293

Susanin's Auctioneers & Appraisers

Garden, Stand, Plant, Square Top, Bentwood, Twig, 2 Layers, 12 x 12 x 30 In.
$68

Hartzell's Auction Gallery, Inc.

Garden, Sundial, Iron, Carved Stone Base, Circular Foot, Virginia Metal Crafters, c.1910, 30 In.
$375

Leslie Hindman Auctioneers

Garden, Windmill, Wood, Wire Mesh Blades, Copper Roof, England, c.1900, 33 x 25 x 13 In.
$351

Thomaston Place Auction Galleries

are pictured on the dishes. There are over 125 recorded patterns. Borders of red, blue, green, gold, brown, or several of these colors were used. Modern reproductions are being made.

Box,	Lid, 3 Geisha In Garden, Rust Border, Japan, 6½ x 3½ In.	19
Mirror,	Geisha In Garden, Silvertone Frame, Faux Jade Handle, 5¼ In.	62
Pin Tray,	6 Geisha, House, Garden, Bridges, Cobalt Blue Border, 4 x 3 In.	25
Sake Set,	Geisha Portraits, Carafe, 3 Cups, Red, Foil Label, Japan	75
Salt & Pepper,	Plastic, Red, Green, 3 In.	32

GENE AUTRY was born in 1907. He began his career as the "Singing Cowboy" in 1928. His first movie appearance was in 1934, his last in 1958. His likeness and that of the Wonder Horse, Champion, were used on toys, books, lunch boxes, and advertisements.

Album,	Vinyl, Columbia Historic Edition, Columbia Okeh Label, c.1982	15
Book,	Redwood Pirates, Bob Hamilton, Hardcover, 1946, 5½ x 8 In., 248 Pages	36
Button,	Portrait, Signature, Blue Ground, Lithograph, 1957, ⅞ In.	12
Comic Book,	City Slickers, No. 81, Dell, 1953, 52 Pages	20
Comic Book,	Outlaw Round Up, Til Goodman Cover, Off-White Pages, March, 1943	236
Comic Book,	Secret Of Skeleton Mountain, Dell, No. 16, 1948	30
Guitar,	Brown Plastic, Tan Accents, Printed Alligator Skin Box, Signature, 1950s, 13 x 33 In.	100
Photograph,	Gene Autry, Doubleday Photo, Sepia, Signed, 5¾ x 3⅞ In.	195
Postcard,	Gene Autry On Horseback, Caravan, Signed, 6 x 4 In.	85

GIBSON GIRL black-and-blue decorated plates were made in the early 1900s. Twenty-four different 10½-inch plates were made by the Royal Doulton pottery at Lambeth, England. These pictured scenes from the book *A Widow and Her Friends* by Charles Dana Gibson. Another set of twelve 9-inch plates featuring pictures of the heads of Gibson Girls had all-blue decoration. Many other items also pictured the famous Gibson Girl.

Dresser Box,	Seafoam Mold, Blue, Cream, Portrait On Lid, Nakara, 5½ x 7½ In.	7800
Vase,	Purple Dress, Feather Hat, Royal Bayreuth, Brocaded Gold Border, Green Ground, 5½ In.	36

GILLINDER pressed glass was first made by William T. Gillinder of Philadelphia in 1863. The company had a working factory on the grounds at the Centennial and made small, marked pieces of glass for sale as souvenirs. It made a variety of decorative glass pieces and tablewares. The company was out of business by the early 1930s.

GILLINDER

Berry Bowl,	Frosted Lion, c.1877, 2½ x 4 In.	25
Bowl,	Maple Leaf, Blue, c.1885, 10 x 6 x 3 In.	60
Compote,	Daisy & Button, Scalloped Rim, c.1890, 7½ In.	90
Salt & Pepper,	Melon Shape, Forget-Me-Nots, c.1875	85
Spooner,	Frosted Lion, 1800s, 5½ In.	50
Sugar & Creamer,	Lion, Pressed Glass	115
Sugar Shaker,	Beaded Twist, 4¼ x 3 in.	59

GIRL SCOUT collectors search for anything pertaining to the Girl Scouts, including uniforms, publications, and old cookie boxes. The Girl Scout movement started in 1912, two years after the Boy Scouts. It began under Juliette Gordon Low of Savannah, Georgia. The first Girl Scout cookies were sold in 1928.

Book,	Leader Guide, Intermediate Program, Hardcover, 1955, 8 x 5 In., 278 Pages	12
Calendar,	1970, Full Color Photographs, Paper Sleeve, 10 x 8½ In.	9
Canteen,	Aluminum, Original Cloth Holder, Box, 1960s, 7½ In.	45

GLASS factories that are well known are listed in this book under the factory name. This category lists pieces made by less well-known factories. Additional pieces of glass are listed in this book under the type of glass, in the categories Glass-Art, Glass-Blown, Glass-Bohemian, Glass-Contemporary, Glass-Midcentury, Glass-Venetian, and under the factory name.

Bowl,	Cased, White Interior, Pink Exterior, Hand Painted, Flowers, 10 In.	81
Creamer,	Clear Body, Millefleur Base, Perthshire, Scotland, 1900s, 4½ In.	120

Gaudy Dutch, Sugar, Lid, Leaf, c.1850, 5½ In.
$3,625

Pook & Pook

Glass, Sculpture, Circus, Tent, Numerous Figures, Alison Ruzsa, 4½ x 7½ In.
$1,107

Skinner, Inc.

Glass, Vase, Green, Sterling Silver Overlay, Hourglass Shape, Garland & Filigree, 10 In.
$484

Fontaine's Auction Gallery

This is an edited listing of current prices. Visit **Kovels.com** to check thousands of prices from previous years and sign up for free information on trends, tips, reproductions, marks, and more.

Glass-Art, Epergne, Pink Cased, Enamel Flowers, Scalloped, Victorian, England, c.1885, 18 In.
$168

Garth's Auctioneers & Appraisers

TIP
Never allow water to evaporate in a glass vase. It will leave a white residue that may be impossible to remove.

Glass-Art, Figurine, Panther, Black, Crouching, Frosted Base, Signed, A. Zavella, 9¾ x 26 In.
$313

Kamelot Auctions

Glass-Art, Fish, Hand Blown, Mouth Open, Blue Crystal, Rainbow, West Virginia, 14 In.
$81

Keystone Auctions LLC

Glass-Art, Sculpture, Cube, Cut, Laminated, Gold Foil, Vladimira Klumpar, 1988, 6½ x 6⅝ In.
$1,500

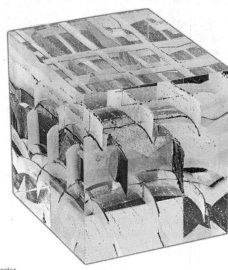

Rago Arts and Auction Center

Glass-Art, Vase, Amber, Moser, Josef Hoffman, c.1900, 6¼ x 8¼ In.
$300

Pook & Pook

Glass-Art, Vase, Amethyst, Moser, Wiener Werkstatte Paper Label, c.1900s, 9 In.
$413

Pook & Pook

Glass-Art, Vase, Iridescent, Trumpet Shape, Peacock Feather, Signed, Stuart Abelman, 15⅜ In.
$108

Thomaston Place Auction Galleries

Glass-Art, Vase, Silver Bead, Blue, Abstract, Marked, Exbor, 1900s, 8½ x 5½ x 2½ In.
$90

Cowan's Auctions

Panel, Stained, Leaded, African Plain, Lion, 2 Giraffes, Back Lit, 44 x 74 In.	250
Sculpture, Circus, Tent, Numerous Figures, Alison Ruzsa, 4½ x 7½ In. ....*illus*	1107
Tankard, Blue, Swirl Design, Ruffled Rim, Enamel Flowers, Victorian, 13 In.	48
Vase, Cylindrical, Tapered Base, Cut Rings, Vertical Vines, Art Deco, France, 14 x 8 In.	537
Vase, Deep Blue Glass, Multicolor, Flowers, Gilt, Victorian, 16 In.	201
Vase, Green, Sterling Silver Overlay, Hourglass Shape, Garland & Filigree, 10 In......*illus*	484
Vase, Pink, Bulbous Body, Amber Feather, England, Victorian, Early 1900s, 7 In.	54
Vase, Silver Overlay, Iridescent, Green To Purple, Art Nouveau, c.1920, 7½ In.	492

GLASS-ART. Art glass means any of the many forms of glassware made during the late nineteenth or early twentieth century. These wares were expensive when they were first made and production was limited. Art glass is not the typical commercial glass that was made in large quantities, and most of the art glass was produced by hand methods. Later twentieth-century glass is listed under Glass-Contemporary, Glass-Midcentury, or Glass-Venetian. Even more art glass may be found in categories such as Burmese, Cameo Glass, Tiffany, and other factory names.

Biscuit Jar, Blue Satin, Bulged Swirls, Silver Plate Lid & Bail, 7¾ In.	72
Bottle, Stopper, Crystal, Signed, Jean Claude, 1900s, 12 In.	188
Bowl, Centerpiece, Blue, Rolled Rim, Pedestal Base, Metal Collar On Stem, 14 In.	184
Bowl, Clear To Amber, Colored Rim, 2¾ x 11½ In.	344
Bowl, Iridescent, Blown Glass, Green, Blue, Signed, 6 x 9 In.	115
Bowl, Multicolor, Line Design, Orange & Red, Art Of Fire, Todd Hansen, 12 x 7 In.	156
Bowl, Yellow Rim, Red, Speckled, Signed, P. O'Reilly, 8 x 18 In.	121
Compote, Circular, Footed Base, Blue, 6½ x 12¼ In.	86
Epergne, Frosted & Clear, Blue Stripe, Red Threading, Ruffled, Brass Stem, Victorian, 19 In. ..	300
Epergne, Pink Cased, Enamel Flowers, Scalloped, Victorian, England, c.1885, 18 In.......*illus*	168
Epergne, Pumpkin, Ruffled Rim, Red, Yellow, Single Horn, Amber, Late 1800s, 17 In.	281
Epergne, Ruffled Rims, 4 Horns, Lime Green, Opalescent, Victorian, 22 In.	96
Figurine, Panther, Black, Crouching, Frosted Base, Signed, A. Zavella, 9¾ x 26 In.........*illus*	313
Fish, Hand Blown, Mouth Open, Blue Crystal, Rainbow, West Virginia, 14 In. ....*illus*	81
Lamp Base, Orange, Bronze Base, Iridescent Threading, 11 x 4½ In.	94
Lamp, Diamond-Quilted, Blue, 5 Toes, c.1800s, 7⅞ x 3⅞ x 2½ In.	329
Lamp, Murano, 3 Dove-Like Birds, Wood Base, Scalloped Edges, 26 x 17 x 21½ In.	211
Pitcher, Apricot Satin, Diamond-Quilted, Frosted, Melon Ribbed Body, 8¾ In.	108
Sculpture, Cube, Cut, Laminated, Gold Foil, Vladimira Klumpar, 1988, 6½ x 6⅝ In.......*illus*	1500
Vase, Amber, Moser, Josef Hoffman, c.1900, 6¼ x 8¼ In. ....*illus*	300
Vase, Amethyst, Moser, Wiener Werkstatte Paper Label, c.1900s, 9 In. ....*illus*	413
Vase, Bulbous Shape, Gilt Decoration, Birds Seated, Branches, 1900s, 10¼ In.	66
Vase, Dancing Nudes, Malachite, Green, Bas Relief, 10 In.	196
Vase, Hand Blown, Green To Purple, Signed, Frederick Carter 48, 7 In.	124
Vase, Iridescent, Trumpet Shape, Peacock Feather, Signed, Stuart Abelman, 15⅜ In.......*illus*	108
Vase, Iridized, Flowers & Lily Pads, Gold, 7½ In.	510
Vase, Koi, Molded, Nickel Silver Collar & Skirt, Unmarked, France, c.1925, 9 In.	277
Vase, Opaque Yellow Glass, Enamel Decoration, Gold Color, France, 7 In.	288
Vase, Silver Bead, Blue, Abstract, Marked, Exbor, 1900s, 8½ x 5½ x 2½ In. ....*illus*	90
Wine, Rhine, Clear, Lavender Highlights, Gold Enamel White Beaded, Red Jewels, 7¼ In.	210
Wine, Studio, Iridescent Cameo Scene Of Dancers, Lautrec, 12 In.	58

GLASS-BLOWN. Blown glass was formed by forcing air through a rod into molten glass. Early glass and some forms of art glass were hand blown. Other types of glass were molded or pressed.

Beaker, Ruby Stain, Etched Stag Scene, Fluted Body, Footed, 7 In. ....*illus*	120
Bell, Industrial, Dome, Mahogany Fitted Circular Base, Victorian, 18 x 12 In.	342
Candlestick, Amethyst, Sausage Turnings, Round Foot, Applied Handle, 4¾ In.	1872
Compote, Ruby, Etched, Ruffled Rim, Deer, Forest Motif, Circular Base, 11 x 7 In.......*illus*	226
Creamer, Shaded Green, Applied Handle, Crimped Foot, Pontil, 4 In.	2340
Decanter, Blue, Multicolor, Enamel Armorial & Border, 1900s, 9½ In. ....*illus*	50
Goblet, Beaker, Enamel Paint, Gilt, c.1850, 5⅛ In. ....*illus*	244
Pitcher, Amberina, Yellow To Amber, Diamond-Quilted, c.1880, 85 In.	120

Glass-Blown, Beaker, Ruby Stain, Etched Stag Scene, Fluted Body, Footed, 7 In.
$120

Fox Auctions

Glass-Blown, Compote, Ruby, Etched, Ruffled Rim, Deer, Forest Motif, Circular Base, 11 x 7 In.
$226

Hartzell's Auction Gallery, Inc.

Glass-Blown, Decanter, Blue, Multicolor, Enamel Armorial & Border, 1900s, 9½ In.
$50

Leslie Hindman Auctioneers

Glass-Blown, Goblet, Beaker, Enamel Paint, Gilt, c.1850, 5 1/8 In.
$244

Glass-Blown, Vase, Flowers, Leaves, Blue & Amber Overlay, Gilt, 1900s, 10 x 5 In.
$360

Glass-Contemporary, Decanter, Magnum, Pointed Stopper, Clear Handle, Turquoise, c.1960, 35 In.
$74

Pitcher, Aqua, Bulbous, Applied Threading On Upper Half, 6 3/8 In.	761
Pitcher, Aqua, Bulbous, Flared Top, Applied Threading, Pontil, 6 3/8 In.	761
Pitcher, Ribbed, Applied Handle, Circular Base, c.1850, 7 In.	469
Salt, Deep Claret Red, Applied Lily Pad Decoration, Folded Rim, Crimped Foot, 3 In.	8190
Salt, Grape Amethyst, Folded Rim, Pedestal Base, Knop, Mantua, Ohio, 2 3/4 In.	3510
Sculpture, Flower, Trumpet Shape, Blue, Purple Speckle, John Leighton, 27 In.	345
Sugar, Lid, Cobalt, Bulbous, Gallery Rim, Inverted Acorn Finial, c.1780, 6 3/4 In.	2340
Urn, Clear, Molded Rim, Circular Base, Footed, 1800s, 10 3/8 In.	375
Urn, Smoke Dome, Clear, Folded Rim, Applied Ring, 1800s, 8 1/2 x 8 In.	63
Urn, Thick Band At Rim, Stacked Ring Support, 1800s, 10 1/2 In.	378
Vase, Clear, Figural Design, Applied Handles, Portland Style, England, Late 1800s, 9 1/2 In.	720
Vase, Flowers, Leaves, Blue & Amber Overlay, Gilt, 1900s, 10 x 5 In. ....*illus*	360
Vase, Green, 2-Masted Ship, Ocean Waves, Continental, 1800s, 8 1/8 In.	63
Vase, Trumpet Shape, Clear, Circular Base, 14 3/4 In.	62
Wine, Ale, Opaque Twist Stem, Ogee Bowl, Spiral, Conical Foot, c.1756, 6 x 2 1/2 In.	234

GLASS-BOHEMIAN. Bohemian glass is an ornate overlay or flashed glass made during the Victorian era. It has been reproduced in Bohemia, which is now a part of the Czech Republic. Glass made from 1875 to 1900 is preferred by collectors.

Adolf Beckert c.1914–1920s	Gräflich Schaffgotsch'sche Josephinenhutte c.1890	J. & L. Lobmeyr 1860+

Compote, Amber, Etched, Deer, Forest Design, Octagonal Base, 12 x 9 In.	90
Compote, Lid, Ruby Cut To Clear, Scene Of Hunter, Stags, Dog, c.1900, 20 In.	540
Mustard Pot, Hinged Lid, Finial, Ear Shape Handle, Cobalt Cut To Clear, 6 x 4 x 2 In.	135
Perfume Bottle, Amber, Cut Glass, Lighthouse Shape, c.1910, 6 x 7 In.	422
Vase, Clear, Etched, Gilt, Domed Base, 9 3/4 In.	111
Vase, Enamel, Gilt, Flute & Scroll Handles, Crimp Rim, Flowers, Gold Ground, 1800s, 12 In.	615
Vase, Raised Red Panels, Gilt Tracery, 1800s, 15 1/2 In.	120

GLASS-CONTEMPORARY includes pieces by glass artists working after 1970. Many of these pieces are free-form, one-of-a-kind sculptures. Paperweights by contemporary artists are listed in the Paperweight category. Earlier studio glass may be found listed under Glass-Midcentury or Glass-Venetian.

Bowl, Azure, Frog Interior, Signed, George Bucquet, 1996, 11 3/4 x 2 In.	151
Bowl, Dark Purple, Iridescent Overlay, Signed, Labino, 1971, 5 x 3 1/4 In.	389
Bowl, Fused, Signed & Numbered, Michael David, 9 x 11 1/2 In.	156
Bowl, Orange, Clear, Brown, Dale Chihuly, 1989, 14 1/2 x 17 In.	8750
Bowl, Yellow Gold Background, Dash Line Pattern, Signed, Lundberg Studios, 1989, 4 1/2 In.	163
Decanter, Magnum, Pointed Stopper, Clear Handle, Turquoise, c.1960, 35 In. ....*illus*	74
Decanter, Rooster Stopper, Incised, K. Franck, Finland, 1967, 12 x 4 In. ....*illus*	812
Flying Pod, Multicolor, Flared Rim, David Goldhagen, c.1993, 13 1/2 x 29 x 23 In. ....*illus*	520
Goblet, Fish, Swirl Pattern, Violet, Alan Goldfarb, 11 In.	163
Scent Bottle, Gilt & Iridescent, Bubbles, Stopper, Signed, Eickholt, 1989, 5 In.	165
Sculpture, Daffodils, Square Lighted Base, Yellow, Signed, Peter Bramhall, c.1988, 10 In. ..*illus*	325
Sculpture, Free-Form, Ariel, Air Traps, Starry Bubbles, Yellow Veil, K. Ipsen, 10 1/4 In.	333
Sculpture, Optochrome, Polarized Glass, Metal, Eric Olson, Sweden, c.1970, 11 x 5 x 3 In.	1647
Sculpture, Yellow Screw, Cast, Rick Beck, 2012, 11 x 7 In. ....*illus*	937
Vase, Amber Cut To Clear, Hobstar Center, Punte, 3 x 3 1/2 In.	36
Vase, Blue Iridescent, Hearts & Vines, Starry Sky, Lundberg, 1979, 10 7/8 In.	248
Vase, Blue Lava, Textured, Organic Shape, Charles Lotton, 1935, 5 x 3 1/2 x 4 1/2 In. ....*illus*	438
Vase, Chartreuse Neck, Multicolor, Hiroshi Yamano, 1989, 9 1/4 x 8 In.	363

Glass-Contemporary, Decanter, Rooster Stopper, Incised, K. Franck, Finland, 1967, 12 x 4 In.
$812

Wright

Glass-Contemporary, Flying Pod, Multicolor, Flared Rim, David Goldhagen, c.1993, 13 ½ x 29 x 23 In.
$520

Susanin's Auctioneers & Appraisers

Glass-Contemporary, Sculpture, Daffodils, Square Lighted Base, Yellow, Signed, Peter Bramhall, c.1988, 10 In.
$325

Heritage Auctions

Glass-Contemporary, Sculpture, Yellow Screw, Cast, Rick Beck, 2012, 11 x 7 In.
$937

Rago Arts and Auction Center

Glass-Contemporary, Vase, Blue Lava, Textured, Organic Shape, Charles Lotton, 1935, 5 x 3 ½ x 4 ½ In.
$438

Abington Auction Gallery

Glass-Contemporary, Vase, Chartreuse, Free-Form, Hand Stretched, Wings & Loops, D. Labino, 6 ¾ In.
$575

Humler & Nolan

Glass-Contemporary, Vase, Cylindrical, Flared Rim, Flared Footing, Feather Pattern, Lundberg, 1900s
$375

Selkirk Auctioneers & Appraisers

Glass-Contemporary, Vase, Face, Zeus, Blown, Sandblasted, Acid Polished, Dan Dailey, 1989, 19 x 13 In.
$5,313

Rago Arts and Auction Center

Glass-Contemporary, Vase, Incalmo, Yellow, Green Rim, Sonja Blomdahl, 1996, 15 x 9 In.
$2,750

Rago Arts and Auction Center

Glass-Contemporary, Vase, Light Green, Dusty Rose Cased, Flowing Sides, Labino, 1978, 6 1/2 x 3 x 3 In.
$512

Aspire Auctions

Glass-Contemporary, Vase, Lobed, Deep Blue, Signed, Labino, 1965, 5 1/2 In.
$374

Blackwell Auctions

Glass-Contemporary, Vase, Multi-Flora, Fuchsia, Pink Flowers, Green Leaves, Charles Lotton, 1990, 11 1/2 In.
$3,025

Humler & Nolan

Vase, Chartreuse, Free-Form, Hand Stretched, Wings & Loops, D. Labino, 6 3/4 In. ....*illus*	575
Vase, Cylindrical, Citron Patterns, Clouds, Christopher Ries, 1976, 10 3/4 In.	182
Vase, Cylindrical, Flared Rim, Flared Footing, Feather Pattern, Lundberg, 1900s...........*illus*	375
Vase, Emerald Brickwall, Stepped Sides, John Conard Lewis, 1988, 18 3/4 x 13 x 5 In.	779
Vase, Face, Zeus, Blown, Sandblasted, Acid Polished, Dan Dailey, 1989, 19 x 13 In...........*illus*	5313
Vase, Fall Leaves, Fronds, Crystal, Engraved, Labino, 1975, 5 3/4 x 4 1/2 In.	575
Vase, Fern, Iridescent Gold, Blue, Green, Ribbed, High Shoulders, Lundberg, 12 In.	230
Vase, Fused Glass Threads, Multicolor, Uneven Rim, Toots Zynsky, 7 1/4 x 12 In.	4725
Vase, Incalmo, Yellow, Green Rim, Sonja Blomdahl, 1996, 15 x 9 In. ....*illus*	2750
Vase, Iridescent, Bulbous Shape, Spherical, Circular Base, 7 1/2 In.	215
Vase, Iridescent, Gold, Pink, Blue, Ribbed Exterior, Polish Base, 1991, 9 1/2 In.	142
Vase, Jack-In-The-Pulpit, Gold, Ruffled Top, Lundberg Studios, 15 In.	238
Vase, Leaf & Vine Pattern, Yellow Background, Signed, David Lotton, 1995, 4 In.	125
Vase, Light Green, Dusty Rose Cased, Flowing Sides, Labino, 1978, 6 1/2 x 3 x 3 In...........*illus*	512
Vase, Lobed, Deep Blue, Signed, Labino, 1965, 5 1/2 In...........*illus*	374
Vase, Multi-Flora, Fuchsia, Pink Flowers, Green Leaves, Charles Lotton, 1990, 11 1/2 In. .....*illus*	3025
Vase, Murrine, Fused, Globular, Stephen Rolfe Powell, Kentucky, 1991, 37 x 19 In.	6875
Vase, Paperweight, Orchid, Pink, Purple, Flowers, Charles Lotton, Signed, 1999, 12 In.	403
Vase, Paperweight, White & Pink Trilliums, Black Stalks, John Lotton, 1997, 13 1/2 In. ....*illus*	847
Vase, Pavonine, Domed Base, Molded Rim, Glazed, Evan Chambers, 8 1/2 In.	126
Vase, Pezzato, Multicolor, Adriano Della Valentina, Signed, Italy, 1998, 13 x 7 In......	523
Vase, Pink & Green Macchia, Orange Lip Wrap, Dale Chihuly, 1989, 19 x 21 In. ....*illus*	10625
Vase, Pink, 3-Sided, Iridescent Glaze Top, Signed, Labino, 1967, 9 1/2 x 4 1/2 In.	425
Vase, Red Lava, Iridescent Gold Bands, Charles Lotton, 1935, 8 x 4 In......	438
Vase, Red, Green Vines, Yellow Flowers, Signed, Charles Lotton, c.1979, 10 3/4 In.	2790
Vase, Sculpture, Ghostly Air Trap, Floating Capsules, Trio Iridescent, Veils, R. Eickholt, c.1976, 10 x 6 In..	169
Vase, Streaked Blue, Yellow, White Interior, 12 In......	288
Vase, Stylized Kite, Orange, Blue, Blown, Dale Chihuly, 1980, 8 1/2 x 6 1/2 In...........*illus*	4375
Vase, Yellow Gold, Green Dash Line, Lundberg Studios, Signed & Dated, 1989, 9 In.	200

GLASS-CUT, *see Cut Glass category.*

GLASS-DEPRESSION, *see Depression Glass category.*

GLASS-MIDCENTURY refers to art glass made from the 1940s to the early 1970s. Some glass factories, such as Baccarat or Orrefors, are listed under their own categories. Earlier glass may be listed in the Glass-Art and Glass-Contemporary categories. Italian glass may be found in Glass-Venetian.

Plaque, Female, Face, Lucite Frame, Signed, Ned Moulton, 1900s, 24 x 12 1/2 x 4 1/2 In.	259
Plate, Square, Aubergine Edge, Woman & Dog, Mailbox, Maurice Heaton, c.1950, 8 In.	96
Sculpture, Cactus, Silicone, Pink, Turquoise, Signed, F. Perkins 1986, 12 1/2 In..........*illus*	720
Server, Arabesque, 2 Tiers, Fusee Glass, Brass, Hickory, Higgins, c.1960, 12 x 16 In..........*illus*	1000
Vase, Iceberg, Tapio Wirkkala, Iittala, Finland, c.1965, 14 1/2 x 12 3/4 x 7 In.	7500

GLASS-PRESSED, *see Pressed Glass category.*

GLASS-VENETIAN. Venetian glass has been made near Venice, Italy, since the thirteenth century. Thin, colored glass with applied decoration is favored, although many other types have been made. Collectors have recently become interested in the Art Deco, 1950s, and contemporary designs. Glass was made on the Venetian island of Murano from 1291. The output dwindled in the late seventeenth century but began to flourish again in the 1850s. Some of the old techniques of glassmaking were revived, and firms today make traditional designs and original modern glass. Since 1981, the name *Murano* may be used only on glass made on Murano Island. Other pieces of Italian glass may be found in the Glass-Contemporary and Glass-Midcentury categories of this book.

Bowl, 2 Birds, Signed, Sandro Frattin, Murano, 7 1/2 x 13 1/2 In.	210
Bowl, Shell Design, Murano, 5 1/2 x 9 In......	94
Bowl, White Cane Slices, Pink Murrines, Fratelli Toso, Murano, 16 3/4 In......	270
Candleholder, Narcissus, Figural, Domed Circular Foot, Murano, 14 In.	94

G

Glass-Contemporary, Vase, Paperweight, White & Pink Trilliums, Black Stalks, John Lotton, 1997, 13 ½ In.
$847

Humler & Nolan

Glass-Contemporary, Vase, Pink & Green Macchia, Orange Lip Wrap, Dale Chihuly, 1989, 19 x 21 In.
$10,625

Rago Arts and Auction Center

Glass-Contemporary, Vase, Stylized Kite, Orange, Blue, Blown, Dale Chihuly, 1980, 8 ½ x 6 ½ In.
$4,375

Rago Arts and Auction Center

Glass-Midcentury, Sculpture, Cactus, Silicone, Pink, Turquoise, Signed, F. Perkins 1986, 12 ½ In.
$720

Eldred's

Glass-Midcentury, Server, Arabesque, 2 Tiers, Fusee Glass, Brass, Hickory, Higgins, c.1960, 12 x 16 In.
$1,000

Wright

Glass-Venetian, Platter, Murrine, Salviati & Co., Murano, 9 ½ x 5 ½ In.
$554

Palm Beach Modern Auctions

Glass-Venetian, Vase, Bulbous, Black Stripes, Lino Tagliapietra, Murano, 1982, 9 ½ x 12 In. $1,239

Aspire Auctions

Glass-Venetian, Vase, Dark Green, Silver Foil Label, Signed, Venini Italia, 20 x 8 In. $293

Thomaston Place Auction Galleries

Goebel, Figurine, Bambi, Porcelain, Disney, String Tag Around Neck, c.1950, 2 ½ x 5 x 7 In. $118

Hake's Auctions

Clock, Wall, Etched Armorial, 8 Panels, Flowers, 1900s, 25 In.	469
Decanter, Phoenix Bird, Red & Green, Italy, 12 x 12 In.	63
Goblet, Gilt, Double Swan Stem, Cobalt Blue, Salviati Style, 9 ¼ In.	127
Goblet, Purple Dragon Stem, Swirled Smoke Glass Bowl, Signed, William Gudenrath, 11 ¾ In.	234
Group, 2 Birds, Branch, Opalescent Heads, R. Anatra, Murano, 11 ½ x 8 ½ x 6 In.	260
Mirror, Leafy Crest, Oval Plate, 1900s, 45 x 27 In.	625
Mirror, Rectangular, Frame, Applied Leaves, 1900s, 41 x 30 In.	813
Platter, Murrine, Salviati & Co., Murano, 9 ½ x 5 ½ In. ....*illus*	554
Sculpture, Swordfish, Gray, Water Form Base, Murano, 14 x 30 x 9 In.	154
Sculpture, Violin, Calcedonia Glass, Blue, Yellow & Red Striations, Dino Rosin, Italy, 25 ¾ x 8 x 4 ½ In.	4750
Vase, Arado, Multicolor Stripes, Alessandro Mendini, Venini, Italy, 1985, 15 x 5 ½ In.	750
Vase, Bulbous, Black Stripes, Lino Tagliapietra, Murano, 1982, 9 ½ x 12 In. ....*illus*	1239
Vase, Clear, Internal Blue Vertical Stripes, Opaque White, Des L. Seguso, 13 x 9 x 6 In.	130
Vase, Dark Green, Silver Foil Label, Signed, Venini Italia, 20 x 8 In. ....*illus*	293
Vase, Glass, Gold Aventurine, Controlled Bubbles, Ercole Barovier, Italy, 9 x 6 In.	200
Vase, Gold Fleck, Air Trap, Signed, M. Asti, Ars Cenedese, Murano, c.1900s, 6 ½ In.	437
Vase, Lid, Amber, Urn, Tripod Feet, Finial, Bulbous Body, 1900s, 19 In.	30
Vase, Moon Flask Shape, Volcanic Style, Seguso, Viro, Murano, 6 ½ In.	115
Vase, Ribbed, Football Shape, Blue, Metallic, Speckles, 1960, 23 x 10 In.	236
Vase, Sculptural, Face & Hand, Renzo Andreon, 19 In.	238
Vase, Translucent White, Signed, Alfredo Barbini, Murano, 15 ¼ x 8 ¾ In.	188
Vase, Weave Design, Green, White, Marked, Flavio Bianconi, For Scozzese, c.1950, 8 ½ In.	1599
Vase, Yellow, Black, Clear, Signed, Luciano Gaspari, Signed Salviati, Italy, 8 ¾ x 6 ½ In.	738
Wine, Gold Enamel, Red, Yellow & Green, Fluted Bases, 8 In., 12 Piece	480

GLASSES for the eyes, or spectacles, were mentioned in a manuscript in 1289 and have been used ever since. The first eyeglasses with rigid side pieces were made in London in 1727. Bifocals were invented by Benjamin Franklin in 1785. Lorgnettes were popular in late Victorian times. Opera Glasses are listed in the Opera Glass category.

Sun, Black, Chanel, Quilted Case	112
Sun, Polaroid 125 Cool-Ray, Caramel Frame, Green Lenses, Woman's, 1960s	16

GLIDDEN POTTERY worked in Alfred, New York, from 1940 to 1957. The pottery made stoneware, dinnerware, and art objects.

Ashtray, High Tide Pattern, Purple, Blue, Black, c.1950, 10 In.	39
Dish, Geometric Pattern, Black, 12 ½ In.	43
Vase, Round, Dark To Light Blue, Speckles, 4 In.	31

GOEBEL is the mark used by W. Goebel Porzellanfabrik of Oeslau, Germany, now Rodental, Germany. The company was founded by Franz Detleff Goebel and his son, William Goebel, in 1871. It was known as F&W Goebel. Slates, slate pencils, and marbles were made. Soon the company began making porcelain tableware and figurines. Hummel figurines were first made by Goebel in 1935. Since 2009 they have been made by another company. Goebel is still in business. Old pieces marked *Goebel Hummel* are listed under Hummel in this book.

Candleholder, Angel, Red Coat & Hat, 4 In.	20
Doll, Bisque, Composition, Glass Eyes, Lace Dress, Pink, 13 In.	90
Egg Timer, Friar Tuck, Brown, Well, 3 x 2 ½ x 1 ½ In.	65
Eggcup, Rooster, Yellow, Red Comb & Beak, 2 ½ x 3 In.	30
Figurine, Bald Eagle, Wings Up, 5 x 5 In.	50
Figurine, Bambi, Porcelain, Disney, String Tag Around Neck, c.1950, 2 ½ x 5 x 7 In. ....*illus*	118
Figurine, Bird, Black, Tan, 3 x 4 In.	24
Figurine, Dog, Bulldog, Brown, Tan, White, 7 x 4 In.	45
Figurine, Mischief Maker, 1960, 4 ¾ In.	88
Lamp, Just Resting, Girl On Fence, c.1979, 16 In.	135
Match Holder, Dog, Brown, 1930s, 2 ½ x 3 ½ In.	248

G

| **Ornament,** Angel, Bell, Green, Blond, 3 In. .... | 28 |
| **Plaque,** Sacrart Angel, c.1960, 4¾ x 3¾ In., Pair .... | 125 |

GOLDSCHEIDER was founded by Friedrich Goldscheider in Vienna in 1885. The family left Vienna in 1938 and the factory was taken over by the Germans. Goldscheider started factories in England and in Trenton, New Jersey. It made figurines and other ceramics. The New Jersey factory started in 1940 as Goldscheider–U.S.A. In 1941 it became Goldscheider–Everlast Corporation. From 1947 to 1953 it was Goldcrest Ceramics Corporation. In 1950 the Vienna plant was returned to Mr. Goldscheider, but it closed in 1953. The Trenton, New Jersey, business, called Goldscheider of Vienna, is a wholesale importer.

Figurine, Young Woman, Lounging Outfit, Seated, Joseph Lorenzl, 11 x 7 x 5 In. ....*illus*	1239
Vase, Nude Female, Standing, Hands Covering Breasts, 27 x 11½ In.	344
Wall Mask, Eve, Apple, Terra-Cotta, Rudolph Knorlein, Signed, c.1930, 13 x 6 x 4½ In. ...*illus*	311

GOLF, *see Sports category.*

GOUDA, Holland, has been a pottery center since the seventeenth century. Two firms, the Zenith pottery, established in 1749, and the Zuid-Hollandsche pottery, made the colorful art pottery marked *Gouda* from 1898 to about 1964. Other factories that made "Gouda" style pottery include Regina (1898–1979), Schoonhoven (1920–present), Ivora (1630–1965), Goedewaagen (1610–1779), Dirk Goedewaagen (1779–1982), and Royal Goedewaagen (1983–present). Many pieces featured Art Nouveau or Art Deco designs. Pattern names in Dutch are often included in the mark.

Gouda / Plateelbakkerij Zenith 1915	Gouda / Kon. Hollandsche Pijpcn–en Aardewekfabriek Goedewaagen 1923–1928	Gouda / Zuid–Holland Platteelbakkerij 1926+

Charger, Rhodian, Radiating Leafy Design, Round, c.1920, 18¾ In. ....*illus*	369
Charger, Rosali, Pottery, Multicolor, Enamel, Bird Perched On Branch, Blossoms, c.1931, 16¾ In..	154
Vase, 2 Handles, Kelat, Flower Head, Scroll Ribbons, 12½ In.	123
Vase, Flowers, Multicolor, Zuid, Holland, c.1900, 9 In.	163
Vase, Glazed, 2 Handles, Round Base, Black Ground, 12¼ In. ....*illus*	86
Vase, Lid, Emmy, Multicolor, Enamel, Leafy Band Border, Holland, c.1923, 14½ In. ....*illus*	338
Vase, Stick, Flowers, Leaves, Curlicues, Multicolor, Signed Zuid Holland Gouda, 1905, 15 x 6 In.	115
Vase, Tapering Shape, Circular Foot, 13½ In.	281

GRANITEWARE is enameled tin or iron used to make kitchenware since the 1870s. Earlier graniteware was green or turquoise blue, with white spatters. The later ware was gray with white spatters. Reproductions are being made in all colors.

Geuder, Paeschke & Frey Co. 1905–c.1972	Iron Clad Manufacturing Co. 1888–1913	Lalance & Grosjean Manufacturing Co. 1877–1955

Pail, Black, White, Marbled, Enamel, Bail Handle, Turned Wood, 5¾ x 9 In.	15
Teapot, Gray Spatter, Pewter Lid, Handle, Spout, 1870s, 10 x 6 In.	35
Teapot, Iron, Trade Sign, Store Display Use, Handle, 1877, 23 x 20 x 18 In.	2205

Goldscheider, Figurine, Young Woman, Lounging Outfit, Seated, Joseph Lorenzl, 11 x 7 x 5 In.
$1,239

Aspire Auctions

Goldscheider, Wall Mask, Eve, Apple, Terra-Cotta, Rudolph Knorlein, Signed, c.1930, 13 x 6 x 4½ In.
$311

Soulis Auctions

Gouda, Charger, Rhodian, Radiating Leafy Design, Round, c.1920, 18¾ In.
$369

Skinner, Inc.

Gouda, Vase, Glazed, 2 Handles, Round Base, Black Ground, 12¼ In.
$86

Skinner, Inc.

Gouda, Vase, Lid, Emmy, Multicolor, Enamel, Leafy Band Border, Holland, c.1923, 14½ In.
$338

Skinner, Inc.

Greentown, Austrian, Saltshaker, Vaseline, Period Metal Lid, 1897, 3 In.
$497

Jeffrey S. Evans & Associates

GREENTOWN glass was made by the Indiana Tumbler and Goblet Company of Greentown, Indiana, from 1894 to 1903. In 1899, the factory became part of National Glass Company. A variety of pressed glass was made. Additional pieces may be found in other categories, such as Chocolate Glass, Holly Amber, Milk Glass, and Pressed Glass.

Austrian, Butter, Cover, Vaseline, 1897, 6¼ x 7¼ In. 293
Austrian, Compote, Jelly, Vaseline, 1897, 4 x 4⅜ In. 152
Austrian, Saltshaker, Vaseline, Period Metal Lid, 1897, 3 In. .... *illus* 497
Austrian, Vase, Vaseline, 1897, 6¼ In. 468
Cord Drapery, Butter, Cover, Green, 1901, 6½ x 7¼ In. .... *illus* 468
Dewey, Mug, Nile Green, Opaque, Beaded Band, Flower Feet, 1898, 3½ In. .... *illus* 152
Dolphin, Condiment, Fish Lid, Golden Agate, Beaded, 4½ x 8 In. 266
Hen On Nest, Dish, Cover, Green, Diamond & Basketweave Base, 4 x 5⅜ In. .... *illus* 105
Herringbone Buttress, Cordial, Green, 1899, 3 In. 152
Herringbone Buttress, Cruet, Green, Tapered Stopper, 1899, 6½ In. .... *illus* 263
Teardrop & Tassel, Berry Bowl, Nile Green, 1900, 1¼ x 4⅛ In. 129
Teardrop & Tassel, Compote, Nile Green, 1900, 5 x 5⅛ In. 527
Teardrop & Tassel, Goblet, Clear, 1900, 5¾ In. 129
Tumbler, Nile Green, 1900s, 3⅞ In. .... *illus* 888

GRUEBY FAIENCE COMPANY of Boston, Massachusetts, was founded in 1894 by William H. Grueby. Grueby Pottery Company was incorporated in 1907. In 1909, Grueby Faience went bankrupt. Then William Grueby founded the Grueby Faience and Tile Company. Grueby Pottery closed about 1911. The tile company worked until 1920. Garden statuary, art pottery, and architectural tiles were made until 1920. The company developed a green matte glaze that was so popular it was copied by many other factories making a less expensive type of pottery. This eventually led to the financial problems of the pottery. Cuerda seca (dry cord) decoration uses a greasy pigment to separate different glaze colors during firing. Cuenca (raised line) decorations are impressed, leaving ridges that separate the glaze colors. The company name was often used as the mark, and slight changes in the form help date a piece.

Paperweight, Scarab, Blue Matte Glaze, Boston, Massachusetts, 1⅛ x 3⅛ In. 677
Tile, Trivet, Ship, Cuerda Seca, Square, Frame, Signed, A.S., 1910, 8¼ In. .... *illus* 2500
Vase, Green Matte Glaze, Applied Stripes, Marked, Early 1900s, 5¼ In. 2214
Vase, Green Matte Glaze, Yellow Buds, Sculpted Leaves, Impressed Mark, 7 x 5 In. .... *illus* 3500
Vase, Green, Yellow Irises, Circular Stamp, Incised ER, c.1905, 11¼ In. .... *illus* 6250
Vase, Leaf, Green Matte Glaze, Terra-Cotta Clay, 11 x 6½ In. 2340
Vase, Leathery Burnt Sienna Matte Glaze, Flared At Base, Tapering To Top, 7 In. 1968
Vase, Leaves, Vertical, Textured, Yellow Buds, Lobed, Label, c.1905, 8¼ In. 4375
Vase, Orange, Long Neck, Bulbous, Glaze, c.1904, 6¾ In. 492
Vase, Paneled, Green, Yellow Blossoms, Stamped, Incised ER, c.1905, 10½ x 7 In. 4375

GUN. *Only toy guns are listed in this book. See Toy category.*

GUNDERSEN *glass is listed in Pairpoint.*

GUSTAVSBERG ceramics factory was founded in 1827 near Stockholm, Sweden. It is best known to collectors for its twentieth-century artwares, especially Argenta, a green stoneware with metallic silver inlay. The company broke up and was sold in the 1990s but the name is still being used

Gustavsberg
1839–1860

Gustavsberg
1940–1970

Gustavsberg
1970–1990s

Bowl, Oxblood Glaze, Undulating Rim, Square Foot, B. Friberg, 1950-70, 3 x 8 In. 625
Vase, Dappled Blue Glaze, Silver Rim, Pencil Neck, Sven Wejsfelt, 5¼ In. 265
Vase, Surrea, 2 Conjoined, Silver Veins, Mottled Turquoise, 9⅜ In. 295

Grueby, Tile, Trivet, Ship, Cuerda Seca, Square, Frame, Signed, A.S., 1910, 8¼ In. $2,500

Rago Arts and Auction Center

Grueby, Vase, Green Matte Glaze, Yellow Buds, Sculpted Leaves, Impressed Mark, 7 x 5 In. $3,500

Treadway

Grueby, Vase, Green, Yellow Irises, Circular Stamp, Incised ER, c.1905, 11¼ In. $6,250

Rago Arts and Auction Center

TIP

Be careful when burning candles in glass candlesticks. If the candle burns too low, the hot wax and flame may break the glass.

Greentown, Cord Drapery, Butter, Cover, Green, 1901, 6½ x 7¼ In. $468

Jeffrey S. Evans & Associates

Greentown, Herringbone Buttress, Cruet, Green, Tapered Stopper, 1899, 6½ In. $263

Jeffrey S. Evans & Associates

Greentown, Dewey, Mug, Nile Green, Opaque, Beaded Band, Flower Feet, 1898, 3½ In. $152

Jeffrey S. Evans & Associates

Greentown, Tumbler, Nile Green, 1900s, 3⅞ In. $888

Jeffrey S. Evans & Associates

Greentown, Hen On Nest, Dish, Cover, Green, Diamond & Basketweave Base, 4 x 5⅜ In. $105

Jeffrey S. Evans & Associates

Halloween, Lantern, Cat Shape,
2-Sided, Paper Insert, Marked, 6 x 7 ½ In.
$181

Hartzell's Auction Gallery, Inc.

Halloween, Toy, Witch, Jack-O'-Lantern,
On Motorcycle, Broom Handle, Rosbro,
c.1950, 6 ½ x 5 In.
$649

Hake's Auctions

Hampshire, Vase, Green Matte Glaze,
Cylindrical, Ruffled Rim, Applied
Bowtie, c.1900, 11 ¼ In.
$246

Skinner, Inc.

HAEGER POTTERIES, INC., Dundee, Illinois, started making commercial artwares in 1914. Early pieces were marked with the name *Haeger* written over an *H.* About 1938, the mark *Royal Haeger* was used in honor of Royal Hickman, a designer at the factory. The firm closed in 2016. See also the Royal Hickman category.

Ashtray, Minnesota Twins, Minnesota Shape, Baseball Players, Teal, 10 ½ x 9 In.	354
Ashtray, Red, Leaf Shape, c.1960, 12 In.	78
Figurine, Panther, Black, c.1970, 6 In.	158
Figurine, Panther, Black, Prepared To Pounce, Rocks, 8 x 14 In.	91
Figurine, Woman, Arm Raised, Knee Out, Long Hair, Head Turned, Nude, White, 24 In.	127
Lamp, Curlicue, Ribbed, Teal To Green, 24 x 9 In., Pair	156
Vase, Olive Green, Urn Shape, Handled, c.1960, 9 x 7 In.	180
Vase, Peacock, Pink, Blue, Pierced Feathers, 15 x 15 In.	124
Vase, Pink, Square, Open Sides, Garden House, c.1950, 14 In.	155

HALF-DOLL, *see Pincushion Doll category.*

HALL'S SUPERIOR QUALITY KITCHENWARE

HALL CHINA COMPANY started in East Liverpool, Ohio, in 1903. The firm made many types of wares. Collectors search for the Hall teapots made from the 1920s to the 1950s. The dinnerware of the same period, especially Autumn Leaf pattern, is popular. The Hall China Company merged with Homer Laughlin China Company in 2010. Autumn Leaf pattern dishes are listed in their own category in this book.

Blue Bouquet, Pepper Shaker, Handle, 7 Holes, 5 In.	54
Cameo Rose, Butter, Cover, Ruffled Grip Handle	399
Cameo Rose, Platter, Serving, Oval, 13 In.	21
Poppy, Reamer, 1933, 7 In.	99
Red Poppy, Mixing Bowl, c.1950, 8 ½ In.	26
Red Poppy, Teapot, Lid, Aladdin, 4 ⅜ In.	229
Teapot, Burgundy, Gold, 6 Cups, 4 x 9 In.	18

HALLOWEEN is an ancient holiday that has changed in the last 200 years. The jack-o'-lantern, witches on broomsticks, and orange decorations seem to be twentieth-century creations. Collectors started to become serious about collecting Halloween-related items in the late 1970s. Old costumes and papier-mache decorations, now replaced by plastic, are in demand.

Cat, Die Cut, Orange & Black, Easel Stand, 1920-30s, 19 In.	102
Jack-In-The-Box, Pumpkin Man, Turnip Nose, Bug Eyes, Plaid Paper Litho Wood Box, 7 In.	346
Lantern, Cat Shape, 2-Sided, Paper Insert, Marked, 6 x 7 ½ In. ....*illus*	181
Lantern, Watermelon, Paper Insert Face, Squat, Wire Handle, Germany, 6 ½ In.	330
Pennant, Jack-O'-Lanterns, Black Cats, Bats, Ghosts, 61 In.	567
Postcard, Bats, Flowers, Jack-O'-Lantern, Children Bobbing For Apples, 1921	28
Pumpkin Man, Bat On Forehead, Root-Shape Legs, Mustache Base, Celluloid, 4 In.	567
Pumpkin, Lantern Mold, Carved Face, c.1900, 8 x 8 In.	59
Toy, Witch, Jack-O'-Lantern, On Motorcycle, Broom Handle, Rosbro, c.1950, 6 ½ x 5 In.....*illus*	649

HAMPSHIRE pottery was made in Keene, New Hampshire, between 1871 and 1923. Hampshire developed a line of colored glazed wares as early as 1883, including a Royal Worcester–type pink, olive green, blue, and mahogany. Pieces are marked with the printed mark or the impressed name *Hampshire Pottery* or *J.S.T. & Co., Keene, N.H.* (James Scollay Taft). Many pieces were marked with city names and sold as souvenirs.

Lamp, Handel, Glass Shade, Green, Landscape, Windmills, Hampshire Pottery Base, 1862, 16 ¾ In.	1230
Pitcher, Green, Pumpkin Shape Bottom, Applied Leaves, Vine Handle, Early 1900s, 8 In.	246
Vase, Green Matte Glaze, Applied Trailing Vine, Early 1900s, 8 ½ In.	369
Vase, Green Matte Glaze, Bulbous, Applied Flowers, 8 In.	240
Vase, Green Matte Glaze, Cylindrical, Early 1900s, 14 ¾ In.	523
Vase, Green Matte Glaze, Cylindrical, Ruffled Rim, Applied Bowtie, c.1900, 11 ¼ In. ....*illus*	246
Vase, Green Matte Glaze, Dandelions, Yellow Flowers, Keene, Early 1900s, 5 ⅞ x 5 In.	308

H

HANDBAG, *see Purse category.*

HANDEL glass was made by Philip Handel working in Meriden, Connecticut, from 1885 and in New York City from 1893 to 1933. The firm made art glass and other types of lamps. Handel shades were made not only of leaded glass in a style reminiscent of Tiffany but also of reverse painted glass. Handel also made vases and other glass objects.

Lamp Base, 5-Light, Griffins, 3 Cast Metal Feet, Gooseneck Socket Cluster, 29 In.	2880
Lamp Base, Bronze, Harp Shape Top, Cloth Label, Single Socket, 57 x 13 ½ In.	275
Lamp Shade, Chipped Ice Finish, Yellow Flowers, Green Leaves, Red Berries, 4¾ x 7½ In.	220
Lamp, 1-Light, Boudoir, Brown, Daffodils, Bronze Ribbed Base, Signed, c.1915, 14¾ In....*illus*	1112
Lamp, 1-Light, Domed Shade, Obverse Painted, Scenic, Valley Landscape, 18 In.	3630
Lamp, 1-Light, Embossed Emerald Case, 8 Panels, Bronze Base, Early 1900s, 28 x 22 In.	1500
Lamp, 1-Light, Flower Shade, Slag Glass, 2 Colors, Bronze Base, 25 In.	825
Lamp, 1-Light, Moonlit River Scene, Bronze Base, c.1920, 30¼ x 11 In.	2520
Lamp, 2-Light, Bronze, 6 Multicolor Slag Glass Panels, Geometric Design, 20 In.	275
Lamp, 2-Light, Leaded Glass Shade, Flowers, Leaf Band, Geometric Amber Glass Panels, 25 x 17 In.	1200
Lamp, 2-Light, Loop Handle, Adjustable, Bronze, Opalescent Glass, 18 In.	1020
Lamp, 2-Light, Patinated Bronze, Figural, Water Bearer, Marked, Early 1900s, 25 In.	1750
Lamp, 2-Light, Slag Glass, Metal Overlay, Hexagonal Shade, Acorn Pulls, 20 In.	825
Lamp, 3-Light, Domed Shade, 4 Clusters Of Stems, Leaves & Vines, Poppy Flowers, 22 In.	4235
Lamp, 3-Light, Leaded Glass Shade, Unique Art Glass & Metal Co., Orange Flowers, Leaves, 24 x 16 In.	1353
Lamp, 3-Light, Mountain Landscape, Domed Shade, Reverse & Obverse Painted, 18 In.....*illus*	8470
Lamp, 3-Light, Reverse Painted, Domed Shade, Lakeside Sunset Landscape Scene, 22 In.	2118
Lamp, 4-Light, Periwinkle Flower Petals, Vine Trunk Base, 32 x 24 In.	4800
Lamp, 5-Light, Tulip, 12-Sided Cone Shade, Caramel Slag Panels, Signed, 65½ In.	3933
Lamp, Birds Of Paradise, Domed Shade, Rich Black Background, Exotic Birds, Signed, 23½ x 17¾ In.	5228
Lamp, Boudoir, Painted Glass Shade, Parrot, Brownish Green Patina, 13 x 8 In.	2360
Lamp, Boudoir, Reverse Painted Shade, Flowers, Bronze Base, Pull Chain, 14 x 7 In.....*illus*	880
Lamp, Bronzed Metal, Slag Glass, Marked, 21 x 14½ In.	1968
Lamp, Desk, Flower Style Glass Shade, Bronze Iron Gooseneck, Adjustable, 14¾ In.	1210
Lamp, Green Glass Cased Shade, Patinated White Metal Base, c.1915, 12½ In. ....*illus*	390
Lamp, Leaded Shade, Yellow Flowers, Leaves, Water Bearer Base, Kneeling Maiden, 18 In.	2596
Lamp, Mushroom Shade, Vertical Panels, Cream Diamond Shapes, Signed, 19 x 11½ In.	1968
Lamp, Piano, Bamboo Overlay, Early 1900s, 16 x 8 In.	360
Lamp, Piano, Reverse Painted Shade, Lakeside Scene, Amber Sky, Moon, 9 x 10 x 15 In.	1210
Lamp, Multicolor, Leaded Glass, Floral Backgrounds, Signed, Early 1900s, 28½ In. ....*illus*	4095
Lamp, Slag Glass, Leaded Shade, Scalloped, Bronze Base, c.1905, 22 x 16¾ In. ....*illus*	492
Lamp, Water Bearer, Maiden, Kneeling, With Water Jug, Leaded Glass Shade, Flowers, 24½ In. .. *illus*	2662
Light, Ceiling, Bell Shape, Filigree Metal, Slag Glass, Stamped, 4¾ x 6¼ In.	156

HARDWARE, *see Architectural category.*

HARKER POTTERY COMPANY was incorporated in 1890 in East Liverpool, Ohio. The Harker family had been making pottery in the area since 1840. The company made many types of pottery but by the Civil War was making quantities of yellowware from native clays. It also made Rockingham-type brown-glazed pottery and whiteware. The plant was moved to Chester, West Virginia, in 1931. Dinnerware was made and sold nationally. In 1971 the company was sold to Jeannette Glass Company, and all operations ceased in 1972. For more prices, go to kovels.com.

Cameoware, Plate, Bread & Butter, Blue, Cream, 6½ In.	18
Corinthian, Plate, Salad, Dark Teal Green, Square, 8⅜ In.	15
Cross Stitch, Bowl, Hotoven, Flowers, 9 x 5 In.	14
Dainty Flower, Plate, Dinner, Blue, White Flowers, 9¾ In.	94
Dogwood, Bowl, Scalloped Edge, Handled, Silver Trim, 10 In.	16
Golden Dawn, Casserole, Round, Yellow, Gray, Specks, 7¼ In.	46
Ivy, Cake Plate, Square, 2 Handles, 12¼ In.	43
Pate Sur Pate, Plate, Dinner, Green, 10 In.	20

Handel, Lamp, 1-Light, Boudoir, Brown, Daffodils, Bronze Ribbed Base, Signed, c.1915, 14¾ In.
$1,112

Jeffrey S. Evans & Associates

Handel, Lamp, 3-Light, Mountain Landscape, Domed Shade, Reverse & Obverse Painted, 18 In.
$8,470

Fontaine's Auction Gallery

Handel, Lamp, Boudoir, Reverse Painted Shade, Flowers, Bronze Base, Pull Chain, 14 x 7 In.
$880

Forsythes' Auctions

Handel, Lamp, Green Glass Cased Shade, Patinated White Metal Base, c.1915, 12½ In.
$390

Garth's Auctioneers & Appraisers

Handel, Lamp, Multicolor, Leaded Glass, Floral Backgrounds, Signed, Early 1900s, 28½ In.
$4,095

Jeffrey S. Evans & Associates

Handel, Lamp, Slag Glass, Leaded Shade, Scalloped, Bronze Base, c.1905, 22 x 16¾ In.
$492

Skinner, Inc.

Silhouette, Pie Plate, Woman In Garden, Hotoven, c.1930, 10 In.	13
White Daisy, Plate, Dinner, 10 In.	28
Wild Rose, Cake & Pie Server, 9⅜ In.	13

HARLEQUIN dinnerware was produced by the Homer Laughlin Company from 1938 to 1964, and sold without trademark by the F. W. Woolworth Co. It has a concentric ring design like Fiesta, but the rings are separated from the rim by a plain margin. Cup handles are triangular in shape. Seven different novelty animal figurines were introduced in 1939. For more prices, go to kovels.com.

Chartreuse, Bowl, Salad, 7 In.	59
Chartreuse, Cup & Saucer	75
Maroon, Nut Dish, Round, Basket Weave, 3 In.	19
Mauve Blue, Creamer, 2 In.	38
Mauve Blue, Figurine, Donkey	179
Medium Green, Ashtray, Basketweave, Scalloped Rim.................*illus*	3835
Red, Ashtray, Stand, Glazed, Round	106
Red, Eggcup, Single, Steamed, 2½ In.	29
Red, Syrup	130
Turquoise, Pitcher, Tankard, 24 Oz.	59
Turquoise, Teapot, Lid, Short Spout, Handle, Finial..............*illus*	35
Yellow, Platter, Serving, Oval, 11 In.	17
Yellow, Syrup	98

HATPIN collectors search for pins popular from 1860 to 1920. The long pin, often over four inches, was used to hold the hat in place on the hair. The tops of the pins were made of all materials, from solid gold and real gemstones to ceramics and glass. Be careful to buy original hatpins and not recent pieces made by altering old buttons.

14K Gold, Filigree, Turquoise Cabochon, 7¼ In. ....*illus*	102
Amethyst Luster Glass, Scarab Bug, 1900s, 11 In.	120
Art Glass, Geometric Patterns, Multicolor, 1¾ In.	20
Brass, Art Nouveau, Winged Nymph, 9 In.	99
Carnelian, Flower & Bead Center, 3⅞ In.	35
Glass, Black, Faceted Border, 8 In.	35
Gold Tone, Sphere, Etched, 4 In.	20
Metal, Sphere, Turquoise Stones, c.1900, 5¾ In.	271
Opal, Teardrop, Bezel Frame, Diamond, 14K Yellow Gold, c.1910, 2¾ In.	275
Porcelain, Pink Roses, Blue Border, Bavaria, 5 In.	87
Rhinestones, Flower, Edwardian, 10 x 2 In.	50
Rhinestones, Square, Art Deco, Gilt, c.1905, 8 In.	109
Sterling Silver, Art Nouveau, Woman's Face, 1930s, 7 In.	60
Wood, Black & White Enamel, Art Deco, 7 In.	20

HATPIN HOLDERS were needed when hatpins were fashionable from 1860 to 1920. The large, heavy hat required special long-shanked pins to hold it in place. The hatpin holder resembles a large saltshaker, but it often has no opening at the bottom as a shaker does. Hatpin holders were made of all types of ceramics and metal. Look for other pieces under the names of specific manufacturers.

Carnival Glass, Grape & Vine, Footed, 6½ x 2½ In.	225
Cloisonne, Heart Shape, Asymmetrical, Enamel, Multicolor, Japan	175
Porcelain, Abstract Flowers, Cobalt Blue, Gilt, Scalloped Edge, 4½ In.	59
Porcelain, Cornucopia Shape, Geisha, Flowers, Gilt, c.1905, 7 In.	95
Porcelain, Maid, Cap, Apron, Blue, Pink, c.1870, 5¼ In.	185
Porcelain, Tapered, Cylindrical, Domed Top, Forget-Me-Nots, Blue, Bavaria, 4 In.	59
Porcelain, White Background, Roses, Gilt Trim, Scherzer, 4¾ x 2¼ In. ....*illus*	90
Porcelain, White, Victorian Santa Claus Head, Hood, c.1870, 4½ x 2 In.	300
Pressed Glass, Scalloped Edge, Footed, 6¼ In.	195

HAVILAND china has been made in Limoges, France, since 1842. David Haviland had a shop in New York City and opened a porcelain company in Limoges, France. Haviland was the first company to both manufacture and decorate porcelain. Pieces are marked *H & Co., Haviland & Co.,* or *Theodore Haviland.* It is possible to match existing sets of dishes through dealers who specialize in Haviland china. Other factories worked in the town of Limoges making a similar chinaware. These porcelains are listed in this book under Limoges.

HAVILAND & Co. Limoges	Théo Haviland Limoges FRANCE	Haviland France
Haviland and Co. 1876–1878; 1889–1931	Theodore Haviland 1893–early 1900s	Haviland and Co. c.1894–1931

Basket, Daisies, Gold Trim, Hand Painted, 1890s, 3 x 5 In.		277
Plate, Deer & Quail, Stream, Fall, c.1890, 9 ½ In.		77
Serving Bowl, Organic Shape, Leafy, Cobalt Blue, c.1890, 3 ¾ x 10 ½ x 8 ⅝ In. ......*illus*		1289
Serving Dish, Lid, Green Panels, Roses, Gilt, 10 x 8 In.		66
Vase, Round, Stick Neck, Trailing Flowers, Leaves, Handles, 12 x 9 In., Pair		222
Vase, Shark, Coiled, Mouth Open, Black, Pink, Edouard Marcel Sandoz, 1940s, 9 ½ In., Pair...		1375
Water Set, Pitcher, 6 Mugs, Handles, Berry, Cherries, Branches, Gilt, Handles, 9 x 5 ¾ In., 7 Piece.		105

HAVILAND POTTERY began in 1872, when Charles Haviland decided to make art pottery. He worked with the famous artists of the day and made pottery with slip glazed decorations. Production stopped in 1885. Haviland Pottery is marked with the letters *H & Co.* The Haviland name is better known today for its porcelain.

HAVILAND & Co Limoges	H & Co L	CFH GDM FRANCE
Haviland and Co. 1875–1882	Haviland and Co. 1875–1882	Charles Field Haviland 1891+

Vase, Ducks, Greenery, Multicolor, Terra-Cotta, c.1880, 10 ¾ x 7 ½ In.		726

HAWKES cut glass was made by T. G. Hawkes & Company of Corning, New York, founded in 1880. The firm cut glass blanks made at other glassworks until 1962. Many pieces are marked with the trademark, a trefoil ring enclosing a fleur-de-lis and two hawks. Cut glass by other manufacturers is listed under either the factory name or in the general Cut Glass category.

Bottle, Vinegar, Intaglio Flower Garland, Signed, 7 ½ In.		48
Bowl, Hobstar & Diamond Panels, Scalloped Rim, Late 1800s, 5 x 10 In.		177
Bowl, Hobstar Center, Hobstar Chain Border, 7 ¾ In.		48
Bowl, Hobstar Chain Border, Intaglio Flower Garland, Signed, 7 ¼ In.		30
Bowl, Millicent, Pedestal, Signed, 3 ½ x 8 ¾ In.		150
Bowl, Ruffled, Hobstar, Clear Edges, Punte Highlights, Signed, 2 x 6 ¼ In.		24
Bowl, Whipping Cream, Minerva, Signed, 2 ½ x 6 In.		48
Carafe, Brunswick, Ray Cut Base, Signed, 7 In.		108
Carafe, Valencian, Flared Rim, 9 ½ In.		1140
Cocktail Shaker, Vernay, Marked, c.1925, 12 ¾ x 4 ½ In.		813
Cologne Bottle, Intaglio Iris, Ray Cut Base, Signed, 6 x 5 In.		240
Cologne Bottle, R.C. Rosalia Pattern, Signed, 5 In.		60
Compote, Caroline, Hobstar Base, Apple Core Stem, Signed, 4 ¾ x 4 ¾ In.		18
Compote, Twist Stem, Ray Cut Base, Signed, 7 ¼ x 6 In.		330
Decanter, Basket Weave, Lid, 16 In.		3600
Decanter, Cayuga, Silver Stopper, Ray Cut Base, Marshall Field, 10 ¼ In.		60
Decanter, Cut Glass, Hobstars, Hobnails, Fans & Ovals, Stopper, 33 ½ In.		380
Decanter, Willow, Bulbous Finial, Curved Handle, 13 ¼ In.		4200
Ferner, Empire, Metal Liner Insert, Signed, 3 ½ x 6 ¼ In.		72

Handel, Lamp, Water Bearer, Maiden, Kneeling, With Water Jug, Leaded Glass Shade, Flowers, 24 ½ In.
$2,662

Humler & Nolan

Harlequin, Medium Green, Ashtray, Basketweave, Scalloped Rim
$3,835

Strawser Auction Group

Harlequin, Turquoise, Teapot, Lid, Short Spout, Handle, Finial
$35

jfhouseofutterclutter on eBay

Hatpin, 14K Gold, Filigree, Turquoise Cabochon, 7 ¼ In.
$102

Soulis Auctions

Hatpin Holder, Porcelain, White Background, Roses, Gilt Trim, Scherzer, 4¾ x 2¼ In.
$90

Soulis Auctions

Haviland, Serving Bowl, Organic Shape, Leafy, Cobalt Blue, c.1890, 3¾ x 10½ x 8⅝ In.
$1,289

Aspire Auctions

Hawkes, Plate, North Star, 7 In.
$420

Brunk Auctions

H

Pitcher, Pressed Irises, Silver Stopper, Repousse, Monogram, 8¾ x 9½ In.	570
Plate, Napoleon Pattern, Signed, 7 In.	108
Plate, North Star, 7 In. ....*illus*	420
Plate, Queens, Marked, 10 In.	720
Rose Bowl, Panel, Bulbous, Marked, 5 In.	3600
Tray, Alhambra, 12¾ In.	1680
Tray, Constellation, 16¼ In.	4200
Tray, Willow, Round, 11¾ In. ....*illus*	5100
Tumbler, Queens, Hobstar Base, Cut Glass, 3¾ In.	60
Vase, Eardley, Pedestal, Signed, 13 In.	60
Vase, Green Cut To Clear, Flowers, Vines, Marked, 6 In. ....*illus*	1200
Vase, Iris, Gravic Cut, Early 1900s, 12¾ In.	270

 HEAD VASES, generally showing a woman from the shoulders up, were used by florists primarily in the 1950s and 1960s. Made in a variety of sizes and often decorated with imitation jewelry and other lifelike accessories, the vases were manufactured in Japan and the U.S.A. Less elaborate examples were made as early as the 1930s. Religious themes, babies, and animals are also common subjects. Other head vases are listed under manufacturers' names and can be located through the index in the back of this book. Collecting head vases was a fad in the 1960s-70s and prices rose. There is less interest now and only a few are high priced.

Clown, Red Nose, Ruffled White Collar, Red Polka Dots, Green Hat, Napcoware, 6 In.	22
Mary Poppins, Holding Umbrella End, Ceramic, Painted, Enesco, 1964, 5½ In. ....*illus*	1955
Moro, Enameled Gold, Piero Fornasetti, 9 x 5 In.	1900
Woman, Bouffant Hair, Black Ruffled Dress, Pearl Jewelry, Green Ring, 7 x 5 In.	99
Woman, Christmas, Poinsettia Flowers, Pearl Earrings, Inarco, c.1961, 6 In.	165
Young Woman, Blue Eyes, Black Hair, Yellow Bow, Flower On Dress, Enesco, 1960s, 5 x 4 In.	75

 HEDI SCHOOP emigrated from Germany in 1933 and started Hedi Schoop Art Creations, North Hollywood, California, in 1940. Schoop made ceramic figurines, lamps, planters, and tablewares. The business burned down in 1958. Some of the molds were sold and Schoop began designing for other companies. She died in 1995.

Figurine, Dancer, Musician, 3-Tiered Riser, Flowing Sleeves, 1950s, 10 In., Pair	175
Figurine, Oriental Woman, Flowers, 12½ In.	49
Planter, Figural, Woman Holding Pots, Green Dress, Bonnet, Yellow Flowers, 13 In.	55
Plaque, Cat, Seated, Black & White Stripes, 7½ x 7½ In.	69

 HEINTZ ART METAL SHOP used the letters *HAMS* in a diamond as a mark. In 1902, Otto Heintz designed and manufactured copper items with colored enamel decorations under the name Art Crafts Shop. He took over the Arts & Crafts Company in Buffalo, New York, in 1903. By 1906 it had become the Heintz Art Metal Shop. It remained in business until 1930. The company made ashtrays, bookends, boxes, bowls, desk sets, vases, trophies, and smoking sets. The best-known pieces are made of copper, brass, and bronze with silver overlay. Similar pieces were made by Smith Metal Arts and were marked *Silver Crest.* Some pieces by both companies are unmarked.

Sterling On Bronze, Box, Peacock, Stamped, Wood Liner, 4½ x 3½ In.	227
Sterling On Bronze, Vase, Cylinder, Flower Stalk, Stamped, 6 x 2 In.	227
Sterling On Bronze, Vase, Iris, Impressed, 11½ x 5 In.	162
Vase, Trophy Shape, Leaves, Vines, Handles, 1912, 9 In.	420

HEISEY glass was made from 1896 to 1957 in Newark, Ohio, by A. H. Heisey and Co., Inc. The Imperial Glass Company of Bellaire, Ohio, bought some of the molds and the rights to the trademark. Some Heisey patterns have been made by Imperial since 1960. After 1968, they stopped using the *H* trademark. Heisey used romantic names for colors, such as Sahara. Do not confuse color and pattern names. The Custard Glass and Ruby Glass categories may also include some Heisey pieces.

Heisey 1900–1957	Heisey Paper label	Heisey Paper label

Animal, Ashtray, Duck, Flamingo, 4 3/4 In.	279
Crystolite, Relish, Shell Shape, 5 Sections, 13 In.	69
Greek Key, Punch Bowl, Clear, 14 7/8 In.	359
Rose Etch, Plate, Center Handle, Dolphin, 14 1/2 In.	80
Rose Etch, Tumbler, Iced Tea, 12 Oz.	29
Toothpick Holder, Simms, Montana, Rosebud, Sawtooth Edge, c.1900, 2 3/8 In.	35

HEREND, *see Fischer category.*

HEUBACH is the collector's name for Gebruder Heubach, a firm working in Lichten, Germany, from 1840 to 1925. It is best known for bisque dolls and doll heads, the principal products. The company also manufactured bisque figurines, including piano babies, beginning in the 1880s, and glazed figurines in the 1900s. Piano Babies are listed in their own category. Dolls are included in the Doll category under Gebruder Heubach and Heubach. Another factory, Ernst Heubach, working in Koppelsdorf, Germany, also made porcelain and dolls. These will also be found in the Doll category under Heubach Koppelsdorf.

Bowl, Nymphs, Coming Out Of Water, Nude, Green, Signed GH, 10 1/2 x 7 1/2 In.	281
Candy Container, Boy, Red Coat, Ball, Scarf, Holly, 5 In.	312
Candy Container, Child On Cotton Ball, Wearing Red Hat & Jacket, Cherries, Fruits, 8 In.	633
Figurine, 2 Boys, Snowy Putz Scene, Wood Hut, c.1910, Germany, 5 In.	288
Pin, Portrait, Woman, Headscarf, Red Necklace, Brass Enclosure, 2 In.	159

HISTORIC BLUE, *see factory names, such as Adams, Ridgway, and Staffordshire.*

HOBNAIL glass is a style of glass with bumps all over. Dozens of hobnail patterns and variants have been made. Clear, colored, and opalescent hobnail have been made and are being reproduced. Other pieces of hobnail may also be listed in the Duncan & Miller and Fenton categories.

Berry Bowl, 3 x 8 In.	30
Bowl, Cranberry Glass, Ruffled Edge, Pontil, Hobb, West Virginia, c.1980, 3 1/4 x 7 1/2 In.	42
Pitcher, Art Glass, Ruby, Reeded Handle, Fire Polished Lip, Victorian, 9 1/2 In. ...*illus*	55
Pitcher, Cranberry, Opalescent, Square Top, Applied Clear Handle, Victorian, 8 In. ...*illus*	60

HOCHST, or Hoechst, porcelain was made in Germany from 1746 to 1796. It was marked with a six-spoke wheel. Be careful when buying Hochst; many other firms have used a very similar wheel-shaped mark. Copies have been made from the original molds.

Group, Gilt Bronze Stand, 4 Putti, Goat, Oval Base, Germany, c.1750, 12 x 14 3/4 x 9 In. ...*illus*	875

HOLLY AMBER, or golden agate, glass was made by the Indiana Tumbler and Goblet Company of Greentown, Indiana, from January 1, 1903, to June 13, 1903. It is a pressed glass pattern featuring holly leaves in the amber-shaded glass. The glass was made with shadings that range from creamy opalescent to brown-amber.

Butter, Cover, Golden Agate, 1902, 5 7/8 x 7 3/8 In.	439
Plate, Golden Agate, Plain Rim, Beaded Top, 1902, 7 1/4 In.	199
Spooner, Golden Agate, Vertical Panels, Beading, Greentown, 1902, 4 In.	322
Toothpick Holder, Golden Agate, Beaded Bands & Rim, Greentown, 1902, 2 1/2 In. ...*illus*	263
Tumbler, Golden Agate, Factory Polished Table Ring, 1902, 3 7/8 In.	293

Hawkes, Tray, Willow, Round, 11 3/4 In. $5,100

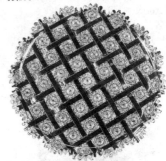

Brunk Auctions

Hawkes, Vase, Green Cut To Clear, Flowers, Vines, Marked, 6 In. $1,200

Brunk Auctions

Head Vase, Mary Poppins, Holding Umbrella End, Ceramic, Painted, Enesco, 1964, 5 1/2 In. $1,955

Van Eaton Galleries

This is an edited listing of current prices. Visit Kovels.com to check thousands of prices from previous years and sign up for free information on trends, tips, reproductions, marks, and more.

H

Hobnail, Pitcher, Art Glass, Ruby, Reeded Handle, Fire Polished Lip, Victorian, 9 ½ In.
$55

Forsythes' Auctions

Hobnail, Pitcher, Cranberry, Opalescent, Square Top, Applied Clear Handle, Victorian, 8 In.
$60

Woody Auction

Hochst, Group, Gilt Bronze Stand, 4 Putti, Goat, Oval Base, Germany, c.1750, 12 x 14¾ x 9 In.
$875

Heritage Auctions

HOLT-HOWARD was an importer that started working in New York City in 1949 and moved to Stamford, Connecticut, in 1955. The company sold many types of table accessories, such as condiment jars, decanters, spoon holders, and saltshakers. Its figural pieces have a cartoon-like quality. The company was bought out by General Housewares Corporation in 1968. Holt-Howard pieces are often marked with the name and the year or *HH* and the year stamped in black. The *HH* mark was used until 1974. The company also used a black and silver paper label. Holt-Howard production ceased in 1990 and the remainder of the company was sold to Kay Dee Designs. In 2002, Grant Holt and John Howard started Grant-Howard Associates and made retro pixie cookie jars marked *GHA* that sold from a mail-order catalog. Other GHA retro pixie pieces were made until 2006.

Candleholder, Igloo, Snow Baby, White, Red Trim, 1950s, 2 ½ In., Pair	40
Salt & Pepper, Cat, Pink Collar, Blue Collar, Marked, 1959, 5 In.	19
Soup & Sandwich Set, Handled Bowls, Lettuce Leaf Plates, 1962, 5 x 9 In., Set Of 4	6

HOPALONG CASSIDY was a character in a series of 28 books written by Clarence E. Mulford, first published in 1907. Movies and television shows were made based on the character. The best-known actor playing Hopalong Cassidy was William Lawrence Boyd. His first movie appearance was in 1919, but the first Hopalong Cassidy film was not made until 1934. Sixty-six films were made. In 1948, William Boyd purchased the television rights to the movies, then later made 52 new programs. In the 1950s, Hopalong Cassidy and his horse, named Topper, were seen in comics, records, toys, and other products. Boyd died in 1972.

Bank, Hopalong Cassidy, Bust, Iowa Trust & Saving, Plastic, Coin Slot On Top, 1950, 4 ¼ In.	31
Bottle Cap, Superior Dairies, Portraits, Red On White, Waxed Paper, 4 In.	25
Cap Gun, Dummy Hammer, Orange Plug, Portrait On Handle, Wyandotte, 1950s	108
Coloring Book, Hoppy, Hitching Post, 48 Pages, Doubleday & Co., 1950, 11 x 14 In.	45
Comic Book, Hoppy, Captain Marvel Cover Cameo, No. 1, February 1943 ....*illus*	414
Dish Set, Hoppy, Blue Outfit, W.S. George, 1950s, 3 Piece, 3-In. Cup, 5-In. Bowl, 9-In. Plate	75
I.D. Bracelet, Silvered Brass, Hopalong Cassidy XX Ranch, c.1950	85
Lunch Box, Metal, Hopalong On Horse, Chuckwagon, Thermos, Aladdin, 1954, 8 ¼ In. ...*illus*	81
Mug, Milk Glass, Red, Cowboy, Handle, 3 In.	5
Night-Light, Electric, Hanging, Pistol & Holster, Milk Glass, Aladdin, 1950s, 10 x 4 In.	90
Pin, Savings Club, Pinback, Round, White Ground, Red & Black Lettering, 1950s, 3 In.	4
Plate, To My Friend, Hoppy, White Ground, Cowboy, Horse, W.S. George, 1950s	9
Pocket Knife, Folding, Can Opener, 2 Blades, Strap & Clip	27
Ring, Metal, Adjustable, Western Movie, Cowboy, William Boyd	13
Stickpin, Hoppy, Star Badge, Gun, Gold Plastic, Sweden, 1 ⅝ In.	70
Tin, Popcorn, Hopalong Image, Lithograph, Mayland Popcorn Co-Op, 5 x 2 ⅝ In. ....*illus*	342
Toy, Camera, Snapshot, Cowboy, Portrait, Galter, Box, 1950s	43
Wood Burning Set, 6 Plaques, Heating Wand, Paint, Box, William Boyd Ltd., 13 x 17 In.	95

HORN was used to make many types of boxes, furniture inlays, jewelry, and whimsies. The Endangered Species Act makes it illegal to sell many of these pieces.

Vase, Flying Cranes, Lotuses, Pond, Inlay, Mother-Of-Pearl, Carved Stand, 1800s, 8 In.	1353

Howard Pierce

HOWARD PIERCE began working in Southern California in 1936. In 1945, he opened a pottery in Claremont. He moved to Joshua Tree in 1968 and continued making pottery until 1991. He made contemporary-looking figurines. Though most pieces are marked with his name, smaller items from his sets often were not marked.

Bowl, Curvilinear Shape, c.1950, 13 x 4 In.	145
Figurine, Cat, Raised Ears, Short Tail, Stylized	95
Figurine, Frog On Stone, 5 ¼ x 4 ¼ In.	95
Figurine, Girl, Long Dress, Holding Bird, Blue, Black Trim, 7 ½ In. ....*illus*	100
Figurine, Goose, Long Neck, Cream To Brown, 1950s, 7 In.	25
Figurine, Mouse, 1950s, 5 In.	80
Figurine, Quail, Mother, 2 Chicks, Brown Matte Glaze, Speckled, Signed, 3 Piece	68
Vase, Quails On Branch, White, 1960s, 9 In.	75

HOWDY DOODY and Buffalo Bob were the main characters in a children's series televised from 1947 to 1960. Howdy was a redheaded puppet. The series became popular with college students in the late 1970s when Buffalo Bob began to lecture on campuses.

Alarm Clock, Talking, Boy & Clown, Painted, Box, 7 In.........................*illus*	130
Bank, Riding Pig, Coin, Shawnee..	56
Bib, Terry Cloth, Red, Yellow, Princess Summerfall-Winterspring, c.1950, 11 x 13 In.	60
Book, How To Make Puppet Show, Punch-Out, Kagran Corp., 1952, 11 x 14 In., 3 Pages	185
Book, Howdy Doody & The Princess, Little Golden Book, Edward Kean, 1952	23
Book, Howdy Doody In The Wild West, Big Golden, Simon & Schuster, 1942, 9 x 11 In.	35
Book, Howdy Doody's Circus, Little Golden Book, 1950, 6½ x 8 In...........................	25
Circus Box, Cardboard, Howdy Doody, Children, 7½ x 6 x 3 In........................	45
Cookie Jar, Lid, Head, Smiling Face, Purinton Pottery, 8 x 6½ In........................	81
Doll, Cloth, Composition Head With Pull String Mouth, c.1950, 26 In.........................	150
Doll, Composition, Cloth, Scarf, Belt, Shoes, c.1948, 20 In..........................	168
Dummy, Ventriloquist, Strings Attached In Mouth, Eegee National Broadcasting, 1972, 30 In...*illus*	74
Dummy, Ventriloquist, Strings Attached In Mouth, Goldberg, 1970s, 12 In.	63
Figure, Howdy Doody, Wood, Red & Blue Paint, 1950s, 12 In.	150
Handkerchief, Red Border, Portrait, Leadworks Inc., c.1988, 21 x 21 In.	25
Marionette, Checkered Shirt, Brown Shoes, Strings Attached To Control, 14 In......................	27
Night-Light, Plug In, Mint, Plastic, Face, Uneeda Ideal, 1950s, 4 In.	11
Ornament, Christmas, Waving, Smiling, Multicolor, Keepsake, 1997	1
Ring, Plastic, Child's, Flicker, Buffalo Bob, c.1950, 4½ In.	13
Sign, Twin Pop, Embossed, Metal, Soda Pop, Gas, Oil, 1950s, 14 In........................	104
Spoon, Silver Plate, Portrait, Kagran, 6⅞ In.	18
Toy, Acrobat, Flips On Bar, Composition Head & Feet, Tin, 12 In.	153
Toy, Squeak, Rubber, Sheriff's Outfit, 13 x 4 In.	89
Washcloth Mitt, Checkered Shirt, Bandanna, 1950s, 8½ In.	15
Wristwatch, Time, Mechanical Movement, Stainless Steel, Colorful Strap, Hand Wind, 1987 ..	10

HULL pottery was made in Crooksville, Ohio, from 1905. Addis E. Hull bought the Acme Pottery Company and started making ceramic wares. In 1917, A. E. Hull Pottery began making art pottery as well as the commercial wares. For a short time, 1921 to 1929, the firm also sold pottery imported from Europe. The dinnerware of the 1940s (including the Little Red Riding Hood line), the matte wares of the 1940s, and the high gloss artwares of the 1950s are all popular with collectors. The firm officially closed in March 1986.

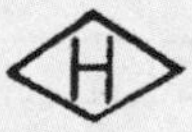

Hull Pottery	Hull Pottery	Hull Pottery
c.1915	1930s	c.1950

Blossom Flite, Teapot, Lid, Pink, Black, Flowers, Rope Shape Handle, c.1955, 4½ In.	129
Bow Knot, Vase, Pink Rim, Blue Scalloped Foot, Floral, Model B-3, 6½ In.	37
Brown Drip, Batter Bowl, Glaze, 8 In...	12
Butterfly, Creamer, Turquoise, Pink & Gold Gilt, 1956, 8¾ In...........................	250
Corky Pig, Piggy Bank, Brown Glazes, Stopper, Footed, 1957	31
Cornucopia, Vase, Wildflower, Footed, Leaves, 6½ In........................	16
Gingerbread Man, Cookie Jar, Brown Drip, Standing, 11⅝ In................................	75
Little Red Riding Hood, Cookie Jar, Figural, Red Cape, Flowers, Basket On Arm, 13 In. .....*illus*	41
Little Red Riding Hood, Creamer, Flowers On Skirt, Handle, High Gloss, 4½ In.	299
Little Red Riding Hood, Lamp, Electric, Floral Dress, 11 x 5½ In.	351
Magnolia, Creamer, Glossy..	55
Pine Cone, Vase, Embossed, Light Blue, 2 Handles, 6¾ In.	18
Serenade, Pitcher, Green Matte, 2 Birds, Handle, Wide Spout, 1950s, 10½ In.	19
Vase, Fan Shape, Wildflower, 2 Handles, 15½ In.	35
Vase, Magnolia, Leaves & Flowers, Ruffled Rim, 2 Handles, Footed, 5 In..................	24
Water Lily, Creamer, Green, Pink, Footed, Handle, Wide Spout, 5½ In.......................	10

Holly Amber, Toothpick Holder, Golden Agate, Beaded Bands & Rim, Greentown, 1902, 2½ In.
$263

Jeffrey S. Evans & Associates

Hopalong Cassidy, Comic Book, Hoppy, Captain Marvel Cover Cameo, No. 1, February 1943
$414

Hake's Auctions

Hopalong Cassidy, Lunch Box, Metal, Hopalong On Horse, Chuckwagon, Thermos, Aladdin, 1954, 8¼ In. $81

Main Auction Galleries, Inc.

Hopalong Cassidy, Tin, Popcorn, Hopalong Image, Lithograph, Mayland Popcorn Co-Op, 5 x 2⅝ In. $342

AntiqueAdvertising.com

Howard Pierce, Figurine, Girl, Long Dress, Holding Bird, Blue, Black Trim, 7½ In. $100

Etsy

Wild Flower, Vase, Dusty Rose, Handles, Marked, 6 In.	22
Wildflower, Vase, Flowers, Pink, White, Yellow, Green Leaves, c.1943, 8½ In.	125
Woodland, Basket, Yellow, Pink, Glossy, 9 In.	18

HUMMEL figurines, based on the drawings of the nun M.I. Hummel (Berta Hummel), were made by the W. Goebel Porzellanfabrik of Oeslau, Germany, now Rodental, Germany. They were first made in 1935. The *Crown* mark was used from 1935 to 1949. The company added the *bee m*arks in 1950. The *full bee* with variations, was used from 1950 to 1959; *stylized bee*, 1957 to 1972; three line mark, 1964 to 1972; *last bee*, sometimes called *vee over gee*, 1972 to 1979. In 1979 the V bee symbol was removed from the mark. *U.S. Zone* was part of the mark from 1946 to 1948; *W. Germany* was part of the mark from 1960 to 1990. The Goebel *W. Germany* mark, called the *missing bee* mark, was used from 1979 to 1990; *Goebel, Germany*, with the crown and *WG*, originally called the *new mark*, was used from 1991 through part of 1999. A new version of the bee mark with the word *Goebel* was used from 1999 to 2008. A special *Year 2000* backstamp was also introduced. Porcelain figures inspired by Berta Hummel's drawings were introduced in 1997. These are marked *BH* followed by a number. They were made in the Far East, not Germany. Goebel discontinued making Hummel figurines in 2008 and Manufaktur Rodental took over the factory in Germany and began making new Hummel figurines. Hummel figurines made by Rodental are marked with a yellow and black bee on the edge of an oval line surrounding the words *Original M.I. Hummel Germany.* The words *Manufaktur Rodental* are printed beneath the oval. Manufaktur Rodental was sold in 2013 and new owners, Hummel Manufaktur GmbH, took over. It was sold again in 2017, but figurines continue to be made in the factory in Rodental. Other decorative items and plates that feature Hummel drawings were made by Schmid Brothers, Inc. beginning in 1971. Schmid Brothers closed in 1995.

Hummel
1935–1949

Hummel
1950–1959

Hummel
2009–present

Ashtray, No. 166, Singing Lessons, Stylized Bee, 1960-72	30
Bank, No. 118, Figurine, Little Thrifty, Full Bee, 5 In.	30
Bell, Annual, With Loving Greetings, 1987, 6 In.	85
Clock, No. 420, Chapel Time, Roman Numeral, Pine Tree, Missing Bee, 11 In.	87
Figurine, No. 59, Skier, Full Bee, 5¾ In.	145
Figurine, No. 71, Stormy Weather, 2 Children, Umbrella, Square Base, Missing Bee, 1980	29
Figurine, No. 127, Doctor, Stylized Bee, c.1960, 4¾ In.	97
Figurine, No. 133, Mother's Helper, Missing Bee, 4¾ In.	76
Figurine, No. 141, Apple Tree Girl, Full Bee, 6½ In.	154
Figurine, No. 172, Angel With Mandolin, Full Bee, 10¾ In.	296
Figurine, No. 175, Mother's Darling, Hummel Mark, 5½ In.	45
Figurine, No. 199/1, Feeding Time, Full Bee, 1948, 5 In.	223
Figurine, No. 218, Birthday Serenade, Full Bee, 4¾ In.	128
Figurine, No. 397/1, The Poet, Hummel Mark, 6¼ In.	95
Figurine, No. 530, Land In Sight, 5 Children, In Boat, Box, 1992, 15 In.	173
Holy Water Font, No. 246, Holy Family, Bird, Wall, Hanging, Missing Bee	11
Lamp Base, No. 227, She Loves Me She Loves Me Not, Missing Bee, 4 In.	21
Plate, Christmas, 1975, Ride Into Christmas, 7½ In.	25
Plate, No. 264, Heavenly Angel, Stars Border, Annual, Three Line Mark, 1971	17
Plate, No. 266, Globe Trotter, 1973, 7½ In.	95
Plate, No. 274, Umbrella Boy, 1981, 7½ In.	60
Plate, No. 276, Postman, 1983, 7½ In.	75
Wall Font, No. 206, Angel Cloud, Full Bee, 2¼ x 4¾ In.	132

HUTSCHENREUTHER PORCELAIN FACTORY was founded by Carolus Magnus in Hohenburg, Bavaria, in 1814. A second factory was established in Selb, Germany, in 1857. The company made fine quality porcelain dinnerware and figurines. The mark changed through the years, but the name and the lion insignia appear in most versions. Hutschenreuther became part of the Rosenthal division of the Waterford Wedgwood Group in 2000. Rosenthal became part of the Arcturus Group in 2009.

LORENZ HUTSCHEN REUTER
GERMANY

Figurine, Mythological Bird, Hand Painted, 1814, 8 ½ In.		427
Group, Dogs, Setter & Pointer, Hand Painted, Marked, c.1950, 18 ½ x 5 ½ In. ....*illus*		300

ICONS, special, revered pictures of Jesus, Mary, or a saint, are usually Russian or Byzantine. The small icons collected today are made of wood and tin or precious metals. Many modern copies have been made in the old style and are being sold to tourists in Russia and Europe and at shops in the United States. Rare, old icons have sold for over $50,000. The riza is the metal cover protecting the icon. It is often made of silver or gold.

Archangel Michael, Oil & Gilt Panel, Russia, 1900s, 13 x 11 x 1 ⅛ In.		720
Blessed Virgin Mary, Traveling, Bronze, Theotokos, Russia, c.1700s, 9 ¾ x 8 ¾ In.		248
Christ Pantocrator, Enamel, Silver Oklad, Ivan Khlebnikov, Russia, 1915, 9 x 7 ¼ In.		2760
Christ Pantocrator, Enamel, Silver Oklad, Turquoise, Pavel Ovchinikov, Russia, 1893, 10 x 8 In...*illus*		3600
Guardian Angel, Oil, Gilt On Panel, Russia, 1900s, 13 x 11 x 1 In.		1230
Holy Mother & Child, Painted Hardwood Panel, Brass Repousse Oklad, 5 x 4 In.		48
Mother & Child, Silver Riza Design, Russia, 1800s, 7 x 9 In.		492
Pieta, Champleve, Bronze, Virgin Mary, Jesus Christ, Gilt Oklad, c.1800s, 13 x 10 In.........*illus*		425
Resurrection, Silver Frame, Cyrillic Mark, D.S., Moscow, Russia, 1908-17, 12 x 10 ½ In.		1440
Saint, Multicolor, Mitrofan Of Voronezh, Frame, 1800s, 6 ¾ x 8 ¼ In. ....*illus*		523
St. Andre, Silver Oklad, Kouznetsov Emelian Alexeivitch, Russia, 1889, 6 x 4 In.		625
St. John, Silver Oklad, Frolov Alexei Fedorovitch, Russia, 1889, 3 ¾ x 3 ¼ In.		300
St. Nicholas, Jesus & Mary, Oil, Wood Panel, Russia, 1800s, 15 ⅝ x 13 ⅝ In.		188
St. Nicholas, Wood, Silver Oklad, Yegor Cheryatov, Russia, 5 ¼ x 4 ¼ In.		484
St. Sergius Of Radonezh, Brown Cloak, Holding Scroll, Gilt, Russia, c.1900, 6 ¾ x 8 ¾ In.		615
St. Zinayida, Silver & Enamel Frame, Moscow Artel, Russia, c.1915, 4 ⅝ x 3 ¾ In.		1800
Virgin Of Kazan, Silver Oklad, Carved Wood Panel, Maker's Mark, K.M., 1856, 12 x 10 In.		1680

IMARI porcelain was made in Japan and China beginning in the seventeenth century. In the eighteenth century and later, it was copied by porcelain factories in Germany, France, England, and the United States. It was especially popular in the nineteenth century and is still being made. Imari is characteristically decorated with stylized bamboo, floral, and geometric designs in orange, red, green, and blue. The name comes from the Japanese port of Imari, which exported the ware made nearby in a factory at Arita. Imari is now a general term for any pattern of this type.

Bottle, Water, Square, Lions, Flowers, Japan, 1627, 7 ½ x 3 ½ x 3 ½ In.		360
Bowl, Barbed Mouth Rim, Diaper & Floral Band, Marked, Mt. Fuji On Base, 3 ½ x 8 ½ In.		431
Bowl, Center Chrysanthemum, Orange, Green, Blue, Sample, Stand, 1900s, 3 ⅝ x 8 ½ In.		363
Bowl, Center, Low, Painted, Double Ring Foot, 1800s, 4 x 12 In. ....*illus*		100
Bowl, Dome Lid, Phoenix & Peony, Carved Hen, Raised Foot, Japan, 1800s, 11 x 13 ½ In. .*illus*		431
Bowl, Foo Dogs, Flowers, Ormolu Mounts, Butterfly Handles, c.1900, 9 x 17 In. ....*illus*		813
Bowl, Immortals In Cartouches, Flower Basket Center, Round, 19 In.		750
Bowl, Octagonal, Landscape & Leaf Panels, 11 ½ In.		184
Bowl, Pine Trees, Prunus, Bamboo Designs, Flowers, Scalloped Edge, 1800s, 12 In. ....*illus*		281
Cachepot, Iris, Birds, Flowers, Japan, 12 x 10 ½ In.		185
Charger, Blue & White Border, Birds, Flowers, Red, White, Green Center, 1900s, 17 In.		295
Charger, Blue & White, Flowers, Bird, Gilt, Hanger, Japan, Late 1800s, 22 ½ x 3 In.		380
Charger, Blue & White, Plums, Pines, Flowers, Leaves, Marked Fuku, Japan, 3 ⅝ x 17 In.		246
Charger, Center Medallion, Flowers, 12 In.		207
Charger, Center, Bird, Landscape Panels, Blue Border, 21 ¾ In.		303
Charger, Flower Rondel, Horse & Falcon In Landscape Ground, Round, 1800s, 18 In.		660
Charger, Flowers & Figures, Center, 6 Panels, 16 ⅝ In.		424
Charger, Flowers, Dragons, Cobalt Blue, Red, Scalloped Edge, Japan, 1900s, 18 ¾ In. ....*illus*		484

Howdy Doody, Alarm Clock, Talking, Boy & Clown, Painted, Box, 7 In.
$130

Milestone Auctions

Howdy Doody, Dummy, Ventriloquist, Strings Attached In Mouth, Eegee National Broadcasting, 1972, 30 In.
$74

rancol0 on eBay

TIP
Think about the problems of owning a cat and a large collection of ceramics.

Hull, Little Red Riding Hood, Cookie Jar, Figural, Red Cape, Flowers, Basket On Arm, 13 In.
$41

peggyburk48zm on eBay

Hutschenreuther, Group, Dogs, Setter & Pointer, Hand Painted, Marked, c.1950, 18 1/2 x 5 1/2 In.
$300

Thomaston Place Auction Galleries

Icon, Christ Pantocrator, Enamel, Silver Oklad, Turquoise, Pavel Ovchinikov, Russia, 1893, 10 x 8 In.
$3,600

Crescent City Auction Gallery

Icon, Pieta, Champleve, Bronze, Virgin Mary, Jesus Christ, Gilt Oklad, c.1800s, 13 x 10 In.
$425

Aspire Auctions

Icon, Saint, Multicolor, Mitrofan Of Voronezh, Frame, 1800s, 6 3/4 x 8 1/4 In.
$523

Skinner, Inc.

Imari, Bowl, Center, Low, Painted, Double Ring Foot, 1800s, 4 x 12 In.
$100

Leland Little Auctions

Imari, Bowl, Dome Lid, Phoenix & Peony, Carved Hen, Raised Foot, Japan, 1800s, 11 x 13 1/2 In.
$431

Skinner, Inc.

Imari, Bowl, Foo Dogs, Flowers, Ormolu Mounts, Butterfly Handles, c.1900, 9 x 17 In.
$813

New Orleans Auction Galleries

Imari, Bowl, Pine Trees, Prunus, Bamboo Designs, Flowers, Scalloped Edge, 1800s, 12 In.
$281

Eldred's

Imari, Charger, Flowers, Dragons, Cobalt Blue, Red, Scalloped Edge, Japan, 1900s, 18 3/4 In.
$484

Leland Little Auctions

TIP
Bone china is a special type of porcelain that has bone ash added to the clay. This makes a stronger, whiter porcelain.

Charger, Flowers, Iron Red, Blue, 1800s, 17 ½ x 2 ¾ In.........	509
Charger, Flowers, Red, Blue, c.1900, 18 ¼ In.	50
Charger, Fruit & Flowers, Patterned Borders, Metal Plate Hanger, 1800s, 15 In.........	431
Charger, Gilt Metal, Floral Border, Grape Bunches, Scrolled Base, Late 1800s, 14 ½ In.........	406
Charger, Gourd Shape, Floral Medallions, Leaf Pinwheel, Japan, c.1890, 2 ⅝ x 17 ⅞ In.........	219
Charger, Lobed Panels, Blue Trellis Ground, Gilt, Japan, 1900s, 2 ⅝ x 18 ⅜ In........*illus*	197
Charger, Phoenix & Crane, Red & Blue Paint, 18 In.........	374
Charger, Prunus Branch, Lotus, Chrysanthemum, Insects, Leafy Border, 1800s, 15 In.....*illus*	1169
Charger, Treasure Ship Center, Geese, Butterflies & Brocade Panels, Round, 18 ¼ In.	200
Dish, Double Fish, Bird, Cherry Tree, Chrysanthemums, c.1880, 11 ½ In.........	216
Jar, Dome Lid, Flowers, Underglaze Blue, Jewel Knob Finial, Bulbous, 1900s, 15 In.........*illus*	123
Jar, Raised Panels, Lid, Houses, Red, Blue, White Ground, 20 In.	390
Lamp, Oil, Electrified, 2-Light, Silver Plate, Copper, Porcelain, Late 1800s, 35 In.........	125
Plate, Landscape, Patterned Diaper Ground, Band Around Rim, Japan, 1900s, 14 ¾ In.........	185
Temple Jar, Dome Lid, Flower Basket, Inverted Pear, Reeded, Onion Finial, 26 In.........	2640
Tray, Flower Garden, Rectangular, Raised & Shaped Sides, 24 x 19 In.........	3600
Vase, Hexagonal Shapes, Top Rim, Flat Sides, Iron Red, Blue, 1800, 17 ¾ x 10 In.........	1017
Vase, Palace, Cranes, Lotus, Blue, Japan, 43 ½ In.........	492
Vase, Vertical Ribbed Body, Floral Panels, Red Blue & White, Late 1800s, 16 In.........	182
Vase, Woman, Seated, Flowers, Flared Rim, Shallow Foot, Ko-Kutani, Late 1800s, 9 x 4 In......	60

IMPERIAL GLASS CORPORATION was founded in Bellaire, Ohio, in 1901. It became a subsidiary of Lenox, Inc., in 1973 and was sold to Arthur R. Lorch in 1981. It was sold again in 1982, and went bankrupt in 1984. In 1985, the molds and some assets were sold. The Imperial glass preferred by the collector is freehand art glass, carnival glass, slag glass, stretch glass, and other top-quality tablewares. Tablewares and animals are listed here. The others may be found in the appropriate sections.

Imperial Glass
1911–1932

Imperial Glass
1913–1920s

Imperial Glass
1977–1981

Atterbury, Dish, Lion On Lacy Cover, Frosted, Clear, 1889, 6 ½ x 7 ½ x 6 In.	20
Candlewick, Pitcher, Ice Lip, Beaded Handle, 80 Oz., 9 In.	30
Cape Cod, Plate, 2 Handle, Flowers, Sterling Silver Overlay, 8 ¾ In.	26
Caramel Slag, Mallard, Wings Down, Mounted	10
Free Hand, Vase, Green Iridescent, Vines, Leaves, 6 ¾ In.	295
Grape, Bowl, Amethyst Iridescent Purple, Carnival Glass, c.1800	71
Lead Luster, Vase, Cache, Green Vines & Leaves, Marigold Rim, 6 ⅜ x 6 ¾ In.	236
Lead Luster, Vase, Trumpet, Cobalt Blue, White Vines & Leaves, 9 ¾ In.	201
Peachblow, Vase, Ruby, Urn Shape Double Knop Neck, c.1965, 10 ½ In.	82
Purple Slag, Cruet, Multicolor, Handle, Stopper, c.1850, 7 In.	30
Star & File, Compote, Iridescent, Clambroth, c.1909, 7 In.	12
Vase, Blue Ripple, Non-Iridized, Fat, Squat, 7 x 5 ¾ x 3 ⅜ In.	153
Vase, Cobalt Blue, Opal Looping, Blue Iridescent Interior, c.1925, 6 ½ In.........*illus*	155
Vase, Iridescent Green, Dragged Loop, Early 1900s, 9 ¾ In.	492
Vase, Iridescent Orange, Black & Green Hearts & Vines, Early 1900s, 11 In.	984
Vase, Trumpet Shape, Variegated Hearts, Orange Iridescent Interior, c.1925, 9 ½ In.........*illus*	538

INDIAN art from North and South America has attracted the collector for many years. Each tribe has its own distinctive designs and techniques. Baskets, jewelry, pottery, and leatherwork are of greatest collector interest. Eskimo art is listed under Eskimo in this book.

Bag, Crow, Hide, Sinew Sewn, Beaded Bands, Multicolor, c.1875, 16 In.........*illus*	780
Bag, Plateau, Beaded, Blue Horse, Red Flowers, Yellow Ground, c.1925, 12 x 9 ¾ In.........*illus*	2280
Bag, Plateau, Parfleche, Hide Fringe, Geometric Designs, Multicolor, c.1875, 19 ¼ In.	900
Basket, Apache, White On Black Animals Figures, c.1910, 20 ¾ In.	3240
Basket, Cherokee, Bent Oak Handle, Walnut Weavers, Blood Root, c.1950, 13 x 9 x 8 In.	83

Imari, Charger, Lobed Panels, Blue Trellis Ground, Gilt, Japan, 1900s, 2 ⅝ x 18 ⅜ In.
$197

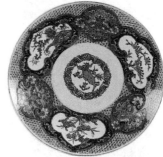

Skinner, Inc.

Imari, Charger, Prunus Branch, Lotus, Chrysanthemum, Insects, Leafy Border, 1800s, 15 In.
$1,169

Skinner, Inc.

Imari, Jar, Dome Lid, Flowers, Underglaze Blue, Jewel Knob Finial, Bulbous, 1900s, 15 In.
$123

Skinner, Inc.

I

Imperial, Vase, Cobalt Blue, Opal Looping, Blue Iridescent Interior, c.1925, 6½ In.

$155

Jeffrey S. Evans & Associates

Imperial, Vase, Trumpet Shape, Variegated Hearts, Orange Iridescent Interior, c.1925, 9½ In.

$538

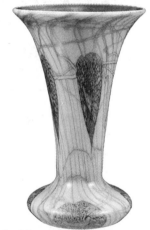

Jeffrey S. Evans & Associates

Indian, Bag, Crow, Hide, Sinew Sewn, Beaded Bands, Multicolor, c.1875, 16 In.

$780

Cowan's Auctions

Basket, Cherokee, Twin, Swing Handle, Weave, 9¼ x 16 In.	75
Basket, Cherokee, White Oak, Walnut Stain, Wrapped Rim, Signed, Wages, c.1950, 18 x 13 In.	319
Basket, Papago, 2 Handles, Flowers, 17 x 8 In.	450
Basket, Pomo, Coiled, Geometric Accents, Beads, Feathers, Early 1900s, 3½ x 8 In.	2460
Basket, Pomo, Coiled, Woven Triangles, Northwest California, 1800s, 4 x 6 In.	492
Basket, Western Apache, 9 Horses, 6 Men, Nesting Flowers, Brown, c.1900, 3¾ x 15 In.	14400
Basket, Wounaan, Macaws, Perched, Ferns, White Ground, 6¾ x 10¾ In.	2280
Bolo, Navajo, Silver, Coral, Bear Claws, Teddy Goodluck, c.1950, 2 x 2¾ In.	254
Bolo, Zuni, Katsina, Silver, Tortoiseshell, Leather Cord, Bennet Pat., 2½ x 2 In.	283
Bolo, Zuni, Road Runner, Cactus, Inlaid Shell, Silver Frame, L. & A. Lonjose, 1970s, 3 In.	540
Bracelet, Navajo, Cuff, Silver, Stamp Work, Turquoise Stone, c.1965, 5½ In. *illus*	900
Doll, Arapaho, Shield, Breast Plate, Coup Stick, Fur, D. Shakespeare-Cummings, 1900s, 16 x 18 In.	338
Doll, Central Plains, Hide, Yellow Quilled Breastplate, Brass Ring, Beads, c.1875, 9 In. *illus*	1200
Effigy, Snake, Woodlands, War Club, Eyes & Bone Inset, Knob, 24 In.	413
Figure, Man, Haida, Ivory, Walrus, Carved, c.1890, 3 In.	281
Figure, Northwest Coast, Seated, Staff & Headdress, Wood, Carved, 1900s, 7¾ In.	210
House Post, Haida, Cedar, Carved, Red, Black, Blue, Patina, c.1890, 34¾ In.	7500
House Post, Haida, Cedar, Carved, Red, Blue, Black, c.1890, 30 In.	3900
Jar, Acoma, Black, White, Geometric, c.1940, 9¼ In. *illus*	660
Jar, Acoma, Red, Black, White, Flower, c.1930, 9¼ In. *illus*	360
Jar, Hopi, Overlapping Geometric Patterns, Jofern Silas Puffer, 17 In.	1560
Jar, Jemez, Carved, Figural Turtle, Corn Accents, Signed, Bertha Gachupin, 5½ x 7 In.	79
Jar, Mata Ortiz, Pear Shape, Geometric, Lucie Zete, Mexico, 11 In. *illus*	660
Jar, Seed, Acoma, Orange, Brown & White Slip, Bulbous, Early 1900s, 4 x 8½ In.	593
Katsina, Hopi, Case, Flowers, Clouds, Bandolier, Armbands, Sio Hemis, 13 In. *illus*	1599
Ladle, Penobscot, Scoop, Carved, Burl Root, 18 In.	270
Moccasins, Central Plains, Sinew Sewn, Beads, Checkered, Multicolor, 13 x 9¼ In.	1320
Moccasins, Cheyenne, Hide, Beaded, Sinew Sewn, 6-Sided Stars, Multicolor, 10½ In.	2583
Necklace, Blackfoot, 20 Claws, Hide Thong, Brass Beads, c.1875, 14½ In. *illus*	8400
Necklace, Navajo, Squash Blossom, Silver, Turquoise, Inlay, Cabochons, 33 x 4½ In. *illus*	5843
Olla, Apache, Geometrics & Animal Designs, c.1910, 18 In.	2160
Olla, Zia, Bird & Flowers, 2 Handles, Signed, L. Concha, 11 x 10 In.	570
Olla, Zuni, Heartline Deer, Birds, Hatching, Crosshatch, Red, White, Black, 11¼ x 13 In. *illus*	3900
Pendant, Cochiti, Silver, Ingot, Lines, Cord, Silver Beads, Cippy Crazy Horse, c.1990, 3 In. *illus*	450
Pendant, Navajo, Sunface Katsina, Inlaid Stones, Silver Frame, A. Yellowhorse, c.1885, 3½ In. *illus*	960
Pipe, Navajo, Stag Horn Bowl & Mouthpiece, Leather & Beaded Shaft, 13 In.	118
Pipe, Tomahawk, Plains, Ash Handle, Iron Blade, Cutout Heart, Curled Flanges, c.1875, 10 x 23 In. *illus*	3900
Pipe, Tomahawk, Western Great Lakes, Brass Collar, Silver Inlay, Hearts, Stars, 19¾ x 2 In.	4800
Purse, Iroquois, Wool, Beaded, Flowers, Wings, Pink, Black, Blue, Green, 5½ x 5 In.	360
Rattle, Northwest Coast, Wood, Carved, 1900s, 7 In.	300
Rug, Navajo, Diamond Pattern, Zigzags, Orange, Cream, Brown, 53 x 86 In. *illus*	1416
Rug, Navajo, Yei Design, 9 Standing Figures, c.1935, 4 Ft. 4 In. x 6 Ft. 6 In. *illus*	938
Saddle Drop, Crow, Hide, Trapezoidal, Beads, Geometric Designs, Multicolor, 9 x 5 In. *illus*	600
Sheath, Cree, Knife, Flowers, Beads, Sinew Sewn, Bone Handle, Pewter Inlay, 13 In.	3900
Sheath, Plains, Yellow Beading, Flowers, 8½-In. Knife, Hide Handle	1140
Spike, Woodlands, Curved Tiger Grain Wood & Brass, Beveled, 19 In.	248
Totem, Northwest Coast, Bone, Carved, c.1940, 2¾ In.	3375
Vase, Laguna, Geometrics, Inscribed Old Laguna, N.M., Signed, Lee Ann Cheromiah, 15 In.	300
Vase, Southwestern, Bulbous, Black, Geometric, Flared Rim, Fito Tena, 9 In.	153
War Club, Penobscot, Root Tips, 8 Carved Animal Heads, Brass Tack, 1934	165
Weaving, Navajo, 10 Figurines, Stepped Diamonds, Red, Black, c.1925, 84 x 47 In.	461
Weaving, Navajo, Banners, Feathers, Tan Ground, Teec No Pos, c.1975, 137 x 62 In. *illus*	4000

INDIAN TREE is a china pattern that was popular during the last half of the nineteenth century. It was copied from earlier Indian textile patterns that were very similar. The pattern includes the crooked branch of a tree and a partial landscape with exotic flowers and leaves. Green, blue, pink, and orange were the favored colors used in the design. Coalport, Spode, Johnson Brothers, and other firms made this pottery.

Bowl, Vegetable, Lid, 2 Handles, Coalport, Oval, 11¼ In.	54
Bowl, Vegetable, Square, Scalloped Rim, Spode, 9¼ In. *illus*	42

Indian, Bag, Plateau, Beaded, Blue Horse, Red Flowers, Yellow Ground, c.1925, 12 x 9¾ In.
$2,280

Cowan's Auctions

Indian, Bracelet, Navajo, Cuff, Silver, Stamp Work, Turquoise Stone, c.1965, 5½ In.
$900

Allard Auctions

Indian, Doll, Central Plains, Hide, Yellow Quilled Breastplate, Brass Ring, Beads, c.1875, 9 In.
$1,200

Cowan's Auctions

Indian, Jar, Acoma, Black, White, Geometric, c.1940, 9¼ In.
$660

Eldred's

Indian, Jar, Acoma, Red, Black, White, Flower, c.1930, 9¼ In.
$360

Eldred's

Indian, Jar, Mata Ortiz, Pear Shape, Geometric, Lucie Zete, Mexico, 11 In.
$660

Eldred's

Indian, Katsina, Hopi, Case, Flowers, Clouds, Bandolier, Armbands, Sio Hemis, 13 In.
$1,599

Cowan's Auctions

Indian, Necklace, Blackfoot, 20 Claws, Hide Thong, Brass Beads, c.1875, 14½ In.
$8,400

Cowan's Auctions

Indian, Necklace, Navajo, Squash Blossom, Silver, Turquoise, Inlay, Cabochons, 33 x 4½ In.
$5,843

Cowan's Auctions

Indian, Olla, Zuni, Heartline Deer, Birds, Hatching, Crosshatch, Red, White, Black, 11¼ x 13 In.
$3,900

Cowan's Auctions

Indian, Pendant, Cochiti, Silver, Ingot, Lines, Cord, Silver Beads, Cippy Crazy Horse, c.1990, 3 In.
$450

Allard Auctions

Indian, Pendant, Navajo, Sunface Katsina, Inlaid Stones, Silver Frame, A. Yellowhorse, c.1885, 3½ In.
$960

Allard Auctions

Indian, Pipe, Tomahawk, Plains, Ash Handle, Iron Blade, Cutout Heart, Curled Flanges, c.1875, 10 x 23 In.
$3,900

Cowan's Auctions

Indian, Rug, Navajo, Diamond Pattern, Zigzags, Orange, Cream, Brown, 53 x 86 In.
$1,416

Hess Auction Group

Indian, Rug, Navajo, Yei Design, 9 Standing Figures, c.1935, 4 Ft. 4 In. x 6 Ft. 6 In.
$938

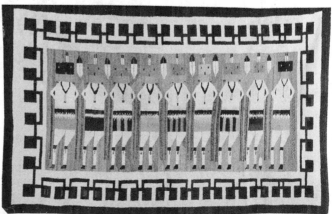

Eldred's

Cake Plate, Footed, Cream Ground, Floral, Red, Green, Copeland, 4¼ x 8¼ In.	76
Cake Plate, Scalloped Edge, Tab Handles, Coalport, c.1871, 10 x 10 In.	26
Cup & Saucer, Coalport	35
Cup & Saucer, Footed, Duchess	16
Cup & Saucer, Meakin	45
Inkwell, Double, Tray, Meissen, c.1900, 8½ In.	950
Plate, Doulton & Co., 8½ In.	50
Soup, Cream, Saucer, Handles, Coalport	25
Teapot, C Handle, Finial, White Ground, Multicolor, Coalport	55
Teapot, Curved Spout, Bronze, Burnt Orange, Spode, 6½ x 11 In.	185
Teapot, Leaves, Multicolor, H. Wood, England, 6½ In.	10
Vase, Footed, Flowers, Gold Rim, Coalport, Miniature, 2¼ In.	7

INKSTANDS were made to be placed on a desk. They held some type of container for ink, and possibly a sander, a pen tray, a pen, a holder for pounce, and even a candle to melt the sealing wax. Inkstands date to the eighteenth century and have been made of silver, copper, ceramics, and glass. Additional inkstands may be found in these and other related categories.

Brass & Horn, Single Well, Pen Rests, Candleholder, Footed, 12 x 12 In.	138
Brass, Tiger, Mouth Open, Posable Penholders, Oval Onyx Base, 1800s-1900s	120
Bronze, Cathedral, Stamp Compartment, Architectural, Gothic Style, 1800s, 7 x 6 In.......*illus*	984
Bronze, Continental, 3 Heads, Paw Feet, Petrarc, Inscribed, Cherub, Late 1800s, 7 In.	250
Bronze, Gilt, Renaissance, Scrollwork, Malachite Stones, Cabochon Garnets, c.1980, 8 x 11 x 8 In.	1188
Bronze, Parrots, Penholder, Letter Opener, Painted, Onyx Base, Vienna, c.1900, 9 x 18 x 18 In..	438
Bronze, Rooster, Figural, Signed, 2 Wells, Red Marble, Footed, 1800s, 6 x 12 In.	184
Cast Lead, Stag Head, Glass, c.1880, 7 In.	106
Gilt Bronze, Tray, Art Nouveau, Nude Female, Maurice Bouval, c.1890, 6 x 10 x 7 In.	2000
Mahogany, 2 Cut Glass Bottles, Hinged Lids, Ebonized Pen Wells, 1800s, 6 x 13 x 9 In.......*illus*	112
Marble, Black, Brass, 2 Cubed Wells, Hinged Lids, Pen Groove, 12½ In.	80
Oak, 2 Glass Inkwells, Pen Tray, Coromandel, 1800s, 10½ x 13 x 12 In.	307
Oak, Swirling Glass, Nickel Silver Trim, 7 x 11 In.	92
Pewter, Central Stand, 6 Quills, Broad Round Base, 1800s, 3¼ x 15⅛ In.	148
Porcelain, French Scenic Panels, Turned Legs, Signed, c.1800, 6¾ x 7 x 14 In.	605
Porcelain, Winged Leopard Feet, Gilt Wings, Turquoise Highlights, France, 1900s, 11½ In.	138
Silver, Tray, Pierced, Footed, Cut Glass Inkwells, Lids, H. Wilkinson, 1875, 9 x 6 In.	510
Walnut, Ram's Horn Dolphin, Silver Plate, Bell, Well, Pen Tray, Drawer, c.1875, 13 x 7 In... *illus*	1320

INKWELLS, of course, held ink. Ready-made ink was first made about 1836 and was sold in bottles. The desk inkwell had a narrow hole so the pen would not slip inside. Inkwells were made of many materials, such as pottery, glass, pewter, and silver. Look in these categories for more listings of inkwells.

Brass, Roundhouse, Dwarfs In Arches, Hinged Lid, Dwarf Finial, 4½ In.	108
Brass, Sailor, Capstan, Coil Of Rope, c.1900, 6½ x 7 In.........*illus*	450
Bronze, Bust, Arab Man, Continental, c.1900, 3¾ In. ....*illus*	120
Bronze, Dante, Book, Savonarola Chair, Onyx Base, Hinged Well, A. Titze, 1900s, 11 x 9 In.	420
Bronze, Figural, Bulldog, Marble Base, Glass Eyes, c.1900	288
Bronze, Figural, Man, Holding Lantern, Oaken Barrel, Floral Base, 1800s, 13 x 5 x 4 In.	136
Bronze, Figural, Man, Sitting, Holding Pot, Patinated, 1800s, 3 x 3 In.........*illus*	311
Bronze, Figural, Rabbit, Musket Slung, Brown Patina, 6 x 3½ In. ....*illus*	545
Cherub, Snail In Center, Satyr Handles, Glass Inserts, 12½ x 7 x 6½ In.	58
Cut Glass, Crosscut & Strawberry Diamond, Prism & Tusks, Flowers, Gorham, 4 x 3½ In.	780
Cut Glass, Silver Cap, Monogramed C.F.R., Marked Gorham, 4 x 3½ In.	172
Fox, Lying Down, Bird In Its Mouth, Impressed 595, c.1900, 10 In.	63
Gilt Bronze, Glass Well, Baccarat Style Swirl, Flowers, Art Nouveau, 3 x 6¾ In.	150
Glass, Brass Lid & Swirl Foot, 1800s, 8 In.	161
Glass, Bronze Mount, Gilt, Women, Wings, Lucien M. Bing, Art Nouveau, France, c.1900, 5 x 5 In.	563
Glass, Owl Head Lid, Glazed Pottery, 4½ In.	600

Indian, Saddle Drop, Crow, Hide, Trapezoidal, Beads, Geometric Designs, Multicolor, 9 x 5 In.
$600

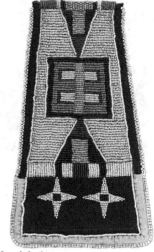

Cowan's Auctions

Indian, Weaving, Navajo, Banners, Feathers, Tan Ground, Teec No Pos, c.1975, 137 x 62 In.
$4,000

Cowan's Auctions

Indian Tree, Bowl, Vegetable, Square, Scalloped Rim, Spode, 9¼ In.
$42

klouyer689 on eBay

Inkstand, Bronze, Cathedral, Stamp Compartment, Architectural, Gothic Style, 1800s, 7 x 6 In.
$984

Skinner, Inc.

Inkstand, Mahogany, 2 Cut Glass Bottles, Hinged Lids, Ebonized Pen Wells, 1800s, 6 x 13 x 9 In.
$112

Leland Little Auctions

Inkstand, Walnut, Ram's Horn Dolphin, Silver Plate, Bell, Well, Pen Tray, Drawer, c.1875, 13 x 7 In.
$1,320

Eldred's

> **TIP**
> Clean a glass inkwell carefully. The old ink may cover a crack. Wash in warm water with mild dishwashing liquid or soap, never dishwasher detergent. Don't use ammonia if the glass is decorated or iridescent.

Inkwell, Brass, Sailor, Capstan, Coil Of Rope, c.1900, 6 ½ x 7 In.
$450

Eldred's

Inkwell, Bronze, Bust, Arab Man, Continental, c.1900, 3 ¾ In.
$120

Eldred's

Inkwell, Bronze, Figural, Man, Sitting, Holding Pot, Patinated, 1800s, 3 x 3 In.
$311

Hartzell's Auction Gallery, Inc.

Inkwell, Bronze, Figural, Rabbit, Musket Slung, Brown Patina, 6 x 3 ½ In.
$545

Fontaine's Auction Gallery

A Standish

A *standish* is an inkstand. Most are figural with inkwells and containers for pens, blotting material, sealing wax, or other things needed to write a letter in the ninteenth century.

Inkwell, Marble, Parian Bust, Benjamin Franklin, 2 Inkwells, Metal Lids, 1800s, 5 ½ x 10 x 5 In.
$800

Skinner, Inc.

Inkwell, Silver Plate, Stag Head, 2 Bottles, Lids, Granite Base, c.1900, 6 ½ x 7 x 4 ½ In.
$84

Thomaston Place Auction Galleries

Glass, Wood Carving, Saint Bernard Dog, Barrel Around Neck, c.1880, 4 In.	210
Goat, White Porcelain, Cart, Gilt Metal, Glass Wells, c.1890, 2 In.	265
Marble, Parian Bust, Benjamin Franklin, 2 Inkwells, Metal Lids, 1800s, 5½ x 10 x 5 In. *illus*	800
Ram's Horn, Bronze Head, Hooves On Horn, Feet, 7 In.	228
Ribbed, Mottled Manganese Glaze, 2 Holes, Oval, c.1850, 1 x 2¾ x 3⅞ In.	222
Silver Plate, Stag Head, 2 Bottles, Lids, Granite Base, c.1900, 6½ x 7 x 4½ In. ....*illus*	84
Silver, Travel, Cube Shape, Spring Driven, Hinged Lid, Russia, 1881, 2 x 2 x 2 In. ....*illus*	1815
Spelter, Donkey, Sitting, Painted, Hinged Lid, Milk Glass, c.1900s, 5 x 2 x 2½ In.	367
Standish, White Metal, Figural Lid, Leopard On Carpet, Austria, 1932, 2 x 9 x 4 In.	124
Stoneware, Cylinder, Tooled Rim, 3 Holes, Cobalt, Smith & Day Norwalk, c.1840, 2 In.	1180
Wood, Bear, Carved, Black Forest, Lift Lid, Revealing Glass, Dark Finish	110
Wood, Carved, Glass Jars, Floral Embossed Flowers, Metal Lids, 13½ x 8½ x 4 In.	127
Wood, Cat, Bust, Glass Eyes & Liner, Black Forest, 3 In. ....*illus*	375
Wood, Eagle, 2 Glass Wells, Green Baize Bottom, S. Siliman & Co., c.1850, 3½ x 6 In.	246

INSULATORS of glass or pottery have been made for use on telegraph or telephone poles since 1844. Thousands of styles of insulators have been made. Most common are those of clear or aqua glass; most desirable are the threadless types made from 1850 to 1870. CD numbers are Consolidated Design numbers used by collectors to indicate shape. Lists of CD numbers and other identifying marks can be found online.

Black Glass, Commemorative, Breakup Of Bell System, Bell Shape, Dec. 31, 1983, 3 In.	29
Brookfield, Continuous Drip, Dark Aqua Glass, Telegraph, No. 3 Transposition	18
CD 100, Hemingray, Babson Bros., Surge, Clear, Embossed, 1850s	10
CD 102, Royal Purple, Smooth Base, Vertical Bar, Diamond, Pony	125
CD 106, C.T.N.E.E.S.A., Ice Green, Clear, Spain	21
CD 154, Dominion-42, R-D, Continuous Drip, Yellow Amber, Diamond, Railroad, Canada	420
CD 162, Hemingray-19, Glass, Cobalt Blue, Embossed, Skirt ....*illus*	238
CD 734, Hat, Threadless, Continuous Drip, McMicking-R, Victoria, B.C. 75, Canada	72
Hemingray, Muncie, Continuous Drip, CD 303 Top, CD 310 Base, Embossed, Aqua, 1893, 12 x 9 In.	302
Patent, Cabletop, Mint Green, Swirled Deep Blue, Continuous Drip 292, 1890	318
Porcelain, Ohio Brass, Dark Gray, U-320, Embossed, 3¼ x 3½ In. ....*illus*	214

IRISH BELLEEK, *see Belleek category.*

IRON is a metal that has been used by man since prehistoric times. It is a popular metal for tools and decorative items like doorstops that need as much weight as possible. Items are listed here or under other appropriate headings, such as Bookends, Doorstop, Kitchen, Match Holder, or Tool. The tool that is used for ironing clothes, an iron, is listed in the Kitchen category under Iron and Sadiron.

Armada Chest, Painted Figural Landscape, Interior Compartments, Continental, 1600s, 18 x 31 In.	3000
Basket, Hanging, Square, Forged, 16 Hooks, Link Chain, 24 x 17¾ In.	72
Boot Scraper, Art Tail Finials, Cast Iron, Hand Wrought, 1800s, 28 In.	52
Boot Scraper, Dragons, Enameled, Samuel Yellin, c.1917, 17 x 16 x 18 In. ....*illus*	1875
Boot Scraper, Figural, Horse, Horseshoe, Cast Iron, Marked, 10 In.	52
Boot Scraper, H Shape, Limestone Block, c.1850, 10½ x 9½ x 9½ In.	556
Boot Scraper, Strap Steel, Hand Wrought, Welded, Riveted, c.1900, 4½ x 11 In. ....*illus*	29
Boot Scraper, Witch, On Broom, Silhouette, Red Paint, Albany Foundry Co., N.Y., c.1900, 10 In. *illus*	510
Boot Scraper, Wrought Iron, Animal Shape, Pierced Eye, Ga., c.1850, 11 x 13 x 12 In.	351
Door Mat, Interlocking Heart Design, Late 1800s, 36¼ x 22¼ In.	360
Figure, Dog, Pointer, Black & White Paint, Straight Head Screw, 9 x 15 In.	58
Figure, Duck, Canvasback, Cast, Red Eye, White, Black, Brown, 6 x 14 In.	118
Figure, Eagle, Spread Wings, Wood Base, Ohio Canal, 1800s, 13 x 31 x 14 In.	480
Figure, Lion, Lying Down, Bronze Green Finish, 1800s, 13¾ x 23 x 5 In.	861
Figure, Rooster, Standing, White Paint, Late 1900s, 35 x 26 In.	300
Safe, Alpine Safe & Lock Co., Hinged Door, 2 Compartments, 25 x 16 x 18 In. ....*illus*	424
Safe, Floor, Black, 2 Oak Drawers, Diebold Safe & Lock Co., 27¾ x 17 x 19 In.	484
Shield, Eagle, Spread Wings, Laurel, Arrows, 1800s, 14 x 31½ In.	1003

Inkwell, Silver, Travel, Cube Shape, Spring Driven, Hinged Lid, Russia, 1881, 2 x 2 x 2 In.
$1,815

Fontaine's Auction Gallery

Inkwell, Wood, Cat, Bust, Glass Eyes & Liner, Black Forest, 3 In.
$375

Leslie Hindman Auctioneers

Insulator, CD 162, Hemingray-19, Glass, Cobalt Blue, Embossed, Skirt
$238

55fultonst on eBay

Insulator, Porcelain, Ohio Brass, Dark Gray, U-320, Embossed, 3 ¼ x 3 ½ In.
$214

55fultonst on eBay

Iron, Boot Scraper, Dragons, Enameled, Samuel Yellin, c.1917, 17 x 16 x 18 In.
$1,875

Rago Arts and Auction Center

Iron, Boot Scraper, Strap Steel, Hand Wrought, Welded, Riveted, c.1900, 4 ½ x 11 In.
$29

Keystone Auctions LLC

Iron, Boot Scraper, Witch, On Broom, Silhouette, Red Paint, Albany Foundry Co., N.Y., c.1900, 10 In.
$510

Garth's Auctioneers & Appraisers

Iron, Safe, Alpine Safe & Lock Co., Hinged Door, 2 Compartments, 25 x 16 x 18 In.
$424

Fontaine's Auction Gallery

Iron, Stringholder, Post Office, Beehive, Marked U.S.P.O. Dept., 1800s, 7 In.
$81

Keystone Auctions LLC

Iron, Windmill Weight, Chicken, Figural, White, Marked, Hummer, Box, 38 Lb., 13 x 17 x 14 In.
$293

Thomaston Place Auction Galleries

Ispanky, Figurine, Abigail, Long Dress, Hat, Carrying Flower Basket, Signed, Goebel, 1980, 9 In.
$10

antiquebutique on eBay

Stringholder, Post Office, Beehive, Marked U.S.P.O. Dept., 1800s, 7 In. ....*illus*	81
Windmill Weight, Chicken, Figural, White, Marked, Hummer, Box, 38 Lb., 13 x 17 x 14 In...*illus*	293

IRONSTONE china was first made in 1813. It gained its greatest popularity during the mid-nineteenth century. The heavy, durable, off-white pottery was made in white or was decorated with any of hundreds of patterns. Much flow blue pottery was made of ironstone. Some of the decorations were raised. Many pieces of ironstone are unmarked, but some English and American factories included the word *Ironstone* in their marks. Additional pieces may be listed in other categories, such as Flow Blue, Gaudy Ironstone, Mason's Ironstone, Staffordshire, and Tea Leaf Ironstone. These three marks were used by companies that made ironstone.

TJ & J Mayer's	W. Baker & Co. (Ltd.)	Wood & Son(s) (Ltd.)
1842–1855	1893+	1910+

Pitcher, White, Diagonally Flowered Band, Alfred Meakin, c.1890, 9 ½ In.	135
Plate, Brazil & River Plate Steam Navigation Co. Ltd., Blue Rim, Company Crest, 9 ⅜ In.	488

ISPANKY figurines were designed by Laszlo Ispanky, who began his American career as a designer for Cybis Porcelains. He was born in Hungary and came to the United States in 1956. In 1966 he went into business with George Utley in Trenton, New Jersey. Isplanky made limited edition figurines marked with his name and Utley Porcelain Ltd. The company became Ispanky Porcelains Ltd. in 1968 and moved to Pennington, New Jersey. Ispanky worked for Goebel of North America beginning in 1976. He worked in stone, wood, or metal, as well as porcelain. He died in 2010.

Ispanky

Bust, Donkey Heads, Mother, Colt, 7 x 5 In.	197
Bust, Joshua, Holding Horn Above His Head, 1975, 19 x 10 ½ x 7 ½ In.	203
Bust, Madonna With Bird, 11 x 7 ½ x 5 In.	138
Bust, Serenity, Flower In Hair, Cape Over Shoulders, 4 ½ In.	45
Bust, Susie, Woman, Blond Ponytail, Pink Top, 6 In.	36
Figurine, Abigail, Long Dress, Hat, Carrying Flower Basket, Signed, Goebel, 1980, 9 In......*illus*	10
Figurine, Autumn, Woman, Plate Of Vegetables, 7 In.	65
Figurine, Awakening, Girl, In Chair, Signed, 8 x 7 ½ In.	40
Figurine, Ballerina Dancers, Male & Female, Round Base, 10 ½ In.	50
Figurine, Ballerina, Cappelia, Wearing Tutu, Sitting On Draped Box, 9 In.	36
Figurine, Cinderella, Woman, Wiping Floor, Signed, 12 x 8 In.	496
Figurine, Horse, Front Legs Up, One Leg & Tail On Base, Light Gray, 10 ½ x 11 In.	188
Figurine, Storm, Man In Long Robe, Leaning Into Wind, 14 x 16 In.	202
Figurine, Winter, Woman, Fence, Cape, 9 In.	60
Medal, Society Of Medalist, Spring Wind, Autumn Wind On Reverse, Bronze, 1974, 2 ⅞ In.......	214
Vase, Seminude Woman, Blond Braided Hair, Paneled, 11 x 6 x 5 In.	125

IVORY from the tusk of an elephant is thought by many to be the only true ivory. To most collectors, the term *ivory* also includes such natural materials as walrus, hippopotamus, or whale teeth or tusks, and some of the vegetable materials that are of similar texture and density. Other ivory items may be found in the Scrimshaw and Netsuke categories. Collectors should be aware of the recent laws limiting the buying and selling of elephant ivory and scrimshaw.

Baton, Vertebra, Baleen Knob & Spacers, 1800s, 21 ¼ In.	168
Box, Lid, Masks, Carved & Stacked, Helmeted Samurai, Court Lady, Sword Finial, 4 In.............	1320
Card Case, Monkey & Men, Frogs & Birds, Signed, Japan, c.1870, 4 ½ x 2 ½ In.	1599
Card Case, Owl, Frog, Carved, 4 x 2 ½ In.	630
Card Case, Pierced, Curved, People In Garden, Different Scenes On Reverse, 4 x 2 In.	630
Figurine, Bagpiper, Carved, Wood Stand, 1800s, 3 ¼ In.	108
Figurine, Buddha Riding Guardian Lion, Gilt, c.1850, 6 ¾ In. ....*illus*	1920
Figurine, Carved, Man Holding Boy, Net, Cardboard & Cloth Box, Japan, 9 x 3 ½ In. ....*illus*	819

Ivory, Figurine, Buddha Riding Guardian Lion, Gilt, c.1850, 6 ¾ In.
$1,920

Eldred's

Ivory, Figurine, Carved, Man Holding Boy, Net, Cardboard & Cloth Box, Japan, 9 x 3 ½ In.
$819

Morphy Auctions

Ivory, Figurine, Man, Carrying Baskets, Carved, Cardboard & Cloth Box, Japan, 1800s, 10 x 7 In.
$720

Morphy Auctions

Ivory, Figurine, Man, Seated, Birdcage, Carved, Wood Base, Japan, c.1890, 5 ½ x 4 In.

$567

Morphy Auctions

Ivory, Group, Musician, Playing Biwa, 2 Large Frogs, Signed, c.1890, 4 ¼ In.

$204

Eldred's

Ivory, Whistle, Naughty Leg, Engraved Garter, Carved Boot, Whale Ivory, c.1850, 4 In.

$960

Eldred's

Figurine, Carved, Skull, Snakes, Cardboard & Cloth Box, Japan, 1800s, 6 x 3 ½ In.	3000
Figurine, Dragon Boat, 25 Passengers, Carved, Cardboard & Cloth Box, 12 In.	630
Figurine, Fertility, Carved, Akua'ba, Africa, 9 In.	403
Figurine, Fisherman, Barefoot, Pulling Full Net From Water, Japan, 5 x 6 ¼ In.	3120
Figurine, Man Holding Boy & Net, Carved, Box, Japan, 7 ½ In.	819
Figurine, Man, Carrying Baskets, Carved, Japan, Signed, 10 x 7 In. ....*illus*	738
Figurine, Man, Seated, Birdcage, Carved, Wood Base, Japan, c.1890, 5 ½ x 4 In. ....*illus*	567
Figurine, Skeleton Man, Holding Beads, Cardboard & Cloth Box, Japan, 4 ¾ In.	523
Figurine, Skull, Snakes, Carved, Cardboard & Cloth Box, Japan, 1800s, 6 x 4 In.	3000
Figurine, Woman Holding Beads, Girl, Carved, Cardboard & Cloth Box, Japan, 14 x 3 ½ In.	504
Group, Mother, Seated, Holding Child, Carved, Possibly Dieppe, France, 5 In.	670
Group, Musician, Playing Biwa, 2 Large Frogs, Signed, c.1890, 4 ¼ In. ....*illus*	204
Kiseru-Zutsu, Pipe Case, Carved, Samurai Fishing, Pheasant, Cylindrical, Japan, 1800s, 8 In. .	438
Lighter, Tusk, Sterling Silver, Osprey, Table, 16 x 5 In.	1107
Ojime, Ball, Carved Dragon, Gyokuzan, Japan, 1800s, ¾ In.	120
Ojime, Ball, Carved, Hawk, Pine Tree, Songbird, ¾ In.	96
Ojime, Ball, Carved, Lotus Seapods, Stem, c.1800, 1 ¾ In.	300
Puzzle Box, Melon Shape, 3 Gourds, Chain, Japan, Late 1800s, 2 ½ x 1 ¼ In.	234
Salt Box, Ship, National Flags, Woman Holding Glass, Whale's Tail Hook, c.1850, 3 ½ In.	812
Tusk, Elephant, Carved, Snake & Leaves, Scalloped Base, Western Africa, 1800s, 23 In.	330
Tusk, Mastodon, Cats Hunting Rats, Black Eyes, Wood, Bamboo, Basket, Asian, 4 x 5 x 4 In.	700
Tusk, Walrus, Undecorated, Custom Iron Base Display, 20 In.	575
Whistle, Naughty Leg, Engraved Garter, Carved Boot, Whale Ivory, c.1850, 4 In. ....*illus*	960

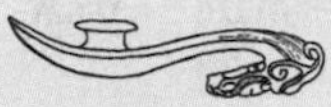

JADE is the name for two different minerals, nephrite and jadeite. Nephrite is the mineral used for most early Oriental carvings. Jade is a very tough stone that is found in many colors from dark green to pale lavender. Jade carvings are still being made in the old styles, so collectors must be careful not to be fooled by recent pieces. Jade jewelry is found in this book under Jewelry.

Belt Hook, Pale, Celadon, Carved Hook, Fungi Shape, Swan Neck, Ruyi Body, 3 ¼ In.	2040
Boulder, Carved, Landscape, Pines & Villas, Wood Stand, Chinese, 9 In. ....*illus*	523
Bowl, Brush Washer, Circular Carved, Green, 2 Handles, Chih Lung Dragons, 4 ⅞ In.	2040
Brush Washer, White, Twins, Figural, Hang On Either End, Fruit, Vines, 2 ¾ x 6 In.	1320
Buckle, White, Carved Foo Dog, Chinese, ½ x ¾ x 1 ¼ In.	246
Censer, Lid, Carved, Foo Dogs, Chinese, 16 ¼ In.	584
Censer, Lid, Carved, Serpentine, Tripod Feet, Chinese, 5 ⅞ x 6 ¾ x 4 In.	425
Censer, Nephrite, Phoenix, Interlocking Rings, 1900s, 10 In.	8960
Cup, Spinach Green, Taotie Designs, Dragon Shape Handle, Footed, Chinese, c.1875, 3 In.	4250
Fan, Stand, Carved, Burmese, Red Base, Chinese, 4 ⅞ x 8 ⅛ x 1 ⅜ In.	425
Figurine, 2 Cats, Nephrite, Oval Shape, Pale Celadon & Gray Stone, 1 ¾ In.	2460
Figurine, Bat, Pale Green, 1 Wing Outstretched, 1 Tucked Under, Pebble Carved, 2 In.	390
Figurine, Bixie, With Pup, White, Chinese, 1900s, 1 ½ x 3 ½ In.	300
Figurine, Boy On Boat, Pale, Celadon, Peaches, Paddle In His Hands, c.1800, 2 ⅜ In. ....*illus*	2000
Figurine, Buddha's Hand, Celadon, Russet Veinings, Leafy Stem Base, 1800s, 3 In.	938
Figurine, Damo, Seated, Curly Hair, Long Beard, Black & White, 1800s, 3 ½ In.	2500
Figurine, Elder, With Vase, Carved, Chinese, 3 ¼ x 5 ¼ x 2 ¾ In. ....*illus*	500
Figurine, Foo Dog, Carved, Rectangular Base, Chinese, 1900s, 3 ½ x 2 ⅜ x 1 ½ In.	325
Figurine, Guanyin, Standing, Holding Flower, Celadon, Light Brown Stone, Wood Stand, 19 In.	2583
Figurine, Immortal, Draped Robes, Left Hand Holding Bucket, Black & White, 3 ½ In. ....*illus*	938
Figurine, Tree, Carved, Prunus, Celadon, Fitted Wood Stand, 2 ½ x 3 ½ In.	300
Figurine, White, Boy, Carved, Riding On Bamboo Horse, c.1800, 2 ½ In.	1625
Figurine, Woman, Dragon, Carved, Archaic Style Birds, 7 x 3 x ¼ In.	472
Group, 2 Elders, Tree, Temples, On Mountain, 7 ¾ x 4 ¾ x 2 ¾ In. ....*illus*	2723
Group, Man, Woman, Seated, Garden, Tree, White, Brown Streaks, 3 ¾ In.	576
Ornament, Openwork, Deer Under Leafy Trees, 2 Holes, Celadon Stone, 1 ⅛ In.	369
Pendant, Koro, Lion, White, Leaves, Lotus, Rings, 6 ½ x 7 ½ In.	2040
Pendant, Medallion, Carved, Tiger & Pine Tree, Russet, Amber Stone, 3 ¼ x 2 ⅜ In.	300
Plaque, Magpie, On Leafy Branches, Reticulated, Celadon, Carved, 1800, 2 ⅛ In.	2250
Plaque, Scholar, Landscape, Poetic Inscriptions, White, Carved, c.1800, 2 ¼ In.	5250

Jade, Boulder, Carved, Landscape, Pines & Villas, Wood Stand, Chinese, 9 In.
$523

Clars Auction Gallery

Jade, Figurine, Boy On Boat, Pale, Celadon, Peaches, Paddle In His Hands, c.1800, 2 ⅜ In.
$2,000

Leslie Hindman Auctioneers

Jade, Figurine, Elder, With Vase, Carved, Chinese, 3 ¼ x 5 ¼ x 2 ¾ In.
$500

Heritage Auctions

Jade, Figurine, Immortal, Draped Robes, Left Hand Holding Bucket, Black & White, 3 ½ In.
$938

Leslie Hindman Auctioneers

Jade, Group, 2 Elders, Tree, Temples, On Mountain, 7 ¾ x 4 ¾ x 2 ¾ In.
$2,723

Fontaine's Auction Gallery

Jasperware, Bough Pot, Square, Paneled, Blue & White, Classical, Neale & Co., Late 1700s, 5 ½ In.
$338

Skinner, Inc.

Jewelry, Belt Buckle, Eagle, Flags, Shield, Bayonets, Liberty, Justice, Flowers, 10K Gold, 1 ¾ x 2 ½ In.
$390

Cowan's Auctions

Jewelry, Necklace, Pendant, Stylized Bird, Silver, Amazonite, Rolph Scarlett, 1960s, 4 x 3 In.
$1,875

Rago Arts and Auction Center

Jewelry, Necklace, Trade Beads, Blue & White, Graduated, New York, 1750s, 22 In.
$120

Allard Auctions

Jewelry, Pendant, Vinaigrette, Ladybug, Jewels, Seed Pearls, Wings Open, 2 x 1 ½ In.
$4,375

Morphy Auctions

Jewelry, Pin, Beetle, Pearl, Ruby Eyes, Enamel Wings, 18K Yellow & White Gold, 1 ¼ In.
$512

Morphy Auctions

> ### Gold Notes
> 24-karat gold is pure gold; 18-karat is 75 percent gold mixed with another metal like nickel or copper; 14-karat is 58.5 percent gold.

Jewelry, Pin, Butterfly, Rose Cut Diamonds, Sapphires, Rubies, Pearls, 10K Gold, 1 ⅛ x ⅞ In.
$1,625

New Orleans Auction Galleries

> ### TIP
> Do not wash rhinestones with water. It will tarnish the foil background. Use a cotton swab or small, soft brush and glass cleaner. Do not hold the jewelry under running water. Rub dry with a soft cloth.

Jewelry, Pin, Ginkgo Leaf, 15 Diamonds In Stem, 18K Gold, Platinum, Tiffany & Co., Box, 1 ¾ In.
$570

Eldred's

Jewelry, Pin, Opals, Diamonds, Baguette, White Gold, Art Deco, 2 x 1 ¼ In.
$826

Aspire Auctions

Plaque, White, Square, Carved, Female Immortal, Holding Covered Base, 1800s, 2 1/8 In.		7500
Scepter, Ruyi, Tourmaline & Hardstone, Enameled, Apple Green Jadeite, Carved, 13 In.		3000
Tea Bowl, Lid, Carved, Green To Yellow, Chinese, 3 x 3 3/8 In.		475
Teapot, Lid, Carved, Bamboo Leaves, Handle & Spout, Sea Green Matrix, Chinese, 5 1/4 In.		338
Teapot, Lid, Spinach, Relief Carved, Flowers, Miniature, Chinese, 3 x 5 In.		300
Tree, Stone, Flowers, Marble Planter, Wood Platform, 25 In.		219
Urn, Carved, Flowers, Fruit, Chinese, 5 1/4 In.		1250
Urn, Flowers, Fruit, Openwork, Wood Stand, Green, White, Purple, Yellow, 1900s, 5 1/4 In.		1260
Urn, Lid, Flowers, Tree, Bird, Carved, Wood Plinth, 1900s, 13 1/2 In.		510
Vase, Flower Form, Liu Hai & Toad Front, Lotus & Bird Back, Wood Stand, Chinese, 5 1/2 In.		615
Vase, Lid, Carved, Footed, Handles, Square Base, Chinese, 5 In.		450
Vase, Lid, Lappet Leaves, Elephant Head Handles, Celadon, c.1900, 10 In.		2125
Vase, Mughal Style, Spreading Foot, Flaring Rim, 1900s, 7 3/8 In.		938

JAPANESE WOODBLOCK PRINTS *are listed in this book in the Print category under Japanese.*

JASPERWARE can be made in different ways. Some pieces are made from a solid-colored clay with applied raised designs of a contrasting colored clay. Other pieces are made entirely of one color clay with raised decorations that are glazed with a contrasting color. Additional pieces of jasperware may also be listed in the Wedgwood category or under various art potteries.

Bough Pot, Square, Paneled, Blue & White, Classical, Neale & Co., Late 1700s, 5 1/2 In......*illus*		338

JEWELRY, whether made from gold and precious gems or plastic and colored glass, is popular with collectors. Values are determined by the intrinsic value of the stones and metal and by the skill of the craftsmen and designers. Victorian and older jewelry has been collected since the 1950s. More recent interests are Art Deco and Edwardian styles, Mexican and Danish silver jewelry, and beads of all kinds. Copies of almost all styles are being made. American Indian jewelry is listed in the Indian category. Tiffany jewelry is listed here.

Belt Buckle, Eagle, Flags, Shield, Bayonets, Liberty, Justice, Flowers, 10K Gold, 1 3/4 x 2 1/2 In..... *illus*		390
Bracelet, Bakelite, Etched Medallion, Caramel, Cream, Chrome Spacers, Josephine Baker, 7 In.		300
Bracelet, Bangle, 5 Diamonds, 18K Gold, Linda Morgan, 7 1/2 In.		805
Bracelet, Bangle, Hinged, Black Enamel, 18K White Gold, Satin, Hidalgo, 6 1/2 In.		660
Bracelet, Cuff, Brass, Cutout Rectangles, Marked, Mary McFadden, 4 In.		450
Bracelet, Cultured Pearls, 3 Strands, Box Clasp, Safety Chain, 1950s, 7 1/2 In.		125
Bracelet, Hinged, Turquoise, Rows Of Cabochons, Center Pearl, Victorian, 6 In.		1500
Bracelet, Link, Textured Goldtone Metal, Brutalist Style, Kenneth J. Lane, 1970s, 7 1/2 In.		192
Bracelet, Link, U-Shape, 14K Gold, Alternating Gold Beads, Marked, AGS, Italy, 7 3/4 In.		540
Clip, 5 Gripoix Glass Cabochons, Goldtone Metal Flower Rim, Dangling Pearls, Chanel, 4 3/4 In.		780
Clip, Asian Princess, Headdress, Enamel, Plique-A-Jour, Rhinestones, Goldtone Metal, DuJay, 3 In.		2280
Clip, Cuckoo Clock, Mechanical, Rhinestones, Chain, Pearl End, M. Boucher, 2 In.		1440
Clip, Flower Basket, Heart Shape Faux Amethysts, Crystals, DeRosa, 2 1/2 In.		660
Clip, Plume, Amber Baguettes, Green Crystals, A. Philippe, Trifari, 5 In.		570
Clip, Swan, Amethyst, Rhinestone Pave, A. Philippe, Trifari, 4 In.		1800
Clip, Wheelbarrow, Moonstone & Opal Fruit Salad, Rhinestones, Trifari, 3 1/4 In.		480
Cuff Links, Antelope Heads, Long Horns, 14K Gold, Diamond Eyes, Box, 1 1/4 In.		570
Cuff Links, Black Jasperware, Horse, Wedgwood, 14K Gold Twisted Rim, England, 1 In.		150
Cuff Links, Hexagonal, 18K Gold, 6 Table-Cut Emeralds, 5/8 In.		1000
Cuff Links, Moon Face, Venetian Glass, Mother-Of-Pearl Ground, 18K Gold, Locke, 1 In.		2500
Cuff Links, Sapphires, Round Cut Diamonds, 18K Gold, 1 In.		2125
Duette, Flowers, Molded Crystals, Rhinestones, Shield Shape, Mazer, 2 1/2 In.		330
Duette, Trembling Flowers, Rhinestones, Pearls, Red Beads, Bronze Enamel, Coro, 1939, 3 In.		300
Earrings, Dangle, Diamond Of 4 Squares, Turquoise, Rhinestones, Kenneth J. Lane, 3 In.		192
Hairpin, 26 Diamonds, 18K Gold, U-Shape, Wavy Ends, Marked, Cartier, 2 1/4 In.		1560
Hatpins are listed in this book in the Hatpin category.		
Man's Dress Set, Onyx Plaque, Diamond Center, Rectangular 14K Gold Mount, 5 Piece		1625
Necklace & Earrings, Pansy, Pave Rhinestones, Enamel, A. Philippe, Trifari, 1940s, 16-In. Chain.		270
Necklace, Beads, Coral, Carved, 2 Strands, Victorian, 19 1/2 In.		360

Jewelry, Pin, Star, Long & Short Points, Textured Disks, Raised Centers, 21K Gold, 2 In.
$510

Morphy Auctions

Jewelry, Pin, Wreath, Crown, Entwined V & A, Rubies, Diamonds, 18K Gold, Victorian, 1 3/8 x 1 In.
$1,250

Neal Auction Company

Jewelry, Tie Pin, Bird Of Paradise, Multicolor, 14K Gold, Spring Push Back, 7/8 x 1/2 In.
$142

Aspire Auctions

J

Judaica, Etrog Box, Patinated, Egg Shape, Hebrew Inscription, Footed Base, 6½ In.
$154

Clars Auction Gallery

Judaica, Platter, Brass, Flared Rim, Hand Chased, Temple, Figures, Animals, Round, 11⅞ In.
$130

Aspire Auctions

Judaica, Tray, Challah, Silver, Relief Design, Hebrew Blessing On Border, Mexico c.1950, 17 x 13 In.
$2,125

Royal Crest Auctioneers

Necklace, Beads, Coral, Single Strand, Graduated, Victorian, 26 In. ... 360
Necklace, Cameo, 3 Graces, Shell, 14K Gold, Discs, Marked Kalo, Chain 16 In. ... 2500
Necklace, Chain, Dangling Clamshells, 3 Rows, Textured Goldtone, M. Haskell, 1950s, 29 In. ... 300
Necklace, Collar, Blue & White Jewels, Silvertone Metal, Trifari, 4¾ In. ... 144
Necklace, Dangle, 3 Pendants, Clear Crystals & Rhinestones, Schreiner, 18 In. ... 480
Necklace, Dangling Beads, Faux Pearls & Sapphires, Miriam Haskell, 16 In. ... 480
Necklace, Diamonds, 14K White Gold, Marked BH, 18 In. ... 374
Necklace, Emerald Beads, 4 Strands, Tumbled, Graduated, Rock Crystal Clasps, Schepps, 17 To 22 In. ... 4750
Necklace, Pendant, Stylized Bird, Silver, Amazonite, Rolph Scarlett, 1960s, 4 x 3 In. ... *illus* 1875
Necklace, Serpent, Gold Wash, Faceted Jewel Eyes, A. Katz, Coro, 20 In. ... 120
Necklace, Trade Beads, Blue & White, Graduated, New York, 1750s, 22 In. ... *illus* 120
Pendant, Vinaigrette, Ladybug, Jewels, Seed Pearls, Wings Open, 2 x 1½ In. ... *illus* 4375
Pin & Earrings, Feather Form, 14K Gold, Marked, Tiffany & Co., Germany, 2-In. Pin ... 660
Pin & Earrings, Pink Flower, Green Leaf, Gripoix Glass, Silver Rim, Nettie Rosenstein, 3-In. Pin ... 780
Pin, Bakelite, Flower, Apple Juice Leaf, Green Rhinestone Cluster, 3 In. ... 84
Pin, Beetle, Pearl, Ruby Eyes, Enamel Wings, 18K Yellow & White Gold, 1¼ In. ... *illus* 512
Pin, Blackamoor, Turquoise Bead Breastplate, Colored Rhinestones, M. Boucher, 3¾ In. ... 450
Pin, Bouquet, Pink Flowers, Ribbon, Enamel, Fred Block, 4¾ In. ... 480
Pin, Bow, Diamante, 4 Flower Heads, Textured Goldtone Petals, M. Haskell, 3½ In. ... 720
Pin, Butterfly, Rose Cut Diamonds, Sapphires, Rubies, Pearls, 10K Gold, 1⅛ x ⅞ In. ... *illus* 1625
Pin, Cameo, Angel, Shell, Carved, Engraved 18K Gold Frame, 2 In. ... 300
Pin, Cameo, Finding Of Moses, Conch Shell, 14K Gold Ropetwist Mount, Seed Pearls, 3 In. ... 540
Pin, Christmas Tree, Red & Green Rhinestones, Candles, Gold Plated, Hollycraft, 1960s, 2 In. ... 75
Pin, Circle, Scotch Agate Plaques, Silver, Open Center, 2⅝ In. ... 216
Pin, Clown, Ball, Clown Spins, 18K Gold, Enamel, Marked, Martin, 1 x 1½ In. ... 480
Pin, Diamonds & Rubies, 14K Gold, Loop & Scroll Design, Mauboussin, 1¾ In. ... 1845
Pin, Diamonds, 3 Interlocking, Red, White & Blue Rhinestones, Mazer, 3½ In. ... 192
Pin, Dragonfly, Multicolor Rhinestones, Goldtone Metal, Monet, c.1980s, 2 In. ... 24
Pin, Dwarf Bonsai Tree, Gold Wash, Enamel, Rhinestones, Boucher, 3 In. ... 3840
Pin, Face, Old Man, Mousta, Moonstone, Silver, 14K Gold, JL Heatwole, Va., c.1990, 3¼ x 2 In. ... 351
Pin, Flower Basket, Molded Glass Flowers, Red, Blue, Green, Rhinestones, Enamel, Mazer, 3 In. ... 420
Pin, Genie, Stars On Pants, Holding Crystal Ball, Goldtone Metal, HAR, 2½ In. ... 270
Pin, Ginkgo Leaf, 15 Diamonds In Stem, 18K Gold, Platinum, Tiffany & Co., Box, 1¾ In. ... *illus* 570
Pin, Hand, Friendship, Goldtone Metal, Enamel, A. Katz, Coro, 4 In. ... 330
Pin, Maltese Cross, Blue Crystals, Pink, White & Blue Rhinestones, Kenneth J. Lane, 4 In. ... 450
Pin, Micro Mosaic, Roman Ruins, Blue Rim, 14K Gold Frame, Ropetwist, Victorian, 2 In. ... 677
Pin, Netsuke, Ebony, Menpo Mask Form, Japan, c.1800, 1¾ In. ... 300
Pin, Opals, Diamonds, Baguette, White Gold, Art Deco, 2 x 1¼ In. ... *illus* 826
Pin, Orchid, 18K Textured Gold, Pearl Stamen, Marked, CC, 3 x 1¾ In. ... 360
Pin, Peas In Pod, 4 Faux Pearls, Mother-Of-Pearl-Enamel, Sandor, 3 In. ... 108
Pin, Praying Mantis, Rhinestones, Green Enamel, Silvertone Metal, M. Boucher, 3 In. ... 1920
Pin, Punchinello, Jester, Mechanical, Enamel, Rhinestones, M. Boucher, 2¾ In. ... 1800
Pin, Rockfish, Aqua Stone In Mouth, Enamel, Rhinestones, Rose Gold Plated, Corocraft, 3 In. ... 330
Pin, Star, Long & Short Points, Textured Discs, Raised Centers, 21K Gold, 2 In. ... *illus* 510
Pin, Stem, 3 Wooden Leaves, Green Crystals, Wired, Silver, Sandor, 4 In. ... 108
Pin, Taurus The Bull, Ivory Color, Jeweled Wreath, Nettie Rosenstein, 3½ In. ... 360
Pin, Turtle, Emerald Eyes, Green Enamel, Lapis Lazuli Legs, 18K Gold, Hammerman, 1 In. ... 2215
Pin, Wreath, Crown, Entwined V & A, Rubies, Diamonds, 18K Gold, Victorian, 1⅜ x 1 In. ... *illus* 1250
Ring, 7 Diamonds, 14K White Gold, Man's, 2½ In. ... 374
Ring, Cat's Eye Chrysoberyl, Diamonds On Sides, 18K Gold, Man's, Size 10 ... 3250
Ring, Moses Head, Yellow Sapphires, Diamonds, 14K Textured Gold, Size 9¾ ... 2750
Tie Pin, Bird Of Paradise, Multicolor, 14K Gold, Spring Push Back, ⅞ x ½ In. ... *illus* 142
Watches are listed in their own category.
Wristwatches are listed in their own category.

JOHN ROGERS statues were made from 1859 to 1892. The originals were bronze, but the thousands of copies made by the Rogers factory were of painted plaster. Eighty different figures were created. Similar painted plaster figures were produced by some other factories. Rights to the figures were sold in 1893, and the figures were

manufactured until about 1895 by the Rogers Statuette Co. Never repaint a Rogers figure because this lowers the value to collectors.

Bust, Abraham Lincoln, Bronze Color, Beveled Marble Base, Signed, 8 ¾ In.	708
Group, School Days, New York, Patent 1877, 21 ½ In.	359

JOSEF ORIGINALS ceramics were designed by Muriel Joseph George. The first pieces were made in California from 1945 to 1962. They were then manufactured in Japan. The company was sold to George Good in 1982 and he continued to make Josef Originals until 1985. The company was sold two more times. The last owner went bankrupt in 2011.

Josef Originals

Bell, Angel, Red Christmas Dress, Holding Baby Jesus, Boot Clapper, 4 ¼ In.	11
Figurine, Boy, Choir, Singing, Christmas, Red & White Robe, 4 ½ In.	24
Figurine, Dog, Poodle, Gilt, Head, Tail, Paw, 1950s, 3 ¾ In.	19
Figurine, Girl, Asian, Holding Musical Instrument, 3 x 3 In.	50
Figurine, Girl, Saturday, Holding Pie, Cream & Blue, 4 In.	50
Figurine, Lamb, Big Eyes, Butterfly On Tail, Japan, 1940s, 3 x 4 In.	28
Figurine, Mouse, Bobbing Head, Ladybug, Yellow Flower, Be Happy, 4 In.	18
Figurine, Owl, Boxing, Champion, Bandages On Head, 1980s, 2 ¾ In.	17
Figurine, Woman, Buying A New Hat, Mother's World, 22K Gold Trim, 1960s, 8 In.	123
Lipstick Holder, Teen Girl, Blond Hair, Pink Flower, Flower Base, 5 Holes, 6 ¾ In.	86
Music Box, Angel, Girl, Red Dress, Gold Trim, Basket, Spins, 6 In.	26
Night-Light, Virgin Mary, Praying, Cream Dress, Blue Ribbon On Waist, 8 ½ In.	13
Pie Bird, Grandma, Mixing Bowl & Spoon, Green Dress, Apron, 3 ¼ In.	23
Planter, Girl, Big Eyes, Blue Dress, Basket Of Flowers, 1960s, 4 ½ In.	10
Salt & Pepper, Santa Claus, Cooking, Green Gloves, Long White Beard, 4 In.	21
Soap Dish, Mermaid Baby, Girl, Blue Tail, Sitting On Brown Shell	43
Vase, Pocket, Molly, Yellow Green Dress, Hat, No. 251, 5 ½ In.	21

JUDAICA is any memorabilia that refers to the Jews or the Jewish religion. Interests range from newspaper clippings that mention eighteenth- and nineteenth-century Jewish Americans to religious objects, such as menorahs or spice boxes. Age, condition, and the intrinsic value of the material, as well as the historic and artistic importance, determine the value.

Candlestick, Traveling, Sabbath, Hinged Box, 2 Holders, Stars Of David, Silver, 2 In.	83
Charm, Mezuzah, 14K Yellow Gold, Scroll, Red & Blue Enamel Beads, 1 ½ In.	255
Etrog Box, Patinated, Egg Shape, Hebrew Inscription, Footed Base, 6 ½ In. ....*illus*	154
Kiddush Cup, Silver, Shmirot, Made From Coins, Boyan Hasidic, Bukowina, Ukraine, 1800s..	2500
Kiddush Cup, Silver, Tripod, Round Bowl, Kurt Marzdorf, 6 In.	2880
Menorah, Wall Hanging, Cast Brass, 8 Wells For Oil, Removable Shamash Cup, 6 ¼ In.	73
Pin, 50th Jubilee Flag, Glassy Enamel, Zionist, Histadruth, 1947	52
Platter, Brass, Flared Rim, Hand Chased, Temple, Figures, Animals, Round, 11 ⅞ In. ....*illus*	130
Postcard, Seder Night, April 17, 1916, Family Around Table, Piano, Candles	50
Sculpture, Star Of David, 18K Gold, Wire, Fitted Box, France, 5 ¼ In.	1875
Seder Plate, Pesach, Lamb, Symbolic Foods, Black Transfer, c.1924, 10 In.	293
Spice Box, Lid, Sterling Silver, 6-Sided, Footed, Viktor Savinkov, Russia, 1873, 3 ½ In.	205
Spice Box, Silver, Fish Shape, Besamim, Marked, 9 ½ In.	177
Torah Pointer, Silver, Hand At Tip, Engraved, Yad, Germany, c.1900, 11 In.	566
Tray, Challah, Silver, Relief Design, Hebrew Blessing On Border, Mexico c.1950, 17 x 13 In. *illus*	2125

JUGTOWN POTTERY refers to pottery made in North Carolina as far back as the 1750s. In 1915, Juliana and Jacques Busbee set up a training and sales organization for what they named Jugtown Pottery. In 1921, they built a shop at Jugtown, North Carolina, and hired Ben Owen as a potter in 1923. The Busbees moved the village store where the pottery was sold to New York City. Juliana Busbee sold the New York store in 1926 and moved into a log cabin near the Jugtown Pottery. The pottery closed in 1959. It reopened in 1960 and is still working near Seagrove, North Carolina.

JUGTOWN WARE

Bean Pot, Lid, Pumpkin Glaze, Grooved Body, 6 x 5 In.	225
Bowl, Mottled Green & Brown Matte Glaze, 5 x 3 In.	125

Jukebox, AMI, Model B, 78 RPM Records, Wood & Plastic, Lock & Key, 1948, 66 x 31 In.
$720

Potter & Potter Auctions

Jukebox, Mills, Hi Boy, Model 802, 5 Cents, Walnut Cabinet, 12 78 RPM Record Selections, 1928
$7,920

Potter & Potter Auctions

Jukebox, Wurlitzer, Model 1015, Multi Coin, Bubbler, Phonograph, 24 x 32 ½ x 59 In.
$6,150

Morphy Auctions

Kate Greenaway, Napkin Ring, Figural, Silver Plate, Teacher, Children, ABCs, Simpson, Hall, Miller, 3 x 3 In.
$2,040

Morphy Auctions

Kelva, Jewelry Box, 6-Sided, Pink Flowers, Green Mottled Background, Marked, 3 x 3¾ In.
$1,320

Woody Auction

Kelva, Jewelry Box, Blue Mottled, Pink Flowers, Reticulated Silver Color Base, 2¾ x 3 In.
$480

Woody Auction

TIP

Carry your keys and use the flashlight on your phone when walking at night.

Bowl, Tobacco Spit Glaze, 6¼ x 3½ In.	120
Jug, Frogskin Glaze, Incised Lines, Applied Handle, 3 In.	85
Pitcher, Lid, Flared Collar, Strap Handles, Orange, Olive Mottled Base, c.1950, 9 In.	148
Sugar, Lid, Lug Handles, Orange Glaze	40
Vase, Red & Blue Drip Glaze, Bulbous, 7 In.	295

JUKEBOXES play records. The first coin-operated phonograph was demonstrated in 1889. In 1906 the Automatic-Entertainer appeared, the first coin-operated phonograph to offer several different selections of music. The first electrically powered jukebox was introduced in 1927. Collectors search for jukeboxes of all ages, especially those with flashing lights and unusual design and graphics.

AMI, JAJ200, 100 Selections, Plays 100 45 RPM Records, 1959, 59 x 33 In.	2016
AMI, Model B, 78 RPM Records, Wood & Plastic, Lock & Key, 1948, 66 x 31 In. ......*illus*	720
AMI, Model JEJ-200, Stereophonic, 200 Selections, 1959, 59 x 53 In.	1625
Mills, Hi Boy, Model 802, 5 Cents, Walnut Cabinet, 12 78 RPM Record Selections, 1928.....*illus*	7920
Rock-Ola, Model 1458, 120 Hi-Fi, Stars, Green, Blue, Orange, 1958, 55 x 30 In.	1375
Rock-Ola, Multi Coin, Magic Glo, 78 RPM Records, Phonograph, c.1948, 8 x 31 x 60 In.	5440
Seeburg, Model 8200, Green Panels, Red Cap, 20 Selections, c.1941, 63 x 33 In.	1968
Wurlitzer, Model 800, Arched Top, Bubble Tubes, 24 Selection, 60 x 38 In.	3997
Wurlitzer, Model 1015, Multi Coin, Bubbler, Phonograph, 24 x 32½ x 59 In. .....*illus*	6150
Wurlitzer, Model 1700, Domed Glass Front, Florescent Lights, c.1954, 55 x 32 In.	3382

KATE GREENAWAY (1846 to 1901), who was a famous illustrator of children's books, drew pictures of children in high-waisted Empire dresses. Her designs appear on china, glass, napkin rings, and other pieces as well as prints and storybooks.

Book, A Apple Pie, Frederick Warne & Co., Hardcover, c.1900, 8 x 10 In.	58
Book, Almanack, Girls, Hats, Flowers, Field, Umbrella, Blue, Orange, 1886	250
Book, Mother Goose, Crisscross Design, Frederick Warne, 1902, 6¾ x 5 In., 48 Pages	235
Bowl, Center, Silver Plate, Glass, Dome Gazebo, Victorian, 1800s, 9 x 11¾ In.	229
Box, Gaming Counter, Silver, Victorian, Coins Lid, George II, 1881, 1¾ x 1 In.	242
Bracelet, Bangle, Hinged, 3 Scenes Of Children, Sterling Silver, 1¼ x 6 In.	485
Button, Glass, Picture, Black, Round, 3 Women, Victorian, 1 In.	8
Button, Wood, Little Bo Peep, Hand Painted, Black, Green, Cream, 1972, 1⅜ In.	7
Coin Holder, Solid Silver, Engraved, Child, George IV, Lid, 1881, 1¾ In.	57
Match Safe, Silver, Girls, Sitting, On Fence, Field, Flowers, Gold Wash Interior, 2 x 1¼ In.	246
Napkin Ring, Figural, Girl, Muff, Coat, Silver Plate, 1850-99, 2⅜ In.	38
Napkin Ring, Figural, Silver Plate, Teacher, Children, ABCs, Simpson, Hall, Miller, 3 x 3 In...*illus*	2040
Ornament, Woman, White Coat, Hat, Figural, Glass, Bottle Shape, 4 x 1½ x 1¼ In.	80
Pin, Boy Whispering To Girl, Fence, Cat, Basket, 18K Gold, c.1890, 6½ x 5 In.	2200
Toothpick Holder, Boy Lighting Cannon, Hat, Nautical Uniform, Silver Plate, 3 x 4¾ In.	300
Trade Card, Fan Shape, Children On Wall, Pink, Silver, H. McAllister & Co., 3 x 3½ In.	12
Tray, Silver Plate, Engraved Couple, Characters Holding Tray, J.W. Tufts, 1880s, 7 In.	879

Kay Finch **KAY FINCH CERAMICS** were made in Corona del Mar, California, from 1935 to
CALIFORNIA 1963. The hand-decorated pieces often depicted whimsical animals and people. Pastel colors were used.

Ashtray, Lamb, Figural, Seated On Top, Brown	6
Bowl, Swan, Flower, Cream, Green, Glaze, Black Eyes, 1940s, 10 x 8 In.	95
Dish, Shell Shape, Scalloped, Purple Glaze, 1960s	50
Figurine, Angel, Hands Crossed, Blue Wings & Collar, 3⅞ In.	30
Figurine, Dog, Cocker Spaniel, Cream & Gray, Sitting, 1950s, 13 x 13 In.	846
Figurine, Dog, Skye Terrier, Sitting, White, 11 x 11 x 8 In.	79
Figurine, Dog, Terrier, White, Gray, 1960s, 11½ In.	225
Figurine, Duck, Baby, Peep, Green Head & Tail, White Body, Brown Feet, 1940s, 4 x 3 In.	45
Figurine, Elephant, Peanut, Pale Pink, Raised Foot, Green Toenails, Flowers On Ears, 1950s	220
Figurine, Hannibal, Angry, Standing, Tail Up, 1940s, 10½ x 8½ In.	130
Figurine, Hen, Sleeping, White, Gold Highlights, 1950s, 5 x 5 In.	30
Figurine, Monkey, Sitting, Smiling, White, Blue Ribbon, 10 x 7½ x 8 In.	256

J

Planter, Santa Claus, Pack Of Toys On Back, Open At Top, 4 ¼ x 4 In.		20
Stein, Turquoise, Dachshund Handle, Brown Glaze, 1950s, 7 ¼ In.		395

KAYSERZINN, *see Pewter category.*

KELVA glassware was made by the C. F. Monroe Company of Meriden, Connecticut, about 1904. It is a pale, pastel-painted glass decorated with flowers, designs, or scenes. Kelva resembles Nakara and Wave Crest, two other glasswares made by the same company.

KELVA

Jewelry Box, 6-Sided, Pink Flowers, Green Mottled Background, Marked, 3 x 3 ¾ In.	*illus*	1320
Jewelry Box, Blue Mottled, Pink Flowers, Reticulated Silver Color Base, 2 ¾ x 3 In.	*illus*	480
Jewelry Box, Lid, Apricot Mottled Background, Violets, 3 ¾ x 6 In.		240
Jewelry Box, Metal, Lavender, Blue Flowers, C.F. Monroe, 3 ¾ x 5 In.	*illus*	480
Jewelry Box, Oval, Dark Green, Pink Poppy, White Bead Scroll, 3 x 5 ½ x 4 In.		210
Memo Spike, 8-Sided, Pink Flowers, Green Mottled, Unmarked, 6 ½ x 3 ½ In.		660
Napkin Ring, Silver Plate Rim, Blue Mottled Glass, Pink Flowers, Unmarked, 2 ½ In.		210
Vase, Gilt Metal Feet & Handles, Blue Mottled, Pink Flowers, 10 x 3 ¾ In.		210
Vase, Lily, Red Mottled, Gilt Metal Feet & Handles, Marked, 14 x 8 In.	*illus*	900

KENTON HILLS POTTERY in Erlanger, Kentucky, made artwares, including vases and figurines that resembled Rookwood, probably because so many of the original artists and workmen had worked at the Rookwood plant. Kenton Hills opened in 1939 and closed during World War II.

Vase, Lamp, Leaves, Llamas, Squeezebag, 10 ⅜ In.		1062

KEW BLAS is the name used by the Union Glass Company of Somerville, Massachusetts. The name refers to an iridescent golden glass made from the 1890s to 1924. The iridescent glass was reminiscent of the Tiffany glass of the period.

Candlestick, Gold, Iridescent, Taper, Steuben Style, 8 ½ In.		175
Vase, Bulbous Flared Base, Gold, Pink, Iridescent, Signed, 5 ¼ x 12 ½ In.		375
Vase, Green, Gold, Iridescent, Pulled Feather Design, Applied Lip, 4 x 3 In.		625

KEWPIES, designed by Rose O'Neill (1874-1944), were first pictured in the *Ladies' Home Journal.* The figures, which are similar to pixies, were a success, and Kewpie dolls and figurines started appearing in 1911. Kewpie pictures and other items soon followed. Collectors search for all items that picture the little winged people. They are still popular with collectors.

Ashtray, Doll On Top, Holding Guitar, Bisque, 1920s-30s, 2 x 2 ½ In.		760
Bisque, Bellhop, Jointed Arms, Blue Uniform Jacket, Hat, Germany, 1912, 3 ¾ In.		367
Bisque, Sitting, Cream Chair, Arms Folded, Rose O'Neill, 3 ¾ In.	*illus*	192
Composition Head, Cloth Body, Side-Glancing Eyes, 22 In.		180
Inkstand, Metal, 2 Containers, Pen, Cream, Marked, 1910s, 8 x 5 ¾ x 6 ½ In.	*illus*	3658
Ornament, Black Baby, Doodle Dog, White Blanket, Red Polka Dots, Hanging, Bisque, 3 ½ In.		26
Pencil Sharpener, Celluloid, Marked, T In Circle, Made In Japan, 3 ¼ In.		325
Pincushion Doll, Bisque, Tan, Seminude, Red Cheeks, c.1900, 6 ½ In.		154
Scootles, Vinyl, Cameo Doll Co., Wrist Tag, LE, 1950s-60s, 9 In.		78
Sugar, Kewpie On Lid, Blue, White, Flowers, Jasperware, Wedgwood, 1920s, 5 ½ In.		119

KITCHEN utensils of all types, from eggbeaters to bowls, are collected today. Handmade wooden and metal items, like ladles and apple peelers, were made in the early nineteenth century. Mass-produced pieces, like iron apple peelers and graniteware, were made in the nineteenth century. Also included in this category are utensils used for other household chores, such as laundry and cleaning. Other kitchen wares are listed under manufacturers' names or under Advertising, Iron, Tool, or Wooden.

Bin, Vegetable, Green, Black, 3 Tiers, Marked Mascot, 1800s, 26 x 13 ¼ In.		984
Butcher Block, Wood, Turned Legs, 1800s, 31 x 18 ½ In.		615

Kelva, Jewelry Box, Metal, Lavender, Blue Flowers, C.F. Monroe, 3 ¾ x 5 In.
$480

Woody Auction

Kelva, Vase, Lily, Red Mottled, Gilt Metal Feet & Handles, Marked, 14 x 8 In.
$900

Woody Auction

K

Kewpie, Bisque, Sitting, Cream Chair, Arms Folded, Rose O'Neill, 3 ¾ In.
$192

Hartzell's Auction Gallery, Inc.

Kewpie, Inkstand, Metal, 2 Containers, Pen, Cream, Marked, 1910s, 8 x 5¾ x 6½ In.
$3,658

Charleston Estate Auctions

Iron Pans Smooth

Vintage cast-iron pans were hand-cast in sand, while modern pieces are made by a different method that leaves a rough surface. The old ones bring the highest prices.

Kitchen, Butter Stamp, 4 Impressions, Carved, Back Handle, Kingwood, 4 In.
$46

Keystone Auctions LLC

Kitchen, Churn, Dazey, Glass Body, Wood Handle, Crank Mechanism, 13 In.
$52

Keystone Auctions LLC

Butter Mold, look under Mold, Butter in this category.	
Butter Stamp, 4 Impressions, Carved, Back Handle, Kingwood, 4 In. ....*illus*	46
Butter Stamp, Lollipop, 3 Stepped Hearts, Serrated Legs, 1800s, 9 x 4⅛ x 4¼ In......	527
Butter Stamp, Lollipop, Cow, Horns & Leaves, Rib Rim, Oblong Handle, 1800s, 13 x 4⅞ In....	222
Butter Stamp, Lollipop, Figural Lyre, Ribbed Rim, Arched Handle, 1800s, 10½ x 4⅜ In........	263
Cake Board, Carved, Mahogany, Basket Of Fruit & Bird, John Conger, 11 x 11 In.	3338
Canister, Spice, Lid, Wood, 8 Interior Canisters, Bentwood, Metal Bands, 3½ x 9½ In.	177
Carrier, Utensil, Pine, Brown Paint, Curved Wood Handle, Softwood, 1800s, 12 x 31 In.	71
Churn, Dazey, Glass Body, Wood Handle, Crank Mechanism, 13 In. ....*illus*	52
Churn, Glass & Metal, Wood Handle, Crank, 8 Qt., 8 x 15½ In.....................*illus*	102
Churn, Pine, Barrel, Rocker, Wrought Iron Mounts, 25 x 34 x 14 In.	106
Churn, Wood, Crank, Stand, Standard Churn Co., 1910, 22 x 38 In.	250
Churn, Wood, Green Paint, Crank, 14 x 14 In.	102
Churn, Wood, Mustard Paint, Circular, Hand Crank, 15 In.	189
Churn, Wood, Round, Side Handle, Mustard Paint, 15 In. ....*illus*	189
Coffee Grinders are listed in the Coffee Mill category.	
Coffee Mills are listed in their own category.	
Coffeepot, Punched Tin, Basket Of Tulips, Gooseneck Spout, c.1850, 11½ x 11 x 7 In.	600
Cookie Board, Wood, Woman, Long Dress, Lace Bonnet, Pitcher, c.1850, 31 x 10½ x 1½ In....	88
Cookie Cutter, Man On Horseback, Tin, 8¼ x 8½ In...................*illus*	354
Cookie Cutter, Soldier, Tin, 10¾ In....................*illus*	177
Dough Box, Oak, Poplar, 2-Board Top, Breadboard Ends, Turned Legs, 1850s, 29 x 46 x 26 In. ..*illus*	750
Dough Box, Pine, Lid, Canted Sides, Turned Legs, c.1875, 30½ x 33½ In.....................*illus*	200
Dough Box, Walnut, Dancing Figures In A Landscape, Louis XV, 1700s, 39 x 61 x 22 In. ...*illus*	750
Doughnut Lifter, Cast Iron, Faschnautt, Scissor Type Mechanism, Patented 1888, 8 In.	52
Eggbeater, Brass, Stainless Steel, Bakelite Handle, USA, 1940s, 11¾ In......................	15
Eggbeater, Green Wood Handle, Marked A & J, c.1920, 12 x 5 In.	25
Flat Iron, Hood's Soapstone, Square Back, Pat. 1867, 6 x 4½ In.	79
Food Chopper, 6 Blade, Metal, Wood Handle, Patina, 1800s, 8 x 3 In.	32
Frying Pan, Copper, Oval, Tin Lined Brass Handles, France, 1¾ In.	54
Ice Chest, Oak, Lift Top, Zinc Washed Tin-Lined Interior, c.1910, 29 x 29 x 20 In..............*illus*	210
Icebox, Oak, 3 Drawers, Nickel Hardware, c.1920, 39½ x 27½ x 16½ In.	215
Icebox, Oak, Lift Top, Door In Front, Label, Leader, 36 x 19 In.....................*illus*	427
Iron, Detachable, Filakovd, Aqua Base, Red Handle, c.1900, 7¾ x 5 In. ....*illus*	226
Iron, Electric, Gabrifer, France, 1940s ....*illus*	51
Iron, Fluter, Brass Rollers, Royal 77, 1876, 5¾ In.	51
Iron, Fluter, Sun Dry, Roller Handle, 6 In...........................	62
Iron, Liquid Fuel Jet, Double Point, I Want U Comfort Gas, 8 x 6 In.	6
Iron, Peerless, Black, Tank Under Handle, 7½ In.	23
Iron, Sleeve, Sweeney No. 4, Pat.1898, 7¼ In.	68
Iron, Turned Chimney, Copper Heat Shield, Fletcher Russell & Co., 7 In.	85
Kettle, Copper, Tin Lined, Blue White Porcelain Handle, France, 8 x 7¼ x 7¼ In.................	55
Kettle, Hot Water, Embossed Lid, Iron, H. Wells & Bro., 1886, 8½ In.	120
Kettle, Sugar, Flared Rim, Deep Bowl, Iron, 1800s, 23½ x 55½ In.	3125
Kettle, Sugar, Flared Rim, Deep Bowl, Iron, 1800s, 31 x 73 In.	5313
Kettle, Tin, Hot Water, 2 Handles, Spout, 1800s, 12½ In.	75
Ladle, Straining, Iron, Wood Handle, 1800s, 43 In.......................	38
Ladle, Wrought Iron & Brass, Lollipop Hanging Ring, c.1797, 22⅝ In................	400
Lemon Press, Handheld, Wood & Metal, Brown, Will & Finck, 1800s, 10 In.	103
Mangle Board, Carved, Rib Surface, 35 x 7¼ In.	23
Match Holders can be found in their own category.	
Match Safes can be found in their own category.	
Milk Jug, Copper, Swing Handle, c.1900, 24½ x 10½, 5 Gal.	240
Mixer, Milk Shake, Cast Iron, Spoked Wheels, Pulleys, Oak Base, Ovaltine, 48 x 14 x 18 In.	1150
Mixer, Milk Shake, Green Porcelain Base, Hamilton Beach Co., c.1940, 18 x 8 x 6 In................	432
Mixing Bowl, Primitive, Wood, Dough, Butter, Tan, 14 x 8 In.........................	139
Mold, Cake, Castle Turret, 5 Tiers, Copper, 1900s, 10 x 9 In.	330
Mold, Cheese, Heart Shape, Punched Tin, Sunburst, Loop Handle, 4 x 6½ In.................*illus*	83

K

Kitchen, Churn, Glass & Metal, Wood Handle, Crank, 8 Qt., 8 x 15 ½ In.
$102

Kitchen, Churn, Wood, Round, Side Handle, Mustard Paint, 15 In.
$189

Kitchen, Cookie Cutter, Man On Horseback, Tin, 8 ¼ x 8 ½ In.
$354

Kitchen, Cookie Cutter, Soldier, Tin, 10 ¾ In.
$177

TIP
Some people say you should shine the chrome on your 1940s toaster with club soda or lemon juice.

Kitchen, Dough Box, Pine, Lid, Canted Sides, Turned Legs, c.1875, 30 ½ x 33 ½ In.
$200

Kitchen, Dough Box, Walnut, Dancing Figures In A Landscape, Louis XV, 1700s, 39 x 61 x 22 In.
$750

Kitchen, Dough Box, Oak, Poplar, 2-Board Top, Breadboard Ends, Turned Legs, 1850s, 29 x 46 x 26 In.
$750

TIP
A paste of baking soda and water can be used to clean old enameled cast-iron pots.

Kitchen, Ice Chest, Oak, Lift Top, Zinc Washed Tin-Lined Interior, c.1910, 29 x 29 x 20 In.
$210

Thomaston Place Auction Galleries

Kitchen, Icebox, Oak, Lift Top, Door In Front, Label, Leader, 36 x 19 In.
$427

Nadeau's Auction Gallery

Kitchen, Iron, Detachable, Filakovd, Aqua Base, Red Handle, c.1900, 7¾ x 5 In.
$226

Hartzell's Auction Gallery, Inc.

Kitchen, Iron, Electric, Gabrifer, France, 1940s
$51

Hartzell's Auction Gallery, Inc.

Kitchen, Mold, Cheese, Heart Shape, Punched Tin, Sunburst, Loop Handle, 4 x 6½ In.
$83

Hess Auction Group

Kitchen, Mold, Pudding, Copper, Round, 1800s, 7½ x 14½ In.
$120

Eldred's

Kitchen, Pie Crimper, Whale Ivory, Carved, Woman's Leg, Pierced Heart, Wheel, c.1850, 6¾ In.
$3,600

Eldred's

Kitchen, Rolling Pin, Walnut, Turned Whale Ivory Handles, Whaleman Made, c.1850, 13 In.
$2,160

Eldred's

Kitchen, Spice Box, Lid, Stencil Spices, 7 Fitted Canisters, Lids, c.1900, 9½ In.
$48

Eldred's

Kitchen, Spoon, Pineapple Shape, Crisscross Carving, Whalebone Handle, Shell Bowl, 1800s, 10 In.
$344

Eldred's

Kitchen, Stand, Cheese Wheel, Painted, Gilt, 1800s, 10¼ x 15 x 5½ In.
$236

Copake Auction

Mold, Chocolate, Bonzo Puppy, F.A. Reiche, c.1940s, 5 x 2 x 2 In.		128
Mold, Copper, VR & Crown, Tiered Sides, Benham & Froud, c.1900, 4 ½ x 5 In.		780
Mold, Fish, Pumpkin Glaze, Scales Interior, 1800s, 11 ½ In.		189
Mold, Heart Shape, Stainless Steel, Fried Egg, Pancake, 3 ¹⁵/₁₆ x 3 ¹⁵/₁₆ x ³/₁₆ In.		3
Mold, Ice Cream, English Crown, Pinned Hinge, Pewter, 2 Handles, 6 ½ x 10 In.		510
Mold, Pudding, Copper, Round, 1800s, 7 ½ x 14 ½ In.	*illus*	120
Mold, Candle, see Tinware category.		
Mortar & Pestle, Wood, Turned, Painted, Putty Color, 1800s, 13 In.		156
Muffineer, Regency, Mahogany, Octagonal Base, 1800s, 28 x 14 ¾ In.		338
Nut Cutter, Indian Brass, Betel, Sarota, c.1900, 2 x 2 ½ In.		115
Pie Crimper, Whale Ivory, Carved, Woman's Leg, Pierced Heart, Wheel, c.1850, 6 ¾ In.	*illus*	3600
Pie Crimper, Wheel Patina, Primitive, Metal, Scroll Handle		26
Potato Masher, Metal, Wood Handle, France		10
Press, Tie Machine, Countess Mara, Blue & Red, England		28
Press, Trouser, Watt's Upright, Wood, Metal, 30 ½ x 17 In.		11
Rack, Pot, Steel, Hanging, Contemporary, Chain, Hooks, 74 x 30 In.		250
Rack, Utensil, Pine, Wrought Iron Hooks, Old Red Surface, c.1800, 13 x 32 ¾ In.		281
Reamers are listed in their own category.		
Rolling Pin, Walnut, Turned Whale Ivory Handles, Whaleman Made, c.1850, 13 In.	*illus*	2160
Salt & Pepper Shakers are listed in their own category.		
Scoop, Ice Cream, Brass Frame, Beechwood Handle, Gilchrist, No. 31, c.1914, 10 ½ In.		48
Spatula, Stainless Steel, White Pearl Handle, Model No. 17, Cutco, 12 ½ In.		18
Spice Box, Lid, Stencil Spices, 7 Fitted Canisters, Lids, c.1900, 9 ½ In.	*illus*	48
Spice Box, Silver, Puffy Fish, Articulated, Glass Eyes, Hinged Mouth, c.1870, 5 x 2 ½ In.		1722
Spice Box, Wood, 3 Tiers, Red Paint, Turned Knobs, Molded Base, 1800s, 12 x 14 x 9 In.		2460
Spit Jack, Tin, Cast Iron Base, Brass Handle, Interior Geared Works, 1800s, 13 x 8 In.		120
Spoon, Pineapple Shape, Crisscross Carving, Whalebone Handle, Shell Bowl, 1800s, 10 In.	*illus*	344
Stand, Cheese Wheel, Painted, Gilt, 1800s, 10 ¼ x 15 x 5 ½ In.	*illus*	236
Sugar Nippers, Steel, Stamped At Throat, Clasp & Spring Handle, 1800s, 9 ⅝ In.		94
Sugar Nippers, Wrought Steel, Spring, Locking Grips, 1800s, 3 ½ x 9 ¼ In.	*illus*	66
Teapot, Brass Top, Copper Bottom, Knob & Handle Porcelain, c.1920, 11 x 8 In.		75
Teapot, Lid, Tetsubin, Loop Handle, Iron, Japan, 9 x 12 In.		83
Toaster, Electric, Art Deco, Edison Hotpoint Gazelle, c.1930, 7 x 8 x 5 In.		154
Toaster, Electric, Nickel Plated, Embossed, Landers Frary & Clark, c.1929, 9 x 8 x 5 In.		288
Toaster, Electric, Toast-O-Lator, Model J, 9 ¾ x 12 x 4 In.		128
Toaster, Wrought Iron, Wood Handle, Rectangular, 1800s, 10 x 15 In.		50
Tray, Utensil, Walnut, Scalloped, 1800s, 7 ½ x 16 x 9 ½ In.	*illus*	100
Trencher, Rough Hewn, Wood, Red Paint, Flowers, Scandinavia, c.1850, 4 x 25 In.		330
Trivet, see Trivet category.		
Waffle Iron, Cast Iron, Handle, Puritan, No. 8, Griswold, No. 975		61
Washboard, Wood Frame, Brass, Scrub Board, Tin, Backing, 12 ⅝ x 23 ½ x 2 ½ In.		17

Kitchen, Sugar Nippers, Wrought Steel, Spring, Locking Grips, 1800s, 3 ½ x 9 ¼ In. **$66**

Forsythes' Auctions

Kitchen, Tray, Utensil, Walnut, Scalloped, 1800s, 7 ½ x 16 x 9 ½ In. **$100**

Pook & Pook

Knife, Bowie, Bone Handle, Brown Sheath, Leather Case, 16 In. **$84**

Martin Auction Co.

KNIFE collectors usually specialize in a single type. In the 1960s, the United States government passed a law that required knife manufacturers to mark their knives with the country of origin. This seemed to encourage the collectors, and knife collecting became an interest of a large group of people. All types of knives are collected, from top quality twentieth-century examples to old bone- or pearl-handled knives in excellent condition.

Bowie, Bone Handle, Brown Sheath, Leather Case, 16 In.	*illus*	84
Bowie, Brass, Wood Handle, Stamped Palmetto Armory, 18 ¼ In.		219
Dagger, Carved Handle, Damascus Blade & Kris, Gilt Figure, Jeweled Brass Knob, 18 x ¾ In.		484
Dagger, Gray, Jade Handle, Mughal Style, 1900s, 15 ½ In.		813
Dagger, Mughal Style, Gilt Blade, 1900s, 19 ¾ In.		2000
Dagger, Steel, Wood, Silver, Brass, Sheath, Jambiya, Morocco, 16 In.		450
Display, 3 Jewels, Gold Gilt, Medallion, Case, 15 ½ In.		35
Folding, Handmade, Jay Bigler Inscribed On Blade, 6 ¼ In.		24
Hunting, Damascus Blade, Stag Handle, Brown Sheath, 8 In.		54
Lock Blade, Sheath, Delrin Handles, Back Packer, Puma, Germany, 1993, 4 ¼ In.		94
Pocket, 14K Gold Case, Tape Measure, Scissors, File, Fisherman's Basket, Reel, Fish, 4 ¼ In.		300

K

Kosta, Vase, Carved, Internal Purple Fishnet, Imitation Minnows, Vicke Lindstrand, 11 5/8 In.
$182

Humler & Nolan

Kutani, Bowl, Dragons, Multicolor, Gilt Lotus Scroll, Marked, Japan, 4 x 9 In.
$86

Skinner, Inc.

Kutani, Figurine, 2 Puppies Playing, White, Gilt Spots, Marked, 1800s, 7 x 7 x 5 1/2 In.
$242

Locati Auctions

Pocket, Doughboy & American Flag Photo, Camping Scene, Wilson, c.1918, 5 1/8 In.	266
Pocket, Eagle Handle, Folding, Single Blade, 4 1/4 In.	24
Pocket, Folding, 3 Blades, Winchester, 3 1/2 In.	36
Pocket, Multi Tool, Saw & Corkscrew, Horn Handle, Folding	30
Pocket, Sky Riders, Black Grips, 2 Blades, Folding, Colonial, 3 In.	95
Steel, Folding, Double, James Barber Sheffield, c.1910, 3 5/8 In.	105

KNOWLES, *Taylor & Knowles items may be found in the KTK and Lotus Ware categories.*

KOSTA

KOSTA, the oldest Swedish glass factory, was founded in 1742. During the 1920s through the 1950s, many pieces of original design were made at the factory. Kosta and Boda merged with Afors in 1964 and created the Afors Group in 1971. In 1976, the name Kosta Boda was adopted. The company merged with Orrefors in 1990 and is still working.

Sculpture, 2 Faces, Signed, Bertil Vallien, Kosta Boda Label, Sweden, 6 1/2 x 5 x 3 1/4 In.	338
Vase, Carved, Internal Purple Fishnet, Imitation Minnows, Vicke Lindstrand, 11 5/8 In.......*illus*	182

K.P.M KPM refers to Berlin porcelain, but the same initials were used alone and in combination with other symbols by several German porcelain makers. They include the Konigliche Porzellan Manufaktur of Berlin, initials used in mark, 1823–47; Meissen, 1723–24 only; Krister Porzellan Manufaktur in Waldenburg, after 1831; Kranichfelder Porzellan Manufaktur in Kranichfeld, after 1903; and the Krister Porzellan Manufaktur in Scheibe, after 1838.

Bottle, German Imperial Navy Flag, Cross, Sailor, White, 6 In.	73
Cake Stand, 2 Parts, Floral, Beaded, Gilt, Gold Rim, c.1950, 6 x 10 1/4 In.	42
Cup & Saucer, Flowers, Rococo Scrolls, Baroque Garden Motif, White	185
Cup, German Imperial Cross, Gilt, White, c.1914, 4 In.	183
Figurine, Europa & The Bull, Riding, Seminude, Both Legs To Side, 15 1/2 x 18 In.	172
Lithophane, see also Lithophane category.	
Plaque, Woman, Giltwood Frame, Signed, E. Volk, c.1900, 20 x 17 x 2 1/2 In.	5250
Plaque, Woman, Standing, Portrait, Gilt Frame, Signed, c.1900, 9 x 6 1/8 In.	2125
Plate, Flowers, Multicolor, Scrolled Edge, Gilt, c.1840, 11 In.	195
Plate, Venus U Amor, Cherubs, Reticulated Rim, Late 19th Century, 9 1/2 In.	950
Platter, Flower Sprays, Butterflies, Gilt Border, 13 x 10 In.	179
Platter, Snowcapped Mountains, Willow Trees, Gilt, c.1900, 13 1/2 x 9 3/4 In.	495
Urn, Cherubim, Architectural Masks, Floral Garlands, 2 Piece, Bolted Together, Painted, 11 x 12 In.	502

K.T.&K. CHINA KTK are the initials of the Knowles, Taylor & Knowles Company of East Liverpool, Ohio, founded by Isaac W. Knowles in 1853. The company made many types of utilitarian wares, hotel china, and dinnerware. It made belleek and the fine bone china known as Lotus Ware from 1891 to 1896. The company merged with American Ceramic Corporation in 1928. It closed in 1934. Lotus Ware is listed in its own category in this book.

Gravy Boat, White, Handle, Footed, 1880s, 9 x 5 In.	50
Jug, Whiskey, Painted, Multicolor Flowers, Gold Gilt Around Handle & Spout, 7 1/2 In.	75
Plate, Blue, Peach & White Flowers, Gilt Rim, 1920s, 10 In.	17
Vase, Tiger Motif, Brown, Green, c.1890, 10 1/2 x 6 In.	425

KUTANI porcelain was made in Japan after the mid-seventeenth century. Most of the pieces found today are nineteenth century. Collectors often use the term *Kutani* to refer to just the later, colorful pieces decorated with red, gold, and black pictures of warriors, animals, and birds.

Bowl, Dragons, Multicolor, Gilt Lotus Scroll, Marked, Japan, 4 x 9 In.................*illus*	86
Charger, Elephant, Figures All Over Surround, Grape & Vine Border, 1800s, 14 1/2 In.	200
Figurine, 2 Puppies Playing, White, Gilt Spots, Marked, 1800s, 7 x 7 x 5 1/2 In. ....*illus*	242
Figurine, Jurojin, Holding Fan & Staff, Wood Stand, Japan, 19 1/2 In.	154
Jar, Lid, Bulbous, Trumpeted Rim, Mouse Finial, 6 1/2 x 6 1/2 In.................*illus*	242
Jar, Lid, Flowers, Salmon Ground, Gilt, Cylindrical, 3-Footed, Figure In Kimono Finial, 9 In.	660
Tray, Samurai, Cherry Tree, Rust Red, Square, Notched Corners, Marked, c.1900, 14 In.	1080
Vase, Urn, Open Handles, Chickens, Herons, Flowers, Landscapes, 1800s, 8 x 18 1/4 In.	303

K

COLLECTING TRENDS:
ICONIC DESIGNERS OF TWENTIETH-CENTURY FURNITURE

**Important designers and companies made—and are still making—
sought-after pieces that can be collected today,
sometimes at attractive prices.**

Modern Design has become one of the hottest areas of collecting. The use of this furniture in today's advertising, television, and movies has added fuel to the interest in this period. Many vintage pieces can be found at house sales, flea markets, antique shops, and even "highbrow" auction houses. American furniture companies such as Knoll and Herman Miller hired great architects, artists, and industrial designers to design contemporary pieces after World War II. These architects and designers were prolific creators of stylish furniture, lighting, clocks, and useful household items.

Herman Miller and Knoll are so important to the boom in midcentury design that original pieces by the companies bring premium prices. When buying midcentury furniture, make sure that reproductions of their pieces are not confused with the originals.

Individual designers became important as well, and collectors today look for their now "classic" designs.

Herman Miller, Inc.

Herman Miller was founded in 1905 in Zeeland, Michigan, as the Star Furniture Company. In 1923, Herman Miller and his son-in-law purchased 51% of the company and renamed it the Herman Miller Furniture Company. In 1960, it became Herman Miller, Inc. Initially the company produced high quality furniture, particularly bedroom suites, in historic revival styles. Until 1930, the company made only traditional wood furniture. With the coming of the Great Depression in 1929, the company was forced to explore new products to survive in a shrinking market and reluctantly hired Gilbert Rohde, a designer who specialized in modernist designs. Rohde turned the company in a totally new direction, and, in 1933, Herman Miller debuted a line of modern furniture at the Century of Progress Exposition in Chicago. In 1941, the company opened a showroom in the Merchandise Mart in Chicago and another in New York City.

Rohde died in 1944 and was replaced by architect George Nelson, who joined the firm as director of design in 1945. Over the next four decades, Nelson had an enormous influence on Herman Miller, not only for his personal design contributions, but also for the talented designers he recruited to its ranks, including Isamu Noguchi and Charles and Ray Eames. Beginning in the late 1940s, the period under Nelson's guidance, Herman Miller produced some of the world's most iconic pieces of modern furniture, including the Noguchi table; the Eames lounge chair; and the Nelson Marshmallow sofa, Ball clock (actually made by Howard Miller Clock Company), and Sling sofa.

Knoll Company

Knoll was founded by Hans and Florence Knoll in 1938. The company has worked with world class industrial designers, architects, and artists for more than 80 years. Eero Saarinen designed the Womb chair in 1948 and the Tulip chair and table about 1956. Mies van der Rohe worked with Knoll beginning in 1953 and designed many pieces including the Barcelona chair. Other important Knoll furniture was designed by Marcel Breuer, Isamu Noguchi, and Frank Gehry.

Charles (1907–1978) and Ray (1912–1988) Eames

Charles and Ray Eames are among the most important designers of the 20th century. The Eameses are best known for their groundbreaking contributions to architecture, furniture design, industrial design, manufacturing, and the photographic arts.

Charles Eames was born in 1907 in St. Louis, Missouri. He attended school there and developed an interest in engineering and architecture. He was thrown out of Washington University in St. Louis, where he was on scholarship, for his advocacy of Frank Lloyd Wright. Eames worked at an architectural office before starting his own firm in 1930. He began extending his design ideas beyond architecture and received a fellowship to Cranbrook Academy of Art in Michigan, where he eventually became head of the design department.

Ray Kaiser Eames was born in 1912 in Sacramento, California. She studied painting with Hans Hofmann in New York before moving on to Cranbrook Academy where she met and assisted Charles Eames and Eero Saarinen in preparing designs for the Museum of Modern Art's Organic Furniture Competition. Eames' and Saarinen's designs, created by molding plywood into complex curves, won the two first prizes.

Charles and Ray married in 1941 and moved to California where they continued their furniture design work molding plywood. During World War II, they were commissioned by the United States Navy to make molded plywood splints, stretchers, and experimental glider shells. In 1946, Evans Products began producing the Eames molded plywood furniture. Their molded plywood chair was called "the chair of the century." Soon production was taken over by Herman Miller, Inc., which continues to make the furniture in the United States today. Vitra International manufactures the furniture in Europe.

Rago Arts and Auction Center

In 1949, Charles and Ray Eames designed and built their own home in Pacific Palisades, California, as part of the Case Study House Program sponsored by *Arts & Architecture* magazine. Their design and innovative use of materials made the house a mecca for architects and designers from both near and far. Today, it is considered one of the most important postwar residences anywhere in the world.

Above: Charles and Ray Eames ESU bookcase, fiberglass, enameled Masonite, birch plywood, zinc-plated and enameled steel, Herman Miller, 1950

Right: Charles and Ray Eames Lounge chair 671 and ottoman 670, rosewood plywood, leather, enameled aluminum and steel, Herman Miller, 1956 / c.1980

Los Angeles Modern Auctions (LAMA)

Above: George Nelson Ball wall clock, enameled brass, wood, enameled aluminum, Howard Miller Clock Co., 1949

George Nelson (1908–1986)

George Nelson was, together with Charles and Ray Eames, one of the founding fathers of American modernism. He was considered "The Creator of Beautiful and Practical Things."

Nelson was born in Hartford, Connecticut, in 1908. He graduated from Yale University, receiving a degree in architecture in 1928 and a second degree in fine arts in 1931. A year later, while preparing for the Paris Prize competition, he won the Rome Prize along with Eliot Noyes, Charles Eames, and Walter B. Ford.

Nelson was part of a generation of architects that found too few architectural projects so turned successfully toward product, graphic, and interior design. Based in Rome, he travelled throughout Europe where he met a number of the modernist pioneers. A few years later he returned to the United States to devote himself to writing. Through his writing in "Pencil Points," he introduced Walter Gropius, Mies van der Rohe, Le Corbusier, and Gio Ponti to North America. At the magazine *Architectural Forum*, he was first associate editor (1935–1943) and later consultant editor (1944–1949). He defended, sometimes ferociously, the modernist principles and irritated many of his colleagues who, he felt, as industrial designers made too many concessions to the commercial forces in industry.

By 1940, Nelson had drawn popular attention with several innovative concepts. In his postwar book *Tomorrow's House*, he introduced the concept of a "family room." Another of his ideas, the "storage wall," attracted the attention of D.J. De Pree, Herman Miller's president. In 1945, De Pree asked him to become Herman Miller's design director, an appointment that became the start of a long series of successful collaborations with Ray and Charles Eames, Harry Bertoia, Richard Schultz, Donald Knorr, and Isamu Noguchi. Although years later both Bertoia and Noguchi expressed regrets about their involvement, it became a uniquely successful period for the company and for George Nelson. He set new standards for the implementation of design in all facets of the company. In doing so, he pioneered the practice of corporate image management, graphic programs, and signage.

George Nelson's catalogue and exhibition designs for Herman Miller show how he made design the most important driving force in the company. From his start in the mid-1940s to his retirement in the mid-1980s, his office worked for and with the best designers of his time. At one point, even Ettore Sottsass worked at his office. Nelson was, without any doubt, the most articulate and one of the most eloquent voices on design and architecture in the U.S.A. of the 20th century. He was a teacher, prolific writer, and organizer of conferences including the legendary Aspen gatherings. Among his best-known designs are the Marshmallow sofa, Coconut chair, Catenary group, colorful clocks, and many other products that became milestones in the history of a profession that he helped to shape.

Above: George Nelson Marshmallow sofa, Naugahyde, enameled and chrome-plated steel, Herman Miller, 1956. The Marshmallow sofa is made of 18 marshmallow-like circles. Each circle was made by hand and, therefore, very expensive to produce. Originally, only 200 were made.

Harry Bertoia (1915–1978)

Harry Bertoia was a gifted artist. Knoll historian Brian Lutz once said, "Bertoia's paintings were better than his sculptures. And his sculptures were better than his furniture. And his furniture was absolutely brilliant."

After studying at the Detroit Technical High School and the Detroit School of Arts and Crafts, Harry Bertoia opened his own metal workshop at the Cranbrook Academy of Art where he taught jewelry design and metal work. In 1946, he moved to California to help fellow Cranbrook alumnus Charles Eames develop methods of laminating and bending plywood. Bertoia's contributions to the famous Eames chairs were crucial even though not well known.

On the suggestion of Herbert Matter, who had worked alongside Eames and Bertoia, Florence and Hans Knoll traveled to California and encouraged Bertoia to move east and set up his own metal shop in a corner of Knoll's production facility. Having studied with Bertoia at Cranbrook, Florence was sure that he would produce something extraordinary if given the time and space to experiment.

Characteristic of the early environment at Knoll, Hans and Florence never demanded that Bertoia design furniture, but instead encouraged him to explore whatever he liked. They simply asked that if he arrived at something interesting, to show them. Bertoia did arrive at something outstanding, his iconic wire furniture collection. Introduced in 1952, it is recognized worldwide as one of the great achievements of 20th-century furniture design.

Los Angeles Modern Auctions (LAMA)

Above: Harry Bertoia Bird chair and ottoman, chrome-plated steel, upholstery, and rubber, Knoll International, 1952 / 1999

Right: Harry Bertoia Diamond chair, chrome-plated steel, upholstery, and rubber, Knoll Associates, 1952

Los Angeles Modern Auctions (LAMA)

Eero Saarinen (1910–1961)

Eero Saarinen was born to famous parents, architect and Cranbrook Academy of Art director Eliel Saarinen and textile artist Loja Saarinen. He was surrounded by design his entire life and he began helping his father design furniture and fixtures for the Cranbrook campus in his teens. In 1929 Eero went to Paris, where he studied sculpture for a year before enrolling in the Yale architecture program. In 1934, he returned to Michigan to teach at Cranbrook, work on furniture designs, and practice architecture with his father.

It was at Cranbrook that Saarinen met Charles Eames. The two young men, both committed to the exploration of potential new materials and processes, quickly became great friends, pushing each other creatively while collaborating on several projects. The most notable outcome of their partnership was the groundbreaking collection of molded plywood chairs for the MoMA-sponsored 1940 Organic Design in

Wright

Above: Eero Saarinen Tulip chair, Model 151, laminate, enameled aluminum, molded fiberglass, and upholstery, Knoll International, 1956

Below Right: Eero Saarinen Womb chair and ottoman, upholstery and enameled steel, Knoll Associates, 1946

Home Furnishings competition. Their collection was awarded first prize in all categories, catapulting the young designers to the forefront of the American modern furniture movement.

Saarinen also met Florence Knoll at Cranbrook, who at that time was a promising young protégé of Eliel Saarinen. Florence spent all her free time with the Saarinen family, including summer vacations to Finland. Florence and Eero developed a brother-and-sister-like relationship that would last the rest of their lives. When Florence joined Knoll in the 1940s, it was an obvious choice for her to invite Eero to design for the company.

Over the next 15 years, Saarinen designed many of the most recognizable Knoll pieces, including the Tulip chairs and tables, Womb chair, and 70 Series seating collection. Eero, who was known for being obsessed with revision, took a sculptural approach to furniture design, building hundreds of models and full-scale mock-ups to achieve the perfect curve, find the right line, and derive the most pleasing proportions. His designs, which employed modern materials in graceful, organic shapes, helped establish the reputation and identity of Knoll during its formative years.

In addition to his achievements in furniture, Eero Saarinen was a leader of the second-generation modernists. Constantly pushing boundaries, Saarinen expanded the modern vocabulary to include curvilinear and organically inspired forms not found in the work of his predecessors. Among his outstanding projects are the Dulles International Airport in Virginia (metro Washington, D.C.); the Gateway Arch in St. Louis, Missouri; the TWA Terminal at Kennedy International Airport; and the CBS Building in New York City.

Los Angeles Modern Auctions (LAMA)

Russel Wright (1904–1976)

Russel Wright was an unusual combination of American craftsman, industrial designer, and naturalist. Born to Quaker parents in Lebanon, Ohio, in 1904, he grew up and began his professional career during a period of profound changes, when Americans began enjoying the benefits of enormous new wealth. This frenzy was obvious in the designs of the 1920s, from costumes to interiors to furniture and accessories. Then came the crash of 1929 and the Depression, when people felt a need for unity and a symbol of hope. "Streamlining" became the American symbol, representing the power and speed of the machine.

Wright was very aware that the Depression brought a totally different way of living. No one could afford household help to polish silver, handle porcelain dishes with care, wash clothes, and serve meals. His insight that Americans wanted homes that were well designed and easy to care for led him to produce a series of housewares and furnishings made of easily maintained materials such as solid wood, spun aluminum, stainless steel, earthenware, paper, and plastic, that made him a household name. As he and his wife Mary, also a designer as well as a businesswoman, noted in their timely 1950 book, *Guide to Easier Living,*

"our main thesis here is that formality is not necessary for beauty."

An independent thinker, not a follower of the newest trends, Wright helped create the concept of the industrial designer, an American phenomenon that emerged during the 1920s. An industrial designer is known for designing everything, for being a problem solver, and for being able to design for mass production. Unlike most industrial designers of his age, Wright designed mainly for the home.

Wright also brought his special talents on the relationship between design and the natural environment. In the 1950s, he began to create an ecologically sensitive woodland garden on his estate, Manitoga, in Garrison, New York. He had already begun building a residence and studio there named Dragon Rock to explore ways of bringing daily life closer to nature. During the 1960s, he became a consultant to the National Park Service and focused on bringing people into the parks to enjoy nature.

Above: Russel Wright Oceana tray, olivewood, Klise Woodworking, 1935

Right: Russel Wright American Modern pitcher, glazed stoneware, Steubenville Pottery, 1939

Etsy

Wright was a craftsman at heart who wanted to make household pieces that were beautiful, useful, reasonably priced, and available to everybody. Every newlywed couple from the late 1930s through the 1950s knew his name, stamped on the bottom of their new china, along with all the other useful and handsome objects that made them proud to be Americans. Today his pieces are prized by museums and avid collectors everywhere.

Wright

Above: Gio Ponti Leggera chair, walnut and jute, Cassina, Italy, 1952

Gio Ponti (1891–1979)

Gio Ponti was an Italian architect, artist, and designer, known for his role in erecting the Pirelli Tower (1956–1959) in Milan, Italy. He brought his modern aesthetic to buildings, interiors, and furnishings, as well as to domestic design, based on the belief that all pieces of a structure should work in harmony. "Industry is the style of the 20th century, its mode of creation," Ponti once said. Born Giovanni Ponti on November 18, 1891, in Milan, his tastes evolved from Neoclassicism toward Modernism over the course of his career. He studied architecture at Politecnico di Milano University, graduating in 1921. The founding editor of *Domus* magazine in 1928, Ponti used the publication to express his own beliefs on architecture and design. Later working within industrial design, the artist created iconic pieces of furniture such as the Distex armchair (1953) and the Superleggera chair (1957). Ponti died on September 16, 1979, in Milan. Today, his works are in the collections of the Museum of Modern Art in New York, the

Victoria and Albert Museum in London, and the Art Institute of Chicago among others.

Ettore Sottsass (1917–2007)

Ettore Sottsass was born in Innsbruck, Austria, in 1917. If you know the name Ettore Sottsass, it is probably because you are aware of Memphis, the design collective he spearheaded in the 1980s. It remains one of his most well-known achievements. But the true force of the designer's character is much bigger than any single movement and was refined throughout various moments of his career.

Bunch Auctions

Above: Gio Ponti Model 2129 cabinet, walnut, Singer & Sons, Italy, c.1950

In December 1980, Memphis was born when a group of designers got together in Sottsass's small Milan apartment. They had been listening to Bob Dylan records, and the group's cheeky name is in part a reference to his song, "Stuck Inside of Mobile with the Memphis Blues Again," as well as the ancient capital of Egypt and the modern city in Tennessee. Though Sottsass has been considered the group's leader, that is not a position Sottsass would have wanted to take on. "He detested any type of institution or hierarchy," the designer's widow, Barbara Radice, once noted. "He didn't like anything that told you what to do. He believed everybody should find their own way of doing things." From its debut at Milan's 1981 *Salone del Mobile*, the movement sent ripples through the design community. In 1982 in New York, Sottsass organized the first stateside exhibition of Memphis, titled "Memphis at Midnight," which opened to an eager crowd of more than 3,000 people waiting to cram inside the Chelsea loft showroom where the works were displayed.

The Milan-based collective of designers banded together to challenge the design principles they had been taught. They employed unexpected forms, bold colors, graphic patterns, and cheap materials—like plastic—to forge a new approach to design. If there was such a thing as a "Memphis style," it was characterized by an attitude more than anything else.

Sottsass left Memphis after a few years, and in 1985 he founded his own practice, Sottsass Associati, a firm that continues to operate today. His focus once again turned to architecture, with projects like the design of Milan's new Malpensa airport in 2000. Though Sottsass

Rago Arts and Auction Center

Left: Ettore Sottsass Carlton bookcase, laminate over plywood, Memphis, Italy, 1981

Below: Ettore Sottsass Valentine typewriter, plastic, enameled steel, and rubber, Olivetti, Italy / Spain, 1969

Palm Beach Modern Auctions

tended to describe himself as first and foremost an architect, he was something of a "Renaissance man." He was also an industrial designer, a painter, a writer, a curator, and a photographer.

If one characteristic defined Sottsass more than others, it was his insatiable curiosity. He drew inspiration from a spectrum of sources, like literature, anthropology, ethnology, geography, and archaeology. He was an avid photographer and took thousands of photographs.

Throughout his work, color played a critical role and was an ongoing preoccupation. He was captivated by its ability to evoke memories and emotions. Red was important to him not just because it carried a bold presence, but for what it symbolized. Red is "the color of the Communist flag, the color that makes a surgeon move faster and the color of passion," he would say.

For Sottsass, designing was a more complex endeavor than just building a house or creating a new consumer object. "Ettore thought that design should help people become more aware of their existence: the space they live in, how to arrange it, and their own presence in it," explained Radice. "That was the core of Ettore."

Gaetano Pesce (1939–present)

Born in La Spezia, Italy, in 1939 and educated in Venice, Gaetano Pesce has become prominent in several fields—architecture, interior design, graphics, and film. He had numerous projects in architecture, including the Hubin apartment in Paris (1986), the Organic Building in Osaka, Japan (1990), the Gallery Mourmans in Knokke-le-Zoute, Belgium (1994), the Schuman residence in New York (1994), the office for the advertising agency TBWA\Chiat\Day in Los Angeles (1994), and monumental glass design elements for the Palais des Beaux-Arts of Lille, France (1996). The architect's reputation has also been built upon experimentation in the area of industrial design and furnishings, including development of a series of now iconic chairs (like the Up series), tables and lamps. In addition to maintaining long-standing relationships with such landmark furniture manufacturers as B&B Italia, Cassina, and Vitra International, Pesce launched the New York City companies Fish Design and Open Sky to develop and manufacture home design objects, lighting, and jewelry for the consumer market. Gaetano Pesce's work is represented in the permanent collections of leading museums internationally, including both the Museum of Modern Art and the Metropolitan Museum of Art in New York City, the San Francisco Museum of Modern Art, the Victoria and Albert Museum in London, and the Musée des Arts Décoratifs and Centre Georges Pompidou in Paris. He was honored in 1996 with a career retrospective at the Centre Pompidou.

Left: Gaetano Pesce UP-5 chair (also called La Mamma) and UP-6 ottoman, stretch fabric over polyurethane foam and rubber, marked Series 2000, B&B, Italy, 1969 / 2000

Right: Gaetano Pesce Feltri chair, felt, upholstery, and rope, Cassina, Italy, 1987

Ahlers & Ogletree Auction Company

Wright

OTHER IMPORTANT 20TH-CENTURY FURNITURE DESIGNERS

Ron Arad (1951–present). British-Israeli industrial designer, artist, and architectural designer. One of the most prolific current designers of mass-produced and limited-edition series of furniture. Well-known designs include the Rover and Pappardelle chairs.

Marcel Breuer (1902–1981). Hungarian born modernist architect and furniture designer. Most famous for his Wassily chair.

Right: Ron Arad Rover chair, enameled steel, Kee-Klamps, Rover car seat, One Off, United Kingdom, 1981

Left: Marcel Breuer Short chair, bent birch plywood, Isokon Furniture Company Ltd., London, c.1936

Rago Arts and Auction Center

Phillips

Left: Wendell Castle Zephyr chair, walnut, 1973

Below: Paul Evans Directional cabinet, patchwork, mixed metals, steel, 1970s

Wendell Castle (1932–2018). American furniture maker and leading figure of the American craft movement. Credited with being the father of the art furniture movement.

Cottone Auctions

Paul Evans (1931–1987). American furniture designer and sculptor. Prominent in the American Craft movement of the 1970s. Best known for his metal-clad furniture, the Cityscape and Patchwork series.

Michael Graves (1934–2015). American architect and industrial designer. Member of the famous New York Five architects and the Memphis group. Best known industrial design was the Whistling Bird Teakettle for Alessi.

Michael Graves Whistling Bird teakettle, stainless steel, Alessi, 1985

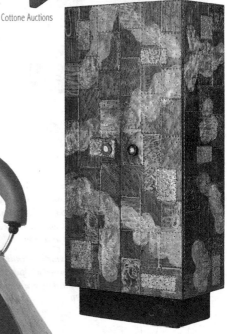

Rago Arts and Auction Center

Rago Arts and Auction Center

Finn Juhl (1912–1989). Danish architect and interior designer best known for furniture design, including his Chieftain chair introduced in 1949.

Vladimir Kagan (1927–2016). American furniture designer, known for very biomorphic sofas and chairs.

Above: Finn Juhl Chieftain chair, teak, leather, Baker, Denmark / USA, 1949 / 1970s

Right: Vladimir Kagan Sculpted rocking chair and ottoman, walnut and upholstery, Kagan-Dreyfuss, Inc., c.1953

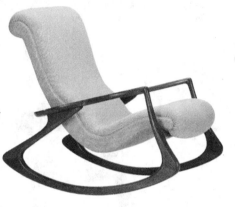

Wright

James D. Julia
(a division of Morphy Auctions)

Warren McArthur (1885–1961). American designer best known for his aluminum furniture which he began to design in 1929.

Alessandro Mendini (1931–2019). Italian designer and architect. Important in Italian, postmodern, and radical design movements. Best known for his Proust chair designed in 1978.

Above: Warren McArthur Biltmore chair, variation, originally designed for the Biltmore Hotel, Phoenix. Aluminum, vinyl, rubber armrests and discs, 1933 and later

Right: Alessandro Mendini Poltrona di Proust armchair, fabric and wood hand painted by Francesco Migliaccio, 1979–80

Phillips

Ludwig Mies van der Rohe (1886–1969). German American architect, considered one of the pillars of modern architecture. Director of the Bauhaus from 1930–1933. Known for his "less is more" style.

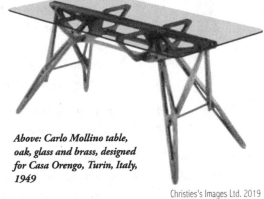

Carlo Mollino (1905–1973). Italian architect and designer. Most famous table is his oak and glass table made for the Casa Orengo in Turin, Italy that sold for $3,824,000 at Christie's in 2005.

George Nakashima (1905–1990). American architect and furniture maker known as one of the fathers of the American craft movement. Best known for his exquisitely made custom designed tables and chairs using exotic woods, often with raw edges.

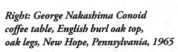

Isamu Noguchi (1904–1988). Japanese-American artist and landscape architect. Best known for his sculptures, furniture, and lamps. Most famous piece of furniture was the Noguchi cocktail table.

Warren Platner (1919–2006). American architect and furniture designer. Designed Windows of the World restaurant in New York City. His famous Platner chairs and tables, manufactured by Knoll, are still desirable today.

Wright

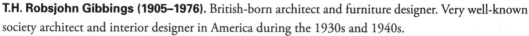

Quittenbaum Kunstauktionen GmbH

Gerrit Thomas Rietveld (1888–1964). Dutch furniture designer and architect. Principal member of the De Stijl artistic movement. Most known for his Red and Blue chair.

T.H. Robsjohn Gibbings (1905–1976). British-born architect and furniture designer. Very well-known society architect and interior designer in America during the 1930s and 1940s.

Philippe Starck (1949–). French designer best known for interior and product design including furniture. He has designed everything from interiors for the president of France to cell phones, speedboats, hotels, and even toilet brushes. Still going strong at 70 years of age.

Robert Venturi (1925–2018). American architect best known as one of the founders of the postmodern movement in the U.S. Known for his saying "less is a bore" as a knock to Mies Van der Rohe's "less is more." Designed wonderful series of chairs for Knoll in the 1980s.

Wright

Hans Wegner (1914–2007). Danish furniture designer considered one of the icons of Scandinavian design. Designed more tha n 500 chairs in his career, including "The Chair," 1949, one of the most elegant chairs of the 20th century.

Skinner, Inc.

Wright

L.G. WRIGHT Glass Company of New Martinsville, West Virginia, started selling glassware in 1937. Founder "Si" Wright contracted with Ohio and West Virginia glass factories to reproduce popular pressed glass patterns like Rose & Snow, Baltimore Pear, and Three Face, and opalescent patterns like Daisy & Fern and Swirl. Collectors can tell the difference between the original glasswares and L.G. Wright reproductions because of colors and differences in production techniques. Some L.G. Wright items are marked with an underlined *W* in a circle. Items that were made from old Northwood molds have an altered Northwood mark—an angled line was added to the *N* to make it look like a *W*. Collectors refer to this mark as "the wobbly W." The L.G. Wright factory was closed and the existing molds sold in 1999. Some of the molds are still being used.

Candy Dish,	Knobby Turtle, Amber Glass, Green Shades, 8 In.	41
Daisy & Button,	Plate, Square, Amberina, Red & Yellow, 5 ½ In.	16
Daisy & Cube,	Lamp, Oil, Amber, Stars & Bars, Button, Miniature, 8 ¾ In.	33
Hen On Nest,	Candy Dish, Amethyst, Purple, Glass, 1967, 5 In.	69
Moon & Stars,	Lamp, Kerosene Oil, Amethyst Glass, Miniature, 9 ¼ x 2 ⅜ In.	91
Moon & Stars,	Toothpick Holder, Vaseline, Satin, Pearline, Yellow	28
Pitcher,	Water, Blue Opalescent, Flared & Crimped Rim, Reeded Handle, 1900s, 9 In.	82
Purple Slag,	Dish, Hen On Nest Cover, Marbled, Milk Glass, 7 x 5 In.	26
Swirl,	Cruet, Cranberry, Opalescent, Stopper, 6 ½ In.	19

LACQUER is a type of varnish. Collectors are most interested in the Chinese and Japanese lacquer wares made from the Japanese varnish tree. Lacquer wares are made from wood with many coats of lacquer. Sometimes the piece is carved or decorated with ivory or metal inlay.

Basket,	Wedding, Lid, 3 Sections, Metal Bail Handle, Chinese, c.1950, 26 x 19 In.	89
Bottle,	Sake, Gold, Fan, Cherry Blossoms, Squared Shoulder, Stopper, 1800s, 8 ¾ In.	480
Bowl,	Sake, Gold, Mons & Leaves, Nashi Ground, River Inside, Flared Foot, 5 x 9 In.	375
Box,	Black, Red Interior, Burmese, 1900s, 6 ½ x 18 x 12 In.	500
Box,	Cherry Tree In Landscape, Calligraphy, Black & Gold, 3 Sections, 5 x 5 In.	594
Box,	Eggplant Shape, Gilt, Grasshopper, Japan, 2 x 3 ⅜ In. *illus*	615
Box,	Hinged Lid, Prince Igor, Scenic, Kholuj, Russia, 2 x 8 x 6 In.	118
Box,	Lid, 3 Drawers, Black, Gilt, Red, Flowers, Fitted Interior, c.1900, 8 x 11 In. *illus*	406
Box,	Red, 2 Parts, Children, Good Luck Symbols, Chinese, 1900s, 5 x 19 x 12 In.	367
Box,	Red, Carved, Flower Shape, Daoist Immortals, Buddhist Emblems, c.1900, 8 In.	4000
Box,	Red, Carved, Landscape, Scholars Underneath Pine, Children Playing, c.1900, 2 In.	1250
Box,	Scene, 2 Men On Top, Gilt Decoration On Sides, Russia, 4 ½ x 4 x 4 In. *illus*	1017
Box,	Waterfall, Burnished, Silver & Coral Inlay, Round, 9 Fruit Shape Jars, 5 In.	3120
Box,	Writing, Suzuribako, Firefly, Plum Blossoms, Black & Gold, 9 In.	780
Butsudan,	Black, Doors, Metal, Inside Doors, Gilt, Drawers, c.1900, 35 x 25 In. *illus*	406
Cabinet,	Black & Multicolor, 4 Doors, Gilt, 1900s, 76 x 27 x 13 In.	188
Cabinet,	Boulle, Marble Top, Ormolu Female Busts, Louis XIV Style, 44 x 38 x 15 In.	431
Cabinet,	Carved, 6 Drawers, 4 Shelves, Scroll Feet, 1800s, 20 x 14 x 9 ⅜ In.	1250
Cabinet,	Corner, Black, 2 Doors, Women Playing Instruments, Chinese, 72 x 37 x 19 In.	384
Cabinet,	Red, Doors, Circular Metal Lock, Block Legs, Chinese, 71 x 44 x 22 In.	500
Figure,	Ebisu, Patron Of Fisherman, Lacquer & Ivory, S. Getsuko, Box, Late 1800s, 4 x 2 In.	252
Inro,	2 Tiers, Dark Brown, Plant & Cricket, Mother-Of-Pearl, Japan, 2 ¼ x 2 ¼ In.	92
Inro,	4 Tiers, Figures & Willow Tree, Black, Japan, 2 ¾ x 2 ¼ In. *illus*	123
Inro,	4 Tiers, Rocky Shore & Tree, Japan, 2 ¾ x 2 In.	62
Inro,	Box, 4 Compartments, Black, Ivory & Metal Samurai, Landscape, Japan, 3 In.	720
Inro,	Box, 4 Compartments, Gold, River Landscape, Hirakawa, Japan, 3 ¼ In.	780
Jardiniere,	Red, Lion Mask, Ring Handles, Figures, Landscape, 19 x 21 In.	1020
Lamp Base,	Electric, 4-Sided Hu Shape, Landscapes, Lotus Scroll, Wood Stand, 1900s, 12 In.	584
Plaque,	Black & Gold, Sparrow, Snail, Frog, Flowers, 18th Century, 15 x 24 In.	720
Shrine,	Buddhist, Pull-Out Doors, Shelf, Japan, 1800s, 48 x 18 x 14 In.	875
Shrine,	Portable, Gold Lacquer, Cylindrical, 2 Doors, Buddha, Standing, 5 ⅛ In.	1046
Table,	Scholar, Mother-Of-Pearl, Inlaid Hardwood, Chinese, 9 x 22 ½ x 14 ½ In.	425
Tray,	Black, Octagonal, Mother-Of-Pearl, 1600s, 13 ⅝ In.	1875

Kutani, Jar, Lid, Bulbous, Trumpeted Rim, Mouse Finial, 6 ½ x 6 ½ In. $242

Fontaine's Auction Gallery

TIP

If you have to deal with a flood from melting snow, pipes breaking, or overflowing streams, it's a mess. Don't store anything cardboard on the floor. Use plastic storage containers with tight lids or make a platform with wooden crates.

L

Lacquer, Box, Eggplant Shape, Gilt, Grasshopper, Japan, 2 x 3 ⅜ In. $615

Skinner, Inc.

LACQUER

Lacquer, Box, Lid, 3 Drawers, Black, Gilt, Red, Flowers, Fitted Interior, c.1900, 8 x 11 In.
$406

Eldred's

Lacquer, Box, Scene, 2 Men On Top, Gilt Decoration On Sides, Russia, 4 ½ x 4 x 4 In.
$1,017

Soulis Auctions

Lacquer, Inro, 4 Tiers, Figures & Willow Tree, Black, Japan, 2 ¾ x 2 ¼ In.
$123

Clars Auction Gallery

Lacquer, Trousseau Chest, Red & Black, Quatrefoil, Bronze, 5 Tiers, Wood, Chinese, 34 x 18 In.
$679

Aspire Auctions

Lacquer, Butsudan, Black, Doors, Metal, Inside Doors, Gilt, Drawers, c.1900, 35 x 25 In.
$406

Eldred's

Lalique, Bookends, Reverie, Kneeling Nude, Female, Frosted, Marked, Box, 8 ½ x 5 In.
$1,708

Neal Auction Company

Lalique, Box, Cigar, Sultane, Frosted, Sepia, Geometrics, Seated Nude Handle, 1928, 6 In.
$3,250

Rago Arts and Auction Center

Lalique, Figurine, Chat Couche, Cat, Crouching, Frosted, 1945, 4 ½ x 9 ¼ x 2 ½ In.
$325

Heritage Auctions

L

Tray, Kimono, Plum Blossom & Zigzags, Black & Gold, Kiriwood Box, 20 x 14 In.	600
Tray, Parcel Gilt, Maroon, Flower, Butterflies, Regency, c.1820, 19 x 29¾ x 22 In.	750
Tray, Social Scene, Vignettes & Medallions, Rectangular, 1800s, 19 x 24½ In.	148
Triptych, Buddha, 2 Acolytes, Moon, Sun & Clouds, Black, Inlaid Metal, c.1860, 5 In.	1560
Trousseau Chest, Red & Black, Quatrefoil, Bronze, 5 Tiers, Wood, Chinese, 34 x 18 In. ...illus	679
Trunk, Storage, 9 Imperial Dragons, Silver Gilt, Iron Red, Chinese, 19 x 45 x 20 In.	366
Vase, Globular, Long Neck, Banded Rim, Marbled, Wood Stand, Chinese, 13¾ In.	338

LADY HEAD VASE, *see Head Vase.*

LALIQUE glass and jewelry were made by Rene Lalique (1860-1945) in Paris, France, between the 1890s and his death in 1945. Beginning in 1921 he had a manufacturing plant in Alsace. The glass was molded, pressed, and engraved in Art Nouveau and Art Deco styles. Most pieces were marked with the signature *R. Lalique*. Lalique glass is still being made. Most pieces made after 1945 bear the mark *Lalique*. After 1978 the registry mark was added and the mark became *Lalique ® France*. In the prices listed here, this is indicated by Lalique (R) France. Some pieces that are advertised as ring dishes or pin dishes were listed as ashtrays in the Lalique factory catalog and are listed as ashtrays here. Names of pieces are given here in French and in English. The Lalique brand was bought by Art & Fragrance, a Swiss company, in 2008. Lalique and Art & Fragrance both became part of the Lalique Group in 2016. Lalique is still being made. Jewelry made by Rene Lalique is listed in the Jewelry category.

R. LALIQUE. FRANCE	LALIQUE FRANCE	Lalique ® France
Lalique c.1925–1930s	Lalique 1945–1960	Lalique 1978+

Bookends, Reverie, Kneeling Nude, Female, Frosted, Marked, Box, 8½ x 5 In. ...illus	1708
Bowl, Caviar Server, Lid, Igor, Dolphin Shape Finial, Silver Plate Frame, 9¾ x 7 In.	498
Bowl, Champs-Elysees, Chestnut Leaves, 7½ x 18 x 10 In.	492
Bowl, Floral, Frosted Glass, Marked Lalique France, 12 In.	213
Bowl, Nemours, Graduated Flower Heads, Concave, 1950, 10 In.	192
Bowl, Ondines, Water Nymphs, Opalescent, c.1921, 3 x 8 In.	431
Bowl, Persepolis, Clear & Frosted, Green, 7 x 11½ In.	1188
Bowl, Pinsons, Finches, Bird & Vine, Frosted & Polished, c.1950, 3½ x 9½ In.	165
Bowl, Poissons, Fish, Blue, Swirls, 10½ In.	450
Box, Cigar, Sultane, Frosted, Sepia, Geometrics, Seated Nude Handle, 1928, 6 In. ...illus	3250
Caviar Set, Cooler, Bowl, Metal Support, 3-Fish Footring, France, 10 x 7¾ In.	531
Clock, Clear & Frosted, Curious Cat, Molded Base, 1945, 7½ x 7⅜ x 2⅛ In.	438
Clock, Clear & Frosted, Iris, Marked, Switzerland, Late 1900s, 6¾ x 8 x 3½ In.	325
Clock, Deux Colombes, 2 Doves, Opalescent, Enameled Metal, Molded R. Lalique, Ato, 8⅝ In.	3750
Compote, Pinsons, Birds On Stem, Incise Signature, France, 1900s, 3½ In.	72
Compote, Virginia Peacock, France, 1900s, 7 In.	313
Dish, Ring, Frosted Etched Figure, Marked, 4 In.	169
Dresser Box, Swan Parade, Frosted, France, 4 In.	127
Figurine, Chameleon, Green, Incised Signature, France, 2½ In.	63
Figurine, Chat Couche, Cat, Crouching, Frosted, 1945, 4½ x 9¼ x 2½ In. ...illus	325
Figurine, Deux Poissons, 2 Fish, Frosted, Round Base, 11½ x 10 x 5½ In. ...illus	1089
Figurine, Elephant, Frosted, Rectangular Glass Base, France, 1900s, 6 In.	132
Figurine, Firebird, Phoenix, Incised Signature, France, 1900s, 4 In.	156
Figurine, Frog, Gregoire, Green Frosted, Signed, France, 3 x 4½ x 4½ In. ...illus	250
Figurine, Horse, Frosted, France, 4 In.	230
Figurine, Liberty Eagle, Standing, Etched, Frosted & Clear, 9 x 5 x 5¾ In.	380
Figurine, Lionne Simba, Lioness, Clear, Frosted, France, Marked, 5½ x 9½ In.	393
Figurine, Nude Woman, Swan, Frosted, France, 4½ In.	104
Figurine, Oceanide, Nude Woman, Frosted, Signed, France, 17½ In.	3750
Figurine, Pigeon, Mounted, Signed, France, c.1934, 4¼ x 11 x 4¼ In.	666
Figurine, Sirene, Mermaid Shape, Incised Signature, 3¾ In.	188
Hood Ornament, Coq Houdan, Rooster, Auto, Clear, 8 In.	6550
Hood Ornament, Coq Nain, Dwarf Cockerel, Topaz, Marked, 8 In.	2750

Lalique, Figurine, Deux Poissons, 2 Fish, Frosted, Round Base, 11½ x 10 x 5½ In. **$1,089**

Fontaine's Auction Gallery

Lalique, Figurine, Frog, Gregoire, Green Frosted, Signed, France, 3 x 4½ x 4½ In. **$250**

Susanin's Auctioneers & Appraisers

TIP
Valuable glass should not be washed in a dishwasher.

Lalique, Paperweight, Elephant, Frosted Body, Clear Base, Signed, France, 6 x 4 x 6 In. **$275**

Forsythes' Auctions

This is an edited listing of current prices. Visit **Kovels.com** to check thousands of prices from previous years and sign up for free information on trends, tips, reproductions, marks, and more.

Lalique, Statue, Suzanne, Woman, Drapery, Yellow Amber, R. Lalique, Etched France, 1925, 9 x 7 In.
$11,875

Rago Arts and Auction Center

Lalique, Vase, Andromeda, Fish Scale, Frosted, Marie Claude, 5 3/4 x 6 In.
$201

Charleston Estate Auctions

Lalique, Vase, Bacchantes, Female Nudes, Clear & Frosted, 1990s, Label, Lalique, Paris, 9 1/2 In.
$1,500

Rago Arts and Auction Center

Hood Ornament, Eagle Head, Frosted, Molded, Marked, 1920s, 5 1/4 x 5 1/2 In.	437
Lamp, Ceiling Fixture, Flowers Background, 4 Silk Ropes, Signed, R. Lalique France, 12 In.	1792
Paperweight, Apple, Stopper Lid, 1900s, 7 In.	113
Paperweight, Elephant, Frosted Body, Clear Base, Signed, France, 6 x 4 x 6 In. ....*illus*	275
Perfume Bottle, 2 Flowers, France, 4 In.	127
Perfume Bottle, Phoenix, Covering Factice, France, 1900s, 7 In.	156
Plate, Algues, Seaweed, Black Frosted, France, Signed, 8 In.	61
Plate, Fleurons, Flowers, Opalescent, Signed Rene Lalique, France, 1 3/4 x 10 In.	375
Platter, Chene, Oak Leaves, Clear & Frosted, 1945, 2 x 24 x 14 In.	1625
Statue, Suzanne, Woman, Drapery, Yellow Amber, R. Lalique, Etched France, 1925, 9 x 7 In. ....*illus*	11875
Vase, 2 Doves, Frosted Oval Spiral, Etched, Signed, France, 5 In.	173
Vase, 2 Lion's Heads, Frosted, Signed, France, 1900s, 6 1/2 x 9 x 3 1/2 In.	300
Vase, Acanthes, Acanthus Leaf, Footed, St. Cloud Pattern, 1900s, 4 1/2 x 4 x 3 7/8 In.	124
Vase, Aigrettes, Egrets, Red Patina, Palm Leaves, Wheel Cut, 1926, 9 5/8 x 8 In.	8125
Vase, Andromeda, Fish Scale, Frosted, Marie Claude, 5 3/4 x 6 In. ....*illus*	201
Vase, Bacchantes, Female Nudes, Clear & Frosted, 1990s, Label, Lalique, Paris, 9 1/2 In. ....*illus*	1500
Vase, Bagatelle, Birds, Vine, Frosted, Signed, France, Late 1900s, 7 In. ....*illus*	248
Vase, Bammako, Clear Spheres, Frosted Ground, Signed R. Lalique, 7 1/4 In.	1476
Vase, Birds & Leaves, Frosted, 6 3/4 In.	207
Vase, Birds In Flight, Frosted, France, 5 In.	127
Vase, Columns Of Leaves, Frosted Upper Portion, France, 1900s, 7 1/4 In.	132
Vase, Cyrus, Clear & Frosted, Turquoise Twisted Band At Neck, 1980, 6 1/4 x 10 In.	1625
Vase, Dampierre, Pedestal, 4 3/4 x 4 1/2 In.	275
Vase, Enamel, Box, Sleeve & Brochure, Tanzania, 1991, 8 x 8 In. ....*illus*	2375
Vase, Esterel, Protruding Birds, Laurel Leaves, Signed, R. Lalique, France, c.1923, 6 1/4 In.	715
Vase, Eucalyptus, Frosted, Crystal, Pink, France, 6 1/2 x 5 5/8 In.	594
Vase, Feather Design, France, 1900s, 6 In.	132
Vase, Female, Green, Engraved, 8 x 5 x 5 In. ....*illus*	281
Vase, Filicaria, Ferns, Turquoise, Willow Leaves, France, 1900s, 4 1/2 In.	263
Vase, Frosted Rose, Isfahan, Pressed Glass, Clear, France, 9 1/2 x 7 3/4 In.	410
Vase, Hirondelles, Swallows, France, 9 1/2 x 6 1/2 In.	615
Vase, Jaffa, Frosted, France, 7 3/4 x 12 1/2 x 5 In.	2000
Vase, Laurier, Leaves, Berries, Opalescent, Signed R. Lalique France, 7 x 4 In.	544
Vase, Martinets, Swifts, Molded, Frosted, Engraved, France, 1900s, 9 1/2 x 6 1/2 In.	469
Vase, Moissac, Overlapping, Leaves, Opalescent, Blue Patina, Molded R. Lalique, 1927, 5 In...*illus*	1500
Vase, Mossi, Protruding Discs, Kaleidoscopic, Cabochons, Frosted Base, 8 1/4 x 6 In.	813
Vase, Nefliers, Molded, Flowers, Frosted, Polished Foot, Signed R. Lalique, c.1923, 5 3/4 In.	260
Vase, Ondines, Water Nymphs, Clear, Signed, c.1960, 9 1/2 x 7 1/2 In.	507
Vase, Perruches, Parakeets, On Branches, Sepia Highlights, 9 1/2 In.	2950
Vase, Piriac, Fish & Waves, Frost & Blue, Wheel Cut Signature, 7 1/4 x 8 In.	767
Vase, Raisins, Frosted, Signed, France, 6 1/8 x 3 5/8 In.	500
Vase, Royat, Vertical Molded Ridges, Marked, France, 6 1/4 In.	543
Vase, Sauge, Sage Leaves, Frosted, Signed, 10 1/4 In.	938
Vase, Scarab, Black, Inset Square Silver Accents, Etched, 1900s, 7 1/2 x 4 1/2 x 3 1/2 In.	585
Vase, Sophora, Feuilles, Leaves, Amber, White Patina, Molded R. Lalique, 1926, 10 In......*illus*	8125
Vase, Sylvie, 2 Doves, Frosted & Clear, Flower Frog, Signed Underside, 8 1/2 x 7 1/2 x 4 In.....*illus*	130
Vase, Tanega, Wrapped In 3-Dimentional Leaf, Fitted Box, Signed, 14 1/2 x 8 x 8 In.	1375
Vase, Tanzania, Enamel, Black, 1991, 8 x 8 In.	2375
Vase, Tourbillons, Whirlwind, Black Enamel Highlights, France, 8 x 7 1/4 In.	1845
Wall Console, Figural Stag Frosted, Semicircle Shelf, Stainless Bracket, 11 1/2 x 20 In.	1265

LAMPS of every type, from the early oil-burning Betty and Phoebe lamps to the recent electric lamps with glass or beaded shades, interest collectors. Fuels used in lamps changed through the years; whale oil (1800–40), camphene (1828), Argand (1830), lard (1833–63), solar (1843-60s), turpentine and alcohol (1840s), gas (1850–79), kerosene (1860), and electricity (1879) are the most common. Early solar or astral lamps burned fat. Modern solar lamps are powered by the sun. Other lamps are listed by manufacturer or type of material.

Adjustable, Cast White Metal, Glass Shade, H.A. Best Lamp Co., Chicago, c.1950, 55 In.	293
Aladdin, Oil, Cream Color Base, Burner, Nu-Type Model B, Chimney, USA, 11 x 23 1/2 In.	44

Lalique, Vase, Bagatelle, Birds, Vine, Frosted, Signed, France, Late 1900s, 7 In.
$248

Leland Little Auctions

Lalique, Vase, Enamel, Box, Sleeve & Brochure, Tanzania, 1991, 8 x 8 In.
$2,375

Royal Crest Auctioneers

Lalique, Vase, Female, Green, Engraved, 8 x 5 x 5 In.
$281

Roland Auctioneers & Valuers

Lalique, Vase, Moissac, Overlapping Leaves, Opalescent, Blue Patina, Molded R. Lalique, 1927, 5 In.
$1,500

Rago Arts and Auction Center

Lalique, Vase, Sophora, Feuilles, Leaves, Amber, White Patina, Molded R. Lalique, 1926, 10 In.
$8,125

Rago Arts and Auction Center

Lalique, Vase, Sylvie, 2 Doves, Frosted & Clear, Flower Frog, Signed Underside, 8½ x 7½ x 4 In.
$130

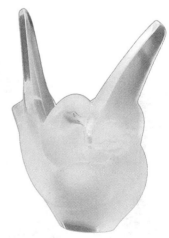

Aspire Auctions

Lamp, Argand, Tin, 2-Light, Brass Base, 29 In.
$113

Pook & Pook

Lamp, Astral, Frosted Globe, Gilt Font, Shaft, Marble Base, Cornelius & Co., c.1850, 21 In.
$330

Eldred's

Lamp, Astral, Oil, Brass, Marble, Glass Prisms, 1800s, 14 In.
$177

Copake Auction

Lamp, Banquet, Ball Shade, Flowers, Red, Yellow, White Metal, Electrified, c.1885, 24 In.
$281

Garth's Auctioneers & Appraisers

Lamp, Banquet, Hand Painted, Rose Design, White Metal Base, Marked M.C. Co., 28 x 14 In.
$60

Garth's Auctioneers & Appraisers

Lamp, Bouillotte, 2-Light, Brass, Wick Trimmer, Handle, Drip Pans, Metal Shade, France, 1800s, 14 In.
$1,404

Jeffrey S. Evans & Associates

Lamp, Bull's-Eye, Brass, Reflectors, Wick Damper, Molry & Ober, London, 1820, 10 In.
$138

Keystone Auctions LLC

The Lamp Shade Is Important

The prices of lamps with painted, blown out, or stained glass shades are based primarily on the shade. A substitute base of the expected quality does not lower the value by much.

Lamp, Chandelier, 1-Light, Modern, 3 Graduated Glass Circles, Chrome, 38 x 23 In.
$300

Burchard Galleries

Lamp, Chandelier, 6-Light, Antler, Candlecups, Painted Surface, 1900s, 18 x 29 ½ In.
$480

Brunk Auctions

Aladdin, Oil, Green Glass, White Metal Base, Chimney, Burner, 26½ In.	165
Aladdin, Pedestal, Green Depression Glass, Marked, Chimney, 23¾ In.	68
Argand, Brass, 1-Light, Frosted Shade, Prisms, c.1850, 15 In.	300
Argand, Tin, 2-Light, Brass Base, 29 In. ....*illus*	113
Astral, Bronze, Frosted & Etched Glass Shade, Faceted Prisms, Leafy Base, Electrified, 1800s, 25 x 9 In.	688
Astral, Frosted Globe, Gilt Font, Shaft, Marble Base, Cornelius & Co., c.1850, 21 In. ....*illus*	330
Astral, Marble Base, Glass, Opaque Cut, Overlay Stem, Brass Collar, 1900s, 15¼ In.	148
Astral, Oil, Brass, Marble, Glass Prisms, 1800s, 14 In. ....*illus*	177
Banker's, Double Green Glass Frosted Shades, 2 Inkwells, Pen Rests, 19 In.	121
Banquet, Ball Shade, Flowers, Red, Yellow, White Metal, Electrified, c.1885, 24 In. ....*illus*	281
Banquet, Blown-Out Lion's Heads, Hand Painted Roses, Matching Shade, 24 In.	92
Banquet, Brass Base, Alabaster Stem, Vaseline Opalescent Shade, 1800s, 25½ In.	144
Banquet, Brass Base, Step Foot, Ball Shade, Blue, 1800s	180
Banquet, Cut Glass, Footed, 27½ In., 6 Piece	9600
Banquet, Hand Painted, Rose Design, White Metal Base, Marked M.C. Co., 28 x 14 In. ......*illus*	60
Banquet, Milk Glass, Lions, Shields, Eagles, Leaves, Flowers, Late 1900s, 35½ In.	156
Bouillotte, 2-Light, Brass, Wick Trimmer, Handle, Drip Pans, Metal Shade, France, 1800s, 14 In.. *illus*	1404
Bouillotte, 3-Light, Empire Style, Bronze, Adjustable, Gilt, Electrified, 1800s, 28 In.	1080
Bouillotte, Empire Style, Gilt Metal, Tole Shade, 1900s, 25 In.	188
Bradley & Hubbard lamps are included in the Bradley & Hubbard category.	
Brass, Floor, Adjustable, Amber Glass Shade, Circular Base, 1900s, 46 In.	50
Brass, Iron Hanger, Morley, Leeds, Marked, Hailwood & Ackroyd, England, 1800s, 10¾ In.	123
Brass, Onion Shape, Reservoir & Burner, Marked, Perkins, Late 1800s, 10 x 18½ In.	660
Brass, Wrigglework Engraved, Iron Swing Lid, Hanger & Hook, Pa., Late 1700s, 4½ In.	400
Bull's-Eye, Brass, Reflectors, Wick Damper, Molry & Ober, London, 1820, 10 In. ....*illus*	138
Candle, Etched Hurricane Chimney, Blue Glass Rim, Brass & Marble Base, 20 In., Pair	96
Candlestick, Table, Silver Plate, Cunard Steamship Co., Ltd., 1900s, 24¾ In.	500
Carriage, Tin, Iron, Brass, Die Cut Piercing, Beveled Glass Lens, c.1975, 21 x 7 x 9 In.	156
Ceiling, Electric, 2-Light, Clear Globes, Adjustable, Nickel Plated, Angle Lamp Co., c.1880, 18 x 23 In..	252
Ceiling, Electric, Brass, Etched Glass Shade, c.1910, 11 x 9 In.	250
Chandelier, 1-Light, Modern, 3 Graduated Glass Circles, Chrome, 38 x 23 In. ....*illus*	300
Chandelier, 3-Light, Brass, Electrified, 23 x 21 In.	325
Chandelier, 3-Light, Brass, Glass, Etched, Globe, Chain, Late 1900s, 24 x 17 In.	649
Chandelier, 3-Light, Bronze, Chains, Ram's Head Mounts, Neoclassical, c.1920, 41 x 24 In.	188
Chandelier, 3-Light, Classical Revival, Argand Style, Scroll Arms, c.1900, 36 x 31 In.	2500
Chandelier, 3-Light, Satin Glass, Grape Clusters, Hanging Chain, 1900s, 18 x 17 In.	1112
Chandelier, 3-Light, Slag Glass, Hanging, 14 x 12 In.	148
Chandelier, 3-Light, Slag Glass, Metal Frame, Openwork Flowers, Leaves, 30 x 20 In.	94
Chandelier, 4-Light, Brass, Leaf & Scroll, Etched Glass Globes, Victorian, 33 x 23 In.	625
Chandelier, 4-Light, Bronze, Patinated Metal, Eagles, Spread Wings, Female Mask Arms, 29 x 19 In.	1250
Chandelier, 4-Light, Cast Metal, Chain, Mount & Brass Wash, Hanging Sockets, 17 In.	52
Chandelier, 4-Light, Electrified, Louis XV Style, Gilt Bronze, Leafy Scrolls, 39 In.	2000
Chandelier, 4-Light, Oil, Milk Glass Shades, Cast Iron, Electrified, Victorian, 32 In.	450
Chandelier, 4-Light, Patinated Metal, Central & 3 Small Frosted Glass Shades, Leafy, 34 x 26 In..	130
Chandelier, 4-Light, Pendants, Slag Glass, Caramel, Green, White, 1900s, 17½ In.	480
Chandelier, 5-Light, Brass, Art Glass Shades, Bell Shape Fitter, 2-Tone Green, 39 x 16 In.	968
Chandelier, 5-Light, Brass, Griffins, Rosettes, Filigree, Faces, Frosted, Etched Glass, 44 x 32 In.	212
Chandelier, 5-Light, Bronze, Cherubs, Grapevines, Gasolier, Mid 1800s, 67 x 31 In.	5625
Chandelier, 5-Light, Electrified Candlearms, 1900s, 30 x 22 In.	240
Chandelier, 5-Light, Gilt Metal, Hung Prism, Electric, France, 1800s, 25½ In.	250
Chandelier, 6-Light, 2 Tiers, Scroll Candlearms, Brass, Late 1900s, 26 x 27 In.	24
Chandelier, 6-Light, Alabaster, Carved Flowers, c.1925, 25 x 24 In.	2560
Chandelier, 6-Light, Antler, Candlecups, Painted Surface, 1900s, 18 x 29½ In. ....*illus*	480
Chandelier, 6-Light, Brass & Crystal, Teardrop, 23 x 24 In.	94
Chandelier, 6-Light, Brass, Delft, Early 1900s, 22 x 27 In.	163
Chandelier, 6-Light, Bronze, Fluted, Female Figures On Column, Leafy Arms, Gasolier, 44 x 38 In..	688
Chandelier, 6-Light, Candleholders, Weighted Tin, 1800s, 25 x 24 In.	584
Chandelier, 6-Light, Cased Glass, Gilt Bronze, Floral, c.1950, 17 In.	250

Lamp, Chandelier, 8-Light, Brass, Tole, Candlearms, Pinecone Pendant, France, c.1850, 27 x 24 In.

$875

New Orleans Auction Galleries

Lamp, Chandelier, 9-Light, Gilt Bronze, Upturned & Downturned Candlearms, France, c.1890, 48 In.

$625

Leslie Hindman Auctioneers

Lamp, Chandelier, 12-Light, Louis XIV Style, Bronze, 37¼ x 32 In.

$1,000

Doyle Auctioneers & Appraisers

Lamp, Chandelier, 16-Light, Cascading, Mule Deer Antler, 3 Levels, 44 x 37 In.
$1,416

Burchard Galleries

Lamp, Chandelier, Bakalowits & Sohne, Miracle, Brass Plated, Glass Rods, 1960s, 15 x 32 In.
$6,250

Rago Arts and Auction Center

Lamp, Chadelier, Fluid, 14 Burners, Painted, Tin, 1800s, 25 x 29 In.
$725

Pook & Pook

TIP
Reverse-painted lampshades should never be washed. Just dust them.

Lamp, Chandelier, Fortuny, Silk, Swirl Pattern, Metal Frame, Glass Bead Drops, 1900s, 30 x 24 In.
$600

Brunk Auctions

Lamp, Chandelier, Wrought Iron, Alabaster Shades, Michael Zadounaisky, France, 1900s, 32 x 30 In.
$1,125

Rago Arts and Auction Center

Lamp, Desk, Bellova Shade, Spelter Stick Base, Socket, Emeralite Frame, 17 x 8¾ x 11 In.
$545

Fontaine's Auction Gallery

Lamp, Electric, 1-Light, Iron, Figural, Guanyin, Octagonal Wood Base, 1940s, 35 x 62 x 21 In.
$531

Neal Auction Company

Lamp, Electric, 2-Light, Art Nouveau, Gilt, Bronze, New York, Signed, E.F. Caldwell, 9½ In.
$2,596

Cottone Auctions

Lamp, Electric, 2-Light, Majestic, Fiberglass, Boomerang, Fiberglass Shade, 24 x 22½ In.
$720

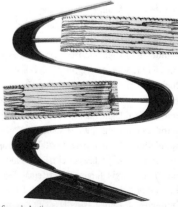

Cowan's Auctions

Chandelier,	6-Light, Chromed Metal, Brass & Glass, 32 ½ x 25 In.	156
Chandelier,	6-Light, Gilt Metal & Glass, Neoclassical, Continental, 39 x 24 In.	875
Chandelier,	6-Light, Gilt Metal, Neoclassical, C-Scroll Arms, Ram Mask, c.1900, 29 x 20 ½ In.	813
Chandelier,	6-Light, Gilt, Metal, Cage Shape, Prism & Swags, 28 In.	406
Chandelier,	6-Light, Giltwood, Rope & Tassel, Leafy Arms, Electrified, Neoclassical Style, 27 x 25 In.	500
Chandelier,	6-Light, Gold Color, Flower Etch, Ornate, 31 x 31 In.	44
Chandelier,	6-Light, Gold, Hanging, Frosted Glass, 36 In.	100
Chandelier,	6-Light, Hanging, Brass, Cobalt Blue Cut To Clear Accent Base, 36 In.	81
Chandelier,	6-Light, Metal, Glass, Knopped Baluster Shape, Hanging Prisms, 1800s, 41 In.	500
Chandelier,	6-Light, Metal, Glass, Luster, 29 x 24 In.	219
Chandelier,	6-Light, Painted & Wrought Iron, 62 x 48 In.	218
Chandelier,	6-Light, Painted, Cut Metal, Amber Glass Teardrops, 1900s, 23 x 21 ½ In.	163
Chandelier,	6-Light, Rectangular, Iron, Hand Forged, Currey & Co., 1988, 40 x 20 x 39 In.	177
Chandelier,	6-Light, Rock Crystal, Gilt & Patinated Metal, Louis XV, 44 x 34 In.	2750
Chandelier,	6-Light, Roses, Leaves, Wrought Metal, Continental, c.1925, 28 x 26 In.	480
Chandelier,	6-Light, Scroll Arms, Crystal Beads, Swags, Continental Style, 17 x 17 ½ In.	123
Chandelier,	6-Light, Woven Reed & Enameled Brass, Mario Garcia Torres, Mexico, 1970, 24 x 40 In.	1125
Chandelier,	7-Light, 6 Tiers, Curved Panels, Glass, Metal, Mazzega, 24 x 24 In.	3150
Chandelier,	7-Light, Scroll Arms, Tiered, Prism, French Classical Style, 1900s, 26 x 24 In.	507
Chandelier,	7-Light, Scroll Candlearms, Silver Gilt Leaves, Flowers, Continental, 39 In.	1875
Chandelier,	8-Light, Alabaster, Shade, Glass, Marble, Balls, Brass, Framework, 22 x 34 ½ In.	750
Chandelier,	8-Light, Black, Beaded Strands, Crystals, 28 x 24 In.	406
Chandelier,	8-Light, Brass, Tole, Candlearms, Pinecone Pendant, France, c.1850, 27 x 24 In...*illus*	875
Chandelier,	8-Light, Bronze, Leafy Arms, Prisms, Electrified, Louis XV Style, 1900s, 32 x 29 In.	1500
Chandelier,	8-Light, Bronze, Candlearms, Acanthus Leaves, Finial Bowknots, c.1980, 41 x 31 In.	1125
Chandelier,	8-Light, Bronze, Scroll Arms, Cut Glass Pendants, Louis XV Style, 54 x 36 In.	7188
Chandelier,	8-Light, Candle, Wire Scroll Arms, Tin Sockets, Late 1900s, 24 x 20 In.	60
Chandelier,	8-Light, Continental, Metal, Crown Shape, Flower Form Sockets, 1900s, 29 x 18 In.	1188
Chandelier,	8-Light, Cut Glass, George III Style, 32 ½ x 25 ½ In.	250
Chandelier,	8-Light, Glass Scroll Arms, Candles, White, 1900s, 18 x 21 In.	188
Chandelier,	8-Light, Pied Piper, Metal, Multicolor, Electrified, 26 x 30 In.	246
Chandelier,	9-Light, 2 Tiers, Tin, Wire, Loop Hanger, Candle Sockets, 1800s, 22 x 28 In.	2337
Chandelier,	9-Light, Brass, Scroll Candlearms, Hexagonal, Electric, 1800s, 37 x 21 In.	1375
Chandelier,	9-Light, Leafy Candlearms, Hung, Gilt Tole, France, 27 ½ In.	375
Chandelier,	9-Light, Gilt Bronze, 3 Cherubs, Grape Bunch, c.1900, 33 In.	2750
Chandelier,	9-Light, Gilt Bronze, Patinated Metal, Empire, 39 x 30 In.	875
Chandelier,	9-Light, Gilt Bronze, Upturned & Downturned Candlearms, France, c.1890, 48 In..*illus*	625
Chandelier,	9-Light, Iron, Copper, Scroll & Lead, c.1940, 42 x 16 In.	94
Chandelier,	9-Light, Louis XV Style, Gilt, Carved, Caffieri, Electrified, 36 x 34 In.	1875
Chandelier,	10-Light, Bronze Leafy Filigree, Rococo, 25 x 25 x 22 ¼ In.	605
Chandelier,	10-Light, Bronze, Cut Glass, Shield Backplate, Pendants, Late 1800s, 45 x 27 x 18 In.	2188
Chandelier,	10-Light, Gilt Bronze, Leafy Scroll Candlearms, Chains, 1800s, 20 x 22 In.	1063
Chandelier,	10-Light, Wrought Iron, Leaf Bobeches, Arts & Crafts, c.1800, 36 x 22 In.	813
Chandelier,	12-Light, Athena, Leaf Molding, Bronze, Baroque Style, 1900s, 25 ½ x 25 In.	500
Chandelier,	12-Light, Baroque, Giltwood, Gilt Metal, Scroll Candlearms, Leaves, c.1950, 47 x 39 In.	2125
Chandelier,	12-Light, Brass Arms, Glass Prisms & Flowers, 12 Candlecups, 1900s, 40 x 21 In.	120
Chandelier,	12-Light, Brass, Shaped Arms, Candlecups, c.1850, 34 x 43 In.	125
Chandelier,	12-Light, Bronze Scroll Arms, Clear, Rose Quartz, Amethyst Pendants, 36 x 29 In.	5313
Chandelier,	12-Light, Candle, Wire Scroll Arms, Tin Sockets, Wood Column, 1900s, 26 x 23 In.	120
Chandelier,	12-Light, Carved Leaves, Bell Shape Finial, Scroll Arms, Candle Sockets, c.1950, 39 x 38 In.	1125
Chandelier,	12-Light, Dutch Baroque Style, Bronze, 2 Tiers, 27 x 26 ⅛ In.	563
Chandelier,	12-Light, Flower Form, Gilded Brass, Acanthus Cap, France, c.1900, 16 x 27 In.	593
Chandelier,	12-Light, Gilt Bronze, Candle Arms, Hanging Flower Sockets, Ram's Heads, 43 x 28 In.	1875
Chandelier,	12-Light, Louis XIV Style, Bronze, 37 ¼ x 32 In.......*illus*	1000
Chandelier,	12-Light, Louis XV Style, Gilt Bronze, Rose Quartz, Rock Crystal, 1900s, 32 In.	3000
Chandelier,	12-Light, Louis XVI Style, Bronze, Scrolled Leaf, Bell Flower, 1900, 39 x 42 In.	900
Chandelier,	12-Light, Neoclassical Style, Patinated Metal, Crystal, 55 x 29 In.	2375
Chandelier,	12-Light, Multicolor Wood, Iron, 1900s, 42 ½ In.	242

Lamp, Electric, 2-Light, Metal Base, Slag Glass Shade, Belle Epoque Janette Style, 28 x 20 In.
$885

Aspire Auctions

Lamp, Electric, 2-Light, Powell, Evans, Walnut, Brass, Tapered, Woven Grass Shade, 1956, 42 In.
$8,750

Rago Arts and Auction Center

Lamp, Electric, 2-Light, Reverse Painted Glass, Scenic, Olive Matte, Jefferson, 22 x 16 In.
$590

Aspire Auctions

Lamp, Electric, 3-Light, Lightolier, Tommi Parzinger, Silver Plate, Floor, 1940s, 61 In., Pair
$2,375

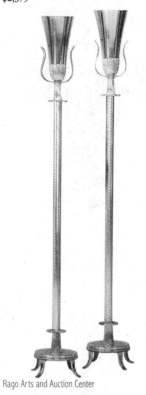

Rago Arts and Auction Center

Lamp, Electric, Art Glass, White Satin, Diamond-Quilted Mother-Of-Pearl, 21½ In.
$3,300

Woody Auction

Chandelier, 14-Light, Oak & Iron, 63 x 38 In.	125
Chandelier, 15-Light, Bronze, Goat-Head Masks, Entwined Snakes, Oil, 1800s, 39 x 28 In.	2500
Chandelier, 16-Light, Brass, Cased Glass, 1900s, 27 In.	531
Chandelier, 16-Light, Cascading, Mule Deer Antler, 3 Levels, 44 x 37 In. ....*illus*	1416
Chandelier, 18-Light, Gilt Bronze, Floral Basket, Neoclassical Style, 47½ x 29 In.	1331
Chandelier, 19-Light, Electrified, Giltwood, Metal, Neoclassical Style, Italy, 43 x 42 In.	938
Chandelier, 20-Light, Lotus Leaf, 2-Tiered Scrolling Frame, 37 x 42 In.	354
Chandelier, 22-Light, Ceiling Plate, Metal, 68 x 58 In.	150
Chandelier, 24-Light, 3 Tiers, Giltwood, Carved & Turned, c.1799, 38 x 35 In.	6000
Chandelier, 24-Light, Stainless Steel, Crystal, Savinel, & Roze For Baccarat, c.1985, 39 In.	5500
Chandelier, Art Glass, Art Nouveau Design, Faux Crackle Glass Ball Shade, Austria, 42 In.	4305
Chandelier, Bakalowits & Sohne, Miracle, Brass Plated, Glass Rods, 1960s, 15 x 32 In. ....*illus*	6250
Chandelier, Baptistry, Silver Plate, Chain, Gothic Revival, 5 In.	531
Chandelier, Brass & Crystal, J & L Lobmeyr, 1900s, 18 x 17 In.	369
Chandelier, Fluid, 14 Burners, Painted, Tin, 1800s, 25 x 29 In. ....*illus*	725
Chandelier, Fortuny, Silk, Swirl Pattern, Metal Frame, Glass Bead Drops, 1900s, 30 x 24 In. ..*illus*	600
Chandelier, Gilt Metal, Alabaster, Decorative Hanging Light, Empire, 16 x 24 In.	375
Chandelier, Gilt Metal, Hung & Swags, Prisms, Empire Style, 1900s, 33 In.	375
Chandelier, Leaded Glass, Birds, Cherries, Striated Blue & White, Striated Green Leaves, 24 x 16 In.	677
Chandelier, Multiple Lights, Fontana Arte, Brass Rods, Colored Glass Dividers, 1950s, 36 x 31 In.	10000
Chandelier, Wrought Iron, Alabaster Shades, Michael Zadounaisky, France, 1900s, 32 x 30 In. ... *illus*	1125
Chandelier, Wrought Iron, Light Fixture, Multi Arm, Acanthus Leaf, c.1940	406
Desk, Bellova Shade, Spelter Stick Base, Socket, Emeralite Frame, 17 x 8¾ x 11 In. ....*illus*	545
Desk, Burnished Brass, White Interior, Domed Shade, c.1950, 23 In.	72
Desk, Chrome Base, Green Shade, Art Deco Style, Hubbell Patd, 1912, 14 In.	68
Electric, 1-Light, Aluminum Body, Cream Shade, Sonneman, 62 In.	59
Electric, 1-Light, Brass Bound Ivory Enamel, Rectangular, Etched R. Kuo, 1900s, 17 In.	409
Electric, 1-Light, Brass, Adjustable Arm & Base, Rounded Base, 49 x 13 x 10 In.	125
Electric, 1-Light, Brass, Bulbous Body, Mica Lamp Company, 14½ x 14 In.	295
Electric, 1-Light, Bronze, Cast, Female, Seated, Holding Light, Signed, M. Le Verrier, 1900s, 9¼ In..	523
Electric, 1-Light, Ceramic, Linen, Lacquered Wood, Dark Brown Shade, c.1970, 35 x 16 In.	437
Electric, 1-Light, Dancers, Flutist, Blue, Marcello Fantoni, Italy, 1900s, 27 x 5½ In.	240
Electric, 1-Light, Flying Saucer, 24 x 14 In.	118
Electric, 1-Light, Hanging, Brass, Glass, Victorian, 35 In.	47
Electric, 1-Light, Hearts & Vines, Favrile Glass, Tiffany Style, 8 In.	219
Electric, 1-Light, Iron, Figural, Guanyin, Octagonal Wood Base, 1940s, 35 x 62 x 21 In. ....*illus*	531
Electric, 1-Light, Leaded Glass Shade, Pansy, Bronze Base, Fine, 19 x 22 In.	403
Electric, 1-Light, Leaded Glass, Circular Base, Linenfold, Tiffany Style, 11½ x 18 In.	250
Electric, 1-Light, Molded Metal, Column Base, Mother-Of-Pearl Glass Shade, 1900s, 29 In.	92
Electric, 1-Light, Painted Wood, Landscape, Fall Colors, Metal Base, 16 x 8 x 4 In.	1100
Electric, 1-Light, Palm Tree, Cold Painted Bronze, Arab Horseman, 1900s, 11 x 5 x 6 In.	375
Electric, 1-Light, Parcel Gilt, Acorn, Jean-Michael Frank, France, 12½ In.	10000
Electric, 1-Light, Porcelain, Urn Shape, Bright Colored Glazes, 1900s, 35 In.	120
Electric, 1-Light, Rose Quartz, Lotus Scrolls, Bird Handle, Footed, Finial, 11 x 27 In.	438
Electric, 1-Light, Spiral Wood Body, Cream Shade, 63 In.	24
Electric, 1-Light, Surveyor's Transit Base, Buff & Buff Mfg. Co., 1900s, 22½ In.	270
Electric, 1-Light, Wallpaper Roller, 33 In.	47
Electric, 2-Light, 7 Caramel Slag Curved Panels, Painted Bronze Frame, 24 In.	1650
Electric, 2-Light, Art Nouveau, Gilt, Bronze, New York, Signed, E.F. Caldwell, 9½ In. ....*illus*	2596
Electric, 2-Light, Boudoir, Calcite Shades, Gold Liners, Gilt & Clear Base, 15 x 14 In.	154
Electric, 2-Light, Chromed Metal, Spherical, K. Springer, c.1985, 30 x 26 In.	2000
Electric, 2-Light, Cloth Shade, Green, Violet, Marked, Makoto Yabe, Boston, 24 x 24 In.	738
Electric, 2-Light, Double Candle, Shade, Metal, Gold Plated, c.1950, 16½ In.	585
Electric, 2-Light, Gilt Bronze, Figural, Cherub, Shade, 1900s, 29 In.	65
Electric, 2-Light, Iron, Twisted, c.1950, 63 x 23 x 16 In.	313
Electric, 2-Light, Mahogany, Urn, Carved, Regency Style, 23 In.	438
Electric, 2-Light, Majestic, Fiberglass, Boomerang, Fiberglass Shade, 24 x 22½ In. ....*illus*	720
Electric, 2-Light, Marble, Baluster, Quartz Finial, 30½ In.	23

Lamp, Electric, Art Nouveau, Figural Maiden, Spelter, Nautilus Shade, 20 x 9 ½ In.
$1,936

Fontaine's Auction Gallery

Lamp, Electric, Beaded Glass Shade, Fruit, White Metal Base, Czechoslovakia, 1900s, 7 x 12 In.
$240

Garth's Auctioneers & Appraisers

Lamp, Electric, Boudoir, Parrot, Agate Glass, Metal Base, Birdcage, Early 1900s, 14 x 8 x 6 In.
$215

Cowan's Auctions

Lamp, Electric, D. Tognon, Dania, Enameled Aluminum, Curved, Artemide, Italy, 1969, 16 In.
$594

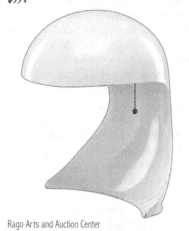

Rago Arts and Auction Center

Lamp, Electric, Desk, Amronlite, Brass, Columnar, Green Case Glass Shade, Early 1900s, 18 In.
$150

Selkirk Auctioneers & Appraisers

Lamp, Electric, French, Iron Base, Tapered Rattan Shade, 20th Century, 24 x 11 In.
$938

Rago Arts and Auction Center

Lamp, Electric, Hanging, 8 Panels, Multicolor Slag Glass, Pierced White Metal, c.1925, 15 x 28 In.
$463

Garth's Auctioneers & Appraisers

Lamp, Electric, Hanging, Duffner & Kimberly, Leaded Glass, Flowers, Leaves, Amber Tiles, 27 In.
$3,690

Morphy Auctions

Lamp, Electric, Jefferson, Poppies, Dragonflies, Bees, Reverse Painted, Textured Base, Signed, 23 In.
$3,383

Morphy Auctions

L

Lamp, Electric, Leaded Glass Shade, Flowers, Leaf Border, Wilkinson Peony, 18¾ In.
$2,478

Burchard Galleries

Lamp, Electric, Loie Fuller, Figural, Patinated Bronze, Art Nouveau Style, 17½ In.
$2,250

Susanin's Auctioneers & Appraisers

Lamp, Electric, Lucite, Natural Leaf, Stepped Metal Base, c.1970, 13 x 7 x 7 In.
$250

Kamelot Auctions

Electric, 2-Light, Metal Base, Slag Glass Shade, Belle Epoque Janette Style, 28 x 20 In......*illus*	885
Electric, 2-Light, Metal Body, Stained Glass Shade, 2 Pull Chains, Ruby Glass Buttons, 26 In..	104
Electric, 2-Light, Nickel Plated, Brass, Philippe Barbier, 1970s, 79 x 8½ In.................	688
Electric, 2-Light, Pittsburgh, Reverse Painted, Indian, Geometric Symbols, 22¾ x 16½ In.....	3840
Electric, 2-Light, Porcelain, Blue, Bronze Mounts, Chain Pulls, c.1920, 21 x 12 x 9¼ In.	360
Electric, 2-Light, Powell, Evans, Walnut, Brass, Tapered, Woven Grass Shade, 1956, 42 In... *illus*	8750
Electric, 2-Light, Reverse Painted Glass Shade, Night Landscape, Bronzed Cast Iron, 22 In.	468
Electric, 2-Light, Reverse Painted Glass, Scenic, Olive Matte, Jefferson, 22 x 16 In...........*illus*	590
Electric, 2-Light, Reverse Painted Landscape, 2 Swans, Pittsburgh, 18¾ In.................	666
Electric, 2-Light, Reverse Painted, Orange Poppy Flower, Dragonflies, Bees, 23 x 18 In.	3383
Electric, 2-Light, Spherical, Black Conical Shade, Karl Springer, 28 x 14 x 23 In.......................	1353
Electric, 2-Light, Statue Of Woman, Rounded Base, August Moreau, 1900s...............	192
Electric, 2-Light, Suess Leaded Glass Shade, White Lilies, Leaves, Cream Color Ground, 26 x 21½ In..	1920
Electric, 3-Light, Blue & White, River Landscape, Mountain, Chinese, 36 In.................	125
Electric, 3-Light, Caramel Slag Glass, Leaves, Urn, Silvertone Base, Vines, Miller, 24 x 15 In. ..	405
Electric, 3-Light, Chrome, Stand, Rounded Base, 64 In.	125
Electric, 3-Light, Leaded Glass Shade, Scrolling Bronze Base, Wilkinson Co., 25 In.	2950
Electric, 3-Light, Leaded Glass Shade, Stylized Yellow Flowers, Signed, Williamson, 25¾ x 20 In...	1920
Electric, 3-Light, Lightolier, Tommi Parzinger, Silver Plate, Floor, 1940s, 61 In., Pair.......*illus*	2375
Electric, 3-Light, Lily Pad, Art Glass Shades, Leaves Base, 1900s, 16 In..................	52
Electric, 3-Light, Peony, Yellow & Salmon Flower Border, Wilkinson, c.1915, 25 In...................	2214
Electric, 4-Light, Slag Glass Shade, Green Verdigris, Fence, Grass, Early 1900s, 22 x 14 In.	1112
Electric, 5-Light, Bronze, Crane, Rocaille Base, Signed, Ant. Amorgasti, 1924, 23 x 13 x 13 In.	688
Electric, 5-Light, Porcelain, Cobalt Blue, Ormolu Mounts, Early 1900s, 33 In.	77
Electric, 6-Light, Bronze, Tree Trunk, Exposed Roots, Arts & Crafts, 26 x 11½ In.	1599
Electric, 8 Caramel Slag Glass Panels, Bronzed & Painted Floral Frame & Base, 17 In.	4400
Electric, Agrafee, Steel, Aluminum, Brass, Serge Mouille, France, 1956, 20 x 11 x 29 In.	10000
Electric, Akari, Bamboo Shaft, Rice Paper Shade, Isamu Noguchi, c.1960, 71 In.......................	2625
Electric, Alabaster, Domed Top, Putti, Basin, Marble, Figural, Continental, Late 1800s, 45 In.	375
Electric, Arredoluce Monza, Brass, Inverted Milk Glass Shade, Italy, 37 x 11½ In.....................	1476
Electric, Art Deco, Figural, Nude Woman, Holding Ball, 25 In...........................	173
Electric, Art Glass Shade, Adjustable Arm, Brass Base, 15 x 7 In.......................	277
Electric, Art Glass, White Satin, Diamond-Quilted Mother-Of-Pearl, 21½ In.................*illus*	3300
Electric, Art Nouveau, Figural Maiden, Spelter, Nautilus Shade, 20 x 9½ In....................*illus*	1936
Electric, Arts & Crafts, Glass & Metal, Wood Base, 22 In.	594
Electric, Banquet, Dying Gaul, Floral Molded, Patinated Metal, 1800s, 35 x 16 x 13 In.	375
Electric, Banquet, Puffy, Red Glass Shade, White Metal Frame, 1900s, 30 In.	252
Electric, Beaded Glass Shade, Fruit, White Metal Base, Czechoslovakia, 1900s, 7 x 12 In..*illus*	240
Electric, Bird & Flowers, Tiffany Style, 26 x 20 In.	94
Electric, Bluebird Shade, Flowering Branches, White Metal Base, Red Highlights, c.1950, 25 In.	240
Electric, Boudoir, Parrot, Agate Glass, Metal Base, Birdcage, Early 1900s, 14 x 8 x 6 In.....*illus*	215
Electric, Boudoir, Reverse Painted Landscape, Cottage, Lake, Bronzed Cast Iron Base, 14 In...	110
Electric, Brass, Floral Shade & Chimney, Victorian, 25 In.	24
Electric, Brass, Shade & Chimney, Flowers, Victorian, 25 In.............................	35
Electric, Bronze, 2 Arabs, Tent, Minaret, Red Glass Panels, Cold Painted, Bergman, 9 x 4 In...	1722
Electric, Bronze, Floor, Disderot, Roger Fatus, France, c.1950, 59 In........................	688
Electric, Bronze, Globular, Dragon Design, 1900s, 8½ x 16 In.	86
Electric, Bronze, Marble Base, Dome Shade, Elk, Art Nouveau Glass, c.1800, 20 x 9 x 6 In.	500
Electric, Bronze, Marble, Silk Pleated Shades, Molded Lotus Leaves, c.1915, 20 In., Pair..........	1125
Electric, Bronze, Slag Glass Shade, Caramel Overlay, Miller, 23 x 18 In........................	221
Electric, Bronze, White Metal, Slag Glass, Octagonal Shade, Swan Form Base, 24 x 19½ In....	369
Electric, Bronze, Woman, Figural, On 3 Animal Form Legs, Claw Feet, White Shade, 1800s, 25 In.	390
Electric, Bulbous, Beaded Fringe Shade, Mackenzie-Childs, 45½ In.........................	475
Electric, Caramel Slag Glass Shade, Panels, Round Base, 23 x 18 In.	165
Electric, Carved Walnut, Paper Shade, c.1960, 38½ x 18⅛ In..............................	500
Electric, Carved, Tusk, Villagers & Animals, Wood Base, Tribal, Africa, c.1920, 9½ In.	173
Electric, Ceiling Light, Enamel Brass, Frosted Glass, Arredoluce, Italy, c.1957, 26½ x 20 x 31 In.	8125
Electric, Chartreuse Glass, Brass Accents, Stilnovo, Italy, 1950s, 34 x 8 In..................	1063

Electric, Cold Painted, Metal, Arab Man On Rug, Silk Shade, Tassels, Austria, 10 3/8 In.	94
Electric, Copper, Beaded Edges, Starbursts, Gold Tone, Black Metal, Cube Base, 50 x 19 In.	225
Electric, Cube Shape, White Frosted Glass, Louis Poulsen, Denmark, 6 3/4 x 5 3/4 x 5 3/4 In.	384
Electric, D. Tognon, Dania, Enameled Aluminum, Curved, Artemide, Italy, 1969, 16 In....illus	594
Electric, Dancer, Figural, Metal, Frosted Green Snow Ball, Marble Base, 11 In.	150
Electric, Desk, Amronlite, Brass, Columnar, Green Case Glass Shade, Early 1900s, 18 In..illus	150
Electric, Desk, French Art Deco, Frosted & Clear Pyramid Shade, Tapered Metal Base, 16 In.	344
Electric, Desk, Metal, Sphinx Figures, Amber Glass, Egyptian Revival, 8 x 13 x 6 In.	378
Electric, Desk, White Metal Frame, Shade, Apollo Electric Co., Chicago, 1900s, 19 x 10 x 13 In.	125
Electric, Double Globe, White Glass Chimneys, Store, 18 In.	144
Electric, Edgar Brandt, Bronze, Cobra Snake Holding Daum Shade, Signed Shade, 21 x 6 1/2 In.	12160
Electric, Egg, Glass, Vetri Murano, Italy, 1900s, 16 1/2 x 13 In.	677
Electric, Elephant, Glass Shade, Onyx Base, Metal, 24 x 12 x 6 In.	344
Electric, Empire Style, Gilt Bronze & Tole, 19 1/2 In.	209
Electric, Enamel Steel & Aluminum, Blue, White, Red, 1951, 17 1/2 x 16 1/2 x 83 In.	2470
Electric, Enamel, Bronze, Birds & Bamboo Shade, Fabric Liner, Japan, Early 1900s, 24 In.	212
Electric, Enameled Aluminum, Teak, Brass, Hans-Agne Jakobsson, Sweden, c.1955, 24 x 22 x 8 In.	625
Electric, Enameled Steel, Brass, Aluminum, Gilbert Watrous, 1951, 15 x 48 x 43 In.	5625
Electric, Figural, Nude, Gilt Tree Trunk, Naturalistic Base, Continental, 38 In.	523
Electric, Figural, Stained Glass Shade, Birds & Trees, Circular Base, 22 In.	92
Electric, Floor, Brass, Adjustable, Cedric Hartman, c.1970, 55 x 24 In.	344
Electric, Floor, Brass, Iron, Wood, Glass Shades, c.1950, 70 In.	531
Electric, Floor, Giltwood, Lotus & Acanthus Leaves, Silk Shade, c.1915, 73 x 25 In.	500
Electric, Floor, Paper & Enameled Steel, Pallucco Company, c.1980, 74 In.	79
Electric, Floor, Stainless Steel, Linen, Beige, Aluminum, c.1970, 46 1/4 x 12 x 25 In.	1500
Electric, Flowers, Golden Paint, Gilt, 2 Glass Beaded Shades, Early 1900s, 8 x 12 In.	69
Electric, French, Iron Base, Tapered Rattan Shade, 20th Century, 24 x 11 In. ...illus	938
Electric, Gherpe, Acrylic, Chromed Steel, Plastic, Superstudio, Italy, 1967, 20 x 11 In.	3500
Electric, Gilt Metal, Agate Torchiere, Iridescent Glass Shade, Gilbert Rohde, 65 In.	354
Electric, Gilt Metal, Cherub, Fluted Stem, Cylindrical Plinth, France, 1900s, 33 In.	250
Electric, Gilt Metal, Circle Base, 54 1/2 x 17 1/4 In.	625
Electric, Ginger Jar, Blue & White, Hand Painted, Brass Cap, Chinese, 1800s, 27 In.	212
Electric, Girl, Gilt, Silver Basket, Glass Grapes, Light Bulb Above, 10 In.	81
Electric, Globe Pink To White, Gold, Plum, Blue Hues, Flowers, Cast, Iron, Brass, 10 x 27 1/2 In.	88
Electric, Good Fairy, Statue Mounted, Early 1900s, 13 x 22 x 11 1/2 In.	83
Electric, Grisaille, Black, Sepia, Oval, Carved Wood Base, Chinese Republic Period, 10 In.	1476
Electric, Hanging Above Seated Old Man, Oriental Rug, Bronze, Bergman, c.1950, 13 In.	156
Electric, Hanging, 8 Panels, Multicolor Slag Glass, Pierced White Metal, c.1925, 15 x 28 In..illus	463
Electric, Hanging, Copper, Frosted Glass, Erik Hoglund, Sweden, c.1965, 32 x 6 x 16 In.	500
Electric, Hanging, Duffner & Kimberly, Leaded Glass, Flowers, Leaves, Amber Tiles, 27 In..illus	3690
Electric, Hanging, Fabric, Wire, Aluminum, Falkland, Bruno Munari, Italy, 1964, 48 x 16 In.	218
Electric, Harris Strong, Tile, Landscape, Teak, 38 In.	115
Electric, J. Adnet, Stitched Leather, Cone Base, 1950s, 58 x 16 In.	3625
Electric, Jefferson, Poppies, Dragonflies, Bees, Reverse Painted, Textured Base, Signed, 23 In..illus	3383
Electric, Leaded Glass Shade, Flowers, Leaf Border, Wilkinson Peony, 18 3/4 In.....illus	2478
Electric, Leaded Slag Glass, Green & Caramel, No. 1163, 20 In.	403
Electric, Leaded, Rectangular Shade, Green & Amber Border Panels, Flowers, 9 3/4 x 32 x 10 In.	242
Electric, Loie Fuller, Figural, Patinated Bronze, Art Nouveau Style, 17 1/2 In. ...illus	2250
Electric, Lucite, Natural Leaf, Stepped Metal Base, c.1970, 13 x 7 x 7 In....illus	250
Electric, M.C. Fouquieres, Acrylic, Resin, Green, Burlap Shade, 1970s, 16 In....illus	1000
Electric, Maison Charles, 12-Light, Tubular Form, Enameled & Chromed Steel, 39 x 12 In.	1250
Electric, Marble Base, Achille Castiglioni, Arco, 96 x 48 x 12 In.	2500
Electric, Metal, Bronze Color, Fringed Shade, Beads, Slag Glass Medallions, Early 1900s, 24 In..illus	182
Electric, Mosaic, Octagonal Pleated Cloth Shade, Round Base, Late 1900s, 13 x 16 In.	74
Electric, Multicolor Stained Glass Shade, 4 Legs, Paw Feet, Adjustable, 45 x 13 x 13 In.	188
Electric, Mushroom Shape, Floral Green Yellow & Pink, Textured Glass, 12 x 11 1/2 In.	375
Electric, Night Watchman, Figural, Lantern, Axe, Carved Wood, 20 In.	115
Electric, Painted Glass Shade, Forest Scene, Ornate Base, 18 x 24 In.	1092

Lamp, Electric, M.C. Fouquieres, Acrylic, Resin, Green, Burlap Shade, 1970s, 16 In.
$1,000

Rago Arts and Auction Center

Lamp, Electric, Metal, Bronze Color, Fringed Shade, Beads, Slag Glass Medallions, Early 1900s, 24 In.
$182

Ahlers & Ogletree Auction Gallery

Lamp, Electric, Reverse Painted, Waterfront Cottage, P.L.B.&G., Pittsburgh, c.1915, 20 x 13 In.
$531

New Orleans Auction Galleries

Lamp, Electric, Rocket, Lacquered Wood, Aluminum, Plastic, Brass, France, c.1950, 9 x 10 In.
$500

Wright

How Bright the Light?

The light from one regular 60-watt lightbulb is equal to the light from twenty-five double-wick whale-oil lamps used in the nineteenth-century.

Lamp, Electric, Student, Brass, Double Arm, Yellow Shade, 1800s, 20½ In.
$75

Pook & Pook

Lamp, Electric, Travelers Aid, Plastic Collar, Milk Glass Inserts, Globe, c.1950, 15 x 17 x 13 In.
$108

Thomaston Place Auction Galleries

Electric, Patinated White Metal Base, Reverse Painted, Snowy Landscape, c.1925, 24 x 16 In...	360
Electric, Pear Shape, Metal Armature, Paper Shade, 4-Footed, Noguchi, 25 x 16 In.	425
Electric, Porcelain, Gilt Bronze Mounted, Vase Shape, Lion Masks, France, 1800s, 26 x 8 In....	625
Electric, Porcelain, Turquoise Glaze, Scrolled Ormolu Mounts, c.1915, 18 In.	142
Electric, Portable, White, Globe Top, Metal Construction Base, Midcentury, 7 x 13 In..............	140
Electric, Pottery, Green Ground, Russian Men On Horseback, 31 In.	124
Electric, Red Glass, Molded Scroll & Grape, Marked, 1800s, 25 In.	153
Electric, Reverse Painted Shade, Blue Birds, Flowering Branches, White Metal Base, c.1915, 24 In.....	150
Electric, Reverse Painted Shade, Church, Lake, Mountains, Forest, White Metal Base, c.1915, 24 In.	252
Electric, Reverse Painted Shade, Landscape, Sunset, Boat, Castles, G. Morley, 21 In.................	1150
Electric, Reverse Painted Shade, Winter Sunset Scene, House, c.1915, 23 x 17 In.	240
Electric, Reverse Painted, Waterfront Cottage, P.L.B.&G., Pittsburgh, c.1915, 20 x 13 In....*illus*	531
Electric, Rocket, Lacquered Wood, Aluminum, Plastic, Brass, France, c.1950, 9 x 10 In....*illus*	500
Electric, Rosewood, Brass Inlay, Carved, Twist, Wire, Satin Lampshade, 12 x 70 In.	50
Electric, Satin Glass, Butterscotch, Diamond Quilted, Brass Fitting, Late 1900s, 17 In.	390
Electric, Slag Glass Shade, Fishing Scene Overlay, Patinated, 1900s, 24½ In.	213
Electric, Slag Glass Shade, Flowers, Multicolor, White Metal Base, 1900s, 24 x 17¾ In.	168
Electric, Slag Glass Shade, Green, Tans Panels, Patinated White Metal Base, 24 x 17 In.	372
Electric, Slag Glass Shade, Multicolor, Bronze Column Base, 1900s, 70 In.	444
Electric, Slag Glass Shade, Tulip, Table, Metal Lily Pad Base, Early 1900s, 15 In.	165
Electric, Smoker's, Brass, Slag Glass Shade, Cigarette Dispenser, c.1920, 20 x 13 x 9 In.	152
Electric, Snowball, Figural, Metal, 2 Children, 11 In.	115
Electric, Sprocket Shape, Glass, Nickel Plate, Desny Paris, France, 8¾ x 5⅞ In.	2000
Electric, Stainless, Steel, Chrome Plated Brass, Cedric Hartman, 1966, 37 x 12 x 11 In...........	1750
Electric, Stoneware, Linen Shade, Marked, Jane & Gordon Martz, c.1960, 26 In.	215
Electric, Student, Brass, 2 White Glass Shades, 22 In.	132
Electric, Student, Brass, Double Arm, Yellow Shade, 1800s, 20½ In.....................*illus*	75
Electric, Student, Brass, Glass Shade, Domed Base, 23½ In.	98
Electric, Table, Cranberry Cut, Clear Font, Metal & Marble, 26½ In.	46
Electric, Table, Grasshopper, Brass, Aluminum, 1949, 6¼ x 15 x 15¼ In.	3000
Electric, Table, J. Camp, Sculpted, Walnut, Carved, Glass, Signed, 1995, 60 x 19 x 30 In.	2500
Electric, Table, Laminated & Turned Wood, Brass, Linen, c.1955, 17 x 34½ In.	687
Electric, Teak, Conical Linen Shade, Round Base, Unmarked, Denmark, 1950s, 58½ x 9 In...	215
Electric, Travelers Aid, Plastic Collar, Milk Glass Inserts, Globe, c.1950, 15 x 17 x 13 In.....*illus*	108
Electric, Tripod Feet, Floor, Black, Greta Grossman, 1947-48, 49½ x 15 x 17 In...........	1000
Electric, Valiglia, Enameled Steel, Signed, Ettore Sottsass, Italy, 1977, 14 x 9 x 13 In.	875
Electric, Vase, Battle Scene, Foo Dog Mask Handles, Porcelain, Wood Plinth, 1900s, 19 In.	189
Electric, Wall Mounted, Walnut, Aluminum Shade, Wharton Esherick, 1969, 21 x 19 In...*illus*	1300
Electric, Walnut, Carved, Paper, c.1960, 38½ x 18 In.	500
Electric, White Metal Frame, Reverse Painted Glass Shade, Cabin Lake Scene, 1925s, 22 In.....	168
Electric, Will Rogers, Wiley Post, White, Airplane, Chip On Base, Collar, 17 In....................	79
Electric, Winter Scene, Purple, Mountains, Lake, Trees, Moe Bridges Co., 23½ x 14½ In.	1815
Electric, WMF, Ikora, Chrome Finish, Marble Glass Dome, Round Base, 9½ x 5¼ In..............	283
Electric, Woman, Figural, Leaves, Patinated Metal, France, 20 In.	92
Electric, Wood Base, Cylindrical, Turned Top, Early 1900s, 5½ In..........................	144
Electrolier, 10-Light, Gilt Bronze, Gas & Electric Arms, Rope Twist Standard, c.1900, 42 In.	625
Fairy, Domed Shade, Pink Ruffled, Glass, Cased, 6½ x 5½ In.	42
Fairy, Embossed Rose, Green Ruffled, 6½ x 5½ In.	30
Fairy, Spangle Glass, Colored Flakes, 2 Base Vents, Clear Cup, c.1850, 5 x 4 In. ....*illus*	176
Figural, 2-Light, Bronze & Gilt, Putti, Column Supports, Linen Shade, France, 31½ In.	263
Figural, Opaline Glass Shade, Female Caryatid, Floor, c.1800s, 36 In.........................	354
Finger, Kerosene, Diamond & Fan, Vaseline Glass, 7 In.	100
Fluid, Brass, Footed, Globe Body, Milk Glass Shade, 18½ In.	13
Fluid, Candlestick, Silver, Cut Glass, Plated Burner, Overlay Shade, 27¼ In.	500
Fluid, Glass Bowl, Metal Spout, Rounded Base, New England, 1800s, 10 In....................	263
Gas, 3-Light, Brass, Glass Shade, Gas Light, c.1870, 30 x 24 In.	313
Gasolier, 6-Light, Brass, Valve Switches, Center Stem, Fleur-De-Lis, 7½ x 4 In.................*illus*	484
Grasshopper, Brass, Aluminum, G. Magnusson Grossman, For Ralph O. Smith, 1949, 15 In....*illus*	3000

Grease, Carved Slate, Spout & Cover, Edge Flakes, c.1850, 5 ½ In.	525

Handel lamps are included in the Handel category.

Hanging, 2-Light, Carved Mermaid, Holding Lights, Frosted Shades, Brass, c.1900, 48 x 28 In...*illus*	1500
Hanging, Blue Aqua Shade, Swirled Pattern, Brass Fixtures, Late 1800s, 15 In.	90
Hanging, Brass, Cylindrical, Opalescent Jewels, Smoke Bell, Miniature, c.1900, 5 x 2 In.	239
Hanging, Brass, Gilt Metal, Frosted Glass, Victorian, 36 x 12 ½ In.	125
Hanging, Diecast, Spun Brass Frame, Cranberry Shade, Clear Prism, Victorian, 14 In.	390
Hanging, Electric, Juno, Brass, Green Tin Shade, 32 In.	57
Hanging, Parlor, Cranberry Shade, Brass Frame, Glass Prism, 1800s	108
Hanging, Silver Bowl, Engraved, Chains, Amethyst Glass Insert, Marks, Russia, c.1880, 16 In.	369
Hanging, Silver, Iron, Mica Shade, Medieval Style, c.1920, 13 x 22 In.	220
Hanging, Slag Glass, Fruit, Cream, Multicolor, c.1950, 13 x 25 In.	52
Kerosene, Amber Glass Base, Hobnail Shade, 1800s, 17 ½ In.	75
Kerosene, Banquet, Clear, Atwood Collar, Nickel Plated, Clarissa, Ill., c.1880, 18 x 4 ½ In.	199
Kerosene, Electrified, Silver Plated, Trefoil Base, Clambroth Glass Shade, Victorian, 22 x 12 In.	72
Kerosene, Glass, Ball Shape, Blue 5-Toed Base, Cut Velvet, Diamond-Quilted, c.1980, 8 x 3 In.	585
Kerosene, Junior, Banquet, Yellow, Ball Shape, Metal Foot, Applied Jewels, c.1750, 18 x 4 In.	410
Kerosene, Opalescent, Blue, Swirl, Globular Font, Footed, 1900s, 10 x 4 x 2⅝ In.*illus*	299
Kerosene, Satin Glass, Pink, Raindrop Ball Shape, Nutmeg Burner, Early 1900s, 8 x 3 In.	129
Kerosene, Student, Double Burner, Brass, Adjustable Height, Late 1800s, 27 x 14 In.	72
Loom, 1-Light, Iron, Wood Base, Curled Hanger, 1800s, 26 In.	197
Motion, Cowboys At Campfire, Marked, LS Goodman, 1956, 10 In.	201
Oil, Blue & White, Porcelain, Flowers, Painted Glass Globe, Germany, 19 In.	94
Oil, Brass, Embossed Medallions, Circular Foot, c.1900s, 8 x 5 x 3 In.	96
Oil, Brass, Footed, Handle, Plume & Atwood, c.1885, 5 In.	75
Oil, Cut Glass, Swirl Pattern, Globe Shape, 15 In.	9600
Oil, Glass, Metal Tray, Floral, Gilt, 11 ¼ In.	12
Oil, Hand Painted, Floral, Royal Burner, 3 Feather Brand Chimney, 30 ½ In.	226
Oil, Iron, Round Cage, Concentric Interior Rings & Font, 1800s, 6 In.	875
Oil, Lantern, Glass Globe, Punched Tin Cap, Removable Burner, 13 In.	226
Oil, Opaque White Glass, Globular Font, 5 Toes, Amber Rim, Miniature, c.1900, 7 x 4 x 3 In.	2988
Oil, Owl, Figural, Opaque White, Ball Head, Orange Enamel Eyes, c.1900, 7 x 4 x 2¾ In.	388
Oil, Owl, Figural, Yellow Glass Eyes, Ruffled Rim, 1881, 4 ½ x 5 ½ In.	508
Oil, Pressed Glass, Cobalt, Lobed Front & Base, Etched Chimney, c.1800, 18 In.	156
Oil, Satin Glass, Yellow, Etched Glass Globe, Victorian, 32 ½ In.	161
Organ, Floral Ball Shade, Pressed Brass Font & Column, Electrified, 1900s, 61 In.	96

Pairpoint Lamps are in the Pairpoint category.

Parlor, Frosted Ruby Glass, Matching Globe, Floral, Brass Base, 21 In.	104
Parlor, Gilt Brass, Blue Cut To Clear Font, Winged Paw Feet, Electrified, 1800s, 39 x 11 In.	500
Parlor, Hanging, Brass Frame & Fittings, Salmon Shade, Victorian, 34 x 15 In.	150
Robsjohn-Gibbings, Marble Column, Brass Fittings, Hansen Lighting, 1960s, 30 In., Pair	1000
Santa Claus, Oil, Miniature, Milk Glass, Painted, 1887, 9 ½ In.	2596
Sconce, 1-Light, Carved Hand, Swags, Painted, Parcel Gilt, Candle Sockets, 32 In., Pair	1250
Sconce, 1-Light, Shell Shape, White, Stacked, Plaster, After Serge Roche, 9 x 19 ¼ In., Pair	2812
Sconce, 2-Light, Electric, Bronze, Ribbon Shape Backplate, Leaf, Acorn Decor, Pair, c.1900, 32 x 14 In.	1125
Sconce, 2-Light, Gilt Metal, Sunflower, Round, 1900s, 21 In.	176
Sconce, 3-Light, Bronze, Rock Crystal, Rose Quartz, Electrified, 1900s, 31 x 16 x 8 In., Pair	2500
Sconce, 3-Light, Mirror, Gilt Metal Mounts, Ribbon Finial, 1800s, 14 In.	75
Sconce, 3-Light, Mirrored, Brass, Circular Shape, 23 x 19 ¾ In.	266
Sconce, 4-Light, Gilt, Bronze, Wing Victory Shape, Empire Style, Late 1800s, 18 In.	469
Sconce, Bronze, Dolphin, Gilt, Pendant Quezal Shade, Early 1900s, 17 x 4¾ x 7 In.	500
Sinumbra, Brass, Frosted Cut, Clear Glass Shade, Marble Base, 26 ½ In.	138
Sinumbra, Brass, Gilt Opalescent, Frosted, Cornelius & Baker, Philadelphia, c.1850, 28 In.	690
Sinumbra, Brass, Marble, White Paint, Frosted Cut Shade, Faceted Prisms, c.1850, 30 In.	1140
Sinumbra, Bronze, Frosted, Blown, Glass Shade, Wheel Cut, c.1825, 24¾ In.	649
Solar, Brass Font, Label, Japanned Stem, Square Marble Base, Ball Shade, 1850s, 22 In.	450
Solar, Bronze, Fluted Column, Frosted & Cut Glass Shade, Marble Base, Hooper, c.1850, 21 In.	1000
Solar, Etched Globe, Prisms, Marble Base, Electrified, Victorian, 22 In.	500

Lamp, Electric, Wall Mounted, Walnut, Aluminum Shade, Wharton Esherick, 1969, 21 x 19 In.
$1,300

Wright

Lamp, Fairy, Spangle Glass, Colored Flakes, 2 Base Vents, Clear Cup, c.1850, 5 x 4 In.
$176

Jeffrey S. Evans & Associates

Lamp, Gasolier, 6-Light, Brass, Valve Switches, Center Stem, Fleur-De-Lis, 7 ½ x 4 In.
$484

Fontaine's Auction Gallery

Lamp, Grasshopper, Brass, Aluminum, G. Magnusson Grossman, For Ralph O. Smith, 1949, 15 In.
$3,000

Wright

Lamp, Hanging, 2-Light, Carved Mermaid, Holding Lights, Frosted Shades, Brass, c.1900, 48 x 28 In.
$1,500

Garth's Auctioneers & Appraisers

Lamp, Kerosene, Opalescent, Blue, Swirl, Globular Font, Footed, 1900s, 10 x 4 x 2 ⅝ In.
$299

Jeffrey S. Evans & Associates

Lamp, Solar, Gilt Bronze, Leafy Standard, Etched Shade, Marble Base, Hooper, Boston, c.1850, 21 In.
$1,125

Neal Auction Company

Lamp, Whale Oil, 2 Wicks, Gilt Bronze, Urn, Lion's Head, Footed Bowl, 1800s, 5 ½ In.
$63

Leslie Hindman Auctioneers

Lampshade, Slag Glass, 6 Petals, Green, Rose, Amber Panels, Metal Rim, Early 1900s, 8 x 4 In.
$59

Jeffrey S. Evans & Associates

Lantern, Hanging, 4-Light, Brass, 6 Glass Panels, 6 Link Chains, 28 ½ x 16 In.
$687

Doyle Auctioneers & Appraisers

Lantern, Kerosene, Tin, Filler & Chimney, 11 x 11 In.
$136

Hartzell's Auction Gallery, Inc.

Solar, Gilt Bronze, Leafy Baluster, Marble Base, Floral Cut Shade, Starr, Fellows, c.1850, 12 In. .	1000
Solar, Gilt Bronze, Leafy Standard, Etched Shade, Marble Base, Hooper, Boston, c.1850, 21 In.. *illus*	1125
Solar, Gilt Bronze, Starr Fellows, Fluted Column, Marble Base, Globe Shade, c.1850, 18 In.......	938
Solar, Reeded Column, Globe Cut Glass Shade, Dietz Brothers & Co., N.Y., c.1850, 27 x 9 In......	2250
Street Light, Kerosene, Sheet Metal Frame, Amethyst Globe, Domed, Wood Finial, 1800s, 25 x 17 In.	59
Tiffany Lamps are listed in the Tiffany category.	
Torchere, Bronze, Milk Glass Shade, Figural Base, 76 In..............	125
Torchere, Edgar Brandt, Iron, Corkscrew Designs, Bell, Glass Shade, 68 x 16 In.	281
Torchere, Twisted Scalloped Shade, Metal Stem, Mirror On Base, 68 x 16 In.	319
Vaseline, Pyriform Font, Pinched Lower Body, Spar Brenner Burner, c.1900, 9 x 4 x 2 In.	2390
Whale Oil, 2 Wicks, Gilt Bronze, Urn, Lion's Head, Footed Bowl, 1800s, 5 ½ In.................*illus*	63
Whale Oil, Blown Glass, Hollow Stem, Flattened Thumbprint, Early 1800s, 10 In.	198
Whale Oil, Opalescent, Font, Ribbed, Scalloped Edge, A&P Gaurdard Burner, c.1900, 10 x 5 x 3 In..	1673

LAMP BASE

Bronze, Empire Style, Gilt, Candlestick, France, 1900s, 23 ½ In...	63
Bronze, Urn Shape Vase, Scrolling Leaves, Gold Gilt, Carved..	549
Bronze, Urn Shape, Neoclassical Style, Green Patina, 14 x 9 ½ x 9 In.	406
Creamware, Rouleau, Tubular, Amethyst Peach Finial, Metalwork Stand, 1900s, 13 In..........	277
Glass, Gold & White Latticinio, Ivory Vertical Bands, Electric, 1-Light, Italy, 25 x 7 In.............	63
Glass & Mesh, 2 Gourd Shape, Filled With Blue Dyed Water, Electric, 28 In......................	123
Metal, Openwork, Oriental Design, Electric, 3-Light, Acorn Chain Pulls, c.1925, 23 x 7 In.	300
Porcelain, Famille Verte, Flowers, Electric, 1800s, 35 In..	1375
Porcelain, Blue & White, Scholars, Landscape, Electric, 1900s, 18 In.	338
Porcelain, Jar Drilled As Lamp, Deer, Bird, Flowers, Electric, Chinese, 11 In........................	187
Porcelain, Urn, Ceres & Jupiter, Baluster, Painted, Mounted As Lamp, Electric, c.1900, 23 In. .	150
Pottery, Painted Flowers, Dark Gloss Glaze, Hole In Base For Cord, 10 ¾ In.	77

LAMPSHADE

Glass, Umbrella Shape, Pink & Yellow Ground, Green Scrolling, Fleur-De-Lis, c.1850, 6 ½ x 10 In..	129
Hanging, Glass, Lantern, Block Shape, Fancy Metalwork Top, 6 In...................................	127
Hanging, Slag Glass, 8 Multicolor Panels, 12 x 16 x 16 In.	127
Hanging, Stained Glass, Dome Shape, Flowers, 20th Century, 13 x 20 In.....................	23
Leaded Glass, Flared Octagonal Shape, Caramel & Amber Glass Panels, 7 ½ x 8 ½ In.	24
Leaded Glass, Grapevine, Trumpeted Crown, Geometric Brick, Cranberry Panels, 16 ½ In.	272
Slag Glass, 6 Petals, Green, Rose, Amber Panels, Metal Rim, Early 1900s, 8 x 4 In. ....*illus*	59

LANTERNS are a special type of lighting device. They have a light source, usually a candle, totally hidden inside the walls of the lantern. Light is seen through holes or glass sections.

Barn Wood, Wire, Tin Smoke Shields, Loop Handle, 4 Glass Panes, Guards, 1800s, 16 In.	923
Bronze, Cage Form, Leafy Finials, Porcelain Flowers, 48 x 19 x 19 In....................................	2125
Bronze, Temple, Lotus Leaf Cover & Finial, Pierced Body, Japan, c.1900, 56 In., Pair	2000
Candle, Tin, Ring Carry Handle, Cone Top, 1800s, 18 In..	250
Candle, Tin, Triangular Shape, 2 Glass Panes, Sliding Panel In Back, 1800s, 18 x 15 In.............	510
Electric, 4-Light, Hanging, Iron, Cast Finials & Masques, Dome Top, 1900s, 72 x 26 x 26 In....	1750
Electric, Tin, Green Glass, Conical Finial, Filigree Border, Early 1900s, 18 x 7 x 7 In.	120
Fluid Burner, Tin Font, Glass Cleat Globe, Mid 1800s, 17 In.	938
Hall, 3-Light, Inverted Bell Shape, Brass & Glass, Empire Style, 1900s, 36 In..........................	375
Hanging, 4-Light, Brass, 6 Glass Panels, 6 Link Chains, 28 ½ x 16 In.............................*illus*	687
Hanging, 4-Light, Gilt Metal, Cylindrical, Glaze Side, 1900s, 22 x 10 ½ In............................	875
Hanging, 6-Light, Copper, 6 Panels, Glass, 50 x 32 In.	1187
Hanging, Candle, Tin Riveted Body, Glass Front, Ring Finial, c.1900, 11 In...........................	127
Hanging, Conical, Hammered Copper, Iron Ring Hanger, Amber Glass Shade, c.1910, 16 In....	143
Hanging, House Shape, Red, Green, Blue, Slag Glass, Geometric, Bronzed Metal Frame, 11 In.	413
Hanging, Lamp, Color Glass, Brass, Turkey, c.1950, 15 x 7 x 7 ½ In..................................	125
Kerosene, Tin, Filler & Chimney, 11 x 11 In...*illus*	136
Metal, 4-Light, Cage Shape, Porcelain Flowers, Mounted, France, 1900s, 47 x 18 x 18 In.	1375
Newel Post, Hammered Copper, Square, Glass Panels, Gustav Stickley, c.1910, 19 x 6 In...*illus*	4062
Pine, Wood Body, Beaded Corners, 4 Rectangular Windows, Pyramidal Top, 1800s, 11 x 6 In. .	1968

Lantern, Newel Post, Hammered Copper, Square, Glass Panels, Gustav Stickley, c.1910, 19 x 6 In.
$4,062

Rago Arts and Auction Center

Lantern, Temple, Hanging, Brass, Lotus Roof, Rice Paper Windows, Hexagonal, Japan, 1900s, 14 In.
$369

Skinner, Inc.

Le Verre Francais, Vase, Stylized Necklace, Mottled Pink Ground, Cameo, Signed, Charder, 12 x 10 In.
$2,768

Morphy Auctions

Leather, Bag, U.S. Mail, City Collection, Canvas, Trim & Buckles, 1900s, 11 x 24 x 14 In.
$219

Rago Arts and Auction Center

Leather, Briefcase, Black, Top Handle, Strap, Caggiano, 14 In.
$338

Clars Auction Gallery

Leather, Paper Shelf, Stepped Serpentine Tiers, Brass Handles, France, 20 x 24 x 18 In.
$1,063

New Orleans Auction Galleries

Sheet Iron, Pierced Top, Blown Glass Globe, Strap Ring Handle, Brass Collar, Mid 1800s, 17 In.	129
Skater's, 3-Sided, Glass, Steel Wire Handle, Brass Font, Burner, Brown Patina, 13 ½ In.	110
Temple, Hanging, Brass, Lotus Roof, Rice Paper Windows, Hexagonal, Japan, 1900s, 14 In. *illus*	369
Tin, Dormer Vents, Horn Panels, Stamped, 6 WR, 1800s, 18 ½ In.	120
Tin, Lamp, Bulbous Globe, Tinned Iron, Whale Oil Burner, England, c.1850, 10 In.	338
Tin, Pentagonal Shape, Tin Reflector, Ring Handle, 4 Glass Panes, Rectangular, 1800s, 12 In.	338
Tin, Punch, Brass, Front Sliding Glass, Ring Finial, 15 In.	115
Tin, Red, 3 Windows, Horn Panes, Conical Top, Hanging Ring, 1800s, 16 In.	984
Tin, Wedding Cake Shape, Black Paint, Embossed Arched Sides, Ring Hanger, 1800s, 16 In.	2520
Travel Light, Tin Lithograph Body, Gold, Loop Handle, Stevens, 6 In.	46
Wood, Square, Leather Hinges, 1-Candle Base, Pyramid Top, 3 Holes, c.1820, 9 ⅝ In.	1920
Wood, Tin Door, Tin Smoke Shield, Wire Handle, 3 Glass Panes, 1800s, 11 In.	2337

Le Verre Francais **LE VERRE FRANCAIS** is one of the many types of cameo glass made by the Schneider Glassworks in France. The glass was made by the C. Schneider factory in Epinay-sur-Seine from 1918 to 1933. It is a mottled glass, usually decorated with floral designs, and bears the incised signature *Le Verre Francais*.

Vase, Blue, Raised On Round Foot, Signed, Charder, 12 In.	406
Vase, Clear To Amethyst, Raised On Round Foot, Signed, Charder, 9 ¾ In.	219
Vase, Clear To Black, Incised, Raised On Round Foot, Marked, Charder, 5 ¼ x 4 In.	125
Vase, Clear To Pink, Raised On Round Foot, Signed, Charder, 10 ½ x 8 ½ In.	563
Vase, Lavender, Mottled, Turned Out Mouth, Cameo, Signed, Charder, 5 ½ In.	677
Vase, Mottled Orange, Flowers, Pink & White Ground, Art Deco Cameo, 24 ½ x 7 In.	2142
Vase, Palmiers, Dark Blue Stylized Palm Tree, Blue, White Ground, Signed, 15 In.	3075
Vase, Stylized Necklace, Mottled Pink Ground, Cameo, Signed, Charder, 12 x 10 In. *illus*	2768
Vase, Tortues, Tortoise, Tile Pattern, Green To Dark Shade, Mottled Orange, Signed, 12 x 4 In.	2142

LEATHER is tanned animal hide and has been used to make decorative and useful objects for centuries. Leather objects must be carefully preserved with proper humidity and oiling or the leather will deteriorate and crack. This damage cannot be repaired.

Bag, Bowler, Prada, Chestnut Brown, Brushed Gold Hardware, Hang Tag, Adjustable Straps	184
Bag, U.S. Mail, City Collection, Canvas, Trim & Buckles, 1900s, 11 x 24 x 14 In. *illus*	219
Briefcase, Black Walnut, Brass Hardware, Box, J. Benjamin, c.1985, 14 x 16 ½ x 3 In.	273
Briefcase, Black, Top Handle, Strap, Caggiano, 14 In. *illus*	338
Briefcase, Brass Mounts, Tan, Divided Interior, Hartmann, c.1980, 17 x 18 x 5 In.	201
Chaps, Adjustable, Bat Wing Leg, Brass Conchas, Embossed Stars, Signed C.P. Shipley, 36 x 26 In.	896
Coat, Wool, Suede, Ivory & Beige, Gold Trim, Claude Montana, 1980-81	1170
Figure, Piglet, Standing, Seam Down Back, Brown, 6 x 10 ½ In.	150
Holster, Gun Belt, Edward H. Bohlin, 42 In.	150
Paper Shelf, Stepped Serpentine Tiers, Brass Handles, France, 20 x 24 x 18 In. *illus*	1063
Saddle, Western, Intertwined Design, 6 Brass Conchos, Signed, Chas. P. Shipley, c.1930, 13 x 26 In.	672
Saddle, Wood, Brown, Western, Black, 96 In.	425

LEEDS POTTERY **LEEDS** pottery was made at Leeds, Yorkshire, England, from 1774 to 1878. Most Leeds ware was not marked. Early Leeds pieces had distinctive twisted handles with a greenish glaze on part of the creamy ware. Later ware often had blue borders on the creamy pottery. A Chicago company named Leeds made many Disney-inspired figurines. They are listed in the Disneyana category.

Basin, Blue, Tan, Flowers, Leaves, Trailing Vine Border, 4 x 14 In.	212
Jar, Perfume, Creamware, Ornate Panel Sides, Raised Foot, Impressed, 1800s, 10 In.	222
Plate, American Eagle & Shield, Blue Feather Edge, 8 ¼ In.	420
Plate, Green Feather Edge, Peafowl, Multicolor, Central Branch, Cream, 8 In.	201
Platter, Green Feather Edge, Shaped, Oval, 13 x 17 In.	177

LEFTON is a mark found on pottery, porcelain, glass, and other wares imported by the Geo. Zoltan Lefton Company. The company began in 1941. George Lefton died in 1996 and the company was sold in 2001 but the mark *Lefton* is still being used. The company mark has changed through the

L

years, but because marks have been used for long periods of time, they are of little help in dating an object.

| Lefton China 1948–1953 | Lefton China 1950–1955 | Lefton China 1949–2001 |

Ashtray, Holiday, Christmas Tree, White Ground, Rectangular, 9 x 4 In. 4
Bank, Blue Bird, Rhinestone Eyes, Sticker, 6 In. 31
Candle Climber, Mrs. Santa Claus, Square Spectacles, Christmas, Red & Gold Base, 3¼ In. 6
Figurine, Candy Cane Toboggan, 4 Angels Riding, Merry Christmas, 10 In. 82
Figurine, Doctor, Listening To Child's Chest, 6¾ x 4½ In. 24
Figurine, Owl, Brown, Perched, 6¼ In. 12
Figurine, Pineapple, Rosebuds, Pink, Gilt, White, 5 x 4 In. 62
Figurine, White Pixie, Elf, Iridescent, Red Foil Label, Hat. 86
Figurine, Woman, Muff, Christmas, Green Coat, Red Dress, 4 In. 22
Nut Dish, Lid, Miss Priss, Kitty Cat, Dish, Cream Ground, Floral, 4½ x 5¾ In. 147
Pitcher, Miss Priss, Kitty Cat, Milk, Creamer, Handle, Wide Spout 16
Planter, Blond Girl, Basket Of Valentine Hearts, 4½ x 11 In. 79
Planter, Bunny Rabbit, Pink, Blue, White, 7½ x 4 In. 49
Plate, Christmas Tree, Cream Ground, Holly & Berries, 1970, 8¼ x 7¼ In. 8
Salt & Pepper, Blue Bird, Marked, 3¾ In. 64
Salt & Pepper, Chintz, Violets, c.1950, 2½ In. 22
Wall Plaque, Cat, Sitting, White 40

LEGRAS was founded in 1864 by Auguste Legras at St. Denis, France. It is best known for cameo glass and enamel-decorated glass with Art Nouveau designs. Legras merged with Pantin in 1920 and became the Verreries et Cristalleries de St. Denis et de Pantin Reunies.

Vase, Autumn Forest, Coppery Leaves, Enamel, Cameo, 5⅞ In. 885
Vase, Bulbous, Enamel Flower Heads, Leaves, Signed, 8 x 6 In. 90
Vase, Flowers, Carved, Off White, Red Brown Flowers, Cameo, Signed, 4½ x 3 In. 500
Vase, Landscape Scene, Barren Trees, Autumn Yellow Shading, Blue, Cameo Cut, Signed, 5⅜ x 3 In. 2304
Vase, Maroon Enameled Blossoms, Cameo, 4¾ In. 188
Vase, Snow Scene, Tapering, Undulating Rim, 4 Colors, Signed, 12 In. 396

LENOX porcelain is well-known in the United States. Walter Scott Lenox and Jonathan Coxon founded the Ceramic Art Company in Trenton, New Jersey, in 1889. In 1896 Lenox bought out Coxon's interest, and in 1906 the company was renamed Lenox, Inc. The company makes porcelain that is similar to Irish Belleek. In 2009, after a series of mergers, Lenox became part of Clarion Capital Partners. The marks used by the firm have changed through the years, so collectors can date the ceramics. Related pieces may also be listed in the Ceramic Art Co. category.

Ashtray, American Cup, Defender, Schooner, Columbia, 1871 21
Bust, Baby Angel Head, Ivory Color, 1935, 4½ In. 21
Candleholder, Tea Light Votive, Pink Roses, Gold Trim, 2½ In. 8
Gravy Boat, Autumn, Attached Underplate, Cream Ground 64
Plate Set, Fish, Gilt, Shaped Rim, 12 Different Fish, W.H. Morley, 1900s, 9⅜ In., 12 Piece 492
Plate, Christmas, 1999, Christmas Trees Around The World, Mexico, Horse, Fish, Flowers, Box 29
Plate, Dinner, White, Great Seal Of United States, Gold Logo & Border 229
Platter, Holly Berry, Gilt Gold Trim, Eggshell Ground, 13 In. 56
Stein, Golfers, Green, Silver Lid, Engraved, Cobble Hill Golf Club, 1899, ½ Liter 570
Stein, Sterling Lid, Toasting Monk, C Handle, c.1890 175
Stein, Victorian Man, Top Hat, Cane, Merry Christmas, Blue, Metal Tiffany Lid, ½ Liter 510
Sugar, Lid, Southern Vista, Flowers, Cream, Gold Trim, c.1992, 5 In. 24
Vase, Flowers, Multicolor, Gilt Trim, J. Nosek, c.1925, 15¼ In., Pair 246

Lenox, Vase, Trumpet, Yellow, Cream Interior, Green Mark, Bailey Banks & Biddle, c.1930, 8 In.
$129

Cordier Auctions

Libbey, Cruet, Green & Brown Staining, Applied Custard Handle, Stopper, 1800s, 7¼ In.
$191

Jeffrey S. Evans & Associates

Libbey, Pitcher, Cut Glass, Curved Handle, Flared Rim, Mark, 12 In.
$840

Brunk Auctions

Libbey, Sugar Shaker, Corn Maize, Opaque Glass, Blue Husks, 6 In. $92

vintagesecrets on eBay

Libbey, Vase, Harvard Pattern, Trumpet, Cranberry Cut To Clear, 14 ¼ In. $1,020

Brunk Auctions

Lighter, Advertising, Sunoco, Figural Gas Pump, 3 ⅝ x 2 x 1 ¼ In. $319

AntiqueAdvertising.com

Vase, Pink Iris, Light Yellow Ground, Gilt Trim, Bulbous Middle, Signed H. Nosek, 15 In.	246
Vase, Trumpet, Yellow, Cream Interior, Green Mark, Bailey Banks & Biddle, c.1930, 8 In. *illus*	129

LETTER OPENERS have been used since the eighteenth century. Ivory and silver were favored by the well-to-do. In the late nineteenth century, the letter opener was popular as an advertising giveaway and many were made of metal or celluloid. Brass openers with figural handles were also popular.

Aladdin, Bronze, Arts & Crafts, Chinese, c.1910, 7 ½ In.	180
Birds, Flower, Bronze, Carved, Art Deco, 7 In.	12
Crocodile, Tail Used To Open Letter, Brass, 1950s, 9 In.	49
Dagger, Knife, Red Gem, Scottish Style, Lion, Steel Blade, 6 ½ In.	9
Dog, Pug, Head, Sterling Silver, 2-Sided, England, c.1906, 9 ¼ In.	498
Dolphin, Silver, George Jensen, 4 ½ x ¾ In.	69
Dragon, Belt Hook, Jade, Silver Engraved Blade, 8 ¼ In.	1000
Dragon, Brass, Cloisonne Carving, Chinese, 1940, 1 ¾ x 7 x 3 In.	22
Flower, Desk, Page Turner, Copper, Art Nouveau, c.1925	38
Kilkenny Design, Wire-Wrapped Handle, Ireland, 1965, 9 ¾ In.	201
Maiden Head, Silver, Art Nouveau, Secessionist, 6 ¾ In.	148
Mermaid, Flowing Hair, Holding Pirate Swords, Pewter	17
Monkey, Tree, Cast Handle, Engraved Blade, Brass, Japan, 1930, 12 In.	51
Owl, Brass, Glass Eyes, Marked, c.1900, 7 ¼ In.	595
Owl, Flying, Sterling Silver, Dominic Haff, 9 ½ In.	151
Panther, Sitting, Bronze, Art Nouveau, 1930s, 12 In.	225
Rabbit, Bone, Ears Back, 8 ¼ In.	31
Rose Point, Sterling Silver Handle, Stainless Blade, Wallace, 7 ¾ In.	22
Sailor Holding Onto Capstan, Bronze, c.1880, 8 ¼ In.	48
Sterling Silver, Solitaire, Gold Lining, Montblanc	86
Swan Handle, Rock Crystal, Gold, Diamond, Enamel, Red, 9 ½ In.	1750

Libbey **LIBBEY** Glass Company has made many types of glass since 1888, including the cut glass and tablewares that are collected today. The stemwares of the 1930s and 1940s are once again in style. The Toledo, Ohio, firm was purchased by Owens-Illinois in 1935 and is still working under the name Libbey Inc. Maize is listed in its own category.

Bottle, Sauce, Harvard Pattern, Ray Cut Base, 8 In.	84
Bowl, Centerpiece, Fruit, Oval, Cut Glass, Footed, 7 x 13 x 7 In.	1050
Bowl, Pedestal, Ruffled, Clusters Of Puntes, Intaglio Flowers, Ray Cut Foot, 4 ¾ x 9 ¾ In.	48
Candlestick, 6-Sided, Ray Cut Base, Clear Blank, Signed, 10 In.	72
Celery Tray, Glenda Pattern, Cut Glass, Signed 12 x 4 ¼ In.	48
Cruet, Green & Brown Staining, Applied Custard Handle, Stopper, 1800s, 7 ¼ In. *illus*	191
Dish, Rourke Pattern, Hobstar, 2 ½ x 10 In.	54
Glass, Old Style Lager, Beer, Red Print, 1940s, 3 ½ In.	200
Goblet, Cat Decoration, Opalescent Stem, Silhouette, Nash, 1930s, 7 x 3 In.	86
Goblet, Venetta Pattern, Cut Notched Stem, Ray Foot, 6 ¼ In.	18
Jug, Rum, Cut Glass, Crystal Strap Handle, Sultana, 7 x 6 ¾ In.	543
Nappy, Cut Glass, Estrella Pattern, Signed, 5 In.	18
Nappy, Harvard Pattern, Cut, Folded Edges, Triple Notched Handle, 7 In.	24
Nappy, Senora Pattern, Cut, Sacre Mark, Signed, 6 In.	60
Pitcher, Cut Glass, Curved Handle, Flared Rim, Mark, 12 In. *illus*	840
Plate, Aztec, Cut, Marked, 7 In.	1920
Plate, Sunset Pattern, Cut, Signed, W.C. Anderson, 7 In.	72
Punch Cup, Pedestal, Ray Cut Foot, Signed, 3 ¼ In.	18
Relish, Ozella Pattern, Cut, Signed, 7 ¾ x 4 In.	48
Rose Bowl, Princess, Ray Cut Base, Notched Rim, 7 ½ x 8 ½ In.	150
Sugar Shaker, Corn Maize, Opaque Glass, Blue Husks, 6 In. *illus*	92
Tray, Empress Pattern, Cut, 11 ¾ In.	180
Tray, Expanding Star Pattern, Cut, 12 ¼ In.	1200
Tray, Ice Cream, Cut Glass, 17 ½ In.	3900

Vase, Bowling Pin Shape, Intaglio Cut Flowers, Signed, c.1912, 11 ½ In.		181
Vase, Harvard Pattern, Trumpet, Cranberry Cut To Clear, 14 ¼ In.	*illus*	1020
Vase, Herringbone, Cut Glass, Handblown, Clear, c.1900, 7 ⅞ x 5 ⅜ In.		128
Vase, Jack-In-The-Pulpit, Amberina, Optical Ribbing, 5 ½ x 6 In.		266

LIGHTERS for cigarettes and cigars are collectible. Cigarettes became popular in the late nineteenth century, and with the cigarette came matches and cigarette lighters. All types of lighters are collected, from solid gold to the first disposable lighters. Most examples found were made after 1940. Some lighters may be found in the Jewelry category in this book.

Advertising, Sunoco, Figural Gas Pump, 3 ⅝ x 2 x 1 ¼ In.	*illus*	319
Atlanta Boat Works, Hana, Black & Red, Boat Shape, Box		106
Azur, Lift Arm, Enameled, Monaco, c.1920, 2 In.	*illus*	125
Camel, Red Kamel Turkish Cigarettes, 10 For 10 Cents, Red, Gold Trim, 8 x 8 ½ x 3 In.	*illus*	1088
Cartier, Gas, Gold Plated, Pentagonal, Cut Design, Swiss, 2 ¾ x 1 x ½ In.		133
Cigar, Eldred Mfg., Oak, Metal Fuel Tank, Battery Operated, c.1900, 14 ½ x 7 ½ In.		540
Cigar, Gorham, Ashtray, Peacock, Burner Lifts Out, Silver Plate, c.1910, 8 x 7 In.		104
Cigar, La Fendrich, Mild Havana Cigar, Iron, Glass Shade, Kerosene, 11 x 8 x 6 In.	*illus*	960
Cigar, Old Sailor, Wood Plaque, Glass Eyes, Wall Mount, Germany, 8 ¾ x 8 x 5 ¾ In.		132
Cigar, S.T. Dupont, Black Enamel, Goldtone, Refillable, Leather Case, 2 ½ x 1 ½ x ½ In.		130
Cut Glass, Hawkes, Silver Wells, Pedestal, Striped Highlights, Pushbutton, Signed, 5 ½ In.		180
Dunhill, Lift Arm, 5 Peseta Coin Body, Pocket, 2 ⅛ In.		125
Dunhill, Pistol, Flintlock, Wood Handle, Table		136
Dunhill, Rollagas, Gold Plated, Crosshatch Pattern, Box & Papers, 2 ⅜ In.		220
Dunhill, Rollalite, Silver, Engraved Shangri Dragon, Gas, Table		248
Figural, Devil, Cigar In His Mouth, 1800s, Desk, 8 ½ x 4 x 5 In.		1140
Flintlock, Steel Body, Compartment Door, Hardwood Grip, England, 1700s, 7 In.		677
Owl, Perched, Spelter, Applied Glass Eyes, 3 x 5 In.		174
Ronson Storm, 100 Yrs. Free Postage, Lift Arm, Petrol, Goldtone Chrome, 1896		28
Ronson, Octette, Touch Tip, Art Deco, Table, 1930-40		113
Silver, Enamel, Pink, Blue Flowers, Leaves, Chevron, Art Nouveau, 1900-40, 2 In.		211
St. Dupont, Andalusia, Line 2, Platinum, Lacquered, 2 ½ In.		469
St. Dupont, Gold Plate, Enamel, Black Stripe, Jeroboam, France, 3 ¾ x 3 In.		756
St. Dupont, Picasso, Faune, Line 1, Lacquered, Box, 2 ½ In.		531
St. Dupont, Solitaire, Platinum, Diamond, Pocket, Box, 2 ½ In.		375
St. Dupont, Statue Of Liberty, Platinum, Lacquered, Box, 2 ½ In.		500
St. Dupont, Stylo Plume, Gold Plate, Lacquered, Stamped, 2 ½ In.		344
Tinder, Brass, Mahogany, Gun Shape, Wood Handle, Flintlock, 1700s, 7 ⅛ In.		1750
Tinder, Pistol Grip, Brass Frame, Lyre Support, Mahogany Grip, c.1880, 5 ½ In.		813
Tinder, Pistol Grip, Engraved Brass Frame & Handle, Ball Foot, c.1880, 8 In.		480
Zippo, Barcroft, 4th Model, B On Monogram, Scott & Patricia On Back, Metal, Table, c.1979		255
Zippo, Joe Biker, Riding Motorcycle, Dark Chrome, Table, Box, 1992		26

LIGHTNING RODS AND LIGHTNING ROD BALLS are collected. The glass balls were at the center of the rod that was attached to the roof of a house or barn to avoid lightning damage. The balls were made in many colors and many patterns. Collectors prefer examples made before 1940.

Glass Ball, Triangular Base, Blue Glass Ball, Marked, Kretzner St. Louis, c.1900, 62 In.		83
Metal, Goose, Glass Ball, Wood Base, 20 x 59 ½ In.		236

LIMOGES porcelain has been made in Limoges, France, since the mid-nineteenth century. Fine porcelains were made by many factories, including Haviland, Ahrenfeldt, Guerin, Pouyat, Elite, and others. Modern porcelains are being made at Limoges. The word *Limoges* as part of the mark is not an indication of age. Porcelain called "Limoges" was also made by Sebring China in Sebring, Ohio, in the early 1900s. The company changed its name to American Limoges China Company after the Limoges Company in France threatened to sue. American Limoges China Company went out of business in 1955. Haviland, one of the Limoges factories, is listed as a separate category in this book. These three marks are for factories in Limoges, France.

Lighter, Azur, Lift Arm, Enameled, Monaco, c.1920, 2 In.
$125

Leslie Hindman Auctioneers

Lighter, Camel, Red Kamel Turkish Cigarettes, 10 For 10 Cents, Red, Gold Trim, 8 x 8 ½ x 3 In.
$1,088

Morphy Auctions

Lighter, Cigar, La Fendrich, Mild Havana Cigar, Iron, Glass Shade, Kerosene, 11 x 8 x 6 In.
$960

Morphy Auctions

This is an edited listing of current prices. Visit **Kovels.com** to check thousands of prices from previous years and sign up for free information on trends, tips, reproductions, marks, and more.

Limoges, Bowl, Grapevine, Gilt, Stand, Claw Feet, 9 ½ x 14 In. $234

Skinner, Inc.

Limoges, Charger, Man & Woman, Mother & Child, On Bench, Gilt Border, Signed, E. Furlaud, 15 In. $424

Fontaine's Auction Gallery

Limoges, Tray, Bronze Mounts, Cobalt Blue Border, 2 Women Kissing, Signed, 3 x 22 x 12 In. $484

Fontaine's Auction Gallery

Lithophane, Fairy Lamp, Panoramic Scenes, Porcelain, 3 Angels, c.1900, 4 ⅝ x 4 In. $168

Jeffrey S. Evans & Associates

A. Klingenberg c.1880s–1890s	D & Co. c.1881–1893	M. Redon c.1882–1896

Bowl, Enameled Flowers, Orange & Red, Mottled Green Ground, Iron Frame, C. Faure, 13 ½ In. — 780
Bowl, Grapes, Vines, T&V, 5 x 12 In. — 59
Bowl, Grapevine, Gilt, Stand, Claw Feet, 9 ½ x 14 In. — *illus* 234
Bowl, Heart Shape, Red & Purple Grape Bunches, 10 In. — 35
Box, Round Lid, Cobalt Blue, Gilt, Portrait, Queen Louise, T&V, 7 x 3 ½ In. — 58
Cachepot, Pate-Sur-Pate, Cameo, Woman & Child, ¾ x 8 In. — 313
Charger, Man & Woman, Mother & Child, On Bench, Gilt Border, Signed, E. Furlaud, 15 In. — *illus* 424
Dish, Lovers, Landscape, Painted, France, 13 ⅜ In. — 70
Plate, Poppies, Gilt Trim, Marked, Alice, c.1915, 12 In. — 145
Platter, Oval, Shaped, Tressemann & Vogt, 9 ½ x 24 In. — 207
Tray, Bronze Mounts, Cobalt Blue Border, 2 Women Kissing, Signed, 22 x 12 In. — *illus* 484
Tray, Rectangular, Molded, Rocaille, Flowers, 20 x 16 ¼ In. — 201
Vase, Birds, Flowers, Green, Brown, Signed Larson, 14 In. — 184
Vase, Elongated Oval, Flowers, c.1920, 21 ½ In. — 125
Vase, Geometric Shapes, Enameled, Art Deco, Camille Faure, 12 ¼ In. — 6150
Vase, Gilt Top Rim, Birds Perched, La Porcelaine Limousine, c.1920, 13 x 5 In. — 48
Vase, Green, Lavender, 3 ½ x 2 In. — 215
Vase, Metallic Luster, Large Crab, Frederic Danton, France, c.1920, 4 ½ In. — 215

LINDBERGH was a national hero. In 1927, Charles Lindbergh, the aviator, became the first man to make a nonstop solo flight across the Atlantic Ocean. In 1932, his son was kidnapped and murdered, and Lindbergh was again the center of public interest. He died in 1974. All types of Lindbergh memorabilia are collected.

Badge, Photo Button, Airplane, American Flag Ribbon, Minnesota's Own, 3 ¼ In. — 144
Badge, Photo Button, Smiling, Welcome Our Hero, Metal Airplane, 1 ¼ In. — 354
Bank, Bust, Metal, Gilt, Lindy Bank, 1928, 6 ½ x 4 In. — 79
Bank, Charles, Bust, Cast Aluminum, Marked, N. Tregor, 1920s — 20
Banner, Spirit Of St. Louis Plane, New York To Paris Flight, Silk, 1927 — 81
Bookend, Propeller, Aircraft Engine, Cast Iron, 8 ¼ x 4 ¾ In. — 106
Bookends, Spirit Of St. Louis, Clouds, First Non-Stop Flight, 4 ¾ In. — 153
Bookends, The Aviator, Portrait, Cast Iron, Bronze Finish, 1920s, 5 ½ x 4 ¾ In. — 225
Box, Pencil, Tin, Spirit Of St. Louis, Lindy, Portrait, Airplane, 1930s, 7 ¾ x 2 In. — 49
Button, Political Campaign, Pinback, Aviation, Welcome Lindy, Whitehead & Hoag — 8
Commemorative Medallion, Bronze, New York, Paris, 1927, 2 ¾ In. — 75
Handkerchief, Sketch Of Lindbergh, So This Is Paris On Top Of Head, 1927, 11 In. — 45
Medal, Lindy's Good Luck Token, Flight, 1927 — 30
Poster, Anti-Tobacco, Featuring Lucky Lindy, No. 1, Broadside, 1920s — 55
Toy, Airplane, Bleirot Monoplane, Spirit Of St. Louis, Tootsietoy, 1910s, 2 ¼ x 2 ¼ In. — 69
Watch, Hour Angle, Automatic, Roman Numerals, Stainless Steel, 1 ½ x ¾ In. — 610

LITHOPHANES are porcelain pictures made by casting clay in layers of various thicknesses. When a piece is held to the light, a picture of light and shadow is seen through it. Most lithophanes date from the 1825–75 period. A few are still being made. Many lithophanes sold today were originally panels for lampshades.

Easel, Frame, Cherubs, Flowers Openwork, Metal, Art Nouveau, 1900s — 313
Fairy Lamp, Panoramic Scenes, Porcelain, 3 Angels, c.1900, 4 ⅝ x 4 In. — *illus* 168
Lamp, 2 Deer, Mountainous Scene, Painted, Porcelain, c.1900, 4 ½ x 3 ⅝ In. — 329
Lamp, Brass, 2 Panels, France, Adjustable Height, c.1930, 19 x 8 In. — 124
Tea Warmer, Military Figures, Woman, Teapot, Marked, JP, Germany, c.1850, 11 In. — *illus* 1989

LIVERPOOL, England, has been the site of many pottery and porcelain factories since the eighteenth century. Color-decorated porcelains, transfer-printed earthenware, stoneware, basalt, figurines, and other wares were made. Sadler and Green made print-decorated wares starting in 1756. Many of the pieces were made for the American market and feature patriotic emblems, such as eagles and flags. Liverpool pitchers are called Liverpool jugs by collectors.

Jug, 3-Masted Ship, Ophelia, Red, White & Blue Pennant, c.1825, 10 In.	840
Jug, Boston Frigate, Flag, Cannon, Battle Verse, Swag, Tassel, 10 ½ x 9 ½ In.	2880
Jug, Clipper Ship, Full Sail, American Flag, Grisaille Wreath, 1800s, 10 In.	720
Jug, Creamware, Classical Scenes, Bird, Fox, 1800s, 7 ¼ In.	237
Jug, Farmer's Arms, Weaver's Arms, Creamware, George Cubbinson, 1800s, 11 ½ x 7 ¾ x 9 ½ In.	277
Jug, Tom Truelove Going To Sea, Jack Spritsail, Herculaneum, Early 1800s, 10 In.	406
Jug, Washington Memorial, Portraits, Sam Adams, John Hancock, Multicolor, 9 x 9 ½ In.	2040
Jug, Washington Memorial, Winged Eagle, Grape Cluster, Ribbon, 9 ½ x 10 In.	780
Jug, White, Black, Trees, Horse, People, Handle, 1800s, 9 In.	300
Mug, Creamware, Transfer, Mariner's Compass, c.1800, 4 ⅝ In.	584

LLADRO is a Spanish porcelain. Brothers Juan, Jose, and Vicente Lladro opened a ceramics workshop in Almacera in 1951. They soon began making figurines in a distinctive, elongated style. In 1958 the factory moved to Tabernes Blanques, Spain. The company makes stoneware and porcelain figurines and vases in limited and unlimited editions. Dates given are first and last years of production. Marks since 1977 have the added word *Daisa,* the acronym for the company that holds the intellectual property rights to Lladro figurines.

Bust, Figurine, Sad Clown, Butterfly On Hat, No. 5611, 1989-97, 8 In.	124
Figurine, A Barrow Of Fun, Girl, Wheelbarrow, Puppies, No. 5460, 1988-91, 8 x 10 In.	372
Figurine, Anniversary Waltz, Man & Woman, Mint, No. 1372, 1978-2004, Box	123
Figurine, Boy Student, Porcelain, Standing, Sandals, Reading Book, 17 ½ In.	104
Figurine, Boy With Dog, Quiet, Hand Painted, No. 4522, c.1970	56
Figurine, Bridal Portrait, Box, No. 5742, 1991-95, 13 ¼ In.	161
Figurine, Clown, Tired Friend, No. 5812, 1991-2007, Box	28
Figurine, Geisha Girl, Sayonara, No. 4989, 1978-96, 10 ½ In.	155
Figurine, Kitty Cart, Girl, Pushing Cart, Cats, Flower, No. 6141, 1994-2004	523
Figurine, Littlest Clown, Holding Balloons, Standing, Circular Base, No. 5811, 1991, Box *illus*	68
Figurine, My Baby, Vatala & Luana Devis, No.1331, 1976-81, 14 x 11 x 7 In.	168
Figurine, My Wedding Day, 2 Women, Jose Puche, 1986-92, 15 ¼ In.	230
Figurine, Mystical Garden, Glaze, No. 6686, 2000-02, 13 ¾ x 6 ¾ In.	560
Figurine, Pearl Mermaid, Fantasy, No. 1348, 1978-83, 11 ⅜ x 9 ¼ In.	460
Figurine, Sancho Panza, Seated On Stool, No. 1031, 1969-89, 12 x 12 x 6 ½ In. *illus*	250
Figurine, Tinkerbell, Peter Pan, Porcelain, Mint, No. 7518, 1992, 10 ½ In.	1137
Figurine, Viento De Primavera, Spring Breeze, Young Woman, Box, No. 4936, 1974-2004, 14 In.	240
Figurine, Woman, 3 Angels, Heavenly Prayer, Fulgencio Garcia, No. 6145, 1994-97, 17 In.	230
Figurine, Young Woman, Picking Bouquet Of Flowers, Matte Finish, 8 In.	60
Group, Impossible Dream, Don Quixote, Sancho Panza, No. 1318, 1976-86, 19 x 22 x 9 In.	438
Group, In The Gondola, Man, Woman, Gondolier, Guitar Player, No. 1350, 1978, 16 x 31 x 7 In.	600
Group, Puppy Love, Boy & Girl, Holding Hands, No. 1127, Box, 1971-96, 10 ½ In.	125
Ornament, Landing Dove, Christmas, Glossy, No. 6266, 1995-97, 3 x 4 In.	31
Vase, Dragon, Yellow & Green, Glossy, Fluted Top, No. 4690, 1970-81, 10 x 3 x 4 In.	133

LOCKE ART is a trademark found on glass of the early twentieth century. Joseph Locke worked at many English and American firms. He designed and etched his own glass in Pittsburgh, Pennsylvania, starting in the 1880s. Some pieces were marked *Joe Locke,* but most were marked with the words *Locke Art.* The mark is hidden in the pattern on the glass.

Pitcher, Grapes & Lines, Etched, Colorless, Unsigned, Late 1900s, 6 ¾ In.	222

Lithophane, Tea Warmer, Military Figures, Woman, Teapot, Marked, JP, Germany, c.1850, 11 In.
$1,989

Jeffrey S. Evans & Associates

Lladro, Figurine, Littlest Clown, Holding Balloons, Standing, Circular Base, No. 5811, 1991, Box
$68

Hartzell's Auction Gallery, Inc.

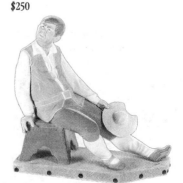

Lladro, Figurine, Sancho Panza, Seated On Stool, No. 1031, 1969-89, 12 x 12 x 6 ½ In.
$250

Garth's Auctioneers & Appraisers

Loetz, Vase, Green Iridescent, Polished Pontil, 4 x 6 In.
$83

Forsythes' Auctions

TIP
Pronounce Loetz correctly. Most Americans pronounce it like "lotes," but it is pronounced "lertz."

Loetz, Vase, Green Iridescent, Silver Overlay, Floral Engraved, 4 ½ In.
$236

Forsythes' Auctions

Loetz, Vase, Green Iridescent, Threaded, Handles, Crete Pampas, 5 ¼ x 5 x 8 In.
$272

Fontaine's Auction Gallery

LOETZ glass was made in many varieties. Johann Loetz bought a glassworks in Klostermuhle, Bohemia (now Klastersky Mlyn, Czech Republic), in 1840. He died in 1848 and his widow ran the company; then in 1879, his grandson took over. Most collectors recognize the iridescent gold glass similar to Tiffany, but many other types were made. The firm closed during World War II.

Bottle, Green Iridescent, Glass, Late 1900s, 11 ¼ x 6 ¾ In.	94
Bowl, Amethyst Threading, Ruffled Rim, Figural Classical Stem, c.1900, 11 ½ In.	156
Bowl, Tango, Orange, Black Enamel, Oval, 8 Lobes, Footed, Dagobert Peche, 1920s, 6 x 6 In.	1125
Bride's Basket, Threaded, Olive Green, Scalloped Rim, Stand, 12 ½ x 9 ½ In.	216
Chandelier, 5-Light, Brass, Corbels, Ram's Heads, Leafy Casings, 18 ½ x 16 ½ In.	4538
Dresser Box, Iridescent, Enameled, Brass, 3-Footed, 4 ½ In.	288
Vase, Blue Iridescent, Green, Ruffled Rim, Polished Pontil, Austria, c.1880, 13 ½ In.	523
Vase, Candia, Aurene, Blue Feathers, 8 Dimples, Polished Pontil, 8 x 5 ½ In.	1331
Vase, Creta Diaspora, Green, Pinched Sides, Tricornered Lip, 4 ¾ In.	126
Vase, Creta Formosa, Green Iridescent, Applied Blue Threading, c.1910, 7 x 8 ½ In.	431
Vase, Crete Pampas, Green Iridescent, Squat Base, Baluster Mouth, Signed, c.1899, 8 ½ In.	413
Vase, Cytisus, Iridescent, Pulled Feather, Austria, Unsigned, 7 x 4 In.	2000
Vase, Diaspora, Platinum Iridescent Overlay, Craters, Applied Gold Iridescent Handles, 6 In.	984
Vase, Flared Inverted Lip, Amber Iridescent, Pulled Feather, 5 x 5 ¼ In.	301
Vase, Glass, Patinated Metal, Wiener Werkstatte Style, Austria, c.1910, 17 In.	1469
Vase, Green Iridescent, Polished Pontil, 4 x 6 In. *illus*	83
Vase, Green Iridescent, Silver Overlay, Floral Engraved, 4 ½ In. *illus*	236
Vase, Green Iridescent, Threaded, Handles, Crete Pampas, 5 ¼ x 5 x 8 In. *illus*	272
Vase, Honey Iridescent, Crackle Glaze, Candia Mimosa, 5 ½ x 3 ½ In.	89
Vase, Iridescent, Flowers, Silver Overlay, 3 ½ x 4 In.	2000
Vase, Iridescent, Green Ruffled Lip, Ausfhurung 44, Random Threading, Handles, 5 ½ In.	284
Vase, Iridescent, Maximia, 3-Sided Top, 3 Elongated Dimples, 8 ½ x 4 In.	2080
Vase, Iridescent, Ruffled Rim, Orange Spots, 5 ½ In.	431
Vase, Medici, Iridescent Oil Spot, Chestnut Ground, 4 ½ x 7 ½ In.	473
Vase, Medici, Iridescent, Combed Oil Spots, Chestnut Ground, 4 ½ x 7 ½ In. *illus*	473
Vase, Melusin Titania, Gray Trailings, Flared Upper Rim, Unsigned, 10 ¾ x 7 In.	1320
Vase, Papillion, Gold Iridescent, Green, 5 Tulip Openings, 6 ½ x 5 ½ In. *illus*	567
Vase, Papillon Genre, Oil Spot, Amber Glass Ground, Mounted Handles, Signed, 11 x 8 In.	738
Vase, PG Zephyr Genre, Translucent, Pinched Sides, Applied Red Tendrils, 11 x 6 ½ In. *illus*	861
Vase, Phaenomen Candia, Gold Waves, Blue, Magenta, Cupped Rim, 5 ⅝ In.	531
Vase, Phaenomen, Iridescent, Multicolor, Uneven Rim, Holes, Pulled, Pierced, 10 x 7 In. *illus*	4375
Vase, Phaenomen, Pink & Silver Iridescent, Bell Form, Flared & Flattened Rim, 5 x 4 In.	1375
Vase, Phaenomen, Wavy Lines, Dimples, Ruffled Rim, Etched Mark, c.1900, 7 x 3 In. *illus*	1125
Vase, Silver Overlay, Pinched, Tooled Rim, La Pierre Mfg. Co., c.1900, 9 ½ In.	1121
Vase, Titania, Bulbous, Cylindrical Neck, Flared, Green Metallic Threads, 7 x 4 In.	1845
Vase, Titania, Cobalt Blue, Feathery Tips, Bubbles, Ribs, 4 In.	2714

LONE RANGER, a fictional character, was introduced on the radio in 1932. Over three thousand shows were produced before the series ended in 1954. In 1938, the first Lone Ranger movie was made. The latest movie was made in 2013. Television shows were started in 1949 and are still seen on some stations. The Lone Ranger appears on many products and was even the name of a restaurant chain from 1971 to 1973.

Action Figure, Tonto, Shoes, Guns, Belt, Clothes, Gabriel, 1973, 10 In.	12
Animation Cell, Lone Ranger, Tonto, Face To Face, Frame, 1981, 14 x 16 In.	425
Badge, Deputy, Secret Compartment, Guns, Brass, 1949, 2 In.	65
Badge, Safety Sentinel, Miami Maid, Membership Pin, 1939, 1 ⅜ In.	59
Book, Lone Ranger & Talking Pony, Little Golden Book, 1958	18
Calendar, 1949, Merita Bread, Tonto, Dan Reid, 12-Month Display, 8 x 15 In.	162
Card, Hand Signed, Matted Display, Clayton Moore, 11 x 14 In.	18
Doll, Lone Ranger, Hat, Mask, Gunbelt, Composition, Dollcraft, c.1937, 15 In.	850
Game, Cardboard Disc, Tokens, Cowboy & Western Theme, Parker Brothers, 1956	33
Lunch Box Thermos, Black Cup Lid, Hard Plastic, Tonto, Multicolor	18
Lunch Box, Red Band, Silver, Pail, Handle, Adco Liberty, 1954	104

Loetz, Vase, Medici, Iridescent, Combed Oil Spots, Chestnut Ground, 4 ½ x 7 ½ In.
$473

Morphy Auctions

Loetz, Vase, Papillion, Gold Iridescent, Green, 5 Tulip Openings, 6 ½ x 5 ½ In.
$567

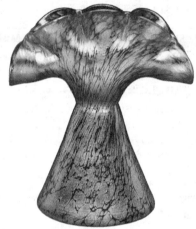

Morphy Auctions

Loetz, Vase, PG Zephyr Genre, Translucent, Pinched Sides, Applied Red Tendrils, 11 x 6 ½ In.
$861

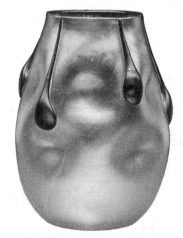

Morphy Auctions

Loetz, Vase, Phaenomen, Iridescent, Multicolor, Uneven Rim, Holes, Pulled, Pierced, 10 x 7 In.
$4,375

Treadway

Loetz, Vase, Phaenomen, Wavy Lines, Dimples, Ruffled Rim, Etched Mark, c.1900, 7 x 3 In.
$1,125

Rago Arts and Auction Center

Longwy, Bowl, Embossed Flowers, Multicolor, Kenilworth Studios, France, c.1920, 3¼ x 10 In.
$90

Soulis Auctions

Lunch Box, Football Helmets, American & National Conferences, Metal, King-Seeley, c.1976
$35

Main Auction Galleries, Inc.

Lunch Boxes

About 650 different children's metal lunch box designs have been made in the United States. The first, a Hopalong Cassidy lunch box, was made in 1951; and the last, a Rambo box, dates from 1985. Now children's lunch boxes are plastic.

Lunch Box, Munsters, Metal, Characters & Scenes, King-Seeley, c.1965
$127

Main Auction Galleries, Inc.

Magazine, Masked Rider's Justice, Freeing Tonto, Trojan Publishing Corp., 1937	261
Magazine, Phantom Rider, Tonto Holding Rifle, Trojan Publishing Corp., 1937, ¾ In.	297
Pen, Black Marble Looking, 14K Gold Filled Point, Stratford, 1938	34
Puzzle, Picture, Frame Tray Inlay, Whitman, 1957, 14½ x 11½ In.	21
Sailor Cap, Hi-Yo Silver, Fabric, Black & White, c.1940, 8 In.	100
Sweater, Lone Ranger & Silver, Blue, Gray, Cotton, 1940s, Child's, 12 x 36 In.	90
Tablecloth, Lone Ranger Galloping Border, Western Graphics, Paper Art Co., 54 x 102 In.	10
Toy, Holster Belt, Leather, Cowboy, Marked	30
Toy, Lone Ranger, Silver, Spinning Lasso, Tin, Windup, Marx, 1938, 8½ x 6 In.	389
Watch, Tonto, 12-Hour Dial, Arabic Numerals, Chrome, Pocket, Smiths, 1950s-60s, 2 In.	50

LONGWY WORKSHOP of Longwy, France, first made ceramic wares in 1798. The workshop is still in business. Most of the ceramic pieces found today are glazed with many colors to resemble cloisonne or other enameled metal. Many pieces were made with stylized figures and Art Deco designs. The factory used a variety of marks.

Longwy Faience Co.
1880–1939

Longwy Faience Co.
1890–1948

Longwy Faience Co.
1951–1948

Bowl, Embossed Flowers, Multicolor, Kenilworth Studios, France, c.1920, 3¼ x 10 In.	*illus*	90

LOTUS WARE was made by the Knowles, Taylor & Knowles Company of East Liverpool, Ohio, from 1890 to 1900. Lotus Ware, a thin porcelain that resembles Belleek, was sometimes decorated outside the factory. Other types of ceramics that were made by the Knowles, Taylor & Knowles Company are listed under KTK.

Ewer, White, Green, Pink Flowers, Gold Interior & Trim, c.1895, 9½ In.	406
Pitcher, White, Fishnet Decoration, Handle, 5 In.	250
Teapot, Lid, White, Gold Accents, Porcelain, 1890s, 7 x 3½ In.	279
Venice, Tea Set, Pot, Sugar, Creamer, Relief Flowers, Gold Accents, 1890s	499

J.&J.G.LOW **LOW** art tiles were made by the J. and J. G. Low Art Tile Works of Chelsea, Massachusetts, from 1877 to 1902. A variety of art and other tiles were made. Some of the tiles were made by a process called "natural," some were hand-modeled, and some were made mechanically.

Bowl, Blue Border, Flowers, Initials, c.1780, 6¾ In.	240
Tile, Arabic Star, Green Olive Glazed, 1881, 4 x 4 In.	100
Tile, Blue, Swirl Design, 1800s, 4¼ In.	199
Tile, Putti, Grapes, Blue, Marked, Chelsea, c.1890, 4 x 4 In.	65

LOY-NEL-ART, *see McCoy category.*

 LUNCH BOXES and lunch pails have been used to carry lunches to school or work since the nineteenth century. Today, most collectors want either early tin tobacco advertising boxes or children's lunch boxes made since the 1930s. These boxes are made of metal or plastic. Vinyl lunch boxes were made from 1959 to 1982. Injection molded plastic lunch boxes were made beginning in 1972. Legend says metal lunch boxes were banned in Florida in 1972 after a group of mothers claimed children were hitting each other with them and getting injured. This is not true. Metal lunch boxes stopped being made in the 1980s because they were more expensive to make than plastic lunch boxes. Boxes listed here include the original Thermos bottle inside the box unless otherwise indicated. Movie, television, and cartoon characters may be found in their own categories. Tobacco tin pails and lunch boxes are listed in the Advertising category.

Barbie & Midge, Dome Lid, Faces, Black Ground, Vinyl, Thermos, 1964	42
Barbie, Pink Ballet Shoes, Ponytail, Black, Vinyl, Strap, Mattel, 1962, 8½ x 8½ x 3½ In.	62

Barbie, Profile, Figures, Black Vinyl, Thermos, King-Seeley Thermos, 1962	175
Buccaneers, Dome Lid, Spanish Coins, Metal, Plastic Handle, Aladdin, 1957, 6 x 4 In.	41
Football Helmets, American & National Conferences, Metal, King-Seeley, c.1976 ....*illus*	35
Hogan's Heroes, Dome Lid, Prison Barracks, Haircut, Yellow, Gray, 1966	409
Jetsons, Mini, Tin, Metal, Multicolor, Dome, Lock & Handle, Hallmark	15
Lost In Space, Dome Lid, Space Rover, Rocky Landscape, Red Cup, 1967	327
Monroes, Metal, Plastic Handle, Cowboy, Horse, Aladdin, 1967	44
Munsters, Metal, Characters & Scenes, King-Seeley, c.1965 ....*illus*	127
Peter Rabbit, Tin, Peter & Friends, Tindeco, 4 ½ In.	149
Rice Krispies Elves, Red & White, Scenes, Plastic, Aladdin, With Thermos, 1984	25
Road Runner, Coyote, Metal, Plastic Handle, King-Seeley Thermos Co.	60
Underdog, Metal, Rectangular, Lock & Handle, Multicolor, 1972	920
Wrangler, Vinyl, Cowboy Roping Cow, Thermos, 1960s, 3 x 7 x 8 In.	145
Yogi Bear, Huckleberry Hound, Lock & Handle, Hanna Barbera, 1961	59

LUNCH BOX THERMOS

Chuck Wagon, Western Theme, Red Cup Lid, Stainless, Multicolor, Aladdin, ½ Pt., 6 ½ x 3 In.	15
Get Smart, Metal, White Cup Cover, Handle, Man & Woman	35
Gunsmoke, Woman, Blue Dress, Cowboy, Red Cup Lid, Metal, Handle	28
Monkees, Portrait, Metal, Hard Plastic, White Cup Lid, 1967	23
Yogi Bear, Quick Draw McGraw, Tug-O-War, Metal, Yellow Cup Lid, 8 Oz., 1961	17
Yosemite Sam, Bugs Bunny, Elmer Fudd, Loony Tunes, Blue Cup Lid, 1971	50
Zorro, Metal Rim Lips, Hard Plastic, Aluminum, Walt Disney, Aladdin	51

LUNEVILLE, a French faience factory, was established about 1730 by Jacques Chambrette. It is best known for its fine bisque figures and groups and for large faience dogs and lions. The early pieces were unmarked. The firm was acquired by Keller and Guerin and is still working.

Vase, Elephant, Howdah, Gilt, Embossed, Majolica, 1800s, 7 x 9 x 3 In. ....*illus*	300

LUSTER glaze was meant to resemble copper, silver, or gold. The term *luster* includes any piece with some luster trim. It has been used since the sixteenth century. Some of the luster found today was made during the nineteenth century. The metallic glazes are applied on pottery. The finished color depends on the combination of the clay color and the glaze. Blue, orange, gold, and pearlized luster decorations were used by Japanese and German firms in the early 1900s. Fairyland Luster was made by Wedgwood in the 1900s. Copies made by modern methods started appearing in 1990. Tea Leaf pieces have their own category.

Copper, Goblets, Redware, Flowers & Leaves, 5 In.	75
Copper, Mug, Alternating Bands Of Blue Enamel, c.1850, 5 x 1 In.	258
Fairyland Luster is included in the Wedgwood category.	
Mug, Cider, Silver Trim, Beige, c.1830, 3 x 3 In.	74
Sunderland Luster pieces are in the Sunderland category.	

LUSTRES are mantel decorations or pedestal vases with many hanging glass prisms. The name really refers to the prisms, and it is proper to refer to a single glass prism as a lustre. Either spelling, luster or lustre, is correct.

Apple Green, Ruffled Top, 8 Hanging Glass Spears, Mantel, 12 x 5 x 5 In.	385
Candleholder, Red, Stained, Etched, Deer, Birds, Castles, Bohemian, 10 x 5 In., Pair	499

MACINTYRE, *see Moorcroft category.*

MAJOLICA is a general term for any pottery glazed with an opaque tin enamel that conceals the color of the clay body. It has been made since the fourteenth century. Today's collector is most likely to find Victorian majolica. The heavy, colorful ware is rarely marked. Some famous makers include George Jones & Sons, Ltd.; Griffen, Smith and Hill; Joseph Holdcroft; and Minton. Majolica made by Wedgwood is listed in the Wedgwood category. These three marks can be found on majolica items.

Luneville, Vase, Elephant, Howdah, Gilt, Embossed, Majolica, 1800s, 7 x 9 x 3 In.
$300

Thomaston Place Auction Galleries

Majolica, Bowl, Pink, Flowers, Lobed Shape, Circular Foot, 9 In.
$138

Leslie Hindman Auctioneers

Majolica, Centerpiece, 2 Cherubs Holding Garland, Reticulated Basket, England, 1800s, 8 x 13 In.
$480

Brunk Auctions

Majolica, Centerpiece, Basket, 2 Pan Figures, Back To Back, Multicolor, 1900s, 17 x 15 In.
$125

Leslie Hindman Auctioneers

M

Majolica, Centerpiece, Scrolls & Berry Clusters, Pedestal Base, Handle, Late 1900s, 12 In.
$129

Jeffrey S. Evans & Associates

Majolica, Cheese Dish, Blue Birds, Pink Flowering Prunus, Water Lilies, 1800s, 9 x 10¼ In.
$90

Soulis Auctions

Majolica, Cheese Dish, Dome Lid, Flowers, Wheat, Blue, Stick Handle, George Jones, c.1880, 10 In.
$615

Skinner, Inc.

George Jones, George Jones & Sons, Ltd.
1861–1873

Griffen, Smith and Hill
c.1879–1889

Joseph Holdcroft, Sutherland Pottery
1865–1906

Ashtray, Boy Smoking Cigar, 8 x 6 In.	210
Basket, Strawberry, Bird, 2 Nests, Joseph Holdcroft, c.1900, 4¾ x 12 x 9½ In.	210
Bowl, Cabbage Leaf Shape, Green & White, c.1951, 3 x 9 In.	125
Bowl, Maple Leaf, Green Leaves, Brown, Cream, High Gloss Glaze, c.1850, 10 In.	311
Bowl, Oval, Dog, Brown, Handle, George Jones, c.1850, 11½ In.	188
Bowl, Pink, Flowers, Lobed Shape, Circular Foot, 9 In. ....*illus*	138
Bread Tray, Fern Leaves On Basket Weave, 10 x 14 In.	196
Butter, Goat Lying On Barrel, Minton, c.1850, 4½ In.	438
Candlestick, Twisted Oak Branches, c.1900, 7½ In.	25
Centerpiece, 2 Cherubs Holding Garland, Reticulated Basket, England, 1800s, 8 x 13 In..*illus*	480
Centerpiece, Basket, 2 Pan Figures, Back To Back, Multicolor, 1900s, 17 x 15 In. .....*illus*	125
Centerpiece, Bohemian, Putti, Multicolor, Footed Pedestal Base, c.1980, 10¼ In.	176
Centerpiece, Scrolls & Berry Clusters, Pedestal Base, Handle, Late 1900s, 12 In. ....*illus*	129
Charger, Multicolor, Yellow Border, Putti, Italy, 1900s, 17½ In.	125
Cheese Dish, Blue Birds, Pink Flowering Prunus, Water Lilies, 1800s, 9 x 10¼ In..........*illus*	90
Cheese Dish, Dome Lid, Cows, Tree, Grass, Blue, Green & Brown, 1800s, 8 x 10 In.	1298
Cheese Dish, Dome Lid, Flowers, Wheat, Blue, Stick Handle, George Jones, c.1880, 10 In...........*illus*	615
Cheese Dish, Dome Lid, Ribbon & Leaf, Blue, Thomas Forester, England, 1800s, 11½ x 10 In. *illus*	578
Compote, Lobed Bowl, 3 Seated Monkeys, Cobalt Blue Base, 1900s, 11¾ In.....................*illus*	240
Dish, Flower Form Vase Center, 3 Leaf Shape Compartments, George Jones, c.1880, 6¾ In. *illus*	123
Ewer, Battle Scene, Grapevine, Footed, Wilhelm Schiller & Sohn, Austria, 18¾ In.	250
Figurine, Hawk, Glass Eyes, Green & Brown Glaze, c.1890, 5 x 12 In.	485
Figurine, Honey Bear, Drum On Back, Detailed Fur, Holdcroft, England, 8¼ x 3½ In.	640
Garden Seat, Passion Flower, Multicolor Enamel, Minton, c.1872, 17 In. ....*illus*	1046
Jar, Tobacco, Child Holding A Pipe, Seated On A Melon, 1800s, 10½ In...........................*illus*	125
Jardiniere, Molded Flower Drop, Leaves, Scroll Handles, c.1885, 16 x 20 In.	1188
Jardiniere, Stag, Boar, Bird, Gun, Frie Onnaing, France, c.1850, 9¾ x 14 x 10 In.	813
Jug, Water, Palissy Ware, Vine Handle, Frogs, Lizards, Moths, France, 1900s, 12 In.	100
Pedestal, Blue & Brown Stylized Flowers, Urn, Tan Ground, 26½ x 11½ In.	81
Pitcher, Ceramic, Handle, Bird, Bamboo Tree, Faux Bamboo Handle, 7½ x 6½ In.	38
Pitcher, Figural Monkey, Seated, Leaves On Back, 11½ In.	150
Pitcher, Frog On Lily Pad, Edward Steele, 1800s, 5¾ In.	125
Pitcher, Mermaids, Putti, Neptune, Ivy Handle, Impressed, Minton, 1873, 17¾ In. ....*illus*	938
Pitcher, Swallow Perched Atop A Mottled Gourd, George Jones, 1800s, 6⅜ In...................*illus*	594
Plate, Decorative, Bird, Berries, Leaves, Blues, Greens, Browns, 1920s, 8 In.	109
Plate, Serving, Strawberry Vine Border, Green, Brown, White, 10 In.	175
Plate, Yellow Starfish, Pink Edges, Green Leaf, c.1950, 9 In.	85
Serving Dish, Fox, Leaves, George Jones, England, c.1869, 3½ x 10 x 8¾ In.	1353
Spooner, Snails, Oak Leaves, 2 Handles, Minton, 1800s, 4⅝ In. ....*illus*	200
Tazza, Figural Cranes, Pond Lily, 3 Storks, Unsigned, 9 x 10 In. ....*illus*	545
Teapot, Seaweed, Shells, Etruscan, Green, Lid, 6½ In.	219
Tray, Asparagus, Leaves, Acorn, Multicolor, 8¾ x 11½ In.	127
Tureen, Game Pie, Lid, Fox Handles, Ducks, Mushroom Finial, Minton, c.1877, 15 In.	4613
Tureen, Lid, Molded Fish, Oval, Impressed Marks, George Jones, 1800s, 18½ In.	813
Umbrella Holder, Tree Trunk, Floral Vines, Pink Interior, Early 1900s, 21½ In.	106
Umbrella Stand, Blue Glaze, Brown, Cream, Bamboo, Birds, c.1898, 24 x 12 In.	7000
Urn, Flowers, 2 Handles, Marble Base, Frederick & Alexander Gerbing, 1900-03, 14 In.	198
Urn, Garden, Leaves, Blue, Green, 1900s, 11 x 13 In.	303

Majolica, Cheese Dish, Dome Lid, Ribbon & Leaf, Blue, Thomas Forester, England, 1800s, 11 ½ x 10 In.
$578

Leland Little Auctions

Majolica, Garden Seat, Passion Flower, Multicolor Enamel, Minton, c.1872, 17 In.
$1,046

Skinner, Inc.

Majolica, Jar, Tobacco, Child Holding A Pipe, Seated On A Melon, 1800s, 10 ½ In.
$125

Leslie Hindman Auctioneers

TIP

We sometimes wonder about the editors of home decorating magazines. Recently we read an article suggesting that you use a collection of nineteenth-century majolica to serve a luncheon. The table pictured was set with over a thousand dollars' worth of majolica. Our advice: don't use valuable old majolica; it chips and stains easily. Antique porcelain dishes can be used; they are not as fragile.

Majolica, Compote, Lobed Bowl, 3 Seated Monkeys, Cobalt Blue Base, 1900s, 11 ¾ In.
$240

Eldred's

Majolica, Dish, Flower Form Vase Center, 3 Leaf Shape Compartments, George Jones, c.1880, 6 ¾ In.
$123

Skinner, Inc.

Majolica, Pitcher, Mermaids, Putti, Neptune, Ivy Handle, Impressed, Minton, 1873, 17 ¾ In.
$938

Onnaing, A City with Majolica
Onnaing is a town in France with several factories that made majolica. One important factory was La Faiencerie d'Onnaing. The most interesting pieces for today's collectors are its figural pitchers. Collectors call the pieces "Onnaing majolica."

Royal Crest Auctioneers

Majolica, Pitcher, Swallow Perched Atop A Mottled Gourd, George Jones, 1800s, 6 3/8 In.
$594

Leslie Hindman Auctioneers

Majolica, Spooner, Snails, Oak Leaves, 2 Handles, Minton, 1800s, 4 5/8 In.
$200

Leslie Hindman Auctioneers

Majolica, Tazza, Figural Cranes, Pond Lily, 3 Storks, Unsigned, 9 x 10 In.
$545

Fontaine's Auction Gallery

Vase, Child Chiseling Face Out Of Rock, Serpent Handles, Italy, c.1900s, 10 1/2 In. ....*illus*	130
Vase, Urn Shape, Flared Shape, Black, Green, Goldenrod, Blue Interior, Continental, 15 In.	92
Wall Vase, Figural Fish, Fontainebleau, Marked, 18 In.	184

 MALACHITE is a green stone with unusual layers or rings of darker green shades. It is often polished and used for decorative objects. Most malachite comes from Siberia or Australia.

Box, Lid, Rectangular, Green, 1 3/4 In. ....*illus*	125

 MAPS of all types have been collected for centuries. The earliest known printed maps were made in 1478. The first printed street map showed London in 1559. The first road maps for use by drivers of automobiles were made in 1901. Collectors buy maps that were pages of old books, as well as the multifolded road maps popular in this century.

America, Copper Plate Engraving, Burl Frame, Emanuel Bowen, 1747, 20 1/4 x 23 1/4 In.	281
Belgian Congo, Fabric Backing, Wood Top & Bottom, Belgium, 1951, 32 x 30 1/2 In.	135
Eastern North America, Mississippi Blue, Engraving, Wood Frame, Matthias Seutter, 29 x 32 In.	1416
Globe, Brass, Chromolithograph, Mahogany Stand, Carved, Adam's Style, c.1925, 12 In.	143
Globe, Bronze & Stone, Inlay, Stand, 1900s, 12 x 10 In.	63
Globe, Celestial, Mahogany Stand, J. & W. Cary, c.1820, 47 x 27 In.	5250
Globe, Celestial, Table, Cartouche, Mahogany Stand, W. Newton, London, 1834, 12 In. ......*illus*	1560
Globe, Gold Wire Longitude & Latitude Lines, Wood Base, Specimen, c.1950, 28 In.	210
Globe, Library, Reeded Tapering Legs, Oval Plinth, Gustav Brueckmann, c.1950, 32 In.	3250
Globe, Mahogany Stand, Williams Pridham, Scotland, c.1920, 40 1/2 x 18 In. ....*illus*	688
Globe, Miniature, Terrestrial, Wood Pedestal, J.L. Co., c.1880, 4 x 9 In.	154
Globe, Paper Covered, Metal Stand, New Terrestrial, C.S. Hammond, c.1915, 14 In. ....*illus*	204
Globe, Revolving Tray, Rope Twist Legs, Shelf, Bun Feet, Casters, Beech, 1900s, 39 x 26 In.	313
Globe, Terrestrial, Brass Stand & Tripod Base, Andrews, C.F. Weber Co., 13 1/2 In.	313
Globe, Terrestrial, Claw Feet, Isothermic Lines, Cast Iron Frame, Flanagan Co., 16 In.	141
Globe, Terrestrial, Paper, Composition, Art Deco, 1920s, 9 x 14 In.	342
Globe, Terrestrial, W. & A.K. Johnson, Mahogany Quatrefoil Base, Claw Feet, c.1900, 46 In.	3540
Globe, Terrestrial, Walnut, Carved, Revolving Tray, Turned Legs, France, 1900s, 39 x 28 In...*illus*	308
Globe, Walnut, Brass, Print Paper Over Plastic, 1953, 20 1/2 x 34 1/2 In.	1625
Jamaica, Burl Wood Frame, Johannem Ogiluium, 1674, 23 1/4 x 27 In.	94
Map Of English Plantations, North & South America, Morden, 1673, 17 x 20 3/4 In.	13200
St. Kitts Island, Carte De L'Isle St. Christophe, Gilt Frame, 11 1/2 x 15 1/2 In.	188

 MARBLE collectors pay highest prices for glass and sulphide marbles. The game of marbles has been popular since the days of the ancient Romans. American children were able to buy marbles by the mid-eighteenth century. Dutch glazed clay marbles were least expensive. Glazed pottery marbles, attributed to the Bennington potteries in Vermont, were of a better quality. Marbles made of pink marble were also available by the 1830s. Glass marbles seem to have been made later. By 1880, Samuel C. Dyke of South Akron, Ohio, was making clay marbles and The National Onyx Marble Company was making marbles of onyx. The Navarre Glass Marble Company of Navarre, Ohio, and M. B. Mishler of Ravenna, Ohio, made the glass marbles. Ohio remained the center of the marble industry, and the Akron-made Akro Agate brand became nationally known. Other pieces made by Akro Agate are listed in this book in the Akro Agate category. Sulphides are glass marbles with frosted white figures in the center.

Latticinio, Swirl White Core, Red, White, Blue, Yellow, Green, Bands, 1 15/16 In.	68
Latticinio, Swirl, Red, Yellow, White Core, In Holder, 1 9/16 In. ....*illus*	102
Lutz, Round, Swirl, Band Of Blue, Gold Glitter, 3/4 In.	60
Lutz, Round, Swirl, Band Of Green, Dark Green, Black, 1 In.	120
Onionskin, Handmade, Round, Yellow, Green, Red, 1 11/16 In.	96
Onionskin, Swirl, Blue, Red, White, 3/4 In.	30
Onionskin, Swirl, Red, White, Blue, 1 1/2 In.	96
Swirl, Handmade, White, Green, Yellow, 1 13/16 In.	84

M

MARBLE CARVINGS, such as large or small figurines, groups of people or animals, and architectural decorations, have been a special art form since the time of the ancient Greeks. Reproductions, especially of large Victorian groups, are being made of a mixture using marble dust. These are very difficult to detect and collectors should be careful. Other carvings are listed under Alabaster.

Buddha, Curled Hair, Sitting, White, Wood Base, Chinese, Late 1800s, 11 x 7 x 4 In.	480
Bust, Caesar Augustus, Laurel Wreath, 1800s, 27 x 22 In.	1375
Bust, Distinguished Gentleman, Henry Weekes, 1837, 29 x 20 In.	4750
Bust, Girl, Square Socle, c.1875, 18 x 10 In.	812
Bust, Marie Antoinette, c.1875, 26 x 16 x 9 In.	1812
Bust, Marie Antoinette, Unsigned, Felix Lecomte, 1800s, 29 In.	3120
Bust, Minerva, Goddess Of Wisdom & War, Rafaelo Batelli, Italy, c.1900, 14 In. ...*illus*	944
Bust, Nymph, Relief, c.1895, 16 x 14 In.	1187
Bust, Satyr, Rectangular Plinth, c.1900, 12 ½ In.	1625
Bust, Woman, Carved, Alabaster, White, Square Base, 19 In. ....*illus*	71
Bust, Woman, Carved, Italian Style, Beauty, Circular Base, 27 x 15 In.	121
Bust, Young Woman, Headband, Ruffled Lace, 17 x 12 ½ x 8 In.	847
Cassolette, Rouge, Bronze Mounted, Leafy Arms, Collar, 20 ½ x 13 x 8 In.	500
Jardiniere, Variegated, Molded Rim, Cream, 6 ½ x 9 In.	52
Model, Temple Of Vespasian & Titus, Yellow, 1800s, 19 x 5 x 5 ¾ In.	4465
Panel, Grape Bunches, Rectangular, 1900s, 38 x 67 x 1 ¾ In.	625
Pedestal, Carved, Slender Shaft, Feather Decoration, Continental, 1900s, 42 ½ x 11 ½ In.	132
Pedestal, Column, Gilt Bronze Mounted, Onyx, 1800s, 39 ½ In.	438
Pedestal, Column, Square Top, Raised Stepped Plinth, 1800s, 42 ½ x 13 x 13 In.	238
Pedestal, Gilt Bronze Mounted, Footed, Empire Style, France, c.1880, 46 x 14 ½ x 13 In.	1500
Pedestal, Gilt Bronze, Claw Feet, Louis XVI Style, 36 x 18 x 13 In.	438
Pedestal, Marble, The Virgin, Gothic Frieze, Alabaster Column, 1800s, 66 In.	480
Pedestal, Pink Marble, Swivel Square Top, Spiral Twist, Reeded Center, c.1985, 42 In., Pair	277
Pedestal, Square Top & Foot, Columnar Stand, 1900s, 44 ¼ x 12 x 12 In.	531
Pedestal, Tapered, Square Column, Veneered, Beige & White, 1900s, 44 In.	360
Reliquary, Faux, Tapered Case, Molded Cornice, Suppressed Ball Feet, Gilt, 17 x 18 In.	375
Statue, Aphrodite, Carved, Unsigned, Italy, 21 ½ In.	1093
Statue, Dying Gaul, Black, c.1900, 9 x 17 In.	1000
Statue, Evita, Mica, Plaque, Milt Paulenoff, 24 x 9 x 8 In.	492
Statue, Faun, Standing, Square Base, 24 x 9 ¼ x 6 ¼ In.	1000
Statue, Guanyin, Standing, Foo Dog, Chinese, 1900s, 43 x 22 x 10 In.	344
Statue, Woman, 2 Children, Multicolor, Signed, 1800s, 31 In.	3000
Statue, Woman, Holding Flowers, c.1900, 60 In. ...*illus*	4000
Statue, Woman, Seated, Wearing Classical Clothing, c.1700s, 12 x 9 ½ x 7 In. ...*illus*	480
Statue, Woman, Seminude, Roman Style, Rectangular Base, 1900s, 42 In.	2750
Statue, Woman, Standing, Ruffled Collar, Box, 2 Birds, c.1900, 30 ½ In.	938
Tazza, Butterscotch, 4 Leafy Feet, 8 x 13 x 9 ½ In.	345
Woman, Undressing, Continental, 1900s, 45 ½ In.	2125

MARBLEHEAD POTTERY was founded in 1904 by Dr. J. Hall as a rehabilitative program for the patients of a Marblehead, Massachusetts, sanitarium. Two years later it was separated from the sanitarium and it continued operations until 1936. Many of the pieces were decorated with marine motifs.

Vase, 5 Colors, Trees & Green Leaf, Blue Fruit, Hennesey & Tutt, c.1915, 7 x 3 ⅛ In.	4680
Vase, Cylindrical, 4 Colors, Vines, Blue Ground, c.1915, 8 ⅝ x 3 ¾ In.	4680
Vase, Dragonfly, Green Matte Glaze, Impressed Mark, Hannah Tutt, 6 x 3 ¼ In.	4375
Vase, Flowers, Matte Glaze, 5 Shades, Arthur Hennesey & Sarah Tutt, 4 ¼ x 3 ¾ In.	4688
Vase, Stylized Fruit Trees, Blue, Rounded Square, A. Hennesey, S. Tutt, 1910s, 4 In.	5313
Vase, Stylized Fruit Trees, Tan, Green Leaves, Tapered, c.1915, 4 ¾ x 3 ½ In.	1875

MARDI GRAS, French for "Fat Tuesday," was first celebrated in seventeenth-century Europe. The first celebration in America was held in Mobile, Alabama, in 1703. The first krewe, a parading or social club, was founded in 1856. Dozens have been formed

Majolica, Vase, Child Chiseling Face Out Of Rock, Serpent Handles, Italy, c.1900s, 10 ½ In.
$130

Freeman's Auctioneers & Appraisers

Malachite, Box, Lid, Rectangular, Green, 1 ¾ In.
$125

Nadeau's Auction Gallery

Map, Globe, Celestial, Table, Cartouche, Mahogany Stand, W. Newton, London, 1834, 12 In.
$1,560

Brunk Auctions

M

Map, Globe, Mahogany Stand, Williams Pridham, Scotland, c.1920, 40½ x 18 In.
$688

Leslie Hindman Auctioneers

Map, Globe, Paper Covered, Metal Stand, New Terrestrial, C.S. Hammond, c.1915, 14 In.
$204

Garth's Auctioneers & Appraisers

Map, Globe, Terrestrial, Walnut, Carved, Revolving Tray, Turned Legs, France, 1900s, 39 x 28 In.
$308

Crescent City Auction Gallery

Marble, Latticinio, Swirl, Red, Yellow, White Core, In Holder, 1 9/16 In.
$102

Soulis Auctions

Marble Carving, Bust, Minerva, Goddess Of Wisdom & War, Rafaelo Batelli, Italy, c.1900, 14 In.
$944

Leland Little Auctions

Marble Carving, Bust, Woman, Carved, Alabaster, White, Square Base, 19 In.
$71

Copake Auction

Marble Carving, Statue, Woman, Holding Flowers, c.1900, 60 In.
$4,000

Kamelot Auctions

Marble Carving, Statue, Woman, Seated, Wearing Classical Clothing, c.1700s, 12 x 9½ x 7 In.
$480

Cowan's Auctions

Martin Brothers, Ewer, Molded Base & Spout, Flowers, Handle, c.1900, 3½ In.
$275

Heritage Auctions

since. The Mardi Gras Act, which made Fat Tuesday a legal holiday, was passed in Louisiana in 1875. Mardi Gras balls, carnivals, parties, and parades are held from January 6 until the Tuesday before the beginning of Lent. The most famous carnival and parades take place in New Orleans. Parades feature floats, elaborate costumes, masks, and "throws" of strings of beads, cups, doubloons, or small toys. Purple, green, and gold are traditional Mardi Gras colors. Mardi Gras memorabilia ranges from cheap plastic beads to expensive souvenirs from early celebrations.

Doll, Jester, Star Tattoo On Face, Purple, Green, Gold, 1980s, 9 x 6 In.	39
Invitation, Cowbellion, 49th Anniversary, Mobile, Alabama, 1879, 7 3/8 x 10 1/16 In.	352
Mask, Venezia La Maschera Del Galeone, Black & White, Hand Painted, Italy	16
Medallion, Pendant, Endymion Krewe, Token Of Youth, Enamel, Gold Chain, 1976, 2 In.	10
Pin, Jester, Sterling Silver, Lang, 1 5/8 In.	46
Pin, Mask, Rhinestone Face, Sapphire Eyes, Red Lips, Golden Bow, 1 x 1 In.	62
Pin, Mask, Swan Crystal Rhinestone, Enamel, Swarovski, 1 x 1 1/4 In.	44
Umbrella, Purple, Green, Gold, Ruffle Edge, Goldtone Beaded Curved Handle, 22 In.	20
Vase, Fluted Top, Crown On Stem, Embossed Base, Metal, Dated 1905, 4 1/2 x 2 3/8 In.	132

MARTIN BROTHERS of Middlesex, England, made Martinware, a salt-glazed stoneware, between 1873 and 1915. Many figural jugs and vases were made by the four brothers. Of special interest are the fanciful birds, usually made with removable heads. Most pieces have the incised name of the artists plus other information on the bottom.

_Martin Bro¹
London_

Ewer, Molded Base & Spout, Flowers, Handle, c.1900, 3 1/2 In. ....*illus*	275
Jug, Eskimo, Fur Wrap, Glaze, Stoneware, c.1912, 12 3/4 In.	2091
Jug, Face, 2-Sided, Salt Glaze, Incised, 1903, 6 3/4 x 6 In. ....*illus*	4062
Jug, Face, Spout, Square Handle, c.1900, 7 In.	5843
Jug, Jellyfish, Glazed, Bulbous Shape, Stoneware, c.1900, 9 In.	1845
Jug, Parrot, Square Handle, Brown Ground, 1880, 10 3/4 In.	431
Jug, Stoneware, Tan Ground, Blue Enamel, Lion Mask, 1896, 9 1/4 In.	2337
Mug, 2-Sided Face, Grinning, Late 1800s, 5 In.	2460
Pitcher, Hummingbirds, Damselfly, Patches Of Blue Flowers, 1882, 8 3/4 In.	708
Pitcher, Sea Creatures, Salt Glaze, 1895, 7 x 6 In.	2125
Spoon Warmer, Boar's Head, Modeled, Scrolled Base, Late 1800s, 8 x 5 3/4 In.	1230
Tobacco Jar, Bird, Salt Glaze, Head Incised, R. Wallace Martin, 1894, 16 3/4 In. ....*illus*	112500
Tobacco Jar, Bird, Salt Glaze, Painted, Robert W. Martin, 16 In.	50000
Tobacco Jar, Creature, Brown, Salt Glaze, 1888, 7 1/2 x 4 1/2 In.	16250
Vase, Blossoms & Birds, Glazed, Enamel, c.1900, 7 3/8 In. ....*illus*	738
Vase, Bottle Shape, Loop Handles, Brown Slip Spots, Amber, Stoneware, 1904, 4 7/8 In.	492
Vase, Cobalt Blue Ground, Incised Flowers, 1897, 9 In.	1107
Vase, Crabs, Anemones, Stoneware, Salt Glaze, Oval, Flattened, 1903, 8 3/4 In.	2625
Vase, Frogs, Brown Tones, Salt Glaze, Signed, 1909, 7 1/2 x 5 In.	3125
Vase, Hexagonal, Sea Creatures, Vegetation, Glazed, 1900, 10 3/4 In.	2583
Wall Pocket, Dragon, Crouching, Indigo, Incised, 5 1/2 x 3 3/4 In.	4800

MARY GREGORY is the name used for a type of glass that is easily identified. White figures were painted on clear or colored glass as the decoration. The figures chosen were usually children at play. The first glass known as Mary Gregory was made in about 1870. Similar glass is made even today. The traditional story has been that the glass was made at the Boston & Sandwich Glass Company in Sandwich, Massachusetts, by a woman named Mary Gregory. Recent research has shown that none was made at Sandwich. In fact, all early Mary Gregory glass was made in Bohemia. Beginning in 1957, the Westmoreland Glass Co. made the first Mary Gregory–type decorations on American glassware. These pieces had simpler designs, less enamel paint, and more modern shapes. France, Italy, Germany, Switzerland, and England, as well as Bohemia, made this glassware. Children standing, not playing, were not pictured until after the 1950s.

Bottle, Barber, Spot Optic, Pale Blue, Woman's Portrait, Flowers, 1950s, 8 In. ....*illus*	176
Dresser Box, Girl Watering Garden, Black Glass, 6 x 2 In.	125
Jewelry Box, Lid, Girl, Amethyst Glass, 1800s, 4 In.	283

Martin Brothers, Jug, Face, 2-Sided, Salt Glaze, Incised, 1903, 6 3/4 x 6 In.
$4,062

Rago Arts and Auction Center

Martin Brothers, Tobacco Jar, Bird, Salt Glaze, Head Incised, R. Wallace Martin, 1894, 16 3/4 In.
$112,500

Rago Arts and Auction Center

Martin Brothers, Vase, Blossoms & Birds, Glazed, Enamel, c.1900, 7 3/8 In.
$738

Skinner, Inc.

M

Mary Gregory, Bottle, Barber, Spot Optic, Pale Blue, Woman's Portrait, Flowers, 1950s, 8 In.
$176

Jeffrey S. Evans & Associates

Match Holder, Columbia Mills Flour, Miss Liberty, Flag Dress, Tin, 5½ x 2 In.
$797

Wm Morford Auctions

Match Holder, Eagle, Lion, Tree Stump, Iron, Metallic Paint, Late 1800s, 3 x 5½ In.
$120

Garth's Auctioneers & Appraisers

Jug, Child Holds Out Arms, Tree, Cobalt Blue, c.1900, 7 In.	47
Syrup, Girl, Bird, White Ferns, Cranberry Glass, Hinged Metal Lid, 6 x 10 In.	90
Vase, Bud, Boy Blowing Horn, Cranberry Glass, c.1890, 6 In.	89

MASONIC, *see Fraternal category.*

MASON'S IRONSTONE was made by the English pottery of Charles J. Mason after 1813. Mason, of Lane Delph, was given a patent for this improved earthenware. He usually called it *Mason's Patent Ironstone China.* It resisted chipping and breaking, so it became popular for dinnerware and other table service dishes. Vases and other decorative pieces were also made. The ironstone was decorated with orange, blue, gold, and other colors, often in Japanese-inspired designs. The firm had financial difficulties but the molds and the name *Mason* were used by many owners through the years, including Francis Morley, Taylor Ashworth, George L. Ashworth, and John Shaw. Mason's joined the Wedgwood group in 1973 and the name was used for a few years and then dropped.

Jug, Hydra, Flowers, Serpent Shape Handle, Marked, 9 x 10 In.	425
Punch Bowl, Imari Pattern, Red Flowers, Gilt Leaves, 1835, 13 x 5 In.	3000
Vase, Mazarine Blue, Oval, Flared Rim, Dragon Handles, c.1838, 22½ In.	1200

J.Massier fils **MASSIER,** a French art pottery, was made by brothers Jerome, Delphin, and Clement Massier in Vallauris and Golfe-Juan, France, in the late nineteenth and early twentieth centuries. It has an iridescent metallic luster glaze that resembles the Weller Sicardo pottery glaze. Most pieces are marked *J. Massier.* Massier may also be listed in the Majolica category.

Plaque, Stylized Dancer, Pink, Blue, Green & Purple Glaze, Round, Signed, c.1900, 15 In.	1250
Vase, Dimpled Body, Metallic Luster, Painted, Plants, Clement, France, 4½ x 3¼ In.	55
Vase, Glazed, Stoneware, Etched Flowers, Multicolor, 13 In.	3250
Vase, Pine Boughs, 2 Wing-Like Handles, c.1900, 19½ x 12 In.	1625

MATCH HOLDERS were made to hold the large wooden matches that were used in the nineteenth and twentieth centuries for a variety of purposes. The kitchen stove and the fireplace or furnace had to be lit regularly. One type of match holder was made to hang on the wall, another was designed to be kept on a tabletop. Of special interest to collectors today are match holders that have advertisements as part of the design.

Alligator, Brass, G. & C. Co., c.1890, 7½ In.	208
Apollinaris, Cobalt Blue, Striker On Body, Porcelain, 3 In.	69
Athletic, 14K Gold, Enamel, Marked, Carter & Howe, c.1896, 2⅝ x 1½ In.	1200
Columbia Mills Flour, Miss Liberty, Flag Dress, Tin, 5½ x 2 In. *illus*	797
Dog, Top Hat, Belmont Glass, Electric Blue, 1880s, 4 In.	195
Eagle, Emblem, 5 Stars, Cast Iron, Black, Gold, 4 x 5 In.	60
Eagle, Lion, Tree Stump, Iron, Metallic Paint, Late 1800s, 3 x 5½ In. *illus*	120
F.B. Thomas, Druggist, Meyersdale, Pa., Wood, 5 In.	83
Figural, Old Mustache Face, Walnut, Carved, Early 1900s, 4¾ In.	388
Fox, Sitting On Barrel, Holding Cup, Black Forest, Carved, 1800s, 6 In.	372
Grumpy Monk's Face, White Hood, Porcelain, Bohne, 3¼ In.	78
Kolumbia Shoe Store, Cardboard, Tin, 6½ In.	83
Lion's Head, Silver, Monogram, Marked, 1900s, 2½ x 1½ In.	461
Louis Bergdoll Brewing Co., Cigar Cutter, On Base, Ceramic, 4 x 5 In. *illus*	330
Majolica, Grapes, Grape Leaves, Bundled Cigars, Underplate, 6 x 3 In.	499
Man Wearing Hat, Wheat & Farm Equipment, Cast Iron, 6 x 4½ In.	57
Merry War Lye, Girl Washing In Tub, Gray Border, 5 In. *illus*	212
Monkey, Standing, Dressed, Butcher Clothes, Etched Apron, Kettle, 2½ x 4 In.	175
Nakara, Gilt Metal Rim, Pink Tones, Blue Flowers, Handles, 1¾ x 3 In.	120
Nest & Eggs, Walnut, Carved, Black Forest Type, Birds, Flowers, Leaves, 16 In.	130
Silver Plate, Bear, Standing, Round Base, Pairpoint, 2¾ x 3 In.	60
Tortoise, Insure In The Old Connecticut Fire, Hinged Lid, Cast Iron, 1 x 5¼ x 3 In. *illus*	100
Usher Whisky, Transferware, Gentleman In Khaki, R. Tuck & Sons, 3½ x 2½ In.	92
Wood, Pine, Fishtail Top, Cut Tack Drawer, Early 1900s, 18 In.	29

M

MATCH SAFES were designed to be carried in the pocket or set on a table. Early matches were made with phosphorus and could ignite unexpectedly. The matches were safely stored in the tightly closed container. Match safes were made in sterling silver, plated silver, or other metals. The English call these "vesta boxes." A large, famous collection of match safes was auctioned in sales this year and many sold for record prices.

Advertising, Liberte, Silver, Enamel, Albert Cohen & Charles Solomon, 1903, 2 x 1 ½ In.	185
Advertising, Thuet Bros. Livestock, Steel, Celluloid Wrapped Body, 2 ¾ x 1 ½ In.	77
Barrel, Brass, Painted, Red, Gold Bands, Bottom Striker, Vesta Lights, c.1890, 2 x 2 In.	45
Castle Door, Silver, Gold Wash, Monogram, 1900s, 2 ⅜ x 1 ⅜ In.	240
Cherub, Kissing Woman, Silver, Enamel, Hinged Top, Striker, London, 1889, 2 x 1 ½ In. ...*illus*	480
Cigars, Bundled Together, Silver Plate, Marked, c.1900, 2 ⅜ x 1 ½ In. ...*illus*	300
Clamshell, Concentric Ribs, Squid, Mollusk, Starfish, Hinged Lid, c.1900, 2 ¾ x 1 ¾ In.	179
Coins, Woman's Profile, Alligatored Surface, Silver, Gorham, 1892, 2 ⅝ x 1 ½ In.	720
Dog, Spaniel, Continental Silver, Enamel, Oval, c.1900, 2 ⅛ x 1 ⅛ In.	277
Dragon, Striker, Silver, Marked, Japan, 2 ⅛ x 3 ⅛ In.	360
Fish, Silver Plate, c.1900, 2 ⅝ x 1 ⅝ In. ...*illus*	720
Flag, Blue Enamel, Striker, Silver, Marked, Birmingham, c.1895, 2 x 1 ¼ In.	420
Foxes, Grapes, Leaves, Scrolls, Silver, Repousse, c.1900, 2 ⅝ x 1 ⅛ In. ...*illus*	180
Girl & Lamb, Mary Had A Little Lamb, Silver Plate, Engraved, 1800s, 2 x 1 ¼ In.	123
Golfer, Lid, Rustic Landscape, Silver, Gorham Manufacturing Co., c.1900s, 2 ¼ x 1 ⅛ In. .*illus*	140
Greek Warrior, Repousse, Silver, Marked, Fairchild & Co., 1919-22, 2 ⅝ x 1 ⅝ In.	180
Horse Head, Silver, Howard Sterling Co., Late 1800s, 2 ⅝ x 1 ⅛ x ⅝ In. ...*illus*	424
Metal, Engraved, Striker Base, Edward J. Hauck, Pat. Aug 14, 83, 3 ¼ x 1 ½ In.	51
Motto, Match, In Me You'll Always Find, Silver, Birmingham, 1892, 1 ¾ x ⅞ In.	240
Nautical, Anchor & Rope, Sailboat, Silver, Marked, 1900s, 2 ½ x 1 ¾ In.	510
Notepad Case, Pencil, Woman, Cornucopia, Silver, Signed, E. Dropsy, France, 1900s, 2 x 1 ⅜ In.	90
Openwork, Pierced, Scrolling Openwork, Silver, Marked, 1900s, 2 ¼ x 2 In.	277
Pierced, Openwork Sides, Cartouches, Monogram, Marked, Gorham, c.1890, 2 ⅜ x 1 ⅞ In.	330
Pig, Brass, Striker On Bottom, Vesta, c.1895, 2 In.	59
Pocket Knife, 2 Blades, Brass, Nickel Plated, Simulated Stag Grips, Flip Top, 1 x 2 ¾ In.	243
Portrait, Gilt Enamel, Classical Figure, Medallion, Silver, 1900s, 2 ⅜ x 1 ⅜ In.	240
Portrait, Woman, Nude, Neoclassical, Silver Ground, JW, Birmingham, 1887, 1 ⅞ x 1 ⅝ In.	600
Punch, Figural, Silver Plate, c.1890, 2 ¼ x 1 ¼ In. ...*illus*	480
Satchel, 3 Straps & Buckles, Silver Plate, Unmarked, 1900s, 1 ⅞ x 1 ⅛ In.	420
Silver, Blue Guilloche, Continental, Marked, 1900s, 1 ⅛ x 1 ½ In.	360
Skull, Gray Metal, Basic Details, Hinged Jaw, Striker, 1 ¾ x 1 ½ In.	243
Snakes, 4 Entwined Snakes, Silver, Marked, 1900s, 2 ½ x 1 ⅜ In.	277
Vulcanite, Brown, Amber, Green, Molded Round Shape, c.1890, 3 x 1 In.	125
Woman, Profile, Art Nouveau, Monogram, Silver, Birmingham, 1903, 2 x 1 ¾ In.	420
Woman's Shoe, Metal, Leather Wrap, Brown, Pushbutton Lid Release, c.1890, 3 x 1 In.	95

McCOY pottery was made in Roseville, Ohio. Nelson McCoy and J.W. McCoy established the Nelson McCoy Sanitary and Stoneware Company in Roseville, Ohio, in 1910. The firm made art pottery after 1926. In 1933 it became the Nelson McCoy Pottery Company. Pieces marked *McCoy* were made by the Nelson McCoy Pottery Company. Cookie jars were made from about 1940 until December 1990, when the McCoy factory closed. Since 1991 pottery with the McCoy mark has been made by firms unrelated to the original company. Because there was a company named Brush-McCoy, there is great confusion between Brush and Nelson McCoy pieces. See Brush category for more information.

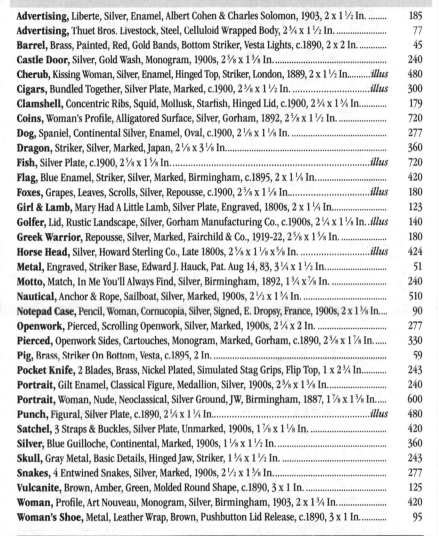

Bank, Seaman's Savings, Sailor, White Uniform, Bellbottom Pants, Carrying Sack, 1940s, 6 In.	10
Bowl, Onion Soup, Lid, Brown, Drip Edge, Handles, c.1910, 4 x 5 ¾ In.	7
Cookie Jar, Barn Shape, Chimney Finial, Pink, 10 In. ...*illus*	403
Cookie Jar, Black Woman, White Dress, Says Cookies On Skirt, Red Cap, 1940s, 11 In.	44
Cookie Jar, Boy On Football, Marked 222, 11 ½ In.	104
Cookie Jar, Drum, Brown, Yellow & White, Cold Paint, Marked, 9 ½ In.	316
Cookie Jar, Kangaroo, Yellow, Tan Gloss, Marked, 11 ¼ In.	184
Cookie Jar, Touring Car, Black & Gold, Marked, 11 x 7 In.	276
Jardiniere, Blue Leaf & Berry, Clay, Footed, 6 x 7 ½ In.	96

Match Holder, Louis Bergdoll Brewing Co., Cigar Cutter, On Base, Ceramic, 4 x 5 In.
$330

Match Holder, Merry War Lye, Girl Washing In Tub, Gray Border, 5 In.
$212

M

Match Holder, Tortoise, Insure In The Old Connecticut Fire, Hinged Lid, Cast Iron, 1 x 5 ¼ x 3 In.
$100

This is an edited listing of current prices. Visit **Kovels.com** to check thousands of prices from previous years and sign up for free information on trends, tips, reproductions, marks, and more.

Match Safe, Cherub, Kissing Woman, Silver, Enamel, Hinged Top, Striker, London, 1889, 2 x 1 ½ In.
$480

Cowan's Auctions

> **TIP**
> Don't try to remove dents in silver or pewter. This is a job for an expert.

Match Safe, Cigars, Bundled Together, Silver Plate, Marked, c.1900, 2 ⅜ x 1 ½ In.
$300

Cowan's Auctions

Match Safe, Fish, Silver Plate, c.1900, 2 ⅝ x 1 ⅝ In.
$720

Cowan's Auctions

Match Safe, Foxes, Grapes, Leaves, Scrolls, Silver, Repousse, c.1900, 2 ⅝ x 1 ⅛ In.
$180

Cowan's Auctions

Match Safe, Golfer, Lid, Rustic Landscape, Silver, Gorham Manufacturing Co., c.1900s, 2 ¼ x 1 ⅛ In.
$140

Jeffrey S. Evans & Associates

Match Safe, Horse Head, Silver, Howard Sterling Co., Late 1800s, 2 ⅝ x 1 ⅛ x ⅝ In.
$424

Aspire Auctions

Match Safe, Punch, Figural, Silver Plate, c.1890, 2 ¼ x 1 ¼ In.
$480

Cowan's Auctions

McCoy, Cookie Jar, Barn Shape, Chimney Finial, Pink, 10 In.
$403

Belhorn Auction Services

McCoy, Planter, Dog, Dachshund, Standing, Stretching, Blue Glaze, 7 ¼ In.
$36

caesar2222 on eBay

Jardiniere, Fin Style, White Matte, 8¼ x 6¾ In.	46
Jardiniere, White Matte, Leaf & Berry, Pedestal Included, 29 In.	518
Mixing Bowl, Pink & Blue Stripes, No. 12, Oven Ware, 12 In.	21
Pin Tray, Hands Shape, Cream Ground, Leaves, Round Base	7
Pitcher, Embossed Donkey & Stars, White Matte Glaze, C Handle, 7 x 7½ x 3 In.	164
Planter, Dog, Dachshund, Standing, Stretching, Blue Glaze, 7¼ In. ....*illus*	36
Planter, Dog, Retriever, Brown, Glaze, Marked, c.1959, 5 x 7 In.	92
Planter, Dog, Setter, Black & White Spotted, Marked, c.1959, 5¼ x 7 In.	104
Planter, Wishing Well, Pink Fairy, Brown Glaze, Marked, 1950s, 8 x 7 In.	1380
Reamer, Juice, Yellow Glaze, Tapered Conical, 8 x 3 In.	35
Sprinkler, Turtle, Green, Figural, Berries, Branch Handle, 10 In.	25
Tray, Baseball Glove, Burgundy Gloss, Duluth, 4¾ In.	63
Trinket Box, Aqua & Pink Iridescent Glazes, Marked, 5¼ x 2⅞ In.	161
Vase, 2 Tulips, Gold Trimmed, Glossy, Marked, 6¼ In.	115
Vase, 3 Lilies, White Glossy Glaze, Gold Trim, Marked, 6¾ In.	69
Vase, Ram's Head, Molded, White Matte, Marked, 9 In.	196
Vase, White Matte, Arrow Leaf, Marked, 10 In.	46
Wall Pocket, Grapes, Leaves, 1950s, 7½ In.	63
Wall Pocket, Magnolia Flower Shape, Underglaze, Hand Incised, Magnolia, 6 In.	196
Wall Pocket, Orange Center, Cold Paint, Green Leaves, 1950s, 7½ In.	104
Wall Pocket, Woman's Head, Gold, Yellow, Flower, Red Lips, Pink Cheeks, 4½ x 2 In.	21

McKEE is a name associated with various glass enterprises in the United States since 1836, including J. & F. McKee (1850), Bryce, McKee & Co. (1850 to 1854), McKee and Brothers (1865), and National Glass Co. (1899). In 1903, the McKee Glass Company was formed in Jeannette, Pennsylvania. It became McKee Division of the Thatcher Glass Co. in 1951 and was bought out by the Jeannette Corporation in 1961. Pressed glass, kitchenwares, and tablewares were produced. Jeannette Corporation closed in the early 1980s. Additional pieces may be included in the Custard Glass and Depression Glass categories.

McKee Glass Co. c.1870	

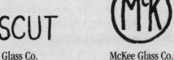

PRESCUT		
McKee Glass Co. c.1904–1935		McKee Glass Co. 1935–1940

Butter, Cover, Red Checkered, Gingham Bow Design, White Glass, 3½ x 6¾ x 3½ In.	282
Canister, Flour, Jar Shape, Jade, Aluminum Screw-On Lid, 7¾ In.	356
Carafe, Green & Clear Glass, Sheraton Hotel, Marked Glasbake, 5½ In.	7
Champagne, Eureka, Flint, Round Base, c.1866, 5¼ x 2½ In.	17
Compote, Pedestal, Bellflower, Fine Rib, Personal Glass, Flint, 1860s, 5 x 8 In.	10
Creamer, Eureka, Flint, Round Base, Handle, c.1866, 6⅛ x 3¼ In.	13
Cruet, Sultan, Wild Rose, Brown Knot, Chocolate, McKee Glass Co., Early 1900s, 7¼ In.	82
Dish, Duck, Chocolate, Ribbed Base, Early 1900s, 4½ x 5½ In. ....*illus*	4095
Mixing Bowl, Blue Polka Dots, Custard Glass, Delphite, 4½ x 9 In.	275
Salt & Pepper, Milk Glass, Tappan, Bakelite Lid, Red & Green, 4 In.	78

MECHANICAL BANKS *are listed in the Bank category.*

MEDICAL office furniture, operating tools, microscopes, thermometers, and other paraphernalia used by doctors are included in this category. Veterinary collectibles are also included here. Medicine bottles are listed in the Bottle category. There are related collectibles listed under Dental.

Cabinet, Apothecary, 8 Drawers, Gouge Carved Knobs, Hanging, 18 In.	92
Cabinet, Apothecary, 18 Drawers, Multicolor Paint, Knob Handles, 31 x 11 x 14 In. ....*illus*	236
Cabinet, Apothecary, Oak Base, 2 Doors, 2 Drawers, 2 Shelves, Cast Iron, 97 x 48 In.	198
Cabinet, Apothecary, Pine, Tabletop, 8 Drawers, Porcelain Knobs, c.1800s, 26 x 8 In. ....*illus*	439
Cabinet, Mahogany, Glass Door, 2 Drawers, Milk Glass Shelves, 66 x 22 x 15 In. ....*illus*	311
Cabinet, Metal, Black Formica Top & Chrome Bottle Holders, c.1940, 34 x 33 In.	79

McKee, Dish, Duck, Chocolate, Ribbed Base, Early 1900s, 4½ x 5½ In.
$4,095

Jeffrey S. Evans & Associates

Medical, Cabinet, Apothecary, 18 Drawers, Multicolor Paint, Knob Handles, 31 x 11 x 14 In.
$236

Copake Auction

Kerosene, the Victorian Wonder Cure

Kerosene was used in the early 1900s not only for lighting but also as a medicine. It was said that kerosene applied to the body could help cure appendicitis, consumption, croup, burns, bunions, rheumatism, and quinsy. It could be swallowed to help cure a cold, toothache, and diphtheria and could even remove dandruff.

Medical, Cabinet, Apothecary, Pine, Tabletop, 8 Drawers, Porcelain Knobs, c.1800s, 26 x 8 In.
$439

Jeffrey S. Evans & Associates

M

Medical, Cabinet, Mahogany, Glass Door, 2 Drawers, Milk Glass Shelves, 66 x 22 x 15 In.
$311

Hartzell's Auction Gallery, Inc.

Medical, Leg Splint, Mahogany, Molded, C. & R. Eames, Label, Evans Products, 1943, 42 In.
$625

Wright

Meissen, Bowl, Schneeballen, Flowers, Birds, Green, Gilt Vines & Leaves, 1800s, 4 x 9 In.
$1,875

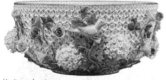

Heritage Auctions

Cabinet, Veterinary, Sergeant's Dog Medicines, Metal, Yellow, Boy & Dog, 14 x 13 x 6 In.	965
Chest, Apothecary, 25 Drawers, Porcelain Knobs, Poplar, Bracket Feet, 1900s, 36 x 68 x 15 In.	1080
Fleam, Brass, Lancet Shape Blade, Spring Mechanism, Leather Box, 2½ In.	103
Fleam, Iron Blades, Horn Handle, Hutchinson Sheffield England, 1800s, 3½ In.	150
Generator, RenuLife, Violet Ray, Model R, Quack Electrotherapy Device, 1920	252
Leg Splint, Mahogany, Molded, C. & R. Eames, Label, Evans Products, 1943, 42 In. .....*illus*	625
Prosthetic Leg, Maple, Leather, Metal Hinges At Knee, Shoe, Brown, c.1900, 31 In.	282
Sign, Dr. S.P O'Brien, Physician & Surgeon, Wood, 1800s, 21¼ x 32 In.	177
Sign, Trade, Optometrist, Giltwood Frame, Octagonal Eyeglass Shape, c.1930, 23 x 10 In.	3456
Suppository Press, Iron, Wheel, Black Paint, Gold Pinstripes, Steel Screw Brass, 12 x 5 In.	72

MEISSEN is a town in Germany where porcelain has been made since 1710. Any china made in the town can be called Meissen, although the famous Meissen factory made the finest porcelains of the area. The crossed swords mark of the great Meissen factory has been copied by many other firms in Germany and other parts of the world. Pieces of Meissen dinnerware in the Onion pattern are listed in their own category in this book.

Basket, Stand, Gilt, Central Vignettes, Late 1800s, 16½ x 20 x 12 In.	11250
Bowl, Gilt, Ivy Leaf, Flowers, Scalloped Edge, 11 In.	103
Bowl, Schneeballen, Flowers, Birds, Green, Gilt Vines & Leaves, 1800s, 4 x 9 In. .....*illus*	1875
Bust, Young Girl, Yellow Ribbon Headband, Blue Crossed Swords, 1800s, 6½ In.	120
Candelabrum, Classical Female, Putti, White Glaze, 1800s, 18 In.	182
Centerpiece, Figural, Woman, Seated, Child, Flowers, Gilt, Late 1800s, 18 x 13 x 7¾ In.	8125
Clock, Figural, Stand, Multicolor Flowers, 3 Cherubs On Top, Gilt, c.1900, 12 x 13 x 9 In...*illus*	4000
Figurine, Abundance, Man, Seated, Dog, Food, Drink, Gilt, Late 1800s, 9 x 5½ x 4 In.	2000
Figurine, Aquarius, Holding Vase, Germany, c.1947, 5½ In.	610
Figurine, Boy, Feeding Ducks, 1800s, 5¼ In.	169
Figurine, Camel, Multicolor, Gilt, Johann Joachim Kaendler, c.1750, 9 x 7 x 4 In. .....*illus*	1438
Figurine, Cupid, Feeding Nightingales, Gilt, Signed, Rudolf Holbe, Late 1800s, 21⅜ In.	4000
Figurine, Cupid, Gloves & Snowballs, Underglaze, Blue, Carl Thieme, c.1900, 5½ In.	188
Figurine, Cupid, Porcelain, Pigeon, Heart, Johann Pollack, c.1900, 12¾ In.	1625
Figurine, Cupid, Underglaze Blue, Heinrich Schwabe, c.1900, 6½ In.	525
Figurine, Dancer, Kilt, Feather Helmet & Cape, Germany, c.1930, 9½ x 6 x 3 In.	875
Figurine, Dog, Bolognese, Black & White, Marked, c.1800s, 9½ In. .....*illus*	938
Figurine, Dog, Pug, Seated, Marked, Pommel-Ended Blue Cross, c.1830, 7 x 7 In. .....*illus*	1063
Figurine, Dog, Pug, Seated, Tan, Dark Brown Face, Paws, Tail, Marked, 6¾ In.	1063
Figurine, Girl Gardening After Michel Victor Acier, c.1900, 7¾ In.	625
Figurine, Girl, Flower Basket, Johann Joachim Kaendler, c.1900, 5¼ In. .....*illus*	200
Figurine, Man, Pantaloon, Standing, Round Base, c.1850, 6¼ In.	1298
Figurine, Scorpio, Zodiac Sign, White & Red, 4¾ In.	793
Figurine, Virgo, Zodiac Sign, White, Yellow & Blue, 1940s, 5⅜ In.	793
Figurine, Woman, Peasant, Sheep, Multicolor, Germany, 1850-99, 12 In.	488
Figurine, Young Woman, Holding Gold Ball, Gilt, Walter Schott, Early 1900s, 15 x 9 x 6 In.	1375
Group, 2 Nude Females, Holding Whippet, White Glaze, 9¾ x 6 In.	133
Group, Earth, Goddess, Putto Digging, Another Feeding Chickens, c.1730, 6¾ In.	813
Group, Europa & Bull, Crossed Swords, Underglaze Blue, c.1900, 10¼ In.	750
Group, Gallant Man Assisting Woman, Rococo Base, 5½ x 4 In.	394
Group, Man & Woman, Birdcage, Basket Of Eggs, Hand Painted, 9½ x 11 In. .....*illus*	316
Group, Man & Woman, Pug Dog, Crossed Swords Mark, Late 1700s, 6¾ x 5½ In. .....*illus*	726
Group, Mother, 3 Boys, Picking Apples, Ladder, 1850-1922, 10 x 5 In.	813
Group, Sense Of Smell, Woman, Child, Dog, Johann Friedrich Eberlein, Late 1800s, 13 x 4 In.	1063
Group, Woman & Cavalier, Dancing, Elegant Dress, Marked, 1800s, 7¾ In. .....*illus*	300
Group, Young Boy & Girl, Seated On Logs, 5½ x 5½ In.	422
Jar, Lid, Lovers, Scenes, Landscape, Wide Rim, Painted, 4 In.	112
Plate, 8-Sided, 2 Birds, Landscape, Painted, 9½ In.	106
Plate, Bird & Fruit, Scalloped Gilt Rim, Marked, 1900s, 9 In.	153
Plate, Central Flowers, Insects, Fish, Earls Coronet, Painted, 9½ In.	169
Plate, Flower Clusters, Painted, 1800s, 9 In.	133
Plate, Gilt, Birds, Scrolls, Central Medallion, 7½ In.	69
Plate, Gilt, Leaves, Purple, Orange, Yellow Flowers, 11 In.	80

Meissen, Clock, Figural, Stand, Multicolor Flowers, 3 Cherubs On Top, Gilt, c.1900, 12 x 13 x 9 In.
$4,000

Heritage Auctions

Meissen, Figurine, Camel, Multicolor, Gilt, Johann Joachim Kaendler, c.1750, 9 x 7 x 4 In.
$1,438

Heritage Auctions

Meissen, Figurine, Dog, Bolognese, Black & White, Marked, c.1800s, 9½ In.
$938

Freeman's Auctioneers & Appraisers

Meissen, Figurine, Dog, Pug, Seated, Marked, Pommel-Ended Blue Cross, c.1830, 7 x 7 In.
$1,063

New Orleans Auction Galleries

Meissen, Figurine, Girl, Flower Basket, Johann Joachim Kaendler, c.1900, 5¼ In.
$200

Leslie Hindman Auctioneers

Meissen, Group, Man & Woman, Birdcage, Basket Of Eggs, Hand Painted, 9½ x 11 In.
$316

Keystone Auctions LLC

Meissen, Group, Man & Woman, Pug Dog, Crossed Swords Mark, Late 1700s, 6¾ x 5½ In.
$726

Ahlers & Ogletree Auction Gallery

Meissen, Group, Woman & Cavalier, Dancing, Elegant Dress, Marked, 1800s, 7¾ In.
$300

Nadeau's Auction Gallery

Meissen, Urn, Molded Snake Handles, Painted, Gilt, Germany, c.1930, 15 x 9 x 5 In.
$594

New Orleans Auction Galleries

M

Meissen, Vase, Lid, Avian, Schneeballen, Birds, Snowball Flowers, Late 1800s, 20 ¼ In.
$15,000

Heritage Auctions

Merrimac, Vase, Pink Volcanic Glaze, Paper Label, c.1905, 7 ¼ In.
$3,500

Rago Arts and Auction Center

Metlox, Cookie Jar, Cabbage, Lid, Green, Rabbit Finial, Red Jacket, 10 ½ x 8 In.
$30

Martin Auction Co.

Plate, Painted, Rocaille & Gilt, Porcelain, Marked, Late 1800s, 11 ½ In.		225
Plate, Parcel Gilt, Vine & Berries, 11 In.		113
Plate, Portrait, Young Woman, Cobalt Blue Border, Leafy Design, 1 ¾ x 11 ½ In.		413
Plate, Watteau Style Scene, Cobalt, Blue Cross Swords, Germany, 10 In.		875
Urn, Cobalt Blue, Double Handles, White Snakes, 19 In.		799
Urn, Molded Snake Handles, Painted, Gilt, Germany, c.1930, 15 x 9 x 5 In.	*illus*	594
Vase, 2 Serpents Handle, White & Gold, Gilt, 1800s, 19 x 12 In.		910
Vase, Flowers, Fruit Encrusted, Green Acanthus, Leaf Handles, 1800s, 10 x 7 ⅞ In.		182
Vase, Lid, Avian, Schneeballen, Birds, Snowball Flowers, Late 1800s, 20 ¼ In.	*illus*	15000

MERRIMAC POTTERY Company was founded by Thomas Nickerson in Newburyport, Massachusetts, in 1902. The company made art pottery, garden pottery, and reproductions of Roman pottery. The pottery burned to the ground in 1908.

Bowl, Silver, 5 x 7 In., Pair		125
Compote, Pale Yellow, Pedestal, c.1940, 5 ½ In.		93
Lamp, 2-Light, Electric, Bulbous, Footed, 30 x 11 In.		212
Vase, Silver, Ribbed, Footed, 12 x 8 In., Pair		150
Vase, Pink Volcanic Glaze, Paper Label, c.1905, 7 ¼ In.	*illus*	3500

METLOX POTTERIES was founded in 1927 in Manhattan Beach, California. Dinnerware was made beginning in 1931. Evan K. Shaw purchased the company in 1946 and expanded the number of patterns. Poppytrail (1946–89) and Vernonware (1958–80) were divisions of Metlox under E.K. Shaw's direction. The factory closed in 1989.

Aztec, Mug, Poppytrail, Handle, White Matte, 1950s	78
Aztec, Serving Dish, Poppytrail, Handle, Ivory, 11 ¾ In.	42
California Ivy, Gravy Boat, Poppytrail, Ivy, Brown Tree Twig Shape Handle, 3 x 10 In.	18
California Ivy, Plate, Salad, Crescent, Vernon, 7 In.	41
California Provincial, Bowl, Salad, Serving, Vernon, 11 In.	69
California Provincial, Coffeepot, Green, Rooster, 1956-82, 11 ½ In.	35
California Provincial, Soup, Dish, Handled, Rooster, 6 ¼ In., 2 Piece	40
Cookie Jar, Cabbage, Lid, Green, Rabbit Finial, Red Jacket, 10 ½ x 8 In.........*illus*	30
Cookie Jar, Teddy Bear, Sombrero & Pancho, Orange Glaze, 13 In.	24
Figurine, Elephant, Walking, Cream Matte, 1938-42, 4 x 6 ½ In.	67
Poppytrail, Figurine, Nude Woman, Doves, Statue, C. Rommanelli, 1825, 11 In.	32
Poppytrail, Pitcher, Slanted, White, Free-Form Design, Eames Era, 1950s, 14 x 7 x 5 In.	104
Provincial Blue, Grandmug, Lid, Poppytrail, 5 In.	55
Provincial Blue, Plate, Dinner, Poppytrail, 10 In.	13
Red Rooster, Match Holder, Poppytrail, Drawer, Hanging On Stand, 7 ¾ x 4 ¼ x 5 In.	32
Red Rooster, Tray, Serving, Poppytrail, 3 Divisions, Basket Weave Border, Cream Ground	76
Red Rooster, Tureen, Soup, Ladle, Lid, Poppytrail, 11 x 16 In.	305
Sculptured Grape, Coffeepot, Lid, Handle, 8 Cup, 8 ⅝ In.	23
Vase, Fish, Marlin, White Matte Finish, Rommanelli, 9 ¼ x 4 ¼ x 8 ¼ In.	82

METTLACH, Germany, is a city where the Villeroy and Boch factories worked. Steins from the firm are marked with the word *Mettlach* or the castle mark. They date from about 1842. *PUG* means painted under glaze. The steins can be dated from the marks on the bottom, which include a date-number code that can be found online. Other pieces may be listed in the Villeroy & Boch category.

Beaker, No. 545, Renaissance Woman, ½ Liter	*illus*	720
Charger, Phanolith, Seated Woman, Attendants, Marked, Late 1800s, 18 In.		875
Goblet, Pilsner, No. 2775, Gnomes Drinking, Footed, 1907, 11 In.		225
Jardiniere, Glazed, Blues, Brown, Flowers, Vines, Marked, Germany, 7 x 16 In.		500
Pitcher, White & Turquoise, 1900s, 11 ¾ In.	*illus*	100
Plaque, No. 1044/5056, Windmill, Painted, Shades Of Blue, 15 ½ In.	*illus*	96
Plaque, No. 1386, Germania, City Shields Around Border, Etched, 20 In.	*illus*	3480
Plaque, No. 2623, Man Carrying Tray Of Drinks, Fritz Quidenus, 10 ⅛ In.		395
Plaque, No. 2697, Elves & Toadstools, Etched, H. Schlitt, 17 ½ In.		3600
Plaque, No. 7047, 3 Figures, Phanolith, Stahl, Modern Frame, 20 x 19 ½ In.		660

M

Mettlach, Beaker, No. 545, Renaissance Woman, ½ Liter
$720

Fox Auctions

Mettlach, Pitcher, White & Turquoise, 1900s, 11¾ In.
$100

Pook & Pook

Mettlach, Plaque, No. 1044/5056, Windmill, Painted, Shades Of Blue, 15½ In.
$96

Fox Auctions

Mettlach, Plaque, No. 1386, Germania, City Shields Around Border, Etched, 20 In.
$3,480

Fox Auctions

Mettlach, Stein, Bicycles & Riders, Metal Lid, Late 1900s, ½ Liter, 8⅝ In.
$164

Jeffrey S. Evans & Associates

Mettlach, Stein, No. 1909/672, 3 Dwarfs With High Hats, Painted, ½ Liter
$115

Fox Auctions

Mettlach, Stein, No. 1997, George Ehret New York Brewery, Etched Portrait, Inlaid Lid, ½ Liter
$132

Fox Auctions

Mettlach, Stein, No. 2235, Schutzenliesel, Barmaid, Rifle, Eagle, Abbey Mark, 1896, 9½ In.
$189

Aspire Auctions

Mettlach, Vase, No. 2462, Art Nouveau Flowers, Etched, Orange Ground, 4½ x 7 In.
$336

Fox Auctions

M

305

Milk Glass, Vase, Boston State House Decoration, Flaring Rim, Hand Painted, 1800s, 9⅝ In.
$227

Skinner, Inc.

Millefiori, Paperweight, Multicolor Canes, White Ground, Clichy, France, 1800s, 3 In.
$777

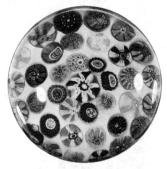

Jeffrey S. Evans & Associates

Minton, Jardiniere, Majolica, Monumental, Stand, Bellflower, Leaf & Fern, 15½ x 21½ In.
$1,250

Rago Arts and Auction Center

Pokal, Lid, Renaissance Figures, Figurehead Handles, Impressed, Abbey, 1785, 18 In.	543
Stein, Bicycles & Riders, Metal Lid, Late 1900s, ½ Liter, 8⅝ In. ....*illus*	164
Stein, Man On High Wheel Bicycle, Engraved, Finial, Signed, c.1885, 9½ In.	351
Stein, No. 406, Soldier, Students, Violin Player, Outside Pub, Pewter Lid, ½ Liter	168
Stein, No. 1108, People Enjoying Party, 1896, 6½ In.	195
Stein, No. 1431, Geruch, Man Smoking, Crested Tapestry, 1915, ½ Liter	215
Stein, No. 1519, School Rowing Teams, Skulling, Wreath, Etched, Inlaid Lid, ½ Liter	288
Stein, No. 1527, Men Drinking, Inlaid Lid, Christian Warth, 1890, ½ Liter	295
Stein, No. 1909/672, 3 Dwarfs With High Hats, Painted, ½ Liter ....*illus*	115
Stein, No. 1909/702, Procession To The Tavern, Tower Finial, Germany, ½ Liter	156
Stein, No. 1915, Koln Cathedral, Etched & Painted, Inlaid Lid, ½ Liter	660
Stein, No. 1997, George Ehret New York Brewery, Etched Portrait, Inlaid Lid, ½ Liter ....*illus*	132
Stein, No. 1999, Medallion, Portraits, Leafy Vines, Hinged Lid, 9 In.	173
Stein, No. 2001E, Books, Science, Inlaid Lid, Metal Owl Finial, ½ Liter	288
Stein, No. 2025, Cherubs Playing, Abandon, Cylindrical, 6½ x 3½ In.	108
Stein, No. 2033, Stags & Tree, Westerwald Style, Relief, Glazed, ½ Liter	600
Stein, No. 2074, Bird In Cage, Etched, Inlaid Lid, ½ Liter	1320
Stein, No. 2086, Peasant Dance, Relief, Terracotta Background, ½ Liter	132
Stein, No. 2121, Children, Leaves, Baby Etched Inlaid Lid, Marked, ¼ Liter, 6½ In.	146
Stein, No. 2140, Newport, R.I., Scene, Inlaid Lid, ½ Liter	720
Stein, No. 2184, Tools, Carpenter, Mason, Painted, Gnome Thumblift, 1896, ½ Liter	192
Stein, No. 2194, 3 Panel Scenes, Inlaid Lid, Turtle, Figural Alligator Handle, 3 Liter	480
Stein, No. 2222, Fraternal, Student Signatures, Inlaid Lid, 1895, ½ Liter	288
Stein, No. 2235, Schutzenliesel, Barmaid, Rifle, Eagle, Abbey Mark, 1896, 9½ In. ....*illus*	189
Stein, No. 2238, Regimental, 7th National Guard Army New York, Etched, ½ Liter	312
Stein, No. 2608, Blue, Cameo, Mandolin Players, Couples, Trees, Inlaid Lid, ⅓ Liter	204
Stein, No. 2631, Cameo, Boar Hunt Scene, Rabbit Band On Base, Inlaid Lid, 2½ Liter	2280
Stein, No. 2722, Occupational, Shoemaker, Etched, Inlaid Lid, ½ Liter	840
Stein, No. 2809, Story Teller, Children, Rip Van Winkle Was A Lucky Man, Inlaid Lid, ½ Liter..	510
Stein, No. 2889, Man On Horseback, Inlaid Lid, 1903, ½ Liter	295
Stein, No. 3344, Fraternal, Students, Verse, Shield, 6-Sided, ½ Liter	276
Stein, Telegrapher, Dome Lid, Train Finial, Eagle, Shield, Impressed, Abbey Mark, 1901, 9 In.	507
Vase, No. 2462, Art Nouveau Flowers, Etched, Orange Ground, 4½ x 7 In. ....*illus*	336
Vase, No. 2505, Brown, Tan, Blue, 2 Handles, Footed, c.1905, 13¼ In.	225
Vase, No. 3040, Cameo Figures In Arches, 4-Sided, Tapered, 11½ In.	120

MILK GLASS was named for its milky white color. It was first made in England during the 1700s. The height of its popularity in the United States was from 1870 to 1880. It is now correct to refer to some colored glass as blue milk glass, black milk glass, etc. Reproductions of milk glass are being made and sold in many stores. Related pieces may be listed in the Cosmos, Vallerysthal, and Westmoreland categories.

Biscuit Jar, Iron Handle, Cream Ground, Flowers Painted, 9 In.	58
Toothpick Holder, Beggar's Hand, 3½ In.	29
Toothpick Holder, Yutec Pattern, 1950s, 2¼ In.	12
Vase, Boston State House Decoration, Flaring Rim, Hand Painted, 1800s, 9⅝ In......*illus*	227
Vase, Hobnail, Crimped Rim, 4 x 4 In.	10

MILLEFIORI means, literally, a thousand flowers. Many small pieces of glass resembling flowers are grouped together to form a design. It is a type of glasswork popular in paperweights and some are listed in that category.

Basket, Tapers, Frosted Handle, Rounded Foot, 8 In.	75
Creamer, Flowers, Red, Blue, White, Yellow, Swirled Clear Handle, 4 In.	50
Epergne, Venetian Glass, Ruffled Edges, 4 Vases Set, Italy, c.1950, 16½ x 11¾ In.	344
Figurine, Fish, Tail Up, Blue, Yellow, Green, Red, 4¼ x 7½ In.	75
Figurine, Gold Fish, Blue, White & Orange Flowers, Standing On Clear Fins, 7 x 5 In.	115
Figurine, Unicorn, White Satin, Horn, Ears, Tail, 7 x 2 x 3 In.	70
Paperweight, Multicolor Canes, White Ground, Clichy, France, 1800s, 3 In......*illus*	777

M

Vase, Round, High Shoulders, Green, Red, Multicolor, Murano, 7¾ In.	94
Vase, Small Mouth, Round, Yellow Orange, Murano Vetro, 6 x 5¼ In.	58
Vase, White Design, Brown Background, 2 Handles, c.1920, 4 In.	370

MINTON china was made in the Staffordshire region of England beginning in 1796. The firm became part of the Royal Doulton Tableware Group in 1968, but the wares continued to be marked *Minton*. In 2009 the brand was bought by KPS Capital Partners of New York and became part of WWRD Holdings. The company no longer makes Minton china. Many marks have been used. The word *England* was added in 1891. Minton majolica is listed in this book in the Majolica category.

Minton
c.1822–1836

Minton
c.1863–1872

Minton
1951–present

Bowl, Vegetable, Haddon Hall, Oval, 10⅝ In.	74
Charger, Portrait, Penelope Boothby, Age 4, Signed E. Broughton 1875, 15¼ In.	431
Charger, Sgraffito, Renaissance Style Portrait, Glazed Redware, Pierced Border, c.1870, 17 In.	308
Cup & Saucer, Ring Handle, Red Flower, Gilt Leaves & Rim, c.1810	74
Ewer, Birds, Butterflies & Fauna, Turquoise Glaze, Bottle Shape, c.1875, 8¾ In.	615
Ewer, Bottle Shape, Yellow, Flowers, Pierced Turquoise Handle, England, c.1880, 9 In.	369
Figurine, Girl Training Her Dog, Parian, Luigi Guiglielmi, England, 1870, 10 In.	246
Figurine, Maiden, Seminude, Standing, White, Circular Base, 18 In.	172
Jardiniere, Majolica, Monumental, Stand, Bellflower, Leaf & Fern, 15½ x 21½ In. *illus*	1250
Tazza, Gilt Dish, 3 Parian Herons On Stem, 5¾ In.	1046
Urn, Dome Lid, Handles, Brown, Maiden, Cherubs, Pate-Sur-Pate, A. Birks, 1914, 13 In. *illus*	7500
Urn, Lid, Cream Ground, 2 Wreath Handles, Ribbon, Cupid, A. Birks, 1911, 12 In.	3500
Vase, Bottle Shape, Turquoise, White Flowers, Faux Wood Base, 1889, 8½ In.	677
Vase, Cupid, Mauve Ground, Pate-Sur-Pate, Loop Handles, Flared Neck, c.1875, 15⅞ In.	2000
Vase, Molded Figures Of People & Snakes, Dragon Handles, Gilt, Chinese Style, c.1873, 8 In.	1046
Vase, Turquoise Glaze, Loop & Ring Handles, Flowers & Butterflies, 1873, 10½ In.	615

MIRRORS *are listed in the Furniture category under Mirror.*

MOCHA pottery is an English-made product that was sold in America during the early 1800s. It is a heavy pottery with pale coffee-and-cream coloring. Designs of blue, brown, green, orange, black, or white were added to the pottery and given fanciful names, such as Tree, Snail Trail, or Moss. Mocha designs are sometimes found on pearlware. A few pieces of mocha ware were made in France, the United States, and other countries.

Bowl, Earthworm Inside & Out, Tan Interior Glaze, c.1825, 5 x 11½ In.	1680
Bowl, Lid, Marbleized, 2 Handles, Acorn Finial, c.1825, 5 x 6 In. *illus*	720
Bowl, Seaweed, Pumpkin Ground, Tooled Yellow Rim, England, 1850s, 2¾ x 5 In. *illus*	960
Creamer, Tobacco Leaf, Tan Ground, Molded Handle, England, 1850s, 3½ In.	3000
Mug, Abstract Pattern, White, Caramel, Blue, Black, c.1825, 4 In.	750
Mug, Rings & Dots, Green, Pink, Red, Handle, 3 In.	240
Pepper Pot, Dots & Fern, Yellow, Green, Black & White, c.1925, 4½ In.	1680
Pitcher, Barrel Shape, Bands, Diagonal Wavy Lines, 7 In.	472
Pitcher, Bulbous, Molded Foot, Handle & Spout, D.G. Carpentier, 7¾ In.	413
Pitcher, Cat's-Eye, Sienna Ground, Tricolor Ferns, Leaf Molded Handle, 1850s, 6 In. *illus*	2280
Pitcher, Stripes, Black, White, Blue, 1930s, 7 In.	395
Vase, Brown, Green Sponge Glaze, Yellow Flared Neck, c.1800, 6½ In.	301

MONMOUTH POTTERY COMPANY started working in Monmouth, Illinois, in 1892. The pottery made a variety of utilitarian wares. It became part of Western Stoneware Company in 1906. The maple leaf mark was used until about 1930.

Ashtray, AFAM, Masonic Symbol, 4 In.	24
Bean Pot, Lid, Loop Handles, Brown, Tan, 7 x 9 In.	35

Minton, Urn, Dome Lid, Handles, Brown, Maiden, Cherubs, Pate-Sur-Pate, A. Birks, 1914, 13 In.
$7,500

Royal Crest Auctioneers

Mocha, Bowl, Lid, Marbleized, 2 Handles, Acorn Finial, c.1825, 5 x 6 In.
$720

Garth's Auctioneers & Appraisers

Mocha, Bowl, Seaweed, Pumpkin Ground, Tooled Yellow Rim, England, 1850s, 2¾ x 5 In.
$960

Garth's Auctioneers & Appraisers

M

Mocha, Pitcher, Cat's-Eye, Sienna Ground, Tricolor Ferns, Leaf Molded Handle, 1850s, 6 In.
$2,280

Garth's Auctioneers & Appraisers

Moorcroft, Bowl, Persian, Flowers, Leaves, Ivory Ground, Marked, W. Moorcroft, c.1916, 3 x 6 In.
$550

Fairfield Auction

M

Moorcroft, Jardiniere, Pomegranate, Seeds & Leaves, Blue Ground, 1924, 9 ¼ In.
$600

Fairfield Auction

Bowl, Lid, Brown Glaze, 8 x 6 In.	14
Jug, Brown Glaze, Maple Leaf, Gal., 10 ¾ In.	150
Jug, Lid, Cattails, Disk Shape, Open Handle, 7 ½ In.	25
Pitcher, Brown, Rings, 4 ¼ In.	21
Pitcher, Sea Foam, Lotus, Embossed, 6 In.	47

MONT JOYE, *see Mt. Joye category.*

MOORCROFT pottery was first made in Burslem, England, in 1913. William Moorcroft had managed the art pottery department for James Macintyre & Company of England from 1898 to 1913. The Moorcroft pottery continues today, although William Moorcroft died in 1945. The earlier wares are similar to the modern ones, but color and marking will help indicate the age.

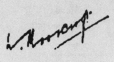

W. Moorcroft Ltd.	W. Moorcroft Ltd.	W. Moorcroft Ltd.
1898–c.1905	1898–1913	1928–1978

Bowl, Columbine, Blue Ground, Footed, c.1950, 4 In.	115
Bowl, Eventide Glaze, Molded Base, 1900s, 3 x 6 ¼ In.	221
Bowl, Leaf & Berry, Green, Purple, Yellow, 1900s, 5 x 2 In.	160
Bowl, Persian, Flowers, Leaves, Ivory Ground, Marked, W. Moorcroft, c.1916, 3 x 6 In. *illus*	550
Bowl, Pomegranate, Multicolor Enamel, Dark Blue Ground, c.1925, 8 ¼ In.	369
Jardiniere, Pomegranate, Seeds & Leaves, Blue Ground, 1924, 9 ¼ In. *illus*	600
Plate, Hibiscus, Flowers, Paper Label, 10 ¼ In.	594
Tobacco Jar, Alhambra, Stylized Flowers, Gilt Ground, Marked, Macintyre, 1903, 4 ¾ In. *illus*	300
Vase, 2 Handles, Cornflower, Signed, Rigg & Son Glasgow, c.1911, 10 In.	400
Vase, Art Deco, Landscape, Blood Orange Ground, c.1920, 4 In.	1695
Vase, Brown Chrysanthemum, Flowers, 2 Handles, c.1915, 10 ⅛ In.	660
Vase, Carp, Swimming Among Vegetation, Multicolor, Signed, 1993, 26 In.	2214
Vase, Cornflower Blue, Flowers, c.1920, 10 ½ In.	390
Vase, Eventide, Landscape, Cylindrical, Flared Top, Silver Plated Foot, c.1925, 7 ¾ In.	523
Vase, Finches, Blue, Tube Liner, Gillian Powell, 1991, 10 ¾ In.	1898
Vase, Flamminian Glaze, Twin Handle, Landscape, Rolling Trees, Wood Stand, c.1915, 12 In.	2723
Vase, Florian, Bottle Shape, Multicolor, Enamel, Poppy, Early 1900s, 9 ¾ In.	123
Vase, Florian, Green, Tan, Pink, Bulbous, Marked, Macintyre, 8 ¾ In.	390
Vase, Florian, Lilacs, Shaded Blue Ground, Tapered, c.1902, 6 ⅜ In. *illus*	1100
Vase, Hibiscus, Yellow & Red Flowers, Green Ground, Impressed Mark, 7 In. *illus*	531
Vase, Kyoto, Cranes, Butterflies & Flowers, Multicolor, 1994, 24 ¼ In.	677
Vase, Moonlit Blue & Green, Trees, Dark Blue Ground, Signed, c.1925, 8 ¼ In.	492
Vase, Moonlit Blue, Flared, c.1934, 4 ½ In.	540
Vase, Orchids, Deep Blue Ground, Bulbous, Signed, c.1940, 12 ½ In.	400
Vase, Pansy, Purple, Yellow, Green, Cream, W. Moorcroft, Macintyre, c.1911, 5 ¾ In. *illus*	1300
Vase, Red, Blue, Green, Yellow, 4 In.	190

MORGANTOWN GLASS WORKS operated in Morgantown, West Virginia, from 1900 to 1974. Some of their wares are marked with an adhesive label that says *Old Morgantown Glass.*

Bottle, Water, Jade Green, Bulbous Body, 1930, 6 x 3 ½ In.	17
Cocktail, Clear, Amber Stem, Figural Jockey, Gulfstream Race Track, 5 ½ In.	123
Cordial, Ruby Cased, Filament Stem, Salem No. 7700, Hand Blown, 1931, 3 ½ x 1 ⅜ In.	23
Decanter, Ice, El Mexicano, Stopper, White, c.1930, 8 ¼ In.	73
Glass, Mai Tai, Clear Bowl & Foot, Topaz Figural Stem, For Trader Vics, c.1960, 5 ½ In.	96
Plate, Salad, Queen Louise, Etched, Silk-Screened Cameos, 1928, 7 In.	39
Vase, El Greco, Ritz Blue, No. 87, 2 Handles, Sticker, 11 x 4 x 8 In.	637

Moorcroft, Tobacco Jar, Alhambra, Stylized Flowers, Gilt Ground, Marked, Macintyre, 1903, 4¾ In.
$300

Moorcroft, Vase, Florian, Lilacs, Shaded Blue Ground, Tapered, c.1902, 6⅜ In.
$1,100

Moorcroft, Vase, Hibiscus, Yellow & Red Flowers, Green Ground, Impressed Mark, 7 In.
$531

Moorcroft, Vase, Pansy, Purple, Yellow, Green, Cream, W. Moorcroft, Macintyre, c.1911, 5¾ In.
$1,300

Moriage, Umbrella Stand, Courtly Scenes, Enamel, Molded, Reticulated Central Band, Japan, c.1950, 25 In.
$185

Moser, Cruet, Octagonal, Green Fading, Gilt, Bronze Mounted, 9⅜ In.
$165

M

Moser, Wedding Cup, Green, Enameled Scrolls, Flowers, Gilt, Woman Form, Myers Neffe, 8 In.
$660

Fox Auctions

M

Mother-Of-Pearl, Lamp, Rainbow Pastels, Square Form Font, 1900, Miniature, 9¾ x 5 x 4¼ In.
$2,629

Jeffrey S. Evans & Associates

Motorcycle, Helmet, Patrolman's, Blue Leather, Buff Canvas, Red Liner, Chin Strap, Everoak, 1956
$144

Thomaston Place Auction Galleries

MORIAGE is a special type of raised decoration used on some Japanese pottery. Sometimes pieces of clay were shaped by hand and applied to the item; sometimes the clay was squeezed from a tube in the way we apply cake frosting. One type of moriage is called Dragonware by collectors.

Bowl, Coralene Lid, Footed, Green, Orange Tones, Nippon, 7 In.	460
Bowl, Jardiniere, Multicolor On Cream Glaze, Japan, Late 1800s, 16⅝ x 12 In.	121
Bowl, Oval, Gold Beaded Swag, Flowers, Green Ruffled Rim, Scalloped Foot, 8 x 4 In.	36
Humidor, Hand Painted Flowers, Green Maple Leaf Mark, Nippon, 5¾ In.	385
Humidor, Indian Chief, Headdress, M In Wreath Mark, Nippon, 7½ In.	1840
Pitcher, Pink & Purple Flowers, Gold, Green Paint, Nippon, 8 x 8 In.	150
Umbrella Stand, Courtly Scenes, Enamel, Molded, Reticulated Central Band, Japan, c.1950, 25 In. *illus*	185
Umbrella Stand, Green, 3 Geisha Girls, Palm Leaves, Floral Border, Japan, 24 x 8¾ In.	118
Vase, Nasturtiums, Painted, Gold Color, Art Nouveau, Nippon, c.1920, 8½ In.	120
Vase, Red Tulip, Steel Blue & Green Ground, Nippon, c.1900, 9 In.	275
Vase, Scene, Palm Trees, Houses, River, 2 Handles, Bulbous, Round Base, Nippon, 6¼ In.	44

MOSAIC TILE COMPANY of Zanesville, Ohio, was started by Karl Langerbeck and Herman Mueller in 1894. Many types of plain and ornamental tiles were made until 1959. The company closed in 1967. The company also made some ashtrays, bookends, and related giftwares. Most pieces are marked with the entwined MTC monogram.

Tile, Hawk, Arts & Craft Mission, Pink, Kindergarten Series, 1930s, 4½ In.	225
Tile, Lion, Shield, Heraldic, Blue Glaze, c.1910, 6 In.	95
Trivet, Nursery Rhyme, Old King Cole, Raised Feet, 1930s, 6 x 6 In.	95

MOSER glass is made by a Bohemian glasshouse founded by Ludwig Moser in 1857. Art Nouveau–type glassware and iridescent glassware were made. The most famous Moser glass is decorated with heavy enameling in gold and bright colors. The firm, Moser Glassworks, is still working in Karlovy Vary, Czech Republic. Few pieces of Moser glass are marked.

Beaker, Amber, Baden, Enameled Multicolor Flowers, 3¼ In.	96
Champagne, Hand Painted, Gilded, Enamel Dots & Flowers, c.1900, 5½ In.	350
Cruet, Octagonal, Green Fading, Gilt, Bronze Mounted, 9⅜ In. *illus*	165
Goblet, Red, White, Gold Gilt, 10 In.	395
Pitcher, Electric Blue, Elaborate Stylized Flowers, Ruffled Rim, Gold Trim, 4 In.	300
Pitcher, Gold Gilt Rim, Handle, Marked, 1900s, 9¼ In.	350
Vase, Elk, Etched Glass, Bulbous, 8 Sided, Alexandrite, Signed, 8 x 4½ In.	605
Vase, Enamel Bug & Leaf, Raised Acorns, 1857, 5½ In.	403
Vase, Enamel, Flowers, White Panels, Trumpet Shape, 1857, 16 In.	259
Vase, Enamel, Gold Trim, Raised Pansies, 1857, 14 In.	460
Vase, Enamel, Pansies, Purple, Yellow, Clear, Green Leaves, c.1915, 14 In.	1295
Wedding Cup, Green, Enameled Scrolls, Flowers, Gilt, Woman Form, Myers Neffe, 8 In. *illus*	660

MOTHER-OF-PEARL GLASS, or pearl satin glass, was first made in the 1850s in England and in Massachusetts. It was a special type of mold-blown satin glass with air bubbles in the glass, giving it a pearlized color. It has been reproduced. Mother-of-pearl shell objects are listed under Pearl.

Helmet, Roman, Perfume Bottle Caddy, Blue Velvet, 2 Square Cut Perfumes, c.1880, 6½ In.	262
Lamp, Rainbow Pastels, Square Form Font, 1900, Miniature, 9¾ x 5 x 4¼ In. *illus*	2629
Magnifying Glass, Rectangular, Case, Velvet Lined, 5¼ In.	693
Toothpick Holder, Sterling Silver, Shield, Leaves, 3 In.	390
Vase, Diamond Quilted, Ruffled, Blue, 10 In.	84
Vase, Herringbone, Crimped Top, Yellow, 6¼ In.	60
Vase, Yellow Satin, Blue Coralene Overlay, 6½ In.	60

MOTORCYCLES and motorcycle accessories of all types are being collected today. Examples can be found that date back to the early twentieth century. Toy motorcycles are listed in the Toy category.

Ashtray, Indian Motor Cycles, Round, 5 ½ In.	36
Badge, Salesman's, Harley-Davidson, Michelin Tires, c.1960, 1 ⅝ In.	101
Clock, King Of The Highway, 8-Sided, Neon Spinner, Harley-Davidson, 18 ½ x 18 ½ In.	509
Helmet, Patrolman's, Blue Leather, Buff Canvas, Red Liner, Chin Strap, Everoak, 1956 ....*illus*	144

MOUNT WASHINGTON, *see Mt. Washington category.*

MOVIE memorabilia of all types are collected. Animation Art, Games, Sheet Music, Toys, and some celebrity items are listed in their own section. A lobby card is usually 11 by 14 inches, but other sizes were also made. A set of lobby cards includes seven scene cards and one title card. An American one sheet, the standard movie poster, is 27 by 41 inches. A three sheet is 40 by 81 inches. A half sheet is 22 by 28 inches. A window card, made of cardboard, is 14 by 22 inches. An insert is 14 by 36 inches. A herald is a promotional item handed out to patrons. Press books, sent to exhibitors to promote a movie, contain ads and lists of what is available for advertising, i.e., posters, lobby cards. Press kits, sent to the media, contain photos and details about the movie, i.e., stars' biographies and interviews.

Lobby Card, Alice In Wonderland, Paramount Pictures, 1933, 11 x 14 In. ....*illus*	463
Lobby Card, Amos 'N' Andy, Check & Double Check, RKO, 1930, 11 x 14 In.	214
Lobby Card, Becky Sharp, Miriam Hopkins, Rouby Mamoulian, 1935, 11 x 14 In.	260
Lobby Card, Charlie Chan At The Circus, Warner Oland, Fox, 1936, 11 x 14 In. ....*illus*	130
Lobby Card, Dodge City, Cowboys, Errol Flynn, Warner Bros., 1939, 11 x 14 In.	393
Lobby Card, Ghost Of Frankenstein, 1948, 11 x 14 In.	350
Poster, Adventures Of Robin Hood, Technicolor, Errol Flynn, 41 x 27 In.	35
Poster, Cat's Paw, Harold Lloyd, Silver Frame, Fox Release, 17 ¾ x 13 ¾ In.	106
Poster, Road To Zanzibar, Bob Hope, Bing Crosby, Dorothy Lamour, 1941, 40 x 26 ¾ In. ....*illus*	292
Poster, Shanghai Chest, Charlie Chan, Monogram Pictures, 1948, 35 ¾ x 14 In.	286
Poster, The Awakening, Vilma Banky, 1928, 14 x 36 In.	450
Prop, 2-Headed Eagle, Dr. Zhivago, Plaster, Ice Palace Scene, 1965, 37 In.	750
Prop, Helmet, Centurion's, Ben Hur, Hinged Guards, Red Bristle Crest, 1959, 16 In. ....*illus*	840
Prop, Tomahawk, From Movie Unconquered, Brass Blade, Nickel Plated, Hardwood Shaft, 1948	1046
Theater Turnstile, Ticket, Movie & Amusement Ride, c.1950, 40 In.	504
Title Card, 3 Stooges, Even As IOU, 65th Short Film, Selling, Columbia, 1942, 11 x 14 In.	2155
Title Card, Adventures Of Robin Hood, Swashbuckler Film, Errol Flynn, 1938, 11 x 14 In.	1696

MT. JOYE is an enameled cameo glass made in the late nineteenth and twentieth centuries by Saint-Hilaire Touvier de Varraux and Co. of Pantin, France. This same company made De Vez glass. Pieces were usually decorated with enameling. Most pieces are not marked.

Vase, Cameo, Serpentine Rim, Acid Cut, Flowers & Butterfly, 3 ½ x 7 In. ....*illus*	189

MT. WASHINGTON Glass Works started in 1837 in South Boston, Massachusetts. In 1870 the company moved to New Bedford, Massachusetts. Many types of art glass were made there until 1894, when the company merged with Pairpoint Manufacturing Co. Amberina, Burmese, Crown Milano, Cut Glass, Peachblow, and Royal Flemish are each listed in their own category.

Dish, Sweetmeat, Melon Shape, Yellow Tones, Pink Flowers, Silver Plate Lid & Bail, 4 x 5 In.	180
Paperweight, Strawberries, Glass Work, Oval, 4 Berries, Blossom, 3 ¾ x 2 ¾ In.	4920
Pitcher, Water, Burmese, Squat, Circular Rim, Marked, c.1880, 6 ¾ x 6 ½ In.	263
Pitcher, Water, Spherical, Fish & Seashells, Twisted Handle, c.1885, 8 ⅛ In. ....*illus*	9560
Saltshaker, Cockleshell, Opaque White, Yellow Shading, Spider Mum, Satin, Lid, 1800s, 2 ¾ In.	322
Saltshaker, Milk Glass, Tomato, Opaque, 8 Lobe Body, Embossed Flowers, 1800s, 2 ¾ In.	60
Saltshaker, Tan, Chick Head, Multicolor, Flowers, 1900s, 2 ⅜ In. ....*illus*	269
Sugar Shaker, Egg Shape, Flowers & Leaves, Pink & White, 4 ¼ In.	60
Sugar Shaker, Egg Shape, White, Flowers, Enamel, 4 x 3 ½ In.	72
Sugar Shaker, Opaque, Milk Glass, Custard & Peach Ground, Multicolor, Floral, 4 In.	956
Toothpick Holder, Hat, Opal, Pink Flowers, Green Leaves, Marked, c.1888, 2 In. ....*illus*	211

Movie, Lobby Card, Alice In Wonderland, Paramount Pictures, 1933, 11 x 14 In.
$463

Hake's Auctions

Movie, Lobby Card, Charlie Chan At The Circus, Warner Oland, Fox, 1936, 11 x 14 In.
$130

Hake's Auctions

TIP
Don't eat or drink while you are working with your paper collectibles.

Movie, Poster, Road To Zanzibar, Bob Hope, Bing Crosby, Dorothy Lamour, 1941, 40 x 26 ¾ In.
$292

Hake's Auctions

M

Movie, Prop, Helmet, Centurion's, Ben Hur, Hinged Guards, Red Bristle Crest, 1959, 16 In.
$840

Mt. Joye, Vase, Cameo, Serpentine Rim, Acid Cut, Flowers & Butterfly, 3 ½ x 7 In.
$189

Mt. Washington, Pitcher, Water, Spherical, Fish & Seashells, Twisted Handle, c.1885, 8 ⅛ In.
$9,560

Mt. Washington, Saltshaker, Tan, Chick Head, Multicolor, Flowers, 1900s, 2 ⅜ In.
$269

Mt. Washington, Toothpick Holder, Hat, Opal, Pink Flowers, Green Leaves, Marked, c.1888, 2 In.
$211

Muller Freres, Vase, Cameo, Flared Shoulders, Floral, Pres Nancy, Early 1900s, 5 ½ In.
$248

Muncie, Lamp Base, Rombic, Empire State Building, Green Matte Glaze, Art Deco, c.1930, 11 In.
$570

Muncie, Pitcher, Elongated Spout, Green Matte Drip Over Green Glaze, 1922-1939, 12 In.
$36

Muncie, Vase, Lovebird, Glossy Peachskin Glaze, c.1930, 9 In.
$360

M

MULBERRY

MULBERRY ware was made in the Staffordshire district of England from about 1850 to 1860. The dishes were decorated with a reddish brown transfer design, now called mulberry. Many of the patterns are similar to those used for flow blue and other Staffordshire transfer wares.

Creamer, Buildings, Trees, Octagonal, Transferware, Podmore, Walker & Co., c.1850, 5 In.	88
Eggcup, Double, Flowers, Scalloped, Charles J. Mason, 1940s	49
Ladle, Bridge, Trees, Black & White, Transferware, 19th Century, 12 ½ In.	75
Pitcher, Flowers, Leaves, Scalloped Rim, Footed, Purple, 10 ¾ In.	99
Pitcher, Giraffes, Palm Trees, Strap Handle, John & Matthew Bell, 1840s, 8 In.	795
Plate, Andrew Johnson Home, Purple, Transferware, 10 In.	42
Plate, Landscape, Buildings, Purple, Podmore Walker Co., 1850s, 10 ¾ In.	44
Plate, Rat & Oyster, Blue & White, Brown Westhead & Moore, c.1880, 10 In.	248
Platter, Pagoda, River, Boats, F & W Co., Transferware, c.1845, 16 x 12 In.	185
Platter, Village, Windmills, Black & Mulberry, 1800s, 8 ¾ x 6 ¾ In.	175

MULLER FRERES

MULLER FRERES, French for Muller Brothers, made cameo and other glass from about 1895 to 1933. Their factory was first located in Luneville, then in nearby Croismare, France. Pieces were usually marked with the company name.

Vase, Blackberries, Cameo, 2 Applied Handles, Signed, 5 ½ x 2 ¾ In.	625
Vase, Cameo, Flared Shoulders, Floral, Pres Nancy, Early 1900s, 5 ½ In. ...*illus*	248
Vase, Double Gourd, Serpentine Vines, Leaves, Berries, Croismare, 6 ½ In.	354
Vase, Lake, Rocky Coastline, Trees, Cameo, Shouldered, Blue, Black, 16 x 9 In.	2124
Vase, Nighttime Scene, Dark Red Cameo Owl, Trees, Earthy Background, Signed, 8 ¾ x 4 ½ In.	7380
Vase, Trumpet, Flowers, Burgundy & Pink Over White Cameo, 9 x 17 In.	1999

MUNCIE

MUNCIE Clay Products Company was established by Charles Benham in Muncie, Indiana, in 1918. The company made pottery for the florist and giftshop trade. Art pottery was made beginning in 1922. Rombic is pottery made by this company and Ruba Rombic is glass made by the Consolidated Glass Company. Both were designed by Reuben Haley. The company closed by 1939. Pieces are marked with the name *Muncie* or just with a system of numbers and letters, like *1A* .

MUNCIE

Basket, Rose Glaze, Green Drip, Handle, 11 x 7 In.	143
Bookends, Flower Basket, Bows, Green Matte, Glaze, c.1930, 5 ½ In.	192
Lamp Base, Rombic, Empire State Building, Green Matte Glaze, Art Deco, c.1930, 11 In.. .*illus*	570
Pitcher, Elongated Spout, Green Matte Drip Over Green Glaze, 1922-39, 12 In. ....*illus*	36
Vase, Lovebird, Glossy Peachskin Glaze, c.1930, 9 In. ....*illus*	360
Vase, Rombic, Falling Triangles, Matte Blue Over Green Glaze, 1930, 7 In. ....*illus*	420
Vase, Rombic, Money Bag, Glossy Black Glaze, 1928-32, 6 In.	840
Vase, Rombic, Stacked Cubes, Green Matte Over Lilac Glaze, 7 In.	5520
Vase, Rombic, Star, Matte White Over Rose Glaze, Angular, 1928-32, 5 In.	120
Vase, Spanish Line, Low Aorta, Orange Peel Glaze, Flattened Handles, 1927-32, 5 In	960

MURANO, *see Glass-Venetian category.*

MUSIC

MUSIC boxes and musical instruments are listed here. Phonograph records, jukeboxes, phonographs, and sheet music are listed in other categories in this book.

Accordion, Black, Ivory Colored Accents, Vents, 2 Octaves, Brass Buttons, Bell, Italy..........*illus*	83
Accordion, Box Shape, Black Paint, Parsifial Melodeon, Germany	115
Accordion, Case, Leather Straps, Rosati, 22 x 17 x 10 In.	200
Altonium, H.N. White, King, Brushed Silver, Removable Bell, Case, Oh., c.1958	300
Balalaika, Triangular Wood, 3 Strings, 27 In.	24
Banjo, Electric, 5 Strings, A.C. Fairbanks, Whyte Laydie No. 7, Rim, Case, c.1908, 12 In.	4305
Banjo, Gibson Mastertone, 5 Strings, Case, 1940s, 14 x 4 x 38 In.	2934
Banjo, Majestic, Mother-Of-Pearl Inlay, Hard Case, c.1920, 33 x 13 In.	976
Box, Ballerina, Wood Case, Mechanical & Singing Birds, Reuge, 19 x 13 ½ x 9 In.	3900
Box, Bells, Drum, Cylinder, 12 Tunes, Spring Driven, 12 ½ x 25 x 14 ½ In.	1452
Box, Burl Walnut, Henry Gautschi & Sons, c.1890, 16 x 30 ⅝ x 15 ¾ In.	2500

Muncie, Vase, Rombic, Falling Triangles, Matte Blue Over Green Glaze, 1930, 7 In.
$420

Ripley Auctions

Music, Accordion, Black, Ivory Colored Accents, Vents, 2 Octaves, Brass Buttons, Bell, Italy
$83

Alderfer Auction Company

Music, Box, Calliope, 12 Discs, 4 Saucers, Walnut, Brass Shield, c.1890, 10 x 9 x 6 In.
$1,133

Charleston Estate Auctions

M

Music, Box, Cylinder, Bell, Marquetry, Cherry, Swiss, c.1880, 10 ½ x 23 ¼ x 12 In. $2,250

Heritage Auctions

Music, Box, Leipzig, 23 Discs, Double Comb, Floral Inlaid Top, 10 x 23 x 18 In. $150

Nadeau's Auction Gallery

Music, Box, Piano Shape, Flowers & Leaf Scrolls, Couples, Bucolic Landscape, 1800s, 6 In. $750

Leslie Hindman Auctioneers

Music, Box, Singing Bird, Gilt, Silver, Austria, c.1890, 4 In. $4,320

Eldred's

Box, Calliope, 12 Discs, 4 Saucers, Walnut, Brass Shield, c.1890, 10 x 9 x 6 In. ....*illus*	1133
Box, Criterion, Hand Carved, Walnut Case, Fern Medallion, 4 Discs, 12 x 22 x 20 In.	708
Box, Cylinder, 8 Tune, Inlaid, Mahogany Case, Swiss, 27 ½ x 12 x 9 In.	920
Box, Cylinder, 8 Tunes, Grain Painted, Inlay, Swiss, c.1850, 6 x 15 ¾ x 7 ⅝ In.	545
Box, Cylinder, Bell, Marquetry, Cherry, Swiss, c.1880, 10 ½ x 23 ¼ x 12 In. ....*illus*	2250
Box, Cylinder, Grain Painted Case, 10 Tunes, 3 Bells, Butterfly Clappers, c.1900, 9 x 19 x 9 In..	900
Box, Cylinder, Sublime Harmony Zither, Mahogany Case, Swiss, c.1885, 9 x 34 x 13 In.	2188
Box, Kingwood Inlay, Burl Walnut, Cabriole Legs, Casters, c.1880, 43 x 47 x 29 In.	6875
Box, Lebell, Cylinder, 6 Bells, 6 Butterflies, Rosewood Case, c.1880, 18 x 9 In.	1475
Box, Leipzig, 23 Discs, Double Comb, Floral Inlaid Top, 10 x 23 x 18 In. ....*illus*	150
Box, Lid, Cylinder, Mother-Of-Pearl Inlay, Veneered, Bone Inlay, Swiss, c.1890, 27 x 12 In.	864
Box, Mira Disc, Mahogany Case, Maryland My Maryland, 6 x 6 x 27 In.	840
Box, Piano Shape, Flowers & Leaf Scrolls, Couples, Bucolic Landscape, 1800s, 6 In. ....*illus*	750
Box, Polyphon Style 104, Walnut Case, Germany, 1900, 50 ½ x 27 ½ x 15 ½ In.	1300
Box, Regina, Disc, Double Comb, Mahogany Case, Drawer, Ball Feet, Roped Edging, 15 ½ In. ..	110
Box, Regina, Double Comb, Mahogany Case, Columns, Inlay, Bun Feet, c.1896, 11 x 21 In.	2520
Box, Regina, Style 35, Walnut, 12 Discs, c.1900, 67 ½ x 26 ½ x 22 In.	5250
Box, Singing Bird, Birdcage, Brass Wire, Giltwood Base, Loop Handle, 22 ½ x 15 x 10 In.	2723
Box, Singing Bird, Birdcage, Brass, Giltwood Base, 1900s, 20 In.	1845
Box, Singing Bird, Brass Cage, Loop Handle, Leafy Perch, K. Griesbaum, c.1950, 11 In.	633
Box, Singing Bird, Brass, Box, Filigree, Hinged Lid, Red Feather Bird, Germany, c.1945, 4 In....	575
Box, Singing Bird, Cage, Blue & Red, France, 10 ½ In.	325
Box, Singing Bird, Cage, Red, Black, Gold, Footed, 9 In.	316
Box, Singing Bird, Domed Cage, Gilt, Yellow, On Stand, 1900, 12 x 7 In.	272
Box, Singing Bird, Gilt, Silver, Austria, c.1890, 4 In. ....*illus*	4320
Box, Singing Bird, Real Feathers, Brass Cage, Perch, Brass Cage, Embossed Trim, Spring Wind, 11 In....	210
Box, Symphonia, Roller, Vacuum Movement, Wilcox & White Organ Co., 1800s, 14 x 20 x 15 In.	252
Box, Symphonion No. 30, Disc, Walnut Case, 100 Teeth, Schutz, c.1900, 24 x 18 x 11 In.	1521
Box, Symphonion, Single Comb, Lacquered Wood, Crank Mechanism, 5 ¾ x 6 ½ In.	156
Box, Thorens, 10 Discs, Brass, Ribbed, Fred Zimbalist, Oh., 4 ½ x 7 ½ x 5 ¾ In.	424
Cabinet, 3 Interior Shelves, Oak Body, Brass Handle, Art Deco, 38 x 25 x 16 In.	58
Clarinet, Eagle Device, Plaque Engraved, A.G. Huttl, c.1870, 16 ¼ In..................................	215
Clarinet, Greville, Silver Plated, Penzell Mueller Mouthpiece, Tweed Case, 1930s...................	120
Clarinet, Lyceum, Rosewood, Case, c.1905, Italy, 26 In.	195
Drum, African, Animal Skins, Doum Palm, Dark Brown, Tan, 17 x 6 In...	150
Drum, Bentwood, Painted, Bass, Mounted, Glass Top, 16 ¼ x 31 In..	369
Drum, Brass, Wood, Leather Ropes, Drumsticks, A.T. Baird, 1870s, 16 x 12 In...................*illus*	531
Drum, Rope Tension, Brown, Carrying Strap, J.W. Pepper, c.1975, 16 x 16 In.	277
Drum, Snare, Black Avalon Pearl Finish, Nickel Plated, Stand, Brushes, 1939	300
Dulcimer, Hammered, Trapezoidal Board, Strings, Wood, Collapsible Stand....................*illus*	130
Dulcimer, Wood, Hand Crafted, S. Anderson, 1980, 37 In.	59
Euphonium, Brass, Double Bell, Lyre, Vincent Bach Mouthpiece, Case, Stand, Pat. 1886..*illus*	2160
Flute, 4 Key, Boxwood, Stamped Firth, Hall & Pond, c.1840	277
Flute, Silver Plate, Bundy, Selmer, Fitted Case, 16 In..	61
Graphophone, Cylinder, Morning Glory Horn, Mahogany Case, Bale Handle, 22 x 3 In.	600
Graphophone, Edison, Black Painted Finish, Crank Key, Horn, Oak Case, 16 ¾ x 30 In.	140
Graphophone, Morning Glory Horn, At Style, Oak, Dome Cover, 12 x 12 x 21 In.	283
Guitar, Acoustic, 6 Strings, Black Lacquer, Domed Back, F Hole Arch Top, Hard Case................	180
Guitar, Acoustic, 12 Strings, Flat Spruce Top, Rosewood Bridge, Soft Case, 1969, 42 In.	330
Guitar, Acoustic, Gibson J-45, Mahogany, Sunburst Finish, 1944......................................*illus*	7200
Guitar, Acoustic, Martin O-18, Flat Top, Bound Spruce Top, Mahogany, Hardshell Case, 1967..	2596
Guitar, Acoustic, Yamaha CG171S, Case, 43 ½ In.	123
Guitar, Acoustic, Yamaha, FG-230, 12 Strings, Rosewood & Spruce, Hard Case, 16 x 42 In.	303
Guitar, Bass, Electric, Ampeg, Red, Black, 4 Strings, Soft Case, 47 ½ In.	2310
Guitar, Bass, Fender Mustang, Bluish Green, Stripes, Orange Felt-Lined Case, c.1970	1298
Guitar, Electric, Fender, Bridge Cover, Hardshell Case, Jaguar, 1962....................................	3444
Guitar, Electric, G&L Comanche, Blue Metal Flake, Black Pickguard, Maple Neck, 40 In. ..*illus*	995
Guitar, Electric, Gibson, Hollow Body, Chet Atkins Model, Sunburst Finish................................	2048
Guitar, Electric, Kent, Rosewood Fretboard, Open Gear Tuners, Hardshell Case, 1970s	216
Guitar, Epiphone Zephyr, Deluxe Regent, Electric, Case, 1953, 20 x 44 In.	4245
Guitar, Flamenco, Rosewood Back & Fretboard, Marcelino Barbero, c.1975, 11 x 9 x 14 In.	726
Guitar, Gibson, Rounded Shoulder, String, Case, 1968, 28 In.	4313

Music, Drum, Brass, Wood, Leather Ropes, Drumsticks, A.T. Baird, 1870s, 16 x 12 In.
$531

Milestone Auctions

Music, Dulcimer, Hammered, Trapezoidal Board, Strings, Wood, Collapsible Stand
$130

Alderfer Auction Company

Music, Euphonium, Brass, Double Bell, Lyre, Vincent Bach Mouthpiece, Case, Stand, Pat. 1886
$2,160

Alderfer Auction Company

Music, Guitar, Acoustic, Gibson J-45, Mahogany, Sunburst Finish, 1944
$7,200

Eldred's

> **TIP**
>
> *If you have an old piano, beware of moths. They sometimes infest the interior fabrics.*

Music, Guitar, Electric, G&L Comanche, Blue Metal Flake, Black Pickguard, Maple Neck, 40 In.
$995

Cordier Auctions

Music, Nickelodeon, Cremona, 5 Cent, Upright Stained Oak Case, Iron Frame, 29 x 65 x 57 In.
$2,700

Morphy Auctions

Music, Piano, Grand, John Broadwood & Sons, Amboyna, Gilt, c.1845, 38 ½ x 98 ½ x 58 In.
$27,500

Heritage Auctions

M

Music, Piano, Grand, Steinway, Model L, Black Lacquer, c.1935
$9,440

Burchard Galleries

Music, Picture, Oil On Metal, Church, Working Clock, Pull String, Frame, c.1850, 19 x 22 In.
$386

Auction Team Breker

Music, Zither, 5 Strings, Drone Section, Bone-Style Edging, Case, Tuners, M. Kraus, Chicago
$35

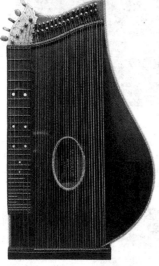

Alderfer Auction Company

Harp, Clark, Irish, Model A, Mixed Wood, Painted Irish Designs, Paw Feet, Stand, 53 In.	492
Harp, Rock Maple, Parcel Gilt, 44 Strings, 7 Pedals, Case, Wurlitzer Starke, 67 ½ In.	3500
Horn, Hunting, Carved, Hunting Dogs, Running Dogs, Palmetto Tree, 1800s, 12 In.	780
Mandolin, Sunburst Top, Mahogany Back, Case, 1939, 25 x 10 In.	295
Nickelodeon, Cremona, 5 Cent, Upright Stained Oak Case, Iron Frame, 29 x 65 x 57 In. *..illus*	2700
Organ, Pump, 3 Beveled Mirrors, Weaver Organ & Piano Co., c.1885, 43 x 24 In.	425
Piano, Baby Grand, Steinway & Sons, Mahogany, c.1935, 39 x 57 x 62 In.	9440
Piano, Baby Grand, Steinway & Sons, Model 280431 M, c.1930, 30 x 58 67 In.	29000
Piano, Baby Grand, Steinway & Sons, Overstrung Scale, Ebonized, 38 x 58 x 69 In.	4200
Piano, Grand, Erard, Rosewood, 85 Keys, Carved, Fluted Legs, c.1890, 38 x 53 x 85 In.	908
Piano, Grand, John Broadwood & Sons, Amboyna, Gilt, c.1845, 38 ½ x 98 ½ x 58 In. *..illus*	27500
Piano, Grand, Steinway & Sons, Mahogany, Model M, Bench, 1956, 57 x 66 In.	12500
Piano, Grand, Steinway, Model L, Black Lacquer, c.1935 *...........illus*	9440
Piano, Grand, Yamaha G2, Walnut Case, Japan, 1970	2714
Piano, Salon Grand, Steinway & Sons, Ebonized, c.1982, 41 x 60 x 72 In.	27500
Picture, Oil On Metal, Church, Working Clock, Pull String, Frame, c.1850, 19 x 22 In. *.....illus*	386
Roller Organ, Oak Case, Glass Lid, Ebonized Base, Crank Handle, 12 ½ x 18 In.	266
Saxophone, Alto, Silvertone, Selmer Case, Stamped, C.G. Conn, Early 1900s	354
Saxophone, Marked, Kalison, Milano, Italy, 12 x 2 ½ In.	666
Saxophone, Tenor, Case, Selmer Mark IV, 1959.	8610
Trumpet, Brass, Stradivarius Model, Mother-Of-Pearl Keys, Vincent Bach, Box	1800
Trumpet, First Slide Trigger, Case, C.G. Conn Constellation 28B, c.1950	400
Trumpet, Tibetan, Black, Metal Decoration, Dragon Shape, 1800s, 4 x 19 x 2 In.	790
Trumpet, Tibetan, Fish Shape, Brass, 19 ¾ In.	105
Ukulele, 4 Strings, Canvas Case, Stamped & Label, C.F. Martin & Co., c.1920	600
Viola, Cornerless, 5 Strings, Case, 1997, 16 In.	308
Viola, Internal Brand, Dominic Excell, Case & Bow, 1986	492
Violin, Branded Internally & Externally, Vincenzo Cavani, Italy, c.1940.	4305
Violin, Elias Howe, Boston No. 178, Anno 1911, Case	502
Violin, Maple, Spruce, Inlaid Flowers, c.1920, 23 In.	1750
Violin, Saquin, Luthier, Rue Beauregard 14, Bausch Bow, Case, 1850	177
Violin, Thumbprint, Case, James Reynold Carlisle, 1924	4305
Violoncello, 2 Bows, Louis Dolling, Wernitzgrun, Germany, 1954.	1230
Zither, 5 Strings, Drone Section, Bone-Style Edging, Case, Tuners, M. Kraus, Chicago *......illus*	35

MUSTACHE CUPS were popular from 1850 to 1900 when the large, flowing mustache was in style. A ledge of china or silver held the hair out of the liquid in the cup. This kept the mustache tidy and also kept the mustache wax from melting. Old left-handed mustache cups are rare and have been reproduced since the 1960s.

Blue Willow, Trees, Saucer, 1920s	117
Flower Petals, White, Gold, Saucer, Germany, 1920s	119
Flowers, Pink, Gold Trim, Saucer, Tressemann & Vogt, c.1905, 5 ¾ In.	230
Flowers, Transferware, Red, Pink, Cream Ground, 1920s, 3 x 3 In.	56
Horse Heads, Brown, White, Roses, Shades Of Blue & Pink, Gold Trim, Bavaria, 3 ½ x 4 ¾ In.	25
Lotus, Water Lily, White Ground, Handle, Saucer, Germany, 1950s, 3 x 3 ¾ In.	33
Metal, Gray, Silver Cut Design, Saucer, Marked, James W. Tafts, 1800s	99
Rose, Tea, Porcelain, Gilt, White, Victorian Style, Haviland, c.1900, 2 ⅜ x 5 In.	21
Roses, Painted, White, Green, Pink, Porcelain, 3 x 6 x 4 In.	14
Victorian, Green, Gold, Footed, Saucer, 3 x 6 In.	185
Violets, White Ground, Gold Rim, Saucer, Marked AKD, France, 2 ¾ x 3 ½ In.	21
Waterlilies, Blue & White, Figural Handle, Girl On Bridge	50

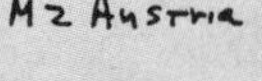

MZ Austria **MZ AUSTRIA** is the wording on a mark used by Moritz Zdekauer on porcelains made at his works in Altrolau, Austria, from 1884 to 1909. The mark was changed to MZ *Altrolau* in 1909, when the firm was purchased by C.M. Hutschenreuther. The firm operated under the name Altrolau Porcelain Factories from 1909 to 1945. It was nationalized after World War II. The pieces were decorated with lavish floral patterns and overglaze gold decoration. Full sets of dishes were made as well as vases, toilet sets, and other wares.

Bowl, Pink & White Roses, Blue Luster Border, 11 In.	80

Nakara, Humidor, Indian Chief, Full
Headdress, Brass Lid, Metal Base,
C.F. Monroe, 8 x 6 In.
$960

Woody Auction

Nakara, Vase, Sailboats In Harbor,
Night, Cobalt Blue, Vermillion, Handles,
17 x 10 In.
$5,700

Woody Auction

Napkin Ring, Silver, Eagle, Swastika,
Greek Key Band, Bruckmann & Sohne,
1¾ x 1¾ In.
$900

Cowan's Auctions

NAILSEA glass was made in the Bristol district in England from 1788 to 1873. The name also applies to glass made by many different factories, not just the Nailsea Glass House. Many pieces were made with loopings of either white or colored glass as decoration.

Centerpiece, Beveled Mirror Base, Stemmed, Ruffled	180
Fairy Lamp, Cranberry Glass, Opal Loopings, Satin Finish, Ruffles, c.1920, 7½ In.	2863
Fairy Lamp, Green, Opal Loopings, Scalloped Rim, c.1875, 5 x 5¾ In.	809
Fairy Lamp, Opaque White, Opalescent Loopings, Ruby Cased Glass, Late 1800s, 7½ In.	480

NAKARA is a trade name for a white glassware made about 1900 by the C.F. Monroe Company of Meriden, Connecticut. It was decorated in pastel colors. The glass was very similar to another glass, called Wave Crest, made by the company. The company closed in 1916. Boxes for use on a dressing table are the most commonly found Nakara pieces. The mark is not found on every piece.

NAKARA

Box, Collars & Cuffs, Embossed, Cherubs Holding Horn, Dolphin Feet, 7 x 7 In.	960
Dresser Box, 2 Women, Pink, Cream, Background, C.F. Monroe, 5½ x 7½ In.	900
Dresser Box, Apricot, Blue Flowers, Pink Trim, White Enamel Beads, Mirror Inside, 5 x 4 In.	210
Dresser Box, Cherubs, Umbrella, Pink, Yellow, Blue Flowers, C.F. Monroe, 3¾ x 8 In.	720
Dresser Box, Hinged Lid, Apricot & Yellow, White Flowers, Lined, 4½ x 7½ In.	480
Humidor, Indian, Headdress, Brown & Rust Tones, Cigars On Lid, 5¾ x 4 In.	1320
Humidor, Indian Chief, Full Headdress, Brass Lid, Metal Base, C.F. Monroe, 8 x 6 In. ......*illus*	960
Humidor, Lions, Brass Lid, Brown, Mauve, C.F. Monroe, 7 x 4½ In.	600
Humidor, Mauve, Blue Floral, Beaded White, Marked, C.F. Monroe, 5½ x 4 In.	300
Jewelry Box, Apricot, Yellow Tones, Enamel Beaded, 6-Sided, 3¼ x 4 In.	210
Jewelry Box, Portrait, Young Woman, Apricot, Yellow, White Beads, 2¾ x 4½ In.	270
Jewelry Box, Portrait, Young Woman, Bishop's Hat Mold, White Beads, 4 x 6½ In.	720
Match Holder, Brass Ormolu Trim, 2 Handles, Marked, 3 In.	81
Ring Box, Green & Pink Glass, Classical Courting Scene, 2½ x 2½ In.	600
Ring Box, Portrait, Woman In Classic Dress, Blue, Lining, Marked, 2¼ x 2½ In.	660
Vase, Pink, Yellow, Blue Orchid Glass, Gilt Metal Handles & Feet, 14½ x 8½ In.	720
Vase, Sailboats In Harbor, Night, Cobalt Blue, Vermillion, Handles, 17 x 10 In. ....*illus*	5700

NANKING is a type of blue-and-white porcelain made in China from the late 1700s to the early 1900s. It was shipped from the port of Nanking. It is similar to Canton wares (listed here in the Canton category), but it is of better quality. The blue design was almost the same, a landscape, building, trees, and a bridge. But a person was sometimes on the bridge on a Nanking piece. The "spear and post" border was used, sometimes with gold added. Nanking sells for more than Canton.

Bowl, Serpentine Edges, Scenic Waterway, 5 x 3 In.	95
Gravy Dish, Crimped Edge, Loop Handle, Blue, White, 7 x 3 In.	145
Plate, Landscape, Pagoda, c.1820, 9½ In.	265
Plate, Pagodas, Walled Compound, Mountains, 1800s, 9 In.	135
Plate, Pagodas, Water, Mountains, Trees, c.1805, 9⅞ In.	135
Platter, Oval, Blue, White, Blue, Birds, Flowers, c.1785, 12 x 9 In.	399
Platter, Pagodas, River, Bridge, Oval, Scalloped Edge, c.1860, 7½ x 6 In.	125
Serving Bowl, Blue Transfer, Landscape, E. Challinor & Co., 1850s, 12 x 4 In.	90
Tankard, Strap Handle, Trees, Birds, Boats, Orange Peel Glaze, 7½ In.	1400

NAPKIN RINGS were in fashion from 1869 to about 1900. They were made of silver, porcelain, wood, and other materials. They are still being made today. Collectors pay the highest prices for the silver plated figural examples. Small, realistic figures were made to hold the ring. Good and poor reproductions of the more expensive rings have been made since the 1950s and collectors must be very careful.

Bakelite, Rabbit, Red, Black Eyes, 2⅛ x 2⅛ x ½ In.	20
Bone China, Carved Dragon, Cattle, Cream, c.1910, 1⅞ x ⅞ In.	11
Cut Glass, Swirled Vesicas, Cane, Strawberry Diamond, Star Highlights, 2¼ x 1¾ In.	180
Figural, Silver Plate, Angel, Cherub, Simpson Hall Miller, c.1900, 3¼ In.	54
Figural, Silver Plate, Bulldog, Dog House, Squared Platform, Scrolled Feet, c.1910, 3 x 3 In.	495

N

Napkin Ring, Table Set, Silver Plate, Cherub, Ring, Open Salt, Pepper, Plate, Bull Dog, Cart, Tufts, 7 In.
$630

Morphy Auctions

Natzler, Bowl, Cylindrical, Mustard Hare's Fur Glaze, Signed, 1966, 3 5/8 x 4 3/4 In.
$4,063

Los Angeles Modern Auctions

TIP
Check wall-hung and glass shelves regularly to be sure they have not loosened or bent.

Natzler, Vase, Speckled, Tan Smudges, Tan Rim, Signed G.O.N., 1 1/2 x 1 1/4 In.
$937

Rago Arts and Auction Center

Nautical, Alarm, Ship's Rattle, Panbone & Wood, Whalebone, Turned Handle, c.1875, 5 x 8 In.
$1,560

Eldred's

Nautical, Clock, Ship's, Silvered Dial, Japanese Characters, 8-Day, Signed, Japan, 6 In.
$212

Fontaine's Auction Gallery

Nautical, Clock, Ship's, U.S. Lighthouse Service, Chelsea Clock Co., c.1900, 5 In.
$1,320

U.S.L.H.Service

Eldred's

Nautical, Clock, Ship's Bell, Schatz, Brass Case, Painted Face, Germany, c.1975, 7 1/2 In.
$75

Garth's Auctioneers & Appraisers

Nautical, Clock, Ship's Bell Helm, Brown Patina, Chelsea Clock Co., 17 x 12 In.
$1,573

Fontaine's Auction Gallery

Nautical, Compass, Mahogany, 8-Sided, Brass Gimbal, S.A.W., Right-On Polarus, c.1890, 14 1/2 In.
$480

Eldred's

Figural, Silver Plate, Cow, Birds, Branches, Leaves, Flowers, c.1895, 3 x 3 In.		295
Figural, Silver Plate, Dog, Collie, Sitting, Pail In Mouth, James W. Tufts, 2 ½ In.		315
Figural, Silver Plate, Dog, Playing, Pairpoint, c.1880, 3 ⅛ x 1 ¾ x 3 ¼ In.		91
Figural, Silver Plate, Giraffe, Palm Tree, Rockford Silver Plate Co., 3 ½ x 4 ½ In.		615
Silver Plate, Bamboo Tree, Engraved, Wood & Hughes, 1 ¾ x 1 ⅞ In.		45
Silver, Eagle, Swastika, Greek Key Band, Bruckmann & Sohne, 1 ¾ x 1 ¾ In.	*illus*	900
Silver, Enamel, Children, Art Nouveau, Victorian, 1884, 1 ¾ In.		105
Silver, Engraved Band, Beaded Rims, Script Name, Will, 1 ⅝ x 1 ¾ In.		153
Silver, Hammered, Japonesque Style, Leaves, Fan, Wood & Hughes, 1850s, 1 ¾ x 2 In.		203
Table Set, Silver Plate, Cherub, Ring, Open Salt, Pepper, Plate, Bull Dog, Cart, Tufts, 7 In.	*illus*	630
Tartanware, Plaid, Yellow Inside, Orange, Green, Gray, Black, Wood, McLean		30

NATZLER pottery was made by Gertrud Amon and Otto Natzler. They were born in Vienna, met in 1933, and established a studio in 1935. Gertrud threw thin-walled, simple, classical shapes on the wheel, while Otto developed glazes. A few months after Hitler's regime occupied Austria in 1938, they married and fled to the United States. The Natzlers set up a workshop in Los Angeles. After Gertrud's death in 1971, Otto continued creating pieces decorated with his distinctive glazes. Otto died in 2007.

G + O
NATZLER

Bottle, Lapis Blue Glaze, Square Body, Paper Label, Signed, 1962, 14 x 3 ½ In.		4375
Bottle, Lip, Round, Turquoise Matte Glaze, Signed, 7 ½ x 6 In.		2813
Bowl, Cylindrical, Mustard Hare's Fur Glaze, Signed, 1966, 3 ⅝ x 4 ¾ In.	*illus*	4063
Bowl, Green, Blue, Volcanic Glaze, Signed, 1 ¼ x 5 In.		2625
Bowl, Hare's Fur Glaze, Interior Swirl, Footed, Paper Label, Signed, 1965, 2 ½ x 5 ½ In.		2875
Bowl, Indented Rim, Turquoise Glaze, Signed, 1957, 2 ⅞ x 6 In.		5938
Bowl, Ivory Crystalline Glaze, Signed, 1963, 3 ¼ x 6 ½ In.		187
Bowl, Lapis Lazuli Glaze, Paper Label, Signed, 1966, 3 x 4 ½ In.		2250
Bowl, Low, Blue Hare's Fur Glaze, Black Rim, Footed, Paper Label, 1963, 2 ¾ x 5 ¾ In.		1500
Bowl, Nocturne Glaze, Melt Fissures, Paper Label, Signed, 1957, 2 ½ x 6 ¾ In.		1500
Bowl, Sang Reduction Glaze, Blue, Signed, 1965, 3 ⅝ x 5 ½ In.		2813
Bowl, Turquoise Glaze, Flared, Footed, Signed, 4 x 6 ½ In.		2625
Vase, Indigo Blue Crystalline Glaze, Paper Label, Signed, 1959, 14 x 5 In.		6250
Vase, Microcrystalline Glaze, Earthenware, Signed, 5 ¾ x 3 ¼ In.		3625
Vase, Speckled, Tan Smudges, Tan Rim, Signed G.O.N., 1 ½ x 1 ¼ In.	*illus*	937
Vase, Yellow, Microcrystalline Glaze, Cylindrical, Wide Neck, Signed, 5 ¾ x 3 ¼ In.		3625

NAUTICAL antiques are listed in this category. Any of the many objects that were made or used by the seafaring trade, including ship parts, models, and tools, are included. Other pieces may be found listed under Scrimshaw.

Alarm, Ship's Rattle, Panbone & Wood, Whalebone, Turned Handle, c.1875, 5 x 8 In.	*illus*	1560
Ashtray, Rosewood & Chrome, Sphere Shape Cup, Pole, Caster Foot, 24 In.		150
Barometer, Marine, Mahogany, Brass, Bone Scales, Beveled Glass, 1800s, 41 In.		3186
Bell, Ship's, Bronze, Cast Iron Clapper, Coastal Schooner, Late 1800s, 8 ½ x 9 In.		132
Bell, Ship's, HMS Voyager, Australian Navy, Bronze, 1918, 10 x 11 In.		2820
Billet Head, Cornucopia Design, Leaves, Pine, Carved, 19th Century, 10 x 14 x 7 In.		1140
Binnacle, Brass, Wood Base, Kelvin White, c.1900, 54 In.		660
Binnacle, Hexagonal, Walnut Base, Brass Ring Handles, Geometric Designs, c.1900, 19 x 12 In.		3000
Blubber Spade, Wrought Iron, Wood Pole, Stamped Dean & Driggs, 20 In.		900
Branding Iron, Cask, Wrought Iron Shaft, Loop Handle, Leonard, 25 In.		1375
Bread Plate, Bowring Brothers Limited Logo, Blue Border, Porcelain, 1800s, 6 ¾ In.		65
Cabin Lamp, Brass, Stamped, Military Broad Arrow, Glass Panels, Australia, 1944, 16 x 8 In.		355
Cask Water Deck, Canvas Tag, Wood, From Whaler Wanderer, c.1875, 10 x 9 In.		1375
Chronometer, Mahogany, Bone Escutcheon, Glass, Barraud, c.1850, 5 x 6 x 5 ¾ In.		4800
Chronometer, Mahogany, Brass Binding, Pennsylvania, 7 ½ In.		1320
Clock, Brass Case, Painted Face, Chimes Bells, Schatz, Germany, 1900s, 7 ½ In.		75
Clock, Brass Case, Steel Face, Seth Thomas, 1900s, 5 ¾ In.		118
Clock, Deck, Mark I, U.S. Navy, Black Dial, White Numbers, Chelsea Clock Co., c.1950, 16 In.		420
Clock, Ship's Bell, Hinged Bezel, External Bell, Seth Thomas, Model 30, 10 In.		277
Clock, Ship's Bell Helm, Brown Patina, Chelsea Clock Co., 17 x 12 In.	*illus*	1573

Nautical, Compass, Ship's, Brass, Liquid Filled, Sestrel, Henry Browne, c.1930, 9 In.
$267

Auction Team Breker

Nautical, Helmet, Navy, Pilot, Protective Eye Shields, Galavitz, c.1950, 10 x 9 x 9 In.
$602

Aspire Auctions

Nautical, Light, Masthead, Brass, Fresnel Lens, Reservoir & Burner, Perko, c.1875, 20 In.
$720

N

Eldred's

Nautical, Model, Beetle Whaleboat, Oars, Paddles, Sails, Lines, Cased, Colin Gray, 1900s, 9 In.
$625

Eldred's

Nautical, Model, Black, Red Painted Wood, 6-Masted, William L. Douglas, 45 x 104 In.
$2,500

Leslie Hindman Auctioneers

Nautical, Model, Cutty Sark, 3-Masted, Wood Hull, Painted, Maple Base, 1900s, 26 In.
$74

Skinner, Inc.

Nautical, Model, Sailboat, Wood, Painted, Cloth Sails, Stand, 40 x 9¾ x 42 In.
$156

Alderfer Auction Company

Clock, Ship's Bell, Blue Spade Hands, Chelsea Clock Co., 10½ x 8½ In.	545
Clock, Ship's Bell, Brass Cases, Seth Thomas, c.1875, 11 In.	240
Clock, Ship's Bell, Rounded, Brass, Brass Sound Plate, Hardy & Hayes Co., 10 x 9 In.	726
Clock, Ship's Bell, Schatz, Brass Case, Painted Face, Germany, c.1975, 7½ In. ....*illus*	75
Clock, Ship's, Brass Footed Case, Steel Face, Roman Numerals, Marked, Frederic A. Ryder	1000
Clock, Ship's, Seth Thomas, U.S. Navy, Black Bakelite Case, 1915, 10¼ In.	330
Clock, Ship's, Silvered Dial, Japanese Characters, 8-Day, Signed, Japan, 6 In. ....*illus*	212
Clock, Ship's, U.S. Lighthouse Service, Chelsea Clock Co., c.1900, 5 In. ....*illus*	1320
Clock, Ship's, Wardroom, Brass, Mounted, Wood Backboard & Base, c.1915, 10 x 10 In.	360
Clock, Ship's, Wheel, Wood, Brass, Beveled Glass Face, 18 In.	100
Clock, Waterbury, Lever, Octagon, Brass Alarm Indicator Disc, L. Hubbell, 10 x 10 In.	121
Compass, Brass, Correction Of Quadrantal Deviation, Pine Box, 10 In.	960
Compass, Brass, Engraved, Fleur-De-Lis, Case, Wm. T. Gregg, 1800s, 7 x 15¾ In.	468
Compass, Mahogany, 8-Sided, Brass Gimbal, S.A.W., Right-On Polarus, c.1890, 14½ In...*illus*	480
Compass, Marine, Henry Hughes Son Ltd., London, 8½ x 7½ x 4 In.	59
Compass, Ship's, Brass, Liquid Filled, Sestrel, Henry Browne, c.1930, 9 In. ....*illus*	267
Compass, Ship's, Gimbal Mounted, Walnut, Slide Top, Case, 1800s, 6 x 7 x 9 In.	117
Dipper, Sailor, Coconut Shell Bowl, Maple Turned Handle, 1800s, 15½ In.	175
Gauging Stick, Oil Barrel, Folding, 10½ In., Folded	125
Harpoon, Macy, Single Flue, Manila Rope, 96 In.	4200
Harpoon, Wrought Iron, Darting Gun Type, Stamped DB & AH, c.1900, 37 In.	875
Harpoon, Wrought Iron, Oliver Allen Type, 4-Point Barb Head, 45 In.	1200
Harpoon, Wrought Iron, Sag Harbor Type, Toggle Head, Rope, 24 In.	812
Harpoon, Wrought Iron, Toggle Head, Double Shank, Shoulder Gun, Iron, c.1875, 27 In.	594
Head Case Bailer, Tin Pail, Iron Rod, c.1850, 42 In.	960
Helmet, Navy, Pilot, Protective Eye Shields, Galavitz, c.1950, 10 x 9 x 9 In. ....*illus*	602
Hull, B.B. Crownshield, Naval Architect, Black & White Paint, 1800s, 12 x 49 In.	720
Hull, Naval Warship, Carved Cannon, Scrolled Acanthus, Theodore D. Wilson, 18 x 78 In.	7200
Lamp, Signaling, Marine Daylight, Brass, Shonan Kosakusho Co., Ltd., 32 x 21 In.	489
Lantern, Docking, Oval Bull's-Eye Front, Marine Signal No. 2, c.1875, 22 x 12 In.	1320
Light, Masthead, Brass, Fresnel Lens, Reservoir & Burner, Perko, c.1875, 20 In. ....*illus*	720
Miniature, Gangway Board, Eagle, Stars & Stripes Shield, Rope, Anchor, 15¾ x 9 In.	720
Model, Beetle Whaleboat, Oars, Paddles, Sails, Lines, Cased, Colin Gray, 1900s, 9 In.......*illus*	625
Model, Black, Red Painted Wood, 6-Masted, William L. Douglas, 45 x 104 In....*illus*	2500
Model, Brass, Anchor, Inscribed Along Shaft, Martin, 13½ In.	1560
Model, Brigantine, Sailing, Black, White, Mahogany Decks, Stand, 1900s, 23 x 27 x 9 In.	120
Model, Builder's Half Hull, Sailing Vessel, c.1850, 10¾ x 51½ In.	1440
Model, Chinese River Junk, Flat Hull, Rounded Sides, 3 Masts, Fabric Sails, 29 x 28 In.	750
Model, Clipper Ship Lightning, Painted Green Bottom, 1900s, 26 x 38¾ x 12 In.	840
Model, Corsair, J.P. Morgan, Painted Hull, Mahogany Deck & Case, 57 x 57 x 16 In.	2750
Model, Cutty Sark, 3-Masted, Wood Hull, Painted, Maple Base, 1900s, 26 In. ....*illus*	74
Model, Golden Hind, 3-Masted, Flag Of England, Wood, Glass Display Case, 27 x 35¾ In.	2125
Model, Green Hull, Black & White Rail, 3-Masted, Fabric Sails, Isaac Webb, 49 x 64 In.	2750
Model, HMS Sovereign Of The Seas, 3-Masted, Wood, Ben Progosh, 1900s, 31 x 39 x 13 In.	1000
Model, John Bull, Riverboat, Black Paint, Trapezoidal Wood Hull, Red Paddles, 18 x 47 In.	875
Model, Longboat, Rudder, Floorboard, Deck Grating, Oar Locks, 13½ In.	1080
Model, Sailboat, Wood, Painted, Cloth Sails, Stand, 40 x 9¾ x 42 In. ....*illus*	156
Model, Schooner, Wood Hull, 2-Masted, 7 Fabric Sails, Wood Base, 18 x 26 In.	1000
Model, Ship Of The Line, Copper Bottom, 2 Gun Decks, 3-Masted, 48 x 35½ x 12 In.	360
Model, Ship, 3-Masted, Wood, San Juan Nepomuceno, Ben Progosh, 1900s, 30 x 36 x 15 In...*illus*	969
Model, Ship, Carved, Painted, Green, Wood, 19½ x 25 In.	308
Model, Signal, Brass, Mahogany, Wheels, Marked, Gregory Marine, c.1885, 20 x 10 x 10 In.	3042
Model, Sloop, Lateen Rigged, Single Mast, Wood, Brass Mounts, Glass Case, 23 x 4 x 13 In.	132
Model, SS Rotterdam, Mounted, Wood Base, Plexiglas Box, 1900s, 9⅞ x 2 x 4 In.	65
Model, Vasa, Wood Hull, 3-Masted, Swedish Flag, Brass Mounted, 31 x 37¾ In.	1875
Model, Wood Ship, Painted, Plexiglas Display Case, 1900s, 28½ x 41 In. ....*illus*	100
Model, Yacht Schemier, Standing & Running Rigging, 1900s, 12 x 12 x 3½ In.	3000
Model, Yacht, Shamrock, America's Cup, Cotton, Metal, Wood, 1898, 25 x 18 In.	400

Nautical, Model, Ship, 3-Masted, Wood, San Juan Nepomuceno, Ben Progosh, 1900s, 30 x 36 x 15 In.
$969

Heritage Auctions

Nautical, Model, Wood Ship, Painted, Plexiglas Display Case, 1900s, 28 ½ x 41 In.
$100

Pook & Pook

Nautical, Pond Boat, Schooner, Hardwood, Brass Fittings, Inlaid Banding, 43 ½ x 36 ½ x 8 In.
$550

Forsythes' Auctions

Nautical, Sailor's Valentine, Double, Shells, Star, Flower, Heart, 8-Sided, 1800s, 12 In.
$3,000

Eldred's

Nautical, Sailor's Valentine, Shells, Sea Grass, Flowers, Lottie, Frame, c.1890, 18 x 14 In.
$7,800

Eldred's

Nautical, Telegraph, Ship's, Brass, Mounted Wood Base, A. Robinson & Co., England, 38 ½ In.
$1,170

Susanin's Auctioneers & Appraisers

Nautical, Tiller, Wood, Monkey's Fist End, Rope Carving, Beaded Edge, England, 1800s, 23 In.
$1,680

N

Eldred's

Netsuke, Ivory Holder, Mixed Metal, Man, Costume, Well, Copper Bucket, c.1850, 2 In.

$192

Eldred's

Netsuke, Ivory, 5 Rats, Inlaid Eyes, Signed, Marked With Seal, Tadaju, c.1850, 1 ½ In.

$2,160

Eldred's

Netsuke, Ivory, 7 Karako Dancing, Oni Mask, c.1810, 1 ½ In.

$875

Eldred's

Netsuke, Ivory, Ball, God Of Happiness, Treasure Sack, ½ In.

$100

Eldred's

Needlework, Schooner Painting, Pine, 6 Boards, Stanley Boat, Maine, 1800s, 14 x 34 x 17 In.	2633
Plate, Cunard, Lion, Royal Mail Steam Packet Co., Gothic Borders, Ironstone, Bodley & Co., 9 In. ..	325
Plate, Great Northern Steamship Company, Logo, Gilt Edge Rim, c.1904, 9¾ In.	26
Plate, Guion Line, Crest, Green Seashells & Coral, Gilding, c.1866, 9¼ In.	1063
Plate, Inman & International Steam Ship Co., Blue Flowers, Gilt, c.1885, 9¾ In.	553
Plate, Lamport & Holt Line, Transfer Print, Gilt Border, c.1934, 9¾ In.	13
Pond Boat, Sailboat, Painted, Wood, Metal Stand, Captain Cox, 93½ x 21½ x 70 In.	108
Pond Boat, Sailboat, Wood, Cloth Sails, Painted, Stand, 36 In.	390
Pond Boat, Schooner, Hardwood, Brass Fittings, Inlaid Banding, 43½ x 36½ x 8 In. ......*illus*	550
Postcard, R M S Titanic, Picture Of Steamer Ship, 1913.	250
Quarterboard, Ship's, Carved Wood, Scrolled Base, Cargo Symbols, c.1850, 74 x 7 In.	527
Rowboat, Lapstrake, Cedar Plank, White Oak, Teak Dressing, Cecil Burnham, c.1971, 188 In.	2223
Sailor's Valentine, Double, Shells, Star, Flower, Heart, 8-Sided, 1800s, 12 In. ....*illus*	3000
Sailor's Valentine, Shells, Flowers, Heart, 2-Sided, Walnut Case, c.1890, 9 x 9 In.	3120
Sailor's Valentine, Shells, Sea Grass, Flowers, Lottie, Frame, c.1890, 18 x 14 In. ....*illus*	7800
Sailor's Valentine, Shellwork, Green Background, Octagonal, Late 1900s, 7 x 7 In.	390
Sailor's Valentine, Shellwork, Mahogany Frame, Octagonal, Debra Callaway, 9 x 9 x 4 In.	240
Sailor's Valentine, Shellwork, Walnut Shadowbox Frame, Oval, 1800s, 21 x 18 x 4 In.	2340
Sea Chest, Schooner, Leonora, 3-Masted, Cotton Sails, Maine, Case, 1871, 79 x 70 x 21 In.	410
Sextant, Double Metal Frame, Mahogany, Brass Degree Scale, Heath & Co., c.1900, 5 x 10 x 10 In.	1020
Ship's Wheel, 8-Spokes, Walnut, Iron Hub, Brass Ring, c.1900, 50 In.	1375
Ship's Wheel, Mahogany, 10 Turned Spokes, Bronze Hub, 58 In.	484
Ship's Wheel, Wood, Brass & Iron, Turn Spindle Spokes, 72 In.	565
Sign, Johnson Sea Horse Outboard Motors, Embossed, Tin Litho, c.1940s, 14 x 20 In.	738
Telegraph, Ship's, Brass, Circular Base, England, c.1940, 42½ In.	431
Telegraph, Ship's, Brass, Mounted Wood Base, A. Robinson & Co., England, 38½ In. ....*illus*	1170
Tiller, Wood, Monkey's Fist End, Rope Carving, Beaded Edge, England, 1800s, 23 In. ....*illus*	1680
Whimsey, Wood, Chain Shape Surrounding Ball In Cage, c.1850, 12 In.	200

NETSUKES are small ivory, wood, metal, or porcelain pieces used as toggles on the end of the cord that held a Japanese money pouch or inro. The earliest date from the sixteenth century. Many are miniature carved works of art. This category also includes the ojime, the slide or string fastener that was used on the inro cord. There are legal restrictions on the sale of ivory. Check the laws in your state.

Boxwood, Shishi Mai Dancer, Carved, 1800s, 2¾ In.	133
Coral & Ebony, Diver, With Splintwork Basket, 1⅝ In.	1625
Hornbill, Nesting Crane, Featherwork, Horn Inlaid Eyes, 1¾ In.	938
Inro, 2 Cases, Bull, Mountains, Pines, Sprinkled Lacquer, Signed, 1800s, 2⅜ x 3 In.	923
Inro, 6 Cases, Landscape, Pines, Rocks, Waterfall, Egg Shape, 3¾ In.	400
Inro, Black Lacquer, 5 Cases, Silver & Gilt Fan, Glass Ojime, c.1900, 3 In.	600
Ivory Holder, Mixed Metal, Man, Costume, Well, Copper Bucket, c.1850, 2 In. ....*illus*	192
Ivory, 2 Carp, Swimming, Yin Yang Symbol Form, 2¾ In.	500
Ivory, 5 Rats, Inlaid Eyes, Signed, Marked With Seal, Tadaju, c.1850, 1½ In. ....*illus*	2160
Ivory, 7 Karako Dancing, Oni Mask, c.1810, 1½ In. ....*illus*	875
Ivory, Ball, God Of Happiness, Treasure Sack, ½ In. ....*illus*	100
Ivory, Child Tying The Obi Of An Elderly Man, 1¾ In.	200
Ivory, Fox, Reclining, Incised Features, Patina, Flattened Form, 1700s, 3¼ In.	360
Ivory, Gourd Form, Relief Leaves & Vines, Sashi, 6 In.	300
Ivory, Man Lying On Partially Unrolled Scroll, c.1820, 1¼ In.	375
Ivory, Monkey, Seated, Holding Banner, Okame Mask, Treasure Sack, Coin, c.1850, 2 In. ...*illus*	1320
Ivory, Reclining Sage With Small Dog, 18th Century, 1½ In.	344
Ivory, Rooster, c.1850, 1½ In.	594
Ivory, Seated Skeleton, c.1890, 1¾ In.	330
Porcelain, Dog, Reclining, Blue, Red, 1800s, 2 In.	150
Seal, Guardian Lion, Sitting On Platform, Calligraphy Base, Ivory, 1700s, 1¼ In.	281
Wood, Bamboo Shoot Shape, Leaf, Ivory Grub Boring Into Tip, c.1820, 2 In.	570
Wood, Blackwood, Dog, Basset Hound, 1900s, 1¾ In.	125

Wood, Child, Shishi Costume, Ivory, Mother-Of-Pearl, Hinged Mask, c.1860, 2 In. ....*illus*		1875
Wood, Decaying Pear, Hole With Worm, c.1900, 2¼ In........................		1200
Wood, Dog, Carved, Japan, c.1900, 2 x 2 x 1⅜ In........................		125
Wood, Female Tatabina Doll, Gold Lacquer Eyes, Kimono, Waves, Grasses, 2 In..................		1200
Wood, Frog, Banana Leaf, Signed, Shugetsu IV, 1800s, 1⅞ In. ....*illus*		333
Wood, Mushrooms, 1800s, 1¼ In.		570
Wood, Rat, Curled Up, Carved, Signed Characters, 1¼ x 1¼ In........................		195
Wood, Sambaso Dancer, Carved, Holding Rattle & Fan, Japan, 1800s, 2¼ In........................		60
Wood, Seated Man, Ivory Head & Hands, c.1850, 1½ In........................		150

NEW HALL Porcelain Works was in business in Shelton, Hanley, Staffordshire, England, from 1781 to 1835. Simple decorated wares were made. Between 1810 and 1825, the factory made a glassy bone porcelain sometimes marked with the factory name. Do not confuse New Hall porcelain with the pieces made by the New Hall Pottery Company, Ltd., a twentieth-century firm working from 1899 to 1956 at the New Hall Works.

New Hall

Bowl, Footed, Flowers, c.1790, 6 In........................		125
Creamer, London Shape, Mother, Child, c.1815, 6¼ x 3¾ In........................		135
Cup & Saucer, Chinese House With Bridge, c.1805		300
Cup & Saucer, Cobalt Blue Ribbons, Sevenfold Symmetry, c.1790		85
Plate, Bird, Flowers, Multicolor, Gilt Rim, c.1805, 8½ In........................		145
Tea Bowl, Boy In The Window Pattern, c.1810, 3½ x 2 In........................		50
Teapot, Flower Sprays, Basket Weave, Notched Spout, 1820s........................		245

NEW MARTINSVILLE Glass Manufacturing Company was established in 1901 in New Martinsville, West Virginia. It was bought and renamed the Viking Glass Company in 1944. In 1987 Kenneth Dalzell, former president of Fostoria Glass Company, purchased the factory and renamed it Dalzell-Viking. Production ceased in 1998.

Bookends, Clipper Ship, Clear Glass, c.1940, 6 x 4 In.		15
Candlestick, Amber, Fan Shape, 1930s, 7¾ In........................		89
Moondrops, Candleholder, 3-Light, Ruby, c.1932, 4¾ x 7 x 5 In........................		36
Moondrops, Cordial, Goblet, Emerald Green, c.1935, 2⅞ In.		8
Perfume Bottle, Apple Green, Frosted Satin Glass, 1930s, 5½ In.................*illus*		73
Perfume Bottle, Green, Wand, Stopper, Marked N Over M, 6 x 1½ In........................		30
Vase, Nautilus Seashell, Clear & Frosted Glass, 5½ x 6 x 2¾ In........................		26
Viking, Candy Dish, Lid, Ruby, 6 Petals, Footed, 8¼ x 13 In.		13
Viking, Figurine, Rooster, Deep Ocean Blue, 10 In. ....*illus*		49

NEWCOMB POTTERY was founded at Sophie Newcomb College, New Orleans, Louisiana, in 1895. The work continued through the 1940s. Pieces of this art pottery are marked with the printed letters *NC* and often have the incised initials of the artist and potter as well. A date letter code was printed on pieces made from 1901 to 1941. Most pieces have a matte glaze and incised decoration. From 1942 to 1952 the Newcomb mark was revived and put on pieces of pottery from the college. New names were used.

Bowl, Pink Flowers, Impressed Mark, Signed, Sadie Irvine, 2¼ x 7 In.		813
Bowl, Yellow Trumpet Flowers, Green & Ocher Glaze, M.W. Butler, 10½ In........................		8125
Mug, Stylized Thistle Blossoms, Leaves, Green Underglaze, Marked, Harriet Joor, 1902, 4 In..*illus*		2432
Plate, Yellow Chrysanthemums, Green, Anna Frances Simpson, 8¾ In., Pair		1875
Tile, Woman With Umbrella, Flowers & Seashells, Square, L. Nicholson, 5 In........................		500
Vase, Banana Palm Trees, Carved, Blue, Green, Alma Florence Mason, 1912, 15½ In. ......*illus*		26840
Vase, Blue & Rose Matte, Carved Leaves, 4 Handles, Signed, Sadie Irvine, 6½ x 5 In........................		1188
Vase, Cypress Trees, Relief Carved, Blue, Pink, Matte Glaze, Anna Frances Simpson, 1928, 7 In.		2815
Vase, Daffodils, White, Blue, Green, Carved, Anna Frances Simpson, 8 x 6 In........................		2813
Vase, Flowers, Leaves, Blue Ground, Ivory Color Interior, c.1915, 6 x 3 In........................		1872
Vase, Freesia, Mauve, Pink, Alma Mason, 1913, 8½ x 5 In........................		2500
Vase, Fuchsia, Blue, Green, Henrietta Bailey, 1904, 8¼ x 7 In........................*illus*		4687
Vase, Hyacinth, Carved, Matte Glaze, Henrietta Bailey, 1915, 7 In........................		2596
Vase, Ivory Color, Blue Trim, Glossy Finish, Roberta Kennon, c.1905, 8¼ x 2¼ In..........*illus*		5265

Netsuke, Ivory, Monkey, Seated, Holding Banner, Okame Mask, Treasure Sack, Coin, c.1850, 2 In.
$1,320

Eldred's

Netsuke, Wood, Child, Shishi Costume, Ivory, Mother-Of-Pearl, Hinged Mask, c.1860, 2 In.
$1,875

Eldred's

Netsuke, Wood, Frog, Banana Leaf, Signed, Shugetsu IV, 1800s, 1⅞ In.
$333

Rachel Davis Fine Arts

N

NEWCOMB POTTERY

New Martinsville, Perfume Bottle, Apple Green, Frosted Satin Glass, 1930s, 5 ½ In.
$73

richardglenn1 on eBay

New Martinsville, Viking, Figurine, Rooster, Deep Ocean Blue, 10 In.
$49

clockpeddler2 on eBay

Newcomb, Mug, Stylized Thistle Blossoms, Leaves, Green Underglaze, Marked, Harriet Joor, 1902, 4 In.
$2,432

Neal Auction Company

Newcomb, Vase, Banana Palm Trees, Carved, Blue, Green, Alma Florence Mason, 1912, 15 ½ In.
$26,840

Neal Auction Company

Newcomb, Vase, Fuchsia, Blue, Green, Henrietta Bailey, 1904, 8 ¼ x 7 In.
$4,687

Rago Arts and Auction Center

Newcomb, Vase, Ivory Color, Blue Trim, Glossy Finish, Roberta Kennon, c.1905, 8 ¼ x 2 ¼ In.
$5,265

Jeffrey S. Evans & Associates

Newcomb, Vase, Jonquil, Matte Glaze, Henrietta Bailey, 1915, 6 ¼ x 3 ½ In.
$1,750

Crescent City Auction Gallery

Newcomb, Vase, Yellow Flowers, Carved, Painted, Green Matte Glaze, Anna Simpson, 5 ½ x 7 In.
$1,500

Treadway

Niloak, Vase, Marbleized, Blue, Brown, Cream, Marked, Partial Label, 17 ½ x 8 ½ In.
$1,950

Treadway

Vase, Jonquil, Matte Glaze, Henrietta Bailey, 1915, 6¼ x 3½ In..........*illus*	1750
Vase, Landscape, Carved, Painted, Matte Glaze, Anna Frances Simpson, 3½ x 3 In..........	1875
Vase, Live Oaks, Spanish Moss, Moon, Anna Frances Simpson, 1927, 5 x 6 In.	3750
Vase, Matte Glaze, Purple, Green, Marked, Sadie Irvine, 1932, 6⅛ x 4⅝ In..........	1500
Vase, Moss Covered Oaks, Moon, Matte Glaze, Signed, Jonathan Hunt, 6 x 6½ In..........	2990
Vase, Nasturtiums, Tapered, Blue Glaze, Sadie Irvine, 1909, 8¾ x 3½ In..........	3375
Vase, Pink & Blue Matte Glaze, Relief Carved Cypress Tree, Marked, 1928, 7 In..........	2750
Vase, Stylized Iris Band, Blue, Green, Oval, Swollen Shoulder, 1903, 9½ x 4¾ In..........	5313
Vase, Stylized Violets, Blue, Green, Sabina Wells, 1904, 4¾ x 3 In..........	2875
Vase, Trees, Moss, Full Moon, Blue, Green, Cream, 1902, 5¾ In..........	3120
Vase, Yellow Flowers, Carved, Painted, Green Matte Glaze, Anna Simpson, 5½ x 7 In. ......*illus*	1500
Vase, Yellow Freesia Band, Green & Yellow Glaze, Tapered, M. LeBlanc, 10 In..........	3125
Wall Pocket, Stylized Paperwhites, Leona Nicholson, 1906, 10½ x 3¾ In..........	3625

NILOAK POTTERY (*Kaolin* spelled backward) was made at the Hyten Brothers Pottery in Benton, Arkansas, between 1910 and 1947. Although the factory did make cast and molded wares, collectors are most interested in the marbleized art pottery line made of colored swirls of clay. It was called Mission Ware. By 1931 the company made castware, and many of these pieces were marked with the name *Hywood*.

Vase, Marbleized, Blue, Brown, Cream, Marked, Partial Label, 17½ x 8½ In..........*illus*	1950

NIPPON porcelain was made in Japan from 1891 to 1921. *Nippon* is the Japanese word for "Japan." The McKinley Tariff Act of 1891 mandated that goods imported to the United States had to be marked with the country of origin. A few firms continued to use the word *Nippon* on ceramics after 1921 as a part of the company name more than to identify things as made in Japan. More pieces marked *Nippon* will be found in the Dragonware, Moriage, and Noritake categories.

Nitto 1890–1921	Nippon 1894–1920	Morimura/Noritake c.1911–1921

Ashtray, Indian Chief, Smoking Peace Pipe, Blown Out..........	345
Ashtray, Tiger, Figural, Lying Down, Marble Base, 3½ x 6 In..........	440
Candlestick, Desert Scene, Gold Trim, M In Wreath Mark, 10 In., Pair..........*illus*	35
Hatpin Holder, Porcelain, Flowers, Swirled Ribbed, Ruffled Rim, 4¾ In..........	49
Hatpin Holder, Stylized Flowers, Gold Relief Leafing, 4¾ In..........	39
Humidor, Bulldog's Head, Shield, Blown Out, Brown & Yellow Swirled Glaze, 6 x 5 In..........	160
Humidor, Lid, Gold Dragon, 3-Footed, Knob Finial, 7 In..........	121
Humidor, Man Playing Accordion, Knob Finial, Cylindrical, Brown Ground, 6½ In..........*illus*	303
Humidor, Tobacco, Indian Warrior On Horseback, Rifle, Porcelain, Morimura Bros., 6¼ In....	384
Jar, Black Man, Strumming Banjo, 5¾ In..........	345
Jug, Wine, Egyptian Scene, Handle, Orange Background, 7 In..........	198
Pitcher, Cottage, Lake, Ice Lip, Marked, 6¼ In.	32
Plaque, Round, Purple Irises, Floral, Leaves, Gold Rim, 10 In..........	99
Platter, Pheasants, Stylized Star Border, Gold Beading, Green Maple Leaf Mark, 17 x 12 In...*illus*	325
Stein, Desert Village Scene, Stylized Animal Border, Gold Beading, Marked, 8 In..........*illus*	40
Vase, 2 Handles, Gold, Floral, Cobalt Blue, Maple Leaf Mark, 6 In.	44
Vase, 2 Women, Outdoor Scene, Roses, Cobalt Blue, 2 Handles, 2 Piece, 12 In.	578
Vase, Cylindrical, Gild Handles, European Country Scene, Japan, c.1915, 11 In..........	60
Vase, Enamel Woodland Scene, 2 Handles, Rounded Base, 5 In..........	209
Vase, Geese Flight, Wetland Setting Sun, 2 Handles, 11½ In..........	661
Vase, Mountain Landscape Scene, Cobalt Blue, Gilt, Marked Imperial Nippon, 12 In..........	58
Vase, Relief Elephant, Molded, 2 Handles, 3-Footed, 7¼ In. ....*illus*	440
Vase, Woman's Portrait, Flowers, Gold Scrolling, Green Mark, 12 In..........	375

Nippon, Candlestick, Desert Scene, Gold Trim, M In Wreath Mark, 10 In., Pair
$35

Harritt Group, Inc.

Nippon, Humidor, Man Playing Accordion, Knob Finial, Cylindrical, Brown Ground, 6½ In.
$303

Forsythes' Auctions

Nippon, Platter, Pheasants, Stylized Star Border, Gold Beading, Green Maple Leaf Mark, 17 x 12 In.
$325

Harritt Group, Inc.

N

Nippon, Stein, Desert Village Scene, Stylized Animal Border, Gold Beading, Marked, 8 In.

$40

Harritt Group, Inc.

Nippon, Vase, Relief Elephant, Molded, 2 Handles, 3-Footed, 7¼ In.

$440

Forsythes' Auctions

Nodder, Porky Pig, Blue Jacket, Red Tie, Black & Yellow Hat, Warner Bros., Japan, 1960s, 6 In.

$143

bear2fish on eBay

NODDERS, also called nodding figures or pagods, are figures with heads and hands that are attached to wires. Any slight movement causes the parts to move up and down. They were made in many countries during the eighteenth, nineteenth, and twentieth centuries. A few Art Deco designs are also known. Copies have been made. A more recent type of nodder is made of papier-mache or plastic. These often represent sports figures or comic characters. Sports nodders are listed in the Sports category.

Ashtray, Woman, Pinup, Lying On Back, Legs Up, Black Skirt, Fan, Beach Design, Japan	26
Baby Snookums, 1 Tooth, Crawling, George McManus, 3 x 3 In.	65
Boy, Unhappy, Brown Cap, White Knee Patches, Composition On Wood Base, 6½ In.	88
Cat, White, Suit, Double Breasted, Bow, Paws On Hips, Pressed Cardboard, Germany, 8 In.	113
Dog, Scottish Terrier, Bobble Head, Papier-Mache, 5 x 6½ In.	17
Donald Duck, Standing, Blue Shirt, Hat, Walt Disney World, 6½ In.	20
Elephant, Wheels, Papier-Mache, Glass Eyes, Green Blanket, 16 x 8¼ In.	840
Fox, Bushy Tail, Brown, Cream, Black, c.1950, 3½ In.	21
Japanese Man, Holding Fan, 4 x 3 In.	189
Mandarin, Man & Woman, Porcelain, Red, Gold Trim, Mottahedeh, N.Y., 15½ In., Pair	203
Policeman, Writing Summons, Gray Uniform, Head & Body Both Nod, 9 In.	88
Porky Pig, Blue Jacket, Red Tie, Black & Yellow Hat, Warner Bros., Japan, 1960s, 6 In. ....*illus*	143
Salt & Pepper Shakers are listed in the Salt & Pepper category.	
Santa, Candleholder, Colorful Dolls, Brown Coat, Kathy Patterson, 14¼ x 5 In.	277

NORITAKE porcelain was made in Japan after 1904 by Nippon Toki Kaisha. A maple leaf mark was used from 1891 to 1911. The best-known Noritake pieces are marked with the *M* in a wreath for the Morimura Brothers, a New York City distributing company. This mark was used primarily from 1911 to 1921 but was last used in the early 1950s. The *N* mark was used from 1940 to the 1960s, and *N Japan* from 1953 to 1964. Noritake made dinner sets with pattern names. Noritake Azalea is listed in the Azalea category in this book.

Berry Bowl, Legendary Secret Love, 5½ In.	6
Biscuit Jar, Lavender Flowers, Green Leaves, Gray Ground, Applied Gold, 7 x 4 In.	145
Bowl, Cereal, Inverness, Lugged, 6½ In.	7
Bowl, Gemini, Women Leaning Back Over Bowl, Holding Hands, Orange Dresses, 6 In. ....*illus*	1277
Bowl, Vegetable, Adagio, Round, 10 In.	40
Bowl, Vegetable, Imperial, Oblong, Handle, 10½ In.	22
Bowl, Vegetable, Inverness, Oval, 9½ In.	12
Bowl, Vegetable, Savannah, Oval, 9⅝ In.	20
Cake Plate, Woman, Long Robe, Reaching Toward Dog, Tree, Art Deco, Luster, 7½ In.	208
Creamer, Homecoming, 3¾ In.	18
Cup & Saucer, Foxboro, Cobalt Blue, Gold, Birds	49
Cup & Saucer, Kelcraft, Ireland, Nature's Bounty	6
Cup & Saucer, Royal Pink, White, Pink Band, Gold Trim, N In Wreath Mark	10
Cup & Saucer, Savannah	7
Dish, Lid, Grand Terrace, Handles, 1970s	35
Dresser Jar, Lid, Figural Finial, Japanese Man, Umbrella, Luster, Green M Mark, 5 x 5 In...*illus*	169
Dresser Tray, Woman, Blond Curls, Flowers, Pearl Luster, M In Wreath, Oval, 8 x 5¾ In.	184
Gravy Boat, Aegean Mist, Underplate, 8¼ In.	40
Gravy Boat, Imperial, Underplate, 9 x 6 In.	30
Gravy Boat, Roselane	49
Gravy Boat, Shenandoah, Underplate, Flowers, 2½ x 7½ x 3½ In.	34
Plaque, 5 Horses, Relief Molded, Green M In Wreath Mark, 10 In. ....*illus*	325
Plate, Bread, Belmont, 6¼ In.	5
Plate, Bread, Helene, 6½ In.	4
Plate, Bread, Sorrento, White Lace, 6½ In.	4
Plate, Dinner, Fairmont, 10½ In.	8
Plate, Lunch, Old Capital Building, Colonial Times Series, 9⅛ In.	10
Plate, Oriental, Gold Trim, 10⅜ In.	19
Plate, Salad, Pleasure, Stoneware, 8¼ In.	6
Platter, Campobello, Primastone, 1972, 14 In.	22

N

Platter, Mystery 14, Oval, 16½ In.		25
Platter, Serving, Adagio, Oval, 16¼ In.		60
Platter, Serving, Sherwin, 15 In.		48
Powder Box, Masquerade, Woman Wearing Mask, Multicolor, White Ground, 3¼ x 3 In.		169
Salt & Pepper, Blue Moon		25
Salt & Pepper, Women, Blue Luster, Gold Trim, 3½ x 1¼ In.		119
Saucer, Blue Hill, 6 In.		3
Sugar, Lid, Imperial, 3 In.		22
Teapot, Lid, Brookhollow, Flowers, White, Handle, Foot Ring		193
Teapot, Progression, Palos Verde, 8 In.		54

NORSE POTTERY COMPANY started in Edgerton, Wisconsin, in 1903. In 1904 the company moved to Rockford, Illinois. The company made a black pottery, which resembled early bronze relics of the Scandinavian countries. The firm went out of business in 1913.

Urn, Coiled Dragons, Incised, Dragon Handles, Serpentine Feet, Marked, 4 x 6 In.		236
Vase, Black Metallic Glaze, Handles, Geometric Design, 12 x 6 In.		427

NORTH DAKOTA SCHOOL OF MINES was established in 1898 at the University of North Dakota. A ceramics course was established in 1910. Students made pieces from the clays found in the region. Although very early pieces were marked *U.N.D.*, most pieces were stamped with the full name of the university. After 1963 pieces were only marked with students' names.

U. N. D.

North Dakota School of Mines
1910–1963

North Dakota School of Mines
c.1913–1963

Bowl, Water Lilies, Carved, Glazed Ceramic, Signed, Sylvia Adams, 1926, 3 x 8 In.		1625
Vase, Birds, Fawn, Rabbits, Carved, Blue & Tan, Signed, Mayks, 1947, 5¾ x 5¾ In.		1875
Vase, Green Matte Glaze, Carved, Signed, Owens, 1937, 5½ x 4 In.		938
Vase, Lid, Blue & Tan Glaze, Carved, Signed, Sarah Hoffman, Stamped, 6½ x 6 In.		813
Vase, Morning Glory, Carved, Green To Tan, Signed, 1953, 8½ x 6 In.		1040
Vase, Prairie Rose, Julia Mattson, Blue Stamp, 4¼ x 4¼ In.		625
Vase, Stylized Waves, Blue, Green, Stamped, 1900s, 3 x 4 In. ....*illus*		1000
Vase, Yellow Flowers, Brown Glaze, Cylindrical, 5 x 3 In.		177

NORTHWOOD glass was made by one of the glassmaking companies operated by Harry C. Northwood. His first company, Northwood Glass Co., was founded in Martins Ferry, Ohio, in 1887 and moved to Ellwood City, Pennsylvania, in 1892. The company closed in 1896. Later that same year, Harry Northwood opened the Northwood Co. in Indiana, Pennsylvania. Some pieces made at the Northwood Co. are marked "Northwood" in script. The Northwood Co. became part of a consortium called the National Glass Co. in 1899. Harry left National in 1901 to found the H. Northwood Co. in Wheeling, West Virginia. At the Wheeling factory, Harry Northwood and his brother Carl manufactured pressed and blown tableware and novelties in many colors that are collected today as custard, opalescent, goofus, carnival, and stretch glass. Pieces made between 1905 and about 1915 may have an underlined *N* trademark. Harry Northwood died in 1919, and the plant closed in 1925.

Northwood Glass Co.
1905–c.1915

Northwood Glass Co.
1905–c.1915

Northwood Glass Co.
1905–c.1915

Blue Opalescent, Pitcher, Water, Lattice, Star-Crimp Rim, Feathers, 1900s, 8¾ In.		140

Noritake, Bowl, Gemini, Women Leaning Back Over Bowl, Holding Hands, Orange Dresses, 6 In.
$1,277

jims340aar on eBay

Noritake, Dresser Jar, Lid, Figural Finial, Japanese Man, Umbrella, Luster, Green M Mark, 5 x 5 In.
$169

bostonsantique on eBay

Noritake, Plaque, 5 Horses, Relief Molded, Green M In Wreath Mark, 10 In.
$325

Harritt Group, Inc.

N

North Dakota, Vase, Stylized Waves, Blue, Green, Stamped, 1900s, 3 x 4 In. $1,000

Rago Arts and Auction Center

Margaret Kelly Cable

Margaret Kelly Cable was the first trained potter who worked at the North Dakota School of Mines. She worked from 1910 to 1949.

Northwood, Christmas Snowflake, Pitcher, Water, Rib, Blue Opalescent, Leaf, c.1895, 8⅞ In. $585

Jeffrey S. Evans & Associates

Northwood, Inverted Fan & Feather, Spooner, Pink Slag, Scalloped Rim, c.1904, 4¼ In. $129

Jeffrey S. Evans & Associates

Christmas Snowflake, Pitcher, Water, Rib, Blue Opalescent, Leaf, c.1895, 8⅞ In. ....*illus* 585
Chrysanthemum Swirl, Toothpick Holder, Cranberry, Opalescent, c.1890, 2⅛ x 1¼ In......... 67
Coin Spot, Sugar Shaker, 9 Panels, Green & White, Ground Glass Rim, 1905, 4½ In............... 43
Daisy & Fern, Pitcher, Water, Ball Shape, Blue Opalescent, Square Rim, c.1894, 8¾ In. 129
Drapery, Rose Bowl, Aqua Opal, Carnival, Iridescent, Pink & Blue, c.1910, 6½ In. 93
Inverted Fan & Feather, Spooner, Pink Slag, Scalloped Rim, c.1904, 4¼ In. ....*illus* 129
Klondyke, Shaker, Opalescent Yellow, Vaseline Glass, c.1890, 3 In. 26
Leaf Mold, Saltshaker, Lid, Cranberry Spatter, White & Red.............................. 89
Peacocks, Dish, Scalloped Crimped Edge, Electric Purple, 8¾ In.............................. 91
Polka Dot, Syrup, Blue Opalescent, Pressed Fan, Lid, c.1894, 6 In............................. 234
Spanish Lace, Sugar, Opaline Brocade, Cranberry Opal, Silver Plate Frame, c.1899, 2½ In..*illus* 153
Swirl, Toothpick Holder, Cased, Opal, Rainbow Swirl, c.1890, 2⅛ In. 263
Vase, Funeral, Green Carnival, Swung, Circular Foot, 8-Sided Panel Body, 17 x 14 x 4 In. 28

NU-ART *see Imperial category.*

 NUTCRACKERS of many types have been used through the centuries. At first the nutcracker was probably strong teeth or a hammer. But by the nineteenth century, many elaborate and ingenious types were made. Levers, screws, and hammer adaptations were the most popular. Because nutcrackers are still useful, they are still being made, some in the old styles.

Brass, Pocket Lever, Hand Worked Design, Late 1700s, 3¾ x 1¼ In.. 99
Dog, Lift Tail, Crack Nut In Mouth, Nickel Plated, 10 In. 246
Eagle, Beak Open, Cast Iron, c.1880, 10 x 4¾ In...*illus* 398
Jolly Black Man, Mechanical, Cast Iron, John Harper & Co., 1939, 8¾ In.................. 80
Lady's Legs, Nude, Brass, Art Deco, Metalware, 4½ In. 38
Man, Standing, Bald, Coat, Hands In Pocket, Jaw Moves, Brass, 8 x 4¾ x 6 In.................. 90
Musketeer, Wood, Feather Cap, Bearded Jaw, Sword, East Germany, 1960, 19 In...... 495
Squirrel, Figural, Hand Carved, Wood, Black Forest, 1900s, 7 In. 20
Squirrel, Painted, Cast Iron, Mounted On Later Base, c.1900s, 9¼ In..............*illus* 594
Woman, Seminude, Standing, Hands Up, Wood, 13 In. 21

NYMPHENBURG, *see Royal Nymphenburg.*

 OCCUPIED JAPAN was printed on pottery, porcelain, toys, and other goods made during the American occupation of Japan after World War II, from 1947 to 1952. Collectors now search for these pieces. The items were made for export. Ceramic items are listed here. Toys are listed in the Toy category in this book.

Ashtray, 4 Cigarette Holders, Drummer, Black, Los Angeles, Porcelain, 4 x 2¾ x 3 In.............. 26
Cigarette Box, Black Lacquer, Mother-Of-Pearl Fish, Woven Green Straps Inside, 3 x 2½ In... 12
Creamer, Cow, Figural, Ceramic, Reddish Brown, Tail Is Handle.............................. 4
Cup & Saucer, Tea, Porcelain, Flowers, Gold Trim, Chubu, 1940s, 2½ x 5 In...................*illus* 16
Dish, Lily Pad, Lime Green, Glazed, Embossed Frog, 4 In. 9
Incense Burner, Gilt, Leaves, Gray, Blue, 3-Footed, 3½ x 3½ In.......................... 100
Pencil Sharpener, Figural, Indian Chief Head, Metal, Painted, 1940s, 1¾ x 1¼ In.................. 31
Salt & Pepper, Flamingo, Wings Spread, Leaves, 2½ In.......................... 16
Toothpick Holder, Devil Head, Porcelain, 2 In................................. 112
Vase, Nude Flapper Girl, Sitting On Book, Leaning Against Vase, Porcelain, Floral, 3 In............ 18

 OFFICE TECHNOLOGY includes office equipment and related products, such as adding machines, calculators, and check-writing machines. Typewriters are in their own category in this book.

Book Press, Cast Iron, Floral Decals, Painted Scrolls, Lever, Victorian, 15 x 10 x 13 In............. 100
Chair, Leather, Chippendale Style, Swivel, 3 Legs, Late 1900s, 43 x 25 x 25 In. 281
Chair, Skeleton, Gray Leather, De Sede, Arms, Key, Switzerland, 52 x 27 In................ 1000
Stock Ticker Machine, Western Union Universal, Edison, Late 1800s, 8¾ x 8⅝ In........*illus* 5000

Northwood, Spanish Lace, Sugar, Opaline Brocade, Cranberry Opal, Silver Plate Frame, c.1899, 2 ½ In.
$153

perryphernalia on eBay

Nutcracker, Eagle, Beak Open, Cast Iron, c.1880, 10 x 4 ¾ In.
$398

RSL Auction

Nutcracker, Squirrel, Painted, Cast Iron, Mounted On Later Base, c.1900s, 9 ¼ In.
$594

Pook & Pook

Occupied Japan, Cup & Saucer, Tea, Porcelain, Flowers, Gold Trim, Chubu, 1940s, 2 ½ x 5 In.
$16

cOllectOr810 on eBay

Lock Your Doors
In half of all burglaries, the thief came in through an unlocked window or door.

Office, Stock Ticker Machine, Western Union Universal, Edison, Late 1800s, 8 ¾ x 8 ⅝ In.
$5,000

Heritage Auctions

Ohr, Inkwell, Pottery, Redware, Inscribed Ohr, Biloxi, 1 ¾ x 3 ¾ x 3 ¾ In.
$1,845

Cowan's Auctions

Ohr, Jardiniere, Diagonal Band, Flowers, Joseph Meyer, Pottery Club, c.1889, 17 In.
$24,400

Neal Auction Company

Ohr, Mug, Puzzle, Pierced, In-Body Twist, Gunmetal Glaze, Signed, c.1900, 3 ½ In.
$2,875

Rago Arts and Auction Center

Ohr, Vase, Maroon, Green, Ribbon Handles, Bulbous Top, Stamped, 1897-1900, 8 In.
$56,250

Rago Arts and Auction Center

O

Ohr, Vase, Twisted Body, Straight Neck, Red Clay, Signed, G.E. Ohr, c.1900, 3 ¾ In.
$1,464

Neal Auction Company

Olympics, Torch, Berlin, 1936, Summer, Walter Lemcke, 11 ½ In.
$1,920

Heritage Auctions

Onion, Tureen, Lid, Leaf Bracket Handles, Crossed Swords Mark, Meissen, 9 ½ In.
$138

Garth's Auctioneers & Appraisers

Opalescent, Diamond Quilted, Vase, Pink, 7 ½ In.
$68

Hartzell's Auction Gallery, Inc.

OHR pottery was made in Biloxi, Mississippi, from 1883 to 1906 by George E. Ohr, a true eccentric. The pottery was made of very thin clay that was twisted, folded, and dented into odd, graceful shapes. Some pieces were lifelike models of hats, animal heads, or even a potato. Others were decorated with folded clay "snakes." Reproductions and reworked pieces are appearing on the market. These have been reglazed, or snakes and other embellishments have been added.

Bowl, Crumpled, Green, Gunmetal, Raspberry, Stamped, G.E. Ohr, Biloxi, 2 ½ x 4 ½ In.	11250
Cup, Tea, Ruffled Rim, Mahogany, Gunmetal, Stamped G.E. Ohr Biloxi, 1895, 2 x 3 ½ In.	2500
Inkwell, Pottery, Redware, Inscribed Ohr, Biloxi, 1 ¾ x 3 ¾ x 3 ¾ In. ....*illus*	1845
Jardiniere, Diagonal Band, Flowers, Joseph Meyer, Pottery Club, c.1889, 17 In. ......*illus*	24400
Mug, Gunmetal Glaze, 3 Ear Shape Handles, 1898-1910, 4 ¾ x 6 In.	6875
Mug, Puzzle, Pierced, In-Body Twist, Gunmetal Glaze, Signed, c.1900, 3 ½ In. ......*illus*	2875
Mug, Snake, Mahogany & Gunmetal Sponged Glaze, Ear Handle, c.1900, 4 ¼ In.	5312
Sculpture, Hat Shape, Black Iridescent Glaze, Stamped, c.1895, 2 ¼ x 4 In.	8125
Vase, Brown, Green & Ocher Sponged Glaze, Speckled, Twisted Shoulder, 6 ½ In.	10625
Vase, Cat Head, Olive Green Glaze, Brown Speckles, Pinched Nose, 2 ⅞ x 4 In.	2360
Vase, Crimped Rim, Footed, Green & Brown Sponged, Late 1800s, 2 ⅜ In.	1416
Vase, Fan, Brown & Blue Speckled Glaze, Flared, Footed, Serrated & Ruffled Rim, 9 x 9 In.	6875
Vase, Green, Ocher & Gunmetal Glaze, Pinched Waist, Oval Bottom, Flared Top, 6 ½ In.	4375
Vase, Gunmetal Glaze, In-Body Twist, Crenellated Rim, c.1895, 4 x 5 ½ In.	5000
Vase, Maroon, Green, Ribbon Handles, Bulbous Top, Stamped, 1897-1900, 8 In. ....*illus*	56250
Vase, Twisted Body, Straight Neck, Red Clay, Signed, G.E. Ohr, c.1900, 3 ¾ In. ....*illus*	1464

OLD PARIS, *see Paris category.*

OLD SLEEPY EYE, *see Sleepy Eye category.*

OLYMPICS memorabilia include commemorative pins, posters, programs, patches, mascots, and other items from the Olympics, even the torch carried before the games.
The Olympics are thought to have started as a religious festival held in Olympia, Greece, in 776 BC. It included a foot race in the stadium. After that games were held every four years until 393 AD and more athletic events were added. The games were revived in 1896 when the first modern Olympics were held in Athens, Greece, with fourteen countries participating. The Olympics were held only in the summer until 1924 when the first Winter Olympics were held in Chamonix, France. The current schedule of an Olympics every two years, alternating between Summer and Winter Olympics, began in 1994. The Olympic flag was introduced in 1908; official Olympics posters were first commissioned in 1912; the Olympic torch first appeared in 1928; and the first relay to light the torch was held in 1936 at the Olympics in Berlin.

Badge, St. Moritz, 1928, Concurrent, Blue Border, Silver Text, Rings, 1 ¼ In.	795
Diploma, Rome, 1960, Embossed Bronze Colored Medallion, Italian Text, 13 x 19 In.	250
Flag, Munich, 1972, White Cotton, 5 Colored Interlocking Rings, 16 Ft.	1059
Medal, Mexico City, 1968, Team Fencing, Inscribed, 2 ⅜ In.	7500
Medal, Netherlands, 1928, Gold, Seated Victory, Laurel Wreath, Palm, Summer, 2 ⅜ In.	9600
Poster, Berlin, 1936, 11th Games, 12 x 36 In.	36
Poster, Berlin, 1936, Athlete Wearing Laurel Crown, Rings, Frame, 33 x 48 In.	1251
Poster, Lake Placid, 1932, Winter, 5 Events Represented, Frame, 25 x 39 In.	1114
Program, Paris, 1900, Summer, International Contests, Hardcover, 6 ½ x 9 ¾ In., 64 Pages	1875
Torch, Berlin, 1936, Summer, Walter Lemcke, 11 ½ In. ....*illus*	1920
Torch, London, 1948, Summer, Aluminum Alloy, Cauldron Shape Top, Cutouts, 16 In.	7500
Torch, Moscow, 1980, Summer, Aluminum, Gray, Red Text, Goldtone Ring, 22 In.	1186

ONION PATTERN, originally named bulb pattern, is a white ware decorated with cobalt blue or pink designs of a vine with buds that look like onions. Although it is commonly associated with Meissen, other companies made the pattern in the late nineteenth and the twentieth centuries. A rare type is called *red bud* because there are added red accents on the blue-and-white dishes.

Compote, Blue & White, Scalloped Edges, Meissen, Early 1900s, 9 x 9 In.	212

O

Tureen, Lid, Leaf Bracket Handles, Crossed Swords Mark, Meissen, 9½ In......................*illus*   138

OPALESCENT GLASS is translucent glass that has the tones of the opal gemstone. It originated in England in the 1870s and is often found in pressed glassware made in Victorian times. Opalescent glass was first made in America in 1897 at the North-wood glassworks in Indiana, Pennsylvania. Some dealers use the terms *opaline* and *opalescent* for any of these translucent wares. More opalescent pieces may be listed in Hobnail, Pressed Glass, and other glass categories.

Cranberry, Dish, Shell Shape, Shaded, Silver-Plate Leaf Shape Base, c.1890, 6 x 8 In.	259
Cranberry, Epergne, Triple Lily, 2 Canes, Victorian, 22½ x 12½ In.	518
Cruet, Handle, Stopper, Victorian, 7½ x 3½ In.	42
Diamond Quilted, Vase, Pink, 7½ In. ....*illus*	68
Lamp, Sandwich, Hexagonal Font & Base, Whale Oil Burner, c.1850, 8½ In.	600

OPALINE, or opal glass, was made in white, green, and other colors. The glass had a matte surface and a lack of transparency. It was often gilded or painted. It was a popular mid-nineteenth-century European glassware.

Decanter, Round Reserve, Red, Roman Profile, Round Foot, France, 1900s, 11½ In., Pair	151
Egg, Dore, Bronze Mounts, Footed, Hinged Lid, France, 1800s, 6 x 3½ In.	406
Inkwell, Pottery, Figural Hut, White, Flowers, Bronze Roof & Insert, France, Late 1900s, 5 In.	199
Vase, Blue, Parcel Gilt Trim, c.1900s, 7¾ In.....................*illus*	25

OPERA GLASSES are needed because the stage is a long way from some of the seats at a play or an opera. Mother-of-pearl was a popular decoration on many French glasses.

Brass, Aluminum, Egyptian Designs, Occupied Japan	88
Enamel & Brass, Garden Scenes, Couples, Gilt, Mother-Of-Pearl, Lemaire Paris	438
Enamel, Bird & Flowers, Translucent Red, Case	138
Enamel, Flowers, Coral Beads, Gilt Embellishments, Cobalt Blue Ground, c.1920	352
Enamel, Red, Gilt Fleur-De-Lis, Mother-Of-Pearl, Telescopic, Peter Engel, France	375
Lemoire, Mother-Of-Pearl Eyepiece Trim, Gold, Adjustable Sizing	50
Mother-Of-Pearl, Ribbed, Handle, 3½ x 4¾ In.	89
Mother-Of-Pearl, Tapered, 4¼ x 3 In.	137

ORPHAN ANNIE first appeared in the comics in 1924. The last strip ran in newspapers on June 13, 2010. The redheaded girl, her dog Sandy, and her friends were on the radio from 1930 to 1942. The first movie based on the strip was produced in 1932. A second movie was produced in 1938. A Broadway musical that opened in 1977, a movie based on the musical and produced in 1982, and a made-for-television movie based on the musical produced in 1999 made Annie popular again, and many toys, dishes, and other memorabilia have been made. A new adaptation of the movie based on the musical opened in 2014.

Badge, Decoder, Telematic, Brass, Star, 1938, 2 In. Diam.	85
Book, In The Thieves' Den, Better Little, Helen Berke, 3¾ x 4¾ In.	21
Button, Decoder, ROA, Radio Orphan Annie, Secret Society, Shield Shape, Brass Color, 1936	28
Doll, Wood, Jointed, Dress & Hat Painted Red, 5 x 1 In.	115
Game, Little Orphan Annie, Chromolithograph, Milton Bradley, Dice, Board, c.1930, 17 x 9 In.	56
Pin, Decoder, Radio Orphan Annie's S.S., Crossed Keys, Round, 1935	37
Ring, Secret Guard, Magnifying, Embossed Face, Radio Premium, Brass, 1940s.....................*illus*	33
Sconce, Annie & Sandy At Table Sharing Ice Cream, Ceramic, Japan, 2 x 3 x 5 In.	95
Toy, Orphan Annie, Skipping Rope, Tin, Windup, Orange Paint, Marx, 5 In.	99

ORREFORS Glassworks, located in the Swedish province of Smaaland, was established in 1898. The company is still making glass for use on the table or as decorations. There is renewed interest in the glass made in the modern styles of the 1940s and 1950s and after. In 1990, the company merged with Kosta Boda and is still working as Orrefors. Most vases and decorative pieces are signed with the etched name Orrefors.

Orrefors

Bowl, Spiraling Fern Leaves, Engraved, Sven Palmquist, c.1950, 4¼ x 6½ In.	30

Opaline, Vase, Blue, Parcel Gilt Trim, c.1900s, 7¾ In.
$25

Freeman's Auctioneers & Appraisers

Orphan Annie, Ring, Secret Guard, Magnifying, Embossed Face, Radio Premium, Brass, 1940s
$33

buyer-askcopperfish on eBay

Orrefors, Vase, Fish, Vegetation, Green, Clear Glass, Edvard Hald, 1958, 4¼ In.
$584

Skinner, Inc.

This is an edited listing of current prices. Visit **Kovels.com** to check thousands of prices from previous years and sign up for free information on trends, tips, reproductions, marks, and more.

Ott & Brewer, Cup & Saucer, Ruffled Gold Rim, Branch Handle, White, Dotted, Belleek, 2 x 3 In.
$65

Owens, Vase, Utopian, White Rose, Molded Base, 11 In.
$150

Paden City, Crow's Foot, Candy Dish, Lid, Section Base, Ruby Red, Elegant, 4 x 7 In.
$26

Vase, Ariel, Blue, Yellow & Clear, Signed, Ingeborg Lundin, 7¾ x 4⅜ In. 813
Vase, Fish, Vegetation, Green, Clear Glass, Edvard Hald, 1958, 4¼ In. ....*illus* 584
Vase, Green, Fish, Vegetation, Colorless, Glass, Marked, Edvard Hald, Sweden, 1957, 6¼ In. 677

 OTT & BREWER COMPANY operated the Etruria Pottery at Trenton, New Jersey, from 1871 to 1892. It started making belleek in 1882. The firm used a variety of marks that incorporated the initials O & B.

Candy Dish, Footed, Belleek, Eggshell, Pink Interior, c.1890, 4 x 5½ x 5 In. 215
Creamer, Branch Handle, Ruffled Rim, Flowers, Cream Ground, Belleek, c.1885, 3 In. 10
Cup & Saucer, Ruffled Gold Rim, Branch Handle, White, Dotted, Belleek, 2 x 3 In. ......*illus* 65
Honey Pot, Dome Lid, Footed, Beehive, Flowers, Leaves, c.1883, 5¼ x 4¾ x 4¾ In. 799
Jug, Fish Scale, Raised Floral & Cloud Designs, Cobalt Blue Bands, 8¾ x 8 In. 51
Pitcher, Ewer, Kidney Shape, Embossed & Gilt, Floral, Belleek, c.1890, 6½ In. 105
Plate, Eggshell, Ruffled Rim, Green Ivy Around Rim, Mint, Belleek, c.1890, 9 In. 60
Teapot, Floral, Branch Handle, Bulbous Body, Multicolor, Belleek, c.1885, 7 x 9 In. 137
Vase, 3 Parts, Pink & Blue Beadwork Flowers, c.1890, 5½ x 4 x 4 In. 89

 OVERBECK POTTERY was made by four sisters named Overbeck at a pottery in Cambridge City, Indiana. They started in 1911. They made all types of vases, each one of a kind. Small, hand-modeled figurines are the most popular pieces with today's collectors. The factory continued until 1955, when the last of the four sisters died.

Vase, 5 Carved Panels, Brown & Green Matte Glaze, Incised, Elizabeth, 4 x 4 In. 2000
Vase, Birds Kissing, Carved, Green & Turquoise Glaze, Incised, Elizabeth, 4½ x 5½ In. 7800

OWENS POTTERY was made in Zanesville, Ohio, from 1891 to 1928. The first art pottery was made after 1896. Utopian Ware, Cyrano, Navarre, Feroza, and Henri Deux were made. Pieces were usually marked with a form of the name Owens. The company continued to make tiles but production of art pottery was discontinued about 1907 and the company was sold. The new owners went bankrupt in 1909. J.B. Owens started the J.B. Owens Floor & Wall Tile Company in 1909. It closed in 1928.

| Owens Pottery 1896–1907 | *J. B. Owens* Owens Pottery 1896–1907 | Owens Pottery 1905+ |

Vase, Utopian, Ewer Shape, Leaves, Glazed, 10½ In. 207
Vase, Utopian, White Rose, Molded Base, 11 In. ......*illus* 150
Wall Pocket, Green, Shell, Horn Shape, Marked Owens, 11¼ In. 63

 OYSTER PLATES were popular from 1840 to 1900. Each course at dinner was served in a special dish. The oyster plate had indentations shaped like oysters. Usually six oysters were held on a plate. There is no greater value to a plate with more oysters, although that myth continues to haunt antiques dealers. There are other plates for shellfish, including cockle plates and whelk plates. The appropriately shaped indentations are part of the design of these dishes.

4 Wells, Batwing, Red, Brown, Black Border, 9 x 6 In. 295
4 Wells, Cornflower Blue Flowers, Sponged Gold Border, c.1870, 7 In. 225
4 Wells, Pink Blossoms, Green Leaves, 1880s, 7⅜ In. 125
5 Wells, Crescent Shape, Shells, Turquoise, Lavender, c.1850, 8¾ x 7 In. 269
5 Wells, Dolphins, Plums, Greens, Browns, Scalloped Center, 9 In. 990
5 Wells, Ferns, Scalloped Border, Interior Gilt Band, Ovington Bros., 7¾ In. 145
5 Wells, Holly, Berries, Scalloped Edge, Tressemann & Voght, 1890s, 8½ In. 275
5 Wells, Turkey, Flower Border, Scalloped Edge, Haviland, 8¾ In. 169
6 Wells, Electroplated Silver, Crossed Tie Border, Gorham, c.1865, 11 In. 300

O

6 Wells, Fan Shape, Ribbed, Pink, White, Yellow, Rudolstadt, 10 In.	375
6 Wells, Sea Life, Plums, Greens, Gilt Edging, c.1850, 9 In.	210
6 Wells, Shell Shape, Fluted, Seaweed, Blue, Green, Beige, c.1870	870
6 Wells, Water Scenes, Rope Border, Marital & Redon, c.1890, 9¾ In.	335

PADEN CITY GLASS MANUFACTURING COMPANY was established in 1916 at Paden City, West Virginia. The company made over 20 different colors of glass. The firm closed in 1951. Paden City Pottery may be listed in Dinnerware.

Ardith, Candy Box, Green, Square, Divided, Etched Glass, Lid, 6⅜ In.	33
Ardith, Sugar, Yellow Topaz, c.1930, 3⅝ x 3 x 4⅞ In.	4
Black Forest, Cake Plate, Open Handle, Black, c.1928, 11 In.	54
Black Forest, Candy Dish, Lid, 3 Parts, Black, c.1928, 4 x 6 In.	180
Black Forest, Compote, Cheriglo, 7¾ x 5½ In.	69
Bookend, Animal Figure, Seahorse, Clear, Shell Base, c.1940, 8¼ In.	27
Bowl, Diana, Console, Ruby, 1920s, 11½ In.	120
Crow's Foot, Cake Plate, Handles, Ruby Red, 14 x 14 In.	38
Crow's Foot, Candy Dish, Lid, Section Base, Ruby Red, Elegant, 4 x 7 In. *illus*	26
Crow's Foot, Orchid, Bowl, Square Rounded Corners, Round Foot, Ruby Red, 1930s, 11 In.	115
Crow's Foot, Plate, Clear, 11 In.	28
Crow's Foot, Soup, Dish, Handles, Footed, Ruby Red, 1920s	19
Diana, Bowl, Open Tab Handles, Amber, 9 In.	55
Figurine, Colt, Standing, Curly Mane & Tail, Clear, Round Base, 11½ In. *illus*	21
Figurine, Pony, Black, 1940s, 11½ In.	245
Figurine, Pony, Tall, Clear, 12 In.	85
Gazebo, Dish, Mayonnaise, Handles, Underplate, Clear	25
Gothic Garden, Handles, Gilt, Clear, 1930s, 11½ In.	40
Largo, Candleholder, 2-Light, Clear, 1940s, 5½ In., Pair	55
Minion, Pitcher, Maroon, Handle, Long & Wide Spout, 64 Oz., 9 In.	50
Peacock & Rose, Compote, Green, Depression, Floral, Footed, 6 x 8 In.	28
Peacock & Wild Rose, Vase, Flared, Black, 12 In.	95
Pouter Pigeon, Bookend, Animal Figure, Clear, Ground Polished Base, c.1940, 5¾ In.	17
Spire, Tray, Center Handle, Round, Clear, Footed, 10½ In.	175
Springtime, Compote, Silver Overlay, Ruby, c.1925, 6 x 6 x 3 In.	55
Top Hat, Vase, Trumpet Flower, Etched, Clear, 4½ x 8½ x 7½ In.	9
Tree, Vase, Black, Deer, Dogs, Moose, Forest Etching Scene, 6¼ In.	26
Triumph, Sandwich Tray, Handle, Flared Sides, Amber, 10½ x 5½ In.	60

PAINTINGS listed in this book are not works by major artists but rather decorative paintings on ivory, board, or glass that would be of interest to the average collector. Watercolors on paper are listed under Picture. To learn the value of an oil painting by a listed artist, you must contact an expert in that area.

Gouache, G. Battista, Fisherman In Bay Of Naples, Italy, 8¾ x 14 In.	316
Miniature On Ivory, Portrait, George Washington, Wood Frame, Carved, 1800s, 1¾ In.	183
Miniature, Reverse On Glass, Oil, Girl, Doll, Brass Frame, 1830s, 3 x 2¼ In. *illus*	2322
Oil On Canvas, Canadian Ship Monrovia, W.H. Yorke, Frame, 31 x 42 In.	7800
Oil On Canvas, Middle East Interior Scene, Douglas Arthur Teed, Gilt Frame, 20 x 24 In.	1062
Oil On Canvas, Nude, Female, B. Schlemm, 16 x 12 In.	173
Oil On Canvas, Parisian Street Scene, Figures, Antoine Blanchard, France, 20 x 25 In.	4840
Oil On Canvas, Portrait, Boy, N. Cook, Saratoga Springs, 1865, 34½ x 27 In.	384
Oil On Canvas, Street Scene Mazatlan, A.S. Clark, c.1923, 7¼ x 9⅛ In.	1452
Oil On Canvas, Street Scene, Figures, Horse, Max Ohmayer, Germany, 26¼ x 34 In.	333
Oil On Canvas, Washer Woman, Abalone, Sea, Boat, W.C. Adam, 24 x 28½ In.	1694
Oil On Canvas, Yosemite Valley, Indian, Horse, Lake, Pine Tree, Unsigned, 1800s, 28 x 42 In.	424
Oil On Ivory, Portrait, Man, Black Coat, White Collar, James R. Lambdin, Gilt Frame, 3 In.	615
Oil On Panel, View Of Coast, J. Isabey, Frame, 14 x 19 In.	687
Oil On Paper, Woman In Black Dress, Lace Cap, Esther Francis Aged 53, 1884, Frame, 8 In.	345
Reverse On Glass, Woman, Hand Mirror, Asian, Carved Frame, 1800s, 26 x 19 In. *illus*	500

Paden City, Figurine, Colt, Standing, Curly Mane & Tail, Clear, Round Base, 11½ In.
$21

yrucello on eBay

Painting, Miniature, Reverse On Glass, Oil, Girl, Doll, Brass Frame, 1830s, 3 x 2¼ In.
$2,322

Skinner, Inc.

Painting, Reverse On Glass, Woman, Hand Mirror, Asian, Carved Frame, 1800s, 26 x 19 In.
$500

Eldred's

P

333

PAIRPOINT

Pairpoint, Cracker Jar, Pink & Blue Flowers, Opaque White, Gilt, Metal Mount, Signed, 8 x 6 In.
$70

Pairpoint, Lamp, Carlisle Shade, Flowers, Frosted, Marble Square Base, c.1915, 21 In.
$1,287

Pairpoint, Lamp, Oil, Russian Pattern, Burner, Metal Base, Quadruple Plate, 13½ In.
$600

Pairpoint, Lamp, 2 Flying Cherubs, Urn Shape Base, White Enamel, Signed, Late 1800s, 21 In.
$586

Pairpoint, Lamp, Electric, 2-Light, Sailing Ships, Lansdowne Style, Signed, F. Chadd, 22 In.
$3,025

Pairpoint, Lamp, Puffy, Peonies, White Tracery, Reverse Painted, Square Shade, 18 x 9 In.
$5,843

Pairpoint, Lamp, 3-Light, Reverse Painted, Egyptian Landscape, Octagonal Foot, 22 In.
$1,100

Pairpoint, Lamp, Flower Band, Painted Stippled Interior, Mahogany, Brass Trim, c.1915, 24 In.
$720

Pairpoint, Lamp, Puffy, Umbrella Shade, Floral Band, Signed, c.1890, 10⅜ In.
$644

P

PAIRPOINT Manufacturing Company was founded by Thomas J. Pairpoint in 1880 in New Bedford, Massachusetts. It soon joined with the glassworks nearby and made glass, silver-plated pieces, and lamps. Reverse-painted glass shades and molded shades known as "puffies" were part of the production until the 1930s. The company reorganized and changed its name several times. It became the Pairpoint Glass Company in 1957. The company moved to Sagamore, Massachusetts, in 1970 and now makes luxury glass items. Items listed here are glass or glass and metal. Silver-plated pieces are listed under Silver Plate. Three marks are shown here.

Pairpoint Corp.
1894–1939

Gunderson–Pairpoint Glass Works
1952–1957

Pairpoint Manufacturing Co.
1972–present

Compote, Jelly, Doris Pattern, 6 1/4 x 4 In.	30
Cracker Jar, Pink & Blue Flowers, Opaque White, Gilt, Metal Mount, Signed, 8 x 6 In.......*illus*	70
Cup, Novelty, Cut Glass, Cambridge Pattern, Reversible, 4 In.	120
Lamp, 2 Flying Cherubs, Urn Shape Base, White Enamel, Signed, Late 1800s, 21 In..........*illus*	586
Lamp, 3-Light, Chipped Ice Shade, Reverse Painted, Silver Plated, Parrots, 22 x 17 In.	1239
Lamp, 3-Light, Reverse Painted, Egyptian Landscape, Octagonal Foot, 22 In..................*illus*	1100
Lamp, Carlisle Shade, Flowers, Frosted, Marble Square Base, c.1915, 21 In.....................*illus*	1287
Lamp, Electric, 2-Light, Sailing Ships, Lansdowne Style, Signed, F. Chadd, 22 In..............*illus*	3025
Lamp, Electric, Hexagonal, Directoire Shade, Chestnut Cluster, 3-Legged Support, 21 In.........	1513
Lamp, Electric, Reverse Painted, Carlisle Style, Green, Amber Dome Top, 21 In.	1210
Lamp, Flower Band, Painted Stippled Interior, Mahogany, Brass Trim, c.1915, 24 In. ....*illus*	720
Lamp, Medial Flower, Painted, Silver Plated Base, Signed, c.1915, 21 In.	498
Lamp, Oil, Russian Pattern, Burner, Metal Base, Quadruple Plate, 13 1/2 In. ....*illus*	600
Lamp, Puffy, Peonies, White Tracery, Reverse Painted, Square Shade, 18 x 9 In..............*illus*	5843
Lamp, Puffy, Umbrella Shade, Floral Band, Signed, c.1890, 10 3/8 In..............................*illus*	644
Lamp, Reverse Painted, Stylized Flowers, Acanthus Leaf, Frosted, Signed, 14 x 9 In.................	544
Lamp, Reverse Painted Shade, Orange Iris, Green, Doulton Base, Signed, CB Hopkins, 23 x 14 In.	9600
Lampshade, Molded Glass, Square, Butterfly, Flowers, Enamel, c.1910, 8 x 12 x 12 In..............	4030
Lampshade, Painted, Flowers, Butterflies, Hexagonal, 15 x 9 In.	99
Pitcher, Green, Cut Glass, Silver Collar & Spout, Monogram, Gorham, 9 3/4 In.	2400
Pitcher, Savoy, Cranberry, Cut Glass, Silver Collar & Spout, Gorham, 10 In. ....*illus*	2640
Server, Cheese & Cracker, Baltic Pattern, 2 x 9 In.	84
Toothpick Holder, Cherub On Tortoise, Umbrella, Gold Plated, c.1894, 6 x 5 1/2 In.	739
Tumbler, Savoy Pattern, Ray Cut Base, 3 3/4 In.	150
Vase, Cranberry, Cut To Clear, 9 3/8 In.	1200

PALMER COX, *Brownies, see Brownies category.*

PAPER collectibles, including almanacs, catalogs, children's books, some greeting cards, stock certificates, and other paper ephemera, are listed here. Paper calendars are listed separately in the Calendar category. Paper items may be found in many other sections, such as Christmas and Movie.

Baptismal Certificate, Green Heart, Text Inside, Elias Braun, c.1820, 12 x 15 1/2 In.	1046
Birth Certificate, Watercolor, Brightly Colored Gowns, Daniel Peterman, 1861, 14 x 12 In......	1968
Bookplate, Wenworth, Armorial, Chippendale, New Hampshire, Signed, N. Hurd, 3 x 2 In.......	660
Family Register, Fatout, Ink & Watercolor, Frame, N.J., Births 1773-1825, 8 x 10 In.	183
Family Register, Rose Vines, Watercolor, Gilt Frame, Almira Edson, c.1810, 18 x 24 In.	1353
Fraktur, Birth, Ink & Watercolor, Frame, Maria Van Ness, B.1804, 8 x 9 In.	3416
Fraktur, Scherenschnitte, Flower Border, Watercolor, Cutwork, Frame, c.1800s, 7 x 12 In........	10980
Fraktur, Watercolor, Heart, Sun, Moon, Flowers, Frame, c.1837, 17 x 20 In..............................	840
Letter, Friendship, Watercolor, Willow Tree, Grain Painted Frame, c.1827, 12 x 8 In.	1476
Magazine, Playboy, Woman Leaning, Donald Trump Cover, 1990 ....*illus*	115

Pairpoint, Pitcher, Savoy, Cranberry, Cut Glass, Silver Collar & Spout, Gorham, 10 In.
$2,640

Brunk Auctions

Paper, Magazine, Playboy, Woman Leaning, Donald Trump Cover, 1990
$115

Keystone Auctions LLC

Paperweight, Advertising, Dr. Daniels' Remedies, Horse, Cattle, Sheep, Don't Gamble, 5 Dice, Glass, 1 1/2 x 3 In.
$472

AntiqueAdvertising.com

P

Paperweight, Advertising, Figural, Pre-Prohibition, Buffalo Springs Distilling Co., 2 x 2 x 1 In.
$120

Soulis Auctions

Paperweight, Advertising, J.H. Turner Wholesale Hay, Photograph, Cruver Mfg., c.1900, $2\frac{1}{2}$ x 4 In.
$90

Soulis Auctions

Paperweight, Boston & Sandwich, Pink Poinsettia, Glass, Granulated Ground, $2\frac{3}{4}$ x $1\frac{3}{4}$ In.
$154

Skinner, Inc.

TIP
Rub tartar-control toothpaste on your scratched snow dome paperweights. It will remove the smaller scratches.

Marriage Certificate, Watercolor, 2 Urns, Painted Red Frame, c.1843, 15 x 12 In. 2460
Penmanship, Poetry, Eagle, Ships, Building, Watercolor, D. Auger, Vermont, c.1850, 10 x 8 In. 2583
Penmanship, Progress Banner, Eagle, Signed, C.P. Zaner, Columbus, Ohio, 1891, $19\frac{1}{2}$ x 25 In. 923
Scroll, Bandit, Watercolor & Ink, Batten & Roller, Taisho, Japan, c.1920, 61 x 21 In. 96
Valentine, Cupid, Heart & Diamond Border, Cutwork, Gilt Frame, 1800s, 12 x 12 In. 1353

PAPER DOLLS were probably inspired by the pantins, or jumping jacks, made in eighteenth-century Europe. By the 1880s, sheets of printed paper dolls and clothes were being made. The first paper doll books were made in the 1920s. Collectors prefer uncut sheets or books or boxed sets of paper dolls. Prices are about half as much if the pages have been cut.

Baby Tender Love, Doll, Plastic Stand, 27-Piece Wardrobe, Whitman, Precut, Box 5
Barbie, Quick Curl, Plastic Stand, 25-Piece Wardrobe, Whitman, Precut, Box 5
Bride & Groom, Book, 6 Dolls & Clothes, Merrill, 1949, 12 x 10 In. 45
Jane Allyson, 2 Dolls, 1 Blond, 1 Brunette, Clothes, Whitman, Uncut, 1956 25
Little Women, 4 Women, 1 Man, Book, Saakfield, Uncut, 1960, 13 x 10 In. 40
Raggedy Ann & Andy, Book, Uncut, 1957, 14 x 11 In. 42

PAPERWEIGHTS must have first appeared along with paper in ancient Egypt. Today's collectors search for every type, from the very expensive French weights of the nineteenth century to the modern artist weights or advertising pieces. The glass tops of the paperweights sometimes have been nicked or scratched, and this type of damage can be removed by polishing. Some serious collectors think this type of repair is an alteration and will not buy a repolished weight; others think it is an acceptable technique of restoration that does not change the value. Printie is the flat or concave surface formed when a paperweight is shaped on a grinding wheel. Baccarat paperweights are listed separately under Baccarat.

Advertising, Brown Wagons, Figural Beetle, Iron, c.1890, $12\frac{1}{2}$ x $4\frac{1}{4}$ x $3\frac{3}{4}$ In. 384
Advertising, Busy Alley Union Stock Yards, Chicago, Sepia Tone, Early 1900s, $2\frac{1}{2}$ x 4 In. 64
Advertising, C.S. Osborne & Co., Harness Tools, Glass, Barnes & Abrams Co., 1882, 4 x 2 In. 115
Advertising, Dr. Daniels' Remedies, Horse, Cattle, Sheep, Don't Gamble, 5 Dice, Glass, $1\frac{1}{2}$ x 3 In. *illus* 472
Advertising, Figural Anchor Logo, North & Judd Mfg. Co., Hames, 3 x 3 In. 256
Advertising, Figural Bear, A.W. Bear Co., Gilt Finish, Embossed, 2 x 4 x $2\frac{1}{2}$ In. 179
Advertising, Figural, Pre-Prohibition, Buffalo Springs Distilling Co., 2 x 2 x 1 In. *illus* 120
Advertising, J.H. Turner Wholesale Hay, Photograph, Cruver Mfg., c.1900, $2\frac{1}{2}$ x 4 In. *illus* 90
Advertising, Lipman, Model Engine, Power Plant, Nickel Plated Wheel, $1\frac{3}{4}$ x 3 In. 124
Ayotte, R., Mother Robin With Baby, Wriggling Worm, 1979, $2\frac{3}{4}$ In. 900
Ayotte, Rick, Egg Shape, Blue, Pink, Yellow, Orange Flowers, Signed, $3\frac{1}{2}$ x $2\frac{3}{4}$ In. 584
Bacchus, Concentric Millefiori, Hollow Cogs, Ruffled Canes, Bubbles, 3 In. 6000
Banford, R., Rose Buds, Pink Aventurine Ground, Gold & Blue Dust, Faceted, $2\frac{1}{4}$ In. 240
Banford, R., Rose, Yellow & Purple Iris, Radiating Leaves, Diamond Cut Ground, 3 In. 1320
Blown Glass, Swirls Of Pink, Yellow & White, Signed Joe Zimmerman, $\frac{3}{4}$ In. 69
Blue & White Primrose, Stardust Center, Green Leaves, Faceted, $1\frac{3}{4}$ In. 600
Boston & Sandwich, Pink Poinsettia, Glass, Granulated Ground, $2\frac{3}{4}$ x $1\frac{3}{4}$ In. *illus* 154
Bottle, Blue, Clear, Charles Wright, Signed, Floral Base, 1994, 5 x 4 In. 79
Brass, Figural, Cast, Sleeping Child, Late 1800s, 6 In. 100
Bronze, Bear, Walking, Wooden Base, $1\frac{1}{2}$ x 3 In. 36
Bronze, Napoleon's Death Mask, Gilded Laurel Wreath, 1800s, 5 x 5 In. 225 to 750
Cape Cod Works, Swirling Red & White Stripes, Bull's-Eye Cane Center, 3 In. 360
Carnival Glass, Bird, Iridescent, Gibson, 3 x 4 In. *illus* 24
Clichy, Millefiori & Roses, Green Stave Basket, $2\frac{1}{2}$ In. 1320
Clichy, Millefiori Quatrefoil Garlands, Interlaced, Ruby Ground, $3\frac{1}{8}$ In. 720
Clichy, Millefiori, Globular, Blue, Green, Red & Rose, C-Scrolls, c.1850, 3 x $2\frac{1}{2}$ In. 2214
Clichy, Pansy, Oval Shape, Flower With Bud, Leaves, $2\frac{1}{4}$ x 2 In. *illus* 615
Clichy, Pinwheel, Pink & White Swirl, Blue Bull's-Eye Cane Center, $2\frac{5}{8}$ In. 780
Clichy, Swirl, Globular, Pink & White, Rose, c.1850, $1\frac{7}{8}$ x $1\frac{3}{8}$ In. 615
D'Onofrio, Snow Owl, Mouse, Mottle Blue Ground, Full Moon, Signed, 3 In. 419
Egerman, Engraved Landscape, Stag In Woods, Red Stained Base, $2\frac{7}{8}$ In. 360

Paperweight, Carnival Glass, Bird, Iridescent, Gibson, 3 x 4 In.
$24

Martin Auction Co.

Paperweight, Perthshire, Honeycomb, Bees, Glass, Globular, 3¾ x 3½ In.
$1,169

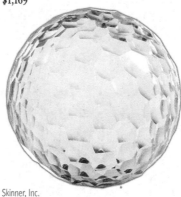

Skinner, Inc.

Paperweight, Stankard, Paul J., Yellow Flowers, Leaves, Roots, Oval, Signed, 3¼ x 2½ In.
$1,476

Skinner, Inc.

Paperweight, Clichy, Pansy, Oval Shape, Flower With Bud, Leaves, 2¼ x 2 In.
$615

Skinner, Inc.

Paperweight, Rosenfeld, Ken, Serpent, Flowers, Lavender, Blue, Yellow, 3 x 2½ In.
$554

Skinner, Inc.

Paperweight, Trabucco, Cut Facet, Bouquet, Green Leaves, Blue Ground, Signed, 1986, 3½ In.
$538

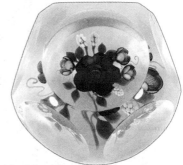

Jeffrey S. Evans & Associates

Paperweight, Kaziun, 2 Blue Petals, 3 White & Amethyst Petals, 3 Green Leaves, 1950, 2⅛ In.
$359

Jeffrey S. Evans & Associates

Paperweight, St. Louis, Glass, Pear Shape, Pillow Square Base, France, c.1850, 2⅛ In.
$431

Skinner, Inc.

Paperweight, Ysart, Flower Bouquet, Stems, Latticinio Twists, Scotland, 1900s, 2¾ In.
$448

Jeffrey S. Evans & Associates

P

Papier-Mache, Bull, Gold Paint, Mounted, Rectangular Base, 26 x 30 x 11 In.
$111

Papier-Mache, Head, Male Mannequin, Bushy Eyebrows, Lifelike Eyes, Mark Ballenget, 8 x 11 ½ In.
$1,200

Parian, Bust, Professor John Wilson, Socle Base, 1800s, 11 x 7 In.
$219

Parian, Figurine, Ariadne, Nude, Seated On Panther, England, c.1860, 11 ¼ In.
$1,230

Paris, Veilleuse, Tea Warmer, Hot Air Balloon, Napoleon III, Manoir De Mont Salvy, 10 In., 3 Part
$67

Paris, Pitcher, Flowers, Central Medallion, Blue Ground, Gilt Accents, 1800s, 10 x 8 ½ In.
$113

Pate-De-Verre, Vase, Multicolor, Flowers, Medallion, Art Deco, Gray Background, 7 In.
$5,750

Pate-Sur-Pate, Box, Silver Lid, Art Nouveau, Portrait, Minerva, Signed, A. Riffaterre, France, c.1903, 5 In.
$563

Pate-Sur-Pate, Vase, Hornberg, Porcelain, Forest Nymph, Flowers, 2 Handles, Germany, 7 x 4 ½ In.
$118

P

F. Whittemore, 2 Candles, Holly & Berry Sprigs, Ruby Ground, Faceted, 2¾ In.	192
Gillinder & Sons, Millefiori, Central Cranberry, White, Cane, Exterior Bands, c.1875, 2½ In.	330
Glass, Owl, Cobalt Blue, White, Square Base, 3½ x 2 In.	24
Glass, Rooster, Blue, 4¼ x 2½ In.	24
Glass, Rooster, Cobalt Blue, Standing, 4¼ x 2½ In.	24
Hansen, R., Purple Peacock, Blue Tail With Orange Spots, Pink Ground, Faceted, 3 In.	120
Kaziun, 2 Blue Petals, 3 White & Amethyst Petals, 3 Green Leaves, 1950, 2⅛ In. ....*illus*	359
Liberty Village, Rounded, Blossom, Pulled Feather Design, 1979, 3 x 3 In.	145
Lundberg, 3 Cherries On Branch, Ribbed Leaves, Clear Ground, D. Salazar, 3⅜ In.	96
Lundberg, Upright Orange Tiger Lily, Black Specks, Leaves, Footed, 1986, 3½ In.	330
Lundberg, Worldweight, Green & Beige Continents, Blue Water, Clear Overlay, 2½ In.	132
Manson, Green Salamander, Yellow Spots, Sandy & Rocky Ground, 1980, 2¾ In.	269
McDougall, P., Cog Cane Circle, 9 Radial Latticinio Twists, Black Ground, 3 In.	60
McDougall, Multicolor, Millefiori, Star & Floral, 1900s, 2 In.	108
Micro Mosaic, Oval, Black Slate Shape, 5 Scenes, 5 x 3¾ x ⅜ In.	594
Millefiori, Clichy, La Garenne, Oval, Concentric Garlands, Pink Canes, c.1850, 3 x 2 In.	861
New England, Nosegay, Millefiori Rim, Red Double Swirl Latticinio Ground, 2½ In.	2040
Orient & Flume, Round Shape, Painted Fish, Blue, Yellow, Purple, Marked, 1975, 2 x 3 In.	295
Perthshire, Honeycomb, Bees, Glass, Globular, 3¾ x 3½ In. ....*illus*	1169
Perthshire, Millefiori Forget-Me-Nots, Green Double Swirl Latticinio, 1976, 3 In.	300
Pinchbeck, Bust, Empress Eugenia, Golden Colored Zinc, 3 In.	600
Pressed Glass, Bohemian, Blue, 3-Feather Crown, Prism Exterior, c.1900, 3 In.	84
Rosenfeld, Ken, Flowers, Ladybugs, Spiders, Globular, Leaves, 3 x 2¾ In.	523
Rosenfeld, Ken, Red Roses, Buds, Green Stems, Green Carpet Ground, 1990, 3½ In.	330
Rosenfeld, Ken, Serpent, Flowers, Lavender, Blue, Yellow, 3 x 2½ In. ....*illus*	554
Sandwich Glass, Clematis, Latticinio, Swirl, Globular, 2½ x 2 In.	123
Scrambled End-Of-Day Millefiori, Copper Aventurine, Venetian, 2½ In.	108
Simpson, Josh, Plant, Blue, Black, Marked, Dated 1989, 3 x 3 In.	250
Simpson, Josh, Undersea, Cane Clusters, Swirl Ground, Pale Blue & Cobalt, 1993, 3¼ In.	277
St. Louis, Apple, Glass, Pillow Square Base, France, c.1850, 2 In.	615
St. Louis, Blue Dahlia, Clear Ground, Faceted, 1970, 3¼ In.	600
St. Louis, Concentric Millefiori, Stave Basket, Ribbed Pistachio Canes, 3 In.	2040
St. Louis, Crown, Red & Green Twisted Ribbons, Blue, Pink & White Canes, 2½ In.	480
St. Louis, End Of Day, Egg Shape, Torsades & Canes, 1¾ In.	123
St. Louis, Glass, Pear Shape, Pillow Square Base, France, c.1850, 2⅛ In. ....*illus*	431
St. Louis, Honeycomb Strawberry, White Flowers & Leaves, 2½ x 2 In.	615
St. Louis, Spaced Millefiori, Yellow Tubes, Blue Jasper Ground, Red Specks, 2 In.	360
St. Louis, Upright Bouquet, Clematis, Serrated Leaves, Amber Torsade, 3 In.	5400
St. Mande, Concentric Millefiori, Star Center, Blue Flower Canes, 2 In.	840
Stankard, Paul J., Botanical, Flowers, Honey Bee, Dragonfly, 2⅝ x 3⅜ In.	3198
Stankard, Paul J., Green Overlay, Apple Branch, Flower, Bee, Signed, 3 In.	1476
Stankard, Paul J., Seedpod, Yellow Flower, Pollen, Bee, Clear Ground, Beveled, 1999, 3 In.	1200
Stankard, Paul J., Yellow Flowers, Leaves, Roots, Oval, Signed, 3¼ x 2½ In. ....*illus*	1476
Tarsitano, Pears On Leafy Branch, 5 Blossoms, Blue Stardust Cane Carpet, 3¼ In.	1000
Trabucco, Coiled Snake, Crimson Rose, Leaves, Speckled Rocks, Sandy Ground, 4 In.	780
Trabucco, Cut Facet, Bouquet, Green Leaves, Blue Ground, Signed, 1986, 3½ In. ....*illus*	538
Trabucco, Globe Shape, Red & White Flowers, Bee, 3 x 2 In.	523
Whitefriars, Cane Angelfish, Concentric Canes Surround, Faceted, 1977, 3 In.	420
Ysart, Flower Bouquet, Stems, Latticinio Twists, Scotland, 1900s, 2¾ In. ....*illus*	448

PAPIER-MACHE is made from paper mixed with glue, chalk, and other ingredients, then molded and baked. It becomes very hard and can be painted. Boxes, trays, and furniture were made of papier-mache. Some of the nineteenth-century pieces were decorated with mother-of-pearl. Papier-mache is still being used to make small toys, figures, candy containers, boxes, and other giftwares. Furniture made of papier-mache is listed in the Furniture category.

Bull, Gold Paint, Mounted, Rectangular Base, 26 x 30 x 11 In. ....*illus*	111
Dog, Seated, Raised Paws, Looking Up, Begging, 28½ x 10 x 14 In.	424

Pate-Sur-Pate, Vase, Porcelain, Green Background, Base, Continental, c.1890, 18¼ x 6½ In.
$575

Heritage Auctions

Pate-Sur-Pate, Vase, Zeus, Hera, Reserves, Leaves, Gilt, Pedestal Base, Porcelain, France, c.1800, 8 x 7 In.
$1,074

Aspire Auctions

Paul Revere, Pitcher, Bobbie, His Pitcher, Yellow Duck, Handle, 1921, 4¼ In.
$277

Skinner, Inc.

P

Paul Revere, Vase, Trees In Landscape Band, Brown, Fannie Levine, 1921, 8¼ In.
$6,875

Rago Arts and Auction Center

Peachblow, Epergne, 4 Holders, Pink, Yellow, Flowers, D. Robinson, Fenton, 1900s, 13 x 12 In.
$240

Garth's Auctioneers & Appraisers

Head, Male Mannequin, Bushy Eyebrows, Lifelike Eyes, Mark Ballenget, 8 x 11½ In. ....*illus*	1200
Rattle, Punch, Head, Tall Hat, Ruffled Color, Stick, 1800s, 4 In.	413
Tray, Battle Scene, Gold Stencil Border, 1812 Ships, Constitution & The Java, 22 x 28 In.	1750

PARASOL, *see Umbrella category.*

PARIAN is a fine-grained, hard-paste porcelain named for the marble it resembles. It was first made in England in 1846 and gained favor in the United States about 1860. Figures, tea sets, vases, and other items were made of Parian at many English and American factories.

Bust, Ophelia, On Column, Plinth, Gilt Trim, c.1850, 16 In.	277
Bust, Professor John Wilson, Socle Base, 1800s, 11 x 7 In. ....*illus*	219
Figurine, Ariadne, Nude, Seated On Panther, England, c.1860, 11¼ In. ....*illus*	1230
Figurine, Omphale, Hercules, Lion's Pelt & Club, Marked, 1800s, 12 x 8 x 5½ In.	219

PARIS, Vieux Paris, or Old Paris, is porcelain ware that is known to have been made in Paris in the eighteenth or early nineteenth century. These porcelains have no identifying mark but can be recognized by the whiteness of the porcelain and the lines and decorations. Gold decoration is often used.

Pitcher, Flowers, Central Medallion, Blue Ground, Gilt Accents, 1800s, 10 x 8½ In. ....*illus*	113
Veilleuse, Tea Warmer, Hot Air Balloon, Napoleon III, Manoir De Mont Salvy, 10 In., 3 Part..*illus*	67

PATENT MODELS were required as part of a patent application for a United States patent until 1880. In 1926 the stored patent models were sold by the U.S. Patent Office. Some were given to the Smithsonian, some were returned to inventors' descendants, and the rest were sold as a group. As groups changed hands in later years in unsuccessful attempts to start a museum individual models started appearing in the marketplace. A model usually has an official tag.

Mowing Machine, Iron, Wood, Folding Blade, Platt & Co., 1875, 22 x 18 In.	3000

PATE-DE-VERRE is an ancient technique in which glass is made by blending and refining powdered glass of different colors into molds. The process was revived by French glassmakers, especially Galle, around the end of the nineteenth century.

Vase, Multicolor, Flowers, Medallion, Art Deco, Gray Background, 7 In.............................*illus*	5750

PATE-SUR-PATE means paste on paste. The design was made by painting layers of slip on the ceramic piece until a relief decoration was formed. The method was developed at the Sevres factory in France about 1850. It became even more famous at the English Minton factory about 1870. It has since been used by many potters to make both pottery and porcelain wares.

Box, Silver Lid, Art Nouveau, Portrait, Minerva, Signed, A. Riffaterre, France, c.1903, 5 In...*illus*	563
Plate, Well & Rim, Blue Floral Band, Early 1800s, 9 In..	369
Vase, Hornberg, Porcelain, Forest Nymph, Flowers, 2 Handles, Germany, 7 x 4½ In. ....*illus*	118
Vase, Porcelain, Green Background, Base, Continental, c.1890, 18¼ x 6½ In. ....*illus*	575
Vase, Zeus, Hera, Reserves, Leaves, Gilt, Pedestal Base, Porcelain, France, c.1800, 8 x 7 In...*illus*	1074

PAUL REVERE POTTERY was made at several locations in and around Boston, Massachusetts, between 1906 and 1942. The pottery was operated as a settlement house program for teenage girls. Many pieces were signed *S.E.G.* for Saturday Evening Girls. The artists concentrated on children's dishes and tiles. Decorations were outlined in black and filled with color.

Dish, Lid, Yellow, Handle On Top, Vent Hole, Saturday Evening Girls, 2½ x 8½ In.	130
Pitcher, Bobbie, His Pitcher, Yellow Duck, Handle, 1921, 4¼ In...*illus*	277
Tray, Yellow, Oval, Raised Rim, Marked S.E.G., 10⅝ x 8 In..	115
Vase, Gunmetal Gray, Clay, Mission Style, PRP Circular Stamp On Base, 4¾ In......................	63
Vase, Trees In Landscape Band, Brown, Fannie Levine, 1921, 8¼ In..............................*illus*	6875

P

PEACHBLOW glass was made by several factories beginning in the 1880s. New England Peachblow is a one-layer glass shading from red to white. Mt. Washington Peachblow shades from pink to bluish-white. Hobbs, Brockunier and Company of Wheeling, West Virginia, made Coral glass that it marketed as Peachblow. It shades from yellow to peach and is lined with white glass. Reproductions of all types of peachblow have been made. Related pieces may be listed under Webb Peachblow.

Bowl, Jewels Bar, Gilt, Floral, Scalloped Lip & Ground, Thomas Webb, 2½ x 4¼ In.	142
Creamer, Plush, Ribbed, Opal Handle, New England Glass Co., c.1880, 2⅝ In.	152
Epergne, 4 Holders, Pink, Yellow, Flowers, D. Robinson, Fenton, 1900s, 13 x 12 In. *illus*	240
Jug, Claret, Mahogany, Red, Yellow, Shell Handle, Rigaree Neck, 9½ In.	295
Jug, Opal Case, Square Rim, Applied Handle, Hobbs, Brockunier & Co., c.1886, 5½ In.	269
Pitcher, Handle, Enamel, White & Pink, Flowers, 4 x 3 In.	30
Vase, Morgan Shape, Ground Top Rim, Polished Pontil, Hobbs, Wheeling, Late 1800s	192

PEANUTS is the title of a comic strip created by cartoonist Charles M. Schulz (1922–2000). The strip, drawn by Schulz from 1950 to 2000, features a group of children, including Charlie Brown and his sister Sally, Lucy Van Pelt and her brother Linus, Peppermint Patty, and Pig Pen, and an imaginative and independent beagle named Snoopy. The Peanuts gang has also been featured in books, television shows, and a Broadway musical. The comic strip is being rerun in some newspapers.

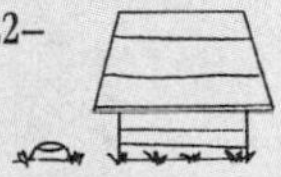

Bank, Snoopy, Lying On Top Of Hamburger, Stopper, Ceramic, 1958	103
Figure, Snoopy, Astronaut, White Suit, Plastic Bubble Helmet, American Flag, 1969	508
Lunch Box, Characters Under Tree, Comic Strip Sides, Red, Yellow Handle, Metal, 1973	46
Mug, Snoopy, Pilot, On Doghouse, Curse You Red Baron, White Ground, Handle, 4 In. *illus*	258
Night-Light, Snoopy, Vinyl, 1960s, 6 In.	70
Ornament, Schroeder, Playing Piano, Ceramic, United Features Syndicate Inc., 1951, 2½ In.	39
Pin, Support Ice Follies, Snoopy Skating, Yellow, 1960s, 1½ In.	118
Snoopy, Lunch Box, Domed, Metal, Have Lunch With Snoopy, American Thermos Products, 1968. *illus*	35
Toy, Snoopy, Space Scooter, Blue, Battery Operated, Box, 9½ In.	460

PEARL items listed here are made of the natural mother-of-pearl from shells. Such natural pearl has been used to decorate furniture and small utilitarian objects for centuries. The glassware known as mother-of-pearl is listed by that name. Opera glasses made with natural pearl shell are listed under Opera Glasses.

Plaque, Nativity Scene, Carved, Flowers, 7½ x 6¾ In.	277
Rattle, 14K Yellow Gold, Pearl, Whistle, 4 x 2 In.	896

Pearl

PEARLWARE is an earthenware made by Josiah Wedgwood in 1779. It was copied by other potters in England. Pearlware is only slightly different in color from creamware and for many years collectors have confused the terms. Wedgwood pieces are listed in the Wedgwood category in this book. Most pearlware with mocha designs is listed under Mocha.

Bowl, Shallow, Ruffled Rim, Blue Feather Edge, Cap. Jones Of The Macedonian, 9⅝ In.	793
Jug, Slip, Bands, Cat's-Eye, Multicolor Bands On Ocher, England, c.1820, 7 In.	861
Mug, Blue, Gray, Black, Bands, White Slip Twigs, England, 1820-40, 4¾ In.	369
Mug, Brown Slip Twigs, Molded Foot, Extruded Handle, Leafy Terminals, c.1830, Qt. *illus*	1476
Pitcher, Multicolor Flowers, Green, Blue, Pink, White, Barrel Form, 1800s, 8 In.	138
Plate, Blue Feather Edge, Washington & Lafayette, 1800s, 9⅞ In.	793
Plate, Peafowl, Green Scalloped Shell Edge, Multicolor, Impressed C, c.1850, 8 In. *illus*	164
Plate, Soup, Flowers, Multicolor, 1800s, 9⅞ In.	819
Plate, Toddy, Eagle, Octagonal, Green Feather Edge, 1800s, 5 In. *illus*	854
Platter, Molded Feather, Flowers, Blue & White, Marked, England, Early 1800s, 19 In.	461
Platter, Oval, Star, White, Blue & Yellow Border, c.1850, 18⅝ x 14¾ In.	351
Punch Bowl, Flower Basket & Swag, Flower Sprigs, c.1850, 10¾ In. *illus*	234
Punch Bowl, Grapevine, Yellow Background, Floral, England, Early 1800s, 4 x 10 In.	308
Teapot, Lid, Veneer, Marbelized Band, Wood & Caldwell, c.1790, 5 x 8 In. *illus*	885

Peanuts, Mug, Snoopy, Pilot, On Doghouse, Curse You Red Baron, White Ground, Handle, 4 In.
$258

philadelphiaeagles52 on eBay

Peanuts, Snoopy, Lunch Box, Domed, Metal, Have Lunch With Snoopy, American Thermos Products, 1968
$35

Main Auction Galleries, Inc.

P

Pearlware, Mug, Brown Slip Twigs, Molded Foot, Extruded Handle, Leafy Terminals, c.1830, Qt.
$1,476

Skinner, Inc.

PEARLWARE

Pearlware, Plate, Peafowl, Green Scalloped Shell Edge, Multicolor, Impressed C, c.1850, 8 In.
$164

Jeffrey S. Evans & Associates

Pearlware, Plate, Toddy, Eagle, Octagonal, Green Feather Edge, 1800s, 5 In.
$854

Pook & Pook

Pearlware, Punch Bowl, Flower Basket & Swag, Flower Sprigs, c.1850, 10¾ In.
$234

Jeffrey S. Evans & Associates

Pearlware, Teapot, Lid, Veneer, Marbleized Band, Wood & Caldwell, c.1790, 5 x 8 In.
$885

Leland Little Auctions

Peking Glass, Vase, Carved Peonies, Prunus Fruit, Yellow, 7 x 3½ In.
$484

Ahlers & Ogletree Auction Gallery

Pen, Cartier, Fountain, Black Resin Barrel, 18K Gold Plated, Diabolo, Box, 4¾ In.
$303

Ahlers & Ogletree Auction Gallery

Pencil Sharpener, Automatic, Spring-Loaded Lever, Auto-Feed, Metal, Model 52/20, Faber Castell
$71

jeffrotools on eBay

Pencil Sharpener, Cast Iron, Mechanical, Mushroom Base, Self-Turning, Desktop, Roneo
$62

getyourown67 on eBay

Pencil Sharpener, F.S. Webster Co., Iron, Tabletop Mount, Hand Crank, Pine, c.1890, 6½ x 5 x 7¾ In.
$424

Soulis Auctions

Pencil Sharpener, Roneo, No. 2, Mechanical, Iron, Automatic Screw Cutting Co., 1913, 4¼ x 8½ In.
$113

Soulis Auctions

P

PEKING GLASS is a Chinese cameo glass first made popular in the eighteenth century. The Chinese have continued to make this layered glass in the old manner, and many new pieces are now available that could confuse the average buyer.

Bowl, Water Lilies, Scalloped Rim, Red Casing, White, 4 ½ In.		69
Cup, White Glaze, Raised Lotus Blossoms, Tendrils Exterior, Chinese, 1800s, 2 In.		86
Vase, Carved Peonies, Prunus Fruit, Yellow, 7 x 3 ½ In.	*illus*	484
Vase, Overlay, Foo Dog, Flowers, Birds, Clouds, Chinese, Marked, 11 In.		496

PENS replaced hand-cut quills as writing instruments in 1780, when the first steel pen point was made in England. But it was 100 years before the commercial pen was a common item. The fountain pen was invented in the 1830s but was not made in quantity until the 1880s. All types of old pens are collected, everything from quill pens to fountain pens. Float pens feature small objects floating in a liquid as part of the handle. Advertising pens are listed in the Advertising section of this book.

Aurora, Fountain, 14K Gold Trim, Celluloid & Metal, Piston, Aquila, 4 ¾ In.		171
Aurora, Fountain, Barrel Blue Green, Nacre, Gold Trims, Optima 365, 14K Gold, 5 In.		303
Bulgari, Fountain, 18K Gold Nib, Cartridge, Certificate, Box, Switzerland		342
Cartier, Ballpoint, Black Composite & Gold Trinity, Blue Ink, 7 ¾ x ½ In.		305
Cartier, Fountain, Black Resin Barrel, 18K Gold Plated, Diabolo, Box, 4 ¾ In.	*illus*	303
Elsa Peretti, Ballpoint, 18K Yellow Gold, Extra Cartridge, Box, Tiffany & Co.		767
Lamy, Fountain, Titanium Barrel, 14K Gold Nib, Persona, Box, Germany		163
Montblanc, Ballpoint, Le Grand, No. 161, Black Gloss, 5 ¾ In.		224
Montblanc, Fountain, 18K Gold Nib, Gray Granite Cap, Box		800
Montblanc, Fountain, Black Barrel Cap, Gold Accents, 14K Monotone, c.1970, 5 ¾ In.		303
Montblanc, Fountain, Marbled Resin Barrel, Brown, 2-Tone Gold, 18K, Alexandre Dumas, 5 ¼ In.		1210
Montblanc, Fountain, Striated Sterling Silver, Gold Accents, c.1990, 5 ½ In.		726
Montegrappa, Fountain, 18K Yellow Gold Resin, Piston, Box, Traviata, 5 ½ In.		4150
Parker, Fountain, Full Snake Cap & Barrel, 2 Hand-Cut Emerald Eyes, Gold, 1905		1446
Parker, Fountain, Marbleized White Resin, 18K Gold Nib, 5 ½ In.		242
Pelikan, Fountain, Black Striped, Anthracite, 14K Gold, Chrome Trim, Germany		248
Pilot, Fountain, Dragon, Chrome Trim, Black Shaft, Namiki		92
Versace, Fountain, Crocodile Skin, Gilt, Dark Brown, Original Box, 5 ¾ In.		272
Visconti, Fountain, Moonlight Red, Arch Shape Mechanism, Tubular Nib, Chromium 18, Italy		103
Visconti, Fountain, Ragtime, Marbleized Brown Resin, 14K Yellow Gold Nib, Italy, Box, 5 In.		333
Waterman, Ballpoint, Serenite, Box & Paperwork, 2 Extra Cartridges, Set		260
Waterman, Fountain, Ideal, Gold Nib, Black Shaft, 38 In.		875
Waterman, Fountain, Octagonal Royal Plate, 14K Gold Trim, Flexible Nib, 1920s		852

PEN & PENCIL

Cartier, Must De, Ballpoint, Mechanical Pencil, Goldtone, C320, Set, Box, 4 ¾ In.		340
Cross, Ballpoint Pen, Mechanical Pencil, 14K Gold Filled, Label On Box		135
Eversharp, Fountain Pen, Mechanical Pencil, 14K Solid Gold, Skyline, Set, Box		572
Montblanc, Mechanical Pencil & Fountain Pen, Gold M Wing Nib, 254 & 274, Zipped Case		203
Parker 51, Aerometric Filler, Signet Style, 14K Gold Filled Barrel & Caps, Box, 1949, 5 In.		262
Parker 75, Cisele, Fountain Pen, Mechanical Pencil, Sterling Silver, 14K Gold Nib, Set, Box, 5 In.		167
Sheaffer, Fountain Pen, Mechanical Pencil, Marine Green & Black, Golden Nib, Set, Box		272
Sheaffer, Fountain, 14K Gold, Palladium Plating Nib, Sentinel Green, Set, c.1949, 5 ½ In.		88
Waterman, Fountain Pen, Mechanical Pencil, 14K Gold Nib, Inkview, Judd, Set		225

PENCILS were invented, so it is said, in 1565. The eraser was not added to the pencil until 1858. The automatic pencil was invented in 1863. Collectors today want advertising pencils or automatic pencils of unusual design. Boxes and sharpeners for pencils are also collected. Advertising pencils are listed in the Advertising category. Pencil boxes are listed in the Box category.

Caran D'Ache, Mechanical, Ecridor, Hexagonal, Sterling Silver, Switzerland		160
Chatelaine, Mechanical, Silver, Extending, Bullet Shape, Edward Barker & Son, 1930s, 4 In.		240
Dixon, Mechanical, Drafting, Wood Holder, Eldorado 164		33
Eversharp, Mechanical, 14K Gold Trim, Hanging Ring At End, Skyline, 1940s, 5 ¼ In.		19

Pepsi-Cola, Bottle Display, Composition, Raised Lettering, Opening At Back, 48 x 15 In.
$678

Rich Penn Auctions

Pepsi-Cola, Cooler, Lid, Drink Pepsi-Cola, Handle, Tray, Blue & White, 18 x 13 x 18 ½ In.
$177

Copake Auction

Pepsi-Cola, Sign, Bottle Cap, Embossed, Die Cut, Metal, Stout Sign Co., 28 In.
$622

Rich Penn Auctions

Pepsi-Cola, Sign, Ice Cold Sold Here, Double Dash, 2-Sided, Metal, Flange, 16 x 17 In.
$1,469

Rich Penn Auctions

Pepsi-Cola, String Holder, Tin Lithograph, Double Dash, For Colonial Bread, c.1940, 16 x 12 In.
$622

Rich Penn Auctions

Perfume Bottle, Boucheron, Jaipur Saphir, Eau De Toilette, Clear, Blue, Ring Shape, France, 12 x 10 In.
$141

Rich Penn Auctions

Montblanc, Mechanical, Gold Plate, Resin, Leather Case, 3¼ x 7¾ In.	315
Montblanc, Propelling, Twist Click, Sterling Silver, Voltaire, 1995, 5½ In.	229
Mordan & Co., Propelling, 9K Gold Barrel, Screw Top Cap, 1920s, 4½ In.	161
Propelling, Silver, Citrine Seal Inset At One End, c.1800, 4¼ In.	94
Rotring 600, Mechanical, Newton, Black Matte, Germany, 1990s	64
Wahl Eversharp, Mechanical, Gold Filled, Nail Shape, 5¼ In.	16

PENCIL SHARPENER

Asis, Mechanical, Desktop, Metal, Self-Turning, 1950s	39
Automatic, Jumbo, 3 Knives, Multicolor Label, Signed, 1911, 5½ x 4 x 2 In.	113
Automatic, Spring-Loaded Lever, Auto-Feed, Metal, Model 52/20, Faber Castell............*illus*	71
Bakelite, Red Catalin, Timothy Mouse, Walt Disney, 1930s	52
Baker's Chocolate, Woman, Holding Tray, Apron, Metal, U.S. Pat. Off., 2 In.	45
Boston Silver Comet, Nickel Plated, Metal Label, 5 x 7 In.	21
Car, Citroen, Figural, Plastic, Diecast, Poland, 1960s	30
Cast Iron, Mechanical, Mushroom Base, Self-Turning, Desktop, Roneo...........*illus*	62
Climax No. 3, Mechanical, Signed, Metal Label, c.1921, 5¼ x 8 x 4 In.	34
Dandy, Automatic Feed, Patent Date, Spengler-Loomis Mfg. Co., 8½ x 2¾ In.	28
Dazey, Gray Metal, Black Hand Crank	34
Dog, Scottie, Green Bakelite, Souvenir Of Enid Oklahoma, 1⅜ x 1½ In.	38
El Casco, Industrial, Chrome & Black, Self-Turning, Desktop, 6¾ x 2⁵⁄₁₆ x 2⅝ In.	128
F.S. Webster Co., Iron, Tabletop Mount, Hand Crank, Pine, c.1890, 6½ x 5 x 7¾ In.......*illus*	424
Ferdinand The Bull, Disney Character, Bakelite, 1¾ x 1⅛ In.	29
Hand Crank, Cover, Metal, Wooden Base, Impressed No. 51, Desktop, Gab	280
Jupiter Pencil Pointer, Rotary Cutter Disc, Guhl & Harbeck Co., 1897, 5 x 13 In.	354
Jupiter, Gilded Lettering, Cast Iron, Guhl & Harbeck Co., Germany, 5 x 13 x 5½ In.	339
Karbonax Ltd., Mechanical, Super Automatic, Metal, Hand Painted, 1920s, 6 In.	207
Planetary Pencil Pointer, Iron, Brass Label, A.B. Dick Co., c.1896, 5 x 5 x 5¾ In.	203
Roneo, No. 1, Mechanical, Cast Iron, Automatic Screw Cutting Co., 1913, 7 x 9 x 4 In.	181
Roneo, No. 2, Mechanical, Iron, Automatic Screw Cutting Co., 1913, 4¼ x 8½ In. ....*illus*	113
Roneo, Victor, Mechanical, Iron, Signed, c.1913, 7 x 9 x 4 In.	181
U.S. Automatic, Cutting Wheel Pointer, Self-Turning, 3 Blades, Steel, Auto Lead Rotation, 1907	157

 PENNSBURY POTTERY worked in Morrisville, Pennsylvania, from 1950 to 1971. Full sets of dinnerware as well as many decorative items were made. Pieces are marked with the name of the factory.

Amish, Ashtray, Such Schmootzers, Couple Kissing, Flowers, Leaves, 5 In.	14
Barbershop Quartet, Mug, 4 Men, Musical Notes, Tan, Brown, 4 x 5 In.	25
Figurine, Bird Of Paradise, Spread Wings, Branch Mounted, Multicolor	294
Pitcher, 2 Couples, Drinking Beer, 1 On Each Side, 1950s, 7¼ x 8 In.	45
Tiger Locomotive Train, Plate, Plaque, Pennsylvania R.R., 1856, 7¾ x 5 x 1½ In.	24

PEPSI-COLA, the drink and the name, was invented in 1898 but was not trademarked until 1903. The logo was changed from an elaborate script to the modern block letters in 1963. Several different logos have been used. Until 1951, the words *Pepsi* and *Cola* were separated by two dashes. These bottles are called "double dash." In 1951 the modern logo with a single hyphen was introduced. All types of advertising memorabilia are collected, and reproductions are being made.

Pepsi-Cola
1903

Pepsi-Cola
1939–1951

Pepsi-Cola
1965

Ashtray, Tin, Round, White Ground, Blue, Red, 1970s, 3½ In.	6
Bank, Delivery Car, 1905 Ford, Blue & White, Die Cast, Ertl, No. 9736	22
Bank, Dispenser, Battery Operated, Tin, Glasses, Box, Linemar, 10 In.	720
Bottle Cap, Double Dash, Cork Lined, Red, White, Blue, 1930s	69
Bottle Display, Composition, Raised Lettering, Opening At Back, 48 x 15 In......*illus*	678
Bottle Opener, Wall Mount, Metal, Embossed, Starr X, Brown Mfg., Box, 1950s	64
Calendar, Say Pepsi Please, Metal Over Cardboard, Months, 1970 & 1971, 12 x 6½ In.	91

Clock, Drink Pepsi-Cola, Double Dash, Light-Up, Metal Case, 1957, 17½ x 25½ In.	1356
Clock, Say Pepsi Please, Bottle Cap, Electric, Light-Up, Square, 16 x 16 In.	133
Cooler, Lid, Drink Pepsi-Cola, Handle, Tray, Blue & White, 18 x 13 x 18½ In....................*illus*	177
Menu Board, Double Dash, Embossed, Metal, Chain Hanger, Self-Framed, 30 x 19½ In.	509
Menu Board, Say Pepsi Please, Metal, Blackboard Surface, Yellow Border, 1960s, 30 x 19 In...	128
Radio, Coin-Operated, AM-FM, White, Red & Blue Trim, Logo, Electric, 1960s, 12 In.	364
Sign, Bigger Drink Better Taste, Metal, Embossed, Self-Framed, 15¾ x 49 In.	904
Sign, Bottle Cap, Embossed, Die Cut, Metal, Stout Sign Co., 28 In.....................................*illus*	622
Sign, Bottle Cap, Have A Pepsi, Tin, Embossed, Marked, 48 x 17 In..	413
Sign, Bottle Cap, Pepsi-Cola, Metal, Embossed, Red, White & Blue, 1966, 28 In....................	372
Sign, Bottle Cap, Red, White, Blue, Metal, Embossed, 1967, 36 In.	800
Sign, Bottle Shape, Red, White, Blue, Tin, c.1960, 37 In.	354
Sign, Drink Pepsi-Cola, Metal, Embossed, Bottle Cap Logo, Self-Framed, 31 x 27 In.	565
Sign, Ice Cold Sold Here, Double Dash, 2-Sided, Metal, Flange, 16 x 17 In. ....*illus*	1469
Sign, Say Pepsi Please, Embossed, Metal, Bottle Graphic, Self-Framed, 46½ x 16½ In.	452
Sign, Take Home A Carton, Oversize Bottle, Tin Litho, Die Cut, c.1930s, 44½ x 12¼ In.	2714
String Holder, Tin Lithograph, Double Dash, For Colonial Bread, c.1940, 16 x 12 In.........*illus*	622
Tap Handle, Soda Fountain Dispenser, Bottle Cap Logo, Red, White, Blue..................................	29

PERFUME BOTTLES are made of cut glass, pressed glass, art glass, silver, metal, jade, enamel, and even plastic or porcelain. Although the small bottle to hold perfume was first made before the time of ancient Egypt, it is the nineteenth- and twentieth-century examples that interest today's collector. DeVilbiss Company has made atomizers of all types since 1888 but no longer makes the perfume bottle tops so popular with collectors. These were made from 1920 to 1968. The glass bottle may be by any of many manufacturers even if the atomizer is marked *DeVilbiss*. The word *factice*, which often appears in ads, refers to large store display bottles. Glass or porcelain examples may be found under the appropriate name such as Lalique, Czechoslovakia, Glass-Bohemian, etc.

Amethyst Glass, Umbrella Shape Stopper, Oroplastic Frieze, Warriors, c.1920, 6 x 2 In.	585
Black Glass, Raised & Recessed Circles, Stopper, Bob Mackie, 11½ x 8 In.	68
Boucheron, Jaipur Saphir, Eau De Toilette, Clear, Blue, Ring Shape, France, 12 x 10 In...*illus*	141
Christian Dior, Poison, Amethyst Glass, Clear Stopper, Factice, c.1986, 11½ x 9 In..................	90
Cranberry Glass, Hinged Gilt Dog Top, Clear Stopper, c.1890, 9¼ In.	552
Cranberry Glass, Stopper, Turquoise, Frosted, Signed Jean Claude, 1993, 12 In.	189
Cut Glass, Intaglio Flowers, Pattern Cut Stopper, 8¼ In..	36
Elizabeth Taylor, Passion, Amethyst Glass, Raised Diamond, Factice, 12½ x 9½ In.	102
Glass, Red, Cameo Style Decoration, Silver Hinged Stopper, 6¼ In...	94
Guerlain, Imperial, Embossed Honey Bee & Hive, Ground Neck & Stopper, 11¾ In.	57
Niki De Saint Phalle, Eau De Toilette Flacon, Snake, Metal Display, Signed, c.1980, 14 x 5 In. .	625
Vera Wang, Pyramid Shape, Metal Collar, Lucite Stopper, Factice, 11 x 7½ In. ....*illus*	141
Vinaigrette, Cut Glass, 18K Gold, Bloodstone Top, Chain & Finger Ring, 3½ In.......................	3520

PETERS & REED POTTERY COMPANY of Zanesville, Ohio, was founded by John D. Peters and Adam Reed in 1897. Chromal, Landsun, Montene, Pereco, and Persian are some of the art lines that were made. The company, which became Zane Pottery in 1920 and Gonder Pottery in 1941, closed in 1957. Peters & Reed pottery was unmarked.

Vase, Brown, Green, Vines, Column Shape, 12 In.	13
Vase, Chromal, Maroon, Blue, Drip, Ring Mouth, 8 In..	57
Vase, Landscape, Castle, Trees, Brown, Green, 21 In.	316

PETRUS REGOUT, *see Maastricht category.*

PEWABIC POTTERY was founded by Mary Chase Perry Stratton in 1903 in Detroit, Michigan. The company made many types of art pottery, including pieces with matte green glaze and an iridescent crystalline glaze. The company continued working until the death of Mary Stratton in 1961. It was reactivated by Michigan State University in 1968.

Vase, Blue Green Over Copper, Metallic Glaze, Detroit Stamp, 5¼ In..	554
Vase, Brown Tan, Turquoise Blue Metallic Glaze, Paper Label, Impressed Mark, 2 x 2 In...*illus*	358

Perfume Bottle, Vera Wang, Pyramid Shape, Metal Collar, Lucite Stopper, Factice, 11 x 7½ In.
$141

Rich Penn Auctions

Pewabic, Vase, Brown Tan, Turquoise Blue Metallic Glaze, Paper Label, Impressed Mark, 2 x 2 In.
$358

Treadway

Pewter, Figure, Eagle & Snake, Architectural Finial, Gilt, Mexico, c.1900, 22 x 14 x 13 In.
$475

Heritage Auctions

Pewter, Porringer, Dolphin Handle, Spline Back Strap, Early 1800s, 4¾ In. $188

Pook & Pook

Pewter, Teapot, Jade Handle, Spout, Finial, Hexagonal Shape, Chinese, 1900s, 3 x 6 x 2 In. $420

Thomaston Place Auction Galleries

Pewter, Teapot, Lid, Finial, Footed, Boardman & Co., Bands, Marked, 1800s, 12 In. $125

Pook & Pook

Vase, Gold & Green, Metallic Glaze, 2 x 2 In.	500
Vase, Orange Matte, Metallic Glaze, Incised Signature, 2½ x 1¾ In.	625
Vase, Red, Blue & Gold, Metallic Glaze, 2½ x 1½ In.	750

PEWTER is a metal alloy of tin and lead. Some of the pewter made after 1840 has a slightly different composition and is called Britannia metal. This later type of pewter was worked by machine; the earlier pieces were made by hand. In the 1920s pewter came back into fashion and pieces were often marked *Genuine Pewter*. Eighteenth-, nineteenth-, and twentieth-century examples are listed here. Marks used by three pewter workshops are pictured.

Thomas Danforth
1727–1733

Timothy Boardman
1822–1825

William Will
1764–1798

Box, Ram's Head Finial, 2 Scroll Side Handles, 4 Footed, Portugal, c.1900, 8½ x 7⅝ In.	132
Candlestick, James Weekes, Bobeche, Circular Base, Marked, c.1830, 7½ In.	180
Coffeepot, Freeman Porter, Repainted Handle, Marked, 11 In.	281
Dish, Blakeslee Barnes, Deep, Plain, Philadelphia, 1800s, 13 In.	438
Dish, Despres Avallon, Overlapping Leaves, Handle, 8 x 18 In.	60
Dish, Edward Danforth, Deep, Plain, Connecticut, 13¼ In.	150
Figure, Eagle & Snake, Architectural Finial, Gilt, Mexico, c.1900, 22 x 14 x 13 In. *illus*	475
Flagon, Engraved, Knights Jousting, Anno 1675, Scroll Handle, Continental, 1800s, 10 In.	175
Lamp, Albin Muller, Electric, 1-Light, Stamped, Early 1900s, 10¾ In.	125
Lamp, Freeman Porter, Fluid Burner, Circular Base, Marked, 3¾ In.	336
Mold, Candle, 18 Molds, Wood Frame, Footed, 1800s, 16½ x 20 x 6½ In.	360
Mug, Preston Edgar & James Curtis, Scroll Handle, Marked, 6 In.	180
Porringer, Dolphin Handle, Spline Back Strap, Early 1800s, 4¾ In. *illus*	188
Tazza, Candlesticks, Tudric, Liberty & Co., Hammered, Triple Stem, Flattened Foot, 3 Piece	1063
Teapot, Jade Handle, Spout, Finial, Hexagonal Shape, Chinese, 1900s, 3 x 6 x 2 In. *illus*	420
Teapot, Lid & Finial, R. Gleason, Bands, Squat, Stamped, 1800s, 9 In.	188
Teapot, Lid, Finial, Footed, Boardman & Co., Bands, Marked, 1800s, 12 In. *illus*	125
Tray, Serving, Tudric, Art Nouveau, Early 1900s, 18 In.	75
Vase, J. Garnier, Mermaid & Waterspout, Scalloped Rim, Signed, c.1890, 15 x 7 x 6 In.	500
Vase, Nude Maiden Handle, Grotesque Mask Spout, Stamped, Art Nouveau, c.1890, 10 x 4 In.	313

PHOENIX GLASS Company was founded in 1880 in Pennsylvania. The firm made commercial products, such as lampshades, bottles, and glassware. Collectors today are interested in the "Sculptured Artware" made by the company from the 1930s until the mid-1950s. Some pieces of Phoenix glass are very similar to those made by the Consolidated Lamp and Glass Company. Phoenix made Reuben Blue, lavender, and yellow pieces. These colors were not used by Consolidated. In 1970 Phoenix became a division of Anchor Hocking, which was sold to the Newell Group in 1987. The factory is still working.

Pitcher, Spot-Optic, Spatter, Blue & White, Lobed, Handle, c.1885, 7½ In. *illus*	82
Pitcher, Water, Blue, Mica Flakes, Flared Crimped Rim, Reed Handle, c.1880, 8¾ In. *illus*	164

PHONOGRAPHS, invented by Thomas Edison in 1877, have been made by many firms. This category also includes other items associated with the phonograph. Jukeboxes and Records are listed in their own categories.

Berliner, Gramophone, Top Crank, Turntable Brake, Oak Case, c.1898, 14 x 25 In. *illus*	1500
Colombia, Cylinder, Horn, Oak Base, American Gramophone Co., c.1900, 11½ x 7 x 13 In.	288
Columbia, Grafonola, 50, Horn, Adjustable Louvers, Case, c.1918, 14 x 21 x 18 In. *illus*	330
Columbia, Graphophone, Model AJ, Oak Case, Metal Horn, Crank, c.1903, 10 x 10 x 6 In. *illus*	780
Columbia, Graphophone, Model BI, Oak, Nickel Plate, c.1915, 30 x 13 x 21 In. *illus*	720
Edison Standard, Morning Glory Horn, Cylinder, Oak Case, 1905, 12 x 13 In.	339
Edison, Diamond Disc, Model A250, Mahogany Case, Windup, 1912-14, 23 x 23 x 51 In.	1275

Phoenix Glass, Pitcher, Spot-Optic, Spatter, Blue & White, Lobed, Handle, c.1885, 7 ½ In.
$82

Jeffrey S. Evans & Associates

Phoenix Glass, Pitcher, Water, Blue, Mica Flakes, Flared Crimped Rim, Reed Handle, c.1880, 8 ¾ In.
$164

Jeffrey S. Evans & Associates

Phonograph, Columbia, Grafonola, 50, Horn, Adjustable Louvers, Case, c.1918, 14 x 21 x 18 In.
$330

Thomaston Place Auction Galleries

Phonograph, Columbia, Graphophone, Model AJ, Oak Case, Metal Horn, Crank, c.1903, 10 x 10 x 6 In.
$780

Morphy Auctions

Phonograph, Columbia, Graphophone, Model BI, Oak, Nickel Plate, c.1915, 30 x 13 x 21 In.
$720

Garth's Auctioneers & Appraisers

Phonograph, Edison, Home, Oak Case, Oak Cygnet Horn, c.1915, 42 x 16 x 9 In.
$1,020

Garth's Auctioneers & Appraisers

Phonograph, Edison, Standard, Model D, Tulip Flower Horn, Golden Oak Case, 25 x 19 In.
$496

Phonograph, Berliner, Gramophone, Top Crank, Turntable Brake, Oak Case, c.1898, 14 x 25 In.
$1,500

Heritage Auctions

Aspire Auctions

P

Phonograph, Victor Victrola, Model VV-330, Mahogany, Hump Back, Cabriole Legs, c.1915, 38 x 38 x 23 In.
$132

Phonograph, Victor, Credenza 13551, Jacobean Style, Mahogany, Spring Wind, 45½ x 31 In.
$312

Phonograph, Victor, Model E, Monarch Junior, Oak Case, Black & Silver Horn, 1900s, 8 x 10 x 11 In.
$702

Phonograph, Victor Victrola, Model VV-XIV, Quartersawn Oak, Decal, c.1915, 47 x 21 In.
$168

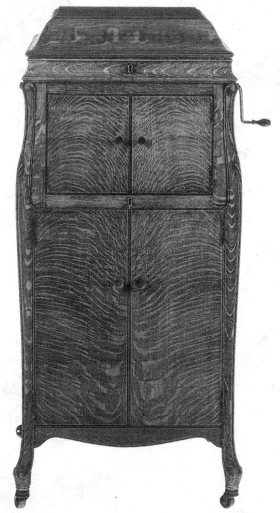

Phonograph, Victor, Schoolhouse, Model XXV, Horn, Quartersawn Oak, Hinged Lid, 1913, 55 x 26 x 20 In.
$4,305

Phonograph Needle Case, Everest, Blue Green, Yellow, Black, Needle, Mountain, Rectangular, 34 Needles
$68

Edison, Diamond Disc, Model B80, Chrome Plated Arm, Mahogany Case, 24 x 17 x 16 In.........	480
Edison, Fireside, Open Works, Oak Case Horn, 20 Cylinders, c.1905, 11 ½ x 11 ¾ x 9 In.	1000
Edison, Home, Cylinder, Oak, Brass Bell Horn, c.1902, 23 x 16 x 18 In.	1125
Edison, Home, Model B, Oak Cabinet, Cygnet Horn, Wing Type, Crank, c.1905, 16 x 10 x 12 In. .	840
Edison, Home, Oak Case, Oak Cygnet Horn, c.1915, 42 x 16 x 9 In.....................*illus*	1020
Edison, Model D, Oak Case, Painted, Horn, 4 Blue Amberol Cylinder Records	452
Edison, Model F, 12 Cylinder, Black Horn, 38 x 12 In..........................	420
Edison, Standard, Model A, Cylinder, Green Oak Case, Decal, c.1901, 11 x 12 ¾ x 8 ¾ In..........	625
Edison, Standard, Model D, Tulip Flower Horn, Golden Oak Case, 25 x 19 In. ....*illus*	496
Lakeside, Tabletop, Oak Case, Record Player, Square, c.1915, 10 x 11 ½ In.	96
Standard, Model A, Cast Iron, Painted Brass Horn, Talking Machine Co., c.1905, 12 x 20 x 8 In.	875
Standard, Model E, Tabletop, Quartersawn Oak, c.1915, 10 x 12 ½ x 16 In.	84
Standard, Style X, Oak, Paneled Tin, Gilt Rim, Front Mount Horn, c.1915, 21 x 17 x 26 In........	180
Victor Victrola, Model M, Gramophone, Oak Horn, Monarch, c.1903, 22 x 27 In.	5950
Victor Victrola, Model VV-50, Oak, Nickeled Hardware, Portable Case, c.1925, 9 x 12 x 17 In...	84
Victor Victrola, Model VV-80, Upright, Mahogany, 39 ½ In...	70
Victor Victrola, Model VV-230, Mahogany, Molded Top, Gold Wash Hardware, 37 x 38 x 23 In.	36
Victor Victrola, Model VV-330, Mahogany, Hump Back, Cabriole Legs, c.1915, 38 x 38 x 23 In.. *illus*	132
Victor Victrola, Model VV-VI, Oak, Lundstrom Converto Cabinet, c.1915, 43 x 18 In.	72
Victor Victrola, Model VV-IX, Oak, c.1915, 15 x 17 x 20 ½ In....................................	192
Victor Victrola, Model VV-XIV, Quartersawn Oak, Decal, c.1915, 47 x 21 In. ....*illus*	168
Victor Victrola, Model VV-XIX, Mahogany, Nickeled Hardware, c.1925, 45 x 21 In.	240
Victor Victrola, Model VV1-90, Mahogany, c.1950, 15 x 19 ½ x 18 In..............................	36
Victor, Credenza 13551, Jacobean Style, Mahogany, Spring Wind, 45 ½ x 31 In. ....*illus*	312
Victor, Golden Oak Case, Turntable, Metal Crank & Tone Arm, 14 ¾ x 17 x 20 ½ In.	201
Victor, Gramophone, Mahogany Case, Heco, Morning Glory Horn, 23 x 15 In............................	660
Victor, Model E, Monarch Junior, Oak Case, Black & Silver Horn, 1900s, 8 x 10 x 11 In. ....*illus*	702
Victor, Schoolhouse, Model XXV, Horn, Quartersawn Oak, Hinged Lid, 1913, 55 x 26 x 20 In. ..*illus*	4305

PHONOGRAPH NEEDLE CASES of tin are collected today by music and phonograph enthusiasts and advertising addicts. The tins are very small, about 2 inches across, and often have attractive graphic designs lithographed on the top and sides.

El Cardenal, Flecha, Bird On Branch Center, Fuchsia, Tan, Black, Square........................	33
Esta, Blue, White, Black, Bird Flying, In Shield, Rectangular........................	34
Everest, Blue Green, Yellow, Black, Needle, Mountain, Rectangular, 34 Needles..............*illus*	68
Floria, Dog, Finest Quality Gramofones Needles, Blue, Yellow, Black, England, 1 ¼ x 1 ½ In.....	218
Herold, Electro, Shimmy, Couple Dancing, Beige, Square, Original Contents	71
Marschall, Starkton-Nadeln, Orange, Gold, Flowers, Germany, Needles, Germany	36
Sem, Town, Castle, River, Multicolor, Prague, Czechoslovakia, Rectangular, 1930s	30

PHOTOGRAPHY items are listed here. The first photograph was a view from a window in France taken in 1826. The commercially successful photograph started with the daguerreotype introduced in 1839. Today all sorts of photographs and photographic equipment are collected. Albums were popular in Victorian times. Cartes de visite, popular after 1854, were mounted on 2 ½-by-4-inch cardboard. Cabinet cards were introduced in 1866. These were mounted on 4 ¼-by-6 ½-inch cards. Stereo views are listed under Stereo Card. Stereoscopes are listed in their own section.

Albumen, Confederate General Thomas Jonathan Stonewall, Boude & Miley, Frame, 11 x 13 In. ...	780
Albumen, Japanese Garden, Hand Colored, 1890s, 8 x 10 ½ In.	96
Albumen, William Swain, Whale Ship Commander, September 14, 1777, 5 x 7 In............*illus*	216
Ambrotype, 2 Railroad Workers, Lanterns, R.H. Vance, ⅙ Plate, Leather Case, 3 x 3 In.	780
Ambrotype, 3 Men, Playing Cards, Drinking Whiskey, Pistol, 2 ½ x 3 In.	885
Ambrotype, Civil War Soldier & Wife, Seated, ⅙ Plate...	59
Ambrotype, Civil War Soldier, Seated, Uniform, ⅙ Plate..	142
Ambrotype, Couple, Niagara Falls, Wet Weather Clothing, Log Bench, Bridal Veil Falls.....*illus*	570
Ambrotype, Horse Drawn Carriage, Man Wearing Hat, Storefront, ¼ Plate, 3 x 4 In.	450
Ambrotype, Lehigh Valley Railroad, Train, Tracks, 10 ½ x 19 In.	18

Photography, Albumen, William Swain, Whale Ship Commander, September 14, 1777, 5 x 7 In.
$216

Cowan's Auctions

Photography, Ambrotype, Couple, Niagara Falls, Wet Weather Clothing, Log Bench, Bridal Veil Falls
$570

Cowan's Auctions

Photography, Ambrotype, Man, Pouring Whiskey, Tinted, Gold Highlights, Leatherette Case, ⅙ Plate
$780

Cowan's Auctions

PHOTOGRAPHY

Photography, Cabinet Card, Curley, Custer's Scout, D.F. Barry, West Superior, Wis.
$1,020

D. F. BARRY, WEST SUPERIOR, WIS.

Cowan's Auctions

Photography, Cabinet Card, Gold Rush, Man, Off To The Klondike, Silver Gelatin, Geo. W. Stitt, 1897
$204

Cowan's Auctions

Photography, Cabinet Card, Leaping Panther Warrior, Shoshone, Baker & Johnston
$1,560

Cowan's Auctions

Photography, Cabinet Card, Tony, American Dollar Dog, Silver Gelatin, Print, G.W. Brown, Wyoming
$60

Cowan's Auctions

Photography, Camera, Studio, Mahogany, Bellows, Brass Lens, Ross Of London, c.1880, 6 x 4 In.
$270

Thomaston Place Auction Galleries

Photography, Carte De Visite, Buffalo Bill, Stamped, Reverse, Warren, Boston
$240

Cowan's Auctions

Photography, Daguerreotype, Postmortem, Man, Bearded, Pressed Paper Case, ½ Plate
$600

Cowan's Auctions

Photography, Photograph, Santa & Girl In Sleigh, Tinted, Frame, 12 x 17 In.
$180

Morphy Auctions

350

Ambrotype, Man, Pouring Whiskey, Tinted, Gold Highlights, Leatherette Case, ⅙ Plate ...*illus*	780
Ambrotype, Union First Lieutenant, Solemn Looking, Union Case, ¼ Plate	330
Cabinet Card, 2 Cowboys, Full Dress, Hats, 3 Indian Women, Child, Ollason Studio	1722
Cabinet Card, American Horse, Oglala Sioux, Headdress, Blanket, L.W. Stilwell, Deadwood, S.D.	270
Cabinet Card, Curley, Custer's Scout, D.F. Barry, West Superior, Wis. ....*illus*	1020
Cabinet Card, Gold Rush, Man, Off To The Klondike, Silver Gelatin, Geo. W. Stitt, 1897 ...*illus*	204
Cabinet Card, Leaping Panther Warrior, Shoshone, Baker & Johnston.........................*illus*	1560
Cabinet Card, Quanah Parker, Comanche Chief, Wife, Tonacy, Sink, Vernon, Texas	1560
Cabinet Card, Silver Gelatin, Rowing, Regatta, Bermuda, Richardson & Astwood, 1898	84
Cabinet Card, Sitting Bull, Hunkpapa Sioux Chief, Standing, Studio Setting, D.F. Barry, 1880	840
Cabinet Card, Tony, American Dollar Dog, Silver Gelatin, Print, G.W. Brown, Wyoming...*illus*	60
Cabinet Card, William Gladstone, British Prime Minster, In Chair, Grandson On His Lap	60
Cabinet Card, Young Girl, With Only 1 Leg, Standing Next To Bench, Kansas, 1870	54
Camera, Daguerreotype, Brown, Wood, Gilt, 1845, 7 x 13 x 6 ½ In.	3540
Camera, Hasselblad, 503CW, Prism Finder, Carl Zeiss Lens	2640
Camera, Kodak, Century Studio, Adjustable Stand, Cast Iron Base, 15 x 24 x 20 In.	1120
Camera, Studio, Mahogany, Bellows, Brass Lens, Ross Of London, c.1880, 6 x 4 In. ....*illus*	270
Camera, Zeiss Ikon Super Ikonta 533/16, Leather Case, 4 ¾ x 6 x 2 In.	259
Carte De Visite, Abner Doubleday, Brigadier General, Brady Negative, 1862	270
Carte De Visite, Abraham Lincoln, Seated At Table, Matthew Brady, c.1862	780
Carte De Visite, Amputees, Civil War Veterans, Trumpet, American Flag, S. Roden	84
Carte De Visite, Buffalo Bill, Stamped, Reverse, Warren, Boston ....*illus*	240
Carte De Visite, Col. Edmund Dana, Pennsylvania Infantry, Mathew Brady	480
Carte De Visite, Colonel Thornton Brodhead, 1st Michigan, Cavalry, Brady, New York	215
Carte De Visite, Hiram Rhodes Revels, First African-American U.S. Senator, 1870-71	584
Carte De Visite, Horse Drawn Streetcar, Welsh Train, Handwritten Ink Registry On Back, 1807	60
Carte De Visite, Interior Of Union Railroad Car, 2 Men At Cannon, Rifles Stacked At Side	1320
Carte De Visite, John Buford, Hero, Battle Of Gettysburg, 1863	360
Carte De Visite, P.T. Barnum's General Tom Thumb, Wife, Child, 1860s	36
Carte De Visite, Sam Houston, Suit, Bowtie, Cane On His Left, Bust Length, 1793-1863	510
Carte De Visite, Samuel Sturgis, Indian, Fighter, Brady, 1880s	210
Carte De Visite, Union Private, Seated, Wife Standing	431
Carte De Visite, Wesley Merritt, Cavalry General, Reserve Brigade, Gettysburg	330
Carte De Visite, West Coast First Nation, Indian Men & Women, Ottawa, James Inglis, Montreal	570
Daguerreotype, Joseph Sillman Edwards, Ohio Minister, With, Book, Standing, ½ Plate	300
Daguerreotype, Man, Holding Cigar, Bust, 4 x 3 In.	148
Daguerreotype, Militiaman, Seated, Shako, Emblazoned Henry's, 1851, ⅙ Plate	840
Daguerreotype, Postmortem, Man, Bearded, Pressed Paper Case, ½ Plate.....................*illus*	600
Daguerreotype, Woman, Seated In Chair, Leather Case, c.1840, ⅙ Plate	60
Gelatin Silver, Foggy Swamp, Signed, Titled, O.L. Gagliani, 1962s, 14 ¼ x 17 ¼ In.	333
Photograph, Christmas Tree, Big Doll, Frame, Victorian, 14 ¾ x 16 ½ In.	90
Photograph, Grand Canyon, End Of Bright Angel Trail, A.W. Dow, 1911, 13 x 10 In.	3625
Photograph, Man Holding Musket, Art Nouveau Style Oval Frame, 19 x 9 In.	189
Photograph, Platinum, Cherokee Chief Two Bulls, J.E. Watson, Mounted, Mat, c.1890, 10 x 13 In.	215
Photograph, Portrait, Family, Christmas Tree, Frame, 11 ¾ x 9 ¾ In.	160
Photograph, Santa & Girl In Sleigh, Tinted, Frame, 12 x 17 In. ....*illus*	180
Photograph, Santa, Children, Filling Stockings, Frame, 13 ¾ x 10 ¾ In.	90
Photograph, Yale College Track Team, 10 Young Men, 2 Older Men, Frame, 1926, 27 x 23 In.. *illus*	180
Photogravure, Woman, Iguanas, Verso, Pencil, Signed, G. Iturbide, Mexico, 29 ¾ x 25 In.	633
Platinum Print, Abraham Lincoln, Ayres, Hesler Negative, 1881, 18 ½ x 21 ½ In.	1680
Platinum Print, Abraham Lincoln, Seated, Moses P. Rice, Gardner Negative, 1863, 17 x 21 In..	3120
Silver Gelatin Print, Buffalo Bill, On Horseback, Arena Show, Regalia, 5 ½ x 8 In.	185
Silver Gelatin Print, Juan Pecheco, San Filipi Man, Blindstamp, Verso, 1914, 6 x 9 In.	300
Silver Gelatin Print, Only North American Red Indians Ever At Lands End, 1904, 5 ¾ x 8 In.	360
Silver Print, Buffalo Bill, Young Fan, Mat, Webster & Stevens, Seattle, 10 x 12 In............*illus*	600
Tintype, Black Woman, Standing, Bonnet, Striped Shawl, 3 ¼ x 4 ¼ In.	540
Tintype, Boys, Girls, Young Woman, Class, Outdoor, Building, Tree, 12 ½ x 14 ½ In.	390
Tintype, Civil War Soldier, Seated, Uniform, Studio, Oval Casing, ⅑ Plate	224
Tintype, Class, Boys, Girls, Woman, Outdoor, Building, Tree, Frame, 12 ½ x 14 ½ In.	390
Tintype, Geo. W. Butler, Sea Captain, Holding Octant, Tinted, Civil War Era	120

Photography, Photograph, Yale College Track Team, 10 Young Men, 2 Older Men, Frame, 1926, 27 x 23 In.
$180

Cowan's Auctions

TIP

Do not use photo albums with plastic or black paper pages. These will damage the photos in time.

Photography, Silver Print, Buffalo Bill, Young Fan, Mat, Webster & Stevens, Seattle, 10 x 12 In.
$600

Cowan's Auctions

P

Piano Baby, Girl, Sitting, Butterfly On Leg, Bisque, c.1800s, 9 ¾ In.
$96

Garth's Auctioneers & Appraisers

Picture, Memorial, Lady Buxton, Daguerreotype In Tin Foil Wreath, Frame, c.1850, 21 In.
$123

Bunch Auctions

Picture, Mourning, Weaving, Human Hair, Tomb, Cross, Willow, Frame, Victorian, 9 x 10 In.
$345

Bunch Auctions

Picture, Needlework, Children, Animals, Roses, Vignettes, Gilt Gesso, Malvina Bates, 1862, 30 x 33 In.
$1,046

Skinner, Inc.

Picture, Needlework, Embroidery, Silk, Basket Of Fruit, Birds & Flowers, Frame
$222

Nadeau's Auction Gallery

Picture, Needlework, Watercolor, Silk, Weeping Woman, Ann Clap, Frame, 1807, 17 x 12 In.
$9,600

Eldred's

Picture, Needlework, White Rose, Butterfly, Maple Frame, Signed, 1835, 7 ¼ x 5 ¼ In.
$263

Thomaston Place Auction Galleries

Picture, Needlework, Woman, Riding Sidesaddle, Buckram Ground, Regency Style, 1800s, 18 x 21 In.
$132

Thomaston Place Auction Galleries

Picture, Pastel, Dog Pulling Drape Cord, American School, Frame, 1800s, 10 x 7 ½ In.
$300

Eldred's

Picture, Scherenschnitte, Heart, Vines, Presentation, Jointed Rabbet Frame, 15 ½ x 15 In.
$708

Hess Auction Group

P

Tintype, Soldier, Standing Pose, Uniform, Thermoplastic Case..	165
Tintype, Union Cavalryman, 1860 Army Revolver, Half Pressed, Paper Case, 2¾ x 3¼ In.	390

PIANO BABY is a collector's term. About 1880, the well-decorated home had a shawl on the piano. Bisque figures of babies were designed to help hold the shawl in place. They usually range in size from 6 to 18 inches. Most of the figures were made in Germany. Reproductions are being made. Other piano babies may be listed under manufacturers' names.

Baby, Kicking, Fussy, Open Mouth, Crawling, Bisque, 4½ x 2 In..	133
Baby, Sitting, Blond, Spiked Hair, Seated, Raised Arm, New Year's Jan. Wrist Band, 4½ In.......	35
Baby, Sitting, Cross Legged, Holding Bottle, Ruffle, Gold Beads, 3¾ In.	100
Baby, Sitting, Holding Blanket On Tummy, Dog, Pacifier, Germany, 1800s, 8½ In.	219
Baby, Sitting, Pink Hat, Blue Bow, Holding Velveteen Rabbit Toy, Germany, 6½ x 4½ In........	75
Boy, Feet In Air, Blond, Romper, Hands On Chin, Hertwig, 2½ In.	38
Boy, Seated, Cuddling Puppy, Holding Glass, 4 In..	85
Boy, Seated, Reading Book, Blue Romper, 4¼ In..	38
Boy, Seated, Shirt Off Shoulders, Side-Glancing Eyes, Gebruder Heubach, 5 In.	175
Boy, Sitting, Pacifier, 1 Sock, Germany, 6 x 5 In.	425
Boy, Standing, Nude, Hands On Hip, Wool Hat, 5 In.	175
Girl, Crawling, Head Up, Blue Collar, Ponytail, Bow, 4 In.	199
Girl, Curly Hair, Tied Up In Cloth, Bow, Raised Gold Dots, Lavender, 5 x 3 x 3 In....................	60
Girl, On Back, Holding Toes, Blond, Gebruder Heubach, 5¾ In.	69
Girl, Shy, Ribbon Bonnet, Ladybug On Knee, 6 In.	225
Girl, Sitting, Butterfly On Leg, Bisque, c.1800s, 9¾ In. ....*illus*	96
Girl, Sitting, Pink Dress, Bow In Hair, Ball, Hand On Cheek, Bisque, 5 In.	45

PICKARD China Company was started in 1893 by Wilder Pickard. Hand-painted designs were used on china purchased from other sources. In the 1930s, the company began to make its own china wares in Chicago, Illinois. The company made a line of limited edition plates and bowls in the 1970s and 1980s. It now makes many types of porcelains.

Pickard/Edgerton Art Studio	Pickard/Pickard Studios, Inc.	Pickard, Inc.
1893–1894	1925–1930	1938–present

Cup & Saucer, 22K Gold, Encrusted, Rosenthal, Ivory, 3 x 2¼ In., 2 Piece..............................	31
Milk Pitcher, Strawberries, Gold Trim, Signed Leroy, c.1903, 5 x 5½ In.................................	187
Plate, Leaf Shape, Cherries, Branches, Leaves, Gold Trim, 6¾ x 6 In.	180
Tea Set, Teapot, Sugar & Creamer, Grapes, Leaves, Flowers, Gilt, c.1950, 3 Piece......................	250
Vase, Red Roses, Yellow Ground, Parcel Gilt, Signed, Limoges, France Stamp, c.1905, 12 In......	2125

PICTURES, silhouettes, and other small decorative objects framed to hang on the wall are listed here. Some other types of pictures are listed in the Print and Painting categories.

Calligraphy, Patriotic, 3 Gentleman, Molded Giltwood Frame, G.N. Eckert, 1800s, 10 x 15 In..	738
Diorama, Children In Nursery, Shadowbox, Oval Gold Frame, Rose Handles, c.1890, 25 In.	460
Diorama, Ship, 3-Masted, Cloudy Sky, Wood, Paint, Paper, Frame, 19 x 28 x 5½ In.	720
Drawing, Prodigal Son, Bistre Pen & Wash, Jacques Callot, 1700s, 2¾ x 4 In.	620
Drawing, Study Of Bull, Graphite, European School, 1800s, 15¾ x 19 In.	24
Engraving, Palace Of Monte Alto-Napoli, Italy, Gold Frame, 1700s, 6½ x 8 In.	35
Etching, Ducks In Flight, Signed, Roland Clark, 16½ x 13¼ In.	151
Lithograph, Dewey's Victory, Naval Battle, National Publishing Co., Frame, c.1800, 24 x 34 In..	54
Memorial, Lady Buxton, Daguerreotype In Tin Foil Wreath, Frame, c.1850, 21 In............*illus*	123
Miniature, Man, Signed, Count D Clermons, Brass Frame, Zippered Pouch, 2½ In....................	92
Miniature, Portrait, Woman With Crown, Gutta Percha Case, Continental, 1800s, 3 x 2½ In. ..	118
Miniature, Young Man, Oval, Brass Frame, Signed, Anton Weissenfeld, Early 1800s, 3 x 2 In..	270

Picture, Watercolor, Pen & Ink On Paper, Adam & Eve, Apple Tree, Frame, c.1850, 13 x 11 In.
$960

Garth's Auctioneers & Appraisers

Pillin, Vase, Plum Colored Glaze, Glossy, Signed, W&P Pillin, Late 1900s, 9 x 5 In.
$311

Soulis Auctions

Pillin, Vase, Portrait, Woman, Horse, Rooster, Greens, Blues, Pink Band, Signed, 1900s, 4 In.
$250

Neal Auction Company

Pincushion Doll, Girl's Head, Bisque, Glass Eyes, Painted Face, Cardboard Base, Germany, 7 x 6 x 5 In.
$102

Soulis Auctions

Pipe, Carved, Painted & Stained Wood Handle, Custom Stand, 1900s, 10 x 18 x 6 In.
$563

Rago Arts and Auction Center

Pipe, Meerschaum, Hunter, 2-Barrel Shotgun, Wood Case, Leather Cover, 9 x 3 ½ In.
$165

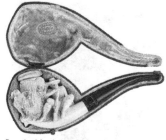

Forsythes' Auctions

Mourning, Watercolor, Men, Women, Children, Black Crepe Draped Urn, Trees, 1800s, 18 x 14 In...	2460
Mourning, Watercolor, Weeping Woman, Cory Family, Obelisks, Arcade, c.1802, 14 x 16 ½ In.	435
Mourning, Watercolor, Weeping Woman, Urn, Jabez Hatch Weld, c.1824, 16 ½ x 16 ½ In.	581
Mourning, Weaving, Human Hair, Tomb, Cross, Willow, Frame, Victorian, 9 x 10 In........*illus*	345
Needlework, 2 Women, Cat, Silk, Rural Scene, Molded Gilt Gesso Frame, 1800s, 5 ½ In.	308
Needlework, Biblical Scene, Black Frame, England, 1700s, 18 ½ x 14 ½ In..............................	400
Needlework, Children, Animals, Roses, Vignettes, Gilt Gesso, Malvina Bates, 1862, 30 x 33 In...*illus*	1046
Needlework, Dragonfly, Fruit, Oval, Gilt & Beaded Frame, 1800s, 9 ¼ x 7 ¼ In.	123
Needlework, Eagle, Shield, E Pluribus Unum, Silver Bullion, Frame, c.1898, 23 x 25 In.	156
Needlework, Embroidery, 2 Young Children In Forest, Silk, Linen, Oval Walnut Frame, c.1820, 13 In.	518
Needlework, Embroidery, Silk, Basket Of Fruit, Birds & Flowers, Frame.................................*illus*	222
Needlework, Watercolor, Silk, Weeping Woman, Ann Clap, Frame, 1807, 17 x 12 In.........*illus*	9600
Needlework, Watercolor, Silk, Woman, Sheep, House, Trees, Frame, Oval Window, 18 In.	570
Needlework, White Rose, Butterfly, Maple Frame, Signed, 1835, 7 ¼ x 5 ¼ In. ....*illus*	263
Needlework, Woman, Riding Sidesaddle, Buckram Ground, Regency Style, 1800s, 18 x 21 In..*illus*	132
Pastel, Damned, Condenado, Paper, Signed, John Valadez, Mexico, 1986, 75 x 59 ½ In.	2420
Pastel, Dog Pulling Drape Cord, American School, Frame, 1800s, 10 x 7 ½ In..................*illus*	300
Pastel, Resblando, Paper, Signed, John Valadez, Mexico, 1989, 68 x 32 In.......................	1210
Pen & Ink, Sailing Ship Carron, 3-Masted, England, Frame, 1800s, 24 ¾ x 31 ½ In.	54
Pencil, Bucolic Scene, Half Dormered House, Stream, Cows, Boaters, c.1850, 23 x 32 In.	108
Portrait, George Washington, Medallion, Transfer, Frame, c.1850, 3 ½ x 2 ½ In.	397
Portrait, Young Man, Oval, Giltwood Frame, Flemish Style, Late 1800s, 7 ½ x 6 In.	120
Scherenschnitte, Heart, Vines, Presentation, Jointed Rabbet Frame, 15 ½ x 15 In. ....*illus*	708
Serigraph, Marilyn, Acrylic, Signed, Steve Kaufman, 19 x 18 ½ In...............................	424
Serigraph, Waiting On Line, 3-D, Pencil, Signed, J. Rizzi, 1986, 4 ½ x 12 ½ In.................	127
Silhouette, 2 Families In Parlor, 9 Figures, Dog, A. Edouart, 1840, Frame, 15 x 35 In..............	6875
Silhouette, Hollow Cut, Watercolor, White Ruffle Collar, Gilt Molded Frame, 1800s, 4 x 3 In. ..	584
Silhouette, Mrs. Emma R. Adam & Children, Auguste Edouart, Frame, 10 x 14 In..................	1250
Silhouette, Susannah Willes Holyoake, Spinning Wheel, Frame, Auguste Edouart, 11 x 7 In...	6000
Theorem, Watercolor, On Paper, Fruit In Footed Bowl, Mica Flakes, 1800s, 16 x 20 In............	1200
Theorem, Watercolor, On Velvet, Fruit On Tray, Grain Painted Frame, 23 x 26 In.................	3360
Watercolor & Crayon, Woman, Portrait, Parrot, Emily Eastman, Gilt Frame, 1800s, 17 x 15 In.	3321
Watercolor & Pencil, Family Record, Man, Burrell-Pratt, Frame, c.1836, 14 ¾ x 12 ⅜ In........	2613
Watercolor, Matador, Man, Signed, L. Roma, Italy, 1800s, 29 x 20 ¼ In.	369
Watercolor, On Ivory, Woman In Black Dress, Black Lacquer Frame, Early 1800s, 2 ¾ x 2 ¼ In.	1169
Watercolor, Pen & Ink On Paper, Adam & Eve, Apple Tree, Frame, c.1850, 13 x 11 In........*illus*	960
Watercolor, Portrait, Woman, Side View, Rufus Porter, Gilt Molded Frame, 4 x 3 In.................	4613
Watercolor, River Scene, Sailboats, W.E. McDougall, 1893, 10 x 14 In.	88
Watercolor, Sherlock Holmes, Dr. Watson, Douglas, Silver Frame, 25 x 17 ½ In.	148
Watercolor, Ship Sailing, Signed, Sandor Bernath, Frame, 17 x 19 ½ In.	266
Watercolor, Woman, Dress, Red & Black Check Necktie, F.W. Fox, Frame, 1824, 8 x 6 In..........	180

PICTURE FRAMES *are listed in this book in the Furniture category under Frame.*

PIERCE, *see Howard Pierce category.*

PILKINGTON TILE AND POTTERY COMPANY was established in 1892 in England. The company made small pottery wares, like buttons and hatpins, but soon started decorating vases purchased from other potteries. By 1903, the company had discovered an opalescent glaze that became popular on the Lancastrian pottery line. The manufacture of pottery ended in 1937. Pilkington is still making tiles.

Vase, 4 Fish, Shades Of Gold, Rose, Purple, Black, Marked, 1910, 7 ⅝ In.	767
Vase, Gold Paint, Lusterware, Royal Lancastrian, William S. Mycock, c.1920, 8 In....................	438

W + P
Pillin

PILLIN pottery was made by Polia (1909–1992) and William (1910–1985) Pillin, who set up a pottery in Los Angeles in 1948. William shaped, glazed, and fired the clay, and Polia painted the pieces, often with elongated figures of women, children, flowers, birds, fish, and other animals. The company closed in 2014. Pieces are marked with a stylized Pillin signature.

Vase, Plum Colored Glaze, Glossy, Signed, W&P Pillin, Late 1900s, 9 x 5 In.......................*illus*	311
Vase, Portrait, Woman, Horse, Rooster, Greens, Blues, Pink Band, Signed, 1900s, 4 In.......*illus*	250

PINCUSHION DOLLS are not really dolls and often were not even pincushions. Some collectors use the term "half-doll." The top half of each doll was made of porcelain. The edge of the half-doll was made with several small holes for thread, and the doll was stitched to a fabric body with a voluminous skirt. The finished figure was used to cover a hot pot of tea, powder box, pincushion, whiskbroom, or lamp. They were made in sizes from less than an inch to over 9 inches high. Most date from the early 1900s to the 1950s. Collectors often find just the porcelain doll without the fabric skirt.

Girl's Head, Bisque, Glass Eyes, Painted Face, Cardboard Base, Germany, 7 x 6 x 5 In.......*illus*	102
Woman, Bisque, Shoulder Head, Sculpted Hair, Dresden Coronet Garland, Germany, 6 In.......	1725
Woman, Porcelain, Pink Tinted Cheeks, Brown Eyes, Black Curls, Germany, c.1860, 6 In.	748

PINK SLAG *pieces are listed in this book in the Slag Glass category.*

PIPES have been popular since tobacco was introduced to Europe. Carved wood, porcelain, ivory, and glass pipes and accessories may be listed here.

Bamboo, Portrait, Henry Clay, 1840s, 21 x 3 In...	145
Bone, Carved, 4 Naughty Scenes, Wooden Bowl Ends, 22 In..	92
Burl, Horn Stem, German Silver Cap, John Boyd, Civil War Cavalryman, 1860s, 5 x 10 In.	236
Carved, Painted & Stained Wood Handle, Custom Stand, 1900s, 10 x 18 x 6 In.................*illus*	563
Ivory, Carved, 2 Elephants, Trunks Up, 6 In...	115
Meerschaum, Cheroot, Figural, Clown, Ruffled Collar, Camera, Carved, Holder, Case, 4¼ In.	172
Meerschaum, Figural, Nude Woman, Standing, Carved, 5¾ In.	308
Meerschaum, Horse's Head, Leather & Wood Stand, Signed, I. Bekler	245
Meerschaum, Hunter, 2-Barrel Shotgun, Wood Case, Leather Cover, 9 x 3½ In...............*illus*	165
Opium, Dragon Shape, Ball In Mouth, Enamel, Silver, Shaped Case, 7 In.................................	488
Wood, Battle Of Camden, Civil War, Laurel Foot, Eagle, Shield, 1862, 2½ x 3½ x 1½ In.	1680
Wood, Carved, Laurel Root, Civil War, Crossed Flags, Frederick, Va., 1862, 3 x 2½ x 1½ In.	3000
Wood, Inscribed, Rob't Welch, 165th Reg't, Geometric Patterns, c.1865, 1¾ x 1¼ In........*illus*	420

PIRKENHAMMER is a porcelain manufactory started in 1803 by Friedrich Holke and J. G. List. It was located in Bohemia, now Brezova, Czech Republic. The company made tablewares usually decorated with views and flowers. Lithophanes were also made. It became Manufaktura Pirkenhammer I.S. Original Porcelan Fabrik Brezova s.r.o. in 2002. The mark of the crossed hammers is easy to remember as the Pirkenhammer symbol.

Pirkenhammer Austria

Figurine, Nude Woman, Kneeling, Arms On Head, White, 1900s, 7 x 4 In................................	75
Vase, Dragon Shape Handles, Perched Birds, Branches, Crossed Hammers, 23 In., Pair............	2125
Vase, Triangular, Cherubs, Clouds, Blue Sky, Leaves, Footed, 5¼ x 13 In.	125

PISGAH FOREST POTTERY was made in North Carolina beginning in 1926. The pottery was started by Walter B. Stephen, who had been making pottery in that location since 1914. The pottery continued in operation after his death in 1961. The most famous Pisgah Forest wares are the turquoise crackle glaze wares and the cameo type with designs made of raised glaze.

Pisgah Forest Pottery
1926+

Pisgah Forest Pottery
Late 1940s

Pisgah Forest Pottery
1961+

Vase, Buffalo Hunt Scene, Cream Glaze, Inscribed, W.B. Stephen, Early 1930s, 9½ In.	2500

Pipe, Wood, Inscribed, Rob't Welch, 165th Reg't, Geometric Patterns, c.1865, 1¾ x 1¼ In.
$420

Cowan's Auctions

Planters Peanuts, Costume, Mr. Peanut, Peephole At Center Of Body, 1960s, 48 In.
$443

Milestone Auctions

Planters Peanuts, Display, Planters Best Peanut 5 Cent Bar, Tin Lithograph, Countertop, 1920s, 12 x 4 In.
$2,714

Wm Morford Auctions

P

Planters Peanuts, Pin, Figural, Lucky Mr. Peanut, Hand On Waist, Cream Ground, 1940s, 2⅝ In.
$38

sadl-ethe on eBay

Planters Peanuts, Tin, Planters Nut & Chocolate Co., Clean Crisp Salted Peanuts, Store Tin, 10 Lb., 10 In.
$366

AntiqueAdvertising.com

Plastic, Poker Chip Holder, Bakelite, Catalin Swirled, Plastic Chips, 1940s, 2¼ x 2½ In.
$17

collegeboy14 on eBay

 PLANTERS PEANUTS memorabilia are collected. Planters Nut and Chocolate Company was started in Wilkes-Barre, Pennsylvania, in 1906. The Mr. Peanut figure was adopted as a trademark in 1916. National advertising for Planters Peanuts started in 1918. The company was acquired by Standard Brands, Inc., in 1961. Standard Brands merged with Nabisco in 1981. Nabisco was bought by Kraft Foods in 2000. Kraft merged with H.J. Heinz Company in 2015. Planters brand is now owned by Kraft Heinz. Some of the Mr. Peanut jars and other memorabilia have been reproduced and, of course, new items are being made.

Bank, Figural, Mr. Peanut, Standing, Cane, Red, Plastic, Round Base, 8½ In.	12
Bookmark, Greetings From Mr. Peanut, Yellow, Black, Cardboard, 3 In.	32
Container, Peanut Shape, Embossed Planters, Papier-Mache, 9 In.	37
Costume, Mr. Peanut, Peephole At Center Of Body, 1960s, 48 In. *illus*	443
Display, Planters Best Peanut 5 Cent Bar, Tin Lithograph, Countertop, 1920s, 12 x 4 In. *illus*	2714
Jar, Display, Clear Glass, Embossed, Lid, Peanut Finial, 13 In.	47
Jar, Display, Lid, Pressed Glass, Peanuts Design, Pennant, Octagonal Finial, 1940s, 12 x 7 In.	30
Nut Dish, Figural Mr. Peanut, Standing In Center, Engraved Planters Peanuts, Goldtone	63
Pin, Figural, Lucky Mr. Peanut, Hand On Waist, Cream Ground, 1940s, 2⅝ In. *illus*	38
Sign, Planters Peanuts, After School, Mr. Peanut, Metal, Brace Mount, Round, 4 x 2½ In.	133
Tin, Pennant, Green, Red, Black, Lithograph, Nut Can, 10 Lb., 10 In.	89
Tin, Planters Nut & Chocolate Co., Clean Crisp Salted Peanuts, Store Tin, 10 Lb., 10 In. *illus*	366
Whistle, Figural, Mr. Peanut, Dark Blue, Plastic, Hand On Waist, 2½ In.	86

 PLASTIC objects of all types are being collected. Some pieces are listed in other categories; gutta-percha cases are listed in the Photography category. Celluloid is in its own category.

Creamer, Red & White, Mini Pitcher, Tableware, Moline Tractor, 2½ x 2⅞ In.	45
Hatpin, Bakelite, Marbled, Jester's Cap Shape, c.1920, 2¾ In.	70
Ice Bucket, Drum, 1st Battalion Seaforth Highlanders, 2½ Pt., 6½ x 5¾ In.	22
Lamp Base, Lucite, Geometric, Electric, Signed, Van Teal, 30 x 7 x 5 In.	144
Poker Chip Holder, Bakelite, Catalin Swirled, Plastic Chips, 1940s, 2¼ x 2½ In. *illus*	17
Salt & Pepper, Globular, Swirled Ribbing, c.1930	55
Sculpture, Lucite, 2 Opposing Pieces, Curved, Beveled, Van Teal, Signed, 24¾ x 24 x 17 In.	2070
Tray, Card Holder, No. 30, Maroon, Holds 2 Decks, Nu-Dell, 1950s	9

 PLATED AMBERINA was patented June 15, 1886, by Joseph Locke and made by the New England Glass Company. It is similar in color to amberina, but is characterized by a cream colored or chartreuse lining (never white) and small ridges or ribs on the outside.

Celery Vase, Pinched Waist, Mahogany To Custard, Ribbing, Opal, 3¾ x 6⅜ In. *illus*	1170
Creamer, Opal Cased, Red To Cream, Ribbed, Amber Handle, c.1886, 2 x 3¼ In.	2614
Pitcher, Red To Cream, Lobed, Amber Handle, Ruffled Mouth, 5 In.	5227
Vase, Lily, Opal Cased, Ribbed, 1886, 3¾ x 3 In.	2460

 PLIQUE-A-JOUR is an enameling process. The enamel is laid between thin raised metal lines and heated. The finished piece has transparent enamel held between the thin metal wires. It is different from cloisonne because it is translucent.

Case, Pheasant, Parrot, Dragonfly, Geometric Border, Ovchinnikov, 4 x 3 In.	2816
Glass Holder, Gadrooned Rim, Flowers, Leaves, Pavel Ovchinnikov, c.1887, 3¼ x 5 In.	3840
Salt Cellar, Chair Shape, Birds, Leaves, Hinged Seat, Gavril Grachev, 2¾ x 2¾ In.	3328
Tea Strainer, Pierced Bowl, Green Leaves, Norway, 4¾ In.	192
Tray, Oval, Leaves, Geometric Patterns, Katherine The Great Coin, Beaded Rim, 10 x 7 In.	6080
Vase, Bud, Green Field, Chrome Base, Top Rim, Flowers, c.1850, 5 In.	96

 POLITICAL memorabilia of all types, from buttons to banners, are collected. Items related to presidential candidates are the most popular, but collectors also search for material related to state and local offices. Memorabilia related to social causes, minor political parties, and protest movements are also included here. Many reproductions have

P

been made. A jugate is a button with photographs of both the presidential and vice presidential candidates. In this list a button is round, usually with a straight pin or metal tab to secure it to a shirt. A pin is brass, often figural, sometimes attached to a ribbon.

Badge, Clinton, Gore, D.C. Metro Police, Bastian Bros., 1993, 2¼ x 2½ In.	173
Badge, Lyndon B. Johnson, Asst. Doorkeeper, Yellow Ribbon, 1964, 2 x 3 In.	64
Badge, McKinley, Col. Wm. A. Stone, Sepia Button, Portrait, Metal Frame, 1¼ In.	118
Ballot, Greeley, Brown, Constitution & Union, Blank Back, Horizontal Fold, 3¾ x 5¾ In.	118
Bandanna, Cleveland, Stevenson, Jugate, Public Office Is A Public Trust, 13 x 14 In. ....*illus*	118
Banner, Franklin Roosevelt, Gallant Leader, Wood Bar At Top, Perskie, 38 x 59 In.	260
Banner, Union Makes Us Strong, Graphic Of Worker, Sledge Hammer, Ax, Felt, 23 x 38 In.	292
Button, Bryan, Clock Face, Baltimore Badge Co., 1¼ In. ....*illus*	571
Button, Jesse Jackson 88, Pinback, 1988, 1½ In.	8
Button, McKinley & Roosevelt, Jugate, 1900, 1¾ In.	140
Button, McKinley, Protection, Expansion, Prosperity, 1¼ In. ....*illus*	355
Button, Mechanical, McKinley, Bryan, Sure Winner, 1896, 1¼ In. ....*illus*	247
Button, Parker, Davis, Portrait, Sepia Tone Photo, Metal Back, Bar Pin, Oval, 1⅜ In.	118
Button, Rutherford B. Hayes, William A. Wheeler, Pinback, 1 In.	335
Button, Uncle Sam, I Am Proud He Is My Uncle, Red Stars On Hat, 1940, 1¼ In.	30
Cabinet Card, Benjamin Harrison, c.1888, 4¼ x 6½ In.	95
Campaign Ribbon, Governor Andrew G. Curtin, Soldier's Friend, Silk, Long, Pa., 1863, 6 In. .	260
Campaign Ribbon, Harrison, Tyler, Banner, Silk, Small Log Cabin, 1840, 7 In.	275
Cane, Parade, Parker, Davis, Jugate, Wood, Applied Paper, c.1904, 34½ In.	118
Cane, William McKinley, Figural Bust, Shield, 1896, 36 In.	260
Cap, Parade, Bryan, Stevenson, Torchlight, Brown, Silver Ink Text, 2¾ x 6 In.	649
Card, Mechanical, Van Buren, Ugly Mug, Log Cabin, Hard Cider, 1840, 3¼ x 5 In.	207
Chair, House Of Representatives, Oak, Leather Back, Seat, Arms, Bembe & Kimbel, c.1857, 43 In. ..*illus*	11520
Cigar Case, Henry Clay, American Statesman, 1844, 2¾ x 5½ x ⅜ In.	1521
Clock, Roosevelt, F.D.R., Man Of The Hour, Ship Of State, United Electric, c.1935, 15 In. .....*illus*	120
Ferrotype, Breckinridge, Lane, Bulbous Copper Shell, Portrait, 1860, 1³⁄₁₆ In. ....*illus*	1298
Ferrotype, Grant, 3 Cutout Color Accent Stars, Oval Rings, Brass Frame, 1868, 1¹⁄₁₆ In.	318
Figure, Elephant, Coolidge, Dawes, Heavy Cast Metal, 1924, 1½ x 3½ In.	584
Flag, McKinley, Portrait, Patriotism, Protection & Prosperity, Silk, Frame, 1896, 15 x 21 In.	454
Hanger, William H. Taft, Portrait, Medallion, Brass, Links, c.1908, 2¼ x 2½ In.	118
Hat, Campaign, Harrison, Reid, Tall Felt Top, Ribbon Hatband, 1892, 7 In.	143
Hat, Kepi, Parade, Taft, Sherman, Felt, Cardboard Bill, Leon Rowe, Child's, 2 x 6 x 7 In. ....*illus*	357
Hat, Parade, Captain's, Cleveland & Hendricks, Felt, Glossy Coat Brim, 4 x 8¾ x 9¼ In.	325
Lamp, Harrison, Kerosene, Fluted Top, Chimney, Oak Leaves & Acorns, 1888, 6 x 13 In. ..	363
Match Safe, Benjamin Harrison, Figural, 2-Sided, Silver Plate, Pushbutton, 3 x 5 In. ....*illus*	236
Medal, Henry Clay Dewitt, Portrait, White Metal, 1844-46, 1⅝ x ¼ In.	452
Medal, Lincoln, Freedom To All Men, White Metal, Portrait, 1864, 1¼ In.	521
Mug, Republican, Elephant, Light Gray, White Sand, Marked GOP, 1996, 4 In.	18
Pail, Dinner, McKinley, Roosevelt, Jugate, Slogan, Wood, Scroll Handle, 1900, 4 In.	344
Pamphlet, Wilson Helped The Jews, Portrait, Paper, Yiddish, 5¾ x 8½ In.	1493
Parade Torch, Kerosene, Glass Ball, Metal Mount, Swivel, c.1880, 4 x 4 x 4 In.	175
Pennant, Keep Cool-Idge, Sewn Letters, Calvin Coolidge, 1924, 25 In.	234
Pennant, Taft, Portrait, Masonic Emblem, Flags, Vertical Format, 14 x 30 In.	326
Pennant, William J. Bryan, Our Choice, For President, Green, 1908, 11¼ In.	173
Pin, Bryan, Silver Bug, Mechanical, Photo, 1¼ x 1½ In. ....*illus*	270
Pin, Harrison & Reform, Hard Cider, Sulphide, Brass Frame, 1840, ¾ x ⅞ In. ....*illus*	552
Pin, Hoover, Portrait, American Flag, Lapel, Brass Frame, 1⅛ x 1½ In.	265
Pin, Kennedy, Campaign, Flicker Flasher, Kennedy For A Better America, 1968, 2½ In.	44
Plaque, E.V. Debs, Wood, Bronze Portrait, Metal Products Mfg. Co. Inc., N.Y., 7 In. ....*illus*	975
Postcard, Bobby Kennedy, 1968	7
Poster, Cox, Roosevelt, Paper, Con. P. Curran Printing Co., St. Louis, 1920, 16 x 20 In.	430
Poster, Dewey, Vote For My Delegates, Cardboard, Milwaukee 59, 14 x 22 In. ....*illus*	118
Poster, Forward With Roosevelt, Thin Paper, Stoic Portrait Of FDR, 13¾ x 21½ In. ....*illus*	162
Poster, Ike For President, Taft For Governor, Portraits, Cardboard, c.1952, 17 x 22 In.	118
Poster, James Cox, Peace, Progress, Prosperity, Campaign, Ohio, 1920, 14 x 21 In.	472
Print, Lincoln, Grave Of The Union, Bromley & Co., 1864, 17½ x 23 In.	1201

Plated Amberina, Celery Vase, Pinched Waist, Mahogany To Custard, Ribbing, Opal, 3¾ x 6⅜ In.
$1,170

Cordier Auctions

Political, Bandanna, Cleveland, Stevenson, Jugate, Public Office Is A Public Trust, 13 x 14 In.
$118

Hake's Auctions

Political, Button, Bryan, Clock Face, Baltimore Badge Co., 1¼ In.
$571

Hake's Auctions

P

POLITICAL

Political, Button, McKinley, Protection, Expansion, Prosperity, 1 ¼ In.
$355

Hake's Auctions

Political, Button, Mechanical, McKinley, Bryan, Sure Winner, 1896, 1 ¼ In.
$247

Hake's Auctions

Political, Chair, House Of Representatives, Oak, Leather Back, Seat, Arms, Bembe & Kimbel, c.1857, 43 In.
$11,520

Neal Auction Company

Political, Clock, Roosevelt, F.D.R., Man Of The Hour, Ship Of State, United Electric, c.1935, 15 In.
$120

Selkirk Auctioneers & Appraisers

Political, Ferrotype, Breckinridge, Lane, Bulbous Copper Shell, Portrait, 1860, 1 ³⁄₁₆ In.
$1,298

Hake's Auctions

Political, Hat, Kepi, Parade, Taft, Sherman, Felt, Cardboard Bill, Leon Rowe, Child's, 2 x 6 x 7 In.
$357

Hake's Auctions

Political, Match Safe, Benjamin Harrison, Figural, 2-Sided, Silver Plate, Pushbutton, 3 x 5 In.
$236

Hake's Auctions

Political, Pin, Bryan, Silver Bug, Mechanical, Photo, 1 ¼ x 1 ½ In.
$270

Hake's Auctions

Political, Pin, Harrison & Reform, Hard Cider, Sulphide, Brass Frame, 1840, ¾ x ⅞ In.
$552

Hake's Auctions

P

Ribbon, Harrison, Morton, Jugate, Raccoon Holding American Flag, Silk, c.1888, 9 In.		118
Ribbon, Henry Clay, Harry Of The West, Silk, Portrait, 1844, 6½ In.		443
Ribbon, Henry Clay, Pride Of America, Silk, Perche Eagle Motif, 1844, 9 In.		157
Ribbon, Hughes, Republican Presidential Notification, July 31 1916, 5 In.		118
Ribbon, Van Buren, Johnson, Democracy, Slogan, Eagle, Silk, 1840, 7½ In.		1103
Sign, Mayor Of Hammtramck, P.C. Jezewski, Gilt Wood, Pencil Shape, 1922, 16 x 3 In.		944
Speech Booklet, Teddy Roosevelt Progressive Party, 1912, 8 Pages, 6 x 9 In.		24
Sticker, Robert F. Kennedy, Oregon, Kennedy Campaign Press, Union Bug, 1968, 2 x 3 In.		118
Stud, Bryan, Portrait, Free Silver, Celluloid, Brass Stud, 1 In.		118
Tankard, McKinley & Hobart, Jugate, Porcelain, 7 In.		175
Textile, Blaine, Logan, Campaign, Fabric Bunting, 6 Stars At Top, 1884, 25 x 40 In.		649
Textile, Woodrow Wilson, Silk Woven, Portrait, France, 17½ x 21¾ In.		118
Thimble, Coolidge & Dawes, Metal, 1924, ¾ In.		15
Ticket, Admission, National Republican Convention, Academy Of Music, 1872, 2¼ x 4 In.		643
Token, Hayes, Wheeler, Honest Money Honest Government, Copper, 1876, ⅞ In.		314
Toy, Uncle Sam, Jumping Jack, Blue & Yellow Jacket, Wood, Carved, c.1910, 10½ In.		750
Tray, Parker, Davis, Jugate, Fearless In Battle, Aluminum, Embossed, 3¾ x 9¼ In.	*illus*	182
Watch Fob, Kansas For Bryan, July 7, 1908, Sunflower Design, 1¾ In.		295
Watch Fob, Taft, Eagle, Shield On Reverse, Celluloid, Leon Rowe, 1½ In.		295
Window Card, George Wallace, Virginia, Screen Print, c.1968, 14 x 22 In.	*illus*	118

POMONA glass is a clear glass with a soft amber border decorated with pale blue or rose-colored flowers and leaves. The colors are very, very pale. The background of the glass is covered with a network of fine lines. It was made from 1885 to 1888 by the New England Glass Company. First grind was made from April 1885 to June 1886. It was made by cutting a wax surface on the glass, then dipping it in acid. Second grind was a less expensive method of acid etching that was developed later.

Celery Dish, Ruffled Top Edge, New England, 6½ In.		35
Celery Vase, Cornflower, Scalloped Base, Polished Pontil, c.1880, 6¼ In.	*illus*	351
Vase, Cornucopia, Green Amber, Yellow Round Base & Rim, Carder Steuben, 11 x 7 In.		202
Vase, Mother-Of-Pearl, Satin Lapierre, Sterling Overlay, Steuben, 7¼ In.		114

PONTYPOOL, *see Tole category.*

POOLE POTTERY was founded by Jesse Carter in 1873 in Poole, England, and has operated under various names since then. The pottery operated as Carter & Co. for several years and established Carter, Stabler & Adams as a subsidiary in 1921. The company specialized in tiles, architectural ceramics, and garden ornaments. Tableware, bookends, candelabra, figures, vases, and other items have also been made. *Poole Pottery Ltd.* became the name in 1963. The company went bankrupt in 2003 but continued under new owners. Poole Pottery became part of Burgess & Leigh Ltd. in 2012. It is still in business, now making pottery in Middleport, Stoke-on-Trent.

CARTER STABLER & ADAMS / POOLE ENGLAND	POOLE ENGLAND	Poole handpainted
Poole Pottery 1921–1924	 Poole Pottery 1924–1950	Poole Pottery Ltd. 1990–1991

Charger, Free-Form, Abstract, Red Lines, Blue Squares, Eames Design, 13 In.		153
Jam Jar, Lid, Bluebird, Earthenware, Multicolor, Art Deco, 1920s, 4¾ In.		63
Lamp Base, African Sky Pattern, Embossed Backstamp, 13½ In.		100
Plaque, His Majesty King Edward VIII, Profile, Harold Brownsword, 11 x 8½ x ¾ In.		85
Plate, Delphis, Stylized Lion, Spear Head Shape, Yellow, Orange, 16¾ In.		94
Plate, Orange Ground, Green & Yellow, Marked, 1960s, 10½ x 10⅝ In.		44
Salt & Pepper, Salt Dish, Pepper Pot, Stopper, Cream Ground, 2½ x 1½ In.		14
Vase, Free-Form, Stretched, Rolling Pin Shape, Blue Spirograph, Eames, 10⅝ In.	*illus*	145
Vase, Squat, Multicolor, Leafy Branches, Claude Smale, 1850s, 4¾ x 4¾ In.		156

Political, Plaque, E.V. Debs, Wood, Bronze Portrait, Metal Products Mfg. Co. Inc., N.Y., 7 In.
$975

Political, Poster, Dewey, Vote For My Delegates, Cardboard, Milwaukee 59, 14 x 22 In.
$118

Political, Poster, Forward With Roosevelt, Thin Paper, Stoic Portrait Of FDR, 13¾ x 21½ In.
$162

P

This is an edited listing of current prices. Visit **Kovels.com** to check thousands of prices from previous years and sign up for free information on trends, tips, reproductions, marks, and more.

Political, Tray, Parker, Davis, Jugate, Fearless In Battle, Aluminum, Embossed, 3¾ x 9¼ In.
$182

Hake's Auctions

Political, Window Card, George Wallace, Virginia, Screen Print, c.1968, 14 x 22 In.
$118

Hake's Auctions

Pomona, Celery Vase, Cornflower, Scalloped Base, Polished Pontil, c.1880, 6¼ In.
$351

Jeffrey S. Evans & Associates

Poole, Vase, Free-Form, Stretched, Rolling Pin Shape, Blue Spirograph, Eames, 10⅝ In.
$145

jamesmiles2012 on eBay

Popeye, Doll, Eugene The Jeep, Composition Head, Painted, Wood Jointed Body, Decal, Cameo, 1935, 12 In.
$414

Weiss Auctions

Popeye, Doll, Popeye, Composition Head, Wood Jointed Body, Decal, 1935, 14 In.
$311

Weiss Auctions

Popeye, Toy, Barrel Walker, Tin Lithograph, Windup, Chein, 6½ In.
$425

Milestone Auctions

Popeye, Toy, Popeye, With Sea Bag, Composition, Wood Jointed Body, J. Chein, 1932, 8 In.
$391

Weiss Auctions

Popeye, Toy, Wimpy, Wood, Jointed Body, 10 In.
$150

Weiss Auctions

P

POPEYE was introduced to the Thimble Theatre comic strip in 1929. The character became a favorite of readers. In 1932, an animated cartoon featuring Popeye was made by Paramount Studios. The cartoon series continued and became even more popular when it was shown on television starting in the 1950s. The full-length movie with Robin Williams as Popeye was made in 1980. KFS stands for King Features Syndicate, the distributor of the comic strip.

Bank, Daily Quarter Bank, Tin, Register, Kalon, Box, 5 In.	180
Bank, Dime Register, King Features, 1929, 2½ In.	145
Bank, Yellow Popcorn, Yellow, Red, Navy Blue, Purity Mills Inc., Dixon, Ill., Tin, c.1964	87
Brush, Aluminum Handle, Black Bristles, Popeye Walking, 1929, 2 x 4 x 5 In.	55
Doll, Eugene The Jeep, Composition Head, Painted, Wood Jointed Body, Decal, Cameo, 1935, 12 In. . *illus*	414
Doll, Popeye, Composition Head, Wood Jointed Body, Decal, 1935, 14 In. *illus*	311
Door Push, Popeye White Hulless Popcorn, Sold Here, White, Blue, Red, 6 x 3 In.	394
Doorstop, Popeye, Full Figure, Yellow Pipe, Cast Iron, Hubley, 1929, 9 x 4½ In.	2400
Eggcup, Swee'Pea, Yellow & White, 1980, 3½ In., Pair	25
Figure, Olive Oyl, Vinyl, Movable Arms & Legs, Fabric Dress, Dakin, 1960s, 9 In.	70
Figure, Popeye, Rubber, Arms Down, Pipe, Hat, King Features Syndicate, 1935, 7 In.	70
Game, The Juggler, Dexterity Puzzle, Olive Oyl, Yellow & Red, 1929	62
Lamp, Figural, Popeye, Leaning On Lamp Post, Polished Silver, 1935, 12½ In.	333
Lunch Box, Olive Oyl, Brutus, Wimpy, Popeye Truant Officer, Metal, Promotional, Baggies, 1964.	645
Party Game, Pin The Pipe On Popeye, Box, 1937	40
Pencil Sharpener, Popeye, Walking, Holding Pencil, 1929, 1¾ In.	65
Pin, New York Evening Journal, Pinback, 1930s, 1¼ In.	13
Pin, Orange, Comics Everyday Journal, Celluloid, Bastain Brothers, 1930s, 1 In.	115
Pin, Penney's Back To School Days, Popeye Carrying Books, 1930s, 1 In.	26
Pin, Popeye, The News Bee, Blue & White, Celluloid, 1930s, 1¼ In.	90
Pistol, Popeye, Pirate, Tin, Clicker, Detailed Graphics, Marx, 10 In.	170
Pitcher, Figural, Popeye, Sitting, Hand On Chin, Ceramic, Japan, 1930s, 4¾ In.	45
Plate, Popeye, Holding Swee'Pea, Olive Oyl, Wimpy, Multicolor, Melmac, 7½ In.	11
Stickpin, Popeye, Aluminum Plate, Igloo, Copyright KFS, Europe, c.1960, 1¾ In. x ¾ In.	10
Tie Bar, Popeye, Anchor Tattoos, Silvered Brass, 1930s, 2 In.	25
Tie, Popeye, I Yam What I Yam, Silkscreen, Blue, 1940s, 36 In.	100
Toy, Barrel Walker, Tin Lithograph, Windup, Chein, 6½ In. *illus*	425
Toy, Popeye Express, Airplane, Cardboard, Tin, Lithograph, Windup, Marx, Box, 9½ In.	885
Toy, Popeye, Carrying Parrot Cages, Tin Lithograph, Marx, Box, 8 In.	510
Toy, Popeye, Motorcycle Patrol, Cast Iron, Painted, Hubley, 9 In., 2 Piece	1440
Toy, Popeye, Waddler, Tin Lithograph, Windup, Chein, 6½ In.	382
Toy, Popeye, With Sea Bag, Composition, Wood Jointed Body, J. Chein, 1932, 8 In. *illus*	391
Toy, Roly Poly Rattle, Popeye, 2 Faces, Wood Beaded Arms, Celluloid, 1930s, 4 In.	125
Toy, Tank, Silver, Red, Blue, Windup, Tin Lithograph, Linemar, 1950, 2 x 4 In.	750
Toy, Tumbler, Popeye, Tin Lithograph, Windup, Linemar, 5½ In.	602
Toy, Turnover Tank, Popeye Lifts, Tin Lithograph, Windup, Linemar, 1950, 4 In.	248
Toy, Wimpy, Wood, Jointed Body, 10 In. *illus*	150

PORCELAIN factories that are well known are listed in this book under the factory name. This category lists pieces made by the less well-known factories. Additional pieces of porcelain are listed in this book in the categories Porcelain-Contemporary, Porcelain-Midcentury, and under the factory name.

Beaker, Repeating HR, Tan, Brown, 4 In.	875
Bottle Stopper, Teardrop Shape, Green, Gilt, Romanesque Medallions, 1800s, 7¾ In.	12
Bowl, Blue & White Transfer, Shaped Panels, 2 Brushwork Scenes, Japan, 1900s, 12⅜ x 18 In.	123
Bowl, Centerpiece, Blue, Nymphs, Figural Gilt Bronze Stand, c.1875, 20 x 18 x 16 In.	3250
Bowl, Famille Rose, Central Medallion, Crown, Floral Rim, Fruit Sprays, 1800s, 3 x 11 In.	188
Bowl, Flowers, Gilt Rim, White Ground, Footed, 5½ In.	46
Bowl, Gilt, Bronze, Mounted, Oval, Maiden, Pierced Base, Early 1900s, 8 x 13¾ In.	1000
Bowl, Ornate, Koi Fish Interior, White Background, Flowers, Wood Base, 29 x 21 In.	35
Box, Figural Scenes, Multicolor, Capo-Di-Monte Style, Continental, 4¾ x 7⅞ In.	246
Box, Gilt, Bronze, Mounted, Rectangular, Hinged Lid, Footed, Sevres Style, 1900s, 16 In.	1875

Porcelain, Cachepot, Sevres Style, Bronze Rim, Base, Ring Handles, Flowers, c.1900, 4 x 6¾ In.
$531

Leslie Hindman Auctioneers

TIP
The word trademark *was used on English wares after 1855, but most of the pieces with the letters* LTD, *the abbreviation for* Limited, *were made after 1880.*

Porcelain, Dish, Fish & Vegetable, Blue Cell & Diaper Band Border, Palissy Type, 1800s, 11 In.
$185

Skinner, Inc.

Porcelain, Figurine, Bald Eagle In Flight, Rock Cliff, Raised On Wood Base, Kaiser, c.1950, 19 In.
$24

Garth's Auctioneers & Appraisers

Porcelain, Figurine, Madame Recamier, Gilt Daybed, Hand Painted, 7¾ x 4 x 6½ In.
$118

Charleston Estate Auctions

Porcelain, Jewelry Box, Egg Shape, Couple, Garden, Cobalt Blue Ground, c.1900, 6¾ x 9½ In.
$156

Selkirk Auctioneers & Appraisers

Porcelain, Plaque, Portrait, Young Girl, Red Head Scarf, Germany, Early 1900s, 8 x 5½ In.
$1,000

Rago Arts and Auction Center

Box, Interior Scene, Fabric Seller & Ladies, Gold Trim, Scalloped, 4 x 5 In.	219
Bread Plate, Richard Ginori, La Veloce, Maroon & Gilt Border, Logo, 1900s, 7½ In.	125
Brushpot, Blue & White, Woman Figure, Rounded Base, 6⅜ In.	780
Bust, Young Napoleon, Bisque, Green & Gold Base, Limoges, France, 8 x 3 x 3 In.	504
Cachepot, Sevres Style, Bronze Rim, Base, Ring Handles, Flowers, c.1900, 4 x 6¾ In. *illus*	531
Cake Plate, Yellow, Blue & Lavender, Violet Flowers, 11 In.	60
Cake Stand, 3 Tiers, Gilt Border, Ivory Ground, 1800s, 11½ In.	100
Casket, Gilt Metal, Ovoid, Hinged Top, Sevres Style, 1800s, 10½ In.	188
Casket, Sevres Style, Gilt Metal Mounts, Lobed Oval, Courting Couple, Landscape, 1900s, 12 In.	406
Centerpiece, Bronze, Hand Painted God, Flowers, Rich Blue Trim, Footed, 1800s, 10 x 14 In.	230
Centerpiece, Gilt Bronze, Putto, Shell Horn, Neptune Head, Flowers, Painted, c.1900, 10 x 4 x 15 In.	1000
Charger, Cornflowers, White, Blue Flowers, Gold Rim, Niderviller, c.1790, 14¾ In.	13
Compote, White, Blue Decoration, Portland Steamship Company, 1900s, 5¼ x 9⅛ In.	63
Creamer, Pink & Brown Border, Company Monogram, Marked, Ellerman Line, 1900s, 3¾ In.	25
Dish, Blue & White Transfer, 7 Sages, Bamboo Grove, 1900s, 1⅞ x 13 In.	123
Dish, Fish & Vegetable, Blue Cell & Diaper Band Border, Palissy Type, 1800s, 11 In. *illus*	185
Dish, Lobster Shape Center, White, Ruffled Rim, Blue Trim, Germany, 13½ In.	38
Dish, Presentation, Clipper Ship, Black Enamel, Anna Decatur, c.1860, 10¼ In.	360
Dresser Box, Amorous Couple, Raised Gilt Flowers, Green, c.1920, 5½ x 10½ x 8 In.	188
Dresser Box, Courting Scene, Burgundy, Gold Trim, Austria, 4½ x 8½ In.	115
Dresser Box, Courting Scene, Flowers, Gold Trim, France, 1800s, 3½ x 5½ In.	230
Figurine, Angel Care, No. 5727, 2 Angels, F. Polope, Spain. 1990-2000, 5 In.	86
Figurine, Bald Eagle In Flight, Rock Cliff, Raised On Wood Base, Kaiser, c.1950, 19 In. *illus*	24
Figurine, Butler Dragooner, Soldier, Blue Coat, White Boots, Allach, Germany, c.1943, 9½ x 4 x 3 In.	5313
Figurine, Cat, Hollow Form, Clear Glaze, Glass Eyes, France, Mid 1900s, 13½ In.	153
Figurine, Lipizzaner Horse & Rider, Karl-Heinz Klette, Germany, 11¼ x 8¾ x 4 In.	132
Figurine, Madame Recamier, Gilt Daybed, Hand Painted, 7¾ x 4 x 6½ In. *illus*	118
Figurine, Man, Riding Goat, Germany, 9¼ In.	150
Figurine, Napoleonic Hussar, Saber, Dressel, Kister & Co., 9½ In.	214
Figurine, Peacock, Multicolor, Enameled, Seated, Folded Tail, Bisque Base, 1900s, 14 In.	246
Figurine, Pelican, Light Green, Blue & Brown Feathers, Gilt Neck, Face, 1900s, 7¼ x 11 x 5 In.	260
Figurine, Woman Dancing, Printed Marks Underside, Hertwig, Germany, Mid 1900s, 8 In.	63
Figurine, Woman, Holding Mask, White, Nymphenburg, Colombine, Germany, 1800s, 8 In.	295
Figurine, Woman, Water Jug, 1920, 28 x 11 In.	85
Figurine, Woodpecker, Blue Scepter Mark, Blanc De Chine, 9½ In.	94
Group, Mother, Carrying 2 Children, Another Child Standing, Blue Mark, Germany, 6 In.	120
Jar, Lid, Baby Head, Pacifier, 6 x 4½ In.	18
Jar, Lid, Famille Noire, Birds, Lotus, Water Plants, Pond, Blue, Black Ground, 1900s, 19 In.	354
Jar, Sang De Boeuf, Bulbous, Waisted Neck, White Base, Unglazed Foot Rim, 1900s, 8 In.	185
Jardiniere, Bowl, Stand, Rococo Style, Cobalt Blue, Picnic, Landscape, House, Sevres Style, 20 x 27 In.	5040
Jardiniere, Pedestal, 2 Parts, Red, Green, Gilt, Lion Mask Handles, c.1900, 34 x 16 x 14 In.	189
Jardiniere, Pedestal, Cat-O'-Nine-Tails Base, Sunburst, Green & Red, 23 In.	52
Jewelry Box, Egg Shape, Couple, Garden, Cobalt Blue Ground, c.1900, 6¾ x 9½ In. *illus*	156
Pedestal, Marble Column, Scenes, Gilt Bronze Mounts, Sevres Style, 44 x 12 x 12 In.	4125
Plaque, Circular, Sistine Madonna, Carved, Giltwood Frame, Signed, Dietrich, 18 x 18 In.	570
Plaque, Frame, Portrait Of Young Woman, Seminude, Germany, 1900s, 7 x 5 In.	750
Plaque, Gilt Metal, Sevres Style, Rectangular, Celeste Bleu Ground, 1800s, 11 x 7 In.	1063
Plaque, Marie Antoinette, Sticker On Reverse, Germany, 1800s, 6¼ x 4½ In.	875
Plaque, Portrait, Young Girl, Red Head Scarf, Germany, Early 1900s, 8 x 5½ In. *illus*	1000
Punch Bowl, People, Multicolor, Giltwood Stand, 3-Legged, 1800s, 7 x 16 In.	5500
Tazza, Dessert, Imperial 2-Headed Eagle, Kremlin, 1800s, 8¾ x 3½ In. *illus*	813
Teapot, Lid, 8-Sided, Queen Elizabeth I, Figures With Royal Titles, Sadler, Marked, 6 In.	94
Tray, American Flag & Shield, Mounted, Brass Stand, Late 1800s, 5¼ x 8½ In.	854
Tray, Champleve, Mounted, Leafy Scrolls & Rocaille, Courting Couple, c.1900, 11⅝ In.	563
Urn, Bronze, Mounted, Painted Scenes, Sevres Style, France, 1900s, 18½ In. *illus*	500
Urn, Lid, Bisque, Cherubs, Gilt Trim, Sevres Style, Pseudo Mark, France, 1800s, 8 x 16 x 13 In.	1250
Urn, Lid, Painted, Flowers, Crossed Lines, Underglaze Blue, c.1900, 29 In.	625
Urn, Lid, Sevres Style, Cobalt Blue, Raised Gilt, Handles, France, c.1900, 42 x 17 In. *illus*	1750
Urn, Lovers, Hand Painted, Bronze Rim & Figural, 16½ In.	288
Urn, Sevres Style, Gilt Bronze Rim, Mounted, Cobalt Blue Ground, Square Base, 1800s, 8⅝ In.	313

P

Porcelain, Tazza, Dessert, Imperial 2-Headed Eagle, Kremlin, 1800s, 8¾ x 3½ In.
$813

Rago Arts and Auction Center

Porcelain, Urn, Bronze, Mounted, Painted Scenes, Sevres Style, France, 1900s, 18½ In.
$500

Leslie Hindman Auctioneers

Porcelain, Urn, Lid, Sevres Style, Cobalt Blue, Raised Gilt, Handles, France, c.1900, 42 x 17 In.
$1,750

New Orleans Auction Galleries

Porcelain, Vase, Squat, Woman Portrait, Ruffled Rim, Vienna, c.1900, 5 In.
$281

Leslie Hindman Auctioneers

Porcelain-Asian, Bento Box, Food Storage, Famille Rose, 3 Tiers, Children, 6¼ x 8½ In.
$94

Susanin's Auctioneers & Appraisers

Porcelain-Asian, Decanter, Liquor, Skulls, Crossed Bones, Marked Poison, 2 Handles, Footed, Japan, 8 In.
$136

Hartzell's Auction Gallery, Inc.

Porcelain-Asian, Figurine, Star God Lu, Ruyi Scepter, Hair Beard, Chinese Republic Period, 25 In.
$861

Skinner, Inc.

Porcelain-Asian, Ginger Jar, 100 Butterfly, Stand, Enamel, Vibrant, 7 x 7 x 10 In.
$177

Charleston Estate Auctions

Porcelain-Asian, Jar, Asparagus, Hand Craft, Earthenware, Au Bon Gout Production, Marks, 5¾ x 7 In.
$2,500

Royal Crest Auctioneers

P

PORCELAIN

Porcelain-Asian, Jardiniere, Blue, White, Quail, Flowering Leaves, 3 Scroll Feet, Japan, 12¾ x 16 In. $878

Thomaston Place Auction Galleries

Porcelain-Asian, Vase, Moonpot, Runny Brown Tones, Glazed, Tiny Mouth, Toshiko Takaezu, 5½ In. $1,000

Rago Arts and Auction Center

Porcelain-Chinese, Bowl, Shallow, Flared Rim, Sang De Boeuf, Qianlong Mark, 18th Century, 2 x 8 In. $2,500

Susanin's Auctioneers & Appraisers

Porcelain-Chinese, Bowl, Yellow Ground, Gilt, Deep Walls, Bamboo Stalks, Gilt Rim, Tongzhi, 7¾ In. $4,250

Leslie Hindman Auctioneers

Vase, 18 Luohan, Lantern, Buddhist Emblems, Wood Base & Lid, Early 1900s, 7 x 11 In.	250
Vase, Birds, Flowers, Metal Holder, Jacob Petit, c.1796, 11 x 7 In., Pair	896
Vase, Bisque Glaze, Neoclassical Masks, France, c.1880, 18 x 12 x 8 In.	625
Vase, Blue & White, Bird & Flower, Lotus Scroll Ground, Wood Stand, 35¾ In.	185
Vase, Double Handles, Leaves, Flowers, Pink, Green, Brown, 13 x 17 In.	69
Vase, Flambe Glaze, 3 Lobes, Double Gourd, 10¼ In.	344
Vase, Flared, Bleu D'Celeste, Dragon Handles, Floral, Jacob Petit, 14 x 8½ x 5 In.	375
Vase, Gilt Handles, Flowers, Art Nouveau, Artist Signed, Gessner, Austria, 1900s, 15½ In.	31
Vase, Gilt, Bird, Brown, Flying, Leaves, Shaped Mouth, Continental, 10¾ In.	141
Vase, Squat, Woman Portrait, Ruffled Rim, Vienna, c.1900, 5 In. *illus*	281
Vase, Turquoise Glaze, Double Handle, Renaissance Revival Base, Late 1800s, 43 In.	260
Vase, Turquoise Glaze, Waisted Neck, Rolled Rim, Flowers, Black Outline, 1900s, 7⅞ In.	62

PORCELAIN-ASIAN includes pieces made in Japan, Korea, and other Asian countries. Asian porcelain is also listed in Canton, Chinese Export, Imari, Moriage, Nanking, Occupied Japan, Porcelain-Chinese, Satsuma, Sumida, and other categories.

Bento Box, Food Storage, Famille Rose, 3 Tiers, Children, 6¼ x 8½ In. *illus*	94
Bowl, Applied Flowers, Putto Supports, C.G. Schierholz Plaue, Germany, 13½ In.	246
Bowl, Fish, Imari Palette, Figures In Low Relief, Japan, 1900s, 13 In.	531
Bowl, Rice, Dome Lid, Brown Sepia, Gilt Finial, Scalloped Rim, Japan, 1900s, 4 x 7 In.	48
Censer, Lid, Octagonal, Reticulated, 3-Footed, Blue, White, Hirado, Japan, 1800s, 2¾ x 4 In.	73
Decanter, Liquor, Skulls, Crossed Bones, Marked Poison, 2 Handles, Footed, Japan, 8 In. *illus*	136
Figurine, Guanyin, Standing, Holding Foo Dog, Wave Base, Foo Dog Fish, 1900s, 14 In.	3480
Figurine, Star God Lu, Ruyi Scepter, Hair Beard, Chinese Republic Period, 25 In. *illus*	861
Ginger Jar, 100 Butterfly, Stand, Enamel, Vibrant, 7 x 7 x 10 In. *illus*	177
Jar, Asparagus, Hand Craft, Earthenware, Au Bon Gout Production, Marks, 5¾ x 7 In. *illus*	2500
Jar, Lid, Multicolor, Gilt Metal Handles, 1900s, 14 x 10 In.	25
Jardiniere, Blue & White, Hawthorne Pattern, Japan, 13¾ x 16 In.	1750
Jardiniere, Blue & White, Quail, Flowering Leaves, 3 Scroll Feet, Japan, 12¾ x 16 In. *illus*	878
Plate, Ducks, Lotus Blossoms, Pond, Blue, White, 15½ In.	570
Urn, Lid, Blue, White, Iron Red, Gilt Floral, Square Base, Japan, 1800s, 11¼ x 5 In.	146
Vase, Moonpot, Runny Brown Tones, Glazed, Tiny Mouth, Toshiko Takaezu, 5½ In. *illus*	1000
Vase, Oxblood & Purple Glaze, 6-Sided, Round Handles, Marked, c.1835, 14 In.	406

PORCELAIN-CHINESE is listed here. See also Canton, Chinese Export, Imari, Moriage, Nanking, and other categories.

Basin, Famille Rose, Flat Rim, Enamel, Floral Sprays To Rim, 1900s, 4⅝ x 13¾ In.	360
Bowl, Central Roundel Shape, Court Life Scenes, 7 x 16½ In.	180
Bowl, Children Surrounding An Immortal, Early 1900s, 4 In.	272
Bowl, Cobalt Blue Dragon, Flowers, 6-Character Mark, 1800s, 7½ In.	173
Bowl, Eggshell, Flowers & Dragon, Marked, 6 x 14 In.	188
Bowl, Famille Jaune, Painted, Landscape, Flowers, 5¾ In.	1230
Bowl, Famille Rose, 9 Peaches & Bats, Carved Rosewood Stand, 1900s, 2½ x 6 In.	150
Bowl, Flared Rim, Dragon, Birds & Butterflies, Blue Rings, Kangxi, c.1700, 2¾ x 5⅞ In.	156
Bowl, Floral, Circular Gilt Rim, White Background, Late 1800s, 2½ x 5½ In.	123
Bowl, Green-Blue Drip Glaze, Circular Foot, Junyao, 7 x 2⅞ In.	303
Bowl, Iron Red, 8 Daoist Immortals, Crashing Waves, Kangxi, 8¼ In.	875
Bowl, Iron Red, Phoenix Medallions, Yongzheng, 5½ In.	2500
Bowl, Leaf Shape, Green, Painted, Wood Stand, Signed, 3 x 8 In.	63
Bowl, Lid, Shishi Finial, Flowers, Kamcheng, Mark, 1900s, 6½ x 6⅞ In.	545
Bowl, Milky White, Translucent, Rolled Rim, Yuan Shufu, 1300s	600
Bowl, Shallow, Flared Rim, Sang De Boeuf, Qianlong Mark, 18th Century, 2 x 8 In. *illus*	2500
Bowl, Shallow, Yellow, Blue Leaves, Green Greek Key, 1½ x 7¾ In.	625
Bowl, Turquoise Glaze, Flowers, Vine & Geometric Bands Inside, Flared, 3 x 6 In.	1180
Bowl, Underglaze Blue, White Porcelain, Bird, Equestrian Scene, 1368-1644, 5¾ In.	84
Bowl, Yellow Ground, Gilt, Deep Walls, Bamboo Stalks, Gilt Rim, Tongzhi, 7¾ In. *illus*	4250
Brush Washer, Cobalt Blue Glaze, White Inner, Scholar, 1800s, 2½ x 9¼ In.	260
Brushpot, 10 Figures, Scenic, Garden Setting, Cylindrical, 6 In.	310
Brushpot, Biscuit, Bamboo Form, Alternate Yellow & Green Glaze, 6¾ In.	250

P

Brushpot, Famille Verte, 2 Women, Landscape, 5 x 4 In.	500
Brushpot, Water Buffalo Scene, Black & White, Carved Wood Stand, 1900s, 6¾ x 5 In.	1020
Charger, Famille Verte, Dragon, Flaming Pearl, Blue Kangxi Mark, c.1700, 2 x 11 In.	2000
Container, Stacked, 4 Containers, White, Coin Shape Medallions, Metal Handles, 1800s, 5⅝ In.	590
Cup, Blue & White, Bell Shape, Flowers & Leaves Frieze, 1½ x 2½ In.	215
Cup, Scalloped Rim, Blue Rings, 2 Chilong Dragons, Cobalt Blue Underglaze, 1800s, 2 In.	120
Cup, Squid, Octopus, Dragons, Hardwood Stand, 18th Century, 3 x 4½ x 2¾ In.	4840
Dish, Quail, Famille Rose, 3 Quails, Yellow Underside, Flared Rim, c.1725, 1⅝ x 6⅝ In.	406
Figurine, Boy, Riding Turtle, Multicolor, c.1900, 15 In.	150
Figurine, Foo Dog, Seated, Paw On Brocade Ball, Turquoise, 1800s, 12 In., Pair	330
Figurine, Guanyin, Blanc De Chine, Dragons Head To Base, 21 x 5½ In.	125
Figurine, Guanyin, Blanc De Chine, Sitting Cross-Legged, Holding Scroll, 7 x 5 x 4 In.	42
Figurine, Guanyin, Famille Rose, Seated, Draped Robes, Beaded Jewelry, 10 In. ....*illus*	469
Figurine, Guanyin, Robes, Beaded Jewelry, Blanc De Chine, Early 1900s, 10¼ In.	5000
Figurine, Immortal, Brown Glaze, Lotus Base, Voluminous Robe, Ruyi Scepter, 10 In. ......*illus*	313
Figurine, Official, On Dragon Throne, Turquoise Aubergine, Holding Scepter, 1800s, 9 In.	438
Ginger Jar, Lid, Peonies & Peacocks, Flowers, Red Finial, 1970, 14 In.	62
Hat Stand, 6-Sided, Medallion Openings, Hand Painted, Birds, Flowers, Late 1800s, 11 In.	236
Jar, Gilt, Fruit, Lapis Lazuli Ground, Blue Circle, 11½ In.	847
Jar, Lid, Famille Noir, Children In Lion Dance, Garden Setting, Marked, Kangxi, 14 In. ....*illus*	185
Jar, Lid, Famille Verte, Robust Body, Floral Scrolls, Lotus Finial, 14 In.	1875
Jardiniere, Bulbous, Relief Bird & Flowers, Blue & White, c.1900, 7⅝ x 10¼ In.	60
Jardiniere, Lotus Blossoms, Vines, Cloud Collar, Lappet Borders, Blue, White, 16 In.	1200
Plaque, Mountain & Lake Landscape, Upper Right Poem, Signed, Frame, 23 x 44 In.	1116
Plate, Black Ground, Green Dragons, Flaming Pearls, Shallow Sides, Circular, 1800s, 8 In.	563
Plate, Gangly Bush, Pink Buds, Stylized Birds, Famille Rose, c.1916, 10 In. ....*illus*	151
Punch Bowl, Owl, Flying Dragons, Blue Ground, Wood Stand, Late 1800s, 16 In.	649
Rice Container, Stacking, Lid, Blue & White, 4 Levels, c.1950, 16 In. ....*illus*	406
Saucer, Cherry Pickers, 2 Women, Late 1800s, 4¾ In.	400
Teapot, Cadogan, Gourd Shape, Bamboo Turned Handle & Spout, 1800s, 6 x 6¼ In.	97
Urn, Floral, Orange, Foo Dogs, Handle, Rounded Base, 14 In.	496
Vase, 2 Handles, Lotus, Clouds, Good Luck Symbol, Famille Rose, 10¼ x 7½ In.	992
Vase, Alternating Panels, Figures In Garden, Floral Reserves, Blue, White, 18 In.	1488
Vase, Aubergine Glaze, Oval, Straight Neck, Bisque Foot Ring, Recessed Base, 1900s, 10 In.	2706
Vase, Blue & White, Bulbous Body, Flared Rim, Leaves, Qianlong, 1700s, 5 x 4 In.	406
Vase, Blue Ground, Saucer Shape Top, 2 Handles, c.1900, 14⅝ x 8 In.	1063
Vase, Bottle Shape, Famille Rose, Blue Yongzheng Mark, 2 Rings, 13 In.	260
Vase, Bottle Shape, Flared Opening, Blue, White, Lotus Blossoms & Leaves, 1800s, 9 In.	726
Vase, Bulbous Shoulder, White, Flared, Footed, Palm Leaf Border, 1700s, 5 In.	1625
Vase, Bulbous, Flared Rim, Phoenix, Flowers, Leaf Borders, Red Glaze, c.1900, 13 In.	300
Vase, Dome Lid, Finial, Hand Painted, Flower Baskets & Butterflies, 1800s, 25 In.	325
Vase, Double Gourd, Garden Scene, Figures, Wucai, Marked, 1800s, 6 In.	123
Vase, Enamel, Scenic, Yellow, Flowers, Gold Border, 1900s, 14⅜ x 5½ In.	375
Vase, Enameled, Trumpet Shape, Long Tail, Peonies, 10¼ In.	338
Vase, Famille Rose, Shaped Panels, Immortals, Light Blue, 1800s, 7 In. ....*illus*	469
Vase, Famille Rose, Bird, Flower, Phoenix, Butterfly, Peacock, Lion Handle, 22 In.	125
Vase, Famille Rose, Globular Body, River Scenes, Dragon Handles, 1900s, 12 In. ....*illus*	1750
Vase, Famille Verte, Warrior Scenes, Kangxi Style, 14⅞ In.	438
Vase, Fish, Horses, Cobalt, Crow's Foot Interior, Signature, 1800s, 16 In. ....*illus*	748
Vase, Flambe, Mottled Copper Red, Green, Elephant Mask Handles, 7⅝ In.	128
Vase, Foo Dog Handles, Floral, Orange, Marked, Square Base, 22 x 4 In.	403
Vase, Foo Dog Mask Handles, Family Life Scene, White Background, 17 In.	840
Vase, Globular, Famille Jaune, Bird, Flowers, Lotus Scroll, Handles, Late 1800s, 8 In.	1230
Vase, Globular, Turquoise Ground, Flowers & Quail, Qianlong, 18th Century, 15 x 8 In.	406
Vase, Iridescent, Birds, Rocks, Prunus Blossoms, Famille Noir, 24 In.	1191
Vase, Mallet Shape, Sancai Glaze, Ruyi Clouds, Green, Yellow, Aubergine, c.1700, 6 In.	531
Vase, Mirror Black Glaze, Wanli Mark, Early 1900s, 10 In.	250
Vase, Moonflask, Blue & White, Arabic Calligraphy, 1900s, 12 x 9 x 5 In.	2500
Vase, Mountain & Ocean Scene, Pine Trees, Clouds & Birds, Blue, White, 18½ In.............*illus*	1116
Vase, Outdoor Scene, Phoenix Birds, Flowers & Leaves, Bulbous, Marked, 10 In.	496
Vase, Powder Blue, Phoenix Tail, Underglaze, Double Ring Mark On Base, 18 In.	1786

Porcelain-Chinese, Figurine, Guanyin, Famille Rose, Seated, Draped Robes, Beaded Jewelry, Early 1900s, 10 In. $469

Porcelain-Chinese, Figurine, Immortal, Brown Glaze, Lotus Base, Voluminous Robe, Ruyi Scepter, 10 In. $313

TIP
Don't soak old ceramic pieces in water for a long time. Old repairs may be loosened.

Porcelain-Chinese, Jar, Lid, Famille Noir, Children In Lion Dance, Garden Setting, Marked, Kangxi, 14 In.
$185

Clars Auction Gallery

Porcelain-Chinese, Plate, Gangly Bush, Pink Buds, Stylized Birds, Famille Rose, c.1916, 10 In.
$151

Locati Auctions

Porcelain-Chinese, Rice Container, Stacking, Lid, Blue & White, 4 Levels, c.1950, 16 In.
$406

Freeman's Auctioneers & Appraisers

Porcelain-Chinese, Vase, Famille Rose, Shaped Panels, Immortals, Light Blue, 1800s, 7 In.
$469

Leslie Hindman Auctioneers

Porcelain-Chinese, Vase, Famille Rose, Globular Body, River Scenes, Dragon Handles, 1900s, 12 In.
$1,750

Leslie Hindman Auctioneers

Porcelain-Chinese, Vase, Fish, Horses, Cobalt, Crow's Foot Interior, Signature, 1800s, 16 In.
$748

Keystone Auctions LLC

Vase, Square Baluster, Famille Rose, Red Archaic, Marked, c.1800, 14¾ In.	375
Vase, Tulip, Blue & White, Lobed Body, 4 Holes For Flowers, Bulb Finial, 1700s 10 x 6 In.	688
Vase, Turquoise Glaze, 4-Sided, Oval, Dragon, Peonies, Bisque Base, Late 1800s, 8½ In.	369
Water Pot, Junware, Lotus Bud Shape, Raised Foot, Grayish Blue, 4½ In.	338

PORCELAIN-CONTEMPORARY lists pieces made by artists working after 1975.

Bowl, Cobalt Blue Oxide, Signed, Rudolf Staffel, Pa., c.1970s, 4¾ x 9 x 8¾ In.	4688
Teapot, Geometric, Triangular Lid, 3 Wheels, Signed, Peter Shire, 1984, 8½ x 9 In.	484
Vase, Ball Shape, Butternut Glaze, Concentric Rings, Viviko & Otto Heino, 5½ x 6 In.	424
Vase, Ball Shape, Closed Mouth, Manganese Drip, Feather Edges, Blue, Signed, Tom Turner, 8 x 7 In.	113
Vase, Incised Fox, Hare, Marked, Miranda Thomas, Quechee, Vermont, 8⅞ x 4¾ In.	246
Vase, Light Gatherer, Thrown, Applied Pieces, Rudolf Staffel, Pa., c.1980, 7 x 7 x 6 In. ......*illus*	2500
Water Cooler, Lid, Green Glaze & Daubs, Brown & Blue, Signed, Tom Turner, 9½ x 7 In.	79

PORCELAIN-MIDCENTURY includes pieces made from the 1940s to about 1975.

Bowl, Midsummer Night's Dream Scene, Signed, Bjorn Wiinblad, Nymolle, Denmark, 9½ x 6 In.	48
Charger, Madoura Visage, Glazed, Round, Blue & White, Pablo Picasso, 16½ In.	10938
Figurine, Vakula, Riding Devil Creature, Hand Painted, 1950-60, 6⅛ In.	580
Ginger Jar, Dark Green Body, 5 Country Scenes, Gold Trim, Gerold, West Germany, 10 In.	24
Tray, Lettuce Leaf Ware, Hand Craft, Jupiter Mark, Dodie Thayer, 17 In.	1625
Tureen, Lid, Figural Goose, Mottahedeh, 1950s, 15 In.	313
Vase, Feelie, Mottled Glaze, Signed, Rose Cabat, 2½ x 2½ In.	531
Vase, Feelie, Turquoise Glaze, Gold Crystals, Signed, Rose Cabat, 6½ In.	2250
Vase, Monumental, Glazed, Cylindrical Form, Signed, Cuno Fischer, Germany, c.1965, 25¾ x 9 In.	156

POSTCARDS were first legally permitted in Austria on October 1, 1869. The United States passed postal regulations allowing the card in 1872. Most of the picture postcards collected today date after 1910. The amount of postage can help to date a card. The rates are: 1872 (1 cent), 1917 (2 cents), 1919 (1 cent), 1925 (2 cents), 1928 (1 cent), 1952 (2 cents), 1958 (3 cents), 1963 (4 cents), 1968 (5 cents), 1971 (6 cents), 1973 (8 cents), 1975 (7 cents), 1976 (9 cents), 1978 (10 cents), March 1981 (12 cents), November 1981 (13 cents), 1985 (14 cents), 1988 (15 cents), 1991 (19 cents), 1995 (20 cents), 2001 (21 cents), 2002 (23 cents), 2006 (24 cents), 2007 (26 cents), 2008 (27 cents), 2009 (28 cents), 2011 (29 cents), 2012 (32 cents), 2013 (33 cents), 2014 (34 cents), 2016 (35 cents beginning January 17 and back to 34 cents beginning April 10, 2016), 2018 (35 cents beginning January 21, 2018). Collectors search for early or unusual postmarks, picture postcards, or important handwritten messages (that includes celebrity autographs). While most postcards sell for low prices, a small number bring high prices. Some of these are listed here.

Brooklyn Bridge, Skyline Of Lower Manhattan, Vintage View, New York, 3½ x 5½ In.	4
Gluckliches Neujahr, Happy New Year, 4 Girls, Champagne, Dog, Austria, c.1918	16
Indian, Smiling Bear Of Lone Ranger Fame, 1950, 3½ x 5½ In.	35
Job Cigarettes, Woman Smoking, 1897 Calendar Series, France, 1914, 3 x 6 In.	28
Miss Arlette Dorgere, Actress, Real Photo, No. 34, Reutlinger, Paris, 1907-15	5
Parker Gun, Shotgun, Gamebird, Parker Brothers Makers, Meriden, Ct., c.1915	143
Pawnee Bill, Buffalo Bill Cody, 1860-1942, Photograph, Signed, G.W. Lillie ......*illus*	228
Promotional, Steve Donovan, Western Marshall, NBC TV, 5½ x 8½ In.	40
St. George Hotel, St. Augustine, Florida, Raphael Tuck & Sons, 1910s	3
St. Patrick's Day, Embossed, Baby Irish, Ellen Clapsaddle, 1916	19
Teddy Roosevelt, Colorado, The Ideal Vacation Land, Rock Island, 3½ x 5½ In.	101

POSTERS have informed the public about news and entertainment events since ancient times. Nineteenth-century advertising and theatrical posters and twentieth-century movie and war posters are of special interest today. The price is determined by the artist, the condition, and the rarity. Other posters may be listed under Movie, Political, and World War I and II.

Art, Nathan Oliveira Exhibition, Figural Work, Offset Print, 1992, 25 x 19 In.	61
Blue Jeans, Will Never Wear Out, 1890s, 29 x 21 In.	1000

Porcelain-Chinese, Vase, Mountain & Ocean Scene, Pine Trees, Clouds & Birds, Blue, White, 18½ In.
$1,116

DuMouchelles

Porcelain-Contemporary, Vase, Light Gatherer, Thrown, Applied Pieces, Rudolf Staffel, Pa., c.1980, 7 x 7 x 6 In.
$2,500

Freeman's Auctioneers & Appraisers

P

Postcard, Pawnee Bill, Buffalo Bill Cody, 1860-1942, Photograph, Signed, G.W. Lillie
$228

Cowan's Auctions

Poster, Concert, B.B. King, King Of Blues, Cardboard, c.1960, 14 x 22 In.
$354

Hake's Auctions

Poster, Mossant, 3 Hats, Black & Yellow, Cappiello, 1938, 60 x 41 In.
$369

Skinner, Inc.

Poster, Gridley, Rain Or Shine, Paper Lithograph, Home Delivery, Blue, White, 26 x 21 In.
$738

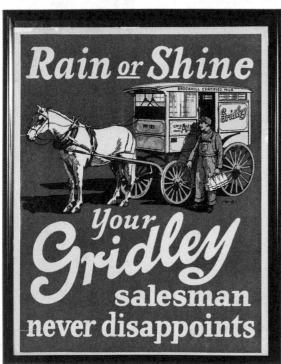

Wm Morford Auctions

Poster, Woman Wearing Red Dress, Signed, Gruan, Frame, 33 ½ x 26 In.
$443

Copake Auction

Boxing, Joe Frazier vs. Muhammad Ali, Madison Square Garden, Leroy Nieman, 1971, 36 x 24 In.	472
Broadside, Fireman, Save My Child, Spike Jones, Mahogany Frame, 1954, 52¾ x 38¼ In.	60
Circus, Cole Bros., Famous Nelson Family, Lithograph, 1935-50, 27 x 21 In.	195
Concert, B.B. King, King Of Blues, Cardboard, c.1960, 14 x 22 In. ....*illus*	354
Concert, Rockin' Blues Record Star Parade, Highland Club, Cardboard, 1960, 14 x 22 In.	472
Concert, Woodstock, An Aquarium Exposition, Orange Ground, 30 x 20 In.	468
Gridley, Rain Or Shine, Paper Lithograph, Home Delivery, Blue, White, 26 x 21 In. ....*illus*	738
Mossant, 3 Hats, Black & Yellow, Cappiello, 1938, 60 x 41 In. ....*illus*	369
Museum, East Asian Art, Fur Ostasiatische Kunst, Germany, 1968, 46 x 17 In..........................	250
Opera, Esclarmonde, Linen Back, France, c.1889, 23 x 31 In..	196
Travel, Messageries Maritimes, Egypt, Syrie, Liban, Par Champollion, Vincent Guerra, 39 x 24 In.	200
Travel, Wagon-Lits, Linen Back, Woman Dreaming, Acropolis, Jean Don, Paris, c.1953, 25 x 39 In.	173
Woman Wearing Red Dress, Signed, Gruan, Frame, 33½ x 26 In. ....*illus*	443

POTLIDS are just that, lids for pots. Transfer-printed potlids had their heyday from the 1840s to the early 1900s. The English Staffordshire potteries made ceramic containers with decorative lids for bear's grease, shrimp or meat paste, cold cream, and toothpaste. Printed advertising and pictures of historical events, portraits of famous people, or scenic views were designed in black and white or color. Reproductions have been made.

Areca Tooth Paste, For Cleansing & Preserving Teeth & Gums, Ironstone, BJL, London..........	47
Atkinson Rose Cold Cream, 24 Bond Street, London	25
Burgess's Genuine Anchovy Paste, For Toast Biscuit Etc., Royal Crest, London......................	24
Celebrated Heal-All Ointment, Mrs. Ellen Hale's, Victorian Woman, London........................	120

POTTERY and porcelain are different. Pottery is opaque; you can't see through it. Porcelain is translucent. If you hold a porcelain dish in front of a strong light, you will see the light through the dish. Porcelain is colder to the touch. Pottery is softer and easier to break and will stain more easily because it is porous. Porcelain is thinner, lighter, and more durable. Majolica, faience, and stoneware are all pottery. Additional pieces of pottery are listed in this book in the categories Pottery-Art, Pottery-Contemporary, Pottery-Midcentury, and under the factory name. For information about pottery makers and marks, see *Kovels' Dictionary of Marks—Pottery & Porcelain: 1650–1850* and *Kovels' New Dictionary of Marks—Pottery & Porcelain: 1850 to the Present.*

Bowl, Lid, Ribbed Handles, Incised Line, Glazed Interior, Boscawen, N.H., c.1850, 7½ In.	312
Bust, Heloise, Red Clay, Pedestal Base, 26 In. ....*illus*	150
Centerpiece, Roses, Gilt, Bronze Mounts, Cupids, Victorian, Austria, 18 x 18½ In............*illus*	121
Jardiniere, Raku, Tapered, Dark Brown, Japan, 39 In.	393
Pitcher, Albany Slip, Drape & Spot, Inscribed, Think Of Me, Tanware, Pa., c.1885, 7⅜ In........	3540
Pitcher, Bulldog Shape, Handle, Painted, 10½ In.	83
Pitcher, Dash Albany Slip, Handle, Flaring Collar, Fuchsia Vine, Tanware, Pa., c.1885, 9 In.....	649
Pitcher, Hand Painted, Side Handle, Figural Scene, Italy, 1800s, 10¼ x 7½ In.	63
Pitcher, La Belle Cider, Flow Blue, White, Ruffled Rim, Wheeling Pottery, 8 x 7 In.	29
Plate, Milkweed, Brown, Green, Blue, Glazed, Henry Varnum Poor, 1920s, 9¾ In.............*illus*	1625
Sugar, Buddha Shape, Sadler, 8½ In.	59
Tea Bowl, Footed, Shino Glaze, Makoto Yabe, Late 1900s, 3 x 4¾ In.	74
Vase, Birds, Wisteria Branches, Caramel & Yellow Glaze, Kyoto, Japan, Early 1900s, 12 In.	113
Vase, Bottle Shape, Blue Lava Glaze, Amalgam Relief, Ceramano, 1960s, 8½ In.....................	162
Vase, Glaze, Incised & Multicolor, Stylized Flowers, Heraldic, c.1930, 36 x 20 In.................	708
Vase, Oxblood, Handle, White Pines, Circular Paper Label, c.1915, 7 x 4 In.	1125
Vase, Red & Blue Fish, Black Ground, Late 1800s, 12¼ In.	270
Vase, Reseau, Network, Green, Gold, Signed, Markham, 1900s, 3 x 6¾ In.	1000

POTTERY-ART. Art pottery was first made in America in Cincinnati, Ohio, during the 1870s. The pieces were hand thrown and hand decorated. The art pottery tradition continued until studio potters began making the more artistic wares about 1930. American, English, and Continental art pottery by less well-known makers is listed here.

Pottery, Bust, Heloise, Red Clay, Pedestal Base, 26 In.
$150

Keystone Auctions LLC

Pottery, Centerpiece, Roses, Gilt, Bronze Mounts, Cupids, Victorian, Austria, 18 x 18½ In.
$121

Fontaine's Auction Gallery

Pottery, Plate, Milkweed, Brown, Green, Blue, Glazed, Henry Varnum Poor, 1920s, 9¾ In.
$1,625

Rago Arts and Auction Center

P

Pottery-Art, Bowl, Octagonal, Black & White, Keramos, Austria, 1900s, 9 In. $2,202

Pook & Pook

China Mark

A mark with the words *Made in the People's Republic of China* was used starting in 1949. The mark appears on baskets, pottery, and other objects. *Made in China* was used from 1891 to 1949 and again starting in 1978.

Pottery-Art, Charger, Interior Scene, Couple & Globe, Floral Border, 18 In. $403

Richard D. Hatch & Associates

Pottery-Art, Vase, Celadon, Russet Crystalline Glaze, Adelaide Robineau, 1915, 3¾ x 4¼ In. $23,750

Rago Arts and Auction Center

Most makers listed in *Kovels' American Art Pottery,* such as Arequipa, Ohr, Rookwood, Roseville, and Weller, are listed in their own categories in this book. More recent pottery is listed under the name of the maker or in another pottery category.

Bowl, Footed, Marked, Multicolor, Austria, Early 1900s, 4 In.	150
Bowl, Octagonal, Black & White, Keramos, Austria, 1900s, 9 In. ....*illus*	2202
Charger, Interior Scene, Couple & Globe, Floral Border, 18 In. ....*illus*	403
Figurine, Fox Lying Down, Multicolor, 1900s, 6½ In.	38
Figurine, Woman, Standing, Long Dress, Circular Base, P. Ipsen Enke, c.1930, 14 x 9 x 5 In....	94
Jardiniere, Earthenware, Raised Flowers, Figures, Enamel, Japan, c.1920, 24 x 11½ In.	123
Pitcher, Hedingham, Earthenware, Mottled Brown Glaze, E. Bingham, 1800s, 14 In.	111
Temple Jar, Blue, White, Lion Finial, Wood Stand, Earthenware, Chinese, 1900s, 28 In.	300
Tile, Victorian Woman, Long Gown, Frame, Russell Crook, 16½ x 9 In.	1888
Vase, 7 Handles, Organic, Green Glaze, Signed Hicks, Ephraim, 1900s, 12½ x 12 In.	525
Vase, Art Deco, High Shoulder, Green Glaze, Inscribed, EB, c.1925, 8 x 5½ In.	271
Vase, Canteen, Flowers, Stippling, Cincinnati, Hungarian Faience, 11 In.	83
Vase, Celadon, Russet Crystalline Glaze, Adelaide Robineau, 1915, 3¾ x 4¼ In. ....*illus*	23750
Vase, Copper Crystalline, Hare's Fur Glaze, Signed, Charles F. Binns, 1930, 9 x 4 In. ....*illus*	4062
Vase, Double Stem Shape, Germany, Early 1900s, 9¾ In.	75
Vase, Floral, Aesthetic Style, Painted, 8 x 9½ In.	38
Vase, Grape Clusters, Flame Painted, Theophilus Brouwer, Incised, 1900s, 13 In. ....*illus*	4062
Vase, Incised Design, Christopher Dresser, Linthorpe, Early 1900s, 5½ In. ....*illus*	75
Vase, Leaves, Buds, Green, William Jervis, Rose Vallery Pottery, 1905, 7 x 3¾ In.	7500
Vase, Limoges Style, Applied Bluebird, Iridescent, Footed, 1880s, 6 In.	295
Vase, Oak Trees, Copper Brown, Blue, Signed, California Faience, 6¼ In.	4375
Vase, Overlapping Leaves, Blue Ground, Incised, Hy-Long Muscle Shoals, 5½ In.	560
Vase, Signed, Andra Petitcily, France, c.1900s, 11 In.	25
Vase, Squat, Green Iridescent, Flowers, Heliosine, Bohemia, c.1900, 5½ In.	300
Vase, Stylized Trees, Incised, Olive Green, Blue Matte Glaze, Zark, 5 x 5½ In.	2250
Vase, Stylized Tulips, Blue, Frederick Rhead, Avon Faience, c.1903, 5½ In. ....*illus*	1625
Vase, Turned Squares, Circles, Black, Emile Lenoble, 1926, 11½ In.	3750

POTTERY-CONTEMPORARY lists pieces made by artists working about 1975 and later.

Basket Shape, Tang Style Glaze, Earthenware, 1970s, Stamped Woodman, 7½ x 15 In.	10625
Bowl, Crater, Tan Glaze, Signed, James Lovera, 2½ x 8 In.	1000
Bowl, Flared, Brown, Red Band, White Clay, Lucie Rie, England, c.1955, 4 x 9 In.	9840
Bowl, Glaze, Green & Brown, Inscribed Beato, Beatrice Wood, c.1960, 2 x 7 In.	1000
Bowl, Landscape, Raku, Earthenware, Wayne Higby, c.1988, 7 x 11 In.	2375
Bowl, Rectangular, Cream Background, Black Rim, Michael Simon, 8½ x 9 In.	207
Chalice, Stylized Flowers, Iridescent, Beatrice Wood, 8 x 5 In. ....*illus*	2250
Charger, Don Quixote, Horseback, Hand Painted, Signed, Puente Arzobispo, 16½ In.	42
Charger, Fish, Fancy Fruit Border, Ron Meyers, 15 In.	81
Charger, Footed, Green Iridescent Glaze, Tony Evans, Late 1900s, 18½ In.	153
Figurine, Storyteller, Woman, Suede Shawl, Holds Children, Robert Rivera, c.1950, 9¾ In.	250
Figurine, Stylized Figure, Multicolor, Glazed, Michael Lucero, 1990, 18 x 14 In. ....*illus*	2375
Jar, Botanical, Hand Painted, Mary Vaughn, 1980, 8 In.	94
Jar, Lid, Plum Tree, Handles, John Parker Glick, 12 In.	115
Jar, Mottled Beige Glaze, Blue Overglaze, Otto Heino, 6¾ In.	369
Jar, Wood Fired, Oval, 2 Strap Handles, Dark Tapered, Mark Hewitt, 11½ x 10 In.	307
Jardiniere, Salt Glaze, Ribbon, Concentric Lines, Drain Hole, Mark Hewitt, 11 In.	177
Jug, 2 Scrolled Handles, Rear Lug Handles, North Carolina, 17½ In.	112
Jug, Face, Devil, Red, Horns, Tongue, Strap Handle, Brown's Pottery, 1994, 15 In. ....*illus*	420
Jug, Swirl Face, Cobalt Blue & Cream Glaze, Bulbous, Inscribed, A.V. Smith, 13¾ In.	688
Tea Bowl, Green Glaze, Footed, Marked, Warren Mackenzie, 2¾ x 4⅞ In.	185
Tea Bowl, Shino, Glaze, Red, White, Artist's Mark, Makoto Yabe, Boston, 3 x 5 In.	431
Tea Bowl, White Glaze, Black Crazing, Footed, Nancee Meeker, Westport, Mass., 2¾ x 5 In.	277
Teapot, Blue, Purple, Green, Pink, Mottled, Makoto Yabe, Boston, c.1990, 6½ In.	461
Vase, Birds, Carved, Painted, Flattened Shape, A. Bohrod, C. Ball, 11 x 5 In. ....*illus*	938
Vase, Blue & Tan, Narrow Neck, Flat Rim, Beatrice Wood, 5 x 4½ In.	1353
Vase, Bottle Shape, Blue, Black Base, Rings, Vivika & Otto Heino, 7¾ x 5 In. ....*illus*	311

P

Pottery-Art, Vase, Copper Crystalline, Hare's Fur Glaze, Signed, Charles F. Binns, 1930, 9 x 4 In.
$4,062

Rago Arts and Auction Center

Pottery-Art, Vase, Grape Clusters, Flame Painted, Theophilus Brouwer, Incised, 1900s, 13 In.
$4,062

Rago Arts and Auction Center

Pottery-Art, Vase, Incised Design, Christopher Dresser, Linthorpe, Early 1900s, 5 ½ In.
$75

Pook & Pook

Pottery-Art, Vase, Stylized Tulips, Blue, Frederick Rhead, Avon Faience, c.1903, 5 ½ In.
$1,625

Rago Arts and Auction Center

Pottery-Contemporary, Chalice, Stylized Flowers, Iridescent, Beatrice Wood, 8 x 5 In.
$2,250

Rago Arts and Auction Center

Pottery-Contemporary, Figurine, Stylized Figure, Multicolor, Glazed, Michael Lucero, 1990, 18 x 14 In.
$2,375

Rago Arts and Auction Center

Pottery-Contemporary, Jug, Face, Devil, Red, Horns, Tongue, Strap Handle, Brown's Pottery, 1994, 15 In.
$420

Brunk Auctions

Pottery-Contemporary, Vase, Birds, Carved, Painted, Flattened Shape, A. Bohrod, C. Ball, 11 x 5 In.
$938

Treadway

Pottery-Contemporary, Vase, Bottle Shape, Blue, Black Base, Rings, Vivika & Otto Heino, 7 ¾ x 5 In.
$311

Soulis Auctions

POTTERY-CONTEMPORARY

Pottery-Contemporary, Vase, Bulbous, Ribbed Neck, Ash Glaze, Marked, Rob Barnard, Late 1900s, 9 1/2 In.
$37

Skinner, Inc.

Pottery-Contemporary, Vase, Crater, Volcanic Glaze, Green, Yellow-Orange, Doyle Lane, 3 1/2 x 4 In.
$2,730

Treadway

Pottery-Contemporary, Vase, Resin, Gaetano Pesce, Fish Design, Italy, 2013, 6 x 9 1/2 In.
$1,750

Wright

Pottery-Contemporary, Vase, Stripes, Beige, Gray, Brown, Small Neck Opening, Antonio Prieto, 12 x 9 1/2 In.
$1,188

Treadway

Pottery-Contemporary, Vase, Sutup, Glazed Stoneware, Slip Coated, Neutral Colors, Claude Conover, 21 x 15 In.
$10,000

Rago Arts and Auction Center

Pottery-Midcentury, Bowl, Drip Glaze, Wide Rim, Lip, Footed, Waylande Gregory, 3 3/4 x 11 1/2 In.
$562

Rago Arts and Auction Center

Pottery-Midcentury, Figurine, Sul Mondo, Nude Girl, Dog, Sitting On Globe, Lenci, 1930s, 19 x 10 In.
$8,750

Rago Arts and Auction Center

Pottery-Midcentury, Planter, Architectural, David Cressey, c.1963, 23 x 23 1/2 In.
$5,625

Los Angeles Modern Auctions

Vase, Bulbous, Handles, White Glaze, Bruno Gambone, Italy, 12 x 15 In.	984
Vase, Bulbous, Ribbed Neck, Ash Glaze, Marked, Rob Barnard, Late 1900s, 9 ½ In...........*illus*	37
Vase, Bulbous, Tapering, Banded Rim & Foot, Otto & Vivika Heino, c.1975, 17 In......................	2583
Vase, Carved & Painted, Molded Base, Michael Sherrill, 9 x 6 ½ In.	161
Vase, Carved & Painted, Tree Shape, Signed, Don Walton, 15 In.	295
Vase, Crater, Volcanic Glaze, Green, Yellow-Orange, Doyle Lane, 3 ½ x 4 In. ....*illus*	2730
Vase, Faces On Rim, Black, Blue On Red Clay, Signed, Beato, 4 ⅜ x 5 In.	1298
Vase, Feelie, Crystalline Glaze, Purple, Green, Blue, Tan, Cabat, 6 In...............................	1298
Vase, Feelie, Glaze, Yellow, Signed On Base, Rose Cabat, 3 ¼ In.	369
Vase, Green, Brown, Black Polka Dots, 2 Handles, Stamped Woodman, 1980s, 9 ¾ x 12 In.	20000
Vase, Iridescent Green, Small Opening, Beatrice Wood, 5 x 6 In.	1845
Vase, Lid, Hand Formed, Orange, White, Makoto Yabe, Boston, c.1990, 8 ⅜ In.	615
Vase, Light Blue, Short Stem, Footed, Charlotte Reith, c.1980, 3 ⅜ x 4 In.	49
Vase, Maal, Tan & Cream Glaze, Signed, Claude Conover, 15 ½ x 13 In.	6875
Vase, Moonpot, Cream To Tan Glaze, Rattle, Signed, Toshiko Takaezu, 6 x 5 In.	1105
Vase, Mossy Green, Gray, Stretched Surface, Lacquer Lid, Marked, Makoto Yabe, Boston, 10 In. .	308
Vase, Odysseum, Figures, Horse, Multicolor, Glazed, Rudy Autio, 1993, 24 x 23 In...................	6875
Vase, Pitcher, Pillow, Tang Style Glaze, Betty Woodman, 1970s, 13 ½ x 14 In.	31250
Vase, Raku Fired, Textured, Signed, Peter Hayes, England, 21 ½ x 16 ½ x 6 In.	625
Vase, Raku, Earthenware, Black & White, Bulbous, Paul Edmund Soldner, 14 x 14 In................	984
Vase, Raku, Earthenware, Brown, Nude Woman, Paul Edmund Soldner, 11 x 11 ¼ x 10 ¾ In....	1230
Vase, Resin, Gaetano Pesce, Fish Design, Italy, 2013, 6 x 9 ½ In.............................*illus*	1750
Vase, Round, Ebonized Pine, Shades Of Gray, David Sengel, c.1996, 5 x 12 In.	208
Vase, Snakes, Climbing, Frog Inside, Blue & Green, Tim Eberhardt, 1995, 9 ½ In.	177
Vase, Stripes, Beige, Gray, Brown, Small Neck Opening, Antonio Prieto, 12 x 9 ½ In..........*illus*	1188
Vase, Sutup, Glazed Stoneware, Slip Coated, Neutral Colors, Claude Conover, 21 x 15 In....*illus*	10000
Vase, Tenmoku Glaze, Cylindrical, Lacquer Top, Malcolm Wright Studio, Marlboro, Vt., 6 x 6 ⅝ In. .	123
Vase, Volcanic Glaze, Painted, Signed, Beatrice Wood, 5 ½ x 4 In.	5000
Vase, White, Gray, Pink, Brick Glaze, Marked, Tom Hoadley Studio, N.Y., 1980, 5 ¾ x 5 ½ In.	123

POTTERY-MIDCENTURY includes pieces made from the 1940s to about 1975.

Bowl, Carved, Reddish Brown Glaze, Signed, Laura Andreson, 3 x 6 ½ In.	390
Bowl, Drip Glaze, Wide Rim, Lip, Footed, Waylande Gregory, 3 ¾ x 11 ½ In.....................*illus*	562
Bowl, Flared, Diagonal Lines, Light Brown Glaze, Lucie Rie, c.1952, 6 x 10 In.	6765
Bowl, Stylized Tree, Earth Tones, Glazed, Harrison McIntosh, 9 In......................................	937
Bowl, Taureau, Glazed, Pablo Picasso, Paris, France, 2 ½ x 7 In...................................	4920
Cornucopia, Yellow Glaze, Signed, Nicodemus, 10 In..	29
Figurine, Bird, Robin, Fero Stone, Golden Bill, Black & Redbreast, Nicodemus, 5 In.	35
Figurine, Dog, Fox Terrier, Wire Haired, Glazed, Signed, Nicodemus, 4 ½ x 5 In.	489
Figurine, Pelican, Cream Glaze, Copper Color Highlights, Signed, Nicodemus, 9 In.................	1208
Figurine, Sul Mondo, Nude Girl, Dog, Sitting On Globe, Lenci, 1930s, 19 x 10 In..............*illus*	8750
Pitcher, Cavalier Et Cheval, Horse & Rider, 1952, 8 x 7 In.	11875
Pitcher, Cruchon Hibou, White, Black, Blue, Madoura, Pablo Picasso, 10 ½ x 7 In.	12000
Pitcher, Green Mottled Glaze, Brown Rim, Handle, Signed, Nicodemus, 16 Oz.	127
Pitcher, Picador, Glaze, Terra-Cotta, Paris, Pablo Picasso, France, 5 ¼ x 4 x 3 ¼ In.	3998
Planter, Architectural, David Cressey, c.1963, 23 x 23 ½ In. ....*illus*	5625
Plaque, Woman, Man, Birds, Incised Harris Strong, 23 ½ In., Pair..	236
Plate, Life Scene, White Glossy Glaze, Blue, Black & Green, Signed, Picasso, Madoura, 10 In. ..	2723
Plate, Toros, Bulls, Black Oxide, Colored Engobe, Madoura Pein Feu, Pablo Picasso, France.....	4920
Platter, Bouquet, Flowers In Vase, Pablo Picasso, 1955, 12 x 14 In.	9688
Platter, Visage De Femme, Engobe, Pablo Picasso, Paris, France, 15 ¼ x 12 ½ x 1 ½ In.	30750
Vase, Abstract Design, Blue Glaze, Aaron Bohrod, Carlton Ball, c.1950, 8 ½ x 7 In.	750
Vase, Earth Tones, Glazed, Round, Maija Grotell, 1940s, 11 x 10 In..................................*illus*	2875
Vase, Flared, Footed, Pale Blue Green Matte Glaze, Signed, Laura Andreson, 6 ½ x 11 In..........	1250
Vase, Gourd, Black Matte Design On Glossy Black, Peter Voulkos, 1950s, 7 ¾ In.............*illus*	1500
Vase, Heartbeat Pattern, Light Blue, Speckled, Bodo Mans, Germany, 21 In.	181
Vase, Ilkil, Glazed, Signed, Claude Conover, Ohio, c.1965, 21 ½ x 17 In..........................*illus*	5625
Vase, Mottle Glazed, Handless, Stahl, c.1936, 7 ¾ In.	325
Vase, Pfaltzgraff, 2 Handles, Brown, Grain Texture, 8 ¼ In..	50
Vase, Tan, Brown Band, Dark Speckles, Vivika & Otto Heino, 12 x 13 In...........................	698

Pottery-Midcentury, Vase, Earth Tones, Glazed, Round, Maija Grotell, 1940s, 11 x 10 In.
$2,875

Rago Arts and Auction Center

Pottery-Midcentury, Vase, Gourd, Black Matte Design On Glossy Black, Peter Voulkos, 1950s, 7 ¾ In.
$1,500

Rago Arts and Auction Center

P

Pottery-Midcentury, Vase, Ilkil, Glazed, Signed, Claude Conover, Ohio, c.1965, 21 ½ x 17 In.
$5,625

Freeman's Auctioneers & Appraisers

Powder Flask, Copper, Brass, Embossed Eagle Both Sides, 4½ In.

$136

Hartzell's Auction Gallery, Inc.

Powder Horn, Engraved, Birds, Ducks, Hunter Dog, Soldiers In Uniform, 1879, 9 In.

$120

Garth's Auctioneers & Appraisers

Powder Horn, Metal Inset Star, Josiah Owens, American, c.1856, 14 In.

$1,125

Leslie Hindman Auctioneers

Vase, Variegated Drip Glaze, Face, Bruce Fontaine, c.1970, 11 x 6 x 6½ In.		148
Wastebasket, Oval, Brown, Glaze, 4-Footed, Signed Wyman, East Weymouth, Mass., c.1970, 14 x 13 In.		523

POWDER FLASKS AND POWDER HORNS were made to hold the gunpowder used in antique firearms. The early examples were made of horn or wood; later ones were of copper or brass.

POWDER FLASK

Copper, Brass, Embossed Eagle Both Sides, 4½ In.	*illus*	136
Jade, Spinach Color, Carved, Mughal Style, 1900s, 7¼ In.		313
Wood, Brass Collar, Eagle, Perched, 4 In.		77

POWDER HORN

Engraved, Birds, Ducks, Hunter Dog, Soldiers In Uniform, 1879, 9 In.	*illus*	120
Engraved, Dark Brown Patina, Stopper, William X. Donald, 1800s, 14 In.		252
Great Seal Of The United States, Reverse Side Tree, E.B. Holden, 1832, 6 In.		469
Horn, Carved, Engraved, Checkerboard Pattern, 3 Stars, A. Wilson, c.1792, 10½ In.		900
Horn, Carved, Engraved, House Above Ships, Heart, Diamond, c.1795, 7½ In.		720
Horn, Engraved, Birds & Ducks, Hunter & Dog, Soldiers, 1879, 9 In.		1500
Horn, Flask Shape, Brown, Engraved, Early 1800s, 7 In.		72
Horn, New York Map, Royal British Crest, Heraldic Crest, Scottish Silver Mounts, 13 In.		9000
Horn, Rural Scene, Branches, Blue & Salmon, Hand Painted, 11 In.		103
Incised Florette Roundel, Ship, Bald Eagle, Various Tools, c.1776, 11½ In.		625
Metal Inset Star, Josiah Owens, American, c.1856, 14 In.	*illus*	1125
Scrimshaw, Woven Carrying Strap, Inscribed, Thomas Browne, 16 In.		136

PRATT FENTON **PRATT** ware means two different things. It was an early Staffordshire pottery, cream colored with colored decorations, made by Felix Pratt during the late eighteenth century. There was also Pratt ware made with transfer designs during the mid-nineteenth century in Fenton, England. Reproductions of the transfer-printed Pratt are being made.

Figurine, Lion, Reclining, c.1825, 4 In.	275
Loving Cup, Turquoise, Country Scenes, c.1850, 4 x 4 In.	360
Mug, Imari, Chinoiserie, 1890s, 3 In.	85
Plate, The Hop Queen, Marbled Border, 1851, 9 In.	145
Potlid, Shottery, Shakespeare's Wife, Frame, c.1850-60, 5 x 3 In.	145
Potlid, The Village Wedding, Watercolors, Frame, c.1857, 6¼ x 1⅛ In.	95
Potlid, Woman, Boy & Goats, Multicolor, Transfer, c.1860, 3 x 1¼ In.	110

PRESSED GLASS, or pattern glass, was first made in the United States in the 1820s after the invention of glass pressing machines. Hundreds of patterns of pressed glass were made in complete table settings. Although the Boston and Sandwich Works was the most famous of the pressed glass factories, there were about sixteen other factories making pressed glass from 1830 to 1850, and still more from 1850 to 1900, when pressed glass reached its greatest popularity. It is now being widely reproduced. The pattern names used in this listing are based on the information in the book *Pressed Glass in America* by John and Elizabeth Welker. There may be pieces of pressed glass listed in this book in other categories, such as Lamp, Ruby Glass, Sandwich Glass, and Souvenir.

Actress, Goblet, Woman On Each Side, Footed, 6⅜ x 3¼ In.	9
Atlas, Pitcher, Clear, 52 Oz., 12 In.	132
Bead & Dart, Mug, Cobalt Blue, Child's	27
Block & Diamond, Compote, Vaseline, 9½ In.	39
Coin Spot, Banana Stand, Blue Opalescent, 5 x 7 x 4 In.	60
Colorado, Toothpick Holder, Green, 3-Footed, U.S. Glass, 2¾ In.	10
Crossed Swords, Nappy, Blue	245
Daisy & Button, Inkwell, Vaseline, Arm Chair Shape, Yellow, 4 x 2 In.	169
Daisy & Button, Whiskbroom, Amber, 7½ x 5 In.	50
Diamond & Leaf, Pitcher, Sawtooth Rim, 9¾ In.	55
Diamond Point, Inkwell, Clear, Square Shape, Marked Made In England, 2 x 3 In.	11

Diamond, Bowl, 6⅝ In.	22
Fan & Diamond, Creamer, 5¼ In.	18
Grapes & Leaves, Mug, Cobalt Blue, Child's, 2½ In.	34
Grasshopper, Bowl, 3 Curled Feet, 8 x 2 In.	50
Hatch Diamond & Fan, Vase, Ruffled Rim, Flared, 12 In.	160
Herringbone Buttress, Tumbler, Green, 1899, 4 In	263
Hobstar & Pinwheel, Ice Bucket, 9¼ x 6¼ In.	425
Hobstar, Bowl, Sawtooth, 3 x 9 In.	55
Holly, Sugar & Creamer	208
Horseshoe Daisy, Pitcher, Ice Lip, 8 x 5 In.	42
Illinois, Strawholder, Emerald Green, 9 x 3 x 3 In.	425
Inverted Thistle, Compote, Clear, 7½ In.	45
Lacy, Open Salt, Diamond & Scroll, RD 17, Boston & Sandwich Co., c.1835, 1⅛ x 2⁷⁄₁₆ In.	80
Loops & Drops, Butter, Cover, 6 x 8 In.	55
Loops & Drops, Sugar, Lid, 6 x 5 In.	40
Manhattan, Bowl, Pink, Handles, 8 In.	22
Marjorie, Cruet, Stopper, 5 In.	42
Moon & Star, Toothpick Holder, Blue, Ruffled, L.E. Smith, 2⅜ x 2 In.	3
Moon & Stars, Compote, 6¾ x 10 In.	38
Petal, Tray, 11 In.	20
Pineapple & Fans, Vase, Trumpet, Scalloped, 9¾ In.	45
Plume, Compote, Ruby, 7¾ x 6 In.	55
Pressed Block, Compote, 4½ x 3⅞ In.	39
Pressed Leaf, Vase, Loop, Canary Yellow, Fluted Rim, Circular Foot, c.1850, 10 x 4 In. *illus*	439
Psyche & Cupid, Pitcher, Footed, 9½ In.	85
Roman Rosette, Cup Plate, Amethyst, Scalloped, 5⅜ In.	300
Slewed Horseshoe, Underplate, For Punch Bowl, Ruffled, L.E. Smith Glass Co., 21 In.	41
Star, Dish, Pear Shape, 7 In.	145
Stars & Bars, Candleholder, Ball Feet, 4 x 1½ In.	15
Swirl, Relish, 4 Sections, 10 In.	23
Traditions, Celery Dish, 9 x 5 In.	25
Twisted Loop, Vase, 8-Sided, Square Base, Cobalt Blue, c.1840, 10 In.	1234
Water Lily, Bowl, Blue Opalescent, 10 In.	115
Westmoreland, Lamp, Cylindrical Font, Clear Chimney, c.1900, Miniature, 7 x 4 x 3 In.	108
Wexford, Relish, 5 Sections, 10¾ In.	17
Wild Rose, Bowl, Footed, 1940s, 9 In.	25

PRINT, in this listing, means any of many printed images produced on paper by one of the more common methods, such as lithography. The prints listed here are of interest primarily to the antiques collector, not the fine arts collector. Many of these prints were originally part of books. Other prints will be found in the Advertising, Currier & Ives, Movie, and Poster categories.

Aquatint, Yellow, Gray, Black, Adolph Gottlieb, Signed, 1972, 31½ x 21 In.	2706

Audubon bird prints were originally issued as part of books printed from 1826 to 1854. They were issued in two sheet sizes, 26½ inches by 39½ inches and 11 inches by 7 inches. The height of a picture is listed before the width. The quadrupeds were issued in 28-by-22-inch prints. Later editions of the Audubon books were done in many sizes, and reprints of the books in the original sizes were also made. The words *After John James Audubon* appear on all of the prints, including the originals, because the pictures were made as copies of Audubon's original oil paintings. The bird pictures have been so popular they have been copied in myriad sizes using both old and new printing methods. This list includes originals and later copies because Audubon prints of all ages are sold in antiques shops.

J.W.Audubon

Audubon, American Widgeon, 2 Birds, Hand Colored, Engraving, 1836, 26 x 39 In.	767
Audubon, Columbian Black Tailed Deer, J.T. Bowen, Frame, 21 x 25½ In. *illus*	768
Audubon, Cow Bunting, Colored, Frame, 1830, 26½ x 39 In. *illus*	1800
Audubon, Mississippi Kite, Havell, Frame, 30½ x 19 In. *illus*	854
Audubon, Traill's Flycatcher, Hand Colored, Engraving, 1828, 34½ x 25 In.	531
Currier & Ives prints are listed in the Currier & Ives category.	
Escher, M.C., Sky & Water I, Fish, Birds, Tessellation, 1938. *illus*	37500

Pressed Glass, Pressed Leaf, Vase, Loop, Canary Yellow, Fluted Rim, Circular Foot, c.1850, 10 x 4 In.
$439

Jeffrey S. Evans & Associates

Print, Audubon, Columbian Black Tailed Deer, J.T. Bowen, Frame, 21 x 25½ In.
$768

Neal Auction Company

Print, Audubon, Cow Bunting, Colored, Frame, 1830, 26½ x 39 In.
$1,800

Eldred's

This is an edited listing of current prices. Visit **Kovels.com** to check thousands of prices from previous years and sign up for free information on trends, tips, reproductions, marks, and more.

P

Print, Audubon, Mississippi Kite, Havell, Frame, 30½ x 19 In.
$854

Neal Auction Company

Print, Escher, M.C., Sky & Water I, Fish, Birds, Tessellation, 1938
$37,500

Bonhams

Print, Japanese, Hasui, Kawase, Snow At Funabori, River, Nagaban, Tate-E, 22 x 10 In.
$406

Eldred's

Icart prints were made by Louis Icart, who worked in Paris from 1907 as an employee of a postcard company. He then started printing magazines and fashion brochures. About 1910 he created a series of etchings of fashionably dressed women, and he continued to make similar etchings until he died in 1950. He is well known as a printmaker, painter, and illustrator. Original etchings are much more expensive than the later photographic copies.

Icart, Desire, Etching, Aquatint, Oval Giltwood Frame, Signed, 1926, 21 x 26 In.	472
Icart, Morning Cup, Aquatint, Wood Frame, Windmill Blindstamp, Signed, 1940, 30 x 28¾ In.	1888

Jacoulet prints were designed by Paul Jacoulet (1902–1960), a Frenchman who spent most of his life in Japan. He was a master of Japanese woodblock print technique. Subjects included life in Japan, the South Seas, Korea, and China. His prints were sold by subscription and issued in series. Each series had a distinctive seal, such as a sparrow or butterfly. Most Jacoulet prints are approximately 15 x 10 inches.

Jacoulet, Chagrin D'Amour, Kusai, 1940, 6 x 4 In.	300
Jacoulet, Le Marie, Seol Coree, Woodblock, Frame, 1950, 18 x 21 In.	2800
Jacoulet, Le Nid, Coree, 1941, 6¼ x 4¼ In.	325
Jacoulet, Le Tresor, Coree, 1940, 18 x 14 In.	1800
Jacoulet, Nuit De Niege Coree, Woodblock, 1940, 8 x 11 In.	425

Japanese woodblock prints are listed as follows: Print, Japanese, name of artist, title or description, type, and size. Dealers use the following terms: *Tate-e* is a vertical composition. *Yoko-e* is a horizontal composition. The words *Aiban* (13 by 9 inches), *Chuban* (10 by 7 ½ inches), *Hosoban* (13 by 6 inches), *Koban* (7 by 4 inches), *Nagaban* (20 by 9 inches), *Oban* (15 by 10 inches), *Shikishiban* (8 by 9 inches), and *Tanzaku* (15 by 5 inches) denote approximate size. Modern versions of some of these prints have been made. Other woodblock prints that are not Japanese are listed under Print, Woodblock.

Japanese, 5 Scenes From Tokaido Road, 10 x 15 In., 5 Piece	688
Japanese, Hasui, Kawase, Atago Hill In Spring, Children, Cherry Tree, 1921, 15 x 10 In.	6000
Japanese, Hasui, Kawase, Hikawa Park, Omiya, Sun-Splashed Trees, 1929, 15 x 10 In.	1875
Japanese, Hasui, Kawase, Shiba Benten Pond, 2 Women, Bridge, Water Lilies, 10 x 15 In.	3000
Japanese, Hasui, Kawase, Snow At Funabori, River, Nagaban, Tate-E, 22 x 10 In. ....*illus*	406
Japanese, Hasui, Kawase, Wheat Farmers, Harvesting Crops, Watanabe Seal, 10 x 15 In.	510
Japanese, Hasui, Kawase, Zentsu Temple, Sanshu, Temple Gate, Rain, 15 x 10 In.	344
Japanese, Hiroshige, Abalone & Peach Blossom, 15 x 10 In.	540
Japanese, Hiroshige, Ichikoku Bridge In Eastern Capital, Figures Crossing, 15 x 10 In.	180
Japanese, Hiroshige, Swamps & Floating Water Reeds Of The Yoshiwara, Frame, 22 x 16 In.	192
Japanese, Hiroshige, True View Of Muro Harbor In Harima Province, Sailboats, 15 x 10 In. *illus*	100
Japanese, Hiroshige, View Of Oi River From Slope Near Kanaya, 15 x 10 In.	180
Japanese, Karhu, Clifton, Fall Farm, Drying Rice, Mountains, 10 x 10 In.	522
Japanese, Koitsu, Tsuchiya, Night In Shinagawa Port, Sailboats, Full Moon, 15 x 10 In.	360
Japanese, Koitsu, Tsuchiya, Sarusawa Pond, Figure In Snow, Willow Tree, 20 x 9 In.	240
Japanese, Koitsu, Tsuchiya, Snow At Gardens, Kiyoto Maruyama, Bridge, 15 x 10 In.	1680
Japanese, Kuniyoshi, 3 Women & Cherry Trees, Triptych, 15 x 10 In., 3 Piece	510
Japanese, Kuniyoshi, Utagawa, Samurai Holding Large Staff, Beach, Waves, c.1840, 15 x 10 In.	147
Japanese, Kuniyoshi, Woman & 2 Children, Rocks, 15 x 10 In.	96
Japanese, Kuniyoshi, Woman At Hibachi, Hides Puppy In Her Kimono, Frame, 20 x 16 In.	240
Japanese, Sacred Bridge At Nikko, Red Lacquer Bridge, Doi Publishing Seal, 10 x 15 In.	270
Japanese, Shoson, Ohara, Mandarin Ducks In Snow, Watanabe Publisher Seal, 15 x 10 In.	300
Japanese, Shoson, Ohara, Snow At Willow Bridge, 2 Figures With Umbrellas, 15 x 10 In.	1140
Japanese, Taisui, Inuzuka, Hydrangeas, Blue Butterfly, Doi Publishing Seal, 15 x 10 In.	660
Japanese, Yoshida, Hiroshi, Cherry Tree In Kuwagoe, Figures At Shrine, Signed, 15 x 10 In.	406
Japanese, Yoshida, Hiroshi, Fujiyama From Okitsu, Water Reflection, Signed, 15 x 10 In.	688
Japanese, Yoshida, Hiroshi, Sailing Boats, Forenoon, Signed, Jizuri Seal, 15 x 10 In.	6875
Japanese, Yoshida, Hiroshi, Sailing Boats, Morning, Signed, Jizuri Seal, 15 x 10 In.	2500
Japanese, Yoshitora, Samurai On Brown Horse, 15 x 10 In.	72
Japanese, Yoshitoshi, Man & Screen With Cranes, Phases Of The Moon, 15 x 10 In.	175
Japanese, Yoshitoshi, Seated Nobleman, Raiden In Sky, 100 Aspects Of Moon, 15 x 10 In.	188
Japanese, Yoshitoshi, Warriors Fighting On Scaffold, Large Buddha, 14 x 18 In.	438
Japanese, Yoshitoshi, Woman With Fan, Wispy Smoke, 32 Aspects Of Women, 1889, 15 x 10 In.	163
Kellogg & Comstock, Death Of Zachary Taylor, Lithograph, Color, Frame, 16 x 12 In.	23

Lithograph, Javier, M., Colors, Pencil, El Festejado, Signed, Mexico, 1980, 32 x 33 ¼ In............	484
Lithograph, Moore, Henry, Figures, Reclining, Yellow & Green, Pencil, Signed, 11 ½ x 8 ½ In.	259
Lithograph, Newton, A.A., Ormond Persimmon, Ink Signature, J. Bien Co., 14 x 10 ¾ In.	61
Lithograph, Rosenquist, J., Abstract, Untitled, Color, Pencil, Unframed, Signed, 1999, 33 x 37 In..	1840
Lithograph, Smith, G.R., Nudes, Women, At The Beach, Signed, 40 x 18 ¼ x 14 ¾ In................	185
Lithograph, Zuniga, F., Pencil, Mujer Con Naranja, Signed, Mexico, 1974, 35 ½ x 27 In............	393

Nutting prints are popular with collectors. Wallace Nutting is known for his pictures, furniture, and books. Collectors call his pictures Nutting prints although they are actually hand-colored photographs issued from 1900 to 1941. There are over 10,000 different titles. Wallace Nutting furniture is listed in the Furniture category.

Wallace Nutting

Nutting, A Canopied Road, 1940s, 12 x 18 In.	63
Nutting, A House Wife Of Yesterday, Frame, 7 x 9 In.	45
Nutting, Hollyhock Cottage, Signed, Frame, 7 x 9 In.	36
Nutting, Tree In Bloom, Signed, Frame, 1900s, 7 ¾ x 9 ¾ In.	120
Nutting, Warm Spring Day, 7 ½ x 12 In.	150

Parrish prints are wanted by collectors. Maxfield Frederick Parrish was an illustrator who lived from 1870 to 1966. He is best known as a designer of magazine covers, posters, calendars, and advertisements. His prints have been copied in recent years. Some Maxfield Parrish items may be listed in Advertising.

Maxfield Parrish

Parrish, Daybreak, Frame, 20 x 12 In.	265
Parrish, Garden Of Allah, Frame, 1920s, 20 x 11 In.	248
Parrish, Lady On Cliff Mountains, Frame, 16 x 13 In.	100
Parrish, Lute Players, 1930s, 7 x 10 In.	115
Serigraph, Hunt, Peter, Owl, Perched On Branch, Don Quixote Figure Eyes, 32 x 26 In.....*illus*	163

Woodblock prints that are not in the Japanese tradition are listed here. Most were made in England and the United States during the Arts and Crafts period. Japanese woodblock prints are listed under Print, Japanese.

Woodblock, Baumann, Gustave, Cordova Plaza, Santa Fe, Signed, Frame, 1943, 7 ¾ x 8 In..*illus*	1625
Woodblock, Baumann, Gustave, October Night, Santa Fe, 1919, Signed, 9 ½ x 11 In.	11875
Woodblock, Huneck, S., Nantucket Ferry, Dogs, Boat, Signed, 27 x 31 In.	1150
Woodblock, Patterson, Margaret, Coast Cedars, Frame, Signed, 7 ¼ x 10 ¼ In.	3000
Woodblock, Rice, W., Lake Merritt, Moonlight, Trees, Color, 1920s, 6 x 5 ¼ In.	1875

PURINTON POTTERY COMPANY was incorporated in Wellsville, Ohio, in 1936. The company moved to Shippenville, Pennsylvania, in 1941 and made a variety of hand-painted ceramic wares. By the 1950s Purinton was making dinnerware, souvenirs, cookie jars, and florist wares. The pottery closed in 1959.

Purinton Pottery

Apple, Bowl, Vegetable, 8 In.	22
Apple, Canister, Flour, 7 ⅝ In.	25
Heather Plaid, Flat Cup & Saucer, 2 ½ In.	9
Heather Plaid, Sugar..	13
Intaglio Brown, Jam Dish, Open...	15
Ivy Red Blossom, Jug, Dutch, 32 Oz., 5 In.	21
Normandy Plaid, Teapot, Lid, 4 ¾ In.	51
Shooting Star, Vase, Tab Handles, 5 In..	28

PURSES have been recognizable since the eighteenth century, when leather and needlework purses were preferred. Beaded purses became popular in the nineteenth century, went out of style, but are again in use. Mesh purses date from the 1880s and are still being made. How to carry a handkerchief, lipstick, and cell phone is a problem today for every woman, including the Queen of England.

Alligator, Box Style, Shoulder, Brown, c.1945, 10 x 3 In......................	210
Alligator, Brown, Brass Top Pushbutton Closure, Front Pouch, 1960, 12 ½ In	199
Alligator, Clutch, Black, Lucite Clasp, 1940s, 12 x 7 In.......................	82
Basket Weave, Blue Rhinestones, Wrist Strap, Black Silk, Tassel, Interior Mirror, 1920s, 14 In..	299

Print, Japanese, Hiroshige, True View Of Muro Harbor In Harima Province, Sailboats, 15 x 10 In.
$100

Eldred's

Print, Serigraph, Hunt, Peter, Owl, Perched On Branch, Don Quixote Figure Eyes, 32 x 26 In.
$163

Eldred's

Print, Woodblock, Baumann, Gustave, Cordova Plaza, Santa Fe, Signed, Frame, 1943, 7 ¾ x 8 In.
$1,625

Rago Arts and Auction Center

Purse, Canvas, Tote, Pink, Leather Handles, Expandable Sides, Pockets, Hermes, 15 x 9 x 5 In.
$281

Leslie Hindman Auctioneers

Purse, Leather, Quilted, Navy, Double Chain, Shoulder Straps, 2 Pockets, Chanel, 12 x 8 x 2 In.
$1,125

Leslie Hindman Auctioneers

Purse, Leather, Shoulder, Black, Medusa Medallions, Gianni Versace, 1900s, 11¾ x 8½ x 3 In.
$625

Leslie Hindman Auctioneers

Purse, Lizard, Black, Single Pocket, Goldtone Frame, Strap, c.1950, 7½ x 8 x 3½ In.
$89

Leland Little Auctions

Purse, Mesh, Beige, Red, Blue, Black Diamond, Whiting & Davis, Picadilly, c.1915, 7 x 4 In.
$390

Garth's Auctioneers & Appraisers

Mesh for Purses
A machine that made metal mesh was invented in 1909. Before that, mesh purses were made from individual pieces assembled by hand.

Purse, Mesh, Silver, Gold, Side Drapes, Whiting & Davis, c.1915, 7 x 3¾ In.
$120

Garth's Auctioneers & Appraisers

Purse, Minaudiere, Paisley, Goldtone Hardware, Pushbutton, Strap, Leiber, 3 x 5 x 1 In.
$813

Leslie Hindman Auctioneers

Purse, Reptile Skin, Shoulder Strap, Converts To Clutch, Red, Skin, Judith Leiber, 7 x 6 x 2 In.
$401

Aspire Auctions

Purse, Suede, 6-Sided, Triangular Patches, Brown, Camel, Fringe, Yves Saint Laurent, c.1970
$4,093

Sotheby's

Purse, Velvet, Flower Shape, Layered Petals, Black, Handle, Jeanne Lanvin, c.1930
$1,023

Sotheby's

P

Basket, Nantucket, Friendship, Lid, Swing Handle, Whale, Jose Formoso Reyes, c.1960, 6 In.	2280
Basket, Nantucket, Lid, Swing Handle, Seagull, Jose Formoso Reyes, 1965, 10 In.	2760
Basket, Nantucket, Lightship, Scrimshaw Lid Plaque, Signed, 7 x 9 In.	125
Basket, Nantucket, Oval, Hinged Lid, Bentwood Handle, Mass., 1972, 6½ x 9 x 7 In.	246
Basket, Nantucket, Oval, Hinged Lid, Handle, Jeanne Reis, Late 1900s, 7 x 9½ In.	1476
Basket, Nantucket, Oval, Hinged Lid, Ivory Plaque, Marked, Michael Kane, 1986, 7 x 9½ In. ..	923
Basket, Nantucket, Whale & Harpoon Medallion, Signed, B.J. Sayle, 1980, 6½ x 10 In.	775
Beaded, Clutch, Gold Leaves, Faux Pearls, Stars, Black Ground, Spain, 8 x 4 In.	66
Beaded, Empire, Black Silk Netting, 3 Gold Beaded Tassels, Green, Apricot, c.1815, 14 In.	595
Beaded, Swag, Gold, Yellow, Crocheted, Chain Handle, 1920s, 5 x 7 In.	105
Black Caviar Leather, Binocular, Tassel, Oval Cylinder, Chanel, 7 x 5 x 4 In.	944
Brocade, Green, Pink, Blue Leaves, Silk, Sterling Silver Frame, Chain Strap, 1920s, 6 x 7 In. ..	89
Canvas, Black & White, Rolled Handles, Pockets, Zip Around Closure, Hermes, 4½ In.	2750
Canvas, Handbag, Brown, Monogram, Top Zipper, Side Handles, Louis Vuitton, 10 In.	800
Canvas, Sirius Model 45 Travel Bag, Monogram, Leather Handles, Vuitton, 17½ x 12½ In.	460
Canvas, Tote, Pink, Leather Handles, Expandable Sides, Pockets, Hermes, 15 x 9 x 5 In....*illus*	281
Crocodile, Red, Clutch, Foldover, Flap Closure, Nancy Gonzalez, 10¾ x 4½ x 2 In.	688
Flame Stitch, Wallet, Yellow, Red, Blue, Scalloped Flap, 2 Pockets, 1700s, 4 x 8 In.	1169
Goat Skin, Tote, Metallic Silver, Chain Strap, Zipper, CC, Chanel, 2005, 11 x 13 In.	1375
Guereza Fur, Black, Mantle, Acetate Clasp, Yves Saint Laurent, Rive Gauche, c.1970	2339
Leather & Suede, Gucci, Black, Red & Green, Shoulder Strap, 1970s, 11 In.	725
Leather, Black, Epsom Evelyne, Leather H Plaque & Strap, Hermes, 6¾ x 7 x 2 In.	1875
Leather, Black, Papers Inside, Adjustable Sling, Coach, 8 x 13 In.	104
Leather, Blue, Double Handles, Swivel Mirror, Marked Lou Taylor, c.1970s, 22 In.	39
Leather, Brown, Bag, Adjustable Shoulder Strap, Zip & Slip Pocket, Hermes, 9 x 12 x 5 In.	2250
Leather, Brown, Storage Bag, Sling, Coach, 9 x 12 In.	115
Leather, Caviar, Tote, Quilted, Stitched Logo, Medallion, Goldtone Hardware, 9 x 12 In.	780
Leather, Cirkin 35, Chocolate Fjord, Gold Hardware, Hermes, 2008, 11 x 14 In.	8750
Leather, Handbag, Black, Medusa Medallion, Gianni Versace, 1990s, 6¾ x 6 x 2½ In.	2125
Leather, Handbag, Monogram, Bucket, Louis Vuitton	575
Leather, Pebbled, Tote, Crocodile Embossed Sides, Valentino, 11 x 20 x 8 In.	625
Leather, Quilted, Navy, Double Chain, Shoulder Straps, 2 Pockets, Chanel, 12 x 8 x 2 In...*illus*	1125
Leather, Satchel, Black, Silvertone Hardware, Tan Logo, Zip Pocket, Cartier, 17 x 9 x 5 In........	813
Leather, Shoulder Strap, Converts To Clutch, Black, Sea Star, Judith Leiber, 9 x 5 x 2 In.........	301
Leather, Shoulder, Black, Medusa Medallions, Gianni Versace, 1900s, 11¾ x 8½ x 3 In...*illus*	625
Leather, Surpique, Turquoise, Top Stitched, 2 Handles, Metal CC, Zip, Chanel, 2003, 7 x 10 In. .	1625
Leather, Tote, Quilted Caviar, Medallion, 12 x 6 In.	1955
Leather, Tote, Quilted, Navy, 12 x 8 In.	677
Lizard, Black, Single Pocket, Goldtone Frame, Strap, c.1950, 7½ x 8 x 3½ In. ....*illus*	89
Mesh, Beige, Red, Blue, Black Diamond, Whiting & Davis, Picadilly, c.1915, 7 x 4 In. ....*illus*	390
Mesh, Chain Link, Fringe, Floral, Clasp Closure, Germany, 6 x 7 In.	30
Mesh, Evening, El Sah, Dark Brown, Birdcage Frame, Whiting & Davis, c.1915, 6 x 3 In.	60
Mesh, Peacock, Blue, Cream, Wine, Silver Chain, Mandalian, Mid 1900s, 7¾ x 3¼ In.	270
Mesh, Silver & Black, Charlie Chaplin, Whiting & Davis, c.1976, 6 x 3 In.	1200
Mesh, Silver, Blue Cabochon Clasp, Black, White, Whiting & Davis, c.1915, 7½ x 4 In.	125
Mesh, Silver, Gold, Side Drapes, Whiting & Davis, c.1915, 7 x 3¾ In. ....*illus*	120
Minaudiere, Crystals, Goldtone Top Handle, Chain Shoulder Strap, Leiber, 6 x 4½ x 2 In.......	1250
Minaudiere, Crystals, Silvertone Frame, Shoulder Strap, Judith Leiber, 6 x 2 x 1 In..................	594
Minaudiere, Paisley, Goldtone Hardware, Pushbutton, Strap, Leiber, 3 x 5 x 1 In.............*illus*	813
Ostrich, Natural, Birkin 40, Gold Hardware, Hermes, 1999, 11 x 16 In.	15000
Plastic, Woven, Gancini, Metal Handle, Mesh Zipper, Salvatore Ferragamo, 8 x 8 x 4 In.	313
Python, Clutch, Jimmy Choo, Gold Tone Hardware, Suede Lining, 9½ x 6 In.	288
Reptile Skin, Shoulder Strap, Beige, Snap Close, Colored Stones, Valentino, 11 x 20 x 8 In.	171
Reptile Skin, Shoulder Strap, Converts To Clutch, Red, Skin, Judith Leiber, 7 x 6 x 2 In. ..*illus*	401
Silk, Clutch, Black, Embroidered, Kiss Lock, Leather Woven Chain, Chanel, 7 In.	688
Silk, Evening Bag, Black, Silver Lift Latch, Corded Rope, Tassel, Judith Leiber, 7 x 5 In............	1380
Snakeskin, Samantha, Envelope Style, Crystal Flap, Chain, Judith Leiber, Box, 5 x 9 In.	2125
Suede, 6-Sided, Triangular Patches, Brown, Camel, Fringe, Yves Saint Laurent, c.1970.....*illus*	4093
Tote, Rolled Handles, Zipper Pocket, Louis Vuitton, France, 15 x 14 x 3 In...............................	413
Velvet, Flower Shape, Layered Petals, Black, Handle, Jeanne Lanvin, c.1930......................*illus*	1023

Quezal, Vase, Flared Rim, White Cased, Green & Gold Pulled Feather, Pontil, 1900s, 6¼ In.
$800

Skinner, Inc.

Quezal, Vase, Green Pulled Feather, Cream, Gold Iridescent, Flared Ruffled Rim, Signed, 6 x 5 In.
$523

Morphy Auctions

Quilt, Amish, Patchwork, Diamond Center, Gray, Blue, Green, Black, Pink, Cotton, c.1950, 28 x 38 In.
$132

Garth's Auctioneers & Appraisers

Quilt, Amish, Patchwork, Princess Feather Stitching, Blue, Burgundy, Black, Ohio, 1930s, 33 x 38 In.
$660

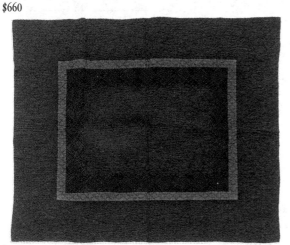

Garth's Auctioneers & Appraisers

Quilt, Appliqued, Rose Of Sharon, Pink, Red, Yellow & Green, Scalloped Border, 72 In.
$443

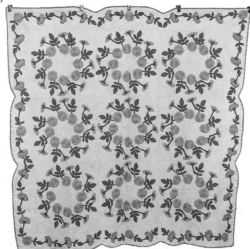

Forsythes' Auctions

Quilt, Patchwork, Basket Pattern, Red & Green, White Ground, Diamond Border, c.1925, 61 x 72 In.
$168

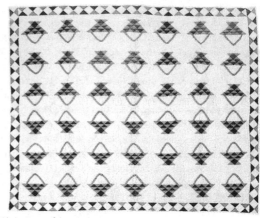

Garth's Auctioneers & Appraisers

Quilt, Patchwork, Log Cabin, Taupe, Yellow & Black, On Stretcher, Late 1800s, Crib, 32 ½ x 36 In.
$246

Skinner, Inc.

Quilt, Patchwork, Star & Block, Beige, Brown, Red, Blue, 74 x 80 In.
$531

Hess Auction Group

P

PYREX glass baking dishes were first made in 1915 by the Corning Glass Works. Pyrex dishes are made of a heat-resistant glass that can go from refrigerator or freezer to oven or microwave and are nice enough to put on the table. Clear glass dishes were made first. Pyrex Flameware, for use on a stovetop burner, was made from 1936 to 1979. A set of four mixing bowls, each in a dfferent color (blue, red, green, and yellow), was made beginning in 1947. The first pieces with decorative patterns were made in 1956. After Corning sold its Pyrex brand to World Kitchen LLC in 1998, changes were made to the formula for the glass.

PYREX

Butter, Milk Glass, Turquoise, Amish Butterprint, Marked	43
Carafe, Clear Glass, Gold Starburst, Black Handle & Lid, Corning	11
Coffeepot, Flameware, Glass, Lid, Percolator, 4 Cup, 1940s	55
Dish, Starburst, Turquoise, Space Saver, Model 575-B, 2 Qt.	331
Gravy Boat, Pink Daisy, Side Handle, White Interior, JAJ, England	77
Loaf Pan, Turquoise, White Interior, 1½ Qt., 5 x 10 x 3 In.	29
Mixing Bowl, Cinderella, Gooseberry, 441, Pink & White, 2 Handles, 1½ Qt.	33
Mixing Bowl, Green Dot, White Ground, No. 23, 4 Qt., 4½ x 10 x 5 In.	74
Platter, Blue Stripe Border, White Ground, Corning, 12½ x 9 In.	6
Teakettle, Clear Glass, No. 8446, Flameware, 6 Cup	30

QUEZAL glass was made from 1901 to 1924 at the Queens, New York, company started by Martin Bach. Other glassware by other firms, such as Loetz, Steuben, and Tiffany, resembles this gold-colored iridescent glass. Martin Bach died in 1921. His son-in-law, Conrad Vahlsing Jr., went to work at the Lustre Art Company about 1920. Bach's son, Martin Bach Jr., worked at the Durand Art Glass division of the Vineland Flint Glass Works after 1924.

Quezal

Lamp Base, King Tut, Gold Iridescent, Purple Ground, 14¾ In.	1845
Lamp, 2-Light, Putti Boudoir, King Tut, Belle Epoque, 12 x 10 x 5 In.	307
Lamp, Hanging, Pulled Feather Glass Shade, Brass Frame, 3 Female Masks, 20 x 10 In.	885
Vase, Blue Iridescent, White Vines, Leaves, Polished Pontil, Shamrock Label, Signed, 11 x 3 In.	2030
Vase, Flared Rim, White Cased, Green & Gold Pulled Feather, Pontil, 1900s, 6¼ In. ...*illus*	800
Vase, Flower Form, Green & Gold, Ivory Ground, Ruffled Top, Signed, 8½ x 6½ In.	938
Vase, Green Pulled Feather, Cream, Gold Iridescent, Flared Ruffled Rim, Signed, 6 x 5 In... *illus*	523
Vase, Jack-In-The-Pulpit, Gold Iridescent, Footed, Signed, 8 x 4 In.	875
Vase, Pulled Feather, Trumpet Shape, Gold Liner, Polished Pontil, 9½ In.	700
Vase, Trifold Top, Pulled, Ribbed, Iridescent, Signed, 7½ x 5 In.	1000

QUILTS have been made since the seventeenth century. Early textiles were very precious and every scrap was saved to be reused. A quilt is a combination of fabrics joined to a filler and a backing by small stitched designs known as quilting. An appliqued quilt has pieces stitched to the top of a large piece of backing fabric. A patchwork, or pieced, quilt is made of many small pieces stitched together. Embroidery can be added to either type.

Amish, Patchwork, Diamond Center, Gray, Blue, Green, Black, Pink, Cotton, c.1950, 28 x 38 In...*illus*	132
Amish, Patchwork, Grandma's Flower Garden, Black Border, Nebraska, Early 1900s, 56 x 78 In..	281
Amish, Patchwork, Princess Feather Stitching, Blue, Burgundy, Black, Ohio, 1930s, 33 x 38 In..*illus*	660
Amish, Princess Feathers, Blue & Burgundy On Black, Crib, c.1930, 33 x 38½ In.	660
Appliqued, Drunkard's Path, Red & White, Handmade, c.1925, 66 x 76 In.	204
Appliqued, Floral Medallions, Flowers & Compass Stars, Late 1800s, 74 x 96 In.	540
Appliqued, Flower & Star, White, Blue, Swag Border, 98 x 89 In.	323
Appliqued, Flower Basket, Red & White, Handmade, Cotton, 1900s, 79 In.	132
Appliqued, Flowers, Red & Green Calico Print, Pieced Bands Of Triangles, c.1860, 80 x 104 In..	468
Appliqued, Flowers, Red & Taupe, Handmade, 1900s, 78 x 79 In.	252
Appliqued, Flowers, Urns, Bud & Vine Border, Red, Yellow, Green, 1850s, 92 x 100 In.	768
Appliqued, Hand Stitched, Oak Leaf, Pinwheels, Late 1800s, 80 x 80 In.	1250
Appliqued, Irish Shamrock, White & Green, Embroidery, Late 1800s, 88 x 82 In.	266
Appliqued, Penny, Various Colors, 1900s, 75 x 90 In.	96
Appliqued, Red Flowers, Green Leaves, White Backing, Cotton, c.1920, 66 In.	192
Appliqued, Red, Green & White Background, Flowers, New York, 1800s, 80 x 91 In.	413

Quilt, Patchwork, Star Square Variant, Red, Blue, Gray, Yellow, 1900s, 84½ x 94½ In.
$156

Garth's Auctioneers & Appraisers

Bad Luck
An old superstition says it is bad luck to break a thread while working on a quilt.

Quimper, Platter, 2 Women, Birds, Floral Borders, Yellow, Octagonal, 8½ x 24 In.
$163

Pook & Pook

Radio, Colonial Radio Corp., New World Globus, Bakelite, Chrome, Gilt, R. Loewy, 1933, 16 In.
$2,720

Auction Team Breker

Radio, Sparton, Model 558, Blue Glass, Chrome, Wood Sled Base, W.D. Teague, 1937, 18 In.
$1,731

Auction Team Breker

Radio, Zenith, Console, Short Wave & Police Bands, Wood Case, c.1941, 42 x 28 x 14¼ In.
$48

Thomaston Place Auction Galleries

Railroad, Chair, Upholstered, Swivel Seat, Centalaska, Wood Legs, Base, c.1928, 27 x 21 x 22 In.
$565

Soulis Auctions

Appliqued, Red, Green, Yellow, Flowers, Vine & Leaves, c.1850, 92 x 100 In.	738
Appliqued, Rose Of Sharon, Pink, Red, Yellow & Green, Scalloped Border, 72 In. ....*illus*	443
Appliqued, Star, Square Pattern, Brown & White, 1800s, 72 x 86 In.	71
Appliqued, Trapunto, Golden Yellow, Red, Faded Green, Cotton, 74 x 80 In.	300
Appliqued, Trapunto, Round Florals, 4 Flowering Urns, Floral Border, c.1850, 83 x 86 In.	935
Appliqued, Tumbling, Blocks, Red, Flower, Green, Line Border, c.1870, 72 x 72 In.	354
Appliqued, White Fabric, 20 Spiral Floral, c.1860, 86 x 72 In.	295
Crazy, Multicolor Silks, Green Velvet Border, Hand Embroidered, Victorian, 65 x 70 In.	154
Crazy, Multicolor, Velvets & Satins, Butterfly, Flowers, Urn, Fan, Victorian, 55 x 44 In.	177
Embroidered, Red On White Ground, Signed & Dated, 1906, 67 x 76 In.	130
Patchwork &, Appliqued, Diamonds, Red Border, c.1900, 80 x 80 In.	138
Patchwork & Appliqued, Branching Flowers, Vining Floral Border, c.1850, 80 x 72 In.	248
Patchwork & Appliqued, North Carolina Lily, Red, Yellow Flowers, White Ground, 81 x 63 In..	1640
Patchwork & Appliqued, Quadruple Pinwheel, Green & Red, Late 1800s, 94 x 80 In.	1107
Patchwork, 29 9-Patch Squares, Cream Ground, Vine & Flower Border, 82 x 77 In.	400
Patchwork, Basket Pattern, Red & Green, White Ground, Diamond Border, c.1925, 61 x 72 In. ..*illus*	168
Patchwork, Compass Stars, Maroon, Red, Blue, Calico Border, Cotton, c.1880, 57 x 35 In.	394
Patchwork, Cotton, Red & White Zigzags, 1800s, 88 x 108 In.	461
Patchwork, Cross-Stitch, Blue & Light, 1900s, 76½ x 93 In.	144
Patchwork, Diamond Shapes, Brown, Blue, Late 1800s, 94 x 88 In.	98
Patchwork, Diamond-Square Variant, Yellow, Salmon, Red, Blue, Green, Cream, 1900s, 70 x 71 In.	312
Patchwork, Green Squares, White Backing, Cotton, Mid 1900s, 76 x 80 In.	168
Patchwork, Linsey-Woolsey, Midnight Blue, Princess Feather, Vining Flowers, c.1800, 77 x 89 In.	1200
Patchwork, Log Cabin, Floral Embroidery, Red, Black & Orange, Early 1900s, 77 x 78 In.	450
Patchwork, Log Cabin, Light & Dark Ray, Cotton, 4 Squares Block, c.1950, 68 x 76 In.	300
Patchwork, Log Cabin, Taupe, Yellow & Black, On Stretcher, Late 1800s, Crib, 32½ x 36 In..*illus*	246
Patchwork, Mennonite, Double Irish Chain, Yellow, Red & Green, Early 1900s, 92 x 94 In.	396
Patchwork, Mennonite, Printed Fabrics, Burgundy, Yellow & Pink, Ohio, Early 1900s, 74 x 87 In.	226
Patchwork, Red & White, 16 Blocks, Red Border, c.1900, 78 x 73 In.	350
Patchwork, Red & White, Star Pattern, c.1900, 72 x 56 In.	94
Patchwork, Seersucker Back, Light Brown Background, 1930s, 62 x 70 In.	69
Patchwork, Star & Block, Beige, Brown, Red, Blue, 74 x 80 In. ....*illus*	531
Patchwork, Star Square Variant, Red, Blue, Gray, Yellow, 1900s, 84½ x 94½ In. ....*illus*	156
Patchwork, Zigzags & Repeating Diamonds, Shades Of Brown, 1800s, 98 x 82 In.	308

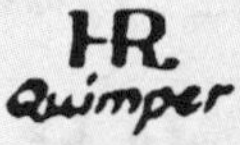

HR
Quimper
QUIMPER pottery has a long history. Tin-glazed, hand-painted pottery has been made in Quimper, France, since the late seventeenth century. The earliest firm was founded in 1708 by Pierre Bousquet. In 1782, Antoine de la Hubaudiere became the manager of the factory and the factory became known as the HB Factory (for Hubaudiere-Bousquet), de la Hubaudiere, or Grande Maison. Another firm, founded in 1772 by Francois Eloury, was known as Porquier. The third firm, founded by Guillaume Dumaine in 1778, was known as HR or Henriot Quimper. All three firms made similar pottery decorated with designs of Breton peasants and sea and flower motifs. The Eloury (Porquier) and Dumaine (Henriot) firms merged in 1913. Bousquet (HB) merged with the others in 1968. The group was sold to an American holding company in 1984. More changes followed, and in 2011 Jean-Pierre Le Goff became the owner and the name was changed to Henriot-Quimper.

Basket, Double Swan, Marked, 1930s, 8 x 8½ In.	84
Basket, Double Swan, Sunflower Necks, Red Flower, Blue Feathers, c.1930, 8 x 8½ In.	86
Bowl, Man, Woman, Seated On Grass, Scroll Handles, 20 In.	212
Coffee Set, Coffeepot, Sugar & Creamer, Yellow, Breton Man, Woman, Yellow Ground, 3 Piece	60
Plate, Woman, Fence, White, Painted, Signed, HB, 9¼ In.	60
Platter, 2 Women, Birds, Floral Borders, Yellow, Octagonal, 8½ x 24 In. ....*illus*	163
Platter, Fish Shape, Cobalt Blue Border, Strolling Couple, 19½ In.	35
Platter, Fish Shape, Couple Dancing, Flowers, Cobalt Blue Rim, Marked, 19½ In.	25
Teapot, Lid, Man On One Side, Woman On Other, Birds, Trees, 7½ In.	106
Vase, Hearts, Curlicues, Ruffled Rim, Brown, Red, Green, Purple, Signed, 6 In.	48
Vase, Man, Woman, Fence, Leaves, Buds, Scrolls, Flared Rim, 13 In.	100
Wall Pocket, Umbrella Shape, Man, Woman, Flowers, 13 x 10 In.	189

Q

RADIO broadcast receiving sets were first sold in New York City in 1910. They were used to pick up the experimental broadcasts of the day. The first commercial radios were made by Westinghouse Company for listeners of the experimental shows on KDKA Pittsburgh in 1920. Collectors today are interested in all early radios, especially those made of Bakelite plastic or decorated with blue mirrors. Figural advertising radios and transistor radios are also collected.

Colonial Radio Corp., New World Globus, Bakelite, Chrome, Gilt, R. Loewy, 1933, 16 In..*illus*	2720
General Electric, Console, Musaphonic, Wooden Case, Model H-116, c.1940, 4 x 32 x 13 In.....	60
Receiver, Sparton, A-C, Model No. 557, c.1925, 18 x 8½ In.	938
Sparton, Model 558, Blue Glass, Chrome, Wood Sled Base, W.D. Teague, 1937, 18 In.........*illus*	1731
Sparton, Neon, AM-FM, Clear Plastic Case, Side Speakers, Model No. NR-8801, 7 x 9½ x 5 In.	121
Zenith, Console, Short Wave & Police Bands, Wood Case, c.1941, 42 x 28 x 14¼ In. ....*illus*	48

RAILROAD enthusiasts collect any train memorabilia. Everything is wanted, from oilcans to whole train cars. The Chessie system has a store that sells many reproductions of its old dinnerware and uniforms.

Bowl, Square, Scalloped Corners, Indian Tree, NY, NH & HRR, Buffalo China, 5 x 4½ In.	26
Chair, Club Car, Wood, Black Leather, Pullman Company, 36 x 23½ x 22½ In............	848
Chair, Upholstered, Swivel Seat, Centalaska, Wood Legs, Base, c.1928, 27 x 21 x 22 In.......*illus*	565
Chandelier, 2 Gas Light Lamps, Acetylene Gas, Gilt, Adams & Westlake Co., c.1900, 29 x 16 x 16 In..	424
Chandelier, 2-Light, Metal Plate, Signed, Hicks & Smith, c.1884, 26 x 22 x 22 In.	961
Chandelier, 2-Light, Milk Glass Shades, Hicks & Smith, c.1884, 26 x 28 x 10 In.	1243
Chandelier, Center Lamp, Oil, Brass, Milk Glass Shade, Dayton Mfg. Co., 20 x 18 x 18 In.........	1413
Chime, Dining Car, 4 Bars, Hammer, 3 x 8 x 12 In....................................*illus*	192
Clock, Electric, Wall, Santa Fe, Plastic Housing, Mid 1900s, 10 In.	90
Ladder, Railcar, Upper Berth, Wood, Carpeted Steps, Pullman Company, 51 x 18 x 9 In.	1130
Lamp, Electric, Switch In Base, Mica Shade, Pullman Company, 18 x 10 In.	1130
Lamp, Oil, Brass, Railcar, Side, Wall Mounted, Signed, Adlake, 1800s, 7 x 5 x 7 In.	57
Lamp, Side, N & W, Oil, Brass, Embossed, 1800s, 4¾ x 6½ x 8 In.	68
Lantern, Brass, Glass Globe, Magnifier, New York, 12½ In.......................................	57
Lantern, Hanging, C & NWRY, Embossed Letters, Glass Globe, 5½ x 6½ In....................*illus*	147
Lantern, Kerosene, Wire Handle, DL & WRR, Adlake, 10½ In.	136
Lantern, Red Globe, Cast Iron, Central, Dietz No. 999	58
Lantern, Signal, Metal, Red & Blue Glass Lenses, Embossed, Gray-Boston, 13 In........................	226
Lantern, Switch, 4-Light, Embossed, Gold & Blue Lenses, Reflectors, 17 In.	226
Mug, Beer, Clear, Side Handle, Santa Fe Script Logo, Enameled, 5½ x 4½ x 3 In.	57
Paperweight, Glass, New York Central, 5 Great Limited Trains, Station, 1893, 4 x 2 In............	147
Paperweight, Pennsylvania RR, Central Knob Handle, Cast Iron, Circular, 1¾ x 2½ In.........	45
Paperweight, Pennsylvania RR, Central Knob Handle, Cast Iron, Oval, 1 x 4 x 3 In................	57
Paperweight, Pennsylvania RR, Pen Stand, Cast Iron, Openwork, c.1875, 1½ x 5 x 2 In..*illus*	147
Plate, Indian Tree, Flowers, White Ground, Dining Car Service, Pullman, Syracuse, 7½ In. ...	11
Plate, Indian Tree, Flowers, White Ground, Pullman, Syracuse, 9 In.	68
Plate, New York Central, Hudson Pattern, GDA Limoges, 9 In. ....*illus*	34
Plate, Soup, Mimbreno, Stamped On Back, Santa Fe, 9 In. ....*illus*	170
Platter, Deer, Mimbreno, Stamped On Back, Santa Fe, 9½ x 6½ In.	124
Platter, Indian Tree, Oval, Flowers, Pullman, Syracuse, 1951, 7¼ x 10½ In.	26
Platter, Union Pacific RR, Harriman Blue Pattern, Maddock's, 1 x 12½ x 9 In.	79
Platter, Union Pacific RR, Historical Pattern, Old Ivory, Syracuse, 8 x 5¾ In.	192
Poster, I'll Wake You In The Morning, Pullman Porter, Lithograph, 1952, 27 x 21 In..............	181
Poster, Lithograph, I'll Shine 'Em While You Sleep, Pullman Porter, 1952, 27 x 21 In..............	136
Poster, Rock Island Rocket, Lithograph, c.1950, 20¾ x 27¾ In.	158
Poster, There's Something Going On All Winter, Pullman, S. Ekman, 27 x 21 In.	136
Rack, Basket, Cast Brass, Adams & Westlake, 1911, 9 x 27½ x 9 In.	819
Rack, Car, Brass, Black Paint, 7 x 62 x 12 In.	124
Sign, Railroad Crossing, White, Lights, Bell, c.1900	383
Sign, Trenton Lawrenceville & Princeton Railroad Co., 2-Sided, 13¼ x 49½ In........................	502
Sign, Union Pacific, Shield Shape, Porcelain Side, Enamel, 144 x 126 In. ....*illus*	2280
Step Stool, Burlington Route, Stainless Steel, Embossed Plaque, 10¼ x 18 x 13 In..................	1639

Railroad, Chime, Dining Car, 4 Bars, Hammer, 3 x 8 x 12 In.
$192

Soulis Auctions

Railroad, Lantern, Hanging, C & NWRY, Embossed Letters, Glass Globe, 5½ x 6½ In.
$147

Soulis Auctions

TIP
Cheesecloth is a good polishing cloth.

Railroad, Paperweight, Pennsylvania RR, Pen Stand, Cast Iron, Openwork, c.1875, 1½ x 5 x 2 In.
$147

Soulis Auctions

R

Railroad, Plate, New York Central, Hudson Pattern, GDA Limoges, 9 In.
$34

Soulis Auctions

Railroad, Plate, Soup, Mimbreno, Stamped On Back, Santa Fe, 9 In.
$170

Soulis Auctions

Railroad, Sign, Union Pacific, Shield Shape, Porcelain Side, Enamel, 144 x 126 In.
$2,280

UNION PACIFIC

Morphy Auctions

Switch Stand, Iron, Crank, c.1920, 58 x 26 In.	236
Table, Parlor Car Or Sleeper, Collapsible, Hinged Leg, Pullman Co., 28 x 22 x 35 In.	170
Tumbler, Cut & Polished Panels, Clear, Santa Fe, 3¾ x 3 In.	113
Whiskey, Santa Fe, Old-Fashioned, Frosted Script Logo, 3½ x 3 In.	57
Wrench, Iron, Stamped N &W, Tools, Early 1900s, 23½ In.	59

RAZORS were used in ancient Egypt and subsequently wherever shaving was in fashion. The metal razor used in America was made in Sheffield, England, until about 1870. After 1870, machine-made hollow-ground razors were made in Germany or America. Plastic or bone handles were popular. The razor was often sold in a set of seven, one for each day of the week. The set was often kept by the barber who shaved the well-to-do man each day in the shop.

Blade Safe, Barber Pole Pixie, Pottery, Painted, 6 x 3 In.	*illus*	30
Blade Safe, Raised Man's Hand, Shaving, Pottery, Domed, Cleminsons, Calif., 1940s, 3 In.	*illus*	26
Celluloid Handle, Metal Inlay, Engraved Pride Of The West, Jack Knife Ben, Germany, c.1910, 6 x 3 In.		218

REAMERS, or juice squeezers, have been known since 1767, although most of those collected today date from the twentieth century. Figural reamers are among the most prized.

Aluminum, Crank, Wood Handle, Quam Nichols Co., 6 In.	20
Ceramic, Blue & Yellow Diamonds, Flowers, Baby's Orange Juice, Japan, 3½ In.	25
Ceramic, Blue, Geometric & Flower Designs, Triangular Shape, Tashiro Shoten Ltd, 8 x 4 In.	35
Ceramic, Clown, Closed Eyes, Blue, Yellow, Red, White, Japan, 5½ In.	58
Ceramic, Green, Brown, Figural Country Cottage, Pulp Strainer, Japan, 1940s, 5 x 6 x 4 In.	28
Ceramic, Yellow, Rust Trim, Bouquet, Embossed Dots, Japan, 1940s, 5¼ x 7 In.	24
Depression Glass, Crisscross, Cobalt Blue, Hazel Atlas, 1930s, 8 In. *illus*	58
Depression Glass, Green, Measuring Cup, Notched Lid, Thick Handle, 1920s, 5 In.	36
Glass, Amber, Thumbprint Handle, Federal Glass Co., 8 x 5¾ In.	18
Glass, Cobalt Blue, Thick Handle, Wide Spout, 3 x 6 In.	14
Glass, Jadeite, Sunkist, Green, McKee	41
Glass, Ribbed Bowl, Shrimp Handle, Anchor Hocking, 8 x 5¾ In.	15
Jadeite, Green, Finger Loop Handle, Swirl Post, Jeannette, 7 In.	25
Milk Glass, Sunkist, U.S.A., 5¾ x 3 In.	28
Plastic, Orange, Tupperware, 4⅜ In.	5
Porcelain, White, Cobalt Blue Flowers, Mini Teapot Shape, Footed, 5 In.	25
Pottery, Pink Spatter Glaze, 5 In.	15
Sterling Silver, Gold Wash, Scroll Handle, Beaded Border, Fuchs, 4¾ x 4 In.	550
Vaseline Glass, Green, Marked, S & H, 6¼ In.	35
Vaseline Glass, Measuring Cup, Transparent Green, Hazel Atlas, 2 Cup	24

RECORDS have changed size and shape through the years. The cylinder-shaped phonograph record for use with the early Edison models was made about 1889. Disc records were first made by 1894, the double-sided disc by 1904. High-fidelity records were first issued in 1944, the first vinyl disc in 1946, the first stereo record in 1958. The 78 RPM became the standard in 1926 but was discontinued in 1957. In 1932, the first 33⅓ RPM was made but was not sold commercially until 1948. In 1949, the 45 RPM was introduced. Compact discs became available in the United States in 1982 and many companies began phasing out the production of phonograph records. Vinyl records are popular again. People claim the sound is better on a vinyl recording, and new recordings are being made. Some collectors want vinyl picture records. Vintage albums are collected for their cover art as well as for the fame of the artist and the music.

American Graffiti, Soundtrack, 41 Songs, LP, Vinyl, 33⅓ RPM, 1973, 12 In.	32
Beach Boys, Pet Sounds, Duophonic, Scranton Pressing, Capitol Records, 33⅓ RPM, 1966, 12 In.	72
Bee Gees, You, Acetate Pressing, Pop, I.B.C. Sound, 45 RPM, 1967, 7 In.	2108
Bill Haley & His Comets, Rock Around The Clock, Decca, 78 RPM, 1950s, 10 In.	29
Bill Haley, Corrine, Corrina, Decca, 45 RPM	19
Bing Crosby, Merry Christmas, Set A-403, Black & Gold, Decca, 78 RPM, 10 In. *illus*	57

Burt Bacharach, James Bond 007, Casino Royale, 1967	60
Don Ellis & The Survival, Star Wars Theme, Atlantic Records, 45 RPM, 1977	9
Doris Day, Highlight, Columbia, Jazz Vocal, LP, 33 ⅓ RPM	13
Elvis Presley, Good Rockin' Tonight, Collectables, Red Vinyl, 45 RPM........................	14
Elvis Presley, Mystery Train, I Forgot To Remember To Forget, 45 RPM, 1955, 7 In. ....*illus*	330
Frank Sinatra, A Jolly Christmas, Vinyl, Capitol W 894, 33 ⅓ RPM, 1957, 12 In.................*illus*	50
Muppet Movie Soundtrack, Atlantic Recordings, 78 RPM, 1979	10
Richard Crean & His Orchestra, Melody Time, 33 ⅓ RPM...............................	45
Rodgers & Hammerstein, Oklahoma, 78 RPM, c.1955	8

RED WING POTTERY of Red Wing, Minnesota, was a firm started in 1878. The company first made utilitarian pottery, including stoneware jugs and canning jars. In 1906, three companies combined to make the Red Wing Union Stoneware Company and began producing flowerpots, vases, and dinnerware. Art pottery was introduced in 1926. The name of the company was changed to Red Wing Potteries in 1936. Many dinner sets and vases were made before the company closed in 1967. R. Gillmer bought the company in 1967 and operated it as a retail business. The name was changed again, to Red Wing Pottery. The retail business closed in 2015. Red Wing Stoneware Company was founded in 1987. It was sold to new owners in 2013. They bought Red Wing Pottery and combined the two companies to become Red Wing Stoneware & Pottery. The company makes stoneware crocks, jugs, mugs, bowls, and other items with cobalt blue designs. Rumrill pottery made by the Red Wing Pottery for George Rumrill is listed in its own category. For more prices, go to kovels.com.

Advertising, Jug, Glasner & Barzen Fine Whiskies, 2-Tone, Black Stamp, Embossed, 1800, 10 In.. *illus*	352
Africa, Vase, Zebra Stripes, Brown, Cream, Marked, c.1940, Pair, 4 x 10 In..........................	375
Apple Shape, Vase, Pink, c.1942, 6 In.	30
Bob White, Butter Warmer, Lid, Metal Stand, Bird, Handle	66
Capistrano, Bowl, Vegetable, Marked, 10 In.	45
Cookie Jar, Chef, Baker, Pierre, Figural, Standing......................................	22
Cookie Jar, King Of Tarts, Figural, Red Face, Crown, 1950s, 9¾ In........................	113
Country Garden, Bowl, Vegetable, 9 In.	68
Flowers, Vase, White Ground, Marked, 10 x 4 x 4 In.	97
Ivory Fleck, Tray, School Lunch, 5 Sections, 12 In.	71
Lotus Bronze, Plate, Dinner, 10½ In.	21
Lute Song, Celery Tray, Musical Instruments, 15¾ In......................	129
Magnolia, Bowl, Lid, Ivory & Chartreuse, 2½ x 4 In.	10
Magnolia, Bowl, Vegetable, Chartreuse, Round, 8 x 2 In.	35
Pepe, Cookie Jar, Lid, Red, Green, Orange, 2 Handles	55
Pompeii, Salt & Pepper	62
Pompeii, Sugar & Creamer..	32
Random Harvest, Bowl, Cereal, 1950s, 7 In.	10
Roundup, Plate, Dinner, Western Scene, 10⅞ In.	179
Smart Set, Beverage Server, Lid, Black, White, Yellow, 15⅛ In.	149
Spongeware, Mixing Bowl, Blue & Rust, c.1901, 8 x 5 In.	32
Stoneware, Crock, Bee Sting, Salt Glaze, 2 Handles, 4 Gal., 11 x 11 In.	153
Stoneware, Crock, Cobalt Blue, 2, Molded Rim, 9½ In.	52
Stoneware, Spongeband, Bowl, Vertical Ridges, Rimmed, Marked, 3¾ x 5 In.	119
Tampico, Mug, Watermelon, Leaves, Ear Handle, Gloss, 12 Oz.	37
Town & Country, Pitcher, Rust Glaze, Eva Zeisel, 48 Oz., c.1947	29
Vase, Turquoise, Black Speckles, 5 Holes, Fan Shape, 9 x 10 In......................	195
Wall Pocket, Violin Shape, Figural, Aqua Matte, Hanging, Tag, Marked	9

REDWARE is a hard, red stoneware that has been made for centuries and continues to be made. The term is also used to describe any common clay pottery that is reddish in color. American redware was first made about 1625.

Bank, Dresser Shape, Scroddled Glaze, Paw Feet, Carved Coin Slot, England, c.1890, 7 x 4 x 6 In..	207
Bird Whistle, Yellow & Brown Glaze, Marked, W. Love, 9½ x 7¼ In........................	124
Bowl, Dough, Glazed Interior, Yellow, Green, Brown Feathers, Meine Fran, c.1850, 5 x 14 In. ...	2520
Bowl, Manganese, Tapered Sides, Crossed Square, Flower Blossoms, 1800s, 3⅞ In....................	148

Razor, Blade Safe, Barber Pole Pixie, Pottery, Painted, 6 x 3 In.
$30

Jack & Jeff Hayes

Razor, Blade Safe, Raised Man's Hand, Shaving, Pottery, Domed, Cleminsons, Calif., 1940s, 3 In.
$26

Jack & Jeff Hayes

Reamer, Depression Glass, Crisscross, Cobalt Blue, Hazel Atlas, 1930s, 8 In.
$58

smw11 on eBay

R

Record, Bing Crosby, Merry Christmas, Set A-403, Black & Gold, Decca, 78 RPM, 10 In.
$57

bartrade on eBay

TIP

To clean a 78 rpm record, use two soft cloths or paper towels. Spray the towels, not the record, with window cleaner. Then clean as if it were a pane of glass.

Record, Elvis Presley, Mystery Train, I Forgot To Remember To Forget, 45 RPM, 1955, 7 In.
$330

kingcreolerecords on eBay

Record, Frank Sinatra, A Jolly Christmas, Vinyl, Capitol W 894, 33 1/3 RPM, 1957, 12 In.
$50

rockin-roll on eBay

Item	Price
Bowl, Moravian, Pale Yellow & Green, Slips & Star Center, c.1825, 2 3/4 x 10 1/2 In.	4680
Bowl, Mottled Glaze, Molded Base & Rim, 1800s, 3 1/2 x 8 In.	165
Bowl, Round Sides, Thin Rolled Rim, Manganese Splotches, Early 1800s, John Bell, 3 x 9 In. ...illus	380
Candlestick, Stepped Base, Olive Green Glaze, 1800s, 7 3/4 In.	420
Cream Jar, Orange, Spots, Covered Rim Molding, Galena, Il., c.1950, 7 1/4 In.	590
Crock, Lead Glaze, Dotted Interior, Shoulder Ring, Shenandoah Co., c.1870, 9 x 8 In. ...illus	47
Crock, Lead Glaze, Iron Oxide Speckles, Shenandoah Co., c.1875, 7 x 5 1/2 In., 2 Gal.	129
Cup, Handleless, Manganese, Lead Glaze, New Market, Va., c.1915, 2 x 3 3/8 x 2 In.	936
Figurine, Lion, Coleslaw Mane, Tail Tip, Yellow, Brown, Signed, LB, Pa., 1982, 9 x 8 In.	502
Flask, Manganese Splotching, Molded Spout, 1800s, 7 In.	250
Flowerpot, Interior, Glaze, Molded Rim, Attached Undertray, 1800s, 5 1/2 In. ...illus	150
Jar, Canning, Lid, Flared Rim, Yellow, Stamped, John Bell, Pa., c.1860, 7 In.	1062
Jar, Copper & Lead Glaze, Incised Shoulder Ring, Shenandoah Co., Va., c.1870, Qt., 7 x 4 3/8 In.	176
Jar, Lid, Tight 2, Lug Handles, Sipe & Son, 2 Gal., 11 1/2 In.	59
Jar, Light Yellow Mottling, Incised Songbird, Green Glaze, New York, c.1850, 10 In.	1140
Jar, Lug Handles, Flaring Rim, Runs & Splotches Of Manganese, Vermont, 1800s, 10 In. ..illus	1742
Jar, Mottled Glaze, Flared Rim, Roulette Neck, Green, Orange, Brown, 1800s, 10 3/4 In.	871
Jug, Curved Pouring Vertical Spout, Handle, Stars, R.C. Mazer, Early 1900s, 14 1/2 In.	148
Jug, Face, Grotesque, Shard Teeth, Applied Handle, Stamped, B.B. Craig, 8 1/2 In. ...illus	216
Jug, Flared Rim, Pouring Spout, Strap Handle, Dark Manganese Splotch, 1800s, 8 1/2 In.	218
Jug, Flat Tooled Rim, Strap Handle, Bulbous Body, Vermont, 1800s, 9 1/2 In. ...illus	254
Jug, Glazed, Bulbous, Reeded Loop Handle, Signed, Thomas Stahl, 1936	153
Jug, Incised Flower, Raised Green Glaze, c.1850, 9 In.	3000
Jug, Oval, Applied Handle, Manganese, Bulbous Body, 1850s, 4 In.	780
Jug, Oval, Manganese Glaze, Handle, 1800s, 9 In.	177
Jug, Squat Bulbous Shape, Scroll Handle, Glazed, Molded, Greybeard Mask, 6 5/8 In.	300
Jug, White & Brown, Panel At Shoulder, C-Scroll Handle, J. Bates, 7 In. ...illus	77
Lamp, Oil, Handle & Spout, Brown Paint, 6 1/2 In. ...illus	35
Loaf Pan, Coggled Rim, Green Squiggle Slip, Mid 1800s, 12 x 17 In.	1200
Loaf Pan, Coggled Rim, Yellow Slip Swirls, Mid 1800s, 9 x 14 In.	1000
Loaf Pan, St. Cecilia, Rectangular, Coggled Rim, Yellow Slip, Early 1800s, 11 3/4 In. ...illus	1451
Milk Pan, Mustard Glazed, Reddish Brown, 1800s, 4 x 17 3/4 In.	160
Mug, Mush, Manganese Splash, Handle, Pennsylvania, 1800s, 5 3/8 In.	344
Pan, Sgraffito, Pale Yellow Slip Ground, Incised Flower, Pa., Early 1800s, 13 In.	5400
Pie Plate, Circular, Yellow Slip, Coggled Rim, Moravian, 1800s, 11 In.	840
Pie Plate, Glaze Flakes, Yellow Slip Linear, Mid 1800s, 12 In.	531
Pie Plate, Sgraffito, Yellow Slip, Green Spots, Urn, Lines, 1792, 12 In.	4920
Pie Plate, Slip Lollipops, Coggled Rim, Green & Brown, Mid 1800s, 8 In.	1680
Pitcher, Lead Glaze, Oval Shape, Beaded Rim, Shenandoah Co., Va., c.1875, Qt., 7 x 3 In.	293
Pitcher, Lid, Tulip, Heart, Yellow, Red & Green, German Inscription, c.1830, 10 1/2 In. ...illus	104
Pitcher, Olive, Handle, Green, Glaze, Bulbous Body, 9 In.	59
Plaque, Eagle, Gold & Green Paint, Full Bodied, Spread Wings, Late 1800s, 11 x 16 In.	210
Plate, Coggled Rim, Yellow Trail Slip Line & Dot At Center, 10 1/2 In.	726
Plate, Slip Design, Black Back, 1800s, 8 In.	207
Plate, Yellow Slip Center, Coggled Wheel Edge, 1800s, 9 In.	236
Platter, Slip, Rectangular, Brown & Yellow Paint, 1800s, 15 1/2 x 21 In.	554
Teapot, Lid, Calligraphic, Cylindrical, Cover, Scroll Border, Chinese, c.1850, 4 In.	360

REGOUT, *see Maastricht category.*

RIDGWAY pottery has been made in the Staffordshire district in England since 1792 by a series of companies with the name Ridgway. The company began making bone china in 1808. Ridgway became part of Royal Doulton in the 1960s. The transfer-design dinner sets are the most widely known product. Other pieces of Ridgway may be listed under Flow Blue.

Item	Price
Creamer, Corey Hill Pattern, Stem-Like Handle, c.1870, 5 In.	50
Cup & Saucer, Cobalt Blue, Salmon, Abstract, Gilt, c.1825	135
Cup & Saucer, Handleless, Mountains, Flowers, Purple Transfer, c.1845	165
Pitcher, Architectural Scene, Horse Scene, Bronze, Brown, Transfer, 4 3/4 In.	29
Pitcher, Horse, Lion, Brown, Silver Luster Trim & Handle, 4 3/4 x 5 In. ...illus	60

R

Red Wing, Advertising, Jug, Glasner & Barzen Fine Whiskies, 2-Tone, Black Stamp, Embossed, 1800, 10 In.
$352

Soulis Auctions

Redware, Bowl, Round Sides, Thin Rolled Rim, Manganese Splotches, Early 1800s, John Bell, 3 x 9 In.
$380

Cordier Auctions

Redware, Crock, Lead Glaze, Dotted Interior, Shoulder Ring, Shenandoah Co., c.1870, 9 x 8 In.
$47

Jeffrey S. Evans & Associates

Redware, Flowerpot, Interior, Glaze, Molded Rim, Attached Undertray, 1800s, 5 ½ In.
$150

Pook & Pook

Redware, Jar, Lug Handles, Flaring Rim, Runs & Splotches Of Manganese, Vermont, 1800s, 10 In.
$1,742

Skinner, Inc.

Redware, Jug, Face, Grotesque, Shard Teeth, Applied Handle, Stamped, B.B. Craig, 8 ½ In.
$216

Garth's Auctioneers & Appraisers

Redware, Jug, Flat Tooled Rim, Strap Handle, Bulbous Body, Vermont, 1800s, 9 ½ In.
$254

Skinner, Inc.

> **TIP**
> It is said creativity comes from a messy, cluttered environment. It inspires ideas. Remember that the next time you rearrange your collectibles.

Redware, Jug, White & Brown, Panel At Shoulder, C-Scroll Handle, J. Bates, 7 In.
$77

Forsythes' Auctions

R

Redware, Lamp, Oil, Handle & Spout, Brown Paint, 6½ In.
$35

Copake Auction

Redware, Loaf Pan, St. Cecilia, Rectangular, Coggled Rim, Yellow Slip, Early 1800s, 11¾ In.
$1,451

Skinner, Inc.

Redware, Pitcher, Lid, Tulip, Heart, Yellow, Red & Green, German Inscription, c.1830, 10½ In.
$104

Freeman's Auctioneers & Appraisers

Ridgway, Pitcher, Horse, Lion, Brown, Silver Luster Trim & Handle, 4¾ x 5 In.
$60

Turners Auctions & Appraisers

Rockingham, Figurine, Dog, Cavalier King Charles Spaniel, Seated, Ornamental Base, c.1975, 10 In.
$384

Crocker Farm

Rockingham, Pitcher, Frog, Relief Hunt Scene, Harriet Armstrong, Reddish Brown, Late 1800s, 8⅝ In.
$767

Crocker Farm

R

Plate, Dollar Pattern, c.1812, 7 In.	65
Plate, Euphrates Pattern, Scalloped Edge, Blue Transfer, c.1834, 10½ In.	55
Plate, Peking Pattern, Blue Transfer, 1845, 9 In.	175
Plate, University Pattern, Blue Transfer, c.1845, 9 In.	30
Platter, Birds, Prunus Tree, Flower Sprays, Scalloped, Blue Transfer, c.1830, 20 x 17 In.	385
Platter, Blue Willow, Buildings, Landscape, Lake, Geometric Border, 19 x 15½ In	84
Tankard, Stagecoach, Horses, Brown Transfer, c.1900, 4⅝ x 3 In.	27
Tureen, Lid, Handles, Pagodas, Trees, Reds & Greens, Transfer, 1800s, 11 x 14 In.	375
Tureen, Underplate, Indian Temple, Blue Transfer, 6-Sided, c.1820, 14 x 7 In.	450

RIFLES *that are firearms made after 1900 are not listed in this book. BB guns and air rifles are listed in the Toy category.*

RIVIERA dinnerware was made by the Homer Laughlin Co. of Newell, West Virginia, from 1938 to 1950. The pattern was similar in coloring and in mood to Fiesta and Harlequin. The Riviera plates and cup handles were square. For more prices, go to kovels.com.

Blue, Soup, Dish, Rimmed	25
Green, Plate, Luncheon, 8¾ In.	20
Ivory, Bowl, Cereal, Rimmed, 6 In.	79
Ivory, Butter, Cover, Insert, Round, 5½ x 8⅜ In.	72
Ivory, Tumbler, Handle, Century Shape	153
Mauve Blue, Butter, Cover, Lug Handles	36
Red, Plate, Dessert, 7 In.	13
Yellow, Butter, Cover, Footed Tray, Fiesta Ware, 1930s	27
Yellow, Cup, Footed, 2¼ In.	17

ROCKINGHAM, in the United States, is a pottery with a brown glaze that resembles tortoiseshell. It was made from 1840 to 1900 by many American potteries. Mottled brown Rockingham wares were first made in England at the Rockingham factory. Other types of ceramics were also made by the English firm. Related pieces may be listed in the Bennington category.

Doorstop, Dog, Spaniel, 10½ In.	396
Figurine, Dog, Cavalier King Charles Spaniel, Seated, Ornamental Base, c.1975, 10 In.....*illus*	384
Figurine, Dog, Spaniel, Curly Haired, Seated, 10¾ In.	85
Figurine, Lion, Standing On Base, Paw On Ball, c.1825, 10 In.	498
Figurine, Rooster, Standing, Head Up, c.1825, 8½ In.	373
Figurine, Sheep, Lying Down, Base, Open Bottomed, c.1825, 4 x 5 In.	404
Loving Cup, Man, Smoking, Drinking, Fighting Dogs, Grapevine Border, 1800s, 7 In.	55
Loving Cup, Traditional Brown Glaze, Bas Relief, Grapevine Border, 1800s, 7 In.	53
Mixing Bowl, Brown, Impressed Sawtooth, 4 x 10 In.	23
Mold, Turk's Head, Spiraled Center Column, Fluted Sides, 6½ x 2¼ In.	110
Pitcher, Brown, Hunter, Hunting Dogs, Trees, Birds, 7½ x 4 In.	35
Pitcher, Figural, Dog, Tricornered Spout, c.1850, 9 x 5 x 3 In.	325
Pitcher, Frog, Relief Hunt Scene, Harriet Armstrong, Reddish Brown, Late 1800s, 8⅝ In. *illus*	767

ROGERS, *see John Rogers category.*

ROOKWOOD pottery was made in Cincinnati, Ohio, beginning in 1880. All of this art pottery is marked, most with the famous flame mark. The *R* is reversed and placed back to back with the letter *P*. Flames surround the letters. After 1900, a Roman numeral was added to the mark to indicate the year. The company went bankrupt in 1941. It was bought and sold several times after that. For several years various owners tried to revive the pottery, but by 1967 it was out of business. The name and some of the molds were bought by a collector in Michigan in 1982. A few items were made beginning in 1983. In 2004, a group of Cincinnati investors bought the company and 3,700 original molds, the name, and trademark. Pottery was made in Cincinnati again beginning in 2006. Today the company makes architectural tile, art pottery, and special commissions. New items and a few old items with slight redesigns are made. Contemporary pieces are being made to

Rookwood, Bookend, Art Pottery, Dutch Boy, Sallie Toohey, 1900s, 6 In.
$125

Pook & Pook

Rookwood, Decanter, Whiskey, Corncob, Husk, Flowers, Maria Nichols Longworth, 1896, 7 In.
$303

Forsythes' Auctions

Rookwood, Mug, Portrait, Indian, Ogallala, Harriet Wilcox, Flame Mark, 1897, 6 x 7½ In.
$1,875

Rago Arts and Auction Center

R

Rookwood, Stein, Sea Green Glaze, Carved Flowers, Pink Highlights, Sallie Coyne, 1905, 5 ½ In.
$385

Forsythes' Auctions

Rookwood, Vase, Autumn Leaves, Brown Shaded To Orange Ground, K. Shirayamadani, 11 x 6 In.
$2,432

Morphy Auctions

Rookwood, Vase, Dogwood Blossoms, Shouldered, Margaret Helen McDonald, 1932, 5 In.
$389

Leland Little Auctions

Rookwood, Vase, Landscape With Trees, Vellum, Sallie Coyne, c.1921, 8 x 3 In.
$1,521

Jeffrey S. Evans & Associates

Rookwood, Vase, Multicolor, Landscape With Trees, Edward Diers, c.1930, 7 x 3 ⅞ In.
$1,112

Jeffrey S. Evans & Associates

Rookwood, Vase, Silver Overlay, Leaf & Berry, Albert Valentien, 1905, 12 In.
$1,169

Skinner, Inc.

complement the dinnerware line designed by John D. Wareham in 1921. Pieces are marked with the RP mark and a Roman numeral for the four-digit year date. Mold numbers on pieces made since 2006 begin with 10000.

ROOKWOOD 1882	RP	RP sun mark
Rookwood 1882–1886	Rookwood 1886	Rookwood 1901

Ashtray, Frog, Green, Brown Matte Glazes, Shirayamadani, 1930, 3 ¼ In.	575
Bookend, Art Pottery, Dutch Boy, Sallie Toohey, 1900s, 6 In...............................*illus*	125
Bowl, Blue, Brown, Matte, Ombrosso Glaze, 3 Handles, 1917, 4 In.	185
Bowl, Flower Border, Beige Interior, Lorinda Epply, 1926, 3 x 8 In...............................	185
Bowl, Pink Matte Glaze, Trumpet Vine, Painted, Margaret Helen McDonald, 3 x 7 ⅝ In...........	454
Bowl, Yellow Matte Glaze, Kataro Shirayamadani, 1911, 1 x 3 In..................................	125
Chocolate Pot, Flowers, Standard Glaze, Josephine Zettel, 9 ½ In..............................	554
Cup, Indian Chief, Buffalo Headdress, Dark Green Background, 1900s, 6 x 8 In.	1920
Decanter, Whiskey, Corncob, Husk, Flowers, Maria Nichols Longworth, 1896, 7 In. ....*illus*	303
Decanter, Whiskey, Silver Overlay, Handle, Chain & Ring, Edward Abel, 1891, 8 In.	1045
Ewer, Nasturtiums, Standard Glaze, Painted, Handle, Sallie Coyne, 8 ⅝ In.	145
Figurine, Carols To You, Mold, Green Glaze, J.D. Wareham, 4 ¾ In................................	200
Humidor, Lid, Brown, High Gloss Glaze, Berries & Holly, 5 Flames, Marked, 1891, 7 x 8 In.	2400
Lamp, 2-Light, Bulbous, 4-Footed, Flaring Lip, Orange Poppies, Dark Brown Background, 22 x 20 In.	277
Match Holder, Bat, Blue Matte Glaze, Marked, Shirayamadani, 2 ⅛ x 6 In..........................	1331
Mug, Ear Of Corn, Standard Glaze, Handle, Lenore Asbury, 1903, 4 ⅝ In.	206
Mug, Gilt Grapevine, W. McDonald, Gorham Silver Overlay, Vines, c.1891, 6 In.	1920
Mug, Portrait, Indian, Ogallala, Harriet Wilcox, Flame Mark, 1897, 6 x 7 ½ In. ....*illus*	1875
Paperweight, Cat, Seated, Tail Curled Across Body, Bronze Glaze, 1837, 4 x 2 x 2 ½ In.	880
Paperweight, Fox, Light Blue Matte Glaze, Shirayamadani, 1923, 2 ¼ x 5 ¾ In.	484
Paperweight, Monkey, Nubian Black Glaze, Square Base, 1934, 4 ½ In.	726
Perfume Jug, Lid, Limoges Style, Bird, Fired-On Gold, Martin Rettig, 4 ½ In.	424
Pitcher, Chains Of Blue Flowers, Green Leaves, 1882, 6 ½ In.....................................	176
Plaque, April Clouds, Vellum, Mary Grace Denzler, Frame, 1914, 14 x 16 ½ In.	2596
Plaque, Vellum, Misty Summer Scene, Wood Frame, Fred Rothenbusch, 7 ¾ x 5 ⅞ In.	1331
Stein, Sea Green Glaze, Carved Flowers, Pink Highlights, Sallie Coyne, 1905, 5 ½ In. ....*illus*	385
Urn, Lid, Blue Band, White Flowers & Butterfly, 2 Purple Bands, Arthur Conant, 7 ¼ In.	726
Vase, Aerial Blue, Swallows, Forest Landscape, 6 ½ x 3 In.	165
Vase, Antelope, Shades Of Gray, Signed, Jens Jensen, 1946, 7 x 7 In.	875
Vase, Art Deco Style, Flowers, Marked, Sarah Sax, 1918, 10 ½ In.	1093
Vase, Arts & Crafts, Burgundy, Crystalline, Ombroso Glaze, 1914, 8 ½ In.	173
Vase, Autumn Leaves, Brown Shaded To Orange Ground, K. Shirayamadani, 11 x 6 In. .....*illus*	2432
Vase, Blue Ground, Flowers, Blue Matte, Charles Stewart Todd, 1914, 8 ½ In.	695
Vase, Boat Shape, Stylized Flowers, A. Valentien, 1888, 9 x 14 In.	295
Vase, Brown & Mustard Glaze, Incised, Signed, Sara Sax, 1905, 6 ½ x 3 ½ In.	1250
Vase, Brown Hombre Glaze, Looping Handle, Flowers To Body, Marked, c.1890, 7 In.	281
Vase, Brown Matte Glaze, Flowers At Shoulders, 1919, 8 In.	143
Vase, Bud, Dark Green Glaze, High Gloss, 1953, 6 ½ In...	75
Vase, Crackle Glaze, Gray, Rose, Grazing Bison Landscape, 1906, 9 In.	2091
Vase, Craquelure Surface, Oval, Ivory Matte Glaze, 1938, 6 ¼ x 4 ½ In.	156
Vase, Dogwood Blossoms, Shouldered, Margaret Helen McDonald, 1932, 5 In. ....*illus*	389
Vase, Fish, Seaweed, Carved, Painted, Electroplated, K. Shirayamadani, 1898, 12 ⅝ In.	9440
Vase, Flowers, Black Opal Glaze, Signed, Kataro Shirayamadani, 1926, 11 x 4 ½ In...............	4688
Vase, Flowers, Ribbed Melon Shape, Matte Glaze, Kataro Shirayamadani, 1940, 5 In.	410
Vase, Flowers, Squeezebag, 3 Nude Women, Elizabeth Barrett, 1935, 8 x 5 ½ In.	2340
Vase, Green Matte Glaze, Carved Geometrics, Incised, 1901, 3 x 4 ½ In.	250
Vase, Incised Ceramic, Flaring Carved, Geometric, Burgundy Highlights, Glaze, 13 ½ x 7 In., 1911	688
Vase, Lamp Base, High Glaze, Celadon, Gray & Yellow Flowers, 1951, 12 In.	108
Vase, Landscape With Trees, Vellum, Sallie Coyne, c.1921, 8 x 3 In...........................*illus*	1521

Rorstrand, Vase, Neutral Tones, Modeled, Glazed, Incised, Gunnar Nylund, c.1950, 24 ½ In.
$3,125

Rago Arts and Auction Center

Rose Mandarin, Bowl, Petal Shape Rim, Hardwood Stand, Chinese, Late 1900s, 4 ⅜ x 9 ¾ In.
$100

Leland Little Auctions

Rose Medallion, Platter, Oval, Flowers, Birds, People, Gilt Rim, Painted, 12 x 14 ¼ In.
$960

Nadeau's Auction Gallery

This is an edited listing of current prices. Visit Kovels.com to check thousands of prices from previous years and sign up for free information on trends, tips, reproductions, marks, and more.

R

Rose Medallion, Punch Bowl, Panels, Figures, Flowers, Birds, Chinese, Late 1900s, 6 x 14 1/2 In.
$210

Cowan's Auctions

Rose Medallion, Tray, Celadon, Bird, Butterfly & Flower, Square, c.1850, 9 In.
$132

Eldred's

Rose Medallion, Vase, Wood Handles, Palace, Flowers, Taoist Symbols, Mid 1900s, 37 x 17 In.
$354

Burchard Galleries

Vase, Leaf & Berry, Albert Valentien, Gorham Silver Overlay, Marked, 1905, 12 In.	1169
Vase, Magnolia Flowers, W.E. Hentschel, 1931, 11 3/4 In.	1046
Vase, Magnolia, Buff Glaze, High Gloss, Kataro Shirayamadani, 1948, 6 In.	125
Vase, Maple Leaves, Reddish Black Matte Ground, Olga Geneva Reed, 11 3/8 In.	1089
Vase, Molded Flowers, Matte Glaze, Charles S. Todd, 1913, 11 In.	1353
Vase, Morning Glories, Leaves, Violet Gray, Glaze, Flared Rim, 1949, 8 1/2 In.	195
Vase, Multicolor Flowers, Vellum, Pink Interior, Edward George Diers, c.1930, 4 7/8 x 3 In.	410
Vase, Multicolor, Landscape With Trees, Edward Diers, c.1930, 7 x 3 7/8 In. ....*illus*	1112
Vase, Ombroso Glaze, Carved & Painted Peacock Feathers, Charles Todd, 10 3/8 In.	1452
Vase, Oval, Art Deco Fish, Jet Black Glaze, Kataro Shirayamadani, 6 In.	194
Vase, Peacock Feather, Matte Glaze, Carved, Signed, Anna Marie Valentien, 5 1/2 x 4 In.	1375
Vase, Poppies, Brown Glaze, Signed, Edith R. Felten, 1899, 9 1/2 In.	316
Vase, Porcelain, White Peonies, Red Sparrow On Reverse, A. Conant, 1918, 6 5/8 In.	708
Vase, Pottery, Yellow Flowers, Multicolor, Elizabeth N. Lincoln, c.1900, 9 In.	234
Vase, Reddish Brown Glaze, High Gloss, Art Deco, 1930s, 5 x 7 In.	650
Vase, Riverscape, Birch Tree, Edward T. Hurley, 8 In.	1353
Vase, Round, Green Glaze, High Gloss, Rectangular Designs At Rim, 1958, 3 x 2 In.	95
Vase, Scenic Vellum, Marked, Sally Coyne, 1920, 7 3/4 In.	923
Vase, Scenic View, Trees, Hills, Leonore Asbury, Marked X For Second, 1918, 9 x 4 In.	330
Vase, Scenic, Vellum, Misty Dusk Landscape, River, Trees, Carl Schmidt, 1918, 14 x 6 In.	885
Vase, Silver Overlay, Leaf & Berry, Albert Valentien, 1905, 12 In. ....*illus*	1169
Vase, Sunset, Vellum, Kataro Shirayamadani, 1912, 11 x 5 In.	1500
Vase, Tulip, Blue Glaze, 1930, 5 In.	175
Vase, Vellum Glaze, Harbor Scene, Signed, Carl Schmidt, 1924, 10 1/2 x 4 1/2 In.	3750
Vase, Vellum Glaze, Scenic Branches & Leaves, E.T. Hurley, 1889, 10 In.	4961
Vase, Vellum, Wild White Rose, Branches, Thorn, Frederick Rothenbusch, 1905, 6 x 4 In.	540
Vase, Water Lilies, Matte Glaze, Kataro Shirayamadani, 1931, 7 1/2 x 7 1/2 In.	1560
Vase, Wax Matte Glaze, Flowers, Blue, Vera Tischler, 1924, 9 3/4 In.	358
Vase, Wax Matte, 6 Running Horses, Sky Blue, Wilhelmine Rehm, 7 1/4 In.	1029
Vase, Winter Landscape, Vellum, Ed Dier, 1909, 15 In.	2070
Wall Pocket, Overlapping Ivy, Marked, 7 3/4 In.	138

RORSTRAND was established near Stockholm, Sweden, in 1726. By the nineteenth century Rorstrand was making English-style earthenware, bone china, porcelain, ironstone china, and majolica. The three-crown mark has been used since 1884. Rorstrand became part of the Hackman Group in 1991. Hackman was bought by Iittala Group in 2004. Fiskars Corporation bought Iittala in 2007 and Rorstrand is now a brand owned by Fiskars.

Bowl, Conical, Blue, Rabbit Fur Crystalline Glaze, Carl Harry Stalhane, 4 In.	350
Vase, Neutral Tones, Modeled, Glazed, Incised, Gunnar Nylund, c.1950, 24 1/2 In. ....*illus*	3125
Vase, Sky Blue Glaze, Speckled Darker Flecks, Granola, Gunnar Nylund, 10 In.	185
Vase, Wild Rose Stalks, Carved, Mela Anderberg, 6 1/4 In.	189

ROSALINE, *see Steuben category.*

ROSE BOWLS were popular during the 1880s. Rose petals were kept in the open bowl to add fragrance to a room, a popular idea in a time of limited personal hygiene. The glass bowls were made with crimped tops, which kept the petals inside. Many types of Victorian art glass were made into rose bowls.

Blue Opalescent, Daisy & Fern, Northwood, c.1900, 4 In.	90
Cut Glass, Atlantic Pattern, Hobstar Base, Notched Rim, Bergen, 5 1/2 x 6 In.	36
Cut Glass, Clear Diamonds, 5-Sided Star-Cut Buttons, Hobstar Base, Fan Border	48
Cut Glass, Hobstar Base, Notched Rim, Monarch Pattern, J. Hoare, 3 1/4 x 3 3/4 In.	60
Enameled, Cranberry Rim, Crimped, Bohemia, 4 In.	68
Opalescent, Cranberry Edge, Beaded Drapes, 3-Footed, Jefferson Glass, c.1905, 4 1/4 In.	64
Pink Herringbone, 1890s, 3 x 4 In.	75
Pink Opalescent, Metallic Specks, 1880s, 3 3/4 x 4 1/2 In.	80
Salmon To Pink, Gunderson Burmese, 1930s, 6 In.	189
Shaded Pink, Shell & Seaweed, Consolidated Glass, 5 In.	165

ROSE CANTON china is similar to Rose Mandarin and Rose Medallion, except that no people or birds are pictured in the decoration. It was made in China during the nineteenth and twentieth centuries in greens, pinks, and other colors.

Compote, Butterflies, Pink, Green, 3 x 8 In.	326
Plate, Center Flowers, Double Dragons, Lucky Symbol Border, 8 In.	145
Vase, Cylindrical, Blue, Green, Gold Accents, 9 ½ In.	425

ROSE MANDARIN china is similar to Rose Canton and Rose Medallion. If the panels in the design picture only people and not birds, it is Rose Mandarin.

Bowl, Petal Shape Rim, Hardwood Stand, Chinese, Late 1900s, 4⅜ x 9¾ In. ....*illus*	100
Candlestick, Flared Base, 1800s, 7¾ x 4 In., Pair	225
Dish, Lotus Shape, Brocade Border, Scenic Panels, c.1830, 10 ½ In.	950
Mug, Court Figures, Flat Twisted Handle, c.1800, 5⅝ x 4 In.	475
Platter, Court Scene, Birds, Flowers & Butterflies Border, 1800s, 23 ½ x 9¾ x 2¾ In.	1150
Punch Bowl, Hunt Scene, c.1800s, 12 In.	813
Vase, Figures, Shouldered, Flared Rim, Foo Dog Handles, 8 In.	175
Vase, Pink, Green, Gilt Handles, Ribbed Panel, 7 x 7 In.	145

ROSE MEDALLION china was made in China during the nineteenth and twentieth centuries. It is a distinctive design with four or more panels of decoration around a central medallion that includes a bird or a peony. The panels show birds and people. The background is a design of tree peonies and leaves. Pieces are colored in greens, pinks, and other colors. It is similar to Rose Canton and Rose Mandarin.

Bowl, Garden Scene, Multicolor, 4 x 10¾ In.	130
Bowl, Shrimp, Orange Peel Glaze, Flowers, Birds, Butterflies, c.1800, 10 x 9 ½ In.	303
Dish, Figures Around Table, Chrysanthemum, Bats, Fruit Border, c.1800, 9 x 9 In.	510
Dish, Round Knob Lid, 4 Quadrants, Birds, People, Pinks, Green Flowers, 1800s	249
Jardiniere, Figural & Floral Panels, c.1875, 13 In.	660
Platter, Figural & Bird Cartouches, c.1875, 16 In.	225
Platter, Oval, Flowers, Birds, People, Gilt Rim, Painted, 12 x 14 ¼ In. ....*illus*	960
Platter, Oval, Flowers, Birds, Scenic, Footed, Early 1900s, 3 x 14¾ In.	177
Punch Bowl, Figures, Courtyard, Flowers, Birds, 4 ½ x 11 In.	270
Punch Bowl, Panels, Figures, Flowers, Birds, Chinese, Late 1900s, 6 x 14 ½ In. ....*illus*	210
Tray, Celadon, Bird, Butterfly & Flower, Square, c.1850, 9 In. ....*illus*	132
Vase, Flared Rim, 1800s, 23¾ In.	1107
Vase, Gourd Shape, Dragons, Imperial Court, Bird, Leaf Scenes, 25 x 15¾ In.	472
Vase, Wood Handles, Palace, Flowers, Taoist Symbols, Mid 1900s, 37 x 17 In. ....*illus*	354

ROSE O'NEILL, see Kewpie category.

ROSE TAPESTRY porcelain was made by the Royal Bayreuth factory of Tettau, Germany, during the late nineteenth century. The surface of the porcelain was pressed against a coarse fabric while it was still damp, and the impressions remained on the finished porcelain. It looks and feels like a textured cloth. Very skillful reproductions are being made that even include a variation of the Royal Bayreuth mark, so be careful when buying.

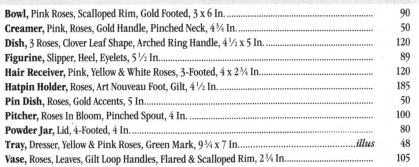

Bowl, Pink Roses, Scalloped Rim, Gold Footed, 3 x 6 In.	90
Creamer, Pink, Roses, Gold Handle, Pinched Neck, 4¾ In.	50
Dish, 3 Roses, Clover Leaf Shape, Arched Ring Handle, 4 ½ x 5 In.	120
Figurine, Slipper, Heel, Eyelets, 5 ½ In.	89
Hair Receiver, Pink, Yellow & White Roses, 3-Footed, 4 x 2¾ In.	120
Hatpin Holder, Roses, Art Nouveau Foot, Gilt, 4 ½ In.	185
Pin Dish, Roses, Gold Accents, 5 In.	50
Pitcher, Roses In Bloom, Pinched Spout, 4 In.	100
Powder Jar, Lid, 4-Footed, 4 In.	80
Tray, Dresser, Yellow & Pink Roses, Green Mark, 9¾ x 7 In. ....*illus*	48
Vase, Roses, Leaves, Gilt Loop Handles, Flared & Scalloped Rim, 2¾ In.	105

Rose Tapestry, Tray, Dresser, Yellow & Pink Roses, Green Mark, 9¾ x 7 In. **$48**

Woody Auction

Rosemeade, Plaque, Fish, Profile, Brown, Plate, Green, Oval, 6 In. **$165**

Strawser Auction Group

Rosenthal, Figurine, Amazon Warrior, On Horseback, Anton Grath, 9¾ In. **$213**

Leslie Hindman Auctioneers

TIP

If a white powder forms on a piece made of lead or glasses or pottery decorated with a lead glaze, immediately remove the piece from your house. The powder is poisonous. Consult an expert conservator if the piece is valuable and should be saved. Do the ecologically correct thing if you must dispose of the piece.

R

Roseville, Apple Blossom, Vase, Twig Handles, Matte Glaze, Coral, Brown, Ivory, Green, c.1935, 18 In.

$150

Garth's Auctioneers & Appraisers

Roseville, Blackberry, Vase, Lobed Body, Green, Brown Band, 2 Handles, 4 1/4 x 6 In.

$176

Forsythes' Auctions

Roseville, Freesia, Jardiniere, Green Ground & Leaves, White Flowers, 2 Handles, 11 1/2 x 8 In.

$77

Forsythes' Auctions

ROSEMEADE POTTERY of Wahpeton, North Dakota, worked from 1940 to 1961. The pottery was operated by Laura A. Taylor and her husband, R.I. Hughes. The company was also known as the Wahpeton Pottery Company. Art pottery and commercial wares were made.

Figurine, Dog, Borzoi, Metallic Bronze, 7 In.	150
Figurine, Fighting Roosters, 5 1/2 x 6 In., Pair	138
Figurine, Nude, Laying On Back, Gold, Signed, 5 x 3 3/4 In.	49
Plaque, Fish, Profile, Brown, Plate, Green, Oval, 6 In. ....*illus*	165
Salt & Pepper, Bison, Brown, Foil Label, 2 3/4 In.	95
Salt & Pepper, Bulldog, Green Glossy Glaze, 2 1/2 x 2 3/8 In.	55
Salt & Pepper, Pig, Sitting, Green	145
Salt & Pepper, Prairie Dog, Tan, Brown & Green Glaze, Foil Label, 3 1/2 In.	75
Vase, Bud, Tapered, Slashed Opening, Speckled Yellow, 5 3/4 In.	33
Vase, Deer, Standing, Flower Shape Opening, Yellow, Pink, 8 In.	55

ROSENTHAL porcelain was made at the factory established in Selb, Bavaria, in 1891. The factory is still making fine-quality tablewares and figurines. A series of Christmas plates was made from 1910. Other limited edition plates have been made since 1971. Rosenthal became part of the Arcturus Group in 2009.

Rosenthal China 1891–1904	Rosenthal China 1928	Rosenthal China 1948

Figurine, Amazon Warrior, On Horseback, Anton Grath, 9 3/4 In. ....*illus*	213
Figurine, Art Deco, Nude Maiden, Holding Basket, White, Marked, 7 1/4 In.	256
Figurine, Clown, Sad Face, Jacket Sleeves Hang To Ankles, Charol, Signed, 11 1/2 In.	221
Figurine, Nude Dancer, Scarf Around Foot & Arm, Marked, 7 In.	570
Figurine, Nude, Female, Hand Painted, Marked, Germany, 9 1/4 In.	580

ROSEVILLE POTTERY COMPANY was organized in Roseville, Ohio, in 1890. Another plant was opened in Zanesville, Ohio, in 1898. Many types of pottery were made until 1954. Early wares include Sgraffito, Olympic, and Rozane. Later lines were often made with molded decorations, especially flowers and fruit. Most pieces are marked *Roseville.* Many reproductions made in China have been offered for sale since the 1980s.

Roseville Pottery Company 1914–1930	Roseville Pottery Company 1935–1954	Roseville Pottery Company 1939–1953

Apple Blossom, Creamer, Pink, Brown Handle, 1940s, 3 x 5 In.	48
Apple Blossom, Vase, Twig Handles, Matte Glaze, Coral, Brown, Ivory, Green, c.1935, 18 In...*illus*	150
Artwood, Planter, Gray, Pink, Crazing, Handles, c.1951, 12 1/2 In.	100
Baneda, Vase, Orange Pumpkins, Pink, 2 Handles, 1932, 4 x 5 In.	360
Basket, Flower Frog, Green Glaze, Pine Branch Handle, 8 x 9 1/2 x 8 In.	266
Blackberry, Vase, Handles, Green, 8 1/4 x 5 1/2 In.	395
Blackberry, Vase, Lobed Body, Green, Brown Band, 2 Handles, 4 1/4 x 6 In. ....*illus*	176
Cherry Blossom, Teapot, Blue, Twig Handle, c.1940, 7 x 11 In.	176
Cherry Blossom, Vase, Brown, White, Green, Yellow, Matte Finish, Handles, 5 x 5 In.	1045
Cherry Blossom, Vase, Handles, Brown, Tan, 5 x 5 In.	195
Clemana, Brown, Cream Flowers, Purple Centers, Basket Weave Motif, 6 1/2 In.	22
Clemana, Vase, Green Ground, White Flowers, 2 Handles, Blue & Pink Center, 12 3/4 In.	110
Cosmos, Rose Bowl, Green, Blue, 1939, 4 x 7 In.	129
Creamware, Pitcher, Green Band, Black Stripes, Handles, 1915-30, 7 x 7 In.	60
Dahlrose, Platter, Jardinere, Daisies, Textured, Mauve, Yellow, Green, 1920s, 6 x 8 In.	149

R

Dahlrose, Vase, Brown & Cream Specks, Handles, c.1930, 6 x 3 In.	69
Dahlrose, Vase, Flat Sides, Sunflowers & Leaves, Stippled Ground, 2 Handles, 6 x 8 ½ x 3 In.	110
Falline, Vase, Tan, Green Blue, Molded Peapod, 2 Handles, 8 x 9 In.	220
Ferella, Vase, Mottled Green To Rose, Open Work Neck & Base, 2 Handles, 4 ¼ x 4 In.	132
Ferella, Vase, Mottled Green To Rose, Open Work Neck & Base, 2 Handles, 6 ¼ x 4 In.	165
Florentine, Ashtray, Brown, Green, Tan, 2 Resting Spots, 5 x 4 In.	55
Freesia, Jardiniere, Green Ground & Leaves, White Flowers, 2 Handles, 11 ½ x 8 In. *illus*	77
Freesia, Vase, Flowers, Leaves, Light To Dark Brown Ground, 2 Handles, 15 ½ In. *illus*	143
Fudji, Vase, Slip Trailed Decoration, 7 ¾ In.	560
Futura, Urn, Football Shape, 9 In.	384
Futura, Vase, Spherical, Balloons, Flared Lip, Green Ground, Pyramid Base, 8 x 5 ½ In. *illus*	1100
Futura, Vase, Violet To Rose Ground, Raised Teasel, 2 Handles, Flared Foot, 8 x 6 In.	413
Gardenia, Platter, Embossed, Signed, 15 x 7 ¾ In.	35
Ixia, Vase, Floral Sprays, Light Green Ground, 12 ½ x 4 ¾ In. *illus*	170
Jardiniere, Columbine, Orange Ground, Blue Flowers, Lug Handles, 3 x 5 ¼ In.	58
Jonquil, Vase, Brown, Green Interior, White Flowers, Green Leaves, Handles, 4 ½ x 4 In. *illus*	55
Magnolia, Basket, Blue, Center Handle, Flowers & Leaves, 10 x 13 In.	60
Morning Glory, Vase, Yellow & Green Matte, Cream Ground, Violet, 2 Handles, 4 x 6 ½ In. *illus*	88
Peony, Vase, Floor, Pink To Green Glaze, Marked, Flowers & Leaves, 18 ½ In. *illus*	94
Pine Cone, Basket, Pine Needles & Cone, Brown Twig Handle, 13 x 9 x 10 ½ In.	275
Pine Cone, Basket, Twig Handle, Blue Ground, Brown Interior, Pine Needles & Cone, 10 x 7 In. *illus*	176
Pine Cone, Bowl, 2 Handles, Green, c.1936, 5 x 3 In.	121
Pine Cone, Bowl, 2 Twig Handles, Pine Needles & Cone, Green Ground, 3 ½ x 11 x 6 In.	99
Pine Cone, Planter, Blue Flower, Leaves, 5 ½ x 6 In.	30
Pine Cone, Planter, Yellow, Pine Cone, Branch, Circular Foot, 6 ½ x 8 In.	83
Pine Cone, Tumbler, Blue, Marked, 5 x 3 In.	245
Pine Cone, Vase, Pillow, Brown, c.1935, 7 x 5 In.	259
Pine Cone, Vase, Twig Handle, Blue Ground, Brown Interior, Pine Needles & Cone, 6 x 7 In.	121
Poppy, Candlestick, Blue Base, White Bud Shape, Green Leaf Handle, 4 x 5 In.	75
Raymor, Bean Pot, Lid, Elongated Handles, 7 ½ x 16 ½ In.	24
Rozane Mongol, Vase, Art Pottery, Red Glaze, Art Deco, c.1925, 13 ½ In.	813
Rozane, Bowl, Cornucopia Shape, Turquoise Matte Glaze, 10 x 12 x 5 ½ In.	44
Rozane, Vase, Pedestal, Jardiniere, Green, Multicolor Flowers, 18 x 11 In.	526
Silhouette, Bowl, White Glaze, Pale Green, 1950s, 4 x 8 In.	120
Silhouette, Vase, Nude Women, Tan, Dark Brown, Footed, 8 x 6 In.	350
Snowberry, Jardiniere, Pink, 2 Handles, 4 x 6 In.	78
Sunflower, Hanging Basket, Leaves, Stipple Ground, Red Interior, 4 ½ x 7 In.	275
Sunflower, Urn, Round, Handles, Blue, Green, Yellow, 4 x 5 In.	323
Sunflower, Wall Pocket, Half Basket, Yellow Flowers, Green Leaves, Stems, 7 x 6 x 3 In. *illus*	358
Teasel, Vase, Blue, Wide Rim, Side Handles, Leaf, 5 x 6 ½ In.	156
Velmoss, Jardiniere, Embossed Leaves, Golden Brown Highlights, Green Matte, 10 x 13 In.	480
Water Lily, Vase, Pink & Green Glaze, Handles, 1940s, 4 x 7 In.	78
White Rose, Bookends, Brown, White, Green, Yellow, 5 x 4 In.	185

ROY ROGERS was born in 1911 in Cincinnati, Ohio. His birth name was Leonard Slye. In the 1930s, he made a living as a singer; in 1935, his group started work at a Los Angeles radio station. He appeared in his first movie in 1937. He began using the name Roy Rogers in 1938. From 1952 to 1957, he made 101 television shows. The other stars in the show were his wife, Dale Evans, his horse, Trigger, and his dog, Bullet. Rogers died in 1998. Roy Rogers memorabilia, including items from the Roy Rogers restaurants, are collected.

Clock, Figural, Horse Trigger, Metal, Wood Base, Dale Evans, 1940-50, 10 x 20 x 5 In.	61
Figure, Linda, Ranch Playset, Cream, Colored Plastic, Marx, 1955, 1 ¾ In.	139
Flashlight, Trigger, Signal Siren, Morse Code, Schylling, 7 In.	12
Fountain Pen, Plastic Barrel, Signature, Stratford, c.1955, 5 In.	75
Hat, Beaded Band, Cowboy, Child's, Tan, Felt, Draw String, Signed Inside	29
Jacket, Leather, Fringed, Western, Chips, Zipper, Brown, Child's, Size 10	14
Lantern, Tin Lithograph, Horseshoe Holder, Bail Handle, Battery, Box, Ohio Art, 8 In.	125
Lunch Box, Double R Bar Ranch, Metal, Thermos, Trigger, Dale Evans *illus*	70
Pin, Corral Member Cowboy, Trigger, Pinback, 1 ¾ In.	13
Pin, Roy & Trigger, Black On Yellow, c.1950, 1 ¾ In.	30
Saddle, Pony, Leather, Wool Cushion, Embossed, Child's	153
Shirt, Orange, Brown, Fringe, Embroidered, Pocket, 1950s, Size 6, 15 x 19 In.	95

Roseville, Freesia, Vase, Flowers, Leaves, Light To Dark Brown Ground, 2 Handles, 15 ½ In.

$143

Forsythes' Auctions

The Monteith Bowl
Mr. Monteith was a Scotsman who wore a cloak with a scalloped hem. A large punch bowl with a similar scalloped edge is called a "Monteith bowl." It is usually at least 12 inches in diameter.

Roseville, Futura, Vase, Spherical, Balloons, Flared Lip, Green Ground, Pyramid Base, 8 x 5 ½ In.

$1,100

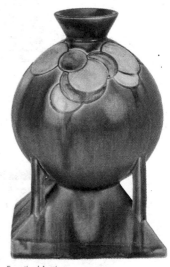

Forsythes' Auctions

R

Roseville, Ixia, Vase, Floral Sprays, Light Green Ground, 12 ½ x 4 ¾ In.
$170

Roseville, Jonquil, Vase, Brown, Green Interior, White Flowers, Green Leaves, Handles, 4 ½ x 4 In.
$55

R

Roseville, Morning Glory, Vase, Yellow & Green Matte, Cream Ground, Violet, Handles, 4 x 6 ½ In.
$88

Roseville, Peony, Vase, Floor, Pink To Green Glaze, Marked, Flowers & Leaves, 18 ½ In.
$94

Roseville, Pine Cone, Basket, Twig Handle, Blue Ground, Brown Interior, Pine Needles & Cone, 10 x 7 In.
$176

Roseville, Sunflower, Wall Pocket, Half Basket, Yellow Flowers, Green Leaves, Stems, 7 x 6 x 3 In.
$358

Toy, Jeep, Test Shot, Hard Plastic, Play Set, Nellybelle, 2 ⅛ In.	51
Toy, Lantern, Horseshoe, Bull, Red, Blue, 7 ¾ x 4 ½ In.	54
Wallet, Faux Leather, Roy, Dale & Trigger, RR Bar Brand, Zipper, 3 ¾ x 4 ½ In.	60
Wristwatch, Trigger, Cowboy Character, Windup, Stainless Steel Band	44

ROYAL BAYREUTH is the name of a factory that was founded in Tettau, Bavaria, in 1794. It has continued to modern times. The marks have changed through the years. A stylized crest, the name Royal Bayreuth, and the word *Bavaria* appear in slightly different forms from 1870 to about 1919. Later dishes may include the words *U.S. Zone* (1945–1949), the year of the issue, or the word *Germany* instead of *Bavaria*. Related pieces may be found listed in the Rose Tapestry, Snow Babies, and Sunbonnet Babies categories.

Royal Bayreuth
1887–1902

Royal Bayreuth
c.1900+

Royal Bayreuth
1968+

Basket, Cattle, Pierced Border, Green, Pink, 4 In.	40
Creamer, Cat, Sitting, Black, Handle, 5 x 4 In.	54
Creamer, Shell Shape, Yellow, White, Blue, Handles, c.1900, 4 x 4 In.	25
Ewer, Pedestal, Girl With Muff, Blues & Greens, 8 In.	30
Relish, Maple Leaf Shape, White, Gilt, 7 ½ In.	30
Salt & Pepper, Figural, Grape Bunches, White, Pink & Yellow Highlights, 3 ¼ In.	17
Stein, Green, Hunt Scene Band, Matching Inlaid Lid, Pewter Thumblift, ½ Liter	96
Stirrup Cup, Figural, Antelope, 4 ¼ In.	70

ROYAL BONN is the nineteenth- and twentieth-century trade name used by Franz Anton Mehlem, who had a pottery in Bonn, Germany, from 1836 to 1931. Porcelain and earthenware were made. Royal Bonn also made cases for Ansonia clocks. The factory was purchased by Villeroy & Boch in 1921 and closed in 1931. Many marks were used, most including the name *Bonn*, the initials *FM*, and a crown.

Cachepot, Mottled Blue Ground, Multicolor, Flower Sprays, 1800s, 13 ½ In. ....*illus*	125
Clock, Mantel, Red & Yellow Flowers, Blue & White Case, Ansonia Works, 10 x 8 In.	40
Urn, Covered, White, Multicolor Rose Garland, Ribbons, Gold Highlights, 2 Handles, 9 ½ In. ..	210
Urn, Dome Lid, Leafy Finial, Side Handles, Baluster, 30 x 15 ½ x 11 In.	847
Vase, Classical Maiden, 2 Colors, Gold Accents, Signed, 10 ¾ x 9 In.	79
Vase, Landscape Scene, Pond, Trees, Sunset, Germany, 11 x 7 ½ In.	94
Vase, Lid, Blue, White, Scroll Handles, Franz Anton Mehlem, 16 x 8 In. ....*illus*	254

ROYAL COPENHAGEN porcelain and pottery have been made in Denmark since 1775. The Christmas plate series started in 1908. The figurines with pale blue and gray glazes have remained popular in this century and are still being made. Many other old and new style porcelains are made today. In 2001 Royal Copenhagen became part of the Royal Scandinavia Group owned by the Danish company Axcel. Axcel sold Royal Copenhagen to the Finnish company Fiskars in December 2012.

Royal Copenhagen
1892

Royal Copenhagen
1894–1900

Royal Copenhagen
1935–present

Bowl, Monteith, Gilt, Botanical Specimens, Primula Nolt, 1940, 5 x 13 x 9 ¼ In.	2750
Bowl, Tenera, Yellow, Black, Gray, Marked, Denmark, c.1970, 8 ¾ In.	65
Bowl, Vegetable, Lid, Flora Danica, Game Series, Twig Handle, 7 x 9 In.	1250
Cachepot, Flora Danica, Gilt Rim, 2 Handles, c.1975, 6 x 10 x 7 In.	2000

Roy Rogers, Lunch Box, Double R Bar Ranch, Metal, Thermos, Trigger, Dale Evans
$70

gotstash4u on eBay

Royal Bonn, Cachepot, Mottled Blue Ground, Multicolor, Flower Sprays, 1800s, 13 ½ In.
$125

Leslie Hindman Auctioneers

Royal Bonn, Vase, Lid, Blue, White, Scroll Handles, Franz Anton Mehlem, 16 x 8 In.
$254

Aspire Auctions

R

Royal Copenhagen, Chocolate Pot, Flora Danica, Porcelain, Wood Handle, 7 x 9 x 5 ½ In.
$3,000

Heritage Auctions

Royal Copenhagen, Figurine, Bulldog, Porcelain, Knud Kyhn, Denmark, 1906, 7 ¼ x 12 ½ x 9 In.
$2,250

Heritage Auctions

Royal Copenhagen, Figurine, Woman, Feeding Cow, Porcelain, Marked, 6 In.
$83

Leland Little Auctions

TIP	
To remove sediment in the bottom of a vase or pitcher, put salt and crushed ice into the vase and stir. The friction will remove the stain.	

Chocolate Pot, Flora Danica, Porcelain, Wood Handle, 7 x 9 x 5 ½ In.	*illus*	3000
Dome, Ice Cream, Flora Danica, Tulip Finial, Stand, Porcelain, 11 x 12 In.		6875
Figurine, Bulldog, Porcelain, Knud Kyhn, Denmark, 1906, 7 ¼ x 12 ½ x 9 In.	*illus*	2250
Figurine, Girl, Looking In Mirror, Gerhard Henning, 1900s, 7 ⅛ In.		732
Figurine, Girl, Yellow Print Dress, Olga Sudejkina, Hand Painted, Russia, Marked, 1920, 11 In.		1098
Figurine, Hawk, Stoneware, Knud Kyhn, 1900s, 10 ½ In.		212
Figurine, Horse, Standing, Head Down, Ribbons, 11 ½ x 13 In.		272
Figurine, Lioness, Lying Down, 1 Paw Facing Up, Glazed, 12 In.		154
Figurine, Nude Girl, Kneeling, Swan, Marked, 6 ¼ In.		671
Figurine, Pheasant, c.1950, 7 ¼ x 12 In.		125
Figurine, Polar Bear, Roaring, Marked, 1900s, 12 ¾ In.		192
Figurine, Satyr Faun, Lizard, Marked, 8 x 3 In.		145
Figurine, Semi-Nude Female Youth, Necklace, 10 ½ In.		305
Figurine, Woman, Feeding Cow, Porcelain, Marked, 6 In.	*illus*	83
Figurine, Workhorse, Painted, Porcelain, Stand, 12 ½ In.		330
Group, Harvest Couple, 3 Waves, Porcelain, Signed, Circular Base, 17 In.	*illus*	130
Group, Skiing Couple, Holding Hands, 1800s, 6 In.		275
Group, Wave & Rock, Couple, Nude, Kissing, Theodor Lindberg, Late 1900s, 18 In.		875
Plate, Christmas 1956, Rosenborg Castle, Copenhagen, 7 ¼ In.		95
Plate, Christmas, 1911, Danish Landscape, Sheaf Of Wheat, Fence		29
Plate, Christmas, 1977, Immervad Bridge, Hunter & Dog, Blue, White, 7 In.		25
Platter, Flora Danica, Marked, Lonicera Periclymenum, 1955, 13 In.		1000
Tureen, Half Lace, Blue, Fluted, Lid, 2 Handles, Mushroom Finial, 7 ½ In.	*illus*	114
Tureen, Lid, Flora Danica, Conforming Stand, 10 ½ x 14 ¼ x 10 In.		4750
Tureen, Lid, Flora Danica, Gilt Accents, Applied Flowers, 14 ½ x 11 x 7 In.	*illus*	3125
Tureen, Soup, Lid, Cobalt Blue Flowers, Blue Fluted, c.1900, 10 x 8 In.		556
Tureen, Underplate, Flora Danica, Porcelain, c.1964, 11 ½ x 16 x 12 ½ In.		3500
Vase, Cream Spots, Tan, Green, Bronze Lid, Nordstrom, Andersen, 1921, 7 x 6 In.	*illus*	1375
Vase, Lid, Oval, St. George & Dragon, Oxblood Glaze, J. Nielsen, 12 x 12 In.		1875
Vase, Lid, Oval, St. George & Dragon, Oxblood Glaze, J. Nielsen, 12 x 12 In.		1875
Vase, Stoneware, Blue Glaze, Sculpted Top, Axel Salto, 1943, 5 x 3 ¾ In.		2625

 ROYAL COPLEY china was made by the Spaulding China Company of Sebring, Ohio, from 1939 to 1960. The best known are the figural planters and the small figurines, especially those with Art Deco designs.

Bank, Pig, Blue Pants, Green Tie, Foil Label, 6 ¼ In.		24
Planter, Bear, Seated, Playing Mandolin, Brown, 6 ½ In.		65
Planter, Finch On Branch, Red, Yellow, Green, 5 x 5 ½ In.		36
Planter, Kitten, Black, Pink Bow, 8 ¼ In.		35
Wall Pocket, Hat, Red Flowers, Bow, 6 ½ x 2 ¾ In.		35
Wall Pocket, Prince Sultan, Turban, Yellow, Gray, Peach, 8 In.		37

ROYAL DOULTON is the name used on Doulton and Company pottery made from 1902 to the present. Doulton and Company of England was founded in 1853. Pieces made before 1902 are listed in this book under Doulton. Royal Doulton collectors pay high prices for the out-of-production figurines, character jugs, vases, and series wares. Some vases and animal figurines were made with a special red glaze called flambe. Sung and Chang glazed pieces are rare. The multicolored glaze is very thick and looks as if it were dropped on the clay. Bunnykins figurines were first made by Royal Doulton in 1939. In 2005 Royal Doulton was acquired by the Waterford Wedgwood Group. It was bought by KPS Capital Partners of New York in 2009 and became part of WWRD Holdings. Beatrix Potter bunny figurines were made by Beswick and are listed in that category. WWRD was bought by Fiskars Group in 2015.

Royal Doulton
1902–1922, 1927–1932

Royal Doulton
1922–1956

ROYAL DOULTON
FINE CHINA MADE IN INDONESIA
© 2000 ROYAL DOULTON
Royal Doulton
c.2000–present

Bowl, Dragon, Climbing Tree, Overhanging Bowl, Gold Trim, Flowers, c.1886, 10 x 12 In........	896
Box, Lid, Sheepherder, Flambe, Oval, 4 x 6½ In..	90

ROYAL DOULTON character jugs depict the head and shoulders of the subject. They are made in four sizes: large, 5¼ to 7 inches; small, 3¼ to 4 inches; miniature, 2¼ to 2½ inches; and tiny, 1¼ inches. Toby jugs portray a seated, full figure.

Character Jug, Dick Turpin, Horse Handle, 1970s, 4 In..	55
Character Jug, General Gordon, Red Hat, Camel Handle, D 6869, 7½ In.	234
Character Jug, Mephistopheles, D 5757, 7 In..*illus*	480
Character Jug, North American Indian, Totem Pole Handle, D 6786, 7 In.	145
Character Jug, Samson & Delilah, 2-Sided, 1987, 7 In..	145
Figurine, Bluebeard, HN 2105, 10 In...	60
Figurine, Good King Wenceslas, HN 2118, 9 In...	40
Figurine, Guinea Hen, Flambe, HN 125, 3 x 5 In...	90
Figurine, Jack Point, Strolling Jester, Embossed, Charles Noke, HN 2080, 1918, 17 In.	210
Figurine, Match Seller, HN 2103, 8¼ In..	30
Figurine, Pensive Moments, Woman Holding Umbrella, Sitting, HN 2704, 5 x 5½ In.	36
Figurine, Punch & Judy Man, HN 2765, 9 In..	60
Figurine, Queen Elizabeth II, 20th Anniversary Of Coronation, HN 2502, 1973, 7¾ In.	133
Figurine, School Marm, HN 2223, 6½ In...	40
Figurine, Sunday Best, Woman, Yellow Dress, Bonnet, HN 2206, 7½ x 7 In.	36
Figurine, Thanks Doc, HN 2731, 8½ In...	125
Figurine, The Auctioneer, HN 2988, 9 In..	125
Figurine, The Jester, HN 2016, 9½ In...	25
Figurine, The Potter, HN 1493, 7 x 7 In...	50
Figurine, The Wizard, HN 2877, 9¾ In...	80
Figurine, This Little Pig, Baby, Sitting, Red Blanket, Toes Out, HN 1793, 4¼ x 3 In.......	48
Loving Cup, Handles, 3 Musketeers, 1930s, 10 x 10 In..	250
Mask, Wall, Madame De Pompadour, Mole, White Hair, Marked, c.1935, 13¼ In.	650
Plate, Automobile Series, Tree Border, D 2406, 10 In.	80
Plate, Luncheon, Gold Encrusted, Ovingtons, Floral Swags, 8½ In.	303
Vase, Flambe, Veined, Shouldered, No. 1617, 13 In..	90
Vase, Globular, Stick Neck, Flambe, Veined, No. 1618, 9 x 7 In.	100
Vase, Trumpet, Wild Rose, Red, Pink & Blue, 8¼ In..	34

ROYAL DUX is the more common name for the Duxer Porzellanmanufaktur, which was founded by E. Eichler in Dux, Bohemia (now Duchcov, Czech Republic), in 1860. By the turn of the twentieth century, the firm specialized in porcelain statuary and busts of Art Nouveau–style maidens, large porcelain figures, and ornate vases with three-dimensional figures climbing on the sides. The firm is still in business. It is now part of Czesky Porcelan (Czech Porcelain).

Centerpiece, 2 Maidens, Clasping Hands, Blue & White, Marked, 7 In.	120
Centerpiece, Seminude Woman, Shell, Art Nouveau, Pink Triangle Mark, c.1910, 15 In. ..*illus*	123
Figurine, Man, Standing, Playing Instrument, 19½ In..	133
Figurine, Parrot, White, Naturalistic Base, 15¾ In.	112
Figurine, Polar Bears, Painted, 12½ In., Pair	216
Vase, Secessionist, Stick Neck, Mottled Yellow, Flowers, Berries, 10½ x 8½ In. ....*illus*	124

ROYAL FLEMISH glass was made during the late 1880s in New Bedford, Massachusetts, by the Mt. Washington Glass Works. It is a colored satin glass decorated with dark colors and raised gold designs. The glass was patented in 1894. It was supposed to resemble stained glass windows.

Biscuit Jar, Roman Medallions, Brown, Raised Gold Lines, c.1890, 5 In.	1187
Ewer, St. George & Dragon, Rope Twist Handle, c.1890, 10½ In.................................	4375
Jar, Crown Finial Lid, Round Medallions, Scrolling Collar, c.1890, 11½ In......................	2625
Vase, 4 Snow Geese, Sunburst, Blue, Teal, Amethyst, Raised Stars & Flowers, 14 x 4 x 2 In.	5750

Royal Copenhagen, Group, Harvest Couple, 3 Waves, Porcelain, Signed, Circular Base, 17 In.
$130

Leland Little Auctions

Royal Copenhagen, Tureen, Half Lace, Blue, Fluted, Lid, 2 Handles, Mushroom Finial, 7½ In.
$114

loft-seeker on eBay

Royal Copenhagen, Tureen, Lid, Flora Danica, Gilt Accents, Applied Flowers, 14½ x 11 x 7 In.
$3,125

Royal Crest Auctioneers

R

Royal Copenhagen, Vase, Cream Spots, Tan, Green, Bronze Lid, Nordstrom, Andersen, 1921, 7 x 6 In.
$1,375

Rago Arts and Auction Center

Royal Doulton, Character Jug, Mephistopheles, D 5757, 7 In. $480

Morphy Auctions

Royal Dux, Centerpiece, Seminude Woman, Shell, Art Nouveau, Pink Triangle Mark, c.1910, 15 In. $123

Cowan's Auctions

Royal Dux, Vase, Secessionist, Stick Neck, Mottled Yellow, Flowers, Berries, 10 1/2 x 8 1/2 In. $124

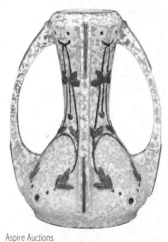

Aspire Auctions

Vase, Coin Medallion, Flower Panels, Gilt Lines, Flared Rim, Ball Feet, Signed, 6 In.	3383
Vase, Round, 3 Applied Feet, 3 Gold Coin Medallions, Flowers, Tan, Pink, 6 x 5 In.	8200

ROYAL HAEGER, *see Haeger category.*

 ROYAL HICKMAN designed pottery, glass, silver, aluminum, furniture, lamps, and other items. From 1938 to 1944 and again from the 1950s to 1969, he worked for Haeger Potteries. Mr. Hickman operated his own pottery in Tampa, Florida, during the 1940s. He moved to California and worked for Vernon Potteries. During the last years of his life he lived in Guadalajara, Mexico, and continued designing for Royal Haeger. He died in 1969. Pieces made in his pottery listed here are marked *Royal Hickman* or *Hickman*.

Dish, Aluminum, RH20, Lobster Shape, Bruce Fox, c.1955, 15 x 8 x 4 1/2 In.	55
Figurine, Leopard, Brown, Tan, Plinth, 1946, 8 x 4 x 13 In., Pair	271
Ladle, Punch, Silver Plated, c.1925, 12 In.	125
Vase, Beehive, Purple To Blue Glaze, 1940s, 8 In.	125
Vase, Bottle Form, Mauve On White, 24 x 10 1/2 In.	162
Vase, Bow, Blue Petty Glaze, c.1938, 11 In.	50
Vase, Free-Form, Coral-Like Shaped Base, Aqua, 1940s, 8 In.	40
Vase, Gladiola, Pierced, Brown, Chartreuse Drip Glaze, 11 x 14 In.	150
Vase, Long Neck, Green Petty Crystal Glaze, c.1930, 8 In.	145
Vase, Swan, Chartreuse Drip Glaze, 13 1/2 x 12 In.	300
Vase, Tan, Light Green, Crystal Glaze, Short Neck, 1930s, 8 x 7 In.	125

 ROYAL NYMPHENBURG is the modern name for the Nymphenburg porcelain factory, which was established at Neudeck ob der Au, Germany, in 1753 and moved to Nymphenburg in 1761. The company is still in existence. Marks include a checkered shield topped by a crown, a crowned *CT* with the year, and a contemporary shield mark on reproductions of eighteenth-century porcelain.

Figurine, Harlequin, Gentleman Dancing, Painted, Germany, 1800s, 7 In.	767

ROYAL RUDOLSTADT, *see Rudolstadt category.*

ROYAL VIENNA, *see Beehive category.*

ROYAL WORCESTER is a name used by collectors. Worcester porcelains were made in Worcester, England, from about 1751. The firm went through many different periods and name changes. It became the Worcester Royal Porcelain Company, Ltd., in 1862. Today collectors call the porcelains made after 1862 "Royal Worcester." In 1976, the firm merged with W.T. Copeland to become Royal Worcester Spode. The company was bought by the Portmeirion Group in 2009. Some early products of the factory are listed under Worcester. Related pieces may be listed under Copeland, Copeland Spode, and Spode.

Royal Worcester
1862–1875

Royal Worcester
1891

Royal Worcester
c.1959+

Ewer, Bottle Shape, Ivory Ground, Scrolled Dragon-Shape Handle, c.1881, 11 3/4 In.	523
Figurine, Br'er Rabbit, Standing, Basket, Base, 4 3/4 In.	225
Figurine, Hindu, Pink, Gilt, Multicolor, 1800s, 6 1/4 In.	225
Figurine, Irishman, Painted Face, 1800s, 7 In.	154
Figurine, Man, Down & Out, Cobbled Base, Hat, 1800s, 6 In.	154
Figurine, Scotsman, Painted Face, 1800s, 6 In.	154
Jug, Kingfisher, Landscape, Painted, 2 1/2 In.	42

Pitcher, Basket Weave Ground, Lizard, Bamboo Handle, 1806, 6 In.	108
Pitcher, Pink & White Flowers, Buds, Branch Handle, England, 1888, 8½ In..................*illus*	210
Potpourri, Lid, Ivory Ground, Japonesque, 3 Elephant Heads, c.1880, 8¼ In.	492
Teakettle, Lid, Alternating Bands Of Flowers, Gilt, Bronze Bail Handle, 1878, 6½ In.	185
Vase, Bottle Shape, Scrolled Handles, Owls, Full Moon, Ivory Ground, c.1883, 11 In.	400
Vase, Cobalt Blue Neck & Foot, Flowers, Gold Trim, 1897, 10 In.	84
Vase, Gilt, Turquoise Enamel, Openwork, Cylindrical, Persian Style, c.1880, 11½ In.	369
Vase, Heron, Landscape, Relief, Gilt, Bronze, Enamel, Lion Ring Handles, Square, c.1880, 11 In..	185
Vase, Heron, Leaves, Marsh, Gilt, Brown, Ivory Ground, c.1880, 6¼ In., Pair.......................	185
Vase, Long Neck, Pierced, Flowers, Leaves, 1800s, 11 In.......................................*illus*	313
Vase, Porcelain, Reticulated Rim, 2 Handles, Flower Sprigs, 1800s, 10¼ In......................	60
Vase, Ring Shape, Pierced Center, Blue, Flower Panels, Gilt, c.1875, 5 In.	215
Vase, Snake Handles, Flower Bouquets, 1800s, 8¾ In...*illus*	240
Vase, Squat, 3 Gilded Snakes, Japonesque, 1882, 7¼ In.	72

ROYCROFT products were made by the Roycrofter community of East Aurora, New York, from 1895 until 1938. The community was founded by Elbert Hubbard, famous philosopher, writer, and artist. The workshops owned by the community made furniture, metalware, leatherwork, embroidery, and jewelry. A printshop produced many signs, books, and the magazines that promoted the sayings of Elbert Hubbard. Furniture by the Roycroft community is listed in the Furniture category.

Bowl, Copper, Arts & Crafts, Aurora Brown, Orb & Cross Mark, c.1930, 2 x 6 In.	79
Lamp, Desk, Copper Base, Hammered, Steuben Shade, Aurene, 14¾ In...................*illus*	5400
Plaque, Be Yourself, Wood, Carved, Orb & Cross Mark, c.1920, 5 x 19 In.	2750
Vase, Bronze, Hammered, Silver Inlay, Geometric, Dard Hunter, c.1915, 6¼ In...........	1200
Vase, Copper, Brass Washed, Hammered, Cylindrical, Etched Band, 1920s, 10 x 3 In...............	1125
Vase, Copper, Hammered, Long Neck, Flared Mouth, Marked, 1920s, 18 x 8 In...........	2125
Vase, Copper, Hammered, Nickel Silver Accents, Buttressed Handles, K. Kipp, 8 In.	4063
Vase, Long Slender Neck, Copper, Hammered, Orb & Cross Mark, c.1915, 21 x 8 In....................	2375

ROZANE, *see Roseville category.*

ROZENBURG worked at The Hague, Holland, from 1890 to 1914. The most important pieces were earthenware made in the early twentieth century with pale-colored Art Nouveau designs.

Vase, Globular, 2 Handles, Multicolor, Enamel, Bird, Holland, c.1900, 13¾ In.	185

RRP, or RRP Roseville, is the mark used by the firm of Robinson-Ransbottom. It is not a mark of the more famous Roseville Pottery. The Ransbottom brothers started a pottery in 1900 in Ironspot, Ohio. In 1920, they merged with the Robinson Clay Product Company of Akron, Ohio, to become Robinson-Ransbottom. The factory closed in 2005.

Bowl, Feeder, Stoneware, Cream, 9½ In.	180
Crock, Lid, Blue & Tan Pattern, Spongeware, 2 Handles, 8½ x 5 x 4 In.	48
Vase, Dark Brown, Mauve, Green, Glaze, Arts & Crafts, c.1920, 23 x 12 In., Pair	250
Vase, Jade Green, Art Deco, Geometric, Accent Lines, High Gloss, 5 x 7¼ In.	35

RS GERMANY is part of the wording in marks used by the Tillowitz, Germany, factory of Reinhold Schlegelmilch from 1914 until about 1945. The porcelain was sold decorated and undecorated. The Schlegelmilch families made porcelains marked in many ways. See also ES Germany, RS Poland, RS Prussia, RS Silesia, RS Suhl, and RS Tillowitz.

Bowl, Centerpiece, Flowers, Purple, Soft Pastels, Gilt, Steeple Mark, 12½ In.	31
Bowl, Oval, Pink Roses, Openwork Handle, 11 x 8 In.	25
Cake Plate, Silhouette, Girl Dancing, Yellow Border, 9¾ In.	40
Candlestick, Chamber, Pink Roses, Stems, Leaves, Scrolled Rim, Gilt, 1910, 5 x 2 In...............	49
Coffeepot, Blackberries In Bloom, White Flowers, Green Leaves, White Ground, 9¾ In............	16
Creamer, Red Poppy Flowers, Looped Handle, 3¼ x 3⅜ x 2¼ In.........................	6
Hair Receiver, Forget Me Knot Flowers, Blue, Green, Gold, S & T, 2 x 5½ x 4⅝ In.	30

Royal Worcester, Pitcher, Pink & White Flowers, Buds, Branch Handle, England, 1888, 8½ In.
$210

Garth's Auctioneers & Appraisers

Royal Worcester, Vase, Long Neck, Pierced, Flowers, Leaves, 1800s, 11 In.
$313

Selkirk Auctioneers & Appraisers

Royal Worcester, Vase, Snake Handles, Flower Bouquets, 1800s, 8¾ In.
$240

Selkirk Auctioneers & Appraisers

R

Roycroft, Lamp, Desk, Copper Base, Hammered, Steuben Shade, Aurene, 14¾ In.
$5,400

Morphy Auctions

RS Germany, Pitcher, Lemonade, Flowers, Green, Gold, Victorian, 6 x 4 In.
$18

richlous.j on eBay

RS Prussia, Chocolate Pot, Lid, Melon Eaters, Children, White, Gold, Purple, c.1890, 10½ In.
$420

dounial on eBay

Pitcher, Flowers, Ruffled Rim, White Interior, Branch Handle, Gloss, Marked	39
Pitcher, Lemonade, Flowers, Green, Gold, Victorian, 6 x 4 In. ....*illus*	18
Shaving Mug, Scroll Handle, Pink Roses, Green Leaves, 2½ In.	30
Sugar, Flowers, Steeple Top Lid, 2 Handles, 4¾ In.	28
Sugar, Red Poppy Flowers, 2 Handles, Lid, 3⅛ x 2¾ x 2⅜ In.	6
Tray, Serving, Golden Owl, Blue Eyes, Gilded, Border, Leaves, Signed D.D., 1945	15
Vase, Cottage, Trees, Cream, Green, Brown, 4 In.	30

RS POLAND (German) is a mark used by the Reinhold Schlegelmilch factory at Tillowitz from about 1946 to 1956. After 1956, the factory made porcelain marked *PT Poland*. This is one of many of the RS marks used. See also ES Germany, RS Germany, RS Prussia, RS Silesia, RS Suhl, and RS Tillowitz.

RS Poland
c.1945–1956

PT Tulowice
After 1945–1956

Sugar & Creamer, Roses, Pink, Yellow, Scalloped Base, Marked	85
Vase, Iris, Leaf & Stem, Cream To Brown, Shouldered, 5¾ In.	110

RS PRUSSIA appears in several marks used on porcelain before 1917. Reinhold Schlegelmilch started his porcelain works in Suhl, Germany, in 1869. See also ES Germany, RS Germany, RS Poland, RS Silesia, RS Suhl, and RS Tillowitz.

RS Prussia
Late 1880s–1917

RS Prussia
c.1895–1917

Bowl, Autumn, Woman, Green, Gilt Highlights, Flowers, c.1900, 3½ x 10½ In.	360
Bowl, Bouquet, White & Blue Border, 11 In.	25
Bowl, Flower Center, White Center, Gold Border, Flower Rim, 10½ In.	72
Bowl, Flowers, Green, Cream & White, 10½ In.	60
Bowl, Flowers, Scroll Mold, White, Pink & Cream, 10 In.	24
Bowl, Flowers, White, Cream & Blue Panels, 10½ In.	48
Bowl, Flowers, Yellow, Green & Lavender, Ribbed & Scalloped Rim, 10¾ In.	60
Bowl, Pink & Peach Roses, Beaded, Scalloped, 10 In.	15
Bowl, Pink Flowers, Leaves, Blue, Cream & White, Hexagonal Base, 10½ In.	36
Bowl, Pink Roses, Green & White Border, 10¼ In.	72
Bowl, Plume Mold, Luster Finish, Water Lilies, 11 In.	60
Bowl, Roses & Snowballs, Pink, Purple, Peach, Satin Finish, Gold Trim, 1900, 11 In.	120
Bowl, Swans, Reflections, Lake Scene, Water Lilies, Blue, 10½ x 2½ In.	94
Bowl, White Satin, White Lilies, 9¼ In.	36
Bowl, Wildflowers, White & Green Border, 10½ In.	36
Bowl, Yellow Roses, White & Green Tones, 10½ In.	48
Cake Plate, Blue & White Flowers, Embossed Poppy Mold, 11 In.	18
Cake Plate, Cobalt Blue, White Flowers, Gold Stenciling, c.1906, 10 In.	250
Cake Plate, Cut Glass Mold, Pink & White, Blue Flowers, 11¾ In.	60
Cake Plate, Flowers, Yellow Gold, Red Star Wreath, 9½ In.	39
Cake Plate, Green & Pink Tulips, Gold Stencil Highlights, 10¾ In.	60
Cake Plate, Pink Roses, Blue & White Tones, Gold Stencil Highlights, 11½ In.	30
Cake Plate, Violets, White Center, 2-Tone Pink Border, Gold Highlights, 10½ In.	60
Celery Dish, Flowers, Blue, White, Green, 2 Handles, 9¼ x 4 In.	72
Celery Dish, Pink & Yellow Roses, White Openwork Border, 12 In.	25

R

Chocolate Pot, Lid, Melon Eaters, Children, White, Gold, Purple, c.1890, 10½ In. ....*illus*	420
Cracker Jar, Stylized Flowers, Gilt, Scalloped Rim, 5 x 6 In....................................	40
Cracker Jar, Swans, Lake, Swag, Tassel, Footed, Handles, 5 x 9 In........................	100
Creamer, Milk Pitcher, Boy Eating Fruit, Late 1800s, 4¼ In.	24
Dresser Tray, Center Flowers, Flower Medallions, Shaped Edge, Clover Mold, 11½ x 7 In.	138
Hair Receiver, Pink Roses, Footed, Green Satin, 4½ In...	25
Muffineer, Pink Roses, Gilt Highlights, Footed, 4½ In...	25
Mustard Jar, White Poppies, Lid, Cream, 3 In...	25
Pitcher, Snowball & Roses, Green & White, 9½ In...	60
Pitcher, Water Lilies, Hand Painted, Rose, White Ground, Multicolor........................	191
Plate, Berries, Flowers, Gilt Trim, 8 In..	35
Plate, Flowers, Daisies, Cream & Blue, Scrolled Rim, 8½ In...................................	25
Plate, Flowers, Iridescent Scalloped Rim, Flowers, Birds, Multicolor, 7¾ In...............*illus*	61
Plate, Roses, White Center, Pink & Green Border, Steeple Mold 3, 12 In..................	36
Relish, Carnation, White, Orange, Lavender, 9¼ In..	15
Relish, Poppies, Pink, Yellow, 9½ In..	30
Sugar & Creamer, Stippled, Green, Cream, Roses...	40
Syrup, Pitcher, Water Lilies, No. 4008, White Ground, Handle, Wide Spout................	62
Tea Strainer, White, Pink Roses, Pierced Star Center, Loop Handle, 5¾ In..............*illus*	30
Teapot, Lid, Pink Roses, White Ground, Raised Scrolls, Footed, 9 In.......................	42
Vase, Burnt Orange Poppy, Pink Flowers, Green Leaves, 1900, 7 In.........................	95
Vase, Landscape, Old Mill, Green & Yellow Paint, 7 In.....................................*illus*	40
Vase, Red Roses, Tapestry, Leaves, 4 Black Scrolled Handles, Footed, 1900, 8½ In......	189

RS SILESIA appears on porcelain made at the Reinhold Schlegelmilch factory in Tillowitz, Germany, from the 1920s to the 1940s. The Schlegelmilch families made porcelains marked in many ways. See also ES Germany, RS Germany, RS Poland, RS Prussia, RS Suhl, and RS Tillowitz.

Dish, Art Nouveau, Flowers, Orange Luster, c.1900, 7 x 8 In.	65
Tray, Art Deco, Flowers, Pink, Gilt Handles, 15 x 5 In..	105
Vase, Arts & Crafts, Roses, Enameled Rose Luster, 6 In.......................................	175

RS SUHL is a mark used by the Reinhold Schlegelmilch factory in Suhl, Germany, between 1900 and 1917. The Schlegelmilch families made porcelains in many places. See also ES Germany, RS Germany, RS Poland, RS Prussia, RS Silesia, and RS Tillowitz.

Vase, Woman, Holding Flowering Branch, Floral Top & Bottom, Gold Handles, 1906, 11 In.	621

RS TILLOWITZ was marked on porcelain by the Reinhold Schlegelmilch factory at Tillowitz from the 1920s to the 1940s. Table services and ornamental pieces were made. See also ES Germany, RS Germany, RS Poland, RS Prussia, RS Silesia, and RS Suhl.

RS Tillowitz
1920s–1940s

RS Tillowitz
1932–1983

Plate, Yellow, White, Passion & Purity, Iris, 9⅝ In...	3

RUBINA is a glassware that shades from red to clear. It was first made by George Duncan and Sons of Pittsburgh, Pennsylvania, in about 1885. This coloring was used on many types of glassware.

Bowl, Scalloped Edge, Silver Plate Stand, Marked, 11 In......................................	144
Pitcher, Bulbous Shape, Side Handle, Polished Pontil, c.1890, 7½ In.	88
Pitcher, Overshot, Pink To Clear, Bulbous Shape, Applied Handle, c.1885, 7½ In. ....*illus*	88
Pitcher, Red To Brown, Peace & Happiness, Frosted, 9¼ In.	189

RS Prussia, Plate, Flowers, Iridescent Scalloped Rim, Flowers, Birds, Multicolor, 7¾ In.
$61

b4y2k! on eBay

TIP
Early plates often have no rim on the bottom.

RS Prussia, Tea Strainer, White, Pink Roses, Pierced Star Center, Loop Handle, 5¾ In.
$30

Woody Auction

RS Prussia, Vase, Landscape, Old Mill, Green & Yellow Paint, 7 In.
$40

Richard D. Hatch & Associates

This is an edited listing of current prices. Visit Kovels.com to check thousands of prices from previous years and sign up for free information on trends, tips, reproductions, marks, and more.

Rubina, Pitcher, Overshot, Pink To Clear, Bulbous Shape, Applied Handle, c.1885, 7½ In.
$88

Garth's Auctioneers & Appraisers

Rubina Verde, Vase, Gilt, Ribbed, 3 Reeded Handles, Flower Scroll, Polished Pontil, 8 In.
$142

Forsythes' Auctions

Rudolstadt, Vase, Roman Chariot, Warriors, Horses, Cream, Figural Handles, 11½ x 8 In.
$180

Woody Auction

Pitcher, Rubina To Cranberry, Inverted Thumbprint, Reed Handle, Footed, c.1900, 8 x 6 In....	45
Pitcher, Water, Cranberry To Clear, Threaded Swirl, 8¼ x 6½ In.	236
Vase, Clear To Red, Melon Shape, 5 In.	20
Vase, Clear To Red, Striped Pattern, c.1900, 5 In.	20
Vase, Ruffled Rim, White Mottling, 7 x 6 In.	42

RUBINA VERDE is a Victorian glassware that was shaded from red to green. It was first made by Hobbs, Brockunier and Company of Wheeling, West Virginia, about 1890.

Bowl, Hobnail, 2¾ x 4¾ In.	70
Bowl, Hobnail, Rectangular, 3 x 7½ In.	80
Vase, Gilt, Ribbed, 3 Reeded Handles, Flower Scroll, Polished Pontil, 8 In. ....*illus*	142

RUBY GLASS is the dark red color of a ruby, the precious gemstone. It was a popular Victorian color that never went completely out of style. The glass was shaped by many different processes to make many different types of ruby glass. There was a revival of interest in the 1940s when modern-shaped ruby table glassware became fashionable. Sometimes the red color is added to clear glass by a process called flashing or staining. Flashed glass is clear glass dipped in a colored glass, then pressed or cut. Stained glass has color painted on a clear glass. Then it is refired so the stain fuses with the glass. Pieces of glass colored in this way are indicated by the word *stained* in the description. Related items may be found in other categories, such as Cranberry Glass, Pressed Glass, and Souvenir.

Decanter, Red, Facet Cut Stopper, Clear Stem, Flowers, Continental, c.1950, 14 In.	90
Vase, Rhyton, Bronze Mounts, Marble Base, D. Clive Hardy, c.1850, 9½ x 5½ x 8½ In.	313

RUDOLSTADT was a faience factory in the Thuringia region of Germany from 1720 to about 1791. In 1854, Ernst Bohne began working in the area. From about 1887 to 1918, the New York and Rudolstadt Pottery made decorated porcelain marked with the RW and crown familiar to collectors. This porcelain was imported by Lewis Straus and Sons of New York, which later became Nathan Straus and Sons. The word *Royal* was included in their import mark. Collectors often call it "Royal Rudolstadt." Most pieces found today were made in the late nineteenth or early twentieth century. Additional pieces may be listed in the Kewpie category.

Candelabrum, 3-Light, Figural Stem, Man, Encrusted Flowers, Eckert, c.1890, 20 x 11 In.	184
Figurine, Country Woman, Basket Of Grapes, Yellow Glaze, Rococo Base, 9½ x 4 In.	62
Figurine, Greek Goddess Of Hunting, Carrying A Wolf, c.1890s, 19 x 7½ In.	312
Figurine, Leda, Swan, Nude, Seated, Drapery, Hand At Ear, 1900s, 17 x 8 In.	150
Figurine, Woman, Walking, Bare Feet, Flowered Dress, Basket, Fish, Multicolor, Bisque, 21¾ In...	110
Group, Man, 2 Women, Flowered Dresses, Big Bows, Stepping In Unison, 1920s, 10½ x 6½ In.....	175
Vase, Flowers, Sky Blue, 2 Handles, Footed, 10 x 4½ In.	25
Vase, Pitcher, Salamander Handle, Violets, 7 x 3¾ In.	35
Vase, Roman Chariot, Warriors, Horses, Cream, Figural Handles, 11½ x 8 In..................*illus*	180

RUGS have been used in the American home since the seventeenth century. The oriental rug of that time was often used on a table, not on the floor. Rag rugs, hooked rugs, and braided rugs were made by housewives from scraps of material. American Indian rugs are listed in the Indian category.

Afghan, Repeating Pattern, Red, White, Black, Orange, Timori-Belouchi, Wool, 3 Ft. 5 In. x 5 Ft. 10 In.	173
Appliqued, Floral, Bold, Berries In Centerfield, Black Ground, 1800s, 2 Ft. 11½ In. x 4 Ft. 9 In..*illus*	871
Ardebil, Indigo, Pink, Medallions, Color Bleeding, 1900s, 4 x 9 Ft.	360
Aubusson, Ivory Medallion, Beige Field, Floral Bouquets, 4 Ft. 10 In. x 1 Ft. 6 In.............*illus*	3198
Bakhtiari, Garden Panel Design, Red, Cream, Orange, Persia, 10 Ft. 3 In. x 5 Ft. 6 In............	612
Bakhtiari, Hand Knotted, Wool, Persian, 6 Ft. 6 In. x 9 Ft. 9 In.	600
Bergama, Burgundy, Medallion, 2 Crosses, Hexagon Border, Turkey, c.1850, 5 Ft. 4 In. x 3 Ft.	300
Bokhara, Red Mogul Medallions, Matching Border, Pakistan, c.1950, 8 Ft. 4 In. x 4 Ft. 11 In..	195
Caucasian, 2-Cross Form, Leaves, Medallions, Red, Ivory, Turkey, c.1960, 4 Ft. 7 In. x 2 Ft. 6 In.	60

Caucasian, Peacocks, Birds, Pitchers, Wool, Hand, Knotted, Persian, 4 x 11 Ft.	375
Contemporary, Flatweave, Optical Concentric Circles, Wool, 8 x 10 Ft.	1250
Hamadan, Latch Hooks, Central Ivory Medallion, Pendants, 6 Ft. 6 In. x 4 Ft. 5 In.	819
Heriz, Center Medallion, Red Field, Ivory Spandrels, Dark Blue Guard Border, 8 x 12 Ft.	856
Heriz, Flowers, Leaves, Vines, Navy Field, Red Medallion, White, Blue Border, 10 Ft. 3 In. x 12 Ft. 9 In.	2829
Heriz, Ivory, Spandrels, Blue Border, 8 x 11 Ft.	960
Heriz, Medallion, 8 Point, Cream Corners, Navy, Ocher Guard Border, 8 Ft. 3 In. x 5 Ft. 11 In.	1200
Heriz, Multicolor, Border, Intricate Design, c.1920, 8 Ft. 6 In. x 11 Ft. 9 In.	1495
Heriz, Red, White, Fringe, Outer, Border, 10 Ft. x 13 Ft. 4 In.	484
Hooked, 2 Cats, Playing With Balls Of Yarn, c.1900, 25 x 53 In. ....*illus*	531
Hooked, 3 Stylized Roses, Leaf Border, 48 x 38 In..	90
Hooked, Cat, On Pillow, Floral Border, Roses, Striated Green Ground, 52 x 30 In.	150
Hooked, Flower Wreaths, Brown, Red, Green, 1900s, 102 x 75 In.	480
Hooked, Geometric, Concentric Rectangles & Roses, 1860-1935, 60 x 41 In.	92
Hooked, Horse, Galloping, Oak Leaf Border, 1860-1935, 36 x 23 In.	570
Hooked, Horse, Running, 1800s, 15 ½ x 24 In. ....*illus*	531
Hooked, Horse, Standing, Leaves, Black, Tan, Scrolling Border, 1900s, 49 x 30 In.	450
Hooked, Horse, Trotting, Geometric Border, Leaves, Flowers, Rectangles, 45 x 30 In.	510
Hooked, Maple Leaves, Stylized Branches, Tan Oval, Green Border, c.1900, 61 x 33 In.	90
Hooked, Penny, Stars, Diamonds, Dots, Fringed Ends, c.1920, 29 x 53 In. ....*illus*	625
Hooked, Reclining Spotted Dog, Flowers, Green & Gold Border, 1900s, 61 x 26 In.	600
Hooked, Rosebud Blossoms, Green, Tan, 1900s, 51 x 36 In.	92
Hooked, Ship, Monitor, American Flag, Brown Border, c.1890, 33 x 56 In. ....*illus*	3690
Hooked, Whaleship Stephania, New Bedford, 1835, Whale, c.1910, 31 x 41 In. ....*illus*	720
Hooked, Winter Scene, Horse Drawn Sleigh, Church, Muted Colors, Black Border, c.1910, 20 x 44 In.	120
Indo Persian, Area, Beige Field, Center Medallion, Red Main Guard Border, 5 x 4 Ft.	342
Karabagh, Cloudband, 3 Medallions, Red Ground, 8 Ft. 9 In. x 4 Ft. 6 In.	615
Kashan, Carpet, Dark Blue Medallion, Red Flower, Iran, c.1970, 13 Ft. 5In. x 9 Ft. 8 In. .....*illus*	523
Kazak, Geometric Design, Red Center, Blue Border, Hand Woven, 6 Ft. x 9 Ft. 6 In.	545
Kerman, Medallion, Lobed Center, Flowers, Spandrels, Animals, 4 Ft. 2 In. x 6 Ft. 2 In.	153
Kerman, Vignettes, Signatures To Panels, 4 Ft. 5 In. x 6 Ft. 9 In.	1652
Khorassan, Medallion, 16 Point, Burgundy Flowers, Iran, c.1920, 6 x 4 Ft.	677
Kirman, Medallion, Floating Pendants, Ivory Field, Persia, 21 Ft. x 11 Ft. 4 In.	226
Kirman, Medallion, Flowers, Burgundy Ground, c.1975, 9 Ft. 8 In. x 13 Ft. 8 In. ....*illus*	720
Kirman, Medallion, Wine Red Ground, Multicolor Flowers, 3 Ft. 8 In. x 10 Ft. 4 In.	848
Kuba Lesghi, Star, Blue, Geometric, 3 Ft. 6 In. x 6 Ft. 7 In.	738
Lut Zweiler, Palmettes & Flowers, Ivory Field, Continental, c.1930, 19 x 13 Ft.	1476
Malayer, Prayer, Flower Urn, Columns, Birds, Blue Border, 4 Ft. 5 In. x 6 Ft.	201
Nain, Vines, Red Border, 16 Ft. 2 In. x 11 Ft. 11 In.	678
Penny, Appliqued Circles, Blue Squares, c.1920, 3 Ft. x 4 Ft. 2 In.............................*illus*	375
Persian, 3 Columns Stepped Hexagonal Medallions, Ivory, Late 1900s, 8 Ft. 10 In. x 4 Ft. 4 In.	120
Qum, Medallion, 16 Point, Ivory Field, Silk, Iran, 1960, 6 Ft. x 3 Ft. 8 In.	215
Sarouk, Flower Sprays, Rose Red Field, Iran, c.1940, 16 Ft. x 7 Ft. 2 In. ....*illus*	615
Sarouk, Flowers, Burgundy Ground, 1900s, 4 Ft. 2 In. x 6 Ft. 4 In.	270
Sarouk, Flowers, Burgundy Ground, Multiple Borders, c.1935, 8 Ft. 4 In. x 11 Ft. 4 In.......*illus*	360
Serab, Runner, Rosettes, Floral Shape, Camel Color, Iran, c.1900, 11 Ft. 8 In. x 3 Ft.................	738
Serapi, Medallions, Ivory, Red Field, Navy Border, 1900s, 6 Ft. 2 In. x 2 Ft. ....*illus*	180
Shag, Rya Danish Modern, Sunset Shaded Circles, Purple Ground, 8 x 11 Ft.	444
Shirred, Flower Basket, Brown Background, Diamond Border, 1800s, 3 x 4 Ft................*illus*	435
Shirred, Flower Urns, Double Serpentine Border, Cotton, 2 Ft. 8 In. x 5 Ft. 2 In...............*illus*	1375
Shirvan, Directional, Repetitive Flowers, Beige Ground, Brown Border, 4 Ft. 1 In. x 3 Ft. 2 In.	216
Tabriz, Medallion, Pole, Repeating Leaves, Cream, Red, Navy Ground, Chinese, 14 x 10 Ft.	1872
Tabriz, Medallion, Red, Dark Blue Arabesque, Birds, Palmettes, c.1950, 13 Ft. x 9 Ft. 10 In......	1599
Tabriz, Silk, Center, White, Fringe, White, Gold, Borders, Flowers, Persia, 5 Ft. 3 In. x 3 Ft.......	272
Tabriz, Trees Of Life Design, Poem, Persian, 1900s, 8 x 11 Ft.	120
Tufted, Stripes, Multicolor, Reciprocating Border, 5 Ft. 5 In. x 7 Ft. 6 In.	212
Turkish, Hereke, Medallion, White Fringe, Orange Field, Green, Spandrel, 5 x 8 Ft.................	303
Wool, Diagonal Stripe Border, Green, Blue, Pink, Cream Field, Edward Fields, 1981, 8 x 8 Ft....	945

Rug, Appliqued, Floral, Bold, Berries In Centerfield, Black Ground, 1800s, 2 Ft. 11 ½ In. x 4 Ft. 9 In.
$871

Skinner, Inc.

Rug, Aubusson, Ivory Medallion, Beige Field, Floral Bouquets, 4 Ft. 10 In. x 1 Ft. 6 In.
$3,198

Skinner, Inc.

Rug, Hooked, 2 Cats, Playing With Balls Of Yarn, c.1900, 25 x 53 In.
$531

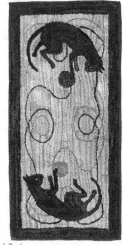

Pook & Pook

R

Rug, Hooked, Horse, Running, 1800s, 15 ½ x 24 In.
$531

Pook & Pook

Rug, Hooked, Penny, Stars, Diamonds, Dots, Fringed Ends, c.1920, 29 x 53 In.
$625

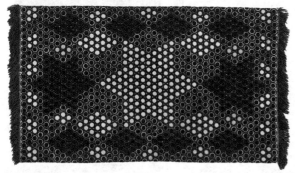

Pook & Pook

Rug, Hooked, Ship, Monitor, American Flag, Brown Border, c.1890, 33 x 56 In.
$3,690

Skinner, Inc.

Patch Up the Sofa

Latest novel decorating idea for a house with antiques: upholster the sofa with pieces of worn Oriental rugs. Then add a few matching patchwork pillows.

Rug, Hooked, Whaleship Stephania, New Bedford, 1835, Whale, c.1910, 31 x 41 In.
$720

Eldred's

Rug, Kashan, Carpet, Dark Blue Medallion, Red Flower, Iran, c.1970, 13 Ft. 5 In. x 9 Ft. 8 In.
$523

Skinner, Inc.

Rug, Kirman, Medallion, Flowers, Burgundy Ground, c.1975, 9 Ft. 8 In. x 13 Ft. 8 In.
$720

Garth's Auctioneers & Appraisers

R

Rug, Penny, Appliqued Circles, Blue Squares, c.1920, 3 Ft. x 4 Ft. 2 In.
$375

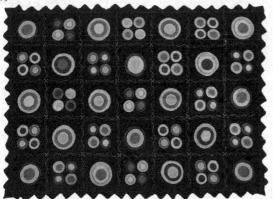

Pook & Pook

Rug, Sarouk, Flower Sprays, Rose Red Field, Iran, c.1940, 16 Ft. x 7 Ft. 2 In.
$615

Skinner, Inc.

Rug, Sarouk, Flowers, Burgundy Ground, Multiple Borders, c.1935, 8 Ft. 4 In. x 11 Ft. 4 In.
$360

Garth's Auctioneers & Appraisers

Rug, Serapi, Medallions, Ivory, Red Field, Navy Border, 1900s, 6 Ft. 2 In. x 2 Ft.
$180

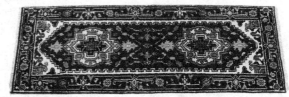

Selkirk Auctioneers & Appraisers

Braided Rugs

The braided rug was first popular from the 1820s to the 1850s. It was made from braided strips of worn fabric that were sewn together, round and round, until a circular rug was made. This type of rug was back in style in the 1890s Colonial Revival rooms and is still popular today.

Rug, Shirred, Flower Basket, Brown Background, Diamond Border, 1800s, 3 x 4 Ft.
$435

Skinner, Inc.

Rug, Shirred, Flower Urns, Double Serpentine Border, Cotton, 2 Ft. 8 In. x 5 Ft. 2 In.
$1,375

Pook & Pook

R

Russel Wright, American Modern, Pitcher, Coral, C-Handle, Steubenville $27

angiedange on eBay

Russel Wright, Chrome, Ice Bowl, Tongs, Art Deco, Chase, 1930s, 6½ x 7 In. $130

riverside17 on eBay

Sampler, Pictorial, Cutouts, Different Subjects, Anna Reinpacke, 1842, Velvet, Frame, 8 x 11 In. $165

Forsythes' Auctions

RumRill

RUMRILL POTTERY was designed by George Rumrill of Little Rock, Arkansas. From 1933 to 1938, it was produced by the Red Wing Pottery of Red Wing, Minnesota. In January 1938, production was transferred to the Shawnee Pottery in Zanesville, Ohio. It was moved again in December of 1938 to Florence Pottery Company in Mt. Gilead, Ohio, where Rumrill ware continued to be manufactured until the pottery burned in 1941. It was then produced by Gonder Ceramic Arts in South Zanesville until early 1943.

Bowl, Cockatiel, Vase, White Matte, Florence Pottery Co., 1939, 8 x 12 In.	49
Bowl, Green, Stacked Rings, Tabs At Shoulders, 7¾ In.	25
Console, Female Nude Handles, Oval Bowl, Pedestal Base, Ecru Matte Glaze, c.1935, 8 x 11 In.	329
Console, Looping Scroll Handles, Pink Matte Glaze, c.1935, 6 x 11 In.	79
Creamer, Peach Cameo Finish, Art Pottery, 3½ In.	26
Planter, Baby Shoe, Sea Spray Green, Ohio, 1940s	34
Planter, Virgin Mary, Madonna, Matte White, 1941, 6 In.	23
Sugar, Deep Rose, Dubonnet, Silver Label, Marked, Handles, 3 In.	12
Urn, Yellow, Aqua Interior, Deco Style, Base, 7 In.	80
Vase, Face, Madonna, White Matte, c.1940, 11 In.	64
Vase, Green Glaze, Mottled, Ribbed Handle, Beaded Shoulder, Footed, 7½ x 6 In., Pair	85
Vase, Green Over Orange, Ribbed Neck, c.1933, 7½ In.	115
Vase, Pinched Waisted, Zigzag Handles, White Matte, 10 In.	18
Vase, Rose, Embossed, Cream, Earth Tones, Medallion Line, Red Wing, 11 In.	51
Vase, Rust Over Green, Dancing Nude, Leaf Handles, 7½ In.	350
Vase, Sphere Shape, Swirling Openings, Salmon Glaze, 5 x 6 In.	100
Vase, Sunflower, Orange, Black, Red Wing, 5½ In.	68

RUSKIN POTTERY WEST SMETHWICK

RUSKIN is a British art pottery of the twentieth century. The Ruskin Pottery was started by William Howson Taylor, and his name was used as the mark until about 1899. The factory, at West Smethwick, Birmingham, England, stopped making new pieces in 1933 but continued to glaze and sell the remaining wares until 1935. The art pottery is noted for its exceptional glazes. It also made ceramic "stones" with the famous glaze to be used in jewelry.

Candlestick, Orange Iridescent, 1921, 6⅞ In., Pair	130
Candlestick, Orange Luster, Knopped Top, Flared Base, 1922, 6¾ x 4¾ In.	74
Ginger Jar, Yellow Lusterware, Bulbous Body, 1915, 13 x 4¾ x 6 In.	1136
Inkwell, Hinged Lid, Blue, Flambe Glazed Pot, Silver Mount, c.1900, 2¾ x 3¼ In.	491
Lamp Base, Mottled Crystalline Glaze, Metal Stand, Mission, 8¾ In.	1464
Vase, Crystalline Orange, Flowers, Molded Base, Scarce Arts & Crafts, 1930s, 5 In.	59
Vase, Dark Blue, Blue & Tan Drips, Round Bottom, Paneled Side, 5¾ In.	185
Vase, Flambe, Red, Art Deco, 1927, 4 x 12½ In.	661
Vase, Multicolor Drip Glaze, Flared Rim, Marked, 7¾ In.	2124
Vase, Purple Luster Glaze, Elongated, 1920, 9½ In.	240
Vase, Purple, Tapered, 1920, 9½ In.	125
Vase, Purple, White, Green, 6½ x 4½ In.	1690
Vase, Tan To Purple To Blue, Foot Ring, 1906, 7¼ x 3¾ In.	2210
Vase, Turquoise Over Amethyst, Flower & Wreath On Shoulder, Semimatte Glaze, 5 x 7 In.	280
Vase, Yellow Lusterware, Art & Crafts, 1915, 8 x 5 In.	350

RUSSEL WRIGHT designed dinnerware in modern shapes for many companies. Iroquois China Company, Harker China Company, Sterling China Co., Steubenville Pottery, and Justin Tharaud and Sons made dishes marked *Russel Wright*. The Steubenville wares, first made in 1938, are the most common today. Wright was a designer of domestic and industrial wares, including furniture, aluminum, radios, interiors, and glassware. A new company, Bauer Pottery Company of Los Angeles, is making Russel Wright's American Modern dishes using molds made from original pieces. Pieces are marked *Russel Wright by Bauer Pottery California USA*. Russel Wright dinnerware and other original pieces by Wright are listed here. For more prices, go to kovels.com.

STERLING CHINA by *Russel Wright*	JUSTIN THARALD & SON *Russel Wright* MADE IN U.S.A.	*Russel Wright* FLAIR *Harker* BOSTON 27
Russel Wright 1948–1950	Russel Wright 1948–1953	Russel Wright 1959–1960

American Modern, Bowl, Gray, Lug Handles, Steubenville, 8 In.		17
American Modern, Flat Cup & Saucer, Gray, 3 ½ In.		8
American Modern, Pitcher, Coral, C-Handle, Steubenville	*illus*	27
American Modern, Pitcher, Water, Lid, Coral, Black Specks, 1930s, 8 In.		239
Ashtray, Yellow, Footed, Sterling China, Glossy		27
Bowl, Lug, Fruit, Olive Green, Steubenville, c.1939, 6 In.		10
Bread Tray, Coral, Oval, Steubenville, 11 x 6 In.		10
Chrome, Ice Bowl, Tongs, Art Deco, Chase, 1930s, 6 ½ x 7 In.	*illus*	130
Clock, Wall, Black & White Glaze, Model 2HA48, General Electric, Harkerware, 8 In.		17
Iroquois Casual, Carafe, White Crazing, 10 ½ In.		165
Iroquois Casual, Mug, Lemon Yellow, Glossy, C-Handle, Marked		89
Iroquois Casual, Saucepan, Lid, Apricot, Hot Pad, 3 ½ x 11 x 6 ½ In.		57
Platter, Suede Gray, Oval, Sterling China, 13 ½ In.		33
Punch, Tumbler, Chartreuse, c.1951, 11 Oz., 4 In.		17

SABINO glass was made in the 1920s and 1930s in Paris, France. Founded by Marius-Ernest Sabino (1878–1961), the firm was noted for Art Deco lamps, vases, figurines, and animals in clear, colored, and opalescent glass. Production stopped during World War II but resumed in the 1960s with the manufacture of nude figurines and small opalescent glass animals. Pieces made in recent years are a slightly different color and can be recognized. Only vintage pieces are listed here.

Sabino France

Figurine, Tanagra, Woman, Nude, Drapery, Arms Out, 1920s, 8 ½ x 4 In.	368
Group, Women, Standing, Opalescent, Illuminated Base, Gilt Metal, Wood, c.1920, 8 ½ In.	1260
Plate, Sirenes, Opalescent, Swimming Nudes, Women, Raised Relief, 11 ¾ In.	625
Vase, La Danse, Opalescent, Women, Dancing, Relief, Marius-Ernest Sabino, c.1929, 14 x 9 In.	843
Vase, Opalescent, Birds, Long Plumes, Round, Squat, 1900s, 10 In.	375

SALESMAN'S SAMPLE *may be listed in the Advertising, Stove, or Toy category.*

SALT AND PEPPER SHAKERS in matched sets were first used in the nineteenth century. Collectors are primarily interested in figural examples made after World War I. Huggers are pairs of shakers that appear to embrace each other. Many salt and pepper shakers are listed in other categories and can be located through the index at the back of this book.

Astronaut & Rocket Ship, Gray, Red, White, c.1969, 1 ½ x 2 In.	49
Bear, Female, Flowers, Male, Bowtie, Standing, Pottery, Brown, Norcrest, 6 ½ In.	41
Bear, Mom In Dress, Hat, Father In Suit, Hat, Holding Cub, Multicolor, Pottery, 1950s, 4 ½ In.	24
Cabbage Heads, Green, Pottery, 2 In.	14
Cat, Figaro, Pink, Blue, Glaze, Pottery, 2 ⅜ In.	50
Chef & Waitress, Waitress In Black Dress, Chef In White & Blue, Pottery, 1940s, 9 In.	77
Coffeepot, Dark Brown Drip Glaze, 3 ¾ In.	12
Corn & Radish, Corn, Flute, Radish, Playing Violin, Cork Stopper, Napco, 4 In.	25
Flower, Face In Blossom, Pink & Yellow, Anthropomorphic, Pottery, 3 In.	33
Fork & Spoon, Pink, Black, Glazed, Waving Arms, Faces, 5 ⅛ In.	14
Maggie & Jiggs, Figural, Glazed, Pottery, 1930s, 3 ¼ In.	125
Milk Glass, White, Red Polka Dots, Fire-King, Anchor Hocking	141
Musicians, Black, Saxophone & Bass, Nodder, 1 & 3 Pour Holes, 4 ¼ In.	66
Raccoon, Holding Shakers, Brown, Porcelain, Hong Kong, 6 In.	18
Rosewood, Pyramid Shape, Scandinavian Modern, 1960s, 4 In.	83

Sampler, Pictorial, Miss Liberty, 1818, Helen White, Age 9, Silk On Linen, Frame, 11 x 14 In.
$523

Forsythes' Auctions

Sandwich Glass, Lamp, Emerald Green, 4-Petal Design, Brass Stem, Marble Base, 1800s, 11 ¼ In.
$330

Eldred's

Sarreguemines, Figure, Female, Nude, Kneeling, Glazed Ceramic, France, 9 x 6 ¾ x 7 ¼ In.
$63

Kamelot Auctions

S

Sarreguemines, Jardiniere, Majolica, Cobalt Blue, Geometric Design, Late 1900s, 6½ x 6½ In.
$59

Jeffrey S. Evans & Associates

Satsuma, Tea Caddy, Lid, Signed, Kozan, c.1880, 6 x 4 In.
$1,107

Morphy Auctions

Satsuma, Vase, Peony Design, Gold, Red, Blue, Marked, Shimazu Crests, Signed, c.1860, 12 In.
$1,375

Eldred's

TIP
When hanging pictures, use your smartphone app for a level to be sure the pictures are not crooked.

Seashells, Conch, White, 1980s, 2 x 4 In.	40
Winnie The Pooh, Rabbit, Enesco Label, 1960s, 3½ In.	90

ABCDE **SAMPLERS** were made in America from the early 1700s. The best examples were made from 1790 to 1840 on homemade fabrics. Long, narrow samplers are usually older than square ones. Early samplers just had stitching or alphabets. The later examples had numerals, borders, and pictorial decorations. Those with mottoes are mid-Victorian. A revival of interest in the 1930s produced simpler samplers, using machine-made textiles, usually with mottoes.

10 Commandments, Angels, Wool, Silk, Linen, Frame, England, c.1750, 19 x 22 In.	469
Alphabet & Sentiment, Emma Fenton, 1869, Wool On Buckram, 19 x 20 In.	210
Alphabet, 2 Federal Style Houses, Trees, Dog, Vine, Anna Hartzell, Ohio, 1847, 16 x 16 In.	450
Alphabet, Floral Border, Jane Walker, Silk Thread, Frame, 1800s, 23¾ x 20 In.	240
Alphabet, Flower Baskets, Birds, Silk Thread, Mary Mallery Pimm, 18 x 16 In.	813
Alphabet, Flowering Vines, Bird Border, Mary Ann Babcock, 1826, Wool On Linen, 17 x 16 In.	6765
Alphabet, Hymn, Flowers, Black Frame, c.1790, 18 x 19 In.	799
Alphabet, Lydia Waterman, 1835, Silk, Linen, Rhode Island, 16 x 17½ In.	406
Alphabet, Numbers, Capital Letters, Dorothea, Silk On Linen, Frame, 1800s, 10 x 9 In.	88
Alphabet, Numbers, Exercise Page, German Text, Frame, Pennsylvania, Late 1700s, 9½ x 9 In.	188
Alphabet, Numbers, Train & Steamship, Henriette Lamay, 1800s, 11½ x 14½ In.	163
Alphabet, Numerical Rows, Vine Border, Frame, 1800s, 12 x 10 In.	123
Alphabet, Pictorial, Vine & Diamond Border, Lucy Leonard, 1834, 13 x 10 In.	94
Alphabet, Potted Plants, Animals, Filigree, French Text, Elizabeth Tibat, 1723, 18½ x 8 In.	242
Alphabet, S. Woodward, Silk On Linen, Wooden Frame, 4⅜ x 3¼ In.	427
Alphabet, Verse, Berry Border, Martha Vinal, 1816, Silk On Linen, Frame, 18½ x 18 In.	300
Alphabet, Verse, Church, House, Amanda Anderson Aged 11 Yrs, 1829, N.Y., Frame, 23 x 26 In.	461
Alphabet, Verse, Flowers, Eleanor Carson, 1830, Frame, 17 x 18 In.	1495
Alphabet, Verse, Flowers, Mary F. Howard, Age 11, 1827, Silk & Wool, Frame, 17 x 16 In.	1170
Alphabet, Verse, Flowers, People, Trees, Ducks, Black Ground, 1800s, 24 x 21 In.	960
Alphabet, Verse, Hannah Adams Stone, Silk On Linen, Frame, Massachusetts, 17¾ x 18 In.	150
Alphabet, Verse, Stag, Harriot Cock, 1816, Frame, 12½ x 11 In.	413
Alphabet, Vine, Ellen Blaine Russell, Dec. 12th 1824, 10th Year, Penn., Frame, 17 x 21 In.	308
Alphabet, Virtues Verse, Flowers, Silk On Homespun Linen, Frame, 19 x 18 In.	339
Alphabet, White Rose, Butterfly, 1835, Maple Frame, 7¼ x 5¼ In.	263
Darning Stitch, Samples, Crowned Initials, 1802, Silk On Linen, Frame, 19 x 18 In.	210
Memorial, Urn, Fruit Branches, Pauline Loder, 1827, Silk On Linen, Frame, 21 x 20 In.	2760
Pictorial, Cutouts, Different Subjects, Anna Reinpacke, 1842, Velvet, Frame, 8 x 11 In. *illus*	165
Pictorial, House, Capital Letters, Margaret Carich, Wool On Linen, 1800s, 16 x 7½ In.	150
Pictorial, House, Red, Green Lawn, Red Flowers, Sunbursts, c.1843, 17 x 17 In.	250
Pictorial, Miss Liberty, 1818, Helen White, Age 9, Silk On Linen, Frame, 11 x 14 In. *illus*	523
Quotation, Lost, 2 Golden Hours, Horace Mann Quote, Frame, Late 1800s, 12 x 15 In.	94
Quotation, Love One Another, Parrots, Flower Basket, Ann Evans, 1850, Frame, 19 x 26 In.	250
Register, Olmsted Family Record, Flower Border, Frame, 1800s, 19 x 21 In.	83
Register, Thompson Family Record, Rose & Vine Border, Silk On Linen, Early 1800s, 18 x 18 In.	363
See Time Steals On, Margaret Bibby, 1827, Silk On Linen, England, Frame, 23 x 23 In.	336
Verse, Bible, Manor House, Landscape, 2 Deer, Mary Farrow, 1835, England, 25 x 27 In.	540
Verse, Industry, Flowers, Vines, Mary Underhill, 1836, Frame, 21 x 20 In.	1062
Wreath, Flowers, Maine, Mary Jane Bangs, Wool Linen, Mahogany Frame, 17½ In.	840

SAMSON and Company, a French firm specializing in the reproduction of collectible wares of many countries and periods, was founded in Paris in the early nineteenth century. Chelsea, Meissen, Famille Verte, and Chinese Export porcelain are some of the wares that have been reproduced by the company. The firm used fake marks similar to the real ones on the reproductions. It closed in 1969.

Bowl, Lozenge Shape, Scalloped, Flowers, Armorial, Footed, 1800s, 3 x 16 In.	108

SANDWICH GLASS is any of the myriad types of glass made by the Boston & Sandwich Glass Company of Sandwich, Massachusetts, between 1825 and 1888. It is often very difficult to be sure whether a piece was really made at the Sandwich factory because so many types were made there and similar pieces were made at other glass factories.

S

Additional pieces may be listed under Pressed Glass and in other related categories.

Bowl, Blown, Cut, Flint, Clear, Round Base, Pa., c.1850, 7¾ x 7⅞ In.	154
Candlestick, Pressed, Flint, Cobalt Blue, Pentagon Footed Base, c.1850, 9¼ In.	125
Cologne Bottle, Flint, Ruby, Mold Blown, Stopper, Cut Panels, Polished Pontil, Boston, 8 In.	31
Compote, Lincoln Drape, Flint, Clear, Round Base, c.1860, 5 x 7 In.	14
Creamer, Gooseberry, Floral, Clear, Round Base, Handle, Wide Spout, 5 x 3 In.	34
Dish, Pekinese Dog Lid, Opaque White, c.1880, 4 In.	59
Hat, Toothpick Holder, 3-Part Mold, Clear, Boston, c.1865	61
Lamp, Banquet, Punty, Cranberry Cut To Clear, Frosted Globe, Marble Base, c.1860, 28 In.	4200
Lamp, Emerald Green, 4-Petal Design, Brass Stem, Marble Base, 1800s, 11¼ In. ....*illus*	330
Lamp, Oil, Amethyst, 4 Printie Block & Monument Base, 1840-65, 12 In.	2460
Lamp, Oil, Canary Yellow, 4 Printie, Block Font, Hexagonal Base, c.1830s, 11½ In.	156
Lamp, Whale Oil, Cobalt Blue, Pentagon Footed Base, 9¾ In.	600

SARREGUEMINES is the name of a French town that is used as part of a china mark for Utzschneider and Company, a porcelain factory that made ceramics in Sarreguemines, Lorraine, France, from about 1775. Transfer-printed wares and majolica were made in the nineteenth century. The nineteenth-century pieces, most often found today, usually have colorful transfer-printed decorations showing peasants in local costumes.

Figure, Female, Nude, Kneeling, Glazed Ceramic, France, 9 x 6¾ x 7¼ In. ....*illus*	63
Jardiniere, Majolica, Cobalt Blue, Geometric Design, Late 1900s, 6½ x 6½ In. ....*illus*	59

SASCHA BRASTOFF made decorative accessories, ceramics, enamels on copper, and plastics of his own design. He headed a factory, Sascha Brastoff of California, Inc., in West Los Angeles, from 1953 until about 1973. He died in 1993. Pieces signed with the signature *Sascha Brastoff* were his work and are the most expensive. Other pieces marked *Sascha B.* or with a stamped mark were made by others in his company. Pieces made by Matt Adams after he left the factory are listed here with his name.

Ashtray, Chimney, Turquoise, Blue Shades, Signed On Side, 7½ x 3 In.	26
Bowl, Hand Painted, Gold Ground, Green & Blue Leaves, Marked Underside, 1¾ x 6½ In.	10
Box, Lid, Sherman Hotel Promo, Hiram Walker, Ceramic, 1958, 9 x 8 In.	25
Container, Lid, Egg Shape, Stripes, Footed, Marked, 8 x 4 In.	11
Dish, Prancing Horse Steed, Bowl, Ivory Ground, Hand Painted, Ceramic, c.1960	15
Dish, Teal, White Horse, Multicolor Accents, Signed, 10 x 9 In.	206
Plate, Serving, Fish Shape, Hand Painted, Ceramic, Indented Sections, 11 x 10¾ In.	65
Trinket Box, Lid, Mermaid, Seahorse, 1950s, 1½ x 5 x 3¾ In.	26
Vase, Gold, Black Interior, Gold Glaze, Stylized Designs, c.1950, 2¾ In.	30

SATIN GLASS is a late-nineteenth-century art glass. It has a dull finish that is caused by hydrofluoric acid vapor treatment. Satin glass was made in many colors and sometimes has applied decorations. Satin glass is also listed by factory name, such as Webb, or in the Mother-of-Pearl category in this book.

Bride's Bowl, Ruffled Edge, Pink, Green, Gilt Scroll, White Flowers, 5½ x 10½ In.	1320
Ewer, Diamond-Quilted, Mother-Of-Pearl, Frosted Handle, Blue, 7½ In.	72
Ewer, Diamond-Quilted, Mother-Of-Pearl, Frosted Thorn Handle, Blue, 13 In.	96
Ewer, Herringbone, Frosted Handle, Rainbow, 5¼ In.	540
Ewer, Pedestal, Apricot, Pansies, Frosted Handle, 13 In.	72
Jar, Diamond-Quilted, Pink, Cased, Dome Lid, Pomegranate Finial, c.1920, 12 In.	510
Lamp, Globular Shape Shade, Ruffled Rim, Pedestal Foot, c.1900, 9 x 4¾ x 2¾ In.	568
Pitcher, Diamond-Quilted, Pink, Handle & Fluted Top, 9 In.	45
Pitcher, Velvet, Pink, Orange, Frosted Ribbed Handle, Victorian, 8 In.	108
Rose Bowl, Moire Mother-Of-Pearl, Frosted Foot, Tricorner Top, Blue, 3 In.	150
Spooner, Herringbone Mother-Of-Pearl, Square, Enamel Flowers, Blue, 5¼ In.	180
Vase, Apricot, Diamond-Quilted, Mother-Of-Pearl, 5¾ In.	60
Vase, Apricot, Enamel Bird, Flowers & Pinecones, Frosted Handle, 12¾ In.	72
Vase, Blossoms, Red Jewel Highlights, Frosted Thorn Handles, Blue, 12 In.	60
Vase, Leaves, Nuts, Branches, Blue Highlights, 10½ In.	60
Vase, Pink, Diamond-Quilted, Mother-Of-Pearl, 7½ In.	72

Satsuma, Vase, Trumpet Mouth, Figural Landscapes, Signed, Nihon Kyoto Yasuda Jo, 24 In.
$246

Skinner, Inc.

Scale, Balance, 2 Brass Bowls, Wrought Iron Base, 13½ x 27 x 10½ In.
$248

Aspire Auctions

Scale, Computing, Standard Computing Scale Co., Barrel Top, Steel, c.1917, 32 x 17 x 21 In.
$615

Morphy Auctions

S

Scale, Postal, Brass, Oak Base,
3 Weights, England, 9½ x 5½ x 4 In.
$60

Cowan's Auctions

Scale, Weighing, Lollipop, O.D.
Jennings, 1 Cent, White Porcelain,
Mirrored, Charts, 69 x 13 x 24 In.
$600

Morphy Auctions

Scale, Weighing, Penny, 1 Cent,
Porcelain Body, Mint Green, Rock-Ola
Mfg., Co., 1930, 42 x 10 x 19 In.
$900

Morphy Auctions

SATSUMA is a Japanese pottery with a distinctive creamy beige crackled glaze. Most of the pieces were decorated with blue, red, green, orange, or gold. Almost all Satsuma found today was made after 1860, especially during the Meiji Period, 1868–1912. During World War I, Americans could not buy undecorated European porcelains. Women who liked to make hand-painted porcelains at home began to decorate white undecorated Satsuma. These pieces are known today as "American Satsuma."

Bowl, Awabi Shell, Hand Painted, Lohans, Seashells, Gilt, 1800s, 12 x 9 x 3 In.	281
Bowl, Pink & Gilt Flowers, Blue Ground, Pheasant & Flowers Inside, 5 Lobes, 3 x 8 In.	344
Bowl, Thousand Faces, Dragon, Pagoda, Gilt Waves & Clouds, Fluted, 4 x 10 In.	840
Box, Lotus Leaves & Flowers, Buddha Design Inside, Round, Jizan, 4 In.	1140
Censer, Lid, Arhats, Gilt, 2 Foo Dogs, Signed, Early 1800s, 15¾ x 13 In.	236
Censer, Oval, Allover Decoration, Asian Man Finial, 3 Figural Legs, 1800s, 14 x 8 In.	375
Jardiniere, Cartouches, Figures, Flowers, Fans, 4 Lobes, Brocade Rim, 9 x 12 In.	192
Sugar & Creamer, Gilt, Moriage, Geisha, Garden Setting, Pagoda, c.1905	125
Tea Caddy, Lid, Signed, Kozan, c.1880, 6 x 4 In. ....*illus*	1107
Vase, 6-Sided, Figures, Arched Panels, Flared Mouth, Imperial Mark, c.1860, 30 In.	2000
Vase, Classical Shape, Embossed Dragon, Men, Gilt, c.1925, 12 In.	360
Vase, Figures In Panels, Brocade Ground, Elongated Pear Shape, c.1900, 14¼ In.	420
Vase, Hardwood Stand, Ruffled Lip, Butterfly Loop Handles, 37½ x 16 In.	625
Vase, Men In Landscape, Flowers, Gilt Highlights, c.1890, 24 In.	406
Vase, Men, Robes, Seated, Arches, Handles, Raised Enamel, Gilt, 6¼ In.	147
Vase, Peony Design, Gold, Red, Blue, Marked, Shimazu Crests, Signed, c.1860, 12 In. ....*illus*	1375
Vase, Samurai In Cartouches, Chrysanthemum & Peacock Ground, Ruffled Rim, 23 In.	570
Vase, Trumpet Mouth, Figural Landscapes, Signed, Nihon Kyoto Yasuda Jo, 24 In. ....*illus*	246
Vase, White Wisteria, Green Leaves, Cream Ground, Inverted Pear Shape, c.1870, 10 In.	750

SATURDAY EVENING GIRLS, *see Paul Revere Pottery category.*

SCALES have been made to weigh everything from babies to gold. Collectors search for all types. Most popular are small gold dust scales, special grocery scales, and tall figural scales for people to use to check their weight.

Balance, 2 Brass Bowls, Wrought Iron Base, 13½ x 27 x 10½ In. ....*illus*	248
Balance, Brass, Milk Glass Tray, Paw Feet, 40 x 30 In.	354
Balance, Butter, Pine, Pegged Handle, 1800s, 27 x 9 In.	480
Balance, Henry Troemner, Brass, 2 Trays, 25½ In.	100
Balance, Otto Fennel Sohne Co., Diamond, Wood Cabinet, Glass, 11½ x 15½ x 20 In.	780
Balance, Painted, Cast Iron, Brass Pans, Silvered, 2 Counterweights, 27 In.	135
Balance, The Computing Scale Co., Ohio, Circular Glass, Platform, 20 x 31 In.	288
Computing, Standard Computing Scale Co., Barrel Top, Steel, c.1917, 32 x 17 x 21 In. ....*illus*	615
Drugstore, Walnut Case, Marble Top, 2 Brass Pans, 1800s	75
Muennighaus, Brass, Black Painted Cast Iron, Wood Base, 11 x 36 x 30 In.	688
Postal, Brass, Oak Base, 3 Weights, England, 9½ x 5½ x 4 In. ....*illus*	60
Weighing, Coin, Chrome Top, 300 Lb. Capacity, Red Body, Menkhaus	127
Weighing, Dayton, Style No. 167, Intl. Business Machine Co., 5 Lb., 5½ x 17 x 15¾ In.	1200
Weighing, Hobart, Market, Copper, Hanging Round Basket, 30 Lb., 15 In.	150
Weighing, Howe Scale Co., Railway Express, Decal, c.1900, 11½ x 20 x 10 In.	250
Weighing, John Chatillon & Sons, Brass, Butcher, Fitted Case, 16 x 13 In.	159
Weighing, Lollipop, O.D. Jennings, 1 Cent, White Porcelain, Mirrored, Charts, 69 x 13 x 24 In...*illus*	600
Weighing, National, Automatic, Lollipop, 1 Cent, Porcelain, Chas. B. Trickey Co., 70 x 16 x 29 In...	6600
Weighing, Penny, 1 Cent, Porcelain Body, Mint Green, Rock-Ola Mfg., Co., 1930, 42 x 10 x 19 In. *illus*	900
Weighing, Salter, Ornate, Cast Iron, Gold Paint, Griffin, c.1880, 5 x 7 x 11¾ In.	154
Weighing, Watling, Freestanding, Octagonal Glass, 1 Cent Tom Thumb Junior, 24 x 17 x 48 In..	277
Weighing, Wrigley's Spearmint Pepsin Gum, Embossed Brass, 7¾ x 10 In.......................*illus*	224

---

scheier **SCHEIER POTTERY** was made by Edwin Scheier (1910–2008) and his wife, Mary (1908–2007). They met while they both worked for the WPA, and married in 1937. In 1939, they established their studio, Hillcrock Pottery, in Glade Spring, Virginia. Mary made the pottery and Edwin decorated it. From 1940 to 1968, Edwin taught at the University of

S

New Hampshire and Mary was artist-in-residence. They moved to Oaxaca, Mexico, in 1968 to study the arts and crafts of the Zapotec Indians. When the Scheiers moved to Green Valley, Arizona, in 1978, Ed returned to pottery, making some of his biggest and best-known pieces.

Bowl, Brown, Gun Metal, Gloss, Mid-Century Modern, Edwin & Mary Scheier, 5 ½ In.	78
Bowl, Figures, Glossy Brown, Tan Glaze, Marked, 5 ¾ x 8 In.	400
Bowl, Human Figure, Fish Sgraffito, Blue Glaze, Marked, 5 ½ x 6 In.	554
Charger, Figures In Canoe, Black & White, Glazed, Incised, 1950s, 19 In.	2375
Dish, Rooster, Clay, Shallow Bowl, Hand Painted, Black & Dark Blue, 6 In.	70
Vase, Avocado Shape, Ovular, Footed, Edwin & Mary Scheier, 15 ½ x 10 ½ In.	420
Vase, Faces, Blue Glaze, Pedestal Base, Edwin & Mary Scheier, c.1950, 12 x 11 ¾ In. .....*illus*	1500

SCHNEIDER GLASSWORKS was founded in 1917 at Epinay-sur-Seine, France, by Charles and Ernest Schneider. Art glass was made between 1918 and 1933. The company went bankrupt in 1939. Charles Schneider and his sons opened a new glassworks in 1949. Art glass was made until 1981, when the company closed. See also the Le Verre Francais category.

Bowl, Tan, Honeycomb, Glass, France, 9 x 10 In.	409
Compote, Gold Leaf Flecks, Footed, Signed, 10 ½ In.	375
Coupe, Flared Bowl, Mottled Pink To Orange Shading, Violet Foot & Stem, Signed, 7 In.	352
Vase, Bijoux, Black Stylized Leaves, Flame Work Threading, Signed, 2 ½ x 4 In.	870
Vase, Round, Textured Body, Flaring Rim, Signed, In Block Letters, 7 ½ In.	188

SCIENTIFIC INSTRUMENTS of all kinds are included in this category. Other categories such as Barometer, Binoculars, Dental, Medical, Nautical, and Thermometer may also price scientific apparatus.

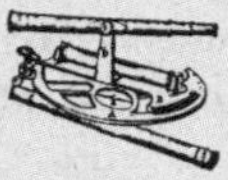

Alidade, Brass, Bubble Level & Compass, Scope, Keuffel & Esser, 8 x 18 x 3 In. .....*illus*	242
Barograph, Short & Mason, Weather Testing, Oak Case, 1915, 15 x 9 In.	196
Galvanometer, Chicago Laboratory Supply & Scale Co., Brass, Mahogany Base, 11 x 7 In.	102
Graphometer, Lenoir, Brass, Silvered Dial, Arc Signed, Paris, 16 In.	360
Kaleidoscope, C.G. Bush & Co., Paper & Brass Case, Walnut Stand, 1875, 15 x 11 x 7 In.	224
Magnifying Glass, Whiting, Silver, Scrollwork, Monogram, c.1890, 8 ¾ In.	113
Microscope, Bausch & Lomb, Horseshoe Base, Iron, Brass Tube, 12 x 4 x 6 ½ In. .....*illus*	113
Microscope, Binocular, Black, White, Carl Zeiss, 15 x 9 x 6 In.	205
Microscope, Brass, Steel, Glass, C. Collins	5168
Microscope, Ernst Leitz Wetzlar, Trinocular, Leica MD Camera, Germany, 16 x 13 x 9 In.	124
Microscope, Queen & Co., Philadelphia, Brass, Late 1800s, Fitted Case, 11 In. .....*illus*	188
Microscope, R&J Beck, Brass, Inscribed London Hospital, Marie Celeste, c.1900, 12 x 6 In.	516
Microscope, Spencer, Boom, 15 Power Lens, Cycloptic Stereo, 13 x 20 x 10 In.	166
Model, Planetarium, Laings Planetarium Co., Cherrywood Stand, 1891, 13 x 21 In.	1770
Orrery, George Philip & Son, England, Earth, Moon, Candle Cup, Reflector, c.1890, 17 In. .*illus*	5428
Orrery, Painted Wood, Metal, Revolving, Sun, Planets, Moons, 3-Step Base, 22 ½ In.	188
Range Finder, A. Barr & Stroud, Brass, Mahogany Case, c.1890, 10 x 46 x 7 In.	396
Spyglass, Shagreen, 4 Draw, Vellum Wrapped, Brass Eyepiece, Sliding Lid, 1900s, 12 In.	160
Spyglass, Walnut, Brass, Decagonal, Focus Threaded Lens, c.1800, 46 In.	1920
Steam Engine, W.M. Welch Scientific Co., Silver Decal, Early 1900s, 6 x 9 x 5 In.	424
Steam Gauge, Ashcroft Mfg. Co., Brass, Silvered Dial, Open Center, 8 x 10 ¾ In.	242
Telescope, Bardou & Son, Brass, Mahogany Tripod, c.1875, 40 In.	960
Telescope, Brass, Adjustable Stand, Mahogany, Fitted Case, Tube, 1900s, 44 x 64 x 74 In.	1750
Telescope, Brass, Mounted, Walnut, Tripod, Tube, Unmarked, England, 1900s, 56 In.	437
Telescope, Decagonal, Mahogany & Brass, Singe Draw Tube, 5 Lenses, 50 In.	3000
Telescope, J. Ramsden, Brass, Tabletop, Cylindrical, 3 Cabriole Legs, London, 38 In.	2040
Telescope, Mahogany, Leather, Single Draw, c.1800, 20 In.	344
Telescope, Tele Vue, Adjustable, Brass, Wood Stand, Renaissance, 1985, 44 ½ x 35 In. .....*illus*	500
Theodolite, A.S. Aloc Co., Brass, Glass Lens, 1800s, 12 ½ x 7 x 9 ½ In.	158
Theodolite, Stanley, Brass, Nickel, Glass, 1900s	5426
Transit, Surveyor's, C.L. Berger & Sons Brass, Magnifiers, Case & Tripod .....*illus*	254
Transit, Surveyor's, Dietzen Surveyor, Wood Case, Lid, Leather Strap, c.1920, 6 x 20 x 10 In.	124
Transit, Surveyor's, Eugene Dietzgen Co., Brass, Box, Marked, N.Y., c.1900, 6 x 13 x 7 In.	215
Transit, Surveyor's, James Foster Jr., Brass, Wood Case, Paper Labels, Ohio, c.1875, 7 x 19 x 3 In.	311

Scale, Weighing, Wrigley's Spearmint Pepsin Gum, Embossed Brass, 7 ¾ x 10 In.

$224

AntiqueAdvertising.com

Scheier, Vase, Faces, Blue Glaze, Pedestal Base, Edwin & Mary Scheier, c.1950, 12 x 11 ¾ In.

$1,500

Rago Arts and Auction Center

Top Ten Pottery & Porcelain Categories
Hundreds of thousands of users visit our website, Kovels.com, each month. There are over 300 pottery and porcelain categories on the site. The most popular among our visitors are:

1. McCoy
2. Bavaria
3. Wedgwood
4. Nippon
5. Haeger
6. Delft
7. Capo-di-Monte
8. Hull
9. Lefton
10. Hall

S

Scientific Instrument, Alidade, Brass, Bubble Level & Compass, Scope, Keuffel & Esser, 8 x 18 x 3 In.
$242

Fontaine's Auction Gallery

Scientific Instrument, Microscope, Bausch & Lomb, Horseshoe Base, Iron, Brass Tube, 12 x 4 x 6½ In.
$113

Soulis Auctions

Scientific Instrument, Microscope, Queen & Co., Philadelphia, Brass, Late 1800s, Fitted Case, 11 In.
$188

Leslie Hindman Auctioneers

Transit, Surveyor's, Keuffel & Esser, Brass, Case, 14½ x 10½ x 7½ In.		367
Transit, Surveyor's, Prandoni Bros., Cast Iron, Case & Tripod, Magnifiers, New Jersey		181
Vacuum Pump, Brass, Glass Bell Jar, 19th Century, 13 In.	*illus*	163

SCRIMSHAW is bone or ivory or whale's teeth carved by sailors and others for entertainment during the sailing-ship days. Some scrimshaw was carved as early as 1800. There are modern scrimshanders making pieces today on bone, ivory, or plastic. Other pieces may be found in the Ivory and Nautical categories. Collectors should be aware of the recent laws limiting the buying and selling of scrimshaw and elephant ivory.

Basket, Whalebone Panels, Wooden Base, Brass Tacks, c.1850, 1½ x 3½ In.	*illus*	1140
Belaying Pin, Turned, Incised Lines At Top & End, Whalebone, 1800s, 15¾ In.		1080
Bodkin, Fish Shape, Articulated Edge & Tail, Baleen Eyes, Tapered Shaft, c.1875, 5 In.		960
Bodkin, Whalebone, 4 Pillars, Carved Ogee Finial, 5 In.		216
Bone, Carved, Shark, Duck, Inuit, 9 In.		316
Busk, Baleen, 3 Ships, American Flag, Lobed End, Stylized Flowers, 1860, 12¾ In.		1140
Busk, Baleen, Plants, Fort, Hearts, Ships, Lighthouse, British Ensign, Leaf Border, c.1850, 15 In.		300
Busk, Carved, Man Holding Sword, Swagged Cartouche, Flowering Plants, c.1850, 12¾ In.		240
Busk, Patriotic, Go Tell The World America Is Free, Sailing Ship, c.1850, 14 In.		960
Busk, Star, Vase Of Flowers, Woman Holding Rose, Tree, c.1850, 15 In.		480
Busk, Whalebone, English Crest, 3-Masted Ship, Anchor, Thistle Border, 15 In.		2760
Busk, Whalebone, Geometric Designs, Basket Of Flowers, Red, Green, Blue, 12 In.		1200
Busk, Whalebone, Star, Sailing Vessel, House, Palm Tree, Red & Sepia, c.1825, 13 In.		1920
Busk, Whalebone, Whaling Scene, Poem, c.1840, 15¼ In.		15600
Candlestick, Whalebone, Tulip Shape Socle, Walnut, Ivory, Mother-Of-Pearl Inlay, c.1850, 8 In.		1560
Candlestick, Whalebone, Turned Feet, c.1850, 7¾ In., Pair		2280
Cane, Whalebone, Clenched Fist Handle, Cuffed Sleeve, Baleen Band Handle, c.1850, 36 In.		1440
Cane, Whalebone, Octagonal Handle, Island Wood Collar, Mid 19th Century, 35 In.		480
Cane, Whalebone, Turned & Carved, Ring & Twist Carvings, 36 In.		1080
Cigar Cutter, Boar Tusk, Silver Plate, 6½ In.		138
Dipper, Walnut Handle, Coconut Shell Bowl, Fist Holding Ring, c.1860, 14¾ In.		1800
Fid, Whalebone, Flattened Knob Terminal, Pierced Hole, Top Of Shaft, c.1800s, 9 In.		300
Figurine, Nude Women, Carved Bone, Toothpick, Folding, 1800s, 2¼ In.		185
Flask, Tapers, Inscribed MR, Wood Plug, 1800s, 5½ In.		123
Ginger Jar, Whalebone, Eagle, Swords, Bugle, Canons, Carved Lid, 2½ In.		85
Horn, Steer, Men & Women, Floral Vines, Late 1800s, 14 x 16 In.		938
Letter Opener, Reindeer Bone, Engraved Reindeer, Norway, 1900s, 7 In.		156
Magnifying Glass, Cow Bone Carved Handle, High Gloss, 6 x 2 In.		125
Pie Crimper, Double Handle, Pierced Hearts, Diamonds, Fluted Wheel, c.1850, 6 In.		2640
Pie Crimper, Ebony Handle, Whale Ivory Banding, Fluted Ebony Wheel, 7½ In.	*illus*	450
Pie Crimper, Oval Handle, Inlaid Mother-Of-Pearl Diamond, Clover, 5-Wheel, 7½ In.		2400
Pie Crimper, Snake Shape Handle, Geometric Inlay, Fluted, 6½ In.		20400
Pincushion Clamp, Whalebone, Geometric Design, c.1850, 3 x 2¾ In.		480
Pipe, Lady's Leg Shape, High Heeled Boot, Sawtooth Border, Garter, c.1850, 2¾ In.		812
Plaque, Panbone, Fighting Ships, British, French Flags, Red, Blue, Mahogany Frame, 10 x 18 In.		3900
Rolling Pin, Acorn Handle, Island Wood, Whalebone Banding, c.1850, 13¾ In.		3000
Sea Elephant Tooth, Confederate Steamer, Waves, 2 Stacks, Smoke, 5½ In.		2125
Seam Rubber, Walnut, Turk's Head Knot, Geometric & Pique Carvings, c.1850, 4½ In.		540
Seam Rubber, Whalebone, Octagonal Handle, Mushroom Finial, c.1850, 4¾ In.	*illus*	480
Seam Rubber, Whalebone, Sawtooth Design On Handle, 5 In.		594
Seam Rubber, Whalebone, Tapered Cut Corner Handle, Patina, c.1850, 5½ In.		360
Sewing Knife, Lady's Leg, Whalebone, 19th Century, 4¼ In.		406
Ship, Portrait Of Sea Captain, Charles Lee, Teak Turntable Base, 1900s, 8 x 4 In.		644
Snatch Block, Rope Cord, Manila Line, c.1850, 5 x 2¼ In.		840
Spoon, Pineapple Shape Terminal, Medial Pineapple Carving, Metal Pins, 1800s, 10 In.		330
Sword Sharpener, Napoleonic Prisoner-Of-War, Hat, Jacket, Hand Crank, c.1800, 5¾ In.		6600
Tea Caddy, 2-Story, Bone Windows, Door, Silver Paint Interior, c.1850, 7 x 5½ x 7 In.	*illus*	1650
Walrus Tusk, Flowers, Wreath, Woman, Gown, c.1900, 12 In.		570
Walrus Tusk, Woman, Children & Stag, 1800s, 18 x 2½ In.		354
Watch Hutch, Gallery, Diamonds, Poles, Banner, String Inlay, Mahogany Cabinet, 9 x 5 In.		1920

Scientific Instrument, Orrery, George Philip & Son, England, Earth, Moon, Candle Cup, Reflector, c.1890, 17 In.
$5,428

Leland Little Auctions

Scientific Instrument, Telescope, Tele Vue, Adjustable, Brass, Wood Stand, Renaissance, 1985, 44 ½ x 35 In.
$500

Rago Arts and Auction Center

Scientific Instrument, Transit, Surveyor's, C.L. Berger & Sons Brass, Magnifiers, Case & Tripod
$254

Hartzell's Auction Gallery, Inc.

Scientific Instrument, Vacuum Pump, Brass, Glass Bell Jar, 19th Century, 13 In.
$163

Leslie Hindman Auctioneers

Scrimshaw, Basket, Whalebone Panels, Wooden Base, Brass Tacks, c.1850, 1 ½ x 3 ½ In.
$1,140

Eldred's

Scrimshaw, Pie Crimper, Ebony Handle, Whale Ivory Banding, Fluted Ebony Wheel, 7 ½ In.
$450

Eldred's

Scrimshaw, Seam Rubber, Whalebone, Octagonal Handle, Mushroom Finial, c.1850, 4¾ In.

$480

Scrimshaw, Whale's Tooth, 3-Masted Ship, Pennant Shape, Carved Gun Ports, c.1850, 6¼ In.

$3,000

Eldred's

Eldred's

Scrimshaw, Tea Caddy, 2-Story, Bone Windows, Door, Silver Paint Interior, c.1850, 7 x 5½ x 7 In.

$1,650

Sevres, Bowl, Gilt Bronze Mount, Figural & Floral Cartouches, 2 Handles, c.1895, 15 x 12 In.

$523

Forsythes' Auctions

Skinner, Inc.

Scrimshaw, Whalebone, Parasol Handle, Carved, Clenched Fist, 10 Bands, c.1850, 6 In.

$120

Sevres, Casket, Pyramid, Landscape Panels, Bronze Figural, 14 x 15½ x 10½ In.

$1,452

Eldred's

Fontaine's Auction Gallery

Whalebone, Carved, Block, Patina & Verdigris, 1800s, 3¾ x ⅞ In.	360
Whalebone, Parasol Handle, Carved, Clenched Fist, 10 Bands, c.1850, 6 In. ....*illus*	120
Whale's Tooth, 3-Masted Ship, Pennant Shape, Carved Gun Ports, c.1850, 6¼ In. ....*illus*	3000
Whale's Tooth, American Eagle, 20 Stars Flag, c.1818, 6 In.	2242
Whale's Tooth, Capitol Building, West Facade, George Washington, Mid 1800s, 7 In.	4209
Whale's Tooth, Dancing Couple, Stylized Arbor, Geometric, 1800s, 6½ In.	1476
Whale's Tooth, Eagle Head, Union Must Survive For Good Of All, Percy Hale, 1900s, 7 In........	2340
Whale's Tooth, Engraved, Brig, Sails, Metal Collar At Base, c.1850, 6¼ In.	1800
Whale's Tooth, House, Sailor, Bottle & Glass, Ship & Seascape Background, Mass., 1800s, 5 In.	1169
Whale's Tooth, Neptune With Sailing Ship, Captain Horn, 1800s, 7½ x 3 In.	826
Whale's Tooth, Portrait, Woman, Hair Bow, Lace Collar, 5½ In.	1159
Whale's Tooth, Sailing Ships, Island, Eagle, Flag, 1800s, 5½ In.	3304
Whale's Tooth, Sailing Ships, Island, Eagle, Flag, Inscribed, Shore Flensing Near Samoa, 5½ In. ...	3567
Whale's Tooth, Sailor, Harpoon, Oval Cartouche, Rope Border, Waves, Bird, c.1900, 6 In.	562
Whale's Tooth, Sailor, Tree, Anchor, 4½ In..	1220
Whale's Tooth, Ship Of The Line, Frigate, Swirling Birds, 3-Story Building, c.1850, 7 In.	3840
Whale's Tooth, Whale, Waves, Ivy, Geometric Pattern, 9½ x 3 In.	7380
Whale's Tooth, Whistle, Diamond & Pique Design, Brass Mouthpiece, c.1825, 3½ In.	780
Whale's Tooth, Wreath Of Palm Fronds, Black Ink, Monogram, NAS, 3¾ In...........................	96

SEBASTIAN MINIATURES were first made by Prescott W. Baston in 1938 in Arlington, Massachusetts. Baston moved his studio to Marblehead, Massachusetts, in 1946 and to Hudson, Massachusetts, in 1976. Figurines at Hudson were made in cooperation with Lance Corporation until 1997, when Lance closed. Baston's son, Prescott W. Baston Jr., began designing figurines in the 1980s. Since 1998 Sebastian Miniatures have been made by Wayland Studio in Wayland, Massachusetts. More than 400 different designs have been made, and collectors search for the out-of-production models. The mark may say *Copr. P.W. Baston U.S.A.*, or *P.W. Baston U.S.A.*, or *Prescott W. Baston*. Sometimes a paper label was used.

Ben Franklin, Figurine, Pen Stand, P.W. Baston, 3¼ x 2⅞ In.....................................	6
Nativity Scene, Manger, Hand Cast & Hand Painted, Round Wooden Base, Multicolor............	37
Uncle Mistletoe, Marshall Fields, Blue Eyes, Black Hat, Red Suit, Marblehead, 1949................	46

SEG, *see Paul Revere Pottery category.*

SEVRES porcelain has been made in Sevres, France, since 1769. Many copies of the famous ware have been made. The name originally referred to the works of the Royal Porcelain factory. The name now includes any of the wares made in the town of Sevres, France. The entwined lines with a center letter used as the mark is one of the most forged marks in antiques. Be very careful to identify Sevres by quality, not just by mark.

Bowl, Gilt Bronze Mount, Figural & Floral Cartouches, 2 Handles, c.1895, 15 x 12 In. ....*illus*	523
Cachepot, Blue Background, Birds & Fruits Portrait, 2 Handles, c.1950, 4 x 5 In.	148
Cachepot, Gold Gilt, Blue Background, c.1750s, 4¼ In.	531
Casket, Pyramid, Landscape Panels, Bronze Figural, 14 x 15½ x 10½ In. ....*illus*	1452
Dish, Bronze Mount, Blue Ground Border, Cherub Center, Late 1800s, 16¾ x 14 In................	246
Dresser Box, Cobalt Blue Background, Gilt, 2 Women Seated, Signed, A. Vigier, 6 x 14 x 9 In. ..	847
Figurine, Cupid Seated, Empire Style Throne, Circular Base, c.1810, 6½ In.....................*illus*	984
Figurine, Deer, Laying Down, Head Up, Green, Oval Base, Black, Paul Milet, 10 x 18 In.	108
Figurine, Woman, Hinged Dress, Erotica, 7½ x 4 x 3 In.	219
Plate, Hand Painted, Cherubs, Cobalt Blue Border, Gold Flashing, 9½ In...........................	81
Plate, Madame Dubarry, Gilt Highlights, Signed Morin, Late 1800s, 9½ In.........................	212
Plate, Portrait, Woman, Burgundy Dress, Gilt Rim, Signed, Chateau De Fontainebleau, 9 In. ..	230
Plate, Portrait, Woman, Diamond Necklace, Signed, JE Toscanne, 1864, 9½ In.	150
Urn, Bronze, Woman, Cupid, Flowers, Putti Handles, Pineapple Finial, 17 In.	553
Urn, Gilt, Bronze Mounts, Cherubs, Temple Of Castor, Pollux, 48 In...............................	4130
Urn, Lid, Lovers, Garden, Bronze Mounts, Enamel, Cobalt Blue, Gilt, Signed, Marant, 29 In. .*illus*	605
Vase, Bronze, Mounts, Green Border, Gilt Enamel, Flowers, 15¾ In..................*illus*	787
Vase, Dancing Couple, Painted, Bronze Mounts, 23 In..	113
Vase, Flowers, Multicolor, Gilt Bronze Mounts, Late 1800s, 21½ In..................*illus*	188

Sevres, Figurine, Cupid Seated, Empire Style Throne, Circular Base, c.1810, 6½ In.
$984

Skinner, Inc.

Sevres, Urn, Lid, Lovers, Garden, Bronze Mounts, Enamel, Cobalt Blue, Gilt, Signed, Marant, 29 In.
$605

Fontaine's Auction Gallery

Sevres, Vase, Bronze, Mounts, Green Border, Gilt Enamel, Flowers, 15¾ In.
$787

Fontaine's Auction Gallery

S

Sevres, Vase, Flowers, Multicolor, Gilt Bronze Mounts, Late 1800s, 21 ½ In. $188

Leslie Hindman Auctioneers

Sevres, Vase, Pate-Sur-Pate, Oval, White Slip, Multicolor Enamel, Marked, 1885, 8 In. $688

Leslie Hindman Auctioneers

Sevres, Vase, Venus, Cupid, Amori, Handles, Bronze Base, Charles Fuchs, Italy, c.1875, 35 In. $2,124

Aspire Auctions

Vase, Pate-Sur-Pate, Oval, White Slip, Multicolor Enamel, Marked, 1885, 8 In. ....*illus*	688
Vase, Purple Flower, Green Leaves, Yellow Gold Background, Stamped, 5 In.	270
Vase, Venus, Cupid, Amori, Handles, Bronze Base, Charles Fuchs, Italy, c.1875, 35 In. ......*illus*	2124
Vase, Woman, Garden, Cherubs, Birds, Rotating Base, Dark Red, 22 In.	1210

SEWER TILE figures were made by workers at the sewer tile and pipe factories in the Ohio area during the late nineteenth and early twentieth centuries. Figurines, small vases, and cemetery vases were favored. Often the finished vase was a piece of the original pipe with added decorations and markings. All types of sewer tile work are now considered folk art by collectors.

Figure, Cat, Lying Down, Molded Redware, Folk Art, Brown Glaze, 9 x 4 ½ x 5 In.	225
Figure, Dog, Spaniel, Seated, Stepped Plinth, 1800s, 9 x 8 ½ x 7 In.	88
Figure, Smokey The Bear, Ranger Hat, Shovel, Brown Glaze, Signed, Roy Blind, 3 ½ In.	350
Planter, Acanthus Leaf Border, Amber Brown Glaze, c.1850, 10 In.	195

SEWING equipment of all types is collected, from sewing birds that held the cloth to tape measures, needle books, and old wooden spools. Sewing machines are included here. Needlework pictures are listed in the Picture category.

Bird, Brass, Old Patina, Pincushion Mount, Clamp, c.1850, 15 In. ....*illus*	88
Box, Burl Walnut, Brass Mount Top, Escutcheon, Lining, Silk, Padded, 1900s, 5 ¾ x 12 In.	101
Box, Burl Walnut, Oval Shape, Handle, Quilted Interior, c.1850, 5 x 11 In.	180
Box, Burl, Coffin Shape, Diamond & Line Inlay, Ring Handles, Paw Feet, 7 ½ x 12 In.	450
Box, Burl, Walnut, Brass Mount, Silk Padded Lining, 1900s, 5 ¾ x 11 ⅞ In.	100
Box, Drawers & Fittings, Lacquered, Gold Gilt, Chinese, 14 x 10 x 7 In.	406
Box, Hinged Lid, Embossed Leather, Fans, Children, Geometric, Brass Trim, Silk Interior, 9 In. *illus*	120
Box, Hinged Lid, Marquetry, Inlaid Design, Mirror Panel, 30 ½ x 26 x 18 In.	250
Box, Mahogany Inlay, Mother-Of-Pearl, Hearts, 5 Stars & Diamonds, Late 1800s, 12 x 14 x 10 In.	212
Box, Mahogany, 2 Tiers, Inlay, Pincushion Top, Whalebone Finials, Drawer, c.1850, 7 x 6 In. *illus*	330
Box, Parquetry, Wood, Inscribed, Annie Eiger, 1886, 13 x 9 In.	113
Box, Red Leather, Floral Exterior, Brass Paw Feet, Drawer, Early 1800s, 6 x 10 x 7 In.	1161
Box, Rosewood & Mother-Of-Pearl Inlay, Fitted Interior, 1800s, 9 x 12 x 5 In.	345
Box, Rosewood, 4 Compartments, Lock, Key, Handles, Bun Feet, c.1870, 9 x 12 x 7 In.	176
Cabinet, Spool, Oak, 2 Drawers, Porcelain Drawer Pulls, 8 x 17 ¼ x 16 ½ In.	62
Cabinet, Spool, Oak, 6 Drawers, Overhanging Top, Brass Pulls, 17 x 24 x 16 In.	151
Cabinet, Spool, see also the Advertising category under Cabinet, Spool.	
Caddy, Mahogany, 3 Graduated Tiers, Whalebone Accents, 1800s, 9 x 8 In.	590
Kit, 18K Gold, Punch, Scissors, Needle Holder, Thimble, Box, Marked, Paris, 1819-38	840
Kit, Flower Lid, Egg Shape, Gilt Copper, Stars, 3 Tools, Scissors, Victorian, c.1850, 4 In.	142
Machine, New Home, Quartersawn Oak Cabinet, Hinged Top, 30 ½ In.	121
Machine, Singer, Featherweight, Black Case, Accessories...	489
Machine, Singer, Treadle, Oak Case, 6 Drawers, Pedal, 1800s ....*illus*	196
Measure, Fabric, Inlaid, Wood, Mother-Of-Pearl, 28 ½ In.	144
Necessaire, Box, Brass Inlay, Flowers, Mother-Of-Pearl, France, 6 ¼ x 4 ¼ x 2 ¾ In.	127
Necessaire, Fan Lid, Wood, Tortoiseshell, Talon Feet, Compartments, C. Sumner, 1815, 9 x 7 In. ..	863
Needle Case, Thread, Solid Silver, Sprung Hinge, George V, Birmingham, 1910, 2 ¾ In.	93
Needle Case, Whalebone, Tulip Shape, Circle Designs, Paper Band, 1800s, 3 ¼ In. ....*illus*	180
Pincushion Dolls are listed in their own category.	
Pincushion, Dog, Mohair, Glass Eyes, Brown, Steiff, Victorian, 5 x 5 x 5 In. ....*illus*	323
Scissors, Knife Edge, G-8, Dressmaker Shears, Chromed, Gingher, 8 In.	22
Scissors, Stork, Figural, Feathers & Wing, Gilded Steel, 2 x 6 ½ In.	38
Sign, Singer Sewing Machine, Porcelain, Germany, c.1920, 23 x 34 ¾ In. ....*illus*	236
Spool Cabinets are listed here or in the Advertising category under Cabinet, Spool.	
Spool Holder, Turned, Hardwood, Pincushion Top, Late 1800s, 12 In.	125
Tape Loom, Standing, Cross Base, England, 1700s, 35 In. ....*illus*	5228
Thimble, 14K Gold, Engraved, Monogram, Leather Case, Saml. Kirk & Son, Md., Size 9....*illus*	625
Yarn Winder, 4 Arms, Birch, Pine, Carved Figure, Sadie Smith, New Eng., c.1835, 41 In.	7200
Yarn Winder, Hand Crank, Bobbin, Sock Knitting, Cast Iron...	27

SHAKER items are characterized by simplicity, functionalism, and orderliness. There were many Shaker communities in America from the eighteenth century to the present day. The religious order made furniture, small wooden pieces, and packaged medicines, herbs, and jellies to sell to "outsiders." Other useful objects were made for use by members of the community. Shaker furniture is listed in this book in the Furniture category.

Basket, Cheese, Splint, Hexagonal, Woven, 23 x 11 In. 47

Basket, Gathering, Splint, Woven, Herb, Wood Handle, 28 x 18 x 7 In. 83

Basket, Herb Drying, Open Wrapped Handles & Rim, Red Dyed Band, 4 x 7¾ In. *illus* 236

Box, 3-Finger, Bentwood, Oval, Winter Landscape, 2½ x 4⅞ x 3¼ In. 248

Box, Bentwood, Margaret G. Van Dyke Mapleton, 2⅞ x 6 In. 125

Box, Oval, Massachusetts, 1800s, 1⅝ x 4 In. *illus* 406

Box, Pantry, 2-Finger, Oak, Cut Tacks, c.1850, 5 x 9½ In. 150

Box, Pantry, 2-Finger, Oval, Lid, 1 x 3⅜ x 2⅛ In. 248

Box, Pantry, 2-Finger, Red Surface Stain, Initials EBS, 1800s, 2½ x 8 In. *illus* 325

Box, Pantry, 3-Finger, Copper Tacks, 1800s, 3½ x 9½ In. 240

Box, Sewing, 3-Finger, Lid, Swing Bale Handle, 3¾ x 9⅜ x 6¾ In. 165

Bucket, Grain Paint & Vines, Wood, Metal Bands, Bail Handle, Late 1800s, 7¼ In. 480

Bucket, Green Paint, Wood, Wire Bail Handle, 2 Metal Bands, 1800s, 4¼ In. 283

Bucket, Salmon Paint, Handle, Late 1800s, 3⅜ In. *illus* 388

Bucket, Wood, Black Paint, Wire Bail Handle, 2 Metal Bands, White Interior, 1800s, 4½ In. 226

Candlebox, Pine, Rectangular, Engraved, 1800s, 2¾ x 13½ x 5 In. 200

Carrier, Mixed Woods, Sections, Arched Handle, Copper Tacks, 1800s, 6 x 12 x 7 In. 192

Peg Rail, Pine, 4 Pegs, 3 x 69 In. 185

Shovel, Wood, Peel, Split Rod Handle, 1800s, 51 In. 48

Sign, Shaker Store, Plain & Fancy Goods, Wood, Stenciled, 13 x 52 In. 3480

SHAVING MUGS were popular from 1860 to 1900. Many types were made, including occupational mugs featuring pictures of men's jobs. There were scuttle mugs, silver-plated mugs, glass-lined mugs, and others.

Cut Glass, Prism Pattern, Ray Cut Base, Sterling Silver Rim, Meriden, 3¼ In. 180

Fraternal, Order Sons Of St. George, Slaying The Dragon, No. 438, 3 x 3½ In. 40

Occupational, Barber, Shop Scene, Hand Painted, T&V, Limoges, France, 3⅝ x 4⅞ In. 349

Occupational, Blacksmith, White Horse, Tools, A. Kern, Gilt, Marked, 4 x 4¾ In. 544

Occupational, Butcher Shop, A.W. Stowell, Gilt, Signed, 4 x 5 In. 77

Occupational, Butcher, Chas. Muetzel, Ox, Gilt, Signed, France, 4 x 5 In. 115

Occupational, Butcher, Meat, F. Bottger, Magenta Wrap, Gold Trim, T&V, 3⅝ In. *illus* 117

Occupational, Furniture Mover, Horse, Wagon, Jos. Werner, Atlanta Estate, 4 In. 136

Occupational, Harness Maker, Bench, Wm. W. Bell, Gilt, 4 x 4½ In. 205

Occupational, Koken Barber Supply, W.H. Mendenhall Jr., White & Gold, Handle, Signature, 4 x 3½ In. 49

Occupational, Slaughterhouse, Geo. W. Dreibelbies, Gilt, Gothic Letters, 4 x 3½ In. 245

Occupational, Sodbuster, Farmer, H.F. Jungblut, Gold Letters, c.1900, 3½ x 4½ In. *illus* 192

Occupational, Tow Truck, C. Wiegand, Royal China, 3 In. 998

Scuttle, Roses, Pink & White Flowers, Foley James Kent Staffordshire, 4 x 6 In. *illus* 9

Shawnee USA

SHAWNEE POTTERY was started in Zanesville, Ohio, in 1937. The company made vases, novelty ware, flowerpots, planters, lamps, and cookie jars. Three dinnerware lines were made: Corn, Lobster Ware, and Valencia (a solid color line). White Corn pattern utility pieces were made in 1945. Corn King was made from 1946 to 1954; Corn Queen, with darker green leaves and lighter colored corn, from 1954 to 1961. Shawnee produced pottery for George Rumrill during the late 1930s. The company closed in 1961.

Cookie Jar, Puss 'N Boots, Figural, White Ground, Red Ribbon, Yellow Bird On Hat 22

Cookie Jar, Smiley Pig, Overalls, Clover, Blue Neckerchief, Beige, White Interior 62

Creamer, Puss 'N Boots, Cat, Cream, Red & Blue, Tail Handle 10

Planter, Burgundy, Fern, Square Base, Marked, 2 x 2¾ In. 19

Planter, Old Chinese Man, Seated, Umbrella, Basket, 1940s, 5 x 5 x 3 In. 10

Teapot, Tom The Piper's Son, Pig Head Spout, Tail Handle, Ivory, 8 x 8½ In. *illus* 15

Vase, Bud, Gray Overall, Footed, 2 Handles, Art Deco, 8 In. 10

Sewing, Bird, Brass, Old Patina, Pincushion Mount, Clamp, c.1850, 15 In.
$88

Forsythes' Auctions

Sewing, Box, Hinged Lid, Embossed Leather, Fans, Children, Geometric, Brass Trim, Silk Interior, 9 In.
$120

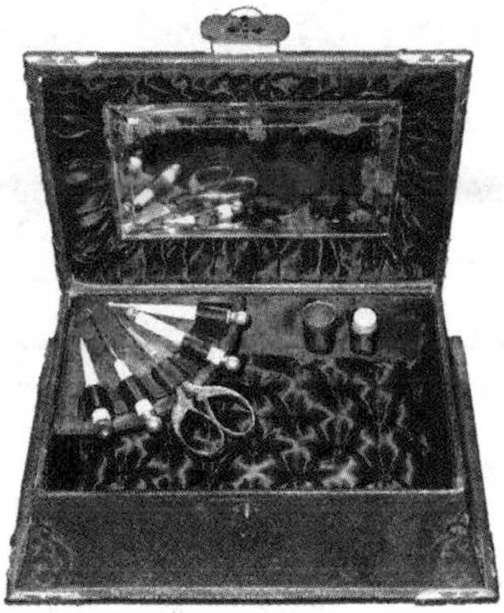

Richard Opfer Auctioneering, Inc.

Sewing, Box, Mahogany, 2 Tiers, Inlay, Pincushion Top, Whalebone Finials, Drawer, c.1850, 7 x 6 In.
$330

Eldred's

This is an edited listing of current prices. Visit **Kovels.com** to check thousands of prices from previous years and sign up for free information on trends, tips, reproductions, marks, and more.

Sewing, Machine, Singer, Treadle, Oak Case, 6 Drawers, Pedal, 1800s
$196

Keystone Auctions LLC

Sewing, Needle Case, Whalebone, Tulip Shape, Circle Designs, Paper Band, 1800s, 3 ¼ In.
$180

Eldred's

Sewing, Pincushion, Dog, Mohair, Glass Eyes, Brown, Steiff, Victorian, 5 x 5 x 5 In.
$323

snailracer500 on eBay

Sewing, Sign, Singer Sewing Machine, Porcelain, Germany, c.1920, 23 x 34 ¾ In.
$236

Hake's Auctions

Sewing, Tape Loom, Standing, Cross Base, England, 1700s, 35 In.
$5,228

Skinner, Inc.

Sewing, Thimble, 14K Gold, Engraved, Monogram, Leather Case, Saml. Kirk & Son, Md., Size 9
$625

Brunk Auctions

Shaker, Basket, Herb Drying, Open Wrapped Handles & Rim, Red Dyed Band, 4 x 7 ¾ In.
$236

Hess Auction Group

Shaker, Box, Oval, Massachusetts, 1800s, 1 ⅝ x 4 In.
$406

Pook & Pook

Shaker, Box, Pantry, 2-Finger, Red Surface Stain, Initials EBS, 1800s, 2 ½ x 8 In.
$325

Pook & Pook

Shaker, Bucket, Salmon Paint, Handle, Late 1800s, 3 ⅜ In.
$388

Pook & Pook

SHEARWATER POTTERY is a family business started in 1928 by Peter Anderson, with the help of his parents, Mr. and Mrs. G.W. Anderson Sr. The local Ocean Springs, Mississippi, clays were used to make the wares in the 1930s. The company was damaged by Hurricane Katrina in 2005 but was rebuilt and is still in business, now owned by Peter's four children.

Candy Dish, Alkaline Glaze, 1970s, 4 In.	45
Figurine, Chesty, Horse, Gray Metallic Glaze, Signed, 11 ¾ In.	121
Figurine, Lion, Aqua Blue, Shoal Glaze, Walter Anderson, 13 ¼ In.	976
Figurine, Lion, Crouching, Curly Mane, Coiled Tail, Blue, 13 ½ In.	1024
Figurine, Lion, Shoal Glaze, Walter Anderson, 13 ¼ In. ....*illus*	1000
Tumbler, Diving Birds, Cream, Gray, Tan, Swirls, 6 x 3 ½ In.	105
Vase, Figural, Fish, Signed, 4 ½ In.	265
Vase, Globular, Flambe Glaze, 7 ½ In.	750
Vase, Goose, Brown & Copper Red Glaze, Walter Anderson, c.1930, 5 ½ In.	1000
Vase, Goose, Brown, Copper, Walter Anderson, c.1930, 5 ½ In.	1024
Vase, Green, Handles, Peter Anderson, Impressed Mark, 5 x 5 ½ In.	82
Vase, Green, Reticulated, Stylized Flowers, James Mac Anderson, c.1940, 4 x 8 ½ In.	1300
Vase, High Shoulders, Metallic Green, Crystallized, 6 In.	192
Vase, Stylized Plants, Blue & Tan, Tapered, c.1935, 10 In.	4429

SHEET MUSIC from the past centuries is now collected. The favorites are examples with covers featuring artistic or historic pictures. Early sheet music covers were lithographed, but by the 1900s photographic reproductions were used. The early sheet music pages were larger than more recent sheets, and you must watch out for examples that were trimmed to fit in a twentieth-century piano bench and should be lower priced.

An Old Fashioned Love Song, Paul Williams, 1970	15
Dixie For The Union, Firth Pond & Co., 1861, 3 Pages	135
Georgia On My Mind, Tommy Dorsey, Southern Music Pub., 1930, 12 x 9 In.	18
Grand March, Major General McClellan, Piano Forte, Musical, 1861 ....*illus*	20
My Fair Lady, Vocal Score, Frederick Loewe, Alan Jay Lerner, 1956	12
Oklahoma, Richard Rodgers, Oscar Hammerstein, 1943, 9 x 12 In.	23
Sweet & Lovely, Van Johnson, Leo Feist Inc., c.1931	10
The Magic Song, Cinderella, Walt Disney Productions, 1948, 12 x 9 In.	14
Tie A Yellow Ribbon Round The Ole Oak Tree, Tony Orlando & Dawn, 1972	10
When Old Bill Bailey Plays The Ukulele, Chas. McCarron & Nat Vincent, 1905, 11 x 10 In.	53
Whistling Rufus, Kerry Mills, 1899, 14 x 11 In.	35
You Needed Me, Anne Murray, 1975	8

SHEFFIELD *items are listed in the Silver Plate and Silver-English categories.*

SHELLEY first appeared on English ceramics about 1912. The Foley China Works started in England in 1860. Joseph Ball Shelley joined the company in 1862 and became a partner in 1872. Percy Shelley joined the firm in 1881. The company went through a series of name changes and in 1910 the then Foley China Company became Shelley China. In 1929 it became Shelley Potteries. The company was acquired in 1966 by Allied English Potteries, then merged with the Doulton group in 1971. Shelley is no longer being made. A trio is the name for a cup, saucer, and cake plate set.

Bowl, Cereal, Coupe, Rose, Pansy, Forget-Me-Not, 6 ¼ In.	35
Cup & Saucer, Blue Daisy, Oleander Shape, Gold Trim, 2 Piece	162
Cup & Saucer, Dainty Blue, Flowers, Blue Trim, 2 ⅜ In.	49
Cup & Saucer, England's Charm, Black, Landscape Scene Inside, White Handle, Gold, 1945-66	95
Plate, Bread & Butter, Dainty Blue, 6 ½ In.	21
Sugar, Lid, Blue Rock, Dainty, Handles, 3 ½ In.	64

SHIRLEY TEMPLE, the famous movie star, was born in 1928. She made her first movie in 1932. She died in 2014. Thousands of items picturing Shirley have been and still are being made. Shirley Temple dolls were first made in 1934 by Ideal Toy Company. Millions of Shirley Temple cobalt blue glass dishes were made by Hazel Atlas

Shaving Mug, Occupational, Butcher, Meat, F. Bottger, Magenta Wrap, Gold Trim, T&V, 3 ⅝ In.
$117

Glass Works Auctions

Shaving Mug, Occupational, Sodbuster, Farmer, H.F. Jungblut, Gold Letters, c.1900, 3 ½ x 4 ½ In.
$192

Soulis Auctions

Shaving Mug, Scuttle, Roses, Pink & White Flowers, Foley James Kent Staffordshire, 4 x 6 In.
$9

annjudg5 on eBay

Shawnee, Teapot, Tom The Piper's Son, Pig Head Spout, Tail Handle, Ivory, 8 x 8 ½ In.
$15

peggyburk48zm on eBay

Shearwater, Figurine, Lion, Shoal Glaze, Walter Anderson, 13 ¼ In.
$1,000

Neal Auction Company

Music from the Movies

Watch out for reprints of old movie sheet music. Music before the 1960s was about 50 cents a copy. Now it is almost $3.00. The reprints are usually made to be sold in a store, not to fool the collector, so the price will be shown.

Sheet Music, Grand March, Major General McClellan, Piano Forte, Musical, 1861
$20

Oxf00 on eBay

Shirley Temple, Carriage, Doll's, Wood, Gray Paint, Leather Sunshade, Decal, Whitney, 1935, 32 In.
$173

Theriault's

Glass Company and U.S. Glass Company from 1934 to 1942. They were given away as premiums for Wheaties and Bisquick. A bowl, mug, and pitcher were made as a breakfast set. Some pieces were decorated with the picture of a very young Shirley, others used a picture of Shirley in her 1936 *Captain January* costume. Although collectors refer to a cobalt creamer, it is actually the 4 ½-inch-high milk pitcher from the breakfast set. Many of these items have been reproduced and are being sold today.

Bowl, Portrait, Cobalt Blue, Scalloped Edge, c.1930, 6 ½ In.	20
Cards, Playing, Double, Bridge, Different Pictures, United States Playing Cards Co., 1935	50
Carriage, Doll's, Wood, Gray Paint, Leather Sunshade, Decal, Whitney, 1935, 32 In. ....*illus*	173
Costume, Doll's, Sailor, Cream Cotton, Blue Striping, Red Scarf, Ideal, 1935 ....*illus*	173
Cowgirl Outfit, Black & Red, Fringe, Hat, Boots, Fits 12-In. Doll, 1950s	75
Doll, Blond, Composition, Mohair Ringlets, Open Mouth, Ideal, Tag, Button, 1938, 13 In.	236
Doll, Composition Socket Head, Sleep Eyes, Mohair, Poor Little Rich Girl Dress, Ideal, 27 In. ...*illus*	3335
Doll, Composition, Jointed, Sleep Eyes, Mohair Wig, Littlest Rebel Dress, Ideal, 20 In. ....*illus*	1955
Doll, Composition, Sleep Eyes, Open Mouth, Red Flowers, Ideal, 1930s, 19 In.	146
Doll, Look-Alike, Painted Features, Composition, 5-Piece Body, Dress, 1930s, 8 In. ....*illus*	46
Doll, Red Dress & Shoes, Ideal Novelty & Toy Co., Box, 15 In.	192
Doll, Red Polka Dot Dress, Blond, Ribbon, Ideal, 1930s, 16 In.	511
Doll, Vinyl, Jointed, Turquoise Corduroy Coat, Cap, Purse, Tag, Ideal, 1958, 12 In..........*illus*	460
Doll, White With Red Polka Dot Dress, Red Bow, Hard Plastic, Rubber, Ideal, 1972, 16 In.	50
Doll, Wig, Brown Sleep Eyes, Open Mouth, Composition, Jointed, Ideal, 1930s, 18 In.	283
Figure, Curtsying, Dress Forms Basket, Pressed Salt, 1930s, 4 ¼ In.	95
Movie, VHS, Littlest Rebel, Color Version	10
Paper Doll Set, 4 Dolls, Dresses, No. 280, Saalfield Publishing Co., 1934	48
Paper Doll, Plaid Frock, Blue, c.1935, 5 x 10 In.	45
Pin, Everybody Loves Me, Miss Charming, Doll, 1930s	21
Pin, Portrait, Sepia Tone, Great Personalities Limited, 1970s, 1 ¾ In.	12
Pitcher, Portrait, Signature, Cobalt Blue, Hazel Atlas, 1930s, 4 ½ In.	36
Pocket Mirror, Portrait, Celluloid, USA, 1930s, 3 x 2 In.	79
Stringholder, Painted Plaster, 1930s, 6 x 7 x 3 In.	250

SHRINER, *see Fraternal category.*

SHEFFIELD, *see Silver Plate; Silver-English categories.*

SILVER DEPOSIT glass was first made during the late nineteenth century. Solid sterling silver is applied to the glass by a chemical method so that a cutout design of silver metal appears against a clear or colored glass. It is sometimes called silver overlay, which is thin designs of sheet metal applied over glass or ceramics.

Vase, Green Glass, Lily Design, c.1900, 6 In. ....*illus*	108

SILVER FLATWARE includes many of the current and out-of-production silver and silver-plated flatware patterns made in the past 125 years. Other silver is listed under Silver-American, Silver-English, etc. Most silver flatware sets that are missing a few pieces can be completed through the help of a silver matching service. Three U.S. silver company marks are shown here.

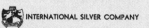

International Silver Co. 1928+	Reed & Barton c.1915+	Wallace Silversmiths, Inc. 1871–1956

SILVER FLATWARE PLATED

Heritage, Punch Ladle, Triple Silver Plate, Gorham, 12 ½ x 1 In.	21

SILVER FLATWARE STERLING

Acorn, Cake Knife, Hallmark, Georg Jensen, 10 ½ In.	113
Alhambra, Ice Tongs, Claw Feet, Whiting Co., 1880, 6 ½ In.	61
Baronial, Slotted Serving Spoon, Monogram Handle, Lion Head, Gorham, 1898, 9 In.	100
Chantilly, Punch Ladle, Handle, Stem, 2-Spout Bowl, Gorham, 13 ¾ In.	153

Shirley Temple, Costume, Doll's, Sailor, Cream Cotton, Blue Striping, Red Scarf, Ideal, 1935
$173

Shirley Temple, Doll, Composition, Jointed, Sleep Eyes, Mohair Wig, Littlest Rebel Dress, Ideal, 20 In.
$1,955

Shirley Temple, Doll, Vinyl, Jointed, Turquoise Corduroy Coat, Cap, Purse, Tag, Ideal, 1958, 12 In.
$460

Theriault's

Theriault's

Shirley Temple, Doll, Composition Socket Head, Sleep Eyes, Mohair, Poor Little Rich Girl Dress, Ideal, 27 In.
$3,335

Silver Deposit, Vase, Green Glass, Lily Design, c.1900, 6 In.
$108

Theriault's

Shirley Temple, Doll, Look-Alike, Painted Features, Composition, 5-Piece Body, Dress, 1930s, 8 In.
$46

Eldred's

Theriault's

Theriault's

S

TIP
If you are having a piece restored, get a written estimate first.

Silver Flatware Sterling, Love Disarmed, Buffet Fork, Reticulated End, Maiden, Cupid Handle, Reed & Barton, 11 In.
$345

Richard D. Hatch & Associates

TIP
Use your silver often.
It will tarnish less.

Silver Flatware Sterling, Love Disarmed, Salad Servers, Reed & Barton, 10½ In., 2 Piece
$576

Neal Auction Company

Silver Flatware Sterling, Marguerite, Ladle, Gold Wash Bowl, Monogram, Gorham, 1907, 13 In.
$130

Charleston Estate Auctions

Cluny, Bonbon Spoon, Gold Wash Bowl, Gorham, 1800s, 5½ In.	168
Les Six Fleurs, Salad Servers, Fork, Spoon, 9¾ In.	192
Love Disarmed, Buffet Fork, Reticulated End, Maiden, Cupid Handle, Reed & Barton, 11 In. ...*illus*	345
Love Disarmed, Salad Servers, Reed & Barton, 10½ In., 2 Piece...*illus*	576
Marguerite, Ladle, Gold Wash Bowl, Monogram, Gorham, 1907, 13 In...*illus*	130
Medallion, Asparagus Tongs, Monogram, John Wendt, Ball & Black Co., 1862, 10 In.	817
Raphael, Asparagus Serving Fork, Alvin, 9½ In.	384
Sir Christopher, Casserole Spoon, Wallace, 1936, 9 In.	92
Tudor, Soup Ladle, Gold Wash Bowl, Engraved, Gorham, 13 In.	115
Tyrolean, Cold Meat Fork, Frank Whiting, 1905, 9¼ In.	83
Versailles, Stuffing Spoon, Button Rest, Monogram, Gorham, 12¼ In.	241

SILVER PLATE is not solid silver. It is a ware made of a metal, such as nickel or copper, that is covered with a thin coating of silver. The letters *EPNS* are often found on American and English silver-plated wares. *Sheffield* is a term with two meanings. Sometimes it refers to sterling silver made in the town of Sheffield, England. Sometimes it refers to an old form of plated silver made in England. Here are marks of three U.S. silver plate manufacturers.

Barbour Silver Co.
1892–1931

J.W. Tufts
1875–c.1915

Meriden Silver Plate Co.
1869–1898

Ashtray, Horseshoe, Green Wood Base, Stitched Leather Trim, Hermes, c.1950s, 5 x 5 x 3 In.	938
Biscuit Box, Castle Tower Shape, Flag Finial, Hinged Lid, 1900s, 9 x 5¾ In.	180
Biscuit Box, Lid, 4-Part, Lion Finial, Mappin & Webb, Late 1800s, 7 x 8 x 7 In.	156
Biscuit Box, Sheffield, Engraved Leaves, Hinged Lid, 1800s, 7½ In.	213
Bowl, Ebony Handles, Maison Desny, 1930s, 4¼ x 11¼ In.	3750
Bowl, Monteith, Footed, Swing Handles, Crenellated Rim, Mottahedeh, 7¾ x 13 x 11¾ In.	330
Bowl, Reticulated Rim, Flowers, Circular, Japan, 1900s, 2½ x 9 In.	29
Bun Warmer, Shell Shape, Israel Freeman & Son, London, 1900s, 10 In....*illus*	192
Caviar Server, Lid, 3-Arm Insert, Glass Bowl, Italy, 4 x 9 In.	358
Centerpiece, Bone, Molded Feet, Cornucopia, Acanthus Leaves, Ram's Head, 12 x 16 x 8 In.	1125
Centerpiece, Leaf, Berry & Blossom Stand, Satin Glass Bowl, Ruffled Edge, 18 In.	344
Chafing Dish, Rolling Dome Lid, Script Monogram, Edwardian, 10 x 13 x 1 In....*illus*	123
Cocktail Shaker, Air Ship, Zeppelin, Wheels, 2 Detachable Parts, England, 12 In.	283
Compote, Enamel Square Bowl, Stand, Middletown Plate Co., c.1875, 10 In....*illus*	413
Compote, Swing Handle, Diamond Cut Crystal Panels, Repousse Foot, 1800s, 7 x 4 In....*illus*	60
Dish, Entree, Double, Lids, Engraved Armorials, Handles, Water Pan Base, 1800s, 5 x 21 x 13 In.	63
Dresser Box, Hunters & Dogs, Footed, Jennings Brothers, 5½ x 7½ x 2½ In.	40
Epergne, Centerpiece, Ornamental, Brass Base, Trumpet Style, 22 x 16½ x 10½ In.	94
Epergne, Central Bowl, Trumpet Vase, 2 Arms, Bowls, James Deakin & Sons, 18½ x 26½ In.	479
Epergne, Glass, Ruffled, Trumpet Style, Footed, 24 In.	177
Fish Set, Knife & Fork, Leaf Decoration, Staghorn Handle, Sheffield, Knife 13½ In.	96
Flagon, Tapering Neck, Bulbous Base, Female Warrior, Germany, 1800s, 21½ x 10¼ In.	4920
Flask, Villagers Dancing, Derby Silver Plate Co., c.1890, 6 x 4 x 1 In.	94
Flower Holder, Insert, Frame, Crossed Torches, Leaves, England, Late 1800s, 7 x 15 x 7 In.	132
Hot Water Urn, Dome Lid, Lion Mask Handles, Sheffield, Early 1800s, 19 In.	188
Ice Bucket, Milk Glass Liner, Handled, Reed & Barton, 6 x 5½ In.	173
Inkwell, Metal Inscription, Shagreen, Birmingham, 1932, 2¾ x 8¾ x 6 In....*illus*	406
Kettle, Hot Water, 4-Legged, Under Burner, Lion Head Handles, Engraved, Sheffield, 14 In.	100
Pitcher, Lid, Inset Irish Coin, Engraved Armorial, 1800s, 6 In.	88
Planter, Young Maiden, Long Flowing Hair, Repousse Flowers, Art Nouveau, 7 x 3¾ In.	960
Plateau, Mirror, Circular, Relief Grape & Leaf, Disc Feet, Early 1900s, 2 x 13 In.	563
Salad Servers, Applied Starfish, Scallops, Openwork Handle, E. Castillo, Mexico, 16 In.	120
Spoon, Souvenir, see Souvenir category.	
Tazza, Figural, Stepped Foot, Reed & Barton, 8 x 9½ In. ...*illus*	175

Tea Tray, Scroll Border, Loop Handles & Feet, Georgian Style, 30 x 20 ⅝ In.	188
Toothpick Holder, Swan's Head Handles, Flowers, Repousse, Pairpoint, 2 In.	45
Tray, Butler's, Shaped, Etched & Chased Flowers, 2 Handles, 1800s, 29 x 23 In.	63
Tray, Circular, Relief Scroll, Leaves, Engraved, Lion Head, England, 1800s, 2 ½ x 22 In.	523
Tray, Round, Raised Sides, Copper, Egg & Dart Rim, Monogram, Stamped, England, 2 x 18¾ In.	18
Tray, Scroll Feet, Handles, Matthew Boulton, Sheffield, Late 1700s, 3 x 12 x 9 In.	246
Tray, Serving, 3 Sections, Scrolling Acanthus Leaf Rim, 2 Handles, 24 In. ....*illus*	62
Tray, Serving, Pierced Gallery, 2 Cutout Handles, Engraved Armorial, 16 ½ In.	138
Tureen, Soup, Dome Lid, Late Georgian Style, Handles, Scroll Feet, Finial, 12 x 14 In. ....*illus*	63
Urn, Classical Figures, Grapevine Band, Laurel Leaves, c.1850, 27¾ In.	540
Wine Cooler, Warwick Vase, Plinth Base, 1800s, 11 ½ In. ....*illus*	875

SILVER-AMERICAN. American silver is listed here. Coin and sterling silver are included. Most of the sterling silver listed in this book is subdivided by country. There are also other pieces of silver and silver plate listed under special categories, such as Candelabrum, Napkin Ring, Silver Flatware, Silver Plate, Silver-Sterling, and Tiffany Silver. The meltdown price determines the value of solid silver items. Coin silver sells for less than sterling silver. These prices are based on current silver values.

INTERNATIONAL SILVER CO.

TRADE MARK / R / STERLING

Gorham & Co.	International Silver Co.	Reed & Barton Co.
1865+	1898–present	1824–2015

Ashtray, Pinkerton Detective Agency, Cigar Rests, Repousse, Gorham, c.1920, 6 ½ In.	575
Asparagus Tongs, Medallion, Ball, Black & Co., 1800s, 10 In.	580
Basket, Flared, Flower Shape Handle, Molded Foot, Washbourne & Dunn, Graff, 1900, 10 In.	360
Basket, Plymouth, Sugar, Swing Handle, Monogram, Gorham, 5¾ x 4 x 3 In.	177
Basket, Reticulated Edge, Engraved D Monogram, R. Wallace & Sons, 10 ½ x 2 In.	130
Bowl, 14K Gold Raised Work, Acid Etched Flowers, Sweeter Co., c.1910, 10 In.	1920
Bowl, Bigelow Kennard & Co., Massachusetts, 8¼ x 11 In.	550
Bowl, Birds, Flowering Trees, 4 Stiff Leaves, Incurved Legs, S. Kirk & Son, c.1890, 9 ½ x 9 In.	5120
Bowl, Cast Rim, Shells & Scrolling Acanthus Leaves, Whiting, 1900, 10 ½ In.	216
Bowl, Charleroi, Baskets Of Flowers, International Silver Co., 6 x 12 In. ....*illus*	660
Bowl, Cut Center, Pedestal, Gold Wash, Whiting Mfg. Co., c.1950, 7 x 9 ½ In.	369
Bowl, Flowers, Scalloped Border, 4-Footed, Signed, Reed & Barton, 2 x 8 In.	237
Bowl, Fluted, Scalloped Rim, Footed, Round Stepped Base, Gorham, c.1946, 4 ½ x 9 In.	570
Bowl, Footed, Marked, S. Kirk & Son, Maryland, c.1930, 4 x 9 In.	575
Bowl, Footed, Scroll Rim, Monogram, Black, Starr & Frost, New York, Early 1900s, 10 In..*illus*	369
Bowl, Hammered, Applied Copper Fruit, Leaves, Birds, Butterflies, 3-Footed, Gorham, c.1890, 8 ½ x 4 In.	4688
Bowl, Oval, Hammered, Allan Adler, Ca., 1900s, 2 x 18 ½ x 6¼ In.	1250
Bowl, Reeded Bands, 2 Panther Head Shape Handles, Dominick & Haff, c.1920, 9 In.	1680
Bowl, Repousse Flowers, Acanthus Leaves, Baltimore Sterling Silver Co., c.1904, 9 x 11 In.	3075
Bowl, Repousse Flowers, Shells & Flower Head Rim, S. Kirk & Son, c.1890, 9 x 7 In.	1845
Bowl, Repousse, Hand Decorated, S. Kirk & Son, 3 x 11 ½ In.	413
Bowl, Reticulated Leaves, Flowers, Marked, Early 1900s, 7 x 15 x 8 In.	1250
Bowl, Revere Shape, Engraved, Monogram, Tuttle Silversmiths, Mass., 1940, 4 ½ x 9 In.	500
Bowl, Scalloped Rim, Dolphin Mask, Leaves Scrolls, Kennard & Co., c.1900, 10 In.	138
Bowl, Scalloped Rim, Repousse Flowers, Fruit, Bird, Domed Foot, S. Kirk & Son, c.1885, 9 x 7 In.	1476
Bowl, Scalloped Rim, Repousse Scrolls, Fruit, Francis I, Reed & Barton, 11 ½ In...............*illus*	615
Bowl, Square, Filigree Border, Signed, Graff, Washbourne & Dunn, 14 x 14 In.	303
Bowl, Trophy, Round Base, Flared Mouth Rim, Engraved, Revere Style, 1900s, 5 x 12 In.	688
Bowl, Vegetable, Lid, 2 Handles, Chippendale, Gorham, 10 ½ x 7¾ x 3 In. ....*illus*	513
Box, Engraved, Indians In Canoes, Semiprecious Stones, Gorham, c.1900, 3 x 2 In...........*illus*	2250
Bread Tray, Lobed Body, Scalloped Edge, Eagle & Lion, Reed & Barton, 12 x 8 ½ In.........*illus*	201
Cake Plate, Griffins, Cupids, Scrolls, Roger Williams Silver Co., Early 1900s, 11 In.	720
Cake Plate, Pierced Border, Scrolling Rose Vines, Bailey, Banks & Biddle, c.1900, 8¾ In.	216
Cake Plate, Reticulated Edge, Engraved Initial In Center, Footed, Gorham, 9 ½ x 1 In.	130
Cake Plate, Wide Rim, Repousse Flowers & Leaves, S. Kirk & Son Co., 1900s, 10 In.	270

Silver Plate, Bun Warmer, Shell Shape, Israel Freeman & Son, London, 1900s, 10 In.
$192

Neal Auction Company

Silver Plate, Chafing Dish, Rolling Dome Lid, Script Monogram, Edwardian, 10 x 13 x 1 In.
$123

Clars Auction Gallery

Silver Plate, Compote, Enamel Square Bowl, Stand, Middletown Plate Co., c.1875, 10 In.
$413

Forsythes' Auctions

Silver Plate, Compote, Swing Handle, Diamond Cut Crystal Panels, Repousse Foot, 1800s, 7 x 4 In.
$60

Thomaston Place Auction Galleries

TIP
You might be able to remove salt spots from your silver-plated saltshakers with olive oil. Rub it on the spots, let stand a few days, then wipe it off.

Silver Plate, Inkwell, Metal Inscription, Shagreen, Birmingham, 1932, 2¾ x 8¾ x 6 In.
$406

Rago Arts and Auction Center

Silver Plate, Tazza, Figural, Stepped Foot, Reed & Barton, 8 x 9½ In.
$175

Kaminski Auctions

Candelabra are listed in the Candelabrum category.	
Candlesticks are listed in their own category.	
Cann, Cup, George II, Molded Foot, Engraved, Scroll Handle, Thomas Moore II, 1700s, 5 In..*illus*	2160
Centerpiece, Plate, Egyptian Motifs, Gorham Mfg. Co., 1800s, 10¾ In.	163
Charger, Maintenon Pattern, Circular, Leaf Rim Border, Plain Center, Gorham, 14¾ In.	1250
Coffeepot, Dome Lid, Baluster, Scroll Handle, Gorham, 1959, 10⅝ x 9⅞ x 4¾ In.	472
Coffeepot, Hot Water, Bulbous, Leaf Motif, Rococo Style, Gorham, c.1917, 10½ x 10 x 5 In.	584
Coffeepot, Lid, Pear Shape, Scrolls, Leaves, Flowers, Gilt, Lincoln & Reed, c.1840, 11 In..*illus*	1088
Compote, Grecian Pattern, Reed & Barton, 11 x 5 In.	594
Compote, Repousse Flowers & Leaves, Marked, S. Kirk & Son, c.1900, 9 x 4½ In..*illus*	469
Compote, Repousse Flowers, Rim & Foot, Monogram, S. Kirk & Son, c.1900, 4 x 11½ In.	600
Confection Spoon, Openwork Bowl, Figural Handle, Gorham, 1800s, 8¾ In..*illus*	293
Creamer, Pedestal, Leaves, Scroll Handle, Joseph Shoemaker, Philadelphia, c.1805, 6 In..*illus*	275
Creamer, Scroll Handle, Coin, William & Archibald Cooper, Marked, c.1836, 4¼ In.	540
Dish, Entree, Lid, Repousse Country Scene, Handles, A.E. Warner, Maryland, c.1850, 6½ x 8½ In.	2500
Dish, Lid, Scrolling Leaves, Flower Handle, Bailey & Co., 1800s, 6½ x 12 x 9½ In.	1770
Dish, Presentation, U.S. Navy, Domed Foot, Fitted Wooden Box, 10 In.	523
Ewer, Pear Shape, Scrolls, Flowers, Leaves, Double Scroll Handle, Gorham, 13 In.	1536
Ewer, Repousse Grapevine, Scroll Handle, Chased, S. Kirk & Son, c.1900, 15 In..*illus*	1416
Fish Server, Fontainbleau Pattern, Marked, Gorham, Late 1800s, 11½ x 2¾ In..*illus*	270
Flower Basket, Oval, Swing Handle, Leafy, J.E. Caldwell & Co., c.1900, 5 In.	420
Flower Basket, Pierced, Engraved, Neoclassical, Monogram, International, 1900s, 12 In.	277
Flower Basket, Scalloped Rim, Lobed, Handle, Scroll Feet, Gorham, 1900s, 16 x 16 x 10 In.	1046
Fruit Bowl, Floral Scroll, Engraved Monogram, Meriden Britannia Co., 8½ x 1¾ In.	118
Goblet, Baltimore Rose Pattern, Repousse, Schofield, 1905, 6¾ In.	938
Goblet, Water, Footed, Marked, S. Kirk & Son, 6¾ In.	106
Gravy Boat, Repousse Flowers, Bird, Hunter, Dog, Twig Handle, A.E. Warner, c.1850, 6 x 8 In..*illus*	938
Ice Bucket, Dome Lid, Urn Finial, 2 Handles, Engraved, Poole Silver Co., Mid 1800s, 8½ In.	469
Ice Bucket, Lid, Hinged Handle, Ice Tong Hanger, Signed, Cartier, 11¾ x 5½ In..*illus*	2118
Ice Tongs, Putnam, Pierced, Watson Co., 1920, 7 In..*illus*	83
Ladle, Poppy, Baker Manchester, 1904, 7½ In.	53
Meat Platter, Scroll Rim, Floral Sprays, Well & Tree, Gorham, 1900s, 20½ In.	984
Mug, Scrolled Handle, Engraved, Marked, Hammond & Company, c.1850, 3¼ In.	113
Napkin Rings are listed in their own category.	
Pitcher, Alphonse La Paglia, Wood Base, International Silver, Meriden, Conn., c.1955, 8 In.	1353
Pitcher, Flowers, Repousse, Coin, Samuel Kirk & Son, c.1850, 9½ In..*illus*	3500
Pitcher, Hammered, Filigree Handle, Signed, Cellini Craft, 8 x 9 In..*illus*	787
Pitcher, Handle & Base Openwork, Floral, Quaker Silver Co., 1900s, 10¾ In.	540
Pitcher, John C. Moore & Son, Engraved, Coat Of Arms, c.1865, 9 x 7 In.	3750
Pitcher, Leaves, Capped Handle, Mark, International Silver Co., 8½ In.	375
Pitcher, Monogram, Floral Handle, Dominick & Haff, 8½ In.	584
Pitcher, Oval, Asian Repousse, Cartouche, Monogram, Samuel Kirk, 1800s, 7 x 8 x 6 In.	1320
Pitcher, Repousse Flowers, Scroll Feet, Marked, Gorham, c.1890, 8¾ In.	938
Pitcher, Royal Danish, Pear Shape, Curved Handle, Footed, International, c.1960, 8¼ In.	738
Pitcher, Scalloped Rim, Beaded Accents, Black, Starr & Frost, c.1900, 8 x 9¾ In..*illus*	813
Pitcher, Split Branch Handle, Flower & Leaves, Quaker Silver Co., 10 x 7¾ x 6 In.	484
Pitcher, Urn Shape, Neoclassical Cartouches, Black, Starr & Frost, Early 1900s, 9 In..*illus*	584
Pitcher, Vase Shape, Scroll Handle, Acanthus Leaves, Rose Borders, F. Marquand, c.1835, 15 x 10 In.	2337
Pitcher, Water, C-Handle, Revere Style, Tuttle Silversmiths, c.1950, 7 x 7 In.	320
Pitcher, Water, Curved Handle, Marked, Gorham, 8 x 7¾ x 5¾ In.	688
Pitcher, Water, Floral & Leaf, Bigelow Kennard & Co., c.1900, 9½ In..*illus*	3068
Pitcher, Water, Leafy Spiral Scrolls, Shell Spout, Gorham, 1890, 7¼ In..*illus*	813
Pitcher, Water, Molded Helmet Mouth, Circular Base, Whiting, 1911, 10 x 9 x 6 In.	513
Pitcher, Water, Openwork Flowers & Leaves, Volute Decoration, Whiting Mfg. Co., 8 In.	688
Pitcher, Water, Repousse Roses, Grapes, Leaves, Coin, Ball, Thompkins, Black, 15¾ In.	1440
Pitcher, Water, Repousse, Serpentine Handle, Monogram, Gorham, 1892, 7 x 8 x 6 In.	1782
Platter, Circular, Cast Leaves, Wide Border, Meriden Britannia, 10½ x ⅞ In.	295
Platter, Round, Serpentine Rim, Leaves, Scroll, Dominick & Haff, 13 In.	590
Platter, Well & Tree Scrolling Leaf Rim, R. Wallace & Sons, Early 1900s..*illus*	570
Pot, Pear Shape, Hinged Lid, Flowers, Scroll Feet, Ivory Connectors, Z. Bostwick, N.Y., c.1850, 11 x 9 In.	1476

Silver Plate, Tray, Serving, 3 Sections, Scrolling Acanthus Leaf Rim, 2 Handles, 24 In.
$62

DuMouchelles

Silver Plate, Tureen, Soup, Dome Lid, Late Georgian Style, Handles, Scroll Feet, Finial, 12 x 14 In.
$63

Neal Auction Company

Silver Plate, Wine Cooler, Warwick Vase, Plinth Base, 1800s, 11 ½ In.
$875

Leslie Hindman Auctioneers

Wash Silver by Hand

Experts say you should never put silverware in a dishwasher for several reasons: eventually the oxidation (black highlights) will disappear, hollow-handled knives are filled with a material that will melt, and if the silver touches stainless steel it will get black spots. Be safe. Wash silver by hand.

TIP

Eighteenth- and nineteenth-century Irish silver is more valuable than English because it is rarer.

Silver-American, Bowl, Charleroi, Baskets Of Flowers, International Silver Co., 6 x 12 In.
$660

Willis Henry Auctions

Silver-American, Bowl, Footed, Scroll Rim, Monogram, Black, Starr & Frost, New York, Early 1900s, 10 In.
$369

Skinner, Inc.

Silver-American, Bowl, Scalloped Rim, Repousse Scrolls, Fruit, Francis I, Reed & Barton, 11 ½ In.
$615

Crescent City Auction Gallery

Silver-American, Bowl, Vegetable, Lid, 2 Handles, Chippendale, Gorham, 10 ½ x 7 ¾ x 3 In.
$513

Charleston Estate Auctions

Silver-American, Box, Engraved, Indians In Canoes, Semiprecious Stones, Gorham, c.1900, 3 x 2 In.
$2,250

Royal Crest Auctioneers

Silver-American, Bread Tray, Lobed Body, Scalloped Edge, Eagle & Lion, Reed & Barton, 12 x 8 ½ In.
$201

Forsythes' Auctions

S

Silver-American, Cann, Cup, George II, Molded Foot, Engraved, Scroll Handle, Thomas Moore II, 1700s, 5 In.
$2,160

Northeast Auctions

Silver-American, Coffeepot, Lid, Pear Shape, Scrolls, Leaves, Flowers, Gilt, Lincoln & Reed, c.1840, 11 In.
$1,088

Morphy Auctions

Silver-American, Compote, Repousse Flowers & Leaves, Marked, S. Kirk & Son, c.1900, 9 x 4½ In.
$469

Royal Crest Auctioneers

Silver-American, Confection Spoon, Openwork Bowl, Figural Handle, Gorham, 1800s, 8¾ In.
$293

Thomaston Place Auction Galleries

Silver-American, Creamer, Pedestal, Leaves, Scroll Handle, Joseph Shoemaker, Philadelphia, c.1805, 6 In.
$275

Pook & Pook

Silver-American, Ewer, Repousse Grapevine, Scroll Handle, Chased, S. Kirk & Son, c.1900, 15 In.
$1,416

Leland Little Auctions

Silver-American, Fish Server, Fontainbleau Pattern, Marked, Gorham, Late 1800s, 11½ x 2¾ In.
$270

Cowan's Auctions

Silver-American, Gravy Boat, Repousse Flowers, Bird, Hunter, Dog, Twig Handle, A.E. Warner, c.1850, 6 x 8 In.
$938

Brunk Auctions

Silver-American, Ice Bucket, Lid, Hinged Handle, Ice Tong Hanger, Signed, Cartier, 11¾ x 5½ In.
$2,118

Fontaine's Auction Gallery

Silver-American, Icc Tongs, Putnam, Pierced, Watson Co., 1920, 7 In.
$83

Charleston Estate Auctions

> **TIP**
> Never store silver in plastic wrap or newspapers or with rubber bands. They will all cause discoloration.

Silver-American, Pitcher, Flowers, Repousse, Coin, Samuel Kirk & Son, c.1850, 9½ In.
$3,500

Rago Arts and Auction Center

Silver-American, Pitcher, Hammered, Filigree Handle, Signed, Cellini Craft, 8 x 9 In.
$787

Fontaine's Auction Gallery

Silver-American, Pitcher, Scalloped Rim, Beaded Accents, Black, Starr & Frost, c.1900, 8 x 9¾ In.
$813

Royal Crest Auctioneers

Silver-American, Pitcher, Urn Shape, Neoclassical Cartouches, Black, Starr & Frost, Early 1900s, 9 In.
$584

Skinner, Inc.

Silver-American, Pitcher, Water, Floral & Leaf, Bigelow Kennard & Co., c.1900, 9½ In.
$3,068

Cottone Auctions

Silver-American, Pitcher, Water, Leafy Spiral Scrolls, Shell Spout, Gorham, 1890, 7¼ In.
$813

Brunk Auctions

Silver-American, Platter, Well & Tree Scrolling Leaf Rim, R. Wallace & Sons, Early 1900s
$570

Selkirk Auctioneers & Appraisers

Silver-American, Punch Ladle, Medici, Oval Bowl, Gold Wash, Scalloped Edge, Gorham, 1900s, 12 In.
$185

Cowan's Auctions

S

Silver-American, Sandwich Plate, Francis I, Repousse Fruit, Leaf Scroll, Reed & Barton, 11 ½ In.
$366

Charleston Estate Auctions

Silver-American, Serving Dish, Royal Danish, Marked, International Silver Co., Ct., 12 ½ In.
$281

Leslie Hindman Auctioneers

Silver-American, Serving Fork, Ornate, Monogram, Simpson, Hall, Miller, 1800s, 8 ½ In.
$130

Charleston Estate Auctions

Silver-American, Tankard, Tapered Body, Molded Lid, Curved Handle, Engraved, John Burt, c.1744, 7 In.
$1,887

Skinner, Inc.

Silver-American, Tea Caddy Spoon, Matte Gilt Bowl, Monogram GBG, Shiebler, 3 ¾ In.
$65

Leland Little Auctions

Silver-American, Tea Urn, Flowers, Leaves, Scrolls, Beaded Rim, Handles, Marked, Philada R. & W. Wilson, 19 In.
$2,700

Jeffrey S. Evans & Associates

Silver-American, Teapot, Drum Shape, Beaded Borders, Straight Spout, Treen Handle, S. Richards, 1800s, 6 In.
$1,440

Northeast Auctions

Silver-American, Teapot, Gooseneck Spout, Lobed Body, Handle, c.1815, 9 In.
$1,375

Pook & Pook

> **TIP**
> *Use your silver often and wash it to keep it clean. Polish it as seldom as possible. Silver polish removes a small bit of silver each time it is used.*

Silver-American, Teapot, Hand Wrought, Hammered, Marked, The Kalo Shop, 9 ¼ x 5 ½ x 7 In.
$1,063

Royal Crest Auctioneers

S

Punch Ladle, Aesthetic Movement, W. Faber & Sons, Late 1800s, 13 In.	154
Punch Ladle, Medici, Oval Bowl, Gold Wash, Scalloped Edge, Gorham, 1900s, 12 In.......*illus*	185
Punch Ladle, Parcel Gilt Bowl, Coin, Marked A.F. Shepard, 3¾ x 13 In.	2415
Sandwich Plate, Francis I, Repousse Fruit, Leaf Scroll, Reed & Barton, 11½ In.......*illus*	366
Sandwich Plate, Repousse Flowers, Half Chased, S. Kirk & Son, c.1940, 10 In.	248
Sauce Ladle, Treen Handle, Towle, 2½ In.	38
Serving Dish, Royal Danish, Marked, International Silver Co., Ct., 12½ In. ....*illus*	281
Serving Dish, Triangular, Engraved, Leaf Tip Design, Coin, J.M. Ford, c.1850, 10⅞ In.	277
Serving Fork, Ornate, Monogram, Simpson, Hall, Miller, 1800s, 8½ In. ....*illus*	130
Serving Spoon, Gilt Wash, Lily Of The Valley, Vine, Starr & Marcus, Gorham, 10½ In.	215
Serving Spoon, Marked Below Tasseled Sword, Wilhelmina Stephan, Early 1900s, 12½ In. ...	300
Serving Spoon, Repousse Flowers & Fruit, S. Kirk & Sons, Early 1900s, 9 In.	60
Serving Spoon, Roses, George W. Shiebler, c.1897, 9 In.	160
Soup Ladle, Engraved, Leafy Design, Marked, Jr., c.1850, 14 In.	156
Soup Ladle, Fiddleback, Monogram, Coin, Kinsey, 9 In.	120
Spoon, Rococo Shell Relief, Monogram, Gray Patina, Charles Hall, Pa., 8¼ In.	900
Stuffing Spoon, Fiddle Back Handle, Marked, E. Whiton, Ma., c.1850, 11⅝ In.	164
Sugar, Lid, Double Handle, Mark Underfoot, Gorham, Early 1900s	120
Sugar, Lid, Finial, Repousse, Leaves, Coin, Robert & William Wilson, c.1840, 9½ x 7¾ In.	720
Table Ornament, Mounted, Horn, Dolphin, Graff, 1900, 14½ In.	813
Tankard, Tapered Body, Molded Lid, Curved Handle, Engraved, John Burt, c.1744, 7 In....*illus*	1887
Tea Caddy Spoon, Matte Gilt Bowl, Monogram GBG, Shiebler, 3¾ In.......*illus*	65
Tea Strainer, Lily Shape, Marked, Webster Co., 1905, 3 In.	250
Tea Strainer, Louvre, Gold Wash Bowl, Handle, R. Wallace & Sons, Late 1900s, 5½ In.	92
Tea Urn, Flowers, Leaves, Scrolls, Beaded Rim, Handles, Marked, Philada R. & W. Wilson, 19 In.....*illus*	2700
Teapot, Boat Shape, Urn Finial, Oval Medallion, 4 Eagles, Isaac Hutton, 1700s, 6⅝ In.	360
Teapot, Bulbous, Swan Neck Spout, Ebonized Handle, Hugh Wishart, 8 x 13 x 5 In.	615
Teapot, Drum Shape, Beaded Borders, Straight Spout, Treen Handle, S. Richards, 1800s, 6 In...*illus*	1440
Teapot, Gooseneck Spout, Lobed Body, Handle, c.1815, 9 In. ....*illus*	1375
Teapot, Hand Wrought, Hammered, Marked, The Kalo Shop, 9¼ x 5½ x 7 In.......*illus*	1063
Teapot, Handle & Spout, Monogram, Reed & Barton, 8½ x 5 In.	484
Tray, 2 Handles, Repousse Flowers, Manchester Silver Co., c.1920, 23¾ x 13¾ In.	1563
Tray, 2 Handles, Round, Marked, Randahl, Illinois, 1900s, 17¼ In.	720
Tray, Egg & Dart Border, Garlands, Cartouches, Reed & Barton, 1900s, 26 x 19 In.	1500
Tray, Flowers, Acanthus, Handles, Dominick & Haff, 32½ x 21 In.	5280
Tray, Hand Hammered, Rose Border, Oval, Flared Rim, Feisa, 19 x 14 x 1 In.	850
Tray, Hand Wrought, Round, Kalo, c.1950, 12 In.	688
Tray, Monogram, Server, Asparagus Spears, Gorham, 1899, 14 In.	2760
Tray, Oval, Footed, Fleur-De-Lis Border, Marked, Theodore B. Starr, 1800s, 14 x 10 In.	960
Tray, Oval, Marked Letter T, Arthur Stone, 1900s, 24½ x 14 x 10 In.	523
Tray, Oval, Raised Edge, Cartier, France, 20 x 13 In.	1815
Tray, Oval, Scrollwork, Leaves & Berries, Gorham, 1899, 13¾ In.	2040
Tray, Reticulated Border, Putti, Flowers, Footed, Gorham, 11⅜ In.	188
Tray, Round, Berries & Leaves, Handles, Jensen Style, Gorham, 14¾ In.	378
Tray, Round, Floral Repousse, Monogram, Ritter & Sullivan, c.1900, 12¼ In.	554
Tray, Serving, Lift Handle, Glass Bottom, George A. Heckel Co., 5¾ x 12 x 10 In.	150
Tray, Serving, Seashell Side Trays, Handle, Wallace, 5 x 15½ x 9 In.	303
Tray, Tea, Plain, Oblong, Reeded Edge, Loop Handles, Gorham, 25¼ x 15 In.	1968
Trophy, Bulbous, Cherubs, Scroll Borders, Horses, Victory Holding Wreath, Pairpoint, 20 x 12 In.	756
Trophy, Military, Pear Shape, 2 Molded Handles, Wallace, 17½ x 13 In.	630
Trophy, Urn Shape, Acorn Branches, 2 Strap Handle, Presentation, Reed & Barton, 26 x 13 In..	2880
Trophy, Vase, Lid, 2 Handles, Flowers, Scrolls, Monogram, Gorham, 15½ In.	2084
Tureen, Beaded, Shoulder & Foot Rims, Marked, Gorham, 1898, 8½ x 14½ In.	875
Tureen, Flowers, Filigree, Loop Handles, Oval Foot, Gorham, 10 x 14 x 8½ In.......*illus*	4235
Tureen, Lid, Urn Shape, 2 Upright Bead Handles, Central Monogram, Gorham, 9½ In.	1107
Tureen, Oval, Ball Finial, Handles, Monogram, Gorham, c.1888, 10½ x 6½ x 7 In.	425
Tureen, Soup, Chantilly Grand, Gorham, Sickle Mark, 1899, 14 x 11 x 8 In.......*illus*	4012
Urn, Cone Shape, Marked, Circular Base, Gorham, 1900s, 18½ In.	688
Urn, Hot Water, Fruit Vines, Removable Lid, 4 Legs, Kidney, Cann & Johnson, N.Y., c.1865, 18 x 9 In.	2432
Vase, Flowers, Repousse, Shreve, Crump & Low, 1900s, 14½ In.	1375

Silver-American, Tureen, Flowers, Filigree, Loop Handles, Oval Foot, Gorham, 10 x 14 x 8½ In.
$4,235

Fontaine's Auction Gallery

Silver-American, Tureen, Soup, Chantilly Grand, Gorham, Sickle Mark, 1899, 14 x 11 x 8 In.
$4,012

Aspire Auctions

TIP
Always repair dented silver. Repeated cleaning of a piece with a dent can eventually lead to a hole.

Silver-Continental, Basket, Floral Panels, Twig Handle, Grapes & Leaves, 8 x 5 In.
$266

Forsythes' Auctions

Silver-Danish, Bowl, Hammered, Openwork Support, Domed Foot, Georg Jensen, c.1975, 5 x 6 In.
$840

Cowan's Auctions

Silver-Danish, Cocktail Shaker, Crown Mark, Georg Jensen, Denmark, 1925-32, 12 In.
$6,250

Rago Arts and Auction Center

Silver-Danish, Ladle, Rosenborg, Anton Michelsen, Denmark, 7½ In.
$83

Charleston Estate Auctions

Vase, Lotus, Marked, Paw Feet, Watson Co., 10½ In.	175
Vase, Trumpet Shape, Vertical Veins, Roses, Signed, Gorham, 14½ x 5 In.	847
Vase, Trumpet, Pierced Rim, Wreath Hallmark, Signed, Watson Co., 18¼ In.	339
Vase, Urn Shape, 2 Handles, Repousse, Bead Rim, Cartouche, Gorham, Mid 1800s, 8 In.	300

SILVER-CHINESE

Bowl, Peonies, Budding & Flowering, Red Glass Liner, c.1900, 4⅞ In.	246
Box, Lid, Circular Shape, Riverscape Scenes, Maker's Marks, Late 1900, 5 In.	125
Mug, Chased Birds, Bamboo Plants, Wang Hing, Shanghai, Canton, 6 In.	1125
Pot, Milk, Armorial, Side Mounted Treen Handle, Cushing, Canton, 1800s, 4½ In.	4080

SILVER-CONTINENTAL

Basket, Floral Panels, Twig Handle, Grapes & Leaves, 8 x 5 In. ....*illus*	266
Spoon, Openwork, Bearded Man, Cherub, Armed Cavaliers, Continental, 1800s, 8¾ In.	84
Vase, Baroque, Applied Shells, Scrolls, Cherub, Lion Heads, Vines, 42 In.	13530

SILVER-DANISH. Georg Jensen is the most famous Danish silver company.

Georg Jensen	Georg Jensen	Georg Jensen
1925–1932	1933–1944	1945–present

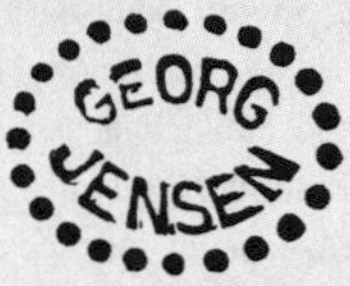

Bowl, Hammered, Openwork Support, Domed Foot, Georg Jensen, c.1975, 5 x 6 In. ....*illus*	840
Cocktail Shaker, Crown Mark, Georg Jensen, Denmark, 1925-32, 12 In. ....*illus*	6250
Compote, Hammered, Openwork, Beaded Bud, Leaves, J. Rohde, G. Jensen, 1945, 4 x 5 In.	677
Compote, Spiral Stem, Pendant Grape Clusters, Georg Jensen, c.1925, 7½ In.	1968
Ladle, Rosenborg, Anton Michelsen, Denmark, 7½ In. ....*illus*	83
Marrow Scoop, Acanthus, Georg Jensen, 7 In. ....*illus*	92
Salt Cellar, Acorn, Enamel, 8 Cellars, 8 Spoons, Cases, Georg Jensen, 1915, Pair	1250
Serving Dish, Marked, Georg Jensen, No. 687, 9½ In.	950
Sugar Castor, Pyramid, Marked, Harald Nielsen, Denmark, 1945, 4¾ x 3 In.	6250
Tray, Blossom Style, Marked, Georg Jensen, 1900s, 25½ x 16¾ In.	3000
Tray, Engraved Steamship, Oval, Molded Rim, Georg Jensen, c.1955, 17 In.	2625

SILVER-DUTCH

Basket, Filigree, Hanging Garland, Leafy Side Handles, 2½ x 7 x 3¾ In.	242

SILVER-ENGLISH. English sterling silver is marked with a series of four or five small hallmarks. The standing lion mark is the most commonly seen sterling quality mark. The other marks indicate the city of origin, the maker, the year of manufacture, and the king or queen. These dates can be verified in many good books on silver. These prices are partially based on silver meltdown values.

Standard quality mark	City mark – London	Date letter mark

Maker's mark	Sovereign's head mark

Basket, Reed, Feather Swing Handle, William Bateman & Daniel Ball, 1841, 11 In.	300
Basket, Repousse, Leaves, Bacchant Faces, Settle & Wilkinson, 1830, 13 x 11 In.	938
Basket, Swing Handle, Oval, Pierced Border, Beaded Rim, George III, 12 x 14 x 10 In.	677
Biscuit Barrel, Geometrics, Flowers, Tray Base, Leaf Feet, Horse Finial, 11 x 11 In.	512
Bowl, Celtic Band, Circular Foot, George V, Wakely & Wheeler, 1935, 5 In. ....*illus*	344
Bowl, Engraved Inscription, Crichton & Co, 5⅝ x 11 In.	812
Bowl, Flower Border, Oval, Spaulding, Victorian, 8½ x 6½ In.	115

Bowl, Fruit, Scrolls, Flowers, Gadroon Rim, Raised Pedestal Foot, c.1800, 5 x 9 In.		1187
Bowl, Grotesque Masks, C-Scrolls, Cartouche, Goldsmiths & Silversmiths Co., 5 In.		584
Bun Warmer, Egyptian Revival Style, 2 Egyptians, Claw Feet, 1800s, 9 x 12 In.	*illus*	138
Cake Basket, Reeded Edge, Wheat Stalk, Oval, Swing Handle, c.1760, 13 x 10 In.		1187
Cake Stand, Grapevine, Openwork, Barkers, England, 1946, 2⅜ x 12 In.		500
Candelabra are listed in the Candelabrum category.		
Candlesticks are listed in their own category.		
Cann, Cup, Scroll Handle, Richard Gurney & Thomas Cook, 4½ In.	*illus*	615
Charger, Scenic, Engraved, Leonard Morel Ladeuil, Elkington & Co., 1876, 20 In.		688
Cigarette Box, Lid, Wood Lined, Asprey & Co., London, 1964, 2 x 7 x 3½ In.		570
Claret Jug, Glass, Curved Handle, Horace Woodward & Co., 1896, 11½ In.		900
Coffeepot, Flowers, Scrolls, Ivory, Wood Finial, John Watson, London, 1821, 9½ In.		615
Coffeepot, Pear Shape, Leaf Spout, Molded Foot, Coat Of Arms, 1765, 10 In.		960
Creamer, Repousse, Roses, C-Scroll Handle, S. Kirk & Son, 4½ In.		190
Cruet Stand, Georgian, Cartouche, Spiderweb, Open Handle, Shell Feet, 9 In.		677
Cup, Lid, George II, Chased Flowers, Coat Of Arms, 2 Handles, W. Cripps, London, 12 In.		3075
Dish, Lid, George III, Benjamin Smith I, James Smith, 1808, 9 x 12 In.	*illus*	1440
Dressing Spoon, Fiddle Thread, Engraved Owl Crest, Wm. Eley & Wm. Fearn, London, 1818, 12 In.		188
Epergne, 6 Arms, George III, Floral Swags, Scroll Legs, D. Smith & R. Sharp, 13 In.		9225
Epergne, Bowl, 4 Arms, Convertible Form, Rococo Style, 9½ x 19 In.		354
Ewer, Classical Figures, Leaf Handle, Vase Shape, Elkington & Co., 1895, 17 x 8 In.		3383
Ewer, Wine, Parcel Gilt, Vase Shape, Edward & John Barnard, Victorian, 11 In.		861
Ewer, Wine, Urn Shape, Wicker Wrap Handle, George III, Joseph Lock, 12 In.		923
Flagon, Lid, Leaves, Scrolls, Deer, Putto Finial, Engraved, R. Hennell, 1848, 15 In.	*illus*	3780
Gravy Boat, George II, Footed, Scroll Handle, 1751, 6 x 9 In., Pair		3198
Ice Bucket, Repousse, Shells, Leaf Ring Handles, Richard Sibley, c.1818, 10 x 9 In.		6563
Jewelry Box, Flower & Vine, Monogram, Velvet Lined, Ring Slots, 2 x 5 In.		341
Jug, Chased, Scrolls, Winged Figures, Scroll Handle, Foot, C.C. Pilling, 1920, 12 x 6 In.		2768
Jug, Hinged Lid, Baluster, Pinecone Finial, Martin Hall & Co., London, 1870, 12 In.		3500
Kettle, Stand, Engraved, Shaped Handle, Crichton Brothers, 13½ In.	*illus*	1770
Marrow Scoop, George II, Engraved, Winged Cow's Head, London, 1748, 8¾ In.		84
Mirror, Table, Angels, King, Knights, Faces, Swords, Heart, William Comyns, 18 x 13 In.		1150
Mug, Christening, Repousse Flowers, Victorian, 1854, 4½ In.		246
Mug, Molded Rim, Footed, Flat Handle, George I, 1726, 3¾ In.		192
Napkin Rings are listed in their own category.		
Pitcher, Water, Engraved Crest, George III, London, 1781, 7½ In.		1020
Pot, Hot Water, George III, Dragon, Craddock & Reid, London, 1812, 9 In.		360
Salver, Chippendale Style, Engraved, 3 Hoof Feet, W. Hutton & Sons, 1915, 14 In.	*illus*	767
Salver, George III, Armorial Cartouche, Gadroon, Shells, John Swift, 1700s, 15 In.		1440
Salver, Round, Engraved, Hutton & Sons, 1900s, 8 In.		138
Salver, Round, Scalloped Border, Rope Edge, Howard & Co., 1¾ x 14 In.		750
Server, Dessert, Pierced Blade, Samuel Herbert & Co., London, 1750, 11¾ In.	*illus*	570
Shoehorn, Aesthetic Movement, Monogram, Hammered, George W. Shiebler, 1886		259
Soup Ladle, Crowned Lion Engraving, Ebenezer Coker, London, 1756, 13 In.		385
Spoon, Strainer, Monogram, Georgian, Solomon Hougham, London, 1805, 12 In.		240
Sugar Nip, Figural, Doll, Dutch, Edwardian, Carrington, London, 1910, 5 In.		461
Sugar, Oval, Marked, Peter, Ann & William Bateman, London, 1799, 8½ In.	*illus*	594
Tea Urn, Threaded Border, Loop Handles, Ball Feet, c.1805, 14¾ In.		180
Teapot, Ebony Handle, Engraved, Marked, Robert Sibley, 1852, 6 In.	*illus*	330
Teapot, Engraved, Neoclassical Swags, Cartouches, George Burrows I, 5 In.	*illus*	369
Teapot, Melon Shape, Edward & John Barnard, Victorian, 5¼ In.		308
Teapot, Oval, Green Pineapple Finial, Wood Handle, George III, 1799, 7 x 12 In.		656
Teapot, Waisted, Scroll Flower Rim, Wooden Handle, Paul Storr, c.1819		1750
Tongs, Toast, Engraved Vines, Flower Border, John Emes, 1807, 10 In.		165
Tray, George III, Ribbon & Shell Border, Monogram, 3 Hoof Feet, c.1746, 7 In.	*illus*	360
Tray, Latin Inscription, Handles, T. Hannam & J. Crouch, London, c.1780, 23 In.	*illus*	4837
Tray, Oval, Shaped Rim, Engraved Crest, John Bache, 1720, 18 x 13 In.		1845
Tray, Round, Engraved Coat Of Arms, Richard Rugg, George III, 1764, 14 In.		1187
Tray, Round, Lion Emblem, Facsimile Signature, G. Bateman & Sons, 6½ In.		250

Silver-Danish, Marrow Scoop, Acanthus, Georg Jensen, 7 In.
$92

Clars Auction Gallery

TIP

Don't soak silver in water overnight. It can cause damage.

Silver-English, Bowl, Celtic Band, Circular Foot, George V, Wakely & Wheeler, 1935, 5 In.
$344

Leslie Hindman Auctioneers

Silver-English, Bun Warmer, Egyptian Revival Style, 2 Egyptians, Claw Feet, 1800s, 9 x 12 In.
$138

Leslie Hindman Auctioneers

This is an edited listing of current prices. Visit Kovels.com to check thousands of prices from previous years and sign up for free information on trends, tips, reproductions, marks, and more.

Silver-English, Cann, Cup, Scroll Handle, Richard Gurney & Thomas Cook, 4 1/2 In.
$615

Skinner, Inc.

Silver-English, Dish, Lid, George III, Benjamin Smith I, James Smith, 1808, 9 x 12 In.
$1,440

Cowan's Auctions

Identifying Old Sheffield from the Nineteenth Century

Scratch your fingernail underneath the border of the silver dish. If it is old Sheffield silver, a thin sheet of silver was rolled over copper and your fingernail will catch the edge of this sheet of silver. If the silver layer has worn off, copper shows through. This is called "bleeding."

Hold the piece and huff at the engraving so your breath clouds the silver. Old Sheffield has an inset piece of solid silver for the engraving. The block of silver should be faintly outlined by your breath.

Tray, Salver, Scalloped Relief Rim, Engraved Border, George III, Richard Brown, 1781, 15 In. .	800
Tray, Square, Cooper Brothers & Sons, London, 1900s, 13 1/2 x 13 1/2 In.	715
Tray, Tea, Gadroon Rim, Leaf Handles, Gibson & Langman, London, c.1895, 28 x 19 In.	5000
Tray, Tea, Gadroon, Scrolls, Loop Handles, William Bateman, London, 1815, 34 x 20 In.	3998
Tray, Waiter, Mermaid Cartouche, Shell Border, Richard Rugg, 1754, 6 1/2 In.	522
Trophy, Military, Engraved, Gibson & Langman, London, 1800s, 18 x 11 In.	2768
Urn, Lid, Beaded Border, 2 Handles, Heraldic, London, 1782, 10 x 18 x 9 In.	4200
Waiter, Piecrust Rim, Flowers, George IV, J. & W. Barnard, London, 24 In.	5228
Wine Coaster, Gilt, Repousse Scenes, George III, Edward Farrell, 1817, 7 In. ....*illus*	1250
Wine Funnel, Bands, George Brasier, 1796, 3 1/4 x 4 3/4 In.	316
Wine Funnel, Clip, Hester Bateman, 4 1/2 In. ....*illus*	413
Wine Funnel, George IV, Fluted, Gadroon, 1823, 5 In.	402

SILVER-FRENCH

Beaker, Rocaille, Flowers, C-Scrolls, Flared Rim, Charles Joseph Fontaine, 1778, 5 In.	500
Bowl, Fluted, Leaf Rim, Marked, Tetard Freres, Early 1900s, 3 1/2 x 5 In. ....*illus*	2000
Bowl, Vermeil, Engraved, Puiforcat, Paris, c.1900, 5 3/4 In.	400
Box, Enameled, Gilt Interior, Engraved, Crown & Crescent, 1900s, 3 x 2 In. ....*illus*	438
Centerpiece, Reticulated, Chased Flowers, Trellis, C-Scroll Handles, 4-Footed, 10 x 17 In.	283
Dish, Square, Rounded Corners, Emile Puiforcat, 1857, 8 3/4 In.	480
Pitcher, Ribbons, Beading, Mermaid Handle, Auguste Louis Fizanine, c.1950, 13 In.	2500
Sauceboat, Rosewood, Rectangular, Bowed Sides, Jean Puiforcat, 1930s, 8 1/2 In.	3437
Stoup, Holy Water, Scrolled Bail Handle, Rococo Repousse, Hallmarks, 1700s, 4 x 6 In.	152
Tray, Allover Rococo, Cartouche, Marked, H. Matthews, 1898, 11 In. ....*illus*	238
Tray, Octagonal, Gustave Keller, Paris, c.1900, 23 5/8 In.	984
Vase, Leaves, Tendrils, Carved, Paint, Bone, Paris, c.1900, 5 1/4 In.	1440
Wine Cooler, Fluted, Coronet, Sword, Banded Rim, Tetard Freres, 1927, 10 In.	6000

SILVER-GERMAN

Basket, Flowers, Cobalt Blue Glass Liner, Otto Hintze, Late 1800s, 8 3/8 In.	124
Beaker, Marked, Wilhelm T. Binder, Early 1900s, 4 3/4 In.	83
Bowl, M.H. Wilkens & Sohne, Crescent & Crown Mark, Germany, c.1850, 3 1/4 x 10 1/4 In.	263
Box, Marie Antoinette & Louis XVI Portraits, Georg Roth & Co., c.1900, 7 x 4 In.	500
Cocktail Shaker, Owl, Feather Detail, Chained Stopper, Strainer, c.1975, 7 x 4 In.	10938
Tea Set, C-Scroll, Finials, Teapot, Coffeepot, Sugar, Creamer, Tray, 5 Piece	1020
Vase, Fluted, Gilt, Art Nouveau, 7 3/4 x 3 1/2 In.	450

SILVER-GREEK

Compote, Gold Finish, Textured, Handles, Lalaounis, 5 1/2 In. ....*illus*	230

SILVER-INDIAN

Group, Elephant, 2 Riders, Mahout, Enamel, Jeweled, Oval Base, Flowers, Late 1800s, 6 In.	420

SILVER-IRISH

Dish Ring, Openwork, Cherubs, Windmill, Grapes, Wakeley & Wheeler, c.1913, 3 x 7 In.	1320
Pitcher, George III, Baluster, Treen Handle, Charles Townsend, 1771, 8 1/2 In. ....*illus*	1800
Pitcher, Hinged Lid, Inset Irish Coin, Monogram, Hammered, 1800s, 6 In.	88

SILVER-ISRAELI

Vase, Trumpet, Scalloped, Beaded Trim & Border, Seashells, Hazorfim, 14 In.	484

SILVER-ITALIAN

Bowl, Fluted Sides, Oval, Box, 17 x 11 3/4 In.	4800
Bowl, Footed, Hand Hammered, Buccellati, 8 x 5 3/4 x 5 In.	688
Bowl, Oval, 2 Putti, Milan, c.1930, 12 x 21 1/2 In.	3690
Lamp, Oil, Finger, Flowers, Geometrics, Scroll Handle, Domed Cap, 5 3/8 x 3 In.	130
Table Ornament, 4 Pomegranates, Leafy Base, Milan, 1900s, 3 1/4 In.	1107
Tray, Oval, Molded, 2 Handles, Fratelli Zaramella, c.1950, 24 x 18 In.	1250
Tray, Rectangular, Marked, Petruzzi Antonio & Branca Ugo, Brescia, 1900s, 10 x 13 In.	283

SILVER-JAPANESE

Teapot, Chrysanthemum Sprays, Textured Ground, Mark, Late 1800s, 9 In. ....*illus*	615
Vase, Globular, Koi, Hammered, Wood Stand, Signed, Shobido, Japan, c.1900, 8 5/8 In.	2337

Silver-English, Flagon, Lid, Leaves, Scrolls, Deer, Putto Finial, Engraved, R. Hennell, 1848, 15 In.
$3,780

Morphy Auctions

Silver-English, Kettle, Stand, Engraved, Shaped Handle, Crichton Brothers, 13 ½ In.
$1,770

Cottone Auctions

Silver-English, Salver, Chippendale Style, Engraved, 3 Hoof Feet, W. Hutton & Sons, 1915, 14 In.
$767

Leland Little Auctions

Silver-English, Server, Dessert, Pierced Blade, Samuel Herbert & Co., London, 1750, 11 ¾ In.
$570

Cowan's Auctions

Silver-English, Sugar, Oval, Marked, Peter, Ann & William Bateman, London, 1799, 8 ½ In.
$594

Leslie Hindman Auctioneers

Silver-English, Teapot, Ebony Handle, Engraved, Marked, Robert Sibley, 1852, 6 In.
$330

Cowan's Auctions

S

Silver-English, Teapot, Engraved, Neoclassical Swags, Cartouches, George Burrows I, 5 In.
$369

Skinner, Inc.

Silver-English, Tray, George III, Ribbon & Shell Border, Monogram, 3 Hoof Feet, c.1746, 7 In.
$360

Northeast Auctions

Silver-English, Tray, Latin Inscription, Handles, T. Hannam & J. Crouch, London, c.1780, 23 In.
$4,837

Grogan & Company

Silver-English, Wine Coaster, Gilt, Repousse Scenes, George III, Edward Farrell, 1817, 7 In.
$1,250

Rago Arts and Auction Center

Silver-English, Wine Funnel, Clip, Hester Bateman, 4½ In.
$413

Pook & Pook

Silver-French, Bowl, Fluted, Leaf Rim, Marked, Tetard Freres, Early 1900s, 3½ x 5 In.
$2,000

Leslie Hindman Auctioneers

Silver-French, Box, Enameled, Gilt Interior, Engraved, Crown & Crescent, 1900s, 3 x 2 In.
$438

Rago Arts and Auction Center

Silver-French, Tray, Allover Rococo, Cartouche, Marked, H. Matthews, 1898, 11 In.
$238

Leslie Hindman Auctioneers

Silver-Greek, Compote, Gold Finish, Textured, Handles, Lalaounis, 5½ In.
$230

Richard D. Hatch & Associates

Silver-Irish, Pitcher, George III, Baluster, Treen Handle, Charles Townsend, 1771, 8½ In.
$1,800

Northeast Auctions

> **TIP**
> *To store silver, wrap it in acid-free paper, then put it in a tarnish-preventing bag.*

SILVER-KOREAN

Warming Dish, Inscribed, To Colonel Russell, 5 ½ In. 448

SILVER-MEXICAN.
Silver objects have been made in Mexico since the days of the Aztecs. These marks are for three companies still making tableware and jewelry.

ChATo CASTiLLo STERLING MEXICO	Matl STERLING MEXICO 925	SANBORN'S STERLING H MADE IN MEXICO
Jorge "Chato" Castillo 1939+	Matilde Eugenia Poulat 1934–1960	Sanborn's 1931–present

Bowl, Flower Shape, Repousse, Sanborns, Mexico, c.1950, 4 In. 60
Bowl, Pedestal, 2 Stylized Handles, Marked, 18 ½ x 6 ¾ In. 649
Box, Lid, Aztec Rose, Etched & Raised, 8-Sided, Maciel, Mexico City, c.1950, 4 x 5 In. 163
Coffeepot, Scroll Handle, Swan Spout, Baluster Finial, 10 ½ In. 590
Compote, Openwork, Twist Stem, Eagle Mark, William Spratling, c.1950, 6 In. ....*illus* 554
Cordial, Flower Band, Baluster Stem, Domed Foot, Maciel, c.1950, 4 ½ In., 6 Piece 330
Fruit Bowl, Scrolling Flower Edge, 4 Matching Feet, 3 x 11 ½ In. 354
Gravy Boat, Fluted, Shell Shape, Arched Handle, Stepped Foot, 6 ½ x 7 In. ....*illus* 130
Humidor, Conquistador, Rectangular, Wood Lined, 9 ½ x 3 ½ In. 366
Pitcher, Lobed, C-Scroll Handle, Wide Spout, Marked, 10 ½ In. ....*illus* 354
Pitcher, Water, Wide Spout, Triangular Handle, 1900s, 8 ¾ In. 441
Teapot, Fluted Sides, Bold, Leaves, Luella, Mexico, 1900s, 10 In. 660

SILVER-PERSIAN

Tray, Rectangular, Engraved, Persian Scene, 5 ⅜ x 9 ⅜ In. 63

SILVER-PERUVIAN

Platter, Oval, C-Scroll Border, Marked 925, 15 ½ In. 344
Tray, Round, Marked, Camusso, 11 ¾ In. 153

SILVER-PORTUGUESE

Ornament, Swan, Articulated Head, Wings, Glass Eye, Mid 1900s, 7 x 8 x 3 In. 594

SILVER-RUSSIAN.
Russian silver is marked with the Cyrillic, or Russian, alphabet. The numbers 84, 88, or 91 indicate the silver content. Russian silver may be higher or lower than sterling standard. Other marks indicate maker, assayer, or city of manufacture. Many pieces of silver made in Russia are decorated with enamel. These prices are based on current silver values. Faberge pieces are listed in their own category.

84 88 91		
Silver–Russian Silver content numbers	Silver–Russian 1741–1900+	Silver–Russian 1896–1908

Basket, Oval, Hinged Handle, Red & Green Enamel, Monogram, 6 x 6 x 6 In. 431
Bowl, Footed, Blue Champleve Enamel Inside, Late 1800s, 4 ⅜ In. ....*illus* 2400
Box, Lid, 2-Headed Eagle, Cupid Finial, 4 x 5 ¼ In. 600
Box, Tea, Square, Engraved, Dome Finial, Ovchinnikov, Moscow, 5 x 3 x 3 In. 1722
Cigarette Case, Enamel, Gold Wash Panels, Flowers, Filigree Borders, 4 x 3 In. 1513
Cigarette Case, Engraved, Sphinx, Portrait, Alexander III, Mikhail Karpinsky, 4 x 3 In. 242
Cigarette Case, Gilt Interior, Zolotnik, Faberge, c.1915, 3 ¾ In. 1800
Cigarette Case, Moscow State University, Gilt Interior, 4 x 3 In. 275
Cigarette Case, Niello, Gilt Interior, Cyrillic Monogram, Button Lock, 4 x 3 In. 244
Cigarette Case, Tree Bark Texture, Gilt Interior, Oval Red Cabochon, 4 ½ x 3 In. 615
Cup, Nautilus Shell, Silver Base, Chased, Cherubs Swimming With Fish, 14 In. ....*illus* 1560
Cup, Peacock, Plique-A-Jour, Knopped Stem, Gadroon Rim, Late 1800s, 5 x 4 In. ....*illus* 4688

Silver-Japanese, Teapot, Chrysanthemum Sprays, Textured Ground, Mark, Late 1800s, 9 In.
$615

Skinner, Inc.

> **TIP**
> Mix baking soda and water into a paste and use it to polish silver.

Silver-Mexican, Compote, Openwork, Twist Stem, Eagle Mark, William Spratling, c.1950, 6 In.
$554

Cowan's Auctions

Silver-Mexican, Gravy Boat, Fluted, Shell Shape, Arched Handle, Stepped Foot, 6 ½ x 7 In.
$130

Forsythes' Auctions

S

Silver-Mexican, Pitcher, Lobed, C-Scroll Handle, Wide Spout, Marked, 10½ In.
$354

Forsythes' Auctions

Silver-Russian, Bowl, Footed, Blue Champleve Enamel Inside, Late 1800s, 4⅜ In.
$2,400

Brunk Auctions

Silver-Russian, Cup, Nautilus Shell, Silver Base, Chased, Cherubs Swimming With Fish, 14 In.
$1,560

Fox Auctions

Dish, Champleve, Scalloped Petal Rim, Ball Feet, Kuzmichev, Oval, 1890, 5¾ x 4¾ In.	1063
Dish, Cut Glass, Silver Mounted, 2 Laurel Wreath Handles, Reeded Edge, 8¼ In.	1845
Figurine, Lion, Seated, Fine Detail, Resin Interior, Marble Base, 9½ In.	288
Glass Holder, Inscription, Memorial, Officers Of 4th Battalion, 1905-08, 4½ In.	397
Glass Holder, Landscape, Tea, Gold Inlay, 1800s, 3 x 2¾ In.	397
Glass Holder, Plique-A-Jour, Cylindrical, P. Ovchinnikov, c.1887, 3¼ x 5 x 3¼ In. *illus*	3750
Helmet, Parcel Gilt, Russian Officer, Kokoshnik Mark, Faberge Style, c.1915, 3 In.	492
Kovsh, Oval, Gadroon Rim, Blue, Red, Green, Pink, White & Yellow, 2⅝ x 5¾ In. *illus*	6250
Kovsh, Scalloped Handle, Amethyst, Bird, Gadroon Border, Konig, Oval, 3 x 7⅜ x 4 In.	7500
Ladle, Imperial, Gilt, Carved, Morozov, 1800s, 13 In.	580
Lamp, Lampada, Cylindrical, Floral Scrolled Crest Handles, I. Saltykov, c.1900, 7 In.	3600
Russian Officer's Helmet, Eagle, Kokoshnik Mark, J. Rappoport, c.1915, 3¼ In., Miniature	431
Spoon, Enamel, Twist Handle, 6¼ In.	307
Spoon, Plique-A-Jour, Inscription, Late 1800s, 7½ In.	1063
Vodka Cup, Cloisonne, Enamel, Birds & Scrolls, Moscow, 2 In. *illus*	5228

SILVER-SCOTTISH

Jug, Gilt, Hardstone Accents, Lion Head Spout, Hamilton Crichton & Co., 5⅝ In.	2460
Mug, Baluster Shape, Molded Foot, S-Scroll Handle, 1737, 4 In.	750
Pitcher, Water, Helmet Form, Lion's Head, Paw Feet, Hamilton, Edinburgh, 1883, 10 In.	1599
Salt Cellar, 3-Footed, Shell Terminals, Hallmark Underneath, c.1846, 3⅜ x 1¾ In.	71

SILVER-STERLING. Sterling silver is made with 925 parts silver out of 1,000 parts of metal. The word *sterling* is a quality guarantee used in the United States after about 1860. The word was used much earlier in England and Ireland. Pieces listed here are not identified by country. These prices are based on current silver values. Other pieces of sterling quality silver are listed under Silver-American, Silver-English, etc.

Basket, Reticulated, Footed, Swing Arm, Top Handle, 10½ x 7¾ x 10 In.	338
Bowl, Flowers, Shells, 3 Chinese Men, William Mann, c.1851, 3 x 4 In.	495
Bowl, Inverse Bell Shape, Flared Rim, Circular Foot, 1900s, 9 In.	480
Bowl, Punch, Relief Grape Leaf, Round Foot, Late 1800s, 20 Pt., 6⅞ x 15 In. *illus*	7995
Bowl, Scalloped Rim, Relief Shell, Floral, Leaf, Bamberger & Gaines, 2½ x 11 In.	215
Box, Lid, Repousse, Marked RC, Early 1900s, 6¾ x 8¾ x 6½ In.	2000
Box, Rectangular, Chased, Repousse Flowers, 1⅝ x 6½ x 3¾ In.	250
Bread Tray, Reticulated Edge, Floral Scroll, 6¾ x 12 x 2 In.	212
Cake Basket, Navette Shape, Swing Handle, Conforming Foot, 10½ x 14 x 10 In. *illus*	325
Cake Basket, Reticulated Handle, Bowl & Foot, Mark, c.1915	420
Candelabra are listed in the Candelabrum category.	
Candlesticks are listed in their own category.	
Card Case, Hinged Lid, Early Auto, Engraved, c.1910, 4½ x 2½ In.	452
Centerpiece, Removable Lid, Swan Handles, Kneeling Women, Footed, Late 1900s, 23 x 23 In. *illus*	8610
Charger, Chased & Repousse, Flowers, Footed, Scalloped Rim	438
Charger, Chased & Repousse, Grape Leaves & Clusters, 17⅝ In.	594
Cigarette Case, Art Deco, Red & Black Inlay, Vermeil Interior	313
Dish, 3 Handles, Footed, Walker & Hall, Marked, 1938, 4 In.	360
Dresser Box, Engraved, Enameled Blue, Champleve Lid, 1⅝ x 6 In.	288
Dresser Box, Malachite, Aztec Style Temple, Heavy Gauge, Wood Lined, 3 x 5 In. *illus*	345
Flask, Napier, Art Deco, Rectangle, Collapsible Jigger Lid, 8¼ x 5 x 1¼ In.	472
Ice Bucket, Hammer Finish, Strapwork Motifs, Monogram, 1900s, 10¾ In.	923
Kettle, Hot Water, Stand, Burner, Top Handle, Early 1900s, 12 x 9 x 5 In.	995
Kettle, Hot Water, Stand, Engrave Armorial, Burner, 14½ In.	738
Ladle, Applied Cast Oyster Shell On Handle, Cleveland, c.1860, 13 In.	563
Napkin Rings are listed in their own category.	
Plate, Fluted Sides, Engraved Crest, Heart & Ribbon Banner, 10½ In.	236
Platter, Flanking Handles, Hallmarks To Underside, Edward J. Dwyer, Mid 1900s, 17 x 26 In.	900
Punch Ladle, Floral Engraved Handle, Bright Cut Bowl, Dr. H. Leahman, c.1850, 12 In.	118
Rattle, Coral, Child, Engraved Monogram, Marked, GU, c.1850, 4½ In. *illus*	677
Serving Spoon, Cast Leaf, Berry Terminus, Bowl Shape, c.1870, 9 In.	112
Spoon, Souvenir, see Souvenir category.	
Sugar Spoon, Spider In Web, Moon, Engraved, 6⅜ In.	98

Silver-Russian, Cup, Peacock, Plique-A-Jour, Knopped Stem, Gadrooned Rim, Late 1800s, 5 x 4 In.
$4,688

Brunk Auctions

Silver-Russian, Glass Holder, Plique-A-Jour, Cylindrical, P. Ovchinnikov, c.1887, 3 1/4 x 5 x 3 1/4 In.
$3,750

Brunk Auctions

Silver-Russian, Kovsh, Oval, Gadroon Rim, Blue, Red, Green, Pink, White & Yellow, 2 5/8 x 5 3/4 In.
$6,250

Brunk Auctions

Silver-Russian, Vodka Cup, Cloisonne, Enamel, Bird & Scrolls, Moscow, 2 In.
$5,228

Skinner, Inc.

Silver-Sterling, Bowl, Punch, Relief Grape Leaf, Round Foot, Late 1800s, 20 Pt., 6 7/8 x 15 In.
$7,995

Crescent City Auction Gallery

Silver-Sterling, Cake Basket, Navette Shape, Swing Handle, Conforming Foot, 10 1/2 x 14 x 10 In.
$325

Soulis Auctions

TIP
Remove egg stains from silver by rubbing the piece with salt, then washing it in dishwashing liquid. Rinse well or the salt will add stains.

Silver-Sterling, Centerpiece, Removable Lid, Swan Handles, Kneeling Women, Footed, Late 1900s, 23 x 23 In.
$8,610

Skinner, Inc.

TIP
Don't clean the impressed hallmarks or names on the bottom of a piece of silver. You may eventually rub them off.

Silver-Sterling, Dresser Box, Malachite, Aztec Style Temple, Heavy Gauge, Wood Lined, 3 x 5 In.
$345

Richard D. Hatch & Associates

Silver-Sterling, Rattle, Coral, Child, Engraved Monogram, Marked, GU, c.1850, 4 1/2 In.
$677

Skinner, Inc.

S

Silver-Sterling, Tray, Tea, Oval, Incised Rococo & Lattice Cartouches, Floral Swags, 1900s, 30 x 19¾ In.
$3,750

New Orleans Auction Galleries

Silver-Sterling, Tureen, Vegetable, Lid, Monogram, Floral Swags, Laurel Leaves, Early 1900s, 10½ In.
$615

Skinner, Inc.

Sinclaire, Tray, Assyrian, Cut Glass, Engraved Floral Border, Marked, Round, 10⅛ In.
$1,140

Brunk Auctions

Tray, Rocaille Scrolls, Floral Sprays, 2 Handles, Early 1900s, 24¾ In.	923
Tray, Round, Monogram, Art Deco, c.1920, 11 x 11 In.	224
Tray, Tea, Oval, Incised Rococo & Lattice Cartouches, Floral Swags, 1900s, 30 x 19¾ In....*illus*	3750
Tureen, Vegetable, Lid, Monogram, Floral Swags, Laurel Leaves, Early 1900s, 10½ In. .....*illus*	615
Vase, Trumpet Shape, Engraved, Pitch Loaded, Scalloped Rim, 20 In.	660
Vase, Trumpet, Etched Floral Scroll, Monogram, 14 In.	130

SILVER-THAI

Bowl, Presentation, Mythological Beings, Masks, Anthropomorphic Plants, 1900s, 5 x 9 In.	192

SILVER-TURKISH

Vase, Repousse, Shells, Lapis Cabochon, Coin, 7½ In., Pair	300

SINCLAIRE cut glass was made by H.P. Sinclaire and Company of Corning, New York, between 1904 and 1929. He cut glass made at other factories until 1920. Pieces were made of clear glass as well as amber, blue, green, or ruby glass. Only a small percentage of Sinclaire glass is marked with the *S* in a wreath.

Bowl, Snowflake & Holly, Cut Glass, Marked, 3¼ x 10¼ In.	1080
Plate, Cut Glass, Flowers, Marked, 3 Leaves Border, Round, 10 In.	125
Tray, Assyrian, Cut Glass, Engraved Floral Border, Marked, Round, 10⅛ In. ....*illus*	1140
Vase, Snowflake & Holly, Cut Glass, Marked, 13 In.	3900

SLAG GLASS resembles a marble cake. It can be streaked with different colors. There were many types made from about 1880. Caramel slag is the incorrect name for chocolate glass made by Imperial Glass. Pink slag was an American product made by Harry Bastow and Thomas E.A. Dugan at Indiana, Pennsylvania, about 1900. Purple and blue slag were made in American and English factories in the 1880s. Red slag is a very late Victorian and twentieth-century glass. Other colors are known but are of less importance to the collector. New versions of chocolate glass and colored slag glass have been made.

Caramel Slag is listed in the Imperial Glass category.

Lamp, Hanging, 8 Panels, White Metal Frame, Early 1900s, 10 x 20 In.	100
Lamp, Urn Shape Base, Ram Head Handles, Finial, 22 x 17 In. ....*illus*	281

SLEEPY EYE collectors look for anything bearing the image of the nineteenth-century Indian chief with the drooping eyelid. The Sleepy Eye Milling Co., Sleepy Eye, Minnesota, used his portrait in advertising from 1883 to 1921. It offered many premiums, including stoneware and pottery steins, crocks, bowls, mugs, pitchers, and many advertising items, all decorated with the famous profile of the Indian. The popular pottery was made by Weir Pottery Co. from c.1899 to 1905. Weir merged with six other potteries and became Western Stoneware in 1906. Western Stoneware Co. made blue and white Sleepy Eye from 1906 until 1937, long after the flour mill went out of business in 1921. Reproductions of the pitchers are being made today. The original pitchers came in only five sizes: 4 inches, 5¼ inches, 6½ inches, 8 inches, and 9 inches. The Sleepy Eye image was also used by companies unrelated to the flour mill.

Pitcher, Blue, Cream, Indian, Teepees, Trees, 8 In.	220
Vase, Indian, Profile, Gray, Blue Cylindrical, 8½ x 4 In.	72

SLOT MACHINES *are included in the Coin-Operated Machine category.*

SMITH BROTHERS glass was made from 1874 to 1899. Alfred and Harry Smith had worked for the Mt. Washington Glass Company in New Bedford, Massachusetts, for seven years before going into their own shop. They made many pieces with enamel decoration.

Biscuit Jar, Opaque, White Glass, Squat, Enamel Flowers, c.1885, 4½ In.	228
Biscuit Jar, Roses, Leaves, Ribbed, Silver Plate Handle, 1880s, 9 In.	300
Bowl, Melon Shape, Cream, Pink Flowers, Beaded Rim, Libby Hallmark, 1918, 3 x 2 In.	38
Bowl, Ribbed, Melon, Pansies, Violet, Pink, Yellow, 5½ x 2¾ In.	140
Vase, Flask Shape, Blue Wisteria, Green & Brown Leaves, c.1890, 6¾ In.	395
Vase, Pink Glass, Stork, Silver Plate Base, Victorian, Simpson Hall & Miller, 8 In.	256

S

SNOW BABIES, made from bisque and spattered with glitter sand, were first manufactured in 1864 by Hertwig and Company of Thuringia. Other German and Japanese companies copied the Hertwig designs. Originally, Snow Babies were made of candy and used as Christmas decorations. There are also Snow Babies tablewares made by Royal Bayreuth. Copies of the small Snow Babies figurines are being made today, and a line called "Snowbabies" was introduced by Department 56 in 1987. Don't confuse these with the original Snow Babies.

Figurine, Babies On Sled, Pulled By Dog, 3 1/2 x 2 1/4 In.	135
Figurine, Baby Sitting On Red Airplane, 1 3/4 x 2 1/4 In.	145
Figurine, Child, Holding Skis, Dog Biting Leg, 2 In.	125
Figurine, Child, Seated, Holding Snowball, 2 1/4 x 2 In.	275
Figurine, Child, Seated, Raised Arms, Wings, 1 3/4 In.	500
Figurine, Children On Brick Slope, Head First, c.1910, 2 x 3 In.	145
Figurine, Santa Claus, Airplane, Hertwig & Co., c.1900, 2 x 2 In.	115

SNUFF BOTTLES *are listed in the Bottle category.*

SNUFFBOXES held snuff. Taking snuff was popular long before cigarettes became available. The gentleman or lady would take a small pinch of the ground tobacco or snuff in the fingers, then sniff it and sneeze. Snuffboxes were made of many materials, including gold, silver, enameled metal, and wood. Most snuffboxes date from the late eighteenth or early nineteenth centuries.

Bone, Carved, Valentine, Lid, Flaming Hearts, 1800s, 4 x 2 In.	420
Hawk, Perched, Carved, Engraved Details, Jet Eyes, c.1820, 4 x 1 3/8 x 1 1/2 In.	384
Lacquer, Black, Portrait, James Lawrence Esq., Transfer Decoration, Round, 1800s, 3 1/2 In.	397
Papier-Mache, Round, Engraved, Woman, Blue Scarf, Puffy Sleeves, c.1805, 3 In.	130
Pressed Wood, Georgian, 3 Horses & Jockeys, Racing, c.1900	375
Silver, Hinged Lid, Stepped Sides, Thomas Street, London, c.1810, 3 3/4 In. ....*illus*	288
Silver, Horn Shape, Black, Removable Lid, 3 1/2 x 3 x 1 1/2 In.	84
Silver, Lid, Engraved Scene Of Woman, Holding Bird, France, Late 1800s, 3 1/4 In.	308
Wood, Lid, Engraved Bone & Horn, Oval, Zigzag Lines, Borders, London, 1851, 2 7/8 In......*illus*	1680
Wood, Man, Standing, Clerical Hat, Carved, 1800s, 4 3/4 In. ......*illus*	200

SOAPSTONE is a mineral that was used for foot warmers or griddles because of its heat-retaining properties. Soapstone was carved into figurines and bowls in many countries in the nineteenth and twentieth centuries. Most of the soapstone seen today is from Asia. It is still being carved in the old styles.

Boulder, Yellow, Carved, Luohan Figures, Mountainous Scene, 3 3/4 In.	1000
Carving, Mountain, Dragon Design, Mottled Gray, Wood Stand, Sienna Mark, 7 1/8 In.	154
Carving, Shou Lao, Standing, Holding Peach & Staff, Carved, Wood, Openwork Stand, 14 In.	923
Group, Rams, Mountain Landscape, Carved, Glazed, Chinese, 12 In. ......*illus*	221
Sculpture, Devilfish, Cocobolo Base, Alan Hamwi, 26 1/2 x 9 x 13 In.	1875
Seal, Carved, Square, Dragon, Mottled Olive Green Stone, Wood Stand, Chinese, 7 In.	123
Seal, Yellow, Carved, Landscape Scene, Mountain, Zhong Mu, Rectangular, 4 1/4 In.	250
Seal, Yellow, Sloping Top, Carved, Wing Bat, 2 Character Mark, Rectangular, 1 3/4 In.	250

SOUVENIRS of a trip—what could be more fun? Our ancestors enjoyed the same thing and souvenirs were made for almost every location. Most of the souvenir pottery and porcelain pieces of the nineteenth century were made in England or Germany, even if the picture showed a North American scene. In the early twentieth century, the souvenir china business seems to have been dominated by the manufacturers in Japan, Taiwan, Hong Kong, England, and the United States. Souvenir china was also made in other countries after the 1960s. Another popular souvenir item is the souvenir spoon, made of sterling or silver plate. These are usually made in the country pictured on the spoon. Related pieces may be found in the Coronation, Olympics, and World's Fair categories.

Ashtray, Ship's Smokestack, SS France, Marked, France, c.1960s, 7 In.	438
Ax, Lodge, Red Handle, Cherries On Blade, Mary A. Haines, Feb. 22nd, 1835, 9 3/4 In.	177

Slag Glass, Lamp, Urn Shape Base, Ram Head Handles, Finial, 22 x 17 In.
$281

Susanin's Auctioneers & Appraisers

Snuffbox, Silver, Hinged Lid, Stepped Sides, Thomas Street, London, c.1810, 3 3/4 In.
$288

Willis Henry Auctions

Snuffbox, Wood, Lid, Engraved Bone & Horn, Oval, Zigzag Lines, Borders, London, 1851, 2 7/8 In.
$1,680

Northeast Auctions

S

TIP
Save your travel souvenirs: the gift shop snowdomes, glasses, key chains, and postcards. They can form the start of a collection.

Snuffbox, Wood, Man, Standing, Clerical Hat, Carved, 1800s, 4¾ In.
$200

Leslie Hindman Auctioneers

Soapstone, Group, Rams, Mountain Landscape, Carved, Glazed, Chinese, 12 In.
$221

Skinner, Inc.

Spatter Glass, Fairy Lamp, Petal Emboss, Opal Flakes, 6 Toes, Pedestal Base, c.1900s, 6 x 4 In.
$717

Jeffrey S. Evans & Associates

Spatter Glass, Lamp, Bubbly Vaseline, Umbrella Shape Shade, c.1900, 7⅜ x 3¾ x 3 In.
$2,032

Jeffrey S. Evans & Associates

Spatterware, Bowl, Shallow, Blue & Purple Bull's-Eye, White Ground, 1800s, 10½ In.
$388

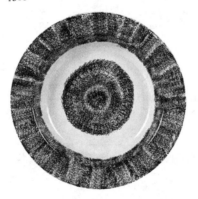

Pook & Pook

Spatterware, Cup & Saucer, Rainbow, 3 Colors, Bands, Saucer 6 In.
$413

Hess Auction Group

Spatterware, Pitcher, Water, Rainbow, 5 Colors, Bands, Double C-Scroll Handle, 11½ In.
$6,490

Hess Auction Group

Spatterware, Plate, Blue Border, Schoolhouse, Tree, White Ground, 1800s, 8½ In.
$1,625

Pook & Pook

Cup, Tennessee Map, Frosted Glass, Marked, Hazel Atlas, 5 x 2¾ In.	76
Pin, New Year Celebration, Woman, Above City, Blowing Horn, Pinback, 1913, 1½ In.	22
Plate, Old Tucson, Arizona, Porcelain, Village Scene, 10 In.	68
Spoon, Silver, Nation's Capitol, Washington, DC, 1861, 5¾ In.	85
Tablecloth, Linen, Europe, Coat Of Arms, 33 Countries, 49 x 60 In.	40

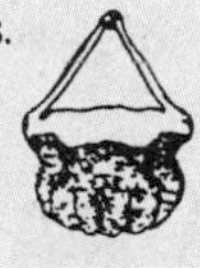

SPANGLE GLASS is multicolored glass made from odds and ends of colored glass rods. It includes metallic flakes of mica covered with gold, silver, nickel, or copper. Spangle glass is usually cased with a thin layer of clear glass over the multicolored layer. Similar glass is listed in the Vasa Murrhina category.

Vase, Rainbow, Flowers, White Interior, c.1800, 5½ In.	94

SPATTER GLASS is a multicolored glass made from many small pieces of different colored glass. It is sometimes called End-of-Day glass. It is still being made.

Fairy Lamp, Petal Emboss, Opal Flakes, 6 Toes, Pedestal Base, c.1900s, 6 x 4 In.	*illus*	717
Lamp, Bubbly Vaseline, Umbrella Shape Shade, c.1900, 7⅜ x 3¾ x 3 In.	*illus*	2032
Lamp, Multicolor, Ball, Raised On 5 Toes, c.1900, 9¾ x 4 x 3⅜ In.		1315
Lamp, Pink Swirls, Barrel, 5 Raised Toes, Crimped Rim, c.1900, 9¾ x 4 x 3⅜ In.		269
Lamp, Ribbed Swirl, Multicolor, Ball Font, 5 Raised Toes, c.1900, 8 x 4 x 3⅞ In.		1793
Lamp, Swirled Beads, Opal & Ruby Flakes, c.1900s, 8 x 3¾ x 2⅞ In.		143

SPATTERWARE and spongeware are terms that have changed in meaning in recent years, causing much confusion for collectors. It is a type of ceramic. Some say that *spatterware* is the term used by Americans, *sponged ware* or *spongeware* by the English. The earliest pieces were made in the late eighteenth century, but most of the spatterware found today was made from about 1800 to 1850. Early spatterware was made in the Staffordshire district of England for sale in America. Collectors also use the word *spatterware* to refer to kitchen crockery with added spatter made in America during the late nineteenth and early twentieth centuries. Spongeware is very similar to spatterware in appearance. Designs were applied to ceramics by daubing the color on with a sponge or cloth. Many collectors do not differentiate between spongeware and spatterware and use the names interchangeably. Modern pottery is being made to resemble old spatterware and spongeware, but careful examination will show it is new.

Bowl, Shallow, Blue & Purple Bull's-Eye, White Ground, 1800s, 10½ In.	*illus*	388
Creamer, Rainbow, Black, Brown, Curved Handle, 4 In.		767
Cup & Saucer, Rainbow, 3 Colors, Bands, Saucer 6 In.	*illus*	413
Cup & Saucer, Rainbow, Black & Brown, 5⅞ In.		212
Pitcher, Milk, Rainbow, 5 Colors, Alternating Bands, 7½ In.		5310
Pitcher, Milk, Rainbow, Green, Yellow, Black, Blue, Red, Scalloped Top, Scroll Handle, 8½ In.		5900
Pitcher, Red Flower, Green Leaves, Brown & Black, 2-Sided, 4 In.		236
Pitcher, Red, Blue, Green Bands, Cream, Handle, Chinese, 3¾ In.		325
Pitcher, Water, Rainbow, 5 Colors, Bands, Double C-Scroll Handle, 11½ In.	*illus*	6490
Plate, Blue Border, Schoolhouse, Tree, White Ground, 1800s, 8½ In.	*illus*	1625
Plate, Mourning Tulip, Red, Green, Yellow, Pennsylvania, 8½ In.		406
Plate, Rabbits Playing Tennis, Stick Spatter, Smith Patterson, Boston, 12 In.	*illus*	608
Plate, Rainbow, Red, Green, 7½ In.	*illus*	325
Plate, Yellow Tulip, Blue, Green, Yellow, Red, White Background, 8 In.		1625
Platter, Rainbow, Green, Blue, Oval, 4⅜ In.		266

SPELTER is a synonym for a zinc alloy. Figurines, candlesticks, and other pieces were made of spelter and given a bronze or painted finish. The metal has been used since about the 1860s to make statues, tablewares, and lamps that resemble bronze. Spelter is soft and breaks easily. To test for spelter, scratch the base of the piece. Bronze is solid; spelter will show a silvery scratch.

Bust, Girl, Bonnet, Necklace, Stand, 1800s, 14 x 8 In.		369
Clock, Gilt, Woman, Green Marble, F. Mauthe, c.1890, 14 x 11 x 7 In.	*illus*	124
Figure, Cupid, Black, Gilt Torch, Sash & Robe, Rococo Style Footed Base, 25 x 7½ In.		192

Spatterware, Plate, Rabbits Playing Tennis, Stick Spatter, Smith Patterson, Boston, 12 In.
$608

Morphy Auctions

Spatterware, Plate, Rainbow, Red, Green, 7½ In.
$325

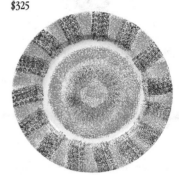

Hess Auction Group

TIP
Clean a clock face as seldom as possible. The brass trim may be coated with colored lacquer, and brass polish will remove the color.

Spelter, Clock, Gilt, Woman, Green Marble, F. Mauthe, c.1890, 14 x 11 x 7 In.
$124

Soulis Auctions

Spelter, Lamp, 3-Light, Scantily Clad Woman, Holding Fan, Wood Base, Victorian, 43 x 22 In.
$509

Soulis Auctions

Spelter, Lamp, Newel Post, Cherub, Marble Base, Frosted Glass Shade, 1900s, 31 In.
$154

Cowan's Auctions

Spinning Wheel, Mixed Wood, 10-Spoke Wheel, Turnings, Splayed Legs, 1800s
$63

Pook & Pook

Figure, Hallali, Bronze Patina, Square Base, Eugene Marioton, Early 1900s, 18 x 10 In.		1125
Figure, Peasant Woman, Standing, Pedestal Base, 22 ½ In.		113
Lamp, 3-Light, Scantily Clad Woman, Holding Fan, Wood Base, Victorian, 43 x 22 In. *illus*		509
Lamp, Cherub, Green Marble Base, Plaque, Enfant Au Lezard, H. Moreau, 1920, 13 x 4 In.		295
Lamp, Newel Post, Cherub, Marble Base, Frosted Glass Shade, 1900s, 31 In. *illus*		154
Newel Post, Cherub, Raised Arm, Silver, Round Base, 22 In.		92
Stringholder, Cat, Hole On Side Of Mouth For String, c.1910, 3 In.		158

SPINNING WHEELS in the corner have been symbols of earlier times for the past 150 years. Although spinning wheels date back to medieval days, the ones found today are rarely more than 150 years old. Because the style of the spinning wheel changed very little, it is often impossible to place an exact date on a wheel. There are different types for spinning flax or wool.

Mixed Wood, 10-Spoke Wheel, Turnings, Splayed Legs, 1800s *illus*		63
Mixed Wood, Turned Legs & Stretchers, Castle, Pennsylvania, 1800s, 55 In. *illus*		590

SPODE pottery, porcelain, and bone china were made by the Stoke-on-Trent factory of England founded by Josiah Spode about 1770. The firm became Copeland and Garrett from 1833 to 1847, then W.T. Copeland or W.T. Copeland and Sons until 1976. It then became Royal Worcester Spode Ltd. The company was bought by the Portmeirion Group in 2009. The word *Spode* appears on many pieces made by the factories. Most collectors include all the wares under the more familiar name of Spode. Porcelains are listed in this book by the name that appears on the piece. Related pieces may be listed under Copeland, Copeland Spode, and Royal Worcester.

SPODE

Spode
c.1770–1790

COPELAND & GARRETT
LATE SPODE

Copeland & Garrett
c.1833–1847

ROYAL WORCESTER SPODE

Royal Worcester Spode Ltd.
1976–present

Cake Plate, Dome Lid, Blue & White, England, 7 ½ In.	245
Cup & Saucer, Demitasse, Cabbage Rose Gold Leaf, Pink, Fluted, c.1885, 11 ½ In.	76
Dish, Entree, Lid, Turquoise, Flowers, Gold Trim, Putti, Scrollwork, 11 In., Pair	562
Footbath, Figures In Landscape, Blue Transfer, 2 Handles, 1800s, 19 x 12 In. *illus*	1829
Tureen, Lid, Imari Pattern, Blue, Brown, White, Gold Trim, 10 x 15 In.	218

SPORTS equipment, sporting goods, brochures, and related items are listed here. Items are listed by sport. Other categories of interest are Bicycle, Card, Fishing, Sword, Toy, and Trap.

Baseball, Ball, Autographed, Babe Ruth, Sweet Spot, Official Reach American League *illus*	21013
Baseball, Ball, Autographed, Branch Rickey, 1953-65	5520
Baseball, Ball, Autographed, Cincinnati Reds, 1940 World Series, Spalding *illus*	660
Baseball, Bat, Autographed, Gabby Hartnett, Game Used, 1939-41, 35 In.	7200
Baseball, Bat, Autographed, Mike Schmidt, MVP, World Champion, Game Used, 1980, 35 ½ In.	4560
Baseball, Bat, Award, National League Batting Champion, Silver, Tony Gwynn, 1988, 34 In.	5040
Baseball, Bat, Barry Bonds, Game Used, 1988, 33 ½ In.	1680
Baseball, Bat, Coach's, Dark Brown, Marked, Yogi Berra, Louisville Slugger, c.1973 *illus*	295
Baseball, Bat, Ernie Lombardi, Game Used, 1942-46	6600
Baseball, Bat, Reggie Jackson, Game Used, 1972, 35 In.	1560
Baseball, Doll, Jackie Robinson, Composition, Dodgers Uniform, 1950, 13 In. *illus*	1093
Baseball, Fan, Cap Anson, Canoe Chewing Tobacco, 1880s, 7 ½ In. *illus*	4080
Baseball, Figurine, Babe Ruth, Leaning On Bat, Composite, Carnival, 1920s, 14 x 6 In. *illus*	320
Baseball, Glove, Batting, Deion Sanders, Black & Red, Nike Swoosh, Game Used, 1997 *illus*	216
Baseball, Glove, Batting, Kirby Puckett, No. 34, Minnesota, 1980s, Large, Pair	216
Baseball, Glove, Fielder's, 18 Autographs, Mantle, Maris, Mays, Berra, Early 1980s	900
Baseball, Glove, Fielder's, Autographed, Fergie Jenkins, Rawlings Pro H-P, Leather, 1978	2880
Baseball, Jacket, Harvey Kuenn, Detroit Tigers, Game Used, 1955-59, 42 In. *illus*	2040
Baseball, Jersey, Jim Catfish Hunter, No. 27, Oakland A's, Game Used, 1974 *illus*	6600

Baseball, Mini Bat, All-American Girls Professional League, Rockford Peaches, 1945, 11 In. ...	153
Baseball, Pants, Bill Dickey, N.Y. Yankees, Game Used, 1939....................	2280
Baseball, Pants, Roy Sievers, Road Gray, Washington Senators, 1959....................	240
Baseball, Pennant, Chief Wahoo, Cleveland Indians, American League Champions, 1948, Frame.... *illus*	177
Baseball, Photograph, Babe Ruth & Lou Gehrig, Barnstorming, Autographed, 1927-28, 10 x 7 In..	2040
Baseball, Photograph, Babe Ruth, Spring Training, Autographed, 1930, 5 x 3 ½ In..........	2760
Baseball, Photograph, Negro League, Detroit Stars & Indianapolis ABCs, 1923, 8 x 37 In..........	1711
Baseball, Scoreboard Sign, Duke Beer, Cleveland Indians, Chief Wahoo, Tin, 26 x 14 In...*illus*	212
Baseball, Statue, Chief Wahoo, Gold Tooth, Cleveland Indians, Pottery, 8 ½ In. ....*illus*	142
Baseball, Stickpin, Mitt, Forbes Field, Pittsburgh Pirates, Opening Day, 1909	2040
Baseball, Trophy, Champions, Chrysler Corporation, 2 Eagles, 1936, 19 x 7 In.	1920
Baseball, Trophy, Pat Donahue, World Series Championship, Silver Plate, 1910, 8 x 6 In. *illus*	7200
Baseball, Wristwatch, Gold, Quartz Movement, Oakland A's, A.L. Championship, 1988	408
Basketball, Ball, Autographed, Milwaukee Bucks Team, Spalding, NBA Game, 1990s.......*illus*	399
Basketball, Jersey, Mark Jackson, No. 13, Indiana Pacers, Game Used, 1995-96	1560
Basketball, Shoes, Autographed, Julius Erving, Converse, Leather, Game Used, 1980-83 ..*illus*	3120
Basketball, Shoes, Autographed, Michael Jordan, Nike, Game Used, c.1995, Size 13 ½......*illus*	7800
Basketball, Shoes, Autographed, Moses Malone, Nike Air Flight, Game Used, c.1988, Size 14...	264
Basketball, Shorts, Kentucky Colonels, Game Used, 1967-70, 38 In.	216
Billiard, Cue Rack, Holds 12 Cues, Mahogany, Locks, Brunswick Balke Collander, 47 x 37 In..	311
Billiard, Scorekeeper, Rosewood, Brass, Brass Slider, Elson & Hopkins, c.1880, 13 x 37 In.	283
Boxing, Belt, USBA Light Heavyweight Champion, James Lights Out Toney, 1995......................	9000
Boxing, Gloves, Autographed, James Lights Out Toney, Fight Worn, 1996, Pair	264
Boxing, Gloves, Autographed, Muhammad Ali, Silver Ink, Everlast, Box, c.1970, Pair........*illus*	900
Boxing, Jacket, James Toney, World Champion, Lights Out, Leather, 1990s, Size XL..........*illus*	204
Boxing, Photograph, Muhammad Ali, Autographed, Thrilla In Manila, Frame, 1998, 25 x 21 In.	2280
Boxing, Photograph, Sugar Ray Robinson, Autographed, 1940s, 10 x 8 In..............................	444
Boxing, Robe, James Toney, Lights Out, Fight Used, Montell Griffin Bout, 1995......................	660
Boxing, Robe, James Toney, Lights Out, Shiny Green, Gold Trim, Embroidered, Fight Used, 1990s	240
Boxing, Robe, James Toney, Losing Is Not An Option, 1995...............................*illus*	444
Boxing, Shoes, Autographed, Ali, Foreman, Spinks, Patterson, Everlast, 1970s, Size 10 ½.........	660
Boxing, Trunks, Autographed, Riddick Bowe, Blue Satin, Fight & Training Used, 1990s	264
Boxing, Trunks, James Toney, Black, Fringe, Fight Used, Iran Barkley Bout, 1993, Large	1800
Football, Ball, Autographed, 1961 Kodak All America Team, Ernie Davis..............................	4800
Football, Ball, Autographed, Green Bay Packers Team, Leather, 1963	1680
Football, Ball, Autographed, Green Bay Packers Team, World Champions, Spalding, 1962...*illus*	660
Football, Ball, Autographed, Notre Dame Team, National Championship, Game Used, 1927....	1560
Football, Cape, New York Giants, No. 31, Bill Winter, Blue Satin, Game Used, 1961-64..............	660
Football, Helmet, Atlanta Falcons, 12-Point Suspension Padding, Game Used, 1969	2880
Football, Helmet, Autographed, Reggie White, Philadelphia Eagles, 1990s............................	1920
Football, Helmet, Autographed, Tom Nowatzke, Baltimore Colts, Super Bowl V, Game Used, 1971 ..	4320
Football, Helmet, Autographed, Tony Canadeo, Green Bay Packers, Arnie Herber, 1930s	4080
Football, Helmet, Carolina Panthers, Silver, Black Panther, Full Size	94
Football, Helmet, Chicago Bears, Black, Game Used, Unidentified Player, 1971	1560
Football, Helmet, George Atkinson, Oakland Raiders, Game Used, Early 1970s.................*illus*	5040
Football, Jersey, Joe Namath, No. 12, Los Angeles Rams, Game Used, 1977 ....*illus*	9000
Football, Nodder, Cleveland Browns, Standing, Red Helmet, Round Base	118
Football, Nodder, Cleveland Indians, Boy, Ball, Mitt, Plastic, Box, Goodman Concessions	71
Football, Nose Mask, Rubber Shield, Cloth Strap, Bite Plate, Morrills Patent......................*illus*	480
Football, Pennant, Cleveland Browns, Mean Elf, Orange, Matted, Frame	153
Football, Pennant, Cleveland Indians, Chief Wahoo, Green, Tassels, Matted, Frame	118
Football, Pennant, Notre Dame, Blue & Gold, Shamrock With Player Passing Ball....................	106
Football, Program, Heisman Trophy, Football Player, Autographed, Nile Kinnick, 1939	6600
Football, Shoes, Autographed, Brett Favre, Green Bay Packers, Practice Used, c.1998, 14 In.....	1080
Football, Trophy, Lombardi, Super Bowl XX, Chicago Bears, Team Staff, 1985, 16 In..............	5760
Golf, Bag, Autographed, U.S. Presidents Cup Team, Logo, American Flag, 1996.................*illus*	312
Golf, Shoes, Ben Hogan, White Bucks, Match Used, c.1950, Pair........................*illus*	1200
Golf, Tray, Award, Boca Raton Pro-Amateur, Sam Snead, Unicorn, 1956, 18 x 13 In.................	240
Hunting, Game Rack, Wrought Iron, 4 Arms, Hooks, 1800s, 15 x 11 In................................	188
Hunting, Rack, Game, Iron, 4 Arms, Hooks For Hanging Game, Rope Twist, 1800s, 15 x 11 In..	30

Spinning Wheel, Mixed Wood, Turned Legs & Stretchers, Castle, Pennsylvania, 1800s, 55 In.
$590

Hess Auction Group

Spode, Footbath, Figures In Landscape, Blue Transfer, 2 Handles, 1800s, 19 x 12 In.
$1,829

Leland Little Auctions

Sports, Baseball, Ball, Autographed, Babe Ruth, Sweet Spot, Official Reach American League
$21,013

RR Auction

S

Sports, Baseball, Ball, Autographed, Cincinnati Reds, 1940 World Series, Spalding
$660

Cowan's Auctions

Sports, Baseball, Bat, Coach's, Dark Brown, Marked, Yogi Berra, Louisville Slugger, c.1973
$295

Milestone Auctions

Sports, Baseball, Doll, Jackie Robinson, Composition, Dodgers Uniform, 1950, 13 In.
$1,093

Theriault's

Sports, Baseball, Fan, Cap Anson, Canoe Chewing Tobacco, 1880s, 7 ½ In.
$4,080

Heritage Auctions

Sports, Baseball, Figurine, Babe Ruth, Leaning On Bat, Composite, Carnival, 1920s, 14 x 6 In.
$320

RR Auction

Sports, Baseball, Glove, Batting, Deion Sanders, Black & Red, Nike Swoosh, Game Used, 1997
$216

Heritage Auctions

Sports, Baseball, Jacket, Harvey Kuenn, Detroit Tigers, Game Used, 1955-59, 42 In.
$2,040

Heritage Auctions

Sports, Baseball, Jersey, Jim Catfish Hunter, No. 27, Oakland A's, Game Used, 1974
$6,600

Heritage Auctions

Sports, Baseball, Pennant, Chief Wahoo, Cleveland Indians, American League Champions, 1948, Frame
$177

Milestone Auctions

S

Sports, Baseball, Scoreboard Sign, Duke Beer, Cleveland Indians, Chief Wahoo, Tin, 26 x 14 In.
$212

Milestone Auctions

Sports, Baseball, Statue, Chief Wahoo, Gold Tooth, Cleveland Indians, Pottery, 8½ In.
$142

Milestone Auctions

Sports, Baseball, Trophy, Pat Donahue, World Series Championship, Silver Plate, 1910, 8 x 6 In.
$7,200

Heritage Auctions

Sports, Basketball, Ball, Autographed, Milwaukee Bucks Team, Spalding, NBA Game, 1990s
$399

Heritage Auctions

Bobbin'-Head Fakes

Bobbin'-head sports dolls have been faked. The only real gold-base college football doll is Wisconsin; the others are fakes. There are also fake basketball dolls for Indiana, Kentucky, and perhaps others.

Sports, Basketball, Shoes, Autographed, Julius Erving, Converse, Leather, Game Used, 1980-83
$3,120

Heritage Auctions

Sports, Basketball, Shoes, Autographed, Michael Jordan, Nike, Game Used, c.1995, Size 13½
$7,800

Heritage Auctions

Sports, Boxing, Gloves, Autographed, Muhammad Ali, Silver Ink, Everlast, Box, c.1970, Pair
$900

Heritage Auctions

Sports, Boxing, Jacket, James Toney, World Champion, Lights Out, Leather, 1990s, Size XL
$204

Heritage Auctions

Sports, Boxing, Robe, James Toney, Losing Is Not An Option, 1995
$444

Heritage Auctions

S

Sports, Football, Ball, Autographed, Green Bay Packers Team, World Champions, Spalding, 1962
$660

Heritage Auctions

Sports, Football, Helmet, George Atkinson, Oakland Raiders, Game Used, Early 1970s
$5,040

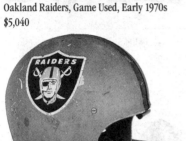

Heritage Auctions

Sports, Football, Jersey, Joe Namath, No. 12, Los Angeles Rams, Game Used, 1977
$9,000

Heritage Auctions

Sports, Football, Nose Mask, Rubber Shield, Cloth Strap, Bite Plate, Morrills Patent
$480

Heritage Auctions

> **TIP**
> *For the best deal on a sports collectible, shop off-season.*

Sports, Golf, Bag, Autographed, U.S. Presidents Cup Team, Logo, American Flag, 1996
$312

Heritage Auctions

Sports, Golf, Shoes, Ben Hogan, White Bucks, Match Used, c.1950, Pair
$1,200

Heritage Auctions

Sports, Tennis, Pin, Cameo, Woman, Tennis Racket, Gold & Diamond Earrings & Bracelet, 2 In.
$6,765

Morphy Auctions

S

Hunting, Sign, Shooting Target, 2 Squirrels, Archer, Sherwood, 8 x 12 In.	215
Hunting, Sign, Winchester, Dawn Of Open Season, Hunters, Dogs, Frame, 1910, 39 x 27 In.	2813
Tennis, Can, Wilson Tennis Balls, Unopened Can Of 12, c.1931	1230
Tennis, Pin, Cameo, Woman, Tennis Racket, Gold & Diamond Earrings & Bracelet, 2 In..*illus*	6765
Tennis, Plate, Wimbledon Championships, Queen Elizabeth II Coronation, Brass, 1953, 5 In..	34
Tennis, Racket, Lawn, Tilt Head, Stamped Sphairistike, French & Co., c.1874, 27 In.	7200
Tennis, Racket, Tilt Head, Wright & Ditson, c.1800, 27 x 8 In.	3900
Tennis, Rocking Chair, Wicker, Woven Tennis Rackct, Balls, c.1900, 36 In..........................*illus*	3690
Tennis, Scorer, Sterling Silver, Repousse Scroll Border, 4 Wheels, Whiting, Victorian...............	2280
Tennis, Skirt Lifter, Metal, Crossed Rackets, Balls, 1880s........................*illus*	1107
Tennis, Trophy, Renshaw Cup, 1913, Winged Mercury, Silver, Elkington, England, 12 In..*illus*	21600
Track, Trophy, Empire City Automobile Track Meet, Silver Plate, 2 Handles, 1903, 18 In.	1800
Wakeboard, Orange, White, Peterborough Canoc Co., Canada, 1920, 28 x 58 In.	335
Wrestling, Poster, Midgets Tag Team Match, Oakland Auditorium, Wood Frame, 1963, 23 x 15 In. ..	170

STAFFORDSHIRE, England, has been a district making pottery and porcelain since the 1700s. Thousands of types of pottery and porcelain have been made in the many factories that worked in the area. Some of the most famous factories have been listed separately, such as Adams, Davenport, Ridgway, Rowland & Marsellus, Royal Doulton, Royal Worcester, Spode, Wedgwood, and others. Some Staffordshire pieces are listed under categories like Fairing, Flow Blue, Mulberry, Shaving Mug, etc.

Basket, Isle Of Wight, Shell Border, Reticulated, Enoch Wood & Sons, c.1830, 11 In.	720
Bidet, Mahogany Base, Asian Scene, Turned Legs, c.1850, 18 x 21 x 18 In.	360
Bowl, Blue, 13 States, Porcelain, Clews, 1800s, 4 x 12 In.	270
Bowl, Cauliflower, Earthenware, Cream, Green Leaves, Molded, England, c.1760, 6 In.....*illus*	1046
Bowl, Peace & Plenty, Fluted, Scalloped Edge, James & Ralph Clews, 1819-36, 9 In................	480
Bowl, Vegetable, Dark Blue Transfer, Enoch Wood & Sons, 1818-46, 11 ⅝ In.	660
Box, Bird, Perched, Enamel, 1800s, 2 ½ In.	281
Box, Hinged Lid, Landscape, Yellow Ground, c.1750, 3 In..............................	150
Coffeepot, Lafayette At Franklin's Tomb, Blue, Early 1800s, 11 In.	944
Coffeepot, Lid, Flowers, Blue & White, Early 1800s, 12 In.	413
Coffeepot, Pearlware, Chinoiserie, Domed Foot, England, 1700s, 12 In...........................*illus*	277
Creamer, Cow, Multicolor, Tail Handle, Stopper, 1880s, 7 In.	495
Dish, Lid, Cobalt Blue, Lion Finial, Chinese Landscapes, c.1800, 6 x 9 x 9 In....................*illus*	142
Figurine, Ben Franklin, Holding Document, Tricorn Hat, 1800s, 14 ½ In.........................*illus*	384
Figurine, Ben Franklin, Standing, White, Gilt, Mislabeled Washington, 1800s, 16 In................	549
Figurine, Couple In Tree, Swan Under Bridge, Square Base, c.1860s, 4 x 7 In.	47
Figurine, Dog, Spaniel, Brown Glaze, Flowers, Morley & Co., c.1885, 10 x 7 In. ....*illus*	142
Figurine, Dog, Spaniel, White, Flower Basket In Mouth, 1850s, 8 x 4 In............................	78
Figurine, Harlequin, Clown, Seated, Birdcage, 1800s, 5 ¼ In............................	472
Figurine, Lion, Lying Down, Beside Bowl, Treacle Glaze, 1800s, 6 ¼ x 4 In.	77
Figurine, St. Cecilia, Holding Book, Flowers, Leaves, Bocage, Early 1800s, 6 In.	313
Figurine, Winter, Red Coat, Standing, Square Base, c.1780, 9 ½ In.	295
Flagon, Brandy Spirit, Deer, Trees, c.1860, 13 x 12 x 8 In.	450
Footbath, Oval, White, Horizontal Bands, 2 Side Handles, Late 1800s, 9 ½ In.	600
Jug, Cock Fighting, Painted, Samuel Roper, 1877, 8 In............................	63
Jug, Great Seal Of U.S., Eagle, Banner, William Adams IV & Sons, c.1830, 6 In.............*illus*	1320
Jug, Welcome Lafayette, Nation's Guest, Ships, James & Ralph Clews, 1800s, 7 In....................	300
Lamp, Figural, Spaniel Puppy, Seated, Black Paint, Composite, 15 ¼ In.	225
Mug, Illusion, 2 Faces, Upside Down, Courtship, Matrimony, c.1820, 6 In..........................*illus*	336
Nutmeg Grater, Enamel, Cobalt Blue, White, Pink Flowers, 2 ¼ x 1 In...........................*illus*	512
Pitcher, American Naval Heroes, Flags, Cannons, Dark Blue Transfer, 1816, 6 ⅜ In.	600
Pitcher, Ships, Constitution, Guerriere, Commodore Perry's Victory, 7 ½ In.	976
Pitcher, State, Washington, Blue, Cartouches, Early 1800s, 9 ½ In......................................	384
Plate, Blue, 3-Story Building, 2 People, 15 States, Washington Medallion, 10 ⅜ In.	123
Plate, Cadmus, Shell Border, Enoch Wood & Sons, c.1850, 10 In.	96
Plate, Cities Series, Quebec, Dark Blue Transfer, 1830-40, 9 In...................................*illus*	360
Plate, City Of Albany, Shell Border, Blue, Enoch Wood & Sons, England, c.1840, 10 In.	204
Plate, Gen. Lafayette, Welcome To Land Of Liberty, 1800s, 6 ⅞ In........................	397
Plate, Lafayette, Jefferson, Washington, Stevenson & Williams, c.1825, 10 In. ....*illus*	2880

Sports, Tennis, Rocking Chair, Wicker, Woven Tennis Racket, Balls, c.1900, 36 In.
$3,690

Morphy Auctions

Sports, Tennis, Skirt Lifter, Metal, Crossed Rackets, Balls, 1880s
$1,107

Morphy Auctions

Sports, Tennis, Trophy, Renshaw Cup, 1913, Winged Mercury, Silver, Elkington, England, 12 In.
$21,600

Morphy Auctions

S

STAFFORDSHIRE

Staffordshire, Bowl, Cauliflower, Earthenware, Cream, Green Leaves, Molded, England, c.1760, 6 In.
$1,046

Skinner, Inc.

> ### TIP
> Transfer-decorated Staffordshire dinnerware was made in many colors—blue, green, mulberry, pink, and others. Two-color pieces are worth more than one-color pieces. Three-color dishes are worth even more.

Staffordshire, Coffeepot, Pearlware, Chinoiserie, Domed Foot, England, 1700s, 12 In.
$277

Skinner, Inc.

Staffordshire, Dish, Lid, Cobalt Blue, Lion Finial, Chinese Landscapes, c.1800, 6 x 9 x 9 In.
$142

Leland Little Auctions

Staffordshire, Figurine, Ben Franklin, Holding Document, Tricorn Hat, 1800s, 14 1/2 In.
$384

Copake Auction

Staffordshire, Figurine, Dog, Spaniel, Brown Glaze, Flowers, Morley & Co., c.1885, 10 x 7 In.
$142

Aspire Auctions

Staffordshire, Jug, Great Seal Of U.S., Eagle, Banner, William Adams IV & Sons, c.1830, 6 In.
$1,320

Northeast Auctions

Staffordshire, Mug, Illusion, 2 Faces, Upside Down, Courtship, Matrimony, c.1820, 6 In.
$336

Pook & Pook

Staffordshire, Nutmeg Grater, Enamel, Cobalt Blue, White, Pink Flowers, 2 1/4 x 1 In.
$512

Morphy Auctions

Staffordshire, Plate, Cities Series, Quebec, Dark Blue Transfer, 1830-40, 9 In.
$360

Northeast Auctions

Plate, Lafayette, Washington, Portraits, Eagle, Stars, Green Rim, 1800s, 6 In.	305
Plate, Lafayette, Washington, Transfer, Stars, Enoch Wood & Sons, c.1830, 6 In. ....*illus*	840
Plate, Marine Hospital, Louisville, Dark Blue, Enoch Wood & Sons, 1800s, 9 In.	187
Plate, Sailing Ship, Cadmus, Fishing, Dark Blue, Floral Border, Unmarked, c.1830, 9 In.	94
Plate, Soup, Blue, Harvard College, Figures & Buildings, Acorn Border, c.1830, 10 In.	187
Plate, Steamship, Chief Justice Marshall Troy, Dark Blue, Enoch Wood & Sons, c.1825, 8 In.	439
Plate, Winter View Of Pittsfield, Mass., Dark Blue, R. & J. Clews, c.1830, 11 In.	234
Plate, Woman & Child, Blue, White, Embossed Flower Rim, c.1810, 7 ½ In.	263
Platter, Bridge & Fishermen, Wild Rose, Blue, Flower Border, 1800s, 15 x 12 In.	1788
Platter, Cape Coast Castle, Africa, Blue Transfer, Enoch Wood & Sons, 1800s, 16 In.	480
Platter, Columbia, Figures, Statue, Flowers, Blue Transferware, 8-Sided, 12 x 15 In.	75
Platter, Coronation, Well & Tree, Flowers, Fruit, Dark Blue, Clews, 14 x 18 In.	413
Platter, Deer, Grassy Knoll, Blue Transfer, Adams, c.1830, 15 ⅜ In. ....*illus*	400
Platter, Esplanade, Castle Garden, New York, R. Stevenson & Son, 1800s, 18 In.	4560
Platter, Hunt Scene, Flowers, Animals, Blue Transfer, Oval, 14 ½ In.	531
Platter, Landing Of Gen'l Lafayette, Blue, 8-Sided, Clews, 1850, 12 x 15 In.....................*illus*	570
Platter, Peace & Plenty, Fruit Border, American Indian Farmer, Dark Blue, 12 x 15 In.	358
Platter, Pennsylvania Hospital, Philadelphia, Flowers, 8-Sided, 1800s, 14 x 18 In.	1063
Platter, Regent's Park, Cumberland Terrace, Blue, 19 x 14 ½ In.	118
Platter, Richard Jordan Residence, N.J., Purple, Joseph Heath & Co., c.1835, 10 x 8 In.......*illus*	322
Platter, Sporting Series, Polar Bear, Blue Transfer, Enoch Wood & Sons, 1800s, 16 In.	1440
Teapot, Cauliflower, White Florets, Green Leaves, 5 In.	1599
Tray, Meat, Cranes, Blue & White, Ironstone, 22 x 17 In.	212
Tureen, Flow Blue, Flower Handles, Don Quixote & The Princess, 7 x 16 x 9 In.	47
Undertray, Deaf & Dumb Asylum, Hartford, Conn., Blue, Oval, England, c.1840, 14 In.	461

STAINLESS STEEL became available to artists and manufacturers about 1920. They used it to make flatware, tableware, and many decorative items.

Ashtray, Zephyr, Streamerica, Tiffany & Co., 1990s, 4 ⅝ In.	750
Cheese Slicer, Cast Iron Handle, Painted Red, Acme MGM Co., USA, 5 ½ x 5 In.	20
Cup, Teddy Bears, Embossed, Selandia, Japan, Baby's, 2 ¾ x 2 ½ In.	6
Dish, Divided, Marked, International Stainless Steel, Alessi, Italy, 1 x 5 x 13 In.	25
Flask, Cigarette Holder, 6 Oz., 4 x 2 In.	35
Food Mill, Foley Mfg. Co., 7 ⅜ x 4 In.	25
Hip Flask, Screw-On Lid, E & J Co., Marked, 3 ½ In.	49
Ice Bucket, Art Deco, Ribbed Band, Handles, Guy Degrenne, France, 7 ⅞ In.	59
Ice Bucket, Penguin, Chrome, Hot Cold, West Bend, 1950s, 8 x 10 In.	39
Pitcher, Oval, Vollrath, 6 ½ In.	20
Sculpture, Biomorphic, Abstract, Jack Arnold, 1970s, 40 x 25 x 27 In.	1895
Sock Stretchers, Cast Iron Hooks, 19th Century, 58 x 8 In.	2250

STANGL POTTERY traces its history back to the Fulper Pottery of New Jersey. In 1910, Johann Martin Stangl started working at Fulper. He left to work at Haeger Pottery from 1915 to 1920. Stangl returned to Fulper Pottery in 1920, became president in 1926, and changed the company name to Stangl Pottery in 1929. Stangl bought the firm in 1930. The pottery is known for dinnerware and a line of bird figurines. Martin Stangl died in 1972 and the pottery was sold to Frank Wheaton Jr. of Wheaton Industries. Production continued until 1978, when Pfaltzgraff Pottery purchased the right to the Stangl trademark and the remaining inventory was liquidated. A single bird figurine is identified by a number. Figurines made up of two birds are identified by a number followed by the letter *D* indicating Double.

Stangl
1926–1930

Stangl
1940s–1978

Stangl
1949–1953

Bird, Crested Goldfinch, No. 3813, On Perch, Yellow, 6 ½ x 4 ¾ In.	68

Staffordshire, Plate, Lafayette, Jefferson, Washington, Stevenson & Williams, c.1825, 10 In.
$2,880

Northeast Auctions

TIP
Stains on porcelains can be removed by soaking them in a mixture of 2 tablespoons denture cleaner in 1 quart tepid water.

Staffordshire, Plate, Lafayette, Washington, Transfer, Stars, Enoch Wood & Sons, c.1830, 6 In.
$840

Northeast Auctions

Staffordshire, Platter, Deer, Grassy Knoll, Blue Transfer, Adams, c.1830, 15 ⅜ In.
$400

S

Skinner, Inc.

Staffordshire, Platter, Landing Of Gen'l Lafayette, Blue, 8-Sided, Clews, 1850, 12 x 15 In.
$570

Garth's Auctioneers & Appraisers

Staffordshire, Platter, Richard Jordan Residence, N.J., Purple, Joseph Heath & Co., c.1835, 10 x 8 In.
$322

Jeffrey S. Evans & Associates

Star Trek, T-Shirt, Spock, Captain Kirk, Dr. McCoy, Donmoor, 1970, Kids Size 16
$56

andgi_74 on eBay

Five *Star Wars* Stars
Look for the five different *Star Wars* cans of Campbell's Soup. Open from the bottom if possible to save as collectibles. There are five different characters in the set.

Cigarette Box, 2 Birds, Blue, Leaves, 4 ½ x 5 ½ x 2 In.	37
Daffodil, Creamer, Yellow & Green, Marked Sample, 3 ¾ In.	78
Dish, Snowman, Brown, Red, Green, White, Signed Mr. & Mrs. J.M. Stangl, 5 In.	208
Dogwood, Serving Bowl, Yellow, Green & White, 8 ½ In.	10
Fruit, Cup & Saucer	27
Jug, Ball Shape, Tangerine Glaze, Handle, c.1940, 2 ¾ In.	24
Kiddieware, Cup, 5 Little Pigs, Pottery, Gold Rim, White Ground, 3 ¾ In.	47
Ranger, Plate, Yellow, Green & Brown, 1939, 8 In.	60
Rooster, Green Body, Yellow Beak, Red Crest, 5 ¼ In.	468
Tray, Condiment, Golden Harvest, Gray Ground, Tan, White, Flowers, Gold, 13 ½ In.	39
Vase, Bud, Light Blue, Gold, Striping Mold, Marked, 1950s	30
Vase, Green Matte Glaze, 2 High Loop Handles, 7 ½ In.	52
Vase, Mountain Goat Head, Blue Green, Tin Glaze, Marked, c.1930, 15 In.	285
Vase, Slanting Handles, Medium Gray Matte Glaze, 7 ½ In.	37
Windfall, Plate, Salad, Leaves, Cream, Yellow, Green, 8 In.	260
Windfall, Saucer.	11

STAR TREK AND STAR WARS collectibles are included here. The original *Star Trek* television series ran from 1966 through 1969. The series spawned an animated TV series, three TV sequels, and a TV prequel. The first Star Trek movie was released in 1979 and eleven others followed, the most recent in 2016. The movie *Star Wars* opened in 1977. Sequels were released in 1980 and 1983; prequels in 1999, 2002, and 2005. *Star Wars: Episode VII* opened in 2015, which increased interest in Star Wars collectibles. *Star Wars: The Last Jedi* opened in 2017. *Star Wars: Episode IX* is scheduled to open in 2019. Star Wars characters also appeared in *Rogue One: A Star Wars Story* (2016) and *Solo: A Star Wars Story* (2018). Other science fiction and fantasy collectibles can be found under Batman, Buck Rogers, Captain Marvel, Flash Gordon, Movie, Superman, and Toy.

STAR TREK

Action Figure, Mr. Scott, Red Top, Belt, Mego, 1974, 8 In.	48
Action Figure, Zaranite, Mego, On Card, 1979, 4 In.	161
Belt Buckle, Star Trek Lives, Mr. Spock, Lee, 1976, Child's, 2 x 1 ¾ In.	6
Figure, Captain Kirk, Quantum Mechanix, 11 ½ In.	535
Figure, Mr. Spock, Poseable, Stuffed Body, Box, Knickerbocker, 1979, 12 In.	35
Ornament, Starship Enterprise, Lights, Keepsake, Hallmark, 1991	245
Photograph, Leonard Nimoy, William Shatner, Autographed, 8 x 10 In.	33
Photograph, William Shatner, Leonard Nimoy, Deforest Kelley, Autographed, 8 x 10 In.	250
Poster, Next Generation, 7th Anniversary, Autographed By Actors, 1994, 20 x 30 In.	175
Poster, Patrick Stewart, William Shatner, Generations, Spiner, Autographed, 1994, 27 x 41 In.	375
Sketch Card, Oil Paint, Charles Hall, 2 ½ x 3 ½ In.	125
T-Shirt, Spock, Captain Kirk, Dr. McCoy, Donmoor, 1970, Kids Size 16 ....*illus*	56

STAR WARS

Action Figure, Yoda, Hand Puppet, Empire Strikes Back, Kenner, 1980	164
Bank, Figurine, Jabba The Hutt, Sigma, 1983, 7 In.	50
Bust, Boba Fett, Arm Out, Head Tilted, Multicolor, 15 In.	138
Cookie Jar, R2-D2, Robot Shape, Ceramic, 1977, 12 ½ x 7 ½ In. ....*illus*	72
Figure, Obi Wan Kenobi, Brown Robe, Kenner, 1979, 12 In.	75
Lunch Box Thermos, Hard Plastic, Red Cup, Cover, Blue, White, 20th Century Fox Corp.	29
Mask, Talking, Darth Vader, Black Plastic, 1977	85
Model, X-Wing Fighter, Icons Master Replicas, 23 x 20 In.	2772
Movie Prop, Han Solo's DL-44 Blaster, Return Of The Jedi, Metal, Resin, 1983 ....*illus*	550000
Poster, Empire Strikes Back Saga Continues, Frame, Signed, 1980, 28 x 42 In.	2000
Poster, Empire Strikes Back, Darth Vader & Luke Skywalker, 1980, 8 x 11 In.	36
Statue, Darth Vader, Empire Strikes Back, Hands On Hips, 85 In.	2079
Toy, AT-AT, All Terrain Transport, Empire Strikes Back, Kenner, Box, 1980	495
Toy, Darth Vader, Star Destroyer, Empire Strikes Back, Kenner, Box.	303
Toy, Imperial Cruiser, Empire Strikes Back, Kenner, Box.	605
Toy, Jaba The Hutt Dungeon, Return Of The Jedi, Kenner, Box.	660
Toy, Rebel Command Center, Empire Strikes Back, Kenner, Box.	605

STEINS have been used by beer and ale drinkers for over 500 years. They have been made of ivory, porcelain, pottery, stoneware, faience, silver, pewter, wood, or glass in sizes up to nine gallons. Although some were made by Mettlach, Meissen, Capo-di-Monte, and other famous factories, most were made by less important German potteries. The words *Geschutz* or *Musterschutz* on a stein are the German words for "patented" or "registered design," not company names. Steins are still being made in the old styles. Lithophane steins may be found in the Lithophane category.

Bohemian Glass, Amber Stain, Cut Spa Views, Inlaid Lid, c.1850, ½ Liter	720
Bohemian Glass, Pink Over White Over Clear, Gilt Spa Views, Lid, Brass Hunter, ½ Liter	900
Character, Barmaid, Holding Stein, Stoneware, Blue Glaze, ½ Liter..............*illus*	240
Character, Boar With Pipe, Wearing Alpine Hat, Porcelain, Schierholz, ½ Liter ....*illus*	3000
Character, Martin Luther Holding Stein, Pottery, Round, ½ Liter	288
Character, Monkey In Top Hat, Reading Book By Darwin, Pottery, ½ Liter	264
Character, Sad Radish, Twisted Face, Porcelain, Radish Lid, Pewter Trim, Schierholz, ⅛ Liter	204
Character, Uncle Sam, Stars On Hat Band, Porcelain, Tan Glaze, Schierholz, ½ Liter ......*illus*	1920
Embossed Figural Scenes, Villeroy & Boch, 10 In.............*illus*	184
Fraternal, Stoneware, Student Shield, PUG, Pewter Lid, ½ Liter...........*illus*	144
Glass, Blown, Faceted, Wheel Cut Spa Scene, Glass Inlay Lid, ⅙ Liter	66
Golf Scene, Lid, Man Swinging, Golf Club, Pewter, Germany, Early 1900s, 9 In.	488
Ivory, Carved Putti, Cart & Wheat, Repousse Silver Mount, Late 1800s, 9 In.	1800
Mettlach Steins are listed in the Mettlach category.	
Milk Glass, Light Blue, Enameled Radishes, Metal Lid, ½ Liter	228
Munich Child, Stoneware, Relief, No. 2784, Sarreguemines, 1 Liter	840
Occupational, Firefighter, Tools, Pottery, Relief, Pewter Lid, ½ Liter	102
Occupational, Ice Cream Delivery Coachman, Jos. Seilsmeier, Porcelain, ½ Liter	324
Occupational, Jockey, Pressed Glass, Cap Lid, Green & Milk Glass Stripes, ½ Liter..........*illus*	115
Occupational, Painter, Maler, Men Painting Murals, Porcelain, Lithograph, ½ Liter	312
Porcelain, Cat With Hangover, Metal Lid, Tail Handle, Musterschutz, Germany, c.1900, 8 In...	295
Porcelain, Skull, Bisque Glaze, Metal Lid, Germany, c.1900, ½ Liter, 5⅞ In...........*illus*	293
Pottery, 5 Musical Clowns, Etched, Hanke, Pewter Lid, ½ Liter	168
Pottery, Drunk Monkeys, Relief, Monkey Handle, Inlaid Lid, Hanke, No. 1741, ½ Liter......*illus*	240
Pottery, German Composers, 6-Sided Medallions, Relief, Inlaid Lid, Hanke, ½ Liter	168
Pottery, King David, Samson, Delila, Noah, Relief, Dumler & Breiden, ¼ Liter	48
Regimental, 12 Inft. Regt. Konig Otto 1870-71, Porcelain, Helmet Finial, ½ Liter	360
Regimental, Regt. Gren Nr. 109 Karlsruhe 1907-09, Roster, Porcelain, Crown, ½ Liter	240
Regimental, Regt. Grenad. Nr. 110 Mannheim 1910-12, City Scenes, Roster, ½ Liter	420
Stoneware, Ludwig III, Konig V. Bayern, Transfer, Painted, Relief Pewter Lid, ½ Liter	78

STEREO CARDS that were made for stereoscope viewers became popular after 1840. Two almost identical pictures were mounted on a stiff cardboard backing so that, when viewed through a stereoscope, a three-dimensional picture could be seen. Value is determined by maker and by subject. These cards were made in quantity through the 1930s.

International Exhibition, State Building, Albumen, 1876, 4¼ x 7 In.	45
Public School Silver Cliff Colorado, Charles Emery, 1880s, 7 x 4 In.	312
West Point Housing, American Views, Albumen, 3⅜ x 6¾ In.	55

STEREOSCOPES were used for viewing stereo cards. The hand viewer was invented by Oliver Wendell Holmes, although more complicated table models were used before his was produced in 1859. Do not confuse the stereoscope with the stereopticon, a magic lantern that used glass slides.

Jules Richard, Desktop Viewer, Wood, Nickle Metal Fittings, Paris, 19 x 11 In.	468
Mechanical, Wood Cabinet, Reel With Cards, Tabletop, Pat. 1874, 16 x 10 x 13 In.	224
Unis France, Wood Case, Hinged Mirror, 5½ x 8 x 7 In.	118
Verascope Richard, Mahogany, Label Reads, Focus Knob On Side, 5⅝ In.	56

STERLING SILVER, *see Silver-Sterling category.*

Star Wars, Cookie Jar, R2-D2, Robot Shape, Ceramic, 1977, 12½ x 7½ In. $72

tashatasha on eBay

Star Wars, Movie Prop, Han Solo's DL-44 Blaster, Return Of The Jedi, Metal, Resin, 1983 $550,000

Julien's Auctions

Stein, Character, Barmaid, Holding Stein, Stoneware, Blue Glaze, ½ Liter $240

Fox Auctions

S

This is an edited listing of current prices. Visit **Kovels.com** to check thousands of prices from previous years and sign up for free information on trends, tips, reproductions, marks, and more.

Stein, Character, Boar With Pipe, Wearing Alpine Hat, Porcelain, Schierholz, ½ Liter
$3,000

Fox Auctions

Stein, Character, Uncle Sam, Stars On Hat Band, Porcelain, Tan Glaze, Schierholz, ½ Liter
$1,920

Fox Auctions

Stein, Embossed Figural Scenes, Villeroy & Boch, 10 In.
$184

Apple Tree Auction Center

Stein, Fraternal, Stoneware, Student Shield, PUG, Pewter Lid, ½ Liter
$144

Fox Auctions

Stein, Occupational, Jockey, Pressed Glass, Cap Lid, Green & Milk Glass Stripes, ½ Liter
$115

Fox Auctions

Stein, Porcelain, Skull, Bisque Glaze, Metal Lid, Germany, c.1900, ½ Liter, 5⅞ In.
$293

Jeffrey S. Evans & Associates

STEUBEN glass was made at the Steuben Glass Works of Corning, New York. The factory, founded by Frederick Carder and T.G. Hawkes Sr., was purchased by the Corning Glass Company in 1918. Corning continued to make glass called Steuben. Many types of art glass were made at Steuben. Aurene is an iridescent glass. Schottenstein Stores Inc. bought 80 percent of the business in 2008. The factory closed in 2011. In 2014 the Corning Museum of Glass took over the factory and is reproducing some tableware, paperweights, and collectibles. Additional pieces may be found in the Cluthra and Perfume Bottle categories.

Basket, Gold Iridescent, Opaque White, Handle, c.1920s, 7 In.	illus	269
Bowl, Aurene, Gold Iridescent, Frederick Carder, 1904, 6 1/2 x 4 1/2 In.		374
Bowl, Blue Aurene, Footed, Splayed Rim, Early 1900s, 4 x 10 In.		461
Bowl, Blue, White, Iridescent, Octagonal, 1 3/4 x 16 In.		151
Bowl, Centerpiece, Round, Footed, 10 3/4 In.	illus	200
Bowl, Low, Blue Jade, Round, 1900s, 12 In.		75
Bowl, Low, Peony, Donald Pollard, 1998, 15 1/4 x 6 1/2 In.		168
Bowl, Marbelite, Opal Iridescent, Signed, F. Carder, c.1925, 2 3/8 In.		48
Candleholder, Blue Aurene, Flowers, Netting, Gold Washed Metal Collar, 7 1/2 In.		272
Compote, Blue Green, Calcite, 8 In.		182
Compote, Celeste Blue, Yellow Stem, Mica Flecks, 1900s, 7 3/4 In.	illus	200
Compote, Rainbow Iridescent, Water Lily, Wind Blown, Waffle Pontil, 6 5/8 x 14 3/8 In.		206
Decanter, Aurene, Gold Iridescent, Pinched, Frederick Carder, 1904, 10 1/2 In.		575
Figurine, Elephant, Clear, Inscribed, 5 1/2 In.		148
Figurine, Tropical Fish, Clear, Inscribed, 1968, 8 1/2 In.		413
Jar, Lid, Jade Over Alabaster, Acid Etched, Chinese Symbols, F. Carder, c.1925, 6 In.	illus	625
Lamp Shade, Calcite, Drizzled Gold Vines, Leaves, 4 1/4 In.		165
Lamp, Gold Aurene Shade, Brass Gimbaled Base, 13 In.		770
Lamp, Gypsy Ball, Controlled Bubble, Black Base, 4 1/2 In.		207
Lamp, Intarsia Border, Red & White Threaded Zigzag, Acorn Pull, 15 3/4 In.	illus	1392
Paperweight, Eagle, Standing, Wings Folded Back, Marked, 5 In.		92
Pitcher, Rosaline, Diamond Quilted, 6 In.		60
Plaque, Pate-De-Verre, Man Holding Bar, Wheeled Cart, F. Carder, 1900s, 11 x 6 In.	illus	4961
Sculpture, Arctic Fisherman, Crystal Iceberg, James Houston, 10 x 18 In.		2460
Sculpture, Seal Rock, 18K Gold Seal Attached, James Houston, Case, Box, 5 3/4 In.		3690
Urn, Lid, 2 Handles, Circular Base, Clear Glass & Finial, 10 1/2 In.		188
Vase, Amphora Shape, Green Jade, Alabaster Handles, F. Carder, 1900, 10 x 7 In.	illus	584
Vase, Aurene, Bulbous, Flared Rim, c.1915, 8 In.		450
Vase, Blue Aurene, Iridescent, Squat, Polished Pontil, 5 x 6 1/2 In.		540
Vase, Blue Aurene, Tapered, Flared, Scalloped, Etched Base, Early 1900s, 7 3/4 In.		923
Vase, Cyprian, Blue Threading, Prunts, 8 3/4 In.		118
Vase, Gold Aurene, Fan Shape, Round Flattened Foot, 8 1/2 In.		1416
Vase, Jade Green, Opaline, Bulbous, Unmarked, 5 x 10 In.		242
Vase, Lotus, Footed, George Thompson, 10 x 6 In.		248
Vase, Lotus, Plum Jade, Double Acid Etched, Cameo, Round, F. Carder, 7 In.		1375
Vase, Red Aurene, Gold Leaves & Vines, Signed, 9 3/4 x 3 1/2 In.		14080
Vase, Rose Quartz, Acid Cut Flowers, Unmarked, c.1927, 14 3/4 x 7 In.		1375
Vase, Tree Trunk, 3-Prong, Pomona Green, Unmarked, 6 1/2 x 4 In.		301
Vase, Tree Trunks, 3-Prong, Blue Aurene, Magenta & Gold Highlights, 6 In.	illus	575
Wine, Gold Aurene, Iridescent, Frederick Carder, 1904, 6 In.		138

STEVENGRAPHS are woven pictures made like fancy ribbons. They were manufactured by Thomas Stevens of Coventry, England, and became popular in 1862. Most are marked *Woven in silk by Thomas Stevens* or were mounted on a cardboard that tells the story of the Stevengraph. Other similar ribbon pictures have been made in England and Germany.

Lady Godiva Procession, Framed, Signed, Nancy Robbins, 2 x 6 In.	50
Portrait, Thomas Edison, Silk, Gilt Edges, c.1883, 4 x 2 In.	125

STEVENS & WILLIAMS of Stourbridge, England, made many types of glass, including layered, etched, cameo, cut, and art glass, between the 1830s and 1930s.

Stein, Pottery, Drunk Monkeys, Relief, Monkey Handle, Inlaid Lid, Hanke, No. 1741, 1/2 Liter
$240

Fox Auctions

Steuben, Basket, Gold Iridescent, Opaque White, Handle, c.1920s, 7 In.
$269

Jeffrey S. Evans & Associates

Steuben, Bowl, Centerpiece, Round, Footed, 10 3/4 In.
$200

Royal Crest Auctioneers

S

Steuben, Compote, Celeste Blue, Yellow Stem, Mica Flecks, 1900s, 7¾ In.
$200

Leslie Hindman Auctioneers

Steuben, Jar, Lid, Jade Over Alabaster, Acid Etched, Chinese Symbols, F. Carder, c.1925, 6 In.
$625

Freeman's Auctioneers & Appraisers

Steuben, Lamp, Intarsia Border, Red & White Threaded Zigzag, Acorn Pull, 15¾ In.
$1,392

Fontaine's Auction Gallery

Steuben, Plaque, Pate-De-Verre, Man Holding Bar, Wheeled Cart, F. Carder, 1900s, 11 x 6 In.
$4,961

Humler & Nolan

Steuben, Vase, Amphora Shape, Green Jade, Alabaster Handles, F. Carder, 1900, 10 x 7 In.
$584

Crescent City Auction Gallery

Steuben, Vase, Tree Trunks, 3-Prong, Blue Aurene, Magenta & Gold Highlights, 6 In.
$575

Humler & Nolan

S

Some pieces are signed *S & W.* Many pieces are decorated with flowers, leaves, and other designs based on nature.

Biscuit Jar, Cobalt Blue Cut To Clear, Bird, Intaglio Flowers, 7 In.	*illus*	9000
Candlestand, Thorn Branch, Ruffled Base, Yellow Cased, Clear, 7 In.	*illus*	666
Goblet, Apricot Cut To Yellow Cut To Clear, 7¾ In.		1800
Pitcher, Blue Opalescent Cased, Amber Fluted, Ribbed Rim & Handle		151
Vase, Flower Form, Vaseline & Clear, Ruffled, Domed Foot, c.1900, 12 x 5 In.		211
Vase, Green, White Flowers, Ring Neck, Fluted, 7 In.		242
Vase, Moss Agate, Maroon, Aqua, Gray, Shouldered, Footed, 8½ In.		413
Vase, Ruby, Blue, Emerald Threading, Distorted Body, Button Pontil, 6 In.		2360

STONE includes those articles made of stones, coral, shells, and some other natural materials not listed elsewhere in this book. Micro mosaics (small decorative designs made by setting pieces of stone into a pattern), urns, vases, and other pieces made of natural stone are listed here. Stoneware is pottery and is listed in the Stoneware category. Alabaster, Jade, Malachite, Marble, and Soapstone are in their own categories.

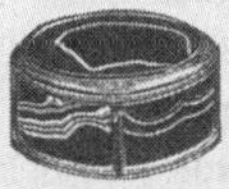

Figure, Bird, Long Tail, Perched, Amber, Red, 11 In., Pair		1062
Figure, Buddha, Seated, Green Hardstone, Carved, Stand, Chinese, c.1900, 6⅜ In.		500
Figure, Dog, Lying, Agate, Red Stone, Wood Curled-Leaf Stand, Chinese, 4 In.		160
Figure, Eagle, Hammered Copper Head & Feet, Wood Base, Signed, 1900s, 15 In.	*illus*	246
Figure, Elephant, Seated, Amethyst, Urn, Handles, Wood Stand, 4 x 3½ In.		210
Figure, Indian Chief, Roger Wermers, 17½ x 22½ In.		660
Figure, Male Nude, Marble Base, Mounted, Glazed, Eleganza, 18½ In.		80
Figure, Torso, Rock Crystal, Carved, Wooden Base, Art Deco, 8⅝ x 3 x 2 In.		575
Fob, Gold & Citrine, Faceted, 3 Flat Panels, Yellow Gold, Victorian, 1 In.		207
Head, Buddha, Carved, Hair In Bun, Gray, Black, 12½ In.		83
Head, Gray Schist, Greco Buddhist, Rosewood Base, Kushan Empire, Gandhara, 6 In.		120
Inkwell, Onyx, Silver Trim, Art Deco Style, English Hallmarks, 4 x 4 In.		127
Pedestal, Agate, 3-Piece, Turned & Polished, 28 x 13 x 13 In.		288
Sculpture, Eagle, Federal Style, Gilt Surface, Rocky Plinth, Late 1900s, 28 x 20 In.	*illus*	378
Seal, Foo Dog, Carved, Tianhuang, Chop Mark Seal, Chinese, 3 In.		92
Vase, Rock Crystal, Lid, Relief Bird & Flower Decoration, Lion Finial, c.1890, 8 In.	*illus*	1320

STONEWARE is a coarse, glazed, and fired potter's ceramic that is used to make crocks, jugs, bowls, etc. It is often decorated with cobalt blue decorations. In the nineteenth and early twentieth centuries, potters often decorated crocks with blue numbers indicating the size of the container. A *2* meant 2 gallons. Stoneware is still being made. American stoneware is listed here.

Ashtray, Impressed X Top, Black Glaze, Signed, Johanna Grawunder, 1997, 8 x 8 In.		62
Barrel, Bristol, Ocher Glaze, Maltese Cross, 1800s, 6 Gal., 18¼ In.	*illus*	84
Batter Jar, Cream Body, Center Handle, Tin Lids, Late 1800s, 8½ In.		100
Batter Jug, Cobalt Blue Flowers, Handle, Signed, Pennsylvania, 1800s, 8½ In.		375
Bowl, Flowers, Blue Slip, 1800, 6½ x 9½ In.		104
Bowl, Organic Form, Oxblood & Blue Glaze, Dalpayrat, c.1900, 4½ x 8 In.		1188
Bowl, Slip Glaze, Tan Shaded To White, Incised, James Lovera, c.1960, 3½ x 6 In.		84
Cake Crock, Cobalt Blue, Lid, Knob Handle, Marked, John Bell, c.1852, 7 x 9 In.		840
Churn, Cobalt Blue Stencil, 2 Handles, William & Reppert, Pa., c.1850, 18 In.	*illus*	270
Churn, Cobalt Blue Wreath, Lug Handles, Burger & Lang, 1800s, 4 Gal., 16½ In.	*illus*	438
Churn, Oval, Cobalt Blue, Lug Handles, Evan R. Jones, c.1875, 4 Gal., 17 In.		492
Cooler, Ice Water, Flower, Metal Spigot, Man's Face, Wingender Pottery, 4 Gal., 17 In.	*illus*	826
Cooler, Water, Lid, 4 Cobalt Blue Bands, Bulbous, Chrome Spigot, 16 In.		69
Crock, Bird, Cobalt Blue, Signed, Vera Berlet, 1800s, 9¾ In.		106
Crock, Blue Bird, Cylindrical, Burley Clay, 11 In.		47
Crock, Blue Flower, Lug Handles, T. Harrington, Late 1800s, 12¾ In.	*illus*	666
Crock, Blue Flowers, Brown Brothers N.Y., 3 Gal.		219
Crock, Blue Letters, A.P. Donaghho, Parkersburg, West Virginia, Gal., 9¾ In.	*illus*	154
Crock, Blue Slip Flowers, 1800s, 2 Gal., 9½ x 10 In.		144
Crock, Brushed Cobalt Blue Bird, Impressed W. Roberts, 2 Handles, c.1850, 10 In.		120

Stevens & Williams, Biscuit Jar, Cobalt Blue Cut To Clear, Bird, Intaglio Flowers, 7 In.
$9,000

Brunk Auctions

Stevens & Williams, Candlestand, Thorn Branch, Ruffled Base, Yellow Cased, Clear, 7 In.
$666

Humler & Nolan

Stone, Figure, Eagle, Hammered Copper Head & Feet, Wood Base, Signed, 1900s, 15 In.
$246

Skinner, Inc.

STONEWARE

Stone, Sculpture, Eagle, Federal Style, Gilt Surface, Rocky Plinth, Late 1900s, 28 x 20 In.
$378

Leland Little Auctions

Stone, Vase, Rock Crystal, Lid, Relief Bird & Flower Decoration, Lion Finial, c.1890, 8 In.
$1,320

Eldred's

Stoneware, Barrel, Bristol, Ocher Glaze, Maltese Cross, 1800s, 6 Gal., 18¼ In.
$84

Thomaston Place Auction Galleries

Crock, Brushed Cobalt Blue Flowers, 1893, Gal., 7 x 8 x 5 In.	142
Crock, Brushed Cobalt Blue Flowers, Incised Ribs, Lug Handles, 1800s, 5 Gal., 16 In.	630
Crock, Brushed Cobalt Blue Leaves, Mid-1800s, 2 Gal., 13½ In.	270
Crock, Brushed Cobalt Blue Stylized Leaves, Squat, Mid 1800s, 2 Gal., 7 In.	1920
Crock, Butter Tub, Blue, Yellow, Round Opening, Handle, 6¾ x 11 In.	106
Crock, Cobalt Blue Bird, Fort Edward, N.Y., 1½ Gal.	414
Crock, Cobalt Blue Bird, J.A. & C.W. Underwood, N.Y., 1800s, 2 Gal., 9 x 9 In.	277
Crock, Cobalt Blue Bird, Lug Handles, 1800s, 3 Gal., 10½ In.	150
Crock, Cobalt Blue Bird, Lug Handles, Marked, Evan H. Jones, 11 In.	150
Crock, Cobalt Blue Eagle, Shouldered, Flared Rim, Lug Handles, c.1850, 2 Gal., 11 In.	617
Crock, Cobalt Blue Flower & Leaf, Lug Handles, Lid, Shenfelder, 6 Gal., 8 In.	266
Crock, Cobalt Blue Flower, Rolled Rim, Remmey, 1800s, 8¼ In.	213
Crock, Cobalt Blue Flowers, D. Weston, Ellen Valley, N.Y., 1800s, 9½ In.	213
Crock, Cobalt Blue Flowers, Marked, Brown Brothers, 1800s, 15 In.	177
Crock, Cobalt Blue Harp, Leaf Spray, Rolled Rim, Lug Handle, 1800s, Gal., 7½ x 8 In.	615
Crock, Cobalt Blue Leaves, Ear Handles, Remmey, 1800s, 12 In.	175
Crock, Cobalt Blue Leaves, Lug Handles, J. Weaver, Pennsylvania, 6 Gal., 15 In.	1188
Crock, Cobalt Blue Lettering, J. Hamilton & Co., Pa., 1800s, 2 Gal., 11½ In.	400
Crock, Cobalt Blue Slip Hand, Lug Handles, W. Hart, Ogdensburg, 2 Gal., 11 In.	1121
Crock, Cobalt Blue Slip Leaves, Molded Rim, Lug Handles, T. Harrington, 3 Gal., 11 In.	325
Crock, Cobalt Blue Tulip, Ear Handles, Remmey, 1800s, 9½ In.	263
Crock, Cobalt Blue Tulip, Shenfelder, Pennsylvania, 1800s, 5 In.	150
Crock, Cobalt Flower Spray, 2 Handles, F. Norton & Co., Vermont, c.1850, 9 In.	300
Crock, Heinz, Blue Incised Letters, Central Mold Line, 5½ In.	216
Crock, Salt Glaze, Eagle In Flight, Hamilton & Jones, Ear Handles, 14 In.	198
Crock, Tulip, Tooled Shoulder, Lug Handles, Lewis Jones, Pa., Gal., 7 In.	708
Cuspidor, Cobalt Blue, Round Rim, Spread Foot, Remmey, 1800s, 5 x 8½ In.	175
Figure, Standing Boar, Light Brown Alkaline Glaze, R. Meaders, Ga., Late 1900s, 12 In.	384
Flask, Ring, Dabbed Cobalt, Rouletted, 1700s, 5½ In.	1968
Jar, Beige, Lug Handles, Edgefield, 11½ In.	9000
Jar, Bird, Flowers, W.H. Farrar & Co., N.Y., Lug Handles, c.1860, 2 Gal., 10 In. _illus_	1230
Jar, Brown Gray Salt Glaze, Marked, J.P. Parker, c.1850, Qt., 5¾ In.	108
Jar, Canning, Cobalt Blue Inscription, A. Conrad, Shinnston, W. Va., 1800s	163
Jar, Canning, Salt Glaze, 3 Cobalt Blue Bands, 8½ In.	132
Jar, Canning, Stenciled Pear, Cobalt Blue, Brushed Stripe, Mid 1800s, 7¾ In.	630
Jar, Cobalt Blue Cherry On Stem, Applied Handle, 1800s, 11 In.	188
Jar, Cobalt Blue Pears On Branch, Gray Glaze, Outward Rolled Rim, Greensboro, 8 In.	1020
Jar, Cobalt Blue Slip Foxglove, Cowden & Wilcox, Gal., 10 In.	153
Jar, Cobalt Blue Tulips, Ear Handles, B.C. Milburn, Va., c.1851, 2 Gal., 13 x 6 In. _illus_	995
Jar, Lid, Cobalt Blue Brushed Flowers & Leaf, 2 Gal., 13½ In.	142
Jar, Oval, Lid, Brown Glaze, Loop Handles, Incised, England, 1900s, 9¾ In.	72
Jar, Water, Lacquer Lid, Hare, Flowers, Miranda Thomas, Quechee, Vt., 8 x 4 In.	523
Jug, Blue Diamond, No. 7, Pittsburgh, W.D. Cooper & Bros., 2 Gal., 14 In.	660
Jug, Blue Folk Art Decoration, Somerset Pottersworks, 1860, 3 Gal., 15¾ In.	390
Jug, Blue Slip Stencil, Established 1873, Glasner & Barzen, Kansas City, 10 x 8 In. _illus_	544
Jug, Blue Stencil, Cream Glaze, Casey Bros., Pa., 11 In.	57
Jug, Bristol Glaze, Blue Stamp, M. Wollstein, Fine Whiskies, Wines & Liquors, 9 x 7 In.	384
Jug, Brushed Cobalt Flower, Speckled Leaves, Applied Strap Handle, c.1850, 13½ In.	300
Jug, Buff Salt Glaze, Cobalt Blue Letters, J. Fisher, Lyons, N.Y., Gal., 11 In.	180
Jug, Cobalt Blue Bird On Branch, J & P Norton, 1800, 2 Gal.	840
Jug, Cobalt Blue Butterfly, Julius Norton, 1800s, 12 In. _illus_	295
Jug, Cobalt Blue Decoration Around Handle, Flowers, Cowden & Wilcox, 13 x 8 In.	351
Jug, Cobalt Blue Diamond, Flat Rim, Lug Handle, J. Darrow & Son, N.Y., 1900s, 4 Gal., 16 In.	338
Jug, Cobalt Blue Feather, Lug Handles, Molded Rim, 1800s, 11 In. _illus_	115
Jug, Cobalt Blue Flower, Handle & Stopper, White's, Binghampton, 11 In.	184
Jug, Cobalt Blue Flowers & Leaves, 1861 Banner, J. Norton & Co., 1½ Gal., 12 In.	1652
Jug, Cobalt Blue Flowers, Cowden & Wilcox, Penn., 1800s, 10 In.	175
Jug, Cobalt Blue Flowers, H.B. Pfaltzgraff, York, Penn., 1800s, 11 In.	288
Jug, Cobalt Blue Message, Connely & Palmer, N.J., Liquor Dealers, 2 Gal., 13 In.	1003
Jug, Cobalt Blue Slip Leaves, Harrisburg, Pa., Gal., 11½ In.	142

Stoneware, Churn, Cobalt Blue Stencil, 2 Handles, William & Reppert, Pa., c.1850, 18 In.
$270

Garth's Auctioneers & Appraisers

Stoneware, Churn, Cobalt Blue Wreath, Lug Handles, Burger & Lang, 1800s, 4 Gal., 16½ In.
$438

Pook & Pook

Stoneware, Cooler, Ice Water, Flower, Metal Spigot, Man's Face, Wingender Pottery, 4 Gal., 17 In.
$826

Bunch Auctions

> **TIP**
> Black lights can detect repairs to antiques that are invisible to the eye, but be sure you use a longwave black light. A shortwave black light could injure your eyes.

Stoneware, Crock, Blue Flower, Lug Handles, T. Harrington, Late 1800s, 12¾ In.
$666

Ahlers & Ogletree Auction Gallery

Stoneware, Crock, Blue Letters, A.P. Donaghho, Parkersburg, West Virginia, Gal., 9¾ In.
$154

Milestone Auctions

Stoneware, Jar, Bird, Flowers, W.H. Farrar & Co., N.Y., Lug Handles, c.1860, 2 Gal., 10 In.
$1,230

Skinner, Inc.

Stoneware, Jar, Cobalt Blue Tulips, Ear Handles, B.C. Milburn, Va., c.1851, 2 Gal., 13 x 6 In.
$995

Jeffrey S. Evans & Associates

S

Stoneware, Jug, Blue Slip Stencil, Established 1873, Glasner & Barzen, Kansas City, 10 x 8 In. $544

Soulis Auctions

Stoneware, Jug, Cobalt Blue Butterfly, Julius Norton, 1800s, 12 In. $295

Copake Auction

Stoneware, Jug, Cobalt Blue Feather, Lug Handles, Molded Rim, 1800s, 11 In. $115

Keystone Auctions LLC

Jug, Cobalt Blue, Oval, Tooled Spout, Impressed 1800s, White's, Utica, 11 In.	163
Jug, Cone Top, 2-Tone, Black Stamp, J.H. Conradt & Co. Wholesale Liquors, 11 In.	416
Jug, Dark Olive Alkaline Glaze, Lanier Meaders, Ga., c.1980, Gal., 10½ In.	384
Jug, Death Of Lord Nelson, 1905, 1½ In.	132
Jug, Face, Olive Matte Alkaline, Painted Teeth, Eyes, Signed, Lanier Meaders, 8 In.	900
Jug, Gray, Bellarmine, Molded Face, Rosettes, Shield, 1800s, 19 In.	1722
Jug, Handle, Brown & Tan Glaze, Incised, Richard Hughes, 1850s, 4 Gal., 18 In.	138
Jug, Horse, Running, M.E. Donally & Co., New York, 9¾ In.	225
Jug, Incised Bird, Oval, 2 Handles, Benjamin Suttles, c.1875	1000
Jug, M. Quinn, Wholesale Grocer, Salt Glaze, Bail Handle, 10 In.	256
Jug, Olive Green Alkaline Glaze, Wide Spout, Handles, N.C., Late 1800s, 5 Gal., 18 In.	472
Jug, Oval, Brown, J. Swank & Co., Johnstown, Pennsylvania, 1800s, 14½ In.	250
Jug, Oval, Wide Band Collar, Strap Handle, c.1850, 4 Gal., 15 In.	1046
Jug, Salt Glaze, Cobalt Blue Letters, C. Welty & Bro., Handle, c.1880, 2 Gal., 14 In.	293
Jug, Salt Glaze, Flowers, Grooved Mouth, Handles, Stamped, J. Miller, Va., 2 Gal., 14 x 6 In.	468
Jug, Salt Glaze, Squared Rim, Arched Handles, Henrico Co., Va., c.1835, 6 Gal., 17 x 9 In.	585
Jug, Salt Glaze, Strap Handle, Stamped, Mt. Crawford, Va., c.1875, Gal., 11 In.	117
Jug, Salt Glaze, Strap Handle, Wilkes Street Pottery, Va., 1847, ½ Gal., 8 x 6 In.	117
Jug, Salt Glaze, Temperance, 4 Snakes, Faces, Head Stopper, D.B. Garner, 1993, 12 In. ......*illus*	175
Jug, Shoulder, 5, Cobalt Blue Keystone, Pfaltzgraff, 1930s, 5 Gal.	28
Jug, Wide Band Collar, Applied Strap Handle, Flower, Tyler & Dillon, Albany N.Y., 15 In.	161
Pitcher, Cobalt Blue Flowers & Feathers, Salt Glaze, Strap Handle, Strasburg, 9 x 4 In.	527
Pitcher, Cobalt Blue Flowers, Cowden & Wilcox Harrisburg, Pennsylvania, 1800s, 8⅜ In.	1750
Pitcher, Cobalt Blue Flowers, Handle, West Troy Pottery, 1882, 6 Qt., 2¾ In.	531
Pitcher, Salt Glaze, Stamped, J. Miller, Georgetown, c.1820, Gal., 10½ x 5½ In.	3276
Plate, Transatlantic Steam Ship Co., Paddle Steamer, Imari Border, 1838, 10 In. ....*illus*	1625
Platter, Well & Tree, Multicolor Flowers, White Ground, Octagonal, 1900s, 20 In.	25
Punch Bowl, Figures, Landscapes, Abrm Jackson, Salt Glaze, Footed, c.1800s, 10 In. ....*illus*	702
Sculpture, Glaze, Mounted On Wood Base, Harrison McIntosh, c.1975, 9¾ x 5 x 5 In.	1125
Vase, Ahpul, Glazed, Signed, Claude Conover, Ohio, c.1965, 16 x 16½ In.	5313
Vase, Amantla, Glazed, Signed, Claude Conover, Ohio, c.1965, 10½ x 16 In.	2625
Vase, Lid, Chartreuse, Gray & Black Bands, E. Sottsass, Bitossi, Italy, c.1955, 7 In. ......*illus*	52625
Vase, Molded Fish, Glazed, Bag Shape, c.1900, 2½ In.	1476
Vase, Oxblood, Speckled, Bottle Shape, Shouldered, Stoneware, Dalpayrat, c.1900, 10½ In.	1125
Vase, Stylized Mistletoe, Turquoise Glaze, Double Gourd Shape, Dalpayrat, 1890s, 10 In.	1000
Vase, White Glaze, Squat, Small Mouth, Incised, Parks, 9½ In.	277
Water Cooler, Cobalt Blue Flowers, 2 Handles, Wooden Spigot, c.1850, 15 In.	300
Water Cooler, Lid, Barrel Shape, Blue Stripes, Crown Stamp, 17½ x 13 In.	94
Water Filter, 3 Part, Cobalt Blue, Lug Handles, Baltimore, 1800s, 24½ In.	1250

STORE fixtures, cases, cutters, and other items that have no company advertising as part of the decoration are listed here. Most items found in an old store are listed in the Advertising category in this book.

Bin, Grain, Pine, 2 Slant Lids, Interior Compartments, Painted, c.1875, 30 x 36 In.	630
Bin, Pine, Painted, Red, Black Greek Key Band, Green Inside, Hinged Lid, 1800s, 30 x 18 In.	153
Bin, Seed, Tower Shape, 2 Parts, 12 Drawers, Brass Label Slots, 1950, 44 x 19 x 17 In.	450
Cabinet, Pine, Grain Painted, 6 Drawers, Mushroom Pulls, 1800s, 9 x 56 x 9 In.	660
Case, Display, Cherry, Side Glass Panels, Mirror Back, Counter, Thos. Moser, 14 x 47 x 24 In.	410
Case, Display, Cold, Metal & Wood, Paint, 2 Doors, Crystal-Fremont, Counter, 34 x 18 In.	141
Case, Display, Notions, Country, Grand Rapids Furniture Co., 38 x 96 x 26 In.	1074
Case, Display, Oak Frame, Curved Glass Top, Wire Shelves, 58 x 20 x 17 In.	396
Case, Display, Oak Frame, Glass Panels, Counter, 1900s, 42 x 11 x 14½ In.	236
Case, Display, Oak Frame, Glass Panels, Slant Front, Counter, 12 x 72 x 24 In.	198
Case, Display, Oak Frame, Glass, Sliding Doors, Casters, 44½ x 34 x 22 In.	102
Case, Display, Oak, Glass, 2 Shelves, Door, Counter, Manhattan Show Case Co., c.1900, 19 x 21 x 30 In.	295
Case, Display, Perfume, Tapered Curved Glass, Wood, J. Giraud Fils, c.1925, 26 x 15 x 14 In.	452
Case, Display, Wood & Glass, 2 Shelves, Bottom Rack, 2 Doors, c.1900, 32 x 22 x 22 In.	246
Chest, Flour, Bin, 5 Compartments, Black Metal, Cylindrical, Complete, 16 x 36 In. ....*illus*	532
Cigar Cutter, Brass, Mahogany, Miniature Guillotine Steel, Early 1900s, 2 x 3 In. ....*illus*	150
Cigar Cutter, Cast Iron, Windup Automatic, Erie Specialty Co., 1889, 6 x 4½ x 4 In.	101
Cigar Cutter, Parrot, Brass, Round Tray, Mechanical, c.1930, 5½ x 9½ x 6 In.	90

S

Coffee Grinders are listed in the Coffee Mill category.

Counter, Country, Oak, Paneled Front & Sides, 2 Cash Drawers, 1 Hole, 34 x 60 x 28 In.	226
Counter, Country, Walnut, Paneled, Painted Column, 13 Drawers, c.1880, 35 x 99 In.	622
Counter, Mercantile, 2 Doors, 4 Drawers, Victorian, 36 x 82 ½ x 27 ½ In.	605
Desk, Slant Front, 5 Drawers, Fitted, Mushroom Pulls, Poplar, 1800s, 40 x 23 x 17 In.	189
Dispenser, Ice Cream Cone, Metal, Glass, Bottom Clamp, 35 x 5 In.	254
Display, Clown, Paper Graphics On Plywood, Holds 24 Lollipops On Back, 25 In. ....*illus*	46
Display, Elephant, Nodder, Papier-Mache, Wood Base, Battery Operated, c.1920, 22 x 27 In.	1368
Display, Glove, Hand Shape, PRO-M, General Porcelain, Trenton, N.J., 12 In. ....*illus*	92
Display, Holds 15 Knives, Wood, Storage Doors On Back, 21 x 18 In.	127
Display, Horse, Wood, Carved, Gold Paint, Late 1800s, 25 x 23 In.	345
Display, Nuts, They're Hot, Salted In The Shell, Metal, Glass, Electric, 10 x 12 x 15 In.	254
Display, Shoelaces, Wood Case, Glass Front, Metal Trays, 17 x 14 In.	170
Meat Slicer, Van Berkels, U.S. Slicing Machine Co., 24 x 36 x 27 In.	1921
Pie Safe, 3 Tiers, Mixed Woods, Late 1800s, 33 x 18¾ x 19 In.	153
Rack, Display, Walnut, Tree Shape, Center Post, 12 Arms, Late 1800s, 39 In.	175
Rack, Sack, Stringholder, Wood, Stenciled Sides & Back, c.1890, 20 x 8 x 16 In.	509
Sign, Groceries, Pine, Black Letters, White Ground, Early 1900s, 13 x 6 x 8 In.	240
Sign, Hair Goods, Black, Vertical Gilt Letters, 1850s, 66 ½ x 13 ¼ In. ....*illus*	1306
Sign, Horse, Running, Oval, Sheet Metal, 29 x 20 ½ In.	502
Sign, Iron, Please Check Your Guns, Brown Background, 3 ½ x 7 ½ In.	42
Sign, Iron, Please Close The Gate, Black, White Letters, Oval, 6 ½ x 3 ¼ In.	42
Sign, Jackknife, Folding Knife, Metal Blade, Walnut Handle, c.1890, 40 In.	2500
Sign, Jewelry, Watch Repair, Watch Shape, Porcelain, Black, Yellow Letters, 15 x 12 In.	360
Sign, Letter G, Plastic, White, 18 x 17 In.	177
Sign, Locksmith, Key Figure, Patina, Wood, c.1910, 53 x 17 ½ In.	1348
Sign, Main Floor, Red Arrow, Wood, Yellow Background, 29 x 24 ¼ In.	94
Sign, Track 21, 2-Sided, White Painted Letters, Black Ground, c.1890, 10 x 38 In.	738
Sign, Wall Paper & Borders, Painted Wood, Ribbon Shape, Red & Gilt, 10 x 151 In.	605
Sign, Welcome, Call Again, Miniature Saddle, Wood, Painted, 15 x 34 In.	281
Stand, Display, 5 Shelves, 4 Legs, 2 Front Wheels, Early 1900s, 25 x 42 x 28 In.	115
String Holder, Cast Iron, Brass, Blade On Top, Thos. Mills, 5 ½ In. ....*illus*	115
Table, Ice Cream, Iron, Marble Top, Wood Swing-Out Seats, Brass Legs, c.1900, 31 x 30 In.	2825

STOVES have been used in America for heating since the eighteenth century and for cooking since the nineteenth century. Most types of wood, coal, gas, kerosene, and even some electric stoves are collected. Salesman's samples may be listed here or in Toy.

Camp, Optimus, Kerosene, 2 Burners	425
Cook, Charter Oak, 6 Burners, G.F. Filley, Pat. 1867, Salesman's Sample, 18 ½ x 19 x 12 In.	203
Cook, Eclipse, Cast Iron, Teakettle, J. & E. Stevens, Salesman's Sample, c.1900, 15 x 9 x 16 In..	396
Cook, Enterprise, 4 Burners, Iron, Phillips & Buttorff, Salesman's Sample, 1800s, 18 x 19 x 13 In..	90
Cook, Godin, Wood Burning, Cast Iron, Oval, France, 36 x 18 ½ In.	225
Cook, Junior, Cast Iron, Nickel, 6 Burners, Bucks Stove & Range, Salesman's Sample, 24 x 15 In. .....*illus*	192
Cook, Kenton, Acme, Black Cast Iron, Salesman's Sample, Early 1900s, 8 x 7 ½ x 13 In.	102
Cook, Kenton, Cast Iron, 7 Burners, 4 Doors, Signed, Salesman's Sample, Early 1900s, 14 ½ x 13 x 6 In.	68
Cook, Optimus, Camping, Portable, 1965	111
Grate, Favorite, Cast Iron, Mounted On Breadboard, 1800s, 10¾ x 14 In.	40
Parlor, Ceramic, Gray Glaze, Rounded Corners, Cherubs, Flowers, 1900s, 34 x 33 x 14 In.	492
Parlor, Ilion No. 4, Cast Iron, Claw Feet, 38 x 23 x 15 In.	136
Parlor, John Clarke, Cast Iron, New York, Miniature, 10 x 7 x 6 In. ....*illus*	124
Parlor, Nesco, No. 12, 4 Legs, Oil, Kerosene, 21 ½ In.	153
Potbelly, Blaze, Cast Iron, Hinged Doors, Ash Pan, Signed, Salesman's Sample, 8 x 4 ½ x 4 ½ In..	40
Stove Plate, Thomas Potts, 1758, Marked, Cast Iron, 24 x 24 In.	922

STRETCH GLASS is named for the strange stretch marks in the glass. It was made by many glass companies in the United States from about 1900 to the 1920s. It is iridescent. Most American stretch glass is molded; most European pieces are blown and may have a pontil mark.

Bowl, Iridescent, Wisteria Purple, Footed, Fenton, 8 x 2 In.	78

Stoneware, Jug, Salt Glaze, Temperance, 4 Snakes, Faces, Head Stopper, D.B. Garner, 1993, 12 In.
$175

Burchard Galleries

TIP
Porcelain and stoneware can be washed, but it is best to hand wash the pieces and not to use the dishwasher.

Stoneware, Plate, Transatlantic Steam Ship Co., Paddle Steamer, Imari Border, 1838, 10 In.
$1,625

Freeman's Auctioneers & Appraisers

S

Stoneware, Punch Bowl, Figures, Landscapes, Abrm Jackson, Salt Glaze, Footed, c.1800s, 10 In.
$702

Jeffrey S. Evans & Associates

Stoneware, Vase, Lid, Chartreuse, Gray & Black Bands, E. Sottsass, Bitossi, Italy, c.1955, 7 In.
$52,625

Wright

Store, Chest, Flour, Bin, 5 Compartments, Black Metal, Cylindrical, Complete, 16 x 36 In.
$532

Morphy Auctions

Store, Cigar Cutter, Brass, Mahogany, Miniature Guillotine Steel, Early 1900s, 2 x 3 In.
$150

Willis Henry Auctions

Tazza, Yellow, Black Trim, Tiffin, 4¾ In.	80
Vase, Iridescent, Gold, Flared Rim, c.1950, 10 In.	295
Vase, Peacock, Purple, Green, Red, Flowers, Flared, Fenton, 7½ In.	112

 SULPHIDES are cameos of unglazed white porcelain encased in transparent glass. The technique was patented in 1819 in France and has been used ever since for paperweights, decanters, tumblers, marbles, and other type of glassware. Paperweights and Marbles are listed in their own categories.

Glass, Dish, Order Of The Garter, Fan Cut Scalloped Edge, c.1830, 6 In.	875
Glass, Farmer Wearing Hat, Standing With Shovel In Hand, Fluted Rim, c.1820, 4 x 2½ In.	812
Glass, Goblet, Prince Albert, 4½ x 3 In.	687
Glass, Plaque, George IV, Portrait, Fan Cut Rounded Corners, 4 x 3 In.	812

 SUMIDA is a Japanese pottery that was made from about 1895 to 1941. Pieces are usually everyday objects—vases, jardinieres, bowls, teapots, and decorative tiles. Most pieces have a very heavy orange-red, blue, brown, black, green, purple, or off-white glaze, with raised three-dimensional figures as decorations. The unglazed part is painted red, green, black, or orange. Sumida is sometimes mistakenly called Sumida gawa, but true Sumida gawa is a softer pottery made in the early 1800s.

Vase, Raised Figures On Sides, Blue, Red, 8¼ x 5½ In.	531
Vase, Relief Dragon On Red Wave, Rectangular, 1800s, 11¼ In. ....*illus*	390

 SUNBONNET BABIES were introduced in 1900 in the book *The Sunbonnet Babies.* The stories were by Eulalie Osgood Grover, illustrated by Bertha Corbett. The children's faces were completely hidden by the sunbonnets. The children had been pictured in black and white before this time, but the color pictures in the book were immediately successful. The Royal Bayreuth China Company made a full line of children's dishes decorated with the Sunbonnet Babies. Some Sunbonnet Babies plates have been reproduced, but they are clearly marked.

Book, Sunbonnet Babies Scenes, Dean's Rag Book Co., 8¼ x 7 In.	35
Playing Cards, Bertha Corbett Illustrations, Merrimack Publishing, 1970s	25
Postcard, Baby Crawling Toward Puppy, Dorothy Dixon, 1905	15
Sugar & Creamer, Monday, Washing, Royal Bayreuth	75
Tablecloth, Days Of The Week, Cotton, 30 x 21 In.	22
Toothpick Holder, Wednesday, Mending, Royal Bayreuth, 3 x 1⅜ In.	22
Trinket Box, Monday, Washing, Royal Bayreuth, 2 x 2 In.	85
Trinket Box, Sunday, Fishing, 4¼ x 2¼ In.	125
Trinket Box, Wednesday, Mending, Spade Shape, Royal Bayreuth, 3 x 3 x 2 In.	49

 SUNDERLAND LUSTER is a name given to a special type of pink luster made by Leeds, Newcastle, and other English firms during the nineteenth century. The luster brothglaze is metallic and glossy and appears to have bubbles in it. Other pieces of luster are listed in the Luster category.

Jug, Pink Luster, Black Transfer, Ship, Three Brothers, 1930s, 8 In.	38
Pitcher, Pink Luster, Ship, Poem, Painted Names, England, 1842, 9¼ x 8 In. ....*illus*	369
Pitcher, Pink Luster, The Sailor's Tear, c.1820, 8 In.	93
Plaque, Pink Luster, Transfer, Portrait, He That Believeth Shall Be Saved, c.1840	125

SUPERMAN was created by two seventeen-year-olds in 1938. The first issue of *Action Comics* had the strip. Superman remains popular and became the hero of a radio show in 1940, cartoons in the 1940s, a television series, and several major movies.

Lunch Box Thermos, Blue Cup Lid, Metal, Plastic, King-Seeley, 1967	56
Pennant, Superman Flying, Blue Ground, White Letters, Tassels, 1966, 29 x 11 In.	104
Toy, Ray Gun, Krypto, 6 Film Strips, Instruction Sheet, Box, 10 In. ....*illus*	2690

S

Store, Display, Clown, Paper Graphics On Plywood, Holds 24 Lollipops On Back, 25 In.
$46

Keystone Auctions LLC

Store, Display, Glove, Hand Shape, PRO-M, General Porcelain, Trenton, N.J., 12 In.
$92

Keystone Auctions LLC

Store, Sign, Hair Goods, Black, Vertical Gilt Letters, 1850s, 66 ½ x 13 ¼ In.
$1,306

Skinner, Inc.

Store, String Holder, Cast Iron, Brass, Blade On Top, Thos. Mills, 5 ½ In.
$115

Keystone Auctions LLC

Stove, Cook, Junior, Cast Iron, Nickel, 6 Burners, Bucks Stove & Range, Salesman's Sample, 24 x 15 In.
$192

Soulis Auctions

Stove, Parlor, John Clarke, Cast Iron, New York, Miniature, 10 x 7 x 6 In.
$124

Hartzell's Auction Gallery, Inc.

S

Sumida, Vase, Relief Dragon On Red Wave, Rectangular, 1800s, 11 ¼ In.
$390

Eldred's

Sunderland, Pitcher, Pink Luster, Ship, Poem, Painted Names, England, 1842, 9 ¼ x 8 In.
$369

Cowan's Auctions

Superman, Toy, Ray Gun, Krypto, 6 Film Strips, Instruction Sheet, Box, 10 In.
$2,690

Milestone Auctions

SUSIE COOPER (1902–1995) began as a designer in 1925 working for the English firm A.E. Gray & Company. In 1931 she formed Susie Cooper Pottery, Ltd. In 1950 it became Susie Cooper China, Ltd., and the company made china and earthenware. In 1966 it was acquired by Josiah Wedgwood & Sons, Ltd. The name *Susie Cooper* appears with the company names on many pieces of ceramics.

| A.E. Gray & Co. c.1925–1931 | Susie Cooper 1932–1934 | Susie Cooper 1932–1964 |

Coffee Set, Coffeepot, 6 Cups, Sugar & Creamer, Stars, Multicolor Interior	950
Cup & Saucer, Gardenia, Thumb Rest, Spur, Green, Gilt, Footed	60
Cup & Saucer, Pink, Roses, Fluted	40
Cup & Saucer, Teal, Roses, Footed	35
Pitcher, Wedding Ring Pattern, Tan, Rust, Green, Earthenware, 3 In.	17
Plate, Flowers, Blue Band, 9 In.	25
Platter, Wedding Ring Pattern, 16 x 12 In.	30
Teapot, Band Of Flowers, Leaves, Orange & Brown, Oval, 6 x 4 ½ In.	40
Teapot, Brown & Orange Flowers, Oval, Art Nouveau, 6 x 4 x 5 In.	40
Teapot, Lid, Tango, Kestral, Art Deco, 5 x 6 ½ In.	228

SWORDS of all types that are of interest to collectors are listed here. The military dress sword with elaborate handle is probably the most wanted. A tsuba is a hand guard fitted to a Japanese sword between the handle and the blade. Be sure to display swords in a safe way, out of reach of children.

Backsword, Basket Hilt, Cone, Wood Grip, Blade, Drury, London, 38 ⅜ In.	10800
Bayonet, Steel, Adjustment Strap, Patinated, 21 In.	57
British Navy, Stamped GR, c.1800, 33 In.	840
Cavalry, Saber, Leather Grip, Stamped, A.E.C. Marca Registrada, Brazil, 1800s, 44 In.	250
Civil War Era Blade, Cast Brass Hilt, Cat Fishscale Grip, 1800s, 3 ½ x 26 x 18 In.	59
Civil War, Sheath, Leather Wrapped Grip, c.1960s, 35 In.	325
Katana, Steel Blade, 2 Characters, Lacquered Wood, Brass Tsuba, Fabric Wrap, c.1950, 24 In.	153
Saber, Cavalry, Scabbard, Iron Ringed, Ribbed, Wooden Grip, Stamped, W. Rose, 1812, 39 In.	780
Samurai, Steel Blade, Decorated Brass Guard, Sharkskin Grip, Japan, c.1945, 39 In.	1452
Samurai, Wakizashi, Ox Bone, Carved Handle, Figures Training, Japan, 20 ¾ x 38 ½ In.	666
Shamshir, Mughal Style, Spinach Jade Ram Handle, 1900s, 36 In.	1063
U.S. Navy, Anchor, Shield, Leather & Brass Scabbard, c.1875, 35 ¾ In.	281

SYRACUSE is one of the trademarks used by the Onondaga Pottery of Syracuse, New York. They also used O.P. Co. The company was established in 1871. The name became the Syracuse China Company in 1966. Syracuse China closed in 2009. It was known for fine dinnerware and restaurant china.

| Syracuse China, Corp. 1871–1873 | Syracuse China, Corp. 1892–1895 | Syracuse China, Corp. 1966–1970 |

Alpine, Coffeepot, Lid, Pink Flower, Platinum Trim, 1950-70, 7 ¾ In.	99
Apple Blossom, Bowl, Vegetable, Oval, 9 ⅞ In.	34
Briarcliff, Soup, Dish, 2 Handles, Cream, Pastel Flowers, Gold Trim, 1949-67	17
Meadow Breeze, Plate, Bread & Butter, 6 ¼ In.	9

Oriental, Pitcher, Gold Trim, Flowers, Leaves, O.P. Co., 1897-1926, 8½ In.		44
Stansbury, Serving Platter, Oval, 16¼ In.		89
Victoria, Creamer, 3½ In.		19
Wedding Ring, Plate, Dinner, 10½ In.		33

Tapestry, Porcelain, see Rose Tapestry category.

TEA CADDY is the name for a small box made to hold tea leaves. In the eighteenth century, tea was very expensive and it was stored under lock and key. The first tea caddies were made with locks. By the nineteenth century, tea was more plentiful and the tea caddy was larger. Often there were two sections, one for green tea, one for black tea.

Black Lacquer, Latticework & Birds, 2 Containers, Glass Bowl, Chinese, 8 x 13 x 7¼ In.	221
Burl & Rosewood Veneer, Rectangular, 2 Interior Compartments, Lids, 1800s, 5 x 9 x 5 In.	108
Burl, Brass Handles, 2 Removable Compartments, Glass Bowl, England, 1800s, 6 x 13 x 7 In.	400
Burl, Coffin Shape, Inlaid, England, 1800s, 8 x 11½ x 6 In.	185
Burl, Dome Lid, 2 Compartments, Brass Mounted, 7 x 9½ In.	200
Burl, Dome Top, Brass Trim, Locking, 5 x 9 x 6½ In.	288
Burl, Hinged Lid, Compartments, Veneer, c.1800, 6 x 12 In.	138
Burl, Lid, Rectangular, Conch Shell & Flower Urn Inlay, 1800s, 4 x 8 x 4 In.	240
Burl, Rectangular, Fruitwood, Lid Shell Inlay, 4 Brass Ball Feet, England, 1800s, 4½ x 9 x 4½ In.	300
Fruitwood, Apple Shape, Steel Lock, George III, c.1800, 4¾ In. *illus*	1875
Fruitwood, Gourd Shape, Brown, Lacquered, Lid, Painted, Late 1700s, 6 In.	2440
Fruitwood, Pear Shape, Wood Stem, England, 19th Century, 6¾ In.	840
Fruitwood, Rectangular, Oval, Flowers, Painted Top & Sides, England, 1800s, 4¾ x 6 In. *illus*	360
Lacquer, Rectangular, Mother-Of-Pearl Inlay, Abalone, Footed, 5½ x 8½ x 6 In.	288
Mahogany Veneer, Oval, Flowered Inlay Top & Front, 1800s, 5 x 5 x 4 In.	240
Mahogany, Box, Brass Handle, Lidded Compartments, Georgian, 1800s, 5 x 8½ x 5 In.	83
Mahogany, Box, Conch Shell Inlay, Top & Front, 1800s, 5 x 5 x 4 In.	360
Mahogany, Routed Edge, Bracket Feet, 3 Lids, Georgian Style, Compartments, 1800s, 7 x 10 x 6 In.	94
Mahogany, Satinwood Border, Brass Lion's Head Handles, Footed, England, c.1840, 6 x 12 x 6 In.	123
Mahogany, Satinwood Patera, Oval Burl Inlay, England, Early 1800s, 5 x 10¼ x 5½ In.	135
Mahogany, Veneer, Brass Fixtures, Coffin Shape, Lift Lid, Continental, c.1850, 9 x 15 x 9 In.	132
Maple, Oval, Lid, Light Wood Inlays, Floral Vine, Ribbon, Tin Lined, 5 x 6 x 3½ In.	460
Rectangular, Mother-Of-Pearl Shell Inlay, Peacocks, Early 1800s, 4½ x 8 In.	472
Rolled Paper, Octagonal, Gold Paint, Floral, Mica & Sanded Ground, England, c.1800, 5 x 6 In. *illus*	210
Rosewood, Coffin Shape, 2 Satinwood Compartments, England, c.1800s, 10 x 16½ x 8 In.	480
Rosewood, Rectangle, Ring Handles, Lock, Ball Feet, Regency, 4½ x 7½ x 6 In.	184
Satinwood, 3 Sections, Rectangular, 1800s, 5 x 11 x 5 In.	120
Shagreen, Pear Shape Containers, Cartouches, Claw Feet, Aldridge & Stamper, 6½ In., Pair	6000
Shagreen, Silver Mounts, Velvet Interior, c.1800, 8 x 13 In.	1800
Silver, Oval Box, Armorial, Ornate Floral Finial, Parker & Wakelin, England, 1760, 4¾ In.	2706
Silver, Oval Box, Landscape Scenery, Anglo Colonial Burmese, 1800s, 4½ x 4½ x 3 In.	475
Silver, Round, Repousse Flowers, Leaves, Fordham & Faulkner, Victorian, 1900, 6 x 3⅝ x 3 In.	550
Silver, Yellow Enamel, Column Shape, c.1905, 5¾ In.	250
Tiger Wood, Rectangular, Hinged Lid, Brass Trim, Locking, 5 x 9 x 5½ In.	230
Tole, Cottage Form, Painted Metal, Vine Around Door, England, c.1920, 7¾ In.	3600
Tole, Tan Chinoiserie, Black Ground, Coffin Lid, 4 Paw Feet, c.1830, 4¾ x 4¾ In.	738
Walnut, Lift Lid, Patera Inlay, Bone Escutcheon, Brass Handle, 1900s, 4½ In.	240
Wood, Apple Shape, Hinged Lid, Stem Finial, 1800s, 5 In.	923
Wood, Apple Shape, Key & Lock, Foil Lined, 6 In. *illus*	367
Wood, Black Forest, Carved, Sheep & Lamb On Top Of Strap, Lock, 1800s, 4½ x 8 In.	207
Wood, Bowfront, Mother-Of-Pearl Shell Inlay, Birds, Flowers, Early 1800s, 6 x 8 In.	885
Wood, Bowfront, Pagoda Shape, 2 Inlaid Compartments, c.1840, 6 x 7 In.	1440
Wood, Dome Lid, Shell Panels, Escutcheon, Lion Handles, Regency, 5 x 4¾ x 4 In.	192
Wood, Dome Top, Boxwood Inlay, Diamonds, Fans, 4½ x 9 x 6½ In.	403
Wood, Hinged Locking Lid, 3 Sections, Pedestal, 4-Legged, Casters, 32 x 22 x 18 In.	944
Wood, Oval, Lid, Landscape, Cowherd, c.1790, 5 x 6 In.	799
Wood, Oval, Lid, Pastoral Landscapes, Bail Handle, England, Late 1700s, 4½ x 4¾ In.	1750
Wood, Pear Shape, Painted Silver Lining, Mother-Of-Pearl Keyhole & Lock, 11 In.	283
Wood, Porcelain Panels, Figures, Garden, Lacquer, Footed, 9¼ In.	126

Tea Caddy, Fruitwood, Apple Shape, Steel Lock, George III, c.1800, 4¾ In. **$1,875**

Pook & Pook

TIP
If your tea caddy or knife box has a silver or brass keyhole don't use a metal cleaner. The cleaner will damage the wood.

Tea Caddy, Fruitwood, Rectangular, Oval, Flowers, Painted Top & Sides, England, 1800s, 4¾ x 6 In. **$360**

Eldred's

Tea Caddy, Rolled Paper, Octagonal, Gold Paint, Floral, Mica & Sanded Ground, England, c.1800, 5 x 6 In. **$210**

Garth's Auctioneers & Appraisers

This is an edited listing of current prices. Visit **Kovels.com** to check thousands of prices from previous years and sign up for free information on trends, tips, reproductions, marks, and more.

T

Tea Caddy, Wood, Apple Shape, Key & Lock, Foil Lined, 6 In.
$367

Hartzell's Auction Gallery, Inc.

Teco, Vase, Squash Blossom, Terra-Cotta, Stamped, c.1910, 10 ½ In.
$1,500

Rago Arts and Auction Center

Telephone, Ericofon, Plastic, Rubber, Thames, Lysell & Blomberg, Ericsson, Sweden, 1954, 8 In.
$133

Wright

Wood, Rectangular, 2 Interior Compartments, Lids, Mother-Of-Pearl Keyhole, 5 ½ x 10 x 6 In.	170
Wood, Rectangular, Banded, Leaf & Vine Inlay, Georgian, 1800s, 4 ¼ x 4 ¼ x 3 ¾ In.	270
Wood, Rectangular, Claw Feet, Brass Decorated, 3 Partitions Inside, 1800s, 10 ½ x 6 x 6 ½ In.	384
Wood, Rosewood, Hardwood, Cut Glass Bowl, Footed, Handled, 7 x 13 x 9 In.	403

TEA LEAF IRONSTONE dishes are named for their decorations. There was a superstition that it was lucky if a whole tea leaf unfolded at the bottom of your tea-cup. This idea was translated into the pattern of dishes known as "tea leaf." By 1850 at least 12 English factories were making this pattern, and by the 1870s it was a popular pattern in many countries. The tea leaf was always a luster glaze on early wares, although now some pieces are made with a brown tea leaf. There are many variations of tea leaf designs, such as Teaberry, Pepper Leaf, and Gold Leaf. The designs were used on many different white ironstone shapes, such as Bamboo, Lily of the Valley, Empress, and Cumbow.

Bowl, Square, Scalloped, Fluted, White, Alfred Meakin, England, 8 x 3 In.	11
Bowl, Vegetable, Lid, Rectangular, Molded Handles, c.1885, 10 x 7 In.	136
Chamber Pot, Lid, Handle, White, Canonsburg, 7 x 4 ¾ In.	13
Coffeepot, Morning Glory, Copper Luster, Bell Shape Flower Finial, c.1875, 10 In.	87
Coffeepot, Morning Glory, Copper Luster, Elsmore & Forstel, c.1875, 10 In.	82
Compote, Red Cliff, 8 x 8 x 4 In.	50
Cup & Saucer, Alfred Meakin	35
Cup & Saucer, Fortune Teller, Witches, White, Icons, Petersyn	325
Gravy Boat, Cable Style, Thomas Furnival & Sons, c.1880, 9 x 5 ½ In.	90
Mug, Lid, Handle, White, Anthony Shaw, 2 ½ x 2 ¾ In., Child's	46
Pitcher, Ribbed Neck, H. Burgess, 1800s, 11 In.	65
Pitcher, Shaped Handle & Rim, Maroon & White, 8 ½ In.	15
Platter, A.J. Wilkinson, 1896, 11 x 16 In.	38
Sugar, Lid, Handles, Mellor, Taylor & Co., c.1900, 6 x 4 x 6 In.	75
Teapot, Lid, Acorn Finial, Chinese Shape, Anthony Shaw, c.1850, 9 ½ x 9 ½ In.	53
Toothbrush Holder, Alfred Meakin, 5 x 2 ¾ In.	70
Tray, Handle, Alfred Meakin, 1880s, 9 x 9 In.	78
Tureen, Lid, Bamboo, Alfred Meakin, c.1875, 11 x 7 x 5 In.	87

TECO is the mark used on the art pottery line made by the American Terra Cotta and Ceramic Company of Terra Cotta and Chicago, Illinois. The company was an offshoot of the firm founded by William D. Gates in 1881. The Teco line was first made in 1885 but was not sold commercially until 1902. It continued in production until 1922. Over 500 designs were made in a variety of colors, shapes, and glazes. The company closed in 1930.

Vase, 2 Handles, Light Brown Matte Glaze Impressed Marl, W.B. Mundie, Chicago, 11 x 5 In.	1250
Vase, Bulbous, Green Matte Glaze, 4 x 4 In.	331
Vase, Buttress, Arts & Crafts, 4 Handles, Green Matte Glaze, 7 ⅜ In.	225
Vase, Flower Form, Bulbous Top, Tall Tapered Base, c.1910, 18 ¾ x 7 In.	1875
Vase, Glossy Metallic Glaze, Brown To Tan, 8 In.	287
Vase, Green Matte Glaze, Fritz Albert, c.1910, 9 ½ In.	565
Vase, Green Matte Glaze, Yellow Speckles, Handles, 11 In.	517
Vase, Pinched Sides, Matte Glaze, 4 x 4 ¼ In.	660
Vase, Reticulated, Leaves, Terra-Cotta, c.1910, 11 x 4 In.	3750
Vase, Squash Blossom, Terra-Cotta, Stamped, c.1910, 10 ½ In. *illus*	1500

TEDDY BEARS were named for a president of the United States. The first teddy bear was a cuddly toy said to be inspired by a hunting trip made by President Theodore Roosevelt in 1902. He was praised because he saw a bear cub but did not shoot it. Morris and Rose Michtom started selling their stuffed bears as "teddy bears" and the name stayed. The Michtoms founded the Ideal Novelty and Toy Company. The German version of the teddy bear was made about the same time by the Steiff Company. There are many types of teddy bears and all are collected. The old ones are being reproduced. Other bears are listed in the Toy section.

Chiltern, Hugmee, Dralon, Plush, Velvet, Beige, United Kingdom, 1950-60, 22 In.	114
Gebruder Bing, Mohair, Light Brown, Glass Eyes, 1920s	2247

Ideal, Mohair, Brown, Shoebutton Eyes, Ribbon, Jointed, 15 In.	401
Knickerbocker, Mohair, Glass Eye, Roaring, Green, 1930s, 28 In.	26
Merrythought, Mohair, White, Red Backpack, Tags, Special Map, England, 10 In.	38
Mohair, Brown, Hermann Style, Ribbon, Tag, Germany, 24 In.	21
Mohair, Golden, Collar Bell, Ear Tag, 12 In.	48
Steiff, Growler, Mohair, Blond, Glass Eyes, Stitched Features, Humped Back, Squeeze, 9½ In.	90
Steiff, Mohair, Fully Jointed, Ear Button & Tag, 6½ In.	69
Steiff, Mohair, Golden, Swivel Head, Amber Eyes, Jointed Hips, Ear Button, c.1945, 4 In.	288
Steiff, Repro Of 1907 Bear, Mohair, Brown, Limited Edition, Box, 25 x 15 x 9 In.	90
Steiff, Repro Of 1908 Bear, Mohair, Blond, Button In Ear, Box, 24 x 14 x 9 In.	57
Steiner, Growler, Brown, Shoebutton Eyes, Stitched Nose, Mouth, England, 16 In.	97

TELEPHONES are wanted by collectors if the phones are old enough or unusual enough. The first telephone may have been made in Havana, Cuba, in 1849, but it was not patented. The first publicly demonstrated phone was used in Frankfurt, Germany, in 1860. The phone made by Alexander Graham Bell was shown at the Centennial Exhibition in Philadelphia in 1876, but it was not until 1877 that the first private phones were installed. Collectors today want all types of old phones, phone parts, and advertising. Even recent figural phones are popular.

Automatic Electric, Monophone, Chrome Trim Front View, Jade Green, 5 x 8 In.	210
Bell System, Paperweight, Glass, Blue, New York Telephone Company	11
Bell, Sign, Flange, 2-Sided, 11 x 11 In.	116
Booth, 2 Glass Doors, Fan, Light, Wooden	203
Ericofon, Plastic, Rubber, Thames, Lysell & Blomberg, Ericsson, Sweden, 1954, 8 In. ...*illus*	133
ITT, Rotary Phone, Red, Desktop, c.1970	52
Kellogg, Switchboard, Station, Quartersawn Oak Case, 31 Audio Cables, 42 x 29 x 35 In. ...*illus*	424
Kellogg, Wall, Hand Crank, Wood Box	168
Kellogg, Wall, Military, Magneto, Wood, Dovetailed, 1945, 12½ In.	41
Monarch Mfg. Co., Crank, Oak, Wall, 1900s, 25¼ In. ...*illus*	96
Northern Electric, Oak, Rotary Dial, Handset, 22 x 8 In.	159
Stromberg-Carlson, Candlestick, Dial, Black & White	86
Tyco, Garfield, Eyes Open & Closes, Plastic, Desktop	25
Wall, Oak Body, Brass, Hand Crank, Lacquered, Wood Case. ...*illus*	127
Western Electric, 202 Bell System, Refurbished Phone, Subset	73
Western Electric, F1, Wall, Metal, Bell System, 9 In. ...*illus*	150
Western Electric, Oak, Writing Ledge, Wall Mount, c.1915, 20½ x 9½ x 12¾ In. ...*illus*	100

TELEVISION sets are twentieth-century collectibles. Although the first television transmission took place in England in 1925, collectors find few sets that pre-date 1946. The first sets had only five channels, but by 1949 the additional UHF channels were included. The first color television set became available in 1951.

Costume, Happy Days, Pair Of Shorts, Blue Suede, Silver Medallions, Fringe, 1977 ...*illus*	180
Emerson, Rabbit Ears Antenna, Cigarette Lighter Plug, Remote, Portable, Off-White, Box, 9 In.	41
Philco, Ford, Blue Screen, Black & White, 14 In.	20

TEPLITZ refers to art pottery manufactured by a number of companies in the Teplitz-Turn area of Bohemia during the late nineteenth and early twentieth centuries. Two of these companies were the Alexandra Works founded by Ernst Wahliss, and the Amphora Porcelain Works, run by Riessner, Stellmacher, and Kessel.

Card Tray, Water Sprite, Lily Pads, Ernst Wahliss, Amphora, 1900, 4 x 13½ x 13 In.	1250
Centerpiece, Figural, Nude, Female, Marked, Riessner, Stellmacher & Kessel, Amphora, 12 x 20 In.	726
Centerpiece, Figural, Woman, Blue & Gold, Signed, RStK Mark, Amphora, 28½ x 19 In.	968
Centerpiece, Shell Shape, 2 Doves, Woman, RStK, Amphora, 22½ x 14 x 12¾ In.	968
Compote, Gres, Art Nouveau, Marked, Amphora, 9½ x 9⅝ In.	1029
Dish, Lid, Figural, Turtle, Frog On Back, Marked, Czecho-Slovakia, 5 x 10 In.	295
Ewer, Art Nouveau, Maidens, Flowing Gowns, Gold Tone, Ernst Wahliss, 12 In., Pair ...*illus*	1107
Ewer, Birch Trees, Mushrooms, Paul Dachsel, Amphora, 1907, 6 x 5½ In.	813

Telephone, Kellogg, Switchboard, Station, Quartersawn Oak Case, 31 Audio Cables, 42 x 29 x 35 In.
$424

Fontaine's Auction Gallery

Telephone, Monarch Mfg. Co., Crank, Oak, Wall, 1900s, 25¼ In.
$96

Garth's Auctioneers & Appraisers

Telephone, Wall, Oak Body, Brass, Hand Crank, Lacquered, Wood Case
$127

Keystone Auctions LLC

T

Telephone, Western Electric, F1, Wall, Metal, Bell System, 9 In.
$150

Keystone Auctions LLC

Telephone, Western Electric, Oak, Writing Ledge, Wall Mount, c.1915, 20½ x 9½ x 12¾ In.
$100

Garth's Auctioneers & Appraisers

Television, Costume, Happy Days, Pair Of Shorts, Blue Suede, Silver Medallions, Fringe, 1977
$180

Potter & Potter Auctions

Ewer, Flowers, Cream & Green Tones, Footed, 6 In.	25
Figurine, Bust, Woman, Stamped RStK Mark, Amphora, 11 x 10 In.	182
Figurine, Dancer, Loie Fuller, Werke Reissner, Amphora, 19 x 17 In.	3630
Figurine, Leaf Woman, Maiden, Long Flowing Hair, Leaves, Amphora, Signed, 21 x 18 In.	3690
Figurine, Loie Fuller, Dancing, Flowing Gown, Scarf, Yellow Gold Glaze, Signed, 20 In. ....*illus*	3075
Figurine, Skiff, Woman Paddling, Daughter Peering, 1900s, 26 x 31 In.	270
Figurine, Young Maiden, Wearing Green Toga, Signed, Ernst Wahliss, 14 x 11 In.	1320
Incense Burner, Raindrops, Paul Dachsel, Amphora, 7 x 6 In.	1125
Jardiniere, Gres-Bijou, Amphora, 12½ x 16 In.	1500
Pitcher, Portrait, Nikolaus Kannhauser, Amphora, 1900, 9 x 5½ In.	2375
Pitcher, Water, Enameled, Handled, Art Nouveau, Signed, Amphora, 11½ x 8 In.	151
Vase, Applied Decoration, 2 Blue Green Handles, Amphora, 1900s, 15 In.	225
Vase, Art Nouveau, Eastern Dragons, Glazed, Eduard Stellmacher, Amphora, 14 x 10½ In.	12100
Vase, Bur Marigold Pattern, Amphora, Marked, Austria, c.1900, 16½ In.	250
Vase, Cobalt Blue Glaze, Long Neck, Gilt, Marked, Amphora, 11⅝ x 7 In.	7260
Vase, Figural Reserve, Gilt Ground, Leaf Scroll Handles, Amphora, Paris, 1800s, 14 In. ....*illus*	313
Vase, Jugendstil, Molded Rose Garlands, Incised Crown, RStK, Early 1900s, 9½ In.	308
Vase, Lady Of The Woods, Maiden, Long Hair, Openwork Handles, RStK, c.1890, 14¾ In.	1074
Vase, Leaf, Art Nouveau, Loop Handles, Marked, Paul Dachsel, Amphora, 12 x 5 In.	575
Vase, Lion Relief, Gres Bijou, Werker Reissner, Amphora, 11 x 10½ In.	1210
Vase, Maiden Portrait, Allegory Of Russia, Amphora, RStK, c.1900, 6 x 4 In. ......*illus*	1375
Vase, Octopus, Seahorse, Eduard Stellmacher, Amphora, 1902, 16 x 7 In.	3750
Vase, Owl & Mice, Matte Glaze, Signed, Bernard Bloch, c.1900, 9½ x 8 In.	1105
Vase, Pterodactyl, Dragon, Red Stamp, Embossed Medallion, Stellmacher, 1906, 26 In.....*illus*	9375
Vase, Rooster Relief, Trees, Marked, Werke Reissner, Amphora, 16 x 10 In.	393
Vase, Stork, Multicolor, Amphora, Art Nouveau, c.1900, 9 In. ......*illus*	250
Vase, Woodland, Rising Sun, Glazed, Marked, Amphora, 13 x 5 In.	726
Vide Poche, Maiden, Long Flowing Hair, Gilt Flower, Art Nouveau, Amphora, 26½ x 20 In.	7380

 TERRA-COTTA is a special type of pottery. It ranges from pale orange to dark reddish-brown in color. The color comes from the clay, which is fired but not always glazed in the finished piece.

Bust, North African Man, Painted, Late 1800s, 18½ In.	813
Bust, White, Wavy Hair, Green Shirt, Blue Tunic, Italy, 1900s, 13 x 11 In.	104
Figurine, Dog, Begging, Wearing Hat, Smoking Cigar, Glass Eyes, Painted, Victorian, 19 In. ...	460
Figurine, Dwarf, Sitting On Log, Painted, 30 In. ......*illus*	1200
Figurine, Horse, Standing, Saddle, Sancai, Flat Base, Tang Style, Chinese, 1920, 17 In. ....*illus*	185
Fountain, Figural, 4 Seminude Maidens Beneath Bowl, Fluted Pedestal Base, 36 In.	3025
Garden Seat, Turtle, White, Pillow Resting On Top, Glazed, Italy, 15 x 22 x 17 In.	344
Jar, Dark Green Glaze, China, 1900s, 14 x 22 In.	800
Jar, Olive, Neutral Color, Round Shape, France, c.1850, 23 x 33 In.	2400
Jar, Seed, Hand Crafted, Painted, Signed, 5 x 12½ In.	3540
Lamp, Concentric Rings, Bands, Black, Green, Blue, White, London Lamp Co., c.1950, 18 x 6 In.	68
Oil Jar, Oval, Remnants Of Later Paint, Molded Foot & Rim, 1900s, 28 x 21 In.	130
Pedestal, 4 Twist Columns, Acanthus Capitals, 48 x 19 In.	1560
Pitcher, Paisley, Clam Glaze, Handle, c.1980, 11 x 10 In.	59
Rosette, Architectural Detail, Center Circular Flower, 4-Point Stars, 10 x 10 x 4 In.	31
Tile, 3 Musicians, Lush Garden, Blue Border, 1800s, 9½ x 15 In. ......*illus*	502
Tureen, Lid, Children Shape, Unglazed Exterior, Clear Glazed Interior, 1970s, 12 x 8 In.	150
Umbrella Stand, Swirling Cloud, Dragons, Ocean Waves, Gilt, Chinese, 23½ x 10 In.	961
Urn, White Glaze, Plinth Base, Double Handled, Lion, Flowers, 33 x 49 In.	250
Vase, Art Nouveau, Figural Crayfish, Stems, Flower Heads, Glazed, Austria, 18 x 11 In.	367
Vase, Carved, Crane Motif, Japan, Late 1800s, 17 In.	266

 TEXTILES listed here include many types of printed fabrics and table and household linens. Some other textiles will be found under Clothing, Coverlet, Rug, Quilt, etc.

Banner, Circus, Giraffe Girl, Canvas, Snap Wyatt, c.1950, 113 x 69 In. ......*illus*	1250
Embroidery, Mourning, William Jackson, Died 1849, Verse, Frame, England, 24 In. ......*illus*	184

Teplitz, Ewer, Art Nouveau, Maidens, Flowing Gowns, Gold Tone, Ernst Wahliss, 12 In., Pair
$1,107

Morphy Auctions

Teplitz, Figurine, Loie Fuller, Dancing, Flowing Gown, Scarf, Yellow Gold Glaze, Signed, 20 In.
$3,075

Morphy Auctions

Teplitz, Vase, Figural Reserve, Gilt Ground, Leaf Scroll Handles, Amphora, Paris, 1800s, 14 In.
$313

Neal Auction Company

Teplitz, Vase, Maiden Portrait, Allegory Of Russia, Amphora, RStK, c.1900, 6 x 4 In.
$1,375

Rago Arts and Auction Center

Teplitz, Vase, Pterodactyl, Dragon, Red Stamp, Embossed Medallion, Stellmacher, 1906, 26 In.
$9,375

Rago Arts and Auction Center

Teplitz, Vase, Stork, Multicolor, Amphora, Art Nouveau, c.1900, 9 In.
$250

Pook & Pook

Terra-Cotta, Figurine, Dwarf, Sitting On Log, Painted, 30 In.
$1,200

Fox Auctions

Terra-Cotta, Figurine, Horse, Standing, Saddle, Sancai, Flat Base, Tang Style, Chinese, 1920, 17 In.
$185

Cowan's Auctions

Terra-Cotta, Tile, 3 Musicians, Lush Garden, Blue Border, 1800s, 9 ½ x 15 In.
$502

Leland Little Auctions

Textile, Banner, Circus, Giraffe Girl, Canvas, Snap Wyatt, c.1950, 113 x 69 In.
$1,250

Garth's Auctioneers & Appraisers

Textile, Embroidery, Mourning, William Jackson, Died 1849, Verse, Frame, England, 24 In.
$184

Bunch Auctions

Textile, Embroidery, Weeping Willow, Woman, Cut Paper Memorial, c.1808, 12½ x 11 In.
$1,200

Eldred's

Embroidery, Weeping Willow, Woman, Cut Paper Memorial, c.1808, 12½ x 11 In...........*illus*	1200
Flag, American, 7 Stars, Confederate Reunion, 1st National Flag, 26¾ x 57 In.	1560
Flag, American, 13 Stars, Confederate Southern Cross, c.1925, 61¾ x 35 In.	720
Flag, American, 13 Stars, Machine Sewn Stripes, Cotton, 65 x 44 In.	3600
Flag, American, 34 Stars, Handmade, Hand Sewn, 71 x 99 In........	2880
Flag, American, 35 Stars, Wool Bunting, Brass Grommets, c.1863, 84 x 162 In.	625
Flag, American, 37 Stars, Silk, 1867, 41¼ x 31 In. ....*illus*	523
Flag, American, 38 Stars, Flower Pattern, Linen, Frame, 13 x 21½ In.	9600
Flag, American, 44 Stars, 13 Stripes, 1891, 16 x 12 In.	594
Flag, American, 45 Stars, Hand Stitched, Double Applique	780
Flag, American, 46 Stars, Annin & Co., Early 1900s, 140 x 83 In.	283
Flag, American, 48 Stars, 7 Flags Of Different Sizes, Frame, 35 x 56 In.	3198
Flag, American, 48 Stars, Crocheted Crepe Paper, Painted Pole, Meta Schmitt, c.1936, 33 x 54 In. ...*illus*	344
Flag, American, 48 Stars, Parade, 34 x 24 In.	81
Flag, Georgian Naval, Red, White, Russia, 38 x 62 In.	18
Flag, Rochester Union Grays, Union Is Strength, 1839, 62 x 71 In........	4425
Obi Sash, Silk, Gilt Embroidery, Cream Ground, Maru, Japan, 1900s, 13 x 12¼ In..........*illus*	48
Panel, Kesi, Silk, Rectangular, Woman & Boy, Frame, Chinese, 42 x 16¼ In.	375
Piano, Scarf, Black Silk, Embroidery Flowers, Early 1900s, 65 x 65 In. .....*illus*	125
Remnant, Woven, Yellow, Flowers, Leaf, England, 62 x 16 In.	148
Silk, Married Couple, Seated, Gold Stick Frame, Floral, Chinese, 1920, 19 x 15½ In.	30
Silkwork, Milkmaid Going To Work, Gilt Cove Frame, Gold Eglomise Mat, c.1820, 19 x 16 In. .	120
Tapestry, Abstract, Woven Fabric, Heart Shape, Signed, Saul Borisov, 24 x 70 In.	288
Tapestry, Circus, Wool, Stylized Figure, After Joan Miro, 1970s, 78½ x 59 In........*illus*	7500
Tapestry, Dragons, Clouds, Silk, Gold Thread, Navy, Frame, 40½ x 78½ In.	7995
Tapestry, Fond De Mer, Wool, Signed, Lars Gynning, Sweden, 77½ x 78 In. ....*illus*	6150
Tapestry, Genre Scene, Flemish, Baroque Style, 1800s, 92 x 49 In.	1250
Tapestry, Panel, Embroidered, Chariot, Horses, People, Wood Frame, Thailand, 27 x 41 In.	125
Tapestry, Printed, Unicorn, Captivity, Metal Rod, 1900s, 64 In.	121
Tapestry, Rambouillet, Red Background, Design After Portique De Junon, 49 x 37 In.......*illus*	250
Wall Hanging, Houses, Cotton, Screen Printed, A. Girard, Herman Miller Fabrics, 1964, 48 In..*illus*	1000

THERMOMETER is a name that comes from the Greek word for heat. The thermometer was invented in 1731 to measure the temperature of either water or air. All kinds of thermometers are collected, but those with advertising messages are the most popular.

Arrow 77 Beer, Printed Metal, Globe Brewing Co., 1950, 27 x 7½ In.	144
Bath Water, Celluloid, Green, Yellow Ducks, c.1950, 4 x 2 x 1 In.	35
Bear, Wood, Black Forest, Glass Eyes, c.1900, 6 In.	222
Blatchford's Calf Meal, Animal Feeds, Wood, Hanging, 21 x 8¾ x ¾ In........	944
Camel Cigarettes, Tin, Lithograph, Box, 5¾ x 13½ In........*illus*	102
Chew Mail Pouch Tobacco & Treat Yourself To The Best, Porcelain, 39 x 8 In.	330
Eagle Topper, Brass, Marble Base, 9 x 4 x 4 In.	219
Empire State Building, Metal, c.1950, 7 In.	42
Esso, Sohio Gas Oil, Embossed, 6½ In.	46
Exide Batteries, Glass Crystal, Red, White, 12 In.	330
Ex-Lax, Blue Enamel, Yellow Letters, c.1915, 38 x 8 In.	175
Ex-Lax, Chocolated Laxative Millions Prefer, Metal, Blue & Red, 1940s, 37 In.	318
Ex-Lax, Keep Regular, The Chocolate Laxative, Porcelain, 36 x 8 In.	390
Farmers Milk, Tin Lithograph, Wall, Graphics, Lettering, 1950s, 15 x 6 In.	125
Figural, Cable Car, Metal, 4 x 5 In.	18
Figural, Rabbit, Ceramic, Yellow, 1950s, 6½ In.	24
Frostie Root Beer, Vintage, Embossed Metal, Tube, 8¼ x 2¼ In.	161
Harp Shape, Bronze, French Champ Le Vie Enameling, Agate Base, c.1900, 2 x 6 In........	165
Hills Bros Coffee, Porcelain, Red & Yellow Paint, 21 x 9 In. ....*illus*	635
Hires Root Beer, Vintage, Porcelain, Blue & White Stripes, Red, 1930-55, 38 x 8 In........	138
L&M Cigarettes, Tin Litho, Yellow, Blue, Red, 11¾ x 5 In.	68
Lighthouse, Edwardian, Cornish Serpentine, Rocky Base, 7 In.	459
Marble, Obelisk, Grand Tour, Negretti & Zambra, London, 14 In.	447
Moxie, Old Fashion, Remember Those Days, Orange, Black, Metal, Round, 1960s, 12 In........	195

470

NuGrape Soda, Figural Bottle, Embossed Tin, 17 x 5 In. ....*illus*	472
Orange Crush, From Natural Orange Juice, 16 x 6 ¼ In.	262
Orange Crush, Tin Lithograph, 1950, 28 ½ x 7 ½ In.	468
Pabst Blue Ribbon Beer, Man At Strength Tester, Metal, 18 x 10 In. ....*illus*	252
Parlor, Hanging, Victorian, 3-Sided, Taylor Bros., c.1887, 8 In.	275
Pratts Veterinary, Stock Fattener & Regulator Product, Brass, 1 ½ x 9 ⅛ In.	826
Quaker State Motor Oil, Glass Crystal, Green, White, Round, 12 In.	240
Ramon's Brownie Pills, Little Doctor, Yellow, Pink, 8 ½ x 21 In.	660
Red Crown Gasoline, Power Service Economy, Red, Blue, White Ground, 74 x 19 ½ In.	2160
Reverse Painted Silhouette, Children's Hour, Poem, Mother Reading, Son, 5 x 4 In.	28
Rolling Rock, Extra Pale, Green, 1900s, 28 x 8 In.	123
Rolling Rock, White Text, Green Background, Box, 27 x 8 ½ In.	79
Sterling Silver, Victorian, Fahrenheit & Centigrade, Velvet Back, c.1898, 6 x 3 In. ...	550
Stihl Chain Saws, Bubble, White Background, 12 In. ....*illus*	260
Williams Shaving Soap, Cow, Children, Metal Frame, Glass, 14 ½ x 3 ¼ In.	502
Wood, Glass Tube, Turned Shaft, Shaped Handle, Strap, 1800s, 12 In.	145

TIFFANY is a name that appears on items made by Louis Comfort Tiffany, the American glass designer who worked from about 1879 to 1933. His work included iridescent glass, Art Nouveau styles of design, and original contemporary styles. He was also noted for stained glass windows, unusual lamps, bronze work, pottery, and silver. Tiffany & Company, often called "Tiffany," is also listed in this section. The company was started by Charles Lewis Tiffany and John B. Young in 1837 in New York City. In 1853 the name was changed to Tiffany & Company. Louis Tiffany (1848–1933), Charles Tiffany's son, started his own business in 1879. It was named Louis Comfort Tiffany and Associated American Artists. In 1902 the name was changed to Tiffany Studios. Tiffany & Company is a store and is still working today. It is best known for silver and fine jewelry. Louis worked for his father's company as a decorator in 1900 but at the same time was working for his Tiffany Studios. Other types of Tiffany are listed under Tiffany Glass, Tiffany Gold, Tiffany Pottery, or Tiffany Silver. The famous Tiffany lamps are listed in this section. Tiffany jewelry is listed in the Jewelry and Wristwatch categories. Some Tiffany Studio desk sets have matching clocks. They are listed here. Clocks made by Tiffany & Co. are listed in the Clock category. Reproductions of some types of Tiffany are being made.

L.C. Tiffany
1848–1933

Tiffany Studios
1902–1919

**TIFFANY STUDIOS
NEW YORK.**

Tiffany Studios
1902–1922+

Bowl, Grapevine, Green Iridescence, Short Wall Shape, 1900s	240
Box, Grapevine, Bronze, Glass, Tiffany Studios, Early 1900s, 3 x 6 ⅝ x 4 In.	1063
Box, Lid, Bronze, 10 Favrile Squares, Bun Feet, Mahogany Lining, c.1890, 3 x 8 x 5 In. ......*illus*	1188
Box, Lid, Pine Needle, Beaded Trim, Bronze, Gold Patina, Signed, 4 ⅜ x 3 In.	738
Box, Pine Needle, Gilt Bronze, Glass, Marked, Early 1900s, 3 x 9 ⅜ x 6 ½ In.	1250
Box, Pine Needle, Green Slag Glass, Stamped Underside, 3 x 6 ¾ x 4 In.	845
Candlestick, Blue Favrile, Twisted Stem, Flared Foot, Marked L.C.T., Early 1900s, 5 In. ...	185
Candlestick, Bronze, Patinated, Blown Out Glass, 3 Legs, Curled Feet, 10 In., Pair	1770
Candlestick, Gold Dore, Puddlestick, Urn Socket, 3 Prongs, Tiffany Studios 1213, 1900s, 20 ¾ In.	500
Candlestick, Gold Favrile, Flared Top, Twist Body, Bulbous, Polished Pontil, 14 ⅞ In.	800
Cane, Silver Handle, Open Crown, Black, Marked Tiffany & Co., Early 1900s, 36 In.	600
Chalice, Iridescent Gold, Twisted Stem, Hand Etched, L.C.T., 6 ½ x 3 ¾ In.	325
Clock, Desk, Bronze, American Indian Symbols, Arched, c.1910, 4 ⅜ x 5 ⅜ In.	1053
Desk Tray, Pine Needle, Brass, 5 ¼ In.	150
Frame, Grapevine Overlay, Bronze, Beaded Border, Green Striated Glass, 10 x 8 In.	2420
Frame, Heraldic, Calendar, Gilt Bronze, Lion Shield Emblem, Faux Leather, 5 ½ x 6 In.	605
Frame, Pine Needle, Bronze, Acid Etched, Slag Glass, Double Frame, Signed, 9 ½ x 8 In.	3900
Frame, Pine Needle, Easel Back, Marked, Tiffany Studios, 14 x 12 In.	2625

Textile, Flag, American, 37 Stars, Silk, 1867, 41 ¼ x 31 In.
$523

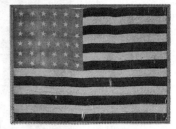

Cowan's Auctions

Textile, Flag, American, 48 Stars, Crocheted Crepe Paper, Painted Pole, Meta Schmitt, c.1936, 33 x 54 In.
$344

Garth's Auctioneers & Appraisers

Textile, Obi Sash, Silk, Gilt Embroidery, Cream Ground, Maru, Japan, 1900s, 13 x 12 ¼ In.
$48

Thomaston Place Auction Galleries

Textile, Piano, Scarf, Black Silk, Embroidery Flowers, Early 1900s, 65 x 65 In.
$125

Leslie Hindman Auctioneers

T I P
*Wash your hands
before handling old
textiles.*

T

Textile, Tapestry, Circus, Wool, Stylized Figure, After Joan Miro, 1970s, 78 ½ x 59 In. $7,500

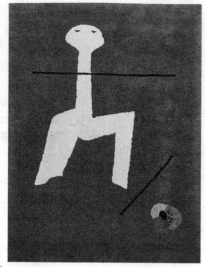

Rago Arts and Auction Center

Textile, Tapestry, Fond De Mer, Wool, Signed, Lars Gynning, Sweden, 77 ½ x 78 In. $6,150

Palm Beach Modern Auctions

Textile, Tapestry, Rambovillet, Red Background, Design After Portique De Junon, 49 x 37 In. $250

Susanin's Auctioneers & Appraisers

Textile, Wall Hanging, Houses, Cotton, Screen Printed, A. Girard, Herman Miller Fabrics, 1964, 48 In. $1,000

Wright

Thermometer, Camel Cigarettes, Tin, Lithograph, Box, 5 ¾ x 13 ½ In. $102

Hartzell's Auction Gallery, Inc.

Thermometer, Hills Bros Coffee, Porcelain, Red & Yellow Paint, 21 x 9 In. $635

midwest-sellitnowstore on eBay

Thermometer, NuGrape Soda, Figural Bottle, Embossed Tin, 17 x 5 In. $472

AntiqueAdvertising.com

Frame, Pine Needle, Marked, Tiffany Studios, 7 x 8¼ In.	406
Frame, Pine Needle, Marked, Tiffany Studios, 9¼ x 7¾ In.	1875
Inkstand, Etched Metal, Favrile Glass, Square, c.1915, 3⅜ x 4 In.	375
Inkwell, Bronze, Urn Shape, Hinged Lid, Roman Style Helmet, Tiffany & Co., 4¾ x 6 In.	545
Lamp Base, 1-Light, Favrile Glass, Gilt Metal Mounted, Signed, c.1915, 11 In.	812
Lamp Base, 3-Light, Bronze, Table, Snake, Basket, Glass Inserts, Marked, 1900s, 15 x 10 In.	1599
Lamp Base, Boudoir, Bronze Gold Dore, Flowers, 10⅛ In.	750
Lamp Base, Bronze, 3-Footed Base, Dark Green, Early 1900s, 55¾ In.	1680
Lamp Base, Iridescent Golden Brown, Yellow Strip, Favrile, Footed, 8½ In.	633
Lamp, 2-Light, Lily, Bronze, Gold Iridescent Glass Shades, 13 x 13⅝ x 5 In.	543
Lamp, 3-Light, Fleur-De-Lis, Geometric Ground, Bronze Ribbed Base, Marked, 22 x 16 In. *illus*	14760
Lamp, 3-Light, Glass Linenfold Panels, Bronze Scroll Rims, Stick Base, 22½ x 18 In. *illus*	31980
Lamp, 3-Light, Lily, Favrile Glass, Green & Gold Feather, Early 1900s, 13 In.	3600
Lamp, 10-Light, Lily, Gooseneck, Bronze, Lily Pad Foot, Signed, 21 In.	25200
Lamp, 16 Panels, Linenfold Panes, Hammered Amber Glass, Bronze Base, 1952, 20 In.	8190
Lamp, Astrological Design, 6 Round Green Turtlebacks, Marked, 1900s, 28 x 22 In.	86100
Lamp, Bronze Base, Teardrop Stem, Bell Shape Shade, Gold Feathered Pattern, 13¼ In.	1815
Lamp, Bronze, Tulips & Scroll Base, Green Shade, Iridescent Ribs, Early 1900s, 55½ In.	5625
Lamp, Brownish Green Patina, 5-Legged Spade Base, 59 In.	1770
Lamp, Colonial, Leaded Glass, Dore Finished Bronze Shade & Base, Marked, 22 x 16½ In.	8450
Lamp, Crocus, Mottled, Cream, Yellow, Orange, Bronze, Cat's Paw Base, 28½ In.	34650
Lamp, Desk, Counterbalance, Pulled Feather Shade, Patinated Bronze, Early 1900s, 12 In.	2829
Lamp, Desk, Damascene, Ribbed Shoulder, Iridescent, Gold Dore, Marked, 12¾ In.	3690
Lamp, Desk, Dore Bronze Shade & Base, Favrile, Marked, L.C.T., 17 In.	6250
Lamp, Desk, Favrile Damascene, Zodiac Harp, Lobe Shape, 13½ x 9½ x 5¾ In. *illus*	4840
Lamp, Desk, Favrile Glass, Bronze, Harp, Signed, New York, 5⅜ x 10½ In.	2250
Lamp, Desk, Linenfold, Bronze, Hexagonal Shade, Brown Patina, Marked, 14 x 6 x 5½ In.	5748
Lamp, Desk, Nautilus Shell Shade, Bronze, Mermaid, Patina, 16½ In.	18450
Lamp, Favrile Glass, Patinated Bronze, 19½ x 8 In.	5310
Lamp, Fish Scale, Yellow & Green Glass, Leaded, Roman Column Base, 32 x 23 In.	44280
Lamp, Gold Iridescent, Dome Shape, Lobed Stem, Bronze Base, Ruffled Platform, 20 In.	7260
Lamp, Green Art Glass Shade, Candlestick, Bronze Dore, Marked, c.1910, 14½ In.	9225
Lamp, Green Damascene Shade, 5-Legged Spade Base, Brownish Green Patina, 54 x 10 In.	5900
Lamp, Hanging, Roses, Lighting, Recreation, Stained Glass, Copper Foil, Late 1900s, 22 In.	198
Lamp, Jonquils & Daffodils, Yellow & White, Green Leaves, Bronze, Applied Tendrils, 28 In.	138600
Lamp, Lily Pad, Art Glass Shade, Marked, Tiffany Studios, 11½ x 7 In.	989
Lamp, Linenfold, Green Panels, Leaded, Bronze, Gold Patina, 19¾ In.	20910
Lamp, Oil, Favrile Glass, Ruffled Shade, Twisted Base, c.1910, 13¼ In.	861
Lamp, Oil, Marked, Brass Base, 14¼ In.	4320
Lamp, Peony, Red & Pink, Leaded, Mottled, Bronze, Stylized Leaf Base, Pad Feet, 24 In.	58405
Lamp, Spirit, Urn Shape, Copper Body, 2 Silver Handles, Monogram, c.1890, 4 In.	360
Lamp, Swirling Leaves, Mottled Green Ground, Bronze Urn Shape Base, Marked, 24 In. *illus*	12600
Lamp, Tyler Shade, Pink Scroll Pattern On Cream, Art Nouveau Bronze Base, 27 In.	18450
Lamp, Wild Carrot, Bronze Base, Relief Leaves, Stamped, Early 1900s, 15 In.	2640
Lighter, Cigarette, Gilt Bronze, Ivory Gold Plated, Victorian	259
Pen Tray, Zodiac, Symbols Of Scorpio & Pisces, 10 x 3¼ In.	189
Pencil, Mechanical, 4K Yellow Gold, Calendar, Engraved	305
Plate, Bronze, Blue, Pink, Gold & Green Glass, Enamel Border, Signed, 1900s, 9¾ In. *illus*	424
Vase, Bud, Trumpet Shape, Pulled Feather, Gold Dora Bronze Base, 12 In.	880
Vase, Bud, Trumpet Shape, Favrile, Opaque Exterior, Gold, Green Pulled Feather, 11½ In.	1089
Vase, Flowers, Ribbed Bowl, Tapered Stem, Flared & Ribbed Base, Favrile, 4 x 10 In.	154
Vase, Jack-In-The-Pulpit, Green To Gold Iridescent, Signed, L.C.T., 16¾ In.	5760
Vase, Trumpet Shape, Flared Base, Engraved Signature, 3¼ x 11¾ In.	523

TIFFANY GLASS

Bowl, Blue Iridescent, Overlapping Petals, Pontil Mark, c.1925, 3 x 7½ In.	793
Bowl, Curled Rim, Gold Favrile, Signed, L.C. Tiffany, c.1910, 3 x 6¼ In.	366
Bowl, Etched Interior, Ribbed Body, Shallow Scallops, L.C.T., Favrile, 1900s, 4 x 10½ In.	600
Bowl, Flared Rim, Gold Favrile, Early 1900s, 5 In.	240
Bowl, Flower, Art Nouveau, Hand Blown, Gold Favrile, 11½ x 4½ In.	245

Thermometer, Pabst Blue Ribbon Beer, Man At Strength Tester, Metal, 18 x 10 In. $252

Matthew Bullock Auctioneers

Thermometer, Stihl Chain Saws, Bubble, White Background, 12 In. $260

Milestone Auctions

Tiffany, Box, Lid, Bronze, 10 Favrile Squares, Bun Feet, Mahogany Lining, c.1890, 3 x 8 x 5 In. $1,188

Garth's Auctioneers & Appraisers

Tiffany, Lamp, 3-Light, Fleur-De-Lis, Geometric Ground, Bronze Ribbed Base, Marked, 22 x 16 In.
$14,760

Morphy Auctions

Tiffany, Lamp, 3-Light, Glass Linenfold Panels, Bronze Scroll Rims, Stick Base, 22 ½ x 18 In.
$31,980

Morphy Auctions

Tiffany, Lamp, Desk, Favrile Damascene, Zodiac Harp, Lobe Shape, 13 ½ x 9 ½ x 5 ¾ In.
$4,840

Fontaine's Auction Gallery

Bowl, Iridescent Gold, Ruffled Rim, Favrile, Early 1900s, 2 ¼ x 6 ¼ In.	615
Bowl, King Tut, Blue Favrile, Signed, Louis C. Tiffany, 11 x 6 ¾ In.	4920
Bowl, Light Amber, Iridescent, Flat Wide Rim, Favrile, Bronze Dore Base, c.1880, 5 x 11 In.. *illus*	510
Bowl, Light Amber, Iridescent, Ribbed, Flared Lip, Polished Pontil, Signed, c.1915, 3 x 7 In.. *illus*	531
Bowl, Quilted, Green Opalescent Body, Fern Design, Favrile, 1925, 4 x 13 In.	492
Cake Stand, Blue, Opalescent Center, Yellow Stem & Base, Marked, 4 x 10 In.	2242
Compote, Bulbous, Ruffled Rim, Pedestal Base, Favrile, New York, 1902-32, 6 ⅜ In.	492
Compote, Diamond Pattern, Green To White, Signed, L.C. Tiffany, Favrile, c.1900, 3 ¾ x 6 ¾ In.	708
Compote, Iridescent Art Glass, Exterior Ribs, Wavy Rim, Teardrop Stem, 6 In. *illus*	333
Decanter, Pale Yellow Opalescent, Tadpole Prunts, Double Gourd, 9 In.	840
Flower Frog, Green Leaf & Vine, Intaglio Carved, Iridescent Gold, Signed, 12 x 4 In. *illus*	1046
Goblet, Tulip, Flat Knop, Favrile, Early 1900s, 8 ¾ In. *illus*	480
Paperweight, Green Damascene Glass, Bronze, Brown Patina, Highlights, Signed, 4 x 2 ¾ In.	3383
Perfume Bottle, Sterling Silver Top, Cut Glass, 4 In.	31
Plate, Stylized Leaves, Radiating, Iridescent, Shades To Yellow, Favrile, Signed, 12 In.	584
Salt Dip, Gold Iridescent, Crimpled Edge, Signed, L.C.T. Favrile, 1 x 2 ½ In.	108
Salt Dip, Gold Iridescent, Footed, Signed, L.C.T., 1 ½ x 2 In. *illus*	120
Salt Dip, Pigtail, Cellar, Favrile, Signed, L.C.T., 1 ⅜ x 2 In.	144
Shade, Domed, Leaded, Acorn, Green, c.1915, 6 ½ x 16 In.	5937
Shade, Hanging, Bronze, Leaded Favrile Glass, Greek Key, Green & White, c.1905, 8 ¾ x 22 In.	1625
Shade, Hanging, Green, Greek Key, 1907, 22 x 9 In.	22140
Tumbler, Gold, Applied Elements, Favrile, Signed, L.C.T., Early 1900s, 4 In. *illus*	240
Vase, 5 Gold Pulled Feathers, 2 Platinum Iridescent Bands, Flared Rim, Favrile, Signed, 5 x 8 In..	3383
Vase, Blue, 3-Corner Pinched Rim, Favrile, Signed, 16 In.	800
Vase, Blue, Iridescent, Favrile, Signed, c.1920, 12 In.	1320
Vase, Bud, Cylindrical, Iridescent Surface, Green Pulled Leaves, Favrile, 13 ¾ In.	847
Vase, Calyx, Green, Yellow, Round Base, c.1905, 19 ½ In.	2500
Vase, Corona, Jack-In-The-Pulpit, Purple, Magenta, Green, Gold, Blue, Stretch Border, 10 ½ x 7 In.	2057
Vase, Cream Color, Pulled Feather, Green, Blue, Purple Iridescent Peacock Eye, 17 x 3 ½ In.	1408
Vase, Flower Form, Saucer Foot, Ribbed Body, Blue Iridescent, Feather Design, Signed, 12 x 4 In.	5228
Vase, Flower Shape, Gold & Rose Iridescent, Ribbed, Folded Top, Favrile, Signed, L.C.T., 11 ½ x 5 In.	813
Vase, Flower Shape, Gold Pulled Decoration, Footed, Favrile, Signed, L.C.T., 12 x 4 In.	2210
Vase, Flower Shape, Ribbed Body, Gold, Amber, Rose Iridescent, Signed, L.C. Tiffany, Favrile, 10 x 4 In.	750
Vase, Flower Shape, Ribbed, Footed, Signed, L.C. Tiffany, Favrile, 15 x 4 ½ In.	1125
Vase, Flower Shape, Saucer Foot, Light Iridescence, Creamy White Background, Signed, 12 ½ x 5 In.	4500
Vase, Flower Shape, Yellow, Ribbed, Red Coral Leaves, Favrile, 12 ½ In.	7080
Vase, Leaf, Golden Iridescent, Pedestal Base, Favrile	518
Vase, Paperweight, White Flowers, Green Leaves, Iridescent, Favrile, Signed, 6 x 3 In. *illus*	8190
Vase, Pinched Neck, Polished Pontil, Blue Iridescent, Favrile, N.Y., Early 1900s, 10 In.	738
Vase, Yellow To Green, Leaves, Bulbous Base, Circular Foot, Polished Pontil, Favrile, 12 In.	1230
Wine, Pastel Blue, Fern Like Pattern, Twisted Stem, Paper Label, L.C.T., 7 x 4 In.	593

TIFFANY GOLD

Cigar Cutter, Retro Design, 14K Yellow Gold, Monogram, Stamped, SL, 1 x 1 In. *illus*	563

TIFFANY POTTERY

Vase, Cypriote, Splotches, Iridescent, Etched, L.C. Tiffany, c.1919, 4 In. *illus*	10625
Vase, Gooseberry Leaves, Favrile, Incised LCT, 1904-19, 12 x 10 In.	9375

TIFFANY SILVER

Baby Spoon, Rabbit Head Shape, 1947-56, 3 ½ In. *illus*	96
Basket, Bellflower Swags, Paterae, Marked, Tiffany & Co., 1900s, 11 In.	500
Basket, Berry Motif, Silver Plate Liner, Bail Handle, Flower Frog, 1900s, 11 In.	3198
Basket, Geometric Grapevine Pattern, Shallow Bowl, Applied Handles, Marked, 11 x 8 In.	523
Berry Spoon, Elaborate Fruit Bowl, 1869, 8 ½ In.	92
Bonbon Spoon, Banana & Palm, Gilt, Early 1900s, 6 ¼ In.	180
Bowl, Art Deco, Vertical Panels, Tomatoes & Leaves, Olaf Wilford, 1940, 2 ½ x 9 ¼ In. *illus*	2106
Bowl, Chrysanthemum Pattern, Monogram, Tiffany & Co, c.1898, 10 In. *illus*	800
Bowl, Cornucopia, Shell, Flowers, Gilt, Footed, Marked, c.1800, 6 ½ x 13 ¾ x 12 In.	2750
Bowl, C-Scroll Frame, Repousse, Scalloped Leafy Rim, 3 x 12 ½ In.	2000
Bowl, Flowers, Turned Down Repousse Rim, Marked, c.1895, 4 x 18 In.	2925

T

Tiffany, Lamp, Swirling Leaves, Mottled Green Ground, Bronze Urn Shape Base, Marked, 24 In.
$12,600

Morphy Auctions

Tiffany, Plate, Bronze, Blue, Pink, Gold & Green Glass, Enamel Border, Signed, 1900s, 9¾ In.
$424

Soulis Auctions

Tiffany Glass, Bowl, Light Amber, Iridescent, Flat Wide Rim, Favrile, Bronze Dore Base, c.1880, 5 x 11 In.
$510

Garth's Auctioneers & Appraisers

Tiffany Glass, Bowl, Light Amber, Iridescent, Ribbed, Flared Lip, Polished Pontil, Signed, c.1915, 3 x 7 In.
$531

Garth's Auctioneers & Appraisers

> **TIP**
> If you have valuable old glass you should keep it in a safe environment. It should be stored or displayed where there is some air movement to dry off the surface. Glass bottles and containers should be stored with the lids and stoppers open.

Tiffany Glass, Compote, Iridescent Art Glass, Exterior Ribs, Wavy Rim, Teardrop Stem, 6 In.
$333

Fontaine's Auction Gallery

Tiffany Glass, Flower Frog, Green Leaf & Vine, Intaglio Carved, Iridescent Gold, Signed, 12 x 4 In.
$1,046

Morphy Auctions

Tiffany Glass, Goblet, Tulip, Flat Knop, Favrile, Early 1900s, 8¾ In.
$480

Eldred's

Tiffany Glass, Salt Dip, Gold Iridescent, Footed, Signed, L.C.T., 1½ x 2 In.
$120

Woody Auction

Tiffany Glass, Tumbler, Gold, Applied Elements, Favrile, Signed, L.C.T., Early 1900s, 4 In.
$240

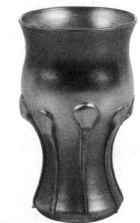

Brunk Auctions

T

Tiffany Glass, Vase, Paperweight, White Flowers, Green Leaves, Iridescent, Favrile, Signed, 6 x 3 In.
$8,190

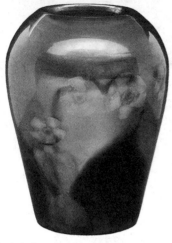

Morphy Auctions

Tiffany Gold, Cigar Cutter, Retro Design, 14K Yellow Gold, Monogram, Stamped, SL, 1 x 1 In.
$563

Brunk Auctions

Tiffany Pottery, Vase, Cypriote, Splotches, Iridescent, Etched, L.C. Tiffany, c.1919, 4 In.
$10,625

Rago Arts and Auction Center

Tiffany Silver, Baby Spoon, Rabbit Head Shape, 1947-56, 3 ½ In.
$96

Eldred's

Tiffany Silver, Bowl, Art Deco, Vertical Panels, Tomatoes & Leaves, Olaf Wilford, 1940, 2 ½ x 9 ¼ In.
$2,106

Thomaston Place Auction Galleries

Tiffany Silver, Bowl, Chrysanthemum Pattern, Monogram, Tiffany & Co., c.1898, 10 In.
$800

Cowan's Auctions

Tiffany Silver, Bowl, Tomato Relief Along Top Edge, 1907-47, 3 ½ x 9 ¾ In.
$688

Rago Arts and Auction Center

Stolen Art & Antiques
It is said that art and antiques worth a total of $6 billion are stolen each year.

Tiffany Silver, Coffeepot, Lobed Body, Dome Lid, Monogram, New York, 9 ¼ In.
$523

Skinner, Inc.

TIP
Don't use brass or other metal polishes on silver.
It is too abrasive.

Tiffany Silver, Bowl, Reticulated Rim, Tiffany, c.1895, 15 ½ In.
$1,770

Cottone Auctions

Bowl, Footed, Filigree, Flower Clusters, Chased Flowers, Claw Feet, 4 In.	3025
Bowl, Hexagonal, Tapered Body & Border, Tiffany & Co., 2 3/8 x 9 3/8 In.	366
Bowl, Melon Shape, Horizontal Lobes, Vines & Leaf Handles, Marked, 1 3/8 x 10 x 5 3/8 In.	400
Bowl, Monogram, Lobed Body & Shell, Scroll Rim, New York, 8 3/4 In.	277
Bowl, Mounted, Cut Glass, Monogram, C-Scrolls & Floral Sprays, Early 1900s, 10 In.	738
Bowl, Palmette, Footed, Marked, 1947-56, 4 3/4 x 10 In.	1000
Bowl, Reticulated Rim, Tiffany, c.1895, 15 1/2 In. ....*illus*	1770
Bowl, Scalloped Rim, Canted Foot Rim, Marked, Tiffany & Co., c.1950, 3 x 10 In.	625
Bowl, Scalloped Rim, Relief Leaf & Berry, Marked, 1900s, 3 x 12 In.	615
Bowl, Stylized Pointed Leaves, Copper Inlay, Tapering Sides, Marked, 1907-38, 7 1/2 x 3 In.	3690
Bowl, Tomato Relief Along Top Edge, 1907-47, 3 1/2 x 9 3/4 In. ....*illus*	688
Cake Slice, Monogram Handle, Tiffany & Co., 2 1/4 x 11 x 2 1/4 In.	156
Casket, Flowers, Leaf Scroll, Oval Cartouche, Tiffany & Co., Early 1900s, 5 1/2 In.	1500
Chocolate Pot, 4 Cast Feet, Floral Ornament, 1800s, 8 1/2 x 6 In.	4613
Cocktail Shaker, Beaker, Hammered, Embossed, Bulrushes, Dragonfly, Turtle, 8 1/2 In.	3250
Coffeepot, Lobed Body, Dome Lid, Monogram, New York, 9 1/4 In. ....*illus*	523
Coffeepot, Queen Anne Style, Ebony Handle, 2 Pt., 9 1/2 In.	431
Compote, Pedestal, Round Top & Base, Monogram, Marked Tiffany & Co., 4 x 9 In.	600
Cup, 3 Scrolled Handles, 6 Chased Sprigs, c.1908, 9 x 7 In.	1638
Dish, Entree, Lid, Oval, Floral Border, Finial, Monogram, Marked, 1873, 5 x 11 1/2 In. ....*illus*	1188
Dish, Figural Leaf, Monogram, 5 x 5 1/2 In.	115
Dish, Folded Down Rim, Flower Shape, 5 1/4 In.	81
Gravy Ladle, Fancy Shell Bowl, English King Pattern, 7 1/2 In. ....*illus*	173
Ladle, Audubon Pattern, Tiffany & Co., 12 1/2 In.	793
Ladle, Cream, Etched Floral & Feather, Monogram, 5 1/4 In.	83
Pitcher, Bulbous, Cylindrical Neck, Applied Handle, Tiffany & Co., 8 x 7 x 6 In.	3449
Pitcher, Curved Handle, Marked, Tiffany & Co., 6 In.	250
Pitcher, Olympian, Water, Marked, Tiffany & Co., 5 1/2 x 7 3/4 x 8 1/2 In.	3000
Pitcher, Water, Figural Handle, c.1864, 9 In.	3186
Pitcher, Water, Silver Plate, Monogram, Tiffany & Co., Early 1900s, 11 In.	90
Plate, Scalloped & Lobed Border, Foot Ring, 9 1/4 In.	310
Punch Bowl, Chrysanthemum, Chased, Ribbed Sides, 4-Footed, c.1900, 17 x 8 1/2 In. ....*illus*	27675
Sauce Ladle, Chrysanthemum, Vermeil, Monogram, c.1885, 7 In.	270
Serving Spoon, Art Deco, Marked, Illustrated, 1937, 10 In.	1063
Serving Spoon, Shell Shape, Giltwash Bowl, Monogram, 1891-1902, 8 3/4 In.	875
Shoehorn, Cut Back Style, Flowers, Monogram, 1887, 7 In.	173
Soup Ladle, Chrysanthemum, Charles Grosjean, c.1880, 12 In.	600
Soup Ladle, Olympian Pattern, W Monogram, Marked, Tiffany & Co., 1873, 13 In.	585
Sugar Sifter, Wave Edge, Tiffany & Co., c.1890, 7 In.	192
Tazza, 3 Figural Griffin Legs, Claw Feet, Cut Glass Tray Top, c.1865, 10 1/2 x 10 In.	5143
Tray, Butler's, Oval, Molded Rim, Reeded Handles, Scrolled Feet, c.1950, 22 In.	2160
Tray, Cherry Blossom Rim, Gilt Handle, c.1880, 11 In.	660
Tray, Round, Reticulated Border, c.1894, 14 In.	1534
Tray, Scalloped Border, Engraved Medallion, Graduate School Of Banking, Round, 12 In.	420
Trophy, Yacht, Hand Hammered, Anchor Handles, Rope Balled Feet, c.1880, 14 In.	8750
Tureen, Bands Of Repousse Flowers & Leaves, Footed, Early 1900s, 12 1/2 In. ....*illus*	1500
Tureen, Lid, Oval Urn Shape, Arabesque Style Handles, Tiffany & Co., 13 x 16 x 9 In.	3250
Vase, Bud, Bottle Shape, Scalloped Rim, 1965, 4 In.	420
Vase, Triple Gourd Body, Leafy Repousse, Marked, Early 1900s, 9 In.	2750
Vinaigrette, 2 Handles, Embossed & Pierced, Signed, c.1840, 3 x 1 In.	615
Water Kettle, Scrolls, Bands, Leaves, Cartouches, c.1870, 2 1/2 x 9 1/4 In.	1920

TIFFIN Glass Company of Tiffin, Ohio, was a subsidiary of the United States Glass Co. of Pittsburgh, Pennsylvania, in 1892. The U.S. Glass Co. went bankrupt in 1963, and the Tiffin plant employees purchased the building and the inventory. They continued running it from 1963 to 1966, when it was sold to Continental Can Company. In 1969, it was sold to Interpace, and in 1980, it was closed. The black satin glass, made from 1923 to 1926, and the stemware of the last 20 years are the best-known products.

Elyse, Double Old-Fashioned, 3 1/2 In.	109
Fuchsia, Goblet, Sherry Stem, 2 Oz., 5 3/8 In.	99

Tiffany Silver, Dish, Lid, Entree, Oval, Floral Border, Finial, Monogram, Marked, 1873, 5 x 11 1/2 In. $1,188

Brunk Auctions

Tiffany Silver, Gravy Ladle, Fancy Shell Bowl, English King Pattern, 7 1/2 In. $173

Richard D. Hatch & Associates

Tiffany Silver, Punch Bowl, Chrysanthemum, Chased, Ribbed Sides, 4-Footed, c.1900, 17 x 8½ In. $27,675

Morphy Auctions

Tiffany Silver, Tureen, Bands Of Repousse Flowers & Leaves, Footed, Early 1900s, 12½ In. $1,500

Leslie Hindman Auctioneers

Tile, Cow, Man, Stylized, Sun, Enameled Copper, Square, Stenvall, c.1950, 6 In. $215

Skinner, Inc.

King's Crown, Flat Iced Tea, Cranberry, 5⅜ In.	39
Rambler Rose, Vase, Fan, Pink, Gold Encrusted Trim, 8 x 6 In.	18
Robin's-Egg Blue, Basket, Cone Shape, Footed, White Handle, 1950s, 10½ In.	75

TILES have been used in most countries of the world as a sturdy building material for floors, roofs, fireplace surrounds, and surface toppings. The cuerda seca (dry cord) technique of decoration uses a greasy pigment to separate different glaze colors during firing. In cuenca (raised line) decorated tiles, the design is impressed, leaving ridges that separate the glaze colors. Many of the American tiles are listed in this book under the factory name.

Cow, Man, Stylized, Sun, Enameled Copper, Square, Stenvall, c.1950, 6 In.	*illus*	215
Girl With Doll, Flower In Hand, Glazed, San Jose Pottery, 6 x 6 In.	*illus*	330
Horse, Standing, Square Base, Tang Style, Sancai, Chinese, 1920, 13½ In.	*illus*	154
Man On Burro, Landscape, Cactus, Mountains, Glazed, San Jose Pottery, 8 x 8 In.		600
Plaque, Norse Ship, Mosaic, Multicolor, Moravian Tile Works, Pa., 1900s, 30 x 24 In.	*illus*	875
Roof, Deity, Riding Ram, Crown, Multicolor, Terra-Cotta, 13 x 4 In.		576
Roof, Sancai Glaze, Mythical Lion, Seated, Carved Wood Base, 15½ In.		277
Roof, Sancai Style, Horseback Warrior, Glaze, 1900s, 15 x 14 In.		234

TINWARE containers for household use have been made in America since the seventeenth century. The first tin utensils were brought from Europe, but by 1798 tin plate was imported and local tinsmiths made the wares. Painted tin is called tole and is listed separately. Some tin kitchen items may be found listed under Kitchen. The lithographed tin containers used to hold food and tobacco are listed in the Advertising category under Tin.

Candlebox, Hanging, Black Paint, Cylindrical, 1800s, 14 In.		113
Cheese Mold, Heart Shape, Punched, Loop Handle, Pennsylvania, 1800s, 6½ In.		85
Coffeepot, Cone Shape, Straight Spout, Round Handle, 1800s, 13 In.		61
Coffeepot, Lid, Punched Tulip Pots, Brass Finial, c.1850, 12 In.	*illus*	540
Coffeepot, Punched, Potted Flowers & Tulips, Brass Finial, 1800s, 11 In.		780
Foot Warmer, Punched Diamond, Pierced Initials, Ball Handle, 1808, 6 x 10 x 8 In.		154
Mold, Candle, 36 Tubes, Wood Stand, Red, 1800s, 11 x 13 x 10 In.		1845
Plate, Painted On Back, Portrait, Woman, 13½ In.		52
Top Hat, Rolled Rim, American Anniversary, 19th Century, 5½ In.	*illus*	570
Watering Can, Galvanized, Spout & Handle, 16 Qt., 17 In.		46

TOBACCO CUTTERS *may be listed in either the Advertising or Store categories.*

TOBACCO JAR collectors search for those made in odd shapes and colors. Because tobacco needs special conditions of humidity and air, it has been stored in special containers since the eighteenth century. Some may be found in Advertising in this book.

Bust, Red Cheeks, Teeth, Scarf, Red Bowtie, Austria, c.1900, 5½ x 5½ In.		89
Colibri Cedar, Metal Medallion, Sailing Ships, 2 Compartments, 5 x 11 x 9 In.		144
Humidor, Cigar, Gustav Stickley Style, Hand Hammered, Aluminum, Early 1900s, 7¾ x 11 In.		238
Humidor, Cigar, Oak, Removable Metal, Floral Mounts, Early 1900s, 10 x 6½ x 4 In.		226
Humidor, Glass, Cranberry, Lobed, Silver Overlay, Swags, Flowers, Whiting, 9 In.		3120
Humidor, Lid, Hammered, Craftsman Workshops, Copper, G. Stickley, Early 1900s, 4 x 7 x 5 In.	*illus*	2583
Humidor, Silver, Repousse, Wood Liner, Georg Jensen, 5 x 3¼ In.		812
Man, Seated, Holding Book & Umbrella, c.1880, 13 In.		237
Redware, Lead Glaze, Bell Shape, John Coffman, Shenandoah Co., Va., c.1850, 8 x 3 x 6 In.		263

TOLE is painted tin. It is sometimes called japanned ware, pontypool, or toleware. Most nineteenth-century tole is painted with an orange-red or black background and multicolored decorations. Many recent versions of toleware are made and sold. Related items may be listed in the Tinware category.

Basket, Scroll Edges, Painted Grapes, Long Handle, c.1930, 13 x 9 x 3 In.	85
Box, Document, Dome Lid, Flowers, Handle, Pennsylvania, 1800s, 7 x 9¾ In.	594

T

Box, Document, Dome Top, Handle, Flowers, Latch, Pennsylvania, 1800s, 7 x 10 x 6 In.	18
Box, Document, Flowers, Salmon Ground, Flowers, Bail Handle, 1800s, 6 x 9 In. ....*illus*	469
Box, Document, Hand Painted, Flowers, Pinstriping, 9 x 6 x 6 In.	113
Box, Document, Lid, Black, Flowers, Red, Yellow, Green Leaves, 1800s, 6 x 9 In.	950
Candle Box, Hanging, Metal, 10 ½ x 8 In.	148
Canister, Fruit & Leaf Bands, Bail Handle, Pennsylvania, 1800s, 6 In.	406
Canister, Spice, Floral Band, Blue Flowers, Japanned, Initials JDS, c.1850, 4 x 8 In.	4200
Coffeepot, Bird Perched, Floral Spray, Black Ground, Pennsylvania, 1800s, 10 ¼ In. ......*illus*	2750
Coffeepot, Dome Top, Peaches On Dark Japanned Ground, Spout, c.1850, 11 In. ....*illus*	480
Coffeepot, Flowers & Berries, Japanned Ground, Red, Side Spout, c.1850, 9 In.	840
Coffeepot, Red & Yellow, Tulips, Green & Yellow Leaves, 1800s, 8 ½ In. ....*illus*	584
Coffeepot, Red Flowers, Green & Yellow Leaves, 1800s, 10 In.	677
Cup, Saffron, Lid, Turned, Painted Flowers, Lehnware, 5 In.	1003
Jardiniere, White, Blue Oriental Scene, Rectangular Black Base, 1800s, 11 x 13 x 8 ¾ In.	250
Lamp, Electric, 1-Light, Red & Gold, Pedestal Base, 19 In.	71
Pail, Scalloped Rim, Black Outline, Stripes, Green, White, Ring Handles, 1900s, 18 In.	239
Sconce, Candle, Red, Flowers, 1800s, 13 In.	531
Tea Caddy, Black Ground, Leaves, Flowers, Green, Yellow, Orange, c.1800s, 7 x 3 In.	120
Teapot, Ship, Flowers, Leaves, Black Ground, Rectangular, C-Scroll Handle, 6 ¾ In.	4420
Tray, Apple, Fruit, Leaves, Red, Green, Yellow, 2 Handles, Bronze, 1800s, 12 ½ In.	275
Tray, Black & Gold, Reticulated, Painted, 1800s, 11 ½ In.	367
Tray, Greek Key Border, Later Stand, Elephant Feet, Regency, 1800s, 16 x 25 x 19 ⅜ In.	313
Tray, Locomotive & Passenger Cars, 3 People, Train, Floral Borders, 9 x 12 In.	121
Tray, Oval, Handles, Landscape, Red Background, c.1850, 21 x 27 In.	180
Tray, Sailing Ship, Sukey, Painted, Gold Trim, Rectangular, 2 Open Handles, 18 x 13 In.	1020
Urn, Italian Chinoiserie, Orange, Red, Gold, Lion Handles, Lion Paw Feet, 6 ½ In., Pair	425

TOM MIX was born in 1880 and died in 1940. He was the hero of over 100 silent movies from 1910 to 1929, and 25 sound films from 1929 to 1935. There was a Ralston Tom Mix radio show from 1933 to 1950, but the original Tom Mix was not in the show. Tom Mix comics were published from 1942 to 1953.

Belt, Plastic, Glow In The Dark, Metal Buckle, Compartment, Cowboy Designs, 1946	400
Comic Book, Trail Of Doom, Stagecoach, No. 17, May 1949, Fawcett ....*illus*	161
Pin, Yankiboy Play Clothes, Advertising, Pinback, 1930s, 2 ⅛ In.	38
Pitcher, Portrait, Cobalt Blue Glass, Paneled, Scalloped Rim, Footed, 4 x 4 In.	30
Silent Film Roll, Rustler's Roundup, 1930s	75
Telescope, Ralston Logo Transfer, Plastic, 1937, 4 x 1 ½ In.	149

TOOLS of all sorts are listed here, but most are related to industry. Other tools may be found listed under Iron, Kitchen, Tinware, and Wooden.

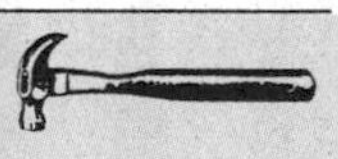

Anvil, Wood Casting, Black Paint, 6-Board Base, Forged Iron Rods, c.1900, 28 x 23 x 11 In.	480
Ax Head, Arm Form, Bronze, Luristan Province, Iran, 8th Century B.C., 7 ½ In. ....*illus*	431
Book Press, Cast Iron, c.1890, 14 x 20 x 10 In.	187
Box, Wood, Late Grain Painting, England, Late 1800s, 8 ½ x 20 ½ x 10 In.	210
Broadaxe, Cast Steel, Hewing, Bentwood Handle, Blodgett Tool Co., 1800s, 12 In.	70
Cabinet, Nuts & Bolts, 96 Drawers, 8-Sided, Porcelain Knobs, Stenciled, c.1890, 39 x 25 In. ....*illus*	1464
Caliper, Man & Woman, In Flagrante, Steel, 1800s, France, 7 In.	3444
Chest, Carpenter's, Wood, Applied Whales, 19th Century, 8 x 35 x 10 In.	1500
Chest, Oak, Pine Paint, Brown, c.1900, 14 ¼ x 33 ¾ x 14 In.	47
Corn Sheller, Red Paint, Wood, Iron, 49 In.	153
Hay Fork, Wood, 5 Prongs, Hickory Construction, Signed, Musser, 1800s, 68 In. ....*illus*	81
Inclinometer, Brass, Mahogany, Iver C. Weilbach & Co., 1900s, 10 ½ In.	240
Ladder, Folding, Leather, Library, England, 1900s, 92 ½ x 12 In.	1500
Ladder, Library, Folds To Single Pole, Leather Bound, Brass Nail, England, 1900s, 81 In.	1625
Mallet, Boxwood, Ebony, Silver Mount, Commemorative Plate, 1872, 8 In. ....*illus*	277
Press, Cider, 2 Molds, Wooden, Iron, Antique, 43 In.	561
Saw, Armorer, Wrought Iron, Wooden Handle, Blade, 1700s, 19 ½ In.	120

Tile, Girl With Doll, Flower In Hand, Glazed, San Jose Pottery, 6 x 6 In.
$330

Treasureseeker Auctions

Tile, Horse, Standing, Square Base, Tang Style, Sancai, Chinese, 1920, 13 ½ In.
$154

Cowan's Auctions

Tile, Plaque, Norse Ship, Mosaic, Multicolor, Moravian Tile Works, Pa., 1900s, 30 x 24 In.
$875

Rago Arts and Auction Center

T

Tinware, Coffeepot, Lid, Punched Tulip Pots, Brass Finial, c.1850, 12 In.
$540

Garth's Auctioneers & Appraisers

> **TIP**
> Don't clean an old painted tin tray or object with any commercial polish. Instead, use your enzymes. Spit on a cotton ball until it is damp. Then lightly wipe the dirt from the painted surface.

Tinware, Top Hat, Rolled Rim, American Anniversary, 19th Century, 5½ In.
$570

Garth's Auctioneers & Appraisers

Tobacco Jar, Humidor, Lid, Hammered, Craftsman Workshops, Copper, G. Stickley, Early 1900s, 4½ x 7 x 5½ In.
$2,583

Skinner, Inc.

Tole, Box, Document, Flowers, Salmon Ground, Flowers, Bail Handle, 1800s, 6 x 9 In.
$469

Pook & Pook

Tole, Coffeepot, Bird Perched, Floral Spray, Black Ground, Pennsylvania, 1800s, 10¼ In.
$2,750

Pook & Pook

Tole, Coffeepot, Dome Top, Peaches On Dark Japanned Ground, Spout, c.1850, 11 In.
$480

Garth's Auctioneers & Appraisers

> **TIP**
> Don't hide all your valuables in one place. Burglars may miss some hiding places.

Tole, Coffeepot, Red & Yellow, Tulips, Green & Yellow Leaves, 1800s, 8½ In.
$584

Skinner, Inc.

Tom Mix, Comic Book, Trail Of Doom, Stagecoach, No. 17, May 1949, Fawcett
$161

Hake's Auctions

Tool, Ax Head, Arm Form, Bronze, Luristan Province, Iran, 8th Century B.C., 7½ In.
$431

Skinner, Inc.

Screwdriver, Metal, Hand Wrought, Wooden Handle, 31 In.	45
Seed Dryer, Circular, Punched Design, 13 x 13 In.	46
Shovel, Carved, Oak, Flat Blade, Rounded Shaft, 1800s, 40¾ x 9⅞ In.	62
Sickle, Wrought Iron, Curved Blade, Spiral End, Wood Handle, France, 13 In. ...*illus*	2091
Step Ladder, Wooden, Horizontal Leg Support, 3 Steps	138
Workbench, Cabinetmaker's, Maple & Pine, Sunken Surface, Clamps, 4 Drawers, 30 x 34 x 95 In.	1870

TOOTHBRUSH HOLDERS

TOOTHBRUSH HOLDERS were part of every bowl and pitcher set in the late nineteenth century. Most were oblong covered dishes. About 1920, manufacturers started to make children's toothbrush holders shaped like animals or cartoon characters. A few modern toothbrush holders are still being made.

Bear, Foil Label, Victoria Ceramics, Japan, 5¼ In.	32
Figural, Bellhop, Wall Mounted, Porcelain, Germany, 3¾ x 5½ x 2⅛ In.	48

TOOTHPICK HOLDERS

TOOTHPICK HOLDERS are sometimes called *toothpicks* by collectors. The variously shaped containers used to hold small wooden toothpicks are made of glass, china, or metal. Most of the toothpick holders are made of Victorian glass. Additional items may be found in other categories, such as Bisque, Silver Plate, Slag Glass, etc.

3 Monkeys, Soapstone, Folk Art, 2¼ x 1⅞ In.	25
Ceramic, Pig, White, Japan, 4 x 2 In.	38
Cut Glass, Barrel Shape, Star, Punte, Prism, Clear Base, 2½ In.	18
Oak, Deer Horn, 2 x 1½ In.	20
Porcelain, Roses, Red, Blue, Pink, Ribbed, Wood Foot, Asian, 3 In.	30
Pressed Glass, Beaded Grape, Emerald Green, US Glass, Square, 2½ x 2½ In.	60
Silver Plate, Dog, Repousse Flowers, James Tufts, 1880s, 2 x 3 In.	225
Silver Plate, Farm Boy, Sheath Of Wheat, Victorian, c.1885	150
Silver Plate, Figural, Atlas, Globe, Victorian, Reed & Barton, c.1850, 3½ In.	222
Silver Plate, Figural, Bulldog, Glass, Eyes, Rogers Brothers, c.1890, 2 x 3 In.	145
Silver Plate, Knight, Crossed Legs, Hand On Hip, Victorian, c.1870, 2¾ x 3⅞ In.	162
Silver, Birds, On Branches, Flying, Flutter Rim, George Shiebler, c.1900, 2¼ In. ...*illus*	238
Sterling Silver, Trash Can, Ribbed, Handles, 2⅛ x 1⅞ In.	165
Vaseline Glass, Book Shape, 3 In.	125
Vaseline Glass, Figural, Conductor's Hat, Button & Daisy, 1¾ In.	125
Wood, Bakelite, Toucan, 2¼ x 2½ In.	295

TORQUAY

TORQUAY is the name given to ceramics by several potteries working near Torquay, England, from 1870 until 1962. Until about 1900, the potteries used local red clay to make classical-style art pottery vases and figurines. Then they turned to making souvenir wares. Items were dipped in colored slip and decorated with painted slip and sgraffito designs. They often had mottoes or proverbs, and scenes of cottages, ships, birds, or flowers. The Scandy design was a symmetrical arrangement of brushstrokes and spots done in colored slips. Potteries included Watcombe Pottery (1870–1962), Torquay Terra-Cotta Company (1875–1905), Aller Vale (1881–1924), Torquay Pottery (1908–1940), and Longpark (1883–1957).

Basket, Handle, Pinched, There Be More In The Larder, Cottage, 5 x 3 In.	60
Bowl, Time Ripens All Things, Cottage, Trees, 2 x 1½ In.	22
Candleholder, Mackintosh Rose, Art Nouveau, Watcombe, 1901-20, 7½ In.	34
Cream Cup, Fresh From The Dairy, Scandy, Ruffled, 3 x 3½ In.	38
Cup, Demitasse, It's An Ill Wind That Profits Nobody, Cottage	20
Dish, Time Ripens All Things, Cottage, Dotted Border, 3 x 3 In.	22
Eggcup, A Stitch In Time Saves Nine, Cottage, Dark Green, 2⅝ In.	35
Eggcup, Stand, Earthenware, Black Cockerel, Longpark Factory, 1918-30, 2½ In.	6
Eggcup, Waste Not Want Not, House, 2¾ In.	45
Hatpin Holder, A Place For Hat Pins, Sailboats, 5 x 3 In.	100
Inkwell, Send Us A Scrape O' Yer Pen, Green, Brown, Flowers, 2¾ In.	75
Jug, White Ground, Red Handle, Cockerel, Puzzle, Aller Vale, 4½ In.	45
Match Holder, Striker, A Match For Any Man, Green, Rust, 2½ In.	40
Mug, Tis A Good Ass That Don't Stumble, Cottage, 4¾ In.	35

Tool, Cabinet, Nuts & Bolts, 96 Drawers, 8-Sided, Porcelain Knobs, Stenciled, c.1890, 39 x 25 In.
$1,464

Neal Auction Company

Tool, Caliper, Man & Woman, In Flagrante, Steel, 1800s, France, 7 In.
$3,444

Skinner, Inc.

Tool, Hay Fork, Wood, 5 Prongs, Hickory Construction, Signed, Musser, 1800s, 68 In.
$81

Keystone Auctions LLC

Tool, Mallet, Boxwood, Ebony, Silver Mount, Commemorative Plate, 1872, 8 In.

$277

Skinner, Inc.

Tool, Sickle, Wrought Iron, Curved Blade, Spiral End, Wood Handle, France, 13 In.

$2,091

Skinner, Inc.

Toothpick Holder, Silver, Birds, On Branches, Flying, Flutter Rim, George Shiebler, c.1900, 2¼ In.

$238

Eldred's

Lithographed Tin Toys

Most lithographed tin toys were made between 1870 and 1915, although some were made later. Collectors like animated groups of animals or people, toys that make noise or music, or toys that move. Makers of special interest include Lehmann, Marx, Chein, Unique, Wolverine, and Strauss.

Perfume Bottle, Earthenware, Dimple Shape, Kentish Violets, 1920-30, 3½ In.	21
Pitcher, Honest Loss Is Preferable To Shameful Gain, Dark Blue, Birds, 5¾ In.	35
Pitcher, Lid, Cobalt Blue, Diving Kingfisher, Devon, 7½ In.	27
Plate, Black, Cat On Brick Wall, Marked, 6⅛ In.	100
Sugar & Creamer, More Haste Less Speed, Ships, Souvenir Of St. Ives.	65
Sugar, Sweeten To Your Liking, Blue, Green, 2 x 3⅜ In.	12
Tray, Sky Blue Ground, Winter Scene, Watcombe, 5 x 2½ In.	80
Vase, Art Nouveau Style, Aller Vale, Floral, Square Base, 8 x 7 In.	56
Vase, Every Blade Of Grass Has It's Own Drop Of Dew, Flowers, Blue, Green, 5 In.	58
Vase, Peacock On Tree Branch, Green, Red, Yellow, Blue Ground, Handles, 6½ In.	450
Vase, To Grieve For That Behind, 4 Openings, 5 x 4½ In.	85

 TORTOISESHELL is the shell of the tortoise. It has been used as inlay and to make small decorative objects since the seventeenth century. Some species of tortoise are now on the endangered species list, and old or new objects made from these shells cannot be sold legally. There is also a Victorian glass that looks like a tortoise shell and is called tortoiseshell glass.

Case, Display, Veneer, Rectangular, Glass Case, 4½ x 26 x 19½ In.	1625
Cigarette Box, Silver Mounts, Cornelius Saunders, Francis Shepard, 1895, 2 x 6 x 4 In.	375
Vase, Floral Ribbed Body, Enameled, c.1890, 7½ In.	58

TOTE, *see Purse category.*

 TOY collectors have special clubs, magazines, and shows. Toys are designed to entice children, and today they have attracted new interest among adults who are still children at heart. All types of toys are collected. Tin toys, iron toys, battery-operated toys, and many others are collected by specialists. Penny toys are inexpensive tin toys made in Germany from the 1880s until about 1914. Some salesman's samples may be listed here. Dolls, Games, Teddy Bears, Bicycles, and other types of toys are listed in their own categories. Other toys may be found under company or celebrity names.

Abacus, 10 Sets Counting Beads, Multicolor, c.1880, 29 x 22 In.	492
Acrobat, Circus, Bisque, Wood, Painted, Wood & Metal Stand, Stool, Schoenhut, 8 In.	1380
Acrobat, Warrior, Holds Clubs, Stands On Slats, Somersaults, Clockwork, Lehmann, 10 In.	570
Acrobatic Gymnast, Formal Uniform, Moves Back & Forth On Bars, Martin, c.1905, 15 In.	15600
Acrobats On Ladder, Tin, Painted, Mechanical, Flip & Tumble Down Rungs, 9 In. *illus*	450
Airplane, Biplane, Engine Noise & Lights, Battery Operated, Japan, Box, 12 In.	212
Airplane, Biplane, Metal, Red, Yellow, Blue Propeller, Distler, Penny Toy *illus*	540
Airplane, Bombardier, Pilot, Battery Operated, Japan, Box, 11 In.	170
Airplane, Bristol Bulldog, Battery Operated, Japan, Box, 14 In.	170
Airplane, Fighter Pilot, Bump & Go, Tin, Windup, Ko, Japan, Box, 5½ In.	212
Airplane, G.B. Model, Balsa & Fabric, Red & White Paint, 78 x 50 In.	570
Airplane, Gray Paint & Decals, Steelcraft, 1900s, 22½ In.	342
Airplane, Jet Flagship, Battery Operated, Stairs, Door, Japan, 21 In.	602
Airplane, Navy, Balsa Wood & Fabric, Gas Engine, Tire Fatigue, 48 x 36 In.	1020
Airplane, Propeller, CKO Logo, Pilot, Tin, Yellow, Red, Kellermann, Germany, Penny, 5 In.	240
Airplane, Rollover, Tin, Windup, Orange, Gray, Marx, Japan, 1930, 6 In.	177
Airplane, Scandinavian Airlines, Viscount, Battery Operated, Japan, Box, 18 x 19 In.	437
Airplane, Super Skyliner, Tin, Windup, Great Britain, 17 In.	708
Airplane, Tin Lithograph, Windup, Air Devil, No. 56, Strauss, Box, 9 x 8 x 4 In.	263
Airplane, Yellow, Black Stripes, No. 574, Tin, Distler, Germany, Penny, 5 In.	210
Airport Tower, Control, Windup, Aerodrome, 3 Planes, Schylling, Box, 1970s, 7 In.	23
Airport, Universal, Tin Lithograph, Windup, Marx, c.1938, 12 x 6¾ x 3 In.	129
Ambulance, Emergency, White, Small Fry Nurse Set, Pressman Hospital, Box, 14 In.	71
Amos 'N' Andy, Andy, Walker, Tin Lithograph, Windup, Marx, 1930, 11 In.	468
Apollo 11, American Eagle Lunar Module, Tin Lithograph, Battery Operated, Box, 9 In.	354
Astroman, Green, Battery Operated, Dux, Germany, Box, 13½ In.	673
Atomic Reactor, Battery Operated, Steam Engine, Linemar, Box, 13 In.	637
Atomic Robot Man, Silvertone, Tin, Occupied Japan, 5 x 2½ In.	192

Baby Bertha, Elephant, Circus, Tin, Battery Operated, Mego, Japan, 12 x 10 In.	130
Badge, Detective, Inspector General Post, General Foods Cereal Premium, c.1933, 1⅝ In.	20
Badge, Marshal, Deadwood, Star, Circle, Metal, Pinback, 2 In.	12
Balancing, 2 Horses, 3-Sided Stand, Weighted Ball, Metal, Paint, 13 In.	900
Balky Mule, Cart, Clown Driver, Tin Lithograph, Windup, Lehmann, Box, c.1905, 7 In. *illus*	389
Barnacle Bill, Sailor, Tin Lithograph, Windup, Brown & Red, Chein, 6½ In.	164
Beany & Cecil, Talking Doll, Mattel, Box, 1961, 18 In. *illus*	130
Bears are also listed in the Teddy Bear category.	
Bear, Black Hat, Tin, Windup, J. Chein & Co., 4½ In.	23
Bear, Climbing Pole, Metal Pole, Rungs, Felt Bearskin, Windup, Martin, France, c.1909, 20 In.	4800
Bear, Mohair, Glass Eyes, Riding Scooter, Tin, Windup, Germany, 5½ In.	153
Bear, Papa, Smoking, Remote Control, Battery Operated, Japan, Box, 9 In.	156
Bear, Playing Ball, Tin, Windup, T.P.S., Japan, Box, 18 In.	130
Bell Ringer, 2 Clowns, Cast Iron, Painted, Wheels, Watrous, 10 In.	130
Bell Ringer, Eagle, Patriotic, Red, White, Blue, Holds Bell In Beak, Embossed No. 50, 6 In. *illus*	840
Bicycles that are large enough to ride are listed in the Bicycle category.	
Bicyclist, Girl Rides Around Track, Clown Waits, Composition, Cloth, Metal, Althof Bergmann, 1877	2700
Billiard Table, 2 Players, Mechanical, Balls, Tin, Windup, Ranger Steel Products, Box, 14 In.	425
Bird In Cage, Tin, Multicolor, Fixed Key, Off-On Switch, Spring Driven, 7 x 5 x 3 In. *illus*	165
Bird, Cage, Tin, Windup, Metal Stand, Germany, 8 In.	201
Bird, Movable Beak, Wood, Yellow, Red, Green, Russia, 1979, 6 In.	27
Bird, Peeking, Tin Lithograph, Multicolor, Windup, 1927, 5¼ In.	39
Black Boy, Composition Head, Hands, Wire Body, Lead Feet, Windup, Germany, 1910, 8 In.	443
Black Man, Porter, Automatic, Wood, Papier-Mache & Fabric, Jigger, c.1865, 10½ x 8 In.	1348
Bo Jangle, Dances, Wood Body, Tin Arms, Hat, Clown Toy Mfg. Co., 1950s, 8 In.	130
Boat, Battleship, Tin Lithograph, Friction, Hess, Germany, 12 In.	384
Boat, Cargo Liner, SS Silver Mariner, Battery Operated, Cragstan, Japan, Box, 16 In.	368
Boat, Flying Yankee, Stained, Pine, Painted, Windup Motor, Jacrim Mfg. Co., 1926, 20 In.	210
Boat, Military, Guns, Cannons, Wood, Battery Operated, Japan, 16 In.	142
Boat, Racing, Driver, Arrow, Crank, Multicolor, Tin, Windup, Japan, 11 In.	127
Boat, River, Queen Mary, Tin Lithograph, Electric, San, Japan, Box, 13½ x 4½ x 4¼ In.	94
Boat, Rocket, Battery Operated, Multicolor, Wood, Japan, 32 In. *illus*	1062
Boat, Speedboat, Driver, Orange, Red, Yellow, Black, Battery Operated, Japan, 11 In.	127
Boat, Speedboat, Nantico 3001, Drivers, Flag & Key, Tin, Windup, Schuco, 18 In.	283
Boat, Speedboat, Painted, Tin, Windup, Lindstrom, 14 In.	184
Boat, Speedboat, Remote Control, Tin Lithograph, With Light, Japan, Box, 7 In.	81
Boat, Speedboat, Yellow & Blue Paint, Tin Windup, Hornby, 12½ In.	83
Boat, Torpedo, Battery Operated, Linemar, Japan, Box, 1950s, 10 In.	120
Boat, Twin Propellers, Geared Transmission, Battery Operated, 1950s, 34 In.	259
Bobby The Policeman, Uniform, Tin Helmet, Billy Club, Raises Arm, Clockwork, Martin, c.1901, 7 In.	3900
Bobo, Juggling Clown, Striped Shirt, Yellow Ball, Windup, 5½ In.	269
Boob McNutt, Black & Red Outfit, Tin, Windup, Strauss, Box, 9 In.	743
Boob McNutt, Small Hat Version, Tin Lithograph, Strauss, Box, 8½ In.	1080
Boy On Scooter, Tin Lithograph, Leg Movement, Clockwork, Victor Bonnet, 1920s, 8 In.	1560
Boy On Tricycle, Composition Head, Holding Top Hat, Tin, Windup, 8 In.	83
Bucking Bronco, Cowboy Rider, White Horse, Windup, Lehmann, Box, c.1925, 6¾ In.	7963
Bulldozer, Marvelous Mike, Tractor, Robot Driver, Battery Operated, Saunders	150
Bus, 6 Rows Of Seats, Working Headlights, Pressed Steel, Cor-Cor, 7 x 24 x 7 In. *illus*	333
Bus, Cannon Ball Express, Push, Black, Red & Yellow, 9 In.	83
Bus, Continental Trailways, Golden Eagle, Tin, Friction, Yellow Paint, Japan, Box, 14 In.	297
Bus, Double-Decker, Arcade, Red Paint, Rubber Tires, Cast Iron, c.1929, 8 In.	170
Bus, Double-Decker, Shell With ICA, Tin Lithograph, Heyashi, Japan, 8 In.	102
Bus, Double-Decker, Tin, Windup, Ferdinand Strauss Co., 6 x 10½ In.	316
Bus, Electric Omnibus Company, Double-Decker, Cutout People, Litho, Meier, Penny Toy *illus*	960
Bus, Green Line, Tin Lithograph, Clockwork, Triang Minic, 7 In.	92
Bus, Greyhound, Painted, Pressed Steel, Windup, Buddy L, 16½ In.	113
Bus, Infants, Animal Graphics, People In Window, Tin, Friction, Japan, 9 In.	57
Bus, Inter-City, Black Paint, Pressed Steel, Wheels, Steelcraft, 1930s, 24 In.	170
Bus, Speedway, 6 Passengers, Tin Lithograph, Wolverine, 14 In.	50
Busy Bridge, Cars, Tin Lithograph, Windup, Marx, 24 x 4 x 8 In.	187

Toy, Acrobats On Ladder, Tin, Painted, Mechanical, Flip & Tumble Down Rungs, 9 In.
$450

Bertoia Auctions

Toy, Airplane, Biplane, Metal, Red, Yellow, Blue Propeller, Distler, Penny Toy
$540

Bertoia Auctions

Toy, Balky Mule, Cart, Clown Driver, Tin Lithograph, Windup, Lehmann, Box, c.1905, 7 In.
$389

Hake's Auctions

This is an edited listing of current prices. Visit **Kovels.com** to check thousands of prices from previous years and sign up for free information on trends, tips, reproductions, marks, and more.

SELECTED TOY MARKS WITH DATES USED

Gebruder Bing Co.
c.1923–1924
Nuremberg, Germany

F.A.O. Schwarz
1914
New York, N.Y.

Louis Marx & Co.
1920–1977
New York, N.Y.

Ernst Lehmann Co.
1915
Brandenburg, Germany

Gebruder Marklin & Co.
1899+
Goppingen, Germany

Nomura Toy Industrial Co., Ltd.
1940s+
Tokyo, Japan

Meccano
1901+
Liverpool, England

Georges Carette & Co.
1905–1917
Nuremburg, Germany

Gebruder Bing
1902–1934
Nuremburg, Germany

Joseph Falk Co.
1895–1934
Nuremburg, Germany

H. Fischer & Co.
1908–1932
Nuremburg, Germany

Ernst Lehmann Co.
1881–c.1947, 1951–2006
Brandenburg, Germany; Nuremburg, Germany

Lineol
c.1906–1963
Bradenburg, Germany

Blomer and Schüler
1919–1974
Nuremberg, Germany

Yonezawa Toys Co.
1950s–1970s
Tokyo, Japan

Butter & Egg Man, Checked Jacket, Duck, Bag, Tin Lithograph, Mechanical, Marx, c.1930, 7¾ In.	395
Cadet, Marching, Celluloid, Tin, Windup, Japan, Box, 6 In.	99
Camel, 2 Humps, Glass Eyes, Cast Iron, Wheels, Fabric Saddle, Steiff, 17 x 13 In. ....*illus*	320
Cannon, Firecracker, Red Paint, Michaelson Mfg. Co., 1920s-30s, 6¾ In.	118
Cap Gun, Butting Match, 2 Men Butting Heads On Top, Ives, 1880s, 5 In.	960
Cap Gun, Luger Repeater, Metal, Plastic Grips, Lincoln Intl., Box, 8 In.	83
Cap Gun, Pecos Kid, Die Cast Metal, Plastic Grips, Lone Star, Box, 8½ In.	493
Cap Gun, Strato Gun, Chrome Plate, Die Cast Metal, Duro Company, 9½ In.	144
Captain Of Kopenick, Cobbler, Dressed As Captain, Moneybag, Lehmann, 7¾ In.	840
Car, Baby Bugatti, Aluminum, Leather Seats, Electric Motor, E. Bugatti Design, 1927, 77 In.	1169
Car, Bluebird, Pressed Steel, 4 Rubber Tires, Windup, U.K., 4 x 18 x 4¾ In. ....*illus*	177
Car, Cadillac, Painted, 2-Tone, Tin, Battery Operated, Plated Tin Trim, 1950s, 13 In.	625
Car, Cadillac, Sedan, Tin, Friction, Blue, Japan, Box, 1959, 12 In.	297
Car, Coo Coo, Red, Yellow & Black, Tin, Windup, Marx, 8 In.	165
Car, Coupe, Electric Light, White Rubber Tires, Red & Black, Wyandotte, 1930, 8 In.	118
Car, Dagwood, Crazy, Wood Hat, Tin, Windup, Marx, 8 In.	602
Car, Driver, Man & Woman, Remote Control, Cable, Green, Arnold Primal, c.1940, 10 In.	105
Car, Fire Chief, Pressed Steel, Headlights, Windup, Battery Operated, Bulbs, 1930s, 14 In.	339
Car, Ford, Galaxie, Rubber Tires, Plastic Underside, Promotional, 1963, 8 In. ....*illus*	195
Car, Ford, Model T, Woman Driver, Black, Tin, Bing, 1920, 6½ In.	153
Car, Ford, Skyliner, Sports Car, Tin Lithograph, Battery Operated, TN, Box.	299
Car, Grand Prix, Alfa Romeo, Orange, Clockwork, Model P2, C.I.J., c.1935, 6 x 21 x 7½ In.	5500
Car, Hot Rod, Driver, Tin, Friction, Red, Japan, Box, 7 In.	198
Car, Jalopy, Driver, Friction Motor, Tin, Linemar, 5 In. ....*illus*	118
Car, Jibby, Green, Music Box, Tin, Windup, Marked, Schuco	177
Car, Limousine, Red, Black, Gebruder Bing, Germany, Late 1920s	1103
Car, Loop, Windup, Red, Yellow & Blue, Arnold, 10 In.	189
Car, Lucky, Driver, Red, Tin Lithograph, Electric, San, Japan, c.1950, 9 x 4 x 5 In.	82
Car, Milton Berle, Hat, Tin Windup, Box, Marx, 6½ In.	319
Car, Milton Berle, Windup, Tin Lithograph, Marx, Box, c.1950, 6¾ x 4 x 6 In.	187
Car, Pedal, Cannonball Express, Red & Black, Casey Jones, 40 In.	316
Car, Police Motorbike, Pro Red, Superfast No. 33, Die Cast, Matchbox, 1960s	133
Car, Porsche, Prototype, Electric, Tin & Clockwork, JNF, Germany, 8 In.	437
Car, Racing, Exhaust Pipes, Wheels, Cast Iron, Hubley, 10 In.	102
Car, Racing, Mercedes SSK, Pressed Steel, Windup, c.1935, 14½ In.	396
Car, Racing, No. 1, Yellow & Red, Tin, Windup, Marx, 13 In.	236
Car, Racing, No. 8, Red, Auburn, Rubber, Yellow Wheels, c.1945, 4½ In.	22
Car, Racing, Plastic Driver, Blue, Red, White & Yellow, Tin, Windup, Marx	142
Car, Racing, Wood, Headlights, Red, Yellow Wheels, Battery Operated, 3½ x 12 x 5 In. ......*illus*	48
Car, Roadster, Green, Red Seat, Tin Lithograph, Mechanical, 9¾ x 3⅝ x 3 In.	82
Car, Roadster, Painted, Tin Lithograph, Hercules Balloon Corp., 16 In. ....*illus*	339
Car, Runabout, Military Man Driver, Meier, Penny Toy, c.1914, 3 In.	210
Car, Shell, Pedal & Wheel, White, Black Tires, 32 In.	259
Car, Speedster, Driver, Pressed Steel, Red Paint, Marx, 6 In. ....*illus*	165
Car, Spotlight, Camouflage, Hand Painted, Marklin, O Gauge, 1930	83
Car, Tacho Examico 4002, Painted, Schuco, 6 In.	248
Car, Touring, Driver, Blue, Silver Spoke Wheels, Passenger, Meier, Penny, 4¼ In.	1020
Car, Tricky, Driver, Red Wheels, Tin Lithograph, Marx, 7¾ x 3 x 6½ In.	263
Car, Volkswagen Beetle, Red, Tin, Friction Motor, Japan, 10 In.	170
Car, Volkswagen Beetle, Space Patrol, Battery Operated, Tin Litho, Japan, 1960s, 12½ In.	3180
Car, Zink Zack, Driver, Tin, Red, White, Blue, Lehmann, 1900s, 5 In.	468
Carousel Horse, Jumper, Carved, Painted, Hair Tail, Stand, 1900s, 17 x 36 In., Child's	125
Carousel Horse, Jumper, Wood, White, Red Saddle, Rolling Stand, 1900s, 36 x 44 x 9 In.	196
Carousel, Children On Horses, Canopy, Tin Lithograph, Germany, 17 In. ....*illus*	480
Carriage, Doll's, Rattan Bassinet, Side Handles, Wood Frame, Folding, c.1920, 26 x 22 x 17 In. *illus*	30
Carriage, Doll's, Wicker, Painted, Iron & Steel Frame, Rubber Tires, c.1915, 33 x 34 x 12 In.	63
Cart, Daredevil, Zebra, Tin Lithograph, Windup, Built-In Key, Lehmann, 1920s, 7 In.	286
Cart, Mule Drawn, Driver, 2 Mules, Tin, Windup, Marx, 10 In. ....*illus*	71
Cash Register, Red, Tom Thumb, Western Stamping Co., 1950s, 7 x 6 x 7 In.	49

Toy, Beany & Cecil, Talking Doll, Mattel, Box, 1961, 18 In.
$130

Milestone Auctions

Toy, Bell Ringer, Eagle, Patriotic, Red, White, Blue, Holds Bell In Beak, Embossed No. 50, 6 In.
$840

Bertoia Auctions

Toy, Bird In Cage, Tin, Multicolor, Fixed Key, Off-On Switch, Spring Driven, 7 x 5 x 3 In.
$165

Forsythes' Auctions

TIP
Don't repaint old metal toys. It lowers the value.

T

Toy, Boat, Rocket, Battery Operated, Multicolor, Wood, Japan, 32 In.
$1,062

Milestone Auctions

Toy, Bus, 6 Rows Of Seats, Working Headlights, Pressed Steel, Cor-Cor, 7 x 24 x 7 In.
$333

Fontaine's Auction Gallery

Battery-Operated Toys
Battery-operated toys were possible after C and D batteries became easily available after World War II. Many of the toys were made in Japan after the war, often using tin from discarded American drink cans left by soldiers.

Toy, Bus, Electric Omnibus Company, Double-Decker, Cutout People, Litho, Meier, Penny Toy
$960

Bertoia Auctions

Toy, Camel, 2 Humps, Glass Eyes, Cast Iron, Wheels, Fabric Saddle, Steiff, 17 x 13 In.
$320

Morphy Auctions

Toy, Car, Bluebird, Pressed Steel, 4 Rubber Tires, Windup, U.K., 4 x 18 x 4¾ In.
$177

Burchard Galleries

Toy, Car, Ford, Galaxie, Rubber Tires, Plastic Underside, Promotional, 1963, 8 In.
$195

Hake's Auctions

Toy, Car, Jalopy, Driver, Friction Motor, Tin, Linemar, 5 In.
$118

Milestone Auctions

Toy, Car, Racing, Wood, Headlights, Red, Yellow Wheels, Battery Operated, 3½ x 12 x 5 In.
$48

Thomaston Place Auction Galleries

Toy, Car, Roadster, Painted, Tin Lithograph, Hercules Balloon Corp., 16 In.
$339

Hartzell's Auction Gallery, Inc.

Castle, 2 Towers & Soldiers, Tin, Wheels, Pull Toy, 13 ½ x 8 ½ In.	252
Cat, Felix, Black Paint, Tin, Windup, Germany, 1924, 6 ½ In.	283
Cat, Felix, Windup, Holding Red Suitcase, 1967, 7 In.	83
Cat, Knitting, White Plush Fur, Wearing Glasses, Windup, Japan, Box, 6 In.	69
Chair, Doll's, Painted, Cane Seat, 1800s, 15 ½ In.	163
Charleston Trio, 3 Figures, Dancing, Tin, Windup, Marx, 8 ½ In.	1097
Charlie The Drumming Clown, Battery Operated, Japan, Box, 9 ½ In.	156
Chef, Roller Skating, Serving Food, Tin, Windup, 6 In. ....*illus*	156
Chest, Doll's, Bombay, Inlaid Flowers, Lift Top, Bronze Ormolu, France, 7 x 12 x 9 In.	230
Chest, Doll's, Empire, Top Drawer Overhanging 3 Lower Drawers, Bun Feet, c.1860, 8 x 16 x 16 In.	863
Chicken Snatcher, Tin, Yellow Hat, Brown Boy, Louis Marx Co., c.1930, 8 In.	1130
Chicken, Hand Painted, Windup, Tin, Germany, 7 In.	83
Child In High Chair, Animal Cards On Tray, Wheels, Tin Litho, Fischer, Penny Toy ......*illus*	240
Clown & Pig, Pig Pulls Clown In Sulky, 2 Wheels, Tin, Penny Toy ....*illus*	1680
Clown In Barrel, Rolls, Head & Feet Stick Out, Tin Lithograph, Germany, Penny Toy ......*illus*	660
Clown Porter, Walking, 3-Wheel Cart, 2 Trapdoors, Clockwork, Hans Eberl, c.1910, 7 In.	10200
Clown, Barrel, Star & Yellow Background, Hat, Tin, J. Chein & Co., 1930, 8 In.	192
Clown, Bell, Painted, Baton, Squeeze, Windup, Tin, Germany, 10 In.	224
Clown, Cart, Donkey, Tin Lithograph, Early 1900s, 9 ¾ x 4 ½ x 6 In.	176
Clown, Composition Head, Wheels, Cymbals, Drum, Pull Toy, 18 In.	522
Clown, Holding A Stick With Bells, Wagon, Glass Eyes, Pull Toy, 7 x 13 In.	450
Clown, Juggling, Windup, Multicolor, Box, Japan, 6 ½ In.	224
Clown, Melody Band, Drums, Battery Operated, Cragstan, Japan, 9 ½ In.	130
Clown, On Motorcycle, Red & White, Blue Hat, Tin Lithograph, Windup, Japan, 5 ½ In.	263
Clown, Papier-Mache Head, Green Hat, Orange Shirt, Windup, Key, Germany, Box, 6 In.	63
Clown, Playing Bugle, Standing On Drum, Tin, Novelty, Germany, c.1895 ....*illus*	424
Clown, Plays Violin, Tin, Windup, Schuco, Germany, c.1930, 4 ½ In.	117
Clown, Spins Upside Down On Hat, Clockwork, Marked, Victor Bonnet, c.1920, 7 ½ In.	6600
Clown, Tambourine, Windup, Red, Yellow & White, Box, Japan, 7 In.	35
Clown, Trainer, Acrobatic Dog, Multicolor, Tin, Windup, Box, 7 In.	170
Clown, Wooden Rocker, Composition Head, Fabric Clothing, 12 ½ x 9 ½ In.	246
Coach, Green, Brown Belt-Line Stripe, Open Windows, Pressed Steel, Buddy L, 7 x 8 x 29 In. ...	2260
Cock Fight, Windup, Tin, Multicolor, Japan, Box, 5 ½ In.	184
Concrete Mixer, Pressed Steel, Paint, Buddy L, c.1928, 14 ½ x 17 ½ In.	509
Confectionary Shop, 3 Walls, Drawers, Shelves, Tables, Tins, Dishes, Gottschalk, 26 In.	330
Cow, On Wheels, Hide Covered, Glass Eyes, Wood Horn, Painted, Brass Rollers, 15 In. ......*illus*	600
Crane, Orange, Hook & Clam, Pressed Steel, Doepke, c.1950, 20 x 6 ½ x 20 In.	211
Cyclist, Clown, High Wheel Bike, Painted, 6 ½ In.	496
Dancer, Dog, Folk Art, Hand Made, Clockwork Mechanism, 13 In.	271
Dancing Couple, Les Valseurs, Boy & Girl Spin, Metal, String, Gyroscope, Martin, c.1885, 4 In.	450
Dancing Couple, Man, Woman, Wheeled Platform, Tin Lithograph, Windup, Germany, 7 In.	1200
Dancing Couple, Windup, Celluloid, Pink, Blue, Occupied Japan, Original Box, 5 In.	48
Dancing Couple, Young Boy & Girl, Gunthermann, 7 In.	900
Dancing Girl, Strutting My Fair Dancer, Tin Lithograph, Battery Operated, Haji, Japan, Box	138
Daredevil Motor Cop, Policeman On Motorcycle, Tin, Windup, Unique Art, Box, 8 ½ In.	920
Dart Gun, Rocket, Embossed, Wyandotte, Box With Space Scene, 10 In.	85
Delivery Truck, Esso, Tin, Windup, Hornby Meccano, 14 In.	189
Delivery Truck, Gasoline, Red Paint, Pressed Steel, No. 16, Tonka, Box, 15 In.	1200
Dog In Kennel, Dog Comes In & Out, Side Lever, Tin Lithograph, Penny Toy ....*illus*	540
Dog, Brindle Bulldog, Wood, Composition, Leather, Glass Eyes, Schoenhut, 6 In.	3450
Dog, Bulldog, Drumming, Celluloid, Windup, Japan, 8 In.	142
Dog, Bulldog, Standing, Plush Over Paper, Painted, Bristle Hair Collar, 13 x 16 x 7 In. ......*illus*	550
Dog, Spotty, Seated, Shaded Cream Mohair, Black Shoebutton Eyes, Steiff, 1930s, 9 In.	518
Dog, St. Bernard, Barrel, Mohair, Shaded Brown, Amber Glass Eyes, Button, Steiff, 10 In.	460
Dolls are listed in the Doll category.	
Doll On Cart, Rings Bell, Parian Head, Mallets Strike Bell When Pulled, Germany, 1870s, 9 In.	900
Dollhouse Furniture, Birdcage, Mahogany, Ornate, Stand, Victorian, Glenowen Ltd.	24
Dollhouse, 2 Story, Arched Lower Front Window, Metal Label, 28 x 18 x 18 In.	384

Toy, Car, Speedster, Driver, Pressed Steel, Red Paint, Marx, 6 In.
$165

Milestone Auctions

Toy, Carousel, Children On Horses, Canopy, Tin Lithograph, Germany, 17 In.
$480

Bertoia Auctions

Toy, Carriage, Doll's, Rattan Bassinet, Side Handles, Wood Frame, Folding, c.1920, 26 x 22 x 17 In.
$30

Thomaston Place Auction Galleries

T

Toy, Cart, Mule Drawn, Driver, 2 Mules, Tin, Windup, Marx, 10 In.
$71

Milestone Auctions

Toy, Chef, Roller Skating, Serving Food, Tin, Windup, 6 In.
$156

Milestone Auctions

Toy, Child In High Chair, Animal Cards On Tray, Wheels, Tin Litho, Fischer, Penny Toy
$240

Bertoia Auctions

Toy, Clown & Pig, Pig Pulls Clown In Sulky, 2 Wheels, Tin, Penny Toy
$1,680

Bertoia Auctions

Toy, Clown In Barrel, Rolls, Head & Feet Stick Out, Tin Lithograph, Germany, Penny Toy
$660

Bertoia Auctions

Toy, Clown, Playing Bugle, Standing On Drum, Tin, Novelty, Germany, c.1895
$424

RSL Auction

Toy, Cow, On Wheels, Hide Covered, Glass Eyes, Wood Horn, Painted, Brass Rollers, 15 In.
$600

Bertoia Auctions

T

Dollhouse, 2 Story, Arched Windows, Double Chimney, Bliss, 14 ½ In.	960
Dollhouse, 2 Story, Wood, Attic, Mullioned Windows, Painted, c.1910, 17 x 12 x 17 In. *illus*	715
Dollhouse, 4 Story, Town House Style, Gray Stucco, 1900s, 45 x 45 x 23 In.	270
Dollhouse, Wood, Brick, Stone, Tile Roof, Metal Windows, Schoenhut, 13 x 17 x 15 In.	330
Dolly Seamstress, Embroidering, Head Turns, Battery Operated, TN, Japan, Box, 7 x 6 ½ In.	224
Dragon, Snappy Happy, Bubble Blowing, Battery Operated, Marx, Japan, 39 In.	2185
Drum, 9 Marching Animals, Instruments, Flag, 6 ½ x 9 In. *illus*	510
Drummer Boy, George, Inn, Windup, Marx, Box, 9 In.	153
Drummer, Bass Drum, Red Jacket, Blue Pants, Windup, Box, Chein, 9 In.	117
Drummer, George The Drummer, Pushing Drum, Front Wheel, Tin Lithograph, Marx, 8 x 8 In.	322
Drummer, Sailor, Celluloid, Windup, Japan, Box, 11 In.	326
Easter Rabbit, Riding Lamb, Lithograph, Cardboard, Wood Platform, Wheels, 5 ½ x 6 In.	1140
Easter Rabbit, Riding Motorcycle, Sidecar, Wyandotte, 9 ½ In.	271
Elephant, Mohair, Shoebutton Eye, Red Saddle, Wheels, Pull Toy, Steiff, 12 x 9 ½ In.	492
Elephant, Squeaks, Composition, Wood Tusk, Trunk Picks Up Tree, Wood Base, Germany, 9 In.	840
Elephant, Stuffed, Wooden Wheels, Shoebutton Eyes, Felt Saddle Blanket, 16 x 13 ½ In.	160
Feeding Chickens, Coop, Box With Sliding Lid, Side Lever, Tin Lithograph, Penny Toy. *illus*	840
Ferris Wheel, Hercules, 6 Baskets, Bell, Tin, J. Chein & Co., c.1930, 16 x 12 x 5 In. *illus*	108
Ferris Wheel, Tin, 12 Gondolas, Seated Figures, Plink Plank Sound, Carette, 20 In.	1020
Fire House, General Alarm, Tricky Fire Chief, Alarm Box, Key, Marx, 17 x 11 In.	140
Fire Truck, 2 Firemen, Tin Lithograph, Battery Operated, TN, Japan, Box, 16 In.	138
Fire Truck, Aerial Ladder, Red, Gold, Pressed Steel, Buddy L, c.1930, 10 ½ x 9 x 39 In.	360
Fire Truck, Coney Island, Steel Panels, Ladders, Pinto Bros Mfg., 26 x 23 x 63 In.	420
Fire Truck, Die Cast Aluminum, Nickel Plate Ladders, Smith Miller, c.1950, 35 x 6 x 7 In.	380
Fire Truck, Ladder, Red, Tin Lithograph, Continental Record, c.1900, 19 In.	106
Fire Truck, Mack Jr., Ladders, Rope, Red Paint, Steelcraft Murray, 1928, 11 x 7 x 26 In.	492
Fire Truck, Mack Jr., Toledo Bulldog, Ladders, Rope, Steelcraft Murray, 1928, 12 x 9 x 31 In.	608
Fire Truck, Red, Cast Iron & Nickel, Pumper, Painted, Marked, Hubley, 5 x 2 In.	125
Fire Truck, Ride On, Ladders & Steering Wire, Red, White, Buddy L, 30 In.	384
Fire Truck, S.F.D., Ladder, Red, Pressed Steel, Structo, 33 x 7 In.	94
Fire Truck, Side Ladders, Hose, Die Cast, Red Paint, Keystone, c.1927, 11 x 9 x 28 In.	313
Fire Wagon, 3 Horses, 2 Firemen, Ladder, Red, Cast Iron, 28 In. *illus*	561
Fire Wagon, Horse Drawn, 2 Firemen, Ladders, Hubley, 1915, 28 In.	212
Fireman, Climbing, Box, Red, Yellow, Blue, Black, Ladder, Windup, Tin, Marx, 1930s, 11 x 3 ½ In.	127
Fisherman, Catches Fish, Pushbutton, Wood, Hand Carved, 6 In.	46
Fisherman, Multicolor, Windup, Stand, Germany, 6 In.	71
Flintstones, Barney Rubble, Riding Dino, Tin, Windup, Marx, Japan, 8 In.	189
Flintstones, Flivver, Fred Driving, Tin, Friction, Marx, 7 In. *illus*	1322
Flintstones, Flivver, Fred Driving, Wooden, Pull Toy, Brio, 8 In.	71
Football Player, Kicks Rubber Football, Red Shirt, Orange Pants, Cast Iron, Helmet, 8 In.	241
Fork Lift, Driver, Tin, Friction, Rubber Tires, Red, Battery Operated, Japan, 11 In.	127
Fox, Golden, Brown Mohair, Amber Glass Eyes, Jointed Limbs, Bushy Tail, Steiff, 1920s, 8 In.	230
Frankie The Roller-Skating Monkey, Battery Operated, Green Hat, Red Jacket, Japan, 13 In.	130
Frog & Toadstool, Frog Jumps Into Container, Tin, Spring Lever, Fischer, Penny Toy. *illus*	1320
Frog, Eater, Whimsical, Mechanical, Germany, 5 x 2 x 5 In.	7200
Frog, Green & Tan Velvet, Amber Glass Eyes, Label, Steiff, 1940s, 3 In.	173
G.I. Joe & K-9 Pups, Soldier, Carrying Dog Crates, Tin Litho, Windup, Unique Art, 8 ¾ In.	105
G.I. Joe, Jouncing Jeep, Tin, Windup, Unique Art, 7 In. *illus*	177
G.I. Joe, Liberators Devil's Brigade, Hasbro, 12 In.	44
Games are listed in the Game category.	
Garage & House, Lights, Metal, Marx, 1960s, 17 In.	145
Gas Station, Pump, Keystone Garage Service, Car Lubricant, 16 In.	83
Gas Station, Universal, Day & Night Service, Tin Litho, Box, Marx, c.1938, 12 x 7 x 3 In.	263
George The Drummer Boy, Tin, Windup, Box, Marx, 9 ½ In.	130
Giraffe, Circus, Wood, Double-Jointed Neck, Glass Eyes, Rope Tail, Schoenhut, c.1905, 11 In.	978
Goat, Pink Collar, Saddle, Wood Platform, Metal Wheels, Victorian, Pull Toy, 12 x 4 x 13 In.	480
Goat, Wheels, Paper Collar, Dresden Trim, 9 x 3 x 9 In. *illus*	352
Go-Cart, Racing, Wood Frame, Red & Silver Finished, Chrome Hardware, 26 x 32 x 75 In.	813
Golfer, Man, Tin, Windup, Rectangular, Strauss, 1920, 12 x 7 In.	260

Toy, Dog In Kennel, Dog Comes In & Out, Side Lever, Tin Lithograph, Penny Toy
$540

Bertoia Auctions

Toy, Dog, Bulldog, Standing, Plush Over Paper, Painted, Bristle Hair Collar, 13 x 16 x 7 In.
$550

Forsythes' Auctions

Toy, Dollhouse, 2 Story, Wood, Attic, Mullioned Windows, Painted, c.1910, 17 x 12 x 17 In.
$715

Forsythes' Auctions

Toy, Drum, 9 Marching Animals, Instruments, Flag, 6 ½ x 9 In.
$510

Morphy Auctions

Toy, Feeding Chickens, Coop, Box With Sliding Lid, Side Lever, Tin Lithograph, Penny Toy
$840

Bertoia Auctions

Legos

It is estimated that over 203 billion Lego parts have been made since 1949. You can combine six eight-stud Lego blocks of the same color 102,981,500 different ways.

Toy, Ferris Wheel, Hercules, 6 Baskets, Bell, Tin, J. Chein & Co., c.1930, 16 x 12 x 5 In.
$108

Thomaston Place Auction Galleries

Toy, Fire Wagon, 3 Horses, 2 Firemen, Ladder, Red, Cast Iron, 28 In.
$561

Copake Auction

Goose, Waddles, Head & Neck Bob, Metal, Embossed, Painted, Clockwork, Martin, c.1899, 6 In.	900
Gorilla, Circus, Wood, Painted, Swivel Head, Cupped Hands, Teeth, Schoenhut, 1910, 8 In.	920
Greyhound Bus, Super Scenicruiser, White & Green, Tin, Friction, Japan, Box, 12 In.	184
Gun, Auto-Magic, Projects Pictures, Casts Metal, Stephens Products, 1939, 6 In.	17
Gun, Space Ray, Tin Lithograph Muzzle & Sight, Red, Wyandotte, 1930, 7½ In.	212
Gun, Space Rifle, Plastic, Sound, Sparks, Friction Motor, Pery Cosmos, 25½ In.	59
Gunboat, USS Farragut, Cap Firing, Tin Litho, Battery Operated, Cragstan, Japan, Box, 16 In.	127
Gymnast, Le Gymnaste, Metal, Cloth, Key Wind, Martin, France, c.1905, 15 In.	15600
Handcar, Hoky Poky, 2 Clowns, Tin Litho, Wyandotte, Windup, 6½ x 6½ In.	187
Handcar, Peter Rabbit, Chick, Mobile, Tin, Glass Eyes, Windup, Lionel, 10 In.	234
Hansom Cab, Horse Drawn, Driver, Wheel Under Horse, Cast Iron, Kenton, 1930, 15½ In.	130
Happy Chef, Bisque Doll, Glass Eyes, Cardboard Kitchen, Accessories, France, 16 x 10 In.	1265
Happy Hooligan, Green, Tin, Windup, Chein, Marx, 6 In.	142
Happy Hooligan, Roly Poly, Papier-Mache, Yellow, Green, Red, Germany, 5 In.	113
Happy Jack, Tapping, Hat, Orange Suit, Tin, Germany, c.1910	254
Happy The Clown, Tin, Windup, US Zone, Box, Germany, 6½ In.	106
Harold Lloyd, Funny Face, Walker, Tin Lithograph, Windup, Marx, c.1920, 10⅝ In. *illus*	222
Hay Rake, Brass, Iron, Maple, Rake Tongs, Spoke Wheels, Salesman's Sample, 10 x 7½ x 6 In.	880
Helicopter, Highway Patrol, B-47, Pilot, Blue & White, Tin, Friction, Box, 16 In.	156
Helicopter, Police, Highway Patrol, Battery Operated, TPS, Japan, 14½ In.	109
Helicopter, Sykorsky, Olive, Tin Rotors, Tootsietoy, 3½ In.	145
Hoisting Tower, Adjustable Delivery Chutes, Cord For Crank, Pressed Steel, Buddy L, 38 In.	283
Honeymoon Express, Turntable, Tunnel, Tracks, Tin Lithograph, Windup, Marx, 9 In.	75
Horse & Jockey, Green Platform, 4 Wheels, George W. Brown Co., c.1870s, 15 In. *illus*	2818
Horse & Rider, Cast Iron, Mounted On Steel Base, Wilkins, 4½ In.	531
Horse & Wagon, Black Horse, Orange Cart, Cast Iron, Ives, Blakeslee Co., 1880s, 10 In.	582
Horse & Wagon, Woman Driver, Surrey, Cast Iron, 17 In.	678
Horse Race, Celluloid Clown, Pink, Windup, Japan, Box, 4½ In.	177
Horse, 4 Wheels, Platform, Cast Iron, Ives, Blakeslee Co., c.1880, 10 In.	4900
Horse, Painted, Pine, White & Green, Pull Toy, 1900s, 22½ In.	100
Horse, Pull, Platform, Wheels, Cloth, Blanket, Saddle, Button Eyes, 15 x 16 In.	535
Horse, Ride-On, Leather Saddle, Iron Stirrups, Wood Platform, Wheels, 1800s, 24 x 20 x 20 In.	1356
Horse, Rocking, Dapple Gray, Red Saddle, Plaid Blanket, Victorian, 30 x 54 x 12 In.	660
Horse, Rocking, Horsehair Mane, Tail, Gray & Black, Harness, Saddle, 1900s, 47 x 66 x 20 In. *illus*	344
Horse, Rocking, Mohair Cover, Paint, 25 x 36 x 12 In.	94
Horse, Rocking, Painted, Carved, Cloth Saddle, Leather, Horsehair, Wood Frame, 35 In.	351
Horse, Rocking, Painted, Wooden, Leather Saddle, 1800s, 33 x 13 x 32 In.	295
Horse, Rocking, Seat Between 2 Horses, Pine, Maple, Painted, 17 x 30½ x 11½ In.	54
Horse, Rocking, Wood, Leather Saddle, Bridle, Horsehair Mane & Tail, 1800s, 31 x 52 In.	677
Horse, Standing, Painted, Wood, Wheels, Pull Toy, c.1900, 16½ x 6 x 12½ In.	71
Humphrey Mobile, Tin Lithograph, Mechanical, Wyandotte, Box, 8⅝ x 7 x 5⅜ In. *illus*	187
Humpty Dumpty, Dog, Carved Wood, Painted Eyes, Nose, Mouth, Schoenhut, 5½ In.	94
Ice Cream Vendor, Driver, White, Red, Tin, Friction, Japan, Box, 8 In.	283
Jazzbo Jim, Dancer On Roof, Arms, Legs, Banjo, Tin, Windup, Strauss, Box, 10 In.	743
Jazzbo Jim, Dancer On Roof, Tin, Windup, Banjo, Unique Art, Box, 1921, 10 In.	413
Jeep, Crazy Car, U.S. Army, Rocket, Tin Lithograph, Vinyl Driver's Head, Battery Operated	115
Jenny The Balking Mule, Old Man Driver, Tin Lithograph, Windup, Strauss, 11 In.	117
Jigger, Somstepa, Standing, Tin, Windup, Painted, Marx, 8 In.	602
Jockey, Horse, Tin, Windup, Platform, Germany, 7 In.	142
Jockey, On Horse, Reddish Brown, Tin Lithograph, Windup, Germany, 1900s, 5 In.	152
Kaleidoscope, Brass, Tin Barrel Mounted, Wood Base, Victorian, Unmarked, 9½ In.	195
Kangaroo, Mama Kate, Brown, Tin Lithograph, Windup, Linemar, Box, 5 In.	113
Kid Samson, Man Hammers Bell, Tin Lithograph, Windup, B & R Co., Box, 9 x 5 x 3 In.	826
Kitty Kat, Mysterious, Wheels, Tin, Windup, Ball, Box, Marx	46
L'Homme Sandwich, Sandwich Man, Walker, Tin Lithograph, Reproduction, Box, 8 In.	900
Li'l Abner Dogpatch Band, Piano, Musicians, Tin Lithograph, Unique Art, Box	420
Limousine, Driver, Tin, Clockwork, Karl Bub, 10 In.	175
Lincoln Tunnel, Traffic, Policeman, Unique Art Mfg., Late 1940s	521
Lion, Circus, Wood, Jointed, Furry Cloth Mane, Teeth, Rope Tail, Schoenhut, 1905, 8 In.	633

T

Little Cook, Man In Chef's Outfit, Peels Carrot, Painted, Tin, Clockwork, Martin, c.1904, 8 In.	1800
Little Logging Set, Tractor, Log Hauler, 3 Logs, Tin Lithograph, Box, 10 x 3 x 2½ In.	129
Locomotive, Sheet Metal, Red, Marked, Stafford Liner 1006, c.1930, 12½ x 1⅜ In.	72
Locomotive, Tender Outdoor Railroad, Pressed Steel Paint, Buddy L, c.1980, 27 x 20 In.	735
Loop The Hoop Whirling Bear, Windup, Key, Paper Tag, Japan, Box, 8 In.	170
Loop-A-Loop, Carnival Scene, Tin Lithograph, Windup, Wolverine, 1930s, 19 In.	83
Main Street, Buildings, People, Tin Lithograph, Key Wind, Marx, 24 In.	176
Mammy, Tin, Green Dress, Yellow Apron, Lindstrom, c.1930.	147
Man, Arab, Hookah Smoker, Handmade, Clockwork, 14 In.	106
Man, Arab, Riding Camel, Windup, White, Red, Blue & Brown, Germany, 6 In.	47
Man, Head, Cloth Clothing, Black, Brown & White, Tin Feet, Windup, 6 In.	47
Merry-Go-Round, 2 Clowns, Twirling, Tin Lithograph, Clockwork, 9 In.	300
Merry-Go-Round, 3 Airplanes, Men & Woman Passengers, Doll Co., Germany, 11 In.	354
Merry-Go-Round, Children In Swings, Tin Lithograph, Windup, Germany, 10½ In.	180
Merry-Go-Round, Millennium, Gondolas, Animals, Bear Riders, Musical, Steiff, 2000, 28 In. *illus*	660
Merry-Go-Round, Plane, Flag, 5 Horses, Tin, Windup, Wolverine, 11 In.	113
Merry-Go-Round, Spaceships, Globe, Tin Lithograph, Clockwork, W. Germany, 8 In. *illus*	270
Merrymaker's Band, 4 Mice, Piano, Music, Tin Lithograph, Windup, Marx, 10 x 10 In.	702
Mighty King Kong, Battery Operated, Handcuffs, Remote, Marx, Box, 12 In.	1416
Milk Wagon, Black Horse, Red & Yellow Truck, Tin Lithograph, Marx, Box, 10 x 4 x 5 In.	222
Mister Bunny, Green Coat, Schuco, Germany, Late 1930s	429
Mixer, Concrete, Tread, Pressed Steel, 16 x 15½ In.	1243
Monkey, Riding Tricycle, Tin Lithograph, Windup, Arnold, Germany, c.1945, 4 In.	117
Monkey, Rock & Roll, Holding Guitar, Battery Operated, Tin, Japan, Box, 12 In.	241
Monkey, Tumbling, Flips Between 2 Chairs, Tin, Windup, Marx, Box, 5 In.	198
Moon Rocket, Rubber Tip, Tin Lithograph, Battery Operated, Japan, Box, 14 In.	779
Motor, Boat, Evinrude Big Twin, Metal, Blue Paint, Decals, 5½ In. *illus*	141
Motor, Boat, Mercury, 55, Thunderbolt Four, Green Paint, Decals, 5½ In.	170
Motorcycle Daredevil, Spins In Cage, Tin, Windup, Arnold, Germany, 11 In.	600
Motorcycle, 2 Riders, Uniforms, Hats, Glasses, Black, Iron, 4 x 5½ In.	42
Motorcycle, Circus Clown, Tin Lithograph, Windup, Japan, Box, 6 In.	118
Motorcycle, Civilian Rider, Blue, Tin Lithograph, Windup, Arnold, 8 In.	472
Motorcycle, Curvo 1000, Red, Man, Green Jacket, Helmet, Windup, Schuco	184
Motorcycle, Driver, Police Highway Patrol, Tin Lithograph, Battery Operated, Japan, 11 In.	299
Motorcycle, Go Round, Windup, Ramp, Germany, 12 In.	342
Motorcycle, Harley-Davidson, Red, Tin, Friction, Japan, 9 In.	326
Motorcycle, Military Police, Tin Lithograph, Friction, Japan, 5½ In.	184
Motorcycle, Motoracer 1006, Tin, Windup, Schuco, Box, 5 In.	120
Motorcycle, Police Patrol, White, Blue, Battery Operated, Japan, 10 In.	227
Motorcycle, Police, Swivel Head Rider, Harley-Davidson, Cast Iron, Hubley, 1930s, 7 In.	402
Motorcycle, Policeman Driver, Cast Iron, Champion, 1930, 7 In.	354
Motorcycle, Policeman Rider, Green Paint, Nickel Spoke Wheels, Cast Iron, Hubley, 7 In.	660
Motorcycle, Rollover, Tin Windup, Japan, 5½ In.	271
Motorcycle, Rubber Balloon Tires, Cast Iron, Hubley, 9 In.	396
Motorcycle, Sidecar, Paya, Tin, Windup, Spain, 1990s, 12 x 6 x 6 In.	95 to 108
Motorcycle, Sidecar, Police Officer, Tin Lithograph, Windup, Marx, 9 x 5½ In. *illus*	211
Motorcycle, Sidecar, Tin Windup, Box, Russia, 9 In.	142
Mr. Fox, Magician, Disappearing Rabbit, Tin, Fabric, Battery Operated, Yonezawa, Japan, 9 In.	196
Mr. Magoo, Car, Yellow, Blue, Tin Lithograph, Battery Operated, Hubley, Box, 9½ In.	326
Naughty Boy, Automotive Coach, Driver, Passenger Sit Face To Face, Box	2940
Noah's Ark, Animals At Windows, Dove On Roof, Tin Lithograph, Germany, Penny, 4½ In.	120
Nodder, Rabbit, Wheels, Side Saddle, Glass Eyes, Pull Toy, 7 x 6 In.	510
Nurse, Red Cross, Painted Face, Cloth Dress & Cap, Clockwork, Martin, c.1913, 7 In. *illus*	6600
Ondine, Swimming Doll, Bisque Head, Cork Torso, Key Wind, S & H, 12 In.	840
Organ Grinder, Composition Head, Painted, Blue Hat, Clockwork, Grotesque, c.1916, 9 In.	1680
Ostrich Cart, Black Man Driver, Zulu, Tin, Windup, Lehmann, Germany, 7 In. *illus*	413
Parade, Bandsman, Airplane, Painted, The Big Parade, Louis Marx & Co., c.1930	1960
Peacock, Tin, Clockwork, Legs Move, c.1890, 6 x 9 In.	325
Pedal Car Trailer, Pressed Steel, 2 Rear Wheels, Rear Door, Winged Logo, 22 x 26 x 38 In.	450

Toy, Flintstones, Flivver, Fred Driving, Tin, Friction, Marx, 7 In.
$1,322

Milestone Auctions

Toy, Frog & Toadstool, Frog Jumps Into Container, Tin, Spring Lever, Fischer, Penny Toy
$1,320

Bertoia Auctions

Toy, G.I. Joe, Jouncing Jeep, Tin, Windup, Unique Art, 7 In.
$177

Milestone Auctions

> **TIP**
> *If the batteries in a battery toy have corroded, remove them and rub an emery board or 0000 steel wool on the contact points. Then put new batteries in the toy and it should work.*

Toy, Goat, Wheels, Paper Collar, Dresden Trim, 9 x 3 x 9 In.
$352

Morphy Auctions

Toy, Harold Lloyd, Funny Face, Walker, Tin Lithograph, Windup, Marx, c.1920, 10⅝ In.
$222

Cordier Auctions

Toy, Horse & Jockey, Green Platform, 4 Wheels, George W. Brown Co., c.1870s, 15 In.
$2,818

RSL Auction

Pedal Car Trailer, Pressed Steel, Orange, White Accents, U Haul, 17 x 34 x 14 In.	330
Pedal Car, Airplane, Pursuit, Orange, Propeller Rotates, Steelcraft, 1940, 25 x 35 x 46 In.	984
Pedal Car, Airplane, Spirit Of St. Louis, Pressed Steel, Wood, Disc Wheels, Gendron, 28 x 53 In.	2825
Pedal Car, Blue, Greyhound Hood Ornament, Steel, American National, 1920, 27 x 21 x 60 In.	900
Pedal Car, Chrysler Roadster, Teal, Black, Red Wheels, Steel, Gendron, c.1920, 27 x 21 x 38 In. *illus*	780
Pedal Car, Fire Dept. Unit 507 Beverly Hills, Decals, Metal, Wood Floor, Bell, c.1950, 41 In.	120
Pedal Car, Lime Green, Orange, Yellow Accents, White Faux, Gendron, 1940, 22 x 20 x 45 In.	923
Pedal Car, Red & Black, Eagle Finial, Toledo Metal Wheel Co., 1930, 32 x 22 x 56 In.	5938
Pedal Car, Steel, Blue, White, Chrome Details, Airplane Hood Ornament, 22 x 35 In. *illus*	254
Pedal Car, Tractor, Cast Metal, Rubber Wheels, Applied Decals, Harvester, 1900s, 24 x 37 In.	188
Pedal Car, Tractor, Green, Yellow Wheels, John Deere, c.1952, 36 x 19 x 27 In.	164
Pedal Car, Tractor, Pressed Steel, Orange, 3 Wheels, BCM Kiddie, 18 x 33 x 26 In. *illus*	177
Pedal Car, Tractor, Red, Cast Metal Body, Farmall, 1960s, 38 In.	259
Penguin, Cyclist, Bell Sounds, Headlight, Remote Control Operated, Japan, Box, 6 In.	127
Peter Rabbit, Pushing Wheelbarrow, Vegetables, Cotton Batting, 1980s, 17 x 7½ In.	640
Phonograph, Jack & Jill, Box, Windup, Joseph Schneider, N.Y., c.1920, 11 x 11 x 4 In.	60
Piano Player, Le Petit Pianiste, Man Sways, Hands Move, Clockwork, Martin, c.1902, 7 In.	1560
Pig, Moves Forward, Head Turns, Squeals, Leather, Metal, Clockwork, Roullet & Decamps, 9 In.	1020
Piggy Cook, Cook Eggs & Ham, Tin, Windup, Japan, Box, 5 In.	106
Pinocchio, Walking, Tin, Windup, Linemar, Box, 6 In.	814
Play Golf, Golfer, 9 Holes, Tin Lithograph, Windup, Ferdinand Strauss, 12 x 7 x 6 In.	129
Policeman, Car, Traffic, B, Dog In Sidecar, Tin Lithograph, Windup, 7 x 3 x 6½ In.	164
Poor Pete, Black Boy, Angry Dog Biting Pants, Tin, Windup, Gunthermann, 6½ In.	708
Porky Pig, Umbrella, Tin Lithograph, Windup, Marx, c.1939, 8 In.	234
Porter, Black, With Wheelbarrow, Tin, Windup, Strauss, 7 In.	227
Porter, Finnegan, Cart, Wheels, Painted, Unique Art, Box, 13½ In.	129
Porter, Great Northern Railroad, Carrying Suitcase, Tin Lithograph, 1930, 7 In. *illus*	1187
Porter, Red Cap, Carrying Suitcases, Windup, Tin Lithograph, Louis Marx, 1930s, 8 In.	263
Puppet Stage, Punch & Judy, 2 Musicians, J.W.S. & S., Bavaria, 55 x 29½ In.	720
Puppet Theater, Wood, Hinged, Lithographed Scenes Of Paris, Pierrot, c.1890, 48 In.	1840
Push Down Cat, Cat & Ball, Rear Wheels, Tin, Windup, Japan, Box, 6 In.	42
Rabbit, Picnic, It Drinks!, Battery Operated, Alps, Japan, Box, 10 In.	118
Rabbit, Walker, Father Pulls Baby Rabbit, Blue Cart, Tin Lithograph, Meier, Penny Toy *illus*	6000
Rifle, Atomic, Space Cadet, Silver & Red, Tom Corbett, 24 In.	177
Ring, Green Hornet, Stamp, Carved, 1960, ⅞ In.	94
Ring-A-Ling Circus, Ringmaster, Lion, Elephant, Monkey, Riders, Tin, Windup, Marx, 8 In.	566
Road Grader, Adams Leaning Wheel, Nickel Plate Copper & Brass, 10 x 21 x 2 In.	5225
Road Roller, Green Body, Red Canopy Roof, Pressed Steel, Large Spoke Wheels, 19 In.	1695
Road Roller, Live Steam, Tin, Fleischmann, Germany, 8½ x 7 In.	130
Robot, Battlin' Robots, 2 Transformers, Durham Industries, Box, 1985, 14 x 14 In.	153
Robot, House, Creature From The Black Lagoon, Tin, Windup, Box, 9½ In.	108
Robot, Mars Attack, Tin Lithograph, Battery Operated, Japan, Late 1960, 12 In.	109
Robot, Moon, Tin, Windup, Japan, Box, 11½ In.	3682
Robot, Red, Magic Mike II, Battery Operated, 10½ x 6 In.	30
Robot, Rosie, Jetsons, Painted, Light Blue, Black, Red, White, Marx	207
Robot, Tommy, Black, Battery Operated, Box, 10½ x 6 In.	36
Rocket Car, Green, Tin, Rod Key Operated, Salco, Box, 1930	212
Rocket Fighter, Sparkling, Ship, Tail Fin, Tin, Windup, Marx, Box, 12 In.	1062
Rocket Gun, Astronaut, Siren & Sparkling, Tin, Friction, Japan, Box, 10 In.	142
Rocket Launcher, Captain Video, Video Rangers, Dumont, 8 In.	297
Rocket Ride, Kiddy City Amusement Park, 3 Rockets, Tin, Windup, Japan, Box, 8 In.	142
Rocket Ship, SS Space Rocket, Tin Lithograph, Battery Operated, KO, Japan, 14 In.	150
Rocket, Apollo X, Moon Challenger, Battery Operated, Box, 16 In.	177
Rocking Chair, Christmas, Bliss, Lithograph Paper, Wood, 13½ x 7 In.	799
Rodeo Joe, Car, Joe Driving, Tin Lithograph, Windup, Unique Art, 7½ In.	115
Roller Coaster, 1 Car, Tunnel, Track, Tin Lithograph, Chein, 20 In.	127
Roly Poly, Clown, Papier-Mache, Bell Shape, Rattle Inside, Weighted, Schoenhut, 12 In.	345
Room, Perfume Store, Parfumerie, Hinged, Paper On Wood, Accessories, France, c.1890, 15 In.	10925
Rooster, Fur Covered, On Wheels, Clockwork, Germany, 4½ In.	75

T

Toy, Horse, Rocking, Horsehair Mane, Tail, Gray & Black, Harness, Saddle, 1900s, 47 x 66 x 20 In.
$344

Garth's Auctioneers & Appraisers

Toy, Humphrey Mobile, Tin Lithograph, Mechanical, Wyandotte, Box, 8 ⅝ x 7 x 5 ⅜ In.
$187

Cordier Auctions

Toy, Merry-Go-Round, Millennium, Gondolas, Animals, Bear Riders, Musical, Steiff, 2000, 28 In.
$660

Garth's Auctioneers & Appraisers

Toy, Merry-Go-Round, Spaceships, Globe, Tin Lithograph, Clockwork, W. Germany, 8 In.
$270

Bertoia Auctions

TIP
Battery-operated toys should be run regularly to keep the parts working. Remove batteries before storing the toy.

Toy, Motor, Boat, Evinrude Big Twin, Metal, Blue Paint, Decals, 5 ½ In.
$141

Rich Penn Auctions

Toy, Motorcycle, Sidecar, Police Officer, Tin Lithograph, Windup, Marx, 9 x 5 ½ In.
$211

Cordier Auctions

Toy, Nurse, Red Cross, Painted Face, Cloth Dress & Cap, Clockwork, Martin, c.1913, 7 In.
$6,600

Bertoia Auctions

493

Toy, Ostrich Cart, Black Man Driver, Zulu, Tin, Windup, Lehmann, Germany, 7 In.
$413

Milestone Auctions

Toy, Pedal Car, Chrysler Roadster, Teal, Black, Red Wheels, Steel, Gendron, c.1920, 27 x 21 x 38 In.
$780

Morphy Auctions

Toy, Pedal Car, Steel, Blue, White, Chrome Details, Airplane Hood Ornament, 22 x 35 In.
$254

Rich Penn Auctionss

Toy, Pedal Car, Tractor, Pressed Steel, Orange, 3 Wheels, BCM Kiddie, 18 x 33 x 26 In.
$177

Copake Auction

Rope Walker, Walks Tightrope, Hand Over Hand, Clockwork, Ives, Patented 1878, 10½ In.... *illus*	1200
Sadiron, No. 2 Hollow Grip, Mark, 3½ x 2¾ In.	34
Sam The Gardener, Man, Pushing Wheelbarrow, Tools, Tin Lithograph, Windup, Marx, 1950s, 8 In.	104
Seesaw, Boy & Girl, Tin, Stencils, Paint, Woman, Flower, Clockwork, Ives, 1873, 18 In.	10800
Seesaw, Metal, Windup, Box, 1930s	225
Sharp Shooter, Windup, Celluloid, Soldier, Gun, Alps, 8 In.	129
Sheep, Green Platform, 4 Wheels, James Fallows, c.1880s, 6½ In.	674
Sheep, Wooly Fur, Glass Bead Eyes, Wheels, Bow, Pull Toy, 1800s, 5 x 5 In.	219
Sheriff, 2 Guns, Vinyl Face, Shifty Eyes, Battery Operated, Cragstan, Japan, Box	170
Showboat, Red, Green, Yellow, Paint, Windup, Lindstrom, 8½ In.	47
Skeleton, Dancer, Mr. McGinty Bones, Wood, Tin, Papier-Mache & Wire, c.1885, 11 x 7 In.	2450
Skier, Boy, Tin, Windup, Chein, Yellow, Red, Blue, 7½ In.	83
Skip Rope, 3 Animals, Tin, Windup, Multicolor, Japan, Box, 9 In.	170
Skippy The Tricky Cyclist, Clown, Unicycle, Windup, Box	142
Skittles Pin Holder, Figural, Rooster, Composition, Holds 9 Pins, Germany, 1920s, 16 In. .... *illus*	1140
Sky Patrol, Flying Saucer, Battery Operated, Japan, Box, 8 In.	312
Sled, Bent Oak, Red Seat, Painted, Flowers, Unmarked, Paris Mfg. Co., c.1905, 33 In........*illus*	108
Sled, Children's, Iron, Runners, Hand Paint, Wood Seat, Victorian, 15 x 42 In.	283
Sled, Flag Holders, Flag, Victorian Child, Painting Of Country Scene, 33 x 12 In.	1152
Sled, Wood Runners & Bed, Painted Trotting Horse, Metal Frame, c.1850, 33 In.	403
Sleigh, 2 Horses, Santee, Tin, Ferdinand Strauss Co., 1920s, 10¾ In.	622
Sleigh, Doll's, Black Paint, Gold Trim, Brass Tack, Cloth Interior, 31 x 21½ In.	126
Soldier, Doughboy, Khaki Uniform, Tin Lithograph, Windup, Chein, 6 In.	187
Soldier, Playing Drum, Windup, Red, Black, Blue & White, Japan, 11 In.	59
Space Capsule, Floating Astronaut, Battery Operated, Japan, Box, 11 In.	227
Space Cruiser, Battery Operated, Brown Box, Japan, 9 In.	106
Space Gun, 007, Linterna Espacial, Green, Light-Up, Argentina, Box, 7½ In.	83
Space Gun, Atomic Disintegrator, Gray, Red Grip, Hubley, 8 In.	212
Space Gun, Moonraker, James Bond 007, Die Cast Metal, Plastic, Lone Star, Box, 11 In.	106
Space Tank, Rex Mars, Multicolor, Tin, Windup, Marx, Box, 10 In.	307
Spaceship, Tom Corbet, Sparkling, Multicolor, Tin, Windup, Marx, Box, 12 In.	1274
Speedboy Delivery, Truck, Driver, Red, Tin, Windup, Marx, 10 In.	156
Stagecoach, R.G. Walls Dry Goods, Wood Wheels, Canvas Sides, Top, 12 x 12 x 7 In.	396
Steam Shovel, Die Cast, Black & Red Details, Keystone, 1925, 14½ x 7½ x 19 In. ....*illus*	224
Steamroller, Brass Boiler, Green, Black Paint, Germany, c.1915, 6 x 9 In.	240
Steamroller, Die Cast, Little Jim, Metal Wheels, Keystone, 1929, 12 x 8 x 19 In.	270
Stove, Metal, Painted, Pots & Pans, 6 Utensils, Marked Western Germany, 1950	170
Strutting Sam, Black Man, Standing, Plaid Jacket, Battery Operated, Japan, Box, 11 In.	150
Suffragette, On Platform, Walking 2 Horses, Flag, Tin, Painted, 4 Ornate Spoke Wheels, 9 In.	1200
Sulky Racer, Horse, Man, Windup, Germany, 6½ In.	46
Sunshine Riding Sparkplug, Tin Litho, 4-Wheel Platform, Pull Toy, J. Chein, 9½ In.	660
Swan, Chariot, Brass, J. & E. Stevens Co., c.1880s, 10½ In.	196
Sweeping Betty, Holding Broom, Yellow & Red, Tin, Windup, Lindstrom, 8 In.	153
Sweeping Mammy, Black Woman, Red Dress, Tin, Windup, Lindstrom, 8 In.	227
Table, Alphabets, Wood, Lithograph, Bliss, 14½ x 9½ In.	480
Tank, Army, Stick Shift, Tin Lithograph, Green, Battery Operated, TN, Japan, Box, 8 In.	75
Tank, Army, Yellow, Soldier, Tin Lithograph, Windup, Marx, 10 In.	152
Tank, Battle, Orange & Blue, Soldier, Latch, Tin Lithograph, Louis Marx	168
Tank, Climbing, Tin, Windup, Marx, 9½ In.	99
Tank, Doughboy, Soldier, Yellow Paint, Tin, Windup, Marx	115
Tank, Midget, Tin, Windup, Marx, 5 In.	94
Tank, Rocket Shooter, M-75, Army, Battery Operated, Japan, Box, 9 In.	58
Tank, Rollover, Casper, Tin, Windup, Linemar, Japan, 4 In.	153
Tank, Sparkling Doughboy, Tin Lithograph, Windup, Marx, Box, 10 In. ....*illus*	200
Tank, Sparkling, Soldier, Tin, Windup, Marx, Box, 10 In.	201
Tank, Turnover, U.S Army, Tin, Windup, Marx, Box, 8 In. ....*illus*	156
Tanker, Shell Chemicals, Red & Yellow, Dinky Toys, 1955, 6 In.	90
Target Game, Knight In Armor, Figure, Battery Operated, Japan, Box, 12 In.	311
Taxi, American Yellow Cab, Doors Open, Windup, Bing, Germany, 7½ In.	300

Taxi, Amos 'N' Andy, Fresh Air, Seated Dog, Windup, Marx, 5 x 7 1/2 In. ....*illus* — 847

Taxi, Cab, Tricky, Limo, Wheels, Tin, Marx, Box, 4 1/2 In. .... — 104

Taxi, Yellow Cab, Driver, Cast Iron, Painted, Arcade Manufacturing Co., c.1925, 9 In. .... — 565

Tea Set, Porcelain, Court Scenes, Cobalt Border, Gold Trim, Leather & Silk Box, France .... — 805

Teddy Bears are also listed in the Teddy Bear category.

Telephone, Flintstones, Hard Vinyl, Die Cut Plastic Dial, Early 1960s, 5 In. ....*illus* — 325

Theater, Clockwork, Dancers, Paper, Lithograph, Wood, Mirror, c.1865, 10 x 9 In. .... — 1063

Tidy Tim, Street Cleaner, Walker, Tin, Windup, Marx, 1930, 7 1/2 x 9 In. .... — 649

Tiger, Cloth, Esso, Tin, Windup, Marx, Japan, 1966, 8 1/2 In. .... — 177

Tiger, Walker, Mechanical, Windup, Marx, Box, 8 In. .... — 212

Tiger, Walker, Remote Control, Holding Hat, Battery Operated, Marx, Japan, Box .... — 242

Toboggan, Tin Track, 2 Trolley Cars, Yellow, Red & Blue, Windup, Germany, Box, 1958, 18 In. — 83

Toonerville Trolley, Tin Lithograph, Windup, Fontaine Fox, 1922, 5 x 2 x 7 1/2 In. ....*illus* — 248

Touchdown Pete, Football Player, Windup, Linemar, Box, 6 In. .... — 271

Tractor, Diesel, Caterpillar, Steel, Cast Iron, c.1936, 7 3/4 In. .... — 452

Tractor, Driver, Yellow, Red, Blue & White, Pressed Steel, Marx, 11 In. .... — 94

Tractor, Industrial, Ford 4000, Backhoe, Battery Operated, Japan, 18 In. .... — 165

Tractor, Red & Green, Gold Painted Driver, Structo, c.1920, 4 1/2 x 14 3/4 x 4 In. .... — 480

Tractor, Steam, Tin, Gebruder Bing, c.1920, 8 1/2 x 11 In. .... — 735

Tractor, Tin, Battery Operated, Driver, White Rubber Treads, Red Paint, Box, Japan .... — 106

Traffic Policeman, Arms Raised, Auto Safety Device, Tin Litho, J.C. Lang, c.1920, 8 1/2 In. ...... — 176

Trailer, Double, Yellow, Green, Red, Cab, Pressed Steel, Buddy L, 9 x 6 1/2 x 16 1/2 In. .... — 330

Train Accessory, Bing, Semaphore Station, Tin Lithograph, House, Red Roof, 9 In. .... — 98

Train Accessory, Lionel, Tunnel, Painted, Standard Gauge, 15 x 9 1/2 In. .... — 47

Train Accessory, Marklin, Castle Tunnel, Walkways, Handrails, Tower, Moss, Rocks, 13 In. ....*illus* — 540

Train Accessory, Marklin, Freight Station, Platform Cranes, Sliding Doors, Embossed, 12 x 6 In. . — 1140

Train Accessory, Marklin, Switch Tower, Embossed Roof, Open Windows, Metal, 12 In. ....*illus* — 1560

Train Car, American Flyer, Switcher, Steam, NPR, Standard Gauge, Back .... — 184

Train Car, Arcade, Pullman, Railplane, Red, Cast Iron, 5 In. .... — 117

Train Car, Buddy L, Locomotive, Tender, Outdoor, Railroad, Pressed Steel, 25 x 18 In. .... — 735

Train Car, Ives, Locomotive, Cast Iron, Painted, O Gauge, No. 3238 .... — 502

Train Car, Lionel, Boxcar, Gray, Red Trim, Electric, Box, c.1929 .... — 748

Train Car, Lionel, Boxcar, No. 814, Sliding Door, Automobile, Furniture .... — 276

Train Car, Lionel, Boxcar, No. 6468, Tuscan B&O, Satin Patina, Box, 1955 .... — 391

Train Car, Lionel, Boxcar, Orange & Tuscan, Matte Patina, c.1942 .... — 265

Train Car, Lionel, Boxcar, Stamped Lettering, Small WP, Blue Feather, Box .... — 391

Train Car, Lionel, Boxcar, Standard Gauge, Yellow Paint, Nickel Trim, Box .... — 345

Train Car, Lionel, Boxcar, Western Pacific, Sentinel, Blue, Silver Wheels, Box, 1956 .... — 483

Train Car, Lionel, Caboose, No. 217, Satin Patina, Red, Blue Roof, Box .... — 288

Train Car, Lionel, Caboose, Pennsylvania, Matte Patina, Light Blue, Box .... — 414

Train Car, Lionel, Caboose, Work, N & W, Box, 1957 .... — 173

Train Car, Lionel, Crane, Gray, White Paint, Box, 1946 .... — 368

Train Car, Lionel, Crane, Yellow Paint, Hook, Line, Standard Gauge .... — 219

Train Car, Lionel, Locomotive, Diesel, Battery Operated, Horns, Black & Orange, Box .... — 138

Train Car, Lionel, Locomotive, Green Paint, Electric .... — 109

Train Car, Lionel, Locomotive, Magne-Traction, Black, Box, 1955 .... — 1955

Train Car, Lionel, Locomotive, Steam, K Line, UP Big Boy, Signal Sounds, Bell, Light, Smoke, Box — 230

Train Car, Lionel, Searchlight, 2 Lights, Box Couplers, Green & Black Base .... — 414

Train Car, Lionel, Searchlight, Nickel Trim, Standard Gauge, Box, c.1934 .... — 230

Train Car, Lionel, Switcher, Navy Yard, New York, Blue, Box .... — 230

Train Car, Lionel, Switcher, Steam, High Coupler, Black .... — 207

Train Car, Lionel, Tank Car, Oil, 215, Green, Standard Gauge, Green, Brass Trim, Box .... — 161

Train Car, Lionel, Tank Car, Shell, Yellow, Standard Gauge, Box .... — 1553

Train Car, Lionel, Tank Car, Sunoco, 215, Ivory, Standard Gauge, Brass Trim, Box, c.1934 ...... — 368

Train Car, Lionel, Tanker, Shell, Yellow, Red Letters, Ladder, Box .... — 299

Train Car, Lionel, Tanker, Standard Gauge, Patina, Green, Box .... — 150

Train Car, Lionel, Track Cleaner, No. 50, Rubber Bumpers, Orange & Black .... — 46

Train Car, Lionel, Traveling Aquarium, Fish In Windows, Green, Yellow Letters, Box .... — 127

Train Car, Lionel, Ventilated Refrigerator, Standard Gauge, Blue Roof Paint, Box .... — 288

Toy, Porter, Great Northern Railroad, Carrying Suitcase, Tin Lithograph, 1930, 7 In.

$1,187

Soulis Auctions

Toy, Rabbit, Walker, Father Pulls Baby Rabbit, Blue Cart, Tin Lithograph, Meier, Penny Toy

$6,000

Bertoia Auctions

Toy, Rope Walker, Walks Tightrope, Hand Over Hand, Clockwork, Ives, Patented 1878, 10 1/2 In.

$1,200

Bertoia Auctions

T

Toy, Skittles Pin Holder, Figural, Rooster, Composition, Holds 9 Pins, Germany, 1920s, 16 In.
$1140

Bertoia Auctions

Toy, Sled, Bent Oak, Red Seat, Painted, Flowers, Unmarked, Paris Mfg. Co., c.1905, 33 In.
$108

Thomaston Place Auction Galleries

Toy, Steam Shovel, Die Cast, Black & Red Details, Keystone, 1925, 14 ½ x 7 ½ x 19 In.
$224

Morphy Auctions

Toy, Tank, Sparkling Doughboy, Tin Lithograph, Windup, Marx, Box, 10 In.
$200

Pook & Pook

Toy, Tank, Turnover, U.S Army, Tin, Windup, Marx, Box, 8 In.
$156

Milestone Auctions

Toy, Taxi, Amos 'N' Andy, Fresh Air, Seated Dog, Windup, Marx, 5 x 7 ½ In.
$847

Fontaine's Auction Gallery

Toy, Telephone, Flintstones, Hard Vinyl, Die Cut Plastic Dial, Early 1960s, 5 In.
$325

Hake's Auctions

T

Train Car, Locomotive, Steam, Williams, Erie Berkshire, Die Cast 2-8-4, Light, Smoke, Black, Box	69
Train Car, Marklin, Beer, Budweiser, Painted, Cream, Blue, Gray, 12½ In.	12000
Train Car, Marklin, Caboose, 8 Wheels, Painted, Hudson River, New York, 11 In.	2160
Train Car, Marklin, Hospital, Painted, Open Vestibule, c.1849, 11 In.	720
Train Car, Marklin, Locomotive & Tender, Painted, Nickel Bell, Cow Catcher, 17 In.	3000
Train Car, Marklin, Locomotive, 4021, Electric, Cow Catcher, Cast Iron, 19 In.	4500
Train Car, Marklin, Passenger, S.P.R.R., Windows, Clerestory Roof, 4 Doors, 11 In. _illus_	5100
Train Car, Marklin, Refrigerator, Painted, Yellow, Green Top, Fruit Express, 11 In.	2040
Train Car, Marklin, Schlitz Beer, Painted, Red & Yellow, Doors Open, Milwaukee, 9 In.	39000
Train Car, Marklin, Tool & Maintenance, Open Gondola, Enclosed Section, 7 In. _illus_	660
Train Car, Tractor On Platform, Box, Battery Operated, Tin Lithograph, Japan, 6½ In.	92
Train Set, Tantet & Manon, Locomotive, Passenger Cars, Train De Plaisir, Paris, c.1890, 15 In.	7200
Train, Ride On, Red, Black, Pressed Steel, Rubber Wheels, Bell, Whistle, Keystone, 27 In.	322
Tree, Whistling Spooky Kooky, Battery Operated, Marx, Japan, c.1960, 14½ In.	552
Tricycle, Good Humor, Red, White, Teal, Ice Cream, Murray, Mid 1950s, 24 x 40 x 18 In.	840
Tricycle, Painted, Carved Wood Seat, Iron, 1800s, 32 x 44 In.	1888
Trolley, Converse, Pressed Steel Clockwork, Marquee, 15½ In.	198
Trolley, Main Street, Side Door Open, Windup, Tin, Nifty, Germany, 1930s, 8½ In.	124
Truck, 5 Ton, Yellow, Red Spoke Wheels, Cast Iron, Hubley, 16 x 5½ x 6 In.	222
Truck, Aerial, Red Paint, Pressed Steel, Nickel Ladders, 29½ In.	339
Truck, Allied Moving Van, Tin, Friction, Linemar, Japan, 14 In.	120
Truck, Army, Yellow, Canvas Cover, Pressed Steel, Keystone, 1929, 11 x 8 x 27 In.	480
Truck, Bell Telephone, Cast Iron, Green Paint, Rubber Wheels, 7 In.	360
Truck, Black Cab, Yellow, Canvas Tarp, Die Cast, Ice Delivery, Buddy L, 1920, 12 x 8 x 26 In. _illus_	861
Truck, Black Police Patrol, Pressed Steel Packard, Keystone, c.1926, 11 x 8 x 28 In. _illus_	640
Truck, Blue, 3 Wheels, Tin, Friction, Japan, 8½ In.	354
Truck, City Sanitation Garbage, Pressed Steel, White Paint, Marx, 2952, 13 In.	81
Truck, Dairy, Toyland, Pressed Steel, Marx, 11 In.	153
Truck, Delivery, Box, Clockwork Mechanism, Marklin, 1992, 17 In.	319
Truck, Delivery, Ford, 1 Ton, Pressed Steel, Red Spoke Wheels, Buddy L, 14 In.	509
Truck, Dump, Pressed Steel, Black & Red Paint, 23½ In.	198
Truck, Dump, Pressed Steel, Die Cast, Red & Black, Keystone, 1920, 8 x 8 x 26 In.	270
Truck, Dump, Pressed Steel, Open Driver's Seat, 9½ x 8¾ x 25 In.	283
Truck, Express Van Lines, Tin Lithograph, Plastic Dual Horns, Marx, 1950s, 12 In.	243
Truck, Ford, Pressed Steel, Red Spoke Wheels, Aluminum Tires, Partial Decals, Buddy L, 11 In.	283
Truck, Horse Box, British Railways, Red Paint, Hire Service, Dinky Supertoys, Box	173
Truck, Lazy Day Farms, Painted, Marx, 1950, 17½ In.	130
Truck, Low Loader, Trailer, Chain, Hook, Red, Tonka, 1955	138
Truck, Lumber, Cab, Driver, 3 Logs, Tin Lithograph, Ferdinand Strauss, c.1930, 18 x 5 x 5 In.	556
Truck, Lumber, Removable Rear Bed, Stake Body, Red, Tonka, 1995	150
Truck, Mack Bulldog, Army, Tin, Flywheel, Drive, Box, Marx	173
Truck, Mack Dump, Arcade, Cast, Iron, Blue Paint, Embossed, c.1926, 12 In.	735
Truck, Packard Model, Black Cab, Red Trailer, Keystone, c.1928, 11 x 8½ x 26½ In.	450
Truck, Packard, Boom, Pressed Steel, Red Paint, Rubber Wrapped Tires, Keystone, c.1925, 28 In.	460
Truck, Packard, Model 78, Pressed Steel, Red, Keystone, 1926, 11½ x 8½ x 27 In.	704
Truck, Patrol, Fire Insurance, Red, Pressed Steel, Brass, Buddy L, 26 In. _illus_	565
Truck, Pickup, State Hi-Way, Orange Paint, Tonka, 1957	219
Truck, Pickup, Tru Scale International, White & Light Blue Paint, 12 In.	307
Truck, Race Car Hauler, Pressed Steel Red & White, Buddy L, 19 In.	283
Truck, Ramp Hoist, Pressed Steel Ramp, Red, White Paint, Tonka, 19 In.	472
Truck, Red Spoke Wheels, Aluminum Tires, Buddy L, 12 In.	311
Truck, Red, Silver Wheels, Moline Pressed Steel, Buddy L, 1924, 12 x 8 x 24 In.	615
Truck, Rexall Drug Fantasy, Good Health To All, Tonka, 12 In.	47
Truck, Sand & Gravel, Pressed Steel, Red, Marx, 13 x 5 x 4½ In.	105
Truck, Sanitation, Hydraulic Lift, Paint, Decals, Green, White, Structo, 18 In.	177
Truck, Semi-Trailer, Pressed Steel, Green Paint, Marshall Field & Company, Tonka	375
Truck, Semi-Trailer, Red Paint, Tin, Friction, Japan, Box, 16 In.	118
Truck, Service, State Hi-Way Dept, Orange Paint, Tonka, Box, 1960	575
Truck, Stake Bed, Pressed Steel, Red & Yellow, Turner, 19 In.	319

Toy, Toonerville Trolley, Tin Lithograph, Windup, Fontaine Fox, 1922, 5 x 2 x 7½ In.
$248

Forsythes' Auctions

TIP
Reproduction cast-iron toys and banks are heavier and thicker than the originals.

Toy, Train Accessory, Marklin, Castle Tunnel, Walkways, Handrails, Tower, Moss, Rocks, 13 In.
$540

Bertoia Auctions

Toy, Train Accessory, Marklin, Switch Tower, Embossed Roof, Open Windows, Metal, 12 In.
$1,560

Bertoia Auctions

This is an edited listing of current prices. Visit **Kovels.com** to check thousands of prices from previous years and sign up for free information on trends, tips, reproductions, marks, and more.

T

Toy, Train Car, Marklin, Passenger, S.P.R.R., Windows, Clerestory Roof, 4 Doors, 11 In.
$5,100

Bertoia Auctions

Toy, Train Car, Marklin, Tool & Maintenance, Open Gondola, Enclosed Section, 7 In.
$660

Bertoia Auctions

Toy, Truck, Black Cab, Yellow, Canvas Tarp, Die Cast, Ice Delivery, Buddy L, 1920, 12 x 8 x 26 In.
$861

Morphy Auctions

Truck, Stake Bed, Red & White, Marx, 13 In.	142
Truck, Stake, Freeport Motor Express, Red & White Paint, Steel, Structo, 1950s, 13 In.	46
Truck, State Hi-Way Department, Metal, Orange, Tonka, 6 x 13 In.	50
Truck, Tanker, 2 Milk Cans, Pressed Steel, Buddy L, 12 x 25 ½ x 8 ½ In. ....*illus*	666
Truck, Tanker, Texaco, Pressed Steel, Plastic Trim & Wheels, Buddy L, Box, c.1964, 27 In.	196
Truck, Telegram, Box, Clockwork Mechanism, Marklin, 15 In.	212
Truck, Tow, Wrecker, Red Paint, Cast Iron, Arcade 4 In.	29
Truck, Transport, Army, Chrome Plastic Bumpers, Green, Buddy L, Box.	276
Truck, U.S. Army Troop Carrier, Marx, 1950, 18 ½ In.	130
Uncle Wiggily Car, Rabbit Driver, Tin Lithograph, Windup, Marx, 8 In.	531
Universal Freight Station, Yellow, Red, Tin Lithograph, Windup, Marx, Box, 12 x 7 x 3 In.	140
Wagon, American Beauty, Red Paint, Handle Extended, 38 In.	47
Wagon, Black, Yellow, White Horse, Sheffield Farms Co., 1900s, 21 In.	338
Wagon, Circus, Band, Horse Drawn, Kenton Overland Circus, Cast Iron, c.1950, 15 ½ In.	198
Wagon, Circus, Bear In Cage, Cast Iron, Kenton, 1942-1952, 14 ½ In.	71
Wagon, Circus, Cage, Humpty Dumpty Circus, Wood, Metal, 2 Horses, Driver, Schoenhut, 31 In.	3220
Wagon, Coaster Express, Wood, Pull Handle, Iron Mounts, c.1890, 19 x 48 x 20 In.	330
Wagon, Coaster, Blue Bird, Wood, Iron Wheels, Blue Paint, 15 x 16 x 25 ½ In. ....*illus*	396
Wagon, Easter Rabbit Riding, 3 Wheels, Tin, Painted, Linemar, 5 ½ In.	59
Wagon, Goat, Wood, Red Paint, 4 Wheels, 36 x 22 x 27 In.	124
Wagon, Wood Stake Body, Rubber Covered Metal Wheels, Handle, c.1950, 20 In.	189
Wagon, Wood, Express, Spoke Wheels, c.1900, 56 In. ....*illus*	384
Wagon, Wood, Green Paint, Yellow Letters, Red Seat, Milk License, c.1800s, 46 x 26 In.	660
Wagon, Wood, Metal Wheels, Marked, Wagner Coaster, 36 x 17 In. ....*illus*	124
Wagon, Wood, Painted, Red, Yellow, Iron Strapping, Bentwood Handle, 1800s, 15 x 27 x 21 In.	240
Weight Lifter, L'Hercule Populaire, Moves Arms, Martin, Box, France, c.1914, 7 In.	11400
Whoopie Car, Tin Lithograph, Clockwork, Box, Louis Marx, 7 ½ In.	360
Windmill, Brass, Wood Wheel, 48 Blades, Salesman's Sample, c.1910, 18 In. ....*illus*	1760
Woman, Chasing Rat, Broom In Hand, Clockwork, Martin, c.1910, 8 In.	1920
Woman, L'Entravee, Felt Skirt, Shawl, Muff, Mechanical, Fernand Martin, c.1910, 8 In.....*illus*	4800
Woman, Pushing Pram, Walking, Tin, Painted, Clockwork, Gunthermann, 8 x 9 In.	1140
Xylophone Player, Celluloid, Windup, Japan, Box, 6 In.	106
Zebra, Circus, Wood, Jointed, Green Glass Eyes, Leather Ears, Schoenhut, 8 In.	345
Zebra, Glass Eyes, Open Mouth, Leather Ears, Cord Tail, Schoenhut Humpty Dumpty Circus, 9 In.	400
Zeppelin, Balloon, Cigar Shape, Painted, Lehmann, Box, 1900.	1470
Zeppelin, Mammoth, Gray, 3 Wheels, Tin, Marx c.1930, 7 x 27 ½ x 5 ½ In.	363

TRAMP ART is a form of folk art made since the Civil War. It is usually made from chip-carved cigar boxes. Examples range from small boxes and picture frames to full-sized pieces of furniture. Collectors in the United States started collecting it about 1970, and examples from other countries, especially Germany, were imported and sold by antiques dealers.

Box, Jewelry, 2 Velvet-Lined Drawers, Early 1900s, 8 ½ x 12 In.	240
Box, Lid, Pedestal, Velvet Interior, Teardrops, 12 x 9 x 9 ½ In.	170
Clock, Shelf, Castle Shape, Lower Drawers, Applied Heart Cutouts, 22 x 15 x 8 In.	212
Dresser Box, Chip Carved, Gold Paint, Velvet Lining, 13 x 8 x 6 In. ....*illus*	147
Dresser Box, Chip Carved, Red Panels, 10 ½ x 7 x 5 In.	90
Frame, Black Paint, Heart Motif, 24 x 28 In. ....*illus*	311
Mirror, Chip Carved, Gold Paint, 23 x 39 In.	181
Table, Giltwood, Crown Of Thorns, Glass Top, 33 x 16 ½ x 16 ½ In. ....*illus*	500

TRAPS for animals may be handmade. One of the most unusual is the mousetrap made so that when the mouse entered the trap, it was hit on the head with a mallet. Other traps were commercially manufactured and often are marked with the name of the manufacturer. Many traps were designed to be as humane as possible, and they would trap the live animal so it could be released in the woods.

Bear, Modified, Duke, Metal, No. 15, Piece, Cabin, 35 In.	265
Bear, Steel, Model No. 15, Oneida Newhouse, 30 In.	835
Cricket Cage, Bronze, Copper Corners, Reticulated Top, Engraved Scene, 8 In.	330

Toy, Truck, Black Police Patrol, Pressed Steel Packard, Keystone, c.1926, 11 x 8 x 28 In.
$640

Morphy Auctions

Toy, Truck, Patrol, Fire Insurance, Red, Pressed Steel, Brass, Buddy L, 26 In.
$565

Rich Penn Auctionss

Toy, Truck, Tanker, 2 Milk Cans, Pressed Steel, Buddy L, 12 x 25½ x 8½ In.
$666

Weiss Auctions

Toy, Wagon, Coaster, Blue Bird, Wood, Iron Wheels, Blue Paint, 15 x 16 x 25½ In.
$396

Rich Penn Auctionss

Toy, Wagon, Wood, Express, Spoke Wheels, c.1900, 56 In.
$384

Copake Auction

Toy, Wagon, Wood, Metal Wheels, Marked, Wagner Coaster, 36 x 17 In.
$124

Hartzell's Auction Gallery, Inc.

Toy, Windmill, Brass, Wood Wheel, 48 Blades, Salesman's Sample, c.1910, 18 In.
$1,760

Forsythes' Auctions

Toy, Woman, L'Entravee, Felt Skirt, Shawl, Muff, Mechanical, Fernand Martin, c.1910, 8 In.
$4,800

Bertoia Auctions

Tramp Art, Dresser Box, Chip Carved, Gold Paint, Velvet Lining, 13 x 8 x 6 In. $147

Hartzell's Auction Gallery, Inc.

Tramp Art, Frame, Black Paint, Heart Motif, 24 x 28 In. $311

Hartzell's Auction Gallery, Inc.

Tramp Art, Table, Giltwood, Crown Of Thorns, Glass Top, 33 x 16½ x 16½ In. $500

Rago Arts and Auction Center

T

Cricket Cage, Gourd, Carved, Deer, Lohan, Sage, Goose, Fish, Wood Lid, Openwork, 1800s, 7 In. *illus*	330
Squirrel Cage, Green Paint, Cottage Shape, Tin, Wood, c.1900, 9½ x 29½ In. ....*illus*	263

TREEN, *see Wooden category.*

 TRENCH ART is a form of folk art made by soldiers. Metal casings from bullets and mortar shells were cut and decorated to form useful objects, such as vases.

Ashtray, Brass, Spitfire Airplane, World War II, 4½ In.	65
Belt Buckle, Silver, Dragons, USMC Logo, 2¼ x 1½ In.	258
Cane, Swagger Stick, Cartridge Shell, Projectile Tip, Boer War, c.1899, 27 In.	71
Coffeepot, Artillery Shell, Bullet Shape Handle, Brass, Stamped, 1941, 4½ In.	36
Frame, Photograph, Royal Air Force Propeller Blade Tip, Brass Eagle, Wood, Glass, 8 In.	28
Inkwell, Royal Air Force, Brass, Glass, 2¼ x 2½ In.	25
Knife, Dagger, Bayonet Tip, Shell Casings, Brass Buttons, 1900s, 6 In.	176
Lamp, Artillery, Hand Tooled, 150-mm Caliber Shell, Wooden Base, World War II, 32 x 7 In.....	159
Shell Casing, German, Brass, Engraved, Monogram, Karlsrue, 1916, 19¾ In.	47
Vase, Cross, Ornate, Lorraine, 75-mm Shell, 1918, 13 In.	133

 TRIVETS are now used to hold hot dishes. Most trivets of the late nineteenth and early twentieth centuries were made to hold hot pressing irons. Iron or brass reproductions are being made of many of the old styles.

Aluminum, Forge, Square, Engraved, Wendell August, 6 In.	32
Brass, Metal, Kitchen Stand, A.K. & Sons, 9 x 4¾ x 4 In.	36
Iron, Brass, Engraved, Wooden Handle, c.1800, 9 x 15½ In.............................*illus*	25
Iron, Heart Shape, Hand Wrought, Rose Head Posts, 10 In................................	52
Iron, Round, Pierced, Heart Tipped Handle, 1800s, 11⅜ In.	246
Steel, Forged, Snake-Like, Twists, Coiled, Stamped, Albert Paley, 1979, 16 x 8 In..............*illus*	2250

 TRUNKS of many types were made. The nineteenth-century sea chest was often handmade of unpainted wood. Brass-fitted camphorwood chests were brought back from the Orient. Leather-covered trunks were popular from the late eighteenth to mid-nineteenth centuries. By 1895, trunks were covered with canvas or decorated sheet metal. Embossed metal coverings were used from 1870 to 1910. By 1925, trunks were covered with vulcanized fiber or undecorated metal. Suitcases are listed here.

Camelback, Interior Tray, Metal & Wood, Key, 22 x 30 x 18 In.	79
Dome Top, Basswood, Sponge Paint, c.1820, 11 x 28 In.	750
Dome Top, Blue Paint, Iron Bail Handles, 1800s, 11½ x 26¾ x 13½ In.	369
Dome Top, Oak, Baroque, Open Interior, Iron Mounts, Wheels, 1700s, 22 x 34 x 18 In......*illus*	300
Dome Top, Oak, Brass Trim, Signed, 4½ x 8½ In.	230
Dome Top, Pine, Nail Construction, Iron Hardware, Grain Painting, c.1850, 14 x 29 In............	938
Dome Top, Pressed Iron, Floral Carvings, Fitted Interior, c.1850, 21 x 28 x 17 In.	66
Dome Top, Storage, Pine, Metal Strapwork, Brass Latch, c.1920.........................*illus*	88
Gary Cooper, Leather, Wood Frame, Tan Border, Brass Tacks, Handle, 17 x 29 In.............*illus*	1320
Goyard, Hat, Leather, Chevrons, Brass Locks, Removable Basket, c.1930, 20 x 18 x 14 In.	2596
Immigrant's, Dome Top, Pine, Dovetail, Iron Hinges, Jans Hansen, 1851, 25 x 48 In........*illus*	390
Jones Bros., Travel, Tole, Painted Steel, Brass Lock, England, 1800s, 14 x 21 x 14 In.	68
Louis Vuitton, Alzer, Monogram, Canvas, Leather Trim, Flip-Lock Latches, 16 x 23 x 8 In.........	1375
Louis Vuitton, Anglais Model, Brown, France, 10 x 31 In................................	4104
Louis Vuitton, Shoe, Lily Pons, Canvas, 30 Compartments, Leather Trim, 1930, 25 x 16 x 45 In.	19470
Louis Vuitton, Steamer, Brass, Brown, c.1920, 25 x 24 x 25½ In.	5625
Louis Vuitton, Suitcase, Canvas, Soft Shell, Zipper, Brown, Monogram, 26 In.	400
Louis Vuitton, Suitcase, Monogram, Bisten 70, Brass Hardware, Tan Leather, France, 16 x 28 In. ...	1200
Louis Vuitton, Suitcase, Monogram, Leather, Brass Straps, Pull-Out Tray, c.1920, 31 x 20 In. ...	1024
Louis Vuitton, Suitcase, Soft Sides, Leather Trim, 2-Way Zip Closure, 18 x 25 x 8 In.	563
Morley & Mason, Carriage, Leather, Embossed, Steel Straps, Brass Bosses, 1800s, 17 x 26 In..	147
Shipping, Wells Fargo & Co. Express, Wood, Walla Leviston, c.1800, 25 x 38 x 22 In..................	3000
Steamer, Wardrobe, Monogram, Louis Vuitton, 11⅜ x 36 x 21½ In.	4000

Wood, Flip Top, Lid Utensil Compartment, Turned Feet, 1800s, 22 x 42 x 18 In.		240
Wood, Metal Strap, Hardwood, 44 x 28 x 24½ In.		177
Wood, Nautical Theme, Green Background, White Text, 47 x 17 x 22 In.		413
Wood, Scene Of Guidoriccio Da Fogliano, Gesso, Italy, 1800s, 26½ x 42 x 18 In.		563

TUTHILL Cut Glass Company of Middletown, New York, worked from 1902 to 1923. Of special interest are the finely cut pieces of stemware and tableware.

Tuthill

Basket, Wild Rose, Handle, 10¼ In.		1000
Dish, Shell Pattern & Shape, 6 In.		660
Plate, Roseacea, Round, Flowers, Marked, 10 In.		480
Tray, Vintage Pattern, Grapes, Leaves, Round, Grapes, 2 x 14 In.		4375
Tray, Wheel Pattern, Faint Mark In Center, 12¼ In.		5700
Vase, Bud, Intaglio Flowers, Signed, 10 In.		72

TYPEWRITER collectors divide typewriters into two main classifications: the index machine, which has a pointer and a dial for letter selection, and the keyboard machine, most commonly seen today. The first successful typewriter was made by Sholes and Glidden in 1874.

Corona, Portable, Gold Text, Cast Iron, Black	*illus*	94
Crate, Underwood, Black Text, 2 Side Graphics, 14 x 21 x 18 In.		81
Hammond, Folding, Multiplex, Enamel, Aluminum Frame, 1921-28		960
Hammond, Oak Cover Case, Keyboard, Decal, 13 x 12 x 7 In.		706
National, Portable, No. 3, Case		134
Remington, Remette Portable, Qwerty Keyboard, Leather Case		236
Smith Corona, Turquoise Blue, Plastic, Portable, Corsair Deluxe, Manual		103
Williams, No. 1, Grasshopper, Metal, Brady Manufacturing Co., 1895		1001

TYPEWRITER RIBBON TINS are now being collected. The lithographed tin containers have been used since the 1870s. Most popular with collectors are tins with pictorial graphics.

Burroughs, Orange & Brown On Silver, 2½ In.		23
Carter's Silver Craft, Silver Wreath, Arrow, 2 In.		17
Gibraltar, Rock, Sunset, 2½ In.		45
Madame Butterfly, Geisha, Miller Bryant Pierce Co., Red, 2 In.		31
Old Town, Hermetic, Self Renewing, Woman Typing At Desk, 2⅝ In.		65
Preferred, Aristocrat Of Typewriter Ribbons, Aetna Products, Crest, Blue, 2½ In.		16

UHL POTTERY was made in Evansville, Indiana, in 1854. The pottery moved to Huntingburg, Indiana, in 1908. Stoneware and glazed pottery were made until the mid-1940s.

Uhl Pottery hand turned since 1849 Huntingburg ind

Bottle, Football, Brown, 2½ x 4 x 2½ In.		6
Cookie Jar, Lid, Hand Painted, Red, Ransburg Rooster, 1940s, 9½ x 7½ x 4⅞ In.		31
Jug, Christmas, Whiskey, Stoneware, Pottery, 1942, Miniature		16
Mug, Barrel Shape, Tan, Speckled, 4½ In.		12
Pitcher, Embossed Grape Cluster & Leaves, Blue, Clay, 5½ In.		5
Pitcher, Grape & Lattice, Blue, 8 In.		60
Vase, Porcelain, Bricks, Twisted, Graduating, c.1960, 7¼ In.		154

UMBRELLA collectors like rain or shine. The first known umbrella was owned by King Louis XIII of France in 1637. The earliest umbrellas were sunshades, not designed to be used in the rain. The umbrella was embellished and redesigned many times. In 1852, the fluted steel rib style was developed and it has remained the most useful style.

Bamboo, Horn Handle, Gold Plated Mounts, James Smith & Sons, 35½ In.		93
Golf, Automatic Open, 2 Canopies, Light Blue, Zomake, 62 In.		18
Parasol, Black Wood Handle, Carved, Tassel, Silk, Lace, 1800s, 41 In.		33

Trap, Cricket Cage, Gourd, Carved, Deer, Lohan, Sage, Goose, Fish, Wood Lid, Openwork, 1800s, 7 In.
$330

Eldred's

Trap, Squirrel Cage, Green Paint, Cottage Shape, Tin, Wood, c.1900, 9½ x 29½ In.
$263

Pook & Pook

Trivet, Iron, Brass, Engraved, Wooden Handle, c.1800, 9 x 15½ In.
$25

Pook & Pook

U V

TIP
Store parasols and umbrellas closed.

501

Trivet, Steel, Forged, Snake-Like, Twists, Coiled, Stamped, Albert Paley, 1979, 16 x 8 In.
$2,250

Rago Arts and Auction Center

Trunk, Dome Top, Oak, Baroque, Open Interior, Iron Mounts, Wheels, 1700s, 22 x 34 x 18 In.
$300

Brunk Auctions

Trunk, Dome Top, Storage, Pine, Metal Strapwork, Brass Latch, c.1920
$88

Selkirk Auctioneers & Appraisers

Parasol, Faux Tortoiseshell Handle, Carved Grapevine, Fringes, Victorian, 28 In.	166
Parasol, Gold Filled Handle, Mother-Of-Pearl, Ornate, Victorian, 8 In.	143
Parasol, Ivory Handle, Carved, Lace, Folding, France, 1800s, 24 1/4 In.	130
Parasol, Ivory, Gold Plated Handle, Engraved, Victorian, 10 In.	58
Sand Anchor, Tilt Telescoping, Tommy Bahama, 7 In.	16
Wood Handle, Brass Logo, Houndstooth, Compact, Polo Ralph Lauren, 37 In.	48
Wood Handle, Canvas Canopy, Ghurka, 33 In.	24

UNION PORCELAIN WORKS was originally William Boch & Brothers, located in Greenpoint, New York. Thomas C. Smith bought the company in 1861 and renamed it Union Porcelain Works. The company went through a series of ownership changes and finally closed about 1922. The company made a fine quality white porcelain that was often decorated in clear, bright colors. Don't confuse this company with its competitor, Charles Cartlidge and Company, also in Greenpoint.

Centerpiece, Basket, Multicolor Flowers, White Ground, c.1866, 7 x 4 1/2 In.	195
Oyster Plate, 4 Wells, Molded Seaweed & Shells, Blue, 8 x 6 x 1 In.	320
Oyster Plate, 6 Wells, Seaweed, Crabs, Shells, 1879, 9 1/2 x 1 1/4 In.	325
Oyster Plate, 6 Wells, Shells, Sealife, Multicolor, 10 x 8 In.	425
Paperweight, Bulldog, Advertising, Perfection Of Quality, c.1880, 2 5/8 In.	187

Val St Lambert **VAL ST. LAMBERT** Cristalleries of Belgium was founded by Messieurs Kemlin and Lelievre in 1825. The company is still in operation. All types of table glassware and decorative glassware have been made. Pieces are often decorated with cut designs.

Biscuit Jar, Swans, Wreaths, Garlands, Green, Finial, Swing Handle, 6 3/4 In.	480
Punch Bowl, Blue Cut To Clear, Hobstar, Strawberry Diamond, 12 x 11 In.	1560
Vase, Blue Cut To Clear, Strawberry Diamond, Star, Fan, Split Vesica, 5 3/4 x 7 In.	420
Vase, Cranberry Overlay, 3 Bands, 10 In.	101
Vase, Vaseline, Cranberry Overlay, Wavy Rim, Cut Lozenges, 8 x 5 3/4 In.	96

Vallerysthal **VALLERYSTHAL GLASSWORKS** was founded in 1836 in Lorraine, France. In 1854, the firm became Klenglin et Cie. It made table and decorative glass, opaline, cameo, and art glass. A line of covered, pressed glass animal dishes was made in the nineteenth century. The firm is still working.

Dish, Boy On Elephant, Opaque Blue, Trunk Up, Ribbons, Tassels, c.1901, 5 3/4 x 7 In.	112
Dish, Boy, Seated, On Turtle, Milk Glass, Multicolor, c.1900, 6 x 4 1/4 In.	381
Dish, Fish, Opaque Blue, Gold Paint Decoration, c.1875, 3 1/4 x 6 1/2 In.	161
Dish, Fly On Walnut, Opaque Brown, Signed, c.1875, 4 x 5 In.	149
Dish, Mouse, On Toadstool, Leaves, Fiery Opalescence, France, c.1900, 4 x 6 In.	149
Dish, Water Buffalo, Lying Down, Seated Person, Milk Glass, c.1875, 6 x 10 In.	3361

VAN BRIGGLE POTTERY was started by Artus Van Briggle in Colorado Springs, Colorado, after 1901. Van Briggle had been a decorator at Rookwood Pottery of Cincinnati, Ohio. He died in 1904 and his wife took over managing the pottery. One of the employees, Kenneth Stevenson, took over the company in 1969. He died in 1990 and his wife, Bertha, and son, Craig, ran the pottery. She died in 2010. The pottery closed in 2012. The wares usually have modeled relief decorations and a soft, matte glaze.

Ashtray, Turquoise, Marked, c.1960, 9 1/2 In.	52
Creamer, Heart Shape, Blue Glaze, 1960s, 3 In.	24
Vase, 3 Graces, Turquoise Matte, Women, Draping Material, Pentagonal Base, 17 x 10 1/2 In.	390
Vase, 3-Petal Flower Head, Green Matte, Carved, 1902, 3 1/2 x 3 In. *illus*	2204
Vase, Arrowroot Leaf, Collared Rim, Matte Glaze, 1919, 17 x 12 In.	1521
Vase, Blue Leaf, Speckled Brown, 1915, 4 x 7 1/2 In.	518
Vase, Blue, Dragonfly, Spread Wings, 3 x 4 In.	147
Vase, Bud, Calla Lily, Mulberry Red, 8 3/4 In.	95
Vase, Fruit Branches, Brown Glaze, Marked, 1906, 8 x 4 3/4 In. *illus*	1250
Vase, Geese, Relief, Yellow Glaze, Oval, Swollen, 1903, 7 x 6 1/2 In.	8750

Vase, Lady Of The Lily, Blue, Green, 11 In.	460
Vase, Mistletoe, Raised On Shoulder, Green Glaze, Oval, Squat, 1902, 3½ In.	1625
Vase, Poppies, Raised, Tan & Green Glaze, Oval, 1904, 9¾ x 8½ In.	6875
Vase, Tobacco Color Glaze, 2¼ x 3 In. .... *illus*	283
Vase, White Glaze, Marked, 1960s, 4 In.	79

VASELINE GLASS is a greenish-yellow glassware resembling petroleum jelly. Pressed glass of the 1870s was often made of vaseline-colored glass. Some vaseline glass is still being made in old and new styles. The glass fluoresces under ultraviolet light. Additional pieces of vaseline glass may also be listed under Pressed Glass in this book.

Cake Plate, Opalescent, Ruffled Edge, Pale Green, 12 In.	30
Celery Dish, Button & Daisy, Canoe Shape, 12 In.	25
Compote, Geometric Hobnail, Hollow Stem, 12 x 8 In.	90
Cruet, Everglades, Clear Stopper, Opalescent, 7 In.	90
Cruet, Meander, Stopper, Flared Base, 8 In.	80
Hat, Button & Daisy, 5 x 6 In.	30
Lamp, Buddha, Patinated Spelter Base, Cloth Shade, 15½ x 6 x 5 In.	480
Pitcher, Hobnail, Globular, 5½ In.	80
Pitcher, Water, Etched Floral Center, Ribbed Body, Side Handle, Footed, 8½ x 7 In.	60
Sugar Shaker, Green Opalescent, 5½ x 3 In.	54
Tray, 4 Scallops, Hobnail Base, 12 x 12¾ In.	80
Tray, Button & Daisy, Shield Shape, Handles, 12 x 13 In.	40
Vase, Opalescent, Round Base, 12 x 4½ In.	36

VENETIAN GLASS, *see Glass-Venetian category.*

VENINI GLASS, *see Glass-Venetian category.*

VERLYS glass was made in Rouen, France, by the Societe Holophane Français, a company that started in 1920. It was made in Newark, Ohio, from 1935 to 1951. The art glass is either blown or molded. The American glass is signed with a diamond-point-scratched name, but the French pieces are marked with a molded signature. The designs resemble those used by Lalique.

Verlys

Bowl, Console, Flower Relief, Key Pattern Base, 10 x 6 x 4 In.	1125
Bowl, Console, Frosted, Sepia Wash, Flying Birds, 11 x 2 In.	275
Bowl, Flying Geese, Green, Frosted, 2½ x 13 In.	60
Bowl, Frosted, Cogwheel Rim Band, 15 In.	1295
Charger, Fish, Waves, Sun, Art Deco, 1940s, 13 In.	450
Cigarette Box, Doves In Clouds, Side Frieze, c.1930, 4¾ x 5 x 2 In.	149
Plate, Dragonflies, Frosted, 3 In., Pair	75
Vase, Alpine Thistle, Shouldered, Rolled Lip, 9 In.	440
Vase, Mandarin, Man, Garden, Greek Key, Frosted, 9½ x 5 In.	74
Vase, Mermaids, Sea Life, Turquoise Blue, 10 In.	1250
Vase, Parakeets, Flared, 9 In.	600
Vase, Relief Roses, Stems, Leaves, Opalescent, 7 In.	770
Vase, Seasons, Spring, Fall, Men, Wheat, Flowers, c.1940, 8 In.	72
Vase, Thistle, Opalescent, Flared Archways, 3-Piece Mold, Signed, 10 x 7 In.	240

VERNON KILNS was the name used by Vernon Potteries, Ltd. The company, which started in 1912 in Vernon, California, was originally called Poxon China. In 1931 the company was sold and renamed Vernon Kilns. It made dinnerware and figurines. It went out of business in 1953. The molds were bought by Metlox, which continued to make some patterns. Collectors search for the brightly colored dinnerware and the pieces designed by Rockwell Kent, Walt Disney, and Don Blanding. For more prices, go to kovels.com.

Coffee Server, Lid, Bakelite Handle, Pastel Green, 8½ In.	29
Fantasia, Figurine, Flute Player, Satyr, 1940, 4½ In.	144
Fantasia, Nutcracker, Cup, Tumbler, Flower, Flared, 1940, 5¼ In.	108
Hawaiian Flowers, Coffeepot, Lid, Maroon, Don Blanding, 8½ x 9 In.	21

Trunk, Gary Cooper, Leather, Wood Frame, Tan Border, Brass Tacks, Handle, 17 x 29 In.
$1,320

Morphy Auctions

Trunk, Immigrant's, Dome Top, Pine, Dovetail, Iron Hinges, Jans Hansen, 1851, 25 x 48 In.
$390

Garth's Auctioneers & Appraisers

Chinese Prices Drop

The wealthy Chinese have been paying high prices for many types of old Chinese art, paintings, scrolls, netsuke, jade, ivory, rhinoceros horn, wood carvings, and furniture—but only the best-quality items. But the Chinese economy is having problems and Chinese collectors are not spending as much as they used to, so prices have dropped since 2011.

Typewriter, Corona, Portable, Gold Text, Cast Iron, Black
$94

Copake Auction

U
V

Van Briggle, Vase, 3-Petal Flower Head, Green Matte, Carved, 1902, 3½ x 3 In. $2,204

Soulis Auctions

Van Briggle, Vase, Fruit Branches, Brown Glaze, Marked, 1906, 8 x 4¾ In. $1,250

Rago Arts and Auction Center

Van Briggle Marks

Van Briggle pottery has been made since 1901. Pieces are usually marked AA and Colorado Springs, sometimes in abbreviated form. "Original," used after 1920, means the piece was turned on a wheel, not made in a mold. "Hand carved" was used on pieces with carved, not molded decorations. "Hand decorated" was used for slip decorated pieces. None of these marks add extra value.

U
V

Melinda, Casserole, Lid, 2 Handles, 4 x 6 In.	12
Souvenir, Ashtray, Plant Visit, Memento, Faye Bennison, Round, 5¾ In.	17
Souvenir, Plate, Clifton's Cafeteria, Blue & White, 10¼ In.	77
Vase, Elephant Head, White, May & Vieve Hamilton, 8 In.	163

 VERRE DE SOIE glass was first made by Frederick Carder at the Steuben Glass Works from about 1905 to 1930. It is an iridescent glass of soft white or very, very pale green. The name means "glass of silk," and it does resemble silk. Other factories have made verre de soie, and some of the English examples were made of different colors. Verre de soie is an art glass and is not related to the iridescent, pressed, white carnival glass mistakenly called by its name. Related pieces may be found in the Steuben category.

Basket, Iridescent, Flowers, Frederick Carder, Steuben, 1905, 16 In.	184
Cologne Bottle, Green Jade Applicator, Painted Red Rose, Steuben, 4 In.	100

VIENNA*, see Beehive category.*

 VIENNA ART plates are round lithographed metal serving trays produced at the turn of the century. The designs, copied from Royal Vienna porcelain plates, usually featured a portrait of a woman encircled by a wide, ornate border. Many were used as advertising or promotional items and were produced in Coshocton, Ohio, by J. F. Meeks Tuscarora Advertising Co. and H.D. Beach's Standard Advertising Co. Some are listed in Advertising in this book.

Plate, Girl, Long Hair, Red Hat, 1905, 10 In.	48
Plate, Woman, Art Nouveau, Ernst Wahliss, c.1890, 9½ In.	16
Plate, Woman, Black Hat, Hand Muff, Meeks & Beach, c.1901, 10 In.	150
Plate, Woman, In Garden, Austria, 1905, 10 In.	10
Plate, Young Woman, Angelo Asti, 1905, 10 In.	46

 VILLEROY & BOCH POTTERY of Mettlach was founded in 1836. The firm made many types of wares, including the famous Mettlach steins. Collectors can be confused because although Villeroy & Boch made most of its pieces in the city of Mettlach, Germany, the company also had factories in other locations. The dating code impressed on the bottom of most pieces makes it possible to determine the age of the piece. Additional items, including steins and earthenware pieces marked with the famous castle mark or the word *Mettlach*, may be found in the Mettlach category.

Stein, Wheat, Brown Ground, Twig Handle, Leaf & Vine, Cartouche, Impressed, 14¾ In.	83
Trivet, Tile, Majolica, Black Lab, Schramberg, Late 1800s, 1⅛ In.	63

VOLKSTEDT was a soft-paste porcelain factory started in 1760 by Georg Heinrich Macheleid at Volkstedt, Thuringia. Volkstedt-Rudolstadt was a porcelain factory started at Volkstedt-Rudolstadt by Beyer and Bock in 1890. Most pieces seen in shops today are from the later factory.

Figurine, Dancer, Arms Up, Veiled, Green, 15¾ x 8 In.	381
Figurine, Woman Bather, Nude, Germany, 1945, 7½ In.	397
Group, Children Presented To Important Lady, Marked, c.1915, 16 x 19 In.	1500
Group, Harpist, Fireplace, Mantel Clock, Rugs, Baskets, 20 x 12 In.	708
Group, Musicians, Lute Player, Piano, Parcel Gilt, 1939-45, 9½ x 13½ In.	684
Group, Woman, Attendant, Vanity, Mirror, Burgundy, Pink, Gold Highlights, 15 x 14 In.	571

 WADE pottery is made by the Wade Group of Potteries started in 1810 near Burslem, England. Several potteries merged to become George Wade & Son, Ltd., early in the twentieth century, and other potteries have been added through the years. The best-known Wade pieces are the small figurines called Whimsies. They were first were made in 1954. Special Whimsies were given away with Red Rose Tea beginning in 1967. The Disney figures are listed in this book in the Disneyana category.

Bank, Piggy, Annabel, Ceramic, Nat. West Money Bank, 1980, 6 In.	16

Candleholder, Cockatoo, White, Black Base, 1957, 2 x 3 In.	35
Creamer, Tower Bridge, Black, Tan, 3 ½ x 2 In.	15
Figurine, Anita Pierette, Harlequin, Plinth, Multicolor, c.1936, 6 In.	554
Figurine, Bear, Seated, Brown, 3 In.	6
Figurine, Budgerigar, Branch, Pink, Blue, Green, 7 x 4 ½ In.	310
Figurine, Dog, Irish Setter, c.1970, 2 ½ x 2 ½ In.	34
Figurine, House, Bloodshott Hall, England, Miniature	9
Figurine, Leprechaun, Seated, Beard, Blue, 1950s, 1 ½ In.	36
Figurine, Mother Goose, Goose	22
Figurine, My Fair Lady, Holding Hat, Roses On Dress, 4 In.	15
Figurine, Paddy Reilly, Dog At Feet, 3 ¾ In.	18
Jug, Felinfoel Quality Ales, 4 ¾ x 5 ¾ In.	17
Mug, Coffee, Irish Porcelain, Green, Hunting Scene, 2 Dogs	11
Open Salt, Dip, Angelfish, Porcelain, Blue, Brown, 4 x 3 ¼ In.	31
Pitcher, Copper Luster, Leaves, Harvest Ware, 1950s, 5 ⅜ x 7 In.	55
Pitcher, Flowers, Multicolor, Footed, 6 ½ x 7 In.	150
Pitcher, Irish Porcelain, Embossed, Signed, James Borsey, 6 x 5 x 4 In.	9
Teapot, Donald Duck, Long Bill, Blue Jacket, Arms Form Handle, c.1930, 4 ⅛ x 5 In.	87

WAHPETON POTTERY, *see Rosemeade category.*

WALL POCKETS were popular in the 1930s. They were made by many American and European factories. Glass, pottery, porcelain, majolica, chalkware, and metal wall pockets can be found in many fanciful shapes.

Cherry, Rosehead & Square Nails, Late 1700s, 15 x 12 x 4 In.	2280
Copper, Round Bowl Shape, Braided Rim, Hammered, Harry St. John Dixon, c.1925, 14 x 3 ¼ In.	510
Fish, White, Blue & Black Swirl, Open Mouth, Akio Takamori, Japan, 11 x 4 ½ In.	1436
Salamanders, Palm Tree, Leaves, Green, Yellow, Brown, Tin Glaze, 8 x 5 ¼ In.	227
Squirrel, Nest, Dove, Leaves, Branch, Belleek, 16 In.	1830

WALLACE NUTTING *photographs are listed under Print, Nutting. His reproduction furniture is listed under Furniture.*

WALRATH was a potter who worked in New York City; Rochester, New York; and at the Newcomb Pottery in New Orleans, Louisiana. Frederick Walrath died in 1920. Pieces listed here are from his Rochester period.

Vase, Stylized Flowers, Yellow Buds, Signed, Incised, c.1910, 7 ¾ x 4 ¾ In.	*illus*	4375

WALT DISNEY, *see Disneyana category.*

WALTER, *see A. Walter category.*

WARWICK china was made in Wheeling, West Virginia, in a pottery working from 1887 to 1951. Many pieces were made with hand painted or decal decorations. The most familiar Warwick has a shaded brown background. The name *Warwick* is part of the mark and sometimes the mysterious word *IOGA* is also included.

Pitcher, Portrait, Young Woman, Flowers In Hair, Brown To Cream, Scalloped Edge, 6 ½ x 4 In.	42
Plate, Dinner, Loch Oich, Scotland, Blue & White, 10 In.	11
Vase, Bouquet, Portrait, Woman, Handles, Shaped Rim, 10 ½ In.	36
Vase, Portrait, Brown Curls, Headband, Handles, Red, Brown, 10 ½ x 5 ½ In.	36
Vase, Portrait, Young Woman, Flower In Hair, 2 Handles, 10 ½ x 5 In.	37

WATCH pockets held the pocket watch that was important in Victorian times because it was not until World War I that the wristwatch was used. All types of watches are collected: silver, gold, or plated. Watches are listed here by company name or by style. Wristwatches are a separate category.

Art Nouveau, 14K Gold, Pansy, Enamel, Purple, 16-In. Pendant Chain	259
Blancpain, Stainless Steel, Sapphire Crystal, Black Dial, Signed, Switzerland, 9 x 1 In.	2460

Van Briggle, Vase, Tobacco Color Glaze, 2 ¼ x 3 In.
$283

Soulis Auctions

Walrath, Vase, Stylized Flowers, Yellow Buds, Signed, Incised, c.1910, 7 ¾ x 4 ¾ In.
$4,375

Rago Arts and Auction Center

Watch, Hamilton, 2 Rollers, 21 Jewel, 10K Gold Plate Case, Pocket, Size 16
$187

Cordier Auctions

W

Watch, Tobias, 18K Gold, Open Face, Keys, Relief, Cherubs, Liverpool, c.1835, 2 In., Pocket
$2,813

Morphy Auctions

Watch Fob, Advertising, Nored-Hutchens Commission Co., 2-Sided, Blue, Red Enamel, Signed, c.1900, 1¾ In.
$352

Soulis Auctions

Waterford, Vase, Starburst, Footed, Clear, Glass, Foil Label, 10 x 6⅜ In.
$86

Bunch Auctions

Elgin, Hunting Case, Gold, Ornate, Pocket, Case, 1⅝ In.	96
Elgin, Hunting Case, Pocket, Open Face, 1⅞ In.	72
Hamilton, 2 Rollers, 21 Jewel, 10K Gold Plate Case, Pocket, Size 16 ....*illus*	187
Hamilton, Open Face, 17 Jewel, Wadsworth, 14K Gold Filled Case, Pocket, 12 In.	105
Howard, 14K Case, 17 Jewel, Swing Out, Monogram, Pocket, 14 In.	322
Illinois, 21 Jewel, Keystone, 10k Gold, Case, Pocket, 16 In.	236
Illinois, Railroad, 21 Jewel, 60-Hour, Bunn Special Model, Gold Filled Case, Pocket	316
Illinois, Railroad, 23 Jewel, Sangamo Special Model, 14K Gold Filled Case, Pocket	374
Tobias, 18K Gold, Open Face, Keys, Relief, Cherubs, Liverpool, c.1835, 2 In., Pocket.........*illus*	2813
Ulysse Nardin, Titanium, Stainless Steel, Sapphire Crystal, Signed, 10½ x 1¾ In.	5228
Vacheron & Constantin, 18K Gold, White Enamel Dial, Hunter Case, c.1880, 1¼ In., Pocket	2460
Vanguard Waltham, 10K Rolled Gold Plate, 23 Jewel, Black Steel Heavy Baton, 2⅛ In., Pocket	180
Waltham, 14K Yellow Gold, Double-Sunk Dial, Arabic Marker, Gold Filled Chain, Pocket, c.1919, 12 In..	677
Waltham, 14K Gold, 15 Jewels, Marked, AWW Co., 1800s, 1¾ In., Pocket.	330
Waltham, Hunting Case, Gold, 1½ In., Pocket.	120
Waltham, Open Face, 17 Jewel, Gold, 2¼ In., Pocket.	60

 WATCH FOBS were worn on watch chains. They were popular during Victorian times and after. Many styles, especially advertising designs, are still made today.

Advertising, Diamond Calk Horseshoe Co., Red Enamel, Embossed Horseshoe, Patented	154
Advertising, Nored-Hutchens Commission Co., 2-Sided, Blue, Red Enamel, Signed, c.1900, 1¾ In. . *illus*	352
Advertising, Tiger, 2-Sided, Thresher, Raised Lettering, Gaar-Scott & Co., 5½ x 1¾ In.	90
Amethyst, Spinner, Gold Filled Chain, 1907, 18 In. Chain, 1¼ x 1 In.	250
Bar Link Chain, Grooved Pattern, 14K Gold, 13 In.	449
Buffalo Bill, Pawnee Bill, Rope Border, Embossed, Uniface, c.1800	179
Carnelian Stone, Locket, Swivel, Scalloped Edge, 14K Rose Gold, 1 x 1½ In.	450
Diamond Shapes, Heart, Twisted Wicker, c.1860, 13 In.	345
Hair, Black, Twists, T Bar, 10K Gold, 1800s, 12 In.	250
Mourning Ribbon, Black, 14K Gold Fob, Monogram, c.1940, 8 In.	190
Sterling Silver, Dolphins, Waves, 1¼ In.	175
Sterling Silver, Rose Gold Applied Shield, Birmingham, 1894, 1¼ x 1½ In.	50
Triple Chain, Medallions, Scroll Design, JMF Co., 4 In.	58
White Agate, Lion & Shield Insignia, 12K Yellow Gold, ⅜ x ⅜ In.	325

 WATERFORD type glass resembles the famous glass made from 1783 to 1851 in the Waterford Glass Works in Ireland. It is a clear glass that was often decorated by cutting. Modern glass is being made again in Waterford, Ireland, and is marketed under the name Waterford. Waterford merged with Wedgwood in 1986 to form the Waterford Wedgwood Group. Most Waterford Wedgwood assets were bought by KPS Capital Partners of New York in 2009 and became part of WWRD Holdings. WWRD was bought by Fiskars in 2015 and Waterford glass is still being made.

Bowl, Console, Clear Glass, Marquis, 9 x 9 x 4½ In.	24
Bowl, Fruit, Master Cutter Series, Etched, 7 x 10 In.	196
Ice Bucket, Cut Glass, Lismore, Signed, 7¼ In.	196
Lamp, Cut Glass, Diamond, Globe Style Shade, 10 x 19 In.	219
Pitcher, Cut Crystal, Lismore, Ice Lip Spout, Signed, 6 In.	81
Vase, Laurel Wreath, Footed, 12 x 6¾ In.	246
Vase, Starburst, Footed, Clear, Glass, Foil Label, 10 x 6⅜ In. ....*illus*	86

 WATT family members bought the Globe pottery of Crooksville, Ohio, in 1922. They made pottery mixing bowls and tableware of the type made by Globe. In 1935 they changed the production and made the pieces with the freehand decorations that are popular with collectors today. Apple, Starflower, Rooster, Tulip, and Autumn Foliage are the best-known patterns. Pansy, also called Rio Rose, was the earliest pattern. Apple, the most popular pattern, can be dated from the leaves. Originally, the apples had three leaves; after 1958 two leaves were used. The plant closed in 1965. Reproductions of Apple, Dutch Tulip, Rooster, and Tulip have been made. For more prices, go to kovels.com.

Apple, Casserole, Individual, No. 18, 8 In.	279
Apple, Mixing Bowl, Ribbed, 3 Leaves, c.1955, 8½ In........	55
Apple, Pitcher, Refrigerator, 2-Leaf, Beige, No. 69, 8 x 7 In......................*illus*	118
Banded Ware, Casserole, Bowl, Eve-N-Bake, Blue Stripe Cream, 7 x 7 In.	13
Butterfly, Pitcher, Refrigerator, Beige, No. 69.................	538
Dutch Tulip, Bean Pot, Lid, Beige, Marked, Oven Ware, No. 76, USA, 8 x 6 In.	96
Pansy, Cut-Leaf, Cookie Jar, Oven Bake Ware, Red & Green, 10 x 7½ In.	66
Pansy, Pitcher, Marked, 5½ In.	45
Rooster, Ice Bucket, Lid, Red, Black, Green Leaves, 5 x 7 In....	250
Rooster, Pepper Shaker, Lance's Dairy In Iowa, Beige, 4¾ In.	66
Rio Rose, see Pansy	
Starflower, Creamer, Clear Glaze, 4 In.	109
Starflower, Mixing Bowl, Ribbed, No. 4, 1950s, 2 x 4 In.	55
Tulip, Creamer Pitcher, Beige, Marked, 4½ x 4½ In.............	31
Tulip, Creamer, No. 62, 4⅜ In.	49

WAVE CREST glass is an opaque white glassware manufactured by the Pairpoint Manufacturing Company of New Bedford, Massachusetts, and some French factories. It was decorated by the C.F. Monroe Company of Meriden, Connecticut. The glass was painted in pastel colors and decorated with flowers. The name Wave Crest was used starting in 1892.

WAVE CREST WARE

Ashtray, Copper Golf Club & Ball, Shell Mold, Gilt Metal Rim, Banner Mark, 1¾ x 4 In.	72
Ashtray, Monkey Seated On Rim, Pink Flowers, Stamped Mark, 4 x 5½ In.	300
Bell, Countertop, Pink, White, Blue Flowers, Gilt Metal, 4 x 3¾ In...................................	1140
Biscuit Jar, Pink Flowers, Gilt Lid, Bail Handle, 8 In.	40
Biscuit Jar, Swirl Mold, Pink Tones, Daisy, Silver Plate Cover & Bail, 7½ In..............*illus*	240
Biscuit Jar, Swirl, White Glass, Multicolor, Metal Mount, C.F. Monroe Co., c.1900, 8 In...........	84
Biscuit Jar, White, Pink Flowers, Green Leaves, Silver Plate Cover & Bail, 8 In.......................	72
Blotter, Ink, Blue & White, Flowers, Scroll Mold, Gilt Metal, 3 x 5½ In.	240
Box, Handkerchief, Floral, Green, Pink & White Panels, Gilt Feet, 4¾ x 8 x 4½ In.	600
Box, Helmschmied Swirl, Ormolu, Silk Lined, Gilt Brass Mounts, Metal Base, 6 x 7 In.	283
Cigarette Jar, Hinged Cover, Front Medallion Raised Enamel, C.F. Monroe, 4 x 3 In.	159
Dish, Open, Cameo Relief Cutting, Mill, Sailboat, Gilt Metal Rim, 2½ x 2½ In.	540
Dresser Box, Apricot Mottled Leaf, Blossom, Swirl Mold, Pink & Yellow, 6 x 7 In.	900
Dresser Box, Clawfoot Stand, Embossed, Pink Flowers On Top, 7 x 7 In.	420
Dresser Box, Couple Walking, Scroll Mold, Cobalt Blue, Pink Flowers, 3¾ x 7½ In.	600
Dresser Box, Cream & Gold, Flowers, Collars & Cuffs, 6½ x 6 In..........................*illus*	420
Dresser Box, Cupids At Play, Light Pink, 5½ In.	78
Dresser Box, Underwater Scene, Fish, Cream, Blue, Gold Stencil, Metal Feet, 6 x 7 In.	7800
Fernery, Blue & White, Pink Flowers, Gilt Metal Rim, Banner Mark, 3¾ x 7¾ In.	60
Fernery, Footed, Flowers, Cream Tones, 3 x 6 In.	50
Fernery, Shipwrecked Sailor Scene, Blue, White, Lavender Enamel Lines, 5 x 8 In.	960
Finger Bowl, Fish, Blue & White Tones, Blossom, Unmarked, 3 x 4½ In.	270
Inkwell, Pedestal, Green Border, White Panels, Flowers, Unmarked, 4½ x 3½ In.................	780
Jar, Lid, White, Blue Flowers, Silver Plate, Unmarked, 6½ x 3¼ In........................	150
Jar, Setting Sun, 10 Storks, 7¼ In.	614
Jar, Stream, Cottage, Trees, Field, 6 x 5½ In........................	96
Jar, Yellowish, Flowers, Silver Plate Mounts & Handle, 7 x 4¾ In.	51
Jardiniere, White, Cottage, Forest & Stream, Beaded Enamel Rim, Unmarked, 7¼ x 10 In.	270
Jewelry Box, Daisy, Pink, Blue Tones, Swirl Mold, Lining, 4½ x 6 In..........................	480
Jewelry Box, Egg Crate Shape, Rectangular, Lavender, Sunflower, 3 x 5¾ x 3 In.	150
Jewelry Box, Embossed Scroll, Seafoam Mold, Blue, White, Pink Flowers, 3¾ x 4½ In.	96
Jewelry Box, Flowers, Yellow & White Scroll Mold, Banner Mark, Lined, 4 x 5 x 3 In.............	180
Jewelry Box, Green Vine, Blossom, Gold Stencil, Scroll Mold, Frosted, 3½ x 5½ In.	720
Jewelry Box, Portrait, Young Woman, Gold Stencil, Tapestry, Banner Mark, 6 x 5 In.	2700
Lamp, Oil, Rust, Brown, Green Tones, 12-Sided, 8 x 6 x 13½ In.......................	150
Letter Box, Egg Crate Shape, Hand Painted, Daisy, C.F. Monroe, 1898-1905, 2½ x 3¾ In........	42
Letter Holder, Egg Crate Shape, Blown-Out, 6 x 3½ x 5¼ In.	98
Matchbox Holder, Hinged Cover, Pink, White Tones, Blue Flowers, 2 x 3½ x 2¾ In.	240
Paperweight, Winged Cherub Finial, Playing Cymbals, White, Flowers, 3 x 3¼ In.	96

Watt, Apple, Pitcher, Refrigerator, 2-Leaf, Beige, No. 69, 8 x 7 In.
$118

martyev on eBay

Wave Crest, Biscuit Jar, Swirl Mold, Pink Tones, Daisy, Silver Plate Cover & Bail, 7½ In.
$240

Woody Auction

Wave Crest, Dresser Box, Cream & Gold, Flowers, Collars & Cuffs, 6½ x 6 In.
$420

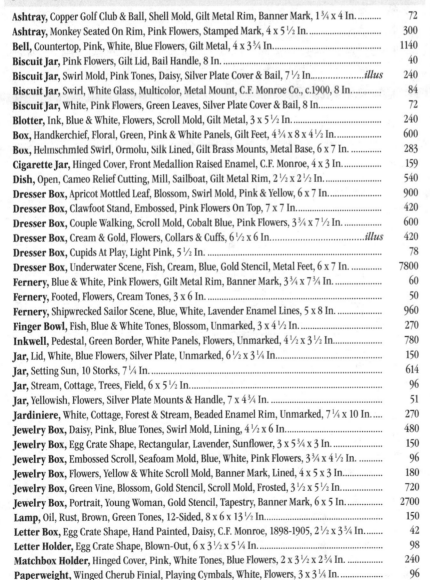

Morphy Auctions

W

Wave Crest, Plaque, Queen Louisa, Green, Pink Border, Scroll Mold, 15 x 12 In.
$9,600

Woody Auction

Wave Crest, Vase, Sea Foam Mold, Enamel Lily, Gilt Metal Feet, Unmarked, C.F. Monroe, 6¼ In.
$600

Woody Auction

Wave Crest, Vase, Sea Wave, Blue, Pink Flowers, Gilt Metal Ormolu, Handles, Dolphin Feet, 15 x 6 In.
$1,320

Woody Auction

Photo Receiver, Gold Stencil, Pink Flowers, Gilt Metal Rim, 5 x 6½ x 3½ In.	210
Pipe Holder, Plaque, Indian, Headdress, Embossed Scroll, Green & Cream, 9½ In.	15600
Plaque, Queen Louisa, Green, Pink Border, Scroll Mold, 15 x 12 In. .....*illus*	9600
Plate, Shell Shape, Leaf, Green, Pink Blossom & Branch, Unmarked, C.F. Monroe, 7½ In.	330
Sugar Shaker, Flowers, Blue & White, Silver Plate Cover, Unmarked, 5 In.	96
Sugar Shaker, Flowers, White, Factory Sample, Unmarked, No Cover, 2½ x 3 In.	36
Vase, Courting Couple, Vermillion Trim, Green, Banner Mark, 17½ x 10 In.	2040
Vase, Flowers, White & Green, Pink Segmented, Unmarked, 9½ In.	180
Vase, Opal, Flowers, Rococo, Footed, Beaded Rim, C.F. Monroe Co., 1900s, 9¾ In.	152
Vase, Scroll Mold, Pink Rose, Green & Cream, Brass Foot & Rim, C.F. Monroe, 16 x 6¼ In.	420
Vase, Sea Foam Mold, Enamel Lily, Gilt Metal Feet, Unmarked, C.F. Monroe, 6¼ In. ....*illus*	600
Vase, Sea Foam Mold, Nude, Field, Flowers, Cobalt Blue, Floral, Gold Stencil, 15¾ x 7¼ In.	5700
Vase, Sea Wave, Blue, Pink Flowers, Gilt Metal Ormolu, Handles, Dolphin Feet, 15 x 6 In...*illus*	1320
Vase, Woman Riding Butterfly, Blue Flowers, Pink Border, Banner Mark, 13½ x 8 In.	840
Vase, Woman, Sea Foam Shape, Cobalt Blue, Iris, Dolphin Feet & Handles, 17 x 7 In...*illus*	3300
Wall Plaque, Maroon Border, Forest Stream, Scroll Mold, 15 x 9½ In.	3600
Wall Plaque, Round, Woman Preparing Bath, Gold Stencil, Cobalt Blue Border, 10 In.	6600

WEAPONS listed here include instruments of combat other than guns, knives, rifles, or swords and clothing worn in combat. Firearms made after 1900 are not listed in this book. Knives and Swords are listed in their own categories.

Pike, Naval Boarding, Wood, Incised US, 54 In.	248
Shield, Targe, Folding, Wood, Leather, Brass, Thistles, Crowns, Hearts, Roses, Scotland, 20 In.	9840
Spear, Fishing, Hand Forge Head, Blacksmith, Cast Iron, Wood Shaft, Silver Cap, 5½ In.	83
Sword, Yakatan, Bayonet Blade, Ornate Brass Hilt, 1800s, 28 x 34 x 1 In.	71
Tomahawk, Inset Steel Cutting Edge, Etched, Silver, Haft Wood, Stamped, A.U. Scovel, 7 x 2 In.	354

WEATHER VANES were used in seventeenth-century Boston. The direction of the wind was an indication of coming weather, important to the seafaring and farming communities. By the mid-nineteenth century, commercial weather vanes were made of metal. Many were shaped like animals. Ethan Allen, Dexter, and St. Julian are famous horses that were depicted. Today's collectors often consider weather vanes to be examples of folk art, even though they may not have been handmade.

Airplane, Directionals, Painted, Iron, 12 x 12½ x 13 In.	406
Angel, Blowing Horn, Full Body, Embossed Detail, Copper, 1900s, 19 x 29 In.	195
Angel, Trumpeting, Topless, Black Hair, Gold Wings, Red Skirt, c.1910, 42 In.	2640
Arrow, Copper, Molded Feathers, Cast Iron, Metal Stand, England, c.1890, 24 In.	800
Arrow, Cow, Decorative Metal, Cast Iron, c.1880, 22 x 7½ In.	58
Arrow, Red Paint, Wood Base, 39½ x 8½ In.	47
Ball, Angel, Painted, Sheet Iron, Stand, 1900s, 74½ In.	325
Banner, Copper, Verdigris, Gilding Traces, 1800s, 19 x 28 In.	1353
Banner, Silhouette, Lyre & Gabriel, Wood, White & Red Paint, c.1980, 7½ x 26 In.	300
Banner, Stylized Flowers, Acorn Finial & Point, Copper, Telescopic Standard, 31 x 51 In.	3600
Beaver, Silhouette, Red Painted Ball, Red, White, Blue, c.1880, 66 x 41½ In.	431
Bicycle, On Arrow, Copper Tubes, Wires, Sheet Metal, Cast Iron, England, 1800s, 8 In.	7995
Bull, Full Body, Rectangular Stand, 25 x 19 In.	3835
Cat, Metal Sheet, Painted, 3 Kittens, 15 x 33 In.	1062
Cat, Squirrel, Wood, Hand Carved, Stand, 23 x 11 In.	547
Chicken, Arrow, Lightning Rod, Primitive Farm, 1800s, 23 In.	862
Clipper Ship, Stand, Cut & Painted Iron, Directionals, Iron, 67 x 27 x 14 In.	319
Codfish, Copper, 1900s, 27 In.	567
Codfish, Sheet Metal, Gilt, E.G. Washburne & Co., N.Y., c.1910, 8 x 25 In.	4200
Cow, Standing, Full Body, Rectangular Stand, 26 x 13¾ In.	3186
Dog, Hound, Brown Paint, Cream, Cast Base, 10½ x 27 In.	60
Dog, Setter, Pointing, Copper, Verdigris, c.1950, 15 x 33 In.	2583
Eagle, 3 Spheres & Arrow, Fiske Style, Verdigris, 1900s, 47 x 24 x 18 In.	439
Eagle, Arrow, Copper, Iron Directionals, Mid 1900s, 81 x 32 In.	30

W

Eagle, Full Body, Directional Arrow, Copper, Gilt & Verdigris, 1800s, 28½ In.	750
Eagle, Full Body, Spread Wings, Arrow & Iron Directionals, Copper, 1950s, 81 x 32 In.	250
Eagle, Molded Copper, Iron Post, Tall Wood, Directionals, Copper Ball, Late 1800s, 81 In.	923
Eagle, On Ball, Spread Wings, Copper, 14 In.	590
Eagle, On Ball, Spread Wings, Copper, Gilt, Molded, England, c.1890, 19 In.	1046
Eagle, On Ball, Spread Wings, Directionals, Roof Mount, 20 x 22 In.	295
Equestrian, Rider On Horse, Sheet Metal, Painted, 1900s, 24 x 29 In.	826
Feather, Finial, Solid Cast Arrow, Patina Paint, Copper, 24 x 16 In.	386
Fireman's Hook & Ladder, Molded Copper, Green Patina, c.1875, 40 In.	7800
Fleur-De-Lis, Directionals, Zinc & Tin, Scalloped, Mounting Bracket, 58 x 36 In.	354
Fox, Bushy Tail, Top Folk Art, Iron, 1900s, 32 x 10½ In.	89
Fox, Running, Copper, Patina, Black Metal Stand, c.1800, 32 In.	7995
Fox, Running, Full Bodied, Copper, Old Verdigris, c.1925, 14 x 31 In.	5100
Gabriel, Painted, Sheet Iron, Signed, S. Kenworthy, 1900s, 80½ In.	250
Gamecock, Copper, Full Body, Tail Feather, 1800s, 17 x 16 In.	4920
Grasshopper, Full Body, Copper, Verdigris, Later Stand, c.1925, 20 x 30 In.	4200
Horse, Copper, Silhouette, Banner, Rosettes, Directionals, c.1880, 44 x 64 In.	6875
Horse, Copper, Zinc Head, Painted, J.W. Fiske, 11 x 26 In.	767
Horse, Galloping, Directionals, Full Body, Copper, Arrow, Horseshoe, Cast Iron, 43 x 46 In.	339
Horse, Race, Zinc Head, Yellow Paint, c.1880, 19 x 34 In.	2400
Horse, Running, Copper Mane, Bob Tail, Flat, c.1880, 18 x 26 In.	3048
Horse, Running, Copper, Cast Iron Head, Gilt & Verdigris, 1800s, 29 In. *illus*	1750
Horse, Running, Copper, Cast Zinc Head, Directionals, Verdigris, 1800s, 29 In.	750
Horse, Running, Copper, Gold, c.1880, 64 x 34 In.	390
Indian, Arrow, Sheet Iron, Red, Black & Yellow Paint, 1800s, 37 x 44½ In.	3750
Lady Liberty, Holding American Flag, Phrygian Cap, Iron, c.1920, 19 x 15 In.	1875
Man, Horseback, Copper, Full Body, Verdigris, Gilt, A.L. Jewell & Co., 1870, 20 x 23 In.	3690
Native American, Massasoit, Holding Bow & Arrow, Old Gilt, 37 x 22 In.	11400
Pig, Copper & Iron, Lightning Rod, Full Body, Heart Scrolled, Arrow Point, 1900s, 21 In.	338
Pig, Topper, Folk Art, Cream Color, Pink Detail, 16 x 10 In.	104
Plaque, Metal, Wave Horizon, Torch Cut Sheet Iron, Stand, 40 x 42 In.	819
Pointing Finger, Gilt Banner, Copper, Zinc, c.1880, 18½ x 52 In.	2440
Quill, Copper, Gilt, Stand, 1800s, 36 x 18¾ In.	2520
Quill, Copper, Leaf, 1900s, 24½ In.	675
Ram, Merino, Molded Sheet Iron, Full Body, Stand, 1800s, 27 x 24 x 5 In. *illus*	938
Rooster, Arrow, Swell Body, Copper & Zinc, 1800s, 33½ x 37 In. *illus*	4000
Rooster, Chicken Farm, Lightning Rod, 22½ x 15½ In.	282
Rooster, Copper, Directionals, Pointed Finial, James Plaque, 32¼ In.	400
Rooster, Copper, Hollow Body, 20 x 21 In.	124
Rooster, Copper, Molded, Feather, Tail, Full Body, Stand, 1800s, 31½ x 29 In.	2177
Rooster, Painted, Aluminum, Kellogg, 30 x 26½ In.	125
Rooster, Painted, Full Body, Square Base, 22 x 18 In.	944
Rooster, Sheet Copper, Full Body, Feather Details, Custom Stand, 1800s, 20 x 20 In.	2032
Seahorse, Sheet Metal, Patina, 17 x 36 In.	584
Serpent, Sheet Iron, Green & Yellow Stripes, Wood Stand, c.1890, 57 x 51 In.	8400
Sheep, Tin, Stand, 21½ x 25½ In.	480
Ship, Wooden, White Sails, Black Hull, Frank Adams, c.1930, 21 x 44 In.	2760
Squirrel, Sheet Copper, Branch Base, Directionals, L.W. Cushing & Sons, 1800s, 62 x 22 In.	6169
Squirrel, Sheet Iron, Black, Marble Eye, Cast Iron Directionals, c.1880, 14 In.	1875
Stag, Leaping, Copper, Cast Zinc Antlers, c.1950, 19 In.	1438
Steer, Full Body, Metal Stand, c.1890, 24 x 26 In.	4800
Swordfish, Painted, Blue & White, Pine & Tin, 39 x 7 In.	1560
Swordfish, Silhouette, Wood, Steel Base, England, 13 x 44½ In.	300
Swordfish, Wood, Painted, Metal Accents, Stand, 20th Century, 12 x 36 In.	123
Whale, Copper, Wood Stand, 23 x 32 In.	625
Whale, Sperm, Copper Mounting Bracket, 29 In.	375
Whale, Sperm, Copper, 20th Century, 17 x 26 In.	187
Witch, Flying On Broom, Sheet Iron, Black Paint, Directionals, c.1940, 29½ In.	775
Woman, Playing Tennis, Copper, Verdigris, 2 Bullet Holes, c.1915	11070

Wave Crest, Vase, Woman, Sea Foam Shape, Cobalt Blue, Iris, Dolphin Feet & Handles, 17 x 7 In.
$3,300

Woody Auction

Weather Vane, Horse, Running, Copper, Cast Iron Head, Gilt & Verdigris, 1800s, 29 In.
$1,750

Pook & Pook

Weather Vane, Ram, Merino, Molded Sheet Iron, Full Body, Stand, 1800s, 27 x 24 x 5 In.
$938

Rago Arts and Auction Center

W

This is an edited listing of current prices. Visit **Kovels.com** to check thousands of prices from previous years and sign up for free information on trends, tips, reproductions, marks, and more.

Weather Vane, Rooster, Arrow, Swell Body, Copper & Zinc, 1800s, 33 ½ x 37 In. $4,000

Pook & Pook

Webb, Vase, Alexandrite, Amber, Pink, Blue, Pull & Tuck Rim, 2 ⅛ x 3 In. $363

Humler & Nolan

Webb, Vase, Spherical Shape, Tricolor, Rose To Frosted, Butterfly, Signed, c.1800, 4 ⅛ In. $956

Jeffrey S. Evans & Associates

TIP

Maroon and yellowish chrome-green colors were never used to decorate porcelain during the eighteenth century.

 WEBB glass was made by Thomas Webb & Sons of Ambelcot, England. Many types of art and cameo glass were made by them during the Victorian era. Production ceased by 1991 and the factory was demolished in 1995. Webb Burmese and Webb Peachblow are special colored glasswares of the Victorian era. They are listed at the end of this section. Glassware that is not Burmese or Peachblow is included here.

Centerpiece, Tricolor, Medallions, Roses, Tulips, Daisies, Strawberry, Cameo, White, Frosted, 3 x 8 In.	1936
Lamp, Brass, Lemon Font, Whale Oil Burner, Marked, Thomas Webb, c.1850, 8 ½ In.	219
Perfume Bottle, Silver Hinged Lid, Albatross, Blue, Cut Feathers, Keller, 1880s, 6 ½ In.	7380
Vase, Alexandrite, Amber, Pink, Blue, Pull & Tuck Rim, 2 ⅛ x 3 In. ....*illus*	363
Vase, Spherical Shape, Tricolor, Rose To Frosted, Butterfly, Signed, c.1800, 4 ⅛ In. ....*illus*	956
Vase, Thorn Branches, Flowers, Oval, Footed, 8 ¼ In.	413
Vase, Tricolor, Cranberry To Butterscotch Ground, Dragonfly, Cameo, Signed, c.1800, 5 In.	1315
Vase, Tricolor, Flowers, Butterfly, Yellow Ground, Wheel Carved, Cameo, 9 In.	1280
Vase, Urn Shape, Branches, Leaves, Butterfly, Signed, c.1800, 7 ¼ In.	1195

WEBB BURMESE is a shaded Victorian glass made by Thomas Webb & Sons of Stourbridge, England, from 1886. Pieces are shades of pink to yellow.

Fairy Lamp, Plush Finish, 3-Part Construction, Scalloped Candlecup, c.1880, 6 In.	172
Vase, Hawthorn Branch, Flowers, Hexagonal Rim, 3 x 3 ½ In.	108
Vase, Lovebirds, Branches, 2 Circles, Satin Glass, 4 ½ x 3 In.	159
Vase, Trumpet, Cased Glass, Pink To Cream, Blue Leaves, 10 x 4 In.	420
Vase, Virginia Creeper, Green Enamel, Gilt, Gold Berry Clumps, 8 In., Pair	1512

WEBB PEACHBLOW is a shaded Victorian glass made by Thomas Webb & Sons of Stourbridge, England, from 1885.

Bowl, Jewels Bar, Scalloped Rim, 4 x 2 ½ In.	144
Rose Bowl, Lilac, Honey Bee, Prunus Branches, Berry Vines, 3 x 3 In.	228
Vase, Butterflies, Asters, 6 x 3 ½ In.	240
Vase, Double Gourd, Branches, Butterfly, Raised Gold, 8 ¼ x 5 In.	944
Vase, Flowers, Dragonfly, White, Cameo, 1875, 5 In.	1369
Vase, Gourd, Fuchsia, Insect, Butterfly, Fir Cones, 8 x 5 In.	996
Vase, Lilac, Flowered Branch, Insects, Globular, Footed, 5 In.	561
Vase, Stick Neck, Butterflies, Flowers, Gold Enamel, 8 ¾ x 4 ½ In.	180

WEDGWOOD, one of the world's most successful potteries, was founded by Josiah Wedgwood, who was considered a cripple by his brother and was forbidden to work at the family business. The pottery was established in England in 1759. The company used a variety of marks, including Wedgwood, Wedgwood & Bentley, Wedgwood & Sons, and Wedgwood's Stone China. A large variety of wares has been made, including the well-known jasperware, basalt, creamware, and even a limited amount of porcelain. There are two kinds of jasperware. One is made from two colors of clay; the other is made from one color of clay with a color dip to create the contrast in design. In 1986 Wedgwood and Waterford Crystal merged to form the Waterford Wedgwood Group. Most Waterford Wedgwood assets were bought by KPS Capital Partners of New York in 2009 and became part of WWRD Holdings. A small amount of Wedgwood is still made in England at the workshop in Barlaston. Most is made in Asia. Wedgwood has been part of Fiskars Group since 2015. Other Wedgwood pieces may be listed under Flow Blue, Majolica, Tea Leaf Ironstone, or in other porcelain categories.

WEDGWOOD & BENTLEY	**WEDGWOOD** OF ETRURIA MADE IN ENGLAND BARLASTON	**W WEDGWOOD** ENGLAND 1759
Wedgwood & Bentley 1769–1780	Wedgwood 1940	Wedgwood 1998–present

Biscuit Jar, Blue, White Classical Figures, Trees & Flowers, 1800s, 6 ⅞ x 5 ⅛ In.	94
Bowl, Butterfly, Octagonal, Early 1900s, 7 In.	63
Bowl, Fairyland Luster, Dana Interior, Octagonal, England, c.1920, 4 ¾ x 2 ¾ In.	2375

Bowl, Fairyland Luster, Elves Sitting On Branch, Insect Encircling Rim, Signed, 6 x 1 ½ In.....	1353
Bowl, Fairyland Luster, Exterior Blue Sky, Interior Daylight Sky, Octagonal, c.1920, 9 In.........	2091
Bowl, Fairyland Luster, Leapfrogging Elves, Octagonal, England, c.1920, 9 x 4 ½ In.	2875
Bowl, Fairyland Luster, Thumbelina & Firbolgs, England, c.1920, 10 ¾ x 4 ½ In..............illus	594
Bowl, Fairyland Luster, Woodland Bridge, Midnight Background, c.1920, 8 x 3 ¾ In.........illus	1000
Bowl, Figures, Black Basalt, Classical, 7 ¼ In.	98
Bowl, Jasperware, Pale Blue, White Classical Figures, Lady Templeton, Late 1700s, 7 In....illus	492
Bowl, Strainer Holes, Painted Upper Rim, Signed, England, 1800s, 7 In.	48
Bowl, Tricolor, Vine, Ribbon, Checkerboard & Star, Impressed, 1900s, 8 In......................illus	250
Bread Plate, Westbury, Flowers, Sliver Trim, 1970s, 6 In.	5
Bust, George Washington, Basalt, Marked, c.1800, 13 In.	6500
Bust, Roman Messenger, Winged Hat, Black Basalt, Pedestal Base, Late 1800s, 18 x 10 In. illus	1638
Charger, Pearlware, Hand Painted, Multicolor, Enamel, Young Girl, c.1877, 15 In.	308
Cheese Dome, Cover, Birds, Flowering Branches, Multicolor, Footed, 1800s, 10 In.	281
Figure, Ariadne, Black Basalt, Titled, Marked, 1800s, 9 ½ x 11 In...illus	1625
Figurine, Elephant, Basalt, Glass Eyes, Ernest W. Light, Marked, c.1913, 5 In.........................	495
Figurine, Mercury, Pedestal, Black Basalt, 11 ½ In.	224
Inkwell, Bronze Base, Filigree, Hinged Lid, Collar, Medallions, Claw Feet, Signed, 5 ¾ x 9 x 9 In.	212
Pitcher, Embossed Scene, Cherubs On Dolphins, Cobalt Blue, Green, 8 ¾ In............................	108
Pitcher, Jasperware, Dark Blue, Light Blue, Green, Handle, Classical Scenes, 1987, 5 x 4 In....illus	63
Plaque, Oval, White Relief Portrait, Green Ground, Light Blue Border, 1800s, 9 ¾ In.	492
Plate, Jasperware, Blue, Neoclassical Scene, Swags, Flowers, c.1885, 8 ½ In., 4 Piece................	1188
Pot, Lid, Fairyland Luster, Malfrey, Woodland Elves, Coral, Bronze, 4 ½ x 3 ¾ In......................	945
Scent Bottle, Jasperware, Light Blue Ground, Floral Swags, Late 1700, 2 x 1 ¾ In..............illus	1404
Scent Bottle, Light Blue Ground, Dipping Of Achilles, Metal Cap, Late 1700s, 4 ⅝ x 2 In..illus	5556
Teapot, Lid, Cobalt Blue, Classical Pate-Sur-Pate, England, 1800s ....illus	36
Tray, Fairyland Luster, Lily, Garden Of Paradise, Gilded Flying Geese, c.1920, 11 In.	2875
Urn, Lid, Blue Jasperware, Classical Scene, Flowers, Bolted, 11 ½ x 7 In.................................	283
Urn, Lid, Jasperware, White, Light Blue, Floral Festoons, England, 1800s, 12 ¼ In. ....illus	1107
Vase, Fairyland Luster, 3 Serpents, Flame Background, England, c.1920, 12 x 5 In.	3250
Vase, Fairyland Luster, Trumpet Shape, Painted, England, c.1920, 9 ½ x 4 ¾ In.	1875
Vase, Jasperware, Acanthus Leaves, White Relief, Early 1800s, 9 In.	431
Vase, Jasperware, Classical Figures, Swags, 2 Handles, 13 ¾ x 8 ½ In.	308

WELLER pottery was first made in 1872 in Fultonham, Ohio. The firm moved to Zanesville, Ohio, in 1882. Artwares were introduced in 1893. Hundreds of lines of pottery were produced, including Louwelsa, Eocean, Dickens Ware, and Sicardo, before the pottery closed in 1948.

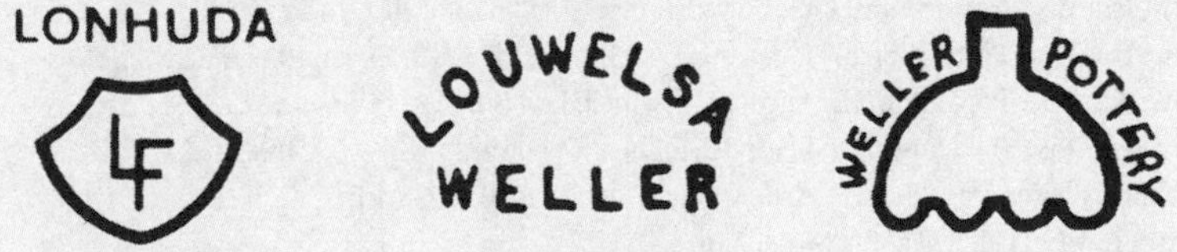

LONHUDA

Weller Pottery
1895–1896

Weller Pottery
1895–1918

Weller Pottery
1920s

Art Nouveau, Jardiniere, Embossed, Peacock Feather, Jewel, 29 In.	120
Art Nouveau, Umbrella Stand, Green & Orange, Glaze, Flower, 21 In.	94
Aurelian, Vase, Bouquet Roses, Yellow Orange, Lillie Mitchell, 24 ¾ In...........................illus	1331
Aurelian, Vase, Nasturtiums & Leaves, Signed, M. Hurst, 10 ⅞ In...	303
Aurelian, Vase, Water Lily, Artist Signed, Glaze, 10 In.	173
Baldin, Vase, Relief Apples, Branches, Green Matte Glaze, Handles, 10 x 9 ½ In.................illus	212
Bowl, Console, Green, Flower, Leaves, 12 ½ x 3 In..	96
Brighton, Figurine, Parrot On Stand, Impressed Mark, 7 ¾ In.	236
Brighton, Figurine, Pheasant, Cobalt Blue, Cream, Green, High Gloss, 7 x 11 In.	275
Burnt Wood, Vase, Round, Modernist Style, Brown, 4 In.	60
Claywood, Jardiniere, 3 Panels, Glossy Brown Interior, Bisque, c.1900, 8 x 9 In................illus	439
Coppertone, Vase, Seated Frog, Water Lily Flower, 4 x 3 ½ x 4 In.	88
Cornucopia, Vase, Double, Blue & Green Glaze, c.1930s, 10 ½ In.	125
Dickens Ware, Mug, Native American Portrait, 5 ⅜ In.	189

W

WELLER

Dickens Ware, Vase, Indian Portrait, Black Bear, Blue Matte, Marked, 10 x 6½ In...........*illus*	938
Dickens Ware, Vase, Tavern Scene, Men Partaking, Incised, Signed, c.1925, 15 In.	250
Duck, Vase, Jug, Green & Yellow Ground, Hand Brushed, Early 1900s, 6⅞ In...........................	47
Echinacea Flowers, Umbrella Stand, Green Matte, 22¼ In.	847
Eocean, Vase, Stems, Green & Pink Flowers, 11 In.	454
Eocean, Vase, Stork, Hand Painted, Green, Embossed, 9½ In.	287
Eocean, Vase, Stork, Standing, High Glaze, Gray, White, c.1925, 9½ In.	225
Figurine, Dog, Pop-Eye, Cream, Tan, Black, Blue Eyes, Incised, 4 x 4 x 3½ In. ....*illus*	201
Flemish, Tub, Matte Glaze, Roses, Basket Shape, Late 1900s, 5½ In.	18
Floretta, Vase, Brown, Green Grapes, Light Brown Vines, c.1905, 9½ In.	200
Forest, Basket, 2 Handles, Trees, Marked, 1920s, 6½ x 3¾ In..	150
Forest, Jardiniere, Trees, Woodsy, Earth Tones, Marked, 1920s, 5 x 6 In.	145
Forest, Teapot, Glazed Porcelain, Brown, Marked, Lid, 6 In.	140
Fru Russet, Lamp Base, Electric, Grapevine, Brown Glaze, Wood Base, c.1904, 29½ x 5¼ In.	125
Fruitone, Vase, Green, Brown, Feathered & Striated Glaze, Rolled Collar, 9 In.	295
Glendale, Bowl, Birds, Net, Branches, Marked, Mae Timberlake, c.1925, 3 In.	359
Hudson, Vase, Flowers, Pink, Green & White, Signed, 1930, 10½ In.	509
Hudson, Vase, Iris, Signed, McLaughlin, 15½ In.	325
Hudson, Vase, Parrot & Butterfly, Hester Pillsbury, c.1925, 27 In. ....*illus*	4687
Hudson, Vase, Wisteria Flower, Blue, Early 1900s, 9¾ x 2⅞ x 6¼ In.	212
Jap Birdimal, Vase, 6 Geese, Stylized Trees, 7½ In.	531
Jardiniere, Pedestal, Parrot & Floral, Ivory Field, 32 x 14 In.	431
Jardiniere, Pink & Green Glaze, Signed, c.1920, 9½ x 11½ In. ....*illus*	68
Jardiniere, White Ground, Moonlit Trees, c.1900s, 11½ In.	125
Jug, Whiskey, Tavern Scene, Man Seated, Serving Girl, Painted, 4 x 5 In.	176
Lasa, Vase, Bamboo Landscape, Signed, 12½ In.	246
Lasa, Vase, Desert Landscape, 9 In.	230
Lasa, Vase, Round, Gold, Green, Red, Palm Tree, Island, 1920-25, 4 x 2 In.	395
Lasa, Vase, Triangular, Marked, 7 In.	461
Lotus, Vase, Yellow Interior, Ivory, Green, 4 x 5 In.	69
Louwelsa, Candlestick, Brown, Green, Flowers, Jug Shape, Loop Handle, Early 1900s, 5 In.	72
Louwelsa, Ewer, Apple Blossom, Bulbous Body, Glaze, Stamped, 7 x 4 In.	110
Louwelsa, Ewer, Flowers & Leaves, Standard Glaze, Handle, Stamped, 5 x 3 In.	110
Louwelsa, Ewer, Painted, Apple Blossom, C-Scroll Handle, 3-Footed, 6 x 5 x 5¼ In.	133
Louwelsa, Jardiniere, Brown, Orange Pansies, Marked, 11 x 14 In.	118
Louwelsa, Vase, 2 Poppies, White & Orange, Footed, 10½ In.	157
Louwelsa, Vase, Flowers, Brown & Green Tones, Glazed, Trumpet Shape, 13 In.	92
Louwelsa, Vase, Nasturtiums, Blue, Flowers, Impressed Bottom, 10¼ In.	333
Louwelsa, Vase, Portrait, Spaniel, Pensive Eyes, Brown, Elizabeth Blake, 10⅝ In.............*illus*	333
Louwelsa, Vase, Portrait, Wolfgang Mozart, Signed, Levi Burgess, 13 In.	424
Louwelsa, Vase, Wild Rose, Hand Painted, Signed, Woodward, 10¾ x 3½ In.	209
Muskota, Flower Frog, Butterfly, Yellow, Pink Flowers, 1920, 3½ x 1 In.	101
Paragon, Vase, Lid, Red Matte Glaze, 7 In.	265
Selma, Bowl, Knifewood, Daisies, 5¾ x 2½ In.	141
Selma, Vase, Brown Owls & Squirrels, Blue Birds, Impressed Bottom, 7 In........................*illus*	363
Sicardo, Lamp Base, Metallic Luster, Electric, 21½ In.	288
Sicardo, Vase, Butterfly, Star, 7¼ x 3¼ In.	263
Sicardo, Vase, Cylindrical, Poppies, Leaves, Iridescent Glaze, 9½ In.................................	460
Sicardo, Vase, Daisies, Signed, 6 In..	826
Sicardo, Vase, Iridescent Glaze, Flowers, Bulbous, Round Base, Signed, 1900s, 5 x 4½ In........	375
Sicardo, Vase, Iridescent Glaze, Leaves Of Ivy, Signed, c.1905, 6 x 4½ In..................*illus*	763
Sicardo, Vase, Neoclassical Style, Iridescent Glaze, Vines, 2 Handles, 3 x 3⅞ In.	283
Sicardo, Vase, Pear Shape, Luster, 6 In.	259
Turada, Jar, Pierced Lid, Light Brown, Dark Green Base, Scrolling Edge, 1900s, 4 In.	151
Tutone, Vase, Stems, Pedestal, Art Deco, Green, Red, 5 x 5 In.	55
Vase, Hand Painted, Flowers, Blue Matte Finish, Double Angular Handles, 9¾ In.	138
Water Lily, Umbrella Stand, Arts & Crafts, Green Matte, 22 x 10½ In. ....*illus*	666
Woodcraft, Jardiniere, Forest, Ohio, 1900s, 26½ x 11 In. ....*illus*	360
Woodcraft, Planter, 3 Foxes, Oak Tree, Embossed, Brown & Green, 5½ x 7 In.	360
Zona, Pitcher, Kingfisher In Tree, Pond, Blues, Browns, 1920-24, 9 In..............................	625

W

Wedgwood, Scent Bottle, Jasperware, Light Blue Ground, Floral Swags, Late 1700, 2 x 1¾ In.
$1,404

Jeffrey S. Evans & Associates

Wedgwood, Scent Bottle, Light Blue Ground, Dipping Of Achilles, Metal Cap, Late 1700s, 4⅝ x 2 In.
$5,556

Jeffrey S. Evans & Associates

Wedgwood, Teapot, Lid, Cobalt Blue, Classical Pate-Sur-Pate, England, 1800s
$36

Selkirk Auctioneers & Appraisers

Wedgwood, Urn, Lid, Jasperware, White, Light Blue, Floral Festoons, England, 1800s, 12¼ In.
$1,107

Skinner, Inc.

Weller, Aurelian, Vase, Bouquet Roses, Yellow Orange, Lillie Mitchell, 24¾ In.
$1,331

Humler & Nolan

Weller, Baldin, Vase, Relief Apples, Branches, Green Matte Glaze, Handles, 10 x 9½ In.
$212

Aspire Auctions

Weller, Claywood, Jardiniere, 3 Panels, Glossy Brown Interior, Bisque, c.1900, 8 x 9 In.
$439

Jeffrey S. Evans & Associates

Weller, Dickens Ware, Vase, Indian Portrait, Black Bear, Blue Matte, Marked, 10 x 6½ In.
$938

Treadway

W

513

Weller, Figurine, Dog, Pop-Eye, Cream, Tan, Black, Blue Eyes, Incised, 4 x 4 x 3½ In.
$201

Weller, Hudson, Vase, Parrot & Butterfly, Hester Pillsbury, c.1925, 27 In.
$4,687

Weller, Jardiniere, Pink & Green Glaze, Signed, c.1920, 9½ x 11½ In.
$68

WEMYSS ware was first made in 1882 by Robert Heron & Son, later called Fife Pottery, in Scotland. Large colorful flowers, hearts, and other symbols were hand painted on figurines, inkstands, jardinieres, candlesticks, buttons, pots, and other items. Fife Pottery closed in 1932. The molds and designs were used by a series of potteries until 1957. In 1985 the Wemyss name and designs were obtained by Griselda Hill. The Wemyss Ware trademark was registered in 1994. Modern Wemyss Ware in old styles is still being made.

Bowl, Lid, Thistles, Painted, Scotland, 7 In.	91
Figurine, Cat, Red Rose, White Background, c.1920, 12 In.	1610
Jug, Rooks In Trees, Rabbits, Painted, Earls Hall, 11 x 8¾ In.	1328

WESTMORELAND GLASS was made by the Westmoreland Glass Company of Grapeville, Pennsylvania, from 1889 to 1984. The company made clear and colored glass of many varieties, such as milk glass, pressed glass, and slag glass.

Westmoreland Glass
c.1910–c.1929, 1970s

Westmoreland Glass
Late 1940s–1981

Westmoreland Glass
1982–1984

Candy Dish, Ribbed, Lace Edge Finial & Foot, Milk Glass, 10 x 5¾ In.	33
Dish, Hen On Nest Cover, Flower, Airbrushed, Painted, Yellow, Milk Glass, 5 In.	31
Doric, Cake Stand, Open Lace, Pedestal, Milk Glass, 1940, 11¾ x 4½ x 4 In.	35
English Hobnail, Cobalt Blue, Champagne Glass, Square Foot, 4⅝ In.	59
English Hobnail, Goblet, Water, Green, Round Foot, 6 In.	31
English Hobnail, Plate, Dinner, Amber, 9 In.	49
Old Quilt, Candy Dish, Lid, Milk Glass, Footed, 6½ In.	17
Owl, Toothpick Holder, Spread Wings, Blue, 2¾ x 2 In.	23
Paneled Grape, Epergne, Opaque White, Pedestal, c.1950, 14½ x 12½ In. ....*illus*	380
Paneled Grape, Milk Glass, Fluted Top Edge, Octagon Knob, 5 x 2 In.	42
Ring & Petal, Cake Stand, Milk Glass, Square, 11 In.	81
Santa On Sleigh, Candy Dish, Nesting, Christmas, Amberina, 4½ x 5 In.	26
Slag Glass, Candy Dish, Camel Lid, Range, 7 x 5½ In.	36
Slag Glass, Candy Dish, Picnic Basket Shape, Jadite, Green, 5 x 5 x 3½ In.	29
Slag Glass, Dish, Lid, Open Neck Swan, Purple Marble, Milk Glass, 4¾ x 5 x 4 In.	37
Thousand Eye, Torte Plate, Ruby, 18 In.	189

WHEATLEY POTTERY was founded by Thomas J. Wheatley in Cincinnati, Ohio. He had worked with the founders of the art pottery movement, including M. Louise McLaughlin of the Rookwood Pottery. He started T.J. Wheatley & Co. in 1880. That company was closed by 1884. Thomas Wheatley worked for Weller Pottery in Zanesville, Ohio, from 1897 to 1900. In 1903 he founded Wheatley Pottery Company in Cincinnati. Wheatley Pottery was purchased by the Cambridge Tile Manufacturing Company in 1927.

Vase, Canteen, Deer Standing In Woods, Winding Road On Reverse, J. Rettig, 1880, 13 In.	4130

WHIELDON was an English potter who worked alone and with Josiah Wedgwood in eighteenth-century England. Whieldon made many pieces in natural shapes, like cauliflowers or cabbages, and they are almost always unmarked. Do not confuse it with F. Winkle & Co., which made a dinnerware pattern marked *Whieldon Ware.*

Jug, Creamware, Tortoiseshell Glaze, Handle, 3 In.	182
Teapot, Lid, Overlaid With Leaves, Tortoiseshell Glaze, 7 In.	534

BELLEEK **WILLETS MANUFACTURING COMPANY** of Trenton, New Jersey, began work in 1879. The company made belleek in the late 1880s and 1890s in shapes similar to those used by the Irish Belleek factory. It stopped working about 1912. A variety of marks were used, most including the name *Willets.*

Weller, Louwelsa, Vase, Portrait, Spaniel, Pensive Eyes, Brown, Elizabeth Blake, 10 ⅝ In.
$333

Humler & Nolan

Weller, Selma, Vase, Brown Owls & Squirrels, Blue Birds, Impressed Bottom, 7 In.
$363

Humler & Nolan

Weller, Sicardo, Vase, Iridescent Glaze, Leaves Of Ivy, Signed, c.1905, 6 x 4 ½ In.
$763

Soulis Auctions

Weller, Water Lily, Umbrella Stand, Arts & Crafts, Green Matte, 22 x 10 ½ In.
$666

Humler & Nolan

Weller, Woodcraft, Jardiniere, Forest, Ohio, 1900s, 26 ½ x 11 In.
$360

Garth's Auctioneers & Appraisers

Westmoreland, Paneled Grape, Epergne, Opaque White, Pedestal, c.1950, 14 ½ x 12 ½ In.
$380

Jeffrey S. Evans & Associates

Window, Leaded, 2 Panels, Multicolor, Flowers, 23 x 17 In.
$138

Keystone Auctions LLC

Window, Leaded, Geometric Shapes, Wood Frame, Early 1900s, 24 x 24 In.
$34

Keystone Auctions LLC

Window, Leaded, Wood Frame, From A. Heurtley House, F.L. Wright, 1902, 43 ½ x 27 In.
$7,500

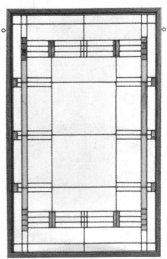

Leslie Hindman Auctioneers

W

Window, Stained, Amber Field, Central Coat Of Arms, Frame, 1900s, 58 x 25½ In.
$438

Garth's Auctioneers & Appraisers

Window, Stained, Wood Frame, Roses, 41 x 46 In.
$254

Hartzell's Auction Gallery, Inc.

Wood Carving, Artist's Model, Arm, Hand, Custom Stand, 26 In.
$590

Copake Auction

Plate, Woman At Shoreline On Right Side, Enameled Raised Gold Fish On Left, 8 In. 94
Vase, White Stork, Plants, Gray Ground, Cylindrical, Marked, 12 x 4 In. 123

WILLOW pattern has been made in England since 1780. The pattern has been copied by factories in many countries, including Germany, Japan, and the United States. It is still being made. Willow was named for a pattern that pictures a bridge, birds, willow trees, and a Chinese landscape. Most pieces are blue and white. Some made after 1900 are pink and white.

Plate, Green, Transfer, John Steventons & Sons Ltd., 1923-36, 10 In., Pair 25
Sugar, Lid, Pink, Handles, White Ground, 3⅝ In. 35
Tureen, Red, Lovebirds, Footed, 6 x 5 In. 50

WINDOW glass that was stained and beveled was popular for houses during the late nineteenth and early twentieth centuries. The old windows became popular with collectors in the 1970s; today, old and new examples are seen.

Circular, Floral, Red & Blue, Cream Background, 24 In. 58
Leaded, 2 Panels, Multicolor, Flowers, 23 x 17 In. ....*illus* 138
Leaded, Colored Glass, Oak Frame, Gothic Arched Top, c.1900, 100 x 43 In. 510
Leaded, Crimson Scroll & Bull's-Eye, Blossoms, Narrow Border, 1900s, 24 x 36 In. 42
Leaded, Flower, Red Rondel Antler, Gothic Arched Frame, c.1800s, 43 x 29½ In. 330
Leaded, Geometric Shapes, Wood Frame, Early 1900s, 24 x 24 In. ....*illus* 34
Leaded, Peacock, Surrounded By Tail Feathers, Signed, Somers, Masotti, 2015, 35 x 45 In. 10240
Leaded, Stained, 8 Oak Lozenges, Crimson Flowers, Diamonds, 1900s, 24 x 43 In. 108
Leaded, Vining Flowers, Geometrics, Slag Glass, Wood Frame, 44½ x 25½ In. 275
Leaded, Wood Frame, From A. Heurtley House, F.L. Wright, 1902, 43½ x 27 In. ....*illus* 7500
Slag Glass, Metal Frame, Center Pane Flanked By Maidens, Late 1800s, 25½ x 47½ In. 313
Stained, 2 Parrots In Center, Arch, Frame, 37 x 18 In. 173
Stained, Amber Field, Central Coat Of Arms, Frame, 1900s, 58 x 25½ In. ....*illus* 438
Stained, Contemporary, Birds, Flying, 3-D Wings, Branches, Pine Frame, 35 x 30 In. 234
Stained, Geometric, Arts & Crafts, Frame, 26½ x 38 In. 150
Stained, Urn Center, Flowers, Wood Frame, 37 x 23 In. 81
Stained, Wood Frame, Roses, 41 x 46 In. ....*illus* 254
Still Life, Peaches In Center, Multicolor, Jeweled, Round, 1800s, 26½ In. 767
Transom, Openwork, Giltwood, Peacock, Chrysanthemums & Clouds, 1900s, 12¾ x 42¼ In. 185

WOOD CARVINGS and wooden pieces are listed separately in this book. There are also wooden pieces found in other categories, such as Folk Art, Kitchen, and Tool.

18 Immortals, Ebony, Painted, Signed, 1700s, 8 In. 138
Artist's Model, Arm, Hand, Custom Stand, 26 In. ....*illus* 590
Artist's Model, Man, Articulated Limbs, Pegged, Carved Face, France, c.1890, 31½ In. .....*illus* 813
Bear, Rectangular, Oak, Table Casket, Black Forest, c.1900, 4⅞ x 5⅝ In. 281
Bird, Carved Bird & Vegetation, Rocks, Ivy & Grass, Signed, Swiss, c.1880, 27 x 8 x 7 In. 1750
Bird, Catching Fish, Painted, Iron Legs, Mounted, c.1900, 7½ In. 800
Bird, Painted, Wood Base, Schtockschnitzler Simmons, 7 In. 8750
Blackamoor, Dancer, On Globe, Zodiac Banner, Pedestal, 1800s, 73 x 18 x 18 In. 1750
Blue Jay, Carved & Painted, Driftwood Base, Signed, R. Morse, c.1950, 2¾ In. 584
Bluebird, Carved, Painted, Wire Legs, Domed Base, Signed, Jess Blackstone, 1900s, 2¾ In. ..*illus* 738
Boat, Olive Pit, Lacquered, Footed Stand, Chinese, 1900s, ¾ x 1¾ In. ....*illus* 123
Bottle Nose Dolphin, Marked, Clark Voorhees Jr. 1900s, 18½ In. 2000
Boxwood, 3 Men At Table Under Tree, 1800s, 6 In. 192
Brushpot, Carved, Relief, 2 Men Playing Game, Chinese, 10 x 7 In. 219
Buddha, Gilt, Red Lacquered, Lotus Throne, Draped Robes, Japan, 1900s, 20 In. 1500
Buddha, Standing, Gilt, Leaf Shape, Mandala, Japan, 1800s, 14 In. 563
Bust, Abraham Lincoln, Painted, White Collar, 1800s, 7 In. ....*illus* 225
Bust, Black Man, Cedar, Mounted, Mahogany Base, 1900s, 12½ In. 277
Bust, Winged Angel, Giltwood, c.1885, Pair, 8 x 4 In. 750

Canada Goose, Painted, Signed, Rubilinos, 1967, 16 x 10 x 10 In.	325
Cat, Seated, Brown, 17¾ In.	177
Crane, Perched On Wood Trunk, Wing Stretching Out, 16½ In.	98
Crow, Glass Eyes, Carved Wing & Feather, Black, Rectangular Base, 1900s, 15½ In.	192
Crucifix, Wood & Gold Gilt, 1800s, 43 x 27 In.	1920
Deity, Scholar, On Socle, Multicolor, Chinese, 1700s, 10¼ In.	270
Dog, Head, Trophy, Hound Mount On Circular Plaque, 1800s-1900s, 11½ In.	240
Dog, Sitting Up, Glass Eyes, Brown Paint, Continental, 1800s, 24 In.	1188
Dog, St. Bernard, 2 Pups, Glass Eyes, Black Forest, c.1900, 6 x 15 In. ....*illus*	4250
Doll, Face & Clothing, Articulated Arms, Polychrome Paint, 1800s, 10 In.	615
Dolphin, Blue & White, Clark G. Voorhees Jr., c.1975, 18 In.	1046
Eagle, Banner, Don't Give Up The Ship, Head, Willard Shepard, 9 x 28 x 4½ In. ....*illus*	1331
Eagle, Gold Detail & Paint, Branch, Black On The Back, 13 x 23½ In.	510
Eagle, Open Wings, Perched, Painted, 1800s, 15 x 12 In.	226
Eagle, Perch, Walnut, Dark Patina, Wings, Tree Trunk, c.1950, 19½ x 23 In.	875
Eagle, Spread Wings, Gilt, Wood Base, Early 1900s, 10¼ x 30½ In.	263
Eagle, Spread Wings, Leafy Branches, Oak Wall Hanging, Weberding, 20 x 36 x 4 In.	605
Eagle, Spread Wings, Perch, Painted, c.1900, 19 x 37 In.	660
Eagle, Spread Wings, Red, White, Blue Shield, Arrows, Gilt, Wall Hanging, 15 x 43 x 5 In.	1573
Fertility, Doll Shape, Ashanti Akua'Ba, Africa, 8½ x 3¾ x 19 In.	71
Giraffe, Rope Tail, Glass Eyes, Leather Saddle, Russ Jacobson, 90 x 48 x 14 In.	726
Guardian, Ruyi Scepter, Stand, Base, Contemporary, Chinese, 27 In.	142
Head, Ekoi, Raffia Fiber Coiffure, Pigmented Eyes & Teeth, 11 In.	246
Head, Painted, Gold & Brown, Haitian, Henri Christophei, 13½ In.	71
Hiker, Woman, Yellow Shirt, Black Shorts, Painted, Early 1900s, 10¾ In. ....*illus*	3048
Hunter, Holding Gamebird, Rifle On Shoulder, Signed, Johann Huggler, 23 In.	1955
Letter Rack, Black Forest, Birds & Nest, Acorns, Square Base, 1800s, 6 x 7½ In.	196
Man, Dancing Black Man, Carved, Painted, Jointed, Metal Stand, Early 1900s, 12¾ In.	1107
Man, Horseback, Painted, Leather Bridle, 1800s, 8⅜ In.	1599
Man's Head, Flat Back, Painted, Bold Facial Features, Red Scarf, 1800s, 14 x 10 In.	1230
Mask, Display, Ngil, White & Orange Pigment, Gabon, Africa, 1900s, 42 x 11 x 7 In.	84
Maternity, Child Seated On Mother's Back, Dogon People, Africa, 27 In.	156
Mermaid, Wings, William Rush, Blue & Brown Paint, 1800s, 60 In.	13200
Model, Leaning Tower Of Pisa, Matchsticks, 8 Layers, Gallery Top, 28 In.	1750
Mountain Climber, Figural, Rope, Black Forest, 23 In.	184
Owl, Perched, Black Forest, Glass Eyes, 9 In.	161
Panel, Carved, Walnut, Lovers Intertwined On Swing, c.1890, 29 x 20 In.	125
Panel, Dog Head, Shield, Crossed Rifles, Flint Pouch, Horn, 34 x 17¾ x 7¾ In.	363
Panel, Walnut, Women Picking Grapes, c.1890, 28 x 21 In.	219
Pedestal, Oak, Floral, Quatrefoil Top, Spiral Turned Column, Acanthus, c.1890, 39 x 14 In.	550
Pedestal, Young Man, Animal Skin, Domed Base, Late 1800s, 37 x 12 In.	385
Plaque, Canada Goose, Flying, Glass Eye, 1900s, 27 x 25 In.	360
Plaque, E Pluribus Unum, Banner, Painted, Gilt, Artistic Company Of Boston, c.1950, 45 In.	2400
Plaque, Eagle, Banner, Don't Give Up The Ship, Bellamy Style, c.1900, 10 x 27 In.	216
Plaque, Eagle, Don't Give Up The Ship, Banner, 1900s, 29 x 10 x 3½ In.	878
Plaque, Eagle, Shield, Gilded, Wall, Banners In Red, White & Blue, 9 x 25 In.	960
Plaque, Eagle, Wall, Red, White & Blue Shield, 1900s, 21 x 18 In. ....*illus*	4080
Plaque, Eagle, Wall, Wing Span, Banner, Painted, Carved & Painted, 20 In.	384
Plaque, George Washington, Pine, Painted, 28 x 15½ In.	325
Plaque, Whale, Open Jaw, Painted, Iron Wire Hanger, Black Patinated, 1900s, 34½ In.	492
Rooster, Iron Wire Legs, Turned Wood Base, Painted, Black, 1800s, 5½ In.	677
Rooster, Painted, Standing, Mounded Base, Late 1800s, 12 In.	2250
Rooster, Softwood, Basket, Mounted On Base, Brown, 6 In.	72
Sakamoto Ryoma, Standing, Leaning On Stump, Zelkova Wood, Lacquer, 14 x 5 In.	201
Santa Claus Head, 1900s, 18½ x 16½ In.	238
Santo, Bearded Robed, Man, Crown, Black Paint, Integral Base, 1800s, 38 x 22½ x 7 In.	1476
Santo, Painted Blue & White, Glass Eyes, c.1800, 42 In.	1062
Scepter, Ruyi, Boxwood, Plum Branch, Relief Carved Sparrow, 11 In.	510
Sconce, Woman, Movie Theater, Candle, Art Nouveau, c.1890s, 18 x 8½ x 9 In.	735

Wood Carving, Artist's Model, Man, Articulated Limbs, Pegged, Carved Face, France, c.1890, 31½ In.
$813

Garth's Auctioneers & Appraisers

Wood Carving, Bluebird, Carved, Painted, Wire Legs, Domed Base, Signed, Jess Blackstone, 1900s, 2¾ In.
$738

Skinner, Inc.

Wood Carving, Boat, Olive Pit, Lacquered, Footed Stand, Chinese, 1900s, ¾ x 1¾ In.
$123

Skinner, Inc.

W

517

Wood Carving, Bust, Abraham Lincoln, Painted, White Collar, 1800s, 7 In. $225

Pook & Pook

Wood Carving, Dog, St. Bernard, 2 Pups, Glass Eyes, Black Forest, c.1900, 6 x 15 In. $4,250

Leslie Hindman Auctioneers

W

Sculpture, Burl, Signed, Sam Markson, 1979, 9¾ x 11 x 8½ In.	338
Sculpture, Figural Scene, People & Animals, Various Poses, R. Jacques, 54 In.	123
Shorebird, Shore, Painted, Signed, H. Buckwalter, 1977, 10 In.	51
Skeleton, Holding Flag, Standing, Painted, Square Base, 16 In. *illus*	750
Soldier, Horseback, Single Block, Hardwood, Painted, 1800s, 11 In.	1599
Sperm Whale, Ashtray, Tooth, Scrimshaw, Signed, 6 In.	196
Sperm Whale, Blue & White Paint, Glass Eyes, 1900s, 21 In.	540
St. Catherine, Holding Bible, Crucifix, Round Base, 63 In. *illus*	605
St. George, Slaying, Dragon, Multicolor, c.1900, 39 In. *illus*	688
Totem, 4 Faces, Painted, Rectangular Base, Early 1900s, 19 In.	450
Turkey, Walking, Painted, A.C. Williams, Oh., c.1925	1103
Vase, Black Cherry, Burl & Resin, Robert W. Chatelain, c.1993, 5 x 8 In. *illus*	91
Vase, Black Palm, Zircote, Antler, Signed, Galen Carpenter, c.1995, 7 x 5 In.	531
Vase, Black Walnut, Turned, Philip Moulthrop, 16½ x 8 In.	2125
Vase, Lid, Tiger Striped Myrtle, Engraved, R.W. Bob Krauss, c.1988, 6 x 6 In.	344
Vase, Smoky Silk, Pink Ivory, Engraved, William Hunter, c.1986, 2¼ x 8½ In.	531
Vase, Tulipwood Lathe, Gloss Finish, Edward Moulthrop, 8½ x 10 In.	885
Vase, Tulipwood, Liriodendron Tulipifera, Ed Moulthrop, c.1990, 9¾ x 14 In.	2500
Virgin & Child, Winged Putti, Clouds, Painted, 23 In.	1488
Wastebasket, Cylindrical, Ash, Teak, Signed, Jens Quistgaard, c.1960, 12 x 12½ In.	585
Watch Holder, Woman Reading Book, Leaning Against Mantel, Painted, 8¾ In.	1020
Whimsy, Tower, Freestanding Spheres, Faces, Base, Signed, Wilfred Coulson, 1932, 27 In.	300
Woman, Holding Bird, Carved Details, Single Block Of Pine, 1800s, 9⅛ In.	2952
Zeus, Gesturing & Holding Globe, Painted, Continental, 36 In.	1220

WOODEN wares were used in all parts of the home. Wood was used for many containers and tools. Small wooden pieces are called *treenware* in England, but the term *woodenware* is more common in the United States. Additional pieces may be found in the Advertising, Kitchen, and Tool categories.

Bag Stamp, Carved, Symbols, J.F. Weaber, 1800s, 8 In.	201
Barrel, Banded, Lid, 1800s, 34½ x 26½ In.	100
Barrel, Brass Bound, Oak, 6-Point Star, The Queen God Bless Her, 1900s, 21 x 18 In. *illus*	660
Barrel, Hornbeam, Carved, Plank Base, 1800s, 26½ x 21 In.	492
Bookstand, Coromandel, Slide, Inset Jewels, Wm. Mansfield, Dublin, c.1860, 7 x 16 x 6 In. *illus*	156
Bowl, Bigleaf, Burl, Maple, Dennis Elliot, c.1994, 29 In.	344
Bowl, Black Walnut, Turned, Ed Moulthrop, 17¾ x 20¾ In.	5000
Bowl, Burl, Carved Handles, Burned Interior, 25 In.	600
Bowl, Burl, Carved, Oval Shape, 1800s, 7 x 17 x 14½ In.	1722
Bowl, Burl, Carved, Rectangular, Rounded Corners, Gold Paint, 1800s, 6 x 16½ In.	4613
Bowl, Burl, Chip Carved, Stylized Compass Roses, 1800s, 2 x 3½ In.	3567
Bowl, Burl, Circular Rim, 1800s, 5¾ x 16½ In.	1968
Bowl, Burl, Molded Rim, Turned, Brown, 6 x 12 In.	177
Bowl, Burl, Treen, Flared, Hole In Bottom, 3½ x 8 In. *illus*	92
Bowl, Burl, Turned, Rounded Rim, 1800s, 7½ x 15 In.	1888
Bowl, Mahogany, Leaf Shape, Carved, Alexandre Noll, France, c.1950, 2¾ x 9½ x 16 In. *illus*	4375
Bowl, Maple, Red, Turned, Wide Rim, Base Ring, c.1801, 6¾ In.	1169
Bowl, Oak, Paduk, Walnut, Bulbous, Signed, Eucled Moore, c.1991, 9 x 14 In. *illus*	91
Bowl, Treenware, Blue Exterior, 1800s, 4½ x 14 In.	1080
Bowl, Tribal, 2 Side Handles, Brown, Black, Shallow Interior, Africa, 14 x 36 In.	92
Bowl, Tropical Hardwood, Carved, Round, c.1950, 5½ x 19 In.	500
Bowl, Turned, Blue Patinated Finish, Brown Interior, 1800s, 24 In.	420
Bowl, Turned, Patina, Natural Hole, 1800s, 6¼ x 17 In. *illus*	1680
Bowl, Turned, Red, Foot Rim, 1800s, 2 x 8 In.	677
Bowl, Walnut, Green Paint, Oblong, New England, Early 1800s, 16¾ x 9 x 3½ In.	339
Bowl, Walnut, Hole, Woodcut, Wharton Esherick, 1962, 2¼ x 7 x 13½ In.	5000
Bowl, Wedding, Carved, Bone Inlays, Female & Male Figure, Solomon Islands, 17 x 4 In.	118
Bucket, 3 Interlocking Bentwood Bands, Handle, Pins, Blue, Stave, 10 x 10 In.	380
Bucket, Lid, Bound, Hand Hewn Straps & Tacks, 1800s, 14½ In.	52
Bucket, Lid, Pine, Wood Straps, Brass Tacks, 10 In.	40

Wood Carving, Eagle, Banner, Don't Give Up The Ship, Head, Willard Shepard, 9 x 28 x 4½ In.
$1,331

Fontaine's Auction Gallery

Wood Carving, Hiker, Woman, Yellow Shirt, Black Shorts, Painted, Early 1900s, 10¾ In.
$3,048

Skinner, Inc.

Wood Carving, Plaque, Eagle, Wall, Red, White & Blue Shield, 1900s, 21 x 18 In.
$4,080

Northeast Auctions

Wood Carving, Skeleton, Holding Flag, Standing, Painted, Square Base, 16 In.
$750

Leslie Hindman Auctioneers

Wood Carving, St. Catherine, Holding Bible, Crucifix, Round Base, 63 In.
$605

Rachel Davis Fine Arts

Wood Carving, St. George, Slaying, Dragon, Multicolor, c.1900, 39 In.
$688

Leslie Hindman Auctioneers

Wood Carving, Vase, Black Cherry, Burl & Resin, Robert W. Chatelain, c.1993, 5 x 8 In.
$91

Freeman's Auctioneers & Appraisers

Wooden, Barrel, Brass Bound, Oak, 6-Point Star, The Queen God Bless Her, 1900s, 21 x 18 In.
$660

Eldred's

Wooden, Bookstand, Coromandel, Slide, Inset Jewels, Wm. Mansfield, Dublin, c.1860, 7 x 16 x 6 In.
$156

Thomaston Place Auction Galleries

Wooden, Bowl, Burl, Treen, Flared, Hole In Bottom, 3 ½ x 8 In.
$92

Keystone Auctions LLC

Wooden, Bowl, Mahogany, Leaf Shape, Carved, Alexandre Noll, France, c.1950, 2¾ x 9½ x 16 In.
$4,375

Wright

Wooden, Bowl, Oak, Paduk, Walnut, Bulbous, Signed, Eucled Moore, c.1991, 9 x 14 In.
$91

Freeman's Auctioneers & Appraisers

Wooden, Bowl, Turned, Patina, Natural Hole, 1800s, 6¼ x 17 In.
$1,680

Garth's Auctioneers & Appraisers

> **TIP**
> Mayonnaise can be rubbed on water-damaged wood to restore the finish.

Wooden, Canteen, Footed, Circular Body, Painted, Leather Strap, 13 In.
$118

Copake Auction

Wooden, Carrier, Cutout Handle, 3 Hearts, Blue Paint, Nail Construction, 6½ x 10¾ In.
$1,062

Hess Auction Group

Wooden, Carrier, Egg Crate, Cardboard Insert, Handle, Ridgecrest Farms, Wilton, Maine, 9 x 7 x 9 In.
$59

Bunch Auctions

Wooden, Easel, Adjustable, Ornate Finial, Lacquered, Tripod Legs, 74 In.
$103

Keystone Auctions LLC

Bucket, Stave Construction, Bentwood Bands, Swing Handle, Pale Yellow, 1850s, 13 x 15 In. ...	480
Canteen, British Navy, Green Paint, Carved DW 1791, 8 In.	687
Canteen, Footed, Circular Body, Painted, Leather Strap, 13 In. ....*illus*	118
Canteen, Iron Bands, Blacksmith, Carved Spout, 1800s, 10 x 5 1/2 In.	165
Canteen, Round, Pine, Red Leather Strap Handle, Interlocking Fingers, 1800s, 10 In.	1080
Carrier, Cutout Handle, 3 Hearts, Blue Paint, Nail Construction, 6 1/2 x 10 3/4 In. ....*illus*	1062
Carrier, Egg Crate, Cardboard Insert, Handle, Ridgecrest Farms, Wilton, Maine, 9 x 7 x 9 In...*illus*	59
Carrier, Lapped Seams, Copper Tacks, Wire Bale Handle, Blue, Round, c.1850, 3 x 4 3/4 In.	1980
Charger, Treen, Dished Rim, Scrubbed Surface, Swirled Grain, Continental, 16 In.	480
Chest, Carved, Coats Of Arms, 2 Portraits, Iron Strap Hinges, Germany, 20 x 53 x 20 In.	800
Compote, Walnut, Round, Rim, Shallow, 1900s, 6 1/4 x 4 In.	236
Container, Kerosene Oil, Red, Handle & Faucet, 3 Gal., 1886, 13 x 12 In.	113
Crucifix, Gilt, Multicolor, Christ Nailed To Cross, Oval Mirror, Italy, c.1780, 37 x 23 1/4 In.	1750
Cup, Bamboo, Libation, Flowers & Branches, c.1900, 5 In.	312
Easel, Adjustable, Ornate Finial, Lacquered, Tripod Legs, 74 In. ....*illus*	103
Firkin, Banding, Bail Handle, Dark Stain, 13 x 15 In.	71
Firkin, Blue & Salmon Paint, Loop Handle, C.1900, 12 1/2 x 12 In.	94
Firkin, Mincemeat, Yellow Painted, Taped Tapered Lap Joints, Bentwood Handle, 10 In.	189
Firkin, Pine, Lid, Stave Construction, Yellow, Bentwood Bands & Handles, 1800s, 12 x 11 1/2 In.	625
Firkin, Pine, Lid, Swing Handle, 1800s, 9 In.	88
Firkin, Pine, Painted, Salmon Surface, Swing Handle, 1800s, 6 1/2 In.	875
Herb Dryer, Carved Frame, Rectangular, Screen Top, Walnut, 1800s, 2 x 16 x 12 In.	277
Hibachi, Copper Lining, Glass Cover, Japan, 1900s, 11 x 25 1/2 x 14 In.	246
Holder, Cheese, Mahogany, Pivoting Stand, Rollers Base, c.1850, 10 x 20 x 9 In.	308
Ice Bucket, Lid, Handle, Dansk, Denmark, 19 In. ....*illus*	151
Keg, Spigot, Stave Construction, 1800s, 16 1/2 x 10 1/2 In.	192
Lightstand, Square Top, Cleat & Chamfered, 3 Splayed Legs, England, 1800s, 27 1/2 In.	800
Mallet, Ash, Baseball End, Silver, Cloth, Leather, Harry Bertoia, c.1973, 6 3/4 x 6 In.	8750
Mirror, Hand, Laminated Teak, Hans-Agne Jakobsson, Sweden, c.1955, 14 x 6 In. ....*illus*	218
Mixing Bowl, Turned, Green Patina Finish, 1800s, 20 1/2 In.	570
Mold, Candle, 24 Pewter Tubes, Pine Stand, 1800s, 18 x 22 1/4 In. ....*illus*	1063
Mold, Candle, Mixed Woods, 18 Pewter Molds, Footed Frame, 1800s, 16 x 20 x 6 In.	360
Mortar, Turned Burlwood, Ring Shape Base, 1800s, 7 x 6 In.	83
Mug, Carved Thumbprint, Handle, Circular Rim & Base, c.1850, 6 1/2 In. ....*illus*	923
Piggin, Painted, Flowers, Round, Handle, 1800s, 6 x 5 1/2 In. ....*illus*	219
Plaque, Eagle, Red, White, Blue, Bellamy Style, Early 1900s, 9 1/2 x 28 1/4 In.	960
Plaque, Patriotic, Wall, Painted, Blue, White & Red, c.1950, 8 x 3 1/2 x 12 1/2 In.	118
Plate Holder, Turned Arms, Central Ball, Late 1800s, 9 x 12 x 12 In.	523
Powder Keg, 4th Co., 3rd Reg., Mustard, Black, Chain Carrying Handle, Late 1800s, 6 In.	420
Rack, Wine, Steel, Oak, Ladder Style, 53 3/4 x 2 x 7 In.	227
Scoop, Carved, Maple, Thin Sides, Curling Handle, Marked, 1800s, 12 x 10 1/4 In.	277
Scoop, Tiger Maple, Carved, Open Handle, 8 3/4 In.	94
Seat, Wagon, Painted, Child's, c.1900, 16 In. ....*illus*	63
Shoulder Yolk, Carved, 2 Handles, Concave, Neck, Vietnam, 1900s, 37 In.	24
Sign, Abacus, Carved, Wooden, Painted, 20 x 40 In.	313
Sign, Codfish, Metal Fins, c.1950, 37 In.	720
Spoon, Treen, Snowflake, Handle, Scandinavia, 1800s, 7 1/2 In.	30
Sugar Bucket, Pine, Bail Handle & Lid, 3 Steel Bands, 7 In. ....*illus*	46
Tabernacle, Doric Columns, Giltwood Shell, Painted, Italy, c.1700, 43 3/4 x 23 x 11 In.	1750
Tankard, Staves, Handle, Burl Lid, 1800s, 13 In.	118
Tantalus, Hunting Dog, Black Forest, Glass Decanters, 6 Cordial Glasses, 16 x 16 x 12 In. *illus*	594
Tray, 2 Compartments, Cutout Sides, Hand Hold, Walnut, c.1850, 5 x 14 x 9 In.	164
Tray, Brass Fence, Deep Floral, Medallions, Gallery Style, Handles, 16 x 32 In.	184
Tray, Mahogany, Brass Handles, Shell Inlay, Cowan, Chicago, Oval, Early 1900s, 17 x 28 In.	113
Tray, Mahogany, Kidney Shape, Gallery Sides, Brass Handles, 14 x 22 In.	161
Tray, Serving, Mahogany, Shell Medallion, Fan Corners, Inlaid, Bronze Handles, 16 x 23 In.	115
Trencher, Chrome, Yellow Painted, Rectangular, Rounded Corners, 1800s, 21 In.	1230
Trencher, Hand Gouged, Iron Braces, 1800s, 12 x 45 In.	805
Trencher, Maple, Oblong, Gray Paint, Handles, Late 1800s, 19 In.	138
Trencher, Maple, Oval, 1800s, 4 x 21 1/2 In.	88

Wooden, Ice Bucket, Lid, Handle, Dansk, Denmark, 19 In.
$151

Clars Auction Gallery

Wooden, Mirror, Hand, Laminated Teak, Hans-Agne Jakobsson, Sweden, c.1955, 14 x 6 In.
$218

Wright

Wooden, Mold, Candle, 24 Pewter Tubes, Pine Stand, 1800s, 18 x 22 1/4 In.
$1,063

Pook & Pook

TIP

For your health and the well-being of your collection, do not smoke. The nicotine will stain fabrics, pictures, and wood.

W

Wooden, Mug, Carved Thumbprint, Handle, Circular Rim & Base, c.1850, 6½ In.
$923

Skinner, Inc.

Wooden, Piggin, Painted, Flowers, Round, Handle, 1800s, 6 x 5½ In.
$219

Pook & Pook

Wooden, Seat, Wagon, Painted, Child's, c.1900, 16 In.
$63

Pook & Pook

Wooden, Sugar Bucket, Pine, Bail Handle & Lid, 3 Steel Bands, 7 In.
$46

Keystone Auctions LLC

Wooden, Tantalus, Hunting Dog, Black Forest, Glass Decanters, 6 Cordial Glasses, 16 x 16 x 12 In.
$594

Susanin's Auctioneers & Appraisers

Wooden, Trencher, Rough Hewn, 2 Notched Handles, Green Paint Traces, c.1850, 5 x 21 In.
$420

Garth's Auctioneers & Appraisers

Non-Smoking Hitler
Hitler was the only important WWII leader who didn't smoke.

Trencher, Pine, 4 Handles, Softwood, Rectangular, 16 ½ x 40 In.	201
Trencher, Rough Hewn, 2 Notched Handles, Green Paint Traces, c.1850, 5 x 21 In. ....*illus*	420
Trencher, South Seas, Carved Figural Handles, 1800s, 4 ½ x 29 In.	420
Urn, Cutlery, Mahogany, George III, Telescoping Lids, c.1890, 25 x 10 In.	1500
Vase, Tulipwood, Small Mouth, Signed, Dan Kvitka, c.1996, 3 x 5 ¾ In. ....*illus*	125
Watch Hutch, Black Forest Style, Waltham Pocket Watch, Hanging, 1800s, Size 16	188

WORCESTER porcelains were made in Worcester, England, from 1751. The firm went through many name changes and eventually, in 1862, became The Royal Worcester Porcelain Company Ltd. Collectors often refer to Dr. Wall, Barr, Flight, and other names that indicate time periods or artists at the factory. It became part of Royal Worcester Spode Ltd. in 1976. The company was bought by the Portmeirion Group in 2009. Related pieces may be found in the Royal Worcester category.

Bowl, Fenced Garden, Painted, Blue & White, 1800s, 5 ⅞ In.	98
Bowl, Landscape, Blue Border, Shell Encrusted, Footed, Chamberlain, c.1830, 8 x 3 In. .....*illus*	154
Cup, Scarlett Japan Pattern, James Giles, 1800s, 2 ½ In.	169
Ewer, Stork Head, Grotesque, Gold Accents, 12 x 8 In.	3520
Jug, Mask Head, Classical Purple Urn, 7 x 5 In.	394
Jug, Sparrow Beak, Old Star Japan, Blue Scale, 4 ¼ In.	253
Plate, Fruit, Painted, Blackberries & Peach, Milwyn Holloway, 8 In.	197
Plate, Painted, Hundred Antiques, White & Blue, 7 ½ In.	155
Plate, Pedestal, Peaches & Grapes, Painted, Moseley, c.1940, 5 ½ In.	125
Platter, Gadroon Rim, Rocaille, Blue Border, Chamberlain, 1800s, 12 ½ In. ....*illus*	250
Vase, Lid, Loop Handles, Bead Borders, c.1909, 10 ⅞ In.	5228

WORLD WAR I and World War II souvenirs are collected today. Be careful not to store anything that includes live ammunition. Your local police will tell you how to dispose of the explosives. See also Sword and Trench Art.

WORLD WAR I

Belt, Steel Buckle, Crown, Gott Mit Uns, Germany, 2 x 4 ½ In. ....*illus*	254
Boots, Motorcycle, Brown Leather, 3 Straps, Dated Inside, 1918	168
Broadside, Jewish Relief, Work Campaign, Home Is Helping Our Boys Over There	36
Flare Gun, Marked JGA, Germany, 1920, 11 ½ In.	144
Medal, Iron, Cross, Black & Silver Ribbon, Germany	58
Photograph, Soldiers, Training Camp Joseph E. Johnston, Names Written On Back	24
Poster, Credit Lyonnais, War Bonds, On Cardboard, France, 31 x 47 In.	148
Poster, Enlist Now & Go With Your Friends, Soldiers, 41 x 28 In.	35
Poster, Invest In The Victory Liberty Loan, U.S. Coast Guard Ship, 1918, 29 x 39 In. ....*illus*	326
Poster, Over The Top For You, Patriotic Image, Ketterlinus, 1918, 30 x 20 In.	292
Poster, U.S. Marine, Be A Sea Soldier, Linen, Clarence F. Underwood, 1917, 40 x 30 In.	292
Poster, Victory Liberty Loan, And They Thought We Couldn't Fight, Mounted, 42 x 31 In.	106
Uniform, Jacket, 4 Pockets, 12 Buttons, Size 42 Breast	48

WORLD WAR II

Ashtray, Chamber Pot Shape, Comic Hitler In Bottom, Handle, 1939-41, 2 x 1 ½ In.	19
Badge, Iron Cross 2nd Class, Eagle, Black & Brown, Ribbon, Germany, 1939	163
Bag, Comfort, Drawstring, Sent To Japanese Soldiers, 12 x 7 ½ In.	162
Bank, Penny On The Drum, For Disabled Vets, Tin, St. Dunstan's, 1948, 7 x 5 x 4 In.	132
Banner, Son In Service, Canadian Army, Maple Leaf Center, Pinked Edges, 12 x 8 ½ In.	69
Boots, Jungle, Impregnated Canvas, Rubber, USMC, 8 ½ In.	148
Bowling Pin, Anti Axis, Tojo, Solid Maple, Brunswick, 1940s, 15 In.	1915
Dagger, German Army Officer's, Leafy Pommel, Celluloid Grip, Eagle Cross Guard, 10 In.	182
Flag, American, 48 Stars, Veteran's Administration, Bull Dog Bunting, 3 x 6 x 8 In.	54
Helmet, Battle For Stalingrad, M40, Steel, Germany, 64 In.	490
Helmet, Japanese Army, Liner, Star, Round	1003
Helmet, Third Reich, Infantry, Decal, 12 ¼ In.	516
Patch, Ranger, Diamond Shape, Shoulder Sleeve, Theater Made, 4 x 2 In.	158
Pin, Torpedo Shape, Blue Stripe, V, Torpedoed, Merchant Marine, Lapel Badge, 1 x ³⁄₁₆ In.	159

Wooden, Vase, Tulipwood, Small Mouth, Signed, Dan Kvitka, c.1996, 3 x 5 ¾ In.
$125

Worcester, Bowl, Landscape, Blue Border, Shell Encrusted, Footed, Chamberlain, c.1830, 8 x 3 In.
$154

Worcester, Platter, Gadroon Rim, Rocaille, Blue Border, Chamberlain, 1800s, 12 ½ In.
$250

> **TIP**
> *German World War II binoculars are very popular with collectors. Second most popular are WW II Japanese binoculars.*

World War I, Belt, Steel Buckle, Crown, Gott Mit Uns, Germany, 2 x 4 ½ In.
$254

World War I, Poster, Invest In The Victory Liberty Loan, U.S. Coast Guard Ship, 1918, 29 x 39 In.
$326

World War II, Poster, Buy War Bonds, Uncle Sam, American Flag, Newell Convers Wyeth, 30 x 40 In.
$649

World War II, Poster, Uncle Sam, Hitler, Dancing Monkey, We Made A Monkey Out Of You, 1943, 20 x 15 In.
$118

Poster, Buy Bonds Every Payday, Aerial Machine Gunner, Martha Sawyers, 1944, 38 x 30 In.	196
Poster, Buy War Bonds, Uncle Sam, American Flag, Newell Convers Wyeth, 30 x 40 In. ......*illus*	649
Poster, Our Carelessness, Their Secret Weapon, Prevent Forest Fires, 28 x 22 In.	177
Poster, Our Fighters Deserve Our Best, Patriotic Art, U.S. Soldier, 1942, 40 x 28 In.	207
Poster, Strong In The Strength Of The Lord, David Stone Martin, 1942, 40¼ x 56 In.	196
Poster, Till We Meet Again, Buy War Bonds, Paper Lithograph, Joseph Hirsch, 1942, 22 x 14 In.	128
Poster, Uncle Sam, Hitler, Dancing Monkey, We Made A Monkey Out Of You, 1943, 20 x 15 In..*illus*	118
Poster, United We Are Strong, United We Will Win, Cannon, Henry Koerner, 1943, 56 x 40 In..	175
Punchboard, Uncle Sam, Ax In Hand, Caricatures, Tojo, Hitler, Mussolini, 1940s, 16 x 11½ In..	161
Sign, Blame Them For Higher Prices & Shortages, Mussolini, Hitler, Tojo, 18 x 15¼ In.....*illus*	422
Sign, Stop Complaining, We're At War, Paper, Frame, 16 x 5 In.	42
Trade Simulator, Penny Drop, Bomb Hit, Wood Case, Novelty Co., Inc., 1940s, 15 x 12 x 7 In..	597

WORLD'S FAIR souvenirs from all of the fairs are collected. The first fair was the Great Exhibition of 1851 in London. Some other important exhibitions and fairs include Philadelphia, 1876 (Centennial); Chicago, 1893 (World's Columbian); Buffalo, 1901 (Pan-American); St. Louis, 1904 (Louisiana Purchase); Portland, 1905 (Lewis & Clark Centennial Exposition); San Francisco, 1915 (Panama-Pacific); Paris (International Exposition of Modern Decorative and Industrial Arts), 1925; Philadelphia, 1926 (Sesquicentennial); Chicago, 1933 (Century of Progress); Cleveland, 1936 (Great Lakes); San Francisco, 1939 (Golden Gate International); New York, 1939 (World of Tomorrow); Seattle, 1962 (Century 21); New York, 1964; Montreal, 1967; Knoxville (Energy Turns the World) 1982; New Orleans, 1984; Tsukuba, Japan, 1985; Vancouver, Canada, 1986; Brisbane, Australia, 1988; Seville, Spain, 1992; Genoa, Italy, 1992; Seoul, South Korea, 1993; Lisbon, Portugal, 1998; Hanover, Germany, 2000; Shanghai, China, 2010; and Milan, Italy, 2015. Memorabilia of fairs include directories, pictures, fabrics, ceramics, etc. Memorabilia from other similar celebrations may be listed in the Souvenir category.

Ashtray, 1939, New York, Carved Tree, Man, Woman, Child, Picnic, Summer, Red	266
Ashtray, 1939, New York, Rubber Tire, Marked, Goodrich Silvertown, 6 In.	29
Bracelet, 1939, New York, Cuff, Silver Plate, Adjustable, 7 In.	30
Clock, 1893, Chicago, Columbus, Bostwick & Burgess, 15 x 6½ In.	114
Elevator Button, 1933, Chicago, Century Of Progress Ride, Otis, 8 In., Pair....................*illus*	1000
Glass, 1901, Buffalo, Pan-American Exposition, Scenes, Pink, 4 In.	42
Lamp, 1939, New York, Trylon & Perisphere, Frosted Glass, H. Rossen, 5½ x 5 x 8 In.	284
Match Safe, 1893, Chicago, Columbian Exposition, Columbus Head, Machinery Hall, 3⅛ In.	90
Needle Case, 1892, Chicago, Columbian Expo, Barrel Shape, 2 In.	69
Pin, 1901, Buffalo, Lancaster, Simplicity & Strength, Hand Drill & Bits, ⅞ In.	68
Plaque, 1904, St. Louis, Tinted Photo Of Cascades, Celluloid, c.1904, 3¾ x 5 In...........*illus*	118
Spoon, 1939, San Francisco, Demitasse, Sterling Silver, 4¼ In.	31
Textile, 1884-85, New Orleans, World's Industrial & Cotton Centennial, Silk, 5⅝ x 7⅜ In.	41
Top, Spinning, 1939, New York, Prototype, Marx Factory, 1939, 4 In....................*illus*	292
Vase, 1904, St. Louis, Green, Gold Trim, 2 Handles, Victoria Carlsbad, 5 x 4 In.	117
Vase, 1939, New York, Yellow, 5¾ In.	443
Watch Fob, 1904, St. Louis, Louisiana Purchase, Medallions, 4 Links, 4 x 1 In.	179

WPA is the abbreviation for Works Progress Administration, a program created by executive order in 1935 to provide jobs for millions of unemployed Americans. Artists were hired to create murals, paintings, drawings, and sculptures for public buildings. Pieces are marked *WPA* and may have the artist's name on them.

Doll, Girl, Indian, Cloth, Leather, Glass Beads, Missouri WPA Project, 1930s, 15 In.	66
Drawing, Pencil Sketch, Railroad Workers, Driving Spikes, Frame, 1930s, 18 x 20 In.	610
Sculpture, John Cabot, Discoverer Of Newfoundland, Papier-Mache, Plaster Base, 17¾ In.	26

WRISTWATCHES came into use during World War I. Wristwatches are listed here by manufacturer or as advertising or character watches. Wristwatches may also be listed in other categories. Pocket watches are listed in the Watch category.

Breitling Navitimer AOPA, Stainless Steel, Black Enamel Dial, c.1954, 1¼ In.	8125
Breitling, Callisto, Stainless Steel Case, Chronograph, Brown Crocodile Strap Band, 9½ In. ..	3068

World War II, Sign, Blame Them For Higher Prices & Shortages, Mussolini, Hitler, Tojo, 18 x 15 ¼ In.
$422

Hake's Auctions

World's Fair, Elevator Button, 1933, Chicago, Century Of Progress Ride, Otis, 8 In., Pair
$1,000

Leslie Hindman Auctioneers

World's Fair, Plaque, 1904, St. Louis, Tinted Photo Of Cascades, Celluloid, c.1904, 3 ¾ x 5 In.
$118

Hake's Auctions

World's Fair, Top, Spinning, 1939, New York, Prototype, Marx Factory, 1939, 4 In.
$292

Hake's Auctions

Wristwatch, Lucien Piccard, Champagne Dial, Quartz, 14K Yellow Gold, Leather Strap
$369

Morphy Auctions

Wristwatch, Van Cleef & Arpels, 18K Yellow Gold, White Dial, Bezel, Round, Black Band, 6 ½ In.
$780

Brunk Auctions

Yellowware, Bowl, Cobalt Blue, Seaweed, White & Brown Bands, 1850s, 4 ½ x 10 ¼ In.
$125

Garth's Auctioneers & Appraisers

Zsolnay, Centerpiece, Shell, Interior Hand Painted Flowers, Blue, 1880-90, 9 ¾ In.
$180

Eldred's

TIP
Replace broken or scratched watch crystals immediately. The crack may let moisture get to the works, and soon your watch will not tell time accurately.

W

Zsolnay, Vase, Flowers, Green Luster, Iridescent, Flared Rim, Stamped, 11 In. $156

Roland Auctioneers & Valuers

Zsolnay, Vase, Tulip, Spreading Foot, Moorish Style, c.1900s, 8 ¼ In. $330

Eldred's

Bulova, Marine, Star, Orange, Bezel & Band	72
Cartier, Panther, 18K Gold, Ivory Dial, Roman Numerals, Brick Links, Pouch	7500
Hamilton, 14K White Gold, Small Diamonds, Numbers, Woman's	120
Hermes, Quartz, Water Resistant, Ostrich Debeer Strap, Goldtone Buckle, 7 ¾ In.	813
Hermes, Stainless Steel, White Dial, Leather Band, Box, Signed, France, 9 ½ x 1 ½ In.	1046
Lucien Piccard, Champagne Dial, Quartz, 14K Yellow Gold, Leather Strap *illus*	369
Lyceum, White Gold, 17 Jewel, 16 Diamonds, Black Strap, Tonneau Case, Woman's, 6 ¾ In.	108
Movado, 14K Gold, Rectangular Case, 10 Diamonds, 5 Jewel, Adjustable, Woman's, 10 ¾ In.	300
Omega, 14K Gold, Black Dial, Bezel, 32 Cut Diamonds, Swiss, Woman's, 6 In.	660
Omega, Seamaster, 300M, James Bond, Stainless Steel, Automatic, Black Face, Blue Bezel	1188
Omega, Seamaster, Date Window, Blue Dial, Stainless Steel, Box, Swiss, 7 ½ In.	1920
Patek Philippe, Calatrava, 18K Gold Case, Bezel, Manual Wind, Goldtone Dial, Woman's, 7 ¼ In.	5664
Van Cleef & Arpels, 18K Yellow Gold, White Dial, Bezel, Round, Black Band, 6 ½ In. *illus*	780

YELLOWWARE is a heavy earthenware made of a yellowish clay. It varies in color from light yellow to orange-yellow. Many nineteenth- and twentieth-century kitchen bowls and jugs were made of yellowware. It was made in England and in the United States. Another form of pottery that is sometimes classed as yellowware is listed in this book in the Mocha category.

Bowl, Cobalt Blue, Seaweed, White & Brown Bands, 1850s, 4 ½ x 10 ¼ In. *illus*	125
Bowl, Mocha Seaweed, White & Blue, 1800s, 5 x 7 ¼ In.	400
Figurine, Cat, Seated, Copper & Manganese, Clear Glaze, c.1860, 10 ¾ x 10 ¼ In.	590
Teapot, Rebekah At The Well, Lid, Green, Brown, Red, Yellow, Blue, S.P. Co., 1888, 4 In.	1534
Vase, Round, Imperial, Glazed, Porcelain, Cliff Lee, Stevens, Pa., 1991, 7 x 8 In.	937

LA MORO — **ZANESVILLE** Art Pottery was founded in 1900 by David Schmidt in Zanesville, Ohio. The firm made faience umbrella stands, jardinieres, and pedestals. The company closed in 1920 and Weller bought the factory. Many pieces are marked with just the words *La Moro*.

Vase, Brown & Green Vulcan Glaze, Stoneware, 11 x 7 In.	225
Vase, Leaf, Green Matte Glaze, Stoneware, 8 x 5 In.	62
Vase, Periwinkle Blue, Bearded Iris, c.1935, 8 In.	42
Vase, Salmon Color, Gold Gilding, Gold Leaves, c.1940, 11 ½ In.	60

ZSOLNAY pottery was made in Hungary after 1853 and was characterized by Persian, Art Nouveau, or Hungarian motifs. A series of new Zsolnay figurines with green-gold luster finish is available in many shops today. Early Zsolnay was not marked, but by 1878 the tower trademark was used.

Zsolnay Porcelanmanufaktura
1871+

Zsolnay Porcelanmanufaktura
1899–1920

Zsolnay Porcelanmanufaktura
1900+

Centerpiece, Shell, Interior Hand Painted Flowers, Blue, 1880-90, 9 ¾ In. *illus*	180
Ewer, Figural Handle, Couple, Iridescent, Raised Mark, 15 ¼ In.	5082
Jug, Eosin Glaze, Turquoise, Flowers, c.1900s, 3 ½ In.	480
Vase, Flowers, Green Luster, Iridescent, Flared Rim, Stamped, 11 In. *illus*	156
Vase, Stand, Baluster Shape, Cobalt Blue Body, Flowers, Signed, 17 x 15 In.	6050
Vase, Tulip, Spreading Foot, Moorish Style, c.1900s, 8 ¼ In. *illus*	330

X
Y
Z

INDEX

This index is computer-generated, making it as complete and accurate as possible. References in uppercase type are category listings. Those in lowercase letters refer to additional pages where pieces can be found. There is also an internal cross-referencing system used in the main part of the book, so if you look for a Kewpie doll in the Doll category, you will be told it is in its own category. There is additional information at the end of many paragraphs about where to find prices of pieces similar to yours.

PHOTO CREDITS

We have included the name of the auction house or photographer with each pictured object. This is a list of the addresses of those who have contributed photographs and information for this book. Every dealer or auction has to buy antiques to have items to sell. Call or email a dealer or auction house if you want to discuss buying or selling. If you need an appraisal or advice, remember that appraising is part of their business and fees may be charged.

Abington Auction Gallery
3251 N. Dixie Hwy.
Fort Lauderdale, FL 33334
abingtonauctions.com
954-900-4869

Ahlers & Ogletree Auction Gallery
715 Miami Circle, Suite 210
Atlanta, GA 30324
aandoauctions.com
404-869-2478

Alderfer Auction Company
501 Fairgrounds Rd.
Hatfield, PA 19440
alderferauction.com
215-393-3000

Allard Auctions
P.O. Box 1030
St. Ignatius, MT 59865
allardauctions.com
406-745-0500

American Glass Gallery
P.O. Box 227
New Hudson, MI 48165
americanglassgallery.com
248-486-0530

AntiqueAdvertising.com
P.O. Box 247
Cazenovia, NY 13035
antiqueadvertising.com
315-662-7625

Apple Tree Auction Center
1625 W. Church St.
Newark, OH 43055
appletreeauction.com
704-344-4282

Aspire Auctions
2310 Superior Ave. #125
Cleveland, OH 44114
aspireauctions.com
216-651-2532

Auction Team Breker
P.O. Box 50 11 19
50971 Köln
Germany
breker.com
207-485-8343 (USA)

Belhorn Auction Services
2746 Wynnerock Ct.
Hilliard, OH 43026
belhornauctions.com
614-921-9441

Bertoia Auctions
2141 DeMarco Dr.
Vineland, NJ 08360
bertoiaauctions.com
856-692-1881

Blackwell Auctions
10900 US Hwy. 19 N
Clearwater, FL 33764
blackwellauctions.com
727-546-0200

Bonhams
bonhams.com

Brunk Auctions
P.O. Box 2135
Asheville, NC 28802
brunkauctions.com
825-254-6846

Bunch Auctions
1 Hillman Dr.
Chadds Ford, PA 19317
bunchauctions.com
610-558-1800

Burchard Galleries
2528 30th Ave. North
St. Petersburg, FL 33713
burchardgalleries.com
727-821-1167

Charleston Estate Auctions
918 Lansing Dr., Suite E
Mt. Pleasant, SC 29464
charlestonestateauctions.com
843-696-3335

Christie's
20 Rockefeller Plaza
New York, NY 10020
christies.com

Clars Auction Gallery
5644 Telegraph Ave.
Oakland, CA 94609
clars.com
510-428-0100

Copake Auction
P.O. Box 47
Copake, NY 12516
copake.com
518-329-1142

Cordier Auctions
1500 Paxton St.
Harrisburg, PA 17104
cordierauction.com
717-731-8662

Cottone Auctions
120 Court St.
Geneseo, NY 14454
cottoneauctions.com
585-243-1000

Cowan's Auctions
6270 Este Ave.
Cincinnati, OH 45232
cowanauctions.com
513-871-1670

Crescent City Auction Gallery
1330 St. Charles Ave.
New Orleans, LA 70130
crescentcityauctiongaller
504-529-5

Crocker Farm
15900 York Rd.
Sparks, MD 21152
crockerfarm.com
410-472-2016

Doyle Auctioneers & Appraisers
175 E. 87th St.
New York, NY 10128
doyle.com
212-427-2730

DuMouchelles
409 E. Jefferson Ave.
Detroit, MI 48226
dumouchelles.com
313-963-6255

eBay
ebay.com

Eldred's
P.O. Box 796
1483 Route 6A
East Dennis, MA 02641
eldreds.com
508-385-3116

Etsy
etsy.com

Fairfield Auction
707 Main St.
Monroe, CT 06468
fairfieldauction.com
203-880-5200

Fontaine's Auction Gallery
1485 W. Housatonic St.
Pittsfield, MA 01201
fontainesauction.com
413-448-8922

Forsythes' Auctions
206 W. Main St.
Russellville, OH 45168
forsythesauctions.com
937-377-3700

Fox Auctions
P.O. Box 4069
Vallejo, CA 94590
foxauctionsonline.com
631-553-3841

Freeman's Auctioneers & Appraisers
1808 Chestnut St.
Philadelphia, PA 19103
freemansauction.com
215-563-9275

Garth's Auctioneers & Appraisers
P.O. Box 369
Delaware, OH 43015
garths.com
740-362-4771

Glass Works Auctions
P.O. Box 38
Lambertville, NJ 08530
glswrk-auction.com
609-483-2683

Goldin Auctions
160 E. Ninth Ave., Suite A
Runnemede, NJ 08078
goldinauctions.com
856-767-8550

Grogan & Company
20 Charles St.
Boston, MA 02114
groganco.com
617-720-2020

Hake's Americana & Collectibles
P.O. Box 12001
York, PA 17402
hakes.com
717-434-1600

Hannam's Auctioneers
The Old Dairy
Norton Farm
Selborne
Hampshire GU34 3NB
UK
hannamsauctioneers.com

Harritt Group, Inc.
4704 Corydon Pike
New Albany, IN 47150
harrittgroup.com
812-944-0217

Hartzell's Auction Gallery, Inc.
521 Richmond Rd.
Bangor, PA 18013
hartzellsauction.com
610-588-5831

Heritage Auctions
3500 Maple Ave., 17th Floor
Dallas, TX 75219
ha.com
214-528-3500

Hess Auction Group
768 Graystone Rd.
Manheim, PA 17545
hessauctiongroup.com
717-898-7284

Homestead Auctions
4217 S. Cleveland Massillon Rd.
Norton, OH 44203
homesteadauction.net
330-706-9950

Humler & Nolan
225 E. Sixth St., 4th Floor
Cincinnati, OH 45202
humlernolan.com
513-381-2041

Jack & Jeff Hayes
Hayes Auction Services
38250 New Market Turner Rd.
Mechanicsville, MD 20659
hayesauctionservices.com
301-861-7738

James D. Julia Auctioneers
Division of Morphy Auctions
2000 N. Reading Rd.
Denver, PA 17517
morphyauctions.com/jamesdjulia
877-968-8880

Jeffrey S. Evans & Associates
P.O. Box 2638
Harrisonburg, VA 22801
jefffreyevans.com
540-434-3939

Julien's Auctions
8630 Hayden Pl.
Culver City, CA 90232
juliensauctions.com
301-836-1818

Kamelot Auction
2216–2220 E. Allegheny Ave.
Philadelphia, PA 19134
kamelotauctions.com
215-438-6990

Keystone Auctions LLC
218 E. Market St.
York, PA 17403
auctionsbykeystone.com
717-755-8954

Leland Little Auctions
620 Cornerstone Ct.
Hillsborough, NC 27278
lelandlittle.com
919-644-1243

Leslie Hindman Auctioneers
1338 W. Lake St.
Chicago, IL 60607
lesliehindman.com
312-280-1212

Locati Auctions
1425 Welsh Rd.
Maple Glen, PA 19002
locatillc.com
215-619-2873

Los Angeles Modern Auctions
16145 Hart St.
Van Nuys, CA 91406
lamodern.com
323-904-1950

Main Auction Galleries, Inc.
137 W. 4th St.
Cincinnati, OH 45202
mainauctiongalleries.com
513-621-1280

Martin Auction Co.
P.O. Box 2
Anna, IL 62906
martinauctionco.com
864-520-2208

Matthew Bullock Auctioneers
421 E. Stevenson Rd.
Ottawa, IL 61350
bullockauctioneers.com
815-220-5005

Milestone Auctions
3860 Ben Hur Ave., Unit 8
Willoughby, OH 44094
milestonesuctions.com
440-527-8060

Morphy Auctions
2000 N. Reading Rd.
Denver, PA 17517
morphyauctions.com
717-335-3435

Nadeau's Auction Gallery
25 Meadow Rd.
Windsor, CT 06095
nadeausauction.com
860-249-2444

Neal Auction Company
4038 Magazine St.
New Orleans, LA 70115
nealauction.com
800-467-5329

New Orleans Auction Galleries
333 St. Joseph St.
New Orleans, LA 70130
neworleansauction.com
504-566-1849

Norman C. Heckler & Company
79 Bradford Corner Rd.
Woodstock Valley, CT 06282
hecklerauction.com
860-974-1634

Northeast Auctions (now Bourgeault-Horan
Antiquarians & Associates, LLC)
93 Pleasant St.
Portsmouth, NH 03801
bourgeaulthoranauctions.com
603-433-8400

Palm Beach Modern Auctions
417 Bunker Rd.
West Palm Beach, FL 33405
modernauctions.com
561-586-5500